Reforming Company and Takeover Law in Europe

Reforming Company and Takeover Law in Europe

Edited by

Guido Ferrarini, Klaus J. Hopt, Jaap Winter and Eddy Wymeersch

OXFORD
UNIVERSITY PRESS

OXFORD
UNIVERSITY PRESS

Great Clarendon Street, Oxford OX2 6DP

Oxford University Press is a department of the University of Oxford.

It furthers the University's objective of excellence in research, scholarship, and education by publishing worldwide in

Oxford New York

Auckland Bangkok Buenos Aires Cape Town Chennai
Dar es Salaam Delhi Hong Kong Istanbul Karachi Kolkata
Kuala Lumpur Madrid Melbourne Mexico City Mumbai Nairobi
São Paulo Shanghai Taipei Tokyo Toronto

Oxford is a registered trade mark of Oxford University Press in the UK and in certain other countries

Published in the United States by Oxford University Press Inc., New York

First published 2004

British Library Cataloguing in Publication Data

Data available

Library of Congress Cataloging in Publication Data

Data available

ISBN 0-19-927380-4

1 3 5 7 9 10 8 6 4 2

Printed in Great Britain
on acid-free paper by
Antony Rowe Ltd, Chippenham

Preface

Reforming company and takeover law in Europe is a task that tops the agenda all over the world. After the American scandals of Enron, WorldCom, and their followers, a veritable reform flood has swept from the United States over to Europe and beyond. The Sarbanes-Oxley Act of July 2002 has set the stage not only for American corporations, auditors, lawyers, and investors, but also very much for non-American ones. Beyond the direct impact of this legislation on those non-American entities and professionals who are listed or are doing business in the United States and therefore cannot escape its reach, there is also an indirect, but hardly less palpable, impact that is not, as in many other instances, simply due to a more or less controversial extraterritorial application of American law. Enron and its consequences are different. They created in Europe as well a radical feeling of uncertainty and actual fear as to the good functioning of corporate governance in these countries. This concern extends beyond concrete corporate governance issues to the possible consequences for the relevant financial and business centers, their international competitiveness, and even the efficiency of their judicial and enforcement systems. If abuses such as Enron can happen in the United States without being detected earlier by a highly sophisticated auditing, financial, and institutional investor community and by a legal and supervisory system which to many Europeans seemed to reach too far, similar dangers are all the more real in Europe. This is why emulation and occasionally even straight imitation of the American reform euphoria and reform measures have stimulated European politicians and legislators in their respective countries as well as in the Council of the European Union to quick and far-reaching company and takeover law reform activities.

This acute, accident-driven reform movement met with a climate in the European Union that was favorable to change. In the European Union as well as in member states such as the UK, Germany, France, Italy, and others, company and takeover law reform has been going on for quite some time. The results have varied, though in the European Union they were much less impressive because of the ongoing federal-state struggle over legislative supremacy in general and also in the field of company and takeover law. European company law harmonization has been promoted by the European Commission for decades, but achievements were varied and showed regular ups and downs. Finally in 2001 the enactment of the Statute of the European Company marked the breakthrough in company law reform, though at the same time it raised the more difficult question of how to proceed from there. On the takeover front, the political struggle continued. For a short while it seemed that the European Council's common position of 21 June 1999 would be the breakthrough in takeover law reform. But, as is well known, on 4 July 2001 the European Parliament voted down the joint text of the Conciliation Committee by a spectacular, unprecedented 273 to 273 vote.

However, what at first seemed to be a disaster for the European Commission and the future of European company and takeover law has turned out to be a unique chance for reflection, for the development of new concepts, and for a promising new start. The European Commission agreed with the Parliament to mandate a High Level Group of Company Law Experts to look into possibilities of improvement and compromise on the 13th directive, but also more generally on the future of European company law. The expert group was deliberately kept small and non-political,[1] combining practical experience with legal expertise and theory and being fully independent of political pressures from any side. This was possible because the group was to make all recommendations in unanimous consensus without acting as representatives of their respective countries, while the European Commission carefully refrained from exercising any influence whatsoever on the outcome of the group's deliberations. The High Level Group presented its First Report on Issues Related to Takeover Bids on 10 January 2002.[2] Enron burst onto the scene while the group's work was going on, and the mandate of the group was extended by the European Commission following the ECOFIN Council meeting in Oviedo and agreed upon by the European Council meeting on 21 and 22 June in Seville to deal specifically with a number of key corporate governance issues. The Final Report of the High Level Group on 'A Modern Regulatory Framework for Company Law in Europe' was presented on 4 November 2002.[3] Both reports, which benefited from extensive consultation both in written submissions and in public hearings, garnered enormous attention in the financial press, in politics, and in legal and economic academia all over the European Union.

As to *takeover law*, the European Commission presented a new draft 13th directive on 2 October 2002[4] that followed many of the recommendations of the expert group but – for political reasons – deviated from it as to the level playing field and the reach of the proposed breakthrough rule. The fierce political struggle between the European Commission, the European Parliament, Germany, and other member states continued, the latter tying together – in varying coalitions along the lines of well-tried horse trading – completely different political issues, remote from any company or takeover law consideration. Though many observers had not thought it possible, on 22 December 2003 the directive was finally adopted by the member states following the Portuguese and Italian compromise

[1] The seven-member group consisted of *J. Winter* (The Netherlands) as chairman and *J. M. Garrido Garcia* (Spain), *K. J. Hopt* (Germany), *J. Rickford* (UK), *G. Rossi* (Italy), *J. Schans Christensen* (Denmark), and *J. Simon* (France).

[2] See infra Annex 2, p 2.

[3] See infra Annex 3, p 2.

[4] COM(2002) 534 final.

proposals.[5] The final version is a typical political solution that bridges over the two key controversial issues – the anti-frustration rule and the level playing field to be reached by the breakthrough rule – by a twofold option right of the member states and the companies themselves. It is hardly astonishing that the end result has been proclaimed by politicians, certain national businesses, and trade unions as politically wise and even liberal, though in reality it is protective against possible hostile takeovers. On the other side, Commissioner Bolkestein, national financial circles, and large multinational enterprises consider the introduction of the opt-outs or (legally more correct and even worse) opt-ins to be the wrong signal to the markets. In summary, however, there is wide agreement that, despite many missed opportunities for a truly European internal market, including the market for corporate control, the mere existence of a framework directive on takeovers is progress. After all, 'politics is the art of the possible.'

As to *company law*, the European Commission moved very quickly as well and presented its Action Plan on 'Modernising Company Law and Enhancing Corporate Governance in the European Union' on 21 May 2003.[6] In this plan the Commission followed closely the recommendations of the second report of the High Level Group with very few exceptions, such as not having the nomination committee of the board consist of a majority of independent directors. The responses received by the Commission in its consultation on the Action Plan[7] showed widespread support of the Commission initiative to modernize company law and enhance corporate governance. The vast majority of respondents considered this an essential step to restore confidence in capital markets and the EU economy, though of course the responses differed as to the specific issues. Therefore, it can be taken for granted that the Action Plan will remain as it stands, and indeed the Commission has already started working on coming up with concrete proposals. Obviously these proposals – mostly directives with some recommendations and occasional studies – will then be subjected to close legal, economic, and political scrutiny. But as the Action Plan puts it, this is the work of the future,

[5] Cf Council of the European Union, Proposal for a Directive on takeover bids, Brussels, 16 December 2003, 16116/03, CODEC 1818 DRS 108.

[6] Communication from the Commission to the Council and the European Parliament, Modernising Company Law and Enhancing Corporate Governance in the European Union – A Plan to Move Forward, Brussels, 21.5.2003, COM(2003) 284 final (Annex 1 in this volume). Background information on a number of corporate governance proposals in this plan is given by KJ Hopt 'Modern Company and Capital Market Problems: Improving European Corporate Governance after Enron' (2003) 3 Journal of Corporate Law Studies 221.

[7] Cf European Commission, Synthesis of the Responses to the Communication of the Commission to the Council and the European Parliament of 21 May 2003, 'Modernising Company Law and Enhancing Corporate Governance in the European Union – A Plan to Move Forward,' A Working Document of DG Internal Market, 15 November 2003.

more specifically 2003-2005 in the short term and 2006-2008 in the medium term.[8]

In November 2002, the second and fourth editors of this book, who have worked together closely since the early 1990s (KJ Hopt and E Wymeersch [eds] *European Insider Dealing* [London 1991], and idem *European Takeovers* [London 1992]), came up with the idea of organizing the first thorough academic discussion of the company and takeover law reforms as recommended by the High Level Group and envisaged by the subsequent Commission initiatives. The first editor, who had already been very helpful in organizing a previous conference in Siena on capital markets and company law, and the third editor, who was the chairman of the High Level Group, enthusiastically agreed to this plan. So this group of four started to assemble a team to discuss the reform measures from different angles: corporate and capital market law and legal policy, company and auditor practice, economic theory and European politics from the side of the European Commission, and others. Particular attention was given to the necessity of having not only Europeans discussing the future of company and takeover law in Europe, but also observers from outside Europe, in particular from the United States. Apart from intellectual and academic curiosity, the driving force for this venture was the aim to discuss thoroughly – and possibly to help solve – questions that may after all be crucial to the economic future of our respective countries on both sides of the Atlantic Ocean and possibly beyond.

This book goes back to an international conference held in Syracuse on May 29-30, 2003, which in turn was a follow-up to two other conferences: the 1997 symposium held at the Max Planck Institute for Foreign Private and Private International Law in Hamburg (KJ Hopt, H Kanda, M Roe, E Wymeersch and S Prigge [eds] *Comparative Corporate Governance: The State of the Art and Emerging Research* [OUP 1998]) and the symposium held in Siena in 2000 (KJ Hopt and E Wymeersch [eds] *Capital Markets and Company Law* [OUP 2003]). Corporate governance – both within the company and, outside the company, at the level of the market of corporate control – and particularly comparative corporate governance, remained the key issue in all three conferences and ensuing books. This is hardly astonishing given the keen international focus on corporate governance. Sometimes one even gets the impression that corporate governance has become an obsession for legislators who want to quickly be doing, or to appear to be doing, anything at all in response to the pressure of the public and the press. It is all the more necessary to accompany this reform rush by more considerate, independent academic thought and scrutiny.

[8] Cf Annex 1 of the Action Plan, infra Annex 1, 24-26. Long-term action, ie, from 2009 onwards, concerns only capital maintenance, ie, the possible introduction in the Second Company Law Directive of an alternative regime, depending on the outcome of the feasibility study.

The aim of this book, while looking at concrete company law, takeover, and corporate governance problems, is more long-term, namely to analyze reform problems and reform options on the basis of international experiences in three continents – Europe, North America, and Australia – from a legal as well as an economic perspective. This is demonstrated in the three parts and 23 contributions to the book: seven contributions to part I, A Framework for a Modern Company and Takeover Law in Europe: Common Regulatory Issues; eight contributions to part II, Corporate Governance: Inside the Corporation; and another eight to part III, Corporate Governance: The Market for Corporate Control and the Level Playing Field. As a more temporal result, we are proud to present this book (to the best of our knowledge) as the first monograph to discuss the Action Plan of the European Commission of May 2003 in a comprehensive, transatlantic, and interdisciplinary way. We hope that it will be a useful tool for the European Commission, the European Parliament, and all those in academia, politics, and business who will work on this plan and on company and takeover law reform during the coming years.

Special thanks are due to the first editor, who was instrumental in organizing the Syracuse Conference; to *Sofie Dejonghe* of Ghent University Financial Law Institute for coordinating the organization of the conference and the editing of the present volume; to *Alexander Hellgardt* and *Patrick C. Leyens* for helping with the case register and the index and in particular to *Ingeborg Stahl,* all three at the Hamburg Max Planck Institute for Foreign Private and Private International Law, who converted the manuscripts and documents into a print-ready format. The fourth editor would also like to thank the Max Planck Gesellschaft for allowing him to fund this further conference with the proceeds of the Max Planck Award for International Cooperation 1998 (see reference in the Siena book).

December 2003

G. Ferrarini, Genova, *K. J. Hopt,* Hamburg
J. Winter, Amsterdam, *E. Wymeersch,* Ghent

Contents

The Contributors

Marco Becht

Marco Becht is a Professor of Finance and Economics at Université Libre de Bruxelles (ULB), a Resident Fellow at the European Center for Advanced Research in Economics and Statistics (ECARES) at ULB and the Executive Director of the European Corporate Governance Institute (ECGI). He teaches at the ULB and, in 2003, at the Said Business School (University of Oxford). Becht graduated from the London School of Economics and Political Science (LSE) and holds a Ph.D. in economics from the European University Institute (EUI). Professor Becht is a member of the European Academic Council of Standard & Poor's, the scientific adviser of the corporate governance committee of APCIMS (Association of Private Client Investment Managers and Stockbrokers), a member of the Belgian Corporate Governance Commission and a board member of the Belgian Foundation of Directors. He has given expert briefings on corporate governance to the Group of Economic Analysis of the President of the European Commission, the senior management of Alcatel, the clients of Hermes Pension Management Ltd., the Euro 50 Group, the Italian Securities Regulator (CONSOB), the OECD, the World Bank and the German Corporate Governance Roundtable, among other. His research currently focuses on empirical corporate finance, corporate governance and business history.

Mike Burkart

Mike Burkart is Associate Professor at the Stockholm School of Economics, joint appointment by the Department of Finance and by the Stockholm Institute of Transition Economics (SITE). He is a research affiliate of the Centre for Economic Policy Research (CEPR) and an associate member of the Financial Markets Group at the London School of Economics. He received a Ph.D in economics from London University (London School of Economics). His research interests are in theoretical corporate finance, and in particular in financial contracting and corporate governance.

John C. Coates IV

John C. Coates IV is Professor of Law at Harvard Law School. He joined the HLS faculty in 1997 after private practice at the New York law firm of Wachtell, Lipton, Rosen & Katz, where he was a partner specializing in mergers and acquisitions, corporate and securities law, and the regulation of financial institutions. He teaches courses on Mergers & Acquisitions, Financial Institutions Regulation, and Corporations. He is a frequent panellist and speaker on M&A, is a consultant to active participants in the M&A market, and was recently invited to join the Legal Advisory Committee of the New York Stock Exchange.

John C. Coffee, Jr.

Professor John C. Coffee, Jr. is the Adolf A. Berle Professor of Law at Columbia University Law School and Director of its Center on Corporate Governance. He is a Fellow at the American Academy of Arts and Sciences, and for the last six years he has been listed by the National Law Journal as among its '100 Most Influential Lawyers in America'. His specialities include complex litigation, corporate governance, securities regulation, and 'white collar crime'. Professor Coffee has been a member of the Legal Advisory Board to the New York Stock Exchange, the Legal Advisory Board of the NASD, the Market Regulation Committee of the NASD, and is currently a member of the Economic Advisory Board to Nasdaq. He served as a Reporter to the American Law Institute for its Principles of Corporate Governance: Analysis and Recommendations, was a member of the SEC's Advisory Committee on the Capital Formation and Regulatory Processes, and served as chairperson of the Section on Business Associations of the Association of American Law Schools. He is the author or editor of several widely used casebooks on corporations, securities regulation, takeovers, and business organization and finance, including Coffee and Seligman, Cases and Materials on Securities Regulation (9th ed. 2000) and Klein and Coffee, Business Organization and Finance (8th ed. 2000). Professor Coffee has also been a visiting professor of law at Harvard, Stanford, Michigan and Virginia law schools and at several foreign law schools and began his teaching career at Georgetown University Law Center. Before entering academia, he practiced corporate law as an associate with the firm of Cravath, Swaine & Moore in New York City. He is a graduate of the Yale Law School and Amherst College.

Kimberley Crook

Kimberley Crook is a senior project manager on the staff of the International Accounting Standards Board. She joined the IASB staff in July 2001, and is assigned to the share-based payment project. Previously, Kimberley was a project director at the UK Accounting Standards Board. She is the principal author of the G4+1 Discussion Paper, *Accounting for Share-based Payment*, published by the ASB, IASC and other G4+1 member bodies in July 2000. Kimberley was seconded to the ASB from PricewaterhouseCoopers in London, where she was a senior manager in the UK national accounting technical department. Kimberley is originally from New Zealand, where she qualified as a chartered accountant. She has a Master of Commerce (Honours) degree in accounting from Canterbury University, NZ.

Paul Davies

Paul L. Davies is Cassel Professor of Commercial Law at the London School of Economics and Political Science. He is a graduate of the University of Oxford (1966) and holds Masters' degrees from the London School of Economics (1968) and Yale Law School (1969). After a short initial teaching spell at the University of Warwick, he joined the Law Faculty of the University of Oxford and eventually became Professor of the Law of the Enterprise. He took up his present post at LSE in 1998. He has held visiting positions at Yale and the universities of Bordeaux, Paris, Bonn and a number of universities in South Africa. He is a Fellow of the British Academy. He is the author of *Introduction to Company Law* (2002) and the editor of the 6th and 7th edition of *Gower's Principles of Modern Company Law* and one of the editors of *Palmer's Company Law*. He was a member of the Steering Group of Company Law Review carried out under the auspices of the Department of Trade and Industry in the UK between 1998 and 2001.

Werner F. Ebke

Werner F. Ebke holds the Business and Tax Law Chair at the University of Konstanz School of Law in Konstanz, Germany, and is the Global Professor of Law at the New York University School of Law in New York. Professor Ebke graduated from the University of Muenster School of Law in Muenster, Germany, where he also received his doctorate in law (Dr. iur.) and his post-doctorate degree of Habilitation. The University of California at Berkeley School of Law (Boalt Hall) awarded him the degree of Master of Laws. Dr. Ebke has published 15 books and over 200 law review articles, book chapters, case notes and book reviews in Europe, the United States, Japan, Mexico and South Africa. He is a member of the Bar of the State of New York and several federal bars. He is also a member of the American Law Institute in Washington, D.C.

Luca Enriques

Luca Enriques is Professor of Business Law at the University of Bologna Faculty of Law, where he teaches courses on securities regulation, financial institutions and corporate governance. Previously, he worked for the Bank of Italy in Rome. His research focuses on corporate law, corporate governance and securities regulation. He received an S.J.D. from Bocconi University, Milan, and obtained an LL.M. from Harvard Law School. He was twice John Olin Fellow at the Cornell Law School and is now an ECGI Research Associate. He advises the Italian Ministry of Economy and Finance on banking and securities law issues and is an independent consultant to Cleary, Gottlieb, Steen, & Hamilton in Rome.

Eilís Ferran

Eilís Ferran is a Reader in Corporate Law and Financial Regulation at the University of Cambridge. Between 1999 and 2003 she was the Director of its Centre for Corporate and Commercial Law (3CL). She is a graduate of Cambridge University (BA, 1983 PhD, 1991) and a qualified solicitor (admitted to the Roll, 1986). She is the author of numerous books and articles on corporate and financial law and is the Editor of the Journal of Corporate Law Studies. She was an adviser to the UK Parliament on the Financial Services and Markets Act 2000 and has provided advice to the British Department of Trade and Industry on the reform of company law.

Guido Ferrarini

Guido Ferrarini graduated from the Genoa Law School in 1972, and obtained an LL.M. from Yale Law School in 1978. He is Professor of Law at the University of Genoa and Director, Centre for Law and Finance. He is Visiting Professor at Columbia Law School (Autumn 2003) and at the University College London (1998 – present). He is the author of various books and articles in the fields of financial law, corporate law, and business law. He is Vice-Chairman of the European Corporate Governance Institute (ECGI), Brussels, member of the Board of Trustees of the International Accounting Standards Committee (IASC), London, member of the Boards of Directors of Autostrade and Telecom Italia and Chairman of TLX (a new Italian investment exchange). He is co-editor of the Rivista delle Società and editor of ECGI Law Working Papers.

Allen Ferrell

Allen Ferrell is a law professor at Harvard Law School. He is also a member of the NASD's Board of Economic Advisors. His research is in the areas of capital market regulation and corporate law. He received his J.D. from Harvard Law School and is a PhD candidate in economics at MIT. His web page, containing his working papers, can be found at http://www.law.harvard.edu/faculty/fferrell/.

Holger Fleischer

Holger Fleischer was born in 1965. He studied law and economic science at the University of Cologne and the University of Ann Arbor in Michigan. His research led him to Brussels (1995), Milan (1996), Paris (1997), London (1998 and 2001) and Valencia (2001). He has taught at the University of Cologne, Bayreuth University, the University of Göttingen and the Friedrich – Wilhelms University of Bonn. Since august 2003, he is director of the Tax Law Institute of the Friedrich – Wilhelms University of Bonn.

Jeffrey N. Gordon

Jeffrey N. Gordon is the Alfred W. Bressler Professor of Law and Co-Director of the Center for Law and Economic Studies at the Columbia Law School, where he teaches and writes on corporate law, mergers and acquisitions, comparative corporate governance, and a course on regulation. Prof. Gordon is a recipient of an Alfred W. Sloan Foundation in personam grant for an ongoing project on the theory and empirics of shareholder value as a basis for corporate governance. His recent publications in professional journals include: What Enron Means for the Management and Control of the Modern Business Corporation; Governance Failures of the Enron Board and the New Information Order of Sarbanes-Oxley; and (with Ronald Gilson) Controlling Controlling Shareholders. He is the co-editor (with Mark Roe) of the forthcoming book, Convergence and Persistence in Corporate Governance.

Sascha Haller

Sascha Haller studied economics and business administration from 1989 to 1994 at the University of Basel, Switzerland. After acquiring a diploma, he started his Ph.D studies at Swiss Central Bank's 'Study Center Gerzensee' and at the University of Basel. In 1996 he joined the institute of Prof. Martin Hellwig at the University of Mannheim. His main fields of research are the financial structure of the firm under incomplete information and bargaining theory. Besides lecturing he also co-ordinates the Center for Doctoral Studies in Economics and Management (CDSEM) at the University of Mannheim.

Gérard Hertig

Gérard Hertig is Professor of Law and Economics at the Swiss Federal Institute of Technology (ETH Zurich), where he is responsible professor for the post-graduate program 'Intellectual Property'. He teaches intellectual property and specializes in corporate law and financial services. He was previously Professor of Administrative Law and Director of the Centre d'Etudes Juridiques Européennes at the University of Geneva Law School (1987-1995). He served as Visiting Professor at UCL (Louvain), ULB (Brussels), University of Liège, Collège of Europe, University of Tokyo and practiced law as a member of the Geneva bar. Recent publications include (in English): *The Anatomy of Corporate Law, A Comparative and Functional Approach*, with Reinier Kraakman et al. (Oxford University Press, forthcoming 2004); 'Four Predictions about the Future of EU Securities Regulation', with Ruben Lee, 3 *Journal of Corporate Law Studies* 359 (2003); 'Regulatory Competition for EU Financial Services', in Esty/Geradin (eds.), *Regulatory Competition and Economic Integration* (Oxford University Press 2001) 218; 'Western Europe's Corporate Governance Dilemma', in Baums/Hopt/Horn (eds.), *Corporations, Capital Markets and Business in the Law* (Kluwer Law International 2000), 265; see also www.hertig.ethz.ch.

Jennifer Hill

Jennifer Hill is Professor of Corporate Law at Sydney Law School, Australia. She also coordinates the Sydney Law School's International Faculty in Corporate, Securities and Finance Law Program. She has been a Visiting Professor in the US on several occasions, at Cornell University (1994), University of Virginia (1998), the University of Texas at Austin (1999) and Vanderbilt University Law School (2003). Professor Hill is a member of the Corporations & Markets Advisory Committee (CAMAC) Legal Committee, which advises the Australian federal government on law reform, and the Law Council of Australia, Corporations Law Committee. She has published widely on topics in corporate theory, corporate liability and comparative corporate governance.

Klaus J. Hopt

Klaus J. Hopt is Professor of law and Director at the Max Planck Institute for Foreign Private and Private International Law, Hamburg/Germany. 1974-95 he was professor of law in Tuebingen, Florence/Italy, Bern/Switzerland, Munich. – *Professional:* Judge Court of Appeals Stuttgart 1981-85; member of the German Takeover Commission 1995-2001, of the High Level Group of Company Law Experts, European Commission 2001-02; vice-president of the German Research Foundation (Deutsche Forschungsgemeinschaft) 2002-; expert for the German Parliament, Central Bank and Constitutional Court, the European Commission and World Bank. – *Visiting prof.:* U. of Pennsylvania 1979, EUI Florence 1981, 1983, Paris I (Sorbonne) 1987, Kyoto U. 1988, U. Libre de Bruxelles 1990, Geneva 1991, Tokyo U. 1991, U. of Chicago 1994, NYU 1999, Harvard 2002, Tilburg/The Netherlands 2003, Paris II (Panthéon-Assas) 2003. – *Recent publications:* Baumbach-Hopt, Handelsgesetzbuch 31st ed. 2003 (together with Merkt); *(Co-)Ed.*: Comparative Corporate Governance 1998 and Capital Markets and Company Law 2003 (both Oxford U.P.); RabelsZ, Zeitschrift für Unternehmens- und Gesellschaftsrecht (ZGR), Int.&Comp. Corp.L.J. *Honors:* Dr. iur. h.c. mult. (U. Libre de Bruxelles 1997, U. Catholique de Louvain 1997, U. de Paris V René Descartes 2000).

Reinier Kraakman

Reinier Kraakman is the Ezra Ripley Thayer Professor of Law at Harvard Law School. He teaches corporate law and corporate finance, and writes widely on topics in corporate liability, corporate governance, and organizational law.

Joseph A. McCahery

Joseph A. McCahery is Professor of International Business Law at Tilburg University Faculty of Law, Research Fellow at the Tilburg Center of Law and Economics, and Research Associate at the European Corporate Governance Institute (Brussels). He holds a visiting appointment at the Leiden University Faculty of Law. Previously, he held an appointment at Warwick University, where he also received a Ph.D. degree. He was also a law clerk for Judge Nathaniel R. Jones of the US Court of Appeals for the Sixth Circuit. His research interests are corporate control, corporate finance, European corporate law, the political economy of federalism, and international banking and securities regulation. He has written extensively on corporate law, corporate governance, securities, and regulation.

Hanno Merkt

Hanno Merkt was born 1960. – *Academic*: Studies in Law, History, and Spanish Philology at the Universities of Bonn, Santiago de Compostela, Münster, Chicago and Hamburg – Dr. iur. University of Münster 1989 – LL.M. University of Chicago 1989 – Research Fellow Max-Planck-Institute for Foreign and International Private Law Hamburg 1990-1996 – Habilitation University of Hamburg 2000 – Professor of Law University of Regensburg 2000 (Lehrstuhlvertretung) – Alfried-Krupp-Chair for German, European and International Private and Business Law, Bucerius Law School Hamburg 2000-2003 – Since 2003 Professor of Law and Director of the Institute for Foreign and International Private Law Albert-Ludwigs-University of Freiburg. *Professional*: Attorney-at-Law (New York Bar) since 1990 – Attorney-at-Law (Hamburg) 1993-2003 – expert amongst others for the German Parliament (Finance Committee) and various German Ministries (Finance, Justice, Economics), Member of the German Takeover Council. *Honours*: Faculty Prize University of Münster 1989; University Prize of the Deutsches Aktieninstitut e.V. 2000; Legal Book of the Year 2001 (Habilitation).

Niamh Moloney

Niamh Moloney (LL.B, Trinity College Dublin (1992), LL.M, Harvard (1993)) is Reader in Law at the School of Law, Queen's University. She is the author of the first book on EC capital markets and investment services law (*EC Securities Regulation*, OUP (2002)) and has published numerous articles on this subject. She is a Research Associate of the European Corporate Governance Institute.

Peter O. Mülbert

Peter O. Mülbert is Professor of Civil, Corporate and Banking Law at the University of Mainz. Previously, he was Professor of Law at the Universities of Heidelberg and Trier. He is Director of the Center for Financial Law at Mainz University and Research Associate of the European Corporate Governance Institute.

Fausto Panunzi

Fausto Panunzi is Professor of Economics at the University of Bologna. He is a research affiliate of the Centre for Economic Policy Research (CEPR) and a research associate of the European Corporate Governance Institute. He received a Ph.D in economics from the Massachusetts Institute of Technology. His research interests are in corporate finance, corporate governance and the theory of the firm.

Michel Prada

Michel Prada studied law, economics and political science in the Universities of Bordeaux and Paris from 1957 to 1962 and graduated from the Ecole Nationale d'Administration in 1966. He was Directeur de la Comptabilité Publique from 1978 to 1985, Directeur du budget from 1986 to 1988 and Président du Crédit d'Equipement des Petites et Moyennes Entreprises 1988 to 1995. He was Président de la Commission des Opérations de Bourse from 1995 to 2002, Chairman of the Executive Committee of the International Organisation of Securities Commissions (IOSCO) from 1996 to 1998 and Chairman of the technical Committee of IOSCO from 1998 to 2000. He is now Chairman of the Inspection Générale des Finances. He has been appointed President of the new Autorité de Marches Financiers.

Luc Renneboog

Luc Renneboog graduated from the Catholic University of Leuven with degrees in management engineering (M.Sc.) and in philosophy (BA), from the University of Chicago with an MBA, and from the London Business School with a Ph.D. in financial economics. He is currently Associate Professor at the Department of Finance of Tilburg University, and a research fellow at the CentER for Economic Research (Tilburg) and Tilburg Law and Economics Center (TILEC). He is also a research associate of the the European Corporate Governance Institute (Brussels). He held appointments at the Catholic University of Leuven and Oxford University, and visiting appointments at London Business School, European University Institute (Florence), HEC (Paris) Venice University, and CUNEF (Madrid). He has published in the Journal of Financial Intermediation, Journal of Corporate Finance, Journal of Law and Economics, Journal of Banking and Finance, Journal of Law, Economics and Organization, Cambridge Journal of Economics, European Financial Management, and others. For Oxford University Press, he co-edited 'Corporate Governance Regimes: convergence and diversity', and 'Venture capital contracting and the valuation of high technology firms'. In addition, he published the book 'Dividend policy and corporate governance', also with OUP. His research interests are corporate finance, corporate governance, dividend policy, insider trading, financial distress, law and economics, and the economics of art.

Peer Ritter

Peer Ritter graduated in Economics from the London School of Economics and the Catholic University of Leuven. After having been a researcher at the University of Mannheim, he was research fellow at the Centre for European Policy Studies, Brussels, where he began work on the takeover-bids directive. In September 2002 he joined the Group of Policy Advisers of the European Commission and now works in its Directorate-General for Economic and Financial Affairs.

Jaap Winter

Jaap Winter is partner at the Dutch law firm De Brauw Blackstone Westbroek and professor of International Company Law at the Erasmus University of Rotterdam. He is the chairman of the High Level Group of Company Law Experts set up by the EU Commission that has produced the reports in 2002 on EU regulation of Takeover Bids and a Modern Regulatory Framework for Company Law in Europe [that are debated in this book]. He is a member of the Corporate Governance Committee of the Netherlands chaired by Mr. Tabaksblat that has prepared a revised corporate governance code. He is also a member of the Advisory Board on Corporate Governance of the World Economic Forum.

Eddy Wymeersch

At present, Chairman of the Banking Finance and Insurance Commission, Belgium; co-chair of the CESR-ECB, working on clearing and settlement; member of the Committees of European Securities Regulators (CESR). Part time Professor of Commercial Law, University of Ghent, Belgium, where he is teaching company law, securities regulation and banking law. Formerly Consultant to EC Commission, World Bank and IFC; member of the corporate governance commission of the Brussels Stock Exchange and chairman of the

SLIM working party (Simpler Legislation for the Internal Market) on the 1st and 2nd directive. He also acted as adviser to the Belgian Government, i.a. as member of the Legislative Branch of the Council of State. He was a member of the board of the National Bank of Belgium and the Belgian Corporate Governance Commission. He was Chairman of the Board of Brussels International Airport Company (BIAC) and adviser on governance issues to several listed Belgian companies. He has published extensively on securities regulation, companies law, especially groups of companies, and corporate governance in the Belgian, European and comparative perspective.

Part I:

A Framework for a Modern Company and Takeover Law in Europe: Common Regulatory Issues

Chapter 1: The Need for a Regulatory Framework

EU Company Law at the Cross-Roads

JAAP WINTER

A. Introduction

When the High Level Group of Company Law Experts (the 'High Level Group') started its work in September 2001, the outlook for EU Company Law was rather bleak. Decades ago, the European Community had started out on an ambitious project to harmonise key areas of the company laws of Member States. The basis for this harmonization process was the freedom of establishment. It was felt that the diversity of national company laws would frustrate the goal of an optimally functioning internal market. It would also distort competition and lead to a race-to-the-bottom: Member States would be encouraged to create as flexible as possible company law, ignoring an appropriate level of protection of shareholders and creditors, in order to attract companies to incorporate in their jurisdictions.[1] The EC Treaty specifically instructed the Council and the Commission to co-ordinate to the extent necessary the safeguards which, for the protection of the interests of members and others, are required by Member States of companies or firms … with a view to making such safeguards equivalent throughout the Community, art. 44 (2) (g). Nine company law directives have come into force since, but the core of company law is still not harmonised. The 5th Directive was first drafted in 1972 to deal with the structure of the company and the powers of the board and the general meeting. But Member States fundamentally disagree on these matters and the 5th Directive has now formally been abandoned. This fate is

[1] V Edwards *EC Company Law* (OUP Oxford 1999) 3.

shared by the draft 9th Directive on group relations, which was based on the German explicit legislation on groups of companies, but was rejected by almost all other Member States. Drafts for the 10th Directive on cross-border mergers and the 14th Directive on cross-border transfers of seat have not resulted into a final text after years of deliberation and disagreement.[2] The key stumbling block is the German insistence on a form of labour co-determination. The same issue held the European Company Statute hostage for decades, until surprisingly agreement was reached on an intriguing Statute and accompanying directive on employee involvement. Finally, the 13th Directive on takeover bids had, after negotiations for more than a decade, reached a rocky stage of agreement between Member States when in early July 2001 the EU Parliament with an unprecedented blocking vote rejected the proposal.

Many felt at that time that the development of EU company law on the basis of the harmonization approach taken in the EC Treaty had come to a grinding halt. There was no sense of direction for the future. This was the background and rationale for setting up the High Level Group. Our mandate was to make recommendations on a modern regulatory framework for company law in Europe, basically to point out a new direction for the future development of company law in the European Union.

During the time and since we worked on our reports other developments influencing the direction of EU company law that were already visible before we started have became more poignant. Three developments have been key: the European Company Statute that was finally adopted on October 8, 2001, the case law of the European Court of Justice on the implications of the freedom of establishment, and the growing impact of capital markets law on company law. All three developments have shaped the work of the High Level Group and are likely to continue to shape the future direction of company law in Europe. I will review these three developments before turning to our reports and what has or may come of them.

B. The European Company Statute

The key rationale for the European Company (SE) was to a large extent the same as the basic reason for harmonization of the company laws of Member States. The SE was intended as a legal form, which could facilitate cross-border cooperation and integration of business in Europe. The SE would do this by offering a legal framework that would be identical in all member states. This would enhance the confidence of businessmen, shareholders and others to engage in cross-border economic activities. Paragraphs 3 and 7 of the Preamble of the European Com-

[2] cf KJ Hopt 'Takeover regulation in Europe – The battle for the 13th directive on takeovers' (2002) 15 Australian Journal of Corporate Law 6.

pany Statute still echo this purpose of the SE: to overcome the psychological difficulties when companies from different Member States engage in restructuring and co-operation and to facilitate the incorporation and management of companies with a European dimension without the impediments of having to deal with differences in company law.

The trouble with the Statute as it has been finally agreed[3] is that it is precisely not doing that. There is no uniform set of rules applying to the SE, as Member States were unable to agree to one set of rules. Instead, after more than thirty years of negotiation the Member States agreed that the SE would only partly be governed by substantive rules in the Statute but that the vast majority of company law matters would be governed by the national company law of the Member State where the SE would be incorporated. As of October 2004 we will witness the incorporation of 15, and shortly after, 25 different types of SEs in the Member States. But this inability to agree on the core rules applicable to the SE has created an intriguing legal form. The SE by inability rather than design deviates substantially from anything the European company law legislator has created so far and in particular from the thrust to harmonise European company law to equivalent standards. The SE offers a system of floodgates, which allows the import and export of national company law between the Member States. There are four such floodgates:

I. Applicable law

An SE is governed by a cascade of rules: first of all by the provisions of the Statute and by the provisions in its articles of association where the Statute allows deviation, then, for matters not provided for in the Statute, by the specific Act each Member State must adopt to implement the Statute, by the general rules applying to public companies in the Member State where the SE has its registered office and finally by its articles of association where the national rules allow deviation, art. 9 Statute. This cascade and the lack of substantive company law rules in the Statute itself will bring on that SEs are primarily governed by the various national company laws. Member States that wish to attract SEs to their jurisdiction are likely to create an attractive, facilitating regime for SEs. In doing so they will have to take account of art. 10 of the Statute, providing that the SE is treated in each Member State as a public company. The purpose of this provision is not altogether clear, but is probably related to par. 5 of the Preamble stating that SEs and national public companies should not be discriminated through unfounded different treatment. This addresses a concern that SEs would be made

[3] Council Regulation (2001/2157/EC) of 8 October 2001, [2001] OJ L 294/1, supplemented by Council Directive (2001/86/EC) of 8 October 2001 with regard to the involvement of employees, [2001] OJ L 294/22.

subject to less attractive rules than national public companies, but the wording of both art. 10 and Preamble 5 is neutral, works both ways. If Member States wish to offer an attractive regime for SEs in their jurisdiction, they may have to offer the same attractiveness to their national companies. If this is the correct understanding of art. 10, then the SE may give an incentive to Member states to review their company laws more generally with a view to making them attractive and flexible, at odds with the original harmonization focus in the Treaty.

II. Transfer of seat, cross-border merger and transformation

The main attractions of the SE are that the SE can be created by a cross-border merger and that it can transfer its seat to another Member State. When a SE transfers its seat to another Member State, it will become subject to the company law of the host state, both its general rules as applicable to public companies and the specific SE legislation. The articles of association of the SE will usually contain a number of provisions that relate to specific elements of the company law of the Member State of incorporation but may be unfamiliar in the company law of the host Member State. It is likely that provisions that contravene company law in the host Member State can no longer be applied and may have to be replaced. But there is no compatibility test before the SE can transfer its seat. Uncertainty will often remain. To the extent the company law of the host Member State is more flexible, with little mandatory provisions, the chances increase that it can accommodate unfamiliar foreign company law mechanisms and as a result become a more attractive jurisdiction for SEs to transfer their seats to. This will apply similarly to cross-border mergers and transformations. These mechanisms will also infuse a certain level of competition between Member States with a view to making their company laws more attractive.

III. Choice between the one-tier and two-tier board system

Europe has never reached agreement on whether a one-tier board system is superior over a two-tier board system or vice versa. This was one of the main problems during the negotiations on the SE. The solution in the Statute was to offer a choice, not to Member States but to users of the SE. Each Member State must offer to SEs to be incorporated in its jurisdiction the choice between a one-tier and a two-tier board. It can provide for this choice either in the specific legislation for the SE or in the general company law applicable to public companies. At least for SEs but possibly for all public companies we will see a more direct competition in each Member State between the two types of board structures. This will give us a chance to learn more about the relative attractions of both systems for which we have little empirical evidence today.

IV. Rules for participation of employees in the managing or supervising body

The Directive accompanying the Statute deals with the information and consultation of employees and their participation in the managing or supervising body of the SE. The latter element is the more troublesome as the views of Member States deviate widely here. The solution provided for in the Directive is very complex and at some crucial places inconsistent. The Directive makes a commendable effort to leave the regime to be applied to the choice of management and employees negotiating on the system for employee involvement. Only if no agreement is reached reference provisions apply. Theoretically a SE incorporated in Germany could elect to have a one-tier board system with a Swedish form of employee participation on the board. The result of the reference rules may also be that a participation regime must be applied, which is unfamiliar to the Member State in which the SE is incorporated. But systems of employee participation do not operate in a vacuum, they are interwoven with other elements of national company law, labour law and the wider rules of civil or common law and laws of procedure. This factor will in practical reality limit the free choice of participation regime that the Directive appears to be offering and may form a serious obstacle for the formation of SEs, at least where companies involved in such formation are subject to various national participation regimes.

The floodgates the SE Statute and the Directive thus offer are complex and in most cases not considered carefully by the European legislator. But they are there and put a certain amount of pressure on Member States to create an attractive, facilitating regime for SEs incorporated in or transferred to their jurisdiction. Unavoidably some Member States will be sensitive to the potential for attracting companies from other Member States. That, by the very nature of the competition accidentally incorporated in the SE Statute, may be enough to force other Member States to follow the example, even though they would not otherwise be inclined to do so.[4]

C. The European Court of Justice

In a groundbreaking series of judgements the ECJ has shown that the freedom of establishment guaranteed by the Treaty not only provides a justification to harmonise company law, but offers much more. In the *Centros* case[5] the Court ruled, building on *Segers*,[6] that companies formed in accordance with the law of a member state and having their registered office, central administration or princi-

[4] J Winter 'De Europese Vennootschap als sluis voor in- en uitvoer van vennootschapsrecht' (2002) 41 Nederlands Juristen Blad 2034-2040.

[5] ECJ C-212/97 [9.3.1999].

[6] ECJ C-79/85 [1986].

pal place of business within the Community are entitled to carry on their business in another member state through an agency, branch or subsidiary. 'The mere fact that a national of a Member State who wishes to set up a company chooses to form it in the Member State whose rules of company law seem to him the least restrictive and to set up branches in other member states cannot, in itself, constitute an abuse of the right of establishment', the Court ruled. Neither does the fact that the company does not conduct any business in the Member State in which it has its registered office and pursues its activities only in the Member State where its branch is established. This clearly indicated a different approach from the one the Treaty writers had in mind when complementing the freedom of establishment with the harmonization process. The Court leaves open that there may be justifications for obstacles to the freedom of establishment, either as set forth in art. 46 of the Treaty (to the extent justified on grounds of public policy, public security or public health) or on the ground of an imperative requirement in the general interest, in which case they are to be applied in a non-discriminatory manner, to be suitable for securing the attainment of the objective which they pursue and do not go beyond what is necessary in order to attain the objective. The refusal by Denmark to register a UK limited company however did not satisfy these tests: the rationale for imposing minimum capital rules does not constitute such an imperative requirement; the refusal to register is not such as to attain the objective of protecting creditors since, if the company would have conducted business in the UK, its branch would have been registered in Denmark, even though Danish creditors might have been equally exposed to risk; and it is possible to adopt measures which are less restrictive, or which interfere less with fundamental freedoms.

The Centros case was followed by the *Überseering* case, in which the Court ruled one day after the publication of the final report of the High Level Group.[7] In this judgement, the Court, following the substance and order of arguments laid out in the Centros case, ruled that a company incorporated in the Netherlands with only German shareholders, cannot be denied legal standing in German courts and cannot be required to re-register as a German company solely because it has moved its real seat from the Netherlands to Germany. In just a few lines the Court quashed the lengthy arguments put forward by Germany and some other member states why it would be justified to impose such a rigid effect on a company that has moved its real seat from the Member State of incorporation to another Member State. The judgement leaves open that other, less rigid measures imposed on companies that have moved their real seat to another Member State could, under circumstances, be justified. Such measures have been reviewed by the Court in the most recent episode of the freedom of establishment-sequel, the *Inspire Art* case.[8] This case involves an English limited company, which has set up a branch

[7] ECJ C-208/00 [5.11.2002] (Annex 3 in this volume).

[8] ECJ C-167/01 [30.9.2003].

in the Netherlands without engaging in activities in the UK. A specific Dutch Act imposes various obligations on a company with legal personality formed under laws other than the laws of the Netherlands, which carries on its activities entirely or almost entirely in the Netherlands and has no real connection with the state in which jurisdiction it was incorporated (such companies indicated as 'formally foreign companies'). Such obligations include additional obligations concerning the company's registration in the commercial register; an indication of the status of formally foreign company in all the documents produced by it; a minimum share capital equal to that required of Dutch limited companies (currently EUR 18,000); the drawing up, production and publication of annual documents. Penalties are imposed, notably personal liability of directors, in case of non-compliance with these provisions. A formally foreign company therefore is registered in the Netherlands (different from Denmark in Centros) and has legal standing in the Netherlands (different from Germany in Überseering), but is subject to certain provisions of Dutch company law. The Court rules that certain disclosure requirements under the Dutch Act are contrary to the disclosure requirements for branches as laid down in the 11th Directive, which is exhaustive, and that there is no justification possible for such extended requirements. The minimum capital requirement and the penalty of personal liability of directors of the company in case of non-compliance are reviewed in the light of the freedom of establishment. The Court rules that these elements of the Dutch Act have the effect of impeding the exercise by formally foreign companies of the freedom of establishment. The reasons for which the company was formed in the other Member State and the fact that it carries on its activities exclusively or almost exclusively in the Member State of establishment, do not deprive it of the right to invoke the freedom of establishment guaranteed by the Treaty, save where abuse is established on a case-by-case basis. The Court then states that the impediments to the freedom of establishment are not justified on grounds within the ambit of art. 46 of the Treaty and that they fail the four-legged test the Court applies to see whether imperative requirements in the general interest justify them. The grounds put forward by the Netherlands to justify the impediments were the protection of creditors, combating improper recourse to freedom of establishment, safeguarding fairness in business dealings and efficiency of tax inspections. The Court, repeating much of its reasoning in Centros discards them all. Exit the special Dutch Act, at least to the extent applied to companies with their registered office in a EU Member State.

The effect of this case law of the ECJ is potentially far-reaching. Under art. 46 of the Treaty and the four-legged test for imperative reasons in the general interest, there appears to be very little, if anything at all, a Member State can do to stop a company incorporated in another Member State to engage exclusively in business within the first Member State's jurisdiction: no refusal of registration, no denial of legal standing, no imposition of key elements of its own company law. This creates a clear competitive advantage for the Member State of which the company law is less restrictive. Nobody wishing to start a small business in for example the Netherlands or Germany needs to set up a Dutch or German company subject to strict minimum capital and capital maintenance rules and relatively severe penalties for directors for non-compliance; one can incorporate an English limited company and do business in the Netherlands or Germany without these burdens. It is to be expected that at least for this lower end of the market for incorporations, a distinct level of competition between the company laws of Member States will follow. Even before the Inspire Art case the Dutch government had already indicated that it would review the Dutch legislation for limited companies with a view to making it more flexible and less restrictive.[9] But the effect of this case law does not have to be limited to smaller companies. The freedom of establishment is not restricted to the lower end of the market for incorporations. It would also apply for example to two companies setting up a substantial joint venture company under the less restrictive company law of one Member State but with its central administration and business activities in another Member State. For that matter, such a joint venture company could take the form of an SE. Art. 7 of the European Company Statute now provides that the SE must have its registered office in the same Member State as its central place of management, and thus forces an SE to transfer its legal seat to another Member State when it moves its central administration there. This provision appears to be directly contravening the freedom of establishment as construed by the Court. This should be clarified beyond doubt by simply striking this element of art. 7 from the Statute.

D. Capital Market Law and Company Law

While the development of company law at EU level has faltered during the last decade, the development of EU capital market law has catapulted. The main driver for this development has been the Financial Services Action Plan (FSAP) set up by the EU Commission and Member States.[10] The aim is to create an integrated European financial market by 2005. A special procedure has been agreed between the Commission, Member States and the European Parliament to allow for a flexible system of law-making. The system differentiates between regulation of principles in directives or regulations, to be elaborated by secondary legislation by the Commission in close co-operation with the EU Securities Commission (ESC) set up by Member States and the Committee of European Securities Regulators (CESR). The FSAP includes such measures as a market abuse directive, prospectus directive, directive on periodic transparency obligations and a full revision of the investment services directive.

[9] cf EDG Kiersch 'Grensoverschrijdende samenwerking en de noodzaak van een eenvoudig BV recht' in *De Beursvennootschap* 40 Instituut voor Ondernemingsrecht 141 and the remarks of Justice Minister Donner in (2003) 11 Ondernemingsrecht 397, expressing that the Netherlands should have the ambition to try to win the competition with legal forms of other states.

[10] FSAP 11 May 1999, COM (1999) 232.

The rapid development of capital market law in the EU begs the question whether, to what extent and how law actually matters for the development of capital markets. The 'Law Matters' school of thought claims that laws that give a better protection to investors on capital markets are instrumental to the development of such markets. This thinking is based on wide empirical research indicating a correlation between levels of development of capital market law and the development of deep and liquid capital markets.[11] However, this correlation as such does not explain what is the cause and what the effect. It may very well be that it is not so much a sophisticated level of capital market regulation and investor protection that brings about a deep and liquid capital market. Capital markets may develop and grow mainly for a complex of economic and financial reasons, which *as a consequence* brings about a need to provide for more sophisticated regulation to deal with the issues that arise on such a market. The development of capital markets in the EU may be an example of this cause-and-effect relationship. The capital markets in many EU Member States have grown almost exponentially during the 1990s, driven by changes in the economic outlook for Europe, the creation of the single market with its single currency, the consequential consolidation of key sectors of European industry, the development of institutional investment in Europe etc. The Financial Services Action Plan and the various regulatory initiatives under it only followed this at the end of the 1990s. Law may matter but maybe not as much as some believe.

Capital market law and company law are closely linked. For both areas of law disclosure and transparency requirements are key elements of the regulatory toolkit. But the rationale for disclosure and transparency requirements in each area of law is different. In company law the key role for disclosure requirements is to serve as an instrument for shareholders to hold the board accountable for its performance. On the basis of the (financial) reporting shareholders can make an informed judgement as to the quality of the management and whether they wish to continue with the current managers, urge them to change strategies or, as an ultimum remedium replace them by others. A secondary role of financial disclosure, in Europe at least, is to determine the extent to which a company can make distributions to shareholders under the capital maintenance rules of the 2nd Directive. In capital market law the rationale for disclosure and transparency is to ensure that the full market is informed timely and accurately of the essential information (financial or otherwise) about the company with a view to investors being able to make informed investment decisions (buy, sell, hold). This rationale presumes a high level of standardisation of information. Capital market law has a

[11] R LaPorta, F Lopez-de-Silanes, A Schleifer and R Vishny 'Law and Finance' (1998) 106 J Pol Econ 1113 and 'Legal Determinants of External Finance' (1997) 52 J Fin. 1131. See also J Coffee 'The future as history: the prospects for global convergence in corporate governance and its implications' (1999) 93 Northwestern University Law Review 641-707 and 'Do norms matter? A cross-country examination of the private benefits of control' (2001) Columbia Law and Economics Working Paper no 183, <http://ssrn.com>.

strong uniforming tendency, probably stronger than classical company law based principally on the free will of those who engage in the setting up and running of commercial companies.

There is more overlap between company law and capital market law. In Europe the most notable area of regulation where this is visible is the draft 13th Directive on takeover bids. Formally, this directive is a directive on company law and part of the company law harmonization process. But at the same time it seeks to regulate an important element of the functioning of capital markets: the public bid for all the shares of a company, and many features of the draft directive have been driven much more by capital market concepts than by company law thinking. From a company law perspective the directive deals with the external side of corporate governance: the disciplinary function of the (threat of) takeover bids and the acquisition of control over a company through a takeover bid.

The reach of capital market law over subjects that traditionally fall within the realm of company law is expanding. One result of the recent crisis of the capital markets has been a growing awareness that the internal governance systems of companies are, to some extent, also a relevant factor for investors to take into account when making investment decisions, and for the confidence of capital markets in general. Consequentially, there is a capital market regulatory response to perceived deficiencies in the corporate governance system. The Sarbanes Oxley Act is the prime example of this development. Apart from its substance the Act is intriguing from a regulatory perspective. It has triggered US domestic questions about the division of powers between the federal government and the states. But it has also laid bare a fundamental complication when capital market law starts to regulate core elements of company law. From a substance point of view regulating corporate governance through capital market law or through company law appears to be of little consequence. It is as with ageing: if you don't mind it doesn't matter. But from a regulatory perspective it does matter, particularly because company law and capital market law make different jurisdictional claims. Company law of a state regulates the governance of companies incorporated in that state or having moved their registered office to that state, regardless of the jurisdiction they conduct their business in. That, as we now know from the case law of the European Court of Justice, is the main jurisdictional claim of company law. In the US this has been understood and applied for a long time. Capital market law of a state on the other hand in principle claims to regulate companies that operate on the capital market of that state, regardless of whether they have their registered office in that state or not. This is all fine when capital market law does not go beyond imposing disclosure obligations. Any company, regardless of its corporate governance structure, can adhere to disclosure obligations. But problems arise when capital market law imposes substantive corporate governance rules on all companies accessing its market. Such rules are likely to be derived from the national company law system. They may not fit well within or may actually contravene corporate governance structures and requirements based on foreign company law. The more detailed these rules become the stronger this effect will be. The Sarbanes-Oxley Act is a showcase.

This in itself would plead for leaving regulation of the substance of corporate governance structures to the company law of states, which do not make conflicting claims of applicability. Good or bad reasons may however drive legislators to choose capital market regulation as the route to regulate (elements of) corporate governance structures. In order for capital markets not to exclude access to companies from other jurisdictions, capital market regulation of the substance of corporate governance must either be principle based, allowing for deviations and requiring at maximum disclosure of (major) deviations by foreign companies,[12] or make explicit exemptions for foreign companies. In either case capital market regulation of the substance of corporate governance requires a thorough understanding of the implications of the proposed rules for foreign companies that are subject to different company law requirements *before* such regulation is imposed. This can only be brought about if legislators and regulators of the states involved discuss regulatory initiatives and the impact on underlying company law systems, again, *before* they choose to regulate.

E. Parenthesis: Competition and Harmonization

From these developments the picture emerges that the original legislative approach to harmonise company laws in Europe in order to avoid 'bad' competition between Member States, has been supplemented by a judicial approach explicitly allowing for competition between the company laws of member states, which has accidentally found a confirmation in legislation through the European Company Statute. Although the original company law harmonization thrust seems to have petered out, competition has not replaced harmonization as the sole regulatory too. They go side by side. The European Court of Justice explicitly referred to this development in the Centros case when stating that the fact that company law is not completely harmonised in the Community is of little consequence for its interpretation of the freedom of establishment. 'Moreover, it is always open to the Council, on the basis of the powers conferred upon it by Article 54 (now 44) (3) (g) of the EC Treaty, to achieve complete harmonization', the Court adds. The challenge for the EU is to find out for what subjects of company law and under what circumstance competition between company law systems may be more beneficial than harmonization and vice versa. Harmonization is no longer the sole option for the EU when confronted with remaining, or potentially new differences between company laws of Member States. I submit that further harmonization of

[12] This is the approach taken by the New York Stock Exchange, cf Amendment no 1 to the NYSE's Corporate Governance Rules Proposals as submitted to the SEC for approval, <http://nyse.com>.

company law actually should only take place if specific company law objectives are to be attained, which cannot be attained through competition, or where there is evidence that harmonization produces a better result than competition. A thorough understanding of the effects of competition of company laws in Europe is required in order to be able to make such judgements.

F. A Modern Regulatory Framework for Company Law in Europe

The final report of the High Level Group reflects these developments. We have indicated in our report that the primary focus of the EU's involvement in company law should be to establish company law that facilitates efficient and competitive business across the EU, rather than focussing on harmonization in order to create similar protection for shareholders and third parties for the sake of it. Further harmonization of company law in Europe is required in some areas because only regulation at the EU level can attain the company law objectives. These areas are mainly:

1. disclosure of the corporate governance regime applied by listed companies. As I said, this is an area of clear overlap of considerations of capital market regulation and company law. For investors on capital markets to have confidence in governance systems of the companies they invest in, it is a prerequisite that the governance systems are fully disclosed. The aim of the EU to create an integrated capital market calls for a high level of standardisation in such a disclosure regime.
2. the ability for shareholders to exercise their voting rights efficiently across borders. This is a core element of the legal infrastructure underlying a good system of corporate governance, which infrastructure Europe does not have today. Many legal, technical and practical problems make it virtually impossible for shareholders in one Member State to exercise voting rights on shares in a company in another Member State. No Member State can solve these cross-border problems on its own. A sub-group of the High Level Group has made specific recommendations how the EU could address these problems.[13] The High Level Group has urged the Commission to produce a directive dealing with these issues on the short term.
3. the ability for companies to engage in cross-border mergers and transfers of seats. This is a key area of company law regulation that would facilitate business to make an optimal use of the European single market. It was part of the original harmonization project but Member States until now have failed to reach agreement on directives which would facilitate the cross-border restructuring of business, mainly because of concerns of some Member States as to the preservation of their particular employee co-determination systems.

[13] See for the report of the Expert Group on Cross-border Voting in Europe <http://wodc.nl>.

This concern has been addressed for the SE in the Directive complementing the Statute, but the result is complex and in key areas inconsistent and therefore difficult if not impossible to apply in practice. Revised drafts for the 10th and 14th Directives on cross-border mergers and transfers of seat are expected to be presented shortly, probably drawing on the solutions for employee involvement found in the SE Directive. Careful reconsideration of these solutions however is needed in order to avoid that the 10th and 14th Directive also become inoperable legal instruments.

Apart from these subjects, the High Level Group in general has been very reluctant to suggest new projects for harmonization of company law at the EU level. Where we did indicate substantive matters for which a common approach in the EU would be beneficial, we were careful to recommend, not imposing one size-fits-all solutions. An example offer our recommendations on the role of non-executive directors, which should be enforced on a comply or explain basis rather than as fixed rules that need to be applied by all. We were critical about the efficiency of certain elements of the harmonization achievements so far, in particular with respect to the 2nd Directive on capital maintenance. The stringent rules of this Directive need to be relaxed in some key area as has been advised before by the SLIM working group. In addition, an alternative system of protection of creditors needs to be developed, which is not based on strict rules of legal capital and distributable reserves defined by annual accounts, but on a system of solvency tests. We expressed strong hesitations to the concept of introducing a Statute for a European Private Company, offering a European legal form particularly suitable for small and medium sized business. Although we acknowledged that the need for such a legal form is expressed widely, in the light of the experience with the creation of the SE Statute we doubted whether Member States could realistically agree to an EPC Statute that would really add value.

The EU Commission has endorsed most of our recommendations in its Company Law Action Plan, which it published in May 2003.[14] There are some differ-

[14] Communication from the Commission to the Council and the European Parliament, Modernising Company Law and Enhancing Corporate Governance in the European Union – A Plan to Move Forward, 21 May 2003 (CLAP) (Annex 1 in this volume). A deviation of substance is the Commission's suggestion that the responsibility for identifying candidates to fill board vacancies should in principle be entrusted to a group composed mainly of executive directors, as they have the knowledge of the challenges facing the company and of the skills and experience of the human resources within the company, CLAP at 15. This goes against our recommendation that a nomination committee consist of non-executive directors only, the majority of whom should be independent, which is in line with all international recommendations and rules on the subject. Naturally, current executive directors are able to identify candidates for future executive board positions, but the point is that they must convince (a majority of) independent outside directors of the quality of the candidates in the broadest sense. The rationale for a decisive role for non-executive directors here is the same as for the audit committee: not because of their superior knowledge and inhouse experience, but to avoid conflicts of interests. It is even more obvious that executive directors should not have the prime

cont. ...

ences as to the priorities on the short, medium and longer term. Most notable among these is that the Commission suggests launching a feasibility study on an alternative system for creditor protection on the medium term only. If such study would indicate that an alternative system would indeed be feasible and needed, drafting, agreeing on and implementing such a system would still take years. I am afraid that the current system of capital maintenance rules of the 2nd Directive will already become inoperable on the short term. Besides all other concerns about the inefficiencies and ineffectiveness of the system the main reason for this is the fundamental change of character of annual accounts as result of application of the International Financial Reporting Standards, as will be required for listed companies as of 2005.[15] IFRS standards on goodwill (impairment), pension fund performance, accounting for derivatives and stock options will render annual accounts highly volatile, regardless of the performance of the underlying business and its cash flow. Such annual accounts are poor yardsticks to measure a company's reserves that it can distribute to its shareholders. The relevance of IFRS annual accounts to the ability of companies to pay its debts after a distribution to shareholders is minimal. The introduction of the requirement to apply IFRS as of 2005 can have far-reaching consequences for the ability of listed companies to pay their regular dividends to shareholders. Considering an alternative solution to the capital maintenance system based on such annual accounts therefore has become urgent and should not be delayed to the medium term.

Another notable difference between the Commission's Action Plan and the High Level Group's report is that the Commission puts forward as its first of two policy objectives the strengthening of shareholders rights and third parties protection.[16] The High Level Group went some length to explain that the primary purpose of company law and the EU's involvement in it should be to facilitate the running of efficient and competitive business enterprises across the Union, which the Commission lists as its second policy objective. We explicitly said that the traditional focus on the co-ordination of shareholder and third party safeguards may have caused us to lose sight of this primary purpose of company law. An adequate level of shareholder and creditor protection should be part of any company law, but should not be the primary focus for the EU now. It is slightly disconcerting to see this focus on strengthening shareholder and third party protection pop up again in the Commission's Action Plan. However, if one reads what specific policy proposals the Commission suggests no harm seems to come from it. The specific proposals put forward are all following up on recommendations of the High Level Group. It may be that the Commission has simply put this policy

responsibility for selecting non-executive who are expected to monitor the executive directors. In view of the substantial criticism the Commission has received on this part of its Action Plan the Commission is expected to return to the original recommendation of the High Level Group.

[15] Regulation (EC) 1606/2002 of 19 July 2002, OJ L 243/1.

[16] CLAP at 8.

objective forward in order to explicitly operate within the Treaty framework of art. 44, charging it with the task to co-ordinate shareholder and third party safeguards in Member States. But there may be a snake in the grass. The Commission intends to undertake a study, in the short to medium term, on the consequences of imposing the one share, one vote principle, or more clearly the principle of proportionality between capital and control. This should help to establish a real shareholder democracy in the EU.[17] Whatever the virtues of such an approach, the debate on the takeover directive shows that Member States already find it extremely difficult if not impossible to reach agreement on the application of the proportionality principle in the extraordinary context of a takeover bid. It is very unlikely that they will agree to full application of the proportionality principle in general, abolishing all deviations. The road to shareholder democracy in the EU for the time being may be a dead end street. It appears much more rewarding for the EU to focus on how to really facilitate efficient and competitive business across the Union through company law.

G. The Takeover Bids Directive

Finally a few words on the 13th Directive on takeover bids. The High Level Group's proposals, in particular the proposed break-through rule dealing with pre-bid defence mechanisms, are discussed at length in other contributions and I need not repeat our arguments and recommendations. I just want to highlight the most recent developments.

In its new draft for the 13th Directive of October 2002, the Commission included a mini-break-through rule. The rule that pre-existing defence mechanisms should be broken through after a bidder, having made a general takeover bid, has acquired a substantial part of the company's share capital, was introduced only for a limited number of mechanisms (transfer restrictions, voting rights restrictions and special rights of shareholders to appoint directors, see art. 11 of the draft Directive). In particular multiple voting rights shares were not made subject to the break-through, although they can have as a result that a bidder having acquired more than 75% of the company's share capital after a takeover bid is unable to exercise control. The exclusion of multiple voting rights shares from the break-through rule is opposed by members of European Parliament and some Member States, as this would not constitute a level playing field. Others, mainly Scandinavian Member States, furiously reject the inclusion of these rights. In the midst of this debate Portugal has suggested a new proposal. The proposal in short introduces a system in which Member States can elect to impose the full application of both articles 9 (shareholder decision taking after a bid has been made; no unilateral frustrating measures by directors) and 11 (break-through rule,

[17] CLAP at 14.

which, under this proposal, would be the full break-through including multiple voting rights) on companies subject to their jurisdiction. But they can also allow their companies to opt-out of application of art. 9 and/or 11. For sake of ease, I refer to companies subject to art. 9 and 11 as 'A-companies' and companies that have opted-out of art. 9 and/or 11 as 'B-companies'. B-companies can at a later stage elect to become an A-company, but A-companies cannot 'fall back' to B-company status. In addition, the proposal introduces a reciprocity rule, which in effect is relevant only when a bid is made on an A-company by a B-company, in which case the A-company (subject to art. 9 and 11) can nonetheless disregard both articles if it wishes to defend against the bid.

As no published text of this Portuguese proposal is available to date, the details cannot be discussed yet. But the proposal raises some interesting general questions. The option for Member States to allow their companies to opt-out of art. 9 and 11 can be seen as an elaborate system of grandfathering. The A-regime sets the benchmark. Companies are not forced into the benchmark; the system relies on market pressure to provide incentives to elect the A-regime. Here, as with the SE Statute, an element of competition is introduced into a directive that sets out to harmonise company law, mainly because Member States are unable to agree on a system to be imposed on all companies. This may still prove to be a significant step into the right direction, with little or no negative side effects. A review could be undertaken after five years to assess the practical results of the system and, depending on the results, eliminate or phase-out the option-system.

A key question is which corporate body is to decide on the election for the A- or B-status if that choice is given to a company. Such a decision is so fundamental for the company that I believe it can only be taken by the shareholders meeting. This would also be consistent with the shareholder decision taking principle underlying art. 9 of the draft Directive.

The troublesome element of the proposal is the reciprocity rule. A company electing the B-regime is not able to enjoy the application of art. 9 and 11 when it makes a bid for an A-company (that it cannot enjoy these rights when it makes a bid on another B-company follows directly from the B-status of that company). Fairness considerations appear to be underlying this rule: 'thou shalt not enjoy the rights in a bid on another company that thou denies to others in a bid on thyself.' This concept of reciprocity is new to EU company law and may be difficult to reconcile with the freedom of establishment and free movement of capital, which do not impose any condition on the party wishing to enjoy rights under national company laws other than having the registered office or central administration in a Member State. It also raises a number of practical issues:

- the rules relevant to a bid on an A-company vary as a result of whether the bid is made by an A-company or a B-company. This causes legal uncertainty and unpredictability;
- the rules can only be applied to companies that have the ability to make the choice between the A-regime and the B-regime. The rules make no sense where a bidder is a non-listed company or a (group of) private individual(s)

or a non-EU company. In particular the risk of bids by US companies certainly is one of the drivers of the reciprocity idea, but it is exactly here that it fails. Are US companies A-companies or B-companies if a choice between two is not available in their jurisdiction? The only way the rule could be made to work practically for non-EU companies, is by determining that all non-EU companies by definition are to be considered B-companies that cannot enjoy the application of art. 9 and 11 when making a bid on a EU A-company. This in all likelihood is in breach of international law obligations of the EU and Member States;

- the rule can easily be evaded by a B-company by incorporating and listing a new A-company under its control to make the bid. A B-company could also induce a friendly A-company to make the bid and sell the target to the B-company after the bid;
- the rule leads to complicated situations where two competing bids are made for an A-company, one by an A-company (for which art. 9 and 11 would apply) and one by a B-company (for which art. 9 and 11 would not apply). This also leaves ample room for manipulation by the target A-company, for example by asking a friendly B-company to make a competing bid.

Many of these problems appear to be insoluble or at least will lead to inconsistencies, discriminatory situations and leave scope for abuse and manipulation. That is a poor result for a concept, which above all is based on a perception of fairness. I would argue that there is no need for the reciprocity rule because the fairness concerns are already addressed in the proposal by Member States being able to allow their companies to elect the B-regime. As a B-company any company can continue to defend against takeover bids from any bidder, regardless of the bidder's constitution.

My understanding is that the Portuguese proposal is still being discussed by Member States. The option system I believe can be made to work and, compare to having no directive at all, would offer benefits in terms of setting a clear benchmark with market incentives to move into the direction of the benchmark. The reciprocity rule however should not be included as it is conceptually flawed, practically very difficult if not impossible to enforce and not essential in addressing fairness concerns. I hope Member States and the European Parliament will exclude it from the directive they finally may agree to.

H. Outlook

The outlook for EU company law has changed fundamentally the last few years, as a result of the SE Statute, the development of capital markets and their regulation and not the least by the case law of the European Court of Justice. Competition and harmonization go together now as two accepted regulatory approaches. But there is little understanding and direction yet to make considered choices between the two approaches: where does competition work best, where is harmonization required? The report of the High Level Group and the Commission's Action Plan based on it may offer a first indication of how such choices could be made. Clearly the real work still needs to begin. The good thing is that at least there is an outlook now that can be developed and challenged.

An Agenda for Reform: Company and Takeover Law in Europe

GÉRARD HERTIG and JOSEPH A. McCAHERY

We evaluate the corporate governance and takeover law recommendations of the High Level Group of Company Law Experts, endorsing those recommendations that are likely to enhance social welfare. We show that the disclosure, board reform and directly liability proposals are unlikely to benefit investors by limiting the central agency problems in the firm. To the extent, moreover, that the reforms aimed at the establishment of a permanent body advising on regulatory initiatives and a director disqualification mechanism lead to increased regulation, the expected benefits of these reforms are not expected to outweigh their costs. Similarly, the key provision of the proposed Takeover Bids Directive designed to create a level playing field for takeovers in the EU, namely the break-through rule, can be expected to hamper the development of a EU-wide market for corporate control. The authors endorse an opt-in/opt-out default rule approach for EU company law reform. The implications of this proposal are discussed in the context of the takeover directive, related party transactions, and minority shareholder protection.

A. Introduction

For more than a quarter century, European company law discussions focused on the process of the enactment of directives in the area of company and accounting law. In the wake of the Maastricht Treaty, however, when the European Commission (EC) sought to expand its initiatives in EU company law, policymakers have been forced to acknowledge that the failure to make significant progress in the harmonization of national law raised questions about the need for a new approach. Proponents of harmonization have taken the lead by mapping out strategies to further harmonize disclosure, board structure, director liability and cross-border reorganizations.

The reinvigoration of the European Union (EU) company law harmonization program is designed to reduce some of the barriers to regulatory reform and provide more effective solutions to many of the policy issues that the EC had dealt with unsuccessfully. The purpose of this article is to address the question whether the EC's 'Action Plan to Modernize Company Law and Enhance Corporate Governance' (Action Plan) to create a more dynamic and flexible mandatory company and corporate law framework can yield effective results. We argue that the use of more diverse regulatory instruments can provide a better solution to some problems that the EC faced attempting to implement its legal harmonization program. In absence of a move toward firms having more freedom to adopt the law they prefer, the EC's Action Plan cannot be expected to provide a practical solution to many of the current implementation and enforcement issues. We suggest that a switch to a default rule approach to EU company law will provide a low cost solution to a range of firms attempting to meet their corporate governance needs. We base our approach on the learning from economic theory that highlights the efficient regulatory response that an *optional regime*, based on a menu of opt out rules and, for some issues, opt-in arrangements, can play in providing the appropriate rule for a diverse range of business parties.

Part B provides an overview of the recent trends in regulatory arbitrage and competition in Europe. Two central trends are clearly beginning to emerge. First, the evidence suggests that, while regulatory competition has yet to play a fundamental role in the development of EU company law, the appearance of new judgments from the European Court of Justice (ECJ) can support the inference that regulatory arbitrage is an imminent possibility. Second, the threat of regulatory competition, which is less attractive to weakly responsive Member States, such as France and Germany, may provide a new impetus for EU harmonization of legal rules. We assert that the Centros, Überseering and Inspire Art cases, and the move toward more flexibility at the Member State level for smaller firms to select their own business statutes, may further encourage the development of competition among states in company law.

Part C critically reviews the EC's Action Plan. It asserts that the EC's new initiative is infirm in several respects. First, the proposed reforms are, to the extent they incorporate the best practices of the Financial Accounting Standard Board (FASB) and the International Accounting Standard Board (IASB), unlikely to make a significant difference in practice; alternatively, in the case where the EC offers new rules on director liability, the proposed reforms will have little impact unless managers have strong incentives to implement these rules. Second, the EC's Action Plan is likely to cause harm, for example, by fostering public enforcement of wrongful trading or establishing centralized oversight of accountants. Moreover, the approach to future law reform, based on the introduction of an organizational scheme that would function to produce uniform legal rules, is likely to be affected by bureaucratic inertia or interest group influences and will tend either to maintain the *status quo* or create vague rules. Third, the current proposals on director nomination and remuneration do not entail more choice for companies and should not be expected to improve upon existing arrangements.

In addition to the discussion of the Action Plan, we provide an analysis of the proposed Takeover Bids Directive. We show that the board neutrality approach would provide an effective way to protect shareholders' interests in takeovers and work to the benefit of business parties by creating a simple EU wide rule on board conduct. Arguments in favour of a board veto are rejected on the grounds that they rest on a misleading view of capital markets and are inconsistent with the empirical evidence which shows that veto power does not yield higher premiums. Here we also explore the case for the proposed mandatory bid rule and argue that it represents a welfare-enhancing strategy and provides minority shareholders with significant protections. Part C ends by discussing the importance of the break-through rule, arguing that the rule does not provide a good basis for shareholder bargaining and appears to conflict with the aims of the mandatory bid rule.

Part D presents the case for an enabling EU company law regime that would introduce a greater expansion of choice for firms in a number of areas. Whereas most EU company and takeover law scholars have presented the case for a legal framework based on mandatory rules, we claim, in contrast, that an optional regime, based on the use of modernized business forms and opt-in/opt-out default rules, will likely yield substantial benefits for stakeholders and firms. We address the implications of the optional approach for company and takeover law reform by considering a menu of default rules that could play an important role in the EU modernization process. In particular, we show that the provision of a default arrangement for hostile takeovers would open up the way for the ratification and implementation of the Takeover Bids Directive. Part E concludes.

B. Reflections on Regulatory Arbitrage and Competition

We begin our examination by discussing, in Part B. I, the recent case law of the ECJ which demonstrates that the court is more likely to favour a policy where Member States are permitted to offer legal rules so as to attract incorporations. In Part B. II, we will first assess whether the EU approach to company law harmonization, which is largely dismissive of competition between Member States, can meet the specific regulatory objectives set by the EC, and then critically consider the costs and benefits of the EC's approach, particularly in light of the expansion of the EU.

I. An Emerging Path

One of the most important debates in European company law is whether a market for corporate law will ultimately emerge within the EU, and if so, whether it will be based on a Delaware-like model in which companies can freely select their state of incorporation.[1] This is, of course, a politically charged question and therefore a somewhat undifferentiated debate. In particular, commentators often fail to distinguish between corporate finance, company formation and restructuring issues (Grundmann 2000:561). Conversely, competition between states in the US is generally assumed to be very active, whereas recent research shows that reality is subtler.[2] However, there is evidence that domicile choices by US corporations can affect their share price and/or provide significant benefits for their managers and controlling shareholders.[3] The absence in Europe of anything resembling American charter competition provides very strong evidence to support the claim that there are significant regulatory and fiscal barriers to jurisdictional competition (Deakin 2001: 190, 205).

To start, EU company law can be viewed largely as an incomplete and rather ineffective set of provisions.[4] Commentators have identified a long list of reasons, including the failure of Member States to repeatedly agree on important substantive issues, the pro-decentralization presumption resulting from the EU subsidiary principle, and the great variation in the implementation of EU directives by Member States (Wouters 2000: 275). This has allowed for continuing diversity in the corporate law systems of the Member States (Berglöf 1997), while fuelling political opposition to regulatory arbitrage and competition.

Despite the persistence of the main (bank-oriented) components underlying the continental European corporate governance regimes, significant changes nevertheless are taking place. There is no denying that the increase in cross-border acquisitions across the EU in the 1990s is broadly consistent with a move toward the Anglo-American 'outsider' model of corporate governance. Similarly, many companies have altered the composition of their boards, established independent audit committees and authorized the substantial issuance of stock options to directors and managers. Moreover, institutional investors have pressured companies to improve auditing practices to enhance transparency. These combined changes suggest increased convergence around the outsider model of corporate governance (Gilson 2001; Hansmann and Kraakman 2001).

Although a strong economic argument for convergence based on increased capital mobility, product market competition and company law practices can be made, it is by now equally clear that there are many path dependent factors

[1] eg Ebke 2000: 625-628 (explaining that competitive lawmaking has become a dominant theme in European company law); Cheffins 1997: 421-51 (explaining the potential role of the market for incorporations for deepening European economic integration).

[2] eg Kahan and Kamar 2002; Bebchuk and Hamdani 2002.

[3] Compare Daines 2001 with Bebchuk, Cohen, and Ferrell 2002.

[4] eg Hopt 2002: 175 (arguing that the EC has done little to enact measures that regulate the relations between shareholders and managers or with minority investors rights); Coffee 1999: 651 (contrasting federal systems that permit a market for incorporation with the different market and institutional environment of jurisdictions that are not committed to a reincorporation regime).

militating against the emerging 'outsider' model which leads us to expect that *regulatory* change may be far slower and ambiguous (Bebchuk and Roe 1999; Bratton and McCahery 1999: 266-271). In this context, it is possible to interpret the failure of the EU to pass a Directive on Takeover Bids as reflecting the continued power and tenacity of the diverse groups that benefit from a traditional corporate governance environment. Similarly, the indifference of Member States to many of the Commission's recent company law initiatives, and the modest support of critical pillars of the Financial Services Action Plan, suggests an even more pessimistic view of the probabilities of regulatory convergence.

Even in the absence of institutional barriers at the EC level, however, EU company law policies are constrained by serious legal obstacles that are biased toward either restrain the free movement of firms within the EU or limit the competitive process between different corporate law regimes. It is well known among policymakers that rules on conflicts of laws, combined with domestic labour, insolvency or tax regulation, serve to block regulatory efforts to allow companies the option to select the corporate law provisions they find desirable.

Under the *siège réel* (real seat) doctrine, which is followed by the majority of EU Member States, a corporation must be incorporated in the Member State where it has its central administration. From the perspective of a firm, the cross-border transfer of the seat is particularly burdensome and unattractive because of the substantial tax implications, especially for corporations that have used conservative accounting to build-up hidden reserves. This obstacle to regulatory arbitrage and competition is compounded by entrenched employee participation structures, German co-determination being the best known but not the only example. These structures consistently favour regulatory conservatism (Wymeersch 1998: 1045), constraining the ability of legislators to respond to managerial or shareholder preferences. As a consequence, there is considerable doubt whether the EU company and takeover law harmonization program can be relied upon to pursue legal reforms aimed at improving the welfare of investors.

It would be wrong, however, to underestimate the tension created by the above mentioned market changes. Prominent US academics have argued that the competitive pressures facing Member States are increasing, which should facilitate the development of regulatory competition in corporate law (Gilson 2001). In our view, ECJ case law is a good indicator, given the Court's record in providing early warning, for significant changes in European Community law (Pollock 2003: 194-202). The ECJ's recent decisions in Centros, Überseering, and Inspire Art[5] could be setting the stage for effective regulatory arbitrage and competition among Member States by their undermining of the real seat doctrine (Wymeersch,

[5] Case C-212/97, *Centros Ltd. v Erhvervs-og Selskabsstyrelsen*, 1999 ECR I-1459; Case C-208/00 *Überseering BV v NCC Nordic Construction Company Baumangement*, 2002 ECR I 9919; Case C-167/01, *Kamer van Koophandel en Fabrieken voor Amsterdam v Inspire Art Ltd* (2003, available at curia.eu.int/jurisp). Compare Case 81/1987, *Regina v H.M. Treasury and Comm'rs of Inland Revenue, ex parte Daily Mail and General Trust Plc*, 1988 ECR 5483.

Chapter I. 3, this volume). Nonetheless, many commentators still take refuge behind a phalanx of obscure and convoluted statements in the ECJ case law in order to defend the real seat doctrine (Halbhuber 2001: 1409). We, on the other hand, expect the ECJ to continue along the doctrinal path it developed in Centros. In this respect, it is worth pointing to the Überseering case, which involves a Dutch close corporation that had moved its headquarters to German. The ECJ ruled that such a corporation could not be denied the capacity to bring legal action before the courts of the Member State in which it has its central administration on the ground that its home/foreign corporate law regime does not satisfy host/domestic corporate law requirements. The Inspire Art case similarly struck down Dutch attempts to limit free choice of legal regime by imposing domestic restrictions on branches of companies formed in accordance with the law of another Member State. As a consequence of Centros, Überseering and Inspire Art, start-up firms should be able to incorporate under the corporate law regime they deem most favourable among the regimes offered by the various Member States. Established firms should be able to take advantage of the newly available European Company Statute to similar effect (Enriques 2004).[6]

In this context, the UK could become the leading jurisdiction for European incorporations (McCahery and Vermeulen 2001: 875-878). Indeed, UK legislators have moved fast to develop a menu of new corporate forms that caters to the needs of entrepreneurs, while its courts are respected and productive – characteristics that have significantly contributed to Delaware's US dominance.[7] Admittedly, charter revenue may not be sufficient to prompt UK legislators to engage in sustained regulatory competition.[8] On the other hand, additional incorporations will mean increased revenue for UK accountants and lawyers – which is one of the main reason why Delaware legislators keep their corporate law in tune with market demands. It is true that UK accountants and lawyers are still rather passive when it comes to making corporate law responsive to the demands of the market place, especially compared to their Delaware counterparts. However, UK lawyers and accountants will adjust fast as soon as it will become clear that regulatory competition magnifies both the benefits of attracting new business and the risks of losing existing clients – especially in an environment that is less mature than the US regulatory market.[9]

[6] Note that *Centros* does not seem to facilitate cross-border restructurings of existing corporations. See Behrens 2001: 503.

[7] eg Black 1990: 590; Romano 1985.

[8] Cheffins 1997: 435 (explaining that the United Kingdom, unlike Delaware, does not impose a franchise tax or an annual fee on incorporated firms and does not charge fees for amendments to the corporate constitution).

[9] Compare Bebchuk and Cohen 2003 (US firms display a substantial home state bias in favour of incorporating in the State in which they are located).

The probability of this scenario is confirmed by early reactions to recent UK company law reforms. Major jurisdictions, such as France and Germany, which are highly vulnerable to the pressures of market competition, have been driven to institute reforms to their corporate law regimes so as to stem the flow of firm migration to the UK.[10] Smaller jurisdictions, such as Ireland and Luxembourg, may join the fray and decide to act entrepreneurial themselves, tempted by what they could see as a chance to get additional chartering revenue.[11] Thus, while it is too early to tell whether the EU is heading toward a US system of state competition, the changes taking place in ECJ case law suggest that new incentives for providing legal rules may be emerging.

II. Harmonization and the Regulatory Competition Debate in the EU

The foregoing discussion of the difficulties firms have to adopt corporate law regimes that meet their needs is crucial to our understanding of European corporate and takeover law reform efforts. As we will discuss in the next section, EC policymakers are attempting, in light of the harmonization process having become bogged down, to adopt new techniques to induce further harmonization of legal rules. Given that there may be significant advantages from the introduction of competition between national corporate law regimes, we examine here whether corporate law regulation should be left to Member States rather than undertaken at the EU level.

Those favouring centralization believe it necessary to eliminate barriers to trade, as well as distortions of competition (Inman and Rubinfeld 1997). A major benefit of centralization is to allow for the internalisation of significant spillovers. Advocates of legal federalism, in contrast, rely on the economic theory of jurisdictional competition to support devolutionary initiatives (Romano 1991; 2001). They claim that regulatory competition shapes a wide range of regulatory outcomes at the Member State and local levels, which tend to correspond to citizen/ firm preferences, since only public goods and regulations for which citizens/firms are willing to pay for will survive (Weingast 1995). Two conditions, however, must be satisfied: (1) lower level regulation must not generate significant externalities; and (2) borders must be open for the free movement of capital and labour.

Debates within the EU aimed at reconciling both positions are strongly affected by the importation of the regulatory competition concept and its race to the bottom and race to the top stories. According to the race to the top story, uniform rules carry the risk of regulatory capture (by managers or controlling share-

[10] For France, see Conac 2002; for Germany, Baums 2003.

[11] Note that double taxation treaties and other tax issues may reduce the charter benefits of regulatory competition. See Cheffins 1997: 435; ECJ *Ponente Carni Spa* [1993] ECR 1947.

holders), while competitive diversity would lead to regulation tailored to the need of local preferences, deter opportunism, and encourage regulatory innovation. According to the race to the bottom story, in the absence of effective harmonization, national level lawmaking would involve complexity, uncertainty, and undesirable deregulation.

By linking together mutual recognition of corporate law systems, subsidiarity (viz. lawmaking takes place at the Member State level unless credible circumstances support harmonization) and minimum requirements, EU lawmakers have created a legal structure that supplies a degree of useful tension between regulatory competition and harmonization. In this context, EU lawmakers have recognized that, while mutual recognition is necessary for the operation of a well-functioning market for legal rules, asymmetric information could undermine the willingness of the relevant actors to participate in that market (Tjiong 2002: 83). To shed light on this problem, we offer an example: if Member States are unable to reject a corporation organized under another Member State's law so as to avoid more restrictive domestic requirements, national regulators can expect problems to arise when it is complicated and costly for investors and creditors to evaluate the quality of the non-domestic corporate law system.

Taken alone, mutual recognition could also make it easier for managers to reincorporate in a Member State that has an anti-takeover regime that suits their interests rather than those of shareholders. Furthermore, following the eastward expansion of the EU in 2004, new Member States will come under increased pressure to make changes in their company law in order to compete for inward investment. This is likely to have a direct effect on the level of minority shareholder and non-trade creditor protection (Berkowitz, Pistor and Richard 2003; Black, Kraakman and Tarassova 2000). In addition, some new Member States are likely to adopt inefficient business forms in order to attract firms that will operate outside their jurisdiction, thus internalising charter and other benefits while externalising costs.

In other words, mutual recognition presupposes that Member States remain empowered to restrain foreign business form that do not offer minimum protections to investors, creditors and other stakeholders. This, in turn, means that 'minimum requirements' must be defined centrally for regulatory competition to have a significant threat value for regulators. As we know from past and current EU experiences, the absence of harmonized minimum requirement leaves ample room for Member States to limit regulatory competition to trivial levels.

Whilst the task of defining 'minimum requirements' can be left to the EU judiciary, this process is often rather slow and piecemeal. Therefore, minimum requirements are mainly developed by the Commission and the Parliament, where regulatory capture generally leads to the adoption of over-inclusive mandatory rules that minimize regulatory arbitrage and competition.

How has the harmonization process impacted the development of EU company and takeover law? The harmonization process has tended to favour the interests of managers and stakeholders such as controlling shareholders and lenders. Yet, in contrast to the US, regulatory capture does not completely distort the agenda-setting process and the production of legal provisions. It is important to recall, however, that centralized rule-making remains incomplete and conservative. This allows for interest groups and other path dependent forces to undermine efforts of policymakers to depart from the *status quo* and consider alternative policies.

Notwithstanding the conservative policymaking scheme for EU company and takeover law, the wave of US corporate governance scandals has also managed to influence EU regulators, who had to appear to be doing something in response and launched a host of reforms intended to protect investor welfare. Yet apart from the need to react to the corporate governance crisis, regulators have also recognized the need to improve the integration of the EU's capital markets. Moreover, they have also been quick to see that the pro-mutual recognition ECJ case law offers a new basis to re-launch EU regulatory efforts to modernize corporate law. We turn now, in Parts III and IV, to analyse these proposed reforms and lays out the case for an alternative to the pre-existing mandatory approach as a way to upgrade EU company law.

C. The Proposed EU Company and Takeover Law Reforms

In this Part, we assess the European Commission's latest efforts to create a modern regulatory framework for corporate law and devise a set of 'level playing field' regulations for takeover bids.[12] Our interest in this section is not, however, the details of the specific reform proposals but rather whether the proposals will improve social welfare in general and have a desirable effect on companies.

The proposed regulatory changes are largely inspired by recommendations made by a group of experts commissioned by the EU to make recommendations for reform (the High Level Group).[13] The objective of the corporate law proposals is to enhance corporate governance while simplify existing rules and improving freedom of choice between alternative forms of organization (Part II/A). The takeover bid proposals aim at setting minimum requirements for corporate conduct and transparency (Part II/B).

[12] European Communities 2003, Action Plan (Annex 1 in this volume); European Communities 2003, Statutory Audit; Draft Takeover Bids Directive (October 2002, available at <www.europa.eu.int>) (Annex 2 in this volume).

[13] See *Report of the High Level Group of Company Law Experts on a Modern Regulatory Framework for Company Law in Europe* (November 2002, available at <www.europa.eu.int>, see Annex 3 in this volume); *Report of the High Level Group of Company Law Experts on Issues Related to Takeover Bids* (January 2002, available at <www.europa.eu.int>, see Annex 2 in this volume).

I. Reforming Corporate Law

The European Commission intends to move forward at four levels. First, it proposes to modernize corporate law by further harmonizing corporate disclosure, board structure and director liability requirements, and by amending capital rules. Second, it plans to adopt rules facilitating corporate restructuring and mobility. Third, the Commission proposes the establishment of a permanent coordination structure, the European Corporate Governance Forum, and of (Member State) agencies to sanction unfit directors. Fourth, it proposes to strengthen the supervision of auditors and to adopt comprehensive rules on the conduct of audits.

We believe, however, that most of the considered changes have important drawbacks and would prove ineffective in practice. More unfortunately, the majority of those considered changes that could prove effective are likely to favour bureaucratic intervention rather than shareholder protection or European economic integration.

1. Harmonization of Disclosure, Board and Capital Requirements

Disclosure. The EU plays second fiddle to more global or powerful bodies when it comes to disclosure requirements for listed firms. For example, EU influence in the accounting area is at best indirect, due to the central role of played by the Financial Accounting Standard Board (FASB) and the International Accounting Standard Board (IASB).[14] Similarly, firms and Member States alike are more concerned by national securities regulators' practices than by EU requirements. In other words, we argue that in absence of a European SEC, lawmaker activism in the area of corporate disclosure will prove especially problematic and only reinforces the argument for an effective enforcement regime (Hertig and Lee 2003).

Moreover, even if one assumes that the EU can play a disclosure role, the proposed rules are unlikely to provide new information to the controlling shareholders that dominate both listed and non-listed EU firms (Barca and Becht 2002; La Porta, et al., 1997; 1999). A far as minority shareholders are concerned, any improvement in their situation presupposes that they can credibly threaten to request a special investigation. This does not seem realistic, however, considering the 5% threshold to be met by shareholders of listed firms, and the limited benefits of transparency requirements for shareholders of non-listed firms.[15]

Board structure and liability. It is unclear whether the board structure and liability proposals will reduce agency costs and decrease risk. For example, mandating that firms must make a choice between one-tier and two-tier boards is

[14] See Regulation (EC) No 1606/2002 on the application of international accounting standards [2002] OJ L 243/1.

[15] For a more optimistic view, see, eg, Hopt 2003.

of limited value, given that one-tier companies can imitate two-tier decision-making by using committees (Hansmann and Kraakman 2004). Similarly, designing provisions that force companies to explain why individual non-executive directors are qualified to serve on the board in their particular role is clearly a requirement that is past its prime. Or, to take another example, harmonizing the definition of 'shadow' directors and requiring Member States to adopt wrongful trading provisions will have little or no effect unless these requirements are coupled with an enforcement mechanism – a topic that we will discuss below.

Moreover, assuming again that EU law could make a difference, for example when it comes to the setting-up of audit committees or director independence and remuneration, such rules are mostly duplicate requirements that already exist at the Member State level and firms therefore are likely to have little to worry about in that case.

Capital requirements. Even though the capital formation and maintenance proposals meet an obvious need, they, nevertheless, are of rather marginal importance overall. For example, the proposals to eliminate current EU expert valuation requirements would only make a difference if they were generally applicable and not merely limited to some contributions in kind (and, should this be the case, the Commission's proposals would significantly increase the risk of opportunistic value diversion unless supplemented by at least equally costly valuation rules). Or, to take another example, extending creditors' rights to require security for all restructuring transactions is unlikely to be useful for those creditors that are not already secured.

More generally, it must be pointed out that capital requirements only apply to open corporate firms (*société anonymes*, *Aktiengesellschaften*), leaving ample room for firms to choose less demanding corporate forms (*sociétés à responsabilité limitée*, *Gesellschaften mit beschränkter Haftung*, etc.).[16]

2. Corporate Restructuring and Mobility

In the short term, the Commission intends to facilitate cross border mergers and the transfer of companies' seat from one Member State to another by tackling the employee participation issues that have up to now prevented the adoption of the relevant directives. Given the EU's track record, it is doubtful that employee participation issues will be solved – the open-ended provisions of the European Company Statute being a recent and telling example. In addition, should an agreement be reached, it is unlikely to be effective. Indeed, it is hard to envisage how EU regulation can go beyond what has already been achieved by ECJ case

[16] For more negative assessments of EU capital requirements, compare Mülbert and Birke 2002; Enriques and Macey 2001.

law without addressing tax issues that are not part of the Commission's reform agenda.

The Commission also intends to facilitate restructurings by relaxing existing shareholder approval requirements and introducing squeeze-out and sell-out rights. Relaxing mandatory EU shareholder approval requirements could make sense, but has rather marginal value – which is also why the Commission does not make such reform a priority. The introduction of squeeze-out and sell-out rights is a more significant change and deserves the Commission's attention. However, such rights only make sense if coupled with expert valuation requirements similar to those that the Commission seems keen to eliminate for contributions in kind. Moreover, a mandatory EU approach to squeeze-out and sell-out rights might not be superior to a default approach, as we will show in Section III below.

3. Coordination Forum and Enforcement Agencies

The High Level Group of Experts has advocated the establishment of a permanent body to provide advice on future EU regulatory initiatives. The Commission has partly endorsed the recommendation by proposing the creation of a European Corporate Governance Forum to encourage the coordination and convergence of Member States corporate governance efforts.

To the extent such a body plays an effective role, it is likely to favour state intervention rather than market-oriented reforms, as its members are likely to be rewarded for regulatory activism. Moreover, various interest groups, by virtue of their expertise and resources, may find it easier to launder their preferences through this structure and thereby influence the content and quality of corporate regulation.

It is also proposed to impose director's disqualification at the EU level. Note that UK practice shows that the disqualification sanction does not sufficiently deter violations of the wrongful trading rule and other fiduciary duties (Ferran, Chapter II. 7, this volume; Cheffins 1997: 548-53). Moreover, as made clear by UK and French experiences, the disqualification sanction is only effective if it is enforced by a well-funded agency (Hertig and Kanda 2004). As a result, there is a risk that the adoption of such a rule, unaccompanied by adequate incentives and enforcement powers, would be problematic and unlikely to achieve the preferred level of deterrence.

4. Audit

The Commission has also proposed ten priorities for improving the quality of statutory audits, in particular to provide better protection against Enron-type scandals. In the short term, the main objectives are to adopt new principles on auditing standards, to require compliance with International Standards on Auditing for all EU statutory audits and to strengthen Member State supervision of auditors.

Proposing to adopt more stringent auditing standards and to reinforce auditor monitoring by replacing self-regulatory regimes through state supervision is a welcome move. To the extent that these reforms are effective, they will tend to reinforce investor confidence and prevent auditor liability becoming prohibitive in the wake of the Enron and similar accounting scandals.[17] The new rules emerging from this reform can play an additional positive role if they are relatively flexible, which should reduce the (excessive) pressure for global unification of audit requirements generated by recent accounting scandals.

On the other hand, the proposed creation of a EU Audit Regulatory Committee may be subject, as long as there is no European SEC, to unhealthy influence activities of pressure groups that cause efficiency problems and would, therefore, yield few benefits.

5. Summary

Our point here is that the proposed EU corporate law reforms are likely to be either ineffective or unnecessary to ameliorate market failures. In addition, they bring the risk of excessive state intervention (supervision of auditors excepted) while ignoring much-needed private action mechanisms. Our own view is that an alternative approach, that addresses corporate law reform in terms of supporting the introduction of a menu of default terms in key areas of company regulation while strengthening the incentives for the enforcement of director's duties, is a much preferable approach for EU company law reform (see Part IV below).

II. Regulating Takeover Bids

We now turn to consider whether the main components of the draft Takeover Bids Directive are likely to be value enhancing and, therefore, promote the development of a cross-border takeover market.

The October 2, 2002 draft Takeover Bids Directive, provides for: (1) strict board neutrality on the part of the target board; (2) a mandatory bid rule that ensures that an offeror cannot obtain a controlling stake without making a controlling bid; (3) break-through rules which stipulate that, during the period of acceptance of a bid, any restrictions on the transfer of securities contained in the articles of association and contractual arrangements (but not in national legislation) are not enforceable against the offeror; (4) disclosure rules according to

[17] Reputation and litigation issues are related, given that the former is eroded by the latter. Conversely, introducing state supervision should enhance auditor reputation as well as induce legislators and courts to keep the liability risk within reasonable limits. See also Coffee 2001.

which the offeror must announce his intention to make an offer and make public an offer document containing at least a minimum of information; and (5) 'squeeze-out' and 'sell-out' rules that would have to be implemented at a fair price.

As with general company law, the central regulatory problem is to determine the optimal balance between harmonization and diversity. One benefit of the proposed Directive lies in the provision of simple common rules (e.g., board neutrality) that avoid some of the costs of having complex and differing national regimes. On the other hand, it is far from clear that Member States with different laws and traditions will be served by some harmonization proposals.

It is worthwhile emphasizing that a key issues in the debate on the proposed Directive relates to whether the 'level playing field' concept is necessary for the regulation of hostile takeovers in Europe (Gilson 1991). To the High Level Group, upon whose recommendations the proposed Directive is based, rules aiming at balancing regulatory advantages are a pre-requisite to the emergence of an integrated market for corporate control. To others, the current Commission proposals may serve to create a level playing field in process but not effect.

While we welcome proposals that aim to restrain managerial discretion and control majority shareholders' extraction of private benefits within acceptable limits, we are sceptical, however, of the promised advantages of the level playing field concept (Hertig and McCahery 2003). More specifically, we submit that while the board neutrality and mandatory bid rules can serve to enhance efficiency, many other rules, such as the equitable exit price rule and the breakthrough rule, are, at best, likely to yield few benefits.

1. Board Neutrality

A recurrent theme in EU takeover policy discussions concerns the balance that policymakers must strike between protecting shareholders from the effects of managerial opportunism (represented in the form of pre and post bid defences) by adopting a board neutrality rule and deferring to the judgment of management.

It has been argued that the policy choice between board neutrality and board discretion depends on the relative efficiency of capital markets (Wachter 2002). The only feasible justification for board intervention is the existence of sufficiently large market externalities that would make it problematic for shareholders, who may be poorly informed about the value of competing bids, to choose the most efficient course of action. The main trade-off entails bad managers entrenching themselves by rejecting value enhancing tender offers against good managers that seek to maximize shareholder value by rejecting value reducing tender offers. While there are good arguments that support both sides of the trade-off, the evidence of the severity of market imperfections impact on the decision-making facilities of target shareholders is insufficient to allow us to properly evaluate the two arguments.

Even in the absence of economic evidence, it may be useful to take into account the role of board neutrality provisions in a key Member State, Germany. The 2002 Takeover Act allows for a general 'duty of neutrality' that prohibits the management from taking any unilateral action to frustrate the hostile takeover offer. However, shareholders can authorize target management to implement defence mechanisms such as: i) issuance of new shares, ii) buy-back of shares (generally limited to ten percent) and iii) sale of key assets and other major transactions.[18] Moreover, the 'duty of neutrality' does not apply to acts that would also have been performed in the ordinary course of performance, such as looking out for a competing offer, and acts approved by the supervisory board of the target company.[19]

Whether and to what extent the German Act constrains management remains unclear. From a capital-market perspective, it would, nevertheless, be preferable for reasons of transparency and coordination to have a single, simple EU rule on board neutrality. Thus, to the extent it does not affect the allocation of decision-making power in the general course of the company's business, the strict board neutrality rule is of sufficient importance to shareholders that it should be adopted.

2. Mandatory Bid and Equitable Exit Price Rules

Article 5 of the draft Takeover Bids Directive is designed to trigger a full mandatory bid when the bidder acquires a percentage of voting rights that confers on him the control of the target. We suggest that Member States should determine both the percentage of voting rights conferring control and the method of its calculation.[20] It is also our view that shareholders would support the adoption of rules on the disclosure of information regarding the bid.[21]

The strongest argument in favour of the mandatory bid rule is that it provides an exit mechanism for shareholders who do not tender in connection with a takeover bid. It also decreases market uncertainty, which enables the bidder and shareholders to capitalize on the cost of the bid and on the cost of exit respectively. On the other hand, if the bidder must obtain control from a blockholder, the mandatory bid rule is likely to prevent the incumbent blockholder from getting compensation for the loss of enjoyment of the private benefits of control. The implication, of course, is that a mandatory bid rule may limit the emergence of value-decreasing takeovers while also restricting some value-increasing takeovers.

[18] See §§71, 186 *Aktiengesetz* (Stock Company Act).

[19] See §33 *Wertpapiererwerbs- und Übernahmegesetz* (Securities Acquisition and Takeover Act, translated in Stohlmeier 2002).

[20] See Art. 5(1), 5(3) Draft Takeover Bids Directive.

[21] See Art. 6(3) Draft Takeover Bids Directive.

The notion of the equitable exit price is thus the key in the proposed mandatory bid context. The draft Takeover Bids Directive adopts the highest price rule recommended by its experts (whereas Member States can grant exemptions under certain circumstances). On this view, minority shareholders must be offered the highest price paid for the shares of the relevant class in a period between six to twelve months prior to the bid in market and over-the-counter transactions.[22]

In our view, imposing a mandatory bid rule at the EU level but leaving the definition of the trigger threshold to Member States is a sensible approach. Under this rule, minority shareholder protection is guaranteed while the differences between Member States rules nevertheless are preserved. On the other hand, mandating the highest price as the equitable exit price restrains regulatory competition that could lead to a substantial reduction in costs (Hertig and McCahery 2003). Arguably, regulatory competition may be restricted if national equitable price rules are complicated. In any event, we submit that there are better ways than mandating the highest price rule to resolve this issue (see Part IV below).

3. The Break-through Rule

The High Level Group also proposed a novel idea called the break-through rule. The rule is intended to eliminate a wide variety of pre-bid defences that are viewed as significant impediments to the emergence of a well-functioning cross-border takeover market.

The major break-through rule provides that a bidder should be permitted, upon the acquisition of 75% of cash flow rights (or any relevant threshold not higher than 75% set forth by the Member States), to convene a general meeting of shareholders at short notice and impose one-share one-vote. Thus, any mechanisms or structures that deviate from the principles of shareholder decision-making and proportionality between risk-bearing and control will be broken through.

So, for example, upon reaching the required threshold, the bidder will be permitted to: (1) amend the articles of association and other constitutional documents; (2) remove any pre-bid takeover defences approved by shareholders; (3) remove voting caps and differential voting rights; (4) remove provisions denying voting rights; (5) remove voting rights on non-risk bearing capital; (6) appoint, suspend, and dismiss the board members other than those appointed by third parties; (7) determine the composition of the board; (8) remove any staggered and/or fixed period provisions; and (9) override special control rights attached to golden shares.

[22] See Recommendation II.2, High Level Group of Company Law Experts 2002b; Art. 5(5) Draft Takeover Bids Directive. Compare Art. 32(4) Swiss Stock Exchange Law (the exit price cannot be less than 75% of the highest price paid by the bidder in the past twelve months).

In the US, most empirical studies have found that takeover defences have limited or no impact on bid outcomes (Hannes 2002; Bebchuk, Coates and Subramian 2002; Brickley, Coles and Terry 1994). This is consistent with practicing lawyers' positions about takeover defences causing little harm and having impact only at the margins. Unlike in the US, there are few empirical studies in Europe that analyse the wealth effects of pre-bid defences by shareholders. A recent study investigates the performance of Danish firms that adopted dual class shares for period between 1995 and 1999 (Rose 2002). It shows that unprotected firms do not outperform firms protected by dual class stock. A potential explanation is that other corporate governance mechanisms, such as blockholder monitoring, appear to limit managerial opportunism. In our view, the efficiency implications of break through rules are inconclusive (Hertig and McCahery 2003). Moreover, Berglöf and Burkart (2002) argue that the break-through rule is inconsistent with the mandatory bid rule.

Indeed, the main effect of the break-through rule is to transform a bid for a company with a concentrated ownership structure into a dispersed bid. If the incumbent controlling shareholders have access to sufficient funds to launch a counter bid, the bidder will in turn be forced to bid at least as much as the incumbent shareholder. The maximum bid of the incumbent shareholder will include the sum total of his private benefits and the stock market valuation of the target firm. But, if the incumbent is financially constrained, the bidder will not offer more than the public value of the target firm after the completion of the takeover. As a result, the bidder's dominant strategy will be to use the cash-flow rights related break-through rule as a means of acquiring control, even if the incumbent management is in principle willing to enter into negotiations.

In legal terms, the break-through rule leads to the acquisition of control not by passing a threshold on voting share holdings but by effecting a change in a corporate charter. It is, however, unclear whether such a control transfer would trigger a mandatory bid. To the extent that a mandatory bid is not triggered, the problems associated with two-tier takeover bids would be reintroduced.

There are other problems as well. For example, if we assume that an incumbent shareholder is not willing to tender, the break-through rule may create special problems by failing to provide an incentive for the new majority shareholders to squeeze out minority shareholders. Another important implication of the break-through rule is that it could alter ownership structures and concentration of voting rights. For example, some predict that the break-through rule might induce firms – particularly new firms – to substitute a dual-class structure with a pyramiding structure.[23] Such a step may in turn give rise, among other things, to problems related to monitoring, managerial incentives, and liquidity.

[23] But cf Gordon 2003: 51 (arguing that pyramids are not a low-cost substitute for firms going public).

To sum up, the introduction of the break through rules will not only likely to result in inconsistency and uncertainty, but is also unlikely to contribute to the emergence of a competitive market for corporate control.

4. Summary

There are some harmonization proposals that are likely to enhance transparency and shareholder protection, namely the board neutrality and the mandatory bid rules. On the other hand, there are good reasons to reject the highest price and the break-through rules. As we will show below, we argue that a better approach would be to offer firms with default arrangements that would serve their needs.

D. An Alternative Approach to Corporate Law Reform

We have argued that the mandatory approach of the EU company law harmonization program is mostly misguided because it provides few incentives to lawmakers to create optimal rules and, to the extent that they disrupt efficient transactions and cause firms to incur high costs, yield few benefits. Whilst there is no shortage of proposals to reforming EU company law, many of the proposals insist on the need for greater flexibility and up to date legislation, while others regard nothing as more important than the fulfilling the European Commission's efforts to harmonize the main areas of company law and corporate governance. Some suggest that the European Commission should respond more forcefully to the crisis in company law harmonization program, while others recommend that lawmakers stand back and allow Member States to undertake the design and implementation of cost-effective default rules that meet the needs of many types of companies.

We are struck by the fact that advocates rarely advance EU reforms that would allow firms to opt out of corporate law rules and substitute private contractual provisions. Let us, therefore, consider the implications of switching to a selective opt-in/opt-out default rule approach in light of our earlier analysis. For those concerned about improving corporate performance, there are good theoretical and practical reasons for allowing firms to either opt *into* EU provisions (and thus opting out of Member State law) or to opt *out* of EU provisions (and thus opting into Member State law). In other words, in some areas, firms that object to the applicable Member State regime's mandatory requirements or find the default regime offered by the EU advantageous from a standardization or signalling perspective, could choose to opt-into the relevant EU provisions and out of the Member State regime. In other areas, firms that object to the directly applicable default EU regime could choose to opt into the relevant Member State provisions, which could be either mandatory or default ones. Allowing more choice encourages both EU and Member State lawmakers to design value-maximizing provisions and, where there is adequate competition, engage in innovative lawmaking.

We illustrate below the potential value of such an approach. The first subsection discusses the limits to centralized rulemaking in the EU. The second subsection focuses on the desirability of creating a menu of opt-in/opt-out default provisions. The final subsection shows how the EU could adopt choice enhancing provisions for both corporate law and the regulation of cross-border takeover bids.

I. The Cost of Mandatory EU Company Law Harmonization

As we have seen, the EU follows a mandatory harmonization approach to company law reform that limits contractual choice of law. To date, policymakers have harmonized a core set of rules for both close and open corporations, albeit the regulatory constraints for closely held corporations are less stringent.

Much of the literature on harmonization relies on the intuition that regulatory choices will have an impact on efficiency or distribution and, consequently, policy makers will choose mandatory arrangements that will benefit some parties better than others (O'Hara 2000: 1564-75). Consider, for example, the EU policy on legal capital. With its bank-centered system of finance, continental European Member States have an incentive to protect creditors' welfare by selecting capital maintenance rules that are deemed optimal for banks even though they may generate significant economic distortions (Enriques and Macey 2001).

Although there is a strong economic argument for harmonization, based on the high information costs required for firms to identify the correct rule to adopt and the advantages of standardization, it is by now equally clear that the introduction of mandatory harmonizing EU directives has resulted in higher costs for many types of firms and has little effect overall on encouraging economic integration. It has also been suggested that the restrictive EU arrangement has minimized the ability of firms to respond effectively to market changes, with potentially negative effects for shareholders.

There is significant evidence that, over the past forty years, EU lawmakers have, by favouring mandatory harmonization, pursued national policy objectives designed to limit regulatory competition between Member States – the ultimate aim being to prevent England or another EU jurisdiction to become the European equivalent of Delaware. Such collusion between Member States has achieved some measure of success in preventing the introduction of competitive pressures in corporate lawmaking. It is true that Member State governments have been unable to prevent key features of the rigid harmonization approach from giving way to a new approach based on mutual recognition, nor have they been able to prevent ECJ case law from increasingly eroding the barriers to free choice of corporate law arrangements. It remains, however, that firms still face significant constraints in their freedom of choice, which continue to prevent most of them from escaping the traditional corporate law regimes and, potentially, improve the welfare of their shareholders.

II. Shifting to an Opt-in/Opt-out Default Approach

Many US corporate law scholars have argued that firms should be free to choose the corporate law rules that they prefer. Early arguments were supplied by scholars who argued that lawmakers should treat corporate law as an exercise in contractual gap-filling pursuant to the 'hypothetical content principle', a universal norm to guide the supply of default terms and gap filling. Under the principle, the legal system supplies the rule that both parties to the contract would have adopted had they addressed the matter *ex ante* in a costless world. Terms that follow the principle will, according to this approach, be efficient for all situations (Easterbrook and Fischel 1991).

Whatever the merits of the hypothetical bargains approach, the law and economics literature has expressed strong scepticism (Ayres 1992; Bratton et al 1996). An alternative incomplete contracts approach suggests that problems arise from attempting to write *ex ante* contracts, due to a diverse range of transaction costs. First, it is difficult for parties to anticipate all the possible contingencies that might arise, and design the contractual provisions to deal with them. Second, even if the parties could specify all the relevant contingencies, there are so many of them that it would be extremely difficult for the parties to write them into a contract. Third, the costs of verifying the performance of the other party may make create disincentives to write a complete contract. Fourth, the enforcement of the contract is expensive.

In general, the understanding of incomplete contracts theory raises many questions about favouring *ex ante* default arrangements. The theoretical literature on default rules has also shown that certain default arrangements can produce undesirable outcomes. For example, it is well known that managers or controlling shareholders may select a default arrangement (either the one provided by lawmakers or a tailor-made one) that not only favours them, but also impose excessive costs on the firm or minority shareholders. This is not too surprising. The default approach's advantage, freedom of choice, also has the inherent disadvantage of providing insiders with room for opportunism.

Nevertheless, this should not lead us to the conclusion that the default approach is inferior to the mandatory approach. First, the default approach inherently constraints the extent to which managers and controlling shareholders can act opportunistically. Indeed, shareholders generally expect the firm's original arrangements to reflect the default rules provided by lawmakers rather than default rules devised by management or controlling shareholders. Moreover, even powerful managers may, due to endowment effects, face shareholder opposition to proposals to amend the original arrangement. (Sunstein 2002: 112-118; Korobkin 2003: 1228). To be sure, such constraints are not strong enough to eliminate opportunistic behaviour. On the other hand, they can be considered a low cost barrier to abusive use of freedom of choice.

Second, lawmakers can adopt default compatible mechanisms to further constrain managers and controlling shareholders. They can, and often do, use the penalty default approach, under which the terms of the default are left open until relevant information is available (Ayres 1989). More importantly, lawmakers can adopt a reverse default rule to reduce the power of managers (Bebchuk and Hamdani 2002: 502). Hence, when faced with the choice between restrictive and less restrictive default rules, lawmakers can be best advised to adopt the arrangement that least favours management. If the restrictive measure turns out to be inefficient, the error should not be too costly since both parties will quickly support replacing the state provided arrangement by a tailor-made one.

Third, lawmakers can reinforce default rules with mandatory provisions. For example, giving shareholders the right to initiate charter amendments could make it more difficult for managers to prevent shareholders from the benefit of opting-in or opting-out opportunities.[24] Similarly, requiring qualified majority voting or even non-controlling shareholders approval to opt out of a EU sell-out rights rule would make reverse default rules effective not only vis-à-vis managers, but also vis-à-vis controlling shareholders.

It follows that, in many areas of corporate and takeover law, EU policymakers would be well served by replacing the current mandatory harmonization regime with an enabling regime based on market experimentation under uncertainty. The adoption of default rules should not only reduce the cost of contracting, but also eliminate the implementation and enforcement difficulties encountered under the mandatory approach. Firms are unlikely to object to or circumvent rules that provide more choice. Similarly, Member States are less likely to oppose regulatory intervention that neither prevents new firms from choosing the existing domestic regime nor forces established firms to abandon the latter – or, at least, leaves firms with the option to revert to the existing domestic regime. As a matter of fact, one would expect EU lawmakers to offer the possibility of using an opt-in rather than an opt-out approach for those corporate law provisions that are most sensitive for Member States. Hence, the optional approach, since it provides less petrifying rules, can serve as a cost-saving alternative to using mandatory rules.

III. Menu of EU Provisions

A shift from a mandatory to an enabling approach implies that regulators will provide a menu of default arrangements that firms will be free to choose, either as a whole or merely in part. Accordingly, three issues face regulators in creating a menu of rules: (1) what sort of provisions should be part of the menu; (2) will they be opt-out or opt-in; and (3) what are the mandatory requirements needed to reinforce provisions on the menu?

[24] Compare Bebchuk and Hamdani 2002: 505-6 (proposing the same rule, but as a default one).

The notion of introducing an enabling regime for EU company law raises complex issues. Indeed, EU regulators addressing these issues face various well-known trade-offs. From a shareholder welfare perspective, they will for example have to balance the advantages of minority protection default rules and the costs they impose on the efficient management of the firm. From a political economy perspective, EU regulators will, amongst other things, have to evaluate whether it is worth applying opt out provisions to both new and existing firms, given the risk of provoking additional Member State opposition to the new approach. It is obvious they will face the same issues when deciding whether to imposing new mandatory requirements that reinforce EU opt-in or opt-out provisions.

There will always be disputes about these and other tradeoffs, notwithstanding the EC's continuing efforts to reach a basis for Member States to pursue policy reform. But the point here is not, in the face of the obvious need to achieve some transformations in corporate regulation, to attempt to resolve these tradeoffs. Our approach, in contrast, is more limited. As we shall see, our aim is not to provide a complete set of default arrangements but rather to identify the main candidates for EU opt-out and opt-in, as well as the mandatory requirements that might be needed to reinforce them. We will also consider how providing a menu of default terms, which has been overlooked by EU regulators until recently, could have the desirable effect of resolving the deadlock over the proposed Takeover Bids Directive.

1. Main candidates for a default approach

Opt-out clauses. Such clauses are especially adapted to situations in which Member State law clearly does not respond to the needs of firms or prevents them from exercising freedom of choice. We submit that, as far as established firms are concerned, opt-out clauses could include provisions on squeeze-out and sell-out rights, mandatory takeover bids as well as on shareholder standing to sue. The later, in particular, could enhance the position of minority shareholders while allowing firms to opt back into Member States law should the interest of shareholders as a class justify a return to the *status quo ante*. We also submit that, as far as new firms are concerned, one share, one vote as well as the prohibition of staggered boards, voting caps and pyramid structures could be prime candidates for EU opt-out provisions.

Opt-in clauses. Providing business parties with a menu of EU default provisions that are especially adapted to situations in which Member States have passed mandatory or default provisions – that they are loath to sacrifice to the benefits of further EU harmonization – can play a productive role in EU law reform.[25] In this view, EU opt-in provisions leave Member State law unchanged,

[25] While relying on a menu of opt-in provisions is not efficiency-enforcing generally, promoting the development of menus of default rules may be a practical way of resolving cont. ...

while permitting firms to escape domestic provisions that are overly constraining or to opt for standardized provisions that are known to shareholders and stakeholders across the EU. Seen from this perspective, there may be a long list of potential candidates for EU opt-in provisions. That said, there is a compelling argument for allowing parties to choose among packages of default rules for approval procedures for related party transactions (including for compensation), board neutrality in takeover situations and employee participation structures.

Mandatory provisions. There may be merits also in reinforcing default rules with four types of mandatory provisions. First, the EU could impose special voting requirements for opt-in or opt-out procedures. For example, special majorities could be required to opt-out from the shareholder standing rule, whereas opting-out of the mandatory bid rule could require minority shareholder approval. Second, the EU could impose state audit supervision, to improve shareholder confidence in the new default regime by reinforcing the legitimacy and reputation of an essential monitor. Third, the EU could adopt standardization provisions in areas where Member State law is too complex or diverse for the needs of a single market. Fourth, the EU could reinforce the shareholder standing rule by facilitating large-scale litigation through the adoption of discovery, attorney fees and cross-border mechanisms.

2. Testing ground: Takeover Law

Another area of company law regulation where the introduction of a menu of default rules can be expected to be beneficial for companies is takeover law. In seeking to fashion a proposal that might win approval for the EU's proposed Takeover Bids Directive, the Italian Presidency of the European Council announced, in October 2003, its endorsement of the proposal of the Portuguese delegation that would allow Member States to permit firms to opt out of Articles 9 and 11 of the proposed Takeover Bids Directive.

The Portuguese proposal has two distinct components.[26] The first is that it allows for Member States to permit shareholders to opt out of the board neutrality (Art. 9) and the breakthrough rules (Art. 11), with the practical effect that their firms will be regulated by Member State takeover rules. Second, the proposal rests on a delicate premise: firms that opt out will not be allowed to launch a hostile bid for firms that are regulated by the EU takeover regime ('reciprocity').

The implicit assumption here is that firms that opt-out of the EU regime may face fewer hostile bids because their defences are insurmountable. However, it is very difficult to predict how many offers will be diverted because of an opt-out. If

problems between Member States. See Cheffins 1997: 253-56; Riley 1999: 82-84; O'Hara 2000: 1574-80.

[26] Directive on Company Law Concerning Takeover Bids, Portuguese Proposal (June 2, 2003).

takeover premiums are significant enough, managers or controlling shareholders may well strike a deal over the distribution of private benefits of control – not least because an opt-out makes it more difficult for shareholders to argue that managers violated their fiduciary duties. The result is that reciprocity might not create a significant barrier to hostile bids deals so long as blockholders and managers have incentives to accept tenders and the transaction costs are not prohibitive.

The value of the new proposal is that it seeks to offer something to the Member States that oppose board neutrality as well as to those Member States supporting a strong directive that would impose both key provisions. At first glance, the Portuguese proposal might seem to be of marginal significance since the inclusion of the reciprocity provisions makes hostile bids more costly and is therefore unlikely to foster far reaching corporate governance changes in some Member States. Still, this framework might prove useful for increasing the number of takeover bids overall. In particular, even if key provisions are optional, the Takeover Bids Directive will create simplified legal rules regarding bids, equitable price, disclosure and squeeze-outs and sell outs that should improve transaction transparency. Generally speaking, the economic analysis indicates, moreover, that even a weak directive can yield benefits for shareholders (McCahery et al 2003). To the extent that lawmakers can promote the goals of increasing cross-border deals and disciplining private benefits extraction while providing desirable flexibility in the face of organizational diversity and information asymmetries, the Portuguese proposal may play an important role for regulating the internal market.

To be sure, there are a number of significant issues that must be addressed before the opt out proposal might be acceptable. In light of the history of the proposed Takeover Bids Directive, two questions are of central importance. First, should Member States or companies decide about the applicability of Articles 9 and 11 of the Takeover Bids Directive? From a shareholder choice perspective, there are a number of arguments derived from finance theory supporting the view that shareholders rather than public officials are best placed to make the decision about what corporate law rules to select. Whatever the explanation for the EC's decision to allow Member States to opt out of either Article 9 or 11, there is little evidence in favour of legislation providing public officials with such powers.

Second, what are the procedural rules regulating the right to initiate and decide about the applicability of the EU regime in Member States that have opted out of Articles 9 and 11? The answer should be straightforward except that Member States have quite diverse requirements. What are the consequences of the EU adopting an optional takeover law? To begin, the flexibility associated with leaving Member States with the powers to decide whether firms can opt-out will resolve some of the conflicts about which rules should govern the role of the board and anti-takeover mechanisms. Second, the opt-out proposal may potentially resolve another key issue that has prevented smooth passage of the Takeover Bids Directive. To the extent that the proposal requires shareholder decision-making in firms allowed to 'opt-out', there is no need for a legal reciprocity clause between firms of different regimes. Unfortunately, Member States opposed to leaving firms' with an opt-out choice are likely to impose the adoption of a legal reciprocity clause that will reduce the number of high quality takeovers by restricting non-EU firms bidding, which in turn will be counterproductive to the Commission's aim of creating an integrated market for corporate control.

Still, the consequences of promoting an optional arrangement involving takeover rules is likely to provide a satisfactory basis for resolving conflicts between Member States and the problems of creating a cross-border market for corporate control will be less acute.

E. Conclusion

In this essay, we have explored the possibility of stimulating a new direction in EU company law reform through the introduction of opt-in/opt-out default rules. We have argued that contractual choice of law is desirable for business parties because it allows them to neutralize the costs of inefficient regulations. Furthermore, we have argued that, according to bargaining theory, parties that have the opportunity to draft their own contract terms are likely to adopt inefficient arrangements because of asymmetries in information and bargaining power. In light of these distortions, there is considerable evidence to support, in some contexts, default arrangements that require opting out or into EU law. We have attempted to examine the areas of company law that would presumptively benefit from EU regulations that allow firms better control over their contracting costs and encourage regulators to design rules that benefit shareholders. In particular, the pervasiveness of distributive politics at the legislative level suggests that allowing companies to opt out of some EU takeover rules could be useful to break the legislative deadlock and provide shareholders with clear alternatives. We conclude by suggesting that a switch to an enabling regime, that permits firms to opt in and out of legal rules, will provide a clear set of benefits for a wide range of companies and supply much needed incentives to lawmakers at the European and Member State level.

References

Ayres, Ian. 1992. 'Making a Difference: The Contractual Contributions of Easterbrook and Fischel', 59 *University of Chicago Law Review* (1992) 1391.

Ayres, Ian and Robert Gertner. 1989. 'Filling Gaps in Incomplete *Contracts: An Economic Theory of Default Rules*', 99 *Yale Law Journal* (1989) 87.

Barca, Fabrizio and Marco Becht (eds). 2002. *The Control of Corporate Europe*. (Oxford: Oxford University Press, 2002).

Baums, Theodor. 2003. 'Company Law Reform in Germany', 3 *Journal of Corporate Law Studies* (2003) 181.

Bebchuk, Lucian A. 2002. 'The Case Against Board Veto in Corporate Takeovers', 69 *University of Chicago Law Review* (2002) 973.

Bebchuk, Lucian A., John C. Coates IV and Guhan Subramian. 2002. 'The Powerful Antitakeover Force of Staggered Boards: Theory, Evidence, and Policy', 54 *Stanford Law Review* (2002) 887.

Bebchuk, Lucian A., Alma Cohen and Allen Ferrell. 2002. 'Does the Evidence Favor State Competition in Corporate Law?', 90 *California Law Review* (2002) 1775.

Bebchuk, Lucian A. and Alma Cohen. 2003. 'Firms' Decision Where to Incorporate', 46 *Journal of Law and Economics* (October 2003, forthcoming).

Bebchuk, Lucian A. and Assaf Hamdani. 2002. 'Vigorous Race or Leisurly Walk: Reconsidering State Competition over Corporate Charters', 112 *Yale Law Journal* (2002) 553.

Bebchuk, Lucian A. and Mark J. Roe. 1999. 'A Theory of Path Dependence in Corporate Ownership and Governance', 52 *Stanford Law Review* (1999) 775.

Behrens, Peter. 2001.'*Centros* and the Proper Law of Companies', in Guido Ferrarini, Klaus J. Hopt and Eddy Wymeersch (eds) *Capital Markets in the Age of the EURO*. (The Hague: Kluwer Law International, 2001).

Berglöf, Erik. 1997. 'Reforming Corporate Governance', *European Economy* (1997) 93.

Berglöf, Erik and Mike Burkart. 2002. 'Break-through in European Takeover Regulation?', Stockholm School of Economics Working Paper (2002).

Berkowitz, Daniel, Katharina Pistor and Jean-Francois Richard. 2003. 'The Transplant Effect', 51 *American Journal of Comparative Law* (2003) 163.

Black, Bernard S. 1990. 'Is Corporate Law Trivial? – A Political and Economic Analysis', 84 *Northwestern University Law Review* (1990) 542.

Black, Bernard S., Reinier Kraakman and Anna Tarassova. 2000. 'Russian Privatization and Corporate Governance: What Went Wrong?', 52 *Stanford Law Review* (2000) 1731.

Brickley, James A., Jeffrey L. Coles and Rory L.Terry.1994. 'Outside Directors and the Adoption of Poison Pills', 35 *Journal of Finance* (1994) 371.

Bratton, William W., Morten Hviid and Joseph A. McCahery. 1996. 'Repeated Games, Social Norms and Incomplete Corporate Contracts', in Chris Willett (ed.), *Aspects of Fairness in Contracts*. (London: Blackstone Press, 1996).

Bratton, William W. and Joseph A. McCahery. 1999. 'Comparative Corporate Governance and the Theory of the Firm', 38 *Columbia Journal of Transnational Law* (1999) 213.

Cheffins, Brian. 1997. *Company Law: Theory, Structure and Operation*. (Oxford: Oxford University Press, 1997).

Coffee, John C. Jr. 1999. 'The Future as History: The Prospects for Global Convergence in Corporate Governance and Its Implications', 93 *Northwestern University Law Review* (1999) 641.

Coffee, John C. Jr. 2001. 'The Acquiescent Gatekeeper: Reputational Intermediaries, Auditor Independence and the Governance of Accounting', Columbia University School of Law and John M. Olin Center of Law and Economics Working Paper (2001).

Conac, Pierre-Henri. 2002. *La Régulation des Marchés Boursiers par la COB et la SEC.* (Paris: LGDJ-Montchrestien, 2002).

Daines, Robert B. 2001. 'Does Delaware Law Improve Firm Value?', 62 *Journal of Financial Economics* (2001) 525.

Deakin, Simon. 2001. 'Regulatory Competition versus Harmonization in European Company Law', in Daniel Esty and Damien Geradin (eds) *Regulatory Competition and Economic Integration.* (Oxford: Oxford University Press, 2001).

Easterbrook, Frank H. and Daniel R. Fischel. 1991. *The Economic Structure of Corporate Law.* (Cambridge, Mass.: Harvard University Press, 1991).

Ebke, Werner F. 2000. '*Centros* – Some Realities and Some Mysteries', 48 *American Journal of Comparative Law* (2000) 623.

Enriques, Luca. 2004. 'Silence is Golden: The European Company Statute as a Catalyst for Company Law Arbitrage', 4 *Journal of Corporate Law Studies* (forthcoming 2004).

Enriques, Luca and Jonathan R. Macey. 2001. 'Creditors versus Capital Formation: The Case against the European Legal Capital Rules', 86 *Cornell Law Review* (2001) 1165.

European Communities. 2003. 'Communication from the Commission, Modernising Company Law and Enhancing Corporate Governance in the European Union – A Plan to Move Forward', COM(2003) 284 final (available at http://www.europa.eu.int) (Annex 1 in this volume).

European Communities. 2003. 'Communication from the Commission, Reinforcing the Statutory Audit in the EU' [2003], OJ L 236/2.

Gilson, Ronald J. 1991. 'The Political Economy of Takeovers: Thoughts on Harmonizing the European Corporate Governance Environment', 61 *Fordham Law Review* (1991) 161.

Gilson, Ronald J. 2001. 'Globalizing Corporate Governance: Convergence of Form or Function', 49 *American Journal of Comparative Law* (2001) 329.

Gordon, Jeffrey N. 2003. 'An International Relations Perspective on the Convergence of Corporate Governance: German Shareholder Capitalism and the European Union, 1990-2000' in Jeffrey N. Gordon and Mark J. Roe (eds) *Convergence and Persistence in Corporate Governance.* (Cambridge: Cambridge University Press, 2004 forthcoming).

Grundmann, Stefan. 2002 'Regulatory Competition in European Company Law – Some Different Genius', in Guido Ferrarini, Klaus Hopt and Eddy Wymeersch (eds) *Capital Markets in the Age of the EURO* (The Hague: Kluwer Academic Press 2002).

Halbhuber, Harld. 2001. 'National Doctrinal Structures and European Company Law', 38 *Common Market Law Review* (2001) 1385.

Hansmann, Henry and Reinier Kraakman. 2001. 'The End of History for Corporate Law', 89 *Georgetown Law Journal* (2001) 439.

Hansmann, Henry and Reinier Kraakman. 2004. 'The Basic Governance Structure', in Reinier Kraakman, Paul Davies, Henry Hansmann, Gerard Hertig, Klaus J. Hopt, Hideki Kanda and Edward B. Rock, *The Anatomy of Corporate Law*. (Oxford: Oxford University Press, 2004 forthcoming).

Hannes, Sharon. 2002. 'The Hidden Virtues of Antitakover Defenses', Harvard University School of Law, Working Paper (2002).

Hertig, Gérard and Hideki Kanda. 2004. 'Creditor Protection', in Reinier Kraakman, Paul Davies, Henry Hansmann, Gerard Hertig, Klaus J. Hopt, Hideki Kanda and Edward B. Rock, *The Anatomy of Corporate Law*. (Oxford: Oxford University Press, 2004 forthcoming).

Hertig, Gérard and Ruben Lee. 2003. 'Four Predictions about the Future of EU Securities Regulation', 3 *Journal of Corporate Law Studies* (2003) 359.

Hertig, Gerard and Joseph A. McCahery. 2003. 'Company and Takeover Law Reforms in Europe: Misguided Harmonization Efforts or Regulatory Competition', 4 *European Business Organization Law Review* (2003) 179.

High Level Group of Company Law Experts. 2002. *Report of the High Level Group of Company Law Experts on Issues Related to Takeover Bids*. (Brussels: The Commission of the European Communities, 2002) (Annex 2 in this volume).

High Level Group of Company Law Experts. 2002. *Report of the High Level Group of Company Law Experts on a Modern Regulatory Framework for Company Law in Europe*. (Brussels: The Commission of the European Communities, 2002) (Annex 3 in this volume).

Hopt, Klaus J. 2002. 'Common Principles of Corporate Governance in Europe', in Joseph A. McCahery, Piet Moerland, Theo Raaijmakers and Luc Renneboog (eds) *Corporate Governance Regimes: Convergence and Diversity*. (Oxford: Oxford University Press 2002).

Hopt, Klaus J. 2003. 'Modern Company Law and Capital Market Problems, Improving European Corporate Governance After Enron', 3 *Journal of Corporate Law Studies* (2003) 11.

Inman, Robert B. and Daniel L. Rubinfeld. 1997. 'Rethinking Federalism', 11 *Journal of Economic Perspectives* (1997) 43.

Kahan Marcel and Ehud Kamar. 2002. 'The Myth of State Competition in Corporate Law', 55 *Stanford Law Review* (2002) 679.

Korobkin, Russell. 2003. 'The Endowment Effect and Legal Analysis', 97 *Northwestern Law Review* (2003) 1227.

Kraakman, Reinier, Henry Hansmann, Gérard Hertig, Klaus Hopt, Hideki Kanda, and Edward B. Rock 2004. *The Anatomy of Corporate Law*. (Oxford: Oxford University Press 2004).

La Porta, Rafael, Florencio Lopez-de-Silanes, Andrei Shleifer and Robert Vishny. 1997. 'Legal Determinants of External Finance', 52 *Journal of Finance* (1997) 1131.

La Porta, Rafael, Florencio Lopez-de-Silanes, Andrei Shleifer and Robert W. Vishny. 1999. 'Corporate Ownership Around the World', 54 *Journal of Finance* (1999) 471.

McCahery, Joseph A. and Erik P.M. Vermeulen. 2001. 'The Evolution of Closely Held Business Forms in Europe', 26 *Journal of Corporation Law* (2001) 855.

McCahery, Joseph A., Luc Renneboog, Peer Ritter and Sascha Haller. 2003. *The Economics of the Proposed European Takeover Directive*. (Brussels: Centre for European Policy Studies, 2003).

Mülbert, Peter and Max Birke. 2002. 'Legal Capital – Is there a Case Against the European Legal Capital Rules?', 3 *European Business Organization Law Review* (2002) 695.

O'Hara, Erin A. 2000. 'Opting Out of Regulation: A Public Choice Analysis of Contractual Choice of Law', 53 *Vanderbilt Law Review* (2000) 1551.

Pollock, Mark A. 2003. *The Engines of European Integration. Delegation, Agency, and Agenda Setting in the EU*. (Oxford: Oxford University Press, 2003).

Riley, Chris A. 1999. 'Managing the Diversity of Business Relationships', in Barry A.K. Rider and Mads Andenas (eds) *Developments in European Company Law, Volume 2/1997: The Quest for an Ideal Form for Small Businesses*. (The Hague: Kluwer Law International, 1999).

Romano, Roberta. 1985. 'The State Competition Debate in Corporate Law', 1 *Journal of Law, Economics and Organization* (1985) 225.

Romano, Roberta. 2001. 'The Need for Competition in International Securities Regulation', 2 *Theoretical Inquiries in Law* (2001) 1.

Rose, Caspar 2002. 'Corporate Financial Performance and the Use of Takeover Defenses', 13 *European Journal of Law and Economics* (2002) 91.

Stohlmeier, Thomas. 2002. *German Public Takeover Law*. (The Hague: Kluwer Law International, 2002).

Sunstein, Cass R. 2002. 'Switching the Default Rule', 77 *New York University Law Review* (2002) 106.

Tjiong, Henri. 2002. 'Breaking the Spell of Regulatory Competition: Reframing the Problem of Regulatory Exit', 66 *RabelsZ* (2002) 66.

Wachter, Michael L. 2002. 'Takeover Defenses when Financial Markets are (only) Relatively Efficient', University of Pennsylvania Institute of Law and Economics Working Paper (2002).

Weingast, Barry. 1995. 'The Economic Role of Political Institutions: Market Preserving Federalism and Economic Development', 1 *Journal of Law, Economics and Organization* (1995) 1.

Wouters, Jan. 2000. 'European Company Law: Quo Vadis?', 37 *Common Market Law Review* (2000) 257.

Wymeersch, Eddy. 1998. 'A Status Report on Corporate Governance Rules and Practices in Some Continental European States', in Klaus J.Hopt, Hideki Kanda, Mark J. Roe, Eddy Wymeersch and Stephen Prigge (eds) *Comparative Corporate Governance: The State of the Art and Emerging Research*. (Oxford: Oxford University Press, 1998).

Trusteeship and Conflicts of Interest in Corporate, Banking, and Agency Law: Toward Common Legal Principles for Intermediaries in the Modern Service-Oriented Society

KLAUS J. HOPT*

'Trusteeship and conflicts of interest' is a problem area in the modern service-oriented society that is simultaneously fundamental and timely. It is a characteristic of our time that complexity is growing everywhere and can only be coped with, if at all, by the help of intermediaries, specialized service providers, and agents. These persons take care of other people's interests and promise to render this service loyally without giving precedence to conflicting self-interest or to the interest of other principals. This is true, for example, for board members, banks, commission dealers and agents, commercial agents, lawyers, auditors, brokers, and many other fiduciaries of various kinds. Conflicts of interest arise everywhere in modern life – in politics, parties, press, business, and banking, as well as in science, as I am unfortunately able to observe as vice president of the German Science Foundation (*Deutsche Forschungsgemeinschaft*). *Guido Rossi,* the father of the Italian antitrust law and a member of the High Level Group of Company Law Experts for the European Commission, is of the opinion that specialization and conflicts of interest are tantamount to a systemic condition of modern society.[1]

[*] Conference held on July 24, 2003, in Karlsruhe in the new library of the German Bundesgerichtshof at the invitation of the German Lawyers' Association, the President of the Bundesgerichtshof, and the Law Society in Karlsruhe. A longer, more dogmatic version in German can be found in Zeitschrift für Unternehmens- und Gesellschaftsrecht (ZGR) 2004, 1-52.

[1] G Rossi *In conflitto epidemico* (Milan 2003). Cf JS Demski 'Corporate Conflicts of Interest' (2003) 17 Journal of Economic Perspectives 51; C Engel 'Causes and Management of Conflicts' (2003) 159 Journal of Institutional and Theoretical Perspective 1 (2 ff).

A. Introduction

The agent who makes a profession out of taking care of other people's interest has to draw an income from this profession. The temptation is high to give precedence, surreptitiously, to self-interest or inappropriately to the interest of third parties over the interest of the principal who may be less knowledgeable or uninformed. In modern economics, this temptation has given rise to the question of the principal-agent relationship, which in turn has led to the development of an entirely new, fast-growing field of research and many schools of thought on how to handle the conflicts arising in this relationship. This research started in the United States and has quickly spread to – and is now also firmly rooted in – Europe.[2] The question is what kind or set of contractual and institutional conditions are necessary in order to enable the principal to control the agent. In corporate law, this question is discussed today under the heading of corporate governance, and this discussion extends more and more to an interdisciplinary and international dialogue, i.e., comparative corporate governance.[3] This was described in a nutshell as early as 1776 by *Adam Smith* in his seminal book 'An Inquiry into the Nature and Causes of the Wealth of Nations.' There it reads: 'The directors of such companies, however, being the managers rather of other people's money than of their own, it cannot well be expected, that they should watch over it with the same anxious vigilance with which the partners in a private co-partnership frequently watch over their own. … Negligence and profusion, therefore, must always prevail, more or less, in the management of the affairs of such a company.'[4] This is illustrated by the leading *Schaffgotsch* decision of the German Federal Bundesgerichtshof,[5] in which the president of the supervisory board got the corporation to issue a bill of exchange to the advantage of his own bank that was in grave financial difficulties. Well-known modern examples include the American cases concerning the conflicts of interest of securities analysts who just seemed to be independent, but in reality acted merely in the interest of their employer banks by recommending securities to be sold by these banks to the public. In Germany, a prominent example has been provided by the president of the Verdi trade union, *Frank Bsirske.* He felt uninhibited to continue to act as vice president of the supervisory board of the Lufthansa corporation while organizing an airport strike in the public service which caused millions of Euro of damages

[2] U Mattei *Comparative Law and Economics* (Ann Arbor 1997); H Fleischer 'Grundfragen der ökonomischen Theorie im Gesellschafts- und Kapitalmarktrecht' [2001] Zeitschrift für Unternehmens- und Gesellschaftsrecht (ZGR) 1.

[3] KJ Hopt, H Kanda, MJ Roe, E Wymeersch and S Prigge (eds) *Comparative Corporate Governance* (Oxford 1998).

[4] Book 5, Ch 1.3.1.2 (5th edn London 1789).

[5] Bundesgerichtshof, [1980] Neue Juristische Wochenschrift (NJW) 1629.

to the corporation. At the general meeting in June 2003, the Lufthansa shareholders reacted by denying to him alone the ratification of the acts of the members of the supervisory board. This was highly unusual and outright spectacular, though no concrete legal consequences follow from such a refusal.[6] Other legal measures – such as a claim for damages – have not been taken.

Conflicts arise not only between the interests of the principal and the agent. Modern professional intermediation often brings about the collision of interests of various principals. There are two main categories of such multiple interest conflicts. First, the agent may act in the interest of more than one principal whose interests lie in and collide on the same side of the market. Examples are the attribution of newly issued, oversubscribed securities to a favourite large client, a practice that unfortunately was common in the late German New Market. Similarly, a particularly good deal – a premise, for example – may be improperly attributed to one of several clients. Second, the conflict may be one between two principals on different sides of the market. Examples for such conflicts are the typical conflicts of interest, which arise for issuing banks between the corporation and the investing public. Similar conflicts exist in the legal profession, for example, for large law firms if a partner changes over to another law firm or in cases of mergers or de-mergers of law firms. In such cases – and more generally if the clients are large international firms – the classes of clients overlap in a way that is hardly manageable.

The question is whether there are solutions for such conflicts of interest that offer better answers than the biblical injunction from St. Matthew 6:24: 'Nobody can serve two masters.' Or is Guido Rossi right in calling for more professional and business ethics, a plea that is certainly important, but, if things get really serious, may often be nothing more than a palliative measure?

B. Duties of Loyalty of Corporate Organs Under Special Contracts and of Professional Intermediaries: A Survey

I. Duties of loyalty of corporate organs, in particular of the members of the board

In private law, the duties of loyalty weighing on corporate organs are in the furthest stage of development, in particular the fiduciary duties incumbent on the board members of a company.[7] These duties are promulgated in detail in many

[6] *Frankfurter Allgemeine Zeitung* no 140, 20.6.2003, at 17, 20. As to the conflicts of interest in the co-determined board, see C. III.

[7] Cf H Fleischer 'Zur organschaftlichen Treuepflicht der Geschäftsleiter im Aktien- und GmbH-Recht' [2003] Wertpapier-Mitteilungen (WM) 1045; TMJ Möllers in P Hommelhoff, KJ Hopt and A von Werder (eds) *Handbuch Corporate Governance* (Cologne/Stuttgart 2003, cited as *Handbuch Corporate Governance*/author) 405; H Merkt 'Unternehmensleitung und Interes-

cont. ...

jurisdictions,[8] e.g., the United States, England, France, Switzerland, and also recently Germany in the German Corporate Governance Code.[9] Even before the broad law and economics movement, the standard work of *Robert Clark* stated in 1986 that the fiduciary duty not only protects shareholders but also the fair competition and the functioning of the markets.[10]

II. Contractual duties of loyalty, in particular of commission dealers, brokers, and other agents

Contractual duties of loyalty can be found in many shapes and forms. Partially, they are regulated by law, e.g., the commission agency, the brokerage contract, and the sales agency. The commission dealer must carry out the business affairs for the account of the principal with diligence, observing the interests of the principal. When the commission dealer's own interests conflict with those of the principal, the agent must disclose the conflict or refuse the agency contract; in the first case, he can accept the agency, but the interests of the principal must take precedence.[11] The broker has a special fiduciary duty *vis-à-vis* his principal,

senkollision [1995] 159 Zeitschrift für das gesamte Handelsrecht und Wirtschaftsrecht (ZHR) 423.

For comparative law, see KJ Hopt 'Self-Dealing and Use of Corporate Opportunity and Information: Regulating Directors' Conflicts of Interest' in KJ Hopt and G Teubner (eds) *Corporate Governance and Directors Liabilities* (Berlin/New York 1985) at 285 (cited as: KJ Hopt 'Conflicts of Interest'). For the UK, see Law Commissions *Company Directors: Regulating Conflicts of Interests and Formulating a Statement of Duties, Law Com No 261* (September 1999), and B Kasolowsky *Fiduciary Duties in Company Law* (Baden-Baden 2003); for the US, see R Clark *Corporate Law* (Aspen Law & Business 1986), s 4 (141 ff), and American Law Institute *Principles of Corporate Governance: Analysis and Recommendations* (St. Paul/Minn 1994) Part V: Duty of Fair Dealing; for France, see D Schmidt *Les conflits d'intérêts dans la société anonyme* (Paris 1999); for Switzerland, see P Forstmoser 'Interessenkonflikte von Verwaltungsratsmitgliedern' in *Liber Amicorum Schulin* (Zurich 2002) at 9.

[8] For references, see H Fleischer [2003] WM 1045 (1047 ff); KJ Hopt in KJ Hopt and H Wiedemann (eds) *Großkommentar zum Aktiengesetz* (4th edn Berlin/New York 1999 cited as: GroßKoAktG/author) s 93 comment 12, comments 526 ff.

[9] German Corporate Governance Code as of 21.5.2003 no 4.3 for members of the management board and no 5.5. for members of the supervisory board; on the Code cf M Peltzer *Deutsche Corporate Governance, Ein Leitfaden* (Munich 2003); H-M Ringleb, T Kremer, M Lutter and A von Werder *German Corporate Governance Code, Kommentar* (Munich 2003); *Handbuch Corporate Governance*/Lutter at 737. See the report on German practice by CH Seibt 'Deutscher Corporate Governance Kodex: Antworten auf Zweifelsfragen der Praxis' [2003] Die Aktiengesellschaft (AG) 465.

[10] R Clark *Corporate Law* s 4.2.1 (151).

[11] Cf the early Reichsgericht, (1901) Juristische Wochenschrift 408; A Baumbach and KJ Hopt *Handelsgesetzbuch (HGB)* (31st edn Munich 2003), s 384 comment 1; as to the conflicts of interest of commission dealers and agents, see KJ Hopt *Der Kapitalanlegerschutz im*

cont. ...

obliging him to comply with the interests of the principal within reasonable boundaries. As a professional and an agent, he has far-reaching disclosure obligations. Conflicts of interests – for example, a personal interest to buy (self interest) or a related but conflicting commission for another principal (dual loyalty), must be disclosed by the broker.[12] In case of an insoluble conflict of interests, he must abandon the contract, except if the principal has full knowledge of the conflict and wishes to pursue the contract anyway.[13] In exceptional cases, such as multiparty representation of a broker, acting according to the rules of the civil law the broker's claim for compensation is even set aside.[14]

When the agent is paid for his business, he fulfils duties generally incumbent on the principal, which the principal has delegated to him. Under the many forms of the agency contract that the modern service-oriented society is familiar with, those in the banking sector have a prominent position. Conflicts between the interests of the client and the individual interest of the bank and between interests of different clients are common and have led to rich case law.[15] The same is true for the commercial agency. The commercial agent must make every effort to support the negotiation and the conclusion of the contracts, and in so doing, he has to take care of the interests of the firm in all his actions. If the commercial agent works for different companies, he owes each of them the safeguarding of their interests. This leads to a special kind of conflict of interests.[16] From the commercial agent's duty of loyalty follows a prohibition of competition during the whole time of his engagement without the need to be stipulated expressly. There are similar principles for modified forms of representation such as authorized dealers, franchisees, trustees, and others.

III. Duties of loyalty of regulated professionals such as investment bankers, auditors, and attorneys

Agency relations, which are also particularly important for the public, have often been handled within public law. This is the case in many countries for banks and

Recht der Banken (Munich 1975) at 478 ff, I Koller 'Interessenkonflike im Kommissionsverhältnis' [1978] Betriebs-Berater (BB) 1733.

12 A Baumbach and KJ Hopt *HGB,* s 93 comment 30.

13 Bundesgerichtshof, [1983] NJW 1848. As to the American law, see American Law Institute, *Restatement of the Law – Second: Agency* (2nd edn St. Paul/Minn 1958) s 389 ff.

14 For Germany, see s 654 of the German Civil Code.

15 For references, see KJ Hopt *Kapitalanlegerschutz* 478 ff.

16 KJ Hopt *Handelsvertreterrecht* (3rd edn Munich 2003) s 86 comment 24. For France, see Y Guyon *Droit des Affaires – Tome 1: Droit commercial général et Sociétés* (11th edn Paris 2001) n° 807, 812.

investment firms, for auditors, and for lawyers. In fact one could distinguish three categories of duties of loyalty: contractual, corporate, and professional.[17]

Examples can be found in capital market law. Article 11 of the Investment Services Directive of 1993, which is about to be reformed, provides for Member State rules of conduct according to which the investment firm is required to try to avoid conflicts of interest and, when they cannot be avoided, ensures that its clients are fairly treated. Supervisory rules of this kind, which can be found in most capital market laws of the world, try to cope with the conflicts of interest in order to protect the investors and to maintain confidence in a well functioning of the capital markets. Conflicts of interest may indeed run against efficient capital allocation.[18]

For auditors, one of the prime professional duties is to maintain independence. The auditor has to behave impartially, especially when rendering reports and expert services. He has to refuse the assignment if during the performance of the mandate partiality could be presumed.[19] The independence of the auditor is being intensely discussed, both internationally and in Germany, because of the business scandals and bankruptcies, in particular the Enron affair.

The attorney may not represent conflicting interests. This express German prohibition is to protect not only the clients of the attorney, but more generally to ensure unimpaired lawyer-client relations and, eventually, confidence in the judicial system. It raises substantial problems in modern legal practice. If it is construed to be applicable to the whole law firm and is to be applied strictly, it could lead to an obstacle to mobility and competition.[20] Other legal systems, such as the British, do indeed clearly provide more flexible regulatory models.[21]

[17] As to the theory and dogmatics of professional law and professional liability, see KJ Hopt 'Nichtvertragliche Haftung außerhalb von Schadens- und Bereicherungshaftung – Zur Theorie und Dogmatik des Berufsrechts und der Berufshaftung' (1983) 183 Archiv für civilistische Praxis (AcP) 608; H Hirte *Berufshaftung* (Munich 1996); V Lang 'Einmal mehr: Berufsrecht, Berufspflichten und Berufshaftung' (2001) 201 AcP 451.

[18] DH Bliesener *Aufsichtsrechtliche Verhaltenspflichten beim Wertpapierhandel* (Berlin/ New York 1998) 39 ff, 169 ff.

[19] Cf s 49 of the Wirtschaftsprüferordnung for Germany; similar provisions are contained in the law of auditing of other countries. As to the reform discussion, see E I 3.

[20] Bundesverfassungsgericht, [2003] NJW 2520.

[21] As to English law, see FMB Reynolds *Bowstead and Reynolds on Agency* (17th edn London 2001) para 6-047. Cf also American Law Institute *Restatement of the Law – Second: Agency 2d*, s 394 comment d. See also E I 2.

IV. Categories of conflicts of interest between principal and agent and between different parallel or opposite interests

In all three categories of agency relations mentioned under B I-III in which the duty of loyalty is addressed, one can distinguish a series of standard examples, although these will differ in form and intensity. Remarkably, these categories are discussed most of the time only in the agency relationship characterizing corporate organs.[22] Moreover, the approach of the courts understandably only takes into account the literature dealing with the specific category put before them, together with the case law and other sources relating to that category. Regarding the standard categories, one must make the earlier-mentioned distinction between two basic kinds of conflicts: self-interest and dual loyalty situations. More generally, there is a fundamental distinction, well known in corporate law, between the duty of care and the duty of loyalty of agents. For the duty of care, a broad and business-oriented judgment standard is applicable (in American law, the business judgment rule). In contrast is the quite severe standard applicable for the duty of loyalty,[23] which is, according to Amcrican courts, of 'uncompromising rigidity.'[24] The most important of these standard categories can be further examined as follows:

1. Duties of loyalty and self-interest

a) *Loyal effort for the company viz. the principal*:[25] At the top of these standard categories is the duty of a director to engage him- or herself loyally for the corporation. Such a duty falls not only on the directors of a corporation, but also more generally on all agents *vis-à-vis* those whose interests they look after. Difficulties can arise to mark the boundary between permitted and not-permitted actions in one's private sphere. Among others, it is not acceptable for a manager to take up functions that will inherently lead to conflicts of interest, for example, acting as the asset manager for a shareholder with a significant holding in the corporation. Dual mandates as a member of management boards in a group of companies must be authorized by the supervisory boards of both companies. Permission from the principal is also required in cases of multiple representations for commercial

[22] But see, eg, M Wellenhofer-Klein 'Treupflichten im Handels-, Gesellschafts- und Arbeitsrecht' (2000) 64 Rabels Zeitschrift für ausländisches und internationales Privatrecht (RabelsZ) 564.

[23] KJ Hopt 'Aktionärskreis und Vorstandsneutralität' [1993] ZGR 534 (542); idem 'Die Haftung von Vorstand und Aufsichtsrat – Zugleich ein Beitrag zur corporate governance-Debatte –' in *Festschrift für Mestmäcker* (Baden-Baden 1996) 909 (922); *GroßKoAktG*/KJ Hopt s 93 comment 145.

[24] Benjamin Cardozo in *Meinhard v Salmon* 249 *NY* 458, 164 *ME* 545 (1928).

[25] *GroßKoAktG*/K J Hopt s 93 comment 156 ff; H Fleischer [2003] WM 1045 (1050 ff).

agents[26] and of brokers working for both parties, at least when the conflict of interest is not in line with the contract provisions.[27]

b) *Self-dealing*:[28] It is accepted that directors may do business with their own company, but transactions are only allowed if the terms of the contract are the same as they would be in transactions with an independent third party. In international practice, this is called 'transactions at arm's length.' There is a different approach for the employment contract as such and especially for the remuneration.[29] A critical and special case is the granting of credit to the agent. There is a specific regulation that only allows the granting of credit by the company to members of its management board after a decision of the supervisory board; it contains remarkable rules against evasion, for example, by extending the rule to spouses or to the use of nominee companies.[30] The agent not only can obtain advantages by doing business with the company viz. the principal, but also by parallel businesses, i.e., transactions that are linked to those of the principal. A well-known banking practice is front-running, which can sometimes cause direct damage to the clients and partly exploits information that cannot always be captured by the prohibition on insider trading of the EC Directive on insider dealing or of the new Directive on market abuse, which will soon replace the first-mentioned Directive.[31]

c) *Competition*:[32] For members of the management board, there is often a statutory prohibition of competing with the own company. It concretely applies the

[26] Court of appeals of Hamm, [1992] Neue Juristische Wochenschrift-Rechtsprechungs-Report Zivilrecht (NJW-RR) 364; KJ Hopt *Handelsvertreterrecht* s 86 comment 30.

[27] The details are highly controversial, cf. for case law H Sprau in Palandt *BGB* (62nd edn Munich 2003) s 654 comment 4.

[28] *GroßKoAktG*/KJ Hopt s 93 comment 159 ff; H Fleischer [2003] WM 1045 (1051); *Handbuch Corporate Governance*/TMJ Möllers at 405 (414 ff); R Clark *Corporate Law* s 4.1 (142 ff): self-dealing; for France, see most recently art. 111, 112 de la loi NRE: conventions réglementées, A Viandier and A Charvériat *Sociétés et la loi NRE* (2nd edn Paris 2002) 320 ff; for comparative law, see L Enriques 'The Law on Company Directors' Self-Dealing: A Comparative Analysis' (2000) 2 International and Comparative Corporate Law Journal 297; for economic analysis, see Z Goshen 'The Efficiency of Controlling Corporate Self-Dealing: Theory Meets Reality' (2003) 91 California L Rev 393.

[29] Cf s 87 of the German Stock Corporation Act; see B IV 1 g.

[30] s 89 of the German Stock Corporation Act. For details, see B IV.

[31] See KJ Hopt 'Insiderwissen und Interessenkonflikte im europäischen und deutschen Bankrecht' in *Festschrift für Heinsius* (Berlin/New York 1991) 289 (293 ff, 307 ff, 316); V Lang *Informationspflichten bei Wertpapierdienstleistungen* (Munich 2003) s 8 comment 5 ff. See also D IV 1.

[32] *GroßKoAktG*/KJ Hopt s 93 comment 164 ff; idem 'Conflicts of Interest' at 285 (300 ff); *Handbuch Corporate Governance*/TMJ Möllers at 405 (418 ff). As to the American law, see American Law Institute *Restatement of the Law – Second: Agency 2d*, s 393.

duty of loyalty of corporate organs. These principles cannot be transferred to the members of the supervisory board because their supervisory function excludes management of the company. Similar prohibitions of competition as applicable to the management board members can be found for other agents, e.g., the commercial agents, and – although limited to front-running and similar violations of customer interests – the commission agents[33] and consequently also the brokers. Often, details of these prohibitions of competition are spelled out in more detail in contractual arrangements.

d) *Use of corporate opportunity*:[34] The prohibition to avail oneself of corporate opportunities was first developed in England and in the United States. In Germany, it was first recognized in the decisions of the German Federal Bundesgerichtshof. Today, in most corporate laws it is an established standard category among the possible infringements of fiduciary duties of directors and owners of the corporation. Details, however, are controversial. As a consequence, there is an explicitly rich body of comparative case law from the American, Canadian, and English jurisdictions.[35] The basic principle, however, is valid for every agent. Commission dealers, brokers, and commercial agents equally may not 'snatch' good businesses away from the principal.

e) *Use of business secrets and inside information*:[36] This subject concerns standard conflicts, which are partly specifically regulated, as is the case in corporate law for the members of the board and for inside information in the EC Directive on insider dealing and the new Directive on market abuse. The forbidden use of business secrets is a serious breach of professional and business secrecy. Until now, forbidden insider dealing in the European Directive has been restricted to the stock market, but it exceeds these boundaries, e.g., for auditors and to some extent for banks.[37]

f) *Use of corporate or business position for personal purposes*: Members of the management board are not allowed to use their position of power for purposes

[33] KJ Hopt *Handelsvertreterrecht,* s 86 comment 26 ff; for commission dealers and agents, see I Koller [1978] BB 1733 (1736 ff).

[34] For example, Bundesgerichtshof, (1986) NJW 584; (1989) NJW 2687; S Grundmann *Der Treuhandvertrag, insbesondere die werbende Treuhand* (Munich 1997) 425 ff; *GroßKoAktG*/KJ Hopt s 93 comment 166 ff; idem 'Conflicts of Interest' 285 (295 ff).

[35] American Law Institute *Principles of Corporate Governance* s 5.05; B Kasolowsky *Fiduciary Duties in Company Law* at 139 ff.

[36] *GroßKoAktG*/KJ Hopt s 93 comment 173 ff; idem 'Conflicts of Interest' at 285 (302 ff). American Law Institute *Restatement of the Law – Second: Agency 2d* s 395.

[37] KJ Hopt in H Schimansky, H-J Bunte and H-J Lwowski *Bankrechts-Handbuch* (2nd edn Munich 2001) s 107 comment 82 ff.

unrelated to the corporation.[38] More specifically, they may not use their influence in the corporation to obtain personal advantages. In case law, this has been decided in the context of consultancy contracts with third parties, for example.[39] Also no corporate means may be used to strengthen the personal position of the director. The same is also true in cases of a takeover bid – no matter whether one recognizes an anti-frustration rule addressed to the directors of the target company or not. Even those who believe that the management board is allowed to frustrate a takeover bid without the prior consent of the general meeting, agree that the management board may only take such measures in the interest of the company.[40] The standard category of using corporate or business positions for personal purposes is quite complex because of the typical mix of motives.[41] There are three typical configurations: 1) the corporation conferring benefits to the directors, 2) third parties conferring benefits to the directors, such as bribery, commissions, and preferential prices, and 3) allowing benefits to be conferred to third parties with whom the director has a special relation.[42] Gray areas are reached when the financial interests of the agent are only affected indirectly, such as in the situation of advantages for third parties with whom the director has a special relation, or when other than pure financial interests are involved.

g) *Excessive remuneration*:[43] An evident conflict of interest for all agents, finally, is their own remuneration. The special feature about remuneration is that, in principle, it must be freely negotiated in the market.[44] For corporate agents, there is a special rule:[45] the supervisory board has to ensure that the total remuneration of a member of the management board stands in a reasonable relation to the tasks of the concerned director as well as to the situation of the

[38] E-J Mestmäcker *Verwaltung, Konzerngewalt und Rechte der Aktionäre* (Karlsruhe 1958) 214 ff; H Wiedemann *Organverantwortung und Gesellschafterklagen in der Aktiengesellschaft* (Opladen 1989) 8; *GroßKoAktG*/KJ Hopt s 93 comment 176; H Fleischer [2003] WM 1045 (1050).

[39] Bundesgerichtshof, [1995] BB 2180 (2182).

[40] The details are controversial, cf M Winter and S Harbarth 'Verhaltenspflichten von Vorstand und Aufsichtsrat der Zielgesellschaft bei feindlichen Übernahmeangeboten nach dem WpÜG' [2002] Zeitschrift für Wirtschaftsrecht (ZIP) 1; H Hirte 'Verteidigung gegen Übernahmeangebote und Rechtsschutz der Aktionäre gegen die Verteidigung' [2002] ZGR 623; KJ Hopt 'Grundsatz- und Praxisprobleme nach dem Wertpapiererwerbs- und Übernahmegesetz' (2002) 166 ZHR 375 (434).

[41] R Clark *Corporate Law* s 4.1 (142, 146 ff): corporate action with mixed motives.

[42] *GroßKoAktG*/KJ Hopt s 93 comment 177 ff, 181, 182; H Fleischer [2003] WM 1045 (1056 ff).

[43] As to s 87 of the German Stock Corporation Act cf. G Thüsing 'Auf der Suche nach dem iustum pretium der Vorstandstätigkeit' [2003] ZGR 457.

[44] Infra D IV 2.

[45] For example, s 87 of the German Stock Corporation Act.

company. However, this has not prevented the practice of excessive remunerations – especially caused by stock options – from finding its way from the U.S. to Germany. At present the subject is highly controversial especially in company law reform discussions. The High Level Group of Company Law Experts has also made some suggestions on this point.[46] The European Commission has adopted these suggestions and has developed a reform proposal.[47] Problems concerning excessive remuneration also exist with other agents, such as banks, where extensive case law can be consulted relating to interest and remuneration.

2. Duties of loyalty and conflicting third-party interests

The first basic category, which was just illustrated, is agency and conflicts of self-interest; the other category consists of conflicts in case of dual loyalty. Conflicts of interests between different clients on the same or on different sides of the market arise for banks[48] as prototypes and are inherent to the system, but they also appear for commission dealers, commercial agents who work for different companies,[49] (commercial) brokers, and other intermediaries.

a) *Conflicts between the interests of several principals on the same side of the market*: conflicts on the same side of the transaction, typically raise distribution issues on the side of the buyer (e.g., oversubscribed securities issues, restricted investment possibilities, issuing of several investment funds); loyal advice on sales and investments (e.g., in case of competition of several issues or investment funds the seller wants to place); and more generally the problem of preferential treatment of clients – important clients compared to others, for example – on information, allocation of securities, and preferential conditions.

b) *Conflicts between the interests of several principals on different sides of the market*: Conflicts of interest between the interests of several principals on different sides of the market are numerous, e.g., in connection with issuing transactions and dealing in securities between issuers and investors, with price stabili-

[46] High Level Group of Company Law Experts, *A Modern Regulatory Framework for Company Law in Europe* (Brussels, 4 November 2002 – Annex 3 in this volume), ch III 4.2 (64 ff) Remuneration of directors.

[47] European Commission, Modernising Company Law and Enhancing Corporate Governance in the European Union – A Plan to Move Forward, 21.5.2003, COM(2003) 284 fin, no. 3.1.3 (p. 19) (Annex 1 in this volume).

[48] As to the following, see KJ Hopt in *Festschrift für Heinsius* at 289 (317); DH Bliesener *Verhaltenspflichten* at 169 ff with case law from the US and the UK at 179 ff, 193 ff. As to English banking law, see EP Ellinger, E Lomnicka and R Hooley *Modern Banking Law* (3rd edn Oxford 2002) Ch 4, Sect 4(i).

[49] KJ Hopt *Handelsvertreterrecht* s 86 comment 24.

sation and manipulation, or with the proxy voting right. Of a special nature are the conflicts of interest that arise when a person has a seat in more than one supervisory board and the relevant corporations are competitors, or the decisions to be taken are, in a specific case, to the benefit of one company and to the detriment of the other company.[50]

c) *Conflicts of interest in takeover situations*: In specific cases, conflicts of interest in takeover situations can lead to real conflicts of duties, which – if they don't constitute a justification – surely excuse the conduct of the member of the supervisory board. I have addressed the subject elaborately elsewhere (see references).[51]

C. Sources, Differences, and Common Features of the Duties of Loyalty of Intermediaries

I. Sources

1. *Contract*: The sources of duties of loyalty of intermediaries are, as demonstrated supra B, very heterogeneous. In principle, in a market economy it is for the contracting parties to create and to specify the extent of the duties of loyalty. The agency contract with an agreed remuneration for the agent is the prototype. Here, a rich variety of modern services with a fiduciary character can be found, especially in the banking and finance sector; but also in sales and distribution; in consultancy, care-taking, and administration. One should refer here to the modern and international contract drafting techniques that are often influenced by Anglo-American practice. This is especially true with regard to secrecy, duties of loyalty, and conflicts of interest.[52]

[50] KJ Hopt '*Conflicts of Interest*' at 304 ff; Karsten Krebs *Interessenkonflikte bei Aufsichtsratsmandaten in der Aktiengesellschaft* (Cologne 2002) at 269 ff (double mandates in competing corporations); *Handbuch Corporate Governance*/TM J Möllers at 405 (415 ff).

[51] KJ Hopt 'Übernahmen, Geheimhaltung und Interessenkonflikte: Probleme für Vorstände, Aufsichtsräte und Banken' [2002] ZGR 333 (359 ff); for a shorter English version, see idem 'Takeovers, Secrecy and Conflicts of Interest: Problems for Boards and Banks' in J Payne (ed) *Takeovers in English and German Law* (Oxford 2002) 33; K Krebs *Interessenkonflikte bei Aufsichtsratsmandaten* at 240, 262 ff, 337 ff; J Semler and A Stengel 'Interessenkonflikte bei Aufsichtsratsmitgliedern von Aktiengesellschaften am Beispiel von Konflikten bei Übernahme' [2003] Neue Zeitschrift für Gesellschaftsrecht (NZG) 1.

[52] W Döser 'Anglo-amerikanische Vertragsstrukturen in deutschen Vertriebs-, Lizenz- und sonstigen Vertikalverträgen' (2000) NJW 1451; H Merkt 'Grundsatz- und Praxisprobleme der Amerikanisierungstendenzen im Recht des Unternehmenskaufs' in *Festschrift für Sandrock* (Heidelberg 2000) 657. For further references, see KJ Hopt 'Gemeinsame Grundsätze der Corporate Governance in Europa?' [2000] ZGR 779 (780 note 2).

2. *Codified and case law*: In Germany, for corporate organs – e.g., members of the management board or the supervisory board – the corporate agency as well as the duty of loyalty are part of the mandatory principles of corporate law. Other jurisdictions are substantially more generous in the granting of contractual freedom in the field of corporate statues.[53] The status and the duties of loyalty (including conflicts of interest) of certain professions such as banks, auditors, and attorneys, are regulated under public law. This is because it concerns not only the protection of the client, but also more generally the protection of systemic goods, like the functioning of the banking system, the confidence in the independence of auditors, and the position of attorneys in the judicature. The utmost limits for intermediaries are marked by criminal law and, for corporate and professional agents, by various corporate, banking, and capital market acts.[54]

3. *Professional rules*: As far as the duties of loyalty of professionals are concerned, more or less distinctive professional rules exist. They have developed historically and certainly have their justification even today, although it cannot be denied that in detail they can be oriented toward the interests of their own professional class and come into conflict with the freedom of competition. The traditional supervision of professions and the practice of disciplinary committees or courts – for instance, for attorneys and auditors – have changed substantially in the last decades.[55] The supervision authorities and the disciplinary tribunals for auditors are especially criticized today. The small number of complaints, the leniency of the sanctions, and the discrete publication of disciplinary measures and judgments stand in sharp contrast to the what happened in recent times to the auditors – some their obvious mistakes having been disclosed immediately before the recent corporate scandals and corporate collapses.

4. *Codes of conduct*: The more recent movement to create codes of conduct follows the international – especially Anglo-American – example, and is rapidly gaining acceptance in Europe including Germany.[56] This movement tries to take

[53] See the comparative law study of KJ Hopt 'Generalbericht' in M Lutter and H Wiedemann (eds) *Gestaltungsfreiheit im Gesellschaftsrecht, Zeitschrift für Unternehmens- und Gesellschaftsrecht -Sonderheft 13* (Berlin/New York 1998) 123; G Spindler 'Deregulierung des Aktienrechts?' [1998] AG 53.

[54] See infra E VI.

[55] For example, Bundesverfassungsgericht, (1988) NJW 191, 194, (2003) NJW 2520. For details see N Sommerschuh *Berufshaftung und Berufsaufsicht: Wirtschaftsprüfer, Rechtsanwälte und Notare im Vergleich* (Baden-Baden 2003) 254 ff, 273 ff.

[56] As to the corporate governance code movement, see KJ Hopt 'Corporate Governance: Aufsichtsrat oder Markt?' in P Hommelhoff, H Rowedder and P Ulmer (eds) *Max Hachenburg, Dritte Gedächtnisvorlesung 1998* (Heidelberg 2000) 9 (20 ff). These codes are compared in detail in a study for the European Commission; see Weil, Gotshal and Manges *Comparative Study of Corporate Governance* (Brussels, January 2002).

countermeasures on these issues. It applies to public corporations in general. We will only mention the German Corporate Governance Code as an example; as mentioned before, it pays special attention to the respective conflicts of interest both of management board members and supervisory board members. It cannot be considered to be a source of law in the true sense of the word since the content is limited to suggestions and recommendations without any qualification as legal norms. However, in 2002, the German legislators adopted the British 'comply-or-explain' principle.[57] According to this principle, the management board and the supervisory board of listed companies do not necessarily have to abide by the code's recommendations, but shall declare once a year 'that the recommendations of the Code have been and are being complied with or indicate which of the Code's recommendations are not being complied with.' The formulation 'are being complied with' has in the meantime led to an extensive and controversial discussion on whether there is a duty of immediate disclosure when a company decides not to apply the recommendations during a year for which the declaration was delivered. This aspect and the general question of liability in case of incorrect statements[58] clash with the optional nature of the compliance and the demand of deregulation of corporate law,[59] are the main topics of the discussion.

II. Fiduciary contracts and fiduciary relationships: The duty of loyalty as correlative of granting increased influence on the principal's sphere of interest

For corporate organs, the legal foundation of their duty of loyalty is no longer considered to be a special relationship based on mutual trust, but the actual and legal power of disposition of other people's pecuniary interests.[60] The members of the management board and the supervisory board are agents of the company and have a special fiduciary relationship with it. This concept, which goes back to early English case law, was first internationally developed and given a consistent

[57] s 161 of the German Stock Corporation Act.

[58] KJ Hopt 'Unternehmensführung, Unternehmenskontrolle, Modernisierung des Aktienrechts' in P Hommelhoff et al (eds) *Corporate Governance, Zeitschrift für das gesamte Handelsrecht und Wirtschaftsrecht Supplement 71* (2002) 27 (51 ff); M Lutter 'Die Erklärung zum Corporate Governance Kodex gemäß § 161 AktG' (2002) 166 ZHR 523; CH Seibt [2002] AG 249 (254 ff); P Ulmer 'Der Deutsche Corporate Governance Kodex – ein neues Regulierungsinstrument für börsennotierte Aktiengesellschaften' (2002) 166 ZHR 150 (168 ff).

[59] The German experiences with self-regulation in the financial sector are rather disappointing; cf KJ Hopt 'Self-Regulation in Banking and Finance – Practice and Theory in Germany' in *La Déontologie bancaire et financière/The Ethical Standards in Banking & Finance* (Brussels 1998) 53.

[60] W Zöllner *Die Schranken mitgliedschaftlicher Stimmrechtsmacht bei den privatrechtlichen Personenverbänden* (Munich/Berlin 1963) at 342 ff; H Fleischer [2003] WM 1045 (1046) with further references.

form by the American law on fiduciary relationships of directors.[61] The position of the director toward the company corresponds to that of the trustee toward the trust.

However, this legal theory, according to which power and responsibility must be in proportion to one another, can also be fruitful beyond the scope of corporate agents.[62] The connection between both is evident to and called for by the contracting parties in the cases of commission agency, brokerage contract, and agency contract. The principle is set down in the law of these contracts; nevertheless, the principal is basically free to deviate from it. Because this connection makes up the heart of the reciprocity for all of these contracts, it can be used to build a separate class of fiduciary contracts.[63]

One should, however, go one step further and see the dogmatic similitude of fiduciary contracts and other fiduciary relationships, i.e., mainly corporate and professional agency. In American corporate, banking, and capital market law, the concept of a fiduciary relationship between the members of the board and the shareholders, and more generally between agents in the capital markets and investors, has proven to be extremely fruitful for the practice of the courts, the SEC, the stock exchanges, and professional associations such as the National Association of Securities Dealers (NASD). The Principles of Corporate Governance of the American Law Institute constitute a veritable gold mine of information for board members and senior executives, with over 100 pages on the duty of fair dealing.[64] The fiduciary relationship, which follows the strict duties of loyalty and care of the trustee, is the underlying idea while the above-mentioned institutions concretize the duties in countless cases and admission requirements because it allows an orientation exceeding the limits of the particular problem in question.[65] It is exactly this orientation found in the category of fiduciary contracts

[61] This was already said very clearly in an early English case – see *Aberdeen Railway v Blaikie* (1854) 1 *Macq.* 461 (HL) – and laid out impressively by the American Law Institute *Principles of Corporate Governance,* see infra in the text. This is also commonly agreed upon in Germany; see KJ Hopt 'Aktionärskreis und Vorstandsneutralität' [1993] ZGR 534 (540 ff).

[62] As to English law, see FMB Reynolds *Bowstead and Reynolds on Agency,* para 6-034. As to US broker-dealer law, cf NS Poser *Broker-Dealer Law and Regulation, Private Rights of Action* (Boston 1995) §2.1 (79).

[63] See KJ Hopt *Kapitalanlegerschutz* at 399, 401; M Wellenhofer-Klein (2000) 64 RabelsZ 564 (583); and as early as M Rumpf 'Wirtschaftsrechtliche Vertrauensgeschäfte' (1921) 119 AcP 1 (53 ff). Cf H Coing *Die Treuhand kraft privaten Rechtsgeschäfts* (Munich 1973); S Grundmann, *Der Treuhandvertrag* 101 ff.

[64] American Law Institute *Principles of Corporate Governance* 209-324; cf KJ Hopt in *Festschrift für Mestmäcker* at 917 ff, 919 ff

[65] R Clark *Corporate Law* s 4.1 (141): 'The general duty permits, and in fact has led to, a continuous evolution in corporate law.'

and fiduciary relationships that could make an essential contribution to the German discussion and practice.

III. Extending the duties of loyalty to related third parties; after-effects of the duty of loyalty

As stated under B IV, conflicts of interest are numerous and can be very subtle. Although it is clearly impossible to cover all conflicts of interest by law, the legal system will nevertheless try to prevent obvious or evident evasions. This applies particularly to two standard categories, as is proven by standard regulations concerning the granting of loans to management board members.[66] On the one hand, these regulations also apply to the granting of loans to spouses, partners, or minor children as well as to loans to undisclosed agents. The *ratio legis* of preventing evasion is clear and so is the legal boundary of the scope of the prevention. In accordance with it, the law also applies to children born out of wedlock and adopted children, but not to divorced spouses. On the other hand, the law also targets loans to companies the management board member belongs to as a statutory representative, as a member of the supervisory board, or as a partner of a partnership. The German Corporate Governance Code records as applicable corporate law that 'all transactions between the enterprise and the members of the Management Board as well as persons they are close to or companies they have a personal association with must comply with the standards as customary in the sector.'[67]

Finally, it must be said that the duty of loyalty may have after-effects beyond the period of office or contract. This surely is the case if the interest that is the subject of the duty of loyalty is related to an event that occurred during the period of office or contract. The German Federal Bundesgerichtshof has described this correctly by stating that the management board member must not cancel the outcome of meeting his official duties after his function expired.[68]

[66] s 89 paras 3 and 4 of the German Stock Corporation Act; as to the interpretation of this provision by case law, see U Hüffer *Aktiengesetz* (5th edn Munich 2002) s 89 comment 6, 7.

[67] German Corporate Governance Code no 4.3.4 sentence 2.

[68] Bundesgerichtshof, [1977] GmbH-Rundschau (GmbHR) 43 (44); cf *GroßKoAktG*/KJ Hopt s 93 comment 183. As to the American law, see American Law Institute *Restatement of the Law – Second: Agency 2d* s 396.

D. Common Legal Principles for Treating Conflicts of Interest

I. Full disclosure: The principle and its reach (e.g., securities analysts, project partners, lawyers, and construction agents)

1. *The principle of full disclosure of conflicts of interest*: Conflicts of interest of the various agents are traditionally handled totally separately by the courts and by academic doctrine, just as they arise coincidentally in corporate, banking or contract law before a court or in a scholar's mind. A synopsis, however, clarifies rather quickly that there is a set of general principles on how to cope with agency and conflicts of interest. First, there is the principle of non-requested disclosure. 'No secret profits' is the principle first put forward by the British Law Commission[69] and further developed by The Company Law Review Steering Group in its pioneering final report from June 2001.[70] As the more flexible legal instrument, disclosure has evolved to take the place of strict prohibitions.[71] In most cases, disclosure for corporate agents is additionally linked to a permission requirement, for instance by the supervisory board or the general meeting..

Like the management board and other directors and monitoring bodies, this basic principle for corporate agents is implemented in most corporate law systems. Members of corporate bodies must disclose all conflicts of interest to the company.[72] This rule even applies even, if after due consideration having been given to the interests involved, .the transaction or the conduct is obviously permitted.

The duty of disclosure is also recognized for the contractual duties of loyalty of agents, e.g., commission dealers,[73] brokers,[74] and commercial[75] and other agents.[76]

[69] Law Commissions *Company Directors: Regulating Conflicts of Interests and Formulating a Statement of Duties, Law Com No 261* (September 1999) Appendix A: Draft Statement of Directors' Duties (5): No secret profits; cf B Kasolowsky *Fiduciary Duties in Company Law* at 296.

[70] The Company Law Review Steering Group *Modern Company Law For a Competitive Economy, Final Report* (London, June 2001) Vol I, Annex C, Schedule 2, General Principles by Which Directors are Bound 5, 6 at 346.

[71] KJ Hopt 'Conflicts of Interest' at 285 (287 ff); L Enriques (2000) 2 International and Comparative Corporate Law Journal 297 at 303 ff.

[72] *GroßKoAktG*/KJ Hopt s 93 comment 185, H Fleischer [2003] WM 1045 (1050) both with further references.

[73] KJ Hopt *Kapitalanlegerschutz* at 478 ff; I Koller in Staub *HGB* (4th edn Berlin/New York 1986) s 384 comment 21, 28; I Koller [1978] BB 1733.

[74] A Baumbach/KJ Hopt *HGB* s 93 comment 27, 33.

[75] KJ Hopt *Handelsvertreterrecht* s 86 comment 20 ff, 40 ff.

[76] As to English law, see FMB Reynolds *Bowstead and Reynolds on Agency* Article 46 ff.

Usually, law sets disclosure obligations for professional agents where there is a lack of contractual relations on this matter. For instance, the recent s. 34 b of the German Securities Trading Act (which came into force in 2002) lays down the duty of disclosure for investment firms within the context of securities analysis. It especially mandates disclosure for three typical conflicts of interest: 1) participation in the company whose securities are the subject of the analysis (already starting from 1%), 2) participation in the underwriting syndicate of the analyzed securities within the last five years, and 3) care-taking of the securities at the stock exchange or on the market based on a contract with the issuer.

2. *The reach of the principle of full disclosure of conflicts of interest as illustrated by prospectus liability case law*: A milestone in the development of the duties of disclosure in the context of conflicts of interest is the ruling of the German Federal Bundesgerichtshof on public partnerships (Publikumsgesellschaften) and other investment schemes, especially because the court could not rely on statutory or literary preliminary work. According to this ruling, material financial or personal links between different parties involved in the project – for example, general partner-corporation, general contractors, chief tenants, and especially the trustees (along with the respective managing directors and controlling shareholders) – must be disclosed in the prospectus or individually upon initiating the negotiations.[77] Special benefits for the incorporators and promoters must as well be disclosed.[78]

This disclosure must happen *ex ante* and helps to enable the investor or client to make an informed decision on whether to give the mandate to the agent anyway or to look for someone else. The case law, however, was quite right to go further and to demand *ex post* disclosure in specific cases,[79] in order to enable the principal to take effective action against the agent. This was decided by the German Federal Bundesgerichtshof with regard to lawyers and tax consultants, for example. They must inform their clients about their own relevant misdemeanors. Violation of these disclosure duties leads to secondary liability for which an independent statute of limitation exists;[80] from a practical point of view, this is often decisive. In this context, the duty to disclose the accepting of bribes

[77] Bundesgerichtshof, *Decisions of the Bundesgerichtshof* (as abbreviated: *BGHZ*) 79, 337; [1980] NJW 1162; [1987] NJW 1815 (1817); A Baumbach and KJ Hopt *HGB* s 347 comment 30.

[78] Bundesgerichtshof, (1995) NJW 130; A Baumbach and KJ Hopt *HGB* s 347 comment 30.

[79] As to English law, see FMB Reynolds *Bowstead and Reynolds on Agency* para 6-059.

[80] Bundesgerichtshof, *BGHZ* 83, 17 (23); *BGHZ* 94, 380; *BGHZ* 114, 150; *BGHZ* 129, 386 (392); (2000) NJW 1263, 1267; (2002) NJW 1117; A Baumbach and KJ Hopt *HGB* s 347 comment 30.

should also be mentioned.[81] In my opinion, this case law applies in general to agents who receive payment from third parties,[82] although this has not been considered so far in German law. One could think of a duty for corporate agents, such as management board members, to disclose former misdemeanors. This would enable the supervisory board and the shareholders to sue upon restitution and damages claims of the corporation, e.g., for a violation of the competition rules, bribery, or other acts damaging the corporation. As these claims are supposed to be accounted for and reflected the annual accounts of the company, this would give rise to a secondary liability with an independent statute of limitation.

In principle, the agent must also disclose secret commissions, such as commissions for auditors and tax advisers;[83] for consultants, creditors' trustees, and future property developers;[84] and the participation of the asset manager in the commission fee paid to the bank.[85] This also applies to payments to a company in which the tax consultant is heavily involved[86] as well as to all-in kickbacks.[87]

However, according to a recent much-criticized decision of the German Federal Bundesgerichtshof, the financing bank must only exceptionally disclose secret internal commissions relating to schemes for tax-efficient construction of residential properties.[88] It is not sufficient to merely note that these internal commissions are included in the purchase price as part of the distribution costs because the same argument could also be raised for public partnerships and other investment possibilities. As a consequence, the prospectus itself can be quite incorrect in such cases, with the resulting liability for the liable for the prospectus. However, it is correct to say that it is not the bank's duty to care about the appropriate price, even if the selling price quite clearly exceeds the fair market value; it is the buyer's responsibility to examine these matters. Surely, though, there is a duty of disclosure on the bank, as is appropriately stated by the court, when the internal commission contributes to such a substantial shift of the relationship between the purchase price and the fair market value that the bank must assume fraud by the seller. Financing, as an independent economic function in an economy based on the division of labour and functions, must not be put into question by exaggerated liability under civil law (i.e., right to put up defence *viz. Einwendungsdurchgriff, culpa in contrahendo,* and prospectus liability). Liability

[81] Bundesgerichtshof, (2001) NJW 1065.

[82] B Kasolowsky *Fiduciary Duties in Company Law* at 296: benefits from third parties.

[83] Bundesgerichtshof, *BGHZ* 78, 263 (268).

[84] Bundesgerichtshof, *BGHZ* 114, 87.

[85] Bundesgerichtshof, *BGHZ* 146, 235.

[86] Bundesgerichtshof, *BGHZ* 95, 81.

[87] Bundesgerichtshof, [1989] WM 1047; [1990] WM 462.

[88] Bundesgerichtshof, [2003] NJW 424.

and profession-related risks should be spread in such a way that a sensible division of functions is achieved.[89] However, whether the spheres and roles are correctly allocated is, of course, the subject of jurisdictional control. These principles can be extended as well to all intermediaries and agents, such as commission agents and brokers.

3. *Disclosure of remuneration*: The general principles for handling conflicts of interest in a market economy reach their limits when the remuneration of the agency itself is concerned. However, the widely accepted and supposedly ethical concept of a fixed and fair price is either medieval – like the theory of *iustum pretium* by Thomas Aquinas – or stems from a state-planned economy. The utmost limit is appropriately set by the legal system for the violations of *bonos mores*.

However, the law imposes stricter limits on professional agents in certain cases. For instance, the directive on rules of conduct for investment firms of the German Financial Supervisory Authority (BaFin) determines that when investment firms are acting as traders for their own account or where fixed prices are agreed upon, they have to inform their clients that this constitutes a sales contract and not an agency; furthermore, when they are acting as traders for third parties, the price must regularly be based on the market price.[90] The American securities regulation has contained a similar and even stricter rule for decades. According to the 5 per cent mark-up rule of the National Association of Securities Dealers, investors have to be informed as soon as that percentage of deviation from the market price is reached.[91]

For corporate agents, disclosure also promotes a control on – or at least the moderation of – excessive remuneration and golden parachutes. These have emerged in Germany following negative American examples[92] and have generated great discussion in general meetings and, in some prominent cases, also in criminal trials. Following the international example, German law tends to impose disclosure of the remuneration of each individual member of the corporate board s. Currently, however, this is not yet an obligation in accounting law. But in May 2003, under great pressure from public opinion and foreign institutional investors, the permanent Government Commission on the German Corporate Governance Code finally adopted such a recommendation.[93] As a consequence, if a corporation chooses not to follow the recommendation, it must explain why, in compli-

[89] KJ Hopt 'Haftung der Banken bei der Finanzierung von Publikumsgesellschaften und Bauherrenmodelle' in *Festschrift für Stimpel* (Berlin/New York 1985) 265 (292 ff).

[90] Wertpapierverhaltensrichtlinie (of the German Financial Supervisory Authority, BaFin), reprinted in A Baumbach and KJ Hopt *HGB* (17) WpHVerhaltensRi, no B.3.3 subpara 6.

[91] Since as early as 1943, cf KJ Hopt *Kapitalanlegerschutz,* 483 with further references.

[92] G Thüsing [2003] ZGR 457 (507) speaks of 'American disease.'

[93] German Corporate Governance Code no 4.2.4.

ance with the statutory 'comply-or-explain' rule. A similar trend toward individual disclosure of remuneration can be detected in Europe, as clearly recommended by the High Level Group of Company Law Experts[94] and, as a result, also by the European Commission in its Plan to Move Forward of 21 May 2003.[95]

4. *Bolstering disclosure by duties of recordkeeping*: It is difficult to control the observance of the duty of disclosure, especially if grounds for suspicion arise only afterward. In this stage, clearing up the matter is only possible by using supporting documents. Therefore, there are statutory duties of recordkeeping for professional agents, for example in Articles 10 and 20 of the Investment Services Directive for investment firms. It is recognised that corporate agents must also enable their corporation to control whether they obeyed their duty of loyalty. If, for instance, the official purposes of expenses are not obvious, the corporate agents must ascertain the facts by recording and presenting supporting documents.[96] Such duties of recordkeeping can be assumed for all agents because of their duty of loyalty.

II. Solving conflicts of interest in the concrete case or more generally

The disclosure of conflicts of interest can constitute a satisfactory solution when the fully informed principal consents to or approves the specific disclosed transaction. In many other cases, however, disclosure by itself will not suffice. Rather, the agent is legally held to solve the conflict of interest in that specific case or in general. Several solutions exist, each with corresponding rights and duties.

1. *Prohibition of self-dealing*: The basic model for legal representatives is s.181 of the German Civil Code, according to which the power of representation does not include the power of self-dealing, no matter whether it is a matter of contracting with oneself or of representation of two or more parties. This rule does not merely constitute a statutory prohibition; it limits the agency power itself, the legal authority of the agent. This rule has led to many debates, and its strictness

[94] High Level Group of Company Law Experts, *A Modern Regulatory Framework for Company Law in Europe* (Brussels 4 November 2002), ch III 4.2 Remuneration of directors.

[95] European Commission Modernising Company Law and Enhancing Corporate Governance in the European Union – A Plan to Move Forward, 21.5.2003, COM(2003) 284 fin, no 3.1.3. at 19 (remuneration of directors).

[96] *GroßKoAktG*/KJ Hopt s 93 comment 186; H Fleischer [2003] Wertpapier-Mitteilungen 1045 (1050).

and rigidity render it unsuitable as a basis for a general analogy for other possible conflicts of interest.[97]

2. *Loss of voting rights*: Instead, for corporate agents – for example, the members of the supervisory board – conflicts of interest can be solved by a loss of voting rights or a prohibition to vote.[98] This is the case when the decision to be taken involves a proposed transaction between the company and that individual board member, or the filing or settlement of a suit between the company and that board member, but also more generally when it involves measures that are legitimately disadvantageous to this board member. This rule is based on the fundamental principles of the prohibition of self-dealing and sitting in judgment over oneself. The loss of voting rights also applies to cases in which the member of the supervisory board is not personally involved but is merely a statutory representative of another company, a personally liable partner of a partnership, or is materially involved in another way in the other company involved in the decision.[99]

3. *Abstention of voting*:[100] Some scholars argue that in cases in which the loss of voting rights does not apply, the member of the supervisory board has a duty to abstain from voting anyway when he finds himself in a conflict of interest. This is not convincing, however, because in fact it would boil down to a loss of voting rights. On the contrary, when the loss of voting rights does not apply, the board member is in principle obliged to exercise his voting rights; only exceptionally does he have the right to withdraw himself from the conflict of interest by abstaining.

4. *Exclusion of attendance*: In specific cases, the corporate agent will not only lose his voting rights but can also be required not to attend the supervisory board meeting when the subject is discussed. For this rule to apply, it is necessary that the mere participation of the member would in fact jeopardize the interests of the company.[101] In very special cases, the exclusion of the supervisory board member from certain information can also be warranted.[102] But here one should keep in mind that the corporate agency functionally differs from the mere two-sided con-

[97] Bundesgerichtshof, *BGHZ* 91, 334 (337); [1991] NJW 982 (983).

[98] K Krebs, *Interessenkonflikte bei Aufsichtsratsmandaten at* 113, 136, 334; *Handbuch Corporate Governance*/TMJ Möllers at 405 (416 ff); J Semler and A Stengel [2003] NZG 1 (3).

[99] This is controversial; see K Krebs *Interessenkonflikte bei Aufsichtsratsmandaten* at 139.

[100] For details, see K Krebs, ibid at 166 ff; cf also P Ulmer 'Aufsichtsratsmandat und Interessenkollision' [1980] NJW 1603 (1605).

[101] KJ Hopt [2002] ZGR 333 (371 ff) for takeover cases; H-J Mertens in Kölner Kommentar zum Aktiengesetz (2nd edn Cologne et al 1996) cited as *KöKo*/Mertens) s 109 comment 8; K Krebs *Interessenkonflikte bei Aufsichtsratsmandaten* at ff, 256 ff.

[102] J Semler and A Stengel [2003] NZG 1 (3 ff).

tractual agency. The exclusion of a board member from participation or even information may solve the problem posed by his own conflicting interests, but only at the price of losing his input in the discussion or decision process of the board, potentially to the detriment of the company. This necessitates some reticence.

5. *Resignation, dismissal*: Even one single conflict of interest may entitle a supervisory board member to resign from office, on the condition that this resignation is not untimely. If the conflict of interest is serious and lasting and cannot be solved in another way, the member of the supervisory board can exceptionally be required to resign.[103] This is also stated in a recommendation of the German Corporate Governance Code: 'Material conflicts of interest and those which are not merely temporary in respect of the person of a Supervisory Board member shall result in the termination of the mandate.'[104] Such a conflict of interest can constitute a good cause for dismissal of the board member by the court at the request of the supervisory board or of minority shareholders.[105] Such a good cause for dismissal was also present in the Hamburg case of *HEW/Jansen*. An energy minister who politically propagates the abandonment of nuclear energy cannot simultaneously function as a member of the supervisory board of a company that predominantly produces its electricity from nuclear sources.[106] If the public authority in particular does not understand this, it amounts to ideological arrogance.

What was said about the resignation of members of supervisory boards is also applicable in principle to members of management boards, with the proviso, however, that here conflicts of interest will occur less frequently than for members of supervisory boards. This is because members of management boards are employed full time and owe the company their complete devotion, which means that other potentially conflicting activities have to yield. On this basis, the German Corporate Governance Code contains no recommendation for conflicts of interest of members of management boards, as opposed to members of supervisory boards.

[103] M Lutter and G Krieger *Rechte und Pflichten des Aufsichtsrats* (4th edn Cologne 2002) s 10 comment 772; KJ Hopt [2002] ZGR 333 (372); *Handbuch Corporate Governance*/TMJ Möllers at 405 (424 ff), each with further references.

[104] German Corporate Governance Code no 5.5.3 sentence 2.

[105] KJ Hopt [2002] ZGR 333 (372); K Krebs *Interessenkonflikte bei Aufsichtsratsmandaten* at 88 ff, 252 ff; M Lutter and G Krieger *Rechte und Pflichten des Aufsichtsrats* s 10 comment 72.

[106] K Krebs *Interessenkonflikte bei Aufsichtsratsmandaten* at 309 ff with further references; M Lutter and G Krieger Rechte *und Pflichten des Aufsichtsrats* s 10 comment 784; cf with the same result Court of Appeals of Hamburg, [1990] ZIP 311 and before Regional Court of Hamburg, [1990] ZIP 102.

III. Application of these principles to all board members, including directors on co-determined boards

In the context of the German system of worker co-determination, it has been argued that a workers' representative in the supervisory board occupies a special position in cases of conflicts of interest.[107] This, however, is *de lege lata* not convincing and constitutes a policy error. This also should have been taken to heart in the case of *Bsirske* mentioned in the introduction.[108] The statutorily imposed system of workers' co-determination does not constitute a license for the workers' representatives to pursue interests other than the company's, and in no way legitimizes the direct harming of the company through a strike organized by a member of the supervisory board. The following principles are binding here. It is no secret that it can be difficult to draw a line in singular cases of conflicts of interest, but this is still no basis for exceptions.

1. *Legitimate passive participation in strikes*: There is no problem with passive participation in a strike. This is not disputed.

The duty of loyalty of a member of the supervisory board, who typically does not hold this position as a full-time function, does not include a prohibition for the bank this member represents to cooperate with the bidder in a hostile takeover;[109] it also does not include a prohibition for the labour union represented by the member to engage in an industrial conflict with the company.

2. *Illegitimate activities (participation in unlawful strikes, violation of board secrecy, actively organizing or supporting strikes against the corporation)*: The previous statement, however, does not mean that an act allowed for the institution represented by the member of the supervisory board is also legitimate behaviour for the actual member or would have no consequences for his activities in the supervisory board. The rights, duties, and consequences of the conflict of interest have to be deduced as previously described in general terms under III 2, i.e., according to the nature and intensity of the conflict of interest, from abstention

[107] For references on the controversy, cf TMJ Möllers [2003] NZG 697 (698 ff); M Lutter and G Krieger *Rechte und Pflichten des Aufsichtsrats* s 10 comment 778; *GroßKoAktG*/Oetker MitbestG s 26 comment 15 ff.

[108] Trade union members in the supervisory board are also bound to pursue the interest of the corporation and may not pursue colliding interests of the trade unions or the trade union members; cf M Lutter and G Krieger *Rechte und Pflichten des Aufsichtsrats* s 10 comment 777, 778 with further references.

[109] KJ Hopt [2002] ZGR 333 (370) contra M Lutter 'Bankenvertreter im Aufsichtsrat' (1981) 145 ZHR 224 (244 ff, 151) idem 'Interessenkonflikte durch Bankenvertreter im Aufsichtsrat' [1987] Recht der Wirtschaft (RdW) 314 (320).

from voting to resignation.[110] Unambiguous breaches of loyalty by a member of the supervisory board would include participation in an unlawful strike, including a breach of a no-strike clause; the use of company information through violation of board secrecy (this does not only include inside information in the technical sense); and the causation of (disproportionately) serious harm to the company by active support of a strike.[111]

Also, consequences are to be drawn in the case of a worker representative on the supervisory board organizing a strike against the company. Such an action is not compatible with supervisory board membership, which requires a loyalty to the company interest and implies a duty of loyal cooperation within the supervisory board, the functioning (and particularly the cohesion essential for the supervisory function) of which is harmed by such an action. During the preparation and implementation of the industrial conflict, the worker representative surely must not only abstain from decisions about how the company will react to the strike, but must also not participate in the parts of the meetings of the supervisory board during which this agenda item is discussed.[112] Under certain circumstances, this duty can become a right of the company to exclude the member from certain information. The behaviour that would be required if the company is not the prime target of the strike but is only indirectly affected is a singular case; among other factors, the degree to which the company is affected and the extent to which it is harmed will be decisive. In any case, when the activities of another firm that are of direct importance to the company are disrupted with the consequence of grave harm for the company – such as an airport strike for airline companies – the same rules apply as in the case of a strike aimed against the company itself. In specific, rather hypothetical cases, a duty to resign from the board can be required. This can be the case for industrial conflicts of long duration that hinder the ordinary functioning of the labour union representative because of the conflict of interest, or when a particular representative is charged as a labour union leader with the organization of industrial actions in general, which would predictably confront him time and again with conflicts of interest with the company.

It remains disputed whether – apart from the actual organization of the strike against the company – every active support of a strike by a member of the super-

[110] Cf for Sweden: 'However, the employee members are barred from participating in the board's deliberations and decisions concerning matters of collective agreements, industrial actions or any other issue, where they may be disqualified because of conflicts of interest between the trade unions and the enterprise.' A Victorin Paper presented to the Heidelberger Symposion on labor co-determination in Europe, 29./30.9.2003.

[111] Of the same view is TMJ Möllers 'Gesellschaftsrechtliche Treuepflicht contra arbeitnehmerrechtliche Mitbestimmung' [2003] NZG 697 (700 ff) with further references.

[112] In agreement *GroßKoAktG*/Oetker, MitbestG s 26 comment 19, but with other reasoning, namely protection of the functioning of free collective bargaining and of the parity of wage battle partners.

visory board also constitutes a breach of loyalty. The better arguments support an affirmative answer.[113] A negative answer from the legislators, allegedly implicit in the introduction of the system of worker co-determination, does not follow as such from the actual language of the statute. The meaning, rationale, and reach of worker participation is not touched by such a limitation, because the strike could just as well be organized by other members of the firm or the labour union as by the member of the supervisory board. Active support of a strike is contradictory to the confidential cooperation within the supervisory board; it jeopardizes its ability to function and hence also harms worker co-determination in general. The principle that all members of the supervisory board should be treated equally also supports this interpretation. If a representative of a bank on the supervisory board cannot simultaneously actively support a hostile take-over of the company, the case of active support of a strike against the company is not essentially different. The argument that co-determination, including the representation of labour unions, is introduced by statute is not convincing. The representation of banks and other business partners of the company on the supervisory board is not only legitimate within the German system, but is also built on elements in history, structure, and positive law.

3. *Duties of the board in cases of illegitimate activities of single board members*: When a member of the supervisory board violates these requirements, the supervisory board or the management board is required to intervene. Ultimately, it must request the court to dismiss the member of the supervisory board. Also, it is possible that in such cases an explanation is necessary (comply or explain).[114] The German Corporate Governance Code recommends that essential and not merely temporary conflicts of interest should lead to the termination of the mandate.[115] If, in the presence of such conflicts of interest, no appropriate measures are taken and this deviation from Code practice is not explicitly disclosed, investors are misled and all the consequences will apply, first among which is liability for potential damage.

4. *Loss of confidence and systemic risks*: Even apart from the question of the compatibility of membership in the supervisory board with active participation in or even organization of strikes, it is regrettably a fact that actions such as those of *Frank Bsirske* have done the German system of co-determination a serious disservice in the eyes of the public in general and foreign investors in particular. In

[113] eg, M Lutter and G Krieger *Rechte und Pflichten des Aufsichtsrats* s 10 comment 778; contra, eg, *GroßKoAktG*/Oetker MitbestG s 26 comment 17. As to the state of the controversy, see TMJ Möllers [2003] NZG 697 (698).

[114] Contra TMJ Möllers [2003] NZG 697 (699).

[115] German Corporate Governance Code no 5.3.3.

the end, this burdens those whose interests allegedly should be protected, that is, all the workers.

IV. Precedence of the interest of the principal over the self-interest of the agent: The principle and its exceptions

1. *The principle*: As a general basic principle, the interests of the principal should prevail over the personal interests of the agent when they come into conflict. This applies equally to corporate agents – such as members of management boards and managing directors – and to contractual agents – such as commission dealers, brokers, and other intermediaries. This basic principle applies in particular also to banks.[116] But it is also clear that this basic principle is no more than a general standard that needs to be specified in each individual case.

For professional fiduciaries this is often done by statute. As was already mentioned, Article 11 of the Investment Services Directive contains special rules on conflicts of interest for investment firms that have been transposed in the national law of the Member States. In Germany, for example, s. 31 para 1 nr. 2 of the German Securities Trading Act contains general rules of conduct and s. 32 of the German Securities Trading Act specifies special rules of conduct regulating the way investment firms have to deal with clients in case of conflicts of interest. S. 32 simply forbids certain types of self-serving behaviour, while s. 31 para 1 nr. 2 requires the banks to try to avoid conflicts of interest and to ensure that when they cannot be avoided 'the client's order will be executed with due care for the interests of the client.' The German directive on codes of conduct of August 2001 specifies this even more. Investment services have to be performed in the best interest of the client and orders that are noticeably not in the interest of the client can only be executed or transmitted when the investment firm has explained the risks to the client.[117] The transactions prohibited by s. 32 of the German Securities Trading Act are also elaborated by specific recommended prohibitions in the German directive, such as for churning, the prohibition of front running, and the expansion of these rules to transactions by employees and other persons.[118] All these duties are part of public law but also reflect on the duties under private law.

2. *The exceptions*: The basic principle that the principal's interest must prevail over the interests of the agent does not apply without limitations. The furthering of personal interests is not per se forbidden, but only significantly limited; pro-

[116] KJ Hopt *Kapitalanlegerschutz* at 440 ff; V Lang *Informationspflichten* s 8 comment 1 with further references; to be distinguished from the (temporal) priority principle, idem at s 8 comment 23.

[117] WpHVerhaltensRi no B.3.3 subpara 1.

[118] WpHVerhaltensRi no E.1-3.

tecting one's personal interests is allowed to the extent that it is legitimate market behaviour and necessary for price setting. As such, the agent remains free to negotiate a beneficial compensation agreement; he is allowed to realize his market value. This is not only true for contractual agents such as commission dealers, brokers, and credit institutions, but also for corporate agents, such as members of management boards[119] and supervisory boards, especially when their dealings and negotiations with the company constitute their main professional activity. For this last category, however, limits should not only be based on *bonos mores*, but also in relation to the duty of loyalty if members of corporate organs wangle compensation for each other that is clearly disproportionate to their services. Regarding stock options, therefore, caps are problematic, preferable are disclosure, co-determination by shareholders, and in particular profit-reducing entries in the company accounts.[120] Finally, it will have to be the institutional investors that impose standards, and they have already partially started doing that.

V. Impartiality in case of conflicting third-party interests, in particular the (temporal) priority principle and the question of equal treatment

1. *Impartiality*: From its very starting point, dealing with different conflicting third-party interests is not as clear and simple as dealing with the conflict of a principal's interests and the self-interests of the agent. Each of the several principals of the agent can expect, in principle, that his own interests will be safeguarded as far as possible. It follows that in case of conflict, the agent must not give arbitrary precedence to one of the conflicting interests. One could therefore speak of a basic principle of impartiality[121] in cases of colliding third-party interests as is formulated by court rulings on commercial brokers and civil brokers, if they are exceptionally allowed to act for both parties. According to this principle, the broker should inform both parties about the circumstances relevant for the conclusion of the contract. This is not a violation of his professional discretion if he does not intervene in the price negotiations.[122]

However, often the basic principle of impartiality has little meaning if one does not declare conflicting multi-party agency to be inadmissible as a preventive measure. When it is allowed anyway, a procedure may be required for deter-

[119] *GroßKoAktG*/KJ Hopt s 93 comments 155, 160, see also comments 146, 154 and 156 ff; H Fleischer [2002] WM 1045 (1047).

[120] High Level Group of Company Law Experts, *A Modern Regulatory Framework for Company Law in Europe* (Brussels 4 November 2002), ch III.4.2 (64 ff).

[121] Bundesgerichtshof, *BGHZ* 48, 344; 61, 17 (22); A Baumbach and KJ Hopt *HGB*, s 93 comment 33.

[122] Bundesgerichtshof, *BGHZ* 48, 344 (347); Bundesgerichtshof, [1968] NJW 150; A Baumbach and KJ Hopt *HGB* s 93 comment 33.

mining which interests among the different third-party interests involved have to be taken into account and in which sequence. The most suitable procedure for most cases is the temporal priority principle. Unless otherwise agreed or statutorily provided, the agent must follow the sequence of reception of orders from his clients.[123] The precise sequence will not only depend on the mere reception of the orders, but also on whether they should be executed immediately, or may also be executed at a later time.

However, the agent is free to follow another procedure with conflicting third-party interests, provided the principal knows about it or is informed in advance.[124] For some professional agents, this rule is expressly laid down in the law. For instance, the German directive on codes of conduct of August 2001 obliges investment firms offering subscription for securities to private clients to inform those clients about the allotment rules for clients, especially in case of oversubscription.[125] The so-called friends and family programs – according to which a certain amount of securities is reserved for beneficiaries provided by the issuer or the bank, e.g., their employees or other business partners – are compatible with the duty of loyalty. But they have to be removed from the so-called free float.[126]

2. *Equal treatment*: Some try to defuse the conflict among several third-party interests by postulating a principle of equal treatment for agents as well.[127] However, there is no general principle of equal treatment in private law, nor can it be derived from European law. The attempts to force such an equal treatment by a general anti-discrimination law even exceeding the European guidelines are very problematic. Also, in the case of agency, equal treatment does not yield the results expected by its staunchest defenders. This is because the principal's interest is normally to obtain the best treatment himself. Special rules apply in cases in which other orders, both from another client or from the agent's own portfolio, may be regrouped with the order of the principal to a large order to obtain better conditions. The benefits achieved by acting in this way should then be evenly spread over all participants.[128]

With agency contracts, a different outcome can arise if the parties agree on equal treatment compared to other clients. An obligation of that kind may derive from the contract between the bank and its clients – especially in the mass bank-

[123] H-D Assmann, UH Schneider and I Koller *Wertpapierhandelsgesetz (WpHG)* (3rd edn Cologne 2003) s 31 comment 49; Lang *Informationspflichten* s 8 comment 23.

[124] See already KJ Hopt *Kapitalanlegerschutz* 447.

[125] WpHVerhaltensRi no B.3.4.

[126] Stock Exchange Experts Commission at the Federal Ministry of Finance, *Grundsätze für die Zuteilung von Aktienemissionen an Privatanleger* (Berlin 7.6.2000) cf W Groß, *Kapitalmarktrecht* (2nd edn Munich 2002) s 1-12 BörsZulV Rdn 11.

[127] eg V Lang *Informationspflichten* 162.

[128] H-D Assmann, UH Schneider and I Koller *WpHG* s 31 comment 47, 60.

ing business – in the sense that one client should not be dealt with arbitrarily on a different basis than all other clients taking part in the same mass transaction.[129]

E. Prevention of Conflicts of Interest, Sanctions, and Enforcement[130]

I. Prevention by duties of organization such as Chinese walls and screening, by duties to avoid the emergence of conflicts of interest, and by independence requirements

1. *Prevention by duties of organization*: The general principles of law dealing with conflicts of interest developed so far are not sufficient in certain conflict situations. The legal system may provide that certain conflicts of interest should be avoided from the outset or be forced back by compliance programs, e.g., in article 11 subsection 1 of the Investment Services Directive. Chinese walls and screens – designed to prevent potential conflicts of interest within the company itself by separating functions and sources of information – have been used for years internationally, especially in the U.S. and in the U.K., and are now increasingly being adopted in several other Western industrial states such as France, Switzerland, and lately also Germany.[131] Many aspects of these organizational preventive measures are still unclear, namely, how these safeguards have to be conceived, and especially whether and what legal consequences these instruments will have apart from the supervisory rights of public authorities on the duties of banks under private law. Apart from affecting the factual evidence in a specific case, these techniques alone will in general not justify conduct that is detrimental to the clients' interests. The prevention of conflicts of interest by duties of organization is being discussed for attorneys[132] and is also to be taken into account for

[129] A Baumbach and KJ Hopt *HGB* (7) Bankgeschäfte comment A/6, controversial. But cf also Bundesgerichtshof, [2002] NJW 3695, a decision which is not convincing, see M Roth 'Der allgemeine Bankvertrag' [2003] WM 480, CP Claussen *Bank- und Börsenrecht* (3rd edn Munich 2003) s 4 II comment 30 c-h.

[130] The problems dealt with in this paragraph are addressed in detail in KJ Hopt 'Prävention und Repression von Interessenkonflikten im Aktien-, Bank- und Berufsrecht' in *Festschrift für Doralt* (Vienna 2004, pending).

[131] C Hollander and S Salzedo *Conflicts of Interest & Chinese Walls* (London 2000); P Buck *Wissen und Juristische Person* (Tübingen 2001) at 499 ff; H-D Assmann, UH Schneider and I Koller *WpHG* s 33 comment 17 ff; G McCormack 'Conflicts of Interest, Chinese Walls and Investment Management' (1999) 1 International and Comparative Corporate Law Journal 5; KJ Hopt [2002] ZGR 333 (367 ff).

[132] M Henssler 'Das Verbot der Vertretung widerstreitender Interessen' [2001] NJW 1521 (1523 ff); M Kilian 'Die Globalisierung der Rechtsberatung – Interessenkonflikte und Chinese Walls –' [2000] WM 1366 (1372 ff). See supra B III and Bundesverfassungsgericht, [2003] NJW 2520 with note M Kilian [2003] BB 2189; contra before Bundesgerichtshof, [2001] NJW 1572 and P Schlosser 'Anwaltsrechtliches Verbot der Vertretung widerstreitender Interessen'

cont. ...

other contractual agents, such as large state-wide brokerage firms. Approaches to this can be found in the doctrine of imputation of knowledge[133] and the doctrine of corporate organizational duties.[134]

2. *Avoiding the emergence of the conflict of interest*: In many cases, prevention by compliance programs is helpful, but it does not hinder the agent in a concrete conflict of interest from favouring his self-interests or that of a conflicting third party in a breach of loyalty that can lead to hardly solvable problems in terms of evidence. In some cases, the legal system then intervenes by stating general or specific prohibitions intended to prevent the emergence of conflicts of interest for agents. This is the case, for instance, for professional agents with the attorney's prohibition to represent conflicting interests, for corporate agents with the statutory prohibition of competition in corporate law, and for contractual agents with the civil broker's prohibition to represent both parties to the deal. Occasionally attempts have been made to extend these prohibitions aiming at the prevention of conflicts of interest by way of analogy. This approach, however, is very problematic.

3. *Independence requirements: Independent directors and auditors*: Even more far-reaching than the rules to reduce or restrict conflicts of interest in special cases are the rules on independence, incompatibility, and rotation for members of the supervisory board and auditors – applicable to the agent and also to his partners – as they have been demanded and implemented in many countries following the recent American corporate scandals such as Enron and WorldCom and as a reaction to the Sarbanes-Oxley Act. One can expect that significant changes will be introduced on behalf of the European Union that will affect the functioning of the German supervisory board, its committees, and the auditors.[135]

[2002] NJW 1376. According to Advocate General Léger Chinese walls are not sufficient at all, Case C 309/99 'Wouters', 10 July 2001, para 194.

133 P Buck *Wissen und Juristische Person* (Tübingen 2001); G Nobbe 'Die Wissenszurechnung in der Rechtsprechung des Bundesgerichtshofes' in W Hadding, KJ Hopt and H Schimansky (eds) *Bankrechtstag 2000* (Munich 2003) at 121.

134 G Spindler *Unternehmensorganisationspflichten* (Cologne 2001).

135 As to the various criteria for independence of board members cf eg (for the UK) The Combined Code on Corporate Governance, July 2003, Section 1, A.3.1. and A.3.2: With the exception of smaller companies at least half of board members should be designated by the board as independent. As to the conflicts of interest of auditors, see R Volhard and D Weber 'Abschlussprüfung und Interessenkonflikt' in *Festschrift für Ulmer* (Berlin/New York 2003) 865.

II. Invalidity of the individual vote, nullity of the resolution

Besides the prevention of conflicts of interest, there is also their repression. As already mentioned,[136] the most immediate reaction of the legal system consists of imposing prohibitions of representation and losses of voting rights. In this case, the given vote is invalid. Defects at the level of the individual vote may lead to deficiencies of the resolution when a majority is not achieved without the invalid vote. Third-party transactions by corporate agents in breach of loyalty or based on void board resolutions are legally effective in general, because they are a matter of external representation of the company.

However, prohibitions of representation and losses of voting rights are exceptional. They cover only a small fraction of the conflicts of interest discussed above, and the applicable rules are only subject to analogy within strict boundaries. This is because the kind of sanction imposed is severe, and therefore must be precisely delineated and certain. This is not just the case for conflicts of interest, which do not end unambiguously but are hard to grasp – especially when affecting indirect financial or immaterial interests and when extending to third parties such as family members or companies of the same group. Therefore, there are good reasons for German law's lack of a general prohibition on exercising voting rights in cases of conflicts of interest.[137]

III. Liability for damages

As with other violations of duties, liability for damages is the usual sanction in the case of a breach of loyalty. In some cases concerning corporate agents such as members of the management board or supervisory board who have violated explicitly regulated duties of loyalty – like the prohibition of competition or of granting loans to board members – the law contains express rules on liability for damages.[138] In other cases of breach of loyalty, the liability for damages will flow from the general rules on corporate law liability for members of the board.[139] Liability for damages serves compensation as well as prevention. The liability rules do not apply or will lapse if the competent organ of the corporation has authorized or approved the conflict of interest or the transaction in question. In

[136] Supra D II 2.

[137] Supra C III, D II; K Krebs, *Interessenkonflikte bei Aufsichtsratsmandaten* at 138 ff, 142.

[138] eg, s 88 para 2, 93 para 3 no 8 of the German Stock Corporation Act.

[139] For details, see *GroßKAktG*/KJ Hopt s 93 comment 144 ff, 156 ff with groups of cases.

liability suits, however, there are difficult problems with causation, the amount of damages, and the burden of proof.[140]

IV. Forfeiture of remuneration

With respect to brokers, s. 654 of the German Civil Code provides a forfeiture of remuneration in cases of a particularly grave breach of contract, i.e., the non-loyal acting for both parties to the deal, regardless of whether the principal has sustained any damage. This rule aims to urge the broker to observe his duty of loyalty.[141] This sanction has been extended in case law and in legal writing to cases in which the broker has seriously harmed the interests of the principal by intentional or grossly negligent violations of essential contractual obligations.[142] Any deliberate or reckless violation of the duty of loyalty in conflicts of interest falls within this category.

On the other hand, the German Federal Bundesgerichtshof has decided that an attorney will forfeit his claim for fees only for an intentional betrayal of a client.[143] From a legal policy standpoint, it was deemed that in cases of conflict of interest it would go too far to impose a general sanction for intentional or grossly negligent breach of loyalty, particularly in cases of long-term agency.[144] At the least, the High Level Group of Company Law Experts, in its report of 4 November 2002, mentioned the forfeiture of a company director's claims for bonuses and profits from distributed shares and stock options as a possible sanction to be enacted by the Member States.[145]

V. Accounting for profits made in the disloyal transaction

Payments the agent receives in breach of loyalty in a case of conflicts of interest should be returned to the principal.[146] This rule applies to bribery[147] or to similar

[140] For details, see KJ Hopt in *Festschrift für Doralt* (Vps na 2004, pending).

[141] Bundesgerichtshof, *BGHZ* 36, 323 (326); H Sprau in Palandt *BGB,* s 654 comment 1.

[142] Bundesgerichtshof, [1981] NJW 280; [1981] NJW 2297.

[143] Bundesgerichtshof, [1981] NJW 1211.

[144] D Reuter in J v Staudinger *BGB* (13th edn Berlin 1995) s 654 comment 3: The breach of contract of one party must not be a windfall profit for the other.

[145] High Level Group of Company Law Experts, *A Modern Regulatory Framework for Company Law in Europe* (Brussels, 4 November 2002), ch III.4.5 (69).

[146] As to American law, see American Law Institute *Restatement of the Law – Second: Agency 2d*, s 403.

[147] For members of the management board, see *GroßKoAktG*/KJ Hopt s 93 comment 181 with further references; for the limited liability company (GmbH), see Bundesgerichtshof, cont. ...

payments that have to be disclosed, as was mentioned earlier.[148] This rule also applies to preferential prices,[149] or as the case may be, to remunerations a member of the management board may claim based on a counselling contract entered into in connection with his office. For bonuses due to credit institutions in connection with the issuing of securities, the same reasoning is being adopted by some legal writers, although it is contrary to the prevailing legal thinking.[150] There is a two-fold justification why the agent is being called to account. On the one hand, this behaviour causes losses to the company or the principal because the counterparty to the transaction is likely to include in its price calculation the amounts due to the board member. But also apart from this, entering into this type of contract and accepting the corresponding fees or payments belongs to the range of activities of the management board.

In German law – in contrast to English law in cases of a breach of fiduciary duty – the legal basis for accounting for profits made in the disloyal transaction is not uniform.[151] In German law, there are several specific rules that concern accounting for profits, e.g., in corporate law, prohibited competition by a member of the management board.[152] Nevertheless, in German law it is more convincing to recognize a general rule that profits from a breach of loyalty have to be accounted for, even outside any fault.[153] According to this rule, the justification of the duty to return unlawfully made profits is the improper exploitation of a dominant position as trustee or – in our cases – as agent. The agent has to return all he has obtained from the agency if there is a danger that the acceptance of the benefit may cause a conflict between his self-interest and that of his principal. Whether the latter's interests have effectively been harmed is of no importance. Rather, the mere existence of a conflict of interest between that of the principal and the self-interest of the agent suffices[154] – and contributes to the preventive effect of the accounting for profits.

[1968] GmbHR 141 (142, obiter), Court of Appeals of Düsseldorf, [2000] WM 1393 (1397); see also Bundesgerichtshof, [1962] WM 578.

148 As to English law, see FMB Reynolds *Bowstead and Reynolds on Agency,* Article 50.

149 Bundesgerichtshof, [1968] GmbHR 141 (142).

150 H-D Assmann, UH Schneider and I Koller *WpHG,* s 31 comment 74.

151 See K Rusch *Gewinnhaftung bei Verletzung von Treuepflichten* (Tübingen 2003) 70 ff.

152 Cf s 88 para 2 sentence 2 of the German Stock Corporation Act, s 667 and s 812 of the German Civil Code (BGB).

153 See K Rusch, *Gewinnhaftung* 70 ff, 229 ff.

154 The sanction of accounting for profits does not work for the large group of cases of conflicts of several parallel or opposite interests (supra B IV 2), because in these cases the question is to whom of the several principals the profit belongs or how it is to be apportioned.

VI. Sanctions under public and penal law

For professional agents such as banks, auditors, and attorneys, sanctions under public and disciplinary law imposed by the public supervisory authorities or by the professional associations should be mentioned. Examples can be found in bank regulation. The non-tax deductibility of remunerations paid to members of the company bodies when certain limits are exceeded can be an effective sanction.

In criminal law, the misconduct of agents related to conflicts of interest may trigger a series of special provisions as are laid down in corporate, banking, and securities laws, or in the insider rules. From the angle of legal policy, these special criminal provisions are often introduced too easily by the legislators, even though they are not the most efficient enforcement instruments. Reference should also be made, however, to the general criminal law prohibition of 'breach of trust.'[155] The difficulties this prohibition raises, especially for conflicts of interest, have been impressively described in legal literature. They spring from the fact that the legal definition of 'breach of trust' was conceived on the model of the asset manager, who merely has to care for the interest of the assets he has to manage. But in cases of conflicts of interest, the 'relatively simple factual situations'[156] – such as the embezzlement of assets trusted to management or the non-restitution of fees paid to the manager – no longer prevail. The cases are much more complex. For members of the supervisory board who are active in a secondary occupation and are entitled to pursue their proper interests, demarcation under criminal law will come close to a nightmare. This is also true if – due to the restrictive interpretation of criminal law provisions – applying the prohibition of 'breach of trust' is limited to specifically defined cases.[157] Therefore, it is fully justified when an expert on the law of economic offences declares that s. 266 of the German Penal Code has been used for palliating the regulatory deficit in the field of business law[158] – in the same sense that criminal law was used to fill in the gaps before the regulation of corporate group law in Germany (and as is still the case in the corporate group law of other jurisdictions, as the 'Rozenblum' concept of the French Cour de Cassation[159] illustrates).

[155] s. 266 of the German Penal Code.

[156] K Tiedemann 'Untreue bei Interessenkonflikten, Am Beispiel der Tätigkeit von Aufsichtsratsmitgliedern' in *Festschrift für Tröndle* (Berlin/New York 1989) 319 (325, with case law at 331).

[157] This is proposed by K Tiedemann in *Festschrift für Tröndle* at 328, 334, but this does not provide for a clear demarcation and application.

[158] ibid at 322.

[159] For details and consequences de lege ferenda see Forum Europaeum Konzernrecht 'Konzernrecht für Europa' [1998] ZGR 672 (705 ff), translated: 'Corporate Group Law for Europe' (2000) I European Business Organization Law Review (EBOR) 165.

Finally, the prohibitions on exercising a function or a profession should also be mentioned. These prohibitions should only be imposed in cases of especially grave and repeated violations of the professionals' duties. The refusal or the withdrawal of a license – such as the prohibition from engaging in banking or investment activities for lack of reliability – prevents the person concerned from taking part in these activities. This remedy is particularly adequate in case of misconduct of agents due to conflicts of interest. It is worthwhile to reflect on the recommendation of the High Level Group of Company Law Experts of 4 November 2002 to introduce within the EU a prohibition from exercising the function of director as a sanction for making false or misleading statements on financial and important non-financial facts or in general for grave misconduct of directors.[160]

F. Summary

I. Intermediation is a characteristic of the modern service-oriented society. As a matter of course, intermediation involves conflicts of self-interest and the interest of others. These conflicts threaten the principal and, more generally, may cause losses of confidence with negative consequences for the market and the economy. In private law, the duties of loyalty of directors – particularly members of the corporate board, both one-tier and two-tier – are the best developed. But in addition to these, the duties of loyalty that arise from service contracts (such as commission dealers, brokers, and other intermediaries) and the duties of loyalty that are standardized by the law of professional intermediaries (such as banks, auditors, and lawyers) must not be neglected. It is possible to categorize a number of case patterns that arise in all three of these groups, though in different frequency, gravity, and shape. It is astonishing to ascertain that case law and legal theory have traditionally focused only on the duty of loyalty of board members and have hardly ever looked beyond the concrete case or the specific legal contract or field into other cases and groups of intermediation. As a result of this focus and – I daresay – narrow-mindedness, the sensitivity for conflicts of interest varies considerably from field to field, as do the legal reactions and solutions offered if the conflict is perceived. It is useful to distinguish between two basic conflict situations: the conflict between the interest of the principal and the self-interest of the agent on the one side, and the conflict among different parallel or opposite interests in multi-principal intermediation on the other side. Examples for the first are self-dealing, competition, use of corporate opportunities, use of business secrets and inside information, use of corporate or business position for personal purposes, and excessive remuneration. Examples for the second are

[160] High Level Group of Company Law Experts, *A Modern Regulatory Framework for Company Law in Europe* (Brussels, 4 November 2002), ch III.4.5 (69 ff).

multiple mandates, multiparty representation, conflicts of allotment, and acting for both sides of the contract.

II. The sources of the duties of loyalties of intermediaries are very different, i.e., contract, codified, and case law; professional rules; and codes of conduct. The rationale for the duty of loyalty in fiduciary contracts and fiduciary relationships is the same, namely, the duty of loyalty as correlative of granting increased influence on the principal's sphere of interest. The emergence of the duties of loyalty in the different fields is accompanied by complicated interactions between public law, private law, and codes of conduct.[161] Particularly in relation to liability for damages, a common question is whether the duty of loyalty arising under a specific public law rule or code of conduct recommendation is meant to also be a legal basis for the principal to recover damages. There are also further questions that arise across the sectors and independently of the source of the duty of loyalty, such as the extension of the duty of loyalty to third parties and the after-effects of such duties of loyalty after the termination of the corporate office or the intermediation contract.

III. The law is called upon to react to these patterns and challenges in modern intermediation by developing common legal principles for treating conflicts of interest beyond the different sectors and sources of rules. This does not mean that the solutions must always be harmonized, but it is hardly convincing that the same conflict of interest is solved or not solved or not even perceived depending on whether it accidentally happens to principals and agents in one or another form of intermediation. At least there must be a similar awareness of such conflicts and a consistent policy in reacting to them. Common legal principles for treating conflicts of interest include the following. a) Full disclosure of the conflict of interest is a minimum requirement. Pertinent case law exists for securities analysts, project development agents, lawyers, and construction agents. b) Beyond mere disclosure, it is often required that the conflict be solved either in the concrete case or more generally. Legal instruments vary and include prohibition of self-dealing, loss of voting right, abstention of voting, exclusion of attendance, resignation, and dismissal. In each case it must be seen whether the legal instrument consists in an outright prohibition, a mere right, or a legal duty of the agent. These principles apply to all board members, including workforce and trade union members in the two-tier board. The German system of co-determination does not justify or even require deviation from these principles. The opinion to the contrary – which is widespread in Germany – is legally unconvincing, economically harmful, and hard to understand internationally. It discredits co-determination itself. Further common legal principles are c) precedence of the interest of the

[161] As to these dogmatic questions, see KJ Hopt 'Interessenwahrung und Interessenkonflikte im Aktien-, Bank- und Berufsrecht' [2004] ZGR 1.

principal over the self-interest of the agent and d) impartiality with conflicting third-party interests. In the latter case, (temporal) priority is usually a good rule. Equal treatment is not generally prescribed, but may provided for by contract or by law in specific situations.

IV. Conflicts of interest may be prevented by duties of organization such as Chinese walls and screening, by duties to avoid the emergence of the conflict (e.g., prohibition for lawyers of representing conflicting interests in the same case, rules against competition with the principal, prohibition of acting on both sides of the contract), and by incompatibility rules and independence requirements (e.g., independent directors and auditors). Conflicts of interest may be repressed by various sanctions such as invalidity of the individual vote, nullity of the resolution, liability for damages, forfeiture of remuneration, accounting for profits made in the disloyal transaction, and administrative sanctions and punishable offences. Administrative and penal law may provide for disqualification from the intermediary's profession, a particularly pungent repressive measure.

V. In spite of all such endeavours by lawmakers and regulators, conflicts of interest remain and violations of the duties of loyalty are a frequent practice. This leads to a certain scepticism toward legal intervention as can be seen from a word of *Truffaldino* from *Carlo Goldoni's* wonderful, wise comedy of 1745, 'Arlecchino, servitore di due padroni.' The servant of two masters says: '*Ho fatto una gran fadiga, ho fatto anca dei mancamenti, ma spero che, per rason della stravaganza, tutti sti siori me perdonerà.*'

A Modern Regulatory Framework for Company and Takeover Law in Europe

MICHEL PRADA

The Syracuse Conference provided us with a most valuable set of remarkable academic studies on the ongoing European debates on the modernisation of the E.U. legislative framework in the field of company and takeover law, as they have been speeded up by the reports issued by the working groups chaired by Pr Jaap Winter and by the negotiations on the draft directives and orientations proposed by the European Commission within the Financial Services Action Plan.

I have been kindly invited by the organisers to react on the reports presented to this Conference, more specifically on the issues of Company law and I am grateful for this invitation.

Being neither an academic nor a professional lawyer, I can only express the personal views and comments of a former securities regulator on these complex issues, without committing in any way French authorities.

It appears that the issues related to company law have been analysed and debated by many participants on the basis of a comparative study of the 'common law' systems and the 'continental law' systems, while the papers on takeovers mainly present economic thoughts and demonstrations on the relevance and efficiency of the rules proposed to monitor the takeover process in Europe.

Accordingly, my comments will address differently the two series of papers.

As for the papers on company law, I have not much to add to the excellent analysis and valuable fact finding provided by the authors of the reports. I must nevertheless confess that I was not convinced by a general tendency to criticise the continental system and to consider the common law system as an incontestable benchmark. In fact, I wonder whether this approach is not flawed, if not counterproductive.

Firstly, it seems to me that there are huge differences within each of these systems and that these differences have been underestimated.

The UK system seems to be very different from the US one (split responsibilities between the Chairman and the CEO, number of executive directors within the boards, role of the shareholders etc...).

Symmetrically, there is no unity within continental Europe (otherwise the Europeans wouldn't have debated for decades on these issues...). The French system is very different from the German or the Dutch one.

It is therefore hazardous to come to affirmative conclusions and take strong views on the merits of the 'basic' systems, as they do differ according to countries, even if they present some common features.

In my view the difference between common law and Roman law is more of a procedural than of a substantial nature. From this point of view, I wonder whether the debate should not focus, if necessary, on the cost-efficiency performance rather than on the rules themselves. This would require an in-depth statistical analysis in order to identify the respective merits of case law versus a more prescriptive system and to analyse the perverse consequences of hypertrophy of litigation, on one side, and hypertrophy of procedure on the other side (which is certainly the case in France, where efficiency is in peril because of a dreadfully lengthy judiciary process).

Secondly, many reports have not taken into consideration the fact that the major scandals that burst out in the recent months took place in a 'common law' environment. Their appraisal of the common law system as the best standard to deliver good corporate governance is based on evidence that is a bit out of date (I refer specifically to the appreciations by La Porta et al. which are explicitly or implicitly referred to by some papers).

On the other hand, many of the messy failures that happened in continental Europe started years ago in an environment of so called 'mixed-economy', where continental corporate laws have not been implemented without some specificities, due to the role of governments in the management of firms. I shall not comment on this, but it is clear that things have recently changed dramatically. As for the private sector, while a few years ago continental capitalism was characterised by concentration of control in the hands of families or friendly companies, recent restructuring, together with securitisation, has favoured openness. This evolution, together with privatisation of state-owned companies, has changed the European landscape and is progressively making the traditional 'clichés' out of date: today, for example, more than one third of market cap of French companies of the 'CAC 40' are in the hands of foreign investors (mainly US and UK pension and mutual funds), which has some significant consequences from the point of view of corporate governance and market behaviour.

It should nevertheless be recognised that there still remains a difference between the US and Europe, but it is also interesting to see the renewal, in the US, of the debates on 'shareholder ownership' and the best ways and means to enhance shareholder's commitment in companies' strategies and control...

Thirdly, when drawing lessons from the recent scandals, one should not consider in the same way strategic failures, due to market conditions, and frauds or misbehaviour by managers. A former regulator should be careful when addressing this kind of issue as many scandals do present both kinds of mismanagement ... but it can be assumed that the Marconi debacle is not comparable to the Enron one and that the loss of value at Aol-Time-Warner (much more significant than the Vivendi one) is not of the same nature as the WorldCom one (even if some fund managers say that it seems that there might also be some irregularities in Aol-Time-Warner accounts). A sound corporate governance system can hopefully address consistently the issue of conflicts of interest and well-balanced internal and external controls; it cannot solve the issue of risk that is at the very basis of entrepreneurship. Even more, it should not be so complicated and adverse to risk that it would make initiative and innovation to become impossible.

Finally, many reports, referring mainly to the US and UK systems, seem to ignore or minimise both excellent rules, which have existed for decades in 'old Europe' (and have recently been implemented in the US, becoming therefore the best rule to be applied worldwide according to the US detailed prescriptions), and recent developments which have brought European companies closer to international recognised standards, quite often inspired by US or UK practice.

As examples of the former, I will mention:

- The prohibition by French company law (since 1966 or, maybe, 1867) of lending by the company to Board members;
- The prohibition by French company law (since 1966) of consulting services by auditors;
- The limitation to a maximum of one third of Board members being paid as executive by the company (whereby the issue of 'independent' directors is obviously of a different nature when compared to the US situation);
- As examples of the latter, I will mention:
- The new provisions by the law on 'Nouvelles Régulations Economiques' (2001) and the law on 'Financial Security' (2003) on Board members' compensation disclosure, limitation of the number of individual directorships, transparency of the rules of governance of the Boards, transparency of trading in company shares by Board members, etc...
- A number of provisions of these two laws which reinforce the powers of shareholders (already very significant according to the corporate law of 1966) in the field of reporting by the Boards, approval of major decisions, capacity to ask for independent expertise and to propose resolutions, and modernisation of voting procedures.

By the way, it is no surprise that an objective analysis of common and continental laws should conclude –as it is too frequently the case– that none is superior to the other as far as substance is concerned. Both systems have the same cultural background and are based on the same values and principles: duty of care ('l'intérêt social') and duty of loyalty (Cour de Cassation 27/02/1996 and 24/02/1998) inter alia, have existed in both systems for decades.

The report by Holger Fleischer has accurately mentioned the French institution of 'abus de biens sociaux' (misappropriation of corporate resources), which is remarkably efficient, even too severe, as some representatives of the community of managers would advocate... One could also mention wrongful trading and its sanction 'l' action en comblement de passif', whereby Board members may be condemned to pay for the company's liabilities, and 'l'interdiction de gérer' which is the equivalent to directors' disqualification.

Therefore it seems to me that drafting a European company law should build on existing systems rather than trying to oppose them or to take one or the other national system as a benchmark. It should also leave room for diversity and flexibility within a framework of strong and comprehensive principles and functional requirements.

A framework directive should establish the main rules and principles. Secondary legislation, preferably through 'rules' (directly applicable) rather than 'directives' should provide for some diversity in the implementation. Mutual recognition would then be the rule for all member states in order to establish a level playing field between them. I understand that this is consistent with the views of the Winter Group and with the 'Lamfalussy process' applicable to some of the directives of the FSAP.

A second remark, which I share with Professor Eddy Wymeersch, is that possibly not all provisions should be enshrined in corporate law and enforced by courts and judiciary procedures. Many provisions should rather be dealt with through securities regulation. It is remarkable that most issues rose since the late nineties are related to the functioning of listed companies, because of the special kind of fiduciary duties management owed to the public at large. Dispersed ownership is from this point of view even more demanding.

These issues deal, in practice, with the good functioning of the markets, i.e. disclosure and transparency requirements, due to the need to compensate the basic 'asymmetry of information', and with consistent reporting and auditing, in order to balance the 'agency' relationship between dispersed shareholders and the management.

In many countries, they fall in the remit of securities legislation and regulations. Securities regulators have the capacity to impose administrative sanctions on wrongdoers. When considering European developments in that field, one can see that many of them are closer to securities legislation than to corporate law (consider, for example, the transparency directive or the market abuse directive).

Finally, it seems to me that we are about to converge towards a set of internationally recognised principles and standards that can – and should – be implemented through possibly different templates. The way forward requires some flexibility and tolerance if we wish to make progress. This is true within the EU. It is also true in the field of transatlantic relationship.

For instance, looking at the Sarbanes-Oxley Act, I can recognise a number of innovations that have existed in France for many years and I certainly welcome them. But does this mean that appointing auditors – at last! – through a decision making process which is independent from the management can be achieved only according to the 'Sarbox' rule? Is their appointment by the general assembly of shareholders upon the proposal of the audit committee unacceptable?

To conclude, let us build a European company framework law on the basis of clear principles and standardised functional requirements; let us leave room for different practical arrangements so that some flexibility is accepted by all member states and implemented through mutual recognition; let's explore all the possibilities of mutual recognition in the transatlantic relationship (as proposed by Dr Benn Steil) and, finally, let's remember the French poet's warning: 'l' ennui naquit un jour de l' uniformité'...

The issues raised by the harmonization of take-over rules are quite different from those related to company law and the process is, of course, at a more advanced stage as the take over directive is about to be adopted, if...

Here we are clearly dealing with two different sets of considerations:

1. Market functioning from the theoretical point of view of maximisation of shareholder value, together with the protection of minority shareholders;
2. National interest from the political point of view of economic and strategic independence.

The High Level Group's report has implicitly addressed both issues and proposed a balanced solution, basically inspired by the necessity to organise an efficient regulatory system in Europe from the point of view of the good functioning of an integrated market (allowing for competition and best allocation of capital) and the necessity to accept, within clear limits, some exceptions to a purely 'free market system'. Hence the proposal to adopt a series of rules that provide acceptable compromises, namely the 'mandatory bid', the 'break-through rule', the 'squeeze-out' option an the 'sell-out option'.

The academic reports presented in Syracuse were fascinating. Most of them provide with a brilliant theoretical analysis of the relevance of these rules and options with regards to the behaviour of market participants, according to their strategic games.

This logical analysis of behavioural patterns is not only useful to enlighten the internal dynamics of financial operations: more than often it demonstrates that an intuitive approach of the legitimacy of some regulatory provisions may be wrong, either because the players react in a way which nullifies the impact of the rule or, even worse, because the rule can have counterproductive effects, as shown with the presentation of the 'free rider' problem.

My only concern is that these reports are either assuming a theoretical environment of 'pure market economy' where market participants are rational and motivated but by maximisation of shareholder value, or inspired by the example of the US market which is probably the closest to this model and does not have – up to a certain point – the same sensitivity to the 'nationalistic' issues and 'minority shareholders' issues which prevail, right or wrong, in (Continental) Europe.

Therefore, considering the European environment, I believe the HLG was well inspired to propose the above-mentioned rules. The main reason is not their intrinsic value, which most reports have shown to be at least debatable. The main reason is that these rules prevent criticism of market functioning by minority and individual shareholders who suffer, in practice, from both asymmetry of information and lack of expertise.

I would add two technical remarks.

Firstly, provided that the breakthrough rule is adopted in principle, in my view the threshold should be consistent with other provisions related to the minority control of the company-namely one third in most countries. If the bidder has gained more than two thirds of the capital (in absolute terms) then the defenders should not be able to oppose the bid and resist the modifications of by-laws. The 75% threshold proposed by the HLG is probably too high and does not have a clear justification (besides the merit of being an acceptable compromise...).

Secondly, there has been a lot of controversy on the relevance and legitimacy of several 'poison pills' such as multiple voting rights etc...Without reopening the debate, it seems to me that these 'poison pills' should be differentiated from the system of 'double voting right' as it functions in France. One should be aware that this system is not meant to organise in advance a specific balance of power between shareholders. These rights are attributed automatically to reward those shareholders who invest for the longer term: once the shares are sold, they lose the rights. Therefore the distribution of these double voting rights takes place 'at random' and cannot be part of a specific strategy of ownership, legitimate or not. Consequently this kind of double voting rights should not be regulated as poison pills.

Finally, I very much hope that the political disputes which have unfortunately delayed the adoption of the takeover directive will finally be settled, even if at the price of some compromises. Building an integrated financial market in Europe aims at a better allocation of capital, at a lower cost. An efficient and fair takeover system is obviously part of this integrated market and must be implemented as soon as possible.

Chapter 2: Regulation of Corporate Governance, in Particular Disclosure

Disclosure and Corporate Governance: An Overview Essay

REINIER KRAAKMAN

Mandatory disclosure obligations perform a range of corporate governance functions in addition to informing share prices. These functions include enforcing proscriptions against self-dealing, informing shareholder votes, and encouraging compliance with extra-legal norms of good corporate governance. The governance functions provide a justification for mandatory disclosure that is independent from its value in informing share prices. But regulators should not expect mandatory disclosure – and concomitant monitoring by shareholders – to substitute for the good governance effects of 'thick' monitoring by proactive directors.

A. Introduction

Mandatory public disclosure, especially of financial data, is an integral aspect of corporate governance in every modern commercial jurisdiction. Rudimentary disclosure requirements date back to the beginning of the last century in the form of stock exchange listing rules. Today, listing rules are augmented by detailed legal disclosure requirements for 'public' or 'listed' companies and, in many jurisdictions, for private companies as well.

A legal regime of mandatory disclosure includes, of course, the rules that specify what information must be disclosed. But it also includes the institutions and ancillary requirements that implement and enforce these rules. Thus, it includes audit requirements and liability rules that ensure the reliability of disclosed information, the accounting methodologies that gives financial disclosure its content, and the range of specialized institutions – internal financial controls, auditors, audit committees, financial analysts, and regulatory agencies – that produce and disseminate information subject to mandatory disclosure.

In this paper, I canvass arguments for mandatory disclosure requirements and attempt to evaluate the potential contribution of these requirements to corporate governance. A minority strand of the law and finance literature – extending from George Benston[1] in the 1970s to Roberta Romano[2] today – questions the benefits of mandatory disclosure. As the High Level Report attests, however, most academics and regulators accept mandatory disclosure as an essential feature of company law and capital market regulation.[3] In part, this consensus reflects a judgment that an unregulated market would undersupply information necessary for the efficient pricing of securities. In large part, however, it reflects concerns unrelated to the efficient pricing of securities, namely, practical concerns associated with the *governance and regulation* of public companies.

More particularly, mandatory disclosure has three governance functions that are independent of its contribution to efficient pricing. The first is an *enforcement function,* insofar as mandatory disclosure discourages opportunism in its own right and permits other legal controls that deter self-dealing decisions by corporate insiders. The second is an *educative function*, insofar as it informs public shareholders whom the law requires to make important governance decisions such as choosing directors or authorizing fundamental transactions. Finally, the third is a *legislative function*, insofar as lawmakers require corporate issuers to comply with certain corporate governance practices or, alternatively, disclose their reasons for not complying (the so-called 'comply or explain' strategy).

This paper develops the twin theses that (1) the governance functions of mandatory disclosure – as distinct from the pricing function – are its most important justifications, but (2) even pervasive disclosure to shareholders is no substitute for active ('thick') monitoring by a motivated board of directors. Section B elaborates on the governance functions of disclosure. Section C reviews the arguments for instituting mandatory rather than voluntary disclosure. Section D examines the question of which companies ought to be subject to a mandatory disclosure obligation. Section E addresses the institutional and enforcement pre-conditions for effective disclosure. Finally, Section F turns to the limits of mandatory disclosure as an instrument of corporate governance.

[1] G Benston 'Required Disclosure and the Stock Market: An Evaluation of the Securities Exchange Act of 1934' (1973) 63 Amer Econ Rev 132.

[2] R Romano 'Empowering Investors: A Market Approach to Securities Regulation' (1998) 107 Yale L J 2359 (1998).

[3] Report of the High Level Group of Company Law Experts on a Modern Regulatory Framework for Company Law in Europe [henceforth High Level Report] Ch II.3 (4 November 2002) ('Disclosure of Information as a Regulatory Tool') (see Annex 3 in this volume).

B. The Governance Functions of Disclosure

The traditional justification for mandatory disclosure is that it assists in the accurate pricing of corporate securities by economizing the information costs of investors. All else being equal, investors should value companies more when valuation information is cheaply available than when it is not. If it is too costly to distinguish between high and low quality companies, rational investors penalize all firms for the risks associated with low quality firms, which leads to a classic problem of adverse selection and unravelling markets. Thus, an informed securities market enhances not only the value of high quality companies, but also the value of the marketable securities of public companies in aggregate.[4]

This pricing function, however, is not the only important rationale for mandatory disclosure. Disclosure also performs three governance functions, which – as I have noted above – might be termed the *enforcement*, *educative*, and *legislative* functions respectively. Each of these functions arguably adds to corporate value in a different way.

Consider the enforcement function first. Much of corporate law can be understood as an effort to control the agency problems that arise either from the opportunism of managers vis-à-vis shareholders, or from controlling shareholders vis-à-vis minority shareholders, or from shareholders vis-à-vis the company's non-shareholder constituencies such as creditors and employees. Particularly in the case of public companies, the legal strategies that are used to contain these agency problems rely heavily on mandatory disclosure. For example, a legal requirement that shareholders must approve mergers, or that they must vote on self-dealing contracts between the company and its directors, would be meaningless without disclosure of the proposed terms of these transactions. Similarly, a shareholder right to enforce the fiduciary duties of corporate directors requires extensive public disclosure to alert public shareholders to possible violations of these duties.

The disclosure rules that target these and other agency problems may not contribute to the accuracy of near-term share prices. For example, the rules requiring disclosure of self-dealing transactions between the company and its directors may be triggered by transactions that are trivial in comparison to the company's asset value or market capitalization. Nevertheless, disclosure of these transactions may be critical for controlling the manager-shareholder agency problem if scrutiny can deter illicit transactions from proliferating. Thus, US securities law requires officers, directors, and their immediate family members to disclose a 'material interest' in all related-party transactions involving amounts

[4] For discussion of the role of mandatory disclosure in economizing on investor information costs, see RJ Gilson and RH Kraakman 'The Mechanisms of Market Efficiency' (1984) 70 Virginia L Rev 549.

greater than $60,000.[5] Since transactions of this magnitude rarely affect the market value of public companies, the $60,000 threshold is clearly about deterring illicit self-dealing rather than informing securities prices. Similarly, the US-UK requirement that public issuers disclose the compensation of individual managers,[6] rather than merely listing the aggregate compensation of senior managers as EU law requires), is almost certainly intended to counter a perceived agency problem rather than to enhance price efficiency.

After enforcement, the second governance function of disclosure is educating public shareholders to make or ratify fundamental corporate decisions. In proxy contests, shareholders require information about the proposed policies and affiliations of competing board candidates. Similarly, shareholders who are asked to approve a merger transaction or respond to a tender offer need information that neither management nor the outside bidder will necessarily supply in the absence of a legal requirement to do so. From the passage of the Securities Exchange Act of 1934 onward, US regulators have justified mandatory disclosure as a means of encouraging the participation of public shareholders in corporate governance. (The hope that disclosure might facilitate 'corporate democracy' remains an important current in US securities law to this day, although the historical evidence suggests that SEC disclosure requirements often *discouraged* shareholder participation in governance in the past.[7])

The third governance function is legislative (or, in the language of the High Level Report, 'regulatory'). Regulators have long appreciated that power over disclosure can be leveraged into power to legislate 'soft' substantive norms of the behaviour for public companies. Corporations need merely be required to report, under penalty of law, whether they follow certain norms of good governance and corporate citizenship (that exceed the law's minimal requirements), or explain why they do not. Depending on the circumstances, these 'supra-legal' norms may be prescribed outright (e.g., 'disclose that the directors on the issuer's nominating committee are independent, or explain why they are not'), or be left to other authorities, or even the company itself, to determine. But no matter how they are set, these norms will be enforced – so the strategy assumes – largely by the reputational cost to companies and managers of confessing unusually lax standards or governance procedures.[8]

[5] SEC Regulation S-K, Item 404(a).

[6] ibid Item 402.

[7] eg J Pound 'Proxy Voting and the SEC' (1991) 29 J Financial Economics 241.

[8] As far as I am aware, the first extensive use of this regulatory strategy in the US occurred in 1979, when the SEC adopted Rule 13e-3 to regulate going-private transactions. Rule 13e-3 requires controlling shareholders who wish to cash-out minority shareholders to disclosure whether their proposed transactions are 'fair' to minority shareholders, and, in the course of this discussion, report on a variety of procedural features – such as independent representation for minority shareholders, approval by a majority of the minority vote, approval by unaffiliated

cont. ...

The High Level Report, in particular, relies heavily on the regulatory use of mandatory disclosure, as the following passage indicates:

> Requiring disclosure can be a powerful regulatory tool in company law. It enhances the accountability for and the transparency of the company's governance and its affairs. The mere fact that for example governance structures of particular actions or facts have to be disclosed, and therefore will have to be explained, creates an incentive to renounce structures outside what is considered to be best practice and to avoid actions that are in breach of fiduciary duties or regulatory requirements or could be criticized as being outside best practice.[9]

Moreover, the Report deftly avoids framing best practice rules itself by proposing that, in lieu of a European-wide governance code, each Member State's public companies should be required to disclose the extent of their compliance with that State's domestic code of corporate governance – or 'explain' why their governance procedures differ from local norms of best practice.[10]

On the other side of the Atlantic, the recently-passed Sarbanes-Oxley Act in the US also makes heavy use of regulatory disclosure by, inter alia, mandating the SEC adopt rules requiring public companies to disclose 'codes of ethics' (or explain why they have not adopted such codes) for senior financial officers that include 'such standards as are reasonably necessary to promote' '(1) honest and ethical conduct. ... (2) full, fair, accurate, timely, and understandable disclosure ... and (3) compliance with applicable governmental rules and regulations.'[11]

C. Why Make Disclosure Mandatory?

Disclosure must be mandatory to serve as a vehicle for legislating substantive norms. Insofar as disclosure serves a pricing, enforcement, or educative function, however, one might ask why companies would not disclose voluntarily, without the prod of legal intervention. Why wouldn't managers who desire to increase share price adopt optimal disclosure policies on their own? Of course, the recent accounting scandals at Enron, WorldCom, and other US companies strongly suggest that market incentives may not ensure adequate disclosure, but *why* might they be inadequate?

Here, several explanations are plausible. The first – and the most persuasive – is the agency problem between shareholders and corporate insiders. In firms with

directors – that the SEC was clearly holding out as indicia of fairness. See Rule 13e-3 and SEC Schedule M-A, Item 1014 ('Fairness of Going-Private Transaction').

[9] High Level Report, Ch II.3, at 33.

[10] ibid at Ch III.6, 72-73.

[11] Sarbanes-Oxley Act, § 406(c).

dispersed shareholdings, bad news hurts managers by reducing their compensation and diminishing their job security. Thus, the worse the news, the less likely managers are to disclose it voluntarily, and the more likely they are tempted to misrepresent the company's finances outright. Moreover, controlling shareholders are equally loathe to disclose bad news that will inevitably reduce the value of their shareholdings and raise the firm's cost of capital. Mandating disclosure of news, whether good or bad, minimizes this agency problem for public investors – providing, of course, that the law's mandate is effectively enforced.

A second reason why firms might disclose too little without legal intervention turns on the private costs of establishing credibility in the market. In the absence of mandatory disclosure, the capital markets would expect corporate insiders to withhold bad news, and would discount the share prices of companies accordingly. To avoid such a discount, confident managers and controlling shareholders might attempt to bond themselves ex ante to reveal all information, good or bad. Under conditions of asymmetric information, however, there is no guarantee that the expected returns from bonding truthful disclosure will exceed the bonding costs, much less the private benefits to insiders that might follow from non-disclosure. In addition, private bonding devices are often costly or unavailable, creating a second obstacle to optimal disclosure. Regulatory intervention can supplement such bonding failures by providing legal liability as an alternative means to assure the market about the quality of corporate disclosure – and about the credibility of commitments to continue to disclose in the future.[12]

The third obstacle to sufficient voluntary disclosure is the divergence between the private benefits of disclosure to the company and the social benefits. Disclosure imposes private costs on firms in many specific situations, even while it enhances the welfare of diversified investors (and social welfare) by improving the accuracy of share prices and reducing agency costs. For example, revealing sensitive information may aid competitors in the product market, reduce financing options in tough times, or invite the unwanted attention of hostile acquirers. It follows that individual managers may disclose too little, as measured by the preferences of diversified shareholders, not only because they have something to hide in their own self-interest, but also precisely because they want to add value to their companies – by thwarting competitors, attracting new capital, or discouraging underpriced takeover bids.

But the rub is that opting out of disclosure regimes creates negative externalities for other portfolio firms. Thus, some firms' competitive gains from opting out are matched by offsetting losses to other (rival) firms, leaving portfolio values unaffected. Similarly, companies that opt out for other 'value-increasing' reasons can be easily mimicked by rogue companies with something to hide. As a result,

[12] eg Gilson and Kraakman (n 4) JC Coffee 'The Future as History: The Prospect for Global Corporate Convergence in Corporate Governance and its Implications' (1999) 93 Northwestern University Law Review 641.

shareholders of honestly-managed opt-outs see only a portion of the benefits of opting out reflected in their share prices (because the market is unsure of the actual reason for opt out), and managers who opt to protect their own interests rather than those of shareholders bear only a portion of the costs (for the same reason). It follow that diversified investors may receive net economic benefits from mandatory disclosure even if managers might be able to increase the value of some particular firms by opting out of the disclosure regime.[13]

Finally, a fourth obstacle to disclosure arises from the fact that information is of less value to investors – and hence incentives to disclose are weaker – to the extent that it is idiosyncratic, without standardized format, content, and quality. At bottom, this is a coordination problem among firms or, alternatively, among shareholders. Standardization improves comprehensibility and comparability, thus increasing the value of information to investors.[14] While firms have surmounted this collective action problem in the past – for example, through stock exchange rules and accounting methodologies – a regime of mandatory disclosure permits immediate standardization without waiting for it to evolve through private ordering.[15]

Of course, all arguments for mandatory disclosure naturally turn on the assumption that the regulators can determine, at least approximately, the appropriate content of what is to be disclosed and the range of companies that ought to be subject to disclosure obligations. As in other areas of the law, it is not enough to point to market failure as a basis for regulation; regulators must also be able to do it better.

D. What Companies Are Subject to Mandatory Disclosure?

The next issue, then, is how to select the companies that should be obligated to comply with a mandatory disclosure regime. This determination requires balancing of the costs and benefits of disclosure. In this regard, the High Level Report

[13] Discussion of the divergence between the private and public benefits of disclosure enjoys a long history in the corporate law literature. Eg MB Fox 'The Securities Globalization Disclosure Debate' (2000) 78 Washington University Law Quarterly 567; id 'Securities Disclosure in a Globalizing Market: Who Should Regulate Whom?' (1997) 95 Michigan Law Review 2498; LA Bebchuk 'Federalism and the Corporation: The Desirable Limits on State Competition in Corporate Law' (1992) 105 Harvard Law Review 1435, 1490-91; JC Coffee 'Market Failure and the Economic Case for Mandatory Disclosure' (1984) 70 Virginia Law Review 717; and F Easterbrook and D Fischel 'Mandatory Disclosure and the Protection of Investors' (1984) 70 Virginia Law Review 669. For a skeptical view, see R Romano (n 2) at 2368.

[14] eg Easterbrook and Fischel (n 13).

[15] An additional obstacle to optimal disclosure arises if investors may simply be too unsophisticated to demand disclosure. If investors refuse to pay for a commitment to disclose in initial public offerings, firms might not undertake such a commitment, even if additional information would enhance share prices in subsequent trading in the secondary market.

divides companies into three classes: widely-traded or 'listed' companies; 'open' companies that might become widely traded someday; and 'closed' companies that cannot be widely traded without changing their legal form.[16] The Report implies that both listed and open companies are plausible candidates for mandatory disclosure, while closed companies are not.[17] Put differently, trading activity is the right trigger for disclosure duties, and the Continental European distinction between the open and closed companies is a useful dividing line between companies that are potentially widely traded and those that are not.

One might argue, however, that the Report gets it wrong. Active trading is certainly correlated with the need for mandatory disclosure, but trading activity per se is the wrong trigger for a disclosure regime that aims at discharging governance as well as pricing functions. In particular, tying disclosure to the distinction between closed and open companies seems unsuitable. It is underinclusive since European closed companies can be quite large, both in assets and numbers of shareholders. Indeed, small shareholders in large closed companies plausibly have an even greater need for mandatory disclosure than investors in open companies who can easily sell their shares in a liquid market. Conversely, forcing disclosure duties on open companies indiscriminately is also overinclusive to the extent that it burdens smaller open companies, and therefore discourages small businesses from adopting the open corporate form.

The alternative to linking a disclosure to the easy transferability of shares that characterizes open companies is to tie it to the governance functions as well as the pricing function of mandatory disclosure. This suggests a different boundary between reporting and non-reporting companies than the one proposed by the High Level Report. More particularly, it suggests that we distinguish between privately-held companies with small numbers of shareholders on the one hand, and all other companies – private or public, with or without controlling shareholders – on the other.

I. Privately-Held Companies

Mandatory disclosure is least attractive for privately-held companies small numbers of shareholders. For these companies disclosure is not cost effective. Because they have relatively few shareholders, individual shareholders are likely to hold large proportional stakes in these firms, and therefore have the ability to contract their own disclosure regimes. In addition, because these shareholders are often managers of their own firms, they are likely to have direct knowledge of the facts. This is why the initial decision to take a company public, whatever its benefits, always has the cost of degrading the collective knowledge of its shareholder

[16] High Level Report, Ch II.4. at 35.

[17] ibid.

base, and thus setting the stage for most of the familiar problems of corporate governance. Outside investors can never understand a company as well as the insiders who have nursed it from the outset and lived with its business plan.

Thus, private companies with small numbers of shareholders don't need mandatory disclosure, no matter how large their assets are. Their shareholders know everything already, and they can structure corporate governance by means of shareholder agreements and provisions in company charters. Anyone who has reviewed the foundational documents of a venture capital financing can attest to the extraordinary care devoted to crafting governance structures.[18] The one-size-fits-all provisions of company laws and governance codes are anaemic cousins to the customized structures that sophisticated parties craft to align interests in their own deals. Moreover, even when private governance is not so sophisticated, mandatory disclosure is not the answer. Formulaic disclosure between managers and shareholders who know one another is silly. Rather, if disclosure in these companies is to be regulated at all, it should be regulated by general standards such as injunctions against fraud, oppression, or breach of the duty of loyalty, which permit courts to redress betrayals of the parties' reasonable expectations about disclosure and fair treatment.[19]

The real issue with private-held companies is line drawing: When does 'private' become 'public' for purposes of mandatory disclosure? Or should there be a bright line at all, as compared to a sliding scale, with a gradual increase in disclosure obligations as firms grow progressively larger?

On the basis of the preceding analysis, I believe that the trigger for mandatory disclosure ought to be a joint function of a company's asset value and number of shareholders. Disclosure grows proportionately less costly as companies increase in asset value, and it grows relatively more beneficial as the number of shareholders increases. But this still does not tell us whether mandatory reporting ought to begin when a company crosses the threshold of $10 million in assets and 100 shareholders, $5 million in assets and 300 shareholders, or some other set of arbitrary lines.[20]

[18] For an overview of venture capital contracts, see, eg S Kaplan and P Strömberg 'Financial contracting theory meets the real world: An empirical analysis of venture capital contracts' University of Chicago Business School Working Paper (2001).

[19] The most famous business law case – although not strictly a corporate law case – in the US jurisprudence concerns the failure of one joint venturer to disclose a lucrative new business opportunity to his co-investor. The case concerns disclosure obligations rather than the illicit taking of a business opportunity precisely because the uniformed partner did not have a claim on the new opportunity as a matter of right, but only a right to compete for the new opportunity. *Meinhard v Salmon* 164 NE 545 (NY 1928) (Cardozo, J).

[20] Current US securities law imposes a federal mandatory reporting requirement on companies with total assets exceeding $10 million and 500 or more holders of a single class of equity

cont. ...

II. Controlled Companies

Given that a trigger for mandatory disclosure ought to be based on a company's asset value and number of shareholders, a remaining issue is whether disclosure policy ought to be conditioned on any other aspect of ownership structure including, in particular, whether there is a controlling shareholder.

Whether or not companies are controlled is profoundly important for company law, since the central agency problem in the modern corporation turns on this fact. In widely-held companies with a controlling shareholder, the chief agency problem is the conflict over the distribution of corporate returns between the controlling shareholder and (minority) public shareholders. In companies with dispersed ownership, the chief agency problem is the conflict between professional management and shareholders as a class. Mandatory disclosure has an important role to play in containing both of these conflicts. Nevertheless, there is a significant difference between these two classes of companies. I conjecture that controlled companies with dispersed minority shareholders can easily survive without mandatory disclosure, while companies with widely-dispersed ownership depend more heavily on effective disclosure.

Minority shareholders play a minimal governance role in controlled companies, and controlling shareholders in these companies have no need for mandatory disclosure, since they are intimately familiar with their companies in any case. Thus, the value added by the educative function of disclosure is likely to be minimal. Similarly, the legislative function of mandatory disclosure is likely to be less significant for controlled companies, if only because well-entrenched controlling shareholders have little to fear from reputational penalties. Apart from informing market prices, then, the real contribution of disclosure in controlled firms is to alert minority shareholders to the company's ownership structure before they invest, and to restrain controlling shareholders from extracting illicit private benefits afterwards.

The High Level Report gives conspicuous emphasis, correctly in my view, to the value of both aspects of mandatory disclosure in the regulation of controlled companies. Thus, Chapter III of the Report includes among its principal recommendations a thorough-going disclosure of major shareholdings, shareholder agreements, and potential shareholder coalitions, as well as an extensive documentation of the economic relationships between companies and their major shareholders.[21] In doing so, the Report refers to prevalence of controlled companies in many European jurisdictions. Indeed, it is fair to say that mandatory

securities. Securities Exchange Act of 1934, § 12(g)(1)(B) and Rule 12g-1. Lighter disclosure obligations reflecting an implicit sliding scale are imposed on so-called small business issuers with revenues less than $25 million and a market capitalization of less than $25 million. Rule 12b-2 and Form 8-K.

[21] High Level Report, Ch III.2, at 46-47.

disclosure is the principal legal control on corporate groups proposed by the Report.[22]

The Report also recognizes that disclosure only benefits minority shareholders who can act on what they learn. In this regard, it proposes adoption of a European Framework Rule granting 'special investigatory rights to minority shareholders[23] as a step toward leveraging the power of disclosure with a suitable enforcement mechanism – a kind of distant cousin to the US class action or derivative suit. It is difficult to evaluate this procedure, however, without knowing what sanctions would attach if controlling shareholders were found to favour themselves in interested transactions with the companies they control.[24] Portions of the Report reflect a concern that rigid the enforcement of conflict-of-interest norms might undermine the legitimate functions of corporate groups.[25] The value of disclosure in the setting of controlled companies will depend in large part on how such legitimate functions are balanced against the interests of minority shareholders.[26]

III. Dispersed Share Ownership

If the value of disclosure in controlled companies depends largely on its usefulness for policing related-party transactions, it has a full complement of other functions in companies with widely dispersed shares, including an important educative function as well as a regulatory function. The educative function follows from the fact that public shareholders matter to the governance of widely-held companies. Shareholders vote on directors and shareholder resolutions; decide on charter amendments and corporate mergers; and, if these shareholders are large enough, lobby top managers and the board for their preferred policies. While mandatory disclosure may not matter much when wealthy contestants cross swords in fully funded proxy fights (since one side or the other can be relied upon to produce all relevant information), it does matter a great deal to less dramatic

[22] Generally id Ch V (Groups and Pyramids).

[23] Id Ch V at 97.

[24] The Report proposes to leave a determination of sanctions to the Member States. Id Ch III.4.4. at 58.

[25] Id Ch V.3 (some Member States believe that conflict of interest rules must be adjusted to reflect the legitimate functions of corporate groups).

[26] Two statements in the Report are disquieting on this score. One is the suggestion that placing investigatory powers at the disposal of minority shareholders can be 'an important deterrent', even if it is rarely used. Id at 58. Just why a rarely used procedure would be a deterrent is unexplained. The second statement is the suggestion that director disqualification might be a useful sanction. Id. Disqualification, which is widely used in the UK, would seem to be better suited for disciplining directors and managers of widely-held companies than for policing the conduct of directors handpicked by controlling shareholders. The issue is: where does the balance of incentives lie?

governance activity, such as the lobbying activity and voting decisions of institutional investors.

The legislative function of mandatory disclosure is important in widely-held companies for a similar reason. In theory, a 'disclose or explain' strategy[27] might reinforce good governance practices in any public company. To a sceptical observer, however, best practices will seem unlikely to matter – one way or the other – in controlled firms. The pervasive domination of controlling shareholders makes everything conditional on their plans and aspirations. By contrast, it is possible to imagine that mandatory disclosure might actually lead to the reality of good governance, as opposed to the mere theatre of good governance, in widely-held companies.

E. The Enforcement of Disclosure Rules

Like all legal rules, mandatory disclosure must be enforced to be effective. But enforcement is not easy because, almost by definition, violations are difficult to detect in the case of rules concerned with information that outsiders don't know or cannot verify in the absence of disclosure. In addition, disclosed information, even if true, may have hidden implications that are difficult to uncover.[28] How, then, can the legal system ensure that the information that companies disclose is reliable?

In the absence of legal intervention, private parties rely on reputation and warranties to reduce verification costs of their interlocutors – in essence, private sanctions – or they can rely on market intermediaries such as investment banks, accounting firms, and even law firms, who undertake an investigation and certify the results to investors with their reputations or their assets. Investors may be able to trust well-reputed intermediaries to report truthfully, even if they do not trust issuing companies themselves, because – the theory goes – these intermediaries are repeat players who face serious sanctions but make no significant gain from misreporting.

As one might expect, legal strategies for enforcing disclosure rules track the market's strategies for ensuring reliability. Issuers can be made liable for misreporting, thereby supplementing reputational and contractual sanctions; or the law can make third parties – 'gatekeepers'[29] in a position to monitor or investi-

[27] This descriptive title for the strategy in question alludes to the 'disclose or abstain' rule that has long governed the regulation of insider trading under Rule 10b-5 in the US.

[28] It is useful to break down information costs into three dimensions: acquisition costs, processing costs, and verification costs. Gilson and Kraakman (n 4) at 597-609. Ideally, mandatory disclosure would reduce each of these cost dimension.

[29] RH Kraakman 'Gatekeepers: The Anatomy of a Third-Party Enforcement Strategy' (1986) 2 J Law, Economics and Organization 53.

gate issuer claims – responsible for their accuracy. Some of the most difficult issues arising from mandatory disclosure regimes revolve around liability questions. Who should be liable for misstatements? What should the standards of liability be? And who should bring enforcement actions?

Consider first the difficulties associated with imposing liability on issuers for the misstatements of their agents. In the classic US fraud-on-the-market case, the managers who misstate a company's earnings or merger prospects are agents who act on behalf of their principal, the corporation. If the agents are liable then, under the rule of *respondeat superior*, so is the principal. But how do shareholders as a class benefit when the corporation compensates one set of shareholders – those who happened to buy or sell after the (intentional) misstatement was made but before it was discovered – with funds that would otherwise belong to the set of shareholders who neither bought nor sold?

One might argue that liability might induce the corporation – or its senior managers – to screen more carefully against misleading statements. This argument, however, overlooks the fact that the corporate agents who misstate information are often the senior managers who control the company.[30] Sanctions against the company are unlikely to deter these managers, who have much at stake in maintaining the company's share price. Thus, company liability for misstatements results in little more than a redistribution of value among shareholders, which no rational investor would prefer ex ante (ie, before she learns whether she will recover or not). Even frequent traders cannot benefit very much from issuer liability, since most issuers with bad news to hide are already bankrupt when the truth is discovered.[31]

Why not, then, sanction the managers who make misrepresentations? We can (and do) sanction them; but we are less successful in deterring them. In the past, major misrepresentation seems to have been most common when companies were on the verge of failure; they were manifestations of a final period problem in which managers, motivated by the high-powered incentive of likely failure and job loss, made a last attempt to save themselves.[32] During the 1990s, however, the widespread increase in equity-based compensation such as stock options greatly expanded the range of occasions under which managers faced high-powered incentives to lie to the market. In today's world in which the bulk of a manager's compensation often derives from options or stock,[33] the power to manipulate market price, even for short periods, generates the possibility of reaping enormous windfalls for managers.

[30] JH Arlen and WJ Carney 'Vicarious Liability for Fraud on Securities Markets: Theory and Evidence' [1992] U Illinois Law Rev 691, 724-727.

[31] Consider the recent US cases of Enron and WorldCom.

[32] Arlen and Carney (n 30).

[33] eg. JC Coates IV and R Kraakman 'CEO Incentives and Merger Activity in the 1990s: Stock Options and Real Options' (Working Paper 2003).

If potential wrongdoers among managers could be forced to pay for all of the damages caused by their misrepresentations, no doubt they would refrain from lying. But their misrepresentations might not be discovered and, in any case, they lack the assets to cover the damages they cause. Moreover, given the money at stake, they may not be deterred by civil sanctions such as disqualification. Of course, criminal sanctions remain possible, but even these might not offset the lure of exercising options and selling shares at artificially high prices. In addition, criminal sanctions impose a heavy burden of proof and threaten to overdeter disclosure by risk-averse but law-abiding managers.

If offending managers cannot be deterred, enforcement depends on enlisting gatekeepers to do the job. Within the firm, potential gatekeepers include officers and directors other than the primary wrongdoers. Outside the firm, they include the same intermediaries that the market relies upon to certify the representations and intentions of corporate issuers: that is, the auditors – and, to a lesser extent, the credit rating agencies, investment bankers, and outside counsel.

The 2001 cohort of US corporate governance scandals – including Enron, WorldCom, Adelphia, and Waste Management – has been blamed on the failure of informational intermediaries,[34] as well as that of inside managers and directors, to faithfully execute their responsibilities. Correlatively, the principal legal response to these scandals – the Sarbanes-Oxley Act of 2002 and related SEC rules – is largely an effort to facilitate gatekeeper enforcement. The measures chosen for this purpose range from a requirement that CEOs and CFOs certify the financial statements and internal controls of their companies,[35] to new rules to ensure the independence and competence of audit committees,[36] the independence of accounting firms,[37] and the responsible advice of outside counsel.[38]

[34] eg JC Coffee 'Understanding Enron: "It's About the Gatekeepers, Stupid"' (2002) 57 The Business Lawyer 1403. Note that Coffee defines "gatekeeper" more narrowly than I have done in earlier articles. For Coffee, a gatekeeper is "a reputational intermediary who provides verification and certification services to investors." Id 1405. I would extend the class of potential gatekeepers to anyone who can be induced to monitor for, and block, potential wrongdoing. In the context of disclosure, there is considerable overlap between these two definitions of gatekeeper.

[35] Sarbanes-Oxley Act §§ 302 ('civil' certification) and 906 ('criminal' certification) and Rule 13a-14(c).

[36] Sarbanes-Oxley Act § 301 (audit committee members must meet new independence requirements), § 407 (company must disclose whether audit committee includes a financial expert and, if not, why not).

[37] Sarbanes-Oxley Act § 201(a) (prohibiting auditors from providing a variety of non-auditor services to client during the audit engagement period); § 303(a) (barring actions to fraudulently influence or mislead auditors).

[38] Sarbanes-Oxley Act § 307 (reporting obligations for attorney where credible evidence of securities violations.

As with other enforcement measures, the value of these reforms turns on the balance of costs and benefits. The costs include, first, the costs to gatekeepers themselves. One of these is the cost of monitoring for misrepresentations. Thus, requiring CEOs and CFOs to certify financial statements forces closer attention to these statements, not only by top management but at lower levels as well, as superiors at every level require their subordinates to certify the areas in which they are expert.[39] Of course, this additional cost of monitoring that managers bear in the first instance is quickly passed on to company shareholders, either in the form of additional compensation or in the form of opportunity costs associated with the diversion of managerial attention from other matters. Much the same can be said about costs of responding to misrepresentations when they are detected (it can't be easy for a CEO to restate her past financials), and the risk-bearing costs that arise whenever legal sanctions are used in the service of ambiguous rules.

A second kind of cost is possible damage to the market in gatekeeper services. Where intermediaries such as accounting firms or underwriters cannot distinguish easily between law-abiding clients and possible wrongdoers, there is always a risk of the market unravelling to the extent that it is no less expensive – but much less profitable – for law-abiding clients to use the services of these intermediaries than for wrongdoers to do so. In this case, wrongdoers earn extraordinary returns by purchasing the services of gatekeepers, even though all clients pay similar prices. While established companies are unlikely to abandon reputable accounting firms, law firms, or investment banks as a result of the additional costs occasioned by gatekeeper liability, it is plausible that smaller issuers will remain private to avoid these costs.[40] In addition, rigorous enforcement of gatekeeper liability can have dramatic effects on the major players in the gatekeeper market. Consider the changes, not all of them good, hat have followed the demise of the accounting firm, Arthur Anderson in the wake of the Enron debacle.

By contrast, on the benefit side of the ledger, legal pressure on gatekeepers might have done much to prevent the debacles of the Enron era. Accounting firms, law firms, and commercial and investment banks were deeply involved in facilitating – and, at times, even suggesting – the business strategies that brought Enron, WorldCom, and other companies into disaster. Additional gatekeeper responsibilities might well prevent a reprise of the Enron-type scandals, particularly because they are accompanied by important new disclosure obligations under the Sarbanes-Oxley Act.[41]

[39] eg M Fedash 'The Buck and the Books: A look at the new world of "disclosure controls"' Business Law Today May/June 2003, at 31-35.

[40] A Hamdani 'Gatekeeper Liability' (2003) 77 USCL Rev 53.

[41] Sarbanes-Oxley § 401(a), which, as implemented by the SEC, requires MD&A disclosure and discussion of off-balance sheet entities and financing devices; and Sarbanes-Oxley § 404, which requires rapid disclosure "in real time" of additional information affecting an issuer's financial condition and operations. See JN Gordon 'Governance Failures of the Enron

cont. ...

My question, however, is whether tomorrow's accountants and lawyers will be able to resist the Enron-type pressures that were exerted on their predecessors. Here I am less optimistic. Large fees in a boom market generate intense agency problems for informational intermediaries, just as they do for the corporations that are their clients. Where agents watch other agents, there is always a risk of collusion at the principal's expense.

F. The Limits of Mandatory Disclosure

What, then, do we conclude about the governance functions of mandatory disclosure – its enforcement, educative, and regulatory roles? First, that mandatory disclosure raises not one issue but many. In addition to determining what must be disclosed, a legal regime must determine when and why disclosure should be mandatory, and how deeply to reach into the organizational fabric of firms and their service providers such as accountants, bankers, and lawyers to enforce disclosure obligations.

As to which firms ought to be required to disclose by law, the key criteria are, first, numbers of shareholders, and second, size of firm. Ownership structure is important for specifying the character of the benefits of mandatory disclosure. In controlled companies, it can aid minority shareholders in exercising whatever levers the law allows them to constrain related-party transactions initiated by controlling shareholders. But mandatory disclosure is more important still for companies with dispersed ownership structures and no controlling shareholder, since in these companies it can play a significant educative and regulatory role.

Nevertheless, the major US scandals of 2001 are an important reminder that one of the world's most extensive regimes of mandatory disclosure is not enough to guarantee transparency in either market prices or corporate governance, still less to serve as a guarantor of good corporate governance.

As several commentators have suggested, there is a deep connection between the disclosure-related Enron cohort of scandals in 2001, and the fundamental changes in management compensation that occurred in the US (and to a lesser extent in the EU) during the 1990s.[42] During the boom decade of the 1990s, financial economists and institutional investors alike applauded a dramatic shift away from cash compensation and toward high-powered, equity-based compensation as a welcome effort to align the incentives of US managers with those of their shareholders. In my view, the proponents of equity-based compensation had a valid point to make. Regardless of the excesses in total compensation that marred the 1990s, it seems unquestionably true that realigned compensation made

Board and the New Information Order of Sarbanes-Oxley' (2003) 35 Conn L Rev 1125, for a helpful discussion of these provisions.

[42] eg Coffee (n 34) at 1413-1414; Gordon (n 41).

managers much more sensitive to shareholder welfare.[43] But the new structure of compensation has also had its costs. In particular, as I noted above, it greatly increased managerial incentives to inflate short-term share prices, and thus increased the pressure on the mandatory disclosure regime. In companies with dispersed ownership structures, equity-based compensation and mandatory disclosure are two important tools for mitigating the principal-agent problem between hired managers and shareholders, but they are not necessarily synergistic tools. The more important stock prices become for managers, the greater the managerial payoffs from manipulating disclosure.

There are three possible responses to the inherent tension between equity-based compensation and mandatory disclosure. One is to use company law to ratchet down the size and volatility of managerial compensation. Sarbanes-Oxley, for example, makes a limited but significant effort to do just this by attempting to bar corporate loans to top managers.[44] But this response (and, a fortiori, more dramatic efforts to control compensation) is undesirable in my view. While numerous companies are now reducing their reliance on stock options to compensate managers – largely in response to shareholder pressure to 'expense' options on the income statement – other forms of equity-based compensation, such as restricted stock grants, are rapidly taking the place of options. These new forms of equity compensation may be less vulnerable to disclosure-based manipulation than stock options, but they still leave managers highly sensitive to share prices.

Moreover, such sensitivity is precisely what we should want. To roll back compensation practices to the cash-and-bonus regimes that dominated in the 1970s and early 1980s would be to sacrifice much of the economic dynamism of the past decade, especially if such a rollback in compensation were not offset by other incentivizing legal changes such as a ban on defensive tactics in hostile takeovers.[45]

A second possible response to the challenge posed by high-powered compensation to disclosure regimes is to strengthen the disclosure regime itself. This is, of course, the principal thrust of the Sarbanes-Oxley legislation in the US Sarbanes-Oxley requires increasingly detailed disclosure; tougher penalties; more attention to codes of conduct and semi-mandated best practices; and, above all, more aggressive gatekeeper measures to regulate the behaviour or accountants and lawyers. But here we must ask about the limits of disclosure as a substitute for more tangible forms of corporate governance. As noted above, extending the disclosure regime – particularly the enforcement of disclosure rules – is costly.

[43] B Holmstrom and SN Kaplan 'The State of U.S. Corporate Governance: What's Right and What's Wrong?' NBER Working Paper 9613 (2002), at 9-12.

[44] Sarbanes-Oxley § 402 (prohibiting insider loans to managers).

[45] M Kahan and E Rock 'How I learned to Stop Worrying and Love the Pill: Adaptive Responses to Takeover Law' (2002) 69 U Chicago Law Rev 871.

Beyond this, as Professor Jeffery Gordon has argued in a recent working paper,[46] there is an irreducible element of discretion in disclosure that will always allow corporate insiders leeway in deciding how much information to reveal, while still complying with the letter of disclosure rules. No amount of disclosure can make a complex business entity like Enron (or GE) entirely transparent. In addition, there are often sound business reasons for shading disclosure, such as attempting to keep strategic information out of the hands of competitors. Finally, even when information is disclosed, the history of the Enron scandal instructs us that the professional investment community is by no means certain to grasp its implications, in part because scepticism may not pay, and it is often safer for fund managers to follow the crowd.[47]

A third response to the tension between disclosure regulation and high-powered incentives is to place an internal monitor on the boards of companies with dispersed ownership. Neither high-powered compensation nor mandatory disclosure can entirely fill the hole in the middle of the governance structure that is left by the absence of an owner or controlling shareholder. That hole – a chasm, really – can be filled in only one way: by introducing full-time directors who unquestionably have the interests of shareholders at heart. This is, after all, precisely the model of the professional board that characterizes firms capitalized by leveraged buyout and venture capital firms, as well as by sophisticated private equity generally.

Put differently, sophisticated mandatory disclosure is essential for widely-traded companies with dispersed share ownership. However, it is unlikely to be a sufficient condition for the proper governance of widely-held companies if their managers are paid like entrepreneurs, rather than with cash salaries and long-term tenure, like trustees (and professors). Even the best regime of mandatory disclosure can only supply a thin sort of monitoring that works to restrain managers only on an ad hoc basis (in addition to its function in informing share prices, of course). Some shareholder or securities analyst must still do her reading to make use of disclosure, and must then ask hard questions, lobby the board, and ultimately initiate a lawsuit or proxy fight if the answers to these questions prove unsatisfactory. And of course, each step in this chain of events that supports outside monitoring based on mandatory disclosure is problematic.

The better alternative to relying too heavily on mandatory disclosure for governance reform is to directly target the board for reform. In my view, this means recruiting professional directors who share shareholder interests and are

[46] Gordon (n 41).

[47] PM Healy and K Palepu 'Governance and Intermediation Problems in Capital Markets: Evidence from the Fall of Enron' Harvard NOM Research Paper No. 02-27 (August 2002). Healy and Palepu argue persuasively that Enron's market valuations were silly on their face, given what Enron had clearly disclosed. In effect, they conclude, many fund managers have weak incentives to demand high quality information about their investments and prefer to follow the crowd.

engaged full-time in the 'thick' supervision of top management because they know their companies almost as well the managers themselves. Ideally, these directors would be a proxy for the missing owner in the middle of the governance structure of companies with widely-dispersed shares.[48] Equity-based compensation and mandatory disclosure are not enough. Until the corporate board becomes a dedicated supervisory organ, the ghosts of Berle and Means will continue to haunt widely-held companies. Indeed, they may come to haunt us as never before, if we continue to sharpen the incentives of hired managers without providing them with professional supervision.

[48] For a proposal for recruiting such directors for large public firms, see RH Gilson and R Kraakman 'Reinventing the Outside Director: An Agenda for Institutional Investors' (1991) 43 Stanford L Rev 863.

Disclosing Disclosure: Europe's Winding Road to Competitive Standards of Publication of Company-Related Information

HANNO MERKT

Disclosure stands right in the centre of the political and legislative debate over the best and most efficient ways to organize companies activities vis-à-vis shareholders, creditors and other market participants. In line with that, the High Level Group of Company Law Experts in its Final Report dated November 4, 2002 strongly advocates disclosure of information as a regulatory instrument. It is that concept of superiority of disclosure over merit regulation that deserves particular attention since it challenges bluntly firm convictions of company regulators as well as academics in many member states of the European Union. In order to place the High Level Group's disclosure approach in context and in order to highlight the pragmatic basis of this approach in market integration rather than in any deeper attachment to the various roles fulfilled by disclosure policy, this paper addresses the subject of disclosure as a regulatory tool in a rather topical way: First, it tries to put disclosure in a broader setting of regulatory alternatives, i.e., in context with more 'radical' alternatives like entirely abstaining from any uniform regulatory interference on one side or limiting company law primarily to substantive regulation on the other side. Second, this paper discusses the choice of level of disclosure regulation, in particular the topics of uniform versus competitive regulation and legislative versus industry self-regulation. Third, the paper tackles the issue of information as marketable good with a look at both the supply side (companies) and the demand side (investors). Fourth, the paper addresses some widely accepted general principles of company disclosure. And finally, it takes a very brief look at the sanctioning of disclosure duties.

A. Introduction

'Publicity is justly commended as a remedy for social and industrial diseases. Sunlight is said to be the best of disinfectants; electric light the most efficient policeman.'[1]

[1] LD Brandeis *Other People's Money – and How Bankers Use it* (Jacket Library New York 1914) 62.

These often quoted words by Justice Brandeis, written some 90 years ago, describe in all brevity and clarity the simple yet utterly efficient way disclosure works. Moreover, these words illustrate the considerable attractiveness of disclosure as a regulatory tool in the context of business law in general and company law in particular. And still, after almost a century of fierce legislative, judicial, and academic debate, disclosure stands right in the centre of the debate over the best and most efficient ways to organize companies activities vis-à-vis shareholders, creditors and other market participants. Regulators literally all over the world, from New Zealand[2] and Australia[3] to the United States[4] and Europe are in the process of addressing whether their domestic disclosure rules are rigorous enough in the light of the problems and implications thrown up by recent corporate collapses – such as HIH and One.Tel in Australia, Enron and WorldCom in the United States, or Ahold and Comroad in Europe to name only few of the most spectacular ones – and the risks associated with inadequate disclosure.

Completely in line with these recent developments, the High Level Group of Company Law Experts in its Final Report dated November 4, 2002 strongly advocates disclosure of information as a regulatory instrument.[5] According to the Report, requiring disclosure of information can be a powerful regulatory tool in company law. It enhances the accountability for and the transparency of the company's governance and its affairs. Therefore, the Group recommends that capital and control structures of listed companies should be disclosed comprehensively and that such disclosure should be updated continuously. However, the Report goes one important step further in stating: 'Disclosure requirements can sometimes provide a more efficient regulatory tool than substantive regulation through more or less detailed rules. According to the Group, such disclosure creates a lighter regulatory environment and allows for greater flexibility and adaptability. Moreover, although the regulatory effect may in theory be more indirect and remote than with substantive rules, in practice enforcement of disclosure requirements as such normally easier.'[6] Hence, the Reports suggests that the European Union, in considering new – and amending existing – regulation of company law, should carefully consider whether disclosure requirements are

[2] eg the recent establishment of a 'Working Group for Improved Product and Investment Advisor Disclosure' of the Securities Commission of New Zealand.

[3] eg the recent establishment of a Roundtable by the Australian SEC examining proposals for better protecting investors by reforming financial disclosure and auditor oversight.

[4] eg SEC Regulation FD (Fair Disclosure) of 24 August 2000, Release No 33-7881, analyzed by Bochner and Bukhari (2002) 7 Stan J L Bus & Fin 225; MI Steinberg and JB Myers (2002) 27 J Corp L 173; Morano (2002) 54 Rutgers L Rev 535.

[5] Report of the High Level Group of Company Law Experts on a Modern Regulatory Framework for Company Law in Europe (hereinafter Winter Report, see Annex 3 in this volume), Brussels, 4 November 2002, 33-35, 45-47, 95-96.

[6] n 5, 34.

better suited to achieve the desired effects than substantive rules. In advocating a disclosure-type approach to company regulation, the Group finds itself in harmony with many respondents to the Group's consultation, who took the view that disclosure was particularly suited as a regulatory tool in the area of corporate governance.

It is that concept of superiority of disclosure over merit regulation that deserves particular attention since it challenges bluntly firm convictions of company regulators as well as academics in many member states of the European Union. In order to place the High Level Group's disclosure approach in context and in order to highlight the pragmatic basis of this approach in market integration rather than in any deeper attachment to the various roles fulfilled by disclosure policy, this paper addresses the subject of disclosure as a regulatory tool in a rather topical way: Part II 1 tries to put disclosure in a broader setting of regulatory alternatives, ie, in context with more 'radical' alternatives like entirely abstaining from any uniform regulatory interference on one side (II 1 a) or limiting company law primarily to substantive regulation on the other side (II 1 b). Part II 1 c discusses the choice of level of disclosure regulation, in particular the topics of uniform versus competitive regulation and legislative versus industry self-regulation. Part II 2 tackles the issue of information as marketable good with a look at both the supply side (companies) and the demand side (investors). Part III addresses some widely accepted general principles of company disclosure. Finally, part IV takes a very brief look at the sanctioning of disclosure duties.

B. Fundamentals of Disclosure

I. The Battle over Disclosure

The following part of the paper aims at putting disclosure into its proper regulatory context. It is astonishing to see that this context varies remarkably from country to country and how different traditions and attitudes exist in various jurisdictions as to voluntary and mandatory disclosure as well as to the choice between disclosure and merit regulation of company law.

1. The American Battlefield: Voluntary versus Mandatory Disclosure

The development of US corporation law can be aptly summarized as a battle between proponents of a more facilitative approach and proponents of a rather mandatory or regulatory treatment of corporations. The influence of modern economic views on the nature of the firm, launched in 1937 by Ronald Coase,[7]

[7] R Coase 'The Nature of the Firm' (1937) 4 Economia 386.

reached mainstream corporate law in the 1980s with the now classic debate on contractual freedom in corporate law. Seen from the perspective of statutory state law, however, this change of perception was not that much dramatic. State Codes had followed almost from their inception a facilitative rather than a regulatory or mandatory approach to company legislation. The reasons are well known: First and foremost, caused by political and historically contingent circumstances corporation law is state law, not federal law. Moreover, American law shares a narrow definition of state corporation law, a definition that limits legislative concern to the relationship of owners and managers, thereby leaving aside the interests of employees and creditors let alone the public at large. In consequence of that, such 'third-party' gained political and regulatory attention only at the federal level, relieving state corporation law from otherwise unavoidable pressures to reconsider this narrow approach. In addition and again for historical reasons, statutory corporation law in the United States has traditionally been unitary law providing identical rules for different types of organizational forms. And finally, the prevailing incorporation rule of conflicts law facilitated from the outset a fierce competition among states to attract incorporations for obvious fiscal and tax reasons by enacting enabling corporation codes with a minimum of regulatory interference with the business of the corporation.

In light of this it is hardly surprising, that the emerging though still contested legal-economic view militates for both a contractarian view of the public owned corporation and for minimally mandatory and maximally facilitative approach to corporation law. That proposition culminates in the provocative question: why law, why not just abolish corporate law and let people negotiate whatever contracts they please? The short answer is that corporate law is a set of terms available off-the-rack so that participants in corporate ventures can save the cost of contracting.[8]

Moreover, this general corporate law debate is accurately mirrored in the long running discussion over mandatory disclosure: Although mandatory disclosure is an established feature of securities regulation in the United States today, there is still a lively debate on the need for mandatory-disclosure policy. This debate circles around the effectiveness and the considerable cost inherent to mandatory disclosure for companies accessing the capital markets. When the Crash of 1929, followed by the Great Depression, finally led to the introduction of the Federal Securities Act of 1933 and the complementary Federal Securities Exchange Act of 1934,[9] the central question was determining what regulatory concept should be chosen in order to effectively protect small investors against false, incomplete and misleading information provided by companies, brokers and dealers. Congress

[8] FH Easterbrook and DR Fischel 'The Corporate Contract' (1989) 89 Colum L Rev 1416.

[9] For mandatory disclosure provisions within these Acts see, eg §§ 11(a), 12(2) Securities Act of 1933, 15 USC §§ 77k(a), 77l(a)(2) and Rule 10b-5 under the Securities Exchange Act of 1934, 17 C.F.R. § 240.10b-5.

had available two different approaches: Under the so-called 'merit regulation' known from state legislatures, only those securities were admissible to trade which met a specific 'fair, just, and equitable'-standard. Here, governmental authorities would have to judge the worthiness of securities to be offered to the public, and could have prevented the sale of 'unfair' securities no matter how sophisticated or risk-inclined the buyer would be.

Opposed to this merit approach was the English history of prospectus disclosure, which relied on the central technique of full disclosure. The Congress opted for the disclosure philosophy over the native merit approach. As a newspaper commentary put it quite vividly: 'Show up the roguery and it is harmless'.[10] Or as a Representative of the Congress stated with respect to the Securities Act: 'The purpose of this bill is to place the owners of securities on a parity, so far as possible, with the management of the corporations, and to place the buyer on the same plane so far as available information is concerned, with the seller.'[11] An observer would later comment that, in passing the 1933 act, Congress did not take away from the citizen his or her inalienable right to make a fool of him- or herself, it simply attempted to prevent other from making a fool of him.[12]

This is, however, not to say that the disclosure philosophy in the area of securities regulation has no critics. There is an economic school that argues powerfully that 'the costs to society of government-required disclosure exceeds the benefits.'[13] In other words: The gain caused by greater party autonomy is outweighed by the additional cost of information. Moreover, the 'Efficient Capital Market Hypothesis' (ECMH), which has occupied a prominent place in the economics and finance literature of the recent decades, implies not only that the SEC's mandated disclosure system is ineffective but also that the very goal of egalitarian disclosure might be inappropriate.[14] This leads to the debate over economic rationales of mandatory disclosure which not surprisingly evolved primarily in the area of securities law.

Intriguingly, when Congress in the early 1930s adopted the Securities Legislation and put in place the statutory basis for extensive periodic reporting require-

[10] Quoted in BC Hunt *The Development of the Business Corporation in England* (Harvard University Press Cambridge MA 1936) 95.

[11] L Loss *Fundamentals of Securities Regulation* (3rd edn Aspen Publications 1995) 33.

[12] Loss, ibid, 32 referring to language from the 1935 Report of the Canadian Royal Commission on Price Spreads (38).

[13] GJ Benston 'An Appraisal of the Costs and Benefits of Government-Required Disclosure: SEC and FTC Requirements' (1977) 41 Law and Contemporary Problems 30, 60; Stigler (1964) 19 Bus Lawyer 721; H Kripke *The SEC and Corporate Disclosure: Regulation in Search of a Purpose* (New York Law and Business 1979).

[14] TR Dyckman, D Downes and RP Magee *Efficient Capital Markets and Accounting: A Critical Analysis* (Prentice Hall Inc Englewood Cliffs NY 1975); EF Fama 'Efficient Capital Markets: A Review of Theory and Empirical Work' (1979) 25 J Fin 25 383; Note (1977) 29 Stan L Rev 1031.

ments, it anticipated a variant of the semi-strong form of the Efficient Capital Market Hypothesis and stated that 'no investor, no speculator, can safely buy and sell securities upon exchanges without having an intelligent basis for forming his judgment as to the value of the securities he buys or sells. The idea of a free and open public market is built upon the theory that competing judgments of buyers and sellers as to the fair price of a security brings [sic] about a situation when the market price reflects as nearly as possible a just price.'[15] Notwithstanding broad acceptance of the semi-strong form of the Efficient Capital Market Hypothesis, and its pivotal role in the United States' regulatory system, the mandatory nature of securities market disclosure requirements has generated substantial controversy. If capital markets appropriately penalize firms that fail to disclose sufficient information to the market, or that fail to provide adequate assurance of integrity and precision regarding their disclosure, the these firms will encounter a higher cost of capital. These increased capital costs should generate an incentive voluntarily to increase the quality and quantity of disclosures until marginal capital costs savings equal marginal disclosure costs. In equilibrium, voluntary disclosures should, by this logic, lead to more efficient information dissemination than a mandatory regime because the mandatory regime would be prone to require too much of some information and too little of other information.[16] Indeed, many firms today routinely supply investors with information that is not required under mandatory disclosure regimes, and that fact suggests that mandatory disclosure regimes do not capture all information that can be efficiently provided.

Initially however, after the enactment of the securities legislation in 1933-34, disclosure was in practical terms aimed at and widely accepted as having a positive effect on the market, with initial and continuous disclosure playing a crucial role in allocating capital efficiently. By the 1960s and 70s, however, the SEC's regulatory disclosure regime was growingly questioned by economists and legal academics as imposing onerous costs on companies which were not counterbalanced by benefits to the individual investor or the public at large.[17] Some commentators have suggested that if mandatory disclosure are beneficial the stock prices should increase when mandatory disclosure regimes are implemented. In particular, stock prices in the United States should have increased in the 1930s in response to the passage of the federal Securities laws. The studies are, however, sharply divided on the United States' market's response to the implementation of mandatory disclosure requirements. And the underlying

[15] United States Congress, House of Representatives, 1934, HR Report No 138.

[16] FH Easterbrook and DR Fischel 'Mandatory Disclosure and the Protection of Investors' (1984) 70 Va L Rev 699.

[17] GJ Benston 'Required Disclosure and the Stock Market: An Evaluation of the Securities Exchange Act of 1934' (1973) 63 Am Econ Rev 132.

empirical and methodological question remains open to heated dispute.[18] Other studies suggest that the dominant effect of a mandatory disclosure regime is to shift the costs of generating information without materially affecting the aggregate quantity or quality of information available in the market, leaving observable stock prices unchanged.[19] If, however, the dominant effect of a mandatory disclosure regime may be to reallocate rents among various market participants without changing observable stock market prices,[20] then the debate about mandatory may have as much to do with law as with economics, and therefore is not susceptible to resolution through event analyses or other types of empirical studies. Moreover, mandatory disclosure regimes are an established feature of our regulatory landscape, and it is quite unlikely that mandatory disclosure as a legislative device will be abandoned. This is particularly true with respect to the situation within the European Union. Although this debate still rages, the SEC still holds firm on its mandatory disclosure policy. Yet, it has taken remarkable steps to streamline the disclosure process in order to integrate different disclosure duties and to avoid inefficient multiple disclosure of identical information.

Looking somewhat closer at the economic rationale for mandatory disclosure, two basic types of justifications can be identified: First, there are various protective functions of mandatory disclosure, which in general are hardly contested today. According to one early analysis, investor confidence in the securities system can be considered as an overriding aim of disclosure, while investor protection, the monitoring of company law, the transparency of the market operations and sales promotion can be considered as subsidiary aims.[21] Other commentators have suggested, that investor confidence and protection (and thereby the promotion of investor confidence) and prevention of fraud are disclosure aims of equal rank.[22] Still other commentators emphasise investor or individual protection and market protection (protection of the functioning of the market) as the two main protective aims of disclosure with a couple of further protective functions subordinated to each of them.[23]

[18] Benston (n 17) 132; idem (1975) 65 Am Econ Rev 473; I Friend and RW Westerfield 'Required Disclosure and the Stock Market' (1975) 65 Am Econ Rev 467.

[19] RJ Gilson and R Kraakman 'The Mechanisms of Market Efficiency' (1984) 70 Va L Rev 559.

[20] SM Phillips and JR Zecher *The SEC and the Public Interes*t (MIT Press Cambridge MA 1981).

[21] E Wymeersch 'Control of Securities Markets in the European Economic Community' Collection Studies Competition – Approximation of Legislation Series No 31 (1977) 139-42; cf also OECD Principles of Corporate Governance, SG/CG (99) 5 sub IV.

[22] N Moloney *EC Securities Regulation* (OUP Oxford 2002) 120.

[23] KJ Hopt *Der Kapitalanlegerschutz im Recht der Banken* (CH Beck Munich 1975); H Merkt *Unternehmenspublizität – Die Offenlegung von Unternehmensdaten als Korrelat der Marktteilnahme* (Mohr Tübingen 2001).

The second type of justification circles around market efficiency and market failure, as already mentioned, and still is far less uncontested among economists and legal academics. Therefore, it is pretty save to say that mandatory disclosure is not a matter of principle (disclosure does have beneficial effects) but a matter of counterbalancing its positive and negative effects (is disclosure too costly in the light of its beneficial effects?). With respect to the fostering of market efficiency through promotion of price accuracy it is argued that, where markets are informationally efficient, in that information is reflected in prices, disclosure serves to ensure that securities are correctly priced, in that they reflect the intrinsic value of the issuer and, in turn, given the role of securities-trading markets in allocating capital, that capital is efficiently allocated. Investment or capital-allocation decisions are therefore made not on the basis of speculation or advertising but in an allocatively efficient manner, based on the value of the security. The role of disclosure in establishing a pricing mechanism has been emphasised as critical, in that behaviour of securities prices has a deep effect on the allocative efficiency of securities markets.[24]

At the centre of the law-and-economics debate over disclosure as regulatory tool stands, as already mentioned, the question whether and to which extent the mere dissemination of issuer information should be mandatory and managed by public rules or left to market forces and the incentives given to companies and other suppliers of information to provide adequate disclosure. The market-failure doctrine teaches that regulation should be imposed on the market only in order to correct a market failure. It operates on the assumption that a perfect market exists which will allocate resources efficiently and that regulation is a corrective to an imperfect market. Information may represent a market failure in this area in that in the absence of public control it will not be disseminated, as a result of its public-good nature,[25] and the efficient allocation of resources will accordingly be prejudiced.[26] Mandatory disclosure regimes can thus be viewed as 'a desirable cost reduction strategy through which society, in effect, subsidizes search costs to secure both a greater quantity of information and a better testing of its accuracy'.[27] Absent mandatory disclosure, investors would also have greater private incentives to invest in the pursuit of information that gives rise to trading gains. As Coffee observes, 'collectivization through mandatory disclosure minimizes

[24] JC Coffee Jr 'Market Failure and the Economic Case for a Mandatory Disclosure System' (1984) 70 Va L Rev 717, 734.

[25] On the public-good nature of information, see A Ogus *Regulation – Legal Forms and Economic Theory* (Clarendon Press Oxford 1994) 33-35; JP Trachtman 'The Applicability of Law and Economics to Law and Development: The Case of Financial Law' in JJ Norton and M Andenas (eds) *Emerging Financial Markets and the Role International Financial Organizations* (Kluwer Law International The Hague 1996) 54.

[26] AC Page and RB Ferguson *Investor Protection* (Northwestern University Press 1992) 36 ff.

[27] Coffee (n 24).

the social waste that would otherwise result from misallocation of economic resources to this pursuit'.[28] In addition, agency problems typically arising in the context of takeovers could give managers a private incentive to manipulate the disclosure of information, either by concealing bad news or exaggerating good news.[29]

Information markets are also subject to signalling problems that that can make it impossible to distinguish high-quality credible information from low-quality information. These difficulties can arguably lead to a 'lemons' type failure. Moreover, even if each issuer had an incentive to provide just the right quantity and quality of information to the market, they could do so using a wide variety of different formats and reporting conventions. These variations could impose significant information processing costs on investors seeking to compare and contrast voluntary reports. Mandatory disclosure conventions economize on these costs.[30]

Recent advances in behavioural economics provide yet another rationale for mandatory disclosure regimes. Executives and promoters are arguably subject to perceptual biases which can cause them to be honestly more optimistic than the proverbial 'prudent merchant' acting under similar circumstances. A mandatory disclosure regime which requires that bad news be revealed along with an insider's honestly held optimistic assessment can arguably help correct for a range of cognitive biases and at the same time promote more accurate pricing in the markets.[31]

Alternatively, it has been argued that, left to their own devices, companies and their management will produce sufficient information for the market ultimately to provide optimum levels of protection and information for investors in that investors will discount the value of securities in respect of which less information is disclosed as those securities represent a riskier investment when compared to securities in respect of which more information is disclosed.[32] Where information would not be produced other than via a mandatory disclosure system the benefits of the information in question are outweighed by the costs of production. As companies compete for investors' funds they are, one might argue, already given adequate incentives to produce information in the extent and quality required by the market. Proponents of this line of reasoning can rely on empirical research

[28] ibid 722.

[29] P Mahoney 'Mandatory disclosure as a solution to agency problems' (1995) 62 U of Chi L Rev 1047.

[30] M Kahan and M Klausner 'Standardization and Innovation in Corporate Contracting (or 'the Economics of Boilerplate')' (1997) 83 Va L Rev 713.

[31] DC Langenvoort 'The Epistemology of Corporate-Securities Lawyering: Beliefs, Biases and Organizational Behavior' (1997) 63 Brooklyn L Rev 629.

[32] Cf HS Scott 'Internationalization of Primary Public Securities Markets' (2000) 63 Duke Journal of Law and Contemporary Problems 71, 75 ff, who challenges the discounting theory.

comparing the disclosure produced by US companies pre and post the introduction of the mandatory federal disclosure regime in 1933 and 34. This research found that companies typically voluntarily produced financial statements (albeit in accordance with a listing obligation) which contained, for the most part, a large proportion of the information which would be required subsequently under the mandatory federal regime.[33] In the US-context, this argument has to far reaching implications: First, voluntary disclosure is preferable over mandatory disclosure. Second, securities regulation is not a proper subject for federal jurisdiction. Hence, it should be returned to the single state legislatures where it was before the federalization of Securities legislation,[34] bringing disclosure regulation back to the realm of competition ('competitive federalism'[35]) and, thereby, ensuring that information is disclosed in such quantity and quality as the market requires. From the perspective of pragmatism, however, it seems that public control over companies and their disclosure policies ensures that disclosure is made available in a standardized manner which facilitates investors in making comparisons. Indeed, the importance of standardization is highlightened in the reforms which have been proposed to the EU's governing disclosure regime.

2. The European Battlefield: Disclosure versus Merit Regulation

Measured by American disclosure-policy standards, it is hard to contest that members of the European Union are – with the exception of UK – developing countries. The battle here is not one over mandatory versus voluntary disclosure, but over disclosure as such versus traditional merit regulation.

a) The Reluctant Position of Domestic Law

This is surprising, since disclosure regulation is a rather traditional and well known regulatory tool in Continental Europe and in particular in Germany. Back in the early and middle 19th century, disclosure was understood and used as an alternative to full substantive or merit regulation. Shareholder and investor protection by disclosure of annual accounts has replaced the requirement of special charter and continuous administrative control of companies limited by shares. This was in essence the Gladstonian reform of 1844 and 1845.[36] But the identical

[33] Easterbrook and Fischel (n 16) 669; R Romano 'Empowering Investors: A Market Approach to Securities Regulation' (1998) 107 Yale L J 2359, 2373 ff.

[34] See the thorough analysis in R Romano *The Advantage of Competitive Federalism for Securities Regulation* (AEI Press Washington 2002).

[35] Romano (n 34) 112-146.

[36] PL Davies *Gower's Principles of Modern Company Law* (6th edn Butterworths London 1997) 38. For a history of disclosure policy and regulation in Europe see Merkt (n 23) 31 ff, 55 ff.

idea flourished all over Europe. The famous Prussian reformer Hansmann asked for disclosure by railway companies limited by shares and gave the following reason: 'Among the means by which the management of a large company limited by shares can be kept law-abiding and efficient, is to be counted that it must be exposed to a certain degree to the public. This is the most effective control. In no State, whichever political constitution it may have, there can be found a reason in the latter which justifies not to allow this kind of control.'[37] Ever since, disclosure has been used as the type of regulation most compatible with a market economy because, the argument goes, it interferes least with freedom and competition of enterprises in the market.[38]

However, a closer look at modern legislation and regulation reveals strong tendencies – in domestic and in European law as well as in statutory and in case law – towards paternalism with respect to disclosure as a regulatory tool.[39] Such paternalism may in part be due to an exaggerated shareholder or investor protection policy. This position is expressed by a recent comment on the Winter Report by the Group of German Experts on Company Law: 'One has to insist that disclosure requirements can replace substantive regulation only in rare instances. Unfortunately, the High Level Group fails to recognize that the main function of disclosure requirements is limited to reinforce and to supply substantive rules. It is only in the area of corporate governance and only with respect to issues of minor importance that substantive regulation is dispensable. The High Level Group is wrong in believing that disclosure requirements would be generally apt to prevent misgovernance and in particular the exploitation of minority shareholders and creditors.'[40] Correspondingly, politicians as well as many academics in Germany like in other Continental countries adhere strongly to shareholder and creditor protection through merit regulation of the minimum-capital-requirement type on the basis of the concept of legal capital,[41] and it is only a minority of

[37] D Hansemann *Die Eisenbahnen und deren Aktionäre in ihrem Verhältnis zum Staat* (Leipzig und Halle 1837) § 108; cf also KJ Hopt 'Vom Aktien- und Börsenrecht zum Kapitalmarktrecht? Teil 1: Der international erreichte Stand des Kapitalmarktrecht Teil 2: Die deutsche Entwicklung im internationalen Vergleich' (1977) 141 Zeitschrift für das gesamte Handels- und Wirtschaftsrecht 389, 411 ff.

[38] Hopt (n 37) 411 ff.

[39] KJ Hopt 'Disclosure Rules as a Primary Tool for Fostering Party Autonomy' in S Grundmann, W Kerner and S Weatherhill (eds) *Party Autonomy and the Role of Information in the Internal Market* (de Gruyter Berlin 2001) 246, 249; cf more generally as to contract law AT Kronman 'Paternalism and the Law of Contracts' (1983) 92 Yale L J 763.

[40] 'Zur Entwicklung des Europäischen Gesellschaftsrechts: Stellungnahme der Arbeitsgruppe Europäisches Gesellschaftsrecht (Group of German Experts on Corporate Law) zum Report of the High Level Group of Company Law Experts on a modern Regulatory Framework for Company Law in Europe' (2003) Zeitschrift für Wirtschaftsrecht 863.

[41] For a critical analysis see PO Mülbert and M Birke 'In Defense of Passivity – on the Proper Role of a Target's Management in Response to a Hostile Tender Offer' (2002) 3 EBOR 695.

commentators that have begun to question the virtues of that traditional concept in light of modern disclosure-based regimes abroad.[42]

From this domestic viewpoint, on might be inclined to ask for empirical proof. Much has been written about the supplementary function of disclosure as an alternative means to massive interference by merit regulation. However, up to now we do lack any substantial and reliable empirical research on the dogma of superiority and its three core questions: First, is it true that disclosure works as efficient as merit regulation does and how could such efficiency be measured? Second, does mandatory disclosure really save costs compared to merit regulation? Third, does disclosure really interfere less with contractual freedom than merit regulation? Affirmative empirical research would make it much easier for proponents of disclosure to convince their opponents.

Moreover, one could argue that there are likely exceptions to the rule of superiority. Consider the case of creditor protection: A disclosure type regime would require permanent creditor information by way of annual publication of audited financial statements, a rather costly technique. A substantive type regulation could limit itself to retrospective application through litigation-related doctrines of the disregard of the corporate entity, a far less onerous mechanism from defendant's perspective.[43] One might argue that the latter type provides less protection because in many cases defendants will lack funds to satisfy claimants. However, this arguments fails for two reasons: First, the mere risk of being held personally liable will have its preventive effect on possible defendants. Second, creditor protection by disclosure is tainted in a comparable way, since financial statements may turn out to be incorrect and creditor confidence therefore unjustified. Again, we still lack sufficient economic and empirical evidence to give clear answers to the question of general superiority of disclosure over merit regulation.

Opposed to what could be fairly described as Continental mainstream is the situation in UK law. Since the early 1990s there has been a broad consensus that the matters covered in the various corporate governance codes which have been issued should not be legally enforceable or governed by merit-type regulation. Instead the codes have been linked to disclosure on a 'comply or explain' basis in the rules of the UK Listing Authority. Breach of these rules can theoretically lead to public or private censure and in extreme cases to fines for the company or individual directors although there has been no case reported in which any of these sanctions has been applied in relation to the corporate governance regime. Disclosure via the 'comply or explain' regime has been accepted as the most

[42] For an early challenge to the traditional legal-capital concept see F Kübler *Aktie, Unternehmensfinanzierung und Kapitalmarkt* (Bank-Verlag Cologne 1989).

[43] Disregard of the corporate entity can historically be seen as remainder of minimal creditor protection through statutory minimal capitalization requirements, an approach that has been abandoned by US-state legislators for many years, RM Buxbaum 'Looking Back' (2002) 50 Am J Comp L 249, 252.

effective means of achieving the greatest possible level of compliance with the corporate governance regime in the UK.[44]

In the meantime, in many EU States compliance with corporate governance codes became voluntary, with disclosure recommended. The different methods of disclosure adopted by the States do not necessarily mean that the various codes lack force and effect. Reputational and market forces, combined with increased disclosure may result in significant pressure for compliance depending on a number of factors including status of the entity responsible for issuing the code and the amount of information about compliance which is available to the market.[45]

b) Pressure by the European Court of Justice

In Europe, it is the European Court of Justice who most strongly and since many years advocates mandatory disclosure laws, thereby favouring information regulation as less restrictive alternative over control and prohibition.

(i) Cassis de Dijon-Case: The priority of disclosure over direct restrictions was spelled out very clearly in the case of Cassis de Dijon.[46] The question before the Court in Cassis concerned the legality under EC law of a German law laying down a minimum alcohol level of 25 % for certain spirits, which included cassis, a blackcurrant-flavoured liqueur. German cassis complied with this minimum, but French cassis, with an alcohol content of 15 through 20 %, did not. Although the German regulation was indistinctly applicable, the result of the measure was effectively to ban French cassis from the German market. The Court stated that certain measures of member state legislatures will not breach Article 30 of the EC-Treaty if they are enacted in the interests of the public and the fairness of commercial transactions and, moreover, are necessary to satisfy mandatory requirements. This rule has come to be known as 'rule of reason'.

In applying the rule of reason to the facts of Cassis the Court found that the German law was in breach of Article 30. Although the measure fell within the categories suggested, being allegedly enacted in the interest of public health (to prevent increased consumption resulting from lowering the alcoholic content of cassis) and the fairness of commercial transaction (to avoid giving the weak imported cassis an unfair advantage over its stronger, hence more expensive, German rival), the measure was not necessary to achieve these ends. Other means, such as labelling, which would have been less of a hindrance to trade, could have been used to achieve the same ends. In the words of the Court: 'As the

[44] Company Law Society for England and Wales, Memorandum, 2001, 8.

[45] European Commission (ed), Comparative Study of Corporate Governance Codes Relevant to the European Union and its Member States, Brussels, January 2002.

[46] Case 120/78, Cassis de Dijon [1979] ECR I-649.

Commission rightly observed, the fixing of limits in relation to the alcohol content of beverages may lead to the standardization of products placed on the market and of their designations, in the interests of a greater transparency of commercial transactions [...] However, this line of argument cannot be taken so far as to regard the mandatory fixing of minimum alcohol contents as being an essential guarantee of the fairness of commercial transactions, since it is a simple matter to ensure that suitable information is conveyed to the purchaser by requiring the display of an indication of origin and of the alcohol content on the packaging of products.'[47] In other words: Under a mandatory disclosure-type regime, it is up to the informed consumer to decide whether he wants to accept a certain offer. At the same time, the state refuses to take responsibility for the decision and its consequences.

This principle of priority of disclosure has two main advantages: First, it urges member state legislators to strive for minimum regulations. Second, mere disclosure regulation can be transferred easily from one national law to another and therefore is more in line with the concept of legal harmonization than prohibition type substantive regulation.[48]

(ii) Daihatsu-Case: In later years, the Court has repeatedly emphasized the role of disclosure for contractual decision-making in the context of corporate contracts. Thus, in the case of Daihatsu the Court provided some guidance as to the type of penalty required for the violation of the duty to properly disclose corporate accounting.[49] Under German law the penalty for failure to disclose the accounts of a GmbH was a fine which may be imposed on application only by a member or creditor of the company or the company's workers' council (Betriebsrat). On a preliminary reference from the Oberlandesgericht (Higher Regional Court) of Düsseldorf, the Court of Justice ruled that Article 6 of the 1th Directive precluded a Member State from so restricting the right to apply for imposition of the penalty for failure to disclose accounts.

The German Government had argued that the coordination of national systems of company law was designed[50] to safeguard the interests of members 'and others' and submitted that the latter comprised solely persons who had a legal relationship with the company. The Court of Justice took a remarkably broader view, stating that Article 54 (3) (g) must be read in the light not only of Articles 52 and 54 of the Treaty, which clearly showed that the coordination of company law formed part of the general program for the abolition of restrictions on freedom of establishment. Rather, it has to be read also in the light of Article 3 (h),

[47] ibid I-664.

[48] S Grundmann *Europäisches Schuldvertragsrecht – Das europäische Recht der Unternehmensgeschäfte* (de Gruyter Berlin 1999) 41.

[49] Case C-97/96, Daihatsu [1997] ECR I-6843.

[50] In accordance with Article 54 (3) (g) of the Treaty.

which provided that the activities were to include the approximation of national laws to the extent required for the functioning of the common market. Furthermore, Article 54 (3) expressly referred to the need to protect the interests 'of others' generally: consequently, the term could not be limited to creditors of the company.[51]

As regards Article 6 of the 1st Directive, disclosure of accounts was primarily designed to provide information to third parties who did not know or could not obtain sufficient knowledge of the company's accounting and fiscal situation.[52] That was confirmed by Article 3, which provided that certain documents and particulars must be entered in a public register and obtainable by any person upon application, and the preamble to the 4th Directive,[53] which referred to the need to establish a minimum equivalent requirements as regards the extent of the financial information to be made available to the public by companies in competition with one another.[54]

(iii) Centros-Case: In 1999, the Court had been vested with yet another opportunity to strongly advocated mandatory disclosure as a superior means to protect market participants as well as markets against the imminent danger of companies with minimum share capital. In Centros the Court upheld the case of a Danish couple against the Danish Companies and Commerce Agency, the authority responsible for registering Danish branches of foreign companies. The Court found that the Agency could not refuse to register a branch of Centros, a private company owned by the couple and registered in the United Kingdom, on the grounds that Centros does not trade in the United Kingdom but conducts all its business in Denmark, and that a British company was chosen in order to avoid the Danish capital requirements for registered private companies. The judgment does not even allow for mitigating circumstances such as the possibility of imposing the Danish capital requirements applying to private companies.[55]

In Germany, this judgment sparked a fierce discussion on whether the individual member state is powerless in the face of de facto circumvention of require-

[51] See also to the same effect the Opinion of Advocate General Cosmas delivered on 3 July 1997, paras 13 through 17.

[52] See also the 4th recital in the preamble to the First Company Law Directive.

[53] In particular the 3rd recital.

[54] The Court unsurprisingly rejected the German Government's preliminary submission that the obligation to provide for appropriate penalties was not yet applicable to the GmbH since the Article provided that in respect of private limited companies, including the GmbH, its application was 'postponed until the date of implementation of a Directive concerning co-ordination of the contents of balance sheets and of profit and loss accounts' and no such Directive had yet been adopted: the Court noted that the legislative lacuna left by the First Company Law Directive had been filled by the Fourth Company Law Directive (para 14 of the judgment).

[55] Case C-212/97, Centros Ltd [1999] ECR I-1459; for an analysis see H Merkt (2001) 3 Int Comp Corp L J 119.

ments which it considers essential such as minimum capital raising and preserving requirements, thereby stripping statutory protection from domestic creditors who suddenly find themselves exposed to the risk of fraudulent bankruptcy due to the insolvency of inadequately capitalized companies. However, the Court itself pointed out that the practice of the Danish Administration was not such as to attain the objective of protecting creditors since, if Centros had conducted business in the UK, its branch would have been registered in Denmark, even though Danish creditors might have been equally exposed to risk.

Moreover, the Court leaves the domestic creditors of Centros far from unprotected against undercapitalization. Again, the Court puts a strong emphasis on mandatory disclosure as less restrictive but suitable equivalent to substantive or even openly 'paternalistic' measures of the minimum capital requirement-type: The possibilities for the company creditors' and contracting parties' to distinguish by way of disclosed information between a foreign branch and a domestic company as well as supportive Community law measures (annual accounts and disclosure requirements) provide most effective protection.

Hence, it can be assumed that the practical significance of Centros will be limited by commercial reality. Most member state company laws provide in accordance with the 11th Directive on branches that in its name, a branch shall include the company name with the addition of the word 'filial' (branch) and a clear indication of the nationality of the company. Branches shall state their name, registered office (head office) and registration number, and, if applicable, any register and registration number of the company in the home country, on all letters and other business documents. If the amount of the share capital is indicated in such documents, amounts for both the subscribed and the paid-up share capital must be stated.

As one Danish commentator has put it, creditors and business partners will by virtue of disclosure duties be able to establish that the company is a foreign one and (by further enquiries) that its financial foundation may be weak or practically non-existing.[56] This psychological barrier created by uncertainty as to the legal nature and financial foundation of the company might therefore prove to be very effective in limiting the use of undercapitalized UK companies in Denmark and elsewhere in the Union, a barrier that so far is not yet subject to the Court's jurisdiction.

(iv) Überseering-Case: In obvious harmony with this line of cases, the ECJ recently argued that minimum capital requirements for investor and creditor protection cannot justify limitations of the freedom of establishment and the free capital movement.[57] As the Court put it: 'It is not inconceivable that overriding

[56] Rasmussen and Ottosen 'Centros judgment undermines national Company law' [1999] Lawyer's Europe Spring 5, 6.

[57] Case C-208/00 Überseering [1999] ECR I-09919.

requirements relating to the general interest, such as the protection of the interests of creditors, minority shareholders, employees and even the taxation authorities, may, in certain circumstances and subject to certain conditions, justify restrictions on freedom of establishment. Such objectives cannot, however, justify denying the legal capacity and, consequently, the capacity to be a party to legal proceedings of a company properly incorporated in another Member State in which it has its registered office. Such a measure is tantamount to an outright negation of the freedom of establishment conferred on companies by Articles 43 EC and 48 EC.'[58]

3. The less Principled Approach of the European Commission

Unlike the European Court of Justice, which, as seen, repeatedly has stressed the dominant role of mandatory disclosure in protecting the market as well as its individual participants, the Commission follows a less principled approach. The role of mandatory disclosure in various areas of regulatory harmonization is most accurately characterized as utterly eclectic. Moreover, it is pretty safe to state that the importance of mandatory disclosure correlates with the impact of Anglo-Saxon legal tradition on individual pieces of regulatory harmonization. In that regard, roughly three types of regulations can be identified.

a) Disclosure only-Directives: The first and smallest group comprises those Directives that apply mandatory disclosure as exclusive remedy for the protection of markets and market participants. The Employee Contract Disclosure Rights Directive of 1991, drawing heavily upon corresponding English regulations,[59] provides for exhaustive information obligations on the part of the employer in order to protect employees.[60] According to its Article 2, the employer is obliged to notify an employee of all essential aspects of the employment contract, thereby vesting employees not only with pre-contractual information rights but first and foremost with a right to information in the course of the ongoing contractual relationship.

Not surprisingly, however, the majority of Directives of this 'disclosure only'-type can be found in the area of securities regulation. The Directive of 1988 on the information to be published when a major holding in a listed company is acquired or disposed of[61] and the Directive of 1989 co-ordinating the require-

[58] ibid paras 92 ff.

[59] s 1 through 6 Employment Protection (Consolidation) Act 1978; RJ Harvey *On Industrial Relations and Employment Law* (Butterworths Tolley London 1995) Q 322-330.

[60] Council Directive 91/533/EEC of 14 October 1991.

[61] Council Directive 88/627/EEC of 12 December 1988.

ments for public offer prospectuses[62] provide for exhaustive disclosure of company related information. Closely connected to this type of Directive is the Directive on Prevention of Insider Trading of 1989.[63] The latter one combines mandatory disclosure (ad hoc-disclosure duties) with a prohibition to contract for securities in cases of non-disclosure ('disclose or abstain'). This regulation makes it particularly clear that disclosure duties and prohibitions do work as substitutes: Wherever the relevant facts are not timely disclosed, any deal is prohibited.

b) Hybrid Directives: The second, most widely employed type of regulation is a hybrid: mandatory disclosure provisions are mixed with prohibitions or other substantive regulations, a patchwork-like technique that in most cases does result from a clash of different regulatory traditions or cultures. For example, the Directive on Consumer Credit of 1986 provides for various substantive consumer rights like the right to discharge the obligation prematurely and the duty of the creditor to specify in writing certain key terms. Identical provisions can be found in the Directive on Package Holiday Tours[64] and the Directive on Time Sharing.[65] Several directives of that type like the Distance Selling Directive[66] and the Doorstep Sales Directive[67] do combine disclosure requirements with a cooling off period allowing the consumer to step back from the deal within a reasonable period of several days after the conclusion of the contract. The Directive on Funds Transfers of 1997 supplements a whole array of information duties with a single non-information regulation, ie a liability rule in case of loss of funds.[68] Identical hybrid solutions can be found in the three Non-Life Insurance Directives.[69]

c) Merit only-Directives: The third type of regulation is the most traditional one: The merit approach limits itself to substantive regulations and direct prohibitions, thus leaving disclosure type provisions completely aside. The role of the legislator in that case could be characterized as a sort of 'guardianship' over consumers. The individual consumer has no choice among various offers, but is limited to what the legislators deems permissible under specific standards. The most notable effect of such legislative preoccupation is that consumer autonomy

[62] Council Directive 89/298/EEC of 17 April 1989.

[63] Council Directive 89/592/EEC of 13 November 1989.

[64] Council Directive 90/314/EEC of 13 June 1989.

[65] Council Directive 94/47/EEC of 26 October 1994.

[66] Council Directive 97/7/EEC of 20 May 1997.

[67] Council Directive 85/577/EEC of 20 December 1985.

[68] Council Directive 97/5/EEC of 27 January 1997.

[69] Council Directive 73/239/EEC of 24 July 1973; Council Directive 88/357/EEC of 22 June 1988; Council Directive 92/49/EEC of 18 June 1992.

becomes severely restrained. A good examples of that latter type of regulation is furnished by the Directive on Liability for Supply of Services which simply provides for certain standards regarding the liability of suppliers of services. Arguably this provision makes it principally impossible for the suppliers of services to limit their liability contractually in order to offer less costly services.[70] Thus, consumer autonomy is constrained. Moreover, it is highly questionable whether this traditional approach is in line with the European Court of Justice's modern principle of priority of disclosure over substantive provisions.[71]

d) The Commission's European Commission Communication of May 2003: The Commission's recent response to the High-Level-Group Report, the so called European Commission Communication,[72] is pretty much in line with what has been said about the Commissions overall position on mandatory disclosure. First and foremost, with respect to a number of issues the European Commission Communication affirms the High Level Group's request for extended and enhanced mandatory disclosure, eg, regarding the inclusion of a coherent and descriptive statement covering the key elements of their corporate governance structure and practices, regarding information about the role played by institutional investors,[73] regarding directors' remuneration,[74] regarding the group structure and intra-group relations[75] and finally regarding information to be submitted by legal entities with limited liability in general.[76] Moreover, the Commission shares the view that disclosure duties should be geared to different types of companies.

However, the Plan avoids carefully to endorse the Winter Report's proposition of general superiority of disclosure over merit regulation. Moreover, the Plan does not even spell out any guideline or principle as to the proper field for merit or disclosure regulation. As a matter of fact, one would not expect such theoretical framework, given that in the end the choice between disclosure and merit regulation would not follow principles but rather political opportunities.

Finally and in summing up what could be observed in the two previous parts of the paper, it is noteworthy that the High Level Group's approach of mandatory disclosure as superior over merit regulation is, in a comparative perspective, by

[70] Grundmann (n 48) 318.

[71] ibid 318.

[72] Commission of the European Communities, Communication from the Commission to the Council and the European Parliament – Modernising Company Law and Enhancing Corporate Governance in the European Union – A Plan to Move Forward (hereinafter: European Commission Communication) Brussels, 21 May 2003 (Annex 1 in this volume).

[73] ibid (n 72) sub 3.1.1.

[74] ibid (n 72) sub 3.1.3.

[75] ibid (n 72) sub 3.3.

[76] ibid (n 72) sub 3.7.

no means 'radical' as it might perhaps appear from a continental viewpoint. Rather, the concept of mandatory disclosure corresponds to what on the international level has become the standard model of regulatory self-restriction.

4. A Common Battleground: The Level of Regulation – Uniform versus Competitive Disclosure Regulation (Harmonization versus Subsidiarity) – Legislative versus Industry Self-Regulation

There is, however, one common transatlantic battleground in the debate over disclosure: the dispute is about the level best suited for disclosure regulation. As already mentioned previously, in the United States economists and legal commentators struggle since long time over this issue. Advocates of decentralized disclosure regulation make the argument, that only regulatory competition might produce the regime most suitable for market participants.[77]

Apparently, the Winter Report challenges this view by advocating centralized disclosure rules on the EU-level in order to achieve harmonization of disclosure requirements within the Union. This conclusion can be drawn implicitly from the Report's proposition that the EU should consider whether disclosure requirements are better suited to achieve the desired effects than substantive rules.[78] In endorsing this concept, the Commission's European Commission Communication states: 'In view of the growing integration of European capital markets, a common approach should be adopted at EU level with respect to a few essential rules [which include mandatory disclosure] and adequate coordination of corporate governance codes should be ensured.'[79] At the same time, the European Commission Communication leaves no doubt, that 'a self-regulatory market approach, based solely on non binding recommendations, is clearly not always sufficient to guarantee the adoption of sound corporate governance practices.'

There are basically three points that deserve being addressed in that context briefly: First and most important, in light of the overriding principle of subsidiarity within the EU, the introduction of a 'common approach' to mandatory disclosure on the EU level requires a sound and convincing justification. Such justification might be derived from the simple fact, that the need to comply with different disclosure requirements imposed by States can serve as a substantial obstacle to multiple listings, as, seen from the opposite perspective, the additional cost of gathering investor information produced under differing standards (with varying language, content etc.) can deter the investment of funds.[80] Moreover,

[77] Romano (n 34).

[78] Winter Report (n 5) 34.

[79] European Commission Communication (n 72) sub 31.1.

[80] This point was acknowledged by the SEC in the context of the disclosure requirements applicable to foreign issuers in 1999, see SEC Release No 33-7637 (1999).

exposure to varying and onerous sanctions and liability regimes can also impair the capital-raising process. Although the former have been addressed by the EU regime, the latter remain subject to Member State control. Given the globalisation of markets, regulators are increasingly cooperating to bring about the convergence of disclosure standards in order to combat the obstacles created by varying disclosure standards. The basis for the US-Canada multi-jurisdictional disclosure system was laid in 1991. In 1998 IOSCO adopted international disclosure standards to be applied to cross-border offerings and initial listings by foreign issuers which were designed to serve as the basis for a disclosure document passport regime which would allow issuers to rely on a document prepared in accordance with the standards for multi-jurisdictional offerings and listings.[81]

Second, assuming that disclosure regulation interferes less with private rights than merit regulation does, a regulatory concept that combines disclosure requirements on the central level with merit regulation on the level of the single States appears to be preferable.

Third, mere disclosure regulation can be transferred easily from one national law to another and therefore is more in line with the concept of legal harmonization than prohibition type merit regulation.[82] In that context, it has recently be argued that directives are not the appropriate legal instruments for implementing disclosure regulation. The process from proposal (by the European Commission) to adoption to implementation, the argument goes, is too slow and reform is even slower. As in the case of merger regulation, regulations are preferable over directives.[83] The validity of this reasoning depends on the character of European disclosure regime envisaged. Certainly, a comprehensive and detailed regime of disclosure duties on the European level requires direct rulemaking without burdensome and time consuming implementation procedures. However, a basic framework leaving sufficient room for individual and competitive membership implementation, as favoured by both the Winter Report and the European Commission Communication, is better served by use of directives. Hence, the choice between directives and regulations is a choice between different basic regulatory concepts and requires careful analysis.

[81] IOSCO 'International Disclosure Standards for Cross-Border Offerings and Initial Listings by Foreign Issuers' (1998).

[82] Grundmann (n 48) 41.

[83] M Becht in KJ Hopt and E Wymeersch (eds) *Capital Markets and Company Law* (OUP Oxford 2003) 87, 89.

II. Disclosed Information as a Marketable Good

1. The Supply Side: Companies

The Winter Report suggests to distinguish between three basic types of companies: listed companies, open companies (whose internal structure would allow for listing) and closed companies (whose shares are not freely transferable). According to the Winter Report 'there may be good reasons why the regulatory approach in company law for these three types of companies should be different. For listed companies, a certain level of uniform, compulsory, substantive rules may be required to sufficiently protect both shareholders (investors) and creditors. On the other hand, disclosure requirements and market forces may provide powerful alternative disciplinary instruments.'[84] This is a pretty formalistic and inflexible concept of threefold disclosure for listed, open and closed companies. First, this approach rather conceals than clarifies the true justification for disclosure. Disclosure is the natural correlative of market participation. Disclosure, therefore, is determined by the market impact of the individual company or issuer of securities.[85] This, however, calls for a much more flexible determination of both the scope and the content of disclosure. Correspondingly, investor protection is not absolute but needs to be differentiated according to the various market segments for different categories of securities. Official markets, regulated markets and new markets present remarkable differences in reputation of the companies listed, in regulation by the competent authority and in protection for the investors. This calls for flexibility, not for simplistic categorization.

Hence, the European Commission Communication is only in part correct in endorsing the Winter Report on that point. According to the Commission 'a proper distinction should be made between categories of companies. A more stringent framework is desirable for listed companies and companies which have publicly raised capital. They should be subject to a certain number of appropriate detailed rules, in particular in the area of disclosure. With respect to other companies, regulatory initiatives should take full account of both their form and size, allowing a more flexible framework for SME's.'[86] The latter distinction and flexibilisation correctly deviates from the too simplistic approach of the Winter Report.

Finally, the European Commission Communication's proposition of increased disclosure requirements for all legal entities with limited liability[87] asks for a brief comment. The Commission advocates such extension of disclosure for two reasons, the preservation of fair competition and the prevention of crime com-

[84] Winter Report (n 5) 35.

[85] For a comprehensive analysis of this concept see Merkt (n 23).

[86] European Commission Communication (n 72) sub 2.1.

[87] ibid sub 3.7.

mitted by use of the company. The first justification appears to be misconceived in that disclosure is not the price to be paid for enjoying limited liability but the price to be paid for participating in the market. Hence, preservation of competition requires inclusion of all forms of businesses that participate to a relevant extent in the market.[88] Second, it is difficult to see how disclosure can efficiently contribute to persecution or prevention of criminal activities. Disclosure itself needs assistance of criminal sanctions in order to effectuate enforcement. Interestingly, the European Court of Justice in its Centros decision quite correctly recognized that the objective of crime prevention would be one of few aims that could justify interference with freedom rights caused by pertinent substantive regulation.[89]

2. The Demand Side: Investors

Corporate disclosure aims not only at investors, but also at creditors, employees, regulatory agencies and the public a large.[90] This is an important yet distinctive feature of disclosure regulation in Europe. Inasmuch as disclosure regulation is designed to substitute merit regulation, it has to cover the same broad range of protective function as merit regulation traditionally does. In that context, it is important to note what the European Court of Justice said in his Centros and Überseering decisions about the effectiveness of disclosure regulation:[91] According to the Court, creditor protection is better and more efficiently achieved by disclosure than by minimum capital requirements and other substantive provisions of the kind. To make that argument more plausible, the Court quotes from two Directives that form central part of the EU's disclosure concept: the Council Directive on annual accounts of certain types of companies (Fourth Company Law Directive)[92] and the Council Directive on disclosure requirements for branches established in Member States by certain types of companies governed by the law of another State (Eleventh Company Law Directive).[93] One could

[88] Surprisingly, footnote 24 to Section 3.7 of the European Commission Communication makes exactly that point. This is particularly true in light of the fact that the traditional distinctions between companies (legal entities) and partnerships as well as between limited and unlimited personal liability are increasingly watered.

[89] Centros (n 55) para 38; Merkt (n 55).

[90] Merkt (n 23) 132 ff.

[91] Merkt (n 55).

[92] Council Directive 78/660/EEC [1978] 25 July 1978.

[93] Council Directive 89/666/EEC [1989] 22 November 1989.

easily have also added the Council Directive on disclosure (First Company Law Directive).[94] Creditor protection is thus achieved through information.

At what audience disclosure should be aimed is a pretty old yet fundamental question, even though it is addressed neither in the Winter Report nor in the European Commission Communication. In theory, three answers are possible: At the unsophisticated, at the financial expert, or at the hypothetical 'reasonable' investor of average sophistication. Throughout its history, the SEC has struggled with this question. It may well be unanswerable. A balance must be struck which reflects, to the extent possible, the needs of all who have a stake in the securities markets. The US regime having been at certain stages preoccupied in making detailed disclosure fully comprehensible to a model retail investor, even though in practice such investors did not understand or even read the disclosed information, has been subject to harsh criticism.[95]

However, the concept of disclosure for reasonably sophisticated investors becomes increasingly questionable. Equity holdings and investment behaviour in Continental Europe is gradually shifting towards the patterns fond in the UK and US markets. In large, publicly listed companies with widely dispersed ownership, individual investors no longer hold controlling blocks the way they did in classical times of owner-managers or family businesses, but rather hold fractional interests. According to the portfolio theory such investors distribute their capital over the entire market. A diversified investor, however, can no longer collect and evaluate all investment relevant information on each company in his portfolio. He turns to support from new players in the market: buy side analysts, asset managers, and intermediaries such as investment companies and pension funds. These players process investment-relevant information regarding the portfolio companies and, on the basis of their findings make recommendations to, or even investment decisions for, the investor. This system certainly does not make it unnecessary to disclose material information to investors. Rather, the addressee of the disclosed information has changed from the investor himself to the buy side analyst or intermediary. Hence, disclosure need not any longer be primarily tailored to the knowledge of the unsophisticated or the average investor. Therefore, under the EC Listing and Reporting Directive an annual financial statement for instance is meaningful to a 'financially literate' investor.[96]

[94] The Directive is not applicable to branches, but only to the companies as such; however, the creditors in the country where the branch is located enjoy the effects of the company's disclosure anyway.

[95] H Kripke 'The Myth of the Informed Layman' (1973) 28 Bus Lawyer 631.

[96] Art 21 (1) of the Council Directive of 28 May 2001 on the admission of securities to official stock exchange listing and on information to be published on those securities (2001/34/EC). Some years ago the German High Court (Bundesgerichtshof) held the 'average investor' the relevant addressee, refusing to attribute to such average investor the ability to understand finan-

cont. ...

3. Hybrid Market Participants

Given the dual role of institutional investors on both the supply and the demand side of the market for company related information, the European Commission Communication quite logically asks for specific disclosure by institutional investors.[97] They should be obliged to disclose their investment policy with respect to the exercise of voting rights in companies in which they invest. Additionally, they should disclose to their beneficial holders at their request how these rights have been used in a particular case.

This is likewise true for holders of majority shares, based on the assumption that extended market impact (majority holding) justifies disclosure. Therefore, the High Level Group is correct in suggesting identification of majority shareholders (with a description of voting rights and special control rights they can exercise and a description of the key elements of the existing shareholder agreements) and, in addition, disclosure of direct and indirect relationships between the company and majority shareholders beyond the shareholding itself.[98]

C. General Principles of Disclosure

An initial and important distinction can be drawn between disclosure requirements designed to provide information to addressees who subscribe to shares in an initial public offering (ex ante disclosure; primary market information) and the continuing disclosure requirement of listed companies (secondary market disclosure). It is important to note that in the context of disclosure both the Winter Report and the European Commission Communication are confined to secondary market disclosure. Correspondingly, the following analysis concentrates on secondary market disclosure.

Traditionally, a shareholder of a stock company obtains the bulk of his information about the company's financial condition and results of operation from the annual shareholders' meeting. For following reasons, however, such information is inadequate for an investor in a publicly held corporation: First, a shareholder's meeting takes places, as a rule, only once in a year. Second, the information presented at the shareholders' meeting usually reaches investors too late. Third, the unconsolidated financial statements presented at the shareholders' meeting are, at least when prepared pursuant to German law, not designed to present a true an fair view of the company, but are designed to protect the interests of creditors and

cial statements, (1992) Wertpapiermitteilungen 901, 904. The decision has been subject to fierce criticism, eg W Groß *Kapitalmarktrecht* (2nd edn CH Beck Cologne 2002) §§ 45, 46 Exchange Act no 25; E Schwark Börsengesetz (2nd edn CH Beck Cologne 1994) §§ 45, 46 no 13; H Fleischer *Gutachten zum 64. Deutschen Juristentag* (Berlin 2002) F 21.

[97] European Commission Communication (n 72) sub 3.1.1.

[98] Winter Report (n 5) 46.

to serve taxation purposes. There is still great need for enhanced disclosure of both group-related financial information and information on group structure and relations. Fourth, management may only be required to provide additional information if an item or request regarding such information has been inserted in the meeting agenda. Fifth, only shareholders, and not individuals interested in investing through the secondary market, are admitted to attend the shareholders' meeting. From that it follows that important information regarding the corporate governance structure of a company is not communicated to the shareholders and the secondary market. Because of these flaws of the current system of shareholders' meetings as a source of information, regulatory requirements and developments in information and communication technology have led to an increased flow of information apart from the shareholders' meeting. Such information consists of a number of elements and serves two main functions: First, to enable shareholders to make a decision regarding their investment on a continuing basis, including when a material change occurs in the company's affairs, and second, to promote the development of an efficient secondary market, ie, to facilitate the decisions of investors interested in acquiring shares that are publicly traded on the secondary market.

In the light of this analysis, it deserves full support that both the Winter Report[99] and the European Commission Communication[100] identify two main areas for law reform in the context of company disclosure: First, the disclosure of corporate governance structures in the form of an annual corporate governance statement; and second, enhanced disclosure of group structures and relations including group-related financial information.

A more detailed review of the debate on the content of disclosure reveals four basic, yet in part overlapping principles of disclosure regulation as to the information disclosed: materiality, comprehensiveness and timeliness.[101]

I. Materiality

As a general principle, disclosure of company related information performs a facilitating function: it is designed to facilitate, assist or enable the decision-making of the addressees. This is particularly true for disclosure directed to addressees making decisions whether to contribute capital, general investors, and

[99] ibid 46 ff, 95 ff.

[100] European Commission Communication (n 72) sub 3.1.1., 3.3.

[101] Cf Winter Report (n 5) 34 with reference to the Winter Report on Takeover Bids, 25-26, (see Annex 2 in this volume) and the new Proposal for a Thirteenth Company Law Directive, in particular its Article 10; for a German reference see W Ballwieser 'Informations-GoB – auch im Lichte von IAS und US-GAAP' (2002) 3 Zeitschrift für kapitalmarktorientierte Rechnungslegung (KoR) 115.

existing shareholders, who are the primary targets of disclosure of material information. According to the economic theory of information, information is material in that sense if it capable of causing an investor to take a different decision than he would have made in the absence of such information. At least three policy considerations arise in connection with material information: First, all material information should be disclosed in its entirety to the market participants. Second, exemptions to this rule of disclosure should be limited, such as for the protection of trade secrets. Third, immaterial information should not be disclosed, since it distract addressees from material information. The goal is optimal disclosure, not maximum disclosure. In other words: It is the quality of disclosure that is important not the quantity. Too much disclosure provides opportunity to 'lose' key information, deliberately or otherwise. As an example Enron's accounts did apparently make reference to the 'contingent' liabilities associated with its partnership arrangements but it was such an insignificant item lost in the morass of information that few picked up on it. Summing it up, the Winter Report is correct in stating that overload of information should be avoided.[102]

II. Comprehensiveness

Article 22 (1) of the EC Listing and Reporting Directive[103] requires that listing particulars produce information in an easily analysable and comprehensible form. Article 5 (2) of the proposed EC Prospectus Directive[104] does reinforce that requirement. A similar proposition has been promoted by the SEC through its 'plain English rule'.[105] This provision spells out six basic principles regarding the language to be used in prospectuses.[106]

Closely linked to comprehensiveness is the issue of standardization, ie, the use of an identical format for disclosure in order to facilitate comparison of the data disclosed. Such standardization of balance sheets, income statements, and interim reporting might contribute to reduce the costs incurred by interested addressees in processing disclosed information. Standardization also presents another characteristic. Because investors are interested in comparing information gathered from various companies, it could be advisable under certain circumstances to disclose a negative piece of information that would not reach the threshold of materiality if the company were evaluated in isolation.

[102] Winter Report (n 5) 34.

[103] 2001/34/EC.

[104] COM (2001) 280 final.

[105] Rule 421(d) under the Securities Act of 1933 as amended, 17 CFR § 230.421.

[106] (i) Short sentences; (ii) Definite, concrete, everyday words; (iii) Active voice; (iv) Tabular presentation or bullet lists for complex material, whenever possible; (v) No legal jargon or highly technical business terms; and (vi) no multiple negatives.

However, the quest for standardization finds itself to a certain degree in conflict with the call for flexible disclosure regulation that takes into account the particular needs of smaller businesses not being capable of steadily publishing large amounts of information. Therefore, standardization should be limited to companies within a certain class of size.

III. Timeliness

Timeliness is a pretty important feature of efficient disclosure. Hence, channels for dissemination of information disclosed are as important as the content of the information itself. While the disclosure of information is often provided for by legislation, filing and access to information can be cumbersome and costly. Within the European Union most countries still prescribe filing with company registers and subsequent paper filing in selected local financial newspapers that a rather expensive and not necessarily circulated throughout the Union. Moreover, many member state have a great number of local or decentralized registers as in the case of Germany where approximately 720 local registers are simultaneously engaged in the administration of company filings.[107] In addition, documents are usually filed in a local language that investors at large or regulators do not readily understand. These and various other obstacles to timely disclosure have led to the proposition that the company's website may be the better place where information is to be published,[108] a suggestion that appears to be supported by both the High Level Group[109] and the European Commission Communication.[110]

However, it should be noted that with respect to reliability the Internet is a pretty unsafe medium for company disclosure. Consider in that context consumers' suspicion and the imperfections of private sector operated electronic systems. Within a few days, the financial press carried reports on Vivendi cancelling of electronic shareholder vote because of inaccuracies due to votes being electronically hijacked by hackers,[111] the threat of KPN Quest shutting down a data network at short notice due to insolvency causing massive disruption[112] and, finally, an 'Online tax service' suspended by UK Inland Revenue because of security breaches.[113] Thus, it still appears important to keep a separate, though

[107] For a comprehensive analysis of the current German system see U Noack *Infobasen für Unternehmensdaten* (Bundesanzeiger-Verlag Cologne 2003) and idem *Unternehmenspublizität* (Bundesanzeiger-Verlag Cologne 2002).

[108] eg Becht (n 83) 89.

[109] Consultative Document of the High Level Group, Question 6 (a).

[110] European Commission Communication (n 72) sub 3.1.2.

[111] *Financial Times* 24 April 2002.

[112] *Financial Times* 31 May 2002.

[113] *Financial Times* 31 May 2002.

centralized, state maintained register on which information will continue to be available after, for instance, the company has ceased to exist or after the company has ceased to be able to fund the maintenance of its website or if, for some reason, the website collapses. At the same time it is indispensable to develop standards for electronic disclosure in order to avoid abuse by misleading publications.[114]

D. Sanctioning of Disclosure Duties

Regulation by disclosure only works if there are resources applied to ensure that proper disclosure is made and that suitable penalties are applied in case of failure.[115] Adequacy and sufficiency of disclosure in practice are typically ensured by imposing sanctions on the issuer and those persons responsible for the disclosure or by making remedies available to the investor.[116] In common with the approach taken towards sanctions and liability across EC securities regulation, liability in respect of inadequate or misleading disclosure is left to the discretion of Member States: remedies are, of course, typically the preserve of the Member States und EC law generally.

Entirely in line with this approach both the Winter Report and the European Commission Communication are silent on the issue of sanctioning disclosure duties, except for the context of co-ordinating national corporate governance efforts, in which the European Commission Communication correctly highlightens the need for Member State procedures to monitor and enforce compliance and disclosure.[117] This does correspond to Article 97 of the Securities Consolidation Directive (SCD) which requires Member States to provide 'appropriate sanctions' in case where those subject to the SCD's large-shareholdings requirements do not comply with its provisions.

A comprehensive overview of sanctions would have to examine market sanctions (such as loss of reputation and impact on stock prices), government imposed sanctions (such as fines and other administrative sanctions)and other mechanisms (such as consolidated financial statements by independent auditors, or judicial actions filed by investors under securities law), and ask whether the principles of disclosure are sufficiently policed by the available sanctions.

With respect to German law on false or misleading secondary market disclosure, liability requires proof of an intentional or morally culpable act or a criminal violation committed by defendant company and resulting in damage to the plaintiff investor. The German legislator has responded to challenges and introduced

[114] Cf Becht (n 83) 90 sub D. (1).

[115] Company Law Society for England and Wales, Memorandum, 2001, 4.

[116] For an extended analysis see MB Fox *Civil Liability and Mandatory Disclosure* (2001).

[117] European Commission Communication (n 72) sub 3.1.4.

legislation imposing liability of issuers who make – by intention or gross negligence – current reports that contain false or misleading information or that are disclosed late, while commentators advocate the additional imposition of personal liability on board members for grossly negligent or intentional publication of information.[118]

E. Conclusion

Both the Winter Report and the European Commission Communication are correct in emphasising the paramount role of disclosure in the Context of company law in general and corporate governance in particular. While the High Level Group's outspoken preference for disclosure over merit regulation is in line with modern international and American standards, the European Commission Communication's rather unprincipled approach diplomatically avoids to strain Continental Member States and their legislatures excessively in advocating a disclosure-first approach. It is unsettled whether such diplomacy will in the end delay the modernization of EU company and securities law to the detriment of European economies and the competitiveness of European markets as well as European companies. Anyway, both propositions need further clarification as well as specification in order to serve as practical guide for European Union rulemaking.

[118] Fleischer (n 96) F 95; Th Baums (ed) Bericht der Regierungskommission Corporate Governance 2001 195.

Chapter 3: Modern Company Law-Making

About Techniques of Regulating Companies in the European Union

EDDY WYMEERSCH

The purpose of this contribution to the study of the Report of the High Level Group of Company Law Experts on 'A modern Regulatory Framework for Company Law In Europe' (the 'Report' or 'Winter Report') is to reflect on the more formal aspects of regulating private companies in Europe. The Report contains some interesting proposals, both for regulating and for deregulating companies, while allowing the use of alternative forms of regulation. As a rule, substantive issues of Company Law in Europe will not be dealt with here.

The first part attempts to give an overview of the main sources of regulation that have an impact on company conduct.

The second part will focus on European law rules that affect the regulation of companies.

The third part will then, in a more general way, outline some ideas for future developments.

A. Regulation of Companies and Their Conduct

1. The subject of regulating companies in Europe raises numerous questions, not only with respect to the type of regulation – public or self regulation, uniform or harmonised rules, model codes, etc – but also with respect to the level at which certain types of conduct are best dealt with. From the Community perspective an increasingly complex apparatus has emerged over time, aimed at Community-wide acceptance of common principles and rules. These efforts have mainly resulted in harmonization directives. The harmonization technique has recently

become the subject of criticism, both from the angle of the policies pursued and from that of the directive as a regulatory device.[1]

Company law harmonization presents some specific characteristics. In other fields, such as the regulation of banking, insurance or in securities regulation, labour relations, and so on, the directives have intervened at the level of detailed national regulatory provisions. As a consequence, government agencies or private regulatory bodies being in charge of applying the national implementing provisions, contribute to the implementation of the directives, and could at an early stage point to deficiencies or call for changes.

In the company law field, there is nothing similar: only as far as listed companies are concerned, market supervisors may be more closely involved in insuring company law orthodoxy. But even there, the attitudes of national supervisors differ from state to state. As to general company law, the majority of the legal provisions have traditionally been laid down in statutes that, by way of mandatory law, or as default rules, have been declared applicable to all entities. Enforcement of the rules is left to the private initiative of the draftsmen of the company documents, of their advisers, including – where applicable – the notaries that draw up the official charter provisions. Previously existing forms of ex ante supervision, as existed eg in the Netherlands or in Italy up to a few years ago, have been abolished.[2] Enforcement most of the time takes place ex post, by way of private litigation, especially through derivative actions[3] and more rarely as a consequence of the intervention of the public prosecutor, acting in the public interest, and this even in the absence of violations of criminal provisions. It will not surprise therefore that implementation of the rules and enforcement is rather haphazard.

Implementing national provisions often are of a general nature, applicable to a heterogeneous population: the Community rules therefore collide with fundamental, cultural or political issues or sensitivities.[4]

[1] For criticism see: L Enriques 'Bad Apples, Bad Oranges: A Comment from Old Europe on Post-Enron Corporate Governance Reforms' (2003) 38 Wake Forest Law Review 911, 918; H Halbhuber 'National Doctrinal Structures and European Company Law' (2001) 38 CML Rev 1385, 1406-07; E Wymeersch 'Company Law in Europe and European Company Law' in *1st European Jurists Forum* (Nomos Verlag 2001) 85; also in 'Gesellschaftsrecht im Wandel, Ursachen und Entwicklungslinien' (2001) ZGR 294.

CWA Timmermans 'Harmonization in the Future of Company Law in Europe' in KJ Hopt and E Wymeersch (eds) *Capital Markets and Company Law* (OUP Oxford 2003) 623-638. Even the ECJ expressed its doubts about some of the Communities Rules: see in the Centros case, infra nr. 21, for the ECJ's analysis of the legal capital rules.

[2] See art 2330 Italian Codice civile. According to the previously applicable law, the tribunal checked whether the company's statutes were in conformity with the law. This was changed by the L 24 November 2000, nr 340: henceforth the registry undertakes a formal verification.

[3] Most European jurisdictions ignore class actions.

[4] The take-over directive and related issues of corporate control are good examples of this type of resistance.

Also, company law harmonization has almost invariably taken the form of full directives.[5] Implementation in national law therefore was in most cases by full legislative act. Flexibility often is absent, leading to more resistance from the member states against any intervention in their legal order. More flexible other forms of intervention – e.g. recommendations, or other alternative techniques of regulation – have not been used.[6] Self-regulation in company law is a rather recent and uncommon phenomenon, and is limited to the world of the listed companies.

Apart form the formal process, the policies underlying these directives have also raised questions: these have not been based on widely discussed policy analyses, whereby both legal, economic, social, and practical arguments would have been taken into consideration, looking at efficiency and cost elements. Harmonization has been most of the time streamlining of the existing national rules, each state pleading for the least change in its own legislation, trying to agree on a common denominator and sometimes 'progressing' but then usually in the sense of stricter regulation. As a consequence, some directive rules are highly controversial and unduly restrictive of business development.[7]

2. Before analysing the ways the European Union could follow to adequately regulate company conduct, it seems useful to dwell for some time on the different types of regulation that are at present applicable to companies. The subject will be dealt with on a Europe wide basis, allowing making abstraction of the details that are specific to any given national system.

The analysis will focus on company law rules, and will not deal with the full range of legal rules or provisions that may be applicable to companies, or their shareholders, directors or auditors. Some of these rules belong to general civil law or common law, to labour law, to criminal law, or to other branches of the legal system. Their understanding may be essential for a precise insight in a national

[5] Except for the European Economic Interest grouping (Council Regulation (EEC) No 2137/85 of 25 July 1985 on the European Economic Interest Grouping (EEIG), OJ L 199, 31/07/1985) and the European Company Statute (Council Regulation (EC) No 2157/2001 of 8 October 2001 on the Statute for a European company (SE).

OJ L 294, 10/11/2001) all European measures in the company law field have taken the form of directives.

[6] See on the subject of alternative regulation in general, the OECD studies on Regulatory Quality and Public Sector Reform, Part of the PUMA project, <http://www1.oecd.org/puma/regref/>, N Lundblad and I Kiefer 'The Economic Efficiency of Self-regulation – Two Case Studies' (2002) available at <http://www.bileta.ac.uk/02papers/lundblad. html>; RD Keleman 'Regulatory Styles: The Diffusion of Adversarial Legalism?' <http://www.upf.es/dcpis/esf/papers.htm>, dealing with several policies at the level of the EU.

[7] One cannot resist to mention the rules on 'financial assistance' in the Second directive: see for an analysis, our paper 'Centros: a landmark decision in European Company Law' in T Baums, KJ Hopt and N Horn (eds) *Corporations, capital markets and business in the law: Liber amicorum Richard M Buxbaum* (Kluwer International London 2000) 629.

legal system, as matters that are dealt with under one set of rules in one jurisdiction, come under a different heading in another.[8] Their analysis would be beyond the scope of the present paper. Also they would be applicable to any form of enterprise, whether organised as a company or not. Only those rules that have a direct impact on the structure or on the functioning of the company as a legal entity will be discussed.

3. In most EU states, company law is laid down in a national Companies Act, a statute dealing with all or most types of companies. Some call these a Companies Code. Other states have specific statutes per company type, rendering the development of general or overriding principles of company law less likely.[9]

In several jurisdictions, these companies acts have been supplemented by implementing decrees, that contain more detailed, often quite technical rules about the functioning of the company or some of its constituent bodies, eg rules on voting in general meetings, use of proxies, mail voting etc. As far as the actual functioning of the company is concerned, no difference has to be made between these two levels of regulation. However, in terms of legislation, these secondary rules usually allow for greater adaptability and flexibility.

At a higher level of regulation, one should also mention international treaties, such as the Friendship and Navigation Treaties[10] that often contain clauses obliging their signatories to mutually recognise their resident companies. These treaties often include 'most favoured nation' clauses, extending the benefit of local regulation to third countries.

Recently the European Court of Justice has drawn the attention to the effect of EU law on companies, especially from the angle of freedom of establishment.[11] The European Convention on Human Rights also may have a bearing on company conduct, in the sense that companies are legal entities that can be considered

[8] A good example are rules limiting majority power, a company law matter in some (under the chapter of group law eg), a criminal matter in other jurisdictions (eg in France under the provisions of 'Abus de biens sociaux' applicable to intragroup dealings: see the Rozenblum and other cases; Cass fr 4 February 1985 (1985) Rev Sociétés 648, note Bouloc (Rozenblum ea); Cass fr 23 April 1991 (1991) Rev Sociétés 785 (Broche); Cass fr 13 February 1989 (1989) Rev Sociétés 693 (Duval); Y Guyon *French Law on Groups of Companies: Current Issues* Forum Internationale (Kluwer Law International 1989) 13.

[9] This methodological subject is not without importance as at the moment of implementation of directives. A certain spill-over effect has been noticed, leading to the application of the directives' provisions to types of companies, or even non-profit organisations other than those intended by the directive. This spill-over effect is especially visible for the rules of the First Company law Directive, addressing third party protection.

[10] See the Friendship, trade and shipping agreements i.a with the US. These agreements usually contain clauses on mutual recognition of companies.

[11] The relatively recent Daily Mail, Centros and Überseering cases have significant impact on company law, and will contribute to more competition between the national companies in the EU member states. See about these cases, further nr 21.

beneficiaries of the treaty's rights and privileges.[12] Also investors or shareholders may be entitled to invoke this Convention's provisions.[13]

Enforcement of these provisions may take different forms[14] depending on the case, sanctioning takes the form of criminal sanctions (fines or imprisonment), civil remedies, declaring null and void any derogation, or imposing civil liability on directors, auditors, or other parties that have contributed to the violation. In all states, substantial case law on these matters exists. Traditionally, sanctions, remedies and enforcement are not dealt with in the EU harmonization directives.[15]

4. Important parts of a company's functioning are governed by related bodies of laws, which, although not exclusively applicable to companies, are mainly targeted at them. Here, one should especially mention the accounting and auditing rules, as addressed only to public and private companies limited. These have to a certain extent been harmonised.[16] The member state's rules will increasingly consist of the International Accounting Standards (or by the International Financial Reporting Standards, or IFRS), after a procedure of 'endorsement' that has

[12] It is generally accepted that the ECHR is applicable to legal entities. This is the case with the rules on fair trial (art 6), free speech, and entitlement to privacy. Article 1 of Protocol 1 specifically refers to 'legal persons'. Important cases in this field are: *Sunday Times v UK* (1979) 2 EHRR 245; *Pine Valley Developments Ltd v Ireland* (1991) 14 EHRR 269; *Air Canada v UK* (1993) 20 EHHR 1550; *Vereinigung Demokratischer Soldaten Österreichs and Gubi v Austria* (1994) 20 EHRR 56; *Agrotexim et al v Greece* (1996) 21 EHRR 250; *British-American Tobacco Company Ltd v the Netherlands* (1995) 10 Interights Bulletin 137; *Pressos Compania Naviera SA and others v Belgium* [1997] IIHRL 68 (3 July 1997). See also MK Addo 'The corporation as a victim of human rights violations' in MK Addo (ed) *Human rights standards and the responsibility of transnational corporations* (Kluwer Law International Den Haag 1999) 187-196; R Clayton and H Tomlinson *The law of human rights* (Oxford University Press New York 2000) 1486-1487, nr 22.20-22.22; S Marcus-Helmons 'L'applicabalité de la Convention européenne des droits de l'homme aux personnes morales' [1996] J T Dr Eur 150-153.

[13] See for the exclusion of shareholders: the French case on squeeze-outs: 10 Cass Com 29 April 1997 (1998) Dalloz 334 comments by Frison-Roche and Nussenbaum; also in Belgium: the Constitutional Court refused to accept discrimination in the rules aplicable to squeeze-outs: Arbitragehof 14 May 2003 nr 64/2003, available at <http://www. arbitrage.be/>.

[14] Companies acts and secondary legislation are enforced by a wide range of instruments, most being ex post such as criminal sanctions, different types of nullity, liability against company organs, while ex ante instruments such as administrative procedures (eg ex ante approval by tribunal, mandatory intervention of a public notary, or of experts, concern specific topics (eg contribution in kind to legal capital).

[15] Often directives only state that appropriate sanctions that have to be provided for by national legislators.

[16] On the basis of the 4th and Seventh Company law directives. However, as to substance, harmonization is quite limited.

been laid down in the EU accounting regulation.[17] However, national accounting rules, based on substantially different domestic principles will continue to apply to consolidated accounts of unlisted groups and to solo accounting.

Many of the rules applicable to the larger companies are directly linked to their status of listed companies. Here one enters the field of securities regulation, in many jurisdictions a complement to traditional company law and applicable only to public issues of securities and to companies whose securities are listed. In the EU, and under the influence of the directives, company law and securities regulation have developed as separate bodies of law, but the dividing line often looks unclear: where take-over bids would be considered to belong to securities regulation in most member states, the EU deals with it from the – apparent – angle of company law.[18] Securities regulation is composed of an often heterogeneous set of national laws, regulations and administrative statements. Its content is partly determined by EU harmonization directives. Technically, and both at the EU level and in the member states' regulation, these two levels of regulation, ie company law and securities regulation are clearly kept separate. In actual company practice however, both sets of rules – and accounting, auditing and tax rules as well – are equally important and are applied simultaneously without regard to the technical difference. From that angle, one could wonder what will be the effects over time of the current approach according to which securities regulation is dealt with according to different, faster and more flexible mechanisms of decision making, implementation and enforcement[19] than company law rules.[20]

Accounting rules – and even more clearly – securities regulatory provisions present a difference v.à.v. traditional company law rules in that dedicated enforcement instruments are available aimed at securing their effective implemen-

[17] On the basis of Regulation 1606/2002 on the application of the International Accounting Standards, OJEC, 11 September 2002, L 243/1. However article 5 allows member states to permit or require these companies to prepare their annual accounts according to IFRS, or other companies to apply IFRS to their consolidated accounts. Endorsement took place on the 29th of September 2003, for all IAS, except for standard 32 and 39. See <http://europa.eu.int/comm/internal_market/accounting/ias_en.htm>.

[18] Under the title of the 13th 'company law' directive.

[19] This would especially apply to the use of Lamfalussy procedures in the field of securities regulation. See Commission Decision 2001/528/EC of 6 June 2001 establishing the Committee of European Securities Regulators (CESR), OJ L 191 of 13/07/2001, 0043 and Commission Decision 2201/529/EC of 6 June 2001 establishing the European Securities Committee (ESC), OJ L 191 of 13/07/2001, 0045. See N Moloney *EC Securities Regulation* (OUP New York 2002) 883 ff; S Mohamed 'A Single Regulator for the E.C. Financial Market' (2001) 8 and 9 JIBL 204; K Lannoo 'Supervising the European Financial System' available at <www.ceps.be>.

[20] One example among many: the MAD directive contains rules on insider trading, or on the repurchase of own shares. Market practices dealing with allotment techniques, claw backs, 'green shoes' and the like are usually considered part of securities regulation, but their effect is of significant importance to the issuers as well. See the CESR paper 'Stabilisation and Allotment – a European Supervisory Approach' of 9 April 2002, available <www.europefesco.org>.

tation. In both cases, implementation in first instance calls for increasingly focused judgment by the company's board. The role of the auditor is essential in insuring that the accounting rules are followed even if the company's management would have mixed feelings about it. This difference is even more striking for securities regulatory provisions, which most of the time are enforced by a public agency, eg by making its approval dependent on the company respecting its interpretation of the general disclosure duties as laid down in the regulation itself. Compared to core company law, both flexibility and strength of enforcement for these sets of rules are significantly higher.[21] In practice however, securities agencies will often extend their action to company law or to accounting rules,[22] which underlines that the distinction between the two sets of provisions is largely historical. It is therefore a question for debate whether it is useful to further differentiate company law and securities regulation, or whether one should not rather distinguish depending on the type of company applying the rules, especially whether the company is listed or not. That subject is discussed infra.[23]

5. A separate class of provisions affecting a company's functioning would be the rules on exchange listing: normally, these would be classified in the section 'securities regulation'. Differences reside in the identity of the body in charge of implementation, often the stock exchange, sometimes even after it has been privatised.[24] Also, at EU level, a different directive – on listing particulars[25] – has dealt with this subject.

[21] One can recently see a tendency for a specialised external agency in charge of reviewing company accounting and disclosure, not only in the US (PCAOB or the Public Company Accounting Oversight Board, see <http://www.pcaob.com>) but also in Europe: see in Belgium, art 4 of the Act of 2 August 2002 on Corporate Governance, also in France: art. 100 of the 'law of 1 August 2003 'sur la sécurité financière' available at <http://ameli.senat.fr/publication_pl/2002-2003/166.html>, instituting a 'Haut Conseil du Commissariat aux Comptes' with extensive disciplinary powers. It organises a very strict separation between auditing and consulting activities.

[22] In some jurisdictions, the securities market supervisor can also intervene in accounting matters, sometimes systematically vetting the accounts.

[23] See nr 30 ff.

[24] This is still the case in the Netherlands – where plans exist for revising the law – and in Belgium, although their stock exchanges have been privatised and are now part of Euronext. In the UK, the FSA acts as listing authority and has provisionally maintained the former listing rules of the LSE. See <http://www.fsa.gov.uk/ukla/1_role.html>.

[25] Originally the 1979 Directive (Council Directive 79/279/EEC of 5 March 1979 coordinating the conditions for the admission of securities to official stock exchange listing OJ L 066 16/03/79 21), later amalgamated in the Directive 2001/34/EC of the European Parliament and of the Council on the admission of securities to official stock exchange listings and on information to be published on those securities (OJ L 184 06/07/2001). For an extensive comment, N Moloney (n 19) 91 ff.

It is useful to make a separate mention of listing rules as these often dig deep into a company's organisational structure and internal affairs.

The rule calling for listing of all of the outstanding shares – only recently made mandatory by some exchanges – may affect the relations between shareholders as these refused to list a certain percentage of their shares in order to render a sale on the market more cumbersome, hence protecting some shareholders against their partners surreptitiously selling out. This was an indirect safeguard against unfaithful signatories of shareholder agreements.

In some states, the UK being the best-known example, listing took place on the basis of an elaborate 'listing agreement'. Hence the listing rules were adapted to the specific characteristics of the individual company. The listing rules contain substantive provisions on control relations, defined as holding 30% or more of the voting stock.[26] Shareholders holding a larger percentage of shares will be under a duty to abstain from exercising significant influence, what one could call 'neutralising control'. This provision is based on the listing agreement and constitutes a conduct rule subscribed by the shareholder towards the market. It is not yet clear to what extent the FSA will continue to impose similar provisions.

In some member states, self-regulatory codes comparable to listing agreements have governed the subject of take-overs, especially mandatory take-overs. These instruments have appeared to be too weak to contain the explosive forces at work in a take-over situation. Hence government regulation was considered indispensable.[27]

6. Agreements among shareholders are direct sources of rights and duties for their signatories. The articles of association constitute the primary agreement among shareholders. The freedom left to the shareholders in their articles of association, and the extent to which they can derogate from the provisions of the companies' act, is the subject of discussion and differences among the EU member states.[28] It is generally known that German AG law has a very strict approach

[26] Compare the similar threshold in the City Code on Take-overs and Mergers: a take-over will be mandated if the shareholder crosses said threshold (§ 9 of the Code).

[27] See the German act on takeovers of 2001. For an extensive commentary see: W Haarmann, K Riehmer and M Schüppen (eds) *Öffentliche Übernahmeangebote – Kommentar zum WpÜG* (Recht und Wirschaft Verlag Heidelberg 2002) Also: ZGR, European Company Law Review – Übernahmerecht, August 2002. Before this act, the subject was dealt with in a voluntary code, the acceptance of which conditioned listing on the Dax (Übernahmekodex der Börsensachverständigenkommission (1997)). See: KJ Hopt 'Auf dem Weg zum deutschen Übernahmegesetz' *FS Zöller* (Heymanns Cologne 1999) 253. A similar attempt was made in Germany with respect to insider transaction rules: it was equally unsuccessful: see KJ Hopt and M Will *Europäisches Insiderrecht* (Enke Stuttgart 1973).

[28] For an overview of the status in some member states, see the series of articles in ZGR, European Company Law Review 'Grenzüberschreitende Sitzverlegung von Gesellschaften in Europa' January 1999, 3-165. See for an overview: E Wymeersch 'The Transfer of the Company's Seat in European Company Law' (2003) CMLR, 661.

severely limiting the parties' freedom to develop rules in the articles of association that would derogate from the companies act's provisions. Many other states allow significant freedom. Therefore standard formulas of articles of association have been developed in notary or attorney practice. These have a value as the 'usual practice', therefore considered acceptable, and could be somehow compared to model acts.

In some states these articles contain significant rules modelling the shareholders legal position: so eg may the benefit of a mandatory take-over bid be made dependent on a provision in the articles of association.[29]

This need for flexibility and the will to free oneself from the strait jacket of the EU directives, has incited some states to introduce a separate form of company that would not be subject to the directives. The case of the French '*société par actions simplifiée*' is well known: it is a more flexible type of limited liability company that is not subject to the strict rules of the EU directives that apply to the '*société anonyme*'. This type of intra-company competition is a phenomenon that deserves a separate analysis that cannot be undertaken here.

Shareholders, mostly the most important ones, often conclude agreements in which they agree on important aspects of company life, such as a pay-out ratio, their representation on the board, matters subject to their approval before the board decision, rights of objection against the appointment of certain staff members, rights relating to transfer of shares, such as rights of first refusal, etc. The validity of these agreements may be open for debate. In practice these agreements often are respected de facto because their signatories have a mutual interest in respecting them.

Usually, most of these agreements remain hidden to the other shareholders, to the public and even to the supervisors. Disclosure would often be required if these agreements relate to control, including transfer of the shares.[30] There are good arguments for widening the scope of this disclosure duty as far as listed companies are concerned.[31]

[29] In Sweden, the 2003 'Recommendation concerning public offers for the acquisition of shares' has recommended a take-over upon crossing the 40% threshold. See JL Hansen (ed) *Nordic Financial Market Law* (Djof Publishing Copenhagen 2003) 299 ff.

[30] cf Council Directive 88/627/EEC of 12 December 1988 on the information to be published when a major holding in a listed company is acquired or disposed of, OJ L 348, 17/12/1988, 62-65, which provides that, where a person acquires or disposes of a shareholding of which the voting rights reach, exceed or fall below one of the thresholds of 10%, 20%, 1/3, 50% and 2/3, he shall notify the company and the competent authority within seven days (Article 4). The directive is in the process of being revised: see proposal for a transparency directive <http://www.europa.eu.int/eur-lex/pri/en/lip/latest/doc/2003/com2003_0138en01.doc>.

[31] This was suggested by the European Commission in 'Modernising Company Law and Enhancing Corporate Governance in the European Union – A Plan to Move Forward' (Communication from the Commission to the Council and the European Parliament, May 2003, COM (2003) 284 final) 12 (see Annex 1 in this volume).

It has been decided that agreements among or with shareholders are not binding on the company: if third parties would derive claims from these agreements, these would not be enforceable against the company, but only against the shareholders.[32]

7. Apart from agreements among shareholders, there may also be agreements among board members, whether or not formally laid down in regulations of the board. Internal board regulations are explicitly recognised in German company law. They are also known in other jurisdictions, as rules on the internal organisation of the board. Usually these rules would not require shareholder approval, and could be modified by a simple board decision.[33] Some boards have eg adopted policies on internal governance matters, conflicts of interest, or on avoiding insider trading by their members.[34]

Of a similar nature are the board's decisions relating to the exercise of its competences. Boards may eg create special board committees, or organise its work through internal working procedures, eg on conflicts of interest. Said committees are merely internal bodies preparing board decisions, and do not have legal competences.[35] They advise the board, the final decision being rendered by the board as a whole. Serious questions about the civil liability of committee members would be raised if final decisions are taken by the committee.

8. Company conduct is also increasingly determined by 'codes of conduct' or similar instruments whether these have been drafted by the board or by third parties. Codes on corporate governance have been issued by the stock exchanges, by business associations, or even international organisations (such as the OECD Principles of Corporate Governance[36]). These codes may deal with a broad range

[32] See Cass B 28 January 1985, RPS, 1987, nr 6430 n 117, note Mougenot; Brussels, 8 January 1986, RW 1986-87, 119; RPS, 1987, nr 6418, 27.

[33] See on this subject: H Laga *Statuten, statutenwijziging en reglement van inwendige orde getoetst aan algemene beginselen van contractenrecht: een toepassing op de coöperatieve vennootschap* (1991) Thesis Faculteit Rechtsgeleerdheid, Leuven.

[34] See the regulation applicable pursuant to art 27 of the Belgian banking Act: C Van Acker 'De wet van 3 mei 2002 tot wijziging van de onverenigbaarheidsregeling voor bestuurders van kredietinstellingen en beleggingsondernemingen' in M Tison, C Van Acker and J Cerfontaine (eds) *Financiële Regulering: op zoek naar nieuwe evenwichten* (Intersentia Gent 2002) 259.

[35] In certain legislations, a shift towards decision-making by board committees is visible: see (§§ 202 or 301 of the Sarbanes-Oxley Act with respect to the Audit Committee; more limited, the Belgian law, where the audit commitee could allow the auditor to cross the 1 to 1 relationship for non-audit fees (art 133, § 5 Companies Act).

[36] Although addressed primarily to governments, the Principles can also be used by private sector parties that have a role in developing corporate governance systems and best practices. See Preamble at 8. The Principles, in the process of revision, can be downloaded at <http://www.oecd.org/EN/home/0,,EN-home-28-nodirectorate-no-no--28,00.html>.

of issues, among which governance is only one of the best known. One also finds codes dealing with ethical conduct in general,[37] with foreign or domestic bribery, ecological policy, timely payments, and so on. Self-regulation is often embedded in professional associations or in contractual relations linking companies to securities markets. Today, the associative structure is less frequently found in relation to securities matters,[38] but it has dominated regulation of securities trading for a large part of the last century.[39]

These codes belong to the wider category of self-regulatory instruments that may be considered applicable to company conduct. Self-regulation is a subject on its own, and will therefore not be dealt with in detail in this overview. Suffice it to say that there are numerous forms of self-regulation. Differences in terms of enforcement constitute an important guiding line for further differentiating between self-regulatory instruments.

9. Enforcement mechanisms for self-regulatory codes are numerous and often quite sophisticated. They would usually depend on the type of self-regulation that has been developed, more specifically the status of the instrument within the legal system.

Self-regulatory instruments that are purely voluntary, ie based on the voluntary adherence of the company to a system of rules or norms[40] would not call for sanctions other than public stigma. However, even this legally weak sanctioning may be effective for companies that are listed and traded on the securities markets, where the company's reputation constitutes a value on its own. In general, listed companies, but also financial institutions such as banks and insurance companies whose business is dependent on their reputation, are keen to present themselves as adhering to good and honourable conduct, inspiring public confidence. Enforcement takes places through the market, whether the securities market or the product or services market, or more widely, public opinion in general.

A special variety of market enforcement occurs through comparative analysis: company practices have been described, analysed and compared in academic or business studies, leading to rankings, eg on disclosure, on accounting or on governance practices. Listed companies are willing to compete for excellence and hence these rankings have an influence on their conduct. This technique has

[37] Especially with conflicts of interest in the broad sense. See <http://www.oecd.org>.

[38] Due to demutualisation of stock exchanges in general.

[39] One could mention here the 1970 German rules on insider trading (*Insiderhandelsrichtlinien*) See Hopt and Will (n 27) at 111. The German Insider Trading code, which although having received some attention in the press, has been considered largely ineffective.

[40] Whether these have been fixed by the company itself, or by a third party, such as a professional association.

recently been taken one step further by rating agencies,[41] large institutional investors or investor protection associations.[42] These organisations include the results of their comparative studies in their rating valuation or investment strategies applicable to listed companies. The actual effect of these techniques is indirect and should be considered part of the impact of the rating agencies, or of the investor organisations' influence on investment strategies.

10. An often used instrument of indirect enforcement is the 'comply or explain' technique, whereby non-adherents have to declare explicitly whether or not they comply with a stated series of principles or rules and state the reasons for not complying. This technique has been applied – with variable effectiveness – to corporate governance codes: companies are invited to state the reasons for which they have abstained from respecting the rules as stated in the code. The advantage is clear: it allows the code to be mildly mandatory, while divergent practices can be maintained, if good reasons underpin them. However, in practice it appears that the motives advanced for not complying are not always credible, while there is no enforcement instrument against those companies that flatly refuse. Public stigma – 'name and shame' – will then be insufficient.

Conduct rules that are part of the listing conditions can be expected to allow more efficient enforcement. Enforcement of listing requirements[43] is obviously quite easy at the moment of listing: in practice, as all exchanges compete for business, upholding the requirements might tend to become flexible. Later on, enforcement may be problematic: fines, 'name and shame' disclosure, and ultimately delisting are the usual enforcement instruments. Delisting however is

[41] See Standard and Poor's Governance Services publishing S&P's Corporate Governance Scores.

[42] <http://www.deminor.org>. The Ratings are allocated on the basis of an extensive analysis grid of over 300 indicators, developed and continuously updated in collaboration with Deminor clients. Clients receive on-line access to 300 extensive Company Reports and Ratings, 17 Country Reports, the Deminor Rating Guidelines and the European Report, an overview of all major findings of the Research and Ratings. On request, the coverage can be extended to companies outside the FTSE Eurotop 300.

[43] This may be the more interesting as some of these listing requirements are the implementation of the EU directive on listing particulars (directive of 1979/2000). Some of these requirements implement the EU directives rules, eg on listing conditions (directive of 1979/2000, see note 14). So eg were the rules on corporate governance applicable to companies traded on Nasdaq Europe (Nasdaq Europe was regulated according to Belgian law) substantially stricter than those officially supported by the market supervisors; also this is the only Belgian market segment that obliges its listed companies to publish quarterly reports. In both cases enforcement takes place by the market organiser. Whether it would give rise to third party liability is a point of controversy.

often more detrimental to the investors than to the unwilling management. Moreover, the company will protest that its shareholders are hurt.[44]

To the extent that the self-regulatory instrument has been introduced with the support of the public authorities, these may also lend their strong arm to promote – but not necessarily ensure – their application. Apart from moral pressure, the securities supervisor may, in individual cases, call attention to these provisions, or publish tables indicating the degree of de facto implementation or compliance with the code by the listed companies. The use of the legal instruments to enforce these codes would call for additional specific rules.[45]

11. In some jurisdictions, government regulation refers to self-regulatory instruments. This intermediate and more effective form of self-regulation may take the form of the law, or a government agency spelling out the principles while referring to internal self regulatory implementation by the company, addressee of the regulation.[46] While the public regulation would call for adequate procedures for the preventing eg insider trading, or for rules dealing with conflicts of interest, the implementation will be effectuated by the addressee companies in its internal procedures and compliance mechanisms. The choice between different approaches (eg trading windows, restricted lists, or others to be developed by the company) is left to the company, while it is made responsible for adequate compliance and, where applicable, disclosure. The government agency reviews the internal rules as to their consistency with its regulation and with respect to the effectiveness of the company's supervision, but does not intervene in its surveillance in practice. In case of violation, apart from the general sanctions, internal instruments, including those based on labour law would be applicable.

12. The international aspects of self-regulation can be referred to only very briefly here. International organisations are frequently making use of regulatory instruments without a legally binding nature. The OECD Guidelines on multi-

[44] See about German Porsche's refusal to publish quarterly reports and the subsequent the lawsuit with Deutsche Börse 'Porsche Faces Delisting from Index As Deutsche Boerse Readies Decision' <http://www.cfo.com/article/1,5309,4480%7C%7CA%7C7%7C1,00. html.

[45] These may be based on the idea of a second line of supervision: without directly enforcing the provision, the supervisor will hold the market organiser accountable for adequately enforcing its own self-regulatory provisions.

[46] This approach has been developed recently in Belgian law (Act of 3 May 2002, for a commentary see C Van Acker at n 30). In a recent example stemming from Belgian banking supervision the following scheme was followed. The law itself laid down the subject matters to be regulated (eg the avoidance of conflicts of interest, extending to insider trading issues). On the basis of the law, the banking supervisor drafted an elaborate instruction. The Companies were urged to draft a self-regulatory code dealing with the subject. This code should respond to the general instruction, without being necessary identical to the instruction. Supervision would relate to the implementation of he instruction, not necessarily to the respect of the substantive obligations flowing from it.

national enterprises and its Codes on bribery[47] and on Corporate Governance can be mentioned as examples.[48] Enforcement takes place through different channels. One can only refer to the abundant legal writing on the first mentioned Guidelines.[49] With respect to the OECD corporate governance code it is useful to mention that its enforcement is supported by the ROSC programmes of the IMF.[50] The impact of these efforts is significant especially in transition economies.[51]

13. The role of the securities markets has already been alluded to. They play an increasingly significant and converging[52] role in moulding company conduct. Here one leaves the field of regulation: market practices, especially in the cross border segments of the markets have a tendency to cross-fertilize and develop 'generally accepted practices' that are often inspired by international – in practice largely inspired by American – market practices. The content of prospectuses, the frequency and timing of other forms of disclosure, alternative financing mecha-

[47] OECD Convention on Combating Bribery of Foreign Public Officials in International Business Transactions, available at <http://www.oecd.org/oecd/pages/home/displaygeneral/0,3380,EN-document-88-3-no-no-7198-88,00.html>.

[48] OECD Principles of Corporate Governance, <http://www.oecd.org/pdf/M00008000/M00008299.pdf>, stating that the principles can be used by government 'as they evaluate and improve their corporate governance laws and regulations' and by private parties 'in developing corporate governance systems and best practices'.

[49] R Blanpain 'Review of the OECD guidelines for multinational enterprises' in *DEELSA/ELSA(99)4* (OECD Paris 1999) 4 – 41; 'Guidelines for Multinational Enterprises, for Ever? The OECD Guidelines, 20 years later' in *The International Journal of Comparative Labour Law and Industrial Relations* (volume 14/4 1998) 337-348; 'Review of the OECD Guidelines for Multinational Enterprises. Possible revisions to the chapter on employment and industrial relations', *DEELSA/ELSA(99)4*, 4-41 (OECD Paris 1999); 'Review of the OECD Guidelines for Multinational Enterprises: Possible revisions to the chapter on employment and industrial relations' in *Multinational Enterprises and the Social Challenges of the XXIst Century, Bulletin of Comparative Labour Relations* (Kluwer Law International The Hague 2000) nr 37, 29-66; 'Guidelines for Multinational Enterprises, Forever? The OECD Guidelines, 20 years later' in *New Trends of Labour Law in International Horizon, Liber Amicorum for Prof. Dr. Tadashi Hanami* (Shinzansya Tokyo 2000); 'Examen des principes directeurs de l'OCDE à l'intention des entreprises multinationales. Propositions de révisions du chapitre sur l'emploi et les relations professionnelles' in *DEELSA/ELSA(99)4* (OECD Paris 2000).

[50] IMF Reports on the Observance of Standards and Codes (ROSCs), <http://www.imf.org/external/np/rosc/rosc.asp>, some of which are expressly dealing with the OECD governance code. See at <http://www.oecd.org/home/>.

[51] See for the OECD Corporate Governance Codes, the conferences organised by the OECD in different former Soviet Union states.

[52] There is wide debate on convergence especially on corporate governance due to the action of the securities markets: see J McCahery, P Moerland, T Raaijmakers and L Renneboog (eds) *Corporate Governance Regimes, Convergence and Diversity* (OUP Oxford 2002).

nisms,[53] company practices dealing with conflicts of interest, procedures to be developed for take-overs, mergers, squeeze-outs and other similar transactions[54] are increasingly streamlined along widely accepted business practices. These practices have not yet reached the status of obligatory 'accepted practices'[55] but are widely followed and tend to become the norm. Enforcement is based on market assessment, on peer pressure, on economic forces (eg refusal of the banks to take part on the basis of a conflict of interest, liability of directors, of auditors,[56] of lawyers) and in some cases even on the support of the public authorities. In some cases, these market driven practices have developed contrary to the general purport of the applicable law, eg in the fields of pre-emptive subscription rights, or financial assistance for the acquisition of shares by the issuer company.[57]

[53] See for the use of equity financing techniques other than provided for by the companies act in France: 'Rapport Lepetit sur les nouvelles formules d'augmentation de capital', available at <http://www.laprofessioncomptable.com/pages/ACTUNORMEDOSS/ CobLepetit.pdf>.

[54] One could mention here the use of 'fairness opinions' and the ensuing issues relating to conflicts of interest, modelled on international practice. With respect to the issues raised by fairness opinions see: MW Martin 'Fairness opinions and negligent misrepresentation: defining investment bankers' duty to third-party shareholders' (1991) 60 Fordham L Rev 133; CM Elson 'Fairness opinions: are they fair or should we care?' (1992) 53 Ohio St LJ 951; TJ Fiflis 'Responsibility of investment bankers to shareholders' (1992) 70 Wash U L Q 497; HM Wachtell 'Investment banker liability to shareholders in the sale-of-control context' (1990) NYLJ 29 March 1990, at 1; LA Bebchuk and M Kahan 'Fairness opinions: how fair are they and what can be done about it?' [1989] Duke L J 27; WJ Carney 'Fairness opinions: how fair are they and why we should do nothing about it' (1992) 70 Wash U LQ 523 (1992); M Schuldt 'A statutory proposal for the regulation of fairness opinions in corporate control transactions' (1991) 56 Mo L Rev 110.

[55] See with respect to the issue whether a due diligence is accepted practice for a eurobond issue: Brussels, Commercial Court, 26 March 1997 (1997) 5 Bank Fin 334-340, in which it was held that a due diligence is no accepted practice in those circumstances. This was confirmed by the Court of Appeal of Brussels on 8 March 2002. The plaintiffs have now taken the case to the Belgium Cour de Cassation.

[56] But recent events in the financial markets may also so much undermine confidence in the system that hard law becomes necessary: see the recent discussion on auditor independence, subject of an EU recommendation (Commission Recommendation of 16 May 2002: 'Statutory Auditors' Independence in the EU: A Set of Fundamental Principles' (notified under document number C(2002) 1873) OJ L 191 19.07.2002, 0022 – 0057 <http://europa.eu.int/smartapi/cgi/sga_doc?smartapi!celexapi!prod!CELEXnumdoc&lg=EN&numdoc=32002H0590&model=guichett>; but already implemented in several states by hard law rules: in Belgium: L. 2 August 2002, art. 4; in France: see the law of 1 August 2003 (n 21). The development is parallel, although different, from the discussion about the same topic under the Sarbanes-Oxley Act.

[57] Significantly, these are two items on which the Winter Reports calls for substantial overhaul of the existing regulation, rooted in the 2nd company law directive. For further details see E Wymeersch 'Company law in Europe and European Company law' (2001) 1st European Jurist Forum (Nomos V 87). The subject of the legal capital has received attention from several

cont. ...

14. Some of the provisions of these codes have a tendency to migrate. The migration however goes both ways. Easily visible is the upside movement: corporate governance codes are being increasingly incorporated in standard company law. This phenomenon can be observed in all fields in which soft law instruments were developed: the soft law phase often is a preliminary maturation and experimentation phase towards final introduction into hard law.

The opposite direction is less visible, as it develops in the margin of the hard law. In some fields, obviously less frequently, practices develop that 'circumvent' the strict provisions of the official statute. In the field of placing of securities, the pre-emptive subscription rights have been largely hollowed out by financial practice placing the shares at market price with institutional investors.[58] The restrictions on companies acquiring their own shares have equally led to creative developments.

The flexibility of soft law instruments allows for an easier incorporation of these evolutionary shifts.

15. Internal company practices are at the lowest level of governing company conduct, but are by no means the least important.[59]

B. The Regulation of Companies at the EU Level

16. Company law in Europe is essentially the national law of the Member states. There is no European company law as such. However, there are some Treaty

legal writers, especially F Kübler *Aktie, Unternehmensfinanzierung und Kapitalmarkt* (Bank Verlag Cologne 1989) 49 and 64; 'Aktienrechtsreform und Unternehmensverfassung' [1994] AG 141; F Kübler, M Mendelson and R Mundheim 'Die Kosten des Bezugsrechts: Eine rechtsökonomische Analyse des amerikanischen Erfahrungsmaterials' [1990] AG 461; F Kübler 'The rules on capital under the pressure of the securities markets' in KJ Hopt and E Wymeersch (eds) *Capital Markets and Company Law* (OUP Oxford 2003). Also E Ferran 'Legal Capital Rules under the Pressure of the Securities Markets – The Case for Reform, as illustrated by the UK Equity Markets' in KJ Hopt and E Wymeersch (eds) *Capital Markets and Company Law* (OUP Oxford 2003) 115-144; P Davies 'Legal Capital in Private Companies in Great Britain' [1998] AG 346; L Enriques 'As simple as it may be: the case against the Second Company Law Directive Provisions on Legal Capital' Manuscript Bologna 2000. For a critical comparative study of European and American rules, see L Enriques and JR Macey 'Creditors versus Capital Formation: the Case against the European Capital Rules' (2001) 86 Cornell Law Review 1165.

[58] See on these E Wymeersch 'Das Bezugsrecht der alten Aktionäre in der Europäischen Gemeinschaft' (1998) 8 AG 382-393; E Ferran 'Legal Capital Rules and Modern Securities Markets – the Case for Reform, as Illustrated by the U.K. Equity Markets' (n 57). See also the French 'Rapport Lepetit sur les nouvelles formules d'augmentation de capital' available at <http://www.laprofessioncomptable.com/pages/ACTUNORMEDOSS/CobLepetit. pdf>.

[59] See for further analysis: E Rock and ML Wachter 'Norms and Corporate Law' (2001) 149 University of Pennsylvania L R.

provisions that directly affect company law, while the Community has enacted secondary legislation directed, most of the time, to national legislators.

Company law being essentially national law, both form and substance differ from member state to member state. Although technically different, the 15 company law statutes present many similarities, whether because they originate from fundamentally similar legal systems, or because the rules have been harmonised pursuant to European company law directives. The outcome remains however an undeniable variety of different company law provisions: practising lawyers would normally not dare to give an opinion on company law matters under another EU jurisdiction than their own. One can identify some legislative 'families': the Nordic states have adopted a significantly identical legislation.[60] German and Austrian law share common roots. The same applies to French, Belgian and Luxembourg law. More generally, the Latin European states – especially Spain, Portugal and Italy – share many common concepts, although formulation and details may be quite different. The UK law is closer to Irish law than to that of any other EU state.

17. The involvement of the European Union in company law matters is a limited one. Apart form the general provisions allowing the Community to harmonise legislation in general,[61] the Treaty does not deal with company law as such, but approaches the position of companies in terms of freedom of establishment in a cross border context. The Treaty's central provision is article 44 (2) (g), (ex art. 54), which is part of the Title III on the 'Freedom of Persons, Services and Capital', under its chapter 2. It provides:

> 44. 2 The Council and the Commission shall carry out the duties devolving upon them under the preceding provisions, in particular: the abolition of restrictions on the freedom of establishment of nationals of a member state in the territory of another member state,
>
> ...
>
> (g) by co-ordinating to the necessary extent the safeguards which, for the protection of the interests of members and others, are required by Member States of companies or firms within the meaning of the second paragraph of Article 48 with a view of making such safeguards equivalent throughout the Community.

[60] This is striking in the Northern states where the rules are largely similar, if not identical. See for a useful comparison between company law statutes of the Northern European States: JL Hansen *Nordic Company Law* (Djøf Publishing Copenhagen 2003).

[61] The Commission could also have used arts 94 and 95 (ex article 100) whereby it is granted broad legal powers to proceed to harmonization of all provisions that directly affect the establishment or functioning of the common market. This provision has not been invoked in company law matters.

In the same chapter, the Treaty identifies the entities that it considers beneficiaries of the freedom of establishment. Paragraph 1 of art. 48 (ex 58) provides:

> Companies or firms formed in accordance with the law of a Member State and having their registered office, central administration or principal place of business within the Community shall, for the purposes of this Chapter, be treated in the same way as natural persons who are nationals of Member States.[62]

On the basis of these provisions, numerous directives and other legal instruments have been enacted that have mandated member states to introduce 'harmonised' rules into their national company laws.

18. From the position of these articles in the overall Treaty one can infer that these essentially deal with removing obstacles to the free circulation of companies and other legal entities within the community thereby contributing to the creation of the internal market. In that perspective, the mandate would have been to ensure that companies are 'recognised' in other jurisdictions, or at least have the same freedom to act in all states, that merge, also on a cross border basis, while having the freedom to move from one state to another, especially by way of transferring their seat.

In fact another approach has been followed consisting of developing largely identical (ie 'harmonised') company law rules that would have resulted in facilitating cross border establishment while resulting in a single company law all over Europe. By imposing similar rules in each of the states, the safeguards for shareholders, creditors and employees would have been largely identical, thereby realising the intermediate objective mentioned in art 44 (3)(g). This article would lead to more or less comparable – albeit not identical – legislation. It would however not open up access to other member states' company law systems, nor markets.

Indirectly this policy aimed at avoiding the risk of regulatory arbitrage and the much feared race for laxity, referred to as the 'Delaware effect'. In the early years of the Community, especially Dutch company law often was referred to as very lax, hence attracting business to the detriment of other states. Paradoxically, the harmonization mandate was interpreted by the founding member states as allowing the introduction of a cartel like mechanism, whereby 'harmonization' was used as an instrument for reducing competition among the states and forbidding them to offer more flexible, less taxing requirements.[63] As time went by and the integration of the markets increased, this policy proved to be fruitless and unrealistic. Indeed it would have called for the harmonization of all provisions of com-

[62] Paragraph 2 adds: 'Companies or firms', meaning 'companies or firms constituted under civil or commercial law, including cooperative societies, and other legal persons governed by public or private law, save for those which are non-profit-making'.

[63] CWA Timmermans *Company Law as Ius Commune* Walter Van Gerven Lecture, Leuven, Centre for Common Law of Europe (Intersentia Antwerp 2002).

pany law, and its implementation, an objective that is unachievable and for policy purposes, ineffective. As a consequence, forty-five years later, company law harmonization has lost its direction. This state of affairs became apparent during the discussions preceding the Winter report, especially at the December 1997 hearing[64] on company law. It led to the installation of the Winter Committee, in an effort to redraw the road map towards integration.

19. The founding fathers of the European Community had a clear view on the matter. In article 293 (ex 220) of the Rome Treaty, the member states are urged to enter into negotiations on a certain number of topics, some of which directly concern company law: the mutual recognition of companies, the maintenance of legal personality in case of a cross border transfer of the company seat or the possibility to enter into cross border mergers. These were – and still are – the principal measures for liberalising the market for companies. However, member states have not been able to agree on these measures. An early attempt to agree on mutual recognition failed, due to the absence of ratification of the Treaty by the Netherlands. The attempt was not pursued after the second wave of member states joined, in 1973.

20. Of crucial importance has proved to be article 48 of the Treaty (ex 58) laying down the basic principle that for the purposes of the chapter on freedom of establishment, companies should be dealt with on the same basis as natural persons that are nationals of the member states. The provision is of importance, not so much because it introduces the rule of equal treatment with natural persons, but especially because it deals with all companies within the EU, irrespective of whether they have their registered office or their central administration or even their principal place of business in the Community. This triple formulation allows to bridge the traditional and long standing controversy between the incorporation and the real seat doctrine, controversy on which the mentioned 1968 treaty on mutual recognition had run aground.

The crucial importance of the triple criterion of art 48 (1) has been illustrated by a series of European Court of Justice cases, in which the Court has taken a deliberate stand on the issue of cross border company transactions, thereby unblocking some of the most controversial subjects and on which member states had not been able to agree, sometimes for decades. Before briefly mentioning these cases, it is useful to mention that all were submitted to the Court by the national judiciary within the framework of a referral for a preliminary ruling (art 234 of the Treaty). The ECJ decisions refer only to the interpretation of rules of European law, not of national law, but confront the latter with the superior European legal order. The Court's decision is binding on the national jurisdiction at

[64] Acts of the Conference on Company Law and the Single Market, 15 and 16 December 1997, Office for Official Publications of the EC, 1998.

least in the case at hand: the national judge has to make a final ruling on the basis of the Court's interpretation. In practice the Court rulings are considered to be generally applicable law.

21. The four important cases that have been rendered up to now in this field are referred to as *Daily Mail*, *Centros*, *Überseering* and *Inspire Art*.

In *Daily Mail*[65], the Court had to decide, in light of the articles on freedom of establishment (52 and 58 at that moment), to what extent a UK company could be refused the transfer of its central management and control to another state. The UK tax authorities had subjected the company's decision to its consent, as the company had planned to transfer its management to the Netherlands, where a more favourable tax regime would have been applicable. On the basis of a very elaborate reasoning, the Court decided that the cited Treaty articles confer no such right, in the absence of a treaty on the basis of article 220 (now 295). It held that 'the Treaty regards the difference in national legislation concerning the required connecting factor and whether the registered office or real head office ... may be transferred ... as problems which are not resolved by the rules of establishment but must be dealt with by future legislation or conventions.'

Although it solved few problems, the decision has long been regarded as stating the Court's opinion on issues of nationality of companies. In fact, as was later clarified in *Überseering*, the Court had been too elaborate in its reasoning, especially in dealing with the conflict of law theories. Furthermore, the case did not involve the transfer of the seat: the company, having been formed in an incorporation state, could not have transferred its seat, but merely established a centre of administration in the other state, not affecting its legal status, but merely its tax position. Later the Court restated its opinion declaring that the treaty rules did not affect the relationship between a state and its corporate entities, formed under its jurisdiction, and that this matter did not concern freedom of establishment. Indeed any legislation is free to deal with its own legal entities and to determine the conditions on which it grants, or refuses legal personality.

22. The *Centros* case[66] was a more typical cross border establishment case. A UK private company limited had been formed in the UK with a minimum legal capital. It exercised no activity there, but applied for opening an office, its principal office, in Denmark. The Danish authorities refused to register the company, as the company had not complied with Danish law, requiring 250 fold more capital. The Court qualified the case under the freedom of establishment rules: therefore the company should be allowed to register and trade in Denmark. However, the

[65] *The Queen v HM Treasury and Commissioners of Inland revenue, ex parte Daily Mail and General Trust plc* Judgment of 27 September 1988, Case 81/87 ECR 1988, 5483.

[66] *Centros Ltd and Erhvervs-og Selskabsstyrelsen* Judgement of 9 March 1999, Case C 212/97, ECR, I-1459.

Court analysed on what grounds the Danish registrar could have refused: fraud and circumvention, or the 'general good' exception were identified as the grounds on which national legislation could validly have imposed additional requirements. The case was considered in legal writing as the first significant step towards the Court's preference for the incorporation doctrine.

23. The *Überseering* case[67] is the most recent one in the row: here a Dutch company sued a German contractor in payment for deficient building works. The company had clearly transferred its centre of business to Germany and its shares had been bought by German citizens. The German court refused the company access to court: it held that the company, having its seat in Germany should have reincorporated according to German law, and in the absence of such re-incorporation, being a Dutch company, German law would consider it inexistent. Here the European Court of Justice clearly held the German theory, based on the strictest reading of the real seat doctrine, contrary to the Treaty as it would have resulted in the negation of the existence of a company, although this company had been validly formed in another member state. There is some discussion in Germany, as some are continuing to argue that the Court merely decided that the company should have access to court, but that the German legal order could have downgraded it to another, much weaker company form. To this reasoning the Court expressly held that the company that the German legal order should have accepted to act in its legal system was the original Dutch company, with all its characteristics under Dutch law.

24. The *Inspire Art* case[68] has taken the subject one step further as it raises the question to what extent a national legislator can impose additional requirements on companies that have been formed under the jurisdiction of a member state where its registered office is located, but without developing any business activity there. The case itself related once more to a UK private company limited, that had applied for registration with the Dutch Commercial Registry where it intended to start its business activity, not having any in the UK. According to a Dutch 'Law on Formally Foreign Companies', these companies must add a suffix to their name, indicating their status as pseudo foreign company. Quite substantial consequences follow from that mention, such as personal liability of the directors for a

[67] Reference to the Court by the Bundesgerichtshof (Germany) for a preliminary ruling in the proceedings between *Überseering BV and Nordic Construction Company Baumanagement GmbH (NCC),* European Court of Justice, 5 November 2002, Case C-208/00, European Court reports 2002 or <http://www.europa.eu.int>.

[68] Reference to the Court by the Kantongerecht of Amsterdam for a preliminary ruling in the proceedings between *Kamer van Koophandel and Fabrieken voor Amsterdam v Inspire Art Ltd* Judgment of 30 September 2003, Case C- 167/01, not yet reported.

sufficient minimum capital, ie an amount equal to the difference between the Dutch minimum capital and the capital actually paid in to the company.[69]

The court followed its previous reasoning by stating that articles 43 and 48 of the Treaty prevent national legislation to impose on companies formed in accordance with the law of another member state certain conditions for the exercise of its freedom of secondary establishment that are provided for in domestic company law in respect of company formation relating to minimum capital, or to director's liability. In the absence of an abuse, established on a case-by case basis, the fact that the company has been formed in the other state or carries on its activity exclusively or almost exclusively in the state of establishment does not deprive it to prevail itself of its right of free establishment under the Treaty.

25. Company law at the European level is constituted first and foremost of a series of 12 directives harmonising company law, including the directives on accounting. For historical reasons a number of directives that are of importance to the largest, ie listed companies have not been included in this series, as they belong to the securities regulation field. Under this heading, matters such as the different types of disclosure – including offering prospectuses, semi-annual, quarterly, and ad hoc disclosure annual reports, the reporting of significant holdings in listed companies – but also the rules on insider trading and market abuse, have been regulated.

The directives are addressed to the member states that have to implement or transpose the directive provisions in their national law[70] (art 249). Hence they do not constitute company law in the national legal order. As transposition is effected by the national legislature in each state, the substantive company law rule in each state may present relatively important different features. Directives therefore differ considerably from uniform acts. Also as to substantive rules, the implementation may lead to quite different results: this is due to the existence of 'options' that are opened up by the directives among which the member states may choose. Especially in the field of accounting, this complex option system has lead to harmonization that is more apparent than real. As a consequence accounting regulation for companies continues to present substantial differences. Further harmonization in this field will be achieved as a consequence of the adoption of the International Accounting Standards.[71]

[69] One clearly sees that continental legislators are dissatisfied with the UK's refusal to extend the application of the second directive to private companies limited.

[70] Art 249 paragraph 3: 'A directive shall be binding, as to the result to be achieved, upon each Member State to which it is addressed, but shall leave to the national authorities the choice of form and methods'.

[71] Accounting Regulation 1606/2002 providing for the application of the IAS, OJ L 243, 11/09/2002, 1-4. It can be downloaded at <http://europa.eu.int/comm/internal_market/accounting/ias_en.htm#regulation>.

26. Being addressed to member states, directives do not directly affect individuals: they do not impose burdens on them nor do they create subjective rights in their favour.

There has been a long-standing discussion as to what extent a directive may have direct effect in the national legal order. The ECJ has repeatedly stated that a directive, being addressed to the member state, is not directly applicable in the national legal order, and therefore cannot be invoked in the relationship among individuals (no horizontal direct effect). This is especially important for purposes of company law, as directives would otherwise affect the relationship within the company, especially between shareholders and the company, or among shareholders.[72] Traditionally, the Court decides that directives do not have 'horizontal direct effect'.

However, states are expected to adapt their legal system to the rules of the directives. Therefore, individuals may raise the directive as a defence against a member state, or against its public bodies including public enterprises[73] ('vertical direct effect'), although the state that failed to adequately implement the directive cannot avail itself of it against an individual. This has been applied in numerous cases, eg when individuals were prosecuted by a member state on the basis of a national provision that might have been contrary to a directive's provision. Provisions of the directive that are sufficiently clear and precise, and do not allow member states to choose between different options, would apply in the relationship of a company to a public authority, such as a securities market supervisor.

Over time the Court has broadened its restrictive attitude, recognising that individuals are entitled to sue a member state for late or deficient implementation of the directive. In these cases, states would normally be liable, not in specific performance, but only for damages. The Court's case law indicates that a Member State may be held liable irrespective of the author of the non-compliance, ie government, parliament or even the judiciary. The conditions under which the Court finds a Member State liable are inspired by the rules prevailing under Article 228; paragraph 2 EC with respect to the liability of Community institutions. Basically, the Court holds that a Member State only incurs liability in case of a serious breach of a rule of Community law that is intended to grant rights to private individuals. Damages will only be granted when there is a direct link with the breach of Community law. There should be a breach by the member state of its obligations under EU law.[74] It is submitted that, as most company law directives are effectively intended to confer rights to individuals, member state liability

[72] eg the principle of equal treatment, as formulated in art 42 of the Second Company Law directive 77/91 cannot be directly invoked within the internal functioning of the company.

[73] *Licensing Authority South Eastern Traffic Area v British Gas plc* [1992] ECR I-4071, 4092.

[74] See in general T Tridimas 'Liability for breach of community law: growing up or mellowing down?' (2001) CMLR 328 ff.

could come into play in case of non-compliance of a member state with the directives.

Finally, even if the directive has not been implemented, the interpretation of the rules of national law should take place in a sense that the directive's provisions are duly taken into account. Although not amounting to declaring the directive applicable in national law, this technique leads to obliging the judiciary to interpret its national law in conformity with directives in force. The bottom line of this approach is, according to recent case law of the Court of Justice, the need to have national law that is akin to interpretation in conformity with the EU provision: where a national provision is clear and unambiguous, though contrary to EU law, a member states judge cannot proceed to interpretation in conformity with EU law if there is no room for interpretation of the national provision. Otherwise, the judge would in fact invalidate the provision of national law and indirectly provide the directive direct applicability in horizontal relations.

27. 'Regulations' on the contrary are directly binding on the citizens in the member states: they are part of the national legal system of each of the states. Regulations do not create self-contained legal instruments, severed from the rest of a member state's legal system. Often provisions of a regulation refer to complementary provisions of the state's legal system, such as the rules on filing documents, on disclosure, etc. Moreover, although the regulation creates a European legal instrument, it will refer to national law as a default rule. Therefore one could infer that regulations constitute a separate, even an autonomous legal instrument within a member state's legal system. This is not always the case: in the two cases in which the Community used the technique of a regulation for enacting company law rules, it has referred, sometimes extensively, to national law for all matters that have not been explicitly provided for in the regulation itself. The case of the Regulation on a European Company Statute is significant in that respect: article 9 provides that the European Company will be governed by the regulation or, where expressly authorised by the regulation, by its 'statutes' or articles of incorporation. For matters that are not or partly governed by the regulation, the SE will be regulated by the provisions of the law adopted by the member state in implementation of community measures relating specifically to SEs, by the provisions of member states' laws which would apply to a public limited liability company formed in accordance with the law of the Member State in which the SE has its registered office, or the provisions of its statutes.[75] The result is that there will be as many SE's as member states.

The Accounting Regulation, introducing the International Accounting Standards has direct effect in all member states: article 11 provides 'This Regulation

[75] Art 9 of the Council Regulation nr 2157/2001 of 8 October 2001 on the Statute for a European Company OJ L 294, 10/11/2001.

shall be binding in its entirety and directly applicable in all Member States.'[76] There would be no room for additional national rules or for 'interpretation'.

C. Which Way Forward?

28. How should future company law in Europe be framed? And as a preliminary question, should there be 'European' company law? Should Europe continue to move towards 'harmonised' law, which obviously has been the broadly defined objective under the harmonization scheme as it has been practiced up to now, or rather move towards more diversity, leaving it to the market forces to create more efficient company law provisions? Or should one rather move in a different direction, towards uniform law, by way of government decision, or on a market driven basis, eg by following some type of model act? What should be determined at the EU level, and what at the State level? And should EU rules introduce a minimum level of regulation, or should it be both minimum and maximum, excluding all forms of regulatory competition? And is maximum harmonization of this type compatible with the EU definition of a directive versus a regulation?

What would be the role of the government and of private regulators- such as securities regulators, stock exchanges, or accounting standard setters in this development? The role of government regulation versus self-regulation needs more detailed discussion, whereby special attention has to be paid to intermediate formulas. Finally, the relationship with securities market regulation should be clarified.

On many of these issues the Report contains interesting views.

I. Matters for EU Action

29. A first question to be raised relates to the involvement of the European Community in company law matters: what should be dealt with at the EU level, and what is better left to the member states? And what are the priorities?

From the angle of the creation of an internal economic area, it seems essential that the Community's main interest lies on the one hand in abolishing all measures that restrict companies to compete with each other on a cross border basis, while on the other in supporting companies' endeavours to spread their activity Europe-wide.

The matter of cross border company transactions has already been referred to: the Community has a primary duty to liberalise cross border establishment by imposing – or organizing – recognition of companies originating from other

[76] It can be downloaded at <http://europa.eu.int/comm/internal_market/accounting/ias_en.htm#regulation>.

member states, by abolishing the restrictions on the transfer of the seat, and by allowing cross border mergers to be fully effective.[77] The Winter Report contains specific proposals to that effect, although some are already obsolete due to the ECJ decisions in *Centros* or *Überseering*, ie the case on the transfer of the seat. The cross border establishment by way of branching should be added to the list: the establishment of a branch in another member state calls for procedures that continue to be quite burdensome.[78] Conceptually, it should be as easy for a company to establish a branch in another state as to create a branch in the home state. This – along with other factors, of course – explains why European groups continue to locate their foreign activities in subsidiaries, rather than by creating branches, thereby continuing the fragmentation of the market. The latter aspect should be investigated from a policy angle: it is striking that companies in Europe use a radically different pattern for establishing themselves in other European states than companies do in the US, where branches are predominant.[79] Tax aspects are sometimes mentioned: however, in principle, taxes should be identical, as they are levied on the economic reality. The SE is based on the concept of

[77] The tax aspects being reserved: it seems that these constitute in practice the major hurdle preventing companies to migrate among jurisdictions, in those cases that company law obstacles would not apply. However, tax harmonization requires a unanimous vote of the 15 EU member states.

[78] See the requirements imposed by the 12th Company law Directive; comp the proposals made in the SLIM working party, European Company Law: The 'Simpler Legislation for the Internal Market' (SLIM) – Initiative of the EU Commission, Nordisk Tidsskrift, November 2000/2, 126-134; C De Vos 'Het SLIM IV Project van de Europese Commissie Harmonisatie door Deregulering van het Europees Vennootschapsrecht' (2000) TBH; E Wymeersch 'Company Law in Europe and European Company Law' 1st European Jurists Forum, 85-163, Nomos Verlagsgesellschaft, Nürnberg 2001.

[79] Anecdotal evidence indicates that companies prefer to use the subsidiary form for several reasons. For banking and financial institutions a survey has being undertaken by the ECB. The following arguments have been submitted. Based on prudential considerations, the supervisor's arguments in favour of forming of a subsidiary relate to the bank's autonomy, the enhanced possibility to supervise the bank, the need to apply local rules, the (possible) poor status of prudential supervision in home state and the (possible) weakness of the parent company capital base. Arguments for a subsidiary from the bank's side can be the will to confer autonomy to the bank, the existence of specialized activities eg private banking, the reputation of the local bank, the position of head of subdivision in a wider group, tax considerations, special tax techniques, tradition, recuperation of previous losses, unsuccessful development strategy in the past.

The banks argued that their preference for a branch were based on the use of a single corporate name, the organisation of the company along business lines cutting across corporate forms, the centralization-specialization of back offices, the local office being only in charge of commercial contacts, the lower cost as a result of the consolidation of own funds and the simpler structure, while internal controls function at group level. Rating of the parent is no longer an argument due to centralization of cash management at parent level. Differences in the deposit protection schemes are sometimes mentioned, even in the advertisements. Also mentioned is the use of free cross border provision of services in the EU. Many banks have double presence.

branching Europe-wide: however, branching can already be realised today, but is rarely practiced.

These subjects are applicable to all types of companies.

II. Ambit of EU Action: Listed v Open v Closed Companies

30. The Community should assess its political interest for involving itself in company law. Should Community law envisage all companies, even small entities that have little, or no relevance for intrastate business? Or should the criterion be the fact that the company is established, or intends to establish itself in another state? Or that it is active in another state, eg in the export markets or by providing cross border services?

Traditionally, and according to the harmonization philosophy, the Community mainly addressed the larger companies. These were identified as the 'public companies limited by shares', the SA or AG types. In several directives, the private companies (Sàrl, GmbH and similar) or other types of companies were not addressed.[80] Unfortunately, what seemed consistent in theory, took no account of practical reality. The use of the different types of companies in each of the Community's jurisdictions is quite diverse: a couple of thousand AGs in Germany, several hundreds of thousands SAs in France, Italy or Belgium. A directive that applies to all companies of the same type in legal terms, covers widely different factual situations. The company type is not a useful factor of discrimination.[81]

Therefore and taking into account the public policy interest, the Community should focus on the most important firms, those with the highest public interest density. In most states these would be the listed companies. Undoubtedly there are very important firms that are not listed, especially those that were formerly, or still continue to be, government owned. Should some of the rules eg on corporate governance not be applied to these entities as well? Critics of state owned firms will certainly observe that good corporate practice is even more needed in those firms. A quantitative criterion is not easy to use, as, apart from technical points, it leads to distortion and evasion.

In any case – and following the recommendations of the Winter Report – the Community's priority in the company law field should first and foremost be

[80] The directives' ambit is quite diverse: the 2nd, 3rd, and 6th directives are applicable to the SAs only. The Accounting directives (4th and 7th) apply to all active companies; while the 1st, and the 11th (branches) apply to both SA and Sàrl types. Finally the 12th directive on one man companies applies to Sàrls only.

[81] For an overview of the different types of companies used in the main industrialized economies of Europe, E Wymeersch 'A Status Report on Corporate Governance in Some Continental European States' in KJ Hopt and others (eds) *Comparative Corporate Governance* (Clarendon Oxford 1998) Table 1, 1049. The number of AGs in Germany has risen to over 15000 in 2003: see: <http://www.dai.de/internet/dai/dai-2-0.nsf/dai_ statistiken.htm>.

addressed to the listed companies. These are most of the time the largest firms, are exposed to the strongest competition within the Community or worldwide, attract the largest amount of capital, and their decisions affect a very large number of shareholders and stakeholders. Moreover, as their shares are traded on the public markets, public policy should take into account the clear need for comparability, transparency and trust building.[82]

31. In the hypothesis that European company law would mainly address the larger – ie the listed firms, including firms regularly traded on publicly accessible markets[83] – the question arises what would be the Community's interest as far as the smaller firms are concerned. On the one hand, there is a wide discussion whether smaller firms should not be better left to the parties' contractual arrangements. Some legislators have understood this message very clearly by allowing companies held by a handful of shareholders to be organised outside the framework of the European directives: the French *Société par actions simplifiée* is the best example of a company the internal organisation of which is largely left to the parties' freedom of association, while the external structure conforms with several of the directives' requirements. Indeed as far as the last mentioned subject is concerned – which is related to these companies taking part in the internal market, hence putting at stake the safety of their contractual arrangements, or the protection of creditors or employees – the Community has an interest to protect contractual parties in the intra European context.[84] If these aspects of company law should therefore be the subject of the EU's attention, it would be preferable to leave other matters, especially the rules on the internal functioning of companies, outside the EU's purview. This opinion is also reflected in the Winter Report, referring to the public consultation.[85]

32. However the Winter Report also calls attention to an intermediate class, ie the 'open' companies. These are 'unlisted' companies that would have qualified for listing, their securities being freely transferable and dispersed among investors. To the extent that they are not listed, nor actively traded, the regulation for listed companies will not apply. It is not clear what rules would be applicable to

[82] The European Commission has endorsed this approach in its Communication '*Modernising Company Law and Enhancing Corporate Governance in the European Union*' (21 May 2003) at 8.

[83] Winter Report (see Annex 3 in this volume), at 35. All markets should be viewed here, whether so-called regulated markets or other publicly accessible markets, as the dividing line is increasingly being blurred (see also under the forthcoming Investment Services Directives, the debate on trading on Electronic Trading Facilities or alternative trading systems within the new ISD).

[84] Several of the matters have been dealt with in the first directive.

[85] Winter Report at 35.

these companies: a balance has to be struck, states the Winter Report, without giving further details.

The issue is well known in several member states that identify in their regulation a separate class of companies that 'have issued securities to the public'.[86] Their legal status is ambiguous. These companies are subject to prospectus disclosure on issuing securities, and enjoy a few of the privileges that are reserved for listed companies.[87] The ambiguity of their legal position should be reconsidered: upon issuing securities to the public they should in principle be obliged to apply for listing of their securities. Those companies that do not voluntarily apply for listing – often companies that started as closed companies, but the shares of which were dispersed over time – should opt either for applying for trading on a market, or make a bid – or have a shareholder make a bid[88] – for their outstanding shares. As access to lightly regulated market segments[89] has become easier these days, there is no reason for these companies not to guarantee a sufficient degree of liquidity and disclosure to their shareholders. As a consequence, once regularly traded, these companies should be subject to a light version of the rules applicable to listed companies.

The position might be different with respect to companies that have issued bonds to the public: these would normally lapse after a certain – minimum – period of time.

III. Matters to be Addressed by the Community

33. Assuming that one subscribes to the proposition that EU company law should only – or mainly – deal with listed companies, the question arises what aspects have to be dealt with and under what conditions.

Harmonization should first deal only with mandatory rules, not with default rules. Indeed, according to the Treaty, it can only aim at serving the protection of shareholders, employees or other parties that may be affected by a company's decisions (art. 43(3)(g) Treaty). These are subjects for which – provided protection is deemed necessary – only mandatory rules will do.

Harmonization would be driven by the needs of the securities markets, not by mere company law motives. The purpose of a Community intervention can only be to make the securities markets more secure, more transparent and hence more efficient. Divergent company law mechanisms make the market less transparent,

[86] One finds this class at least in Belgium and in France.

[87] eg the rules on squeeze out would apply to them: see under Belgian law, art 513 Companies Code.

[88] Sell-out procedures are dealt with in the future 13th directive (art 15).

[89] Some market segments impose very lights requirements: see the 'marché libre' in Paris – and planned in Brussels, – or the 'unregulated market' in Germany.

as special features (eg special classes of publicly traded securities, information asymmetries) are difficult to price, and hence will normally lead to a discount. Liquidity may be affected if introduction of special features would lead to placing too small series of securities. Also intercompany comparability would facilitate price formation: large investors buy into industry sectors, and less in individual stocks. Level playing field considerations are also significant: they have appeared to be at the centre of the debate about the 13th directive on take-overs. Hence, from an overall market perspective there are good reasons for the Community to be involved in company regulation, more specifically in those aspects that have a direct influence on the markets.

However, there are also drawbacks: more uniform regulation reduces the company's autonomy, and hence its flexibility to adapt to the needs of the financial markets. Limiting the use of specific types of financial instruments for instance might be prejudicial to financial creativity and appropriate financing conditions.

Also cultural and historical differences will necessarily have to be taken into account.

Therefore, a balance has to be struck between general rulemaking at the EU level and flexibility at the state level, or even at the level of the individual companies. To strike this balance, the role of – less flexible – Community legislation may usefully be supplemented by some form of – more flexible – self-regulation.

Community legislation should be addressing the general objectives of the law, while the small print is better left to contractual arrangements, possibly with some self-regulatory restraining measures. Corporate governance matters are a good example for this approach: the principles are to be laid down in a European instrument, the detailed measures should be adapted to the individual legal systems.[90] The legislation should allow reviewing the latter in the light of the general principles. Hence direct effect of community measures including directives should be considered in the sense that the judiciary should be entitled to review the implementing measures against the background of the Community's general principles. Enforcement of the principles should thus be made possible both vertically and horizontally.[91]

IV. Comitology Procedure and Expert Advisory Committees

34. Before further analysing self-regulation, it is useful to deal briefly with some of the recently more widely used techniques of regulation within the Community, frequently referred to as the 'comitology' procedures. These procedures are used

[90] This is also the approach of the Commission in its Communication (at 10 ff).

[91] On direct effect of directives see nr 26.

in an increasing number of domains of Community action and have led in 1999 to a regulation restating the existing mechanisms.[92] Among the several types of committees, some serve to expedite the legislative process by conferring some of the legislative powers to specialised committees. In the field of securities regulation this approach has been successfully used by the institution of the European Securities Committee (ESC) and the European Securities Regulators Committee (CESR), leading to a considerable shortening of the legislative procedures. The same techniques are now being considered in the fields of regulation of banking, insurance and financial conglomerates, while a general Financial Services Committee has been installed, in charge of coordinating the remit of the different specialised committees.

The Winter Report mentions the possibility to call on comitology procedures, but does not clearly come out in favour of these. It rather calls for a 'broader use of alternatives to primary legislation, including secondary regulation'.[93] In certain fields, such as more detailed disclosure requirements, electronic voting rules, different disclosures rules, rules relating to other uses of modern technology, it would be very practicable to be able to call on more flexible procedures, that would allow the Community to enact specific and detailed provisions for rather technical matters. With respect to the application of these rules to listed companies, it seems logical to designate the market authorities – ie the securities supervisors – as being in charge of these comitology competences. This is already the case for specific subjects such as disclosure upon offering of securities ('prospectuses') or interim disclosure, but also for matters describing insider information, or rules on the acquisition of own shares under the market abuse directive.[94] This approach would include wide market consultations, as is already standard practice today.[95] It may also allow the implementation of these detailed rules by the listed companies to be further monitored as part of the supervisory action of the market regulators while exchange of information and peer review will ensure that the rules are applied on an equal footing in all member states.[96]

From the angle of European rulemaking, the use of comitology for rulemaking raises the question what will be the legal standing of these rules: will they be

[92] See 1999/468/EC: Council Decision of 28 June 1999 laying down the procedures for the exercise of implementing powers conferred on the Commission, OJ L 184, 17/07/1999, 23. These rulemaking procedures has been in place for a long time in agricultural matters.

[93] Recommendation, Item II.2 Winter Report.

[94] See on the basis of art 11 of the Market Abuse Directive (Directive 2003/6/EC of the European Parliament and the Council of 28 January 2003 on insider dealing and market manipulation) and the documents published by CESR <http://www.europefesco. org>.

[95] CESR's 'Public Statement on Consultation Practices' (Brussels, December 2001). The Statement can be downloaded from <http://www.europefesco.org>.

[96] CESR charter provides that it will 'Work to ensure more consistent and timely day to day implementation of Community legislation in the Member States'. Self-assessment, review and evaluation procedures are undertaken.

'directives', being based on Council and Parliament directives, and calling therefore for further implementation by the member states, leaving some degree of diversity in the ultimate shaping of the rules? Or could they also be regulations, directly applicable in the member states, and leading to a degree of full identical rulemaking within the states? The question has not yet been decided at the EU level, but some deem it contrary to the definition of the directive that it is being implemented in a form that bypasses the states' freedom to decide on 'form and methods' (art 249, §3).[97]

34 BIS. The Report also proposes the creation of an independent standing advisory committee 'on future regulatory initiatives' at the EU level. The matter should be discussed in more detail.

If the remit of this committee would extend to issues specifically involving listed companies, the creation of a 'company matters committee' alongside with the European Securities Committee creates the risk of double track regulation, and hence of conflict between the two approaches. The Securities Committee would be acting on the advice of the CESR and therefore can rely on a longstanding tradition and expertise of the market regulators dealing with the issues of listed companies, which are developing at a pace different from that of general company law.[98] Finally by maintaining and even supporting the dividing line between securities regulation and company law matters, the already existing conflict between the two sets of rules would, rather than being integrated, risk to be aggravated.

On the other hand, a 'Company Law Committee' should be based on another reasoning. A few member states excepted,[99] most states within the EU do not have a policy body in charge of analysing, researching and advising on policy guidelines relating to company law. As a consequence, central issues remain undiscussed and harmonization is being carried forward along the lines of the existing and sometimes erroneous national company law provisions. This approach has been practiced since the beginning of the harmonization, often resulting in member states defending their national legal systems rather than formulating a company law that is adapted to the needs of our times.

The Second company law directive is an example at hand: it was adopted on the basis of a comparative law study, but without in depth investigation neither of

[97] This subject calls for a substantive revision of rulemaking techniques in the EU. The draft Convention contains some radical proposals to that effect.

[98] KJ Hopt and E Wymeersch (eds) *Capital Markets and Company law* (OUP Oxford 2003).

[99] One exception would be the Dutch Commissie Vennootschapsrecht or the Sociaal-Economische Raad. But even there, activities seem to be of a more technical nature. In most other jurisdictions temporary committees were installed to review specific company law matters (eg corporate governance in Belgium) or a more complete overhaul of company law (United Kingdom, Italy).

The Second company law directive is an example at hand: it was adopted on the basis of a comparative law study, but without in depth investigation neither of the objectives to be pursued, nor of the adequate character of the instruments proposed. As a consequence, thirty years later, illogical rules like the one on 'financial assistance'[100] are on the statute book in all fifteen member states, with significant negative effects on company law and economic structure.[101] Another striking policy lacuna relates to the already mentioned persistent use of subsidiaries by companies in Europe, there where branches would be more effective: no in depth analysis has been undertaken. Other interesting subjects: should conflicts of interests in company matters not be an important item on the Community's agenda?[102]

Rather than a 'committee on future regulatory initiatives', one would prefer to see a high level think tank on the economic issues underlying company law regulation. This committee would have in its remit to develop company law 'for a competitive economy'.[103]

Also, any committee in charge of fixing policy guidelines should develop an integrated view on a company's functioning, and not be stopped by the existing subdivision of the subject matters in accounting, financial disclosure, insolvency, securities regulation, etc.

V. Framework Directive

35. On several occasions, the Report refers to the legal instrument to be used, whether at the EU or at national level, to attain the objectives put forward. Several hypotheses can be taken into consideration.

In several instances, the report is based on the assumption that the rules can only be laid down in a traditional directive, because the rules have to be generally applicable to all companies of the specified type. This is the case with the rules – to be revised – relating to the legal capital, or to the mergers and reorganisations

[100] Art 23 of the Second directive, forbidding a company to grant credit or to subscribe to guarantees aimed at supporting the acquisition of the company's own shares, by a third party.

[101] The rule renders straightforward MBOs illegal. Hence intricate – but often risky – evasion techniques have been invented by smart lawyers.

[102] See for an overview: <http://www.oecd.org/pdf/M00018000/M00018919.pdf>. And what about conflicts of law in company law?

[103] This refers to the UK Company law Reform. The foreword to the Final report clearly illustrates that 'Company law can encourage entrepreneurship, promote growth, enhance international competitiveness and create the conditions for investment and commitment of resources, whether of savings or employment. Or it can frustrate entrepreneurs inhibit growth, restrict competitiveness and undermine the conditions for investment. .... Too much of British company law frustrates, inhibits, restricts and undermines'. See Foreword to Modern Company law For a Competitive Economy, Final Report, vol 1, at IX (June 2001).

nature of the present directives that are to be revised, the proposed choice for a directive cannot be avoided. Unfortunately, national legislation will continue to diverge even for matters that have been laid down in the directive. Also, this approach will not lead to reduce the regulatory burden, as the revision will probably limit itself to remove the clearest dysfunctions, but leaving aside the fundamental issues.

In the field of accounting, a totally different approach has been followed. In order to achieve its political objectives, the Community has adopted an even stricter form of rulemaking: the mechanism is laid down in a regulation, and the rules will be directly applicable after a mechanism of 'endorsement' consisting of declaring rules agreed upon by an international private body – the International Standards Board – applicable within the Community. Although the regulation gives the Commission the right to select among the proposals made by the IASB, it seem accepted that at least for the first series of accounting standards, the Commission has proceeded to a bulk endorsement. This type of co-regulation constitutes a novum in the company law or securities field, but not in other fields of Community action

More interesting are the proposals for mixed rulemaking, where the report outlines an approach that is based on several layers of regulation. At the EU level, a 'framework directive' is put forward, aimed at harmonising the high level principles. This approach is especially advocated in connection with the Corporate Governance Statement,[104] although is could be applied for stating other general principles as well, such as the ones relating to minority protection[105] or to parent-subsidiary relations.

Further implementation would take place at the level of the member states, in order to allow them to take account of the differences and specificities of their national company law. The EU would be ensuring the coordination 'to improve corporate governance by changes in their companies laws, securities laws and their codes of corporate governance' and 'to monitor and enforce compliance and disclosure'. A structure has to be put in place aimed at 'facilitating the co-ordination of the member states' efforts to improve corporate governance'; 'co-ordination should not only extend to the making of codes, but also to the procedures ... to monitor and enforce compliance and disclosure'.[106]

Flexibility and adaptability are stressed: over time 'a general framework ... can be expected to emerge'.[107]

36. The above description of the proposed methodology raises a number of questions. Is the proposed 'framework' directive to be implemented by EU

[104] See in general chapter III of the report, more specifically 72.

[105] In fact some of these have been included in the proposed 13th company law directive.

[106] Winter Report at 77.

[107] Winter Report at 73.

comitology procedures, or by member state legislation only, and is there room for self-regulatory instruments or even mixed[108] approaches? What is the status of the coordination structure? Is this a comitology procedure, as referred to above or a new type of supervisory body: according to the Treaty, the implementation of the directives is undertaken by the Commission. Would this co-ordination structure assist the Commission, or rather serve as a liaison between the Member states? These questions have largely been left unanswered.

VI. Implementing the Framework Directive

37. The proposed use of a framework directive illustrates that the Report does not advocate detailed governance rules at the EU level nor does it resort to any specific technique of implementation at the level of the member states. The Report rather adheres to an in between way, based on a mixture of EU and national rules, and for the latter allowing involvement of some self regulation, depending on the decision made by the member state.

It seems wise, taking into account the still considerable diversity of governance rules and practices, that a directive would be limited to very general principles, leaving it to the member states to determine how these have to be implemented. At the level of the member states, the choice for the most adequate instrument is left to the state: in many legal systems, principles of governance are already embedded in present legislation (eg the need for independent directors, for audit committees). Whether self-regulation may be called upon to supplement national legislation depends on the specific national context. At least, self regulation should not be excluded: to this line of reasoning further corresponds the report's call for involvement of market participants in the drafting of the rules and the preference for disclosure as a regulatory device.[109] In the field of governance the report sees no room for detailed rulemaking at the EU level. The absence of any reference to comitology procedures is significant for the intention of the draftsmen not to regulate the entire subject at EU level. Further supplementing provisions or more detailed rules belong to the task of the national bodies, whether state or self-regulatory. At least as far as corporate governance is concerned, implementation by way of full government regulation would not be considered the only, neither the best option. This opinion, as formulated by the experts, is widely shared at the national level.

108 See n 45.

109 Winter Report at 72.

VII. Self-regulation

38. There are numerous forms of self-regulation, going from purely self-proclaimed conduct to government-backed regulation. Self-regulation has been used as a technique for implementing European directives. This approach is better known in the field of labour relations than in financial regulation.[110] The subject could be broadened to the general matter of alternative techniques of regulation, of which self-regulation is one example.

Self-regulation has often been used in the field of financial regulation. It was a privileged technique of regulation by stock exchanges and trade associations, who detailed in their listing or access conditions rules relating to the governance of the companies that were proposed for listing or to the members trading in the exchange. As an increasing number of exchanges have been privatised, one could expect the self-regulatory tradition to be continued on the basis of the exchange's contractual relationship with the listed companies. Some exchanges have drafted corporate governance codes, or are referring to governance codes drafted by other parties, especially specialised 'corporate governance committees'. However, todays privatised exchanges would not consider it their primary duty today to fix corporate governance standards, nor would they like to be involved in the enforcement of those standards that are widely recommended on their market. The markets, especially the institutional investors, require governance codes, and the absence of a similar instrument has been reported as an argument for not investing.

In the late 1990s elaborate 'Corporate governance codes' or conduct of business rules have been developed by exchanges, or by private associations in which the exchanges often played a significant role. These codes are applicable on a voluntary basis or on a 'comply and explain' basis.

These codes have suffered from several weaknesses: often they did not express the common opinion among business leaders, but only of part of the business community; their legal status was unclear; their formulation was often vague and incomplete, implementation scant, while enforcement was often weak and haphazard and mainly occurred in case of negative press reports. Furthermore the codes were not updated not even after the legislation affecting governance has been changed. Notwithstanding all these defects, these codes have had – and continue to have – a significant influence on actual corporate governance practice, and have contributed to steer it in the sense of more transparency and more accountability. Moreover, they present the great advantage of flexibility.

[110] For an overview, see K Sisson and P Marginson '" Soft Regulation" Travesty of the Real Thing or New Dimension?' available at <http://www.one-europe.ac.uk/pdf/w32marginson.pdf>.

39. The Report rightly limits the EU's intervention in this field to the formulation of general principles. It refrains from proposing a Europe-wide corporate governance code, which, due to the large diversity of national laws, traditions and factual situations, could only lead to a very general statement without much added value. By allowing the implementation to take place at the national level, it allows national diversity, innovation, flexibility, all inciting to competition for excellence.

However, the value of self-regulatory instruments very much depends on the enforcement thereof. On this point, the report remains silent, probably considering that enforcement is a matter for national regulation to be taken care of. There are at least two sides to enforcement: on the one hand there is the enforcement of the framework directive: this is a matter for the EU Commission, but market participants will take a strong interest as to whether the implementing rules sufficiently take into account generally accepted governance rules. It is equally important that the national measures are being sufficiently implemented by the companies to which the national code is addressed. Here self-regulatory systems are notoriously weak. Among the avenues that could be followed for ensuring effective implementation one could consider giving authority to the securities supervisors, in charge of supervising the correct functioning of the market and of its participants. As self-regulatory instruments are normally not within the purview of the securities supervisors, one could state that their enforcement instruments would be limited to enforcing the 'comply or explain' principle, while sanctioning would be limited to the 'name and shame' technique.

The absence of an effective enforcement technique will be a weakness in pleading the equivalence of European corporate governance practices with the American prescription under the Sarbanes-Oxley Act. Europe would be at a definitive disadvantage if it were not able to demonstrate that its self-regulatory instruments are effectively equivalent to hard American legislation. Although the substance of the rules may not be so different, if the enforcement is weak to inexistent, the pressure on European firms to simply adhere to the American rules will increase.

The Report paid some attention to the use of voluntary uniform rules, such as a 'Model Codes', but indicated that this path could only be followed in specific fields.[111] It mainly pointed to the wide diversity of legal systems, rendering uniform rules quite difficult. The use of model codes could be advocated for introducing new legal forms.[112] Apart form the question whether new legal forms are needed, one could imagine that the operators of securities markets – the former stock exchanges – may have an interest in streamlining the way the companies

[111] The use of Model Acts, as used in the US has been strongly advocated by W Ebke 'Company law and the European Union: Centralized versus Decentralization Law Making' [1997] The International Lawyer 961-986

[112] Winter Report at 32.

traded on their market are organised. In that sense they have enacted, or more frequently supported corporate governance codes. Whether that approach could be extended to the entire organisation of the companies by way of model acts, seems doubtful. Moreover the competition for new listings is sufficiently strong to avoid any stock exchange being able to impose this type of requirement.

D. Conclusion

How to deal with company law in the European Union? The answer to this methodological question cannot be solved by following examples from the US, Canada, or Australia. The Union is based on too diverse legal systems while integration is only gradually taking place. Also subsidiarity – article 5 of the Treaty – should avoid the Community being too intrusive. Rather, company law will be the result of an interplay of European and national rules.

Company law interventions of whatever nature should be driven by clearly understood policy objectives. Here the Commission should call on the best experts available: the High Level Group was the example of how policies have further to be developed.

Harmonization for harmonization's sake is not needed. As company law has a direct impact on the functioning of the business firms, and the investors' willingness to commit risk capital, one should analyse what means can best be used to ensure efficient functioning and financing of companies. For those that are traded on the securities markets, the markets will exercise a guiding influence: here competitiveness, especially with outside markets is the key element. Adherence to widely accepted international standards in the fields of accounting, auditing, disclosure and corporate governance is needed.

In the field of unlisted companies, intra-European mobility should be formally introduced: the recent developments in ECJ case law, even if welcomed, still leave too much room for discussion and yield too little legal certainty. Whether harmonization in other fields is needed, is a question of – in our view rather low – priority.

Part II:

Corporate Governance:

Inside the Corporation

Chapter 4: Board Structure, in Particular the Role of Non-Executive and Supervisory Directors

Post-Enron Developments in the United Kingdom

PAUL DAVIES

This chapter identifies the defects in governance which are perceived in the United Kingdom to have underlain the demise of Enron and other companies in the United States and to analyse the responses on the part of the UK authorities. It analyses in particular the strengthening of the Combined Code of Corporate Governance and the nature of the (unsuccessful) opposition on the part of British management to those proposed reforms. It contrasts that strengthening of the 'soft law' of corporate governance with a significant shift towards the use of mandatory legislative rules in the area of directors' remuneration, albeit in pursuance of the traditional policies of disclosure and shareholder approval. Attention is also given to the reform of the regulatory structure for audits and auditors, although in this area the influence of Community and international policies has been more marked than in the other two areas just referred to. Finally, the issue of conflicts of interests among the producers of securities research within investment banks is touched on.

A. The Enron Issues and the British Response

The collapse of the Enron company and the contemporaneous demise of some other large corporate entities in the United States might be thought to reveal the following flaws in the applicable governance systems.[1]

[1] From the welter of writing about Enron and the other collapses I have found particularly useful JC Coffee 'What Caused Enron? A Capsule Social and Economic History of the 1990s' cont. ...

1. The adoption by senior management of opaque financial reporting conventions, notably, in the case of Enron, the failure to consolidate the financial results of the special purpose vehicles through which a significant part of its activities were carried on.
2. The failure on the part of the companies' auditors to bring to the attention of either the board or of the shareholders the fact that the financial reports did not present a 'true and fair' view[2] of the companies' financial position or, in those cases where the inadequate reporting was the result of good, old-fashioned failure on the part of management to abide by the established accounting rules, to detect these failures and to report them. These failures raise questions not just of competence but also of loyalty, given the incentives, arising out of the high level of non-audit services provided to the companies, for the auditors not to jeopardise their relationship with the audit client.
3. The failure of the board, and especially its independent members, to have in place controls which were likely to reveal the shortcomings of either the senior management or the auditors.
4. The adoption by the board of remuneration systems for the senior management, especially stock option plans, which generated high-powered incentives for the latter to produce short-run increases in the companies' earnings and stock price.
5. Finally, the continued issuance of buy recommendations by analysts until immediately before the collapses, even though thorough reading of the published material would have indicated grounds for caution and even though there was some evidence that, internally, those grounds for caution were understood by the analysts. Again, this activity raised questions of loyalty rather than of competence, the suggested conflict of interest arising out of investment banks' desire to continue lucrative corporate finance work for the companies whose shares the analysts were scrutinising.

The purpose of this paper is to analyse the response to these developments in the United Kingdom. That response has been a substantial one, in the sense that a number of important initiatives were triggered directly by the Enron and associated collapses, whilst other on-going reform initiatives were give an extra impetus by the US developments. The main elements of that response were as follows.

A. The most direct response was the establishment by the Government, the Financial Services Authority (FSA) and the accountancy professions of a Co-ordinating Group on Audit and Accounting Issues (hereafter 'Co-ordinating

(available on ssrn) and JN Gordon 'Governance Failures of the Enron Board and the New Information Order of Sarbanes-Oxley' (ditto).

[2] It is not suggested, of course, that 'true and fair' is, in terms, a requirement of the US accounting rules.

Group'), which produced both interim[3] and final[4] reports. Two particularly important spin-offs from the interim report of this Group should be noted in this context. First, the Financial Reporting Council (FRC), which has responsibility for the content of the Combined Code on corporate governance (CC), appointed Sir Robert Smith, chairman of a major industrial company, to produce recommendations to strengthen the CC in the area of audit committees.[5] Second, the Secretary of State at the Department of Trade and Industry (DTI) herself appointed a group of civil servants to review the regulatory regime for the accountancy profession (hereafter 'Review Group').[6] Between them, the Co-ordinating Group, Sir Robert Smith and the Review Group addressed issues 1 and 2 above and parts of issue 3.

B. On the same day, and in the same speech,[7] that the Secretary of State at the DTI, Patricia Hewitt, announced the establishment of the Co-ordinating Group, she also announced the appointment of an 'independent review of the role and effectiveness of non-executive directors in the UK', a review ultimately carried out by Derek Higgs.[8] Although that speech, rather coyly, did not specifically characterise the review as a response to Enron, but rather put it in the broader context of 'strengthening the UK's framework for how companies operate', the two enquiries were in fact closely linked. Thus, the Higgs Report[9] was published on the same day as the Smith Report; the Smith recommendations on the CC were amalgamated with the Higgs recommendations and were presented in the Higgs report as a seamless whole;[10] and the Higgs Report refers to close liaison with the Smith Review.[11] Thus, Higgs and Smith between them covered issue 3 above.

C. Executive remuneration, in terms of both its levels and the design of remuneration systems, has been a running sore in British public debate for at least a decade. With Government backing, the Confederation of British Industry

[3] Co-ordinating Group on Audit and Accounting Issues, Interim Report, URN 02/1092, July 2002.

[4] Co-ordinating Group on Audit and Accounting Issues, Final Report, URN 03/567, January 2003.

[5] Sir Robert Smith 'Audit Committees: Combined Code Guidance' FRC, January 2003.

[6] 'Review of the Regulatory Regime of the Accountancy Profession: A Consultative Document' October 1992, URN 02/1340.

[7] DTI Press Release, P/2002/128, 27 February, 2002.

[8] The appointment of the review was jointly with the Treasury. The Treasury has responsibility for the regulation of financial markets; the DTI for company law. Certain rough edges and territorial rivalry result from this division of functions.

[9] D Higgs 'Review of the role and effectiveness of non-executive directors' DTI, January 2003.

[10] ibid, Annex A.

[11] ibid, para 2.2.

sought to defuse the issue through the appointment of the Greenbury Committee, which reported in 1995[12] and whose recommendations were ultimately incorporated, with some amendments, partly in the Listing Rules and partly in the Combined Code. However, by 1999 the DTI was already consulting on reforms,[13] which would both move some of the relevant rules into legislation and enhance the intensity of the regulation. These reforms bore fruit in the Directors' Remuneration Report Regulations 2002,[14] which amended the Companies Act 1985. In this case, therefore, Enron et al did not trigger reform but they undoubtedly added to the pressures behind the reform process. Thus, there was a response to issue 4.

D. Finally, the issue of conflicts of interest within investment banks was taken up by the FSA,[15] both in relation to analysts' recommendations and the allocation of shares in IPOs (the latter aspect not being dealt with here). The FSA specifically mentioned that its efforts were 'driven largely by high-profile investigations and corporate failures in the United States'.[16] This can be seen as the response to issue 5 above.

B. General Points

I. Transnational Corporate Governance

Before making some comments on these developments individually, some general remarks are in order. First, it is a remarkable thing that a series of corporate collapses in a foreign jurisdiction should have triggered such an extensive review in the UK of its own governance provisions.[17] The direct impact of these collapses in the UK was minor. The UK assets of Enron and of the other companies seem to have passed into new hands relatively smoothly and certainly without the major loss of jobs with which those collapses have been associated in the United States. So it is not because these foreign collapses had significant adverse consequences in the UK that government action was triggered, but rather because the foreign corporate failures were thought to raise questions about the efficacy of

[12] 'Directors' Remuneration: Report of a Study Group chaired by Sir Richard Greenbury' Gee, 1995.

[13] DTI 'Directors' Remuneration' URN 99/923.

[14] SI 2002/1986.

[15] FSA 'Investment Research: conflicts and other issues' Discussion Paper 15, July 2002 and 'Conflicts of Interest: Investment Research and Issues of Securities' Consultation Paper 171, February 2003.

[16] Consultation Paper 171, para 1.1.

[17] This review is to be sharply distinguished from the separate exercise of negotiating with the US regulators, notably the SEC, either bilaterally or through the European Commission, to contain the extra-territorial impact of the US own responses to Enron etc.

the British system of corporate governance, taking corporate governance in a broad sense. That these questions should be regarded by the British Government as compelling[18] is perhaps a tribute to the convergence of corporate governance systems in developed economies. Had the US governance system been thought to be very different from the British one, then it is difficult to see why the US collapses should have triggered such an extensive domestic review. Moreover, this is not merely an Anglo-American point. Similar responses to Enron, to a greater or lesser extent, can be seen across Europe, and the force of the convergence point is thus enhanced.[19]

II. National and Community Regulation

Second, in designing their responses the authorities in the UK are did not have a free hand. Company law and capital markets law, albeit patchily and even incoherently, are areas where the European Community legislature has exerted its competence. For example, the Community presence is long-standing in relation to accounting standards and the regulation of auditors.[20] Thus, it is easy to detect the influence of the EC Recommendation on auditor independence[21] on the contents of the Smith Report, whilst the setting of accounting standards for large companies will shortly cease to be a matter for the Member States. From 2005 publicly traded companies, governed by the law of any Member State, will be required to produce group accounts on the basis of international accounting standards in so far as these have been adopted by the European Community, through the Accounting Regulatory Committee (ARC).[22] The ARC's endorsement function in effect gives the EC Commission the power to negotiate on behalf of all the Member States with overseas standard setters about reciprocal acceptance of international standards. Thus, for such companies, the crucial ones in the current context, national standard-setting will be replaced by international standard-setting through the International Accounting Standards Board; and the spill-over effect of

[18] The DTI's web-site contains a heading 'Post Enron Initiatives': <http://www.dti.gov.uk/cld/post_enron.htm>.

[19] KJ Hopt 'Modern Company and Capital Market Problems: Improving European Corporate Governance after Enron' ECGI Law Working Paper 05/2002 (available on ssrn).

[20] The Fourth Directive (Council Directive 78/855/EEC) on accounts dates from 1978; the Seventh Directive (Council Directive 83/349/EEC) on group accounts from 1983 and the Eighth Directive (Council Directive 84/253/EEC) on the approval of auditors from 1984.

[21] O J L 191/22, 19.07.2002.

[22] Regulation (EC) No 1606/2002 on the application of international accounting standards, OJ L 243/1, 11.09.2002. In July 2003 the ARC endorsed all the existing international standards except IAS 32 and 39, dealing with financial instruments, on which further work is being done.

the EC Regulation may catch an even wider range of companies.[23] One can see, too, the prospect of a parallel development in relation to international standards of auditing constraining the UK government's response to the Co-ordinating Group's recommendations, for fear that domestic reform will soon be overtaken by a Community initiative.[24] Indeed, a substantial part of the area covered by the Co-ordinating Group's report is likely to subject to EU regulation as a result of the Commission's proposals radically to revise and extend the Eighth Directive so as to embrace topics such as public oversight of auditors, external quality assurance, auditor independence, ethical standards and discipline, even if the Member States would continue to play a major role in the implementation of the new EU rules.[25]

Accounting and audit are, thus, the two areas where national action is most constrained by Community law, hard or soft, and further developments at Community level post-Enron are to be expected. Outside the areas of accounts and audit, the Community's power to regulate financial markets has recently been brought to bear on the position of financial analysts in article 6.5 of the Market Abuse Directive.[26] Thus, whatever the FSA proposes[27] in this area will need to be consistent with whatever the Commission produces by way of 'Level 2' rules under the Directive. The field in which Member States retain the greatest freedom of action is that of board structure and composition, where the failure to adopt the Fifth Directive has left the Member States in principle in control. The recent Final Report of the High Level Group of Company Law Experts, appointed by the Commission to identify the future direction of company law reform at Community level,[28] did not recommend the resuscitation of the Fifth Directive and, indeed, thought that the production of corporate governance rules should be primarily a task for the Member States and for markets, with only a co-ordinating role for the Community. This approach seems to have been accepted by the Commission. Thus, whereas EU-level 'hard law' regulation of auditing seems

[23] DTI 'International Accounting Standards: A Consultative Document' URN 02/1158, August 2002, raising the question of whether national law should either require or permit the use of international standards by a very much wider range of British companies than those covered by the Regulation, even small and medium-sized enterprises.

[24] DTI 'Review of the Regulatory Regime of the Accountancy Profession: Legislative Proposals' URN 03/717, March 2003, pp 7-8. The Commission's Communication on the statutory audit (see following note) contemplates the use of international auditing standards (ISAs) for all statutory audits in the EU (ie not just by listed companies) from 2005 onwards.

[25] Communication from the Commission on reinforcing the statutory audit in the EU, Brussels, May 2003, ch 2.

[26] Directive 2003/6/EC on insider dealing and market manipulation, OJ L 96/16, 12.4.2003 and Working Document ESC 13/2003 on the implementation of art 6.5.

[27] n 15.

[28] 'A Modern Regulatory Framework for Company Law in Europe' Brussels, 4 November 2002, especially ch III (see Annex 3 in this volume).

likely to be substantially extended via a revised Eighth Directive, the Community rules on audit committees within companies will be subject only to 'soft law' controls by means of a Commission Recommendation.[29]

The overall pattern which seems to be emerging, therefore, is one of Community as prime mover in the regulation of financial reporting by listed companies and of auditing (in relation to all companies where audit is required). Further, the objective of creating a pan-European capital market gives the Community another secure basis for legislation which is only in the process of being brought to bear on Enron-related issues. Otherwise, the Member States will be the prime movers in core company law, but subject to the competitive pressures generated by enhanced freedom of establishment for companies.[30]

III. Moving the Domestic Reform Agenda Forward

The third general point is how quickly Enron changed the reform agenda for company law in the UK and, in consequence, how reactive that reform process can be thought to be. In the middle of 2001 the Company Law Review (CLR), after three years' hard labour and many consultative exercises, delivered its two-volume final report to the Secretary of State at the DTI.[31] It was well received by the Government. And yet within six months the Government had appointed bodies to review central areas of corporate governance and to produce substantial reform proposals. Does this not suggest that the initial CLR project was too narrowly focussed or too narrowly conducted? In part, this sequence of events can be shown to have been anticipated by Government from the beginning. Thus, executive remuneration was largely excluded from the CLR's deliberations because the Government already had the topic in hand when the Review was established. The CLR thus confined itself on this matter largely to the issue of payments to executives upon the termination of their office.[32] Other matters brought into contention by Enron were simply outside the CLR's terms of reference. Thus, the regulation of analysts' conflicts of interest was not within the CLR's remit at all, because it was a financial markets, not a company law, matter.

However, both the Higgs and Smith Reports proposed substantial additions to the CC, on which the CLR had declared, after consultation with interested groups,

[29] Communication from the Commission on Modernising Company Law and Enhancing Corporate Governance, COM(2003) 284 final, 21.5.2003, 15 (see Annex 1 in this volume).

[30] Eddy Wymeersch 'The Transfer of the Company's Seat in European Company Law' ECGI Law Working Paper 8/2003 (available on ssrn). The enhanced commitment to freedom of establishment is more the result of decisions by the European Court of Justice than of legislative action at Community level.

[31] 'Modern Company Law for a Competitive Economy: Final Report' July 2001, URN 01/942 and 943. The writer was a member of the Steering Group for the Review.

[32] ibid, paras 6.10-6.14.

that 'there was a widely held view that the Code needed more time to prove itself and that major change was premature.'[33] More cautiously, the CLR also approved[34] the new arrangements for profession-based regulation of the audit and accounting professions, which were just being introduced, which the Review Group[35] later overturned in favour of more independent regulation via the FRC. However, since the profession-based system had just been agreed by the professional bodies with the Government, it is difficult to see what other line the CLR could have adopted in the absence very strong evidence that the new arrangements would not work.

Overall, however, one can conclude that the substantial external shock which Enron delivered to the governance system opened up, in a practical political sense, reform possibilities which were not available to the CLR when it sought consensus on changes to the rules of corporate governance. In any event, it is certainly the case that the reform agenda in the UK now consists not only of the CLR's Reports but also of the significant body of reform proposals referred to above. Moreover, many of the proposals generated post-Enron are likely to be implemented before the CLR reforms, because, as we shall see below, they are not dependent upon the adoption of new legislation by Parliament. Moreover, where the post-Enron proposals do require minor legislative changes for full effectiveness, the government intends to introduce such legislation in advance of the comprehensive changes suggested by the CLR.[36] However, this is not to say that the post-Enron proposals have had an easy ride. As we shall see below, the Higgs proposals in particular generated significant opposition. By contrast, Enron et al had the effect of giving some of the central proposals of the CLR an even higher profile, notably its recommendations for a tighter reporting cycle for public companies; an expansion of the annual reports to include qualitative, forward-looking, relational data as well as the traditional historical, quantitative, financial information; and for a statutory statement of directors' duties and for a more rational set of rules on derivative actions.[37]

[33] CLR 'Completing the Structure' November 2000, para 4.44 (URN 00/1335).

[34] ibid. paras 6.71 and 12.114ff.

[35] n 6.

[36] UK Parliament, Written Ministerial Statements, 10 July 2003, 'Company Law' (Jacqui Smith).

[37] Final Report (n 31) 39-59 and 161-193. The expansion of the content of the annual report through an 'operating and financial review' is to be one of the accelerated pieces of legislation (see previous note), though in this case the reform can be implemented by secondary legislation.

C. Board structure

I. The Higgs Approach

It is proposed to start the analysis of the particular proposals by dealing with those relating to the structure of the board, ie the Higgs and Smith recommendations. As noted, this is an area of regulation where the Member States retain considerable freedom of action and where the Higgs side of the proposals in particular proved controversial. At one level this controversy was surprising. The Higgs report places itself firmly in the tradition of regulation established in 1992 by the first, and still by far the most important, of the modern governance reports, that of the committee chaired by Sir Adrian Cadbury.[38] Taking Cadbury as a starting point seems entirely rational, for the establishment of the Cadbury Committee was prompted by events in the UK which bore some substantial resemblance to the later Enron and other collapses in the US, though the former were generally on a smaller scale. Cadbury was a response to 'some unexpected failures of major companies'[39] and those who set it up 'were concerned at the perceived low level of confidence both in financial reporting and in the ability of auditors to provide the safeguards which users of company reports sought and expected. The underlying factors were seen as the looseness of accounting standards, the absence of clear framework for ensuring that directors kept under review the controls in their business and competitive pressures both on companies and on auditors which made it difficult for auditors to stand up to demanding boards.'[40] The report also referred to concerns about directors' remuneration.

So, a review of Cadbury was the obvious starting point for Mr Higgs. From that review Cadbury emerged with a strong endorsement. 'I am clear that the fundamentals of corporate governance in the UK are sound, thanks to Sir Adrian Cadbury and those who built on his foundations.'[41] Thus, Higgs did not recommend that board structure should become the subject of legislative regulation. The traditional amnesia of the Companies Acts in this regard should continue and the applicable regulatory instrument, he proposed, should continue to be the Combined Code. Nor should the regulatory 'bite' of the CC be altered. The Listing Rules should continue to require companies to disclose the extent of their compliance with the CC and to explain areas of non-compliance ('comply or explain')[42] but explained non-compliance with the CC would be no breach of the Listing Rules. Action, if any, in response to explained non-compliance should continue to

[38] Report of the Committee on the Financial Aspects of Corporate Governance, Gee, 1992.

[39] ibid para 2.2.

[40] ibid para 2.1.

[41] Higgs Report, 3.

[42] Listing Rule 12.43A.

be a matter for the shareholders.[43] Implicit as well in this approach was the proposition that the rules should apply only to listed companies, though the CLR had taken the view that there was a good case for applying them to all publicly traded companies.[44]

II. The Higgs Proposals

Turning to the substance of the structure rules, Higgs and Smith again stayed with the parameters of the existing CC, in the sense of not introducing any new elements of regulation. What was proposed was the strengthening of the existing elements. Before turning to the question of why that strengthening has proved controversial, it will be useful to identify the main changes proposed. These can be listed as follows.

i. The roles of chairman of the board and chief executive should not be exercised by the same person.[45] (Previous provision: Decision to combine the posts of chairman and chief executive should be publicly justified.)[46] In addition, a chief executive should not go one to become chairman of the same company;[47] and, on appointment, the chairman should meet the tests of independence.[48]
ii. At least half the board, excluding the chairman, should comprise independent non-executive directors (NEDs).[49] However, there should continue to be 'a strong executive representation on the board'.[50] (Present provision: NEDs should comprise not less than one third of the board;[51] and a majority of the NEDs should be independent.[52])
iii. A more precise definition of independence, designed to replace the varying interpretations drawn up by institutional shareholders to express their understanding of the provisions of the present version of the Code. In particular,

[43] ibid.

[44] n 33 at para 4.44.

[45] Proposed Code Provision A.2.1.

[46] [Old] Code Provision A.2.1. The term 'old' is used to refer to the provisions of the CC in its 1998 version. Later on in this article the term 'new' is used to refer to the CC as revised in July 2003.

[47] Proposed Code Provision A.2.3.

[48] Proposed Code Provision A.2.4.

[49] Proposed Code Provision A.3.5.

[50] Proposed Code Provision A.3.2 (so that boards consisting almost wholly or mainly of NEDs would need justification).

[51] [Old] Code Provision A.3.1.

[52] [Old] Code Provision A.3.2.

the new definition requires a lapse of five years between the end of employment with the company and qualification as 'independent' and three years' lapse in the case of material business relationships. Participation in an incentive payment scheme or even membership of the company's pension scheme would disqualify the person from being considered independent. The representative of a significant shareholder would not be independent, nor would a person who had served more than ten years on the board.[53]

iv. There should be a formal induction process for new members of the board, organised by the chairman of the board, which would include meetings with major investors.[54] (No current provision.)

v. NEDs should normally serve two terms of three years and should be subject to annual re-election after nine years.[55] (No current provision, except for three-year terms.)

vi. The nomination committee should consist of a majority of independent NEDs, one of whom should chair it.[56] Crucially, the latter requirement seems to exclude the chairman of the board from chairing the nomination committee. Although the chairman of the board must be independent on appointment, as we have seen, the Higgs view was that the nature of the chairman's duties thereafter disqualify that person from counting as independent, even though he or she should not take up executive duties.[57] The analysis of the chairman of the board as someone who acts as a link between the executive directors and the NEDs, without being fully in either camp, is a significant addition to thinking in this area. (Present provision: majority of the nominating committee should be NEDs and it may be chaired by the chairman of the board.[58])

vii. The remuneration committee should consist exclusively of independent NEDs. (Present provision: the same.)[59]

viii. There should be an audit committee of at least three independent NEDs, at least one of whom should have 'significant, recent and relevant financial

[53] Proposed Code Provision A.3.4.

[54] Proposed Code Provision A.5.6.

[55] Proposed Code Provision A.7.3.

[56] Proposed Code Provision A.4.1.

[57] Report, paras 5.8-5.10. The analysis of the chairman of the board as someone who acts as a link between the executive directors and the NEDs, without being fully in either camp, is a significant addition to thinking in this area.

[58] [Old] Code Provision A.5.1.

[59] [Old] Code Provision B.2.1. As we have noted, the area of directors' remuneration has been substantially occupied by the Directors' Remuneration Regulations, but those regulations do not require the board to establish a remuneration committee. Other ways in which the CC supplements the Regulations will be dealt with in the discussion of the Regulations.

experience'.[60] (Current provision: audit committee of at least three NEDs, the majority of whom should be independent. No provision on financial experience.[61]) Substantial expansion of the specified duties of the audit committee, so as to include: recommending to the board the appointment of the external auditors and their remuneration; monitoring and reviewing the auditors' effectiveness and independence; developing a policy on the supply of non-audit services to the company by the auditors; reviewing the significant financial reporting judgements contained in the company's financial statements; and reviewing the company's internal financial control and risk management systems.[62]

ix. The chairs of the appointment, remuneration and audit committees should be present at the AGM to answer questions. (Present provision: the same)[63]

x. Companies should enter into a dialogue with major investors and report in the annual report the steps taken to develop an understanding of the views of major investors.[64] (Current provision: companies should be ready 'where practicable' to establish such a dialogue.[65] No reporting provision.)

xi. 'The senior independent director should attend sufficient regular meetings of management with a range of major shareholders to develop a balanced understanding of the themes, issues and concerns of shareholders. The senior independent director should communicate these views to the non-executive directors and, as appropriate, to the board as a whole. Non-executive directors should be able to attend regular meetings with major investors and should expect to attend them if requested by major shareholders.'[66] (Present provision: no equivalent.) 'A senior independent director should be identified in the annual report. He should be available to shareholders if they have reason for concern on which contact through the normal channels of chairman or chief executive is inappropriate or has failed to resolve.'[67] (Present provision: 'There should be a strong and independent non-executive element on the board, with a recognised senior member other than the chairman to whom concerns can be conveyed.'[68]).

60 Proposed Code Provision D.3.1.

61 [Old] Code Provision D.3.1.

62 Proposed Code Provision D.3.2.

63 [Old] Code Provision C.2.3.

64 Proposed Code Principle C.1 and Code Provision C.1.1.

65 [Old] Code Principle C.1.

66 Proposed Code Provision C.1.2.

67 Proposed Code Provision A.3.6.

68 [Old] Code Provision A.2.1.

xii. The board should periodically review its own performance[69] (currently no provision).

Probably enough has been said to show that Mr Higgs proposed (a) a considerable strengthening of the CC, but (b) through the mechanisms already put in place by Cadbury. Even if Higgs were fully implemented, the central techniques of the CC would remain those of increasing the number and significance of the independent NEDs and enhancing the role of the chairman of the board. The nature and scope of the Higgs proposals is perhaps most graphically illustrated by looking at the impact of the Higgs Report on the text of the CC.[70] The CC consists of two types of provision: Principles of Good Governance and a Code of Best Practice (CBP) (though it is usual to refer to both elements together as the 'Code'). The division between Principles and Code Provisions relates to the nature of the listed company's reporting obligation. In the first part of its report, the company has to give a narrative account of how it has implemented the high-level principles (without that report having to take any particular form). In the second part, the company has to state whether it has complied with the rule-like provisions of the Code, giving explanations for the areas of non-compliance.

At present the Principles are 17 in number; on the Higgs' proposals just one more would be added ('Boards should evaluate their performance') and a further one would be substantially expanded (to take account of recommendation (iv) above on induction).[71] By contrast, 42 extra paragraphs are proposed to be added to the Code, 31 of which are to be found in Part A of the CBP, dealing with Directors. Part D of the CBP (Accountability and Audit) appears to gets away lightly with a mere 5 extra paragraphs. However, that is supplemented by 12 pages of guidance, the passages of which that are printed in bold (on a rough estimate, some 25% of the guidance) 'should be regarded as essential for compliance with the Code'.[72] This strongly suggests that the Higgs proposals remained within the conceptual structure of the existing CC.

[69] Proposed Principle 6.

[70] Annex A to the Higgs report provided a draft re-write of the CC, which formed the basis of the FRC consultation.

[71] Proposed Principle 5. This is not to say that the wording of the remaining principles remains identical.

[72] Smith Report, 6-17 for the guidance, and the statement at end of proposed Part D of the CBP for the status of the guidance. That little was proposed to be added to Part B of the CBP (Remuneration) should not surprise us, since that topic has now moved firmly into the legislative sphere (see below), whilst relations with shareholders (Part C) and institutional investors (Part E) were not the main focus of the Higgs and Smith enquiries, though institutional investors, as again we shall see below, had already been subject to a separate enquiry.

III. The Managerial Critique of Higgs

Despite the fact that Higgs remained within the Cadbury tramlines, the reform proposals were heavily attacked by senior management of companies and their representative organisations. Particular objects of criticism were the requirement not merely to split the roles of chair of the board and chief executive but also to prevent retiring chief executives from moving immediately into the chair role;[73] that the chair of board should not chair the nomination committee;[74] and that the senior independent NED keep him- or herself informed of the views of major investors.[75] On the other hand, the Higgs report was been supported by institutional investors,[76] and by the Government.[77]

None of this is very surprising. One of the major purposes of Cadbury was to constrain the power of chief executives, more politely put in the CC as the proposition that 'no individual or small group of individuals can dominate the board's decision taking.'[78] The presence of independently-minded directors on the board who do not owe their position to the CEO is likely to constrain the senior management to some degree. For this reason, although Cadbury now appears as part of the landscape in the UK, it was not whole-heartedly welcomed by senior managers at the time, and they mounted something of a counter-attack, ultimately unsuccessfully, when, as Cadbury recommended, the Hampel Committee was set up in 1995 to review the operation of the Cadbury Code. The Preliminary Report of the Hampel Committee,[79] struck a distinctly sceptical note, asserting that 'there is no hard evidence to link success to good governance', a phrase which was not repeated in the Final Report, and implicitly criticising Cadbury for giving rise to a 'box ticking' approach to corporate governance. Past debate on corporate governance, it said, had focused too much on accountability and not enough on the governance contribution to business prosperity, and the Committee wished to 'see the balance corrected.'[80] Only in the final report could the Hampel Committee bring itself to say that it endorsed the 'overwhelming majority'[81] of the recommen-

[73] Chairman and chief executive of Carnival *Financial Times* (5 April 2003).

[74] Chairman of British American Tobacco *Financial Times* (16 April 2003); CBI (see following note).

[75] Confederation of British Industry *Financial Times* (15 February 2003).

[76] See notably a letter signed by 15 pension funds and fund managers in the *Financial Times* (14 April 2003).

[77] Speech of the Secretary of State for Trade and Industry *Financial Times* (11 April 2003).

[78] [Old] Code Principle A.3.

[79] Committee on Corporate Governance 'Preliminary Report' August 1997.

[80] This sentiment does survive to the Final Report: Committee on Corporate Governance 'Final Report' Gee, January 1998, para 1.1.

[81] ibid para 1.7.

dations of the Cadbury Committee.[82] The re-emergence of managerial criticism in the light of the Higgs' proposals to enhance Cadbury's recommendations was thus not surprising, even though those proposals contained no radical innovations.

IV. Higgs in the Context of Myners

However, it is suggested that the level of managerial opposition to Higgs was driven by something more that a general antipathy to the overall Cadbury agenda. Under Cadbury, the constraining impact of the NEDs is limited so long as the NEDs have no independent power base within the company. The strength of the incentives of isolated NEDs by themselves effectively to constrain a powerful CEO may be open to doubt, but less so if independent NEDs become the channel for bringing institutional investor power to bear within the board-room.[83] Executive management has always seen the development of an effective linkage between NEDs and institutional shareholders as the major threat to their autonomy which could emerge from the 'corporate governance' movement of the 1990s. Perhaps conscious of this sensitivity, one proposal which Cadbury went out of its way to turn down was the suggestion that shareholders should be more closely involved in the appointment of directors through the formation of shareholder committees.[84] This presumably was a proposal aimed at giving shareholders greater influence over the process of nomination of directors, thus going beyond their present role of accepting or rejecting in general meeting those nominated by the board.[85] Some elements of the Higgs report could be seen as coming back to this general issue from a different direction.

[82] For the argument that the Cadbury Report successfully established a *functional* division between strategy setting and supervision within the single board structure of British companies, see Davies 'Struktur der Unternehmensführung in Großbritannian und Deutschland: Konvergenz oder fortbestehended Divergenz?' [2000] ZGR 268 (also in English in (2000) 2 ICCLJ 435). That piece also argues, within the British context, in favour of having both executive and non-executive directors together in significant numbers on a single board, as against their separation either through a typical Continental two-tier structure or through the virtual exclusion of the executives from the board, as in many US companies. The Higgs Report takes the same view (at 21).

[83] R Gilson and R Kraakman 'Re-inventing the Outside Director: An Agenda for Institutional Shareholder' (1991) 43 Stanford L R 819; G Hertig 'Western Europe's Corporate Governance Dilemma' in Th Baums, KJ Hopt and N Horn (eds) *Corporations, Capital Markets and Business in the Law* (Kluwer Law International The Hague 2000) 265.

[84] Cadbury Report, para 6.1.

[85] Since the articles of association normally make it impossible for the shareholders to nominate their own alternatives to the board's nominees at the meeting (and very difficult to do so beforehand), the approval of the board's candidates is usually a formality. Note, however, the meeting's power by ordinary resolution at any time and for any reason to remove all or any of

cont. ...

Management fears that Higgs would generate a heightened level of institutional shareholder activism in relation to portfolio companies were compounded by the Government's declared policy of encouraging greater use by institutional investors of their corporate governance powers. As a result of a pre-Enron initiative taken by the Government, in March 2001 Paul Myners delivered a report to the Treasury entitled *Institutional Investment in the UK: A Review*. Although prompted by Government fears that institutional investors were devoting 'insufficient' of their resources to non-listed companies, the Myners report, rather in the style of Cadbury, developed into a general analysis of decision-making by institutional investors, especially pension fund trustees and fund managers acting on their behalf. Although some may have expected otherwise, the Myners report avoided saddling institutional investors with public interest duties and instead adopted the approach of asking whether the institutions were acting in the best interests of those on whose behalf they invested. Our interest is in what Myners had to say about institutional shareholder activism in relation to portfolio companies.

It is generally accepted that levels of institutional shareholder intervention to secure policy changes in portfolio companies are sub-optimal because of (i) conflicts of interest within fund managers and, to some degree, within institutional shareholders themselves, and (ii) collective action problems of both managers and institutional investors. The conflict of interest analysis was advanced in particular by the CLR,[86] ie the argument that intervention was substantially constrained where the fund manager was also supplying financial services to the companies in which it invested on behalf of institutional clients. Building relations with the incumbent management so as to promote the former activity would often be inconsistent with active intervention to change the business policies of management in order to discharge the latter function. The CLR's proposed remedy was enhanced disclosure of potential conflict situations in the annual reports of portfolio companies, but Myners, free to range outside company law, went further by proposing the incorporation into the constitutive documents of pension funds (the trust deed) and the mandates of fund managers an obligation, explicitly derived from the US rules under the Employment Retirement Income Security Act (ERISA),[87] to intervene where there was 'a reasonable expectation that activities by the plan alone, or together with other shareholders, are likely to enhance the value of the plan's investment, after taking account of the costs involved.'[88] It is clear that Myners anticipated that this obligation would extend beyond simply

the directors, irrespective of anything to the contrary in the articles or in the director's contract (other than his or her compensation entitlements): CA 1985, s.303.

[86] Final Report, Volume I, para 3.52-54.

[87] 29 USC §§ 1001 ff.

[88] Myners Report, 92, quoting a US Department of Labor Interpretative Bulleting relating to statements of investment policy, 1994.

voting on resolutions at general meetings and beyond even taking action where the portfolio company's non-compliance with the CC was not accompanied by an adequate explanation. Intervention should embrace the instigation of policy changes. This would require 'persistence and a thick skin, perhaps raising issues repeatedly over a period of time with firmness until concerns are addressed. Merely meeting senior management and expressing polite reservations about strategy is not sufficient, if it is not effective.'[89]

Cadbury-like, Myners proposed the incorporation of the activism principle as one of a set of principles which should either be adopted in trust deeds and investment mandates or an explanation given for not adopting it. Unlike Cadbury, however, it was unclear in the Myners report how the 'comply or explain' obligation was going to be created (ie what was the equivalent of the Listing Rules in the Myners scheme). The Government proposed[90] simply to make activism a legal duty of trustees and managers, but at least for the time being the institutional investors, through the newly-revived Institutional Shareholders Committee (ISC), fought off legislation by the adoption of a voluntary statement of principles.[91] Under this, institutional investors and their agents undertake to set out a policy on activism, up to and including seeking to change the board, and to evaluate the operation of the policy and, in the case of agents, to report to their clients on its operation in practice. In the end, therefore, 'comply or explain' has not been adopted in this field; the driving force behind the ISC's statement of principles is the threat of legislation, if the statement proves ineffective.

Quite how effective the statement of principles will be in re-balancing the institutional investors' decisions as between voice and exit, ie between intervention and sale (either on the market or to a bidder) is difficult to predict. The statement is explicit that, as Myners proposed, the touchstone for intervention is beneficiary welfare, not the wider public interest;[92] and the right to sell 'where this is the most effective response to such concerns'[93] is maintained. However, the institutional investors and fund managers will also be aware that the question whether beneficiaries over a period of time would have been bettered served by a policy of intervention or of sale may not be susceptible of clear proof; and since the government's starting position is that intervention levels at present are sub-optimal, some change of practice will be required to satisfy governmental concerns. Thus, the threat of legislation may operate so as to overcome, at least temporarily, the inducements to inaction generated by conflicts of interest and

[89] ibid para 5.79.

[90] HM Treasury & Department for Work and Pensions 'Myners Review: the Government's Response' para 59 and 60.

[91] Institutional Shareholders' Committee 'The Responsibilities of Shareholders and Agents – Statement of Principles' October 2002.

[92] '...resources should be commensurate with the benefits to beneficiaries': ibid at 2.

[93] ibid.

collective action problems of institutional investors and their agents, even if it cannot be shown that beneficiaries thereby have had their welfare increased.[94]

V. Managerial Attitudes to Smith

Thus, it was not fanciful for management's representatives to see the Higgs proposals, in the Myners' context, as potentially constraining of the autonomy of executive directors. The Smith report as well held out the promise of greater control in the area of audit and accounting. Indeed, its tone at times, in contrast to that of the Higgs Report, was noticeably combative. Thus, the Smith Report accepted that its recommendations 'can put the committee into an adversarial relationship with both the external auditors and the executive, and audit committees must be ready to accept that role if necessary.'[95] The committee may have to 'pit its judgement ... perhaps on a technically complex issue' against both senior management and the auditors.[96] Nor should it confine itself to a fire-fighting role. Its 'work should be more pervasive and seek to build into the organisation a culture of compliance and fair reporting, an environment in which issues are openly discussed and resolved before they become matters of real concern.'[97]

However, whilst recognising the conflicts which may arise, the Smith Report was less persuasive in providing grounds for thinking that the audit committee would not just give in under the 'enormous pressures' it would face. The Report relied, seemingly, on exhortation and 'the personal qualities of the audit committee members. They need to be tough, knowledgeable and independent-minded.'[98]

[94] Note the re-emergence of talk of 'case committees' in which the institutional investors act jointly in relation to problem companies: *Financial Times* (14 March 2003). On the earlier experience with, and the demise of, case committees see GP Stapledon, *Institutional Investors and Corporate Governance* (OUP New York 1996) 135-138. The conflicts of interest of fund managers could be avoided by the institutional investor not delegating voting and other corporate governance activities to the manager but retaining them itself. There is some evidence that very large pension funds, with presumably adequate resources for the task, may be contemplating this step: *FTfm* (28 April 2003) 1. However, large, private-sector corporate pension funds may also be in conflicted positions, with representatives of the sponsoring company being unwilling to see action taken against portfolio companies which they as managers would not want taken against themselves.

[95] Report, at 22. Also: 'While all directors have a duty to act in the interests of the company the audit committee has a particular role, acting independently from the executive, to ensure that the interest of shareholders are properly protected in relation to financial reporting and internal control.' (3)

[96] ibid at 23.

[97] ibid.

[98] ibid at 24. Despite this language, the Smith side of the Smith/Higgs reform proposals has received less public attack from management, perhaps because the Government has already

cont. ...

Perhaps not surprisingly, the Smith report dealt with investor relations only in terms of reports to the AGM, which, however, should include an account of differences between the committee and the board as a whole. It did not suggest a continuing dialogue between the audit committee and major investors. It is one thing for NEDs to act as a conduit for the concerns of major investors and another for the audit committee to take its internal conflicts to the investors for resolution. As the Report said of audit committee resignation in the face of irreconcilable internal conflicts, that would be the 'nuclear option'.[99] Perhaps because of its lesser potential for linking NEDs to major investors, the Smith aspects of the proposed revisions to the CC were the subject of much less public criticism, the main one being the difficulty of finding the requisite number of financially literate NEDs.[100]

VI. Institutional Investors and Government

The expressed opinions of institutional investors to the Higgs proposals have been varied. Those in favour of intervention welcomed them, for they saw Higgs making it easier to implement the Myners agenda. Others, perhaps feeling pushed into greater intervention than they thought desirable and perhaps also fearful of the application of investor power to their own institutions, were more reserved. As to Government, its support for the Higgs/Smith agenda was not surprising. Government has seen good corporate governance as one of its responsibilities at least since Cadbury, even if it has chosen, usually, to operate through committees formally appointed by other bodies whose recommendations have been implemented through mechanisms other than legislation. The hand of the DTI has always been visible in the background of the corporate governance reports of the 1990s. Thus, senior DTI officials provided the secretariat for to the Cadbury Committee and acted as observers on it, whilst the Higgs enquiry was actually commissioned by the Government (DTI and Treasury) rather than the conglomeration of non-governmental organisations which had set the previous enquiries in motion. It has always been understood that the ultimate political sanction behind the 'comply or explain' mechanism was the threat of legislation by government, and so one of the items on the CLR's terms of reference was 'to consider the proper relationship between company law and non-statutory standards of corporate behaviour.'[101] That threat was explicitly articulated in the Final

committed itself so firmly to the Smith reforms in the Final Report of Co-ordinating Group on Audit and Accounting Issues (n 4) ch 2. See below.

[99] The impact of potential legal liability in this situation is discussed below.

[100] The Smith guidance appears on audit committees appears, little changed, as an addendum to the new CC (at 43-57).

[101] DTI 'Modern Company Law for a Competitive Economy' 1998, para 5.2.

Report of the Co-ordinating Group.[102] Rejecting the proposal that the audit committee should be established on a legislative basis, the Group nevertheless states that 'this option should be considered again if the best practice, market-driven approach of the Combined Code proves ineffective in delivering the changes identified in the Smith Group Report and endorsed by us.'[103] Similarly, Higgs recommended progress on its recommendations be reviewed by the Government and the FRC after two years. That these are not idle reviews is demonstrated by the fate of the Greenbury recommendations on remuneration (below) in the light of the Government's dissatisfaction with their implementation.

On the other hand, Higgs was given a pretty clear steer that government did not think that the time had arrived for the adoption of a predominantly legislative approach and that a strengthening of the existing mechanisms was seen as the best way forward.[104] To that extent, the Higgs Report constituted a vote of confidence by Government in the present way of doing things. Such a policy would have been threatened, however, by a substantial failure on the part of the FRC to adopt the Higgs proposals, and the governmental noises, supportive of Higgs, were fully understandable in this context.

VII. Adoption of a New Combined Code

Although the FRC, which is the body responsible for the CC, began consultation on the implementation of the Higgs proposals in the expectation that this would be a largely technical exercise and with the aim of bringing the revised version of the CC into force for reporting periods ending in or after July 2003, it was forced into a more substantive consultative exercise because of the managerial opposition discussed above.[105] However, in the end the delay was relatively short: a new CC was adopted by the FRC in July 2003, for reporting periods from 1 November, 2003 onwards.[106] Moreover, the new Code was greeted with expressions of support from the CBI,[107] and if individual business leaders still harboured dissenting views, they kept quiet about them. This was perhaps surprising, since the new CC is very close to the Higgs proposals.

In part, the support of management seems to have been acquired by the adoption of a new classification device. As pointed out above, the old CC contained

[102] n 4.

[103] ibid para 2.31.

[104] The terms of reference of the Higgs enquiry stated: 'Though the Government has an open mind, its preferred starting-point in this area is, if possible, an approach based on best practice, not regulation or legislation.': Higgs Report, Annex K, p. 117.

[105] *Financial Times* (8 May 2003).

[106] FRC 'The Combined Code of Corporate Governance' July 2003, Preamble, para 3.

[107] *Financial Times* (24 July 2003).

principles and code provisions, and Higgs operated almost wholly by adding provisions to the code.[108] Some of the Higgs proposals have been moved out of the Code Provisions and into the Principles, through the device of the creation of a category of 'Supporting Principles'. This is probably where these proposals should have been in the first place, since the particular proposals in question are closer to standards than to rules, for example, the requirement that 'non-executive directors should scrutinise the performance of management.'[109] Business has welcomed this development as giving them additional flexibility, though it is not clear that it does so. The argument appears to be that the Supporting Principles fall within the narrative section of the listed company's report rather than the section in which it has to confirm whether it has complied with the Code Provisions and to explain areas of non-compliance.[110] To that extent the reporting function in relation to Principles may be less constraining.

Apart from this classificatory innovation, the substantive content of the new Supporting Principles and Code Provisions is not much different from what Higgs proposed. There are two areas in which significant amendments have been made compared with the Higgs' proposals noted above. First, the chairman of the board is no longer excluded from chairing its nomination committee (except when the committee is dealing with the chairman's successor);[111] and the role of the senior NED in dealing with investors has been clarified by stating that the primary responsibility for conveying investors' views to the board lies with the chairman and that the senior NED's role is normally simply to listen to those views at meetings with investors.[112] Further, an addition has been made to the principle which was in the former CC and which stressed that institutional investors should not assume, without proper examination, that non-compliance with the Code Provisions on the part of management is to be criticised (the so-called 'box ticking' approach). A new Supporting Principle spells out in more detail what is required in this regard.[113] It amounts to no more than an insistence that the relevant requirement is 'comply or explain', not 'comply or be condemned.' Finally, a concession has been made to small listed companies (ie those outside the FTSE 350). The requirement that half the board should be independent NEDs is not applied to such companies (at least two is enough to satisfy the CC);[114] and, in consequence, smaller companies may make do with two independent NEDs on

[108] See text attached to nn 72-73 above.

[109] [New] Supporting Principle A.1.

[110] See text attached to n 70 above.

[111] [New] Code Provision A.4.1.

[112] [New] Code Provision D.1.1.

[113] [New] Supporting Principle E.2.

[114] [New] Code Provision A.3.2.

the audit committee, though one of them still has to have 'recent and relevant financial experience'.[115]

Overall, however, it is difficult to believe that these, essentially minor, changes produced by themselves the consensus which now seems to prevail between management and shareholders about the acceptability of the new CC. One suspects that the support for change from Government was seen as a clear indication by all concerned that failure to agree on something close to the Higgs proposals would generate the risk that, sooner or later, legislation would be deployed.

D. Auditor Independence

This issue was addressed by the Co-ordinating Group on Audit and Accounting Issues, which was established by the DTI and the Treasury and had among its members junior ministers from both those departments as well as representatives of other regulators. It was thus clearly a government-driven review, as is appropriate, given the Government's responsibility under the Eighth Directive for the rules on the independence of auditors.[116] However, under the provisions of the Companies Act 1989 the Government has hitherto discharged its responsibilities with regard to the independence (and competence) of auditors largely by delegating them to the professional accountancy bodies, provided those bodies meet certain standards set by the DTI. One question which naturally emerged post-Enron was the adequacy of this system of delegation to the profession. The Co-ordinating Group in its Final Report not surprisingly concluded that such extensive delegation to the accountancy profession was unlikely to continue to be internationally acceptable and that a strengthened element of public interest representation in the regulatory structure was necessary.[117]

However, the issue of how to provide independent oversight and monitoring of auditors proved inseparable from similar questions which were already being raised domestically in relation to the accounting profession as a whole. Outside the area of audit, Community law imposed no requirements and, until recently, these matters had been almost wholly the responsibility of the profession. Thus, on the same day that the Co-ordinating Group produced its final report, a review carried out by the DTI of the regulatory regime for the accounting profession was also published.[118] It is not proposed to analyse these proposed institutional changes in detail or to stray very far into the area of accounting, as opposed to

[115] [New] Code Provision C.3.1.

[116] Directive 84/253/EEC, art 24.

[117] Above n 5. ch 5. For similar views at Community level see n 25 above at 6.

[118] DTI 'Review of the Regulatory Regime of the Accountancy Profession' URN 03/589, January 2003.

audit, regulation. Suffice it to say that the professions will lose some of the control over their own regulation which they had hoped to maintain through the Accountancy Foundation (AF), which had just recently been established. The more important of its functions will be transferred to the FRC, which emerges as the real institutional winner in the reform process. A hitherto obscure and limited regulator, the FRC, or at least its subsidiary bodies, will acquire significant powers in relation to both auditing and accounting when the reforms are implemented. Despite the focus in the reforms on listed companies, the role of the FSA is not proposed to be enhanced in this area to the same extent as that of the FRC.

I. Prohibiting Relationships Carrying the Risk of Conflict

The Co-ordinating Group recognised that conflict of interest on the part of auditors was the major problem revealed by the Enron case. '[T]he perception was that there was an interdependent economic relationship between the Houston office of Andersens and the Enron management, which was far too cosy. Enron was the principal client of the Houston office; former Andersens staff worked for Enron; Andersens provided significant (if not exceptional) non-audit services to Enron; and Andersen appears to have worked closely with the management to develop arrangements for keeping liabilities off the balance sheet, arguably against the interests of shareholders.'[119] There were two main sets of strategies discussed by the Group to deal with this conflict: prohibiting the creation, or continuance, of the relationships in which the conflict was inherent and providing structures and mechanisms for monitoring and managing the conflict. By and large the emphasis is on the second strategy. Let us look first at the possible prohibition strategies.

The conflict of interest generated for auditors by the provision of non-audit services to audit clients is by no means a new issue.[120] One possible strategy is polarisation. Firms either provide audit work or non-audit work, but not both. The strongest argument against such a rule, largely accepted by the Co-ordinating Group,[121] is that the provision of both sorts of service can be efficient, in the sense that knowledge obtained from audit work can feed into the non-audit work and vice versa. Thus, it rejected polarisation. In line with the 'principles' approach to rule-making, the Group also rejected the strategy, followed in Sarbanes-Oxley, of producing a list of prohibited non-audit services. Instead, following the

[119] n 4 at para 1.1.

[120] E Stamp and C Marley *Accounting Principles and the City Code: the Case for Reform* (Butterworths London 1970). By 2001 it was estimated that the FTSE-100 companies paid non-audit fees of £675 to their auditors, whose audit fees were £216, a ratio of 3:1 in favour of non-audit income: Co-ordinating Group, Interim Report, para 3.12.

[121] n 4 at para 1.34.

European Commission Recommendation,[122] it adopted three tests to be applied to determine whether non-audit services were acceptable. Auditors should not provide such services where they would involve the auditor in taking management decisions, auditing its own work or acting as advocate for the client in an adversarial situation. These principles have already been incorporated by the recognised audit bodies into their ethical guidance. What the Group added to this was the proposal that Auditing Practices Board (APB – a proposed subsidiary of the FRC) should develop guidance on how these principles apply to the provision of certain sensitive categories of non-audit services – a sort of half-way house between the list approach and control by unelaborated standards. These services were: internal audit services (presumption strongly against), valuation services, taxation services and the design and supply of IT and financial information technology systems (on most of which matters the Commission's Recommendation already provides a framework of analysis).[123]

An alternative strategy is based on the argument that the risk of conflict of interest (or simply of complacence) increases with the duration of the audit/client relationship.[124] This can be addressed by mandatory rotation of the audit firm or of the senior figures involved in the audit. The Co-ordinating Group rejected mandatory firm rotation on the grounds of its associated inefficiencies (increased cost and likely reduced effectiveness of the first audits by the new firm), a conclusion bolstered by experience in Italy (requiring firm rotation every nine years) and Spain (which had abandoned such a requirement in 1995).[125] Instead, the thrust of the recommendations lies in a strengthening of the already existing professional rules on partner rotation. The rotation period for the engagement partner should be reduced from seven to five years and, following the Commission Recommendation, rotation should be introduced for other key audit partners (but on a seven-year cycle).[126]

A third strategy for the regulation of conflicts focuses on the level of economic dependence of the auditor on a particular client. Existing professional rules on independence prohibit the creation of a situation in which fees from any one client exceed ten per cent. of total firm fees from public interest companies. A reduction of that figure to five per cent was rejected on the grounds that it would make the entry of new firms into the listed company audit market more difficult

[122] Commission Recommendation of 16 May 2002, Statutory Auditors' Independence in the EU: A Set of Fundamental Principles, OJ L 191/22, 19.7.2002.

[123] This would become an international, rather than just a national exercise, if the EU's move to International Accounting Standards were followed by a move to International Standards of Auditing. n 24.

[124] n 4 at para 1.26.

[125] ibid para 1.27. Cadbury had rejected this proposal also.

[126] ibid para 1.22.

(whilst having little impact on the big players).[127] Nor did the Group consider the setting of such percentage figures for particular partners rather than for firms as a whole.

Finally, the Group at least partially addressed conflicts arising out the same personnel in effect appearing on both sides of the process by adopting the Commission's recommendation that there be a two-year cooling off period where an audit partner wished to join an audit client as a senior employee or director.[128]

II. Managing Conflicts of Interest

The relatively light approach to the prohibition of situations of potential conflict of interest necessarily implies a more elaborate structure for the management of conflicts (assuming the issue is to be addressed at all). We have already seen this in the recommendation from the Group that the APB develop guidance on the provision of non-audit services. However, the Co-ordinating Group's approach to such management was not to rely on a single mechanism but to deploy a package of measures to this end.

An obvious regulatory technique is disclosure of the conflict or potential conflict of interest. This was deployed by the Co-ordinating Group in a number of ways, both in relation to audit firms and the audited companies. Thus, it was proposed that audited companies should provide more detail about the nature and value of non-audit services provided by auditors,[129] whilst audit firms should have to disclose situations where total fees from a single listed company or 'public interest client' exceeded five pre cent. of total fees from such clients.[130] However, in a notable development, audit firm disclosure was proposed to be extended on a much broader front. Although most audit firms are partnerships and so not subject to the mandatory financial disclosure rules of the Companies Act, the Co-ordinating Group proposed that auditors of listed companies should be made subject to the Limited Liability Partnership (LLP) disclosure rules, ie essentially to the company regime, even if they are still ordinary partnerships.[131]

[127] ibid para 1.65.

[128] ibid para 1.61.

[129] ibid para 1.55. The aggregate of the amount so paid has been required to be disclosed in the annual accounts since 1991 (S I 1991/2128).

[130] ibid para 1.65. This information should also be communicated to the relevant company's audit committee and perhaps to its shareholders. A ban on fees at this level was rejected: see above. A 'public interest' client would include major pension funds and charities, which, of course, are not be listed companies.

[131] Some of the large firms take the LLP form (eg PricewaterhouseCoopers) and this proposal will presumably encourage others to do so, since the trade off of privacy for unlimited liability will no longer be available.

This would include the obligation to produce an OFR[132] when this is introduced. The proposal was grounded by the Co-ordinating Group in the statutory monopoly which audit firms have been granted and the proposition that there is 'a legitimate public interest in the organisational structure, audit practices and processes and international links of the firms. Disclosure should act as an added spur to audit firms to ensure that their processes and practices continue to be effective.'[133] The disclosures required by audit firm's OFR would include 'the basis of partner remuneration, including in particular remuneration related to the provision of non-audit services to audit clients' and 'the firm's requirements and procedures to ensure that auditors act with independence and integrity.'[134] Such reporting is proposed to be 'voluntary', but with the clear threat of a legislative requirement being imposed, if the voluntary system is judged not to be working satisfactorily.[135]

The second technique deployed by the Co-ordinating Group, again unsurprisingly, was monitoring of independence issues on the basis, among others, of the information disclosed. The Group proposes both demand-side and supply-side monitoring. On the demand side, this will be one of the major responsibilities of the audit committee under the Smith proposals, discussed above. In particular, the audit committee will be charged with the responsibility 'to monitor and review the external auditor's independence, objectivity and effectiveness ... and to develop and implement policy on the engagement of the external auditor to supply non-audit services...'[136] On the supply side, the disclosure rules just discussed clearly reveal an expectation that audit firms will monitor this issue and, as we have noticed, the APB is to develop guidance on the supply of non-audit services.

The third element in the structure was the monitoring of audit work, including, but not confined to, the issue of auditor independence. At present, this is an area where responsibility has been delegated to the professional bodies, subject to regular reporting to the DTI.[137] The Review Group not surprisingly concluded that such delegation was no longer acceptable in the case of listed companies and public interest clients. There was a need a monitoring mechanism which as 'more self-evidently independent – both because of steps being taken in other jurisdictions and because of a heightened focus on the credibility of financial informa-

[132] n 37.

[133] n 4 at para 3.3.

[134] ibid para 3.7.

[135] ibid para 3.6.

[136] Proposed CC provision D.3.3. Near-final proposals for new rules are contained in CP 205, October 2003.

[137] Report of the Review of the Regulatory Regime of the Accountancy Profession, January 2003, URN 03/589, para 5.8. The reporting obligation is in s 37 of the Companies Act 1989.

tion.'[138] The review concluded that an inspection unit independent of the profession should be created which would report to a Professional Oversight Board, which would be a subsidiary of the FRC.[139] As important, the monitoring process should undergo a shift in emphasis so that it concerned itself as much with the judgements made by auditors as with processes and systems.[140] The monitoring process would carry sanctions, including the imposition of conditions on the audit firm and the initiation of disciplinary action. In terms of auditor independence, the proposed reforms can be seen as creating a counterweight to the incentives auditors might have not to challenge with sufficient rigour the reporting choices made by the directors of the audited company. The less radical course of greater independent oversight of a monitoring process which remained with the professions was regarded as 'tenable' but less appropriate than the independent inspection process.[141]

With the rejection of polarisation and mandatory firm rotation, the reform proposals discussed above, like Higgs/Smith, operate within the existing parameters of regulation, except that there is proposed to be a significant shift away from professional self-regulation towards independent control, at least in relation to the audits of listed companies. Also unlike with the Higgs/Smith proposals, there is a statutory framework in place for auditor regulation, into which the current proposals can be fitted with relatively little alteration.[142] The main query over these proposals arises out of the European Commission's Communication on the statutory audit, which could cause some issues to be re-opened. However, the basic structure of the Government's proposals seem to fit well with the framework which the Commission has in mind.[143]

E. Executive Remuneration

The risks associated with the opacity of Enron's financial statements were exacerbated by the fact that its management's remuneration packages were highly sensitive to the company's share price. Management thus had a strong incentive, at least at particular times, to manipulate that price.[144] This strand of the Enron

[138] ibid para 5.14. See also para 5.15: continuation of the present system 'risks undermining the credibility of the monitoring process.'

[139] ibid ch 5.1.

[140] ibid para 5.9.

[141] ibid para 5.28. This expressed in effect a preference for the new Canadian approach over reform proposals in Ireland and Australia.

[142] Review of the Regulatory Regime of the Accountancy Profession: Legislative Proposals, March 2003, URN 03/717. See also n 36.

[143] See n 25.

[144] Gordon (n 1).

debate gave extra power to a domestic British debate on executive remuneration which was already long under way and which produced amendments to the Companies Act 1985 by way of the Directors' Remuneration Report Regulations 2002.[145] Indeed, there has probably always been a debate in modern company law about the proper regulation of directors' remuneration, but it was given an extra dimension by the explosion of managerial pay in the 1990s at a time when the labour market position of lower level workers was moving in a manner adverse to them and trade union power had been restrained by Governmental action. Two elements in that debate are long-standing: the overall level of directors' remuneration and the payment of compensation to directors upon termination of office (the so-called 'rewards for failure').[146] The third element is more recent: the question of the linkage between pay and performance under incentivised pay arrangements. Since, it is the last which is germane to the Enron debate, we will concentrate as far as possible on it.

I. Structure of Regulation of Executive Remuneration

It is important to make clear at the outset that directors' remuneration has never been left solely to be governed by the 'comply or explain' principle. There have always been fully mandatory rules in the Companies Act (and, to some degree, the in common law) on some aspects of the remuneration issues, and the mandatory provisions of the Act have for many years been supplemented by additional mandatory rules in the Listing Rules. So, the structure of regulation is (or, rather, was) tripartite: Act rules applying to all companies,[147] Listing Rules and the CC (or its predecessors), both the latter applying only to listed companies. The regulatory techniques used in the Act and the Listing Rules are essentially two-fold: disclosure and shareholder approval. The CC uses these techniques, as well, but adds to them substantive criteria for the design of remuneration packages, including performance-related remuneration,[148] and structuring the decision-making process on remuneration issues (principally, the remuneration committee, discussed above).

By 2002 the disclosure provisions were pretty advanced as far as remuneration packages were concerned. The Act had moved from (a) the pre-Second World War stance of requiring only aggregate directors' fees to be disclosed to

[145] SI 2002/1986, applying to financial years ending on or after 31 December, 2002.

[146] Despite the reforms, discussed below, to the legislation on directors' remuneration, the government is pursuing the idea of further changes, not necessarily legislative, to deal with termination payments: DTI, '"Rewards for Failure" Directors' Remuneration – Contracts, Performance and Severance' June 2003.

[147] Sometimes, though not often in this area, to all public companies.

[148] CC, Section B1 and Schedule A.

(b) disclosure of aggregate remuneration, including executive remuneration (to take account of 'a growing tendency to include in boards of directors men who hold managerial positions in the company')[149] to (c) giving in addition to the aggregate the individual remuneration of the highest paid director (normally the chief executive) and of the chairman of the board[150] to (d) a comprehensive disclosure of the remuneration and benefit packages of each director by name, in the case of listed companies.[151] Shareholder approval requirements had advanced less rapidly, being required in three particular areas: gratuitous payments to directors upon retirement fromrvifice;[152] approval of service contracts not capable of being terminated by the company within five years[153] (both these provisions being aimed at the 'rewards for failure' debate); and the approval of long-term incentive schemes, including stock option schemes, in the case of listed companies.[154] The recently introduced shareholder approval requirement in this last case had permitted the expression of what Lucian Bebchuk has termed 'shareholder outrage'[155] in a number of cases in the latter half of the 1990s. No company seems to have been defeated on a shareholder vote, but a number thought it prudent to re-design incentive remuneration packages in the light of investor hostility.[156]

II. The Failure of Greenbury

Despite the recent review of this area by the Greenbury Committee[157] in 1995, which had led to a strengthening of the provisions of the Listing Rules and the CC, by 1999 the Government was already consulting on reforming the legislative

[149] Report of the Committee on Company Law Amendment, Cmd. 6659, 1945, para 89; recommendation implemented in 1947.

[150] Introduced by the Companies Act 1967.

[151] Listing Rule 12.43A(c)(ii)-(x).

[152] Introduced in 1947. Now CA 1985, s 312.

[153] Introduced by the Companies Act 1980; now CA 1985, s. 319. For proposals to reduce the relevant period to one year, see n 146 above.

[154] Listing Rule 13.13(b), subject to the exception in 13.13A(b), introduced as a result of the 'Greenbury Report': 'Directors' Remuneration: Report of a Study Group chaired by Sir Richard Greenbury' Gee, 1995, para 5.33. The Association of British Insurers has adopted a policy of voting against such proposals if, under all share schemes, the company's commitments exceed 10% of the issued share capital over any rolling ten-year period (the 'anti-dilution' rule).

[155] LA Bebchuk 'Managerial Power and Rent Extraction in the Design of Executive Compensation' (2002) 69 U Chi L R 731, 786.

[156] See, example, the 29% vote against the C&W incentive scheme in 2001 (*Financial Times* 21 July 2001) and the re-design in that year of incentive schemes at Marconi (ibid, 30 June) and BHP Billiton (ibid).

[157] Above n 154.

framework on remuneration,[158] and legislative change arrived with the Directors' Remuneration Report Regulations 2002. So, this was an area where, in the government's eyes, the use of non-governmental review bodies (Greenbury was established by the Confederation of British Industry) whose recommendations were to be implemented by non-legislative means had not been successful. This was not because Government disagreed with the principles which Greenbury had laid down (and which Hampel had later reviewed). It did not seek to resile, for example, from the Greenbury proposition that 'the key to encouraging enhanced performance by Directors lies in remuneration packages which link rewards to performance, by both company and individual; and align the interests of Directors and shareholders in promoting the company's progress.'[159] The Consultative Document of 1999 did not seek to prohibit performance-related pay or even to control certain types of incentive, for example, stock options. On the contrary, it positively insisted that performance-related elements of remuneration packages 'should form a substantial proportion of the total remuneration packages of executive directors'.[160] In short, the government was prepared to accept the heightened risk of conflict of interest (arising out of the possibility of executive manipulation of the reward criteria) because of the heightened potential for alignment of shareholder and director interests which such remuneration arrangements seemed to offer.

Equally, Government accepted the methods put forward by Greenbury for dealing with the heightened conflict of interest in incentivised payment systems (and, indeed, payment systems as a whole) ie transparency and accountability. The Government's criticism was that the Listing Rules and the CC had not implemented the whole of the Greenbury reforms or had done so in a grudging way. There were two main criticisms. First, whilst there was 'an acceptable level of transparency in respect of the disclosure of individual directors' remuneration packages ... [the Government] does not believe that there has been adequate compliance with the Greenbury recommendations on the disclosure of remuneration policy.'[161] In particular, the Government concluded that 'very few companies are providing adequate information to shareholders on the linkage between rewards and performance'.[162] A notable omission in the transposition of the Greenbury recommendations was that neither the Listing Rules nor the CC picked up the Greenbury proposal that the remuneration report contain information on the performance of comparator groups of companies.[163] Second, whilst Greenbury did

[158] DTI 'Directors' Remuneration: A Consultative Document' 1999, URN 99/923.

[159] Greenbury, para 1.15. This view was later reflected in the CC, Principle B1.

[160] n 142 at 15.

[161] DTI 'Directors' Remuneration: A Consultative Document' 2001, para 2.12 (URN 01/1400).

[162] n 158, para 4.8.

[163] n 161 at 15.

not recommend that the remuneration policy be subject to shareholder approval each year, it was said that the remuneration committee should consider each year whether the circumstances were such that shareholder approval should be required. This did get translated into the CC,[164] but seems to have become a dead letter: only four listed companies sought shareholder approval of remuneration reports in 1998.[165]

These defects in the implementation of Greenbury might not have mattered, had that implementation taken the issue of directors' pay off the public policy agenda. But, it did not, and so the 2002 Regulations shift the Listing Rule requirements into legislation and strengthen them so as to deal with the points mentioned above. However, the board structure provisions (notably the remuneration committee) remain in the CC (as reformed by Higgs), so that the structure of regulation will become largely bipartite (legislation and CC) rather than tripartite. Board structure continues to be regarded in the UK as a subject inappropriate for regulation by 'hard law', even though the Government's 'expectation' is that quoted companies will establish such committees.[166]

III. The Aims of the 2002 Reforms

However, the requirements of the Listing Rules as to the disclosure of directors' remuneration are to be deleted.[167] Taking the Listing Rules largely out of picture has two minor advantages. First, it reduces the difficulties the UK will face if the EC harmonization of Listing Rules (or whatever replaces them) makes it more difficult for member states to add requirements of their own. The requirements on remuneration reports and shareholder approval, which, even in the present Listing Rules, apply only to UK-incorporated listed companies, can be safely lodged in the companies legislation. Second, the obligations of report and approval can be extended to UK-incorporated companies which are listed outside the UK, thus avoiding the generation of an incentive for UK companies to avoid the regulation by listing elsewhere.[168] Under the Disclosure Regulations the regulated companies are those incorporated in the UK[169] which are 'quoted' – defined as a

[164] CC, B.3.5.

[165] n 158, para 2.3.

[166] n 161, para 2.6.

[167] n 161 at para 2.3. However, it seems that the requirement for shareholder approval of long-term incentive schemes, including share options, will remain in the Listing Rules (subject to the review which the FSA is carrying out into the future role of the Listing Rules).

[168] Though they could escape the regulation by *re-incorporating* elsewhere.

[169] Technically, the regulations – like, normally, the Companies Act 1985 which they amend – apply only to companies incorporated in Great Britain. Northern Ireland will presumably develop its own rules in due course for companies incorporated there. The Listing Rules did apply to UK incorporated companies.

company listed in the UK or any other EEA state or admitted to trading on the New York Stock Exchange or Nasdaq.[170]

However, the main objectives of the regulation were greater disclosure of remuneration policy and greater involvement of shareholders in the development of such policies. The Act now[171] requires disclosure, for each director, of a 'detailed summary' of any performance criteria for stock option or long-term incentive schemes (but not annual bonuses), plus an explanation for their absence if there are none. Proposed amendments to such incentive schemes must also be explained and justified; ditto the methodology used to establish whether the criteria have been met. Finally, where the criteria deployed involve a comparison with factors external to the company, these factors must be identified.

However, on the compulsory provision of comparative information, the absence of which had been stressed in its consultation documents, the Government had a late failure of nerve. The Act requires a graph to be provided in the remuneration report which shows total shareholder return (TSR) on a broad index of equity shares[172] over a five-year period and which compares that with TSR on the company's listed equity shares. However, in the consultative draft of the regulations, issued only seven months previously,[173] the comparison based on the TSR on the broad index was presented simply as the fall-back rule, to be applied in the rare case where the incentive scheme was not subject to performance criteria. Where, as would be expected, there were such criteria, and these criteria were comparative in nature, comparison was to be provided, in graphical form, between the company's performance and that of the comparator, by reference to each of the relevant criteria. Although then presenting this approach as one likely to give the British disclosure requirements 'a sharper edge' than those of the SEC, upon which they were otherwise based, it did not survive into the final version of the reform, seemingly because it was thought, on reflection, that it would generate overly-complex and potentially confusing information.[174]

[170] CA 1985, s 262(1).

[171] New Schedule 7A, inserted by the Regulations. Disclosure is dealt with in regs 3 and 4.

[172] Chosen and justified by the board.

[173] n 161 para 3.34-3.39.

[174] Interestingly, the consultative document did not formally consult on the requirement to provide comparative material for each performance condition, and so the government's summary of the responses to the consultation is not very forthcoming on the point: DTI 'Directors' Remuneration: Summary of Responses to the Consultative Document' URN 01/1400, 2002, last page.

IV. Likely Impact of the Reforms

The requirement for approval by the shareholders of the remuneration report, which includes the statement of remuneration policy,[175] extends only to an advisory vote.[176] No director's entitlement to remuneration is dependent on the result of the vote (for fear that the hiring process would become impossibly drawn-out and uncertain) nor is the board required to resign if its report is defeated. On the other hand, it is difficult to believe that defeat or consistent substantial adverse votes on the board's remuneration report would not have an impact on the company's remuneration practices and policies. The question is what that impact is likely to be. Cheffins and Thomas[177] have argued that it is unlikely that the enhanced disclosure and shareholder approval requirements will exert a general downward pressure on executive salaries. This seems undoubtedly to be true if one is thinking of the 'n-x' variety of formula beloved of utilities regulators. The main controllers of votes at general meetings are, as we have seen, the fund managers and the executives of large financial institutions are unlikely to be in favour of such an incomes policy which might impact on their own remuneration.[178] Nor is it at all clear that it would be in the shareholders' own interests to rule out rewards for success in this way.

In any event, it would be wrong to attribute the object of general downward pressure on executive pay to the Government. Its main concern was with the linkage of pay to performance,[179] both in relation to incentivised pay and compensation upon loss of office (not dealt with here). Are the reforms likely to be more successful in this direction? Will the enhanced use of the traditional technique of disclosure, coupled with a formal opportunity for the shareholders to express an opinion on the material disclosed, increase the constraints operating on executive directors not to give free reign to their 'positional power' in remuneration setting?[180] In particular, will these rules enhance the impact of the 'outrage'

[175] The other main element in the report is the disclosure of remuneration packages of each director, ie the requirements previously in the Listing Rules. That is subject to audit, whereas the statement of remuneration policy is not, though presumably the auditors will check that nothing is said in the statement of policy which is inconsistent with what has been found in the audit.

[176] New s 241A.

[177] 'Should shareholders have a greater say over executive pay? Learning from the US experience' (2001) 1 JCLS 277.

[178] See the criticism of the bonus policy of Amvescap, a fund manager, and of the remuneration of the chief executive of Schroders at the AGMs of those companies: *Financial Times* (1 May 2003).

[179] n 142, Foreword.

[180] J Hill and Yablon 'Corporate Governance and Executive Remuneration: Rediscovering Managerial Positional Conflict' 2003 (available on ssrn).

factor[181] (and its associated reputational costs) in constraining abnormal upward shifts in executive remuneration? The new regulations have certainly got off to a high-profile start in this respect. They seem to have moved executive remuneration up the scale of significance in AGMs in 2003.[182] The most dramatic development was the defeat of an approval resolution at GSK, a multinational pharmaceutical company, though the main issue exercising shareholders there seems to have been the size of potential termination payments (albeit that these can be regarded as an aspect of the debate about incentives).[183] A number of companies, anticipating difficulties, discussed their plans with investors in advance of the meeting and modified them to take account of objections.[184] The longer term impact of the reforms, however, is more difficult to predict. In particular, what remains to be seen is whether the reputational costs of a substantial vote against fall as such votes become more common or whether those anticipated costs will lead to a general (if informal) policy of agreeing remuneration policy with major investors in advance of the AGM.

F. Analysts' Conflicts of Interest

This can be dealt with quite quickly, partly because this topic takes us outside the core of corporate governance and partly because the analysis of the problem and the remedies proposed by the regulator (in the case the Financial Services Authority)[185], very closely track those taken in the United States, but operate at a lower level of intensity. The FSA gave events in the US as the trigger for its investigation and proposals and accepts that 'the same potential conflicts and pressures do exist in UK investment banking.'[186] The lower intensity of response can be explained by three factors. There is statistical evidence that conflicts of interest have affected research recommendations in the UK in the FSA's finding that buy recommendations from firms acting as brokers/advisers for the company subject to the recommendation are twice as high as where this is not the case.[187]

[181] n 155.

[182] 'Protest call over executive pay' *Financial Times* (14 April 2003) listing the companies at which the National Association of Pension Funds had recommended that its members vote against or abstain on the remuneration reports; and 'Shareholders seize their power' ibid, 26 April 2003.

[183] 'Investors reject GSK executive pay policy' *Financial Times* (20 May 2003).

[184] See n 182.

[185] To date, its two relevant documents are Discussion Paper 15 (DP 15) 'Investment Research: conflicts and other issues' July 2002 and Consultation Paper 171 (CP 171) 'Conflicts of Interest: Investment Research and Issues of Securities' February 2003.

[186] CP 171, para 1.4.

[187] DP, para 1.4.

However, no charge of illegality has been brought home against any particular investment bank and so there was no basis for imposing, for example, the requirement firms sponsor independent research as part of a settlement, whilst as a regulatory rule it is not clear that such a requirement would pass the Financial Service and Markets Act's cost/benefit requirement.[188]

Further, the FSA's response was a little tentative because the regulation of financial analysts' reports is partly a matter for Community law whose dispositions on the matter are still in a state of development. (The matter is being dealt with by the Level 2 rules under Market Abuse Directive[189] and in the proposed revision of the Investment Services Directive.) Thus, there was a natural reluctance not to commit to national regulatory rules unless it is tolerably clear that they would be consistent with the soon-to-emerge EC regulation. Third, although the FSA accepted that the risk of conflicted research existed, it took the view that the addressees of the research were less likely to be misled in the UK than in the US, because of 'the overwhelmingly institutional nature of the investment research market in the UK.'[190]

A second set of considerations producing a somewhat different response to the regulation of analysts in the UK was the desire of the FSA, as with other regulators, to stick to 'principle-based' regulation. This means that the regulatory structure consists of high-level principles, some of which are highly abstract indeed (such as: FSA's Principle of Business 8: 'a firm must manage conflicts of interest fairly'), guidance from the FSA on what the principles might imply in particular situations, but relatively few bright-line rules. Guidance consists of 'information and advice'[191] and so, in the normal case, neither creates legal obligations nor delineates firmly obligations created elsewhere in the Act, though in practice it may come close to doing both. The FSA's proposed response to the regulatory problems posed by analysts' conflicts of interest was substantially to add to its guidance on what investment banks are required to do to implement Principle 8, and other relevant principles, in the areas of supervision of analysts, analysts' involvement in investment banking and equity sales, their compensation and reward structures and their exposure to pressure from client companies.[192]

However, relatively few new rules were proposed and even fewer of them went beyond disclosure obligations. Disclosure is to be required, as part of the

[188] s 155 and CP 171, paras 4.43-4.46.

[189] See Working Document ESC 13/2003 of the DG Internal Market.

[190] CP 171, para 3.7. The FSA does, however, propose a set of protections for retail investors, whose value does not depend so much upon counteracting conflicts of interest as on combating ignorance on the part of such investors (for example, ignorance that the institutional investors will undoubtedly have extracted the value from a recommendation by action in the market before retail investors become aware of it).

[191] S 157(1).

[192] CP 171, para 4.4.

research report, of any financial interest the analyst has in the subject of the research, any shareholding above 1% or other significant financial interest or relationship on the part of the firm or an associate in the subject of the research, whether the firm is a market-maker in the relevant security and, just to make sure, any other 'material interest' of the analyst or the firm.[193] The research must also reveal, in respect of a twelve month period, comparative data on the recommendations the firm has given which distinguishes those cases where the firm has conducted corporate finance business in relation to the investment and those where it has not.[194] New rule proposals, going beyond disclosure, are confined, as far as analysts are concerned, to the introduction of mandatory 'quiet periods' around IPOs (but not secondary offerings),[195] a prohibition on analysts engaging in own account dealings in companies which they cover (or possibly in any company in the market segments they cover),[196] a reduction of the exceptions to the prohibition on front-running research,[197] and a requirement that the analyst certifies that the views expressed in the research accurately reflect his or her personal views.[198]

G. By Way of Conclusion: The Non-Barking Dog

As we have seen, in all the above cases the main thrust of the regulatory response has been the intensification of regulation along established lines. This effect of Enron and associated events should not be underestimated. It is, for example, quite clear that, without Enron, it is much less likely that a review of the board structure rules of the CC would have taken place at this time or that self-regulation of the accountancy profession through the Accountancy Foundation would have been subject to a partial dismantling. On the other hand, the impact of the scandals was not enough to produce the adoption of new regulatory strategies, such as the mandatory unbundling of the activities of professional service firms or investment banks. Investment banks may still carry on both corporate finance business and the production of research-based recommendations (though the latter may be a less remunerative activity in the future than in the past). With some restrictions, audit firms may still provide non-audit services to clients. In both cases, faith has been placed in much more rigorous management of the potential conflicts of interest rather than their elimination.

[193] Proposed COB 7.16.13.

[194] Proposed COB 7.16.12.

[195] Proposed COB 7.16.14.

[196] Proposed COB 7.13.4 and 7.13.7.

[197] Proposed COB 7.3.4.

[198] Proposed COB 7.16.12.

However, one traditional technique which has not featured in the reform proposals is that of liability rules. At one level this is surprising, since the Enron story is in large part one of the failure of 'gatekeepers', notably auditors and non-executive directors. A part of the answer may be that many of the reforms lie in the area of soft law, which are not apt to generate changes in legal liability. However, the answer probably goes deeper than that and involves considerable doubt about the value of liability in rules in producing efficient solutions in the areas of incompetence or loyalty, despite these being their traditional areas of operation.

As far as auditors are concerned, whose their liability for negligence derives from the general common law rules on liability for negligent misstatements, the dominant tendency in the current case-law[199] is to make the auditors liable only to (a) the company itself and (b) to individual shareholders of the company in respect of the exercise of their corporate governance rights. Thus, reliance on the accounts by shareholders when taking investment decisions and decisions by non-shareholder investors and creditors, even where such reliance is foreseeable on the part of the auditors, will not normally generate liability. In order for the wider liability to arise, the auditors must assume responsibility to the claimant for the statements in the accounts by some act additional to simply certifying the accounts.[200] Although initially contemplating creating a wider liability by statute, the CLR eventually endorsed the common law position, partly because of the potential for 'abusive exploitation by claimants' of the extended liability.[201] In fact, the general thrust of the CLR's final recommendations was to continue the tendency to confine the liability of auditors, partly by clarifying the scope of the auditors to reduce their liability where there was contributory negligence (or worse) within the company and partly by making it easier for the auditors to disclaim liability.[202]

[199] *Caparo Industries plc v Dickman* [1990] 2 A.C. 605 (HL), but contrast *Royal Bank of Scotland v Bannerman Johnstone Maclay* 2003 SLT 181 (reliance by a creditor), where a Scottish court seemed to turn the current law on its head by finding an assumption of responsibility in the failure by the auditors to issue a disclaimer of liability with the accounts. See further below.

[200] For more detail, See Gower and P Davies *Principles of Modern Company Law* (Sweet & Maxwell London 7th edn 2003) 580-589.

[201] CLR, Final Report I, para 8.128 (2001). 'one major risk of such abuse arises from the possibility of actions to recover losses from major failed investment decisions made by professional investors who should rely on their own judgement in such cases. It would be relatively easy for them to identify perhaps quite minor negligent failures by the auditors which they could assert had caused them, in reliance on the accounts and the auditors' report to incur the loss.' (para 8.129)

[202] ibid paras 8.139-8.144. The second of these is likely to be particularly controversial. See the adverse reactions of the SEC and the European Commission to the introduction of disclaimers by some auditing firms in the light of the *Bannerman* decision (above): see *Financial Times* (22 January 2003 and 25 March 2003) and n 25 at 14.

As far as non-executive directors are concerned, historically they have been sheltered from negligence liability (as with all directors) by a uniquely favourable and subjective standard of care. Only a failure to achieve the standard of competence of which the particular director is personally capable with trigger liability. Both at common law and under the reform proposals of the CLR that subjective duty of care is being replaced by an objective duty of the standard type (duty of care of the reasonable person).[203] What this may mean in practice has still to be worked out. In particular, the shift to an objective standard of care does not mean that the range of persons to whom the duty is owed has been expanded and the traditional view is that the directors' duty of care is owed only to the company[204] and derivative actions have not been easily available.[205] However, it is highly likely that what the law requires in the future by way of standards of care of non-executive directors or of companies in respect of the functions of non-executive directors will be strongly influenced by the provisions of the CC. The use of non-legal standards to determine the standard of care required at common law of professional and quasi-professional persons is well established.[206] In this way, the provisions of the CC may have an indirect, but real, impact upon the liability rules applying to non-executive directors, especially in the light of the reforms proposed in relation the induction and training of directors and evaluation of board performance. Mr Higgs in his report clearly regarded this expanded liability as negative potential development, as likely to discourage appropriate persons from putting themselves forward as non-executive directors of large companies.[207] Apart from making it easy for companies to insure or indemnify directors against the costs of litigation, Mr Higgs proposed to go the heart of the problem by introducing language into the CC which, it was hoped, would discourage courts from imposing unrealistic standards upon non-executive directors.[208]

Overall, four points emerge:

[203] CLR, Final Report I, 346, Principle 4.

[204] In respect of the accounts, the range of potential claimants should presumably track that adopted in the case of the auditors.

[205] Thought that too may be about to change to some extent as a result of Law Commission and CLR recommendations: Gower and Davies (n 200) ch 17.

[206] For example *Lloyd Cheyham & Co Ltd v Littlejohn & Co* [1987] BCLC 303 (failure by auditors to following relevant accounting standards).

[207] Higgs Report, ch 14.

[208] Proposed new schedule, now Schedule B of the [new] CC, stressing the limited time commitment of non-executive directors to the company and their lower level of detailed knowledge of the company. On the other hand, the schedule also contains language which stresses the positive duties of non-executive directors in relation to induction, professional development, making enquiries and taking advice and action, so that its overall impact may be different from what the Higgs Report expects. On the willingness of Commonwealth courts to distinguish between the standards of care of executive and non-executive directors see *Daniels v Anderson* (1995) 16 ACSR 607 (NSWCA).

1. The central issues in the post-Enron debate have been seen as revolving around conflicts of interest, rather than competence.
2. Despite the breadth of the reform effort, the changes in mandatory rules (whether contained in legislation or rules laid down by the FSA) have put the emphasis on the traditional prophylactics: disclosure and approval by those likely to be affected adversely by the conflicts of interest.
3. The main thrust of the reforms is to be found in an expansion of the 'comply or explain' provisions of the CC. However, the above analysis carries some warnings for the Cadbury approach of having management and investors negotiate the content and implementation of the structural rules of corporate governance, under the aegis of government. Management and investors must be able to agree and hold in place a structure which meets the Government's minimum requirement that the issue is taken out of public controversy. Otherwise, as with executive remuneration, legislation may follow (which is not to say that legislation will necessarily defuse the controversy, but at least the government can be seen to have acted).
4. It is difficult to present professional self-regulation as an effective response to pressure for change and it is not surprising that, as far as accounting and auditing is concerned, it has been one of the major casualties of Enron.

Corporate Scandals Across the Globe: Regulating the Role of the Director

JENNIFER HILL*

At the beginning of this decade, many commentators assumed that international corporate regulation was inexorably directed towards convergence, in the form of a standardised model of corporate governance. This assumption needs to be reassessed, in the light of the concentration of corporate collapses around the world, including Enron and WorldCom in the US, and HIH and One.Tel in Australia, and the evolving international regulatory response to those collapses. The chapter examines a number of corporate governance reforms and developments in Australia concerning the role of the board of directors, comparing these responses to those in other jurisdictions, such as the US and UK.

A. Introduction

> *The triumph of the shareholder-oriented model of the corporation over its principal competitors is now assured...*
>
> Hansmann and Kraakman (2001)[1]

Comparative corporate governance is at a fascinating juncture. For more than a decade, scholars have been interested in the structural differences and implications of a dispersed shareholding or 'outsider' system of corporate governance, exemplified by the UK and US, and 'insider' systems with more concentrated

* I would like to thank a number of friends and colleagues for helpful comments and support in relation to this research, including Carlo Amatucci, Mark Brandon, John Coffee, Paul Davies, Deborah DeMott, Alan Dignam, Steve Schwarcz, Randall Thomas, Robert Thompson and Charles Yablon. Thanks also to Christopher Demko and David Rolph for excellent research assistance. Financial support for this research was provided by the University of Sydney Law School and Vanderbilt University Law School.

[1] H Hansmann and R Kraakman 'The End of History for Corporate Law' (2001) 89 Geo LJ 439, 468.

ownership structures, traditionally found in continental Europe[2] and Asia.[3] Major international organisations have also engaged in the dissection and classification of comparative corporate governance laws.[4] Whereas outsider systems have typically been associated with a shareholder-centred paradigm of corporate governance, insider systems have been linked to a stakeholder model.

Recent comparative corporate governance scholarship has postulated that 'law matters' in the development and performance of financial markets.[5] And, if law matters, then so, too, does law reform.[6] Two waves of international corporate law reform have recently occurred. Under the first wave, a number of countries with concentrated ownership structures[7] instituted reform programs to replicate aspects of the legal and structural patterns of countries with dispersed shareholding and deep liquid capital markets.

Yet, while some insider legal systems implemented reforms of this kind, the corporate governance rules and norms in jurisdictions with outsider systems of corporate governance are themselves now changing. In the wake of recent corporate collapses, countries such as the US, UK and Australia have embarked upon reform programs designed to rectify perceived governance weaknesses in their legal systems. The Report of the High Level Group of Company Law Experts[8]

[2] For example, G Visentini 'Compatibility and Competition Between European and American Corporate Governance: Which Model of Capitalism?' (1998) 23 Brooklyn J Int'l L 833.

[3] Australia provides an interesting perspective on the comparative corporate governance debate, beause it exhibits characteristics of both the outsider and insider models of corporate governance. Although its system of corporate governance is traditionally treated as reflecting the US/UK model, in fact Australia constitutes a hybrid of the two systems, since its publicly listed corporate sector contains a mix of diversified and controlling blockholder ownership structures. See generally S Lamba and G Stapledon 'The Determinants of Corporate Ownership Structure: Australian Evidence' (2001) Working Paper, University of Melbourne.

[4] See generally AN Licht 'The Mother of All Path Dependencies: Toward a Cross-Cultural Theory of Corporate Governance Systems' (2001) 26 Del J Corp L 147.

[5] For example R La Porta, F Lopez-de-Silanes and A Shleifer 'Corporate Ownership Around the World' (1999) 54 J Fin 471; BR Cheffins 'Does Law Matter? The Separation of Ownership and Control in the United Kingdom' (2001) 30 J Legal Studies 459. The oft-cited McKinsey survey also found that global investors were prepared to pay a large premium for the stock of companies which were governed by effective corporate governance regimes (McKinsey Investor Opinion Survey, June 2000).

[6] For an early discussion of the extent to which comparativism may be useful as a 'tool of law reform', see O Kahn-Freund 'On Uses and Misuses of Comparative Law' (1974) 37 Mod L Rev 1.

[7] These include countries such as Italy, Germany and Japan. See generally HJ Gregory 'The Globablisation of Corporate Governance' Weil, Gotshal and Manges, ((2000) available at <http://rru.worldbank.org/documents/globalisation of corporate governance.pdf>.

[8] J Winter (Chair), *Report of the High Level Group of Company Law Experts on a Modern Regulatory Framework for Company Law in Europe* (European Commission, Brussels November 2002) (Winter Report, see Annex 3 in this volume).

('the Winter Report') has now addressed the issue of corporate governance reform on a European-wide basis.

By the beginning of this decade, many commentators assumed that international corporate regulation was inexorably directed towards a single point of convergence, in the form of a standardised Anglo-US shareholder-centred model of corporate governance.[9] The convergence assumption[10] needs to be reassessed, however, in the light of the concentration of corporate collapses and the evolving international regulatory responses to those collapses.

B. A Tale of Two Australian Corporate Collapses

All happy families resemble each other, but each unhappy family is unhappy in its own way.

Tolstoy, *Anna Karenina* (1875-7)

So intense has been the brouhaha surrounding the collapses of Enron and WorldCom in the US,[11] that it is easy to forget that these financial scandals mirror a global phenomenon. The scandals and collapses, for example, involving Independent Insurance[12] and Marconi[13] in the UK, Elan in Ireland, Kirch[14] in Germany, Royal Ahold[15] in the Netherlands, and HIH Insurance and One.Tel in Australia, pose analogous questions about the efficacy of corporate governance practices and financial regulation.[16]

[9] For example H Hansmann and R Kraakman (n 1) 439.

[10] The Winter Report, while advocating that the EU should co-ordinate the efforts of Member States to facilitate convergence, nonetheless accepted differences in aspects of European corporate governance, such as board structure, which have developed along 'specific paths of legal and cultural development'. See Winter Report 59, 72.

[11] Other US financial scandals have, of course, unfolded more recently, including the scandal at HealthSouth Corp, which is the subject of an SEC prosecution. See 'Close relations: Inside alleged fraud at HealthSouth, a 'family' plot'' *Wall St Journal* (3 April 2003) A1.

[12] Plender 'Missed Signals' *Financial Times* (20 June 2001).

[13] Durman 'Banks prepare to take control of Marconi' *Sunday Times* (London 24 March 2002) 9.

[14] Wagner 'How the mighty have fallen' *The Banker* (1 April 2002) 30.

[15] C Matlack, J Rossant, D Fairlamb and Capell 'The Year of Nasty Surprises' Business Week (10 March 2003) 48.

[16] Plender (n 12). Reactions vary considerably to the corporate scandals across different jurisdictions. While the collapses of HIH and One.Tel have resulted in intense public backlash and law reform in Australia, it has been claimed that the European response to the collapses has been more muted and sanguine. See L Enriques 'Bad Apples, Bad Oranges. A Comment from Old Europe on Post-Enron Corporate Governance Reforms' (paper delivered at the 2003, Wake

cont. ...

International scandals add an important dimension to the current debate in the US on what caused the collapses at Enron and WorldCom. A number of theories are in circulation. A prevalent assumption is that a major factor in the corporate collapses was the inadequacy of US boards,[17] however Professor Coffee has outlined at least three other possible explanations for the outbreak of US financial scandals.[18] It is possible that the existence of shared features in recent international collapses[19] may provide insights into the relative strength and plausibility of competing explanations. Alternative regulatory responses to the corporate collapses also implicitly reflect different theories about their causation.

Two recent Australian corporate collapses, HIH Insurance ('HIH') and One.Tel, form a factual backdrop to the discussion in this paper. HIH is the largest collapse in Australian corporate history, and has been the subject of an A$40 million Royal Commission, which reported its findings in April 2003.[20] One.Tel has spawned extensive proceedings in the Australian courts.

Superficially, at least, HIH and One.Tel appeared to be very different companies. At the time when HIH was placed in provisional liquidation in March 2001,[21] it was Australia's second largest general insurer. The chief executive officer ('CEO') of HIH, Ray Williams, had founded the corporate predecessor of HIH more than thirty years earlier.[22] In contrast, One.Tel was a new player in the telecom market, with 'extravagant aspirations'[23] to become the foremost telco in

Forest Corporate Law Conference), *5ff* examining some reasons for the difference between the public response to the collapses in the US and Europe.

[17] J Sonnenfeld 'What Makes Great Boards Great' (2002) 80 (9) Harv Bus Rev 106.

[18] These possible explanations are: 'the gatekeeper story', focusing on conflicts of interest in reputational intermediaries, such as auditors and analysts; 'the misaligned incentives story', focusing on the role of executive pay; and 'the herding story', focusing on the incentives of fund managers in relation to quarterly performance. See generally, JC Coffee 'What Caused Enron?: A Capsule Social and Economic History of the 1990s' Working Paper No 214, Columbia Law School, 20 January 2003.

[19] For example GP Miller 'Catastrophic Financial Failures: Enron, HIH and More' (Speech delivered at the Ross Parsons Lecture 2002, The Global Regulation of Banking and Insurance: From HIH to Enron, University of Sydney Law School, 11 July 2002) (forthcoming, 2003 Cornell L Rev).

[20] HIH Royal Commission *The failure of HIH Insurance* (National Capital Printing Canberra 2003). The Royal Commission investigation lasted for 18 months. See generally Buffini and others 'Business hits back over HIH reforms' *Australian Financial Review* (22 April 2003) 1.

[21] Two weeks earlier, the Australian Prudential Regulatory Authority ('APRA') issued notice to HIH to show cause why an inspector should not be appointed under the Insurance Act 1973 (Cth). HIH Royal Commission, ibid 30.

[22] ibid 20.

[23] Jay 'The Day of Reckoning' in J Adams, A Bristow, J Cannings and others (eds) *Collapse Incorporated: Tales, Safeguards and Responsibilities of Corporate Australia* (CCH Australia Ltd Sydney 2001) 1.

Australia and a major player in the European market. Ultimately One.Tel had a short shelf-life, surviving less than four years after it was floated on the Australian Stock Exchange in late 1997.

In terms of corporate governance, however, the collapses of HIH and One.Tel display a number of similarities. Both companies had charismatic and dominating CEOs. Both companies engaged in high-risk practices in extremely competitive markets. In the case of HIH, these practices included failure to carry prudential insurance margins;[24] activities in the difficult London reinsurance market and the 'murky' world of film finance;[25] and serious losses in the Californian workers' compensation market.[26] HIH also undertook a takeover of another insurance company, FAI Insurance, which, according to the HIH Royal Commission, exhibited an unusual lack of due diligence checks, was 'impetuous and based on completely inadequate information',[27] and ultimately resulted in disastrous losses for HIH.[28]

Australia has had a system of continuous disclosure for public listed companies since 1994.[29] One interesting post-Enron reform in the US has been a shift away from the traditional American model of periodic disclosure towards a system of 'real time' or continuous disclosure, more akin to the model that has applied in Australia for the last decade.[30] Nonetheless, in spite of the existence of a continuous disclosure rule at the time of the collapses of HIH and One.Tel, there seems little doubt that some investors and insiders were better informed about the true financial position than others, and benefited from that knowledge.[31]

[24] According to the HIH Royal Commission Report, under-reserving was the major cause of HIH's collapse. See HIH Royal Commission (n 20) 13, 21. HIH thus appeared to be an example of the classic problem in the insurance industry, described by John Plender, whereby '[i]t is easy for entrepreneurs to convince themselves that their efforts to increase market share at their competitors' expense are a demonstration of marketing genius, not a symptom of imprudent underwriting and under reserving'. Plender (n 12).

[25] Jay (n 23) 1.

[26] HIH Royal Commission (n 20) 17-18, describing HIH's re-entry into the Californian workers' compensation market as 'a debacle', costing the group approximately A$620 million.

[27] ibid 17.

[28] ibid 18, 23. According to the Royal Commission Report, the FAI Insurance acquisition resulted in a loss to HIH of approximately A$590 million.

[29] Australian Stock Exchange (ASX) Listing Rule 3.1; s 674 Corporations Act 2001 (Cth).

[30] The SEC has already proposed a significant expansion of matters requiring immediate disclosure. See Release #33-8106, Additional Form 8-K Disclosure Requirements and Acceleration of Filing Date (available at <http://www.sec.gov/rules/proposed/33-8106. htm>). See also s 409 of the Sarbanes-Oxley Act 2002.

[31] For example, it has been claimed that although the collapse of HIH came as no surprise to sophisticated investors, many of whom had exited from HIH prior to its collapse, it was wholly unexpected for many other groups, including employees and professional groups, such as the NSW Law Society, which had insurance with HIH. See Jay (n 23) 13. The HIH Royal Commission also found that, in the final days before HIH's collapse, millions of dollars flowed

cont. ...

Nor, it seems did the directors of these companies have more information as a result of the continuous disclosure regime. As in the case of Enron and WorldCom, these collapses also involved aggressive and questionable accounting practices.[32]

In contrast to the characteristic dispersed shareholding associated with outsider systems of corporate governance, HIH and One.Tel both had substantial block shareholders. 50% of HIH was held by another company, Winterthur Swiss Insurance Company, which had a strong international reputation and credit rating. Winterthur Swiss was a passive investor in HIH, but was apparently so concerned about the company's performance, that it ultimately sold its entire shareholding to the public in 1998.[33]

The major shareholders in One.Tel were more high profile and more active in the One.Tel's affairs. One of the reasons for the great level of interest in Australia in One.Tel's collapse was that leading players in the saga were James Packer and Lachlan Murdoch, young heirs to large fortunes. Packer and Murdoch sat on the board of One.Tel as non-executive directors. Their appointment followed a major investment by News Ltd and PBL (the public listed companies controlled by the Murdoch and Packer families respectively) in exchange for a 40% stake in One.Tel.[34] Following the collapse of One.Tel, Lachlan Murdoch swore an affidavit to the Australian Securities and Investments Commission ('ASIC'), claiming that he had been 'profoundly misled' about the state of One.Tel's financial position.[35]

With the benefit of hindsight, the collapses in HIH and One.Tel seem inevitable. Although the HIH Directors' Report for the year ended 30 June 2000 reported consolidated profit of A$18.4 million, a subsequent report by KPMG[36] advised that the company had been on the edge of insolvency for a number of

to a favoured few insiders. HIH Royal Commission (n 20) 30. In the case of One.Tel, see P Barry *Rich Kids: How the Murdochs and Packers lost $950 million in One.Tel* (Bantam Books Milsons Point NSW 2002) 292.

[32] In relation to HIH and FAI Insurance, for example, it appears that the companies entered into a number of transactions, which although described as reinsurance, did not genuinely shift risk, but were merely loans. The companies' classification of the transactions as reinsurance contracts substantially boosted profits. See HIH Royal Commission, ibid, 22-24, 33. In relation to One.Tel, see Barry ibid 361, suggesting that a change to One.Tel's accounting policy helped it to transform a $25 million loss into an A$ 9.8 million profit in its annual results in August 1999.

[33] HIH Royal Commission, ibid 21. According to the Royal Commission, the sale by Winterthur was detrimental to HIH, since it eroded market confidence engendered by the presence of 'a strong shareholder of global repute'.

[34] Barry (n 31) News Ltd and PBL agreed to invest A$430 million immediately and invest a further A$280 million in the future.

[35] Affidavit lodged by Mr Lachlan Murdoch, Supreme Court of NSW (Lacy and Hepworth 'One.Tel: ASIC bombshell' *Australian Financial Review* (15 June 2001, 1).

[36] This report was commissioned by the new CEO of HIH, Randolph Wein, who replaced Ray Williams in December 2000. See Jay (n 23) 10.

years and should be placed in provisional liquidation.[37] A true picture of One.Tel's parlous financial state only emerged after an anonymous warning email was sent to the chief finance adviser of One.Tel's major shareholder.[38]

Like Enron and WorldCom in the US, HIH and One.Tel raise puzzling questions about what caused the collapses, and how boards of directors (and others within the corporate governance ecosystem, such as auditors, shareholders and regulators)[39] can miss crucial warning signs of impending corporate disaster. This is a particularly intriguing question in relation to One.Tel's board, given the close involvement of sophisticated major shareholders in the business and their representation on the board. Like other major international corporate collapses, the events at HIH and One.Tel have prompted a series of significant corporate governance reforms in Australia.

The general regulatory response to corporate collapse in Australia includes, to date: (i) proposed legislative reforms; (ii) governance changes to self-regulatory organisations; and (iii) judicial decision-making. Within the first category, the Corporate Law Economic Reform Program Issues Paper No 9 ('the CLERP 9 proposals'),[40] which the federal government released in September 2002,[41] foreshadows increased regulation of gatekeepers, such as auditors[42] and analysts.[43] The CLERP 9 proposals also address a number of other aspects of corporate governance, such as disclosure,[44] shareholder participation in governance,[45] and enforcement issues.[46]

[37] HIH Royal Commission (n 20) 30.

[38] The email was sent by a senior accountant at One.Tel, code-named 'Ghostdogperil', to Packer's chief finance adviser, Geoff Kleeman, who had gone into One.Tel four months earlier to examine the company's books. See Barry (n 31) 272-273.

[39] On the role of the regulators, including APRA, and the role of the auditors and other advisers in the collapse of HIH, see HIH Royal Commission (n 20) 36-38 and 39-41.

[40] Corporate Law Economic Reform Program, Issue Paper No 9, Corporate Disclosure: Strengthening the Financial Reporting Framework (September 2002) (available at <http://www.treasury.gov.au/documents/403/PDF/Clerp9.pdf>).

[41] Draft legislation under CLERP 9 is due for release in September 2003. Its release was delayed to take into account the findings of the HIH Royal Commission.

[42] A major theme in the CLERP 9 proposals is improvement of the audit function. See Corporate Law Economic Reform Program, Issue Paper No 9 (n 40). While a number of the proposals deal with similar concerns to those addressed in the US under the Sarbanes-Oxley *Act* 2002, the reforms under the CLERP 9 proposals are far less stringent and less prescriptive than the US reforms. For discussion of the scope of the US reforms, see generally, RB Thompson 'Corporate Governance After Enron: The First Year' forthcoming (2003) Houston L Rev 2003.

[43] See Corporate Law Economic Reform Program, Issue Paper No 9 (n 40). See also ASIC, Research Analyst Independence: ASIC Surveillance Report (August 2003).

[44] See Corporate Law Economic Reform Program, Issue Paper No 9 (n 40).

[45] ibid Part 11.

[46] ibid Part 10.

There have also been significant amendments to the Australian Stock Exchange ('ASX') Listing Rules, concerning best practice in corporate governance and enhanced disclosure under Australia's continuous disclosure regime. Finally, there have been some important judicial decisions relating to breach of directors' duties. This chapter predominantly focuses on reforms relating to the role of the board and the responsibilities of directors and managers. It compares the Australian regulatory responses to corporate collapse with those in other jurisdictions, such as the US and UK.

C. Board Structure and Composition as a Contemporary Corporate Governance Tool

I. The Big Picture – Norms and Laws in Corporate Governance

> *I am becoming less and less comfortable with the phrase 'corporate governance' – not because of its content but because it has been so widely used that it may become meaningless.*
>
> The Hon. Justice Neville Owen,
> HIH Royal Commission Report (2003)[47]

Historically, corporate scandals have produced increased levels of regulation in the US,[48] UK,[49] and Australia,[50] and the current regulatory surge is therefore entirely predictable. One of the key subjects, on which reforms in these jurisdictions have refocused attention, is the board of directors, suggesting that board inadequacy, or corruption, was a significant contributing factor to the corporate collapses.[51]

Since at least the 1970s, the board of directors has occupied a central role in monitoring and legitimising managerial conduct within the corporation.[52] Of the

[47] HIH Royal Commission (n 20) 24.

[48] JC Coffee (n 18) 3.

[49] R Smerdon *A Practical Guide to Corporate Governance* (Sweet & Maxwell London 1998) 1 ff, examining the interrelation between a series of UK corporate scandals in the late 1980s and early 1990s, such as Polly Peck, the Maxwell Group, Allied Lyons and Barings Bank, and the introduction of more stringent corporate governance principles.

[50] The introduction of the shareholder consent rules for related party rules under Australian corporate law, for example, was directly attributable to a spate of corporate scandals in the late 1980s, such as Bond Corp and the Qintex Group. See generally, J Hill 'Visions and Revisions of the Shareholder' (2000) 48 Am J Comp L 39, 69ff.

[51] Sonnenfeld (n. 17) 106. This assumption is shared by the Winter Committee. See Winter Report at 60.

[52] For discussions around that time of the evolving significance of the board, see MA Eisenberg *The Structure of the Corporation: A Legal Analysis* (Little Brown & Company

cont. ...

panoply of modern governance techniques,[53] the board of directors is viewed as the dominant accountability mechanism. This perception led to major changes in both the role and structure of the board over recent decades. These changes have in the past been driven, not by legislative intervention, but by the development of commercial practices and norms.[54]

These norms generally emanated from voluntary adoption of guidelines from a range of different sources. A recent comparative study of corporate governance codes in Europe identified such sources as including governmental or quasi-governmental entities; committees organised by governments or by stock exchanges; business, industry and academic associations; directors' associations and investor-related groups.[55]

Thus, for example, in Australia, the Investment and Financial Services Association ('IFSA'), has been an important source of corporate governance norms. IFSA, comprising leading institutional investors, publishes a set of influential guidelines for investment managers, which contain detailed provisions concerning boards.[56] These guidelines relate to matters such as composition of the board, board committees, election of non-executive directors, performance evaluation, allocation of the roles of the board and management, and remuneration policies.[57]

There is, nonetheless, an interrelation between governmental regulation and voluntary corporate governance codes of this kind. The development of self-regulatory codes of conduct has tended to be either a response to the lack of specific governmental regulation in particular areas or, in some cases, a justification for the absence of such regulation.[58] IFSA's guidelines arguably reflect the

Boston 1976) 149-185; V Brudney 'The Independent Director – Heavenly City or Potemkin Village?' (1982) 95 Harv L Rev 597. See also *In re Caremark International Inc Derivative Litigation* 698 A. 2d 959, 970 (1996), stating that 'in recent years the Delaware Supreme Court has made it clear…the seriousness with which the corporation law views the role of the corporate board'.

[53] Such as takeovers, institutional investors, reputational intermediaries like auditors and analysts, and techniques to align managerial interests with those of shareholders via, for example, performance-based pay.

[54] For example, JC Coffee 'Do Norms Matter? A Cross-Country Evaluation' (2001) 149 U Pa L Rev 2151. See also H Hansmann and R Kraakman (n 1) 455, who state that '[w]e expect that the reform of corporate governance practices will generally precede the reform of corporate law, for the simple reason that governance practice is largely a matter of private ordering that does not require legislative action'.

[55] Weil, Gotshal & Manges LLP, 'Comparative Study of Corporate Governance Codes Relevant to the European Union and its Member States, Final Report & Annexes I-III' (on behalf of the European Commission, Internal Market Directorate General (January 2002) 2.

[56] IFSA *Corporate Governance: A Guide for Fund Managers and Corporations* ('Blue Book') (4th edn December 2002).

[57] ibid Guidelines 3, 6, 7, 9, 10, 12 and 13.

[58] This interrelation between government regulation and corporate governance was recognised by Sir Adrian Cadbury in the early 1990s, who argued that inadequate enforcement of

cont. ...

former position. Recent action by IFSA's UK counterpart, the Institutional Shareholders' Committee ('ISC'),[59] however, demonstrates the latter, pre-emptive role of some codes of conduct. The ISC recently published a comprehensive statement of best practice concerning shareholder activism.[60] The adoption of these principles appears to have been a direct attempt to forestall the introduction of stringent government legislation[61] imposing a statutory duty on institutional investors to intervene in corporate governance.[62]

There has also been a global trend for stock exchanges to be more involved in corporate governance regulation. In Australia, the Australian Stock Exchange ('ASX') has played a role in corporate governance since 1996,[63] when it introduced a rule requiring listed companies to disclose certain corporate governance practices in their annual reports.[64] The rule was criticised by institutional investors as lacking regulatory teeth,[65] however, since it avoided any prescriptive rules on content, merely requiring a company to disclose its main governance practices, if any. The ASX argued in favour of a non-prescriptive approach at the time of the introduction of the listing rule, on the basis that it would enhance corporate governance flexibility and allow Australian companies to adopt international best practices.

good governance practices could lead to the renewal of onerous government regulation in the UK. See JB Holland 'Self Regulation and the Financial Aspects of Corporate Governance' [1996] J Bus L 127, 131, n 12.

59 The ISC represents major UK institutional investors.

60 Institutional Shareholders Committee 'The Responsibilities of Institutional Shareholders and Agents – Statement of Principles' (2002) (available at <http://www.investmentuk.org/investment uk/press/2002/20021021-01.pdf>).

61 Government legislation had been canvassed following the influential Myners Report in 2001. See Paul Myners (Chair) *Institutional Investment in the United Kingdom: A Review* ('the Myners Report') (2001), which criticised the reluctance of fund managers to take an activist stance (2).

62 The ISC principles merely recommend, as a matter of best practice, that institutional investors 'intervene where necessary' in matters of corporate governance. See generally Plender 'A curious window on the way it used to be: Cats' cradles and conflicts' *Financial Times* (20 January 2003) 24.

63 At the time of the ASX's entrée into the realm of corporate governance, for example, a Government representative stated 'In Australia, we have…a regulatory framework, whereby the regulator has developed an effective partnership with the Stock Exchange. The importance of self-regulatory organisations should not be underestimated. A self-regulatory organisation has the ability to impose rules for market conduct which are acceptable to market participants'. Senator Gibson, Address at 15th East Asian & Oceanic Stock Exchange Federation General Assembly (1996).

64 ASX Listing Rule 4.10.3.

65 IFSA was particularly critical of the structure and effectiveness of the rule adopted.

This regulatory approach can be contrasted with the more stringent approach under the London Stock Exchange Listing Rules[66] and the London Combined Code 1998, which derived from the recommendations of leading UK corporate governance reports[67] and operates as a blue-print for Stock Exchange rules in many jurisdictions. Under the UK model, a company which does not adopt the governance practices contained in the Combined Code is generally required to provide a public explanation for non-conformity – the now familiar 'comply or explain' model of corporate governance regulation.

In the period prior to the HIH and One.Tel collapses, there was some backlash against Australian corporate governance practices.[68] Stan Wallis, the influential chair of the Wallis Committee on the Australian Financial System, publicly criticised 'the formalised edicts' of Australian corporate governance norms, which he regarded as contributing to a compliance-based system, in comparison with the performance-based focus of US corporate governance principles.[69]

Nonetheless, the collapses of HIH and One.Tel have resulted in a hardening of norms in Australia. The ASX has recently adopted a more prescriptive approach to corporate governance following these collapses and criticism about the credibility of the ASX as a regulatory body.[70]

Thus, at the beginning of 2003, in response to public pressure, Australian Stock Exchange introduced new Listing Rules,[71] under which Australia will adopt a UK-style 'comply or explain' model.[72] One of the goals of the introduction of this enhanced disclosure regime is clearly to forestall stricter legislative regula-

[66] United Kingdom Listing Authority Rule 12.43A(b).

[67] Committee on Corporate Governance (Hampel Committee), *Final Report* (1998); Committee on the Financial Aspects of Corporate Governance (Cadbury Committee), *Report* (1992); Study Group on Directors' Remuneration (Greenbury Committee), *Directors' Remuneration: Report* (1995).

[68] There was parallel backlash in the UK. See, for example, P Burton 'Antecedents and Consequences of Corporate Governance Structures' (2000) 8 Corporate Governance 194, 194-5.

[69] Wallis was particularly critical of the prevalence of a separation between CEO and chair in Australia, in contrast to the US, and argued that slavish adherence to corporate governance norms was stifling managerial risk-taking and performance in Australian companies, in comparison with their US counterparts. Wallis, 2000 Corporate Public Affairs Oration, 'Corporate Governance – Conformance or Performance'.

[70] Criticism in this regard focused on the argument that, as a demutualised corporation in its own right, a conflict exists between the ASX's twin goals of regulation and profit maximisation. See, for example, 'The best way to restore faith' *Australian Financial Review* (23 July 2002) 62.

[71] 1 January 2003.

[72] See address by Richard Humphrey, Managing Director and Chief Executive Officer ASX, 'If Not, Why Not?' (AICD forum, 2 April 2003).

tion.[73] Detailed principles of best corporate governance practice recommended by the ASX Corporate Governance Council, which form the basis of the enhanced disclosure regime, were released in March 2003.[74] The majority of these principles deal directly with the board's role, structure and effectiveness.[75] Australian listed companies are required to comply with, or explain their divergence from, these principles, from their 2004 annual reports onwards. In contrast to this principle-based approach, it appears that under the CLERP 9 proposals, the Federal Government will introduce a mandatory requirement for the top 500 listed Australian companies to have an audit committee.[76]

It is unclear how significant these changes will be. The new 'comply or explain' regime has already been criticised on the basis that the boards of some of Australia's most successful family controlled corporations, such as News Ltd,[77] do not comply with its principles, and that the regime lacks sanctions for non-compliance.[78] It appears that many Australian companies are choosing to follow the explanation, rather than the compliance, route.[79] Also, as a result of HIH and One.Tel, there is scepticism about the gap between rhetoric and reality in corporate governance statements. The anodyne statements in HIH's final annual report in 2000 presented the company as a paragon of corporate governance virtue, in terms of board member experience,[80] committee structure,[81] attention to ethics

[73] See Humphrey, ibid, stating that '[t]hrough a disclosure based approach, the ASX is keen to avoid a US style Sarbanes-Oxley legislative solution...However, it has become clear that our federal politicians are prepared to legislate if business cannot get its house in order'.

[74] ASX Corporate Governance Council 'Principles of Good Corporate Governance and Best Practice Recommendations' (March 2003) (available at <http://www.asx.com.au/about/pdf/ASXRecommendations.pdf>).

[75] ASX Corporate Governance Council (n 74) comprise ten Principles, most relating directly to the board. See, for example, Principle 1 (roles and responsibilities of board and management); Principle 2 (structure of board); Principle 3 (promoting ethical and responsible decision-making); Principle 4 (safeguarding integrity in financial reporting); Principle 7 (establishing a sound system of risk oversight); Principle 8 (encouraging enhanced board and management effectiveness); Principle 9 (determination of remuneration policies); Principle 10 (recognition of legitimate interests of stakeholders). Each Principle includes a number of specific recommendations designed to achieve the goals of the Principle.

[76] Corporate Law Economic Reform Program, Issue Paper No 9 (n 40) Proposal 8 'Audit Committees'.

[77] Kohler 'Try telling Frank, James or Rupert to stand down' *Australian Financial Review* (1 April 2003) 6.

[78] For example, Elliot 'ASX Rules: Shut up and you're sweet' *The Australian* (1 April 2003) 21.

[79] Buffini 'Companies roll out the excuses' *Australian Financial Review* (28 July 2003) 4.

[80] 'The Board remains comprised of directors with a wide range of experience necessary for the complex, international business HIH now represents. Drawing on a diverse range of professionals, HIH's board of directors includes high-level experience in insurance, financial

cont. ...

and a code of conduct.[82] Nonetheless, court proceedings relating to the collapse of HIH, which resulted in a deficit of approximately A$5.3 billion, found that major breaches of directors' duties occurred in the lead-up to the collapse. Thus, in *ASIC v Adler*,[83] Santow J found that, in a series of related party transactions, instigated by the non-executive director, Rodney Adler, and resulting in substantial loss to HIH, there had been 'a serious departure from HIH's own investment safeguards…[t]hat may well have reflected a lax attitude prevailing in HIH's affairs concerning its investment safeguards'.[84] The lesson here is the same as that at Enron[85] – the existence of a corporate governance procedure, such as investment guidelines and an investment committee, is of little use, when the procedures are by-passed.

There has also been a hardening of corporate governance norms in the UK, as a result of the *Review of the Role and Effectiveness of Non-Executive Directors* ('the Higgs Report'), which was released in January 2003.[86] The Higgs Report recommended strengthening requirements concerning composition of the board, independence of directors, recruitment and appointment of directors and audit committees within the framework of the existing UK 'comply or explain' regulatory model, rather than prescriptive governmental legislation.[87] The substance of the recommendations in the Higgs Report has now been adopted and incorporated into the UK Combined Code.[88]

management, legal, accounting and investment areas'. HIH Directors' Report, 1999/2000 Annual Report, 18.

[81] The four main committees at HIH were the audit, human resources, reinsurance and investment committees. ibid.

[82] Pierpont 'Governance as a Form of Art' *Australian Financial Review* (8 June 2002) 84. According to the HIH Royal Commission, the existence of a corporate governance model was negated by the failure of HIH's board to assess periodically its practical effectiveness. HIH Royal Commission (n 20) 25.

[83] (2002) 41 ACSR 72; (2002) 20 ACLC 576.

[84] (2002) 41 ACSR 72, 144. For other examples of deviation from published guidelines at HIH, see HIH Royal Commission (n 20).

[85] SL Schwarcz 'Enron and the Use and Abuse of Special Purpose Entities in Corporate Structures' (2002) 70 U Cincinnati L Rev 1309, 1312.

[86] Higgs (Chair) *Review of the Role and Effectiveness of Non-Executive Directors* (January 2003).

[87] According to Derek Higgs, the 'brittleness and rigidity of legislation cannot dictate the behaviour, or foster the trust, I believe is fundamental to the effective unitary board and to superior corporate performance'. Letter from Derek Higgs to the Chancellor of the Exchequer and the Secretary of State for Trade and Industry, 20 January 2003.

[88] The Combined Code on Corporate Governance (July 2003). See Financial Reporting Council ('FRC'), PN 75, 'FRC issues revised Combined Code' 23 July 2003. Some specific recommendations of the Higgs Report (for example, that the chairman should not be allowed to chair the nomination committee) were wound back in the revised Combined Code amendments. The requirement in the Higgs Report, that at least half the members of the board should be

cont. ...

The regulatory response in the US to the collapse of Enron has focused on governance by self-regulatory organisations and federal legislation and regulations.[89] These US reforms ('the 2002 reforms'), under the New York Stock Exchange (and NASDAQ) proposed listing requirements[90] and the *Sarbanes-Oxley Act* of 2002 ('the *Sarbanes-Oxley Act*'), represent an interesting contrast to the Australian and UK regulatory responses in several respects. First, the US 2002 reforms constitute a shift towards a legislative rules-based approach to corporate governance, with a higher level of mandatory governance standards. The NYSE corporate governance rule proposals,[91] for example, introduce a range of new mandatory requirements concerning board structure,[92] to reflect generally accepted best practice in corporate governance. The reforms deviate from the traditional US state-based model of corporate law as essentially 'facilitative'. While some provisions in the *Sarbanes-Oxley Act* are framed as disclosure provisions

independent, was also ultimately restricted to companies in the FTSE 350. See generally, FRC, PN 74, 'The Higgs and Smith reports: next steps towards a revised combined code following consultation', 14 May 2003.

[89] Generally RB Thompson 'Corporate Governance After Enron: The First Year' (forthcoming (2003) Housten L Rev).

[90] For a useful comparative review of a number of recent corporate governance reform proposals, including the NYSE and NASDAQ proposals, see *Report of the American Bar Association Task Force on Corporate Responsibility* (31 March 2003) 62ff.

[91] The NYSE corporate governance rule proposals will be codified into a new s 303A of the Stock Exchange's Listed Company Manual. The background to the NYSE corporate governance rule proposals is as follows. On 13 February 2002, the then-Chairman of the Securities and Exchange Commission, Harvey Pitt, requested that the NYSE review its corporate governance listing standards. The NYSE appointed a Corporate Accountability and Listing Standards Committee ('the Committee') to review the NYSE's current listing standards. On 6 June 2002, the NYSE released the Committee's report. The NYSE Board of Directors approved the Committee's corporate governance rule proposals on 1 August 2002. The rule proposals become effective upon SEC approval.

[92] For example, the NYSE proposals provide that listed companies must have a majority of independent directors (subsection 1); must have separate executive meetings of non-management directors (subsection 3); must have a nominating, corporate governance and compensation committee composed entirely of independent directors (subsection 4 and 5); must vest responsibility in the audit committee for retention and termination of the company's independent auditors (subsection 7); must adopt corporate governance guidelines and a code of business conduct and ethics (subsection 9 and 10); and that the CEO of a listed company must certify to the NYSE each year that he or she is not aware of any violation by the company of the NYSE corporate governance listing standards (subsection 12).

only,[93] it has been argued that the likely impact of these provisions will be to mandate compliance.[94]

Second, the substance of many of the NYSE rule proposals is stricter than its counterparts in other jurisdictions, such as Australia.[95] Third, the reforms under the *Sarbanes-Oxley Act* have a greater emphasis on criminal liability in corporate governance,[96] than reforms in the UK and Australia. Finally, the reforms constitute an important reallocation of power in relation to the regulation of US corporate law. Against the traditional backdrop of corporate governance regulation via state-based enabling legislation, the *Sarbanes-Oxley Act* introduces prescriptive rules relating to corporate governance at a federal government level. It is this aspect of the *Sarbanes-Oxley Act*, which has been described as creating a 'shadow corporation law'.[97] In contrast to the rapid regulatory changes at federal level, US state-based law has remained essentially unchanged in the post-Enron period.[98]

The 2002 US corporate governance reforms are controversial. Derek Higgs, the author of the UK Higgs Report, for example, strongly criticised the shift from commercial norms to legislation under the US reforms, as creating an overly complex and prescriptive regime, which will be difficult to enforce.[99]

[93] For example, s 406 Sarbanes-Oxley Act, which requires a company to disclose whether it has adopted a code of ethics for senior financial officers (and if not, why not), and s 407 Sarbanes-Oxley Act, which requires an issuer to disclose whether at least one member of the audit committee is a financial expert (and if not, why not).

[94] Thompson (n 89).

[95] For example, the definition of 'independence' is stricter under the NYSE corporate governance rule proposals than under the ASX Corporate Governance Council (n 74). Also, while the NYSE proposals require that the audit committee, nominating committee, corporate governance committee and compensation committee should be composed entirely of independent directors, the Australian governance rules require only that such committees comprise a majority of independent directors.

[96] For example, the Sarbanes-Oxley Act, Title VII ('Corporate and Criminal Fraud and Accountability'); Title IX ('White Collar Crime Penalty Enhancements'); Title XI ('Corporate Fraud and Accountability').

[97] WB Chandler and LE Strine 'The New Federalism of the American Corporate Governance System: Preliminary Reflections of Two Residents of One Small State' (paper presented at Symposium on Control Transactions, University of Pennsylvania, 2003) 29.

[98] Thompson (n 89).

[99] Parker and Tassell 'US Corporate Reform Efforts Come Under Attack in Britain' *Financial Times* (21 January 2003) 1. See also Bruce 'Hope of calmer waters: After the tumult and shouting of last year, 2003 is likely to be less dramatic – though many challenging issues have to be faced' *Financial Times* (9 January 2003) 2, stating that there is strong resistance in Europe to the Sarbanes-Oxley Act, which is seen as 'a back-door attempt to enmesh Europe in the morass of rules-based legislation'. Nonetheless, it now appears that France and Germany are planning to transplant much of the Act into their own corporate legislation. See L Enriques 'Bad Apples, Bad Oranges. A Comment from Old Europe on Post-Enron Corporate Governance Reforms' (paper delivered at the 2003, Wake Forest Corporate Law Conference), 10ff.

US commentators are divided on the impact and wisdom of the 2002 reforms. Some view the reforms as a watershed in US corporate law. Professor Bainbridge, for example, describes them as 'the most dramatic expansion of federal regulatory power over corporate governance since the New Deal', and argues that the reforms will significantly undermine traditional board autonomy.[100] Other commentators, however, view the reforms as essentially political window-dressing, with extravagant rhetoric unmatched by the promise of significant deterrence or effective enforcement.[101]

Yet, the ultimate influence of the 2002 reforms could be more subtle than this. Whereas traditionally, corporate governance norms have preceded law, current developments suggest that the reverse may now be occurring in the US. Law may now be driving norms.

Corporate governance reforms at General Electric Company ('GE') are indicative of such a trend. The NYSE corporate governance rule proposals will require half of all board members to be independent. In late 2002, however, GE announced that the company had adopted a new policy, whereby two-thirds of its board members were independent,[102] and that pursuant to this policy, two directors (who did not satisfy the requirement of independence)[103] would leave the board at the end of 2002. This policy requiring a supermajority independent board formed part of a broader corporate governance reform program voluntarily adopted by GE.[104]

[100] SM Bainbridge 'The Creeping Federalization of Corporate Law' (2003) 26(1) Regulation 26. Professor Bainbridge views the 2002 reforms as 'deeply flawed' and lacking in 'empirical support or economic justification'. See also Thompson (n 89) who argues that the enduring legacy will be to make federal law an equal partner with state law in the area of corporate governance.

[101] For example, L Cunningham 'The Sarbanes-Oxley Yawn: Heavy Rhetoric, Light Reform (And It Might Just Work)' (2003) 35 Conn L Rev 915; MA Perino 'Enron's Legislative Aftermath: Some Reflections on the Deterrence Aspects of the Sarbanes-Oxley Act of 2002' (2002) 76 St Johns L Rev 671; LE Ribstein 'Market vs Regulatory Responses to Corporate Fraud: A Critique of the Sarbanes-Oxley Act of 2002' (2003) 28 J Corp L 1, expressing scepticism about the extent to which the 2002 reforms will effect significant changes to existing US law.

[102] In 2001, a survey by the Investor Responsibility Research Center, which advises fund managers of corporate governance issues, found that GE had the lowest level of independent directors from the top 20 largest companies by revenue. See 'GE says it is dropping 2 directors from board' *New York Times* (8 November 2002) 4.

[103] See 'General Electric appoints 2 independent directors' *New York Times* (29 October 2002) 4.

[104] The changes are available on GE's corporate governance website (available at <http://www.ge.com/governance>).

II. 'Independence' and the Director

'Cause you know sometimes words have two meanings.

Stairway to Heaven

One area where there appears to be a high level of convergence between the US, UK and Australian corporate governance reforms is in relation to independent directors. Quite simply, the idea of the independent director has become the new 'Holy Grail' under the reforms, and will resonate through the entire board structure. For example, the US 2002 reforms will require listed company boards to have a majority of independent directors and to have compensation, nominating/governance and audit committees composed entirely of independent directors.[105]

The Winter Report also supports the role of non-executive/supervisory directors, to ensure more independent monitoring. The report considers that this is important, not only in companies with dispersed shareholding, but also in companies with a controlling shareholder, where non-executive directors perform an important role on behalf of minority shareholders, particularly in relation to nomination and remuneration of directors, and auditing the company's financial position.[106] Nonetheless, under the US 2002 reforms, there is an exception to the independence requirements in the case of 'controlled companies'.[107]

The concept of the independent director is a seductive one.[108] It is one of at least three basic techniques used by corporate law to control conflicts of interest, particularly in areas such as executive remuneration.[109] International committees[110]

[105] See s 301 Sarbanes-Oxley Act; NYSE Corporate Accountability and Listing Standards Committee, *Corporate Governance Rule Proposals* (as approved by the NYSE Board of Directors, August 1, 2003), s 303A (4)-(6).

[106] Winter Report 59-60.

[107] The exception relates to 'controlled companies', in which 50% or more of voting power is held by an individual, group or another corporation. NYSE Corporate Accountability and Listing Standards Committee, *Corporate Governance Rule Proposals* (as approved by the NYSE Board of Directors, 1 August 2002) s 303A(1).

[108] A Banks 'What do we want strong boards to achieve?' *Financial Times* (18 November 2002) 6.

[109] Other techniques are fiduciary duties (comprising self-constraint, with judicial enforcement), and alignment of managerial self-interest with the interests of shareholders. See generally, J Hill and CM Yablon 'Corporate Governance and Executive Remuneration: Rediscovering Managerial Positional Conflict' (2002) 25 UNSWLJ 294, 301.

[110] In the UK, see for example, *Report of the Committee on the Financial Aspects of Corporate Governance* (1992) (chaired by Sir Adrian Cadbury), [4.11]. In Australia, see *Report of the Working Group on Corporate Practices and Conduct* (chaired by Henry Bosch) (3d edn 1995), 14. In the US, see 1 American Law Institute, *Principles of Corporate Governance: Analysis and Recommendations* 110 (1994).

and standards of best practice on corporate governance[111] have for some time recommended that there should be a sufficient proportion of outside directors to exert a real level of influence on the board and therefore enhance accountability.

The rise of the independent director has been dramatic in the US, where it has been said that the 'most noticeable aspect of American corporate governance is the law's repeated resort to the independent director as a cleansing agent'.[112] For example, in the area of self-dealing transactions, the US regulatory approach shifted from outright prohibition to use of independent directors as a filtering device.[113] This structural, legitimising role for independent directors has been far less apparent in the UK and Australia, where there was often no clear distinction between non-executive directors and the stricter concept of independent directors, and where shareholders perform a more important role in addressing conflicts of interest.[114]

The assumption is deeply embedded in corporate governance literature that independent outside directors (as opposed to 'affiliated' outside directors) make better monitors. While empirical studies are yet to prove a positive connection between independent boards and corporate performance,[115] this assumption lies at the heart of the current reforms in the US, UK and Australia.

The definition of 'independent director' under the US 2002 reforms has been described as 'relatively pristine'.[116] A recent survey of annual reports of the top 200 Australian companies makes it clear that Australian non-executive directors would generally fail to meet the stringent standards imposed by the NYSE definition.[117] One aspect of the NYSE reforms, however, which is less than pristine is that it enables a director, who is not a member of the audit committee, to qualify as 'independent', in spite of the presence of consulting or other arrangements, so

[111] For example, IFSA (n 56).

[112] JD Cox 'Corporate Governance in the United States: the Evolving Role of the Independent Board' in CK Low (ed) *Corporate Governance: An Asia-Pacific Critique* (Sweet & Maxwell Hong Kong 2002) 379, 388. See generally L Lin 'The Effectiveness of Outside Directors as a Corporate Governance Mechanism: Theories and Evidence' (1996) 90 Nw U L Rev 898, 904-912.

[113] For example, H Marsh 'Are Directors Trustees? Conflicts of Interest and Corporate Morality' (1966) 22 Bus L 35; Brudney (n 52) 608-609.

[114] On contrasts between US and UK law in this regard, see DA DeMott 'The Figure in the Landscape: A Comparative Sketch of Directors' Self-Interested Transactions' (1999) 62 LCP 243, 245.

[115] Bainbridge (n 100) 29.

[116] Chandler and Strine (n 97) 48. Indeed, Lynn Turner, former chief accountant, stated that the NYSE definition was so strict that 'God would have a tough time qualifying' (quoted in Buffini 'Australia fails NYSE audit test' *Australian Financial Review* (25 September 2002) 10).

[117] Buffini, ibid.

long as the other board members conclude that the director does not have a 'material relationship' with the listed company.[118]

An element of the definition of the 'independence' in the US 2002 reforms, which has already caused some angst, is its seemingly ambivalent attitude to directors who have a connection to major shareholders. Some would regard directors who represent major shareholders as possessing ideal characteristics and incentives to serve as effective monitors. Nonetheless, it has been argued that the US 2002 reforms implicitly adopt a view that ownership by a director (or affiliation with the owner) of a significant block of shares taints a director's independence.[119] It would positively disentitle any such an affiliated director from serving as a voting member of the audit committee under the *Sarbanes-Oxley Act*.[120]

The vision of independence under the US 2002 reforms is interesting, since it seems to encompass not only independence from management, but also independence from stakeholders, who may have strong incentives to monitor. From this perspective, it cuts across much accepted wisdom in contemporary corporate governance, concerning capacity and incentives[121] of outside directors to function as effective monitors.[122] Particularly problematical is the danger that genuine independence may often be accompanied by ignorance and ineffectiveness.

The US 2002 reforms, which require that the compensation, nominating/governance and audit committees of listed companies must be composed entirely of independent directors,[123] go further than parallel reform and reform proposals in other jurisdictions. The new ASX *Principles of Good Corporate Governance and Best Practice Recommendations*, for example, recommend only that a majority of directors on these committees should be independent.[124] The Winter

[118] Chandler and Strine (n 97) 45, 46.

[119] ibid 51. Nonetheless, the Commentary to the NYSE Corporate Governance Rule Proposals states that in relation to board membership, it does not take the view that even a significant amount of stock is 'by itself' a bar to an independence finding.

[120] Section 301 Sarbanes-Oxley Act.

[121] Much contemporary corporate governance literature has stressed the benefits of aligning the interests of non-executive directors with those of shareholders by, for example, paying non-executive directors in shares. See, for example, CM Elson 'Director Compensation and the Management-Captured Board – The History of a Symptom and a Cure' (1996) 50 SMU L Rev 127. As Robert Monks has stated, 'nothing makes a director think and act like a shareholder more than being a shareholder' (quoted in H Parker 'Reempowering the Board: A Proposed Agenda for Action' in RAG Monks and N Minow *Corporate Governance for the 21st Century: Watching the Watchers* (Blackwell Oxford 1996) 289, 306).

[122] For example, RJ Gilson and R Kraakman 'Reinventing the Outside Director: An Agenda for Institutional Investors' (1991) 43 Stanford L Rev 863, recommending a shift from independent directors to outside directors, selected by and beholden to, institutional investors.

[123] See s 301 Sarbanes-Oxley Act; NYSE Corporate Accountability and Listing Standards Committee, *Corporate Governance Rule Proposals* (as approved by the NYSE Board of Directors, 1 August 2003) s 303A (4)-(6).

[124] See ASX Corporate Governance Council (n 74) Recommendations [2.4], [4.3] and [9.2].

Committee explicitly rejects the US paradigm of exclusively independent committees as inappropriate in the European context, where controlling shareholders and employee co-determination are both common features of the corporate governance landscape.[125]

The recommendations under the UK Higgs Report provide an interesting contrast to the US 2002 reforms, and a deceptively radical reform agenda. Like the NYSE proposals, the Higgs Report recommended that at least half the board should be independent non-executive directors,[126] and included a high standard of independence. Indeed, the definition of independence in the Higgs Report is arguably more 'pristine' than that of the NYSE proposals, since the Higgs Report required the board to determine that the director is independent, not only in the sense of being free from material relationships with the corporation, but also 'in character and judgement'.[127] The definitions of independence under the NYSE proposals and the Higgs Report are both more stringent than that adopted in Australia by the ASX corporate governance principles.[128]

Although under the Higgs Report, the fact that a director represents a particular 'significant shareholder' constitutes a relationship or circumstance which could undermine independence,[129] the report nonetheless strengthened the position of independent directors, by envisaging a close relationship between with major shareholders and directors after their appointment to the board. Thus, for example, the Higgs Report recommended the appointment of a senior independent director, who should be available to shareholders with concerns 'that have not been resolved through the normal channels of contact with the chairman or chief executive'.[130] In a section entitled, 'Relationships with Shareholders', the Higgs

[125] According to the Winter Report, it would go 'too far' to exclude such affiliated persons from participating in key areas. See Winter Report 61.

[126] Higgs (n 86) [9.5]. Note, however, that this requirement was subsequently restricted under the revised Combined Code to companies falling within FTSE 350, on the basis that compliance would be difficult for smaller companies. See Combined Code on Corporate Governance (July 2003) A.3.2.

[127] ibid Annex A, Part 2, Section 1, A3.4. Cf Combined Code on Corporate Governance (July 2003) A.3.1.

[128] ASX Corporate Governance Council (n 74) Recommendation 2.1. For example, unlike the Higgs Report, the ASX definition of independence contains no explicit reference to family ties, cross-directorships or board tenure of more than 10 years, as a circumstance that could undermine independence. It appears these provisions were removed from earlier drafts of the ASX Principles. See Gettler 'ASX rules to rein in corporate cowboys' *The Age* (31 March 2003) 1.

[129] Higgs (n 86) Annex A, Part 2, Section 1, A3.4.

[130] ibid 6, [7.4]-[7.5]; Combined Code on Corporate Governance (July 2003) A.3.3; D.1.1.

Report advocated a range of techniques for establishing close contact and a relationship between non-executive directors and major shareholders.[131]

The UK Higgs Report also endorsed the recent Institutional Shareholders Committee's (ISC) Code of Activism, which adopts a norm requiring institutional investors to intervene in the affairs of underperforming companies 'when necessary'. The relationship between non-executive board members and major investors under the Higgs Report appears to be a variation of John Pound's political theory of the corporation, which envisaged a high level of interaction between management and major investors.[132]

In contrast to the Higgs Report, shareholder participation in corporate governance appears to have been somewhat overlooked in the US 2002 reforms. For example, two members of the Delaware judiciary have asked whether a greater role for shareholders in the director election process could be the 'forgotten element' of the 2002 reforms.[133] For example, while the proposed amendments to the NYSE and NASDAQ listing standards require listed to companies to have an independent nominating committee, they do not require the nominating committee to consider sharcholder nominees.[134] Nonetheless, in recent times some US institutional shareholders have attempted, with mixed success, to use shareholder proposals to increase channels of communication with the board,[135] and have threatened to commence a radical agenda of corporate governance litigation – so-called 'governance at gunpoint' – if boards do not address their concerns.[136]

The lack of attention to shareholder participation evident in the US 2002 reforms may, however, be about to change. The SEC recently conducted a review of policies on elections for corporate boards and shareholder proposals under

[131] Some of the recommendations in this regard included proposals that the senior independent director should attend regular meetings with management and 'a range of major shareholders' to develop an understanding of shareholder concerns [15.15]; that non-executive directors should be able to meet with major investors and should expect to do so if requested by the major investors [15.16]; that non-executive directors should meet with major investors as part of their induction into the company [15.17]; that a company should state what steps it has taken 'to ensure that members of the board, and in particular the non-executive directors, develop a balanced understanding of the views of major investors' [15.18].

[132] J Pound 'The Rise of the Political Model of Corporate Governance and Control' (1993) 68 NYU L Rev 1003. See also Combined Code on Corporate Governance (July 2003) D.1 ('Dialogue with Institutional Shareholders') and E.1 ('Dialogue with companies').

[133] Chandler and Strine (n 97) 65 ff.

[134] SEC Staff Report: *Review of the Proxy Process Regarding the Nomination and Election of Directors*, Division of Corporation Finance, 15 July 2003, 18.

[135] The SEC Staff Report provides some examples of this development. For example, in 2003, the AFSCME Employee Pension Plan sought to amend the Kroger Company's bylaws to establish a shareholder committee to communicate with the board regarding certain shareholder proposals. SEC Staff Report, ibid 25.

[136] Targett 'US activists turn up the heat: Radical shareholder champions team up for 'governance at gunpoint'' *Financial Times* (4 November 2002) 1.

Exchange Act Rule 14-a(8), in order to increase shareholder democracy.[137] The review followed a ruling by the SEC, which permitted Citgroup Inc to exclude shareholder nominations for board elections.[138]

The SEC published its Staff Report on 15 July 2003.[139] The Report recommended some key reforms in two areas – enhanced disclosure and improved shareholder access to the director nomination process.[140] Professor Bebchuk has argued that the case for changes to the proxy rules under US law to improve shareholder access to the director nomination process is 'compelling'.[141] The very existence of the SEC review is further indication of the increasing federalism of corporate governance in the US.[142]

The specific reliance on independent directors under the reform proposals in the UK, US and Australia represents a continuation of the 'proceduralisation' of corporate law. Sections of the business community have already complained that the shift to mandatory or quasi-mandatory independent boards will create logistical problems in relation to finding directors and an increase in levels of remuneration for directors.[143]

To what extent will independent directors provide a panacea to the international corporate malaises that have occurred and restore trust to the market? In relation to the Australian corporate collapses, there is no doubt that the boards of HIH and One.Tel both displayed deficiencies in the level of independence of board members. It is, nonetheless, open to doubt whether differently structured boards would have altered the outcomes.

At HIH, five of the seven directors were outside non-executive directors, yet their independence was compromised by a number of factors. For example, three of the board members, including the chairman, were former partners of Arthur Andersen, which was HIH's auditor.[144] Two other non-executive directors, who

[137] SEC, Press Release No 2003-46, 15 July 2003; Solomons 'SEC plans comprehensive look at rules for proxy exclusions' *Wall St Journal* (15 April 2003) C9.

[138] According to SEC chairman, William Donaldson, although the Citigroup Inc ruling was in accordance with existing rules, the 'time has come for a thorough review of the proxy rules and regulations to ensure that they are serving the best interests of today's investors and fostering sound corporate governance and transparent business practices'. ibid.

[139] SEC Staff Report: *Review of the Proxy Process Regarding the Nomination and Election of Directors*, Division of Corporation Finance, 15 July 2003.

[140] ibid 30.

[141] LA Bebchuk 'Shareholder Access to the Ballot' (forthcoming (2003) 58 Bus Law).

[142] See generally R Thompson and H Sale 'Securities Fraud as Corporate Governance: Reflections Upon Federalism' (2003) 58 Vanderbilt L Rev 859.

[143] Kohler 'Try telling Frank, James or Rupert to stand down' *Australian Financial Review* (1 April 2003) 6.

[144] The HIH chairman also continued to receive financial benefits from Andersen through a consultancy arrangement. HIH Royal Commission (n 20) 39.

were clearly affiliated rather than independent, were Rodney Adler, the former CEO of FAI Insurance, and HIH's legal adviser.[145]

At One.Tel, the role of non-executive directors, James Packer and Lachlan Murdoch, is interesting. It is less common for representatives of major shareholders to sit on the board of directors in Australia than in other parts of the world.[146] Professor Langevoort has said that good boards provide a crucial link with the outside world, enabling the corporation to claim and protect 'its share of external resources' by legitimising the company in the eyes of key resource holders.[147] James Packer and Lachlan Murdoch, as representatives of One.Tel's major investors, arguably fulfilled this function, giving One.Tel credibility in the marketplace. Such a role, however, conflicts with the emerging definitions of independence.

Yet, it is by no means clear that lack of independence of directors at HIH and One.Tel actually contributed to the collapses. Similar financial scandals have occurred at companies, such as Sunbeam,[148] where the majority of board members would have satisfied the strict independence requirements under the NYSE proposals.

One of the key problems in the case of both HIH and One.Tel was management's ability to block, filter or distort information reaching the board.[149] This is not necessarily solved by having a high proportion of independent directors. Prior to the 2002 reforms, there had been a strong increase in the US in 'super-majority-independent boards', with only one or two insiders on the board.[150] This is in contrast to the UK, where historically, boards of public companies have had a higher percentage of executive directors.[151] Although the US 2002 reforms mandate only a *majority* of independent directors on the boards of listed US companies, it is generally assumed that the rules will actually result in supermajority independent boards, due to the need to ensure that major board committees are wholly independent. Alternatively, the 2002 reforms may prompt a shift back to

[145] HIH Directors' Report, *1999/2000 Annual Report*, 13.

[146] According to Egon Zehnder International, *Board of Directors Global Study* (2000) Table 18, only 18% of Australian respondents reported that representatives of major shareholders sat on the board. This contrasted with 76% in Asia, 42% in Europe and 28% in North America.

[147] DC Langevoort 'The Human Nature of Corporate Boards: Laws, Norms, and the Unintended Consequences of Independence and Accountability' (2001) 89 Georgetown LJ 797, 802.

[148] See, generally, J Hill 'Deconstructing Sunbeam – Contemporary Issues in Corporate Governance' (1999) 67 U Cin L Rev 1099, 1104 ff; Sonnenfeld (n 17) 108.

[149] HIH Royal Commission (n 20).

[150] For example S Bhagat and BS Black 'Board Composition and Firm Performance: The Uneasy Case for Majority Independent Boards' (1998) 1053 PLE/CORP 95, 106.

[151] Committee on Corporate Governance, *Final Report*, [5.1] (1998) (Sir Ronald Hampel, chair); DeMott (n 114) 248.

larger boards, which have been discouraged in recent principles of best practice in corporate governance.

Yet, insiders can perform a valuable role, and the single-minded focus on the need for independent directors under the US 2002 reforms may be misguided. Research shows, for example, that boards dominated by independent directors may be more effective in performing certain tasks, such as removal of CEOs for underperformance,[152] than in a general monitoring and advisory role. It seems that independent outside directors are also often reluctant to take an activist stance while publicly available performance criteria remain 'respectable',[153] yet one of the most potent messages of the recent collapses has been the ability of management to use earnings management to create an illusion of respectability.[154] This reasoning also applies in relation to board committees. One study, for example, finds a positive relation between firm performance and the percentage of inside directors on finance and investment committees, suggesting that inside directors can play a valuable role in ensuring that the board is well-informed.[155] In situations, such as at HIH and One.Tel, where there is distortion or withholding of information by management to the board, the presence of a super-majority of outside independent directors may only exacerbate the problem. This is clearly recognised by the UK Higgs Committee. While advocating a majority independent board, the Committee also recommended that there should also be a strong executive presence on the board, to act as an informational check.[156]

Another problem with the touchstone of independence is that it is a slippery concept. Even when directors technically qualify as 'independent', there are a range of familiar psychological factors, which can erode genuine independence, such as: – loyalty to an appointor on the board; 'groupthink', which can result in conformity of ideas and approach;[157] aversion of board members to adopting an adversarial role; similarity of executives' and outside directors' backgrounds and

[152] For example MS Weisbach 'Outside Directors and CEO Turnover' (1988) 20 J Fin Econ 431, 433-434.

[153] Bhagat and Black (n 150) 101.

[154] See generally G Rowland 'Earnings Management, the SEC, and Corporate Governance: Director Liability Arising from the Audit Committee Report' (2002) 102 Columbia L Rev 168.

[155] A Klein 'Firm Performance and Board Committee Structure' (1998) 41 JL & Econ 275.

[156] According to the Higgs Committee, 'There is a greater risk of distortion or withholding of information, or lack of balance in the management contribution to the boardroom debate, when there is only one or a very small number of executive directors on the board'. Higgs (n 86) [8.6]. See also the Combined Code on Corporate Governance (July 2003) A.3.

[157] See generally Bainbridge (n 100) 32.

social circles.[158] The One.Tel scenario provides a good example of these more subtle factors.[159]

There is no doubt that effective checks and balances were both lacking, and desirable, in the cases of HIH and One.Tel. Ray Williams at HIH, and Jodee Rich at One.Tel had notoriously dominating and charismatic personalities – both had started the businesses from scratch, and were regarded as visionaries. And behavioural literature suggests that it is particularly important to have effective governance constraints for such business leaders,[160] who are prone to the psychological trait of 'overconfidence'[161] in their company. A supermajority independent board will not necessarily be effective in this role.

One corporate governance device to deal with the problem of the charismatic CEO is the technique of separating the role of CEO and chair of the board. Most publicly listed companies in Australia[162] and the UK adopt this practice.[163] Most listed US corporations do not, and this position is not altered under the 2002 reforms. In January 2003, however, the US Conference Board Blue-Ribbon Commission on Public Trust and Private Enterprise recommended that this technique should be implemented as a direct curb on excessive managerial power in

[158] For example JD Cox and HL Munsinger 'Bias in the Boardroom: Psychological Foundations and Legal Implications of Corporate Cohesion' (1985) 48 LCP 83.

[159] The financial press has made much of the fact that the CEO, Jodee Rich and two of the non-executive directors, James Packer and Rodney Adler, attended the same exclusive private Sydney boys' school.

[160] For an interesting analysis, see M Maccoby 'Narcissistic Leaders: The Incredible Pros, the Inevitable Cons' (2000) 78(1) Harv Bus Rev 69. According to Maccoby, narcissistic leaders thrive in chaotic times (ibid 77) and have 'compelling, even gripping, visions for companies, and they have an ability to attract followers' (ibid 72).

[161] Bainbridge (n 100) 29-30, who states that '[a]lthough individuals may well be better at devising a brilliant plan [than groups], individuals often become wedded to their plans and fail to see flaws that others might identify….The board serves to constrain subordinates who have become wedded to their plans and ideas, rather than developing such plans in the first instance'.

[162] According to the Egon Zehnder International survey, *Board of Directors Global Study* (2000), 94% of Australian respondents separated the role of chair and CEO, compared to 42% in North America. Egon Zehnder International, *Board of Directors Global Study* (2000) 12, Table 23.

[163] According to the Higgs Report, approximately 90% of UK listed companies currently split the role of chair and CEO. Separation of the positions of chair and CEO is viewed as a fundamental element of good corporate governance in both the Australian Stock Exchange principles and the Higgs Report. See ASX Corporate Governance Council (n 74) Recommendations [2.2] and [2.3]; Higgs (Chair), *Review of the Role and Effectiveness of Non-Executive Directors* (January 2003) [5.3] and [5.7]; Combined Code on Corporate Governance (July 2003), A.2.1.

the US context.[164] Nonetheless, historically, there has been far less resistance to centralised power in US corporations, than in Australian and UK companies.[165]

III. An Evolving Role for the Board?

The corporate collapses have resulted in a reconsideration of the appropriate role of the board, and the nature of its interaction with management. A tension exists between the perception that boards require a sense of collegiality to perform well, and the belief, expressed by Warren Buffett, that 'dissent is needed in the boardroom'.[166]

Backlash against corporate governance practices and criticism, such as that expressed by Wallis in Australia, reflects a deep ambiguity concerning the role of the board and corporate governance generally. It derives from a shareholder-centred perception of corporate governance, in which the role of the board is to improve corporate performance and efficiency.

In spite of the dominance of this model in countries like the US and Australia, it is it is only one of a range of possible roles for the board. As Professor Brudney once noted there are at least three possible roles for the board and independent directors – as monitors of integrity, efficiency or social responsibility.[167] The Cadbury Committee report in the UK stressed the integrity rationale and the importance of directors as a check on managerial misconduct, arising from lack of public confidence in the financial reporting system.[168] The subsequent Hampel Committee report, on the other hand, focused on an efficiency performance-based role for the board.[169] Many of the current corporate governance reforms in the US, the UK and Australia, dealing with, for example, internal corporate controls and the audit committee, represent at least a partial reversion to the image of the board as monitor of managerial and financial integrity.[170]

[164] Lublin 'Drive to divide top corporate roles advances' *Wall St Journal* (9 January 2003) A3; Lublin 'Separating top posts will hurt CEO's authority, some believe' *Wall St Journal* (10 January 2003) C11; Michaels 'The Americas – Panel urges curbs on corporate stars' *Financial Times* (10 January 2003) 2.

[165] In the recent UK Combined Code, for example, one of the Main Principles states that '[n]o one individual should have unfettered powers of decision'. Combined Code on Corporate Governance (July 2003) A.2.

[166] 'Dissent is needed in the boardroom; Higgs' critics have failed to grasp why change is needed' *Financial Times* (10 March 2003) 20.

[167] For example, Brudney (n 53) 658.

[168] Committee on the Financial Aspects of Corporate Governance (Cadbury Committee) *Report* (1992) [4.5].

[169] A Dignam 'A Principled Approach to Self-Regulation? The Report of the Hampel Committee on Corporate Governance' (1998) 19 Company Law 140.

[170] For example, the UK Combined Code on Corporate Governance (July 2003) C.3.2.

The corporate collapses have also focused attention on the plight of stakeholders, such as employees, and social responsibility issues. When General Electric Company[171] announced its new corporate governance policy, it explicitly referred to the interests of stakeholders.[172] In Australia, there has, for some time, been a tension between the shareholder-centred nature of Australian corporate law, and laws in other areas that effectively impose obligations on directors vis-à-vis a broader range of stakeholders. This tension is, for example, apparent in relation to Australia's corporate criminal regime, which introduces elements of a social responsibility monitoring role for directors. While under corporate law, the duty of directors to monitor diligently (or to implement compliance programs) has been relatively undemanding in both Australia and the US,[173] Australian criminal law provides stronger incentives for directors to practice risk-management and introduce compliance programs. This is due to the fact that a corporation can be liable under the *Criminal Code*[174] if it had 'a corporate culture' which encouraged or tolerated the commission of the crime.[175]

Several reform proposals in the US, UK and Australia, such as the requirement under the NYSE that listed companies must adopt and disclose a code of business conduct and ethics,[176] implicitly recognise that directors play an important role in shaping the culture of an organisation.[177]

The Winter Report also stressed the need to strengthen the accountability of directors vis-à-vis creditors when a company is near to insolvency, recommend-

[171] n 103.

[172] According to GE, the announced changes to its corporate practices were designed 'to strengthen the board of directors' oversight of management and to serve the long-term interests of shareholders, employees and other stakeholders'. The changes are available on GE's corporate governance website (available at <http://www.ge.com/governance>).

[173] In Australia, see for example, *AWA v Daniels* (1992) 7 ACSR 759; *Daniels v Anderson* (1995) 16 ACSR 607. In the US, see *Graham v Allis-Chalmers Manufacturing Co* 188 A 2d 125 (Del 1963) and *Re Caremark International Inc Derivative Litigation* 698 A 2d Del Ch 959 (1996).

[174] The Criminal Code commenced operation in 1997, however it had only limited application until December 2001, when it commenced general application to all Commonwealth criminal offences.

[175] See generally J Hill 'Corporate Criminal Liability in Australia: An Evolving Corporate Governance Technique?' [2003] JBL 1, 16-20.

[176] NYSE Corporate Accountability and Listing Standards Committee, *Corporate Governance Rule Proposals* s 303A(10). Many of the reforms also pay greater attention to risk management and stakeholder interests. See, for example, ASX Corporate Governance Council (n 74) Principle 7 ('Recognise and manage risk') and Principle 10 ('Recognise the legitimate interests of stakeholders').

[177] DA DeMott 'Organizational Incentives to Care About the Law' (1997) 60 LCP 39, 41. See also the UK Combined Code on Corporate Governance (July 2003) A.1, which states that the board should set the 'values and standards' of the company.

ing the introduction of a European 'wrongful trading' rule.[178] Under this rule, the risk borne by creditors under the separate legal entity doctrine is shifted to directors, if the company incurs a debt in circumstances where the directors ought to have foreseen that the company could not continue to pay its debts. The rule reflects an enhanced monitoring role for directors.

One of the benefits of a European wrongful trading rule, identified by the Winter Committee, is that it could enhance creditor confidence and protection, without the need to harmonise the entire body of directors' liability rules.[179] An analogous 'insolvent trading' regime was introduced into Australian law in 1992.[180] Whereas the UK wrongful trading regime appears to have had limited significance and suffered from enforcement problems,[181] the Australian insolvent trading regime has had a considerable impact on corporate law.[182] Indeed, the relationship between the statutory insolvent trading provisions and directors' duties has been a symbiotic one.[183]

In the early 1990s, a series of insolvent trading cases[184] represented the first indication by the Australian courts that more would now be expected of directors, as a result of changes to the corporations legislation and increasing community expectations. These insolvent trading decisions established that directors must display a sufficient level of financial competence and knowledge to enable them to monitor adequately the company's financial capacity.[185] The cases also stressed that the law would no longer tolerate passive directors.[186] The reasoning in these insolvent trading cases was subsequently adopted and transplanted by the

[178] Winter Report 68-69.

[179] ibid 69.

[180] The insolvent trading provisions were introduced under the Corporate Law Reform Act 1992 and became operative in June 2003. The provisions were based upon the reform recommendations of the Australian Law Reform Commission, Report No 45, *General Insolvency Inquiry*, Canberra 1988 ('The Harmer Report').

[181] P Davies *Gower and Davies Principles of Modern Company Law* (7th edn Sweet & Maxwell London 2003) 199.

[182] The key provisions of the insolvent trading regime are ss 588G and 588H Corporations Act 2001 (Cth).

[183] *Deputy Commissioner of Taxation v Clark* [2003] NSWCA 91, [52]ff and [92]ff, for a useful discussion of the policy behind the insolvent trading regime, its development and its interaction with judicial decisions on directors' duties.

[184] For example, *Commonwealth Bank of Australia v Friedrich* (1991) 5 ACSR 115 and *Statewide Tobacco Services Ltd v Morley* (1990) 2 ACSR 405 (*aff'd* by the Full Court of the Supreme Court of Victoria in *Morley v Statewide Tobacco Services Ltd* (1992) 8 ACSR 305.

[185] See generally, J Bird and J Hill 'Regulatory Rooms in Australian Corporate Law' (1999) 25 Brooklyn J Int'l L 555, 562-563.

[186] *Commonwealth Bank v Friedrich* (1991) 5 ACSR 115, 126.

courts in a number of directors' duties cases on the duty of care, which had traditionally been very low.[187]

The scope of the insolvent trading regime in Australia is extended by virtue of the fact that it also applies to 'shadow directors'. *Standard Chartered Bank of Australia Ltd v Antico*[188] reflects the danger to third parties of the conjunction of the extended definition of 'director'[189] with the insolvent trading regime. In that case, a shareholder, which owned 42% of the shares in Giant Resources Ltd, and exercised a high level of dominion over Giant, was held to be a shadow director for the purposes of an insolvent trading claim.[190]

An even more direct route, by which liability for insolvent trading may be attributed to a shareholder, is under s 588V of the *Corporations Act* 2001 (Cth) ('the *Corporations Act*'), which imposes liability on a parent company, where there has been insolvent trading by a subsidiary.[191] In contrast to liability under the 'shadow director' rubric, a high level of control or domination by the parent company is not a prerequisite to liability under s 588V. The section presumes that a parent company has an obligation to monitor the financial health of its subsidiary for the benefit of creditors.

D. Director and Officer Liability as an Accountability Mechanism

The fish rots from the head
Greek proverb

One corporate governance mechanism which could improve accountability is greater judicial enforcement of director and officer liability.

Historically, the focus of corporate law in both the US and Australia has been on liability of directors. Professors Thompson and Sale have recently argued that this position is rapidly changing in the US context, where the expansion of federal law has resulted in a new focus on the liability of corporate officers, who 'have become the fulcrum of governance in today's corporations'.[192] The

[187] For example *AWA v Daniels* (1992) 7 ACSR 759, 864-865; *Vrisakis v ASC* (1993) 9 WAR 395, 405; *Daniels v Anderson* (1995) 16 ACLR 607, 661-664.

[188] (1995) 13 ACLC 1381.

[189] As defined in s 9 Corporations Act 2001 (Cth).

[190] (1995) 13 ACLC 1381, 1436 ff.

[191] Under s 588V of the Corporations Act 2001 (Cth), which was introduced in 1992, a parent company may become liable for debts incurred by a subsidiary if, at the time the debt is incurred, the holding company or its directors were aware of reasonable grounds for suspecting that the subsidiary was, or would become, insolvent, or should have been aware given the 'nature and extent' of the parent company's control over the subsidiary.

[192] Thompson and Sale (n 142) 859.

Sarbanes-Oxley Act clearly reflects this trend, by imposing an explicit obligation on chief executive officers and chief financial officers to certify their company's financial reports.[193]

In Australia the events at HIH and One.Tel have resulted in increased attention executive officers' liability. The level of legal actions against directors and officers in Australia traditionally tended to be low. First, the standard of care and diligence imposed on directors was undemanding, although there has been an increase in the standard since the series of insolvent trading cases in the 1990s.[194] Also, as in the UK, there existed substantial procedural barriers to minority shareholders bringing proceedings against directors in Australia. While reforms in 2000 introduced a more liberal form of statutory derivative suit,[195] the absence of contingency fee litigation in Australia, makes it unlikely that this form of litigation will be widely used. The 2000 reforms also introduced a statutory business judgment rule,[196] based on the US model, for the benefit of directors.

Nonetheless, one development in Australia, which may strengthen the effectiveness of directors' duties, is the increasingly strategic use by Australian Securities and Investments Commission ('ASIC') of the civil penalty regime as an enforcement mechanism.[197] The civil penalty regime under the *Corporations Act* was introduced in 1993, however, in its early years of operation, it was little used by used by the regulator,[198] and commentators pointed to deficiencies and structural weaknesses in the regime.[199] More recently, however, ASIC has radically increased the number of actions brought under the civil penalty regime.

The scope of the civil penalty regime was extended under the *Financial Services Reform Act* 2001 to cover market misconduct offences, such as insider trading and continuous disclosure. Part of the reason for this expansion was, according to the Explanatory Memorandum, the fact that ASIC had experienced particular difficulty in prosecuting for these offences.[200] The CLERP 9 proposals

[193] Section 302 Sarbanes-Oxley Act 2002.

[194] (n 184).

[195] Part 2F.1A Corporations Act 2001 (Cth).

[196] Section 180(2) Corporations Act 2001 (Cth).

[197] According to a recent Australian Law Reform Commission ('ALRC') Report, there are approximately 2,400 federal civil and administrative penalty provisions under Australian law, mainly in areas related to commercial activity. See ALRC, ALRC Report, *Civil and Administrative Penalties: Civil and Administrative Penalties in Australian Federal Regulation* (December 2002) [2.16].

[198] ASIC commenced only 14 civil penalty actions in the first 6 years of the operation of the civil penalty regime. See G Gilligan, H Bird and I Ramsay 'Civil Penalties and the Enforcement of Directors' Duties' (1999) 22 UNSW LJ 417.

[199] For example, Gilligan, Bird and Ramsay, ibid; H Bird 'The Problematic Nature of Civil Penalties in the Corporations Law' (1996) 14 Company and Securities LJ 405.

[200] See generally G Moodie and I Ramsay 'The Expansion of Civil Penalties Under the Corporations Act' (2002) 30 ABLR 61.

will further strengthen the regulator's power in this regard.[201] The CLERP 9 proposals recommend that the regulator be granted power to impose direct financial penalties and issue infringement notices for contravention of the continuous disclosure regime.[202] Such penalties and infringement notices could be issued, not only against the disclosing entity itself, but also against any other persons, including directors and officers, who are involved in a contravention.[203]

Although part of the original rationale for the introduction of the civil penalty regime in Australia was to create a clearer line between criminal and non-criminal conduct, recent developments suggest that there is increasing blurring of the boundaries between civil penalties and criminal liability.[204] This blurring is also apparent in the dramatic increase in the quantum of civil penalties against companies and officers.[205]

The recent case concerning related party transactions in HIH, *ASIC v Adler*[206] is a good example of the trend towards greater use of civil penalty proceeding under the *Corporations Act.*

ASIC v Adler[207] involved an action against three former directors of HIH. These were the non-executive director, Rodney Adler; the CEO, Ray Williams; and the Chief Financial Officer, Dominic Fodera. ASIC alleged that the directors had breached their fiduciary duties to HIH, in relation to a payment of A$10 million by an HIH subsidiary to Pacific Eagle Equities Pty Ltd, of which Adler was a director and certain subsequent transactions. The transactions resulted in a loss to HIH of A$6 million in less than six months.

Santow J held that breach of fiduciary duty had been established in relation to all three directors, yet found that Mr Adler's contraventions were 'the most serious of all',[208] since, in bypassing of proper corporate safeguards, such as

[201] Corporate Law Economic Reform Program (n 40) 109.

[202] ibid Proposal 22.

[203] ibid Proposal 23.

[204] This blurring was recently identified in a Victorian Supreme Court decision of *ASIC v Plymin (No 3)* (2002) 42 ACSR 670, 678, where Mandie J suggested that the civil penalty proceedings in that case were strongly analogous to criminal proceedings. Nonetheless, one of the advantages to the regulator of proceeding under the civil penalty regime is that a lower standard of proof applies in civil actions than in criminal actions.

[205] Although traditionally it was thought that criminal penalties should be higher than civil penalties, many Australian courts appear to have adopted the reverse assumption in relation to civil penalties in the commercial realm. See, for example, *ACCC v Roche Vitamins Australia Pty Ltd* (2001) ATPR 41-809, where the court ordered civil penalties of A$26 million against pharmaceutical companies for price-fixing and *ACCC v ABB Transmission and Distribution (No 2)* (2002) 190 ALR 169.

[206] (2002) 41 ACSR 72; (2002) 20 ACLC 576.

[207] ibid.

[208] Mr Adler's contraventions were also the most numerous. Santow J found that, whereas Mr Williams and Mr Fodera had contravened the Act seven and five times respectively,

cont. ...

vetting by the Investments Committee, Mr Adler showed consciousness of impropriety.

ASIC v Adler has a number of interesting features. First while the duty of care and diligence has not previously been interpreted to impose a positive monitoring duty on directors to ensure that appropriate compliance systems are in place. Santow J's judgment suggested that such a duty exists under the *Corporations Act*, and may therefore point to a stricter approach in the future.

Secondly, the penalties imposed were relatively stringent. Under the civil penalty provisions of the *Corporations Act*, it is possible for the court to impose disqualification orders, compensation orders for loss, and pecuniary penalties of up to A$200,000 for individuals. ASIC successfully sought each form of remedy.

There has been growing interest in the operation of disqualification orders as a regulatory technique. The Winter Report, for example, considered that, in the light of problems with criminal and civil sanctions,[209] disqualification orders could present a more practicable and efficient form of regulatory sanction.[210]

The court's power to impose disqualification orders under the civil penalty regime has become a particularly potent regulatory tool in Australia. In *ASIC v Adler*, for example, Santow J imposed a 20 year disqualification against Mr. Adler.[211] The disqualification order applied to any involvement by him in the management of both and private corporations.[212] Santow J stressed that the policy rationale for disqualification orders is not punitive in nature, but rather is based upon protection of the public.[213] This new focus on 'protection of the public', and the need for public confidence in the market, is a common theme underlying the current international shift towards a stronger regulatory approach to corporate law.

Another high profile Australian decision, where a disqualification order was made but ultimately reversed on appeal, was *ASIC v Whitlam*.[214] The case involved an action against Nicholas Whitlam, who was president, chairman and a

Mr Adler had committed 101 contraventions. There were also found to be 84 contraventions by Adler Corp. *ASIC v Adler* (2002) 42 epoR 80, 89.

[209] Winter RfVçrt 69.

[210] ibid 69-70.

[211] (2002) 42 ACSR 80, 111. A 10 year disqualification order was made against Mr Williams. (ibid 121). Santow J held that no disqualification order was justified against Mr Fodera. (ibid 124).

[212] Santow J stated, 'It is simply nonsense to suppose that the private status of a company represents some kind of safety zone for members of the public in their dealings; that some kind of *cordon sanitaire* can be placed around private companies so members of the public never deal with them…One might moreover reasonably argue that the public need even greater protection dealing with private companies'. ibid [85].

[213] The 'protection of the public' rationale trumped Mr Adler's claim of 'personal hardship'.

[214] (2002) 169 FLR 383.

director of NRMA Ltd, based upon his failure to sign a poll paper. The unsigned poll paper related to 3,973 proxy votes, which had been given to Mr Whitlam, as chairman of the company's annual general meeting, by members of NRMA Ltd.[215] These proxies directed the chairman to vote against a resolution to increase directors' remuneration. At first instance, Gzell J, held that the chairman's failure to sign the poll paper constituted a deliberate attempt to disenfranchise members, and amounted to a breach of his fiduciary duties to the company. Gzell J imposed a five year disqualification order against Mr Whitlam under the civil penalty provisions relating to breach of directors duties.[216]

This decision was reversed in a controversial decision of the New South Wales Court of Appeal.[217] In a highly technical judgment, the Court of Appeal held that the trial judge's conclusion, that the chair's failure to sign the poll papers was deliberate, was vitiated by certain errors of fact.[218] The Court of Appeal also held that in failing to sign the relevant poll paper for the proxy votes, the chairman was not exercising powers or discharging duties *qua* director,[219] and therefore was not subject to the civil penalty regime relating to breach of directors' duties.[220] ASIC has now lodged an appeal to this decision with the Australian High Court.

There has been debate on whether reform to Australia's proxy rules is needed in the light of the Court of Appeal decision, to provide greater protection for shareholder voting rights. Ultimately, however, technological changes in the context of company meetings may provide a solution to the problem that emerged in the *Whitlam* litigation. The Winter Report stressed the role of modern technology in company meetings and recommended that listed companies should be required to offer shareholders the right to vote *in absentia*, either by direct vote or

[215] Section 250A(4)(c) Corporations Act 2001 (Cth) provides that if the proxy is the chair, the proxy must vote on a poll, and must vote in the way directed.

[216] Gzell J also imposed a pecuniary penalty of A$20,000 on the chairman.

[217] *Whitlam v Australian Securities and Investment Commission* [2003] NSWCA 183.

[218] Although overruling the first instance decision, the members of the Court of Appeal (Hodgson, Ipp and Tobias JJA) acknowledged that the result was 'not entirely satisfactory' (ibid [170]) and that there was 'strong evidence supporting the primary judge's ultimate finding' (ibid [134]).

[219] The Court of Appeal considered that Gzell J was wrong to adopt a general principle that '[t]he failure of any director appointed as proxy to vote in accordance with the instructions of the member appointing him or her is in breach of duty *qua* director'. ibid [151]. Nonetheless, the appellate court acknowledged that, in certain circumstances, it might be argued that a director holding proxies could have dual roles as agent for the appointing member and as director, acting on behalf of the company. This argument had not, however, been made in the Statement of Claim. ibid [156], [158], [161].

[220] *Whitlam v ASIC*, *id*, [148]*ff*.

by proxy, by electronic means.[221] Direct voting by electronic means could ultimately obviate the need for proxies as a voting mechanism at all.

The findings of the HIH Royal Commission[222] focused further attention on the potential liability of executive officers and directors. The Commission's Report identified 56 possible breaches of civil and criminal law by a number of HIH's directors and executive officers (including the CEO and CFO), which the Australian Government immediately referred to ASIC and the Director of Public Prosecutions.[223] Criminal proceedings were commenced against Rodney Adler in relation to the Pacific Eagle Equities transaction, which formed the basis of the civil penalty action in *ASIC v Adler*.[224] In these criminal proceedings, which have been adjourned to the New South Wales Supreme Court, ASIC has alleged that Mr Adler is guilty of offences under the *Corporations Act* of market manipulation and making false and misleading statements in relation to securities.[225]

ASIC has also commenced an A$93 million civil penalty claim in relation to the One.Tel collapse. The focus of this litigation is on the executive officers, including Mr Rich,[226] since ASIC declined to commence proceedings against the outside directors of One.Tel, James Packer, Lachlan Murdoch and Rodney Adler. *ASIC v Rich*,[227] which was heard in the New South Wales Supreme Court in February 2003, involved the status of the former chairman of One.Tel, John Greaves for the purposes of the primary litigation.

Mr Greaves, who is a defendant in the civil penalty proceedings, made an application to the Supreme Court arguing that he should not be held accountable to the same standards as the executive directors, such as Jodee Rich.[228] Rather Greaves claimed that he should be viewed by ASIC as analogous to One.Tel's non-executive directors, and therefore be excluded from the civil penalty proceedings. Austin J disagreed, and held that Mr Greaves had special duties beyond

[221] Winter Report, 52. See also Corporate Law Economic Reform Program (n 40) recommending facilitation of improved shareholder participation in meetings by electronic means.

[222] HIH Royal Commission (n 20).

[223] The Hon. Peter Costello MP, *Report of the HIH Royal Commission*, Press Release, 16 April 2003.

[224] (2002) 20 ACLC 576.

[225] Lampe 'Adler to stand trial over share deal' *Sydney Morning Herald* (11 July 2003) 2.

[226] The defendants' indemnity insurer, CGU, recently argued successfully in the NSW Court of Appeal, that it was entitled to refuse to pay up-front legal expenses on behalf of the defendants, on the basis that the defendants could not be legally indemnified by 'reason of any wrongful act committed by them in their capacity as a director or officer'. See *Silbermann v CGU Insurance Ltd* [2003] NSWCA 203, [7].

[227] [2003] NSWSC 85.

[228] Lampe 'Chairman of the board is now fair game in court' *Sydney Morning Herald* (25 February 2003) 5; Pheasant 'Chairmen face greater legal burden, court rules' *Australian Financial Review* (25 February 2003) 1.

those of the non-executive directors, leading to a higher standard of care and diligence, reflected in contemporary community expectations.

Austin J's decision in *ASIC v Rich*[229] explicitly reflects the approach of the Higgs Report in the UK, viewing the role of the chairman as 'pivotal' in contemporary corporate governance.[230] The chairman, according to the Higgs Report, has 'the responsibility of leading the board in setting the values and standards of the company'.[231] There is an interesting tension between the recognition of heightened responsibilities evident in *ASIC v Rich*[232] and the approach in *Whitlam v ASIC*,[233] where the New South Wales Court of Appeal treated the chairman like any other person receiving proxies and disregarded the powerful role of the chairman within the corporation. The approach in *ASIC v Rich*[234] is more attuned to contemporary corporate governance debate.

In March 2003, Brad Keeling, one of the joint managing directors of One.Tel entered into a landmark settlement with ASIC, in which he agreed to a 10 year disqualification from acting as a manager and accepted liability for a proportion of the A$ 93 million loss sustained by One.Tel.[235]

E. Executive Remuneration

If *possible*, *honestly*, if not, somehow, make money.

Horace, *Epistles*

Many of the current international reforms are premised on an assumption that the predominant area of corporate governance failure in the 1990s was at the level of the board of directors. A contrary view is that it is highly unlikely that boards in the US and around the world suddenly deteriorated in the 1990s.[236] If anything, there was a significant improvement in general board practices during this period, as a result of corporate governance norms advocated by activist institutional investors, which now form the basis of current reforms.

One is left with the uncomfortable proposition that concern about the board of directors may operate as a trompe-l'oeil, disguising other contributing factors in

[229] [2003] NSWSC 85.

[230] Higgs (n 86) [5.1].

[231] ibid [5.2].

[232] [2003] NSWSC 85.

[233] [2003] NSWCA 183.

[234] [2003] NSWSC 85.

[235] Main 'Keeling disqualified for 10 years' *Australian Financial Review* (22 March 2003) 16.

[236] Coffee (n 18) 3.

the recent corporate collapses. The new faith in the 'independent director' as a panacea for corporate governance ills, fails to recognise inherent limitations in the ability of any board to constrain dishonest management. It may therefore be important to look more closely at systemic incentives for the 'fulcrum'[237] of governance, the managers, to engage in dishonest conduct.

The Winter Report identifies remuneration as 'one of the key areas where executive directors have a conflict of interests'.[238] Executive remuneration has been a pervasive governance theme in many of the recent corporate collapses in all jurisdictions.[239] In the range of possible factors contributing to recent corporate failures, the impact of the transformation of executive remuneration is therefore worthy of consideration.[240] Yet, interestingly, executive remuneration receives almost no attention in the US 2002 reforms. One exception, however, is s 403 of the *Sarbanes-Oxley Act*, which provides for the forfeiture of bonuses or incentive-based remuneration received by the CEO and CFO, if corporation is required to restate its financial results due to misconduct and non-compliance with financial reporting requirements. Executive remuneration receives only slightly more attention in the recent Australian corporate governance reform proposals.[241]

In the 1990s, strong convergence of corporate governance practices was evident in the area of executive remuneration.[242] The dramatic rise in the US of performance-based pay coupled with large option grants, which led to sharp pay rises for American CEOs during the 1990s,[243] was widely emulated abroad, in

[237] Thompson and Sale (n 142) 859.

[238] Winter Report, 64.

[239] For example GP Miller 'Catastrophic Financial Failures: Enron, HIH and More' (Speech delivered at the Ross Parsons Lecture 2002, *The Global Regulation of Banking: From HIH to Enron*, University of Sydney Law School, Sydney, 11 July 2002 (forthcoming, 2003 Cornell L Rev).

[240] See generally, Coffee (n 18).

[241] The ASX Corporate Governance Council principles (n 74) contain Principle 9, which deals with best practices in director and executive remuneration. A similar provision to s 403 of the Sarbanes-Oxley Act is embodied in the Corporations (Repayment of Directors' Bonuses) Amendment Act 2003, which permits liquidators to reclaim unreasonable payments made to directors within four years of a company's liquidation.

[242] The levels of pay were, however, far higher in the US than in other countries. See generally M Becht, P Bolton and AA Roël 'Corporate Governance and Control' Finance Working Paper No 02/2002 (October 2002) 97ff.

[243] According to Standard & Poor's data, the median CEO compensation in the US rose from US$1.8 million in 1992 to US$6.1 million in 2000, and there has been a 340% rise in CEO compensation over a 10 year period in comparison with a 36% rise for general employees: The Conference Board Commission on Public Trust and Private Enterprise, 'Findings and Recommendations, Part 1: Executive Compensation' Briefing Paper (2002), 4, (available at <http://www.conference-board.org/PDF_free/756.pdf>). Recent figures, however, suggest that average

cont. ...

countries such as Australia.[244] It was less common, however, in Europe, where stock options tended to be regarded with greater suspicion. It is interesting to note that one European company which used large stock options to reward its managers was the Dutch company, Royal Ahold NV.[245]

Two main factors contributed to the rise of performance-based pay and option grants in the US context – first, the existence of favorable treatment under US tax law for performance-based remuneration, and secondly, the absence of any requirement to expense fixed price options against company earnings.[246]

The emergence of this form of executive remuneration constituted a radical paradigm shift in corporate law, from a fiduciary model of executive remuneration to an alignment of interests model.[247] Previously, executive remuneration had been viewed as a classic corporate governance problem, necessitating a range of suggested regulatory techniques to reduce or eliminate managerial self-interest (such as fiduciary duty liability, use of independent directors, remuneration committees or greater shareholder control). Under the new paradigm, however, executive remuneration was seen, not as a corporate governance problem, but as a solution – it was recast as a corporate governance technique in its own right.[248] Rather than seeking to control or eliminate managerial self-interest, the new paradigm sought to legitimise and harness managerial self-interest, through alignment of the interests of management and shareholders.[249]

The events at One.Tel, which reignited public concern about executive remuneration in Australia, raised fundamental questions about the role of executive remuneration in the recent corporate collapses and the efficacy of the alignment of interests paradigm. Mirroring the events at Enron, where executives were paid

executive pay in the US has declined by 33%. See generally L Lavelle, FF Jespersen and others 'Special Report: Executive Pay' Business Week, 21 April 2003, 86ff.

244 See generally Johnston 'American-style pay moves abroad: Importance of stock options expands in a global economy' *New York Times* (3 September 1998) C2; S Clyne 'Modern Corporate Governance' (2000) 11 Australian Journal of Corporate Law 276, 280-282.

245 Matlack et al 'The year of nasty surprises' Business Week, 10 March 2003, 48; McCartney 'Food baron's fall shakes Dutch; 'Superman' CEO leaves Ahold empire in jeopardy' *Washington Post* (1 March 2003) AO1.

246 DeMott 'Shareholder Challenges to Executive Remuneration' (2000) 74 Australian LJ 576.

247 Yablon 'Bonus Questions – Executive Compensation in the Era of Pay for Performance' (1999) 75 Notre Dame L Rev 271, 279-80.

248 E Johnson 'Waste Not, Want Not: An Analysis of Stock Option Plans, Executive Compensation, and the Proper Standard of Waste' (2000) 26 Journal of Corporations Law 145, 148; RD Ellis 'Equity Derivatives, Executive Compensation, and Agency Costs' (1998) 35 Houston L Rev 399, 402.

249 See generally, J Hill and CM Yablon 'Corporate Governance and Executive Remuneration: Rediscovering Managerial Positional Conflict' (2002) 25 University of New South Wales L Rev 294, 301.

large cash bonuses shortly before the company's collapse,[250] it was revealed in September 2000 in One.Tel's annual report that the joint CEO's, Rich and Keeling, had received cash bonuses of A$6.9 million each. The bonus payments, which were tied to the market capitalisation of One.Tel, prompted public outrage and caused One.Tel's share price to plummet.[251] The liquidator of One.Tel has now commenced legal proceedings, not only against Rich and Keeling to recover the bonuses, but also against the members of One.Tel's remuneration committee, on the basis that they breached their duties in approving the bonus package.[252]

The gap between the theory and practice of performance-based pay has become increasingly apparent in corporate tales such as One.Tel and Enron.[253] They clearly demonstrate a range of common problems relating to executive compensation generally, and performance-based pay specifically. First, the procedures for the payment of the One.Tel bonuses raise concerns about conflict of interests and lack of arm's length dealing. For example, it appears that the structure of the bonuses was suggested by the CEOs themselves, that there was no discussion by the board about the reasonableness of the payments and no advice from independent external compensation consultants.[254] Whereas the two board representatives of the major shareholders were aware of the bonus structure, most shareholders only learned of the existence of the bonuses after they had been paid.

Australian corporate law uses shareholder consent as a regulatory device to screen a range of related party transactions, which may be detrimental to the company's interests. Arguably the One.Tel bonus packages should have been approved by shareholders under Australian law, on the basis that one of the related party provisions exempt remuneration from the requirement of shareholder consent only if the remuneration is 'reasonable'.[255] It appears that the board of One.Tel failed to seek shareholder approval on the basis that it considered the $6.9 million bonuses to meet the standard of 'reasonableness', indicating the regulatory deficiencies of such a provision.

[250] Eichenwald 'Enron's many strands: Executive Compensation' *New York Times* (1 March 2002) 1.

[251] Barry (n 31) 364.

[252] Main 'Liquidator sues One.Tel directors' *Australian Financial Review* (18 February 2003) 7.

[253] The bonuses paid to One.Tel's executives pale in contrast to the US$140 million, which was paid to Kenneth Lay for his work at Enron in 2000. See Report prepared by the Permanent Subcommittee on Investigations of the Committee on Governmental Affairs, United States Senate, *The Role of the Board of Directors in Enron's Collapse* (2002) 8, 52.

[254] Lacy 'Board didn't approve bonuses' *Australian Financial Review* (23 April 2002) 3. The HIH Royal Commission found similar problems to exist at HIH, where the performance of the CEO was subject to 'only the most perfunctory review' by the chairman, Cohen. See HIH Royal Commission (n 20) 26.

[255] Section 211 Corporations Act 2001 (Cth).

The One.Tel story also exemplifies the extent to which the alignment of interests rhetoric in performance-based pay often fails to match reality. There has, for example, been much public condemnation of the reliance on One.Tel's market capitalisation (which was ephemeral and unsustainable) as the criterion for assessing performance of the CEOs. This is a recurrent theme in academic literature in this area. The structures of performance-based pay have often been criticised on the basis that they use inappropriate criteria, are unduly favourable to management, provide little downside risk for executives, or create perverse incentives for short-term gain.[256]

More recent research suggests, however, that even in well-structured performance-based pay packages, the inherent powers and discretions of executive officers over, for example, disclosure and financial reporting, may enable them to influence their own pay by manipulating and distorting the indicia of performance.[257] There has also been a growing recognition of danger whereby option grants inflate corporate earnings and stock prices, and present a misleading picture of a company's profitability. This has led to pressure for reforms to require that options are treated as expenses in corporate accounts, and such reforms now seem inevitable.[258] In the US, a number of companies have already announced that they will voluntarily expense options against company profits, and the Commission on Public Trust and Private Enterprise of the Conference Board has recommended introducing a mandatory requirement to expense fixed-price options.[259]

The events at One.Tel, like those at Sunbeam[260] and Enron[261] suggest that the confluence of performance-based pay and option grants contributed to a corporate

[256] See, for example, GS Crystal *In Search of Excess: The Overcompensation of American Executives* (WW Norton New York 1991) 98; JA Kreinberg, Note 'Reaching Beyond Performance Compensation in Attempts to Own the Corporate Executive' (1995) 45 Duke LJ 138.

[257] LA Bebchuk, JM Fried and DI Walker 'Managerial Power and Rent Extraction in the Design of Executive Compensation' (2002) 69 U Chi L Rev 751; CM Yablon and J Hill 'Timing Corporate Disclosures to Maximize Performance-Based Remuneration: A Case of Misaligned Incentives?' (2000) 35 Wake Forest L Rev 83.

[258] For, example, the Federal Government has recommended the adoption by the Australian Accounting Standards Board ('AASB') of the International Accounting Standards Board ('IASB') standards to require expensing of share options. Corporate Law Economic Reform Program (n 40) 102ff.

[259] The Conference Board Commission on Public Trust and Private Enterprise, 'Findings and Recommendations, Part 1: Executive Compensation' Briefing Paper (2002) 4.

[260] Hill 'Deconstructing Sunbeam – Contemporary Issues in Corporate Governance' (1999) 67 U Cin L Rev 1099, 1127.

[261] When the news of the Enron bonuses emerged, a former federal white-collar crime prosecutor was reported as saying, '[t]he levels of compensation that we are talking about here would certainly seem to provide a powerful incentive to do anything'. Eichenwald 'Enron's many strands: Executive compensation' *New York Times* (1 March 2002) 1. See generally

cont. ...

culture, which stressed short-term profit maximisation for shareholders and provided strong incentives to insiders that controlled the flow of information to engage in manipulation of accounting records.

Yet, while these corporate collapses have led to some soul-searching about the *structure* and fine-tuning of executive pay, the alignment of interests rhetoric underlying performance-based pay has remained essentially intact. Alignment of interests between management and shareholders is still viewed as both desirable and possible – the devil is simply in the detail.

This assumption is evident in Australia in the recent ASX Corporate Governance Council guidelines on corporate governance.[262] The dominant focus of Principle 9, dealing with executive remuneration, is to ensure that there is 'a clear relationship between performance and remuneration'. The guidelines also promote improved disclosure about executive remuneration to investors. Although Australia introduced more stringent rules relating to disclosure of executive remuneration in 1998,[263] paralleling SEC disclosure requirements, there was continuing concern about the adequacy of disclosure under the rules, particularly in relation to disclosure of the value of options.[264] The ASX Corporate Governance Council guidelines seek to address this issue, by clarifying the elements of remuneration, which must be disclosed.[265] The guidelines explicitly require disclosure of the value of shares and options granted, and termination payments. In addition, ASIC recently released guidelines detailing how Australian companies should value options.[266]

Termination payments have become particularly controversial in Australia[267] and the UK.[268] There was public backlash in Australia in 2000 over a payment of

JN Gordon 'What Enron Means for the Management and Control of the Modern Business Corporation: Some Initial Reflections' (2002) 69 U Chi L Rev 1233.

[262] ASX Corporate Governance Council (n 74) Principle 9, 'Remunerate fairly and responsibly'.

[263] See s 300A Corporations Act 2001 (Cth).

[264] In the CLERP 9 proposals, the Federal Government affirmed that it would amend the Corporations Act 2001 (Cth) to require explicitly that the value of stock options must be disclosed. See Corporate Law Economic Reform Program (n 40) 109. See also HIH Royal Commission (n 20) Recommendation 1.

[265] ASX Corporate Governance Council (n 74) Principle 9, 'Remunerate fairly and responsibly', Box 9.1.

[266] ASIC, Media and Information Release 03-202, *Valuing options for directors and executives*, 30 June 2003; ASIC, *Guidelines to valuing options in annual directors' reports*, 30 June 2003. See also, Buffini 'ASIC closes options loophole' *Australian Financial Review* (8 May 2003) 3.

[267] It appears that the problem of termination pay is exacerbated in Australia, by the fact that employment contracts for executives tend to be longer in Australia than in other jurisdictions, such as the US or UK. See International Corporate Governance Network, Sub-Committee on Executive Remuneration, 'Executive Remuneration – The Caucus Race' [31], <http://www.icgn.org/documents/ICGNExecRem.pdf>.

A$13.2 million, one of the largest severance payments in Australian commercial history, to George Trumbull, the former chief executive of AMP Ltd.[269] The most significant aspect of the ASX Corporate Governance Council guidelines relates to up-front disclosure of termination payments. The guidelines suggest that Australian companies may be required to disclose the details of termination payments at the time of entering into the agreement with executives (as opposed to the time of payment), as part of the general continuous disclosure obligation under Australian corporate law.[270]

There is a growing international trend supporting greater participation by shareholders in aspects of corporate governance relating executive remuneration.[271] Yet, to date, the power of shareholders to block or challenge executive remuneration plans has generally been weak.[272] The focus on greater fine-tuning of executive remuneration plans, following collapses like those at Enron and One.Tel, however, create a tension in this regard. One of the dangers of such finetuning, is that executive remuneration packages are becoming increasingly complicated and abstruse, which creates substantial barriers to effective disclosure[273] and use of shareholder approval as a governance technique in relation to executive pay.[274]

[268] For example, Department of Trade and Industry, 'Rewards for Failure': Directors' Remuneration – Contracts, Performance and Severance, A Consultative Document (June 2003).

[269] Termination and retirement benefits continue to be controversial. In 2003, AMP refused to pay Paul Batchelor, Mr Trumbull's successor as CEO, A$18 million, which he claimed in termination benefits. See Ryan 'Rich pickings' *Australian Financial Review* (24 April 2003) 38. Also, Brian Gilbertson, chief executive of BHP Billiton, left office with reported benefits of A$50million. Ryan and Howard 'For the record, Gilbertson leaves BHP with $50m' *Australian Financial Review* (23 May 2003) 1.

[270] ASX Listing Rule 3.1. See Power 'Seven first to meet ASX rules and reveal CEO pay' *Australian Financial Review* (15 April 2003) 55.

[271] For example, the NYSE corporate governance rule proposals, which include a provision requiring a shareholder vote on equity compensation plans (s 303A(8)). In the UK, see also the Directors' Remuneration Report Regulations 2002 (SI 2002 No 1986), introducing an annual shareholders' vote on the directors' remuneration report. In Australia, the ASX Listing Rules were amended in 2001 to require shareholder consent as a precondition to stock option repricing (ASX Listing Rule 6.23).

[272] See generally, RS Thomas and KJ Martin 'Litigating Challenges to Executive Pay: An Exercise in Futility?' (2001) 79 Washington University Law Quarterly 569.

[273] On the general problem of effective disclosure in relation to highly complex transactions, see SL Schwarcz, 'Enron and the Use and Abuse of Special Purpose Entities in Corporate Structures' (2002) 70 U Cincinnati L Rev 1309, 1316-1317.

[274] See International Corporate Governance Network, Sub-Committee on Executive Remuneration, *Executive Remuneration – The Caucus Race* [43], (<http://www.icgn.org/documents/ICGNExecRem.pdf>).

F. Conclusion

No-one yet knows the answer to why we have recently witnessed such a concentration of corporate collapses across the globe, yet these collapses raise a number of fundamental questions. For example, did the collapses occur because of massive corporate governance failure? Or did they occur in spite of corporate governance, suggesting the impotence of corporate governance to deal with such problems?[275] The recent regulatory responses, which focus on strengthening corporate governance monitors such as the board of directors, appear to adopt the former explanation. However, a more problematical explanation, which receives little attention in the reforms, is that these corporate collapses occurred because reforms to corporate governance practices in the 1990s (including the rise of performance-based pay) increased both the pressures and the incentives for management to engage in dishonest conduct.[276] Under this interpretation, the collapses of companies, such as HIH, One.Tel and Enron represent 'the dark side of shareholder value'.[277]

There are many common themes emerging from an examination of the regulatory responses to the corporate collapses in countries such as Australia, the UK and US. Yet, the corporate governance 'systems'[278] in these countries are by no means identical, and inevitable differences in focus and detail emerge in the reforms. Further reflection on the fundamental question of what caused the corporate collapses will undoubtedly drive new species of reform. The current regulatory environment is therefore highly fluid, and suggests that predictions of complete convergence of corporate governance were premature. While globalisation may have led to convergence of capital markets, there is as yet no regulatory convergence.[279]

[275] See generally JR Coffee (n 18) 4.

[276] ibid.

[277] See Bratton, 'The Dark Side of Shareholder Value' (2002) 76 *Tulane L Rev* 1275; Blair, 'Post-Enron Reflections on Comparative Corporate Governance' (2002) (available on Social Science Research Network Electronic Library: http://www.ssrn.com/).

[278] See Winter Report, 7, stressing that corporate governance is a system based partly in company law, wider laws and practices and market structures.

[279] See Bruce, 'Hope of calmer waters: After the tumult and shouting of last year, 2003 is likely to be less dramatic – though many challenging issues have to be faced', *Financial Times*, 9 January 2003, 2.

Chapter 5: The Remuneration of Executive and Non-Executive Directors

Executive Remuneration and Corporate Governance in the EU: Convergence, Divergence, and Reform Perspectives[*]

GUIDO FERRARINI and NIAMH MOLONEY

This chapter examines the current controversy as to the effectiveness of executive remuneration as a tool of corporate governance but places the analysis in the particular context of the dispersed ownership/blockholding ownership faultline which runs across European corporate governance. It reveals that there is a close relationship between governance systems and the sophistication and rigour of the regulatory response to executive remuneration.

To place the European responses to the executive remuneration question in context, Part A sets out the main theoretical arguments which frame the executive remuneration debate and examines the link between remuneration and corporate governance. Section II examines the supporting theory, with particular reference to the principal/agent incentive model. Section III examines the structural problems raised by incentive pay, and, in particular, share options. Section IV covers governance problems, with particular reference to the board of directors, the remuneration committee, remuneration consultants, shareholders and institutional investors. Section V deals with disclosure of executive remuneration as a remedy for agency costs. Section VI outlines the fairness argument and section VII further examines the interaction between executive remuneration and corporate governance systems.

Part B examines, in the light of the preceding discussion, the regulatory strategies adopted by EU Member States with regard to executive remuneration and reveals the extent to which responses track corporate governance systems in terms of sophistication and degree of intervention in remuneration practices, particularly with respect to disclosure. Overall, regulatory strategies focus on company disclo-

[*] Part B of this paper is based on the answers given to a questionnaire on the national laws relating to directors' remuneration in the EU. We are grateful to Ingalill Aspholm, Paulo Câmara, Jan Schans Christensen, Daniel Dax, Alessandra De Cantellis, Sonja D'Hollander, Jesualdo Domínguez-Alcahud, Diego Escanero, Jose M. Garrido, Steven Hijink, Susanne Kalss, Björn Kristiansson, Marco Leonardi, Jacques Loesch, Evanghelos Emm. Perakis, Markus Roth, Joëlle Simon, Kelley Smith, Georgios D. Sotiropoulos, João Sousa Gião, Tiina Visakorpi, Anne Wilschut, Ingrid De Poorter and Andrea Zanoni for either answering or reviewing the answers to the questionnaire. The full text of the answers can be downloaded at <http://www.ecgi.org>.

sure and corporate governance structures, and are grounded both in public regulation and in corporate governance best practices. Sections II and III of Part B analyze the rules applicable to annual disclosure in the different Member States. These sections distinguish between two groups of countries, depending on whether the publication of detailed or summary information is required under national rules and practices. Sections IV and V examine, again with reference to each Member State, the role of corporate governance structures in executive pay, and focus on remuneration committees and the shareholders' powers concerning remuneration policy. Section VI concludes on convergence and divergence of European laws in this area.

Part C discusses reform perspectives with particular reference, in section I, to the 2002 Winter Report and the 2003 Company Law Action Plan. Section II examines reform problems more generally, and suggests that regulation should only be imposed to reset the market mechanism. Section III concludes the chapter.

A. Theoretical Foundations

I. Introduction

Executive remuneration is a classic concern of corporate governance and has important normative and practical implications for the shareholder/manager relationship and the optimum alignment of interests. At present, executive remuneration practices are experiencing a high profile as a *cause célèbre* of international corporate governance in the financial media,[1] among regulators,[2] in the marketplace,[3] and in academia,[4] in the UK, continental Europe, and the US. This development coincides with popular unease with levels of executive remuneration.[5] Executives are now paid at very high levels due, for the most part, to a dramatic increase since the early 1990s in equity-based performance-linked pay and, in particular, the use of share options. Other remuneration practices such as the award of 'rewards for failure' (compensation payments made on termination of a directors service contract) are also generating unease, particularly in the UK.[6] The argument that high levels of remuneration reward corporate performance and so benefit shareholders, and are set by market dynamics, which is traditionally wielded by supporters of the status quo, is not always compelling. Recent evidence of corporate failure appears to support the view that senior management can destory shareholder value and that remuneration should, accordingly be restrained.[7] In particular, the US pay model which, via its emphasis on option

[1] eg the special supplement on executive remuneration published in the UK *Independent* on 20 May 2003.

[2] Reforms were introduced in the UK in 2002, eg which require considerably greater disclosure on executive remuneration practices via a mandatory annual Directors' Remuneration Report, published as part of the corporate financial reporting cycle (Part B, section II.2 below). In Germany, moves are underway to force more extensive disclosure of individual directors' pay: B Benoit 'German executives may be forced to publish salaries' *Financial Times* (20 May 2003).

[3] See the International Corporate Governance Network's Report on executive pay, which includes a ten point Code of Conduct, designed to improve transparency and accountability in pay-setting: ICGN 'The Caucus Race' July 2002.

[4] A vast, predominantly US-based, empirical literature examines executive remuneration under the principal/agent model. For admirable surveys see: K Murphy 'Executive Compensation' in O Ashenfalter and D Card (eds) *Handbook of Labor Economics* (Elsevier Amsterdam 1999) 2485; J Abowd and D Kaplan 'Executive Compensation: Six Questions that Need Answering' (1999) 13 J Economic Perspectives 145 and L Bebchuk, J Fried and D Walker 'Managerial Power and Rent Extraction in the Design of Executive Compensation' (2002) 69 U Chi LR 751.

[5] The rejection of the GlaxoSmithKline Remuneration Report by the shareholders dominated the press, radio, and television media and led to widespread condemnation of perceived 'rewards for failure' in the UK. See eg the 20 May 2003 editorials in the *Independent* ('A vote that marks the beginning of the end of rewards for corporate failure') and the *Financial Times* ('Parachute holed: GSK must respond to shareholder concerns on executive pay').

[6] See the UK Department of Trade and Industry's Consultation Document 'Rewards for Failure' – Directors' Remuneration – Contracts, Performance, and Severance' June 2003.

[7] Less drastically, the evidence suggests that outstanding performance is not required for high levels of remuneration. In 2000, eg 85% of corporate leaders received the maximum bonus, 40% received long term pay outs for median performance, and 43% were awarded options plans for meeting growth targets of only 2-3% above inflation: Andersen Directors' Remuneration Report, September 2001, cited in O Gadiesh and M Blenko, 'The Weapon of Executive Pay' *Financial Times* (27 November 2002).

remuneration, generated often stratospheric payouts to executives who reaped huge rewards from the long bull market run of the 1990s, is coming under harsh review in the face of striking evidence of poor corporate performance in a post Enron/WorldCom economic environment.[8] Similarly, the market dynamic argument can be countered by the existence of severe governance weaknesses in the contracting-for-remuneration process which generate a deeply conflicted pay-contracting process and which, together with inefficiencies in the market for information on pay, may have the effect of allowing executives to control their own remuneration.

The purpose of this paper is to examine the different approaches taken across Europe to the regulation of executive remuneration practices in listed companies in light of current controversies, in light of corporate governance distinctions, and in light of recent EU initiatives, in particular the November 2002 Winter Report and the May 2003 Company Law Action Plan.[9] But in order to expose the fault-lines of the remuneration debate and to highlight the complexity of the area, Part A first sets out the main features of the remuneration controversy. There are three core elements to that controversy: the structure of remuneration; governance, or the process whereby remuneration contracts are adopted; and disclosure. Specifically: section II examines the supporting theory and its implications for dispersed ownership and blockholding systems; section III examines structural difficulties with incentive pay and, in particular, the problems raised by share options; section IV covers governance problems; section V deals with disclosure; section VI outlines the overarching fairness arguments; and section VII further examines the interaction between executive remuneration and corporate governance systems.

The outstanding feature of the regulation of executive pay across the EU is, arguably, the extent to which it reflects the interconnection between pay and corporate governance. As discussed in section II, executive pay, regarded as a performance-based incentive contract, is a key agency-cost control mechanism in dispersed ownership systems. Legal controls on pay are accordingly at their most sophisticated, in terms of seeking to ensure the adoption of an optimal contract for shareholders, in those EU countries where dispersed ownership dominates.[10]

[8] Reference is made to the 'discredited' share-option-driven US model in a *Financial Times* editorial: 'An executive pay package too far' *Financial Times* (22 November 2002.

[9] *Report of the High Level Group of Company Law Experts on a Modern Regulatory Framework for Company Law in Europe* (European Commission November 2002) (hereafter Winter Report, see Annex 3 in this volume) and *Modernising Company Law and Enhancing Corporate Governance in the European Union – A Plan to Move Forward* (Communication from the Commission to the Council and the European Parliament, May 2003, COM (2003) 284 final) (hereafter European Commission Communication) COM (2003) 284 (see Annex 1 in this volume).

[10] The European debate is not confined to the classic dispersed ownership systems. French shareholders, and particularly minority shareholders, are expressing concerns as to executive remuneration: J Johnson 'France Inc closes ranks on dispirited rebel investor' *Financial Times* (26 May 2003).

In systems characterized by blockholding, controlling shareholders can, in theory, monitor management directly without the need for an incentive contract. Pay controls are accordingly less sophisticated. Concerns arise, however, as to the protection of minority shareholders. A shift to more pervasive equity ownership across the EU (section VII) may bring with it the structural, governance, and disclosure problems currently associated with remuneration practices in dispersed ownership systems. But at present EU executive remuneration cannot be regarded in a monolithic fashion given the current sharp differences in corporate governance, as well as diverging cultural attitudes towards wealth and pay transparency.

II. The Agency Model of Executive Remuneration: Implications for Dispersed Ownership and Blockholding Systems

1. Competing Characterizations

A number of different characterizations of executive remuneration converge in the debate as to current structures and levels of executive remuneration. Executive remuneration can be placed in the traditional legal paradigm of the company as a single entity to which directors owe fiduciary duties, including duties not to engage in self-dealing and to avoid secret profits.[11] More generally, executive remuneration can be regarded as a wealth transfer question. In this context, the debate becomes couched in the language of fairness and wealth inequality and the law is cast as a mechanism for curbing executive greed and excess.[12] Executive remuneration is also, in the context of dispersed ownership corporate governance, widely analyzed in terms of agency theory and as a governance mechanism which resolves agency costs. Legal mechanisms play a minimal role in this analysis: the optimal contract is adopted as a matter of market dynamics. There is also the related argument that executive remuneration in itself is not a problem: it is simply the outcome of a wider failure to address defects in corporate governance in dispersed ownership systems, particularly with respect to board passivity,[13] and a symptom of the intractable conflicts at the heart of the separation of ownership and control.

[11] The two models of analysis can be seen as fundamentally misaligned: '... under legal concepts of fiduciary duty, the corporate executive who feathers his own nest at the expense of the corporation is acting aberrantly and improperly, under the economic concept of agency costs, that same behavior is simply the expected utility maximising function of a poorly monitored agent': C Yablon 'Bonus Questions – Executive Compensation in the Era of Pay for Performance' (1999) 75 Notre Dame LR 271, 279.

[12] eg M Loewenstein 'Reflections of Executive Compensation and a Modest Proposal for (Further) Reform' (1996) 50 Southern Methodist University LR 201.

[13] C Elson 'The Duty of Care, Compensation, and Stock Compensation' (1995) 63 U Cinn LR 649, 651 and 661.

2. Executive Remuneration and Dispersed Ownership: The Principal/Agent Incentive Model

The dominant model for executive remuneration in the dispersed ownership context is the principal/agent incentive model. This model generates two competing characterizations of executive remuneration: remuneration as remedy for agency costs; and remuneration as a further cost of the dispersed ownership company.

a) Remuneration as a Remedy for Agency Costs

Under the first model, executive remuneration is a remedy for the agency costs generated by the misalignment of management incentives and shareholder interests in the dispersed ownership company. At the core of the principal/agent model is a simple question: how do wealth-maximizing shareholders ensure that managers with conflicting goals act in their interests?[14] In the dispersed ownership company, with a separation of ownership and control,[15] shareholders have only a fractional interest in firm profits, are not incentivized individually to a significant extent to discipline management, and have limited opportunities to observe management's actions. Management's unobserved actions can, however, have a considerable bearing on shareholder wealth.[16] In particular, management does not bear the full cost of privately beneficial activity which hurts the firm, conflicts with the wealth maximizing agenda of shareholders, and gives rise to agency costs. These activities could include the taking of perquisites, such as corporate jets.[17] They could also extend to less egregious behaviour, such as following risk-averse management strategies which do not maximize shareholder value but which a manager, with salary and career prospects tied up in one company, might be incentivized to follow. Managers also require incentives to expend effort on behalf of the company given that while they enjoy all the benefits of their leisure time, they receive only a fraction of the value their work generates for the company.[18]

Whether, and the extent to which, a manager will fully pursue the shareholders' wealth maximization agenda depends on if, and how, that manager is

[14] The seminal discussion of agency theory with respect to the company is M Jensen and W Meckling 'Theory of the Firm: Managerial Behaviour, Agency Costs and Ownership Structure' (1976) 3 J Fin Econ 305.

[15] A Berle and G Means *The Modern Corporation and Private Property* (Transaction Publishers New York 1932). As discussed below, not all corporate governance systems follow this model, with implications for the executive remuneration analysis.

[16] R Aggarwal and A Samwick 'Executive Compensation, Strategic Competition, and Relative Performance Evaluation: Theory and Evidence' (1999a) 54 J Fin 1999.

[17] eg B Hall and J Liebman 'Are CEOs Really Paid Like Bureaucrats' (1997) NBER Working Paper Series Working Paper No 6213, 1, 5 and Bebchuk and others (n 4) 763.

[18] Bebchuk and others (n 4) 763.

incentivized to take decisions which maximize shareholder wealth. The agency theory analysis suggests that, in a dispersed ownership company, the executive remuneration contract provides an effective way of structuring incentives to minimize agency costs and the conflict between managers and shareholders.[19] Where the appropriate actions which executives should take are known and observable, the optimal contract will simply pay a fixed salary and charge for sub-optimal behaviour. But shareholders do not have complete information about all the manager's actions, the contract cannot cover all contingencies,[20] leading to the need for an incentive contract.[21] The incentive contract therefore generates management incentives in the form of remuneration and aligns them with the interests of shareholders, specifically shareholder wealth.[22] The simplest way of doing this is to link remuneration to shareholder wealth via performance indicators such as share prices or accounting-based targets. If a manager's remuneration is linked to shareholder returns in this way, that manager should take action in accordance with shareholders' interests. Executive remuneration and wealth can be linked to shareholder wealth either directly (equity-based remuneration in the form of shares or share options) or indirectly (accounting-based bonuses). Bargaining in this way to minimize agency costs occurs, in theory, between the shareholders and the managers, with the board of directors acting as a somewhat flawed proxy for the shareholders and in the interests of shareholder-value maximization.

Executive remuneration typically comprises a number of elements, balanced, ideally, to ensure maximum shareholder wealth generation and minimum risk aversion behaviour by management They include: fixed base salaries; annual cash bonuses, often linked to accounting targets; share options which, in effect, link remuneration to share price performance; and long term incentive plans which may involve awards of shares or cash over a medium term period (3-5 years) subject to the achievement of particular performance targets.[23]

[19] Hall and Liebman (n 17) 5.

[20] On the difficulties of complete contingent contracts see M Jensen and K Murphy 'Performance Pay and Top Management Incentives' (1999a) 98 J Pol Econ 225, 226.

[21] B Holmstrom 'Moral Hazard and Observability' (1979) 10 Bell Journal of Economics 74.

[22] M Conyon and D Leech 'Top Pay, Company Performance and Corporate Governance' (1994) 56 Oxford Bulletin of Economics and Statistic 229, 230.

[23] M Conyon and K Murphy 'The Prince and the Pauper: CEO Pay in the United States and in the United Kingdom' (2000) 110 Economic Journal F640, F644. The weighting of these elements can vary considerably. In 1997, for example, UK CEOs received their remuneration in the form of 59% salary, 18% bonuses, 10% share options and 9% long term incentive plan shares. In the US, CEO remuneration weightings included 29% salary and 42% share options: ibid F646-F647.

b) Executive Remuneration as an Agency Cost

The incentive model for remuneration has, in the dispersed ownership context, dominated the remuneration debate and remuneration practices since the early 1990s and lead to an explosion in equity-based remuneration.[24] Part of its appeal lies in a certain compelling simplicity and in the degree of abdication it permits of regulators, but there is also considerable support for its role in making managers more sensitive to shareholder interests and increasing shareholder value.[25] It does, however, present myriad problems in terms of structure and process which are discussed in the remainder of Part A. In particular, difficulties with the agency model have lead to executive remuneration being characterized as an agency cost in itself and as a potential mechanism for self-dealing.[26] As remuneration is set by the board of directors, which is not a neutral arbiter, remuneration contracts are, potentially, not the outcome of adversarial arms' length bargaining by parties seeking to maximize their interests, but give scope to executives to influence remuneration and extract rents in the form of remuneration which is in excess of that which would be optimal for shareholders and which does not generate appropriate incentives.

The view of remuneration as the outcome of a deeply conflicted pay process, and as an expression of self-dealing, is gaining momentum. An analysis of executive remuneration which argues that remuneration can be shaped by, and for the benefit of, directors who exert managerial power to extract pay in the form of rent and are limited only by the 'outrage constraint', or the likelihood of outcry against excessive payments, has recently been presented in the context of the US board of directors and US remuneration practices.[27] It suggests that inefficiencies in pay structures and suboptimal incentive effects, which are otherwise puzzling under the agency model, can be explained by expressing pay as a function of managerial power.[28] Agency theory is also weakened in that it does not grapple

[24] On the impact of the incentive model see Yablon (n 11) 279-280. Share option remuneration began to increase in the early 1990s in the US, urged on by shareholder groups and academics who called for better performance sensitivities, favourable tax reforms, and a climb down by the FASB on the accounting for options as an expense: Conyon and Murphy (n 23) F666.

[25] B Holmstron and S Kaplan 'The State of US Corporate Governance: What's Right and What's Wrong?' (2002) NBER Working Paper No 9613.

[26] M Becht, P Bolton and A Röell 'Corporate Governance and Control' (2002) ECGI Finance Working Paper No 02/2002, 46 and 101-103.

[27] n 4, see 754, 756, 784, and 786-788 for a summary.

[28] J Hill and C Yablon 'Corporate Governance and Executive Remuenration: Rediscovering Managerial Positional Conflict' (2000) 25 NSW LR 294, which places the executive remuneration debate in the context of governance weaknesses, and, in particular, the positional conflicts of interests which management is exposed to given the wide discretion and autonomy conferred on management in public companies.

effectively with the danger that high-powered, equity-based contracts can generate perverse incentives to manipulate share prices and earnings over the short term, as appears to have happened to catastrophic effect in Enron.[29]

3. Executive Remuneration and Blockholding Governance

The agency-driven incentive model as a justification for executive remuneration is at its most powerful where ownership is dispersed and separated from control in the classic Berle-Means or market-based company. But executive remuneration takes on a different complexion in the context of relationship-based corporate governance which is characterized by concentrated shareholdings and long term shareholder commitment to the company.[30]

A wide-ranging study of corporate control in Europe has recently concluded that there is a very high concentration of control among continental European companies.[31] In Belgium for example, the average largest direct shareholding amounts to 45%.[32] In Germany, more than 50% of all listed companies are controlled by a single majority block and only 17.4% are without a blockholder with a veto power.[33] In Italy, the top blockholding for recently listed companies is

[29] eg J Gordon 'What Enron Means for the Management and Control of the Modern Business Corporation: Some Initial Reflections' (2002) 69 U Chi LR 1233 and J Coffee 'What Caused Enron? A Capsule Social and Economic History of the 1990s' (2003) Columbia Law School, Center for Law and Economics Working Paper No 214. In this volume, see also the chapters by Coffee, Hill, and Kraakmann. More generally, Bebchuk and others note that the reductions in shareholder value generated by pay inefficiencies arise from the perverse incentives (and the suboptimal incentives) generated by power-driven pay structures, rather than from the specific rents which excess pay represents (n 4, 757).

[30] Different characterizations are used to the describe these two form of corporate governance such as, eg governance based on control-oriented finance v arms' length finance (E Berglöf 'Reforming Corporate Governance: Redirecting the European Agenda' (1997) 24 Economic Policy 93, 94); market-based v relationship-based governance (S Kaplan 'Top Executive Incentives in Germany, Japan, and the USA: A Comparison' in J Carpenter and D Yermack (eds) *Executive Compensation and Shareholder Value* (Kluwer Boston 1999) 3); dispersed ownership and outsider/arms' length control governance v concentrated ownership and insider/control governance (B Cheffins 'Does Law Matter? The Separation of Ownership and Control in the UK' (2001a) 30 J Legal Studies 459, 460-461); and market governance v blockholder governance (W Bratton and J McCahery 'Comparative Corporate Governance and the Theory of the Firm: The Case Against Global Cross Reference' (1999) 38 Columbia Journal of Transnational Law 213, 218).

[31] F Barca and M Becht *The Control of Corporate Europe* (OUP Oxford 2001).

[32] M Becht, A Chapelle and L Rennoboog 'Shareholding Cascades: The Separation of Ownership and Control in Belgium' in Barca and Becht (n 31) 71, 71.

[33] M Becht and E Böhmer 'Ownership and Voting Power in Germany' in Barca and Becht (n 31) 128, 142-143.

40%.[34] Overall, in 50% of non-financial listed companies in Austria, Belgium, Germany, and Italy, a single blockholder controls more than 50% of the voting rights. In 50% of Dutch, Spanish, and Swedish companies more than 43.5%, 34.5% and 34.9%, respectively of all votes are controlled by a single blockholder. By contrast, the average blockholder in the UK controls 9.9% of votes, while in the US the average blockholding for NYSE and NASDAQ companies is 5%. Small concentrations of voting power below the most dominant blockholder also make it easier for the dominant power to exert control, given the absence of other voting blocks.[35] Concentrations of direct voting power by shareholders in continental companies are intensified into blockholdings and control groups by the common phenomena of cross shareholdings between dominant blockholders (particularly in Germany),[36] the exercise of control through complex pyramidal ownership structures which allow control to be exercised through cascades of companies and without the need to hold substantial cash flow rights (particularly in Italy),[37] proxy voting by financial institutions connected to the company, and voting pacts. Legal devices which separate ownership from control, such as voting caps, multiple voting rights, transfer restrictions, and non-voting shares are also in operation.[38] While family shareholdings form a significant component of continental blockholdings,[39] bank influence remains pronounced. In Germany, for example, there are four dimensions to the central role played by banks: connections to the company via financing activities given the primacy of bank-based finance; blockholdings;[40] supervisory board membership; and exercise of proxy votes.[41] The proxy votes held by banks also means that German blockholders can rely on banks to consolidate their voting power.[42]

This concentration of control and the close relationship between blockholding shareholders and between shareholders and management in continental Europe recasts the management-monitoring agency problem, which executive remuneration, in the Anglo-American system, is designed to resolve. In theory, the agency

[34] M Bianchi, M Bianco and L Enriques 'Pyramidal Groups and the Separation Between Ownership and Control in Italy' in Barca and Becht (n 31) 154, 167.

[35] Becht and Mayer 'Introduction' in Barca and Becht (n 31) 1, 18-20.

[36] Becht and Böhmer (n 33) 142-143.

[37] Bianchi, Bianco, and Enriques (n 34) 170.

[38] For the German experience with these devices see Becht and Böhmer (n 33) 129-134.

[39] Becht and Mayer (n 35) 30-32

[40] The average block held by banks in Germany is 24%: Becht and Böhmer (n 33) 140.

[41] K Hopt 'Common Principles of Corporate Governance in Europe?' in J McCahery, P Moerland, T Raajmakers and L Renneboog (eds) *Corporate Governance Regimes. Convergence and Diversity* (OUP Oxford 2002) 175, 186-187.

[42] Becht and Böhmer (n 33) 129 and 135. On banks as monitors eg B Black and J Coffee 'Hail Britannia? Institutional Investor Behaviour Under Limited Regulation' (1994) 92 Mich L Rev 1997, 2073-2077.

costs which trouble the dispersed ownership company are reduced and shareholders are in a position to monitor managers more directly and effectively and without high-powered incentive contracts.[43] In practice, as is revealed in Part B, European approaches to the management of executive remuneration, and in particular the rigour and sophistication of controls, do appear to track closely the corporate governance system in operation and the availability of alternative management monitors.[44] Concerns remain, however, as to the management of conflicts of interests in the setting of remuneration, particularly with respect to the protection of minority shareholders.

The following analysis focuses, in particular, on the problems as to structure (section III), governance (section IV), and disclosure (section V) raised by remuneration as a remedy for agency costs in the dispersed ownership company: as such it has a particular resonance for the UK and Ireland. As discussed in Part B, regulatory responses in these States are directed to broadly non-interventionist governance and disclosure controls, rather than to controls on the particular structure of remuneration which is broadly left to company discretion and market dynamics, although performance-based pay is explicitly called for by the UK Listing Rules' Combined Code, which applies on a comply or explain basis. But if European corporate governance systems converge towards dispersed ownership (Part A, section VII), European regulatory responses should also converge, broadly, in terms of Anglo-American best practice, adjusted to reflect the particular features of continental governance, such as the two-tier board and the need to protect minority shareholders. Indeed, as discussed in Part B, some convergence in legal responses is emerging, particularly with respect to the centrality of controlling managerial conflicts of interests and governance weaknesses in pay-setting and the importance of disclosure. Certainly, the Commission's recently unveiled approach to executive remuneration is largely couched in terms of eliminating conflicts of interests in remuneration-setting, which is the classic agency problem, although it is calibrated to reflect corporate governance systems (Part C). The implications the continental European form of corporate control holds for the theoretical underpinning of executive remuneration and, in particular, the incentive model, are discussed further in section VII.

[43] eg Kaplan (n 30) 3, Bratton and McCahery (n 30) 226; J Garrido and A Rojo 'Institutional Investors and Corporate Governance: Solution or Problem?' in K Hopt and E Wymeersch (eds) *Capital Markets and Company Law* (OUP Oxford 2002) 427, 433; and Becht and others (n 26) 78 and 100.

[44] For an analysis of how the composition and levels of remuneration packages vary across the EC see G Ferrarini, N Moloney and C Vespro 'Executive Remuneration in the EU: Comparative Law and Practice' (June 2003) ECGI Law Working Paper No 9/2003.

III. Problem (1): The Structure of Remuneration

1. Introduction

The structure of equity-based pay reveals a number of inherent inefficiencies which seem to damage the performance link and thus the incentive mechanism which justifies high levels of pay. In particular, structural difficulties heighten the need for effective governance and disclosure in pay-setting. Much of the evidence, particularly with respect to share options, is grounded in the dispersed ownership context, and US based. Nonetheless, the structural difficulties raised by equity-based pay potentially represent problems for the UK given the internationalization of pay and, if dispersed ownership becomes more prevalent, continental Europe. This discussion highlights four difficulties: the link between remuneration and performance; risk allocation; proxies for company performance; and the problems raised by share options. Other structural weaknesses in remuneration practices include the prevalence, in some systems, of service contracts of over one year which generate long notice periods and large pay-offs (and the related phenomenon of contractually guaranteed termination payments which can amount to 'rewards for failure,')[45] and the sheer complexity of pay contracts which renders effective monitoring difficult.

As discussed in Part B, European regimes tend not to intervene in the particular structure of remuneration contracts (although some rules apply, particularly in the UK and Ireland, on the duration of service contracts as a matter of company law as well as best practice). Instead, they adopt, to widely varying degrees, a matrix of supporting rules on disclosure and governance which seek to maximize the likelihood of optimum contracts being adopted, notwithstanding the inherent inefficiencies of equity-based pay.

2. The Link Between Remuneration and Company Performance

Linking remuneration to indicators of shareholder wealth such as share price is widely regarded as the most effective and direct way to mitigate agency costs in the dispersed ownership company.[46] Management is incentivized to take decisions which increase shareholder wealth as, in so doing, personal wealth is also increased. More intangible factors also strengthen the appeal of the performance-linked remuneration contract: human incentives such as peer approval may come

[45] In the UK eg one in five FTSE 100 companies employs directors on services contracts of more than one year, despite a campaign by institutional investors, particularly the National Association of Pension Funds, to end these contracts: J Boxell 'One in five big companes has directors on long deals' *Financial Times* (14 July 2003).

[46] eg Hall and Liebman (n 17) who have argued that without this link managers would act like bureaucrats rather than entrepreneurs.

into play as better company performance leads to visible success by inclusion in 'highest paid' lists.[47]

Notwithstanding the analytical power of the model, the empirical evidence does not unequivocally support the theory. In their seminal 1990 article Jensen and Murphy found, between 1969 and 1983 and for a sample of US companies, only a very weak link between company performance and remuneration. The weakness of the link suggested that remuneration did not appear to provide sufficient incentives to divert managers from promoting their own self-interests at the expense of shareholders. They attributed this failure to third party political forces impacting adversely on remuneration bargaining.[48] More recently, Hall and Liebman have found a closer correlation in the US between remuneration and performance.[49] Another recent US study has shown that shareholders gain from a positive market reaction on the announcement of performance-linked pay plans.[50] The earlier empirical evidence includes the finding of links between remuneration and performance in financially-distressed firms.[51] In addition, there is some evidence that firms that link remuneration to share returns outperform firms which do not.[52] A positive relationship has also been found between firm performance and the percentage of equity held by managers and the percentage of their compensation which is equity based.[53] The recent explosion in stock option certainly suggests a desire by boards to sharpen the relationship between pay and performance, expressed in terms of the company's share price.[54] Whether the company performance which generates remuneration under incentive contracts actually reflects heightened efforts by senior management, and thus vindicates the incen-

[47] Hall and Liebman (n 17) 10.

[48] Jensen and Murphy (n 20) 250. Similar findings were made in the UK. Between 1983 and 1986 eg a very small positive relationship between pay and performance was observed from a sample of large UK listed companies, while sales was found to be a critical factor in determining pay: Conyon and Leech (n 22). See also P Gregg, S Machin and S Szymanski 'The Disappearing Relationship Between Directors' Pay and Corporate Performance' (1993) 31 British Journal of Industrial Relationships 7 who noted that in the UK between 1983 and 1991 'directors continued to receive high pay irrespective of their companies' performance' (at 2).

[49] n 17.

[50] A Morgan and A Poulsen 'Linking Pay to Performance' (2001) 62 J Fin Econ 489.

[51] S Gilson and M Vetsuypens 'CEO Compensation in Financially Distressed Firms: An Empirical Analysis' (1993) 48 J Fin 426 (using a US 1981-1987 sample). They reported that CEOs retained by such companies sustained large salary and bonus reductions.

[52] E Jenkins and R Seiler 'The Impact of Executive Compensation Schemes upon the Level of Discretionary Expenditures and Growth in Shareholder Wealth' (1990) 17 J Bus Fin and Acct 585.

[53] H Mehran 'Executive Compensation Structure, Ownership, and Firm Performance' (1995) 38 J Fin Econ 163. The study also found that managers are motivated to increase firm value by the form of compensation rather than by its level.

[54] Hall and Liebman (n 17) 33.

tive contract model, is another question, however, which is proving difficult to answer.

3. Risk Allocation and Relative Performance

There are limits to the amount of remuneration which can be linked to company performance and, in particular, share performance, as difficulties arise with risk allocation. In effect, there is a trade-off between the degree to which executives can be induced to engage in wealth-maximizing activities and the amount of risk executives will bear with respect to remuneration.[55] Executives are likely to be slow to accept remuneration which is entirely dependent on incentive or performance criteria as they will carry the risk that the indicators for performance (and remuneration) become subject to changes beyond their control (such as interest rates, market movements, and industry-sector problems). The effect of otherwise high-powered incentives will therefore be lessened by the extent to which firm performance is effected by random shocks.[56]

The risk-burden problem is aggravated where remuneration is in the form of shares or share options. Managers are risk averse and have already invested human capital (in the form of reputation, time, and training), as well as remuneration capital, in the company.[57] Remuneration which is linked to shares or share options requires managers to take on the risk of an undiversified holding and may incentivize them to be risk-averse and avoid company-specific risk.[58] By contrast, shareholders are diversified. The shareholder is risk neutral, having diversified away company risk under portfolio theory. Share and share option remuneration aside, where cash-based remuneration is tied to company performance and, in particular, share price performance, the undiversified manager, already heavily invested with respect to human capital, is likely to be unhappy at having personal wealth tied directly to the company's fortunes.[59] Managers will, therefore, be resistant to more performance pay, particularly pay linked to share price performance or in the form of share options, as it exposes them to market

[55] R Aggarwal and A Samwick 'The Other Side of the Tradeoff: The Impact of Risk on Executive Compensation (1999b) 107 J Pol Econ 65, 67.

[56] Aggarwal and Samwick (1999a) n 16. Share performance indicators raise considerable problems in this regard as an 'executive will understandably have reservations about a remuneration scheme under which his pay can fall dramatically through no fault of his own': B Cheffins *Company Law: Theory, Structure, and Operation* (OUP Oxford 1997), 686.

[57] Risk-averse managers will typically over-emphasize down-side risk to their human capital (or career prospects) and, as a result, will take decisions which are least likely to put career prospects at risk but which do not reflect the risk calculations of diversified investors. See T Nohel and S Todd 'Stock Options and Managerial Incentives to Invest' SSRN (2001) 3.

[58] Holmstrom (n 21).

[59] Cheffins (1997) n 56, 686.

irrationalities and other factors outside their control and exacerbates their difficulty in diversifying their interest in the firm.[60] In particular, performance euro for fixed salary euro swaps are unlikely to be acceptable to managers.[61]

One solution to this problem is to compensate for the risk burden by paying more and by retaining the fixed salary component.[62] High-powered incentives are therefore more costly than lower ones, as pay will rise to a high average level.[63] Another solution is to rely on relative performance pay structures. Contracting theory, relying on Holmstron's moral hazard insight, suggests that pay should not be based on factors beyond the executive's control but on relative, rather than absolute, performance measures,[64] although arguably executives should not be insulated from outside factors against which they can take action to reduce losses.[65] Adoption of an optimal remuneration contract becomes more likely, therefore, when remuneration is not based on measures beyond the control of the executive and performance is measured relative to the market or to a particular peer group. Relative performance can be measured via, for example, the returns of other firms in the same industry such that, all things being equal, an executive's remuneration will drop if executives at competing firms deliver higher shareholder returns and vice versa.[66] If attempts are not made to deal with the risk problem, the danger arises that management will pursue diversification strategies which reduce the market, economy, and sector-wide risks to remuneration. This risk reduction is, however, additional to the risk reduction exercise which shareholders will already have engaged in via portfolio diversification and may run counter to shareholder interests.[67]

The risk allocation inherent in performance pay therefore seems to generate intractable problems for the adoption of an optimal contract. A company which insists on a very close linkage between remuneration and performance may risk losing executives. But greater costs will be imposed on the shareholders if that

[60] See Cheffins (1997) n 56 at 687 who has pointed to the evidence that the resulting equity is sold immediately after the vast majority of share options are exercised.

[61] K Murphy 'Politics, Economics, and Executive Compensation' (1995) 63 U Cinn L Rev 713, 722.

[62] Murphy (n 61) 721 and E Iacobucci 'The effects of disclosure on executive compensation' (1998) 48 U Toronto L J 489, 494.

[63] Hall and Liebman (n 17) 7.

[64] eg Hall and Liebman (n 17) who have argued that managers should be rewarded for outcomes over which they exercise control but insulated from economy, industry, or market-wide shocks.

[65] G Baker, M Jensen and K Murphy 'Compensation and Incentives: Practice v Theory' (1988) 43 J Fin 593, 611.

[66] Aggarwal and Samwick (1999b) n 55, 68.

[67] Loewenstein (1996) n 12, 208, citing J Coffee 'Shareholders Versus Managers: The Strain in the Corporate Web' (1986) 85 Mich LR 1, 16-24.

company, in an attempt to deal with the risk aversion problem, offers richer rewards if the company does well, such that it pays the executive to take the risk of more performance-based remuneration.[68] Popular hostility may also follow in that restructuring pay to reflect performance and increased risk is likely to increase pay.[69] Political pressures may therefore result in the adoption of sub-optimal contracts. Finally, notwithstanding the attraction of relative performance pay and its role in ensuring the adoption of an optimal contract, there is some (US) evidence that it is not used in practice where it might be expected.[70] There appear to be limits therefore on the amount of performance pay that is feasible.[71]

4. Proxies for Firm Performance

Proxies are needed for firm performance. The choice of indicator or performance standard is a complex one.[72] Indicators should, for example, reflect the contribution of the executive and the particular responsibilities carried: share price performance, which reflects total firm performance, may not be an appropriate indicator for an executive with divisional responsibilities who does not have oversight responsibilities for the company as a whole.[73] At a minimum, however, the standard chosen should be sufficiently robust such that it can withstand manipu-

[68] A Rappaport 'New Thinking on How to Link Executive Pay with Performance' [1999] March/April Harvard Business Review 91, 95.

[69] Loewenstein (1996) n 12, 208.

[70] Hall and Liebman (n 17) have found that relative performance is lacking in current remuneration contracts (at 31). Aggarwal and Samwick 1999b (n 55) have also found little evidence that relative performance criteria are incorporated into remuneration contracts. For a review of current research, which concluded that relative performance pay is 'surprisingly absent from US executive compensation practices' see Abowd and Kaplan (n 4) 156-157. Relative performance criteria are, however, common in UK remuneration contracts, particularly with respect to Long Term Incentive Plans and share options.

[71] Hall and Liebman (n 17) 8.

[72] One study has shown that the relative use of accounting and share performance measures depends on the amount of noise in the two indicators and their sensitivity to managerial action: R Lambert and D Larcker 'An analysis of the use of accounting and market measures of performance in executive compensation contracts' (1987) 25 J of Accounting Research 85. For similar conclusions see also S Kole 'The Complexity of Compensation Contracts' (1997) 43 J Fin Econ 79 and D Yermack 'Do Corporations Award CEO Stock Options Effectively' (1995) 39 J Fin Econ 237.

[73] See R Aggarwal and A Samwick 'Performance Incentives Within Firms: The Effects of Managerial Responsibility' (1999) NBER Working Paper No 7334 1999c who have shown that the performance sensitivity depends on how precisely performance is measured for the area for which the manager is responsible.

lation by management.[74] This is not always easy to achieve, particularly given the perverse incentives which can be generated by a focus on share price which can result in short termism and manipulation of the share price.

a) Problems with accounting targets

Typically, accounting indicators include net income, pre-tax income, revenues, operating profits, or earnings per share.[75] Accounting indicators have an advantage over share price targets in that they are not subject to the vagaries of stock market performance and can reward performance more accurately. But they are historical and do not reflect the future impact of management actions. They also carry the danger of manipulation and may incentivize management to engage in creative accounting techniques. Perverse incentives may also be created in that managers may take short term decisions in order to reach accounting targets which are not necessarily in the interests of long term shareholder value. The point has been made that targets such as earnings per share and accounting indicators can prevent management from engaging in downsizing, even where such a strategy may be appropriate for a company in particular company, sector, and economic cycles.[76]

b) Problems with share price targets

Under the Efficient Capital Market Hypothesis (ECMH), share price is ordinarily the best available proxy for share value and shareholder wealth. This is because the actual value of a share is related to the future stream of income, such as dividends, which will accrue to shareholders, discounted to present value. Under the ECMH, the market price is the best estimate of actual value that can be based on publicly available information. Remuneration which links managerial return to share price increases is, as a result, most likely to lead shareholder-wealth maximizing decisions.[77] Share prices are also easily verifiable and easy to work with.[78]

It could, of course, be argued that the market is not efficient, given, for example, the presence of noise traders who are influenced by sentiments which are not fully justified by fundamental news and considerations such as liquidity require-

[74] One US study has shown, with respect to the use of performance standards in the award of bonuses, that internally determined standards (based on managerial action or performance in the previous year) are directly affected by management actions. Managers will manage earnings to meet, but not exceed, budgeted performance, will smooth income accordingly, and, as a result, tend to achieve bonuses which are close to the targeted bonuses: K Murphy 'Performance Standards in Incentive Contracts' (2000) 30 J Acc and Econ 245, summarized at 246-247.

[75] Murphy (2000) n 74, 246 and 250.

[76] Murphy (1995) n 61, 718-720.

[77] M Fox 'A Unified Theory of Section 16(b)' (1994) 92 Mich LR 2088, 2101.

[78] Cheffins (1997) n 56, 680.

ments. Another critical difficulty with share price as an indicator is that its movement is affected by factors outside management's control. The danger also arises of over-compensation of executives who preside over a period of market growth and under-compensation of those who are caught in a down market cycle.[79] This is a particular problem where performance is linked to share performance, remuneration is in the form of options, and the market is pushing the share price up. Share price indicators are also not sensitive to the efforts of senior management who are not concerned with overall firm performance or strategy.[80]

Notwithstanding the weaknesses in the share price indicator which prevent it being a perfect proxy for wealth creation, it is, however, difficult to construct a better alternative for shareholder wealth given that it does reflect the market's perception of the company's current and future cash flows, and so its perceptions of management performance and investment opportunities.[81] The risk of management inflating the share price and manipulating disclosure in order to generate short term share price increases, however, demands that the governance matrix which monitors management and supports the remuneration contract, whether it be independent directors, institutional investors, or controlling shareholders, is robust.

5. Share Options

a) Incidence

Much of the increase in executive remuneration, particularly with respect to US remuneration, can be attributed to the explosion in share option grants[82] over a

[79] C Yablon 'Overcompensating: The Corporate Lawyer and Executive Pay' (1992) 92 Co L R 1867, 1888.

[80] The example has been given of a finance director's equity-based remuneration suffering as a result of a disastrous marketing campaign over which that director had no control: Cheffins (1997) n 56, 682.

[81] Murphy (1995) n 61, 722. He has stated at 736 that: 'while not a perfect measure of shareholder wealth creation, [share price] is a robust estimate of long-run value creation that applies to declining as well as expanding industries, in small as well as large firms.'

[82] Senior US executives receive approximately 58% of their remuneration in the form of options: Hay Group mid-2002 study cited in M Skapiner 'After Garnier: Why executive rewards in the US and UK are unlikely to converge' *Financial Times* (May 21 2003). There has also been an increase in grants initially valued at more than US $10 million: R Thomas and K Martin 'The Determinant of Shareholder Voting on Stock Option Plans' (2000) 35 Wake Forest LR 31, 34. They have also pointed to the increase in 'mega-grants of stock options' or grants initially valued at more than US $10 million (at 35). See also B Hall 'A Better Way to Pay CEOs' in Carpenter and Yermack note 30, 35 who has referred to the dramatic increase in US share options grants and the 700% increase in the value of awards between 1980 and 1994 (at 35).

period of stock market growth which massively increased the value of executive options.[83] Equity-based pay also increasingly forms a significant part of pay structures in the UK.[84] The alternative monitoring mechanism provided by block-holders seems, however, to have limited the degree of reliance on high-powered equity-based contracts in continental Europe, although equity-based performance pay is used (see section VII).

b) Incentive Alignment

In the wake of the recent series of high profile corporate scandals and collapses, which have challenged the effectiveness of executive performance, vocal and increasing criticism of large share option grants has been roused. Criticism has not been limited to the US. In the UK, large option grants to the CEOs of newly privatized utilities in the early 1990s led to public and political hostility and paved the way for equity-based remuneration packages predominantly in the form of share-based Long Term Incentive Plans rather than share options.[85] While the headline size of option grants generates considerable public hostility, share options have, however, a complex profile of advantages and disadvantages which must be considered in any reform of executive remuneration.

A share option gives the grantee of the option the right to buy a particular number of shares at a given price (the exercise price), which is fixed on the day of the option grant, at a point in the future after the option's vesting date and before the option's expiry date. If the share price moves above the exercise price, the grantee can make an immediate profit by selling the share. As managers are financially-motivated to take decisions which will increase the share price above the exercise price, options can create potentially powerful incentives which align otherwise diverging shareholder and executive interests by linking remuneration

[83] One commentator has noted that almost 100% increases in the major stock market indices between 1995 and 1997 resulted in 'executives with fixed price options enjoy[ing] a huge windfall from the long-running bull market that was fueled not only by corporate performance but also by factors beyond management control, such as declining inflation and lower interest rates': Rappaport (1999) n 68, 92. See also Hall and Liebman (1997) no 17, 29 and Conyon and Murphy (2000) who have referred to the 300% increase in the S&P Index in the 1990s, as compared to the 150% increase in the FTSE, as a partial explanation for the large gulf between US and UK CEO packages: n 23, F666.

[84] Share option awards became initially popular in the UK post-1984 when favourable changes were made to the taxation system, and grew dramatically until the early 1990s when the focus shifted to performance-driven Long Term Incentive Plans: B Main 'The Rise and Fall of Executive Share Options in Britain' in Carpenter and Yermack (1999) n 30, 83, 84 and Conyon and Murphy (2000) n 23, F649. There are large divergences in CEO pay between the US and UK as a result of the differing use of option remuneration. Share options represent a smaller percentage of CEO pay in the UK (in 2002, 24%) than in the US (in 2002, 58%), while the average US CEO compensation is $2.5 million as compared to $1.5 million in the UK: Hay Group Study n 82.

[85] Main (1999) n 84, 90-91 and 100-102.

to shareholder returns expressed via the share price.[86] Share options, like any share-price linked remuneration, can also incentivize managers to take decisions which may be personally costly and stressful, such as decisions to lay-off staff and close businesses, but which may ultimately strengthen the company's competitive position and share price.[87] They may also exert a bonding function among senior management and promote greater team efforts to increase the global value of the company and the share price.[88] Share options also have, on first glance at least, an attractively asymmetrical pay structure in that they reward success but do not appear to penalize failure.[89] If the share price does not exceed the exercise price, the manager is not required to exercise the option and can fall back on the cash element of remuneration, which is not always scaled back to reflect the option grant. Managers are not likely to equate the failure to make a gain with an actual loss.[90] Share options can also act as a powerful inducement to join a company and, where the plan is structured over an appropriate length of time, incentivize management to stay.[91] By contrast, fixed salaries are set in advance and thus have limited incentive effects. Cash bonus arrangements are often tied to manipulation-vulnerable accounting indicators,[92] can lead to short term decision-making, and can be structured by boards in a manner which ensures that executives receive high remuneration.[93] Cash payments are also highly visible and transparent and may therefore generate backlash effects which prevent them from acting as effective incentive alignment devices.[94] By comparison, options appear to provide an attractive way of aligning interests.

[86] Hall and Liebman (1997) n 17, 5-6 and 31.

[87] eg Gordon (n 29), 1245.

[88] ibid 1245-6.

[89] Thomas and Martin (2000) n 82, 40.

[90] See n 147 below, however, on the challenges to the theory that share options do not carry downside risk.

[91] Thomas and Martin (2000) n 82, 37. This is particularly the case with small companies who may not be able to afford headline salaries and was key in staff retention in 'high tech' companies during the dotcom boom.

[92] Managers can also, of course, engage in manipulative conduct to meet analysts' expectations and maintain high share prices and thus the value of options: Thomas and Martin (2000) n 82, 44. The perverse incentives generated by option remuneration which can lead to share price manipulation and earnings distortion is emerging as a strong feature of the post-Enron governance reform discusion.

[93] S Stabile 'Viewing Corporate Executive Compensation Through a Partnership Lens: A Tool to Focus Reform' (2000) 35 Wake Forest LR 153, 204-206.

[94] Large cash bonuses and salaries are, unlike share options, completely transparent, and may generate political difficulties for a company even where the cash payments are of an order of magnitude lower than the shareholder gain. See Hall (1999) n 82, 42 who has found, as a result, that they are unlikely to provide the same high-powered incentives as share options. As

cont. ...

There are a number of difficulties with share option grants, however, which suggest that the incentive justification for large grants cannot go entirely unchallenged, and which might support regulatory intervention, particularly with respect to the governance structures which underpin the granting of options. In particular, share options appear to display a number of features, discussed below, which might suggest that in practice they may give management, when it can influence the pay-setting process, scope to skim wealth from shareholders and to disguise the skimming through the structure of option remuneration. As a result, options may amount to rent extraction, and so an agency cost, rather than an agency cost remedy. In particular, the Bebchuk *et al* thesis suggests that while executives may gain control of the remuneration-setting process as a result of governance failures, they are restricted in extracting rents in the form of remuneration by an 'outrage constraint', or the danger that outrageous pay awards may generate embarrassment, damage reputations, and ultimately lead to removal. Executives are, as a result, inclined to legitimize or obscure pay decisions via 'camouflage' mechanisms. As discussed further in this section, options appear to display a number of structural features which lend themselves to camouflage practices.[95]

At the core of the problem is the extent to which share options are performance-based and align incentives: as discussed below, the theoretical and empirical evidence is equivocal. There are, however, ways of structuring option grants to avoid or minimize the inherent agency costs which they seem to generate. Companies can choose from a wide range of options in structuring a remuneration package:[96] that they choose in certain ways is important. This suggests that the share option problem may be a governance problem rather than a problem with the option as a tool of executive remuneration *per se*.

c) Defects in the Performance Link

Notwithstanding the oft-repeated mantra that options align shareholder and management interests and incentivize management to improve performance, the evidence is equivocal.[97] One leading proponent of the principal/agent incentive

discussed below, however, the very opacity of options, and their complexity, makes it easier to hide remuneration which does not pursue shareholder interests.

[95] The characterization of options as potentially representing rents is now appearing in the financial media. The *Financial Times* has commented that: 'During the 1990s bubble, stock option schemes allowed some US executives to loot their companies at the expense of shareholders': Editorial, 'Fair Pay for CEOs: A five point plan for investors on executive remuneration' *Financial Times* (Weekend April 27/26 2003).

[96] S Johnson and Y Tian 'The value and incentive effects of nontraditional executive stock option plans' (2000a) 57 J Fin Econ 3, 4. They examine the different incentive effects of nontraditional options, such as indexed and reload options.

[97] Criticism has been robust: '... the talk of alignment is a myth that sanitizes management compensation packages that conflict with shareholder and labour interests' (L Cunningham 'Commonalities and Prescriptions in the Vertical Dimension of Global Corporate Governance'

cont. ...

model has acknowledged that the empirical basis for justifying share options as a pure incentive mechanism is weak and has noted that it is difficult to show that the increase in share-based incentives had led US CEO's to work harder, better and in the interests of shareholders.[98]

One particularly acute performance problem concerns the extent to which option grants are linked to clear and challenging performance criteria. Specifically, the relative performance problem is exacerbated with respect to share options. Fixed price options, the exercise price of which is fixed for the term of the option grant, can deliver very large gains for executives whenever the market is rising, even if the company is underperforming its competitors. The gain to executives, which becomes greater with the volatility of the shares, may be unrelated to long term company performance.[99] Performance criteria can be met independently of the company's actual performance and with any increase in share price, regardless of the increase's size or underlying cause: this amounts to a waste of the incentive contract. Windfall gains from traditional options are increasingly generating concern among shareholders and even the management community.[100] Shareholders typically expect management to achieve returns ahead of those achieved by the company's peer group, or a particular indicator such as a stock market index.[101] This is reflected, for example, in the prevalence of peer group or index performance disclosure in the detailed remuneration reports required in the US and, as discussed in Part B, the UK. The performance-based justification for large options grants begins to look somewhat vulnerable, therefore, where large gains are transferred to management due to factors beyond the control of management.

One way of curbing massive gains unrelated to specific company performance is to fix the timing of option exercise in order to prevent an executive from generating speculative gains by picking a sell date with maximum effect.[102]

SSRN (1999) 39); and 'options are often not so much an incentive device as a somewhat covert mechanism of self-dealing' (A Schliefer and R Vishny 'A Survey of Corporate Governance' (1997) 52 J Fin 737, 745).

[98] Murphy (1999) n 4, 2555-6. One study has found, however, that the probability of a voluntary liquidation which creates shareholder value increases with the percentage of company shares held by the CEO and with the pay for performance sensitivity of CEO share options outstanding: H Mehran, G Nogler, and K Schwartz 'CEO Incentive Plans and Corporate Liquidation Policy' (1998) 50 J Fin Econ 319.

[99] M Conyon, P Gregg, S Machin 'Taking Care of Business: Executive Compensation in the United Kingdom' (1995) 105 The Economic Journal 704, 706. See also the UK Greenbury Report (The Study Group on Directors' Remuneration, *Directors' Remuneration: Report of a Study Group Chaired by Sir Richard Greenbury* (1995)) which referred to the windfall gains, unrelated to performance, which can be conferred by share options as a drawback to option schemes: para 6.28.

[100] eg Johnson and Tian (2000a) n 96, 4.

[101] Rappaport (1999) n 68, 93.

[102] Conyon et al (1995) n 99, 709.

Another way, which has the advantage of insulating executives from economic and market shocks over which they have no control, is to link the option's exercise price to a market or peer group index such that managers are rewarded only when they outperform the competition.[103] The exercise price, and the executive's gain, would be relative to the company's performance, with the exercise price rising or falling in accordance with the relevant index. Gains from options would become highly sensitive to company performance as the manager would only gain where the company's share price rose ahead of the index, and would not be penalized unfairly in a general economic down turn when the company outperformed its peer group or a particular index. Shareholders would benefit from the extra effort required of management to outperform the index. Larger grants of benchmarked option grants at lower exercise prices to compensate risk averse executives may, however, become necessary.[104] A related difficulty with benchmarked options concerns the potential for dilution if more indexed options are issued to compensate management for increased risk, although given the more testing exercise criteria, less options should be exercised.[105] A further potential difficulty concerns the choice of index. Stock market indices have the advantage of being easily measurable and trackable, while peer group indices will incorporate factors specific to the relevant industry, although diversification in corporate activities may make it difficult to construct an accurate index.[106] Finally, sector-linked performance may generate perverse incentives in that a management team, which is consistently outperforming a peer group, may be reluctant to change strategy, even though the business has become structurally unattractive and uncompetitive.[107]

Options could also be issued at a premium, or 'out-of-the-money' price, which is in excess of the fair market value of the shares on the date of the option grant. These options are more sensitive to performance as they require additional effort on the part of management before a gain is realized and are argued to be more effective at aligning shareholder and management interests.[108] In addition, shareholders alone benefit from share price gains up to the premium price. A variant of the premium option is to fix the exercise price at a premium (such as 25, 50, or 100%) above the market price, or to link the vesting date to the achievement of a particular share price level, which is usually set considerably

[103] Hall and Liebman (1997) n 17, 31-32 and S Johnson and Y Tiang 'Indexed Executive Stock Options' (2000b) 57 J Fin Econ 35. See also Rappaport (1999) n 68, 92 and 93-95.

[104] Rappaport (1999) n 68, 95-96. Adjustments to the number of options granted is, however, a feature of granting a nontraditional option. See Johnson and Tian (2000a) n 96, 6-13.

[105] Rappaport (1999) n 68, 94.

[106] Rappaport (1999) n 68, 93.

[107] Cheffins (1997) n 56, 685.

[108] See Johnson and Tian (2000a) n 96, 4; and Hall (1999) note 82, 43 who has reported that premium options would increase pay/performance sensitivity by 15-38%.

above the share price on the date of the grant.[109] While the premium induces management to achieve performance ahead of the market, it does not, however, protect managers who are performing well with respect to their peer group when the market is in decline.[110]

Notwithstanding their shareholder appeal and their attractions in reducing agency costs by enhancing the performance relation, share options are rarely indexed to the market in the remuneration market which is generating most controversy, the US.[111] Accounting rules may account for this anomaly in that options which carry performance conditions must be accounted for as an expense rather than being covered by footnote disclosure.[112] Out-of-the-money options are also not very common.[113] While the US experience shows the potential for difficulties and skimming problems, benchmarked options and options linked to performance targets are, however, popular in the UK.[114]

d) The Repricing Problem

The likelihood of option grants permitting executives in control of the pay-setting process to skim from the company becomes more possible when their capacity to be repriced is considered. In some cases, share option plans have been replaced with new plans which cancel and replace options whose exercise price has risen sufficiently above the market price of the share such that the manager is unlikely to exercise the option (underwater options), or which reprice underwater options,

[109] Johnson and Tian (2000a) n 96, 4. Firms may require that the share price keep the relevant level for a particular time period before the option can be exercised.

[110] Rappaport (1999) n 68, 93-94.

[111] M Bertrand and S Mullainathan 'Do CEOs Set Their Own Pay? The Ones Without Principals Do' (2000) NBER Working Paper No 7604 2000a, 9.

[112] eg Rappaport (1999) n 68, 94. He has argued that disclosure of indexed options as an accounting expense does not, in itself, make indexed options more costly and, therefore, of concern to shareholders: 'investors are not fooled, and boards should not use the '[i]nvestors won't understand the earning hit' excuse to avoid implementing value-creating compensation arrangements': ibid.

[113] The very low US incidence of indexed options and options issued other than at-the-money, has been characterized as a 'puzzle worth understanding': Murphy (1999) n 4, 2539. See also Hall (1999) n 82, 43 For the view that the failure to index and the almost uniform use of at-the-money options in the US supports a characterization of the remuneration-setting process as potentially one of rent extraction in that shareholders' interests in ensuring that remuneration is sensitive to market and sector movements are not met, see Bebchuk et al (2002) n 4, 758 and 817-821.

[114] B Cheffins 'The metamorphosis of 'Germany Inc.': the case of executive pay' (2001b) 49 AJCL 497, 523 and Lex 'Executive Pay' *Financial Times* (12/13 October 2002) (noting that performance criteria have allowed UK companies to fend off the criticism of share option remuneration faced by US companies). The use of performance criteria in the UK is linked to regulatory policy.

but retain the original vesting and expiry dates of the option. While not a very common occurrence,[115] this practice has attracted widespread criticism.[116] The difficulty here is not, in principle, with the repricing itself, as in some cases repricing may be appropriate to restore managerial incentives to continue to increase shareholder value.[117] The problem arises where repricing damages or removes incentives.

Many of the justifications for repricing might suggest skimming or rent-seeking behaviour by management rather than a real attempt by the board to fine-tune managerial incentives to increase shareholder value. Where the repricing reflects downward market movements or other factors beyond the control of management, and is regarded as an exceptional event, repricing can be justified in that incentives are maintained. As management does, however, benefit from market and industry upswings, particularly where options are not indexed, this justification might also suggest that companies should reprice upwards after very strong industry or market gains.[118] It is also argued that repricing enables companies to retain management who may be poached by competitors.[119] One might well query, however, whether there is a relationship between resetting and common industry or market shocks, and, if not, whether managers who have presided over company-specific poor performance should be retained.[120] Indexing might also provide a more effective way of dealing with market movements. In addition, if management are led to expect that poor share price performance will result in the repricing of an option's exercise price downwards, and no attempt is made, by, for example, readjusting other components of remuneration or readjusting the

[115] For the US data see M Brenner, R Sundaram and D Yermack 'Altering the terms of executive stock options' (2000) 57 J Fin Econ 108 and D Chance, R Kumar and R Todd 'The 'repricing' of executive stock options' (2000) 57 J Fin Econ 129, 153.

[116] In the US context, see Chance et al (2000) n 115; Johnson and Tian (2000b) n 103, 36 and M Carter and L Lynch 'An examination of executive stock repricing' (2001) 61 J Fin Econ 207, 208. US shareholders, and particularly institutional investors, regard the repricing of underwater options as objectionable. See J Heard 'Executive Compensation: Perspective of the Institutional Investor' (1995) 63 U of Cincinnati LR 749, 759 and Thomas and Martin (2000) n 82.

[117] See Brenner et al (2000) who quote one compensation consultant as stating that out-of-the-money options are disliked by managers, even though they do possess potential future value, and that boards regard them as carrying negative incentives with the potential to demoralize the workforce (n 115, 122).

[118] Chance et al (2000) n 115, 131-132.

[119] eg Johnson and Tian (2000a) n 96, 4.

[120] Brenner et al (2000) n 115, 120. They have argued that the retention justification should result in a relation between common negative shocks and repricing and no relation between repricing and firm performance adjusted for industry returns. They have found, however, from a US sample, that repricing does not, as a rule, occur as a result of industry-wide shocks. They have also found no evidence that repricing is concentrated in industries where managerial talent is particularly important (at 120-122).

vesting period of the option, to remove that moral hazard, there is little incentive to improve share price performance. It might also be argued that options which have a long exercise period provide sufficient management incentives to increase the share price over that period.[121] More generally, repricing can strike at the heart of the performance/incentive justification for share options. Given the risk of performance pay (a risk for which the executive is compensated), managers should face the possibility of losing financial rewards when the share price falls. Repricing in effect rewards managers when their firm underperforms, given that it arises on a share price decline.[122] The repricing of options, which weakens, if not entirely destroys, the performance justification for share option gains, might therefore be regarded as a form of wealth skimming from shareholders.[123]

e) Global Incentives

Remuneration packages should be structured in terms of their total incentive effects. More incentives may be needed as executives get older as younger managers have promotion incentives.[124] In addition, given that the interests of managers who hold shares in the company are aligned more closely with shareholders, equity-based performance pay should drop with higher levels of share ownership by management.[125] Share option grants should also, however, take into account the executive's risk profile and in particular, the impact of an executive's wealth and potentially risk-avoidance-generating holdings of shares on the overall incentive effect of a share option grant.[126] The marginal effect of additional share option grants should also be taken in account in assessing total incentive effects: will the award of another million share options generate incentives substantially

[121] One US study has found that even a steep decline in share price can leave incentive levels intact and concluded that restoring incentive-alignment is seldom a good justification for resetting share prices or issuing new options: L Jin and L Muelbroek 'Do Underwater Executive Stock Options Still Align Incentives? The Effect of Stock Price Movements on Managerial Incentive-Alignment' (2001) Harvard Business School Working Paper No 02-002 2001. See also Chance et al (2000) who have found that, of their sample, over half the options would have been at-the-money, without repricing, within 19 months (n 115, 131).

[122] Brenner et al (2000) find that repricing is 'overwhelmingly associated with negative returns.' (n 115, 120).

[123] According to Bebchuk et al (2002), repricing suggests that compensation plans are designed in the interests of managers' rather than shareholders' welfare (n 4, 759-760 and 821-824).

[124] See Becht et al (2001) note 26, 47.

[125] One US study has found that the proportion of equity-based pay will drop given higher levels of share ownership by managers and cites this as evidence that boards do consider the total incentive effects of remuneration packages: Mehran (1995) n 53, 179.

[126] Nohel and Todd (2001) note 57, 4 who have noted that companies should restrict executive share holdings which may counteract the effect of share options by discouraging risk taking.

additional to the upfront and hidden cost of those options where the grantee already holds, and is incentivized by, 1 million options?[127] Finally, share option remuneration, linked to share price performance, is appropriate only for executives with broad company oversight responsibilities: executives with divisional responsibilities will not be appropriately incentivized by share option/share price remuneration.[128]

f) Adverse Impact on Dividends

The hidden costs of share options include their impact on dividend policy. If share options appropriately align shareholder and management incentives, one consequence should be that management is incentivized to allocate cash flow in order to maximize shareholder value. Dividend policy forms part of this analysis in that optimal incentive alignment would see funds being returned to shareholder via dividends and share repurchases rather than being dispersed in value-destroying investments.[129] Share options can distort this alignment in that they can incentivize management to reduce dividends, as the value of options drops with dividend payments.[130] It is possible to protect against this incentive by offering dividend-protected options.[131]

There is some empirical evidence to suggest that executive share options can reduce dividend distributions to shareholders.[132] Reductions in dividends can be offset by repurchases which return value to shareholders without impacting on the value of options, and it appears that executive share options can result in a shift away from dividends and towards repurchases.[133] While managers may therefore be perversely incentivized in their choice of payout method, another explanation

[127] Thomas and Martin (2000) n 82, 40.

[128] Aggarwal and Samwick (1999c) n 73, 2 and 4.

[129] G Fenn and N Liang 'Corporate Payout Policy and Managerial Stock Incentives' (2001) 60 J Fin Econ 45, 46.

[130] eg M Arnold and R Gillenkirch 'Stock Options as Incentive Contracts and Dividend Policy' SSRN (2002) 1.

[131] Dividend protected options are rare in the US. This is usually explained by the accounting rules which require such options to be disclosed as an expense.

[132] For US evidence see R Lambert, W Lanen and D Larcker 'Executive Stock Options Plans and Corporate Dividend Policy' (1989) 24 J of Financial and Quantitative Analysis 409; S Weisbenner 'Corporate Share Repurchases in the 1990: What Role Do Stock Options Play' SSRN (2000) 1, 3, and Fenn and Liang (2001) n 129, 47-48.

[133] For US evidence see Fenn and Liang (2001) n 129, 48, Arnold and Gillenkirch (2002) n 130, 1-2, and K Kahle 'When a buyback isn't a buyback: open market repurchases and employee options' (2002) 63 J Fin Econ 235, 236. Kahle finds evidence that share options have encouraged firms to repurchase in order to maximize managerial wealth (by avoiding dividend payouts) and to fund employee share option plans.

for this may be that firms with investment opportunities and less predictable cash flow require more flexibility in their financing arrangements and will prefer sporadic repurchases to regular dividend payouts.[134] Repurchases can also, of course, mitigate agency costs, by, under the free cash flow hypothesis, returning free cash flow to shareholders. Ultimately, however, the evidence suggests that the impact of share options on dividend policy reveals a potential agency problem. Share option programmes impact on how management sets dividend policy: it is not, therefore, being set in the interests of shareholder.

g) Dilution

Share options carry the risk of dilution of shareholder wealth, as the company must issue further shares to meet the option grants. The risk of dilution is not, of itself, a fatal flaw in share option grants, but it does suggest that they carry costs for shareholders which should be taken into account when remuneration is set.

There are a number of costs associated with dilution. Further issues of shares reduce the earnings per share ratio and shareholder wealth.[135] Where management retains the shares on exercise of the options, the voting power of management increases and may become entrenched, distorting the market for corporate control,[136] which remains a possible monitor for agency costs for dispersed ownership companies. Finally, as the share price increases and options are exercised, shares are issued to cover options, but this may result in a depression of the share price and losses for shareholders.[137] There is some US evidence that the large numbers of shares subject to option plans is generating shareholder unhappiness as to the consequent dilution:[138] US institutional investors recently revealed their unhappiness with the potential dilution represented by share option programmes at the 2003 BAE Systems AGM.[139] It might be argued, however, that agency-cost reductions are not free, and that one cost is the dilution of equity.[140]

[134] Fenn and Liang (2001) n 129, 48. See, however, Weissbenner (2000) n 132, 2-3 who has found that the relationship between dividends and stock options does not appear to be explained by differences in investment opportunities.

[135] Weisbenner (2000) n 132, 1.

[136] Thomas and Martin (2000) n 82, 36.

[137] Thomas and Martin (2000) n 82, 36.

[138] Heard (1995) n 116, 759 and Thomas and Martin (2000) n 82, 59-61. For similar evidence see Morgan and Poulsen n 50. See also K Chauvin and C Shenoy 'Stock Price Decreases Prior to Executive Stock Option Grants' (2001) 7 J Corp Fin 53 who have noted that the announcement of a stock option plan might be considered bad news because of the dilution which will occur on exercise of the options (at 62).

[139] S Mesure 'BAE confirms Boeing talks as US investors stage protest over pay' *The Independent* (20 April 2000).

[140] M Loewenstein 'The Conundrum of Executive Compensation' (2000) 35 Wake Forest LR 1, 19.

h) Balancing the Remuneration Package

A difficulty often cited with share options as evidence of their failure to align shareholder and manager interests is that the proportion of remuneration which is fixed or cash-based does not seem to drop as share option, or performance-based, pay is increased. The principal/agent model suggests that when options are granted, other elements of remuneration should be adjusted downwards, to leave the grantee indifferent.[141] The absence of such rebalancing might suggest that share option remuneration is vulnerable to management influence and skimming. It may, however, simply be a cost of risk-averse management in that more compensation is needed to compensate for the additional risk of performance pay, or may arise a result of the natural bias of management against giving up fixed compensation.[142]

i) Defects in Incentive Alignment: Risk Aversion and Risk Allocation

The unequal distribution of risk between management option-holders and shareholders suggests that share options may not align shareholder and manager interests effectively.

High-powered option contracts may induce an entrenched and undiversified CEO or senior manager to avoid high-risk, high-return projects which are likely to be attractive to diversified shareholders.[143] The converse could also be argued in that share option values rise with the volatility of the share price. Managers may therefore be incentivized to pursue projects which increase the volatility of the company's value in the interests of diversified shareholders.[144] The pendulum may, however, swing too far. Executives holding very large share option grants may be incentivized to engage in very risky and even fraudulent activity to maintain a high share price over a short time frame.[145] In the pursuit of risk-aversion, executives may also, while paying lipservice to the performance pay theory, and particularly where the board is passive or captured, seek to reduce the risks of performance pay, and defeat the incentive effects of options in a variety of ways.

[141] Bertrand and Mullainathan (2000a) n 111, 5.

[142] Iacobucci (1998) who examines to the 'endowment effect' which generates a bias against trading what is already possessed (n 62, 507-510).

[143] Hall and Liebman (1997) n 17, 7 and 10. See also Yablon (1999) n 11, 208 and Mehran (1995) n 53, 165-166.

[144] There is US-based empirical evidence to support this view. See S Rajgopal and T Shevlin 'Empirical Evidence on the Relation Between Stock Option Compensation and Risk Taking' (2002) 33 Journal of Accounting and Economics, who have found, in the oil and gas industry, that share options appear to motivate managers to take on exploration risk. See also Nohel and Todd (2001) n 57 who have found that at-the-money options maximize an executive's incentive to take risk, but that over-investment problems can also arise with share options.

[145] For this analysis in the context of the Enron collapse see Gordon (2002) n 29, 1246-7.

These may include manipulating options via repricing and the use of derivatives to dilute the incentives and risks.[146]

More generally, it might be argued that while, in theory, managers carry more risk when their pay is linked to performance, the additional risk is inconsequential when compared with the shareholder's risk burden. Although options are designed to incentivize managers to think like shareholders, the asymmetric pay structure means that managers are not exposed to downside risk in the same way as shareholders. If share prices drop below, or do not rise above, the exercise price, managers have the choice not to exercise the options,[147] but shareholders will suffer from the drop in share price. As share options rarely replace the fixed salary component of remuneration they represent an additional gain and any downside risk attached to that additional gain can be blunted via hedges and repricing techniques.[148] If management's interests were to be fully aligned with shareholders via the device of share ownership, they would, arguably, be required to purchase shares with their own money, hold the shares for a substantial period of time, and receive limited other compensation.[149] Indeed, the evidence suggests that managers will usually sell all the shares acquired through the exercise of options,[150] destroying any long term effect of the equity incentive.

j) Share Options or Shares?

A more effective alignment of interests via the equity mechanism might occur if share options were combined with share awards, particularly where management is required to hold the shares for the long-term. This could be achieved by Long Term Incentive Plans (LTIPs).[151] It appears that the interests of shareholding

[146] eg D Schizer 'Executives and Hedging: The Fragile Legal Foundation of Incentive Compatibility' (2000) 100 Col LR 440. Bebchuk et al (2002) have queried why companies generally do not prevent managers from hedging away equity exposure, noting that the optimal incentive contract should prevent managers from unwinding incentives without restriction. They have suggested that the lack of restriction evidences options being used to permit rent-seeking activities by managers (n 4, 758-759 and 824-831).

[147] For a challenge to the view that executives do not carry downside risk with options see Hall (1999) n 82 39-41 and, examining non-exercised options as foregone pay, Main (1999) n 84, 97-98.

[148] eg M Benz, M Kucher and A Stutzer 'Are Stock Options the Managers' Blessing? Stock option Compensation and Institutional Controls' (2001) Working Paper Series, Institute for Empirical Research in Economics, University of Zurich, Working Paper No 61, 5-6.

[149] Financial Times Editorial (2002) n 8.

[150] E Ofek and D Yermack 'Taking Stock: Equity-based Compensation and the Evolution of Managerial Ownership' (2000) 55 J Fin 1367.

[151] LTIPs are popular in the UK and are encouraged by the Combined Code which forms part of the London Stock Exchange's listing rules (see Part B). Under an LTIP, an award of shares is typically made at no cost to the executive but the number of shares awarded, which is usually linked to a proportion of salary, is conditional on achievement of performance targets,

cont. ...

management are aligned more closely with shareholders: there is some evidence that equity-based performance pay drops with higher levels of share ownership by management.[152] Performance conditions can also attach over a longer period of time where shares are awarded on a longer time scale than the usual yearly award cycle of options.

There are, however, difficulties with share-based pay, as with share options. Increased voting power may lead to an entrenchment of management with distortions to, for example, the corporate control market. There is some evidence that dividends may reduce with higher levels of management share-ownership.[153] There also appears to be a difficulty concerning the link between share ownership by management and performance. One US study has examined the performance consequences of mandatory share ownership plans and found an improvement in firm performance, with increases in excess accounting returns and share returns after adoption of the plan.[154] There appears to be a lack of consensus, however, on the extent of the link between management share ownership and performance.[155] Share ownership by managers can also carry costs for diversified shareholders by leading to entrenchment effects and risk-avoidance behaviour by non-diversified managers.[156] These effects could, however, be counter-balanced by reducing the amount of share remuneration and awarding larger amounts of fixed salary or performance-linked cash bonuses.

often peer-group related. Once shares are awarded, they are typically subject to vesting conditions of 2 years or more.

[152] Mehran (1995) n 53, 179.

[153] M Rozeff 'Growth, Beta, and Agency Costs as Determinants of Dividend Payout Ratios' (1982) 5 J of Financial Research 249, 249. For a different perspective see Fenn and Liang (2001) n 129 who have found that share ownership by management carries incentives to increase dividends at companies with potentially the most severe agency problems, but has no effect on other firms.

[154] J Core and D Larcker 'Performance Consequences of Mandatory Increases in Executive Stock Ownership' (2002) 64 J Fin Econ 317. See also R Morck, A Schliefer and R Vishny 'Management Ownership and Market Valuation' (1988) 20 J Fin Econ 293 and J McConnell and H Servaes 'Additional evidence on equity ownership and corporate value' (1990) 27 J Fin Econ 595 which show a positive connection between share ownership and performance at certain levels of ownership. Industry sector appears to impact on the strength of the relationship between performance and managerial share ownership. See in the context of R & D firms, H Ciu and Y Mak J Corp Fin (2002) 313.

[155] No relation between between management share ownership and performance was reported in H Demetz and K Lehn 'The structure of corporate ownership: causes and consequences' (1985) 93 J Pol Econ 1155 and (in the context of a comparison of ownership in bankrupt and nonbankrupt companies) C Loderer and and D Sheehan 'Corporate bankruptcy and managers' self-serving behaviour' (1989) 44 J Fin 1059. For the view that larger shareholdings by management does not improve performance, but that executives hold more shares in line with firm performance see C Loderer and K Martin 'Executive Stock Ownership and Performance: Tracking Faint Traces' (1997) 45 J Fin Econ 223.

[156] See Nohel and Todd (2001) n 57, 4 and Cui and Mak (2002) n 154, 315.

k) A Complex Problem

Share option remuneration represents a minefield into which the legislator should step warily, if at all.

They display many structural defects which may damage the incentive alignment or performance link. Their complexity, in terms of incentive effects and structure, combined with their invisibility as an accounting expense in certain accounting regimes, may make it easy for vast wealth transfers to be hidden from shareholders. But design problems are largely in the hands of the board and its allied structures. If the board is acting for the shareholders and bargaining in an adversarial manner, design and structure problems can be mitigated. Defects in the contract-setting process can, however, result in a manipulation of that process. While the connection between bad governance and suboptimal remuneration structures is not entirely clear,[157] it does appear that good governance is central to the adoption of optimal share options and that good governance can exert control on any potential skimming activities to which options may be vulnerable. The European response, discussed in part B, certainly suggests that, even in those systems where the focus on remuneration as a device to monitor management is reduced, governance controls are becoming increasingly important, in some continental legal systems, at least as a protection for minority shareholders.

Part B also makes clear that, across the EU, remuneration is managed by disclosure and governance controls, and not by structural requirements as to the form of remuneration: this approach has also been adopted by the Commission in its Company Law Action Plan (Part C). This is arguably the correct approach. While it is relatively easy to attack the alignment which options, in particular, are supposed to bring to shareholder and management interests, the removal of share options altogether as a form of executive remuneration would be an overly blunt response, to a governance, rather than a structure problem. What may be needed is a more calibrated mix of performance-sensitive, equity-based incentives (including long-term share plans) and cash remuneration which is set at a level which reflects the demands of senior management responsibilities. As a company moves through its life cycle, risk-taking and gambling, which are rewarded by share and share option remuneration, will be more appropriate at certain points, while steadiness and rationality, which is best rewarded by high fixed salaries and bonuses linked to a wide range of performance criteria, will be critical at other

[157] Chance et al (2000) n 115, eg have noted a link between poor governance and repricing. See also Brenner et al (2000) n 115 who point to an 80% higher frequency in repricing where there is disclosure of a conflict of interest in the compensation committee, and to the greater incidence of repricing in small firms which tend to be monitored less closely by the financial press and to have less institutional investor ownership (at 123-127). Carter and Lynch (2001) n 116, by contrast, have not found a connection between repricing and agency problems.

points.[158] Flexibility in choice of remuneration structure is therefore key. The very complex issues which options generate with respect to design, structure, and how they incentivize management suggest that this is not an area in which bright line rules on permissible types of option remuneration are possible or desirable.

IV. Problem (2): Governance and The Pay Setting Process

1. The Inherent Conflict

Adoption of the optimal remuneration contract is therefore dependent on the remuneration-setting process taking place in an adversarial manner between self-interested parties seeking to maximize their interests. If this happens, it becomes difficult to find the market failure justifying controls on the remuneration process: market dynamics set levels of pay.

In dispersed ownership systems, remuneration is not set at arms' length, as the board, composed of or aligned to senior management and not a perfect agent for shareholders,[159] negotiates on both sides of the pay bargain in an inherently conflicted situation in which it is incentivized not to maximize the shareholders' interests.[160] Defects in the negotiation process strike at the heart of the incentive-alignment argument which justifies a hands-off approach to remuneration under Anglo-American corporate governance. An incentive contract which emerges via a flawed process in which the board has lost control of the paysetting process to management might be better regarded as an expression of wealth-skimming (or rent extraction) by self-interested executives, rather than of arms-length contracting.[161] If this is the case, governance controls 'matter' in that they can increase the possibility of the pay-setting process being a contracting one, in which shareholder interests are maximized, rather than a skimming one, in which the board is captured by management. In effect, governance can promote the presence of an active principal in the remuneration negotiations with the execu-

[158] The *Financial Times* has noted that established companies need neither an entrepreneur or a stock market gambler, and has suggested that remuneration for such companies should include a high basic salary, bonuses linked to relative performance targets, and long term shares: Financial Times Editorial (2002) n 8.

[159] Baker et al (1988) n 65, 614.

[160] Yablon (1999) n 11 has noted that it would be surprising if executives were not using governance systems to maximise their remuneration (at 273). This defect in the bargaining process makes it possible to justify the pop star's inflated salary as a result of arms' length bargaining and market dynamics, but not the CEO's (at 306). On similar lines see also Iacobucci (1998) n 62, 495, and Loewenstein (1996) n 12, 201and 203.

[161] See generally Bebchuk et al (2002) n 4. See also M Bertrand and S Mullainathan 'Agents With and Without Principals' [2000b] American Economic Review 203 who have emphasized the significance of control of the pay process passing to management.

tive agent.[162] A key question then arises: what is good governance in the remuneration context? Arguably it is that which ensures that shareholders stay in control of the pay process, whether through disclosure, the presence of institutional investors and independent directors, or the use of remuneration committees, such that the pay-setting body ensures that the contract is optimal from shareholders' perspective.[163]

The following discussion of the interaction between governance structures and the remuneration-setting process is placed primarily in the context of Anglo-American/dispersed ownership corporate governance. In listed continental companies, however, the Anglo-American focus on the effectiveness of governance controls allied to the incentive contracts, such as independent directors, shifts towards the effectiveness of monitoring via large blockholders, financial institutions which provide debt financing, and long-standing, interlocking relationships between management, shareholders, financiers, and other stakeholders (see section VII).[164] The role of the board of directors and outside monitors in the form of independent directors can therefore be viewed as more limited in concentrated ownership companies.[165] Two fundamentally different board structures are also found in Europe: the Anglo-American one-tier board (found in the UK, Ireland, and southern European countries), which includes independent directors, and the two-tier board (Germany is the paradigm example but it is also found in German-speaking countries and in Northern Europe), in which management and supervision is split between the two tiers, with the supervisory board (all members of which must, in Germany, be independent of management)[166] elected by shareholders and empowered to remove the management board. Nonetheless, as shown in Part B, attempts are being made to impose good board governance in pay-set-

[162] eg Bertrand and Mullainathan (2000a) n 111 who have found that there is evidence to suggest that well-governed firms with active principals face lower agency costs with respect to executive remuneration. In particular, the authors have found that CEO pay responds less to luck (which should not be a feature of the optimal incentive contract as it is outside the influence of the CEO and adds risk) in better governed firms, particularly those with a large shareholder. See also J Core, R Holthausen and D Larcker 'Corporate Governance, Chief Executive Officer Compensation and Firm Performance' (1999) 51 J Fin Econ 371 who have found that US CEOs earn greater compensation when governance structures are less effective.

[163] Bertrand and Mullainathan (2000b) n 161, 208.

[164] For a review of the different concerns of Anglo-American and continental corporate governance and the defining characteristics of the two systems see eg Bratton and McCahery (1999) n 30, 222-228 and M Bradley, C Schipani, A Sundaram and J Walsh 'The Purposes and Accountability of the Corporation in Contemporary Society: Corporate Governance at a Crossroads' (1999) 62 L & CP 9, 61-64.

[165] eg Berglöf (1997) n 30.

[166] Supervisory board members will typically, however, not be independent as it is regarded under the UK governance system as they will represent personal and business connections between the company and the business and finance community as well as large blockholdings and cross shareholdings. See Hopt (2002) n 41, 178.

ting, particularly with respect to remuneration committees, although the transplantation of the remuneration committee reflects blockholding governance, particularly with respect to the independence of committee members. The Commission's pan-EU approach to remuneration also appears designed to remove core conflicts from the pay-setting process via the remuneration committee, albeit calibrated again to reflect the particular features of continental corporate governance (Part C).

2. The Board of Directors

The remuneration process is weakened in the first instance where the board of directors, which is assumed to take an arms' length approach to remuneration setting, is passive or captured by management, poorly incentivized to bargain for optimal pay, and not an effective agent for the shareholders. In effect, the pay-setting process can be examined as potentially missing the principal who negotiates in a self-interested manner with management. This gap represents a stiff challenge to the adoption of the optimal incentive contract. There are a number of reasons for the missing principal which include: a lack of private benefits;[167] directors forming the senior management group; board dynamics which often result in deference and politeness towards the CEO;[168] social ties; and the influence of the CEO over the appointment of directors.

The addition of independent directors, as independent monitors, to the board (or remuneration committee) may provide a solution. Independent directors should be able to withstand any overbearing influence of senior management on the board of directors.[169] As they are less close to the company, they are more likely to judge senior management performance objectively and with respect to the company's performance.[170] Independent directors may, however, be reluctant

[167] While the board personally bears a disproportionately large share of the non-pecuniary costs (stress, disapproval etc) of punishing poorly performing CEOs financially, it receives essentially none of the pecuniary benefits, given that it holds only a small proportion of company shares: Baker et al (1988) n 65, 614.

[168] Bebchuk et al (2002) have noted that unless directors believe that a CEO should be fired, 'they…are expected to support their CEO. Those who cannot do so in good faith are expected to step down. Overall, board meetings and processes are characterised by an emphasis on courtesy, politeness, and deference to the CEO' (n 4, 767).

[169] The UK Cadbury Committee eg highlighted the contribution independent directors could make in areas where potential conflicts arise between executive management and the wider interests of the company, particularly with respect to remuneration: Committee on the Financial Aspects of Corporate Governance, *Report on the Financial Aspects of Corporate Governance* (1992) paras 4.4-4.6.

[170] For a review of the literature see J Lawrence and G Stapledon 'Is Board Composition Important? A Study of Listed Australian Companies' SSRN (1999).

to disturb the status quo.[171] They are often friends of the CEO and senior management and may owe their appointment, and directors' salaries, to the CEO. They may often be ex-CEOs and may set compensation in a manner which they would have liked.[172] Alternatively, they may be serving directors or senior managers at other companies and may be incentivized to set pay at levels, and using pay structures, beneficial to them.[173] Independent directors are typically chosen because their outlook sits easily with that of the senior management team and so they may be unlikely to adopt an aggressive approach on sensitive remuneration questions.[174] They may lack expertise on remuneration questions or have insufficient time to become expert.[175] As they lack the level of inside knowledge of company performance and management behaviour possessed by inside directors, they may not be in a position to assess the importance of market, economy, and sector-wide factors and to come to a realistic appreciation of the contribution of a manager. Social influences may be at play which encourage independent directors to placate management.[176] Reputational factors, which may result in an independent director who is regarded as 'tough on pay' being blacklisted from other boards (and in economic costs for the director) may also blunt a director's enthusiasm for rigorous review of remuneration practices. More generally, the majority of the US studies undertaken into the relationship between board independence and performance do not find a positive relationship and there is some evidence that independence is correlated with poor performance.[177] With specific reference to executive remuneration, it has been suggested that independent

[171] For a discussion of independent director weakness in the context of the Enron collapse (the Enron board contained only 2 executive directors and 12 non-executive directors) see Gordon (2002) n 29, 1241-42). The independence of virtually every member of the Enron board was comprised by payments of some kind and 'independence was also compromised by bonds of long service and familiarity' (at 1242).

[172] S Bhagat and B Black 'The Uncertain Relationship between Board Composition and Firm Performance' SSRN (1999) 13.

[173] Cheffins (2001b) n 114, 533. See also Bebchuk et al (2002) n 4, 769 who have raised the less egregious possibility that serving CEOs may be engaging in a form of cognitive dissonance and internally justifying their own pay through the remuneration committee.

[174] The point has also been made that reputational concerns and personal pride in being regarded as an independent decision-maker are likely to incentivize independent directors not to side with management without cause, particularly given the wide media attention in this area: Cheffins (1997) n 56, 695.

[175] Stabile (2000) n 93, 175. A survey of UK directors by KPMG has revealed widespread deficiencies in the knowledge of non-executive directors, although the majority receive some training in corporate governance issues: T Tassell 'Non-executive directors admit to deficiencies in training' *Financial Times* (5 November 2002).

[176] Stabile (2000) n 93, 177.

[177] See generally Bhagat and Black (1999) n 172 and R Romano 'Less is More: Making Institutional Investor Activism a Valuable Mechanism of Corporate Governance' (2001) 18 Yale Journal of Regulation 174, 192.

directors have not controlled executive remuneration, but rather presided over its explosion, although the evidence is equivocal.[178] A particular difficulty here concerns the trade-off between independence and incentives. Independent directors typically own only small amounts of company shares and so have limited incentives to monitor carefully.[179] There are also difficulties in ensuring that independent directors are truly independent given that, for example, they may serve as advisors and consultants to the company, or be members of institutions such as universities or other foundations which depend on the company for funding.

One way out of this impasse is further disclosure of the ties between independent directors and the board of directors/CEO.[180] Another is to readjust the process by making directors bigger shareholders, thereby enhancing their incentives and remedying the inherent defects in the remuneration process.[181] Requiring directors to hold a large equity stake carries the advantage of re-aligning directors' interests with shareholders and readjusting their motivation to monitor executive remuneration accordingly, particularly if a significant shareholding is built up.[182] But the danger of entrenching directors and a loss of their independence due to their financial interest in the company then arises.[183] Another solution is to impose rigorous controls on the independence of nominally independent directors.[184]

[178] Bhagat and Black (1999) n 172, 4 have noted that US CEO remuneration exploded over the period when independent directors became dominant on the boards of large firms and that this has continued with the trend towards independent remuneration committees and supermajority independent boards. Mehran (1995) n 53, has argued, however, that while firms with more outside directors do have a higher proportion of their executive remuneration in equity, insider dominated boards are more likely to be responsive to the interests of management and to use more fixed cash compensation, which is preferred by risk-averse management. Core et al (1999) n 162 have found higher remuneration with a higher proportion of independent directors on the board and that CEO compensation is higher when a greater proportion of the board is composed of outside directors whose independence or effectiveness is prejudiced in some way. Lawrence and Stapledon (1999) n 170 have found, using an Australian sample, however, that an insider-influenced remuneration committee is not statistically more likely to provide greater remuneration than an independent committee, and that there is no evidence that insider-influenced committees are less sensitive to the pay performance relation than independent committees.

[179] Loewenstein (1996) n 12, 208. See also Bhagat and Black (1999) n 172, 35 on the empirical evidence as to the connection between director share ownership and enhanced performance.

[180] Bhagat and Black (1999) n 172, 36.

[181] See generally Elson (1995) n 13. This strategy would require the payment of directors' fees in the form of shares restricted as to resale and the adoption of longer terms of office for directors (at 691-695).

[182] Elson (1995) n 13, 652 and 691.

[183] Loewenstein (2000) n 140, 8.

[184] Conyon et al (1995) n 99, 711.

3. The Remuneration Committee

Other procedural safeguards, allied to the board of directors, can reduce the risk of management taking control of the remuneration-setting process. The remuneration committee is one of the most prominent of these. Composed primarily of management-independent, non-executive directors, and exercising pay-setting functions delegated from the board of directors, it can act as an objective control on the pay-setting process.[185] The influence of management and the CEO on the directors which sit on the committee may, however, damage its effectiveness. While the evidence is equivocal, some studies suggest that there is little evidence that independent remuneration committees do a better job than inside directors.[186]

4. Remuneration Consultants

The remuneration consultant who advises the remuneration committee on pay trends and on the structure of remuneration packages is often cited as a key governance mechanism. Remuneration consultants provide expertise in the complex area of remuneration design, particularly where share options are concerned. They also improve the disclosure available to the remuneration committee on pay practices. There are a number of obstacles, however, to their acting as effective monitors. In particular, they are vulnerable to capture by the board, which may, in turn, be captured by the CEO and senior management. Consultants may be hired by the board, rather than by the remuneration committee, and incentivized as a result to please the board, by justifying or legitimizing remuneration practices, in order to protect their salaries and future business.[187] The consultant's firm may also offer other services, such as human resource management, to the company, further incentivizing the consultant to maintain a good relationship with man-

[185] A remuneration committee should act as 'an independent arbiter of executive compensation on behalf of shareholders' (Conyon et al (1995) n 99, 711).

[186] Bhagat and Black (1999) n 172, 13. An earlier survey of UK listed companies found that companies with a remuneration committee paid more, and were not more sensitive to performance, than companies without such committees: B Main and J Johnston 'Remuneration Committees and Corporate Governance' [1993] 23 Accounting and Business Research 351. By contrast, see Lawrence and Stapledon (1999) n 170, and see D Yermack 'Good Timing: CEO Stock Option Awards and Company News Announcements' (1997) 52 J Fin 449 which reported that the independence of the remuneration committee reduces the tendency of companies to increase executive wealth by awarding share options shortly before the company share price increases

[187] For an early discussion of this problem in the US context see generally GS Crystal *In Search of Excess: the Overcompensation of American Executives* (WW Norton New York 1991). See also Core et al (1999) n 162 who have noted, in the US context, that boards usually rely on consultants often hired by the CEO, which may lead to interest maximization for the CEO (at 373).

agement.[188] If a remuneration consultant develops a reputation for being 'tough on pay', appointment to other companies becomes less likely. Remuneration consultants may, as a result, exercise their expertize and discretion in a manner favourable to management and choose bench marks and remuneration formulae which will deliver high awards[189] In these circumstances, the consultant may become a camouflage mechanism to legitimize sub-optimal pay decisions by management in control of the pay process.[190]

5. Shareholders and Institutional Investors

If the board of directors is the primary, if flawed, monitor of remuneration-setting, shareholder monitoring is a key secondary line of control. Where shareholders are unhappy with remuneration practices, they have the option of exiting, particularly where securities markets are efficient and liquid. Costs and diversification pressure make this an unattractive option for most small investors, in particular.[191] Indirect shareholder control mechanisms from within the company can be expressed as a function of governance mechanisms such as independent directors and objective remuneration committees. Shareholders can, however, represent an important direct monitor on whether an optimal incentive contract is adopted. The direct mechanisms available to shareholders include the removal of directors who preside over inappropriate pay decisions and voting on pay policy or particular pay packages (typically share option programmes). Advisory votes on remuneration packages have a particular attraction in that they serve to send clear signals to management while causing minimal disruption to contracts and contract negotiation. In order to monitor effectively, however, shareholders require knowledge, power, and independence to review decisions in a meaningful manner.

As effective monitors, shareholders suffer from the collective action problem, and from a lack of information. Shareholders are rationally apathetic in that the benefits of their monitoring activities are shared by all shareholders, while the costs are carried by the individual shareholder monitors. Shareholders are therefore incentivized to free ride on the efforts of others. This is exacerbated in the case of executive remuneration as shareholders are unlikely to see much individual gains from alterations to profits arising from a reduction of the costs of ex-

[188] Loewenstein (1996) n 12, 203.

[189] Hall and Liebman (1997) n 17, 30. The *Financial Times* has argued that remuneration consultants should be dispensed with as they 'act as an engine of executive pay inflation' by eg placing all clients in the top quartile of executive remuneration and developing complex schemes which few outsiders can understand. Financial Times Editorial (2003) n 95.

[190] Bebchuck et al (2002) n 4, 756 and 789-791.

[191] Stabile (2000) n 93, 188.

ecutive remuneration,[192] and may suffer if management incentives are damaged. In addition, an examination of the optimality of executive remuneration decisions requires careful case-by case analysis of disclosure which, even where it is made available, can be difficult for shareholders.

Institutional investors are often regarded as potentially strong corporate monitors.[193] The extent to which institutional investors can bear on the remuneration process is, however, doubtful. Institutional investors have not always been active with respect to executive remuneration, although, as discussed below, there is some evidence of change.[194] The collective action problem arises and is aggravated by the need for institutions to have holdings across different companies. Institutions may not communicate effectively as a group and so fail to influence management.[195] Agency problems can arise within an institutional investor, such

[192] Cheffins (1997) n 56, 671.

[193] They are typically knowledgeable and not overawed by management. They have larger holdings which increase the private benefits of monitoring, notwithstanding the collective action problem. They suffer less from co-ordination costs than do retail investors and can agree more readily on common approaches. Their holding of large blocks makes it more difficult for them to exit and more likely that they will challenge management. Action by an institutional shareholder in respect of one company has the advantage of signaling the need for good behaviour to other companies in which the institutional investor has a stake. See generally: B Black 'Shareholder Passivity Reexamined' (1990) 89 Mich LR 520. On the spillover reputational or signaling benefit available to institutional investor monitors see also Conyon and Leech (1994) n 22, 233-234.

[194] See Heard (1995) n 116 who has found, in the US context (at 758), that shareholder voting is not a very strong influence on remuneration as pay plans can be complex, difficult to decipher, and are not ratified very often. A 'hands-off' approach has typically been adopted by shareholders in the UK on remuneration until recently. See B Black and J Coffee 'Hail Britannia? Institutional Investor Behaviour Under Limited Regulation' (1994) 92 Mich L Rev 1997. See also Cheffins (1997) n 56, 670 and 697. While UK institutional investors have tended, up to now, not to challenge individual company decisions, they have had significant input, via the work of the Institutional Shareholders Committee, the National Association of Pension Funds, and the Association of British Insurers (ABI), into the overall design of remuneration by adopting codes of practice. See Main (1999) n 84, 85 and Conyon and Murphy (2000) n 23, F667. Overall, the US and UK evidence suggests that shareholder votes only act as an effective control on remuneration where remuneration deviates considerably from the norm: B Cheffins and R Thomas 'Should shareholders have a greater say over executive pay?: Learning from the US experience (2001c) 1 JCLS 277.

[195] There is a considerable literature on the effectiveness of institutional investors as corporate monitors. See eg Black (1990) n 193; M Roe 'A Political Theory of American Corporate Finance' (1991) 91 Co L Rev 10; J Coffee 'Liquidity versus Control: the Institutional Investor as Corporate Monitor' (1991) 91 Col L Rev 1277; B Black 'Shareholder Activism and Corporate Governance in the United States' in Newman (ed) *New Palgrave Dictionary of Economics and the Law* 459 (3rd edn Macmillan New York 1998); and Garrido and Rojo (n 43). For a challenge to the collective action and organizational problems faced by institutional investors see Romano (2001) n 177 who refers ia to the nontrivial blocks held by institutions and the networking organizations on corporate governance which alleviate collective action difficulties (at 179).

as a fund management company, as those exercising votes need to be incentivized to take action.[196] There is some US evidence, however, that large shareholders (5% and over) can act as an effective governance mechanism with respect to remuneration.[197]

It may be that executive remuneration is an inherently difficult problem for shareholders to manage directly. Activist shareholder monitoring traditionally concerns process issues which are common to many companies. As executive remuneration demands firm-specific knowledge and should relate to firm-specific effects, it may be inherently less amenable to effective direct shareholding monitoring. In particular, the range of finely calibrated factors which determine whether an option grant is optimal in aligning incentives might suggest that shareholders will rarely be in a position to monitor option grants effectively. The failure of institutional investors to impact on executive remuneration packages may, however, simply be a reflection of other shareholders' perception that high, option-based remuneration is key to incentivizing management and strong corporate performance.[198]

Strong evidence of increased institutional investor activism has, however, recently emerged.[199] UK institutional investors, in particular, seem increasingly

[196] The smaller incidence of activism in US private pension and mutual funds, as compared to public pension funds, has been explained as reflecting the decreased likelihood that managers in private institutions will obtain personal benefits from activism, whereas political gains may accrue to officials in public institutions: Romano (2001) n 177, 179 and 181.

[197] Bertrand and Mullainathan (2000b) n 161, 204. They have found statistically significant increases in CEO pay in firms without a 5% or more shareholder and insignificant increases in pay where a 5% shareholder was present and, with respect to performance sensitivity, an increase in sensitivity in firms with a large shareholder and no increase in sensitivity for firms without. See also Core et al (1999) n 162 who have found that CEO compensation is a decreasing function of the existence of an external blockholder who owns at least 5%.

[198] See generally Romano (2001) who argues that the failure of institutional activism to impact positively on share price stems from a misdirection of activism. She argues that proposals which seek to limit executive remuneration are not supported by empirical evidence that such action will improve corporate performance and deliver value to shareholders: n 177, 180 and 201-205.

[199] The *Financial Times* has reported that shareholders are voting in greater numbers and on a wide variety of issues, including executive remuneration. Pensions Investment Research Consultants has reported that the average voting level for FTSE 350 companies has risen to 55% from 51%, the largest increase in 6 years: N Cohen 'Activism by shareholders put pressure on directors' *Financial Times* (10 October 2002). Referring to research by the US Investor Responsibility Research Centre, the *Financial Times* has also reported that 2003 is set to be break all records for shareholder activism. Nearly half of the motions being proposed by institutional shareholders such as public pension funds, charitable foundations, and unions concern executive remuneration and, in particular, the treatment of share options as expenses and the closer linkage of existing share option plans to performance: A Hill and E Wine 'US boardrooms shake to tread of shareholders on the march' *Financial Times* (18 February 2003). In April 2003 the *Financial Times* reported that 'Shareholders on both sides of the Atlantic are

cont. ...

ready to intervene on a company-specific basis and to challenge and reject remuneration packages. Law, and particularly mandatory disclosure, appears to matter in this context. The changes to UK company law in 2002 which require (for listed companies) the production of a new and detailed Remuneration Report and which also require that approval of the Report be put to an advisory shareholder vote (see Part B) appear to be galvanizing institutional investors into action. The 2003 AGM season in the UK, which is the first effected by the changes, shows evidence of a new militancy on remuneration. At the Reuters and Granada AGMs, for example, more than 20% of shareholders objected to the Report.[200] Shareholder dissatisfaction with remuneration was also expressed at the Shell, Schroeders, BAE Systems, and WPP AGMs.[201] Most dramatically, the Report was rejected at the GlaxoSmithKline meeting, generating a veritable tidal way of media reaction.[202] One factor driving this movement is the decision by the National Association of Pension Funds (whose members own approximately 20% of the UK stock market) to challenge remuneration policy more aggressively, using the new shareholder vote on remuneration.[203] It remains to be seen whether the 2003 AGM season represents a profound change in institutional investor behaviour in terms of the time and expense they are prepared to give to pay monitoring, and, if so, whether the direct shareholder vote is emerging as a new and effective way of managing executive remuneration in the dispersed owner-

seething over boardroom pay and fat severance packages for departing executives. Challenges at annual meetings have reached record levels' Financial Times Editorial (2003) n 95.

[200] K Griffiths 'The Face of Corporate Britain' *The Independent* (24 April 2003).

[201] 22.8% of shareholders voted against the Shell remuneration report (by contrast, there was a 92% vote in favour of a new long term incentive plan): D Gow 'Shell shareholders rebel on board pay' *The Guardian* (24 April 2003). They objected to a 55% pay rise to the chairman in the face of a 23% drop in share price. Less than 60% of shareholders endorsed remuneration policy at the Schroeders AGM: ibid. See M Harrison 'Shell board faces barrage of protest' *The Independent* (24 April 2003). At the BAE Systems AGM, US rather than UK investors lead the attack on the remuneration report (694 million votes against and 712 million votes in favour of the report), concerned as to the dilutive impact of the employee share option policy. By contrast, neither of the two main UK institutional shareholder advisory bodies, the Association of British Insurers and the National Association of Pension Funds, objected to the report: S Mesure 'BAE confirms Boeing talks as US investors stage protest over pay' *The Independent* (20 April 2003). At the WPP AGM, the vote of 46% of shareholders against the report is regarded as one of the most significant since the seismic rejection of the GSK report earlier in May 2003: C Harris 'WPP pay package angers shareholders' *Financial Times* (1 July 2003).

[202] n 5.

[203] The National Association of Pension Funds lobbied for a no vote on the Shell remuneration policy, eg, and called the result 'a shot across the bows as far as shareholders are concerned': Gow (2003) n 201. It recommended absentions on remuneration at 32 UK AGMs in April 2003 but called for only four no votes in that time, although critics have argued that abstentions are ineffective in that only no votes make an impact: A Senior, R Miles, and C Merell 'How much difference do these shareholder campagins make?' *The Times* (25 April 2003).

ship context. It also remains to be seen whether companies will react to shareholder anger.[204] Institutional shareholders are, however, also engaging more actively and positively with the remuneration-setting process by calling for closer links between pay and performance and a more even-handed sharing of risk between shareholders and management,[205] setting tougher performance targets, and querying the basis on which remuneration is granted, by, for example, challenging the use of particular peer group comparisons. There is also evidence of clear institutional investor policies on executive remuneration which, rather than focusing on headline remuneration levels, acknowledge the benefits of performance pay while attacking remuneration which represents a wealth transfer from shareholders.[206]

The difficulties faced by institutional investors in monitoring the incentive contract against suboptimality and management influence are a particular feature of Anglo-American corporate governance. In concentrated ownership systems, by contrast, the existence of strong blockholders lessens the need for monitoring by an incentive contract and reduces the incidence of high-powered incentive contracts as well as the potential agency costs which these contracts can generate when governance is flawed. Part B reveals that the use of advisory shareholder votes on remuneration is a feature of dispersed ownership systems, particularly the UK. Voting rules do apply to share option programmes on a pan-EU basis, but, here, the focus tends to be on approving option programmes as an aspect of the company's capital structure, rather than on monitoring remuneration. While the Commission does support shareholder approval of share option plans, as an instrument of shareholder voice rather than as a capital maintenance mechanisms, it has not presented dramatic proposals for remuneration votes.

[204] One *Financial Times* leader is pessimistic: 'many more [companies] have reacted sulkily or even defiantly to shareholder disquiet, trying to justify the indefensible by arguing they are special cases' ('No confidence vote for British business' *Financial Times* (30 June 2003). In one high profile example, however, the CEO of Cable & Wireless agreed to a substantially reduced payoff following concern expressed by leading institutional investors: J Hart 'C &W chief's payoff cut' *The Times* (19 June 2003) while the GSK board has engaged in extensive discussions with its main institutional shareholders.

[205] A study by management consultants Bain has shown that more than 50% of institutional investors (of a US and UK sample) were ready to approve remuneration plans which gave senior executives a larger share of the value they created for shareholders, as long as executives shared in the downside. Cited in Gadiesh and Blenko (2002) n 7. In the US, a major public pension fund, TIAA-CREF, has consulted with 50 companies about reforming their remuneration practices and aligning packages more closely with shareholders' interests. Most (not all) the companies targeted agreed to reforms following the threat of a shareholder vote on remuneration: G Morgensen 'Some executives under fire still battle to keep their options' *Int Herald Tribune* (21 April 2003).

[206] Shareholders are, eg, unhappy with repricing, (Heard (1995) n 116, 759 and Gadiesh and Blenko (2002) n 7) and with practices which provoke dilution (Heard ibid and Cohen (2002) n 199).

6. Governance and the Control of Remuneration

It appears, therefore, that governance does impact on remuneration and its structure, although the evidence is equivocal. Much of the evidence originates in the US, however, and considerable dangers attach to transplanting evidence given the complexities of the remuneration process and cultural attitudes to governance and remuneration.[207] It may be also that certain of the defects in the remuneration process are intractable: performance pay carries certain advantages and reduces certain agency costs, but the trade-off may be that it opens up or sharpens conflicts which are already unavoidable in the governance of companies with a widely dispersed ownership.

The point has been well made that the optimal board structure will vary across companies according to their needs.[208] The same may be true of the remuneration-setting process which should not, as a result, be tied into a regulatory straitjacket: this is all the more the case in the EU where governance systems differ, and the centrality of the remuneration contract, and its monitoring by the board and its supporting/supervising structures, varies. Problems certainly exist in the dispersed ownership context. Not only are the procedures under which remuneration is set and controlled subject to inherent weaknesses, but the evidence, particularly from the US, that remuneration is not optimal, suggests that governance defects are blocking the adoption of remuneration contracts which maximize shareholder value. Reform could proceed via the remuneration committee, which provides a visible form of control, and a strengthening the role of independent directors:[209] this is the approach adopted by the EU and by many Member States. It could also, given the rise in shareholder activism, address the role of shareholders by formally strengthening the role they play in the remuneration-setting process via shareholder votes,[210] although this reform has not, to date, been a major feature of

[207] See, on executive remuneration, Lawrence and Stapledon (1999) n 170 and, more generally, R Romano 'A Cautionary Note on Drawing Lessons from Comparative Corporate Law' (1993) 102 YLJ 2021. The split between US and UK investors on the BAE Systems Remuneration Report provides a recent example of transatlantic differences with BAE noting that 'obviously UK investors don't feel the same concerns on this subject [dilutive effects of share options]': Mesure (2003) n 201.

[208] Romano (2001) n 177, 194

[209] Cheffins (1997) n 56, 673.

[210] The *Financial Times*, eg has called for shareholders to 'vote early and often' on remuneration: Financial Times Editorial (2003) n 95 Greater input by shareholders has also been supported by the UK corporate governance expert and former chairman of Gartmore Investment Management, Paul Myners, who has called for shareholders to challenge bad management more vigorously on remuneration and for fund managers to address corporate governance at appropriately senior levels with their institutions: N Cohen 'investors told to be more vigiliant' *Financial Times* (8 May 2003). For the view that institutional shareholder concern is one of the elements most likely to lead to reform of executive remuneration see

cont. ...

continental governance, save with respect to share option programmes. Disclosure (section VI) might be the least costly way to cross both these reform lines by ensuring that investors have sufficient information on how remuneration is set as well as on any potential conflicts in the remuneration-setting process. It would also cross the EU governance line, as a limited form of intervention which would increase transparency in remuneration-setting and allow minority shareholders, via the AGM, whether generally or in the context of a share option programme vote, the opportunity to challenge remuneration before blockholders and management.

V. Problem (3): Disclosure

1. Disclosure and Executive Remuneration

Effective disclosure may therefore represent one way of dealing with defects in the remuneration-setting process which obstruct the adoption of an optimal remuneration contract. The complexities of the executive remuneration problem are, however, equally apparent in the disclosure sphere. The discussion fractures across two faultlines: (i) whether disclosure can act as an effective remedy to, or whether it aggravates, the perceived difficulties in how executive remuneration is structured and the process under which it is granted and (ii) whether executive remuneration generates an additional agency cost by distorting the effective channeling of disclosure to shareholders and the marketplace.

2. Disclosure as a Remedy for Agency Costs

Disclosure can be an effective mechanism for solving the agency problems produced by dispersed ownership.[211] Assuming that share-based remuneration is an effective remedy for agency costs, disclosure can be regarded as reducing these agency costs in that it results in more accurate share prices, reduces the risk attached to share-based remuneration, and thereby induces risk-averse managers to accept such remuneration.[212]

More specifically, disclosure can address the procedural and structural problems raised by executive remuneration. A recurring theme in the literature concerns the role disclosure plays in counterbalancing defects in the decision-making

Yablon (1999) n 11, 275 who has, however, observed at 293 that the captured board problem is likely to limit their success in restraining increases or demanding higher performance standards.

[211] P Mahoney 'Mandatory Disclosure as a Solution to Agency Problems' (1995) 62 U Chi LR 1047.

[212] M Fox 'Required Disclosure and Corporate Governance' (1999) 62 L & CP 113, 121.

process.[213] It may, for example, sharpen shareholder monitoring (as appears to be occurring in the UK, although with the caveat that the new disclosure rules are coupled with new voting powers). Where internal governance has failed in that the board is an imperfect principal in the pay-setting process, management skimming may be only restrained by costs and the danger of arousing the attention of shareholders.[214] But the information asymmetry between shareholders and the board hampers shareholders in monitoring pay-setting. If full information is provided on remuneration packages and their relationship to performance, as well as on remuneration policies and procedures, shareholders can assess whether the board is negotiating effectively and take appropriate action, whether it be in the form of dismissing directors, or the adoption of resolutions.[215] As setting executive remuneration is a highly complex process, opaque disclosure will not generate effective shareholder activism or oversight. In particular, aggregated disclosure concerning total firm executive remuneration which does not explain remuneration policy and the often highly complex performance conditions applicable or set out the specific components of the remuneration packages of particular and named senior executives will not allow shareholders to assess remuneration policy effectively. It is not entirely clear, however, that shareholders will use disclosure to monitor pay-setting. Enhanced disclosure may, however, induce institutional shareholders who have greater incentives to monitor management to play a more activist role, in their own self-interest. Disclosure of remuneration lowers the cost of monitoring by raising the reputation of institutional investor monitors by signalling or publicizing, in effect, the results of their activism and generating greater deterrence effects.[216] It also makes it easier for institutional investors to communicate with one another and with management.[217]

Disclosure also impacts directly on the board itself, which is induced to justify remuneration choices publicly and with more care.[218] The increase in the use of options, for example, may simply be a consequence of boards wanting to pay executives more as share options provide an easier way of keeping very high remuneration out of the public eye.[219] More disclosure concerning option packages would, however, keep them exposed to shareholder scrutiny and render them less attractive for boards which have fallen under the control of management. The credibility of decision-making should also be enhanced if shareholders gain in

[213] See generally J Hill 'What Reward Have Ye? Disclosure of Director and Executive Remuneration in Australia' (1996) 14 Company and Securities Law Journal 232.

[214] Bertrand and Mullainathan (2000a) n 111, 3.

[215] Comments of L Quinn, Director, Division of Corporate Finance SEC, 1994 Corporate Law Symposium: Presentation and Panel Discussion, (1995) 63 U Cinn LR 770, 773.

[216] Iacobucci (1998) n 62, 498-499.

[217] Stabile (2000) n 93, 196.

[218] Iacobucci (1998) n 62, 500.

[219] Hall and Liebman (1997) n 17, 32-33.

confidence that any divergences in shareholder and management interests with respect to executive remuneration are disclosed. By highlighting the role of remuneration committees, disclosure can also ensure its visibility and enhance its accountability.[220]

In terms of structure, disclosure is likely to result in a shift to performance pay. Greater activism by shareholders and closer scrutiny of the board and remuneration committee suggests more reliance on performance-based pay.[221] Remuneration may as a result increase to compensate risk-averse managers. It may also increase as remuneration committees and consultants can establish the market rate for remuneration easily. Companies are unlikely to pay below the norm given the danger of managers defecting to rivals.[222]

3. Disclosure and Executive Remuneration: the Costs

Disclosure is traditionally associated with minimal regulatory intervention. There are, nonetheless, costs involved in using disclosure to address executive remuneration problems. In particular, the benefits of greater shareholder activism must be weighed against popular and political reaction to enhanced disclosure of executive remuneration. As additional disclosure concerning remuneration reaches the public domain, and particularly if it only contains disclosure on remuneration levels, public curiosity and hostility can generate large costs for a company. Remuneration contracts stop being a private company matter but are played out in the media, influenced by labour, captured by private interests (such as those of political activists and union personnel), and politically-infused. The board may become distracted by these interests, which do not pursue shareholder value, from setting optimal remuneration contracts.[223] If the function of disclosure is to ensure that incentives remain aligned, it must be carefully calibrated to send the correct signal. Disclosure which focuses on 'headline' pay levels, invites popular hostility, and does not facilitate shareholders in assessing remuneration structures and the pay-setting process is destabilizing.[224] By contrast, disclosure which makes is easier to assess the pay performance relation/incentive structure can remedy some of the structural and process weaknesses of executive remuneration.

[220] Murphy (1995) n 61, 737 and Hill (1996) n 213, 239.

[221] Iacobucci (1998) n 62, 501.

[222] Cheffins (2001b) n 114, 536.

[223] M Jensen and K Murphy 'CEO Incentives: It's Not How Much, But How' [1990b] Harvard Business Review 138) have observed that popular protests over levels of executive remuneration which follow disclosure can be damaging as they result in 'uninvited but influential' guests to the negotiations: 139, 144, 145.

[224] Murphy (1995) n 61.

Increased remuneration levels, consequent on disclosure, which reflect greater board focus on incentive effects, can be justified if performance pay is regarded as a remedy for agency costs. Disclosure may, however, result in an increase in pay due to a ratcheting effect. Pay surveys may become distorted by very high individual awards and, as they are relied on by remuneration consultants, feed into executive remuneration generally.[225] Increases driven by ratcheting are more difficult to justify and can lead to fairness challenges to remuneration.[226]

Disclosure rules can also have an adverse effect on remuneration by biasing remuneration awards towards particular forms which would not be adopted in an optimal contract. The best known example of this concerns the impact of US accounting rules on the expensing of options.[227] Current accounting rules mean that options are not expensed as a cost against profits as long as they are granted with a pre-determined exercise price and expiry date, and that the exercise price exceeds the fair market value of the relevant shares on the grant date. Footnote disclosure is required instead. An argument often raised against the use of indexed options, for example, is that, unlike 'plain vanilla' options, these options have to be disclosed as an expense.[228] Options can therefore be used to hide large pay awards and the board is disincentivized to use more performance-sensitive option devices, such as premium options, given the prejudicial impact of such devices on profits.[229]

Finally, performance-based remuneration can generate new agency costs by mis-aligning the interests of shareholders in accurate and timely disclosure and management's interest in maximizing remuneration, and so creating a new forum for management/shareholder conflict.[230] A manipulation of disclosure can arise following this misalignment. Where performance-based remuneration is linked to accounting indicators, for example, management is incentivized to manipulate accounting figures to maximize remuneration. Where remuneration is share-option-based, management is incentivized, and has the opportunity, to manipulate the market price of shares downwards around the dates of share option grants, as

[225] One remuneration expert has recently noted, in the context of the 2002 UK remuneration round, that remuneration is ratcheted up by companies wishing to pay executives in the upper quartile level of their peers – 'Each time a company raises its pay for its executives, this leads to a review at another company': T Tassell 'Corporate Restraints failing as board pay jumps 23%' *Financial Times* (7 May 2003).

[226] Iacobucci (1998) n 62, 519-520.

[227] See Murphy (1999) n 4, 2514-2515.

[228] See, for example, Hall and Liebman (1997) n 17, 31.

[229] For a recent review of the option-expensing controversy see A Parker and A Hill 'Standard-setters are targeting stock options again. After Enron, reform will be harder to resist' *Financial Times* (11 November 2002).

[230] C Yablon and J Hill 'Timing Corporate Disclosures to Maximise Performance-based Remuneration: A Case of Misaligned Incentives' (2000) 35 Wake Forest LR 83.

the exercise price of an option is usually the share price on the date of the grant. This manipulation can be achieved by the disclosure, shortly before the grant, of news which depresses the share price and, as a result, the option's exercise price or, conversely, the withholding of good news, spinning news in a negative manner, or failing to confirm good news.[231] Management is also incentivized to disclose news which raises the share price shortly before the option's exercise date in order to maximise the profit made on exercise of the option. There is some evidence to suggest that manipulation of this kind occurs.[232] Manipulation of disclosure in this way represents an agency cost as it can damage corporate prospects, value, and credibility.[233] More egregiously, disclosure in the form of highly market-sensitive information such as earnings can be fraudulently manipulated to increase the value of share options.

As discussed in Part B, disclosure is emerging as a key mechanism for managing remuneration across the EU and across the dispersed ownership/blockholding faultline, albeit to different degrees particularly with respect to individual and aggregate remuneration. Disclosure is also strongly supported in the Commission's Company Law Action Plan (Part C) which emphasizes the importance of shareholder understanding of the link between company performance and remuneration. As a regulatory mechanism, it has considerable appeal as a non-aggressive form of intervention in bridging the difficult divide between governance systems and responses to remuneration across the EU. It also acts as a bulwark against the core conflict of interest dilemma which remuneration potentially generates in dispersed ownership and blockholding systems (which is recognized by the Commission – see Part C). Nonetheless, as the varying responses to remuneration examined in Part B reveal, disclosure also exposes deep cultural divides as to the primacy of personal privacy in pay across the EC.

VI. Beyond the Incentive Alignment Justification: Is There a Role for Fairness?

Unqualified acceptance of the validity of the link between performance-based remuneration and shareholder interests can lead to an abdication by the board of any responsibility to exercise restraint in setting remuneration and the removal of any upper limit on remuneration, subject only, in effect, to the restrictions of the

[231] See K Chauvin and C Shenoy 'Stock Price Decreases Prior to Executive Stock Option Grants' (2001) 7 J Corp Fin 53, 59-60 on the various ways executives can manipulate information.

[232] eg Chauvin and Shenoy (2001) n 231. Similar results are found in D Aboody and R Kasznik 'CEO Stock Option Awards and Corporate Voluntary Disclosures' (2000) 29 Journal of Accounting and Economics 1. Where option grant dates are variable and manipulation of disclosure thus more difficult, there is evidence that CEOs time the award dates before positive news announcements: Yermack (1995) n 72 and Aboody and Kasznik, ibid.

[233] Yablon and Hill (2000) n 230, 89 and 115.

'outrage constraint'. The quantum of pay is, however, increasingly under review. In particular, fairness and equity might suggest that, even accepting the value of performance-based pay, executives should not garner such a high proportion of the gains generated by incentive contracts and that some consideration should be given to the appropriate proportion of the gain which should be allocated to management.[234] Very high levels of executive remuneration can also damage employee relations, particularly in an economic downturn when cuts are imposed on a labour force.[235] Salary negotiations with employees can be disrupted and, more seriously, productivity and, ultimately, the share price damaged when employee morale is prejudiced by a huge differential between executive and other remuneration.[236] It has also been suggested that very high levels of executive remuneration are a problem for social policy generally[237] and provoke greater and growing inequality of income.[238]

More generally, economic growth can be prejudiced if fewer talented managers engage in entrepreneurial new business activity if it seems that greater returns are available in the management of established companies. Very high levels of executive remuneration may distort the traditional distinction in risk/reward structures as between entrepreneurs/investors and managers. Traditionally, managers of established companies take smaller risks and reap smaller rewards. Very high payouts to executives may, however, change this balance and result in the creation of a privileged corporate class, which has not had to pay for shares, is protected to a considerable extent from downside risk, and disincentivized toward entrepreneurship.[239] There may also be societal implications if the

[234] The view that there is a dimension other than market dynamics to executive remuneration seems to be gaining currency. The President of the New York Federal Reserve, eg, has asked, with reference to the gap between executive and average worker pay, whether or not there should be 'both economic and moral limitations on the gaps created by the market-driven system' and stated that huge increases in executive compensation were 'terribly bad social policy and perhaps even bad morals': A Hill 'Rations and rewards after a year of turbulence' *Financial Times* (24 February 2003). Conversely, recent research suggests that CEOs 'are not constrained by common ethical norms' and that they have 'a different sense of fairness from that of the person in the street': Research by the Academy of Management, reported in M Skapinker, 'CEO: (n) greedy liar with personality disorder *Financial Times* (2 July 2003).

[235] Loewenstein (1996) n 12, 223.

[236] Cheffins (1997) n 56, 658. On the lowering of morale problem see L Barris 'The Overcompensation Problem: A Collective Approach to Controlling Executive Pay' (1992) 68 Indiana Law Journal 59, 67, 69-70. It is not entirely clear, however, whether management remuneration does impact on employee morale: see generally B Main 'Top Executive Pay: Tournament or Teamwork' (1993) 11 J of Labour Econ 606.

[237] Loewenstein (1996) n 12, 216.

[238] Yablon (1999) n 11, 274. One reason for the disparity in remuneration packages between the US and UK may be the historically greater tolerance of income disparity if it is driven by hard work, talent, and entrepreneurialism: Conyon and Murphy (2000) n 23, F667.

[239] Yablon (1999) n 11, 274, 295, and 299-301.

most talented and energetic pursue managerial careers, as opposed to entrepreneurial projects, or, indeed, socially beneficial careers in, for example, the public services, but become frustrated at their failure to make it to the very top of a managerial pyramid where rewards for the senior management group might appear limitless.[240]

As revealed by Part B, quantum and fairness issues are not generally addressed by EU Member States, which leave such issues, and structural pay questions generally, to be determined by market forces. The sharp difference in approaches to pay between dispersed ownership and blockholding systems (section VII) also weaken the applicability of the fairness/outrage argument on a pan-EU basis, particularly when the cultural distaste of high pay in some Member States, particularly Germany, is factored in.[241] The focus currently remains, at both Member State and EU level, on the supporting governance/disclosure matrix, rather than on the details of particular pay structures.

VII. Executive Remuneration as a Particular Problem of Dispersed Ownership

The problems with remuneration discussed above are particularly acute in the dispersed ownership company, where remuneration is used to remedy the agency costs inherent in the divergence of interests between management and shareholders. While information asymmetries with respect to management behaviour also exist in the blockholding-based companies which are a feature of continental governance, blockholding shareholders with long term commitments to the company should wield sufficient influence and power to access information on performance and on operations and to control management. They should also be motivated to do so in that they suffer less from the collective action problem faced under the dispersed ownership governance model.[242]

Remuneration which is linked to share price is also less likely to be attractive to managers where a publicly traded, but closely held, company has only a small 'free float'. In such circumstances, the problemmatic link between managerial performance and share price becomes even more opaque as there is a greater possibility of the share price being influenced by noise.[243] While an increasing number of continental companies are being publicly traded, core concentrated ownership is not being fully dismantled through initial public offerings and list-

[240] Yablon (1999) n 11, 295, 301-303.

[241] See generally Cheffins (2001b) n 114.

[242] For a discussion of the dynamics of blockholder monitoring see, eg, M Roe 'Some Differences in Corporate Structure in Germany, Japan, and the United States' (1993) 102 YLJ 1979-1981.

[243] B Cheffins 'Will Executive Pay Globalise Along American Lines' 11 (2003) Corporate Governance 8, 12.

ings. In many continental European countries (but particularly Belgium) the public offering has been limited to what is necessary to meet listing requirements.[244] One study has reported that, from a sample of 55 initial public offerings (IPOs), pre-IPO shareholders retained 76.4% of the voting rights in Germany and, within 6 years of offering, the original shareholders still retained 45% of the voting rights.[245] Concentrated ownership should also, as long as the CEO and senior management do not form part of the controlling shareholder group, limit the possibility for remuneration-setting to be captured by managerial power and transformed into a process of rent extraction.[246] In addition, the supervisory board which features in a number of two-tier continental governance systems provides an important management-control mechanism and, in particular, provides financial institutions with a forum for monitoring management. Labour co-determination, or the mandatory (in Germany and the Netherlands) representation of labour on the supervisory board, is also likely to keep executive remuneration at politically acceptable levels.

The sharp differences in their degree of reliance on high-powered incentives, particularly share options, between UK, US, and continental companies seem to bear out the link between remuneration and the reduction of the agency costs generated by dispersed ownership.[247] The difference with US pay is particularly striking: one review has reported that, for a typical US CEO, the basic pay pack-

[244] Becht and Mayer (2001) n 35, 8.

[245] M Goergen *Corporate Governance and Financial Performance: A Study of German and UK Initial Offerings* (Elgar London 1998), cited in Becht and Mayer (2001) n 35, 7. The comparable statistics for the UK, by contrast, were 62.8% and 30%.

[246] Bebchuk et al (2002) n 4, 844-845. They note, however, that where there is a controlling group (which may include the CEO) other possibilities for rent extraction, such as self-dealing and the taking of business opportunities, arise and that restricting remuneration may provide a mechanism for camouflaging the overall rent which is being extracted. Under dispersed systems of ownership, specifically the US, maximizing remuneration is the only means available to executives to extract rents.

[247] eg M Conyon and J Schwalbach 'Corporate governance, executive pay, and performance in Europe' in Carpenter and Yermack n 30, 13, 24 who find (based on 1995 data) that across Europe the value of long-term incentives as a percentage of total remuneration is highest in the UK and that long term incentives are not used to any extent in other European economies. For an extensive pan-EC analysis of remuneration practices in the context of the blockholder/dispersed ownership faultline, based on the 2001 disclosure made available by publicly quoted companies, see Ferrarini et al n 44. For Germany specifically, see generally Cheffins (2001b) n 114. For evidence from Italy that the presence of strong shareholders tends to decrease the likelihood of high-powered incentive contracts being adopted see G Brunello, C Graziano, and B Parigi 'Executive Compensation and Firm Performance in Italy' (2001) 19 International Journal of Industrial Organization 133. For a similar perspective see R Crespi and C Gispert 'Board Remuneration, Performance and Corporate Governance in Large Spanish Companies' SSRN (1998) who have found evidence that ownership concentration can act as a substitute for monitoring via the incentive contract and thus lower the pay/performance relation (at 9-11).

age (excluding variable/performance elements) is higher than the total package in Germany, Spain, Sweden and Switzerland.[248] As is clear from Part B, the correlation between governance and remuneration also appears in legal responses in terms of the degree of rigour with which regimes pursue conflict of interest management, good governance, and disclosure, and how they prioritize the concerns potentially raised by executive remuneration. In common with all areas of the executive remuneration debate, the picture is, however, cloudy. The link between share price and remuneration, which lies at the root of many of the criticisms directed at Anglo-American remuneration, is not absent from blockholding systems. One study has shown that managers in both the US and in Germany are more likely to lose their jobs following poor share price performance, while compensation for executives in Germany is also tied to short-term measures such as share price performance and cash flow.[249] Another study has concluded that, across Europe, CEO cash compensation is higher in countries with two-tier boards, notwithstanding the higher level of monitoring that might be expected, although the gap closes when non-cash compensation is factored in, and that countries with two-tier boards have an 'ambiguous relationship' with CEO remuneration.[250]

The 'excessive' remuneration problem and the danger that executive remuneration represents rent-seeking by management may therefore be a cost of the dispersed ownership company and thus not amenable to pan-EC responses. While executive remuneration does not appear to have posed, so far, a significant problem for continental European corporate governance, that system does, however, pose a different set of problems, particularly with respect to the conflict of interest between large, blockholding shareholders and minority shareholders.[251] The picture may be changing, which suggests that the degree of convergence which is emerging on the matrix of governance controls which support the remuneration process, and the Commission's decision to address remuneration as a core conflict of interest and shareholder information problem (Part C), is to be welcomed. A number of factors, including the growing equity culture and focus on shareholder value in Europe which is encouraged by the securities market reforms contained in the EC's Financial Services Action Plan, activism by Anglo-American institutional investors and by a new generation of EC institutional investors in the form of collective investment schemes, international competition in the market for executives, evidence of some movement towards more widely held companies and a (limited) loosening of control by family and government block-

[248] Towers Perrin Worldwide Remuneration Survey (2000), reported in Becht et al (2001) n 26, 97.

[249] Kaplan (1999) n 30, 6-9. He does, however, concede the very sharp divergence in incentive structure that opens up when share option remuneration is considered (at 11).

[250] Conyon and Schwalbach (1999) n 247, 26 and 29.

[251] eg Garrido and Rojo (2002) n 43, 433-434.

holders as continental companies increasingly access the equity markets,[252] may all provoke greater convergence in corporate governance and, where dispersed ownership asserts itself, in remuneration practices along Anglo-American lines.[253] Nonetheless, the faultline between both systems calls for particular care in the adoption of pan-EC reforms to executive remuneration and, in particular, in the transplanting of reforms based on the Anglo-American experience.

B. Comparative Overview

I. Introduction

EU Member States, broadly speaking, adopt a twin-track approach to executive remuneration and focus on company disclosure and on corporate governance structures and procedures. The purpose of Part B is to analyse these strategies with reference to both public regulation and corporate governance best practices (as set out in national reports and private codes). Section II and III concentrate on annual disclosure and consider whether a report, or similar information, must be published on remuneration policy. The analysis also includes a review of whether disclosure as to executive pay must be detailed and individualized, or, less rigorously, general and aggregated. The review distinguishes between particular groups of countries, depending on the approach followed by the relevant national rules or practices. Section IV and V examine the role of corporate governance structures in executive pay and focus, in particular, on remuneration committees and shareholders' powers concerning remuneration policy. Section VI concludes.

II. Annual Disclosure (1): Member States Requiring Detailed Information

1. General

The role of disclosure as a remedy for agency costs has been analysed in Part A, section V above. Firstly, disclosure may sharpen shareholder monitoring. The

[252] See G Hertig 'Western Europe's Corporate Governance Dilemma' in T Baums, K Hopt and N Horn (eds) *Corporations, Capital Markets and Business in the Law* (Kluwer London 2000) 265, 267.

[253] With respect to the link between greater dispersal of ownership and executive remuneration practices see: Cheffins (2003) n 243 and Hertig (2000) n 252. The extent to which convergence towards dispersed ownership is likely to happen, and the dynamics of the driving legal, political, and market forces, is a multi-faceted and controversial subject outside the scope of this discussion. For a recent view from one of the debate's leading commentators see J Coffee 'The Rise of Dispersed Ownership: The Roles of Law and the State in the Separation of Ownership and Control' (2001) 111 YLJ 1.

publication of detailed information on remuneration packages, policies, and procedures empowers shareholders (particularly institutional investors) in reviewing board decisions on pay and enhances their ability to react to abuses effectively. Secondly, exposure to public scrutiny should also induce the board of directors to exercise care in setting executive remuneration, particularly with respect to performance links. This section's analysis of EU disclosure will be limited to annual disclosure. All the Member States considered accept the principle of maximum transparency as to disclosure of directors' pay. They implement this principle with varying degrees of intensity, however, which may reflect the different ownership structures of listed companies and thus the distinct ways in which the core agency costs problem is perceived across the different jurisdictions.

2. United Kingdom and Ireland

The UK and Ireland are, witbout doubt, considerably the most advanced of all the States considered with respect to remuneration disclosure. In the UK, following the 2002 revisions to the Companies Act 1985 (set out in the Directors' Remuneration Report Regulation 2002), directors are now required to prepare a Directors' Remuneration Report for each financial year, which contains the detailed information specified in the new Schedule 7A to the Companies Act 1985 (Companies Act s234B(1)). The Report must be approved by the Board of Directors and signed on behalf of the Board by a director or the secretary of the company (s234C(1)). The company's auditors must also include in their report on the annual accounts a report on the auditable part of the Directors' Remuneration Report and state whether, in their opinion, that part of the Report has been properly prepared in accordance with the Companies Act (s235(4)).

The Directors' Remuneration Report must be published on a yearly basis (Companies Act s234B(1)) and laid before the general meeting of shareholders for approval (s241 and s241A). Like the annual accounts, the directors' report, and the auditor's report on the accounts, wide publication is required: the Report must be sent to every member of the company, every holder of the company's debentures, and every person who is entitled to receive notice of general meetings, within 21 days of the general meeting before which these documents are laid (s238). A copy of the Directors' Remuneration Report, together with the annual accounts, the directors' report and the auditors' report must also be filed with the Registrar of Companies before the end of the period for 'laying and delivering' accounts, which for public companies is 7 months after the relevant accounting reference period (Companies Act s242 and s244).[254]

[254] Instead of sending the accounts, directors' report, and Directors' Remuneration Report to the entitled persons listed in Companies Act s238, listed companies are permitted to send such persons a summary financial statement of the relevant documents (s251). The summary

cont. ...

The Remuneration Report is subject to very extensive disclosure requirements. In particular, it should include the following information (Companies Act 1985, Sch 7A, Part 3, s2-5):

(i) *Remuneration Committee*. Where a committee of the directors has considered directors' remuneration for the relevant financial year, the Directors' Remuneration Report must name each director who was a member of the committee at any time when the committee was considering remuneration (s2(1)(a)). Significantly, given the difficulties raised by conflicts of interests with remuneration consultants, the Report must also name any person who provided the committee with advice or services that materially assisted the committee and state the nature of any other services that person provided the company with during the relevant financial year and whether that person was appointed by the committee (s2(1)(b) and (c)).

(ii) *Remuneration Policy*. The Report must also include a statement of the company's remuneration policy for the following financial year and for subsequent financial years (s3(1)). This statement must include, for each director, a detailed summary of any performance conditions to which any entitlement to share options or under a long term incentive scheme is subject, an explanation of why such performance conditions were chosen, and a summary of the methods used in assessing whether the conditions are met (s3(2)). The policy statement must also, in respect of each director's remuneration terms and conditions, explain the relative importance of those elements which are, and are not, related to performance (s3(3)). Finally, the statement must summarise and explain the company's policy on the duration of contracts with directors and on notice periods and termination payments under such contracts.

A significant innovation in the Directors' Remuneration Report, which seems to institutionalize the link between remuneration and share performance, is the requirement for a performance graph,[255] which sets out the total shareholder

financial statement must include the following from the Directors' Remuneration Report: the statement of the company's policy on remuneration; and the Performance Graph (see below).

[255] Under s4(1)(a) and (b), s4(2), and s4(3), a line graph must show for (i) a holding of shares of that class of the company's equity share capital whose listing or admission to dealing has resulted in the company being listed for the purpose of the application of the remuneration report requirement and (ii) a hypothetical holding of shares, made of shares of the same kinds and number as those by reference to which a broad equity market index is calculated, a line drawn by joining up points plotted to represent for each of the financial years over a five year period, of which the last is the relevant financial year (to which the Report relates), the total shareholder return on that holding. It must also state the name of the index used and the reasons for choosing it. Where the company has been reporting for less than five years, the period is 2, 3, or 4 years, as the case may be. In its first financial year, the period is the relevant financial year.

return[256] of the company on its equity capital (s4(1)). In addition, the following information must be provided, under s5, in respect of the contract of service or contract for services of each person who served as a director at any time during the relevant financial year: the date of the contract, the unexpired term, and details of any notice periods; any provision for compensation payable upon early termination; and details of other provisions in the contract as are necessary to enable members of the company to estimate the liability of the company in the event of early termination. Section 5 has important implications for disclosure, and institutional investor activity in particular, given the current controversy as to rewards for failure in the UK.

(iii) *Detailed Audited Financial Information*. Detailed, individual disclosure is required, for each person who has served as a director at any time during the relevant financial year, as follows:

- emoluments (Companies Act 1985, Sch 7A, Part 3, s6(1)-(4));[257]
- share options (s7-9): detailed information is required.[258] This information must, however, be aggregated and simplified where the directors are of the

[256] Total shareholder return is calculated (s4(4)) using a 'fair method' which: takes as its starting point the percentage change over the period in the market price of the holding; makes specified assumptions as to reinvestment of income and funding of liabilities (see s4(5) and 4(7)); and makes provision for any replacement of shares in the holding by shares of a different description. The same method must be used for each of the holdings.

[257] In tabular form in respect of each director: total amount of salary and fees (s6(1)(a)); total amount of bonuses (s6(1)(b)); total amount of expenses chargeable to UK tax (s6(1)(c)); total amount of compensation for loss of office and other payments in connection with termination of qualifying services (s6(1)(d)); total estimated value of non-cash benefits not covered elsewhere (s6(1)(e)); total amount of (a)-(e). In addition, the total amount from (a)-(e) must be shown for each director for the previous financial year (s6(2)). The Report must also specify the nature of any non-cash elements of the remuneration package (s6(3)).

[258] In tabular form in respect of each director: (a) the number of shares subject to a share option at the beginning of the relevant financial year (or, if later, on the date of the director's appointment as a director) and at the end of the relevant financial year. A distinction should be made between share options with different terms and conditions (s8(a)); (b) information identifying: those share options awarded in the relevant financial year; those exercised in that year; those that have expired unexercised; and those whose terms and conditions have been varied in that year (s8(b)); (c) for each unexpired share option: the price paid, if any, for its award; the exercise price; the exercise date; and the expiry date (s8(c)); (d) a description of any variation made in the relevant year to the terms and conditions of a share option (s8(d)); (e) a summary of any performance criteria upon which the award of an option is conditional, including a description of any variations made to these criteria during the relevant financial year (s8(e)); (f) for each option exercised during the relevant financial year, the market price of the shares in relation to which it is exercised at the time of exercise (s8(f)); and (g) for each unexpired option at the end of the relevant financial year: the market price at the end of the year; and the highest and lowest market price during that year of each share subject to the option (s8(g)).

opinion that full disclosure would result in 'excessively lengthy' reports (s7(2) and s9(1));
- long term incentive plans, excluding any information already provided under the share option rules (s10-11);
- pensions (s12);
- sums paid to third parties in respect of directors' duties (s15).

By contrast with the UK regime, a specific remuneration report is not required as matter of Irish company law, although the UK Listing Authority's Listing Rules, which also apply to companies listed on the Irish Stock Exchange (with minor revisions) do require that the Board reports, in the annual report and accounts, to shareholders on remuneration.[259] In particular, under Listing Rule 12.43(c), the annual reports and accounts must contain a remuneration report from the board, which includes individual disclosure, to shareholders. The 12.43(c) Report must contain:

- a statement of the company's policy on executive directors' remuneration;
- for each director by name and for the period under review, the amount of each element in the remuneration package for the period under review;
- in tabular form, and for each director by name, information on share options;
- details of any long-term incentive schemes, other than share option schemes previously disclosed;
- explanation and justification of any element of salary, other than basic salary, which is pensionable;
- a statement of the company's policy on the granting of options or awards under employee share schemes and other long term incentive schemes;
- detailed disclosure on defined benefit pensions schemes, particularly with respect to transfer value.

3. France and Italy

Under French law, while a specific remuneration report is not required, the directors' annual report must indicate the total amount of compensation and benefits awarded to each corporate officer (*Code de Commerce*, Art. L225-102-1 – it also applies to non-listed companies). In addition, best practice recommends that the annual reports of listed companies include a chapter, drafted with the compensation committee's assistance, on corporate officers' compensation (see *Viénot 2nd Report* p. 23, and *Bouton Report* p. 13). The board of directors must also submit to the shareholders' AGM a special report concerning stock options and stock grants to directors. The report must indicate the number of options or

[259] The Listing Rules on remuneration disclosure are likely to be repealed in the UK, however, following the 2002 Remuneration Report regime.

shares which executive directors are allowed either to exercise or purchase during the year, their expiration date, and exercise price. The same information is required for options and shares bought or subscribed by directors during the year (*Code de Commerce*, Art. L225-184 – also applicable to non-listed companies). These rules also apply to the company's ten most senior employees.

A specific remuneration report is, likewise, not required in Italy. The Italian Exchange recommends, however, the inclusion, in the corporate governance report, of summary information on the remuneration system adopted which specifies whether the remuneration paid to executive directors and senior managers is linked to the company's results or the achievement of specific objectives. Similar information should also be provided on stock option plans, if any. In addition, listed companies must indicate in the notes to the accounts the remuneration paid to each director, member of the board of auditors, and general manager (Consob Regulation 11971/1999 art. 78). Such information must be presented in tabular form and include: fees, including those fixed by the shareholders' ordinary meeting, contingent profit sharing, attendance money, and flat expenses refunds; non-monetary benefits, including fringe benefits and insurance policies; bonuses and other rewards (not including stock options); and other fees, including those received from subsidiaries, salaries, and retirement bonuses (Consob Regulation 11971/1999 Annex 3C Scheme 1).

Details of stock options and stock grants to each director and general manager by name must be disclosed in the notes to the accounts (Consob Regulation 11971/1999 art. 78). This information must be presented in tabular form and include: options held at the beginning of the period under review; options granted and options exercised during that period, together with the spot price at the moment of the exercise; options expired in that period; and options held at the end of that period. A description is also required of the major elements of the company's stock option plans in order to provide full disclosure as to the principles and aims which characterize the plans. The disclosure requirements also apply to directors and general managers employed by the company. Stock grants are to be accounted for as options vested, and immediately exercised, with a strike price equal to zero (Consob Regulation 11971/1999 Annex 3C Scheme 2). Consob (the Italian stock exchange regulator) recommends that the company's management report include disclosure concerning stock option plans which have been adopted, including, but not restricted to: the reasons for the plan; a short description of the plan; the amount of shares involved; the offerees; the terms and the conditions of grant and exercise; and, if the plan is particularly important, its duration, together with an indication of the options held and vested at the end and beginning of the period under review, options granted, exercised and expired during the period, and strike prices and the spot prices (Consob Communication 11508/2000).

4. Netherlands and Sweden

Since 1 September 2002 Dutch 'open' public companies[260] must disclose the amount of each director's remuneration for the relevant financial year in the explanatory notes to their annual financial statements (Art. 283c, Book 2, Civil Code).[261] The amount of each type of remuneration should be specified, such as periodic remuneration, long-term schemes, termination payments, profit sharing schemes and bonuses.[262] Additional requirements apply where members of either the management board or the supervisory board are granted the right to acquire shares in the company's capital (Art. 283d). In this case, the company must disclose, for each member: the strike price and the price of the company's shares at the time of the grant (if lower than the strike price); the number of unexercised rights at the beginning of the financial year; the number of rights granted in the course of the financial year and the relevant conditions (any change of conditions should also be reported); the number of rights exercised together with the number of shares purchased and the relevant strike price; the number of unexercised rights at the end of the financial year, the relevant strike price, the time for the exercise of those rights and other data useful for their valuation; and the conditions, if any, applicable to the granting and exercise of those rights. In addition, Art. 391, para. 2, Civil Code, requires that the company's annual financial statements include a report on remuneration policy with respect to directors and supervisory board members, and disclose how this policy was implemented in the relevant financial year.

In Sweden, listing agreements require disclosure of senior executives' remuneration by incorporation of a recommendation of the Swedish Industry and Commerce Stock Exchange Committee (*Näringslivets Börskommitté – NBK*)[263] to this effect. This recommendation is directed to Swedish and foreign companies whose shares or depository receipts are listed on a Swedish stock exchange or authorized marketplace.[264] The recommendation is incorporated as a binding

260 'Open' public companies include all companies of the NV type, with the exclusion of NVs who (1) only have registered shares (and so do not have bearer shares) (2) have restrictions on the transfer of shares and (3) whose articles do not allow for the issue of depository receipts of shares in bearer form.

261 This provision also requires a report on each former director's remuneration, to the extent it was paid in the relevant financial year. For former members of the management board, long-term payable remuneration and termination payments should also be specified.

262 If the company paid a bonus which is (partly) based on the achievement of stated targets, information must be given on whether these targets were achieved in the relevant financial year. If the company made a profit sharing or bonus payment to members of the supervisory board, the reasons for granting this type of remuneration must be reported separately.

263 Available in English at <www.naringslivetsborskommitte.se>.

264 Foreign companies listed in Sweden can, however, obtain an exemption from these rules and will often do so.

annex to the listing agreements, so that non-compliance with the same is sanctionable. Listed companies' annual reports must provide information concerning remuneration and other benefits which senior executives receive from the company.[265] 'Senior executives' are: the chairman of the board; other directors who receive remuneration from the company in addition to the customary director's fee and who are not employed by the company; the managing director; the group chief executive (if any); and certain salaried executives in the company's senior management team. The disclosure must include the remuneration and benefits provided by all group companies, whether Swedish or foreign. The company must specify the criteria adopted for senior executives' remuneration, with particular regard to fixed and variable remuneration and the proportion of the same. Information must also be provided for each 'top manager'[266] regarding: the total amount of remuneration and other benefits; all remuneration items which are not of minor importance; the fixed and variable components of remuneration, including the main criteria applied for the calculation of variable remuneration;[267] financial instruments, options or entitlements received during the year in connection with incentive programmes linked to share prices, and the estimated market value on the date of allotment and the acquisition price;[268] financial instruments, other options or entitlements received during previous years in connection with incentive programmes linked to share prices; and agreements concerning future pensions and severance payments.

Information shall also be provided on the preparatory and decision-making process followed by the company when determining remuneration for top management. Such information should include whether or not a compensation committee has been appointed and, if so, its mandate and composition. If a compensation committee has been established, it is required, nonetheless, that deci-

[265] If the benefits received by senior executives change significantly during the year, this must be made public in the first interim report.

[266] In the NBK's recommendation, the chairman of the board, relevant members of the board, the group chief executive and the managing director are defined as 'top management'. The expression 'other senior executives' refers to persons who are not members of this group. Normally, this applies to persons employed by the company who constitute the group management team or corresponding unit, which also includes the managing director.

[267] In the case of variable remuneration (bonuses, earnings-related payments and similar remuneration), the total amount is to be stated in the form of information regarding the amount charged against the company's profits for the year, and the main principles for calculating and determining the variable remuneration must be disclosed.

[268] This information must indicate whether or not the allotment involves a benefit (subsidy) for the individual concerned. If there is no established market value for the instrument in question, a theoretical value should be computed, in accordance with a generally recognized valuation model. In this connection, information must be provided concerning the major assumptions that have been applied.

sions regarding the managing director and the group chief executive, if any, be taken by the board.

III. Annual Disclosure (2): Member States Requiring Summary Information

1. General

In several European countries little disclosure is required as to executive remuneration and/or only aggregate data are published as to directors' pay. This practice is based on a long tradition of opacity in remuneration which is generally motivated by confidentiality concerns. The costs of disclosure, highlighted in Part A, section V.3, may also explain the publication of only summary information on executive pay. Firstly, enhanced disclosure may trigger political reactions and public hostility to the company if the level of pay is perceived as excessive. In addition, labour and unions may try to interfere with the remuneration setting process and the board may, as a result, become distracted by these pressures from setting optimal remuneration. Secondly, disclosure may result in an increase in pay due to a ratcheting effect. All this may have determined most of the disclosure rules and practices that are described below, on the increasingly questionable assumption that the benefits of full transparency in remuneration would be overwhelmed by its costs. Recent corporate governance codes adopted in some of the countries considered, however, go in the direction of full disclosure, as shown in the following paragraphs.

2. Germany and Austria

In Germany, information on directors' remuneration (management board and supervisory board) is included in the notes to the consolidated financial statements in aggregate form. According to section 285, number 9, Commercial Code, companies must publish the total, aggregate remuneration (salaries, profit sharing, dividend rights, expense allowances, insurance payments, commissions, and fringe benefits of every kind) of the management board membership separately from the aggregate remuneration figure for the supervisory board membership. Pension payments are disclosed separately for all former members of the management and supervisory board.

With respect to German best practice, the Cromme Code specifies in 4.2.4 that the compensation of management board members which is reported in the notes to the financial statements be subdivided according to fixed, performance-related, and long-term incentive components, and disclosed on an individual basis. The same information should be published (in the notes) with respect to the compensation of members of the supervisory board. All remuneration should be subdivided according to its components and regard should be had to payments made by the company or advantages extended for services provided individually.

These payments and advantages are to be listed separately (Cromme Code 5.4.5). The Cromme Code also provides (7.1.3) that the consolidated financial statements contain specific information on company stock option programs and similar securities-based incentive schemes. Details of stock option plans or comparable compensation systems should also be disclosed in a suitable form (4.2.3). The most controversial aspect of the Cromme Commission's conclusions concerns the publication of management board members' individual remuneration in the financial reports. German business circles have traditionally avoided discussing executive remuneration. As a result, even blue chips like Allianz and Daimler-Chrysler do not comply with the relevant provision of the Code and explain that this would either level or prevent differentiated remuneration. Daimler-Chrysler also refers to the principle of collective responsibility.

Similarly, under Austrian law, the annual report must contain the total aggregate remuneration of the management board members (as a group) and of the supervisory board members (section 239 Commercial Code). Remuneration comprises salary, profit participation, reimbursement of expenses, insurance premiums, commissions and additional benefits of any kind. In addition to the statutory requirement to report the total remuneration of the management board, the Corporate Governance Code states that the fixed and performance-linked components of remuneration are to be disclosed in the annual report (para. 30). The Code also specifies that the management board's remuneration be reported on individually for each board member (para. 31). With respect to stock options, the annual report must indicate for members of the management board and the supervisory board, employees, and senior managers: the number and distribution of options granted and related shares; their essential terms, such as the exercise price or how it is to be computed, and the respective estimated values at the time they are issued; the transferability of options; and the periods in which the options can be granted and exercised and the period of lock up. Further disclosure is required as to the number, the distribution, and the exercise price of options exercised during the period under review (Corporate Governance Code para. 29; section 239 Commercial Code).

3. Spain, Belgium and Luxembourg

Section 200.12 of the Spanish Law on *Sociedades Anónimas* (LSA) requires aggregate disclosure of board members' remuneration.[269] The Olivencia Report

[269] The Transparency Act of 2003, No. 26 amended the LSA and the Securities Exchange Act of 1988, No. 24. The new section 116 of the Securities Exchange Act provides that listed companies shall annually publish a report on corporate governance including, among others, the identity and remuneration of the members of the board of directors and its committees. The contents of the annual report will be indicated by the Economic Ministry or by the Securities and Exchange Commission if so delegated by the Ministry.

(1998) recommended, however, the disclosure of directors' individual remuneration packages and specific disclosure, to the greatest extent possible, of the individual components of remuneration.[270] The recent Aldama Report (2003) noted the slow implementation of this recommendation, reiterating that full disclosure of directors' remuneration is a clear indicator of the quality of corporate governance. The Committee suggested that the annual report disclose each director's remuneration, breaking it down into its various components. With respect to executive directors, however, the Report stated that the amount received as a director (to be disclosed on an individual basis in the annual report) could be separated from the amount received as a manager: that amount would be included in the total remuneration of top management and reported as an aggregate amount. This amount would be specific as to cash salary, salary in kind, stock options, bonuses, pension schemes, indemnification provisions, and other compensation.

In Belgium, the Corporate Governance Recommendations issued by Euronext Brussels and the B.F.C. recommend the inclusion of a corporate governance section in the annual report[271] which should specify the total amount of the executive management's remuneration and the fixed and variable parts of the same. In addition, the principles, if any, governing the calculation of the variable part should be disclosed (para. 3.1). Under Belgian law, only the aggregate amount of directors' remuneration must be reported in the notes to the financial statements (Royal Decree of 30 January 2001).

In Luxembourg, listed companies are not required to publish a remuneration report or similar information. The annual accounts must specify the board's remuneration in aggregate, without providing the details of each director's pay. If, however, the board delegates the day to day management of the company to one of its members (which boards generally do), the remuneration paid to this executive director must be disclosed to the annual general meeting.

[270] The Olivencia Commission recommended that the policy of disclosing director remuneration should be inspired by the principle of maximum transparency which requires full and detailed disclosure of directors' remuneration, including fixed fees, per diems, profit-sharing, bonuses, incentives, pensions, insurance premiums, payments in kind, etc. The Commission recommended that companies choosing to implement transparency in stages should publicly disclose their reasons in the company's annual report. Companies should at least, however, disclose each director's remuneration. Executive directors' remuneration could be disclosed as an overall figure, with an indication of the number of directors in receipt of such remuneration under each of the remuneration headings. All this information should be included in the annual report.

[271] If the annual report constitutes a 'reference document' (shelf-registration procedure), it will also contain the information required by the Royal Decree of 18 September 1990 (prospectus).

4. Denmark and Finland

Under Danish law, the annual report must disclose the aggregate remuneration paid to the board of directors in the relevant financial year (Art. 69 of the Annual Accounts Act). The report must also disclose any incentive programs that include members of the board of directors or board of management, including the categories of members included, the kinds of benefits involved, and the information necessary to evaluate the program. In addition, according to the rules issued by the Copenhagen Stock Exchange,[272] the annual report must contain information on any parts of the program that have not been exercised by the expiry of the relevant financial year and disclose the non-exercised parts which relate to members of the board of directors, members of the management board, and other members of senior management, respectively. According to the Nørby Committee's recommendations, the remuneration of each board member and member of management under share-based incentive programs should be disclosed, individually, in the annual report.

In Finland, a remuneration report is not required. Information on the collective remuneration of the board members is published in the annual report, as required by general company law[273] and by the law relating to listed companies.[274] The guidelines of the Helsinki Stock Exchange recommend, however, additional disclosure with respect to the chairman of the Board concerning the general principles applicable to bonus programmes and pension plans; termina-

[272] Under the listing rules issued by the Copenhagen Stock Exchange, Part II, paragraph 3, section 19, issuers that adopt share-based incentive programs must immediately disclose certain information with respect to such programs. The disclosure obligation must include, as a minimum, information on (i) the type of the share-based incentive program used, (ii) the categories of individuals included in the program, (iii) the time of the grant of rights, (iv) the aggregate number of shares underlying the program and the allocation of such shares among the categories of individuals included, (v) the goals pursued by the program, (vi) the period within which rights under the program may be exercised, (vii) the exercise price, (viii) any particular conditions that will have to be met in order for the beneficiaries to exercise their rights, and (ix) the market value of the share-based incentive program, including a description of the valuation method and the basic assumptions underlying the valuation. Also, the adoption of extraordinary bonus programs must be disclosed.

[273] Chapter 2, para 8, of the Accounting Ordinance, which applies to all companies (including listed companies), provides that the following information should be published with respect to the members of the board of directors collectively: salaries and other compensation for their duties; total amount of loans granted to them and relevant conditions; total amount of guarantees and contingent liabilities; and pension commitments related to their duties.

[274] Chapter 2, para 5, of the Regulation of the Ministry of Finance (538/2002), which applies to listed companies, provides that information must be given with respect to members of the board of directors collectively on salaries and other compensation, benefits in kind, stock options and similar plans.

tion payments, terms of notice etc.; and stock options (amount of share capital to which the options refer, vesting date, price).

5. Greece and Portugal

A remuneration report is neither required nor recommended in Greece. Companies limited by shares (whether listed or not) must include in the notes to the financial statements details of the compensation paid to all members of the board of directors and managers. No distinction is made as to the nature of the compensation. Termination payments must also be indicated. This information may be omitted if, through its disclosure, a member of the board of directors and his or her income may be identified (Section 43a of the Law 2190/1920).

In Portugal, listed companies subject to the Portuguese 'lex societatis' are required to publish a report on corporate governance, to be presented either as a chapter of the annual management report or as an appendix to the same report. This chapter must include details as to the remuneration of members of the board of directors' as a whole, distinguishing between executive and non-executive members, and between the fixed and variable parts of their remuneration (article 1/1/d of CMVM's Regulation nº 7/2001).

IV. Corporate Governance (1): the Remuneration Committee

1. The Remuneration-Setting Process

As argued in Part A, section IV, adoption of an optimal remuneration contract is dependent on the remuneration-setting process taking place in an adversarial manner between self-interested parties seeking to maximize their interests. Governance controls should increase the possibility that this process maximizes shareholder interests, and does not become a skimming process in which the board is captured by management. In Anglo-American corporate governance two devices have been developed to reduce the risk of a board's capture: the appointment of independent directors to the board and the creation of a remuneration committee composed of non-executive/independent directors. The merits and limits of these institutions were analysed in sections IV.2 and IV.3 of Part A. In this section, the rules and practices governing remuneration-setting will be analysed with reference to those EU Member States in which listed companies are recommended to form remuneration committees within their board of directors or supervisory board (depending on whether a one-tier or two-tier system or both are in place under national law). This analysis will show that the institutions of the independent director and the remuneration committee have been transplanted to continental corporate governance, albeit in forms which do not always correspond to the original model. In this respect, the ways in which the institutions in question were adapted to different contexts such as concentrated ownership and two-tier governance structures presents an interesting study of the transplanting of governance structures across governance systems.

2. United Kingdom and Ireland

In both countries listed companies should, in accordance with the Listing Rules' Combined Code, (which operates on a comply or explain basis) establish a formal and transparent procedure for developing policy on executive remuneration and for fixing the remuneration packages of individual directors. In particular, no director should be involved in deciding his or her own remuneration (Combined Code B.2). A remuneration committee should make recommendations to the board on the company's framework of executive remuneration and its cost and should determine on behalf of the board of directors specific remuneration packages for each of the executive directors (B.2.1) More generally, the chairman of the board should ensure that the company maintains contact as required with its principal shareholders with respect to remuneration, in the same way as for other matters (B.2.6). The remuneration committee should also consult the chairman and/or managing director about its proposals relating to the remuneration of other executive directors and have access to professional advice inside and outside the company (B.2.5). The committee should consist exclusively of non-executive directors who are independent of management and free from any business or other relationship which could materially interfere with the exercise of their independent judgement (B.2.2).

With regard to remuneration policy, the remuneration committee should provide the remuneration packages needed to attract, retain and motivate executive directors without paying more than is necessary for this purpose, and should be aware of what comparable companies are paying and take account of relative performance (B.1.1 and B.1.2). But they should use such comparisons with caution, in view of the risk that they can result in an upward ratchet of remuneration levels with no corresponding improvement in performance (B.1.2). Remuneration committees should also be sensitive to the 'wider scene', including pay and performance conditions elsewhere in the group, particularly when determining annual salary increases (B.1.3). The Code also recommends that the performance-related elements of remuneration should form a significant proportion of the total remuneration package of executive directors and should be designed to align their interests with those of shareholders and to give these directors keen incentives to perform at the highest levels (B.1.4).

3. France, Italy and Spain

Under French law, the board of directors can create special committees for specific purposes (Art. 93, *Décret* n. 67-236) while best practice recommends the creation of a remuneration committee (Bouton Report). In the one-tier governance system, the executive directors' remuneration is fixed by the board of directors acting on a proposal from the compensation committee (Art. L.225-45, L.225-47 and 225-53, *Code de Commerce*; Art. 93, *Décret* n. 67-236; Bouton Report, p. 13 f.). In the two-tier system, the '*directoire*' members' remuneration is fixed by the supervisory board acting on a proposal from the compensation committee (art. L. 225 63). The remuneration committee should not include any corporate officers and should have a majority of independent directors. (Bouton Report, p. 14). A director is independent when he or she has no relationship of any kind whatsoever with the corporation, its group, or the management of either that is such as to colour his or her judgment. (Bouton Report, p. 9).[275]

The main task of the remuneration committee concerns the determination of the performance-related aspects of directors' compensation. It should fix general rules for its determination and verify every year if these rules are followed by the board of directors. The Bouton Report also recommends that the general policy governing option grants be discussed within the remuneration committee and that this committee issue recommendations to the board of directors. This policy, which should be reasonable and suited to the needs of the company, should be presented in the annual report and during a general meeting of shareholders when a resolution on the granting of stock options is on the agenda (Bouton Report, p. 16). Further, the committee should be kept informed of policy governing the remuneration of the main executive managers who are not corporate officers. The committee may call upon the participation of the corporate officers in this area. (Bouton Report, p. 15).

Similarly, in Italy the board of directors determines executive directors' remuneration upon a proposal of the remuneration committee, after consulting the board of auditors (Art. 1.2 Corporate Governance Code).[276] This committee also submits proposals on the remuneration framework for the company's senior

[275] The Bouton Report lists the criteria that the committee and the board should examine in order to determine whether a director can be called 'independent' and to avoid the risk of conflict of interests between the director and executive management. With respect to the appointment of independent directors, the Code Bouton recommends that the board of directors should always create a nominating committee, that may or may not be distinct from the remuneration committee, which 'should organize a procedure designed to select future independent directors, and carry out its own research on potential candidates before they have been approached in any way' (Code Bouton, p. 17). The board of directors should review on a case by case basis the situation of each member with regard to the criteria mentioned above, then make known to the shareholders, in the annual report and at any general meeting of shareholders at which any directors are to be elected, the results of its review, so that the designation of independent directors is not carried out only by the company's executive management but by the board itself (Code Bouton, 8).

[276] The recent company law reform (which will enter into force on January 1 2004) has introduced two new governance systems (one-tier and two-tier), in addition to the system, traditional in Italy, of a board of directors and a board of statutory auditors. The Corporate Governance Code has yet to be amended to reflect the new system.

management (Corporate Governance Code art. 8.1). The Corporate Governance Code specifies that the majority of the remuneration committee's members should be non-executive directors. Executive directors could, therefore, also be members of the committee. They will, however, abstain from voting on resolutions concerning their own remuneration. As a matter of practice, in some companies most of the remuneration committee's members are independent, in the sense that they have no material relationships with the company which may influence their objectivity (Corporate Governance Code artt. 3.1, 8.1).[277]

In Spain, the Olivencia Report recommended the formation of a remuneration committee to assist the board in setting and supervising remuneration policy for directors and senior executives. This Report suggested that board committees, such as the remuneration committee, should consist only of non-executive directors with a proportion between 'domanial' (i.e. non-executive directors representing the controlling shareholders) and independent directors similar to that found on the board. The Aldama Report also recommends that listed companies establish an appointment and remuneration committee (*Comisión de Nombramientos y Retribuciones*) whose members should be chosen in accordance with the proportion of non-executive directors (Domanial and Independent) on the board. This committee should report to the board on appointments, re-elections, dismissals and remuneration of directors and on the remuneration policy for the board and top management. The board of directors is to adopt rules for the operation of the remuneration committee, which are included in its by-laws (*Reglamento del Consejo de Administración*).

4. Belgium, Luxembourg and Netherlands

The Belgian Corporate Governance Recommendations suggest the formation of a remuneration committee composed of a majority of non-executive directors. Executive directors can, therefore, also be members of the committee, the formation of which should be disclosed in the annual report. Similarly, in Luxembourg the appointment of a remuneration committee by the board of directors is strongly recommended by the Stock Exchange and is becoming common practice for

[277] A director is independent if he has, or has recently had, no direct or indirect business relationships, including on behalf of third parties, with the company, its subsidiaries, the executive directors or the shareholder or group of shareholders who controls the company of a significance such that his objective judgement is influenced; furthermore he should not own, directly or indirectly or on behalf of third parties, a quantity of shares enabling him to control the company or exercise a considerable influence over it nor participate in shareholders' agreements to control the company; he is also not allowed to have immediate family relations with members of executive directors of the company or of persons in the situations referred above (Corporate Governance Code 3.1).

listed companies.[278] In the Netherlands a similar approach applies. The Dutch Peters report recommends the establishment of a remuneration committee to assess all forms of remuneration, stock options, pension rights, termination payments and liability insurance. This committee should consist of supervisory board members and report its findings and make recommendations to the full supervisory board. Its existence should be reported in the annual financial report. It is expected that the 2003 Corporate Governance Committee will further elaborate on the role of the remuneration committee and its membership.

5. Austria and Germany

The Austrian Corporate Governance Code generally provides that the supervisory board is to set up expert committees from among its members, depending on the specific circumstances of the enterprise and the number of supervisory board members. The human resources committee, if any, will be responsible for the remuneration of the management board.[279] The chair of the human resources committee will always also be the chair of the supervisory board. Where there are less than six members of the supervisory board (including employees' representatives), this committee's function may be assumed jointly by the board. The human resources committee may also act as the strategy committee. The Code provides that the rights of co-determination of employees' representatives are to apply to all committees of the supervisory board; the committee responsible for employment contracts with management board members may, however, be set up without employees' representatives.

Similarly, in Germany the Cromme Code does not expressly require that a remuneration committee be created; it indicates, however, that this is good practice for many corporations. Depending on the individual company and the number of its members, the supervisory board is to form committees (5.3.1 Cromme Code). The subjects which can be delegated to and handled by one or several committees include the compensation of the members of the management board (Cromme Code 5.3.3). All members of the supervisory board are independent, but only to the extent that they cannot be, at the same time, members of the management board. Former members of the management board or employees may, however, be members of the supervisory board. According to the Cromme Code (5.4.2) not more than two former members of the management board can be members of the supervisory board and members of the supervisory board may not

[278] Remuneration committees comprise one or more independent directors and either make proposals to the board or, if so entrusted by the board, set executive remuneration directly.

[279] The committee deals with human resources issues relating to management board members and with succession planning. In particular, the committee decides on the terms of employment contracts with management board members and on their compensation.

hold directorships or similar positions or engage in advisory tasks for important competitors of the enterprise. In addition, all committees that handle contracts with members of the management board are to be chaired by the chairman of the supervisory board (Cromme Code 5.2).

V. Corporate Governance (2): Shareholder Monitoring

1. Role of the Ownership Structure

Section IV.5 of Part A argued that shareholders could represent an important direct monitor on whether an optimal incentive contract is adopted and that the mechanisms available to shareholders include removing directors (in the case of inappropriate pay decisions) and voting on pay policy or particular pay packages. This form of monitoring is particularly relevant for diffuse ownership companies, where institutional investors are often regarded as potentially strong corporate monitors, despite the well-known problems of shareholder activism. In the case of concentrated ownership companies, strong blockholders can influence the setting of executive pay through mechanisms such as the control of the board's majority and close ties with the executive directors. Therefore, the minority shareholders need to be protected from the abuses of controlling shareholders, particularly when they are also managers of the company. Clearly, discussion of company remuneration policy in the shareholder general meeting can benefit minorities by exerting pressure on the dominant blockholders. However, the role of the general meeting is different when ownership is diffuse and institutional investors own a large percentage of the share capital. This may explain why continental countries attribute a limited function to the general meeting with reference to executive pay, while the UK has recently enhanced the role of this meeting, as shown below.

2. United Kingdom and Ireland

As discussed in Part B section II.2, the UK Companies Act now provides that a directors' remuneration report must be published on a yearly basis and laid before the general meeting of shareholders for approval. The fact that shareholders can exercise an advisory vote on the company's remuneration policy is likely to enhance shareholder activism in this area, as confirmed by recent actions taken by institutional investors in the annual meetings of large UK companies (see Part A, section IV.5 above).

In addition, both in the UK and in Ireland, employees' share schemes and long-term incentive schemes are subject to shareholder approval, and detailed procedural and disclosure requirements, under the Listing Rules. The following schemes must be approved by an ordinary resolution of the shareholders of the company in general meeting prior to their adoption: (i) an employees' share scheme if the scheme involves or may involve the issue of new shares; and (ii) a long-term incentive scheme in which one or more directors of the issuer is eligible to participate (Listing Rule 13.13). With respect to these schemes, a number of disclosure rules apply under Listing Rule 13.14.[280] A resolution approving the adoption of an employees' share scheme or long-term incentive scheme may authorise the directors to establish further schemes.

With regard to discounted option arrangements, a listed company may not, without the prior approval by an ordinary resolution of the shareholders of the listed company in general meeting, grant to a director or employee of the issuer or of any subsidiary undertaking of the issuer an option to subscribe, warrant to subscribe or other similar right to subscribe for shares in the capital of the issuer or any of its subsidiary undertakings, if the price per share payable on the exercise of such an option, warrant or other similar right to subscribe is less than whichever of the following is used to calculate the exercise price: the market value of the share on the date when the exercise price is determined; the market value of the share on the business day before such date; or the average of the market values for a number of dealing days within a period not exceeding 30 days immediately preceding such date (Listing Rules 13.30).

[280] The circular to shareholders in connection with the approval of an employees' share scheme or a long-term incentive scheme must: include either the full text of the scheme or a description of its principal terms (13.14(a)); include, where directors of the company are trustees of the scheme, or have a direct or indirect interest in the trustees, details of such trusteeship or interest (13.14 (b)); state that the provisions (if any) relating to: the persons to whom, or for whom, securities, cash or other benefits are provided under the scheme (the 'participants'); limitations on the number or amount of the securities, cash or other benefits subject to the scheme; the maximum entitlement for any one participant; the basis for determining a participant's entitlement to, and the terms of, securities, cash or other benefit to be provided and for the adjustment thereof (if any) in the event of a capitalisation issue, rights issue or open offer, sub-division or consolidation of shares or reduction of capital or any other variation of capital: cannot be altered to the advantage of participants without the prior approval of shareholders in general meeting (except for minor amendments to benefit the administration of the scheme, to take account of a change in legislation or to obtain or maintain favourable tax, exchange control or regulatory treatment for participants in the scheme or for the company operating the scheme or for members of its group) (13.14(c)); state whether benefits under the scheme will be pensionable and, if so, the reasons for this (13.14(d)); if the scheme is not circulated to shareholders, include a statement that will be available for inspection: from the date of the dispatch of the circular until the close of the relevant general meeting, at a place in or near the City of London or such other place as the FSA (the UK regulator, which incorporates the UK Listing Authority) may determine; and at the place of the general meeting for at least 15 minutes prior to and during the meeting (13.14(e)); and comply with the relevant requirements of the contents of all circulars (13.14(f)). The resolution contained in the notice of meeting accompanying the circular must refer either to the scheme itself (if circulated to shareholders) or to the summary of its principal terms included in the circular. (Listing Rules 13.15).

3. Continental Europe

In continental Member States, the role of the shareholder meeting, as a mechanism for shareholder remuneration monitoring, is generally limited to the adoption of stock option plans. A shareholder resolution is mainly required to the extent that the plan involves the issue of new shares when the options are exercised.[281] Similarly, stock grants need to be approved by the shareholders if new shares are issued. Therefore, it is the issue of new shares and not the adoption of an incentive scheme that requires shareholder approval. The fact that shareholders are called to a vote, however, may have an impact on the company's remuneration policy, particularly where the board must justify the incentive plan proposed to the shareholders and this requires *ex ante* disclosure of the main elements of the plan.[282]

French law, however, is distinctive in this context, as it requires a shareholder resolution (to be adopted on the basis of a report by the auditors) for all stock option plans, independently of whether the share capital is to be raised or not. The general meeting of shareholders authorizes the granting of options, sets their maximum number, and determines the main conditions of the same (Art. L. 225-177). The board of directors specifies the conditions of the stock options program.[283]

[281] For instance, in Germany stock options are subject to the power of the general meeting to raise capital. Section 192 Stock Corporation Act provides that the general meeting may adopt a resolution on a contingent capital increase to grant employees and members of the management board rights to new shares. However, the par value of contingent capital may not exceed ten per cent of the share capital as at the date of the adoption of the resolution. In addition, section 193 provides that in the case of a contingent capital increase the general meeting determines the purpose of the contingent capital increase, the persons entitled to subscribe the new shares, the issue price or the basis on which such price is to be computed and, if the persons entitled to subscribe are directors, the performance that shall be achieved, the periods in which the options can be granted and exercised and the period of lock up (at least two years).

[282] For instance, in Italy, where a resolution by the shareholders' meeting is required, a directors' report on the relevant operations must be available to the public at the registered office of the company and at the stock exchange company at least fifteen days before the shareholders' meeting. Consob recommends that the report specify the reasons for the transaction, the offerees, the price of the issue, the specific conditions of the plan, and the amount of the increase, enclosing the plan, where available, in the report (Consob Regulation 11971/1999 Artt 66, 72, 73, Annex 3A Schemes 2-4; Consob Communication 11508/2000).

[283] These conditions can prohibit the immediate resale of the shares or part of them. The prohibition must not last for more than three years from the exercise of the options (*Code de Commerce*, Art L225-177).

VI. Convergence or Divergence?

Overall, in terms of regulatory devices, the role of public regulation is relatively important, on a pan-EU basis, for disclosure of executive pay, while best practices and private codes generally have some impact on the way in which executive compensation is set for listed companies. The ownership structure of European companies is also, to a considerable extent, reflected by regulation, particularly given that the remuneration problem is more acute in diffuse ownership systems. This may help to explain why both public and private rules on executive pay appear to be more developed in the UK and Ireland than in continental Europe. Similarly, the lower level of ownership concentration in France may explain why the French regulatory model in this area is closer to the British model than to the German one.

On the whole, there is some convergence in continental Europe towards the Anglo-American model. The merits of full disclosure of executive remuneration are increasingly acknowledged in corporate governance codes and reports, while the use of remuneration committees is on the rise in the continent. This is not to say that corporate executive remuneration practices will soon be uniform. On the one hand, many companies still refuse to implement the principle of full disclosure, even in countries where the same is recommended as best practice; on the other, institutions like the remuneration committee are not easily transplanted in systems which are characterized by concentrated ownership or two-tier governance structures. In addition, the role of the shareholder meeting in the remuneration-setting process is still debatable, particularly with respect to concentrated ownership structures. Furthermore, adopting principles such as full disclosure and institutions like the remuneration committee also requires the introduction of detailed and effective regulations in the relevant areas as well as their consistent implementation. Otherwise, convergence will be purely nominal and path dependence will prevail, as often seems to be the case in corporate governance.

C. Reform Perspectives

I. The 2002 Winter Report and the 2003 Company Law Action Plan

While individual Member States are, therefore, making some progress in this field, executive remuneration has recently emerged as a question of pan-EU corporate governance in two important reports. The 2002 Winter Report (Annex 3 in this volume) presented proposals on corporate governance in the EU and, specifically, the modernisation of company law, including executive remuneration controls. The Commission's response, and its plan for specific legislative action, is set out in the May 2003 Company Law Action Plan (Annex 1 in this volume). Common to both reports is a concern with the core conflicts of interests problem generated by the remuneration-setting process, as well as an awareness of the dangers in transplanting corporate governance control mechanisms between blockholding and dispersed ownership systems. The Company Law Action Plan, for example, characterizes executive remuneration as a key conflicts of interests problem with respect to executive directors, and calls for remuneration to be set exclusively by non-executive directors who are, reflecting the prevalence of strong blockholders in continental governance, in the majority independent (para 3.1.3).

Process rules, designed to re-adjust the bargaining process, are a common feature of the reform agenda. The Winter Group followed a similar approach, noting that 'the level and form of remuneration of executive directors should be left to the companies and their shareholders' and insisting on 'appropriate governance controls, based on adequate information rights' (Chapter III, para.4.2). Specifically, the Group suggested that the creation of remuneration committees, composed of 'non-executive or supervisory directors who are in the majority independent', be required (para.2). The Group rejected, however, the Anglo-American requirement that remuneration committees should consist entirely of independent directors, noting that 'in Europe, we have to take account of particular situations relevant to board structures, like the existence of controlling shareholders and boards which are partly co-determined by employees.' The Group also argued that the EU should not adopt binding legislation in this area, as it would be 'inflexible and not responsive to local and changing needs and conditions'. It argued that a Commission Recommendation be issued stating that either national company laws or corporate governance codes should adopt provisions concerning remuneration committees, their composition and functioning.

The Group's generally light touch with respect to governance is reflected in its reliance on disclosure, and particularly individual disclosure, as a further control on remuneration. The Report recommended, in particular, that directors' remuneration policy should be disclosed in the financial statements of the company. In addition, the remuneration of individual directors, both executive and non-executive or supervisory directors, should be disclosed in detail in the annual financial statements of the company. Disclosure should cover all financial and non-financial benefits derived from the company, including golden parachutes and pension rights. Finally, the Report called for the effective accounting of share option plans and recommended that the costs to the company of these schemes should be accounted for in the annual accounts, as also proposed by IASB.[284]

Direct shareholder monitoring mechanisms were also addressed, albeit on a limited scale. Inclusion of the remuneration report as an explicit item on the AGM agenda was recommended, but, reflecting the governance faultline in the EU, the Group did not suggest that a vote on remuneration policy, as provided by UK company law, be required. It considered that 'the effects of such a vote can be different from Member State to Member State' and felt that 'the important thing is that shareholders annually have an opportunity to debate the [remuneration] policy with the board.' The Report recommended, however, that share

[284] See the chapter by K Crook in this volume chapter II. 5.

grants and share options schemes, other share incentive schemes, and any substantial change in the same, be subject to the prior approval of the shareholders' meeting. This approval would relate to the scheme as such and not to the individual remuneration of directors under the scheme.

The Commission's Company Law Action Plan broadly reflects the Winter Group's approach and proposes a governance/disclosure matrix designed to minimise conflicts of interests in remuneration setting and inform shareholders (para 3.1.2). The Commission has recommended that listed companies, on a comply or explain basis, should devolve remuneration-setting to a committee composed exclusively of non-executive directors, who, following the Winter Group's approach, would be, in the majority, independent. The Commission is to establish minimum parameters for 'independence', which will include a consideration of interlocking directorships and the number of non-executive mandates which may be held concurrently. The remuneration committee proposals, which will cover its creation, form, and composition, will take the form of a Recommendation, a non-interventionist form of Community measure (supported by the Winter Group) which allows sensitivity to Member State governance systems and culture, but should also further promote the convergence in good governance currently underway, among certain Member States at least.

Disclosure is the second key element in the Commission's approach. Undercutting the disclosure proposals is the Commission's support of the need for shareholders to 'appreciate fully' the relationship between company performance and remuneration. A Recommendation is to be proposed which will cover four key disclosure requirements: disclosure of remuneration policy in the annual accounts; disclosure of individual directors' remuneration in the annual accounts; proper recognition of the costs of shares and share options schemes in the annual accounts; and prior approval by the shareholders' of share and share option schemes. Additional rule-making on remuneration is, expressly, not ruled out.

The share/share option scheme requirement also represents, as in the Winter Report, the Commission's limited coverage of direct shareholder monitoring, clearly reflecting the different roles played by the AGM and blockholders across the EU governance faultline. More generally, however, the Commission has proposed revising the financial services directives to strengthen the role played by institutional investors in good corporate governance and, thus, the control of remuneration (para 3.1.1). They will be obliged to disclose their investment and voting policy and to disclose to their beneficial holders, at their request, how voting rights have been used in a particular case. The Commission has decided against, however, requiring institutional investors to vote, presumably concerned as to the risk of a 'box-ticking' culture, particularly where investors are not sufficiently informed on governance issues.

These proposals appear reasonable, particularly given the limits imposed by the EU's cultural and governance faultline in executive pay, in that they reflect Anglo-American best practices, while taking into account some of the particular features of continental corporate governance. The use of remuneration committees is already common in a sizeable number of EU countries, as shown in Part B, section IV. A Commission Recommendation could enhance this practice and contribute to its extension to the remaining Member States. Disclosure of remuneration policy is likewise already required in some Member State, although particular national requirements differ. The implementation of the Commission's approach will require the selecting of disclosure standards for remuneration policy which are acceptable at the European level if the new regime is to be effective. These standards should also be compatible with capital market conditions and with the corporate governance structures of all Member States. From this perspective, the standards recently adopted by UK company law appear to be too demanding for other countries. While the disclosure of individual remuneration is a requirement in several Member States, in other States a tradition of opaqueness dominates and only aggregate data are published. The publication of detailed and individualized information in all countries may, therefore, only be achieved if required by EU legislation. In this regard, the Commission's reliance on a Recommendation may not be sufficient to dislodge the entrenched distrust of individualized disclosure in some Member States.

II. Reform Problems

There are, however, limits to the reform process, including those reforms suggested by the Winter Group and the Commission. Shareholder-focused solutions, be they via direct mechanisms or indirect disclosure requirements, face the general difficulty of how to promote shareholder activism given the collective action problem. Disclosure requires careful consideration of the nature of the information disclosed to shareholders and the market. Process reforms may only improve the extent to which remuneration contracts are adopted in the interests of shareholders: they cannot eliminate all the difficulties from an inherently conflicted process.

Other reforms address structural problems (an approach not followed by the Winter Group or the Commission) and seek a better alignment of shareholder and management interests by, for example, a closer focus on performance targets through the use of indexed options and the linking of option exercise to performance targets, a clearer demarcation of downside risk burdens via the elimination of repricing, and greater reliance on share, as opposed to option-based remuneration, by the grant of restricted shares rather than options. There is, however, a need for flexibility.[285] Arguably the problem is not with types of remuneration, but with the process under which it is adopted. If the process is secure, remuneration contracts should contain incentives which align incentives appropriately.

[285] Kole (1997) has stressed the importance of board flexibility in designing remuneration: note 72.

Another reform strategy is to reject the basic premise of the performance-based incentive contract and reduce levels of remuneration artificially. Direct government intervention in the remuneration market in the form of caps on remuneration, such as a mandatory linking between executive pay and multiples of an average employee salary, has been raised as a reform strategy.[286] Difficulties abound with this approach, however, including the risk that employee salaries become distorted to deliver high remuneration levels.[287] The tax system can also be used via higher rate taxes and caps on the deductibility of remuneration.[288] The complexities and difficulties of this area suggest, however, that it is not possible to specify a particular form for, much less the appropriate amount of, remuneration.[289]

Ultimately, remuneration should be set by a correctly functioning market and reflect the particular requirements of the company's ownership and monitoring structure, and not be imposed artificially by government. To the extent that regulation is imposed, it should seek to reset the market mechanism. Regulation of process or structure carries the danger of entrenching structural aspects of remuneration which are more appropriately left to the market, which will fine-tune them over time.[290] Requiring, for example, the disclosure in remuneration reports of relative performance graphs which show how share values compare against peer groups (see Part B, section II.2), may entrench share performance as the correct indicator of performance.[291] While it may be the most effective way of aligning incentives, problems remain with share values as performance indicators, particularly given the danger of generating perverse short-termist incentives to distort the share price. Law is also less adaptable. Any changes made through the tax system will prove difficult to unravel if they prove damaging to executive performance and incentives. The debate on executive remuneration also continues to shift. With respect to share options, while the focus in the 1980s in the US was on the greater use of share options in order to link remuneration more closely to shareholder wealth, it has now shifted to how to ensure that executives do not

[286] Paul Myners has suggested that companies compare executive remuneration over time with growth in average employee salaries, rather than with remuneration of executives at other companies: Cohen (2003) n 210. A number of legal systems intervene more gently, with rules requiring that remuneration be 'reasonable': Cheffins (2003) n 243.

[287] See Murphy (1995) n 61, 727-728 and Cheffins (1997) n 56, 701-705. Caps rarely work in practice. Cheffins (2003) points to the Argentinian experience. While remuneration is limited to a proportion of profits, Argentinian CEOs are among the world's most highly paid. N 243, 15.

[288] Yablon (1999) n 11, 274-275.

[289] Yablon (1992) n 79, 1867.

[290] Yablon (1992) n 79, 1889.

[291] Murphy (1995) n 61, 736.

benefit unfairly from windfall market gains as opposed to company-specific performance. Legal solutions may therefore entrench, rather than solve, problems.

III. Conclusion

The executive remuneration problem can be characterized in a number of different ways which are difficult to reconcile when it comes to identifying whether there is a problem in need of reform and the appropriate solutions, particularly on a pan-EU basis. If problems with executive remuneration are regarded as aspects of the core agency problem of dispersed ownership, light-touch regulation which addresses the incentive contract structure and process may be called for. But if the incentive anchor is removed, and the concern is with wider fairness and wealth distribution, difficult balancing questions come into play. The different constituencies involved, employees, shareholders, the public and so on, have different and often irreconcilable concerns. In the EU context, executive remuneration can also be analyzed as exposing another fissure in the faultline between dispersed ownership and blockholding ownership corporate governance systems. In this regard, it forms part of a much wider debate as to the competing advantages and disadvantages of market-based and relationship-based corporate governance.

It is easier to find problems than solutions in this field,[292] particularly on a pan-EU basis where remuneration plays different roles and is subject to different controls according to the governance system. In principle, remuneration contracts are needed to encourage the risk-taking and value-generating entrepreneurs which shareholders want and economies need. There is certainly some doubt that the appealing theory underpinning incentive contracts is not always reflected in practice. This is particularly the case where gains from large share option grants appear unrelated to performance and governance problems exist. The costs of monitoring via remuneration contracts may, however, include the inevitability of a certain level of self-interested behaviour by directors and management which cannot be completely removed.[293] In the absence of some clear evidence of a market failure it seems dangerous to pull down the edifice of performance-related pay, particularly given that there is some evidence of a link between incentive pay and company performance.[294] Ultimately, from the agency/dispersed ownership perspective, minimizing agency costs is not cost-free, but a properly structured

[292] Cheffins (1997) n 56, 706. The point has been well made that executive remuneration is 'the most intractable conundrum in global corporate governance': J Plender 'An assault on boardroom excess' *Financial Times* (14 March 2002) cited in Cheffins (2003) n 243, 8.

[293] Yablon (1999) n 11, 275.

[294] Loewenstein (1996) n 12, 205. The leading study in support of the rent extraction argument (Bebchuk et al (2002) n 4) has acknowledged that the potential for rents does not mean that remuneration schemes never serve shareholders' interests (755).

performance-based contract, balanced as to equity-based and cash remuneration and buttressed by appropriate controls on the negotiation process, may represent one of the best ways to align shareholder and management interests in the context of dispersed ownership. Similarly, while conflicts of interests in remuneration-setting can also arise at board level in blockholding companies, and while remuneration may become an instrument to oppress minority shareholders, incentive contracts remain critical to corporate success, particularly if blockholding control diminishes across the EU.

Overall, a focus on an effective governance/disclosure matrix, as proposed by the Winter Report and the Commission, and as reflected across most EU Member States, may be the best way to calibrate remuneration appropriately. Effective disclosure as to structure and process, allied to greater shareholder activism, may be the least costly approach, as the excesses of the 1990s may be about to be consigned to history as share prices remain depressed and, post Enron *et al*, executive performance remains under the close scrutiny of the financial press. Closer scrutiny of remuneration practices by shareholders can also be expected if company share performances continue to be poor. Managers may also start negotiating for a greater proportion of their remuneration to be in the form of fixed pay, as a bulwark against the poor state of the equity markets.[295] There certainly seems to be some evidence of a move away from US-style option-based remuneration packages in the UK and of a more aggressive focus on performance standards. Even in the US, remuneration committees appear to be exercising restraint.[296] In particular, the dominance of share options may be weakening as companies move towards aligning interests more closely by granting restricted shares, which tie managers more closely to sustained share price performance.[297]

The time may not be right for dramatic intervention given that a shift appears to be underway with respect to remuneration. Further, the complexities of this area, the opacity of the empirical data, and fundamental differences between dispersed and concentrated ownership-based governance systems, caution against any wholesale transplanting of remuneration structures and rationales, empirical evidence, and regulatory responses between the US, the UK, and continental Europe.

[295] See Cheffins (2003) n 243, 11. Annual cash bonuses are increasing in the UK: Tassell (2003) n 225.

[296] In February 2003 the *Financial Times* reported that: 'compensation experts, governance activists and unions all agree that the composition of senior executives' remuneration will change this year. Some companies ... have already announced cuts in bonuses, stock option awards or perks': Hill (2003) n 234.

[297] Hill (2003) n 234.

Accounting for Share-Based Remuneration

KIMBERLEY CROOK*

Although accounting for share-based remuneration is controversial, national and international accounting standard-setting bodies have consistently concluded that all forms of share-based remuneration, including employee share options, result in expenses that should be recognised in an entity's financial statements. The IASB has recently issued proposals to that effect. This paper sets out the background to the IASB's project on the topic – including the accounting issues involved, current US accounting requirements, and recent changes in the political environment surrounding the topic – and outlines the IASB's progress to date in developing an accounting standard on share-based remuneration.

A. Introduction

'The most egregious case of let's-not-face-up-to-reality behaviour by executives and accountants has occurred in the world of stock options. In Berkshire's 1985 annual report, I laid out my opinions about the use and misuse of options. But even when options are structured properly, they are accounted for in ways that make no sense. The lack of logic is not accidental: For decades, much of the business world has waged war against accounting rulemakers, trying to keep the costs of stock options from being reflected in the profits of the corporations that issue them…It seems to me that the realities of stock options can be summarized quite simply: If options aren't a form of compensation, what are they? If compensation isn't an expense, what is it? And if expenses shouldn't go into the calculation of earnings, where in the world should they go?'[1]

Accounting for share-based remuneration, and employee share options in particular, is controversial, as indicated by Mr Buffett's comments above. Yet national and international accounting standard-setting bodies have consistently

* Any views expressed in this paper are those of the author. Official positions of the IASB are found in International Financial Reporting Standards and other IASB publications.

[1] Warren E Buffett, 1992 Letter to the Shareholders of Berkshire Hathaway Inc.

concluded that all forms of share-based remuneration, including employee share options, result in expenses that should be recognised in an entity's financial statements.[2] However, at present, few countries have accounting standards on the topic and many believe those standards that do exist are inadequate or outdated. The IASB sees its project as an opportunity to provide leadership and a basis for convergence.[3]

This paper is set out as follows. The first section gives an overview of the accounting issues considered by standard-setters. The following section sets of the US accounting requirements, because the US is one of the few countries to have accounting guidance on share-based remuneration. Next, the IASB project is outlined. During the course of the IASB's project, there have been changes to the political environment surrounding the topic, which are noted in this section. In the final section, some concluding comments are given.

B. Overview of the Accounting Issues

The main issues when developing an accounting standard on share-based remuneration can be summarised as follows:

- Whether it is appropriate to recognise share-based payment transactions in an entity's financial statements, in particular, transactions involving employee share options
- if such transactions are recognised, what measurement basis should be applied
- at which date that measurement basis should be applied.

As noted earlier, accounting standard-setters have consistently concluded that entities should recognise share-based remuneration in their financial statements. In reaching that conclusion, standard-setters have considered various arguments

[2] eg US Accounting Principles Board (APB), Opinion no 25 'Accounting for Stock Issued to Employees' (1972); US Financial Accounting Standards Board (FASB), Statement of Financial Accounting Standards no 123 'Accounting for Stock-Based Compansation' (1995); G4+1 Group, Discussion Paper 'Accounting for Share-Based Payment' IASC (2000) (The G4+1 Group comprised members of the national accounting standard-setting bodies of Australia, Canada, New Zealand, the UK and the US, and the International Accounting Standards Committee (the IASB's predecessor body); Danish Institute of State Authorised Public Accountants (FSR) 'The Accounting Treatment of Share-Based Payment' (2000); German Accounting Standards Committee (GASC) 'Accounting for Share Options Plans and Similar Compensation Arrangements' (2001); Canadian Accounting Standards Board 'FYI' October 2001 at <www.cica.ca/multimedia/Download_Library/Standards/Accounting/English/e_FYI1001.pdf>; UK Accounting Standards Board, Financial Reporting Exposure Draft FRED 31 'Share-Based Payment' (2002) and International Accounting Standards Board (IASB) ED 2 'Share-Based Payment' (2002) at <www. iasb.org.uk>.

[3] IASB, Press Release 2 August 2001 'IASB Announces Agenda of Technical Projects'.

made against such recognition. These arguments include conceptual arguments, in which respondents to standard-setters' proposals argue against expense recognition in principle, and practical arguments, in which respondents argue against recognition in practice. These arguments, and the IASB's conclusions thereon, are set out in the Appendix.

The issue of recognition is linked to both measurement issues. For example, if a transaction in which share options are granted to employees is measured at the intrinsic value of the share options (the difference between the market price of the underlying shares and the exercise price of the options) at the date the options are granted, the resulting amount 'recognised' is typically zero, because often the exercise price of employee share options is set at the market price of the shares at the date of grant.[4] Hence, in many cases, valuing share options at their intrinsic value at grant date is equivalent to attributing no value to the options.

However, as noted by the IASB,[5] the intrinsic value of an option does not fully reflect its value. Options sell in the market for more than their intrinsic value. This is because the holder of an option need not exercise it immediately and benefits from the right to participate in future gains from increases in the share price. In addition, the option holder benefits from the right to defer payment of the exercise price until the end of the option term. These benefits are commonly referred to as the option's 'time value'.

For many employee share options, time value represents a substantial part of their value. As noted earlier, many employee options have zero intrinsic value at grant date, and hence the option's value at that date consists entirely of time value.

Since the development of option pricing models, which take into account both the intrinsic value and time value of options, accounting standard-setters have consistently concluded that share options should be measured at their fair value.[6] In reaching that conclusion, standard-setters have considered and rejected the argument that it is not possible to measure reliably the fair value of employee share options. The IASB's conclusions on this issue are set out in the Appendix.

There is one point on measurement reliability that is not addressed in the IASB's conclusions[7], because it is a corporate governance issue rather than an accounting issue, although it is noted by the G4+1 Group:[8]

[4] IASB, ED 2 'Share-Based Payment' (2002).

[5] ibid.

[6] eg US FASB 'Accounting for Stock-Based Compensation' (n 2); G4+1 Group 'Accounting for Share-Based Payment' (n 2); FSR 'The Accounting Treatment of Share-Based Payment' (n 2); GASC 'Accounting for Share Options Plans and Similar Compensation Arrangements' (n 2); Canadian ASB, 'FYI' (n 2); UK ASB 'Share-Based Payment' (n 2); and IASB 'Share-Based Payment' (n 2).

[7] IASB 'Share-Based Payment' (n 2).

[8] G4+1 Group 'Accounting for Share-Based Payment' (n 2).

'...there seem to be strong grounds for arguing that the fiduciary duties of directors should prevent them from issuing instruments whose value cannot be established within reasonable parameters' (paragraph 4.38).

A similar point has been made by other commentators, for example:

'The worst argument – the absolute worst – is the one most executives think is their best...the executive will say something like, 'I have not seen an accurate way of determining what value should be put on stock options.'...This is the most ridiculous thing I've ever heard. Why? Because the argument has to cut both ways. If there is no way to value these [options], then why in the world is he handing them out? How can he possibly know how many to hand out, and it whom... It's an admission that the CEO has no idea what the true expenses of the company are, and yet he insists on continuing to be allowed to operate in this fashion. Why did he give an employee 30,000 options as opposed to 3 million of just 300? He doesn't know... His own argument starkly reveals his complete incompetence in watching costs, and his unwillingness to ever do so. There's no possible way he should be left in charge...'.[9]

The other main issue noted above is the date at which to measure the fair value of share options, shares or other equity instruments granted. The dates considered by the IASB and other standard-setters were grant date, service date, vesting date and exercise date. In the context of an employee share option, grant date is when the entity and the employee enter into an agreement, whereby the employee is granted rights to the share option, provided that specified conditions are met, such as the employee's remaining in the entity's employ for a specified period. Service date is the date when the employee renders the services necessary to become unconditionally entitled to the option.[10] Vesting date is the date when the employee has satisfied all the conditions necessary to become entitled to the option. For example, if the employee is required to remain in the entity's employ for three years, vesting date is at the end of that three-year period. Exercise date is when the option is exercised.[11]

Most standard-setters have concluded that the fair value of share options and other equity instruments should be measured at grant date.[12] The exception is the G4+1 Group[13], which concluded that vesting date is the appropriate measurement

[9] Tim Picks 'CEOs as Central Bankers (Part 2)' *Financial Sense Online* 19 February 2003.

[10] Service date measurement theoretically requires the entity to measure the fair value of the option at each date when services are received. For pragmatic reasons, an approximation would probably be used, such as the fair value of the option at the end of each accounting period, or the value of the option measured at regular intervals during each accounting period.

[11] IASB 'Share-Based Payment' (n 2).

[12] eg FASB 'Accounting for Stock-Based Compensation' (n 2); FSR 'The Accounting Treatment of Share-Based Payment (n 2); GASC 'Accounting for Share Option Plans and Similar Compensation Arrangements' (n 2); IASB 'Share-Based Payment' (n 2).

[13] G4+1 Group 'Accounting for Share-Based Payment' (n 2).

date. In response to the IASB's invitation for comment on the proposals by the G4+1 Group, most respondents supported grant date as the appropriate measurement date. Amongst users of accounts, the majority supported grant date, but there was also a significant amount of support for exercise date, and also some support for vesting date. No respondents supported service date measurement.[14]

In general, arguments for these various measurement dates focus on determining the date at which an employee to whom a share option has been granted becomes an equity participant in the entity (ie is considered to be part of the ownership group). For example, supporters of grant date measurement argue that the granting of an option conveys to the employee an equity (ownership) interest in the entity at grant date; hence any subsequent changes in the value of the option are borne by the option holder in the capacity of an equity participant, not an employee. Supporters of vesting date measurement argue that an equity instrument is created only once performance by the employee (the fulfilment of the vesting conditions) is complete; hence it is only at vesting date that an equity instrument is created, giving the employee an equity (ownership) interest in the entity. Supporters of exercise date measurement regard option holders as merely potential owners of the entity. Hence, in their view, share options should be treated as liabilities rather than equity instruments; it is only when shares are issued upon exercise of the options that the option holder becomes part of the ownership group.[15]

The measurement date issue is therefore related to the distinction between liabilities and equity. The IASB based its conclusion that share options are equity instruments, which should be measured at grant date, on the definitions of liabilities and equity in its *Framework for the Preparation and Presentation of Financial Statements.*[16] It also noted that some support other measurement dates because they believe that the definitions in the IASB Framework should be revised. However, it concluded that such a revision should take place only after the implications of these suggested changes have been explored fully as part of a broader project to review those definitions.[17]

[14] IASB Website project summary page for share-based payment 2003, <www.iasb.org.uk>.

[15] G4+1 Group 'Accounting for Share-Based Payment' (n 2). Exercise date measurement also ensures the same accounting result for options and cash-settled share appreciation rights, which some regard as economically similar (IASB 'Share-Based Payment' (n 2)).

[16] IASB 'Framework for the Preparation and Presentation of Financial Statements' published by the IASC in 1989 and adopted by the IASB in 2001.

[17] IASB 'Share-Based Payment' (n 2).

C. U.S. Accounting Requirements

The main pronouncements of US GAAP on share-based remuneration are contained in Accounting Principles Board Opinion No. 25 *Accounting for Stock Issued to Employees* (APB 25), Statement of Financial Accounting Standards 123 *Accounting for Stock-Based Compensation* (SFAS 123), and related interpretations.

I. APB 25

APB 25 was issued in 1972. It deals with employee share plans only, and draws a distinction between non-performance-related (fixed) plans and performance-related and other variable plans.

For fixed plans, an expense is measured at intrinsic value (the difference between the share price and the exercise price), if any, at grant date. Typically, this results in no expense being recognised for fixed plans, because most options granted under fixed plans are granted 'at the money'.

For performance-related and other variable plans, an expense is measured at intrinsic value at the measurement date. The measurement date is when both the number of shares or options that the employee is entitled to receive and the exercise price are fixed. Because this measurement date is likely to be much later than grant date, any expense is subject to uncertainty and, if the share price is increasing, the expense for performance-related plans would be larger than for fixed plans.

In SFAS 123, the FASB noted that APB 25 is criticised for producing anomalous results and for lacking any underlying conceptual rationale. For example, the requirements of APB 25 typically result in the recognition of an expense for performance-related options but usually no expense is recognised for fixed options. This result is anomalous because fixed options are usually more valuable at grant date than performance-related options.

The G4+1 Group[18], in its discussion of US GAAP, noted that the different accounting treatments for fixed and performance-related plans had also had the perverse effect of discouraging entities from setting up performance-related employee share plans; there are relatively few performance-related plans in the US.

II. SFAS 123

SFAS 123 was issued in 1995. It requires recognition of share-based payment transactions with parties other than employees, based on the fair value of shares

[18] G4+1 Group 'Accounting for Share-Based Payment' (n 2).

or options issued. Entities are also encouraged, but not required, to apply the fair value accounting method in SFAS 123 to employee share-based remuneration. Generally speaking, SFAS 123 draws no distinction between fixed and performance-related plans.

If an entity applies the accounting method in APB 25 rather than that in SFAS 123, SFAS 123 requires disclosures of pro forma net income and earnings per share in the annual financial statements, as if the standard had been applied. Until recently, few entities had chosen to adopt SFAS 123 for transactions with employees (recent events are discussed in the following section).

The FASB regards SFAS 123 as superior to APB 25, and would have preferred recognition based on the fair value of employee options to be mandatory, not optional. The FASB decided to permit the disclosure-based alternative for political reasons, not because it thought that it was the best accounting solution:

> 'The debate on accounting for stock-based compensation unfortunately became so divisive that it threatened the Board's future working relationship with some its constituents. Eventually, the nature of the debate threatened the future of accounting standards setting in the private sector ... the Board decided that the extent of improvement in financial reporting that was envisaged when this project was added to its technical agenda ... was not attainable because the deliberate, logical consideration of issues that usually leads to improvement in financial reporting was no longer present. Therefore, the Board decided to specify as preferable and to encourage but not to require recognition of compensation cost for all stock-based employee compensation, with required disclosure of the pro forma effects of such recognition by entities that continue to apply Opinion 25... However, the Board ... continues to believe that disclosure is not an adequate substitute for recognition of assets, liabilities, equity, revenues and expenses in financial statements...The Board chose a disclosure-based solution for stock-based employee compensation to bring closure to the divisive debate on this issue – not because it believes that solution is the best way to improve financial accounting and reporting.'[19]

The political pressure on the FASB came not only from its constituents, particularly the corporate sector, but also from the US Congress. Congressional opposition, driven by major companies and special interest groups representing small high-tech companies, included the introduction of a bill that would have effectively destroyed the FASB's authority to set accounting standards.[20]

The result of the above requirements is that the accounting treatment of share-based remuneration differs, depending on whether the other party to the transaction is an employee or a party other than an employee, whether the remuneration is in the form of shares or options, and whether the entity chooses to apply SFAS 123 or APB 25 to transactions with employees.

[19] SFAS 123, paragraphs 57-62.

[20] MH Granof and SA Zeff 'Unaccountable in Washington' *The New York Times* (23 January 2002).

Having a choice of accounting methods is considered undesirable, because it reduces the comparability of financial statements.[21] US research finds that this choice has a significant impact on the reported income of companies. For example, research by Bear Stearns on the S&P 500 shows that, had the fair value measurement method in SFAS 123 been applied for the purposes of recognising an expense for employee stock-based compensation, the reported earnings of the S&P 500 companies would have been significantly lower, and that the effect is growing. The effect on reported earnings is substantial in some sectors, where companies make heavy use of options.

Table

The reduction in operating income of the S&P 500 when employee share-based remuneration is included, using the fair value measurement method in SFAS 123:

	1999	2000	2001
S&P 500 in total	5%	8%	12%
Networking Equipment (2)*	25%	41%	794%
Semiconductors (18)*	16%	23%	510%
Application Software (9)*	69%	102%	216%
Electronic Equipment & Instruments (10)*	11%	23%	101%

* number of companies in sector

In 2001, the reported total diluted earnings per share of the S&P 500 drops by 20 per cent when stock-based compensation is included (8% in 2000, 6% in 1999).

For the S&P 500 in total, pre-tax stock-based compensation increased by 30 per cent, from US$61.3 billion in 2000 to US$80 billion in 2001. There were 13 companies with pre-tax stock-based compensation exceeding US$1 billion.

Source: Bear Stearns, July 2002

D. IASB Project

The IASB added a project on share-based payment to its agenda in July 2001. In September 2001 the IASB invited additional comment on the proposals developed by G4+1 Group, as set out in the Discussion Paper *Accounting for Share-*

[21] For example, the IASB Framework notes: 'Users must...be able to compare the financial statements of different enterprises in order to evaluate their relative financial position, performance and changes in financial position. Hence, the measurement and display of the financial effect of like transactions and other events must be carried out in a consistent way...for different enterprises' (paragraph 39).

based Payment, published by the IASC, the IASB's predecessor body, and other members of the G4+1 Group in July 2000.

The IASB received over 250 comment letters. The majority of letters were from preparers of accounts, mostly from the US. There was a sharp contrast between the views of investors and other users of accounts, and the views of preparers of accounts (ie the corporate sector).

Investors and other users of accounts unanimously agreed with the proposal that share-based payment transactions should be recognised in the financial statements, including recognition of an expense in the income statement. Many explicitly refuted the arguments made by others against recognition. Users also expressed concern that current accounting requirements created a lack of transparency and caused economic distortions, which were detrimental to investors' interests.

In sharp contrast to the views of users, preparers were strongly opposed to the proposals in the Discussion Paper. Some disagreed with any form of recognition of employee share options. But most focused on practical issues rather than conceptual issues. In particular, most preparers disagreed with measuring employee share options at fair value. They stated that there is no reliable method to measure the fair value of employee stock options.

On a more general level, many US preparers were critical of the Board's decision to put share-based payment on its agenda, saying that the USA had already been through this debate. Most preparers urged the Board to develop a standard based on US generally accepted accounting principles.[22]

In contrast, users commended the Board for tackling this topic. Users that commented on US GAAP were critical of it. Furthermore, users regard the Board's project as an opportunity to improve financial reporting on a worldwide basis.

The IASB took these comments into account when it developed an Exposure Draft of an IFRS on share-based payment. ED 2 *Share-based Payment* was published on 7 November 2002, and comments were invited by 7 March 2003. ED 2 proposed that all share-based payment transactions should be recognised in the financial statements, measured at fair value, resulting in the recognition of an expense when the goods or services received are consumed. Therefore, the proposals in ED 2 do not follow the same approach as US accounting requirements, ie under the proposed IFRS, entities are not permitted a choice between a fair value measurement method and an intrinsic value measurement method for transactions with employees, and are not permitted a choice between recognition and disclosure of expenses arising from employee share-based payment transactions.

The Exposure Draft was also published for comment by national standard-setters in Australia, Hong Kong, New Zealand, South Africa and the UK. The US FASB issued an Invitation to Comment, which sought respondents' views on the

[22] US GAAP.

similarities and differences between the proposals in ED 2 and the requirements of SFAS 123.

During 2002 when ED 2 was being developed, there was a significant change to the political environment surrounding the project, in the wake of the collapse of the US company Enron. Various prominent commentators began calling for a mandatory requirement for companies to recognise expenses in respect of employee share options. Some major US companies have now accepted that expense recognition is preferable, and have voluntarily adopted such an accounting policy. (At the time of writing, there are around 175 companies who have voluntarily begun applying SFAS 123 to employee share-based remuneration, including over 70 companies in the Standard & Poor's 500 stock index, representing more than 30 percent of the index's market value[23]). The present accounting treatment of employee share options is seen as having contributed to the perceived overuse of share options to remunerate employees, caused economic distortions through the overstatement of reported profits, and raised various other related corporate governance concerns. For example:

> 'The use of questionable accounting methods for stock options has several negative results:
>
> - Explosive growth in the use of stock options since 1995—huge, indeed, incredible awards to CEO's and in some companies awards to every employee…
> - The serious distortion of earnings statements…
> - Unprecedented focus on the stock price by all the employees of the company, to the point where serious ethical dilemmas are posed for employees…
> - The dramatic decline in dividends is a direct result of so much recent attention to stock options…'[24]

> 'Enron's reported exploitation of financial-reporting rules is a deplorable but all too natural consequence of the erosion of the US financial-reporting system…At times, under pressure by corporate lobbyists, legislators have inappropriately interfered in standard-setting to get rules based not on the needs of *users* of accounts but on the preferences of *issuers*…For the past 20 years, AIMR has advocated that issuers should *not* be allowed to tailor transactions to get an accounting treatment that suits them. We have repeatedly asked for accounting rules that would require issuers to…measure and record compensation expense for employee stock options…'.[25]
>
> 'In an economy as large, diverse, and complex as ours, sound corporate governance – including the accurate measurement of corporate performance – is essential

[23] C Bryan-Low 'Accounting Panel Faces Puzzle: How to Measure Options' Value' *Wall Street Journal* (24 April 2003).

[24] John Biggs, Chairman and CEO, TIAA-CREF; testimony before the US Senate Committee on Banking, Housing and Urban Affairs, 27 February 2002.

[25] Thomas A Bowman, President and CEO, Association for Investment Management and Research, *Wall Street Journal* and *Washington Post* (15 February 2002) emphasis in original.

> if our nation's resources are to be directed to their most efficient uses...In that regard, the increasing use of stock option grants to employees has raised new challenges for our accounting system...As I noted earlier, critics of option expensing...[have] argued that expenses will make raising capital more difficult. But we need to remember that expensing is only a bookkeeping transaction. To repeat, nothing real is changed in the actual operations or cash flow of the corporation. If investors are dissuaded by lower reported earnings as a result of expensing, it means only that they were less informed than they should have been about the true input cost of creating corporate revenues. Capital employed on the basis of misinformation is likely to be capital misused...'.[26]
>
> 'We, as leaders of America's foremost financial services firms, will expense stock options granted to employees under Generally Accepted Accounting Principles. This is not required by the new reform legislation. However, we feel it is an essential step towards restoring the public's trust in corporate America'.[27]

This change in the political environment surrounding the accounting treatment of employee share-based remuneration is likely to be significant, given the political pressures that have thus far hampered standard-setters' efforts to improve this aspect of accounting.

The IASB is currently re-deliberating the proposals in ED 2, taking into account comments received from respondents to the ED. The majority of respondents agreed with the basic principle proposed in the ED, ie all forms of share-based remuneration, including employee share options, result in expenses that should be recognised in the financial statements. The IASB is currently considering a variety of issues raised by respondents relating to the application of this basic principle. It plans to issue the finalised IFRS by the end of 2003.

At the same time, the FASB is reviewing its accounting requirements on share-based remuneration (stock-based compensation). In March 2003, the FASB announced the addition to its agenda of a project on stock-based compensation:

> 'Recent events have served as a reminder to all of us that clear, credible and comparable financial information is essential to the health and vitality of our capital market system. In the wake of the market meltdown and corporate reporting scandals, the FASB has received numerous requests from individual and institutional investors, financial analysts and many others urging the Board to mandate the expensing of the compensation cost relating to employee stock options...While a number of major companies have voluntarily opted to reflect these costs as an expense in reporting their earnings, other companies continue to show these costs in the footnotes to their financial statements. In addition, a move to require an expense treatment would be consistent with the FASB's commitment to work toward convergence between U.S. and international accounting standards. In

[26] Alan Greenspan, Chairman of the US Federal Reserve, remarks at the 2002 Financial Markets Conference of the Federal Reserve Bank of Atlanta, 3 May 2002.

[27] Financial Services Forum *Wall Street Journal* (14 August 2002).

taking all of these factors into consideration, the Board concluded that it was critical that it now revisit this important subject.'[28]

E. Concluding Comments

As noted at the beginning of the paper, accounting standard setters have consistently concluded that all forms of share-based remuneration, including employee share options, result in expenses that should be recognised in the income statement. Recent events have demonstrated the importance of high quality financial reporting. Investors and other users of financial statements require transparent, neutral and comparable financial information to assist them in making economic decisions. The omission of expenses in respect of employee share options, and the resulting overstatement of reported profits, significantly impairs the quality of financial statements. However, this situation seems about to change. In the author's view, it is highly likely that this major gap in accounting standards is about to be closed.

Appendix

Extracts from the IASB's Basis for Conclusions on ED 2 *Share-based Payment*

RECOGNITION OF EQUITY-SETTLED SHARE-BASED PAYMENT TRANSACTIONS

BC25. The Board first considered conceptual arguments relating to the recognition of an expense arising from equity-settled share-based payment transactions, including arguments advanced by respondents to the Discussion Paper and other commentators. Other respondents who disagreed with the recognition of an expense arising from particular share-based payment transactions (those involving employee share options) did so for practical, rather than conceptual, reasons. The Board considered those practical issues later (see paragraphs BC278-BC294).

BC26. The Board focused its discussions on employee share options, because that is where most of the complexity and controversy lie, but the question whether expense recognition is appropriate is broader than that – it

[28] Robert Herz, FASB Chairman, FASB News Release (12 March 2003).

covers all transactions involving the issue of shares, options or other equity instruments to employees or suppliers of goods and services. For example, the Board noted that arguments made by respondents and other commentators against expense recognition are directed solely at employee share options. However, if conceptual arguments made against recognition of an expense in relation to employee share options are valid (eg that there is no cost to the entity), those arguments ought to apply equally to transactions involving other equity instruments (eg shares) and to equity instruments issued to other parties (eg suppliers of professional services).

BC27. The rationale for recognising all types of share-based payment transactions – irrespective of whether the equity instrument is a share or a share option, and irrespective of whether the equity instrument is granted to an employee or to some other party – is that the entity has engaged in a transaction that is in essence the same as any other issue of equity instruments. In other words, the entity has received resources (goods or services) as consideration for the issue of shares, options or other equity instruments. It should therefore account for the inflow of resources (goods or services) and the increase in equity. Subsequently, either at the time of receipt of the goods or services or at some later date, the entity should also account for the expense arising from the consumption of those resources.

BC28. This rationale is explained further below, in the course of the discussion of the following arguments commonly made against expense recognition:

(a) the transaction is between the shareholders and the employees, not the entity and the employees.

(b) the employees do not provide services for the options.

(c) there is no cost to the entity, because no cash or other assets are given up; the shareholders bear the cost, in the form of dilution of their ownership interests, not the entity.

(d) the recognition of an expense is inconsistent with the definition of an expense in the conceptual frameworks used by accounting standard-setters, including the IASB's *Framework for the Preparation and Presentation of Financial Statements.*

(e) the cost borne by the shareholders is recognised in the dilution of earnings per share (EPS); if the transaction is recognised in the entity's accounts, the resulting charge to the income statement would mean that EPS is 'hit twice'.

(f) requiring the recognition of a charge would have adverse economic consequences, because it would discourage entities from introducing or continuing employee share plans.

'The entity is not a party to the transaction'

BC29. Some argue that the effect of employee share plans is that the existing shareholders transfer some of their ownership interests to the employees and that the entity is not a party to this transaction.

BC30. The Board did not accept this argument. Entities, not shareholders, set up employee share plans and entities, not shareholders, issue options to their employees. Even if that were not the case, eg if shareholders transferred shares or options direct to the employees, this would not mean that the entity is not a party to the transaction. The equity instruments are issued in return for services rendered by the employees and the entity, not the shareholders, receives those services. Therefore, the Board concluded that the entity should account for the services received in return for the equity instruments issued. The Board noted that this is no different from other situations in which equity instruments are issued. For example, if an entity issues warrants for cash, the entity recognises the cash received in return for the warrants issued. Although the effect of an issue, and subsequent exercise, of warrants might be described as a transfer of ownership interests from the existing shareholders to the warrant holders, the entity nevertheless is a party to the transaction because it receives resources (cash) for the issue of warrants and further resources (cash) for the issue of shares upon exercise of the warrants. Similarly, with employee share options, the entity receives resources (employee services) for the issue of the options and further resources (cash) for the issue of shares on the exercise of options.

'The employees do not provide services'

BC31. Some who argue that the entity is not a party to the transaction counter the points made above with the argument that employees do not provide services for the options, because the employees are paid in cash (or other assets) for their services.

BC32. Again, the Board was not convinced by this argument. If it were true that employees do not provide services for their options, this would mean that entities are issuing valuable share options and getting nothing in return. Employees do not pay cash for the options they receive. Hence, if they do not provide services for the options, the employees are providing nothing in return. If this were true, by issuing such options the entity's directors would be in breach of their fiduciary duties to their shareholders.

BC33. Typically, shares or options granted to employees form one part of their pay package. For example, an employee might have a pay package consisting of a basic cash salary, company car, pension, healthcare benefits, and other benefits including shares and options. It is usually not possible to identify the services received in respect of individual components of that pay package, eg the services received in respect of healthcare benefits. But that does not mean that the employee does not provide services for those healthcare benefits. Rather, the employee provides services for the entire pay package.

BC34. In summary, shares, options or other equity instruments are granted to employees because they are employees. The equity instruments granted form a part of their total pay package, regardless of whether that represents a large part or a small part.

'There is no cost to the entity, therefore there is no expense'

BC35. Some argue that because share-based payments do not require the entity to sacrifice any cash or other assets, there is no cost to the entity, and therefore no expense should be recognised.

BC36. The Board regards this argument as unsound, because it overlooks that:

(a) every time an entity receives resources as consideration for the issue of equity instruments, there is no outflow of cash or other assets, and on every other occasion the resources received as consideration for the issue of equity instruments are recognised in the financial statements; and

(b) the expense arises from the consumption of those resources, not from an outflow of assets.

BC37. In other words, irrespective of whether one accepts that there is a cost to the entity, an accounting entry is required to recognise the resources received as consideration for the issue of equity instruments, just as it is on other occasions when equity instruments are issued. For example, where shares are issued for cash, an entry is required to recognise the cash received. If a non-monetary asset, such as plant and machinery, is received for those shares instead of cash, an entry is required to recognise the asset received. If the entity acquires another business or entity by issuing shares in a business combination, the entity recognises the net assets acquired.

BC38. The recognition of an expense arising out of such a transaction represents the consumption of resources received, ie the 'using up' of the resources received for the shares or options. In the case of the plant and machinery mentioned above, the asset would be depreciated over its expected life, resulting in the recognition of an expense each year. Eventually, the entire amount recognised for the resources received when the shares were issued would be recognised as an expense (including any residual value, which would form part of the gain or loss on disposal of the asset). Similarly, if another business or entity is acquired by an issue of shares, an expense is recognised when the assets acquired are consumed. For example, inventories acquired will be recognised as an expense when sold, even though no cash or other assets were disbursed to acquire those inventories.

BC39. The only difference in the case of employee services (or other services) received as consideration for the issue of shares or options is that usually the resources received are consumed immediately upon receipt. This means that an expense for the consumption of resources is recognised immediately, rather than over a period of time. The Board concluded that the timing of consumption does not change the principle; the financial statements should recognise the receipt and consumption of resources, even when consumption occurs at the same time as, or soon after, receipt. This point is discussed further in paragraphs BC40-BC48.

'Expense recognition is inconsistent with the definition of an expense'

BC40. Some have questioned whether recognition of an expense arising from particular share-based payment transactions is consistent with accounting standard-setters' conceptual frameworks, in particular, the *Framework*, which states:

> Expenses are decreases in economic benefits during the accounting period in the form of outflows or *depletions of assets* or incurrences of liabilities that result in decreases in equity, other than those relating to distributions to equity participants. (paragraph 70, emphasis added)

BC41. Some argue that if services are received in a share-based payment transaction, there is no transaction or event that meets the definition of an expense. They contend that there is no outflow of assets and that no liability is incurred. Furthermore, because services usually do not meet the criteria for recognition as an asset, it is argued that the consumption of those services does not represent a depletion of assets.

BC42. The *Framework* defines an asset and explains that the term 'asset' is not limited to resources that can be recognised as assets in the balance sheet (*Framework*, paragraphs 49 and 50). Although services to be received in the future might not meet the definition of an asset,* services are assets when received. These assets are usually consumed immediately. This is explained in FASB Statement of Financial Accounting Concepts No. 6 *Elements of Financial Statements*:

> Services provided by other entities, including personal services, cannot be stored and are received and used simultaneously. They can be assets of an entity only momentarily – as the entity receives and uses them – although their use may create or add value to other assets of the entity… (paragraph 31)

BC43. This applies to all types of services, eg employee services, legal services and telephone services. It also applies irrespective of the form of payment. For example, if an entity purchases services for cash, the accounting entry is:

Dr Services received

Cr Cash paid

BC44. Sometimes, those services are consumed in the creation of a recognisable asset, such as inventories, in which case the debit for services received is capitalised as part of a recognised asset. But often the services do not create or form part of a recognisable asset, in which case the debit for services received is charged immediately to the income statement as an expense. The debit entry above (and the resulting expense) does not represent the cash outflow – that is what the credit entry was for. Nor does it represent some sort of balancing item, to make the accounts balance. The debit entry above represents the resources received, and the resulting expense represents the consumption of those resources.

BC45. The same analysis applies if the services are acquired with payment made in shares or options. The resulting expense represents the consumption of services, ie a depletion of assets.

BC46. To illustrate this point, suppose that an entity has two buildings, both with gas heating, and the entity issues shares to the gas supplier instead of paying cash. Suppose that, for one building, the gas is supplied through a pipeline, and so is consumed immediately upon receipt. Suppose that, for the other building, the gas is supplied in bottles, and is therefore consumed over a period of time. In both cases, the entity has received assets as consideration for the issue of equity instruments, and should therefore recognise the assets received, and a corresponding

* eg because the entity might not have control over future services.

contribution to equity. If the assets are consumed immediately (the gas received through the pipeline), an expense is recognised immediately; if the assets are consumed later (the gas received in bottles), an expense is recognised later when the assets are consumed.

BC47. Therefore, the Board concluded that the recognition of an expense arising from share-based payment transactions is consistent with the definition of an expense in the *Framework*.

BC48. The FASB considered the same issue and reached the same conclusion in SFAS 123:

> Some respondents pointed out that the definition of expenses in FASB Concepts Statement No. 6, *Elements of Financial Statements*, says that expenses result from outflows or using up of assets or incurring of liabilities (or both). They asserted that because the issuance of stock options does not result in the incurrence of a liability, no expense should be recognised. The Board agrees that employee stock options are not a liability—like stock purchase warrants, employee stock options are equity instruments of the issuer. However, equity instruments, including employee stock options, are valuable financial instruments and thus are issued for valuable consideration, which …for employee stock options is employee services. Using in the entity's operations the benefits embodied in the asset received results in an expense... (Concepts Statement 6, paragraph 81, footnote 43, notes that, in concept most expenses decrease assets. However, if receipt of an asset, such as services, and its use occur virtually simultaneously, the asset often is not recorded.) [paragraph 88]

'Earnings per share is "hit twice"'

BC49. Some argue that any cost arising from share-based payment transactions is already recognised in the dilution of earnings per share (EPS). If an expense were recognised in the income statement, EPS would be 'hit twice'.

BC50. However, the Board noted that this result is appropriate. For example, if the entity paid the employees in cash for their services and the cash was then returned to the entity, as consideration for the issue of options, the effect on EPS would be the same as issuing those options direct to the employees.

BC51. The dual effect on EPS simply reflects the two economic events that have occurred: the entity has issued shares or options, thereby increasing the number of shares included in the EPS calculation

– although, in the case of options, only to the extent that the options are regarded as dilutive – and it has also consumed the resources it received for those options, thereby decreasing earnings. This is illustrated by the plant and machinery example mentioned in paragraphs BC37 and BC38. Issuing shares affects the number of shares in the EPS calculation, and the consumption (depreciation) of the asset affects earnings.

BC52. In summary, the Board concluded that the dual effect on diluted EPS is not double-counting the effects of a share or option grant – the same effect is not counted twice. Rather, two different effects are each counted once.

'Adverse economic consequences'

BC53. Some argue that to require recognition (or greater recognition) of employee share-based payment would have adverse economic consequences, in that it might discourage entities from introducing or continuing employee share plans.

BC54. Others argue that if the introduction of accounting changes did lead to a reduction in the use of employee share plans, it might be because the requirement for entities to account properly for employee share plans had revealed the economic consequences of such plans. They argue that this would correct the present economic distortion, whereby entities obtain and consume resources by issuing valuable shares or options without accounting for those transactions.

BC55. In any event, the Board noted that the role of accounting is to report transactions and events in a neutral manner, not to give 'favourable' treatment to particular transactions to encourage entities to engage in those transactions. To do so would impair the quality of financial reporting. If expenses are omitted from the income statement, profits are overstated. The financial statements are less transparent. Comparability is impaired, given that expenses arising from employee share-based payment transactions vary from entity to entity, from sector to sector, and from year to year. More fundamentally, accountability is impaired, because the entities are not accounting for transactions they have entered into and the consequences of those transactions.

(...)

Recognition versus disclosure

BC271. A basic accounting concept is that disclosure of financial information is not an adequate substitute for recognition in the financial statements. For example, the *Framework* states:

> Items that meet the recognition criteria should be recognised in the balance sheet or income statement. The failure to recognise such items is not rectified by disclosure of the accounting policies used nor by notes or explanatory material. (paragraph 82)

BC272. A key aspect of the recognition criteria is that the item can be measured with reliability. This issue is discussed further below. Therefore, this discussion focuses on the 'recognition versus disclosure' issue in principle, not on measurement reliability. Once it has been determined that an item meets the criteria for recognition in the financial statements, failing to recognise it is inconsistent with the basic concept that disclosure is not an adequate substitute for recognition.

BC273. Some disagree with this concept, arguing that it makes no difference whether information is recognised in the accounts or disclosed in the notes. Either way, users of accounts have the information they require to make economic decisions. Hence, they believe that note disclosure of expenses arising from certain employee share-based payment transactions (those involving awards of options to employees), rather than recognition in the income statement, is acceptable.

BC274. The Board did not accept this argument. The Board noted that if note disclosure is acceptable, because it makes no difference whether the expense is recognised or disclosed, then recognition in the financial statements must also be acceptable for the same reason. If recognition is acceptable, and recognition rather than mere disclosure accords with the accounting principles applied to all other expense items, it is not acceptable to leave one particular expense item out of the income statement.

BC275. The Board also noted that there is significant evidence that there is a difference between recognition and disclosure. First, academic research indicates that whether information is recognised or merely disclosed affects market prices (eg Barth, Clinch and Shibano, 2002).* If information is disclosed only in the notes, users of accounts have to expend time and effort to become sufficiently expert in accounting to know (a) that there are items that are not recognised in the financial

* ME Barth, G Clinch and T Shibano 'Markets Effects of Recognition and Disclosure' (2002) Working Paper Stanford University, Graduate School of Business.

statements, (b) that there is information about those items in the notes, and (c) how to assess the note disclosures. Because gaining that expertise comes at a cost, and not all users of accounts will become accounting experts, information that is merely disclosed may not be fully reflected in share prices.

BC276. Second, both preparers and users of accounts appear to agree that there is an important difference between recognition and disclosure. Users of accounts have strongly expressed the view that all forms of share-based payment, including employee share options, should be recognised in the financial statements, resulting in the recognition of an expense when the goods or services received are consumed, and that note disclosure only is inadequate. Their views have been expressed by various means, including:

(a) users' responses to the Discussion Paper

(b) the 2001 survey by the Association for Investment Management and Research of analysts and fund managers – 83 per cent of survey respondents said the accounting method for all share-based payment transactions should require recognition of an expense in the income statement

(c) public comments by users of accounts, such as those reported in the press or made at recent US Senate hearings.

BC277. Preparers of accounts also see a major difference between recognition and disclosure. Many preparers who responded to the Discussion Paper strongly opposed recognition of expenses arising from awards of share options for employees, while advocating disclosure of such information instead, for a variety of reasons. For example, some preparers were concerned that unless expense recognition is required in all countries, entities that are required to recognise an expense would be at a competitive disadvantage compared with entities that are permitted a choice between recognition and disclosure. Comments such as these indicate that preparers of accounts regard expense recognition as having consequences that are different from those of disclosure.

Reliability of measurement

BC278. One reason commonly given by those who oppose the recognition of an expense arising from transactions involving grants of share options to employees is that it is not possible to measure those transactions reliably.

BC279. The Board discussed these concerns about reliability, after first putting the issue into context. For example, the Board noted that when estimating the fair value of options, the objective is to measure that fair value at the measurement date, not the value of the underlying share at some future date. Some regard the fair value estimate as inherently uncertain because it is not known, at the measurement date, what the final outcome will be, ie how much the gain on exercise (if any) will be. However, the valuation does not attempt to estimate the future gain, only the amount that the other party would pay to obtain the right to participate in any future gains. Therefore, even if the option expires worthless or the employee makes a large gain on exercise, this does not mean that the grant date estimate of the fair value of that option was unreliable or wrong.

BC280. The Board also noted that accounting often involves making estimates, and therefore reporting an estimated fair value is not objectionable merely because that amount represents an estimate rather than a precise measure. Examples of other estimates made in accounting, which may have a material effect on the income statement and the balance sheet, include estimates of the collectability of doubtful debts, estimates of the useful life of fixed assets and the pattern of their consumption, and estimates of employee pension liabilities.

BC281. However, some argue that including in the accounts an estimate of the fair value of employee share options is a different matter from including other estimates, because there is no subsequent correction of the estimate. Other estimates, such as employee pension costs, will ultimately be 'trued up' to the amount of the cash paid out. In contrast, because equity is not remeasured, if the estimated fair value of employee options is included in the accounts, there is no 'truing up' of the fair value estimate – unless exercise date measurement is used – so any estimation error is permanently embedded in the accounts.

BC282. The FASB considered and rejected this argument in developing SFAS 123. For example, for employee pension costs, the total cost is never completely 'trued up' unless the scheme is terminated, the amount attributed to any particular year is never 'trued up', and it can take decades before the amounts relating to particular employees are 'trued up'. In the meantime, users of accounts have made economic decisions based on the estimated costs.

BC283. Moreover, the Board noted that if no expense (or an expense based on intrinsic value only, which is typically zero) is recognised in respect of employee share options, that also means that there is an error that is permanently embedded in the accounts. Reporting zero (or an amount based on intrinsic value, if any) is never 'trued up'.

BC284. The Board also considered the meaning of reliability. Arguments about whether estimates of the fair value of employee stock options are sufficiently 'reliable' focus on one aspect of reliability only – whether the estimate is free from material error. The *Framework*, in common with the conceptual frameworks of other accounting standard-setters, makes it clear that another important aspect of reliability is whether the information can be depended upon by users of accounts to represent faithfully what it purports to represent. Therefore, in assessing whether a particular accounting method produces reliable financial information, it is necessary to consider whether that information is representationally faithful. This is one way in which reliability is linked to another important qualitative characteristic of financial information, relevance.

BC285. For example, in the context of share-based payment, some commentators advocate measuring employee share options at intrinsic value rather than fair value, because intrinsic value is regarded as a much more reliable measure. Whether intrinsic value is a more reliable measure is doubtful – it is certainly less subject to estimation error, but is unlikely to be a representationally faithful measure of remuneration. Nor is intrinsic value a relevant measure. Many employee options are issued 'at the money', so have no intrinsic value at grant date. An option with no intrinsic value consists entirely of time value. If the option is measured at intrinsic value at grant date, zero value is attributed to the option. Therefore, by ignoring time value, the amount attributed to the option is 100 per cent understated.

BC286. Another qualitative characteristic is comparability. Some argue that, given the uncertainties relating to estimating the fair value of employee share options, it is better for all entities to report zero, as this will make financial statements more comparable. They argue that if, for example, for two entities the 'true' amount of expense relating to employee share options is CU500,000, and estimation uncertainties cause one entity to report CU450,000 and the other to report CU550,000, the two entities' financial statements would be more comparable if both reported zero, rather than these divergent figures.

BC287. However, it is unlikely that any two entities will have the same amount of employee share-based remuneration expense. Research (eg by Bear Stearns and Credit Suisse First Boston) indicates that the expense varies widely from industry to industry, from entity to entity, and from year to year. Reporting zero rather than an estimated amount is likely to make the financial statements much less comparable, not more comparable. For example, if the estimated employee share-based remuneration expense of Company A, Company B and Company C is CU10,000, CU100,000 and CU1,000,000 respectively, reporting zero for all three companies will not make their financial statements comparable.

BC288. In the context of the foregoing discussion of reliability, the Board addressed the question whether transactions involving share options granted to employees can be measured with sufficient reliability for the purpose of recognition in the financial statements. The Board noted that many respondents to the Discussion Paper asserted that this is not possible. They argue that option pricing models cannot be applied to employee share options, because of the differences between employee options and traded options.

BC289. The Board considered these differences, with the assistance of the project's Advisory Group and other experts, and has drawn conclusions on adjustments that should be made to the inputs to option pricing models, or to the values produced by these models, to allow for these differences.

BC290. In estimating the fair value of employee stock options, it is necessary to estimate several inputs, including expected volatility, expected life and the probability of vesting. But does that make the estimate so unreliable that it should not be included in the financial statements, particularly in comparison with other estimates already included in the accounts, such as liabilities for post employment benefits? And are measurement uncertainties likely to result in understatement or overstatement in practice?

BC291. The Board noted that there is evidence to support a conclusion that it is possible to make a reliable estimate of the fair value of employee share options. First, there is academic research to support this conclusion (eg Carpenter 1998, Maller, Tan and Van De Vyver 2002).[*] Second, users of accounts regard the estimated fair values as sufficiently reliable for recognition in the financial statements. Evidence of this can be found in a variety of sources, such as the comment letters received from users of accounts who responded to the Discussion Paper. Users' views are important, because the objective of financial statements is to provide high quality, transparent and comparable information to help users make economic decisions. In other words, financial statements are intended to meet the needs of users, rather than preparers or other interest groups. The purpose of setting accounting standards is to ensure that, wherever possible, the information provided in the financial statements meets users' needs. Therefore, if the people who use the financial statements in making economic decisions regard the fair

[*] JN Carpenter 'The Exercise and Valuation of Executive Stock Options' (1998) 48 Journal of Financial Economics 127-158; RA Maller, R Tan and M Van De Vyver 'How Might Companies Value ESOs?' (2002) 12 (1) Australian Accounting Review 11-24.

value estimates as sufficiently reliable for recognition in the financial statements, this provides strong evidence of measurement reliability.

BC292. The Board also noted that, although the FASB decided to permit a choice between recognition and disclosure of expenses arising from employee share-based payment transactions, it did so for non-technical reasons, not because it agreed with the view that reliable measurement was not possible:

> The Board continues to believe that use of option-pricing models, as modified in this statement, will produce estimates of the fair value of stock options that are sufficiently reliable to justify recognition in financial statements. Imprecision in those estimates does not justify failure to recognize compensation cost stemming from employee stock options. That belief underlies the Board's encouragement to entities to adopt the fair value based method of recognizing stock-based employee compensation cost in their financial statements. (SFAS 123, Basis for Conclusions, paragraph 117)

BC293. In summary, if expenses arising from grants of options to employees are omitted from the financial statements, or recognised using the intrinsic value method (which typically results in zero expense) or the minimum value method, that means that there is a permanent error embedded in the accounts. So the question is, which accounting method is more likely to produce the smallest amount of error and the most relevant, comparable information – a fair value estimate, which might result in some understatement or overstatement of the associated expense, or another measurement basis, such as intrinsic value, that will definitely result in substantial understatement of the associated expense?

BC294. Taking all of the above into consideration, the Board concluded that the estimated fair value of employee share options at grant date can be measured with sufficient reliability for the purposes of recognising employee share-based payment transactions in the financial statements. The Board therefore concluded that the IFRS on share-based payment should require a fair value measurement method to be applied to all types of share-based payment transactions, including all types of employee share-based payment. Hence, the Board concluded that the IFRS should not allow a choice between a fair value measurement method and an intrinsic value measurement method, and should not permit a choice between recognition and disclosure of expenses arising from employee share-based payment transactions.

Chapter 6: The Responsibility of the Management and of the Board and Its Enforcement

The Responsibility of the Management and Its Enforcement

HOLGER FLEISCHER

A. Introduction

'The directors of such companies, however, being the managers rather of other people's money than of their own, it cannot well be expected that they should watch over it with the same anxious vigilance with which the partners in a private company frequently watch over their own. Like the stewards of a rich man, they are apt to consider attention to small matters as not for their master's honour, and very easily give themselves a dispensation from having it. Negligence and profusion, therefore, must always prevail more or less, in the management of the officers of such a company'.[1] When painting this gloomy picture, Adam Smith referred to the joint stock companies of the late 18th century. Modern company law legislation tackles the same problem with stringent standards of care and loyalty coupled with a regime of civil liability that varies from country to country. The German Stock Corporation Act, for example, stipulates in § 93 (1) that in conducting business the members of the management board shall employ the care of a diligent and conscientious manager, and adds in § 93 (2) that members of the management board who violate their duties shall be jointly and

[1] A Smith *An Inquiry into the Nature and Causes of the Wealth of Nations* (Random House Inc London 1776) 741.

severally liable to the company for any resulting damage.[2] English courts have elaborated similar rules under common law principles.[3] This article explores recent developments in the field of directors' duties and addresses some of the most important issues on the reform agenda: The role of fiduciary duties in different legal systems (B.), the duties to creditors and the responsibility for wrongful trading (C.), the management responsibility for financial statements (D.), and the directors' disqualification (E.).

B. Fiduciary Duties in Different Legal Systems

Being asked to map out the standards of directors in public companies, one can confidently point to a basic bifurcation: the duty of care and the duty of loyalty.[4] While the former has been the object of much scholarly debate, most often with a view to the intriguing business judgment rule,[5] the latter has received less attention, at least in continental legal systems.

I. Comparative Overview of Fiduciary Duties

1. Anglo-American Origin

a) United Kingdom

From an international perspective, English company law has been a pioneer in the field of fiduciary duties. It developed the influential concept of the director as a trustee[6] having its historical origin in the fact that, in the earliest companies, the director *was* a trustee in the full technical sense.[7] Later, when property was owned by

[2] KJ Hopt in KJ Hopt and H Wiedemann (eds) *Großkommentar Aktiengesetz* (4th edn de Guyter Berlin 1999) § 93 comments 72 ff; for a detailed comparative analysis TE Abeltshauser *Leitungshaftung in Kapitalgesellschaften* (Heymanns Carl Verlag Cologne 1998).

[3] PL Davies *Gower & Davies: The Principles of Modern Company Law* (7th edn Sweet & Maxwell London 2003) 370 ff; B Pettet *Company Law* (Longman Harlow 2001) 173 ff; for a comprehensive analysis BS Butcher *Directors' Duties: A New Millennium, A New Approach?* (Kluwer Law International The Hague 2000).

[4] H Fleischer in H Fleischer (ed) *Handbuch des Vorstandsrechts* (2003, forthcoming) § 7 comments 1 ff with many comparative references.

[5] H Fleischer 'Die "Business Judgment Rule" im Spiegel von Rechtsvergleichung und Rechtsökonomie' in Wank and others (eds) *Festschrift für Herbert Wiedemann zum 70 Geburtstag* (CH Beck Munich 2002) 827 ff with many references.

[6] *Great Eastern Rly Co v Turner* (1872) 68 Ch App 149 at 152: 'The directors are the mere trustees or agents of the company, trustees of the company's money and property and agents in the transactions which they enter into on behalf of the company.'

[7] PL Davies *Principles of Modern Company Law* (n 3) 380; for an extensive historical account LS Sealy 'The Director as Trustee' [1967] Cambridge Law Journal 83.

the company in its own right as a result of general incorporation, courts continued to use the label 'trustee' by analogy since the company's assets were still under the director's close control. Over the years, however, it became more and more apparent that, in important respects, directors' duties required a notable departure from trust principles: Unlike trustees who must be careful to preserve the trust property and avoid exposing it to unnecessary risks, directors have to encounter risks and decide whether a risk is worth taking.[8] Today, it is generally held that directors are not trustees, but that they owe strict fiduciary duties to the company.[9] As a consequence, directors are required to act bona fide in the best interests of the company and must not exercise their power for an improper purpose.[10] Moreover, they cannot, without the consent of the company, fetter their future discretion and have to avoid placing themselves in a position in which there is a conflict between their duties to the company and their personal interests.[11] According to a long-standing tradition, the fiduciary duties are owed to the company and not to individual shareholders.[12] However, recent cases have called into question whether this general (and severely criticised[13]) principle still stands.[14]

b) United States

In the States, the law of fiduciary obligations, originating in equity, fell on fertile grounds.[15] Its continued evolution in the corporate context was furthered by the

[8] Pettet (n 3) 173: 'From one angle the director can be seen as a trustee, whose role it is to protect and preserve the assets of the beneficiary. From the other angle, he is seen as a dynamic entrepreneur whose job it is to take risks with the subscribed capital and multiply the shareholders' investment.'

[9] *Regal (Hastings) Ltd v Gulliver* [1967] 2 AC 134 at 139: 'Directors, no doubt, are not trustees, but they occupy a fiduciary position towards the company whose board they form.'; E Ferran *Company Law and Corporate Finance* (Oxford University Press Oxford 1999) 156-157; S Mayson, D French and C Ryan *Company Law* (17th edn Blackstone Press OUP Oxford 2000) 480.

[10] Ferran (n 9) 157; PL Davies (n 3) 385-389; S Mayson, D French and C Ryan (n 9) 499-501.

[11] PL Davies (n 3) 389-391.

[12] *Percival v Wright* [1902] 2 Ch 421.

[13] Sharp criticism was voiced by the Cohen Committee Cmd 6659, paras 86 ff, and by the Jenkins Committee Cmnd 1749, paras 89 and 99 (b).

[14] *Brunninghausen v Glavanics* (1999) 32 ACSR 294; comment by R Goddard 'Percival v. Wright. The End of a Remarkable Career?' (2000) 116 Law Quarterly Review 197; see also PL Davies (n 3) 374-376.

[15] In chronological order A Scott 'The Fiduciary Principle' (1949) 37 California Law Review 539; AG Anderson 'Conflicts of Interest: Efficiency, Fairness and Corporate Structure' (1978) 25 UCLA Law Review 738; T Frankel 'Fiduciary Law' (1983) 71 California Law Review 795; KB Davis 'Judicial Review of Fiduciary Decisionmaking – Some Theoretical Perspectives' (1985) 80 Northwestern Law Review 1.

fact that the most prominent corporate law court – Delaware's Court of Chancery – was (and still is) a separate court of equity.[16] As a general rule, the directors' fiduciary duties go beyond mere fairness and honesty. Often-cited is Benjamin Cardozo's assertion in *Meinhard v Salmon*: 'Many forms of conduct permissible in a workaday world for those acting at arm's length, are forbidden to those bound by fiduciary ties. A trustee is held to something stricter than the morals of the market place. Not honesty alone, but the punctilio of an honour the most sensitive, is then the standard of behaviour.'[17] Courts and academic writers agree that the director's paramount fiduciary obligation is to subordinate his individual and private interests to his duty to the corporation whenever the two conflict.[18] However, no consensus has emerged as to whether the fiduciary duties are owed to the company alone. At least in certain circumstances, courts have recognised fiduciary relationships between directors and individual shareholders.[19] In recent years, the elaboration of directors' fiduciary duties has profited much from the 'Principles of Corporate Governance' published by the American Law Institute in 1994. The 'Principles' dedicate a separate part consisting of almost 200 pages to fiduciary duties analysing in turn the duties of directors (Chapter 2) and controlling shareholders (Chapter 3) and the particular responsibilities in transfer-of-control-situations (Chapter 4).[20] With respect to terminology, it is noteworthy that the 'Principles' avoid the use of the term 'duty of loyalty', when dealing with the obligation of a person who acts with a pecuniary interest in a matter, and instead use the term 'duty of fair dealing'.[21]

2. Reception on the Continent

a) France

On the continent, the concept of fiduciary duties proved to be highly influential. Nowadays, most civil law jurisdictions impose a general duty of loyalty upon

[16] DA DeMott 'Beyond Metaphor: An Analysis of Fiduciary Obligation' [1988] Duke Law Journal 879 at 882.

[17] *Meinhard v Salmon* (1928) 249 NY 456 at 464.

[18] eg *Bayer v Beran* (1944) 49 NYS 2d 2 at 5; similarly *City Bank Farmers Trust Co v Gannon* 51 NE 2d 674 at 675-676: 'Undivided loyalty is the supreme test, unlimited and unconfined.'

[19] The classic case is *Strong v Repide* (1909) 213 US 419; for a comparative overview H Fleischer 'Informationspflichten der Geschäftsleiter beim Management Buyout im Spannungsfeld von Gesellschafts-, Kapitalmarkt- und Vertragsrecht' [2000] Die Aktiengesellschaft 309 at 313-314.

[20] American Law Institute, Principles of Corporate Governance: Analysis and Recommendations (1994) Part V 199-382.

[21] ibid 200.

directors.[22] A recent example is to be found in French company law where commentators have discerned a close connection between the 'Principles of Corporate Governance' and two judgments of the *Cour de cassation*[23] explicitly recognising a *devoir de loyauté* of directors.[24] In the first case, the president of a public, but unlisted corporation bought shares from shareholders for 3.000 F. each and sold them a few days later for 8.800 F. The *Chambre commerciale* held that, by not disclosing the shares' true value, he had violated his duty of loyalty which a director owes to each individual shareholder.[25] The second case dealt with a director who resigned, formed a new company and persuaded key employees of his former company to join him. Unlike the appellate court, the *Cour de cassation* granted damages to the company on the theory that the director had violated his duty of loyalty *vis-à-vis* the company.[26] Commentators emphasise the general convergence between American and French corporate governance principles[27]

[22] For a detailed analysis H Fleischer 'Zur organschaftlichen Treuepflicht der Geschäftsleiter im Aktien- und GmbH-Recht' (2003) Wertpapier-Mitteilungen 1045 with many comparative references.

[23] Cass com 27 February 1996 JCP éd G 1996 II, 22665; Cass com 24 February 1998 JCP éd E 1998 no 17, 637.

[24] B Daille-Duclos 'Le devoir de loyauté du dirigeant' (1998) 39 La Semaine Juridique Entreprise et Affaires 1486: 'Le devoir de loyauté du dirigeant est une création jurisprudentielle de la Chambre commerciale de la Cour de cassation (...) Le devoir de loyauté du dirigeant apparait directement issu des 'principles of corporate governance' définies aux États-Unis par l'American Law Institute (...).' For a thoughtful analysis also V Magnier 'Réception du droit américain dans l'organisation interne des sociétés commerciales' (2001) 45 Archives de philosophie du droit 213 at 219-221.

[25] Cass com 27 February 1996 (n 23) 22665 with the key sentence: 'M. Bernard V a manqué au devoir de loyauté qui s'impose au dirigeant d'une société à l'egard de tout associé.', see also D Freedman 'L'américanisation du droit francais par la vie économique' (2001) 45 Archive de philosophie du droit 207 at 209: 'Les 'fiduciary duties' américaines (duty of loyalty, duty of care, business judgment rule), qui constituent le coeur de la corporate governance américaine, se développent dans le droit des sociétés francais sous la forme de concepts juridiques classiques, propres au droit francais comme la bonne foi, la confiance, la loyauté. La Cour de cassation a par ailleurs, dans un arrêt du 27 février 1996, consacré avec fermeté le devoir de loyauté à la charge du dirigeant de tout associé.'; for a comparative account and the contractual foundation of the case H Fleischer *Informationsasymmetrie im Vertragsrecht* (CH Beck Munich 2001) 706-707 with many references to French contract law, in particular to the concept of *dol par réticence.*

[26] Cass com 24 February 1998 (n 23) 637 with the key sentence: 'Monsieur K. avait exercé successivement les functions de gérant puis après sa transformation en société anonyme de directeur général de la société P., ce dont il découlait qu'il était tenu à une obligation de loyauté à l'egard de cette entreprise.'

[27] F Peltier 'La convergence du droit francais avec les principes de la "corporate governance" américaine' (1997) 23 La Semaine Juridique 245; WL Baker 'L'américanisation du droit par la finance: mythe ou réalité?' (2001) 45 Archives de philosophie du droit 199 at 200-203; for a comprehensive analysis Dion 'Les obligations fiduciaires des dirigeants de sociétés commerciales: droit des Ètats-Unis d'Amérique et droit francais' thèse Orleans (1994).

and regard the recent case law as further support for the continuing *moralisation du droit des sociétés*.[28] Moreover, the evolving civil responsibility is welcomed as a complement to the strict criminal sanctions against directors.

b) Germany

The German Stock Corporation Act has codified the duty of loyalty only in a rudimentary fashion: § 88 (1) AktG prohibits management board members from competing with the company in its line of business, and § 93 (1) AktG stipulates a statutory duty of confidentiality. The general concept, however, is not mentioned in the Act which caused considerable difficulties in shaping the duty of loyalty.[29] Over the years, contributions from comparative law scholarship have helped to fill in the gaps and to flesh out the law of fiduciary obligations.[30] Meanwhile, the duty of loyalty is firmly entrenched in the case law,[31] and the recently introduced 'German Code of Corporate Governance' highlights some of its most important features.[32] Academic writers characterise the director's position almost unanimously as fiduciary[33] or trustee-like[34]. The legal vocabulary, however, is limited and not entirely clear: German lawyers are forced to use the term 'Treuhänder' interchangeably where their Anglo-American counterparts are able to differentiate between 'trustees' and 'fiduciaries'.[35] Substantially, it is gen-

[28] B Daille-Duclos (n 24) 1486 at 1489-1490.

[29] KJ Hopt 'Die Haftung von Vorstand und Aufsichtsrat – Zugleich ein Beitrag zur corporate-governance-Debatte' in UH Immenga, W Möschel and D Reuter (eds) *Festschrift für Ernst-Joachim Mestmäcker zum 70 Geburtstag* (Nomos Verlag Baden-Baden 1996) 909 at 921; H Wiedemann *Organverantwortung und Gesellschafterklagen in der Aktiengesellschaft* (Broschiert Wiesbaden 1990) 12.

[30] Pathbreaking E-J Mestmäcker *Verwaltung, Konzerngewalt und Rechte der Aktionäre* (Karlsruhe 1958) 152 ff, 209 ff; UH Immenga *Die personalistische Kapitalgesellschaft* (Athenäum Verlag Frankfurt 1970) 180 ff.

[31] For details and references, see recently H Fleischer 'Zur organschaftlichen Treuepflicht der Geschäftsleiter im Aktien- und GmbH-Recht' (2003) Wertpapier-Mitteilungen 1045 with all references.

[32] German Code of Corporate Governance, s 4.3: 'Conflicts of interest', explained by M Peltzer *Deutsche Corporate Governance. Ein Leitfaden* (CH Beck Munich 2003) comments 98 ff.

[33] BGHZ 129, 30, 34: 'selbständige treuhänderische Wahrnehmung fremder Vermögensinteressen'; KJ Hopt in KJ Hopt and H Wiedemann (n 2) § 93 comments 12, 72, 144; H-J Mertens in *Kölner Kommentar zum Aktiengesetz* (2nd edn C Heymanns Verlag Cologne 1988) § 93 comment 57.

[34] OLG Hamm AG (1995) 512, 514; U Hüffer *Aktiengesetz* (5th edn CH Beck Verlag 2002), § 93 comment 4.

[35] For a detailed analysis S Grundmann *Der Treuhandvertrag* (CH Beck Verlag Munich 1997) 26 ff 127 ff; critically PO Mülbert in KJ Hopt and H Wiedemann (n 2) §§ 118-147 comments 191 ff.

erally agreed on that the duty of loyalty calls for a more demanding standard of conduct than the general obligation to act in good faith in contractual settings.[36] Commentators explain that the stricter standards mirror the far-reaching influence and power of directors.[37] As the law now stands, the director owes fiduciary duties to the company and to the company only.[38]

3. Conclusions

a) The Law and Economics of Fiduciary Duties

The duty of loyalty is now a well-accepted body of law in almost all jurisdictions. In search for an explanation, one is intuitively inclined to resort to economic reasoning. Economists tend to analyse the separation of ownership and control in public companies through the lens of the principal-agent-model: Shareholders are regarded as principals who have delegated the management of the company to the directors as their agents.[39] Central to the principal-agent-relationship are three characteristics: (1) In conducting the company's affairs, the directors enjoy broad discretion; (2) the directors' duties cannot be precisely specified in advance; (3) direct monitoring of the directors by the shareholders is often prohibitively costly.[40] As a consequence, there are incentives for directors to take advantage of their superior information and to misappropriate corporate resources.[41] In economic parlance, the terms 'hidden gains' and 'hidden actions' are used to characterise the directors' disloyalty. At this point, the duty of loyalty comes into play and serves a valuable function: It must be understood as the law's attempt to ameliorate the agency problem and to establish an incentive structure in which the directors' self interest directs them to act in the interests of the shareholders.[42] Moreover, it helps to economise on transaction costs by stipulating a general

[36] KJ Hopt in KJ Hopt and H Wiedemann (n 2) § 93 comment 72; U Hüffer (n 34) § 93 comment 5; H-J Mertens (n 33) § 93 comment 57.

[37] Pathbreaking W Zöllner *Die Schranken mitgliedschaftlicher Stimmrechtsmacht bei den privatrechtlichen Personenverbänden* (Munich 1963) 342-343.

[38] BGHZ 83, 122, 134; BGHZ 110, 323, 334; KJ Hopt in Hopt and Wiedemann (n 2) § 93 comment 469.

[39] M Jensen and W Meckling 'The Theory of the Firm: Managerial Behaviour, Agency Costs and Ownership Structure' (1976) 3 Journal of Financial Economics 305.

[40] R Richter and EG Furubotn *Neue Institutionenökonomik* (Mohr-Siebeck Tübingen 1996) 163-171.

[41] RD Cooter and BJ Freedman 'The Fiduciary Relationship: Its Economic Character and Legal Consequences' (1991) 66 New York University Law Review 1045 at 1048, speaking of an 'appropriation-incentive model'.

[42] H Fleischer 'Grundfragen der ökonomischen Theorie im Gesellschafts- und Kapitalmarktrecht' [2001] Zeitschrift fuer Unternehmens- und Gesellschaftsrecht 1 at 7-8.

principle that restricts the directors' opportunity to cheat without the costly drafting of elaborate rules while leaving them free to make use of their special skills.[43] From a law and economics viewpoint, therefore, the duty of loyalty pursues a double goal: Ex ante, it seeks to work as a necessary deterrent against managerial misconduct;[44] ex post, it seeks to raise the enforcement probability in cases of misappropriation.[45] However, fiduciary duties alone are not an adequate safeguard and must be supplemented by other devices since violations of fiduciary duty are frequently very difficult to detect.

b) Distinguishing Duty of Loyalty and Duty of Care

Economic reasoning also helps to understand the different legal treatment of care and loyalty in many jurisdictions. First, the affirmative case for insulating management decisions from judicial review by a broad business judgment rule does not apply to directors' disloyalty.[46] Second, it is easier for courts to detect appropriations than to detect negligence, so that the costs of inquiry and error are lower.[47] Third, duty-of-loyalty problems often involve spectacular, one-shot-appropriations in which subsequent penalties through markets are inadequate.[48] Classical examples include hostile takeovers and management buyouts. Restraints from capital markets or job markets which may influence managerial behaviour in repeated transactions[49] remain ineffective due to the last-period-nature of such fundamental transactions.[50]

c) Legal Transplants and Economic Efficiency

As has been pointed out, Anglo-American law has greatly influenced the shaping of fiduciary duties in civil law jurisdictions. The duty of loyalty, therefore may be

[43] AS Anderson 'Conflicts of Interest: Efficiency, Fairness and Corporate Structure' (1978) 25 UCLA Law Review 738 at 760; RA Posner *Economic Analysis of Law* (5th edn Aspen New York 1998) [14.8] 452.

[44] Bainbridge *Corporate Law and Economics* (Foundation Press New York 2002) 305; FH Easterbrook and DR Fischel *The Economic Structure of Corporate Law* (Harvard University Press Cambridge 1991) 95.

[45] Cooter and Freedman (n 41) 1055.

[46] Fleischer (n 5) 829-832.

[47] Bainbridge (n 44) 306; Easterbrook and Fischel (n 44) 103.

[48] ibid.

[49] For an instructive overview E Ferran (n 9) 118-122: 'Controlling Managerial Performance by Market Forces'.

[50] M Ruffner *Die ökonomischen Grundlagen eines Rechts der Publikumsgesellschaften* (Schulthess Zürich 2000) 238-240.

referred to as a 'legal transplant', a phrase linked to the name of Alan Watson.[51] Despite a long tradition of comparative scholarship on both sides of the Atlantic, the general concept of legal transplants in company law has not been fully explored yet[52] although some progress has been made recently in the US scholarship[53] and the French *Archives de philosophie du droit* dedicated a complete volume to the topic.[54] It is submitted that in the corporate context legal transplants can be partly explained on efficiency grounds. Conversely, efficiency may be used to evaluate legal transplants.[55] The duty of loyalty is a nice illustration of how the tools of law and economics together with those of comparative law shed new light on well-known company law problems. The theoretical underpinnings of comparative company law and economics deserve further research.[56]

II. Case Studies

As Justice Frankfurter famously formulated, 'to say that a man is a fiduciary only begins analysis, it gives direction to further inquiry'.[57] Four recurring situations deserve closer scrutiny.[58]

[51] A Watson *Legal Transplants. An Approach to Comparative Law* (2nd edn Scottish Academic Press Edingburgh 1993).

[52] For pioneer approaches in the field of antitrust H Fleischer 'Zum Einfluß des amerikanischen Kartellrechts auf das europäische Kartellrecht' in FIW (ed) *Konvergenz der Wettbewerbsrechte – Eine Welt, ein Kartellrecht* (FIW Cologne 2003) 85; in the field of mergers and acquisitions H Fleischer '*Due Diligence* und *Best Konwledge* beim Unternehmenskauf' in B Dauner-Lieb and M Henssler (eds) *Unternehmenskauf und Schuldrechtsmodernisierung* (CH Beck Verlag Munich 2003) 103.

[53] L Stout 'On the Export of U.S.-Style Corporate Fiduciary Duties to Other Cultures: Can a Transplant Take?' UCLA School of Law Research Paper no 02-11 (May 2002); H Kanda and CJ Milhaupt 'Re-examining Legal Transplants: The Director's Fiduciary Duty in Japanese Corporate Law' Columbia Law School Working Paper no 219 (March 2003).

[54] Archives de philosophie du droit, L'américanisation du droit, Tome 45 (2001).

[55] U Mattei *Comparative Law and Economics* (University of Michigan Press Ann Arbor 1997) 123 ff.

[56] For a more detailed analysis see H Fleischer (n 5) at 846-848; more generally U Mattei and F Cafaggi in P Newman (ed) *The New Palgrave Dictionary of Economics and the Law* (MacMillan London 1998) 346: 'Comparative Law and Economics'.

[57] *SEC v Chenery Corp*, 318 US 80 at 85-86 (1943).

[58] Comparative studies mostly focus on self dealing; see in chronological order: KJ Hopt 'Self-Dealing and Use of Corporate Opportunity and Information: Regulating Directors' Conflict of Interest' in KJ Hopt and G Teubner (eds) *Corporate Governance and Directors' Liabilities* (de Gruyter Berlin 1985) 285; DA DeMott 'The Figure in the Landscape: A Comparative Sketch of Directors' Self-Interested Transactions' (1999) 3 Company Financial

cont. ...

1. Self Dealing

Directors frequently contract with or otherwise transact businesses with their company. In recent years, the American expression 'self dealing' is used to describe this kind of situations that give rise to an apparent conflict of interest: On the one hand, the director is acting in his own self-interest; on the other hand, he is a fiduciary and has to act in the interests of the company.

a) From Flat Prohibition to Policed Permission

At early common law, conflicted interest transactions could per se be annulled by the company without regard to whether they were fair to the company or not. The leading English authority was *Aberdeen Ry v Blaikie*,[59] and US courts originally ruled along the same lines.[60] This outright ban, however, has not survived the evolutionary common law process which has been recounted several times.[61] Today, Anglo-American company law permits interested directors transactions subject to judicial review.[62] In Germany, a strict prohibition against self dealing has not been accepted either.[63] Single proposals to return to the old rule[64] or to a combination of flat prohibition with a variance system[65] have hardly received any attention. A key argument against such a strict rule is that many transactions between the company and a director prove beneficial to both sides.[66] For example,

and Insolvency Law Review 190; L Enriques 'The Law on Company Directors' Self-Dealing: A Comparative Analysis' (2000) 2 International and Comparative Corporate Law Journal 297.

[59] (1854) 1 Macq HL 461, 471-472: '[I]t is a rule of universal application that no one, having such duties to discharge, shall be allowed to enter into engagements in which he has, or can have, a personal interest conflicting, or which possibly may conflict, with the interests of those whom he is bound to protect (...) So strictly is the principle adhered to that no question is allowed to be raised as to the fairness or unfairness of a contract so entered into.' However, that prohibition on self dealing has always been just a default rule which could be opted-out of by shareholder approval; see Enriques (n 58) 297 ff.

[60] *Wardell v Union Pacific RR Co* 103 US 651 (1880).

[61] H Marsh 'Are Directors Trustees?' (1966) 12 Business Lawyer 35; for a different interpretation of the case law see NP Beveridge 'The Corporate Director's Fiduciary Duty of Loyalty: Understanding the Self-Interested Director Transaction' [1992] DePaul Law Review 655; in support of Marsh's reading of the cases *Cary/Eisenberg Corporations, Cases and Materials* (7th edn 1995) 650-651.

[62] RC Clark *Corporate Law* (Little Brown Boston 1986) 160-166.

[63] H Wiedemann *Organverantwortung und Gesellschafterklagen in der Aktiengesellschaft* (Broschiert Wiesbaden 1990) 9.

[64] GH Roth Das Treuhandmodell des Investmentrechts (Athenäum Frankfurt 1972) 286: 'kompromißloser Purismus'.

[65] RC Clark (n 62) 188-189.

[66] Bainbridge (n 44) 308; Wiedemann (n 63) 9.

a director may own a valuable piece of property which would be useful to the company, or he may turn out to be the lender of last resort in financial distress.[67] Obviously, this will more often be the case in the context of smaller companies.

b) Procedural and Substantial Safeguards

In modern company law, the focus has shifted from prohibiting conflicted interest transactions to policing them. Analytically, one can distinguish procedural and substantial safeguards, mirroring the development of modern contract law which also oscillates between procedural and substantial fairness.[68]

aa) United Kingdom

The Joint Stock Companies Act of 1844 had expressly recognised the need for approval in general meeting. However, this provision soon disappeared and was replaced by a more flexible approach. Today, art. 85 of Table A adopted by most companies provides that a director can be interested in a contract with the company, provided that he has disclosed that interest to the board.[69] In addition to disclosure under the articles, s 317 Companies Act 1985 makes disclosure to the board a minimum statutory duty. Compliance with the articles is essential for the validity of the contract whereas compliance with s 317 Companies Act 1985 is necessary to avoid a fine.[70] The exact relationship between these two provisions, however, has not been fully explored by the courts,[71] and company law reform may lead to future changes in this respect.[72] Finally, disclosure in itself will not validate transactions which have been entered into by a director in breach of his duty to act bona fide in the interest of the company.[73]

[67] Historically, the latter cases paved the way for a general relaxation of the old rule; see eg *Twin Lick Oil v Marbury* 91 US 587 (1875).

[68] A Farnsworth *Contracts* (2d edn Little Brown Boston1990), 332; H Kötz *Europäisches Vertragsrecht* (Mohr Tübingen 1996) 191.

[69] JH Farrar and B Hannigan *Company Law* (4th edn Butterworths London 1998) 397: 'It is extremely common for companies to use the articles in this way (...).'

[70] ibid 399; PL Davies (n 3) 613-614.

[71] *Hely-Hutchison v Brayhead Ltd* [1968] 1 QB 549, 595; *Guiness plc v Saunders* [1990] 2 AC 663, 697.

[72] Company Law Review Steering Group 'Modern Company Law for a Competitive Economy – Completing the Structure' (2000) paras 4.11 – 4.16; Final Report (2001) para 6.8.

[73] *Neptune (Vehicle Washing Equipment) Ltd v Fitzgerald (No 2)* [1995] BCC 1000, 1017; Farrar and Hannigan (n 69) 401-402.

bb) United States

American courts have begun, by 1960, to recognise contracts with interested directors as generally valid unless found to be unfair by a court if challenged.[74] Since 1970, most jurisdictions have adopted so-called safe-harbour-statutes for conflicted interest transactions, using § 41 of the old Model Business Corporation Act as a model.[75] The new Model Business Corporation Act, revised in 1988, deals with directors' conflicting interest transactions in a separate subchapter.[76] A similar approach has been presented by the ALI-Principles: According to § 5.02, a director who enters into a transaction with the corporation fulfils the duty of fair dealing if disclosure concerning the conflict of interest and the transaction is made to the corporate decision maker who authorises in advance or ratifies the transaction, and either (1) the transaction is fair to the corporation when entered into; (2) the transaction is authorised in advance by disinterested directors who could reasonably have concluded that the transaction was fair to the corporation at the time of such authorisation; (3) the transaction is ratified by disinterested directors under the same conditions, provided that the failure to obtain advance authorisation did not adversely effect the interests of the corporation in a significant way; (4) the transaction is authorised in advance or ratified by disinterested shareholders, and does not constitute a waste of corporate assets.[77] A party who challenges the transaction has the burden of proof unless the transaction has not been approved by disinterested directors or shareholders. In such a case, the director has the burden of proving that the transaction was fair to the corporation.[78]

cc) France

French company law can look back to a long tradition of policing transactions between directors and their company. As early as 1867, the Companies Act had introduced a provision prohibiting directors to place themselves, without explicit approval of the general meeting, in a position in which there is a conflict between the duties to the company and their personal interest.[79] In 1966, the revised Companies Act introduced a special procedure for policing conflicted interest trans-

[74] RC Clark (n 62) 160.

[75] A Bulbulia and AR Pinto 'Statutory Responses to Interested Directors' Transactions: A Watering Down of Fiduciary Standards?' (1977) 53 Notre Dame Law Review 201.

[76] See Revised Model Business Corporation Act, Subchapter F: Directors' Conflicting Interest Transactions, §§ 8.60 – 8.63.

[77] American Law Institute 'Principles of Corporate Governance' (1994) § 5.02 (a).

[78] ibid § 5.02 (b).

[79] For a detailed analysis see Bizot Espiard 'Étude de l'art. 40 de la loi de 1867' thèse Paris (1945).

actions[80] which has been amended and enlarged by recent reform legislation in 2001.[81] Pursuant to the basic rule in art. L. 225-38 C. com., any convention between a public company and its directors needs prior approval of the board of directors.[82] A small exception covers conventions in the ordinary cause of business and at usual business conditions (*conventions courantes*).[83] Looking at the details, the control procedure consists of five stages: (1) information to the board of directors about the conflict of interest and the details of the transaction; (2) prior approval of the board of directors, (3) information to the internal auditors by the president about the envisaged transaction, (4) report of the internal auditors about the transaction submitted to the general meeting, (5) approval by the general meeting.[84] Sanctions for a violation depend on the respective stage at which the violation occurred.[85] In a private company, the policing procedure is less extensive.[86]

dd) Germany

In coping with conflicted interest transactions, the German Stock Corporation Act makes use of the two-tier-structure of the board: According to § 112 AktG, contracts with members of the management board are transferred for decision to the supervisory board.[87] This provision is based on the legislative concern that the other members of the management board are not disinterested if one of their colleagues transacts with the company.[88] Although not expressly articulated in the Act, it is now widely recognised that all self dealing transactions must also pass the test of dealing at arm's length.[89]

[80] For a detailed analysis see Balensi 'Les conventions entre les sociétés commerciales et leurs dirigeants' thèse Paris (1975); for a comparative study K Huffmann *Kontrolle schuldrechtlicher Austauschgeschäfte zwischen Gesellschaftern und ihren Mitgliedern* (CH Beck Verlag 1996) 5-109.

[81] A Viandier *Sociétés et Loi NRE* (F Lefebre Levallois 2001) [320] ff.

[82] For details see M Germain in G Ripert and R Roblot *Droit commercial* (18th edn Librairie générale de droit et de jurisprudence Paris 2002) tome 1 vol 2, [1647].

[83] P Le Cannu *Droit des Sociétés* (Dalloz Paris 2002) [708].

[84] For details see M Cozian, A Viandier and D Deboissy *Droit des sociétés* (15th edn Litec Paris 2002) [728].

[85] Le Cannu (n 83) [711-712].

[86] Ripert and others (n 82) [1326].

[87] T Abeltshauser *Leitungshaftung in Kapitalgesellschaften* (1998) 337; U Hübner *Interessenkonflikt und Vertretungsmacht* (Munich 1977) 230.

[88] BGHZ 103, 216 at 217; Hüffer (n 34) § 112 comment 1.

[89] KJ Hopt (n 2) § 93 comment 159; H Fleischer 'Zur organschaftlichen Treuepflicht der Geschäftsleiter im Aktien- und GmbH-Recht' (2003) Wertpapier-Mitteilungen 1045 with a more detailed exposition of the problems in private companies.

c) Specific Types of Transactions

In most legal systems, there are statutory provisions for certain types of transactions that are particularly dangerous for the company. According to sec. 330 Companies Act 1985, companies are prohibited from making a loan to a director or shadow director.[90] Exceptions to the general prohibition include loans not exceeding 5000 £, intra-group transactions and money-lending companies. Moreover, sec. 320-322 Companies Act 1985 seek to reduce the potential damage flowing from substantial property transactions with the company; and sec. 323-329 Companies Act 1985 seek to regulate certain share dealings by directors and their families. In the States, sec. 402 of the Sarbanes Oxley Act, adding subsection 13 (k) to the Securities Exchange Act 1934, has recently introduced a ban on loans to executive officers and directors overlapping the more lenient treatment in almost all state jurisdictions.[91] French company law prohibits the extension of credit to and standing surety for directors in art. L. 225-43 C. com. In Germany, § 89 (1) AktG permits companies to extend credit to members of the management board only pursuant to a resolution of the supervisory board, and § 43a GmbHG provides for additional safeguards in private companies in order to strengthen creditor protection.

2. Corporate Opportunities

A core feature of the director's duty of loyalty is the strict prohibition to use corporate opportunities for himself. In all jurisdictions, the difficult issue is to determine what should be deemed, as between company and director, to belong to the company.

a) Judicial Tests

aa) United States

The classic test adopted by American courts is the so-called interest or expectancy test focusing on whether the corporation has an interest or tangible expectancy in a certain business opportunity.[92] Other courts have given primary weight to whether the opportunity is related to or in the corporation's line of business.[93] The ALI-Principles offer a comprehensive definition of a corporate opportunity

[90] Farrar and Hannigan (n 69) 402-406.

[91] For an overview of state law provisions JW Barnard 'Corporate Loans to Directors and Officers: Every Business Now a Bank?' [1988] Wisconsin Law Review 237 at 238, 240-244.

[92] *Lagarde v Anniston Lime & Store Co*, 28 So 199 (Ala 1900).

[93] *Guth v Loft, Inc*, 5 A 2d 503 (Del 1939).

combining elements of both traditional tests.[94] A recent decision of the Delaware Supreme Court, however, has shattered the elusive goal of clarity by evaluating the director's conduct under the totality of the circumstances.[95] The court identifies four relevant considerations insisting that they are mere factors not elements: (1) Is a corporation financially able to take the opportunity? (2) Is the opportunity in the corporation's line of business? (3) Does the corporation have an interest or expectancy in the opportunity? (4) Does a director create a conflict between his self-interest and that of a corporation by taking the opportunity for himself?[96]

bb) United Kingdom

English company law has enriched the corporate opportunities doctrine with cases in which directors resign, form a new company and take up business opportunities in their own capacity.[97] Traditionally, the courts did not hesitate to hold the directors liable for breach of fiduciary duties under such circumstances.[98] However, recent cases seem to indicate a change of approach making it easier for directors to set up their own business profiting from the accumulated knowledge and experience in their former position.[99] Much attention has also been devoted to cases where the company rejected the opportunity from which the directors subsequently profited.[100] In this respect, English courts have followed (and still follow) a hard line[101] whereas other Commonwealth jurisdictions prefer a more

[94] American Law Institute 'Principles of Corporate Governance' (1994) § 5.05 (b).

[95] *Broz v Cellular Information Systems, Inc*, 673 A 2d 148 (Del 1996). For recent academic treatment see PL Davis 'Corporate Opportunities and Comparative Advantage' (1998) 84 Iowa Law Review 211; RA Epstein, 'Contract and Trust in Corporate Law: The Case of Corporate Opportunity' (1996) 21 Delaware Journal of Corporate Law 5; Gelb 'The Corporate Opportunities Doctrine: Recent Cases and the Elusive Goal of Clarity' (1997) 31 University of Richmond Law Review 371; EL Talley 'Turning Servile Opportunities into Gold: A Strategic Analysis of the Corporate Opportunities Doctrine' (1998) 108 Yale Law Journal 277.

[96] *Broz v Cellular Information Systems, Inc*, 673 A 2d 148 (Del 1996); see also WT Allen and RH Kraakman, *Commentaries and Cases on the Law of Business Organization* (Foundation Press Aspen 2003) 329-336.

[97] For a detailed analysis see Ferran (n 9) 192-194; PL Davies (n 3) 422-423.

[98] *Industrial Developments Consultants v Cooly* [1972] 2 All ER 162.

[99] *Canadian Aero Services Ltd v O'Malley* (1973) 40 DLR (3d) 371; *Island Export Finance Ltd v Umunna* [1986] BCLC 460; *Balston Ltd v Headline Filters Ltd* [1990] F.S.R. 385; *Framlington Group Plc v Anderson* [1995] 1 BCLC 475; *Dranez Anstalt v Hayek* [2002] 1 BCLC 693; for a comparative analysis H Fleischer 'Die Gegenwartsfragen der Geschäftschancenlehre im englischen und deutschen Gesellschaftsrecht' in *Festschrift Kilian* (forthcoming).

[100] Farrar and Hannigan (n 69) 418-410.

[101] *Regal (Hastings) Ltd v Gulliver* [1942] 1 All ER 378.

flexible approach.[102] Ongoing company law reform may lead to changes in this area.[103]

cc) Germany

German company law has begun to shape its own concept of corporate opportunities in the 1970s,[104] relying heavily on comparative insights.[105] By now, there is a rich body of case law[106] and extensive academic writing.[107] In defining a corporate opportunity, similar tests have emerged as under U.S. law. An often-cited decision of the *Bundesgerichtshof* has rejected a distinction between business opportunities offered to the director in his corporate capacity and those offered to him in a private context pointing to the indivisibility of fiduciary duties.[108] The same judgment also establishes rather strict rules for directors who leave the company and take with them business opportunities.[109] Despite some criticism in the literature,[110] there is no indication that the courts will strike a balance in future cases that is considerably more in favour of directors than hitherto.

b) Economic Explanations

From a law and economics standpoint, vesting the company with a property right to the corporate opportunity is a well-founded concept: The director is contractually bound to search for business opportunities in the interest of the company, and he receives in return the agreed on compensation for his efforts.[111] The executive compensation which may vary according to the director's success

[102] *Queensland Mines Ltd v Hudson* (1978) 52 ALJR 399 (Australian High Court); *Peso-Silver Mines Ltd v Copper* (1966) 58 DLR (2d) 1 (Supreme Court of Canada).

[103] Company Law Review Steering Group 'Modern Company Law for a Competitive Economy – Final Report' (2001) paras 3.21 – 3.27.

[104] For a detailed exposition H Fleischer 'Verdeckte Gewinnausschüttung: Die Geschäftschancenlehre zwischen Gesellschafts- und Steuerrecht' [1999] Deutsches Steuerrecht 1249 ff.

[105] See especially Mestmäcker (n 30) 166 ff; Immenga (n 30)156 ff.

[106] Cases collected by Hopt (n 2) § 93 comments 166 ff.

[107] N Polley *Wettbewerbsverbot und Geschäftschancenlehre* (Nomos Baden Baden 1993); R Schuhknecht *Schranken der Geschäftschancenwahrnehmung und Wettbewerbsverbot beim GmbH-Geschäftsführer* (Tübingen 1992); J Weisser *Corporate Opportunities* (Heymanns Cologne 1991).

[108] BGH NJW 1986, 585, 586.

[109] BGH NJW 1986, 585, 586.

[110] Hopt (n 2) § 93 comment 169; for a detailed treatment H Fleischer 'Gegenwartsfragen der Geschäftschancenlehre im englischen und deutschen Gesellschaftsrecht' in *Festschrift Kilian* (forthcoming).

[111] H Fleischer 'Verdeckte Gewinnausschüttung: Die Geschäftschancenlehre zwischen Gesellschafts- und Steuerrecht' [1999] Deutsches Steuerrecht 1249 at 1251.

explains why the corporate opportunity doctrine does not significantly discourage the production of new information.[112] Around the edges, however, the scope of the property right is a debatable matter, especially in cases where the director resigns and forms a new company making use of his know how accumulated over the years (nota bene: not a maturing business opportunity actively pursued by the company). Under such circumstances, a more lenient attitude towards the director may be advisable in order to foster entrepreneurial activity and to avoid undue restraints of trade.[113]

3. Misappropriation of Corporate Resources

A similar fact pattern involves the misappropriation of corporate resources. In this regard, courts and academic writers draw a dividing line between unilaterally usurped and consensually granted benefits.[114] To borrow an impressive phrase by Judge Easterbrook: 'It is a violation of duty to steal from the corporate treasury; it is not a violation to write oneself a check that the board has approved as a bonus.'[115] Illustrations from German case law include the free use of corporate personnel for building one's own home[116] and private holidays or invitations at the expense of the company.[117] A recent judgment of the *Bundesgerichtshof* offers some guidance as to whether the use of the company's car for private purposes is part of the director's official compensation package in private companies.[118] The ALI-Principles emphasise that the scope of the misappropriation doctrine goes well beyond the taking-of-corporate-property paradigm: 'A director

[112] H Fleischer 'Grundfragen der ökonomischen Theorie im Gesellschafts- und Kapitalmarktrecht' [2001] Zeitschrift für Unternehmens- und Gesellschaftsrecht 1 at 8; see also Beveridge *Corporate Law and Economics* (2002) 322; more generally Posner (n 43) § 4.6, 126: 'The agent is paid to treat the principal as he would treat himself; to be his alter ego. The fiduciary principle is the law's answer to the problem of unequal costs of information. It allows you to hire someone with superior information to deal on your behalf with others having superior information.'

[113] Along the same lines Pettet (n 3) 183: 'If he [ie: the director] has a lifetime of general entrepreneurial activity in various markets, it will not be possible for a company which hires him for a few years of that lifetime to argue that all future business in that area becomes the business of the company.' See also PL Davies (n 3) 423.

[114] H Fleischer 'Zur organschaftlichen Treuepflicht der Geschäftsleiter im Aktien- und GmbH-Recht' (2003) Wertpapier-Mitteilungen 1045 with many comparative references.

[115] *Jordan v Duff & Phelps Inc,* 815 F 2d 429 at 436 (7th Cir), *cert dismissed,* 108 S Ct 1067 (1988).

[116] BGH WM 1976, 77 at 78.

[117] KG NZG 2001, 325 at 326-327.

[118] BGH NJW 2003, 431 at 432.

(...) may not use corporate property, material, non-public corporate information, or corporate position to secure a pecuniary benefit.'[119]

4. Benefits from Third Parties in Connection with Corporate Transactions

Finally, directors may not, in connection with their work, demand nor accept from third parties payments or other advantages for themselves. Typical examples from the rich US-American case law include securing undisclosed commissions[120] that are regarded as a misuse of corporate position.[121] English illustrations involve bribes on which the courts have always taken a strict line.[122] The German experience is not much different ranging from commissions and bribes to special conditions for private transactions.[123] As a universal rule, it is not necessary for the company to show harm in order to invalidate the contract.[124] Moreover, courts tend to regard side payments as prima facie evidence that the company suffered a loss at least to the amount of the side payment.[125]

5. Common Features

a) Indirect Benefits

The four conflict-of-interest paradigms discussed above frequently involve situations in which the director's advantage is deliberately concealed: The favourable transaction takes place between the company and the director's spouse (self-dealing); the business opportunity to buy an attractive piece of property is taken up by a company wholly owned by the director (corporate opportunity); the dinner invitation at the company's expense includes the director's relatives (misappropriation of corporate resources); the undisclosed commission is paid to a director's nominee (benefits from third parties in connection with corporate transactions). Most company law legislators have foreseen such strategies and put additional safeguards into place. Sec. 346 Companies Act 1985 stipulates that the

[119] American Law Institute 'Principles of Corporate Governance (1994)' § 5.04 (a).

[120] Cases collected in Annotation, Liability of Corporate Officer or Director for Commission or Compensation Received from Third Person in Connection with that Person's Transaction with Corporation, 47 ALR 3d 373.

[121] American Law Institute 'Principles of Corporate Government' (1994) § 5.04, 255.

[122] *Industrial and General Mortgage Co Ltd v Lewis* [1949] 2 All ER 537; PL Davies (n 3) 423-424.

[123] RGZ 96, 53 at 54; BGH WM 1983, 498 at 499; BGH WM 1992, 691 at 693; BGH NJW 2001, 2476 at 2477.

[124] OLG Düsseldorf WM 2000 1393, 1397.

[125] BGH NJW 2001, 2476 at 2477; OLG Düsseldorf WM 2000, 1393 at 1397.

fair dealing provisions are also applicable to connected persons (spouse, child, step-child) and to associated or controlled bodies corporate (ownership of at least one-fifth of the share capital).[126] Likewise, § 5.08 of the ALI-Principles extends the scope of the duty of fair dealing to cases in which the pecuniary benefit accrues to an associate as defined in § 1.03 (spouse, child, grandchild, sibling, parent of director; individual having the same home as a director; person with respect to whom a director has a business, financial, or similar relationship that would reasonably be expected the person's judgment with respect to the transaction in question). Similarly, art. L. 225-38 C. com. requires a policing of self-dealing transactions in which the director participates through an intermediate person (*personne interposée*) or in which he is indirectly interested (*indirectement interessée*).[127] German company law, unfortunately, lacks a general provision. Courts and commentators tend to broaden the concept of § 89 (3) AktG by analogy, thus extending the rules of self dealing to the spouse, a minor child and any third party acting on behalf of the directors.[128]

b) Post-Contractual Duties

As a general matter, it is now widely recognised that the duty of loyalty does not necessarily cease when the director's appointment ends. A dogmatic explanation has been provided by German courts drawing a parallel to the well-accepted doctrine of post-contractual duties in contract law.[129] English illustrations stem from the area of corporate opportunities;[130] a recent French example involves the enticing away the company's personnel by a former director.[131]

III. Conclusions

On a more general level, one can distil two guiding principles from the rich comparative case law and literature on fiduciary duties. These principles are the avoidance of conflicts of interest and the prohibition of special benefits for directors to the detriment of the company. They correspond with two fundamental

[126] Farrar and Hannigan (n 69) 402-403.

[127] Le Cannu (n 83).

[128] H Fleischer 'Zur organschaftlichen Treuepflicht der Geschäftsleiter im Aktien- und GmbH-Recht' (2003) Wertpapiermitteilungen 1045 with further references.

[129] BGH WM 1977, 194; for a detailed analysis C Palzer 'Fortwirkende organschaftliche Pflichten des Geschäftsführers der GmbH' (Heymanns Cologne 2001).

[130] *Island Export Finance Ltd v Umunna* [1986] BCLC 460; PL Davies (n 3) 601.

[131] Cass com 24 February 1998 (n 23) 637.

concepts elaborated by English courts and academic writers: the no-conflict rule and the no-profit rule as separate, but overlapping concepts.[132]

1. Avoiding Conflicts of Interest (No-Conflict Rule)

The director's duty of loyalty primarily aims at avoiding conflicts of interest. Clearly, this is the common thread running through the international and comparative literature: Anglo-American textbooks address the variety of fact patterns in a chapter on 'Conflicts of Interest';[133] the French legislator has introduced new provisions on self dealing under the heading 'Prévention des conflits d'intérêt';[134] the German Code of Corporate Governance explains the fiduciary duties in a separate part entitled 'Interessenkonflikte'.[135] In achieving this ambitious goal, two basic principles are generally agreed upon. The most prominent one, already articulated by Berle and Means in their seminal study on the topic,[136] is that a director must disclose conflicts of interest to the board or the general meeting. It is supplemented by a second rule requiring a director to render account and to keep records so that the shareholders are able to supervise his conduct.

2. Prohibiting Unjustified Benefits (No-Profit Rule)

While the no-conflict rule primarily envisages bilateral (most often: contractual) relationships, the no-profit rule chiefly deals with one-way transactions. The basic idea is that a director, being in a fiduciary position, is not entitled to profit from that position, unless otherwise expressly provided. In practice, the main concern of the no-profit rule is with secret profits.[137] Such clandestine benefits include the

[132] Farrar and Hannigan (n 69) 396 ff, 415 ff; Ferran (n 9) 189: 'Thus, while some judges treat the no-profit rule as being a sub-category of the no-conflict rule, others regard no-profit and no-conflict as separate, but overlapping rules.'

[133] Clark (n 62) Chapter 4: 'Introduction to Conflict of Interest'.

[134] Le Cannu (n 83) no 700: 'Sous cet intitulé très général, la Loi NRE traite de ce que la pratique a coutume d'appeler les conventions réglementées et les conventions interdites'; for a detailed analysis D Schmidt *Les conflits d'intérêts dans la société anonyme* (Joly Paris 2000).

[135] German Code of Corporate Governance s 4.3; for a comment HM Ringleb in HM Ringleb, T Kremer, M Lutter and V Werder *Deutscher Corporate Governance Kodex. Kommentar* (Beck Munich 2003), comments 591 ff.

[136] A Berle and GC Means *The Modern Corporation and Private Property* (Hein Buffalo NY 1932) 307: 'The one ethical point on which everyone is agreed is that the adverse interest, if any, must be disclosed. There appears to be a general feeling that where a man represents adverse interests without letting that fact be known, he has created a situation so dangerous as not to be tolerated in the business community.'

[137] Farrar and Hannigan (n 69) 415.

misappropriation of corporate assets and business opportunities as well as the receiving of bribes and undisclosed commissions in connection with corporate transactions. Other classical illustrations, most notably profits from insider trading,[138] are meanwhile regulated in special national provisions transforming the EU Directive on Insider Dealing. Finally, an important comparative observation is that the scope of the no-profit rule goes well beyond a technical property-rights approach in the narrow legal sense and also includes the misuse of corporate information and position.

C. Duties to Creditors and the Responsibility for Wrongful Trading

It is a widespread belief among company law scholars that the accountability of directors needs to be strengthened when the company is threatened by insolvency. Drawing on earlier proposals,[139] the High Level Group of Company Law Experts recommends the introduction of a wrongful trading rule at EU level.[140] Existing national rules, argues the Group, are very similar across Member States: They make directors liable for not reacting when they ought to foresee the company's insolvency.[141] As a general rule, this is undoubtedly true. However, a closer look reveals considerable divergences in salient points which may have a great impact on the efficacy of a wrongful trading regime.

I. Directors' Duties and Creditors' Interests

Before turning to the technicalities of corporate insolvency law, it is highly instructive to consider an issue which ties together directors' fiduciary duties and directors' responsibility for wrongful trading. That issue is whether directors owe fiduciary duties to creditors.

[138] As to insider dealing as breach of fiduciary duties see Farrar and Hannigan (n 69) 421-422; Hopt (n 3) § 93 comments 173-175.

[139] See Forum Europaeum 'Konzernrecht für Europa' [1998] Zeitschrift für Unternehmens- und Gesellschaftsrecht 672 at 752-766; commented on by H Fleischer 'Neue Entwicklungen im englischen Konzernrecht – vergleichende Notizen im Lichte der Empfehlungen des Forum Europaeum Konzernrecht' [1999] Die Aktiengesellschaft 350.

[140] Report of the High Level Group of Company Law Experts on a Modern Regulatory Framework for Company Law in Europe (European Commission November 2002) (hereafter Winter Report, see Annex 3 in this volume) Recommendation 3.13.

[141] Winter Report 68-69.

1. United Kingdom

In the UK, there is considerable support for the position that directors, in some circumstances, owe the fiduciary duties to the company's creditors.[142] This approach has its origin in a number of Australian and New Zealand decisions.[143] A clear recognition in the English courts is to be found in *West Mercia Safetywear Ltd v Dodd* where Dillon L.J. explained that in insolvency the creditors 'become prospectively entitled, through the mechanism of liquidation, to displace the power of the directors and the shareholders to deal with the company's assets'.[144] A recent judgment has further elaborated on that doctrine and has summarised it as follows: 'Where a company is insolvent or of doubtful solvency or on the verge of insolvency and it is the creditors' money which is at risk the directors, when carrying out their duty to the company must consider the interests of the creditors as paramount and take those into account when exercising their discretion.'[145] The value of this judicial approach is still unclear. While there has been support for the view that the directors owe a direct duty to creditors[146] the predominant opinion is that directors rather owe a duty to their companies to take into account the creditors' interest.[147] Under this view, the duty cannot be enforced by creditors so that they have to wait until a liquidator is appointed and able to champion their claims.[148] A number of commentators argue that the duty to act in the best interests of creditors is ill-focused[149] and no longer needed, since s 214 of the Insolvency Act 1986 permits liquidators to claim compensation from directors for what has come to be known as wrongful trading[150] – a cause of action that is explored in greater detail below. In its Final Report, the Company

[142] For a recent study see A Keay 'The Duty of Directors to Take Account of Creditors' Interests: Has It Any Role to Play?' [2002] Journal of Business Law 370.

[143] For references see Farrar and Hannigan (n 69) 383.

[144] *West Mercia Safetywear Ltd v Dodd* [1988] BCLC 250.

[145] *Colin Gwyer & Associates v London Wharf (Limehouse) Ltd* [2002] All ER (D) 226 (Dec) at n° 74.

[146] Sappideen 'Fiduciary Obligation to Corporate Creditors' [1991] Journal of Business Law 365.

[147] Ferran (n 9) 139; PL Davies (n 3) 372-374.

[148] Keay (n 142) 379 at 380 with note 11.

[149] S Sealy 'Directors' Duties – An Unnecessary Gloss' [1988] Cambridge Law Journal 175 at 177.

[150] PL Davies (n 3) 604: 'Perhaps, because of these statutory provisions, the common law developments have not proceeded very rapidly.'; also Ferran (n 9) 140: 'In the absence of a direct duty to creditors the primary significance of the cases (...) is that this leads to a powerful limitation on the power of the shareholders to authorise the directors to behave in a manner which conflicts with the duties that they owe to the company under the general law, or to ratify wrongdoing after it has occurred.'

Law Review Steering Group took the view that a principle requiring directors to have regard for creditors' interests should be included in the statutory statement of directors' duties.[151] The Government's White Paper, however, has concluded that the weight of the argument is against the inclusion of any duties in relation to creditors.[152]

2. United States

Traditionally, US courts have refused to extend fiduciary duties for the benefit of creditors and have repeatedly held that creditors' rights are limited by the terms of their contracts with the corporation.[153] Under this general rule, directors need not take creditors' interests into account in their decision-making process. The indenture thus both defines and confines the scope of the corporation's obligations to its bondholders.[154] There is, however, support for an exception to the legal primacy of shareholders interests. Several courts have held that once a corporation becomes insolvent, directors owe a fiduciary duty to creditors.[155] The leading precedent is *Credit Lyonnais Bank Nederland, N.V. v Pathe Communication Corp* where Chancellor Allen asserted: 'At least where a corporation is operating in the vicinity of insolvency, a board of directors is not merely the agent of the residue risk bearers, but owes its duty to the corporate enterprise.'[156] He elaborated his view in a famous footnote explaining that '[t]he possibility of insolvency can do curious things to incentives, exposing creditors to risks of opportunistic behaviour and creating complexities for directors'.[157] Upon closer examination, however, many of the cases cited for this view involve fraudulent conveyances or preferences that can be annulled under bankruptcy law.[158] Because creditors can seek redress for those transactions under special provisions, it is not entirely clear what a cause of action based on breach of fiduciary duties adds to the current statutory scheme.

[151] Company Law Review Steering Group 'Modern Company Law for a Competitive Economy – Final report' (2001) paras 3.12 – 3.20.

[152] Modernising Company Law, White Paper (2002), paras 3.8 – 3.14.

[153] *Metropolitan Life Ins Co v RJR Nabisco, Inc*, 716 F Supp 1504 at 1524-1525 (SDNY 1989); *Simons v Cogan*, 549 A2d 300 at 304 (Del 1988).

[154] Bainbridge (n 44) 431.

[155] For references see L Lin 'Shift of Fiduciary Duty Upon Corporate Insolvency: Proper Scope of Directors' Duty to Creditors' (1993) 46 Vanderbilt Law Review 1485 at 1511.

[156] 1991 WL 277613 (Del Ch 1991) = [1992] 17 Delaware Journal of Corporate Law 1099 at 1155. See also B Nicholson Recent Delaware Case Law Regarding Directors' Duties to Bondholders (1994) 19 Delaware Journal of Corporate Law 573.

[157] (1992) 17 Delaware Journal of Corporate Law 1099 at 1155 note 55.

[158] Beveridge (n 112) 431; Lin (n 155) 1485 at 1514-1515.

3. Germany

Under German law, extra-contractual duties to creditors are sometimes mentioned in passing as a sub-species of the larger controversy over corporate social responsibility. The central question, however, has never been up for discussion, and the Anglo-American case law in this regard has hitherto been neglected by comparative scholarship. To be sure, § 18 (1) of the Insolvency Code (InsO) has introduced the concept of imminent inability to pay debts as they fall due (*drohende Zahlungsunfähigkeit*) as a cause for bankruptcy proceedings, but limits the right to file a bankruptcy petition under such circumstances to the company and the company only.[159] The creditors' right to petition for the institution of insolvency proceedings is reserved to cases of actual inability to pay debts.

II. Responsibility for Wrongful Trading

The general concept of wrongful trading is well-known in many EU Member States. The details of the national rules, however, differ markedly. Crucial points include the relevant time when wrongful trading rules come into play and the scope of protection for new creditors who contracted with the company after the critical date. Illustrations are taken from English, German and Swiss law. The rich French and Belgian experience with the *action en comblement du passif* can only be mentioned in passing.[160]

1. United Kingdom

a) Legal framework

In England, wrongful trading liability is dealt with in sec. 214 of the Insolvency Act 1986. Under that provision a court can, on application by a company's liquidator, declare that a director has engaged in wrongful trading and therefore must contribute to the assets available to creditors. Following the recommendations of the Cork Committee,[161] wrongful trading was introduced as an attempt to discourage and penalise abuses of limited liability which stemmed from negligent

[159] J Schulze-Osterloh, in A Baumbach and G Hueck *GmbH-Gesetz* (17th edn Beck Verlag 2001) § 64 comment 9.

[160] For France see Cozian, Viandier and Deboissy (n 84) no 371-372; for Belgium see J-M Van Hille *La Société Anonyme* (Bruylant Brussels 1990) no 333-336.

[161] Report of the Review Committee on Insolvency Law and Practice (the Cork Report) Cmnd 8558 (1982) Chap 44.

rather than fraudulent conduct.[162] It is based on the idea that, in a company's precarious state of affairs, a reasonable director should realise the point of time at which the company cannot recover and should cease to operate as a going concern. Early commentators heralded the enactment of the wrongful trading rules as 'one of the most important developments in company law this century'.[163] Today, the enthusiasm has evaporated. Some academic writers doubt whether wrongful trading provides much assistance to creditors[164] and point to the small number of proceedings under sec. 214 Insolvency Act 1986.[165] Others disagree and emphasise the role of wrongful trading liability as a deterrent against managerial underperformance.[166]

b) Relevant time

Wrongful trading liability is triggered when the company has gone into insolvent liquidation and it appears that the company continued trading after a point in time before the commencement of the winding up when the director knew or ought to have concluded that there was no reasonable prospect that the company would avoid going into insolvent liquidation. In identifying this crucial point of time, English courts have been rather conservative.[167] They seem to give directors the benefit of the doubt[168] and hesitate to find that date too far back from the advent of insolvent liquidation.[169] However, due to a lack of jurisprudence there are still

[162] Pettet (n 3) 35-36; also PL Davies (n 3) 151, describing it as 'probably the most extreme departure from the rule in Salomon's case'.

[163] DD Prentice 'Creditors' Interests and Directors' Duties' (1990) 10 Oxford Journal of Legal Studies 265 at 277.

[164] BR Cheffins *Company Law. Theory, Structure and Operation* (Clarendon Oxford 1997) 539-541.

[165] Schulte 'Enforcing Wrongful Trading as a Standard of Conduct for Directors and a Remedy for Creditors: The Special Case of Corporate Insolvency' [1999] Company Lawyer 80.

[166] Ferran (n 9) 216; similarly Pettet (n 3) 39: 'On the other hand the infrequency of proceedings is probably not an accurate pointer to the effectiveness of the provision. In many situations the wrongful trading provisions are probably operating on the minds of directors, who will have been warned by their accountants about the dangers they face once the company becomes insolvent and it will have been put to them that they should consider putting the company into creditors' voluntary liquidation.'

[167] Keay (n 142) 379 at 388.

[168] Cooke and Hicks 'Wrongful Trading – Predicting Insolveny' [1993] Journal of Business Law, 338 at 341.

[169] An important example is *Re Purpoint Ltd* [1991] BCLC 491 at 498, per J Vinelott: 'I have felt some doubt whether a reasonably prudent director would have allowed the company to commence trading at all. It had no capital base (...) However, I do not think that it would be right to conclude that [the respondent] ought to have known that the company was doomed to en in an insolvent winding up from the moment it started to trade. That would, I think, impose too high a test.'

considerable uncertainties with respect to the exact scope of s 214 Insolvency Act 1986.[170]

c) Compensating creditors

In determining compensation the English legislator confers broad discretion onto the judiciary. According to sec. 214(1) Insolvency Act 1986, the court may order the directors to make such contribution (if any) to the company's assets as it thinks proper. In contrast to the fraudulent trading provision in s 213 Insolvency Act 1986 where a penal element may be appropriate,[171] jurisdiction under s 214 Insolvency Act 1986 is primarily compensatory in nature.[172] The outer boundaries of the compensation are set by the amount by which the company's assets have been depleted by the director's conduct.[173] A recent judgment, *Re Continental Assurance Company of London plc*, uses the label 'increase in net deficiency' and defines it as the loss to the company itself as result of the liquidation being delayed.[174] This approach seems to exclude further harm suffered by the class of creditors who entered into transactions with the company after the point at which insolvency proceedings should have been triggered.[175] An earlier judgment points to the same direction: In *Re Purpoint Ltd* the Chancery Division outrightly rejected the liquidator's contention that the 'new' creditors should be compensated in full: 'The purpose is to recoup the loss to the company so as to benefit the creditors as a whole. The Court has no jurisdiction to direct payments to creditors or to direct that moneys paid to the company should be applied in payment of one class of creditors in preference to another. Moreover, creditors whose debts are incurred after the critical date in fact have no stronger claim than those whose debts were incurred before that date. The former class also suffers to the extent that the assets of the company are depleted by wrongful trading.'[176]

[170] DD Prentice 'Corporate Personality, Limited Liability and the Protection of Creditors' in C Rickett and R Grantham (eds) *Corporate Personality in the 20th Century* (Hart Publishing Oxford 1998) 119: 'inherently elusive'; Cheffins (n 164) 542.

[171] *Re A Company* [1991] BCLC 197.

[172] *Re Produce Marketing Consortium Ltd (No 2)* [1989] BCLC 520.

[173] *Re Produce Marketing Consortium Ltd (No 2)* [1989] BCLC 520 at 553e: 'Prima facie the appropriate amount that a director is declared to be liable to contribute is the amount by which the company's assets can be discerned to have been depleted by the director's conduct which caused the discretion under sub-s (1) to arise.'

[174] *Re Continental Assurance Company of London plc* [2001] BPIR 733, commented by A Walters 'Wrongful Trading: Two Recent Cases' [2001] Insolvency Lawyer 211.

[175] PL Davies (n 3) 155: 'It seems that the contribution from the directors is to the assets of the company generally and not for the particular benefit of those who became creditors of the company during the period of wrongful trading.'

[176] [1991] BCLC 491, 499; approving comment by DD Prentice 'Creditors' Interests and Directors' Duties' (1990) 10 Journal of Oxford Legal Studies 265 at 272-273.

2. Germany

a) Legal framework

The functional equivalent of wrongful trading in Germany, the so-called *Insolvenzverschleppungshaftung* (literally: liability for delaying insolvency) is based on a combination of company law and tort law. The key provisions are to be found in § 92 (2) Stock Corporation Act (AktG) and in § 64 (1) Limited Liability Corporation Act (GmbHG). They stipulate in almost identical terms for public and private companies that the managing directors should file a petition for the institution of insolvency proceedings in the case of inability to make payments (*Zahlungsunfähigkeit*) and over-indebtedness (*Überschuldung*). Both provisions are regarded as protective norms (*Schutzgesetze*) under German tort law, ie § 823 (2) of the Civil Code (BGB).[177] As a consequence, their violation can give rise to damage claims against the directors.[178]

b) Relevant time

German company law operates with two alternative concepts to designate the time when wrongful trading starts: Inability to make payments and over-indebtedness. Both concepts which correspond in some respects (though not fully) with the English cash flow test and balance sheet test have received a statutory definition in the Insolvency Code (InsO). According to § 17 (2) InsO, inability to make payments means inability to pay debts as they fall due;[179] and pursuant to § 19 (2) InsO, over-indebtedness means excess of liabilities over assets.[180] Either of those two concepts trigger the legal duty to file a petition for the institution of insolvency proceedings 'without undue delay', as §§ 92 (2) AktG, 64 (1) GmbHG put it. Both norms, however, provide for a grace period of three weeks in which rescue efforts may take place.[181] After the expiry of that period, there is no discretion left: The directors are forced to file for insolvency and the company's state of affairs becomes public.

c) Compensating creditors

The German concept of compensation is based on a fundamental distinction between 'new' creditors (*Neugläubiger*), ie those who contracted with the com-

[177] RGZ 73, 30; BGHZ 29, 100.

[178] K Schmidt *Gesellschaftsrecht* (4th edn Heymanns Cologne 2002) 1003 ff with many references.

[179] For details see Schulze-Osterloh (n 159) § 64 comments 4 ff.

[180] ibid § 64 comments 11 ff. Under this test, assets are valued on a going concern basis if the continuation of business is more likely than not.

[181] M Lutter and P Hommelhoff *GmbH-Gesetz* (15th edn Schmidt Cologne 2000) § 64 comments 25-27.

pany after the directors should have duly filed for insolvency, and 'old' creditors (*Altgläubiger*), ie those whose claims predate the relevant time. In an earlier decision, the *Bundesgerichtshof* had ruled that § 64 (1) GmbHG protected both classes of creditors, but saw the protective ambit of the provision as being limited to the loss resulting from the diminution of the insolvency dividend.[182] Accordingly, the new creditors did not receive compensation for their reliance loss.[183] This solution soon proved to be impracticable,[184] but was nevertheless confirmed on several occasions[185] until the *Bundesgerichtshof* finally overruled it in a landmark decision in 1994.[186] According to this judgment, old creditors and new creditors are protected in different ways. The old creditors are still compensated for their so-called *Quotenschaden*, a method of calculating damages that compares two positions: the hypothetical insolvency dividend that would have been payable to the creditors at the time when the company should have filed for insolvency and the actual dividend. The difference is being referred to as *Quotenschaden* and may only be recovered by the liquidator.[187] The new creditors, in contrast, receive compensation for their reliance on the company's continued solvency. In reaching this conclusion, the *Bundesgerichtshof* interpreted the protective ambit of § 64 (1) GmbHG much more widely than in earlier cases: The directors duty to file for bankruptcy shall secure the elimination of insolvent companies.[188] Violating this duty renders the directors liable to compensate the new creditors for their damage caused by their entering into legal relationships with the insolvent company. The reliance loss is recoverable by each new creditor individually outside the insolvency proceedings.[189] As the law now stands, the basic distinction between *Altgläubigern* and *Neugläubigern* is firmly established and supported by most academic writers,[190] although it is not unanimously accepted.[191]

182 BGHZ 29, 100 at 103-105.

183 BGHZ 29, 100 at 106.

184 See references in BGHZ 126, 181 at 197: 'beängstigende Schwierigkeiten bei der Schadensschätzung'; 'juristische Spielerei'; 'ebenso ästhetisch anziehend wie praktisch undurchführbar'.

185 BGH WM 1962, 527 at 530; BGHZ 100, 19 at 23-24.

186 BGHZ 126, 181.

187 BGHZ 126, 181 at 190.

188 BGHZ 126, 181 at 184: 'Der Normzweck der gesetzlichen Konkursantragspflichten besteht darin, konkursreife Gesellschaften mit beschränktem Haftungsfonds vom Geschäftsverkehr fernzuhalten, damit durch das Auftreten solcher Gebilde nicht Gläubiger geschädigt oder gefährdet werden.'

189 BGHZ 138, 281.

190 Lutter and Hommelhoff (n 181) § 64 comments 40 ff with many references.

191 For a different approach K Schmidt (n 178) 1085-1086 with references.

3. Switzerland

a) Legal framework

In Switzerland, the general obligation to file for bankruptcy in case of actual insolvency is to be found in Art. 725 (2) OR. It requires that directors prepare an interim balance sheet when there is serious concern of over-indebtedness. If upon preparation of that balance sheet it becomes apparent that the liabilities exceed the assets, the board of directors is obliged to report to the judge who opens insolvency proceedings according to Art. 725a (1) OR. If there is prospect of rescue the judge may delay the commencement of insolvency proceedings. Directors who violate their reporting duties may be held liable under the general liability provision in Art. 754 OR.[192]

b) Relevant time

The legal duty to report to the judge is triggered in the case of over-indebtedness. As Art. 725 (2) OR specifies, the interim balance sheet has to be prepared both on a going concern and a liquidation value basis. If in either case the liabilities exceed the assets of the company, the board of directors has to file for the institution of insolvency proceedings.

c) Compensating creditors

Compensation issues have been a battleground in Swiss company law for more than a decade.[193] In two major decisions in 1991[194] and 1996[195] the *Bundesgericht* laid the ground for a much-criticised doctrine distinguishing between direct and indirect damages. The application of that dichotomy in the insolvency context leads to the following results: Old creditors whose claims predate the relevant time receive a lower dividend reflecting losses incurred by the company due to the violation of Art. 725 OR. These losses are regarded as indirect damages. They are equated with the damage of the company and can only be recovered by the liquidator pursuant to Art. 756 OR.[196] New creditors who seem to have suffered a direct damage are nonetheless denied a right to sue individually for that kind of damage. In dogmatic terms, the Bundesgericht argues that Art. 725 OR serves a double-goal, namely protecting the creditors and the company, and for that reason

[192] H Bärtschi *Verantwortlichkeit im Aktienrecht* (Schultess Zurich 2002) 149-176; 248-249.

[193] For an excellent overview recently Böckli 'Verantwortlichkeit der Organmitglieder' in Baer (ed) *Aktuelle Fragen der aktienrechtlichen Verantwortlichkeit* (2003) 27 ff.

[194] BGE 117 II 432.

[195] BGE 122 III 176.

[196] BGE 117 II 423 at 436-438.

new creditors cannot pursue individual claims once insolvency proceedings have begun.[197] On policy grounds, the court defends its solution by two interrelated arguments: First, new creditors should not be privileged over old creditors; second, economy of procedure calls for a uniform cause of action on behalf of all creditors.[198] There is, however, a small backdoor for new creditors if directors have violated duties which aim exclusively at protecting creditors. This may be the case, explains the *Bundesgericht*, when creditors are induced to extend new credit to the company on the basis of misleading information about its precarious state of affairs.[199] In the literature, the somewhat strenuous reasoning of the court has been heavily criticised.[200] Moreover and more importantly, most commentators disagree with the result that the new creditors are barred form pursuing their individual claims although they have injected new assets into the company and thereby benefited the old creditors. Treating them on an equal footing with all creditors is regarded as an undeserved windfall for the latter.[201]

III. Conclusions

Comparing the different legal regimes, it seems that English law offers less creditor protection than German law in two important respects: First, the 'moment of truth' at which wrongful trading liability is triggered sets in at a rather late stage; second, the new creditors receive no compensation for their reliance losses when entering into new transactions with the company during the period of wrongful trading. Those divergences should not be overlooked when shaping a European framework rule on wrongful trading. It is suggested that such a rule can only succeed when two conditions are met: It must be drafted as precisely as possible in defining the point of time at which a wrongful trading rule begins to operate; and it must provide for effective civil sanctions. Gathering form the rich German experience with § 64 (1) GmbHG, this includes the necessity of compensating new creditors for their reliance losses.

[197] BGE 122 III 176 at 193.

[198] BGE 122 III 176 at 194.

[199] BGE 122 III 176 at 194-195.

[200] P Umbach 'Neue bundesgerichtliche Rechtsprechung zur Unterscheidung zwischen mittelbarem und unmittelbarem Schaden bei aktienrechtlichen Verantwortlichkeitsansprüchen' [1997] Schweizerische Zeitschrift für Wirtschaftsrecht 175; Hirsch 'La responsabilité des organes en cas d'insolvabilité de la SA: dommage direct et dommage indirect des créanciers' [2000] Schweizerische Zeitschrift für Wirtschaftsrecht 94.

[201] Böckli (n 193) 27 at 45-46.

D. Management Responsibility for Financial Statements

With respect to listed companies, one of the most pressing problems is to secure the probity of financial statements. In addressing this problem, the High Level Group persuasively highlights the vital importance of trust in financial statements.[202] It recommends that board-members be held collectively responsible for financial and key non-financial statements.[203] For the sake of clarity, the following analysis distinguishes between misleading primary and misleading secondary market information.

I. Directors' Liability for False Securities Prospectuses

Primary market disclosure seeks to give to the investing public all material information about the company needed to make a reasoned investment decision. The primary tool for disclosure in this regard is the securities prospectus.

1. Comparative Overview

The civil liability of directors for false prospectuses is rarely discussed.[204] In Germany, those who issued the prospectus or who caused it to be issued are jointly liable under § 44 (1) of the Exchange Act (BörsG), if they knew the inaccuracy or were grossly negligent in ignoring it. According to the prevailing doctrine, this provision is applicable to directors only if they are personally interested in the public offering.[205] Case law is scare and obscure.[206] The Anglo-American law of securities regulation takes a stricter stance: Pursuant to sec. 11 (a) (2) of the Securities Exchange Act 1933, investors may sue every person who was a director of the issuer at the time of the filing of the false registration statement.[207] Equally, sec. 152 (1) (b) of the new Financial Services Act 1986 listed

[202] Winter Report 67.

[203] Winter Report Recommendation III. 12.

[204] For a comparative survey see H Fleischer 'Gutachten F zum 64'. Deutschen Juristentag (2002) F62 – F64; more extensively H Fleischer 'Die persönliche Haftung der Organmitglieder für kapitalmarktbezogene Falschinformationen' [2003] Zeitschrift für Bank- und Kapitalmarktrecht 608 at 609-610.

[205] U Hamann in FA Schäfer (ed) *WpHG/BörsG/VerkProspG* (1999) §§ 45, 46 a.F. BörsG comment 43; E Schwark *Börsengesetz* (2nd edn CH Beck Munich 1994) §§ 45, 46 BörsG comment 7.

[206] BGHZ 123, 106, 110, arguably extending the scope of directors' liability.

[207] TL Hazen *The Law of Securities Regulation* (4th edn West Group St Paul, Minn 2002) 350; L Loss and J Seligman *Fundamentals of Securities Regulation* (4th edn Aspen 2001) 1152 with references to a possible exception for outside directors.

the directors of the issuer among those persons responsible for misleading listing particulars and prospectuses, and commentators predict that the approach will remain the same under the Financial Services and Markets Act 2000.[208] In Switzerland, civil liability is extended to board members as well;[209] an early judgment of the *Bundesgericht* confirms that this is at least the case, when the false prospectus was inspired by the directors and they also participated in its publication.[210] Austria lacks a specific provision, thus narrowing down civil liability of directors to extraordinary cases.[211] France, finally, seems to favour criminal liability sanctions for violations of corporate disclosure rules (*atteintes à la transparence des marchés*): Art. L. 465-1 C. mon. et fin. stipulates a catch-all provision for misleading market information obviously inspired by the US model in rule 10 (b)(5).[212] Due to a lack of special liability provisions,[213] a civil cause of action has to be based on general tort concepts, in particular art. 1382 Code civil,[214] which has caused commentators to call for improvement.[215]

2. European Harmonization

Hitherto, the EU has not provided rules for civil liability with respect to false securities prospectuses in the two Directives applicable in this area. Recently, the proposed Prospectus Directive requires Member states, albeit in very general fashion, to ensure that appropriate liability sanctions be imposed in respect of

[208] A Alcock *The Financial Services and Markets Act 2000* (Jordan Bristol 2000) 211. For a comparative Analysis H Fleischer 'Der Financial Services and Markets Act 2000: Neues Börsen- und Kapitalmarktrecht für das Vereinigte Königreich' [2001] Recht der Internationalen Wirtschaft 817.

[209] H Bärtschi *Verantwortlichkeit im Aktienrecht* (Schultess Zurich 2001) 114-115; V Roberto and Th Wegmann 'Prospekthaftung in der Schweiz' [2001] Schweizerische Zeitschrift für Wirtschaftsrecht 161 at 174.

[210] BGE 47 II 272 at 286.

[211] S Kalss (2000) Österreichisches Bankarchiv 641 at 654 with note 169.

[212] Th Bonneau and F Drummond *Droit des marchés financiers* (Economica Paris 2001) no 504: 'Ce délit a été introduit en droit français en même temps que le délit d'initié par loi du 23 décembre 1970. Comme ce dernier, il est directement inspiré par le droit américaine, et plus précisément par la règle 10-5(5)(...)' For a detailed comparative analysis H Fleischer and Jänig, Verantwortlichkeit für falsche Kapitalmarktinformation in Frankreich – das droit des marchés financiers' [2002] Recht der Internationalen Wirtschaft 729.

[213] Bonneau and Drummond (n 212) no 515: 'silence du législateur'.

[214] Cass crim 15 May 1993 Rev soc 847 at 852, 854.

[215] H de Vauplane and O Simart 'Délits boursiers: Propositions de réforme' [1997] Revue de droit bancaire et de la bourse 85 at 96: 'Des améliorations sont donc vivement souhaitables en ce domaine'.

inadequate or misleading disclosure. As has been explained elsewhere, harmonization measures in this regard are highly desirable.[216]

II. Directors' Liability for Misleading Secondary Market Information

Secondary market disclosure seeks to provide the investor with all material information needed to make a reasoned decision whether to hold or sell the securities. It consists of a number of elements: consolidated and unconsolidated financial statements, interim reports, current reports (Ad-hoc-publicity) and disclosure of shareholdings.

1. The German Example

In Germany, the recent discussion about civil liability in this area has very much focused on false current reports. A string of first instance and appellate court cases illustrates that liability exists only if the plaintiff investor can prove that the defendant company damaged him through a wilful or morally culpable act (§ 826 BGB) or violated prohibitions of criminal law (eg, §§ 263, 264a StGB).[217] Responding to sharp criticism of this state of affairs, the German legislator enacted new provisions in a comprehensive Reform Act (*Viertes Finanzmarktförderungsgesetz*).[218] The newly introduced §§ 37b, c of the Securities Trading Act (WpHG) impose liability on issuers who publish current report that – through a wilful act or gross negligence – contain false information or that are published in an untimely manner.[219] However, these provisions refrain from imposing personal liability on board members. The German Lawyers Association (*Deutscher Juristentag*), by contrast, recommended that the liability be extended to board members as well if they intentionally or through gross negligence disclose false information to the capital markets; in the case of gross negligence it is recommended that the liability be capped.[220] These resolutions were prepared and supported by two expert opinions rendered by the Government's Commission on

[216] H Fleischer 'Gutachten F zum 64. Deutschen Juristentag' (2002) F 75.

[217] See LG Bonn AG 2001, 484; LG Kassel, DB 2002, 2151; AG München WM 2002, 594; LG Augsburg NZG 2002, 429; LG München ZIP 2001, 1814; OLG München ZIP 2002, 1989; OLG München ZIP 2002, 1727. For a recent summary of the case law T Holzborn and M Foelsch 'Schadensersatzpflichten von AG und Management bei Anlegerverlusten' [2003] Neue Juristische Wochenschrift 932.

[218] H Fleischer 'Das Vierte Finanzmarktförderungsgesetz' [2002] Neue Juristische Wochenschrift 2977 ff.

[219] For an overview H Fleischer 'Der Inhalt des Schadensersatzanspruchs wegen unwahrer oder unterlassener unverzüglicher Ad-hoc-Mitteilungen' [2002] Betriebs-Berater 1869.

[220] Verhandlungen des 64. Deutschen Juristentages, Band II/1 (2002) P88 – P89.

Corporate Governance[221] and the reporter to the German Lawyers Association in this area.[222] Most recently, the Government has signalled consent and has set management responsibility for misleading information on its reform agenda.[223]

2. The Case for Management Liability

With respect to misleading secondary market information, a legislator can chose between entity liability, manager liability or a combination of both. According to law and economics orthodoxy, entity liability is generally a preferable concept,[224] because a company will have an incentive to police its managers more carefully in the future if it is forced to pay the losses of damaged stockholders.[225] However, this does not necessarily exclude personal liability of board members. Even if managers tend to be risk-averse,[226] there are at least four convincing arguments to hold them liable as well. First, personal liability serves as a strong deterrent against misleading information without stifling entrepreneurial initiative: The affirmative case for shielding management decisions from judicial second guessing by a broad business judgment rule does not carry over to corporate reporting.[227] Second, personal liability contributes to the compensation of investors since it is usually covered by D&O-insurance. This is particularly important in cases of corporate insolvency where plaintiffs have to look for alternative and still solvent defendants.[228] Third, personal liability helps to solve last-period problems at the brink of corporate insolvency: Evidence from the U.S. and Germany suggests that management is inclined to lie in such situations to gain time during which some turnaround in fortunes might occur, or at least to retain

[221] Th Baums (ed) 'Bericht der Regierungskommission Corporate Governance' (2002) comments 186-190.

[222] H Fleischer 'Gutachten F zum 64.' Deutschen Juristentag (2002) F 95 – F 118.

[223] U Seibert 'Das 10-Punkte-Programm "Unternehmensintegrität und Anlegerschutz"' [2003] Betriebs-Berater 693 at 694; H Fleischer 'Die persönliche Haftung der Organmitglieder für kapitalmarktbezogene Falschinformationen' [2003] Zeitschrift für Bank- und Kapitalmarktrecht 608 at 612.

[224] See generally R Kraakman 'Corporate Liability Strategies and the Costs of Legal Controls' (1984) 93 Yale Law Journal 857; LA Kornhauser 'An Economic Analysis of The Choice between Enterprise and Personal Liability for Accidents' (1982) 70 California Law Review 1345; CD Stone 'The Place of Enterprise Liability in the Control of Corporate Conduct' (1980) 90 Yale Law Journal 1; with respect to securities regulation JD Cox 'Making Securities Fraud Class Actions Virtuous' (1997) 39 Arizona Law Review 497 at 511-515.

[225] Posner (n 43) 489.

[226] Easterbrook and Fischel (n 44) 340.

[227] H Fleischer 'Gutachten F zum 64.' Deutschen Juristentag (2002) F 102.

[228] H Fleischer 'Persönliche Außenhaftung der Vorstandsmitglieder für fehlerhafte Kapitalmarktinformation' [2002] Zeitschrift für Rechtspolitik 532.

their perquisites for a bit longer.[229] Fourth, personal liability eliminates strong incentives for directors to profit personally from producing false information before selling their shares: In a corporate world of (often abused) stock option programs, this is no longer a negligible danger.[230] The frequent counter-argument that manager liability will invite strike suits[231] is a serious objection, but it should not be over-emphasised: Limiting personal liability to cases of gross negligence and introducing a liability cap[232] are appropriate safeguards to rein strike suits and to avoid over-deterrence.

3. The Case for Collective Responsibility

With regard to the persons responsible for the probity of financial statements, notable divergences have emerged between the American and the European approach. Under sec. 302 of the Sarbanes-Oxley-Act, the Chief Executive Officer and the Chief Financial Officer shall certify in each 1934 Act annual or quarterly report facts including the following: That they have reviewed the report; that based on their knowledge, the report does not contain any untrue statement of a material fact; and that the report fairly presents in all material respect the issuer's financial condition and results of operations. Under the company laws of EU member states, by contrast, the responsibility for the probity of financial statements is primarily a collective responsibility of the board. Comparing both regimes, the European approach is clearly preferable. To begin with, collective responsibility is the basic principle covering all kinds of board activities and duties. As such, it is firmly entrenched in Germany with its two-tier-structure,[233] and it is equally recognised in England within a one-tier-system.[234] Adopting this

[229] H Fleischer 'Gutachten F für den 64.' Deutschen Juristentag (2002) F 102; GM Gulati 'When Corporate Managers Fear a Good Thing is Coming to an End: The Case for Interim Disclosure' (1999) 46 UCLA Law Review 675; DC Langevoort 'Capping Damages For Open-Market Securities Fraud' (1996) 38 Arizona Law Review 639 at 653-657; J Arlen and W Carney 'Vicarious Liability For Fraud on Securities Markets: Theories and Evidence' [1992] University of Illinois Law Review 691 at 701-704.

[230] Th Baums 'Haftung wegen Falschinformation des Sekundärmarkts' (2003) 167 Zeitschrift für das gesamte Handelsrecht und Wirtschaftsrecht 139, 174; H Fleischer 'Die persönliche Haftung der Organmitglieder für kapitalmarktbezogene Falschinformationen' [2003] Zeitschrift für Bank- und Kapitalmarktrecht 608 at 612.

[231] PO Mülbert 'Empfiehlt es sich, im Interesse des Anlegerschutzes und zur Förderung des Finanzplatzes Deutschland das Kapitalmarkt- und Börsenrecht neu zu regeln?' [2002] Juristenzeitung 826 at 832.

[232] Langevoort (n 229).

[233] RGZ 98, 98 at 100; BGHZ 133, 370 at 376-377; BGHSt 37, 106 at 123.

[234] *Re Westmid Packing Services Ltd* [1998] 2 BCLC 646 at 653: '(...) the collegiate or collective responsibility of the board of directors of a company is of fundamental importance to corporate governance under English company law.'

principle, is particularly advantageous from an agency perspective: As has been explained elsewhere in greater depth, collective responsibility adds a dimension of horizontal monitoring to board decision making and avoids undue influence or biased decisions by single board members.[235] Therefore, the High Level Group's recommendation to extend collective responsibility to all financial statements is well-founded and deserves full support.

4. The Case for a Comprehensive Scope of Liability for Misleading Market Information

Finally, it should be underlined that misleading secondary market disclosure occurs in various forms: In the US, recent corporate law scandals focus primarily on false annual accounts and financial statements whereas in Germany false current reports are at the heart of the discussion. A coherent legislative approach in this area cannot include some types of information and exclude others. Instead, it must be drafted in a comprehensive manner and include at least all kinds of information that are part of the EU mandatory disclosure system.[236] Given the increasing importance of investor relations, it is advisable to extend civil liability also to voluntary information, such as shareholder newsletters, voluntary interim reports or postings on the company's website, if deemed to be material.[237]

E. Directors' Disqualification

The civil liability regime is only one mechanism to prevent and compensate for managerial misconduct. Another device of enforcing appropriate standards of conduct is a disqualification of a person from serving as a director of companies. This enforcement weapon has recently been discussed and recommended by the German Lawyer's Association (*Deutscher Juristentag*) with respect to misleading financial statements,[238] and the High Level Group also encourages further review whether directors' disqualification should be introduced as a sanction at EU level.[239] Valuable insights can be gleaned from English company law where a disqualification order is imposed, inter alia, for wrongful trading, and from US

[235] For a detailed analysis H Fleischer 'Zum Grundsatz der Gesamtverantwortung im Aktienrecht' [2003] Neue Zeitschrift für Gesellschaftsrecht 449 with references to the economic literature.

[236] H Fleischer 'Gutachten für den 64. Deutschen Juristentag' (2002) F 109 – 111.

[237] ibid F 111 – 115.

[238] Verhandlungen des 64. Deutschen Juristentages Band II/1 (2002) P89.

[239] Winter Report 69-70.

securities regulation which provides for director bar orders in cases of misleading information.[240]

I. United Kingdom

1. From the Companies Act 1928 to the Companies Directors Disqualification Act 1986

The paradigm case of directors' disqualification in company law is to be found in the UK. Its prohibition on undischarged bankrupts to serve as directors in the management of companies can be traced back to the Companies Act 1928. Subsequently, the provisions were steadily extended by legislation over the years until the Insolvency Act 1985 produced its current form, now contained in the Companies Directors Disqualification Act 1986 (CDDA).[241] The consolidation of various prior enactments was primarily motivated by a growing concern about the abuse of limited liability. The Cork Committee on Insolvency Law and Practice noted in its report: 'It has been made evident to us that there is a widespread dissatisfaction at the ease with which a person trading through the medium of one or more companies with limited liability can allow such a company to become insolvent, form a new company, and then carry on trading much as before, leaving behind him a trail of unpaid creditors, and often repeating the process several times.'[242] In applying the CDDA, courts have gradually elaborated a tripartite purpose, namely the protection of the public (1) by means of prohibitory remedial action, (2) by anticipated deterrent effect of further misconduct and (3) by encouragement of higher standards of honesty and diligence and corporate management.[243] Today, the CDDA is one of the most productive areas of case law and a frequent object of academic writing.[244]

[240] For a detailed comparative study H Fleischer 'Bestellungshindernisse und Tätigkeitsverbote von Geschäftsleitern im Aktien-, Bank- und Kapitalmarktrecht' [2003] Betriebs-Berater (forthcoming).

[241] For details see Farrar and Hannigan (n 69) 344-361; PL Davies (n 3) 211-224.

[242] Report of the Review Committee on Insolvency Law and Practice Cmnd 8558 (1982) para 1813.

[243] Lord Woolf in *Re Blackspur Group plc* [1998] 1 BCLC 676 at 680.

[244] See recently A Hicks 'Director Disqualifcation: Can It Deliver?' [2001] Journal of Business Law 433 with many references.

2. Grounds for Disqualification

a) Overview

The CDDA divides the numerous grounds for disqualification into three groups. A first group collects cases of general misconduct in connection with companies: Sec. 2 authorises the court to make a disqualification order against a person who is convicted of an indictable offence in connection with the promotion, formation or management of a company; sec. 3 allows disqualifying directors for persistent breaches of companies legislation; sec. 4 covers cases of fraud in the winding up of a company. A second group is concerned with disqualification for unfitness: Under sec. 6, the court shall make a disqualification order against a director of an insolvent company if his conduct as a director of that company makes him unfit to serve; sec. 8 adds that a disqualification order should also be made against a person whose unfitness was discovered after an official investigation of the company. The third group includes various grounds for disqualification: Under sec. 10, the court may disqualify any person against whom a contribution order has been made under the fraudulent or wrongful trading provisions; and sec. 11 provides for an automatic disqualification in the case of an undischarged bankrupt.

b) In Particular: Unfit Directors of Insolvent Companies

The most commonly relied on ground for disqualification is that the director of an insolvent company has been found to be unfit in the sense of sec. 6 CDDA.[245] Guidance on whether he is unfit or not is given in Schedule 1 of the CDDA. It lists the matters which the court must have particular regard to, such as: misfeasance, breach of duty, misapplication of property or conduct giving rise to a liability to account, the extend of his responsibility for any transaction set aside under the avoidance provisions in the insolvency act. In practice, applications for disqualification typically focus on three recurring fact patterns: (1) Poor accounting records usually coupled with the failure to file accounts and returns to Companies House; (2) continued trading while insolvent in disregard of creditors' interests; (3) personal benefits accruing to directors including the granting of preferences to themselves and personal friends, the use of the company's assets for inadequate consideration, undisclosed conflicts of interests resulting in personal gain.[246]

[245] Farrar and Hannigan (n 69) 347.

[246] ibid 353-357; for a different classification of the case law PL Davies (n 3) 218-221.

3. Sanctions, Procedure and Practical Importance

The imposition of a disqualification order is mandatory only in the case of unfit directors of insolvent companies (sec. 6 CDDA); otherwise it is up to the discretion of the court. The leading role in initiating applications for disqualification orders is played by the Insolvency Agency of the Department of Trade and Industry.[247] After sharp criticism of the efficiency of the Insolvency Agency in administering the CDDA in a 1999 report[248], the Government improved its enforcement procedure. As a result of this change of policy, the number of disqualification orders has increased drastically in recent years: Between 1995 and 2000 a total of 5.808 disqualifications were imposed, and in 2000 the annual total had risen to 1.548 cases.[249] The minimum period of disqualification on grounds of unfitness is two years. Guidelines as to the appropriate period of disqualification were laid down by the Court of Appeals dividing the cases into three brackets: (1) The top bracket of 10-15 years should be reserved for particularly serious cases; (2) the middle bracket of 6-10 years should apply to serious cases which do not merit the top bracket; (3) the bottom bracket of 2-5 years should be applied where the case is, relatively, not very serious.[250] In order to avoid evasions, the disqualification order also extents to de facto directors. Pursuant to sec. 18 CDDA, Companies House maintains a register of disqualification orders which is available for inspection by the public. Any disqualified person involved in the management of the company commits a criminal offence and becomes personally responsible for the debts and liabilities of the company.[251]

II. United States

1. Legal Framework

US law makes use of the sanction of officer and director bar orders in the field of securities regulation. The key provisions are sec. 20 (e) Securities Act 1933 and sec. 21 (d) Securities Exchange Act 1934. The origin of these provisions can be traced back to the 1987 Report of the National Commission on Fraudulent Reporting (Treadway Commission), which recommended, among many other items, that 'the SEC (...) seek congressional authority to bar or suspend corporate officers and directors involved in fraudulent financial reporting from future

[247] PL Davies (n 3) 216-217.

[248] National Audit Office, The Insolvency Service Executive Agency: Company Director Disqualification, HC 907 (1993).

[249] For more details see A Walters [2001] Company Lawyer 290.

[250] *Re Seven Oaks Stationers (Retail) Ltd* [1991] Ch 164.

[251] Sections 13 and 15 CDDA.

service in that capacity in a public company.'[252] Following this recommendation, the legislator enacted the Securities Enforcement Remedies and Penny Stock Reform Act of 1990, but reserved the imposition of a corporate bar order for the federal courts.[253] In particular, sec. 20 (e) of the 1933 act provides for the primary market: 'In any proceeding under subsection (b), the court may prohibit, conditionally or unconditionally, and permanently or for such period of time as it shall determine, any person who violated sec. 17 (a) (1) from acting as an officer or director if the person's conduct demonstrate substantial unfitness to serve as an officer or director of any such issuer.' Sec. 21 (d) (2) of the 1934 Act in almost identical terms for the secondary market: 'In any proceeding under § (1) of this subsection, the court may prohibit, conditionally or unconditionally, and permanently or for such period of time as it shall determine, any person who violated sec. 10 (b) or the rules or regulation there under from acting as an officer or director (...) if the person's conduct demonstrate substantial unfitness to serve as an officer or director of any such issuer.'

2. Statutory Elements

a) Violation of Specific Disclosure Provisions

To begin with, corporate bar orders require a violation of the 'hard core' fraud provisions in securities regulation: Sec. 17 (a) (1) of the 1933 Act and sec. 10 (b) of the 1934 Act.[254] Both provisions are only applicable upon a showing of scienter.[255] Thus, mere negligence is not sufficient; the courts usually require intend to defraud or, in some circumstances, reckless behaviour.

b) Substantial Unfitness to Serve

A violation of the fraud provisions alone does not form an adequate basis for a bar order. In addition, the wrongdoer's conduct must demonstrate substantial unfitness to serve as an officer or director in the management of a company. The statutes do not define 'substantial unfitness', and the legislative history of the 1990 act provides little guidance as to what Congress may have intended by the phrase. An influential law review article has proposed to consider seven factors (1) the 'egregiousness' of the underlying violation, (2) the defendant's 'repeat

[252] Report of the National Commission on Fraudulent Financial Reporting (October 1987) 66.

[253] E Ferran, Ferrigno and DS Darland 'Hardball! The SEC's New Arsenal of Enforcement Weapons' (1991) 47 Business Lawyer 33.

[254] For details see Hazen (n 207) 574-577.

[255] *Ernst & Ernst v Hochfelder* 425 US 185 at 2001 (1976): s 10 (b) SEA; *Aaron v SEC*, 446 US 680 at 697 (1980): s 17 SA.

offender' status, (3) the defendant's role in the scheme to defraud, (4) the defendant's degree of scienter, (5) the defendant's economic stake in the violation, (6) the likelihood that misconduct will recur (7) the defendant's appreciation of an executive's fiduciary obligations.[256] Subsequent judgment have frequently adopted this test.[257] In applying the bar orders, courts do not hesitate to impose a lifetime ban in particularly serious cases,[258] but they usually require past violations and a likelihood of recurrence for that draconian sanction.[259]

c) Legislative Changes by the Sarbanes-Oxley Act

The Sarbanes-Oxley-Act has lowered the threshold for corporate bar orders: Sec. 1105 adds sec. 8A(f) to the Securities Act 1933 and sec. 21C(f) to the Securities Exchange Act of 1934 providing for SEC power to prohibit a person who has violated the core antifraud provisions from acting as an officer or director of a publicly reporting issuer if his conduct demonstrates 'unfitness to serve', as distinguished from 'substantial unfitness' under the prior standard.[260]

III. Conclusions

1. Comparative Advantages of Disqualification Orders

Corporate bar orders focus on directors as the key figures in the management of public and private companies. They operate as a supplementary enforcement weapon in addition to criminal and civil liability sanctions. The latter are indispensable as cornerstones in company law, but they struggle with characteristic weaknesses: The director's liability *vis-à-vis* the company is rarely enforced, at least in civil law jurisdictions. Moreover, it requires a damage to the company which may be missing. Finally, even if the company has suffered harm from the director's misconduct, the liability rules may often come too late. Disqualification orders, on the contrary, perform a useful screening function by removing unfit

[256] J Barnard 'When is a Corporate Executive 'Substantially Unfit to Serve?' (1992) 70 North Carolina Law Review 1489.

[257] eg *SEC v First Pacific Bancorp*, 142 F 3d 1186, 1193 (9th Cir 1998).

[258] *SEC v Posner,* 16 F 3d 520 at 522 (2nd Cir 1994): 'The Posners seem to be shocked by what they see as the draconian remedy of eternal board room banishment. We intend our affirmance of Judge Pollack's judgment in this respect as a sharp warning to those who violate the securities laws that they face precisely such banishment.'

[259] *SEC v Patel*, 61 F 3d 137, 142 (2nd Cir 1995): 'Although it is not essential for a lifetime ban that there be past violations, we think that it is essential, in the absence of such violations, that a district court articulate the factual basis for a finding of the likely hood of recurrence'.

[260] See generally L Ribstein 'Market vs. Regulatory Responses to Corporate Fraud: A Critique of the Sarbanes-Oxley Act of 2002' (2003) 28 Journal of Corporation Law 1.

directors from the temptation and the likelihood of renewed misconduct. Also, they offer a more expeditious enforcement mechanism than lengthy shareholder suits. Similarly, they serve as an even stronger deterrent against misconduct than civil liability which is frequently covered by D&O insurance. Whether a disqualification regime may also actively influence the standards of corporate behaviour, remains to be seen: In the UK, the CDDA has been successfully used to refashion the duty of care and skill,[261] but this experience may not be representative since the baggage of cases like *Re City Equitable Fire Insurance Company Ltd*[262] seemed no longer bearable in modern times. To sum up, directors' disqualification offers a number of comparative advantages which merit further review of this enforcement mechanism in company law and securities regulation. It is submitted, however, that a more precise evaluation must differentiate between these two distinct areas of application.

2. Areas of Application

a) Securities Regulation: Misleading Market Information

The first regulatory approach is conceptually one of securities regulation: It aims at the directors of listed companies and seeks to secure the probity of primary and secondary market information, A legislative model is to be found in the US law of securities regulation. The recent resolution of the German Lawyers Association and the recommendation of the High Level Group point to the same direction. Their case for introducing directors' bar orders in that area is convincing for a variety of reasons: First, investor protection against misleading market information is particularly important, and the established sanctions of civil and criminal liability do not fully succeed to curb those kinds of violations. Second, the institutional environment of capital markets provides for optimal enforcement conditions: With the national securities regulators, there is already an agency in place which may administer and police the disqualification provisions. In addition, the transparency of capital markets and the extensive press coverage both contribute to the compliance with directors' bar orders. Third, disqualification has a very serious effect on professional managers whose human capital decreases drastically with a disqualification order: Once disqualified, they should be unable to obtain managerial employment in a major company of the type to which they are

[261] A Walters 'Directors' Duties: The Impact of the Directors Disqualification Act 1986' [2000] Company Lawyer 110; also PL Davies (n 3) 690: 'Although the workings of the Insolvency Agency are still not beyond improvement, its activities probably do far more to protect the interests of shareholders and creditors than the recent developments in the common law of directors' duties, whether by recognition of the interests of the creditors or by way of the development of an objective standard of care.'

[262] [1925] 1 Ch. 407.

accustomed to.[263] This powerful deterrent effect is supported by evidence from the German banking industry where a 'fit and proper' requirement is successfully administered by banking regulators.[264]

b) Company Law: Abuse of Limited Liability

The second regulatory approach is conceptually one of company law: It envisages the directors of private companies and seeks to prevent the abuse of limited liability.[265] The leading example of such misconduct described by the Cork Committee is the so-called 'Phoenix syndrome',[266] the English counterpart of the German 'GmbH-Stafette'. Unlike the CDDA 1986, the German legislator has been more modest in addressing that problem: Following the recommendation of an expert group on white collar crime,[267] he introduced new provisions in the Reform Act of 1980 (*GmbH-Novelle*) covering only the most egregious cases: According to §§ 76 (3) AktG, 6 (2) GmbHG a person convicted of a criminal offence pursuant to §§ 283 to 283d of the Penal Code may not be a director for a period of five years from the date on which the judgment has become final and may not be appealed. In addition, a person who has been prohibited by judicial decision or an enforceable administrative order from engaging in any profession or trade, may not, during the period of such prohibition, be a director of a company whose corporate purpose encompasses, in whole or in part, such prohibited activity.

Whether the more resolute English approach in that area is preferable, is a matter for debate since its dashing attitude is not without drawbacks. To begin with, the investigation and prosecution of disqualification cases requires considerable administrative resources.[268] Moreover, enforcement will be much more difficult in the area of private company directors than in the field of listed companies board members;[269] and a decreasing enforcement probability will be inevitably reflected in a decreasing deterrent effect. Finally, overly rigorous standards of disqualification could discourage the formation and expansion of new business

[263] Hicks (n 244) 442.

[264] H-J Hellwig in 'Verhandlungen des 64. Deutschen Juristentages' (2002) Bd II/1 P 82.

[265] PL Davies (n 3) 210; Hicks (n 244) 454.

[266] PL Davies (n 3) 200-202.

[267] Bundesministerium der Justiz (ed) 'Tagungsberichte der Sachverständigenkommission zur Bekämpfung der Wirtschaftskriminalität' Vol I – III (1973); also K Tiedemann *Wirtschaftsstrafrecht und Wirtschaftskriminalität* (Westdt Wiesbaden 1976) Bd 1 Allgemeiner Teil 72-73.

[268] Cheffins (n 164) 552-553.

[269] For references to strategies of evasion see Stein § 6 Abs 2 Satz 2 GmbHG, § 76 Abs 3 Satz 2 AktG: Verfassungswidrige Berufsverbote?' [1987] Die Aktiengesellschaft 165 at 172; Hicks (n 244) 442.

ventures.[270] Striking an appropriate balance in this regard and further considering the operative costs of a disqualification regime, may well lead to the conclusion that the more cautious German approach in §§ 76 (3) AktG, 6 (2) GmbHG has its benefits when slightly modified and effectively enforced.[271]

[270] For a similar concern Ferran (n 9); Hicks (n 244) 459; Pettet (n 3) 452-453.

[271] H Fleischer 'Bestellungshindernisse und Tätigkeitsverbote von Geschäftsleitern im Aktien-, Bank- und Kapitalmarktrecht' [2003] Betriebs-Berater (forthcoming) with references also to questions of constitutionality.

Chapter 7: The Role of the Shareholder

The Role of the Shareholder in Internal Corporate Governance: Shareholder Information, Communication and Decision-Making[*]

EILÍS FERRAN

European corporate law policy is the focus of this paper. Europe has historically lagged behind the USA in viewing company law's primary role as being to facilitate the operation of business in corporate form. However, the report by the High Level Group of Company Law Experts (Winter Report) to the European Commission in November 2002 marks a distinct break with the past in this respect. This chapter reviews aspect of the Winter Report concerning the role of shareholders in internal corporate governance.

In systems of corporate law that are orientated towards facilitation, disclosure is a key mechanism for the regulation of corporate governance agency problems. This paper argues for Europe to adopt a regulatory structure in which responsibility for monitoring and enforcement of corporate governance disclosure is located with securities regulators. Disclosure is an area where company law and securities regulation come together and making securities regulators the primary regulators of corporate governance disclosure would, it is suggested, promote pan-European consistency in monitoring and enforcement. Making the securities regulator in each Member State the responsible body for corporate governance disclosure would secure the benefits of securities regulators' enforcement expertise, and it could open up a wider range of sanctions. The importance of standardisation with regard to the identity of competent authorities is already accepted in Europe with regard to prospectuses and continuing obligations. The suggestion here is thus complementary to and consistent with developments in very closely related fields. This proposal fits well with US developments where corporate governance disclosure requirements are increasingly part of the federal securities regulatory framework rather than state corporate law. For Europe and the US to adopt broadly similar positions with regard to the allocation of regulatory responsibility for corporate governance disclosures is appealing in that this could secure at a broader international level, as well as within the EU, the benefits of greater consistency in

[*] I am grateful for comments from Rod Cantrill, Richard Nolan, James Palmer, Jonathan Rickford, Len Sealy and participants at *A Modern Regulatory Framework for Company and Takeover Law in Europe,* conference 29 – 31 May 2003. The usual disclaimer applies. An earlier version of this paper was published at 4:4 (2003) European Business Organization Law Review.

regulatory policy and supervisory practices, and could promote international co-operation. A further pragmatic advantage offered by the suggestion that European securities regulators should be responsible for the monitoring and enforcement of corporate governance disclosures is that pan-European mechanisms for co-operation and sharing of information between securities regulators are already in place.

The chapter is sceptical about the merits of the Winter Report's suggestion for the introduction, on a pan-European basis, of a disqualification sanction for non-compliance with disclosure requirements. It points to evidence of dissatisfaction with the operation of the British directors' disqualification regime. It also doubts whether a broad measure of pan-European consistency in the operation of a disqualification sanction is realistically achievable.

Looking beyond disclosure to the actual exercise of internal control by shareholders, the chapter welcomes some of the Winter Report's proposals for improving internal corporate decision making processes. It takes issue with the Winter Report's views on investor disfranchisement arguing that, from the British perspective, the case for legal intervention to address problems that the market has proved unable to solve is limited to possible reinforcement of the regulatory obligations on financial intermediaries.

The chapter concludes by observing that there remains work to be done to build upon the admirable start made by the HLG in spelling out modern objectives of, and rationales for, European corporate regulation.

A. Introduction

Corporate governance is a term that lacks a single, universally accepted definition but it will suffice here to use the OECD description of corporate governance as being 'the internal means by which corporations are operated and controlled'.[1] Using the OECD description, the discussion in this paper is limited to internal corporate governance mechanisms for dealing with principal/agency problems that arise within the corporate framework. In particular the paper concentrates on shareholders' voting rights and associated entitlements such as access to information and ability to activate the corporate decision-making machinery by convening meetings.

The focus of the paper is European corporate law policy. Company and securities lawyers are accustomed to grappling with complex arguments for and

[1] *OECD Principles of Corporate Governance* (OECD 1999) preface.

against State intervention in the operation of the markets. There is voluminous literature recognising the hard policy choices facing national lawmakers on what they should include in their company laws and on whether these laws should be mandatory or default rules, or in some other form. All of these issues are relevant to the debate about European corporate law but there is a further dimension concerning the roles of, and relationships between, European and national Member State lawmaking bodies. Whilst the European subsidiarity principle makes it necessary to consider whether any case for regulatory intervention supports the formulation of Europe-wide rules rather than rules made at national level by Member States,[2] this issue would still demand attention even if this were not an obligatory part of European policy discussions. Around the world contemporary debate on the regulation of economic activity is much concerned with questions about the regulatory challenges presented by the transnational character of modern business and markets. Do the potential benefits for companies and investors operating internationally that could flow from ironing out differences in the legal rules in different countries outweigh the potential drawbacks that could flow from loss of diversity? Where standardisation is desirable, is it best achieved through a process in which States come together to agree upon a set of common standards or by a form of natural selection in which individual States choose to model their laws on what has worked well in other countries? These are fundamental and controversial questions to which those who are interested in the development of European corporate law must, and do, pay attention.

Without wishing to retread a well-worn path, this paper begins in Section B with a brief review of the development of European company law since the 1960s. We are now at a point where there are indications of a distinct break with the past and of a stronger recognition of the need to spell out the justification for regulatory intervention. Section C examines corporate governance disclosure requirements and the institutional infrastructure through which they are best developed, monitored and enforced. It is doubtful about the merits of singling out directors' disqualification as a pan-European sanction for enforcement of disclosure obligations. It suggests that regulatory responsibilities for the monitoring and enforcement of corporate governance disclosure should be located primarily with agencies responsible for securities regulation. Disclosure is an area where company law and securities regulation come together. Making securities regulators the primary regulators of corporate governance disclosure would, it is suggested, promote pan-European consistency. Section D looks at ways in which the effective operation of internal corporate governance could be improved by enhancing the processes and mechanisms whereby shareholders make decisions and receive

[2] The principle of subsidiarity means that in areas outside its exclusive competence, the Community can take action only if, and to the extent that, the objectives of the proposed action cannot be sufficiently achieved by the Member States and can therefore, because of its scale or effects, be better achieved by the Community: P Craig and G deBúrca *EU Law Text, Cases, and Materials* (3rd edn Oxford University Press Oxford 2003) 132 – 137.

information. Section E concludes. The structure and approach of the paper is shaped by reference to the work of the High Level Group of Company Law Experts (Winter Group) which reported to the European Commission in November 2002.[3] The Commission's response to the Winter Report indicates that the Group's recommendations are likely to be highly influential in shaping the development of European regulation of companies in the coming years.[4]

B. The Development of European Company Law

From the foundation of the European Community, company law has been regarded as having an important role to play in promoting economic integration.[5] Alongside this, and linked to it, early European initiatives in company law were characterised by a paternalistic desire on the part of the lawmakers to protect those who dealt with companies from the dangers that lurked in such activities. Europe-wide co-ordination of these protections was required, it was thought, as a response to the spreading activity of companies outside their national borders.

After an initial burst of enthusiasm in the 1960s and 1970s for the creation of harmonised European company laws, things slowed down considerably. Whilst there were some new company law initiatives in the 1980s many of these tended to be narrowly focused. In the 1990s European company law stagnated virtually to the point of standstill.[6] The adoption of the European Company Statute in 2001, although a noteworthy event in itself, is not something that we should regard as signalling a reversal of the trend. That it took some 30 years of negotiations before the European Company became a legal reality, by which time it was doubtful whether the commercial need for it that was thought to exist when the process started still remained,[7] is something that is best regarded as a demonstration of the failure, rather than the success, of the initiative as originally conceived.

[3] *Report of the High Level Group of Company Law Experts on a Modern Regulatory Framework for Company Law in Europe* (European Commission November 2002) (Winter Report) (see Annex 3 in this volume).

[4] *Modernising Company Law and Enhancing Corporate Governance in the European Union – A Plan to Move Forward* (Communication from the Commission to the Council and the European Parliament, May 2003, COM (2003) 284 final) (Modernising Company Law – European Commission Plan) (see Annex 1 in this volume).

[5] RM Buxbaum and KJ Hopt *Legal Harmonization and the Business Enterprise* (Walter de Gruyter Berlin 1988) ch 3.

[6] WF Ebke 'Company Law and the European Union: Centralized Versus Decentralized Lawmaking' (1997) 31 International Lawyer 961, 963; KJ Hopt 'Company Law in the European Union: Harmonisation and/or Subsidiarity' (1999) 1 International and Comparative Law Journal 41.

[7] Hopt, ibid, 50 ('most of them [enterprises affected by the *Societas Europa*] seem to have found other ways to arrange themselves').

With the benefit of hindsight, observers have been able to identify many factors that contributed to the decline of the original European company law harmonization project. At the outset of the programme there was undoubtedly a degree of naivety and over-optimism about what could be achieved at the European level. The challenges involved in securing political agreement for changes in controversial areas, such as worker participation, were certainly underestimated. At least to some extent the European authorities brought trouble upon themselves in this respect by putting forward poor quality proposals that borrowed heavily from the domestic laws of one Member State and, as such, did not fit comfortably within the established legal and economic environments of other European countries.[8] Over time, it became clear that the slow-moving European lawmaking machinery was very poorly adapted to respond to the needs of changing markets and as a result people became increasingly concerned about the risk that anything adopted at European level would remain in force indefinitely. This growing awareness of the risk of petrification chilled enthusiasm for adding to the corpus of European company laws. All of these factors created an environment in which, by the 1990s, the time was ripe for a reassessment, not just of processes and mechanisms, but also the underlying premises of the company law harmonization programme.

The assumptions of the founders of the European Community about the existence of connections between law and economic development and about how corporate and other business laws could be used to achieve desired economic goals have withstood the test of time. Indeed, an important line of contemporary scholarship provides powerful support for the significance of such connections.[9] But the notion pervading early European initiatives that protecting those who deal with companies should be regarded as company's law primary function has fared less well. In the USA, the idea that company law should focus primarily on facilitating the operation of businesses in corporate form rather than seeking to direct people's conduct has, since the 1980s, crossed over from being a controversial topic much debated in the leading journals into the largely uncontested mainstream. Europe has lagged behind the USA in this respect but it clear from the Winter Group's work that company law's facilitative role is now in the ascendancy as the starting point for policy discussions about the direction of European corporate law.[10] This is not to say that rules that control parties' actions can never

[8] Ebke (n 6) 976 – 977.

[9] Leading articles are: R La Porta and others 'Legal Determinants of External Finance' (1997) 52 Journal of Finance 1131; R La Porta, F Lopez-De-Silanes and A Shleifer, A 'Law and Finance' (1998) 106 Journal of Political Economy 1113; R La Porta, F Lopez-De-Silanes and A Shleifer 'Corporate Ownership Around the World' (1999) 54 Journal of Finance 471; R La Porta, F Lopez-de-Silanes and A Shleifer 'Investor Protection and Corporate Governance' (2000) 58 Journal of Financial Economics 4.

[10] Winter Report, 29.

have a legitimate place in company law but simply that we now recognise the need for sophisticated and careful examination of when and why regulatory intervention is more appropriate than simply leaving parties to their own contractual devices and to the operation of market forces. It is from this perspective that this paper considers the issues.

C. Shareholder Information

I. Mandatory Disclosure: a Brief Review of Familiar Territory

It is axiomatic that the effectiveness of internal corporate governance mechanisms and the availability of accurate, up-to-date information are interlinked. Poorly informed shareholders simply cannot make good use of internal governance mechanisms.[11] Although recent practice has to some extent challenged received wisdom about shareholders' willingness to participate in internal governance, such as the established view of UK institutional investors as passive investors who either did not vote or exercised their voting rights simply as a rubber stamp on management proposals,[12] it is self-evident that institutional and other investors are unlikely to vote against management in the absence of information that alerts them to possible difficulties with the view recommended by management.

Should lawmakers concern themselves with whether the flow of information to shareholders is adequate to enable them to make well-informed use of their

[11] MB Fox 'Required Disclosure and Corporate Governance' in KJ Hopt and others *Comparative Corporate Governance – The State of the Art and Emerging Research* (Clarendon Press Oxford 1998) ch 9.

[12] GP Stapledon *Institutional Shareholders and Corporate Governance* (Clarendon Press Oxford 1996). Part II details institutional involvement in corporate governance in the UK. But whilst acknowledging an increase in institutional investor activism, a fairly recent influential review of institutional investment in the UK expressed continuing concern about the sufficiency of such initiatives: *Institutional Investment in the United Kingdom: A Review* (London, HM Treasury) paras 5.73 – 5.94 (Myners Report).

The Spring 2003 AGM season in the UK witnessed unprecedented levels of investor activism over, and accompanying media interest in, the issue of directors' pay. This is a highly-charged and politically contentious issue. We will have to wait for the dust to settle before we can tell whether it was just an instance of 'noise' in the system or whether it heralds a radically new era in which institutional investors actively embrace confrontation as part of their strategy for active, internal monitoring of corporate management. The costs of active and, if circumstances dictate, occasionally aggressive shareholder monitoring remain an important, constraining factor with regard to the further development of this form of corporate governance control. Regulators are pressing for greater accountability of fund managers to end-investors, one element of which is that fund managers should not incur costs for services additional to dealing without the customer's express agreement (eg *Bundled Brokerage and Soft Commission Arrangements* (London, FSA, CP 176, 2003)). Greater transparency on commissions may tell a revealing story about the willingness of end-investors to pay a premium for active monitoring.

internal governance rights? Evidence of connections between the quality of a country's corporate governance mechanisms, its ability to attract investment capital and its economic growth give legitimacy to the inclusion of information disclosure issues on the regulatory public policy agenda since information is pivotal to the effective exercise of shareholder governance control. It is not proposed here to reopen the well known debate on voluntary versus mandatory disclosure but instead simply to accept the case for some State intervention in the form of disclosure requirements to improve the workings of internal corporate governance control mechanisms. In this context the argument that commercial incentives on managers to make voluntary disclosures to their shareholders may well be too weak to outweigh managerial self-interest in keeping information that reflects badly on themselves out of the public domain is particularly powerful.[13]

Mandatory disclosure requirements can sit fairly easily within a regulatory strategy that is primarily facilitative in its orientation on the basis that they promote better-informed decision-making but do not restrict individual autonomy. To be sure, disclosure requirements can change the behaviour of those whose conduct is disclosed as well as promoting informed responses to such conduct, an obvious illustration of this being that the prospect of disclosure will deter reputation-conscious corporate managers from conduct that is likely to attract negative publicity when it is publicly disclosed.[14] But rather than the State banning the conduct – a step that could well have been highly contentious – all that regulatory intervention in the form of disclosure requirements does is to force managers to make choices about the reputational risks they are prepared to take. Sometimes disclosure requirements can be a stepping stone to substantive regulation. One way of interpreting the passage from 'soft' (disclosure) to 'hard' (substantive) regulation of a particular matter which is consistent with a facilitative approach is to say the operation of the disclosure requirements provides the lawmaker with information which enables it to make better-informed choices about its substantive laws. Using the example above, if the market responds negatively to those managers who not deterred by disclosure requirements from engaging in 'risky' conduct, this can be seen as informing the lawmaker that tougher regulation of that conduct may well be in line with the preferences of market participants.

Disclosure requirements have costs implications. This (obvious) point needs to be emphasised as a counterbalance to the positive aspects of a disclosure-based regulatory strategy just outlined. Disclosure requirements are commonly viewed as being less burdensome than substantive rules but if this feature makes law-

[13] JC Coffee 'Market Failure and the Economic Case for a Mandatory Disclosure System' (1984) 70 Virginia Law Review 717, 738 – 743; MB Fox 'Retaining Mandatory Securities Disclosure: Why Issuer Choice is not Investor Empowerment' (1999) 85 Virginia Law Review 1335, 1355 – 1356.

[14] On the behavioural consequences of disclosure: J Parkinson 'Disclosure and Corporate Social and Environmental Performance: Competitiveness and Enterprise in a Broader Social Frame' [2003] Journal of Corporate Law Studies 3, 4 – 5.

makers more willing to experiment with innovative disclosure requirements without giving sufficient attention to costs considerations, paradoxically, the 'light touch' nature of regulation by disclosure rather than by substantive rule could prove very damaging.[15]

II. Mandatory Disclosure, Corporate Governance and the High Level Group

'Disclosure has a pivotal role in company law … corporate governance in general is a particular area where disclosure should be a key component of a regulatory regime.'[16]

In placing disclosure at the heart of its preferred regulatory strategy, the Winter Report is thus in line with mainstream international contemporary thinking on company law and corporate governance. On the face of it, requiring companies to disclose their corporate governance structures and practices does not force companies to modify their operations in any way. It simply enables existing shareholders and external market participants to make better-informed choices in their dealings with companies. However, disclosure requirements can have an indirect catalytic effect on internal corporate governance in that managers may choose to adapt their structures and practices in order to secure a more favourable market response or to avoid a negative reaction. The Winter Report's views about the benefits of disclosure in corporate governance, expressed in terms of the generalities that are appropriate to a 'high level' project, are ones that command wide support in legal and economic literature, and this is confirmed by the Group's own consultation exercise.[17] But, although it may be a cliché, the devil does lie in the detail and, as discussions shift from broad generalities to detailed analysis of how a European corporate governance disclosure regime can best be developed, various potentially problematic issues will surely emerge. Much-discussed issues are likely to include: (1) the content of mandatory disclosure requirements; (2) the sanctions for misleading disclosure: and (3) the institutional arrangements for the monitoring and enforcement of disclosure obligations.

[15] A recent study of SEC regulatory change requiring firms on the OTC Bulletin Board to comply with the reporting requirements under the Securities Exchange Act of 1934 has shown, for example, that for the majority of firms quoted on the OTCBB the costs of this change outweighed its benefits and they were forced out of this market. The authors suggest that their result suggests that an important consequence of mandatory SEC disclosure is to push smaller firms with lower financing needs into less regulated markets: BJ Bushee and C Leuz 'Economic Consequences of SEC Disclosure Regulation' Wharton Financial Institutions Center Working Paper 02 – 24 – B, SSRN abstract_id=307821.

[16] Winter Report, 45.

[17] Winter Report, 45 and Annex 3.

1. Content of mandatory disclosure requirements

The content of disclosure requirements is an obvious area where controversy is likely. Identification of issues that are genuinely transnational and, as such, appropriate subjects for European, rather than national level, regulation is the first hurdle. If there are matters on which the national laws of Member States already contain broadly comparable disclosure requirements, these would be obvious frontline candidates for European-level regulation, on the basis that this could remove minor variations and inconsistencies thereby promoting greater efficiency in the development of the internal market. But beyond formalisation and tidying up of areas where national requirements laws have already converged towards a common position, those responsible for setting the European regulatory policy agenda should tread warily and, in particular, should learn the lessons from the past with regard to the pitfalls that can be involved in 'lifting' rules from one Member State and seeking to apply them across Europe. The Winter Report's views on corporate governance disclosure appear to have been strongly influenced in certain areas by the British model, for example in relation to disclosure of executive compensation. Whilst mandatory disclosure of executive pay is increasingly commending itself to EU Member States as a desirable regulatory strategy,[18] imposition of such requirements from the centre would still represent a significant change for some European countries which have not yet moved as far in this direction as the UK. Should other Member States be forced towards the British (and American) approach with regard to remuneration? Equally should UK companies be required to make disclosures about relationships with their shareholders where the underlying concerns prompting the need for such disclosure relate to corporate ownership structures which are not common in the UK? The answers to such questions may well be yes, perhaps because this is the best way of ensuring that desirable information is provided across Europe in an easy-to-read, standardised form that facilitates cross-country, cross-sectoral comparative assessment of corporate governance practices; but until the case for this is clearly articulated a sceptical approach is warranted. Moreover, to the extent that the case for regulation at the European level rests on its superior ability to ensure standardisation of information disclosure across Europe, then managing the ten-

[18] Germany is a case in point. Provision for disclosure of executive pay is now contained in the Corporate Governance Kodex, para 4.2.4 (February 2002). On the development of German regulation in this respect: BR Cheffins 'The Metamorphosis of "Germany Inc.": the Case of Executive Pay' (2001) 49 American Journal of Comparative Law 497, 533 – 536 which provides a brief comparative assessment of the evolution of disclosure requirements relating to executive pay in the USA, UK and Germany. Further on German disclosure requirements see T Baums 'Changing Patterns of Corporate Disclosure in Continental Europe: the Example of Germany' (2002) ECGI Working Paper No 4/2002. [Cross-reference also to G Ferrarini and N Moloney 'Executive Remuneration and Corporate Governance in the EU: Convergence, Divergence, and Reform Perspectives' [chapter 5 in this book.]

sion between achievement of this goal and allowing individual Member States to retain discretion with regard to the detailed aspects of disclosure requirements must be addressed.

2. Enforcement of disclosure: directors' disqualification sanction

Whether the achievement of a truly pan-European corporate governance disclosure regime is threatened by the decentralisation of responsibilities to individual Member States with regard to liability standards and monitoring and enforcement practices needs also to be considered. In line with recent literature that emphasises that laws 'on the books' have little value if they are not supported by effective enforcement, this paper sees the achievement of credible consistency in monitoring and enforcement as being pivotal to the delivery of an effective European disclosure regime.[19]

One might envisage an 'ideal' world in which European corporate governance disclosure requirements would be accompanied by identical pan-European liability standards. The procedural rules governing standing, production of evidence, costs and so forth would be same regardless of the location within Europe of the parties. Investigators, prosecutors, judges and others involved in the enforcement process would all operate independently, free from political or corrupting influences and according to the same standards of professional expertise and ethics. Broadening out this vision still further, there would be no differences in the legal rules, and accompanying processes that are intended to ensure that information intermediaries, such as lawyers, accountants and bankers, perform effectively the role of filtering out inaccurate or incomplete information.[20] But we are very far from this 'ideal' model. Since the imminent emergence of a dedicated pan-European corporate governance monitoring and enforcement regime is not likely (I return later to 'piggy-backing' corporate governance disclosure monitoring and enforcement onto general securities law enforcement), it is more sensible to concentrate on the relatively modest steps that might be taken to move forward in an incremental fashion by ironing out inconsistencies and divergences in approach.

In this respect, the Winter Report's suggestion that there is a case for examining the possible introduction of a directors' disqualification sanction across the EU, at least for misleading financial and key non-financial disclosures, is deserving of particular attention. Logically, rules and the sanctions for breaches

[19] Members of the Winter Group appear to share this concern about the importance of achieving effective enforcement of disclosure obligations across Europe. As Garrido put it: 'What it is not allowed is to mislead the public by giving incorrect information: if a company does not follow governance guidelines, it cannot fool shareholders and investors that it is complying with them' Letters to the Editor, *Financial Times* (15 November 2002) 20.

[20] Generally, HS Scott 'Internationalization of Primary Public Securities Markets' [2000] Law and Contemporary Problems 63, 71.

of those rules are so closely intertwined that it makes sense to put co-ordination of sanctions next on the list of priorities for consideration behind co-ordination of the rules themselves. Indeed, if one were starting with a blank sheet of paper one might put the question of sanctions at the top of the list, on the basis that one of the most effective ways in which the law can assist and support the operation of market forces is by imposing tough, clear sanctions with claimant-friendly burdens of proof against those who provide misleading information.[21] However, the current agenda is necessarily influenced and shaped by the past and by political considerations. Historically, the European Commission has held back from regulating on liability in the corporate and securities disclosure field, although the inclusion of provisions on liability in the Prospectus and draft Transparency Directive are signs of change.[22] Against this backdrop and in recognition of continuing political sensitivities, it seems inevitable that if the idea of a pan-European disqualification regime were to be implemented (and this is something which itself may well be politically contentious), detailed aspects of the scheme would still be left to national discretion. Moreover continuing variation between Member States with regard to vigorous use of enforcement powers would seem inevitable.

What are the features of a directors' disqualification regime that might commend it for adoption as a general European sanction for disclosure breaches? Disqualification is a powerful sanction in that it can severely damage, if not destroy, a person's reputation and career prospects. But the same could be said of criminal sanctions for serious offences and at least in some circumstances a finding against a director in a civil case could be very damaging both to reputation and to career. So it is not that disqualification is inherently superior to other possible sanctions by reason of its impact on the wrongdoer.[23] Is it that a disqualification sanction is easier to obtain and so likely to be a more effective deterrent than other sanctions? Superficially the British experience, where disqualification

[21] R La Porta, F Lopez-de-Silanes and A Shleifer 'What Works in Securities Laws?' (October 2002) (unpublished manuscript available at <http://post.economics.harvard.edu/faculty/shleifer/papers/securities_10_10_02.pdf>).

[22] Prospectus Directive (insert full reference when published), art 25 provides for an adequate sanctioning mechanism to be put in place in each Member State. It states that such sanctions, including administrative ones, must be effective, proportionate and dissuasive. The Proposal for a Directive of the European Parliament and of the Council on the Harmonisation of Transparency Requirements with Regard to Information about Issuers whose Securities are Admitted to Trading on a Regulated Market and Amending Directive 2001/34/EC (March 2003) (draft Transparency Directive), art 24 is to similar effect. On the historical reluctance of EC authorities to grasp the sanctions nettle in the area of issuer disclosure and the limitations imposed by European law in this respect: N Moloney *EC Securities Regulation* (Oxford University Press Oxford 2002) 153 – 154, 197.

[23] Cf Winter Report, 9, which claims that, as compared to criminal and civil sanctions, disqualification 'is an alternative sanction which may be easier to effectuate and has a powerful deterrent and longer disabling effect'.

is an established sanction for failings by directors across a range of circumstances,[24] appears to support this line of thinking. Whereas criminal proceedings against directors for serious offences are rare[25] and civil actions against directors are hampered by poor laws on shareholder standing to bring derivative suits, unfavourable rules on costs and broader collective action problems, successful disqualification proceedings, which are commenced by a government department and judged according to civil standards of proof, are comparatively common. Proceedings against unfit directors of insolvent companies tend to attract the most attention and it is for these proceedings that statistics are most readily available. In 2001 – 2, some 1,761 directors of insolvent companies were disqualified for unfitness,[26] the majority of them for a period of between two and five years but in the case of 38 individuals for a period of between 11 and 15 years.[27] What are we to make of such figures? Andrew Hicks, a specialist on the practical operation of the British disqualification regime argues that these numbers pale into insignificance when set against the total director population, estimated to be about three million.[28] On the basis of his empirical work, Hicks is sceptical about the disqualification regime's effectiveness in deterring improper conduct and in promoting good standards of practice in corporate management. He also expresses concern about the effectiveness of monitoring of compliance with disqualification orders. Overall, his sobering conclusions are that: 'The politicians have placed disqualification at centre stage in a regulatory role it is manifestly incapable of playing … disqualification still does not achieve the protection, deterrence and education of directors that is expected of it'.[29] Others are more positive: Adrian Walters and Malcolm Davis-White, for example, claim that 'there is a strong case for saying that the law relating to disqualification of directors has become one of the most significant parts of company law'.[30] It is certainly true that the directors'

[24] The Company Directors Disqualification Act 1986 is now the main statute providing for disqualification but the origins of disqualification provisions relating to bankruptcy and fraudulent trading can be traced back to the Companies Act 1928: A Walters and Davis-White *Directors' Disqualification: Law and Practice* (Sweet & Maxwell London 1999) ch 1.

[25] Enquiries by the Law Commissions of England and Wales and of Scotland found that in the period 1990/6, practically no prosecutions had been recorded under the Companies Act 1985, Part X (Enforcement of Fair Dealing by Directors): *Regulating Conflicts of Interests and Formulating a Statement of Duties* (Law Commission Consultation Paper 153, Scottish Law Commission Discussion Paper No 105 (1998)), para 10.2.

[26] Under Company Directors Disqualification Act 1986, s 6.

[27] Insolvency Service *Annual Reports and Accounts 2001 – 02* (DTI London 2002) 31.

[28] A Hicks 'Director Disqualification: Can it Deliver?' [2001] Journal of Business Law 433.

[29] ibid 459.

[30] Walters and Davis-White *Directors' Disqualification* (n 24) 1. But elsewhere Walters has also expressed some concerns about the operation of the directors' disqualification regime in insolvency circumstances: A Walters 'Directors' Disqualification after the Insolvency Act 2000:

cont. …

disqualification regime has claimed some notable, high-profile scalps and that prominent disqualification cases have helpfully clarified certain substantive company law issues relating to directors' duties.[31] Continuing political confidence in the effectiveness of the disqualification sanction is demonstrated by the recent extension of the disqualification regime to cover breaches of competition law.[32] Media coverage of that change inclined towards the view that disqualification is a particularly tough sanction and that its extension into competition matters was likely to have a significant impact on corporate behaviour.[33]

This is not the place for a detailed examination of the attributes and failings of the British directors' disqualification regime. It is a domestic regime and as such its operation is shaped by local factors that would not necessarily apply to a regime that derives from European law. Moreover under British law the disqualification sanction is closely, though not exclusively, associated with failed companies and with the protection of the public from persons who have abused the privilege of trading with limited liability. A disqualification sanction attaching to failure to comply with corporate governance disclosure requirements would be aimed at serving different shareholder-orientated purposes thus suggesting that criticism of the British system's ability to achieve its rather different goals may have limited relevance to the European discussion. Nevertheless, the mixed reports on the effectiveness of the British regime are worth highlighting as meriting some attention in the European debate envisaged by the Winter Report on the merits of introducing a disqualification sanction for non-compliance with disclosure requirements.

Another issue to which those involved in this debate should pay attention is whether a broad measure of pan-European consistency in the use of a disqualification sanction is realistically achievable against an established background in which there appear to be significant variations between the expertise and experiences of the administrative and judicial authorities of different Member States

The New Regime' [2001] Insolvency Law 86. See also V Finch *Corporate Insolvency Law: Perspectives and Principles* (Cambridge University Press 2002) 531 – 538.

[31] *Re Barings plc* [1999] 1 BCLC 433 (affirmed [2000] 1 BCLC 523) qualifies on both counts: a case on unfitness brought under s 6 which concerned high-profile directors and which in the first instance judgment provides the clearest modern judicial statement of the directors' duty of care and skill and their power to delegate and rely on others. For comment on this 'seminal' decision see A Walters 'Directors' Duties: The Impact of the Company Directors Disqualification Act 1986' (2000) 21 Company Lawyer 110. See also *Secretary of State for Trade and Industry v Deverell* [2000] 2 WLR 907 (CA) (interpretation of the definition of 'shadow director').

[32] Enterprise Act 2002, s 204 inserting ss 9A – E into the Company Directors Disqualification Act 1986.

[33] 'Competition: Take the Strain' *The Lawyer* (2 September 2002) 23; 'Danger Lurks Beneath the Director' *Financial Times* (7 October 2002) 13.

with regard to the use of disqualification as a primary sanction against directors.[34] There is a risk that experienced authorities which are confident users of disclosure sanctions against directors could pursue tougher enforcement policies than their less experienced counterparts in other Member States, hence undermining the standardising effect meant to be achieved by the introduction of the sanction on a pan-European basis.

3. Promoting consistency: locating institutional responsibility for monitoring and enforcement of disclosure obligations

The concern about consistency in the operation of a disqualification sanction merges into a broader concern about enforcement of corporate governance disclosure obligations. The Winter Report recommends that Member States should be free to implement corporate governance disclosure requirements as they think fit, through company law, securities law, listing rules or otherwise.[35] This recommendation implies that there could continue to be a diverse range of organisations involved in the processes of monitoring compliance with disclosure requirements and taking enforcement action in the event of default.[36] Diversity of responsibilities at national level is an acceptable result judged against the criterion of favouring 'bottom up' based regulation, but it does have certain disadvantages when it is set against the potential benefits that could be secured by regarding corporate governance disclosure requirements as a matter of securities law, and shaping institutional arrangements for monitoring and enforcement on that basis.

Any theoretical attempt to draw a sharp, firm boundary line between corporate law territory and securities law territory is doomed to fail. Securities law and

[34] Ireland has a similar disqualification regime under its Companies Act 1990 and also a regime for the imposition of restrictions on involvement in corporate management on persons who were directors of insolvent companies: R Keane *Company Law* (Butterworths Dublin 2000) 371 – 377. There are provisions in French law for disqualification of directors in solvency-related circumstances: PJ Omar *Directors' Duties and Liabilities* (Ashgate Publishing Aldershot 2000) 46 – 47; but apparently these are not enforced: R Kraakman and others *The Anatomy of Corporate Law: A Comparative and Functional Approach* (Oxford University Press (forthcoming)) ch 4. In other Member States, too, disqualification from serving as a director may follow from a finding of personal bankruptcy or from conviction of certain offences (eg the German Stock Corporation Act, §76 (3)), but the use of disqualification as a primary sanction for corporate mismanagement or wrongdoing, as opposed to a secondary sanction that is consequential upon some other legal proceeding, appears to be uncommon.

[35] Winter Report, 61 – 62.

[36] Weil, Gotshal & Manges *Comparative Study Of Corporate Governance Codes Relevant to the European Union And Its Member States* indicates the wide variations that currently exist across Member States with regard to institutional responsibility for corporate governance disclosure.

corporate law are best seen as complementary and mutually reinforcing.[37] Disclosure requirements are specifically singled out by the Winter Report as an area where company and securities law come together.[38] So in raising the question of allocation of regulatory functions relating to corporate governance disclosures, there is little point in becoming preoccupied with conceptual niceties. Instead it is more fruitful to be pragmatically and practically focussed. The suggestion here is that in thinking about the location of regulatory responsibilities there are distinct practical benefits that could be secured by decoupling substantive corporate governance from disclosure about corporate governance. Securities regulators may not have the appropriate skills and experience to be the arbiters of best practice on matters of board composition, board committees and other substantive corporate governance concerns. On the other hand, national securities regulators are accustomed to dealing with corporate disclosures in prospectuses and listing particulars, and the continuing obligations regime for listed companies. Extending their role to cover corporate governance disclosures would be an incremental step but not a radical departure into wholly unfamiliar uncharted territory.[39]

To vest responsibility for corporate governance disclosure in national securities regulators in the foreseeable future would presumably require European intervention to oblige Member States to take this step. Would this intervention to override national diversity be justified? If the concern is to achieve greater consistency with regarding to monitoring and enforcing compliance across Europe then it could be. Making a securities regulator in each Member State the responsible body for corporate governance disclosure would ensure a greater degree of common regulatory philosophy and approach amongst the relevant authorities than would be possible in a mixed system where the authority in some States could be a securities regulator, in others a body responsible for overseeing financial accounts and in others some other entirely different organisation. It would allow the corporate disclosure regime across Europe to benefit from securities regulators' enforcement expertise, and it could open up a wider range of sanctions by making available administrative sanctions that can only be imposed by the securities regulator. The importance of standardisation with regard to the identity

37 DC Langevoort 'Seeking Sunlight in Santa Fe's Shadow: the SEC's Pursuit of Managerial Accountability'(2001) 79 Washington University Law Quarterly 449.

38 Winter Report, 34. In the European context, the draft Transparency Directive provides a good illustration of the way in which the boundary lines are increasingly blurred. This draft directive includes provisions on communications with shareholders and the operation of company meetings, matters which traditionally might be regarded as becoming squarely within the company law field.

39 The issue of regulatory responsibility for corporate governance disclosures was raised, though not fully answered, in the context of the review of EU transparency obligations: *Towards an EU Regime on Transparency Obligations imposed for Issuers whose Securities are Admitted to Trading on a Regulated Market. Second Consultation by the Services of the Internal Market Directorate-General of the European Commission* (European Commission 2002).

of competent authorities is already accepted in relation to prospectuses and continuing obligations. The suggestion here is thus complementary to and consistent with developments in very closely fields. This proposal would still not guarantee consistency because significant differences remain in the powers and authorities enjoyed by the large number of securities regulators operating in individual Member States[40] and they each operate in different legal, economic, political and cultural environments; but it could be at least an incremental step in that direction. This proposal fits well with US developments where corporate governance disclosure requirements are increasingly part of the federal securities regulatory framework rather than state corporate law.[41] For Europe and the US to adopt broadly similar positions with regard to the allocation of regulatory responsibility for corporate governance disclosures is appealing in that this could secure at a broader international level, as well as within the EU, the benefits of greater consistency in regulatory policy and supervisory practices, and could promote international co-operation.

A further pragmatic advantage offered by the suggestion that European securities regulators should be responsible for corporate governance disclosures is that pan-European mechanisms for co-operation and sharing of information between securities regulators are already in place. The evolution of a centralised co-operation and information-sharing infrastructure for European securities regulation has moved at a faster pace than for European company law. As a result of initiatives following from the Lamfalussy Report in 2001,[42] the Committee of European Securities Regulators (CESR) was established in 2001 to advise the European Commission on the development of securities legislation and regulation.[43] CESR also acts as a forum in which the principal EU securities regulators meet to formulate common approaches on regulatory issues and to share experiences. CESR feeds into the work of the European Securities Committee (ESC), the second

[40] Or, as the Lamfalussy Report puts it (at 17): 'Competencies are mixed. Responsibilities are different. The result at European level is fragmentation and often confusion'. The formal title is *Final Report of the Committee of Wise Men on the Regulation of European Securities Markets* (Brussels, European Commission, February 2001).

[41] RB Thompson and HA Sale 'Securities Fraud as Corporate Governance: Reflections Upon Federalism' (2003) 56 Vanderbilt Law Review (forthcoming), SSRN abstract_id=362860.

[42] YV Avgerinos 'Essential and Non-essential Measures: Delegation of Powers in EU Securities Regulation' (2002) 8 European Law Journal 269. On the operation of the Lamfalussy process: Inter-Institutional Monitoring Group First Interim Report Monitoring the New Process for Regulating Securities Markets in Europe (The Lamfalussy Process (May 2003) <http://www. europa.eu.int/comm/internal_market/en/finances/mobil/docs/lamfalussy/2003-05-monitoring-summary_en.pdf>.

[43] Although formally established in June 2001, CESR can trace its roots back to the Forum of European Securities Commission which was in place between 1997 and 2001 until its replacement by CESR: M McKee 'The Committee of European Securities Regulators: Is it Working?' (2002) 4 Journal of International Financial Markets 111.

post-Lamfalussy organ, which has been established to advise the Commissions and to work with it in the process of writing detailed technical rules supplementing framework directives, such rules to have legal force under EU comitology procedures. Extending CESR's established channels of communication to cover corporate governance disclosure practices could speed up the process for convergence of requirements and facilitate the sharing of accumulated knowledge, experience and expertise so as to promote greater consistency in the implementation of supervision and in relation to enforcement practices. This concentration of responsibilities could also potentially offer savings with regard to infrastructure support costs.

It may be, however, that the characterisation of vesting corporate governance disclosure responsibilities in securities regulators as a relatively modest step that would complement measures in related fields is wrong and that in some Member States this would be a seen as a highly controversial idea touching upon deep sensitivities and provoking defensive reactions from agencies concerned not to suffer a diminution in their fiefdoms. Moreover more detailed examination of pragmatic benefits that could be secured by treating corporate governance disclosure as an aspect of securities law would entail looking at whether regulatory agencies or other actors in the securities markets, in particular stock exchanges, are best placed to perform the regulatory role.[44] And writing from the British perspective it must be acknowledged that the trend in the UK, where there are proposals to divest the securities regulator of its current responsibilities for corporate governance disclosures and vest them instead in a new Standards Board, is hardly consistent with the model advocated here.[45] Such considerations serve as a check on enthusiasm for this proposal. In view of the notorious difficulties involved in securing political agreement on European measures that touch upon sensitive national interests concerning company law, it would be futile to press the argument for a model that would simply be a target for controversy that could overshadow and possibly block the attainment of other more politically acceptable goals. So, again taking a pragmatic stance, it may well be that HLG's decision to support Member State diversity with regard to supervision and enforcement of corporate governance disclosures represents the sensible and realistic choice at this time. Across the board the HLG's recommendations resonate with an awareness of the need to consider political sensitivities, unsurprisingly so given that the Group was first established to deal with the fallout of political deadlock over the Takeover Directive. Yet to permit uncontrolled Member State diversity in this respect would be at best a political compromise. The position

[44] PA Mahoney 'The Exchange as Regulator' (1997) 83 Virginia Law Review 1453.

[45] *Modernising Company Law* (London DTI Cm 5553, 2002) para 5.11. But note *Review of the Listing Regime: Feedback on DP 14* (London FSA 2003) paras 3.5 – 3.6 which note support from respondents for the current position and indicate that the FSA agrees that the 'comply or explain' provision in the *Listing Rules* is a valuable support to the Combined Code.

would be distinctly unsatisfactory when measured against the criterion of designing arrangements so to promote pan-European consistency in the practical operation of corporate governance disclosure regimes and achieving 'competitive neutrality' in supervision. If estimations that it is in the area of corporate disclosures that political resistance to European centralisation is weakest are right,[46] it could well make political sense to re-open this issue before too long.

III. A Different Structure for Substantive Corporate Governance

It Is worth reiterating the point that the previous parts of this section are based on the premise that, in thinn og about the allocatio 6Vf regulatory responsibilities, it is appropriate to decouple disclosure about corporate governance from substantive corporate governance requirements. This paper does not argue that securities regulators should be generally responsible for substantive corporate governance.

With regard to that, the Winter Report suggests that, beyond key requirements laid down by directive, the EU's role should not be prescriptive. Rather it should actively seek to co-ordinate the development by Member States of corporate governance rules and accompanying monitoring and enforcement procedures through the establishment by the European Commission of a structure for the facilitation of co-ordination.[47] The Winter Report appears to be treading very carefully here, presumably mindful of political sensitivities and tensions. A cynic might dismiss this rather vague proposal as amounting to nothing more than the establishment of a 'talking shop', particularly since it is envisaged that any results from the co-ordination process would be voluntary and non-binding. But a fairer assessment (and one with which the European Commission evidently agrees[48]) is that, in view of the wide variations in corporate ownership patterns and national corporate law cultures across the EU, generally speaking it is sensible for the EU to view its role in relation to corporate governance as being that of co-ordinator of 'bottom up' convergence driven by the activities of Member States. For the EU to attempt to impose 'top down' corporate governance would be politically unfeasible, arguably at odds with the subsidiarity principle and fundamentally undesir-

[46] G Hertig and R Lee 'Four Predictions about the Future of EU Securities Regulation' (2003) Journal of Corporate Law Studies (forthcoming).

[47] Winter Report, 72 – 73 outlines the general framework. It is intended that disclosure requirements should be part of this framework: ibid, 46.

[48] 'The Commission regards it important to encourage the co-ordination and convergence of national codes through regular high level meetings of the European Corporate Governance Forum. Participants to such a Forum, which could meet once or twice a year, will comprise representatives from Member States, European regulators (including CESR), issuers and investors, other market participants and academics. Interested MEP's will also be invited to present their views. The Forum will be chaired by the Commission': extract from European Commission Communication.

able as being a misguided attempt to impose a veneer of centralised uniformity that would sit very uneasily on top of the diversity of corporate structures in Member States. A new heavyweight, centralised Euro structure for corporate governance would have little to commend it.[49]

Whilst the establishment of a corporate governance co-ordination structure might not make 'headline news', over time it could prove to be very significant. There are obvious potential benefits to be secured by promoting the sharing of knowledge between Member States about the regulatory challenges presented by the different patterns of corporate ownership and other structural variations in the wider business context across the EU. Moreover experience has shown that the emergence of a consensus amongst influential participants on what is good practice can have a powerful impact on behaviour despite its voluntary status. 'Behaviour' in this context can certainly include decisions by sovereign states on the content of their national laws.[50] So it is entirely plausible to envisage the co-ordination process envisaged by the HLG acting as a catalyst for legal change in certain Member States with their example in turn then prompting other States to follow suit. As it developed its own authority and influence, the existence of a transnational forum for European deliberations on corporate governance could be a counterbalance to entrenched national interest groups and could dilute their influence over the development of European corporate governance policy.

[49] In view of the significant inter-institutional tensions generated by the Lamfalussy proposals (see, generally, N Moloney *EC Securities Regulation* (Oxford University Press, 2002) ch 15) it seems unlikely that the central European bodies will be keen to rush into a 'son of Lamfalussy' for company law. Moreover achieving EC-wide political agreements on areas of 'core' company law is notoriously difficult and Member States are unlikely to support proposals for infrastructure change that could dilute their ability to block controversial initiatives. Generally, the increasing prevalence of of committees and agencies within the regulatory structure raises issues of constitutional significance for the EU concerning their position, powers and accountability: G deBúrca 'The Institutional Development of the EU: A Constitutional Analysis' in P Craig and G deBúrca (eds) *The Evolution of EU Law* (Oxford University Press 1999) 55, 69 – 81.

[50] The best known illustration is the work of the Basel Committee on Banking Supervision. Voluntary capital adequacy standards developed by the Basel Committee have acquired legal force around the world by being transplanted into the national laws of sovereign states. On the development of international economic and financial law through voluntary codes and standards see generally: C Jordan and G Majnoni 'Financial Regulatory Harmonization and the Globalization of Finance' in JA Hanson, P Honohan and G Majnoni (eds) *Globalization and National Financial Systems* (Washington: International Bank for Reconstruction and Development/World Bank, 2002-2003) SSRN abstract_ id=343260; M Giovanoli 'A New Architecture for the Global Financial Market: Legal Aspects of International Financial Standard Setting' in M Giovanoli (ed) *International Monetary Law* (Oxford University Press, 2000) ch 1.

D. Beyond Disclosure: Active Exercise of Internal Control by Shareholders

I. Limits of Disclosure

Mandatory disclosure makes for better-informed decision-making by shareholders. Yet whilst this statement reflects a central aspect of contemporary thinking about regulatory strategies in relation to companies, we can readily see that disclosure, on its own, plays only a limited role because it has no real impact unless shareholders are empowered to make significant decisions and have access to good decision-making processes that enable them to make effective and meaningful use of their powers. From a securities law perspective, the decisions that are the focus of concern in this respect are investment decisions about whether to buy, sell or hold securities. From an internal corporate governance perspective, questions about the scope of shareholders' decision-making powers – which matters should be for shareholders to decide, what type of shareholder majority should be required, and so forth – the processes for decision-making, and the ways in which shareholders and companies can communicate with each other are complex and wide-ranging. This paper concentrates on decision-making processes and communication mechanisms, in this respect reflecting the emphasis and approach of the Winter Report. Without good processes and mechanisms, shareholders are unlikely to be willing to use whatever internal control powers are vested in them, and such willingness is necessarily a necessary precondition to the effective use of power.

II. Corporate communications outside the general meeting: communications between shareholders amongst themselves, and between shareholders and their company

Where corporate ownership is widely dispersed it is important for the meaningful exercise of internal shareholder influence and control that shareholders should be able to communicate effectively with each other outside the general meeting to facilitate the emergence of standard responses to issues of common concern. It is also important to have good two-way communication between management and shareholders because dialogue should reduce agency problems by facilitating prompt identification of issues where management views are at odds with those of shareholders and perhaps allowing for compromise and reconciliation before the difference of opinion escalates into hostility and conflict at a general meeting. Good communication should nurture trust and co-operation between interested parties.[51] The existence of alternative fora for debate should reduce the pressure

[51] CA Villiers 'Disclosure Obligations in Company Law: Bringing Communication Theory into the Fold' [2001] Journal of Corporate Law Studies 181.

on the general meeting to perform this role.[52] However, as ever, there is a need for balance and a sense of proportionality so that valuable corporate resources are not wasted in responding to complicated, but fundamentally trivial, or largely irrelevant queries.

It is possible for shareholders to develop their own channels of corporate communication without legal intervention. The various investor guidelines agreed between representatives of the major groups of institutional investor in the UK illustrate what can be achieved through private initiative. These guidelines are examples of institutional shareholders coming together to agree a common position which, in turn, is helpful to management because management can predict, with reasonable certainty, the response of their major investors to proposals on matters covered by such guidelines. For example, UK companies can be confident of institutional shareholder support for resolutions to authorise new share issues for cash on a non pre-emptive basis so long as they observe the limits and restrictions on such authorisations that are specified in the voluntary pre-emption guidelines agreed between representatives of industry and institutional investors.[53]

Broadly speaking,[54] institutional investors in the typical UK public company, where ownership is widely dispersed but the predominant investors are institutions, and blockholders in the typical Continental company, where majority ownership remains concentrated,[55] can look after themselves so far as corporate communications are concerned (the difficult question of communications between companies and underlying beneficial owners of shares registered in the name of custodians is dealt with separately, later).[56] The same is not true of retail and minority shareholders who cannot individually exert significant commercial pres-

[52] E Boros 'Corporate Governance in Cyberspace: Who Stands to Gain What from the Virtual Meeting?' [2003] Journal of Corporate Law Studies 149.

[53] The pre-emption guidelines are available at <http://www.ivis.co.uk/pages/gdsc4_1.html>.

[54] The text draws a stark distinction between institutional and retail investors which is convenient for expository purposes but which is admittedly simplistic and crude. For example, smaller institutional investors may lack the commercial clout to secure ready, and continuing, access to informal channels of communication with corporate management.

[55] M Becht and P Bolton 'Corporate Governance and Control' (2002) ECGI Finance Working Paper 02/2002. 31. But note, ibid, 81 on the existence of significant blockholders in UK companies

[56] According to the Higgs Report, it is 'common practice for chief executives to have regular contacts with major shareholders. Chairmen often also participate. According to my telephone survey, three-quarters of chairmen discuss company business with some of their investors at least once a year. Through such meetings, these members of the board gain a clear insight into the views, and on occasion concerns, of the company's major shareholders. For their part, shareholders develop a better understanding of a wide range of issues from the point of view of management. These channels of communication are now widely accepted as both desirable and useful. *Review of the Role and Effectiveness of Non-Executive Directors* (London DTI 2003) para 15.4.

sure on corporate managers to engage in two-way dialogue and who may not, unlike institutional investors, have trade associations and informal contacts to promote co-ordinated responses amongst themselves on matters of corporate governance. There are obvious risks that institutional shareholders and blockholders will exploit their superior position for their own benefit or will collude with management in arriving at solutions that are inimical to the interests of smaller shareholders. Or large shareholders may over-monitor management with the result that managers become overly cautious in their decisions about potentially profitable investment opportunities. Even if exploitation, collusion or over-monitoring does not in fact occur, awareness of their inferior position with regard to corporate communications could discourage retail investors from investing in the corporate sector, thereby reducing the size of the pool of investment capital available to business which, in turn, could impact on productivity.[57]

Policy questions about improving the participative involvement of shareholders, especially retail shareholders, inevitably involve consideration of the use of the internet, email and other forms of electronic communication. Changes to facilitate the use of electronic communications as a mechanism for corporate disclosure have already been made to legal systems around the world.[58] Corporate use of electronic media to enhance the process by which they disclose information to shareholders is already extensive. For example, 83% of the Fortune 100 companies and 30% of FTSE 250 companies now provide corporate web-casts.[59] Online publication of annual reports and accounts is commonplace. Making information promptly available online to all investors is one way in which companies have responded to the concerns of securities regulators about market transparency and selective disclosure of information. However, more radical change permitting companies to use electronic communications to the exclusion of other forms of communication regardless of their shareholders' preferences, looks a long way off. Such a change would be unwarranted until internet usage becomes virtually ubiquitous, and we are far from this at present in Europe.

[57] *Modern Company Law for a Competitive Economy Company General Meetings and Shareholder Communication* (London DTI URN 99/1144 1999) paras 20 and 61 – 63 note longstanding British concerns about uneven access to corporate information as between institutional and retail shareholders.

[58] E Boros 'Corporations Online' (2000) 19 Company and Securities Law Journal 492 provides an overview of relevant legislative developments in Australia, the USA and the UK. The draft Transparency Directive, arts 13 – 14 are in line with this trend.

[59] 'Getting the Message Across: Shareholder Communications: The Internet has Transformed Investor Relations but More Changes are Coming' (*Financial Times* 4 December 2002) 14. However, in the UK there are regulatory problems about corporate webcasts because of concerns that they could be caught by the very broad financial promotions regime imposed under the Financial Services and Markets Act 2000, s 21. The breadth of this regime has come in for strong criticism: J Crosthwait 'Financial Promotion – Time for a Policy Re-think' [2002] Journal of Corporate Law Studies 245.

According to recent European Commission research, in 2002 only around 40% of EU households had an internet connection, in contrast to businesses and schools of which more than 90% were online. There were wide disparities between Member States with regard to household connectivity with three countries with above 65% penetration and, at the other extreme, one with less than 14%.[60] Moreover companies are unlikely to press for legal change permitting them to force shareholders to accept electronic communications so long as shareholders continue to express a strong preference for the delivery of traditional shareholder information, such as annual accounts, in print form, with web-based publication welcomed as a complementary medium which, as well as duplicating information published in traditional form, can also provide additional, more time-sensitive information.[61]

Improving general investor access to corporate information by using electronic media to make more of it available more quickly is, however, only part of the story about the impact of technological development on corporate activity. Another part of the story, which is particularly relevant here, is the role of electronic media in promoting better interactive communications between companies and shareholders, such as through the use of email and bulletin boards. Companies are beginning to explore using investor relations websites as a medium for direct interactive communications. For example, General Electric is reported to be developing plans for shareholders to communicate with its non executive directors through a website.[62] It seems likely that this is part of trend and that, with the use of information technology as a business tool for communicating *to* shareholders now well established, companies will be increasingly alert to exploiting its potential for interactive communication *with* their shareholders. They will weigh the commercial advantages offered by good online shareholder interactive communication facilities against the variety of costs, including those involved in developing and maintaining systems, in ensuring their effective and efficient operation and in keeping them secure and policing them against abuse, that such systems entail. Powerful market forces are likely to result in the emergence of good practices from the 'bottom up'. Accordingly there is nothing to indicate that this is an area where government intervention is either necessary or desirable.

Broadly speaking the Winter Report shares the view that the role of the law is to facilitate the use of electronic communications but not to compel their use. However, an exception to this is the Winter Report proposal that listed companies should be required by European law to maintain a specific section on their websites containing all legal and other information they are required to file and disclose, and to update this information on a continuous basis. The Winter Report

[60] *eEurope 2002 Final Report* (Brussels, European Commission) <http://www.europa.eu.int/information_society/eeurope/2002/news_library/documents/acte_eEurope_2002_en.doc>.

[61] 'Getting the Message Across' (n 59).

[62] 'GE Hires Former Watchdog Member' (*Financial Times* 29 October 2002) 30.

recommends this as an efficiency-enhancing measure. As we have seen, many companies already publish this information on their websites, and this practice is likely to become increasingly common. Therefore a mandatory requirement to include this information on websites would be more a reflection of market practice than a change dictated by the legislature. As such this is a situation where a mandatory rule can be regarded as justifiable because it reflects general expectations and/or relates to an uncontroversial 'housekeeping' matter on which it is convenient to establish a common position.

Good housekeeping is also a justification for the Winter Report's eminently sensible proposal that companies should be required by EU law to inform shareholders about how they can ask questions, how and to what extent the company intends to answer questions and how and under what conditions they can submit proposals to the shareholders' meeting. If an annual corporate governance statement becomes mandatory, this would be a logical place for such information to be set out because pan-European standardisation of the source would promote quick, efficient discovery of shareholder entitlements.

Should officially filed information also be available from a central register, 'central' for this purpose meaning, at least for the moment, a central national register within each Member State although it could, in time and with erosion of national differences that currently stand in way of pan-European standardisation, mean a European central electronic filing system?[63] This is an area where there is considerable overlap between corporate governance and investor protection considerations. Improved facilities for comparative assessment of companies should enable investors to make better informed investment decisions. At the same time they should enable shareholders to discern trends in corporate governance from which they can make more informed assessments of whether the situation in any particular company warrants special attention. The establishment of a central information access point in each Member State could particularly benefit cross-border investors and shareholders for whom searching through a range of different, unfamiliar sources in other countries might be especially challenging. As with corporate governance disclosure, it is appropriate for securities law to lead the way in this respect. The advancement of centralised national filing systems via securities regulators is already on the European securities law reform agenda.[64] The prospect of forthcoming changes to European law may galvanise

[63] E Wymeersch 'Factors and Trends of Change in Company Law' (2000) 2 International and Comparative Corporate Law Journal, 481, 499.

[64] The draft Prospectus Directive, art 14 provides for approved prospectuses to be filed with the competent authority and made available to the public on the authority's website or via a link to the issuer's own site. The draft Transparency Directive also contains provisions for facilitating better public access to regulated information via the developments of appropriate networks: arts 17-18.

national authorities in individual Member States to speed up their efforts to move in this direction.[65]

III. Making General Meetings More Effective

Whilst better communication between companies and shareholders outside the general meeting may reduce the pressure on the general meeting, the general meeting remains vital to the operation of internal corporate governance for two key reasons. First, and of primary significance, the background threat of managerial proposals being defeated when they are put to the general meeting or of management being voted out of office reinforces the commercial incentives on corporate management to engage in meaningful dialogue with their major shareholders. Secondly, smaller shareholders who do not control sufficient votes to exercise formal control by voting down managerial proposals can still make good use of the general meeting by treating it as an opportunity to draw public, especially media, attention to their concerns and/or ideas for improvement. As Boros notes, the possibly fiery setting of a contentious face-to-face general meeting is much more likely to be effective in this respect than an intangible exchange of electronic communications.[66]

Electronic communications technology does, of course, have considerable significance in relation to the effective operation of general meetings even if we put the possibility of the entirely virtual meeting to one side as being undesirable at this time because it would result in the loss of face-to-face accountability.[67] It is increasingly common for companies to offer their shareholders electronic communications facilities for transmission of meetings' material, including notices of meetings and proxy appointment forms.[68] In the UK the use of electronic technology for this purpose has been formally endorsed as 'best practice' by the

[65] In 1999 the UK FSA announced its intention to move as early as possible to electronic filing of documentation from issuers, maintaining a central database of all information filed, with links back to listed companies: *The Transfer of the UK Listing Authority to the FSA* (London FSA CP 37 1999) para 5.11. However, progress towards achievement of this goal has been slow. A modest step forward – electronic submission of draft documentation to the UKLA – became possible in February 2002. According to its Plan and Budget for 2002/3 the FSA is still at the stage of assessing the demand for, and feasibility of, providing a single repository for documents issued by listed companies: <http://www.fsa. gov.uk/pubs/plan/pb2002_03.pdf>.

See also *Review of the UK Mechanism for Disseminating Regulatory Information by Listed Companies* (London FSA CP 92 2001).

[66] E Boros 'Corporate Governance in Cyberspace' (n 52).

[67] ibid 171 – 172.

[68] Winter Report, 49 – 50.

Institute of Chartered Secretaries and Administrators (ICSA)[69] and the law has been changed to facilitate its usage.[70] With practice having lead the way in this respect, the HLG's proposal for EU law to compel companies to use modern technology for meetings' material is not a cause for concern because a mandatory rule here would largely reflect, rather than direct, practice and could enhance uniformity. It is to market initiatives that we should look also for the development of direct electronic shareholder voting processes and electronic communications facilities that allow shareholders who are not physically present at meetings to participate in discussions. Lawmakers are not well placed to assess the technological and practical challenges and costs involved in making such facilities available. There is thus a serious risk that regulatory intervention ahead of the market would be misguided and inappropriate. On the other hand, lawmakers should be alert to the possibility of existing legal rules hindering the evolution of good market practices in these areas and should make provision for the speedy removal of such rules as and when their deficiencies become apparent.[71]

However, whilst modern electronic communications technology can help to make meetings more effective, such as by making relevant information available more quickly and smoothing the voting process for shareholders not physically present at meetings, as Winter notes technological developments alone may not remove fundamental problems about the effectiveness of the shareholder vote as a mechanism for internal shareholder control.[72] This remaining parts of this section concentrate on two such possibly fundamental problems, namely: (i) empowering shareholders to initiate formal decision-making processes; and (ii) ensuring that investors do not become disfranchised because of modern securities markets' structures for investing in equity securities.

1. Shareholder Rights to Initiate Formal Decision-making Processes

Most European countries allow shareholders to file proposals that must be put to the vote at shareholders' meetings.[73] Areas where there are already broadly com-

[69] Electronic Communications Order 2000 – ICSA's Guide to Recommended Best Practice <http://www.icsa.org.uk/products/e_comms.php>.

[70] By the Companies Act 1985 (Electronic Communications) Order 2000 (SI 2000/3373).

[71] For example the UK Government is proposing to include reserve powers in its new companies legislation to ensure that companies will be able to take advantage of further advances in communications technology: *Modernising Company Law* (London DTI Cm 5553 2002) para 2.15 and *Modernising Company Law – Draft Clauses* (London DTI Cm 5553-II 2002) cl 207. The draft Transparency Directive suggests that the EC is, helpfully, moving in the same direction: see eg art 13.

[72] JW Winter 'Cross-border Voting in Europe' in KJ Hopt and E Wymeersch *Capital Markets and Company Law* (Oxford University Press 2003), 387, 416 – 417.

[73] Becht and Bolton 'Corporate Governance and Control' (n 55) 91.

parable rights across the EU are in principle relatively strong candidates for European regulation. The EU should be wary of introducing alien concepts into the national laws of Member States but need not be quite so cautious where all that is involved is the ironing out of inconsistencies that, in one sense, are minor but which could hinder the efficient operation of the internal market (though the risk of petrification if the rule is adopted EU-wide should not be overlooked). Changes in areas where there is already much common ground between Member States also merit attention on practical grounds because the fact that they do not involve significant policy shifts for Members States means that political objections to their adoption should be relatively slight. The linking of the thresholds for the exercise of resolution proposal rights with squeeze-out/sell-out rights would be logical and readily understandable. A minimum threshold is an essential safeguard against companies being burdened with requests for shareholder votes on matters for which there is no meaningful support within the shareholder body.

2. Ensuring Effective Exercise of Voting Rights in Modern Equity Securities Trading Systems

Are investors at risk of disfranchisement because of the nature of modern equity securities trading systems? Are the risks exacerbated for investors residing in countries outside those where the companies in which they hold shares are registered? Can these risks for domestic and foreign investors be addressed through the market? Does the law stand in the way of market-based solutions? Are market-based solutions adequate, assuming that legal impediments to their adoption can be removed, or is there a case for stronger legal intervention? If there is, should this intervention be at national level or should it be directed by the EC? These are very big questions and it is impossible to do them full justice here. Instead, the following section confines itself to examining from the British perspective whether there are problems of investor disfranchisement that the market has proved unable to solve. Admittedly, the position may be different in other Member States because of differences in their domestic company, contract and property laws, the existence of different national systems for the clearing and settlement of securities transactions, and the different levels of investor sophistication and market transparency. But the existence of these differences can be viewed as an important consideration militating against top down EC intervention on the grounds of serious risk of incompatibility between the euro-solution and the domestic position in individual Member States. Moreover if the risks of investor disfranchisement have been adequately addressed through the ingenuity of market participants in certain Member States and this is something that is valued by investors, this should create competitive pressures for other States to follow suit by devising solutions tailored to their domestic legal and business environment. If this is so, then the case for regulatory intervention is weak.

In a system of registered shareholdings, as applies in the UK, it is the registered shareholder who is the member of the company entitled to vote.[74] Communications about company meetings – the notice of the meeting, proxy appointment forms, and so forth – must be sent by the company, or more commonly, the registrars to whom it has delegated these functions, to its registered shareholders. Nowadays, the registered shareholder is likely to be a custodian or other financial institution which is holding the shares on behalf of someone else. In the UK a common reason for this structure is that the registered shareholder is a member of CREST, the electronic securities settlement system, and the shares are being held in this way so as to facilitate dealings through the CREST system.[75] Custodians may pool their clients' holdings in a particular company and rely on their internal records to determine underlying beneficial entitlements. Fund managers are typically interposed between the institutional investors which are the ultimate beneficial owner of shares and the custodians in whose name they are registered. A network of contractual and property law arrangements between the parties will govern the exercise of voting rights attaching to shares. The common pattern until recently has been for the documentation to vest this authority in the fund manager but with some provision for the ultimate beneficial owner to give directions to the fund manager.[76] Recent practice has seen the emergence of specialist voting service providers which, for a fee, assume the role of exercising voting rights in respect of shares.

The British system is very helpful to companies in that it makes the process of checking voting entitlements relatively easy: the register of members as at the relevant record date determines who is entitled to vote, and the registrars do not need to look beyond it. Complex legal documentation governing the chain of relationships back to the ultimate beneficial owner are not the company's concern; it can thus avoid becoming embroiled in disputes as to the exact location of authority to exercise voting rights. These are important practical advantages that facilitate the smooth and efficient operation of the vote execution process. However, whilst these important advantages should not be discarded lightly,[77] there are competing corporate governance considerations. The company law system appears to be poorly aligned with the promotion of good corporate governance in that by focusing on registered shareholders, who often are simply custodian-

[74] Generally, RC Nolan 'Indirect Investors: A Greater Say in the Company?' [2003] Journal of Corporate Law Studies 73, 78 – 80.

[75] V Knapp 'CREST Impact on Corporate Transactions' (1996) 7 (10) Practical Law for Companies 23. Nolan 'Indirect Investors' (n 74) discusses in detail another situation where division of registered ownership and economic interests commonly arises, namely under ADR programmes which has been designed by companies to facilitate investment in their shares by foreign (typically US) investors. This section draws heavily on Nolan's work.

[76] GP Stapledon and JJ Bates 'Unpacking the "Interest-Holders" in a Share: Reducing the Costs of Voting' [2000] Company Financial and Insolvency Law Review, 293, 297 – 298.

[77] Nolan 'Indirect Investors' (n 74) 86 – 90.

nominees, it does not facilitate participation in governance by those who have the economic incentives to do so effectively. Company law pays no attention to whether or not voting rights have been exercised in accordance with the private bargains amongst those involved in the chain from registered owner to ultimate beneficiary. This means that as far as company law is concerned, the risk of possible disfranchisement of the real controllers of the voting rights is simply not an issue, even though from a corporate governance perspective this represents a major problem.

This misalignment of the company law system and corporate governance considerations merits attention in policy discussions[78] because of increasing political emphasis on the importance of active, informed use of voting rights by institutional investors.[79] Pension funds and other institutional investors are coming under increasing pressure from the UK government to exercise their voting rights at general meetings.[80] Although there is no specific legal obligation on institutional investors to exercise their voting rights,[81] under political pressure a climate of opinion has developed in which it is widely considered that they could fail their clients if they do not actively monitor the companies in which they invest, including by exercising voting rights attaching to shares.[82] Institutional investors

[78] This issue was much discussed by the UK Company Law Review Steering Group, an independent review body established by the government to examine British company law generally and to suggest change. The Steering Group produced its final report in June 2001. At the time of writing the government is in the process of producing a new Companies Bill which is intended to replace the existing companies legislation. On the rights of persons other than registered holders: *Modern Company Law for a Competitive Economy Developing the Framework* (London DTI URN 00/656 2000) paras 4.7 – 4.18; *Modern Company Law for a Competitive Economy Completing the Structure* (London DTI URN 00/1335 2000) paras 5.2 – 5.12; *Modern Company Law for a Competitive Economy Final Report* (London DTI URN 01/942 2001) paras 7.1 – 7.4.

[79] Stapledon and Bates 'Unpacking the "Interest-Holders" in a Share' (n 76).

[80] There are parallels here with the political pressures on US pension funds that were highlighted by commentators a decade ago: R Romano 'Public Pension Fund Activism in Corporate Governance Reconsidered' (1993) 93 Columbia Law Review 795. Later work by Romano surveying empirical data casts doubt on the impact of greater institutional investor activism on targeted firms' performance: R Romano 'Less is More: Making Institutional Investor Activism a Valuable Mechanism of Corporate Governance' (2001) 18 Yale Journal on Regulation 174. Romano suggests that activist institutions need to refocus their agenda in order to use their resources more effectively. For other empirical surveys casting doubt on the effectiveness of shareholder activism in the US see B Black 'Shareholder Activism and Corporate Governance in the U.S' in P Newman (ed) *The New Palgrave Dictionary of Economics and the Law* (Macmillan Reference Limited London and Basingstoke 1998); S Gillan and L Starks 'A Survey of Shareholder Activism: Motivation and Empirical Evidence' (1998) 2 Contemporary Finance Digest 10.

[81] Pension funds are required to disclose their voting policies under the Pensions Act 1995, s 35.

[82] eg Myners Report, paras 5.89 – 5.94; Developing the Framework (n 78) para 4.11.

have reacted to this pressure by developing 'best practice' principles for voting and intervention more generally,[83] a move that can be interpreted as an attempt to stave off more heavy-handed intervention by the government in the form of specific legal duties regarding the exercise of voting rights.[84] (Whether this preemptive action will succeed is a moot point but the argument made by the Winter Report (amongst others) that mandatory voting could be counter-productive because it could encourage a mechanistic 'box ticking' approach to voting is compelling.[85]) However, there is little point in governments pressuring institutions to be active shareholders if the system does not ultimately enable their voice to be heard.

There is evidence of UK market participants devising their own solutions to the misalignment of the registered shareholder system with location of economic incentives to make good use of voting rights. These solutions involve using the mechanism of proxy appointments. Registered shareholders can appoint the real controllers of the voting rights, as determined by private bargains, as their proxies with full discretion to vote as they think fit.[86] Alternatively the right to give instructions to a proxy on the exercise of voting rights can simply be passed down the chain from the registered holder to the real controller. Technology plays a role here by allowing information about proxy appointments and proxy instructions to be transmitted electronically between the various participants in the chain. There are various commercial providers of electronic proxy voting services.[87] Since January 2003 the CREST system has offered its own electronic proxy service whereby information about proxy appointments and instructions can between transmitted electronically between issuers and investors which are CREST members. The CREST service allows proxy appointments to be made either by the CREST member itself or by another CREST member, such as a voting service provider, which has been specifically appointed to do so on its behalf.

Although it is early days, there are high hopes for the CREST service on the basis that it should standardise and streamline vote execution procedures.[88] Legal

[83] Institutional Shareholders' Committee *The Responsibilities of Institutional Shareholders and Agents – Statement of Principles* <http://www.abi.org.uk/Display/File/38/Statement_of_Principles.pdf>.

[84] 'Electronics may end plight of paper voting' (*Financial Times* 30 December 2002) 18.

[85] Winter Report, 57. The European Shadow Financial Regulatory Committee has also made the point that mandatory voting could result in funds having to take positions on matters where they do not have appropriate expertise: *Corporate Governance In Europe* (London 2 December 2002, Statement No 15) <http://www.ceps.be/2002/ESFRCCorpGov.pdf>. The Committee's further point that requirements on institutional investors to disclose voting policies would be best located in investment services regulation rather than company law is well made.

[86] Developing the Framework (n 78) para 4.12.

[87] eg the MANIFEST service described at <http://www.manifest.co.uk/services/voteplus.html>.

[88] 'Electronics may end plight of paper voting' (*Financial Times* 30 December 2002) 18.

impediments to these solutions, in the form of doubts about the legal effectiveness of proxy appointments and instructions sent electronically, were swept away by appropriate changes to the law in 2000.[89]

In 1999 a study of the UK vote execution process found that the voting intentions of those who control the exercise of voting rights were being lost in the system because of the multiplicity of parties involved in the process and the unavailability of modern communications technology.[90] The removal of legal obstacles to the use of modern technology is changing the picture. Developments such as the establishment of the CREST service should certainly reduce the problems, although no system that involves communications along a possibly quite long chain of parties can be guaranteed to work perfectly at all times because it is inevitably prone to human error and at least occasional technological failure. Moreover the CREST service only improves the system at the top of chains involving securities held within CREST where issuers have opted into its use. The overall effectiveness of the vote execution process is still heavily dependent on private arrangements below or outside the scope of the CREST service.

If we return at this point to the questions posed at the start of this section, we might see a case for further regulatory intervention. There are contractual and fiduciary obligations attaching to the parties involved in chains to ensure that their arrangements concerning the exercise of voting rights are fulfilled. These obligations are reinforced by the general conduct of business obligations on those in the chain that are subject to regulation by the Financial Services Authority (FSA) under the Financial Services and Markets Act 2000. If further legal underpinning of the system is desirable, a sensible way forward would be to reinforce the financial regulatory regime through the development of conduct of business rules that spell out in more explicit terms the obligations of regulated financial intermediaries with regard to ensuring that investor voting instructions are sought and then accurately transmitted through the system.[91] This would be an initiative outside the field of company law but one that could usefully bolster the operation of effective internal corporate governance.

[89] By the Companies Act 1985 (Electronic Communications) Order 2000 (SI 2000/3373).

[90] As reported in G Stapledon and J Bates 'Reconceptualising the Nature of Modern Shareholding (and Making Voting Easier) (2000) 18 Company and Securities Law Journal 155. For more recent data see Institutional Design *Cross Border Proxy Voting Case Studies from the 2002 Proxy Voting Season* (report commissioned by International Corporate Governance Network, 2003) <http://www.icgn.org/documents/ICGN-crossborder. pdf>.

[91] Nolan 'Indirect Investors' (n 74) 99. *Cross-border Voting in Europe* (Final Report of the Expert Group on Cross-Border Voting in Europe, August 2002) acknowledges that 'to a large extent ...[the issues] boil down to the role and obligations of securities intermediaries in securities holding systems in Europe'. The Winter Report's recommendations on cross-border voting were based on the Expert Group's work (two members of the Winter Report group participated in the Expert Group).

Beyond changes that might be made to the financial services regulatory regime, is there a case for regulatory intervention given that the market has shown itself to be quite ingenious in using the proxy mechanism to achieve functional, if not formal, enfranchisement of the indirect investor? Even if the scope for mistakes within the system is reduced to fairly trivial levels by a combination of technological developments and legal changes to bolster their use, it might still be said that a shareholder voting system that is dependent on proxy voting appointments and instructions passing through a multiplicity of parties is fundamentally unsatisfactory because of its artificiality. For example, the Steering Group in charge of the UK's company law review reported evidence of overseas investors finding the mechanism of the registered shareholder appointing the investor as proxy 'unattractive and hard to understand' because it sat uneasily with their perception of themselves as the owners of the shares.[92] In the absence of public empirical data on the point, it is difficult to assess the seriousness of the problem of artificiality. However, it is plausible to suggest that so long as they have access to a vote execution system which is easy to use, cost-effective and accurately records voting intentions, investors are unlikely to be unduly concerned about the technicalities of the legal devices that are used to make the system work. In practice the distinction between direct voting and voting that relies on using proxies is already blurring: media coverage of the new CREST service tended to describe it simply as an electronic voting service.[93] Lawyers may bemoan the lack of linguistic clarity[94] but, like the swan whose calm appearance on the surface belies the hard work going on in the water, in commercial terms the deployment of increasingly sophisticated technology and advanced technical legal ingenuity so as to create the appearance of a simple system for the transmission of the intentions of those who are entitled to exercise voting rights to companies, has much to commend it.

For the sake of argument let us, however, accept that artificiality may be a problem. Bypassing the links in the chain between the company's registrars and the person who controls the exercise of voting rights would remove artificiality and avoid complexity. There is undoubtedly an attractive superficial simplicity about proposals to the effect that persons who control the voting rights attaching to shares should be directly enfranchised. However, it is doubtful whether this goal is realistically achievable. It is essential to the efficient operation of the corporate decision-making processes that companies can ascertain with certainty and at a reasonable cost that the persons who participate in that process are in fact entitled to do so. Clearly this would be impossible if companies were expected to

[92] Developing the Framework (n 78) para 4.12.

[93] eg 'Electronics may end plight of paper voting' (*Financial Times* 30 December 2002) 18.

[94] eg *Crest Consultation Document On Electronic Proxy Voting* (London Law Society Company Law Committee Memoranda 424) <http://www.lawsoc.org.uk/dcs/fourth_tier.asp?section_id=6171&Caller_ID=NS75>.

examine all of the private contractual arrangements relating to voting entitlements in respect of its shares (even if we assume away problems of companies gaining access to arrangements that those with an interest in their shares may wish to keep private). To be workable, any system of direct enfranchisement would necessarily require rules for identifying voting entitlements. These rules would need to operate independently of, and indeed be capable of overriding, private bargains. The result of applying these rules could therefore be to enfranchise someone other than the person who is actually entitled under the parties' private bargain to exercise the voting rights.[95] In that event, it would still be open to the parties to give effect to their private bargain through the mechanism of proxy appointments between the person enfranchised under the general rules and the person who is really entitled to control the voting rights. But if that is result, then it is obviously open to question whether abandoning reliance on the registered shareholder system in favour of a different approach to ascertaining voting entitlements would actually achieve very much. The fundamental problem would still remain: the location of the voting entitlement attaching to a share under a rule established by the general law might not be the same as the location established by private arrangements relating to that share. At best, the adoption of a different general rule might shorten the chain from the person entitled to vote under the general law to the person with the contractual voting entitlement, and in some instances eliminate it altogether. But if technological developments can deliver a system in which the risks of communication problems between the links in chains are reduced to low levels, securing this benefit would be an insignificant advance in practice. Against this benefit are two new problems that the change would engender. First, from the corporate viewpoint a major drawback of the adoption of a new rule governing voting entitlements is that it would require the maintenance of two registers, one to determine title to shares for transfer purposes and the other to determine voting entitlements. Maintaining corporate registers is an expensive process and in the absence of substantial clear benefits the imposition of this new burden on companies would be hard to justify.[96] Secondly, companies could become embroiled in disputes about voting entitlements under the general law. However, this may be a less serious concern than the additional costs burden of the voting entitlement register because it would presumably be possible to enact

[95] Broadly speaking this is acknowledged in the Report of the Expert Group on Cross-Border Voting in Europe (n 91). This Group suggests a mandatory European rule whereby the last accountholder in a chain within a securities holding system is designated the 'ultimate accountholder' and, as such, entitled to exercise voting rights. However, the Group recognises that this person may not be the person with the real economic interest in the shares and suggests a supplementary rule for such situations, whereby the 'ultimate accountholder' may designate its clients in its place, thus making these clients entitled to control the voting rights.

[96] The ICSA has voiced particular concerns about the increased costs that would be involved in maintaining an additional register: *Re: Consultative Document on Cross Border Voting in Europe* (June 2002) <http://www.icsa.org.uk/news/consults/con02_05. php>.

appropriate statutory protections against companies being dragged into such disputes.[97]

To summarise the position described here in relation to British law and practice, the key points are these. Although there is a real risk of investors becoming disfranchised because of the way in which equity securities and trading systems are nowadays structured, market participants are alert to this problem and have actively sought to devise solutions. These solutions rely on the use of the proxy mechanism and involve the passing of information and instructions up and down chains of registered shareholders, financial intermediaries and investors. Lengthy chains do exacerbate the risks that information will go astray and that instructions will fail to get through accurately. However, whilst these risks cannot be completely eradicated, technological developments should reduce their occurrence in practice. Imaginative use of the proxy mechanism is a pragmatic response to the problem of possible investor disfranchisement; a more elegant solution is practically unattainable because of the open-ended variety of ways in which the various rights attaching to a share can be distributed around a range of parties and the need to protect companies from becoming embroiled in all these arrangements.

It is evident from this summary that my view is that from the British perspective there is no convincing case for sweeping changes to company law to enfranchise indirect investors. My view is consistent with that of some market participants. According to the influential ICSA, regulation to solve problems associated with cross-border voting would be premature because of indications that the market may find its own solution to these issues long before any new EC law could be put into effect. Moreover the ICSA considers that there is no significant problem as regards the ability to vote across borders in UK registered companies.[98]

Companies should not be prevented from recognising voting entitlements, and associated rights to receive information, of persons other than their registered shareholders if they wish to do so. There is some precedent for this in other countries.[99] The abolition of laws that inhibit companies from doing so is therefore a desirable step forward.[100] But the justification for sweeping changes to law that would force companies to enfranchise indirect investors directly, and thereby

[97] Contrast Nolan 'Indirect Investors' (n 74) 89 who suggests that even if the company is protected from any dispute or claim, it (or a registrar acting for it) will inevitably incur a significant time cost because of the dispute or claim, which would simply never have happened under the existing law.

[98] ibid. But contrast the *Position Paper by the Association of British Insurers on the Winter Group Report on Modernising European Company Law*, section 3 which does support speedy progress on implementation of the recommendations of the Cross- Border Voting Group to provide a solution to the problem of identifying at EU level the identity of the holder with whom the voting entitlement resides <http://www.abi.org.uk/Display/File/ 85/winterpaper.doc>.

[99] Stapledon and Bates 'Unpacking the "Interest-Holders" in a Share' (n 76).

[100] Nolan 'Indirect Investors' (n 74) 80 and 93-96.

assume the significant costs of maintaining an extra register indicating voting entitlements, is much harder to establish.[101] Even the Expert Group on Cross-Border Voting in Europe, whose influential report, adopted by the Winter group, presents a much more pessimistic view of the pan-European position with regard to voting than that outlined here with regard to the UK, does not go so far as to insist upon direct enfranchisement of indirect investors by companies. Its suggestion that, at a minimum, the registered shareholder should be obliged under European law to accept voting instructions from lower down the chain, is, in broad terms, not that far removed from the British proxy vote system, although closer examination of this proposal does of course reveal a (by now) familiar problem: that the person from whom the registered holder would be obliged to accept instructions under such a rule would not necessarily be the person from whom the registered holder would be obliged by contract, fiduciary duty or some other private obligation, to accept such instructions.

Where there could be a stronger case for regulatory intervention is with regard to more pragmatic changes to support the operation of the operation of vote execution process. There are good arguments for mandatory rules that promote effective administration and setting them at the European level could promote efficiency. Although it may not seem terribly ambitious or imaginative for the EU to concentrate its efforts on rules that promote better corporate housekeeping, as Nolan notes, it is through practical processes that rights acquire substance.[102] So rules that promote better processes, though seemingly modest in themselves, could make a real difference to the operation of internal corporate governance. For example, standardisation of the proxy appointment process by means of mandatory Euro-wide rules could greatly smooth the process whereby investors, particularly those outside the Member State in which a company is situated, participate in voting.[103]

In thinking about obstacles to the exercise of voting rights the basis on which companies identify the persons the persons who are formally entitled to exercise voting rights as a matter of general company law[104] is another area that deserves

[101] Nolan suggests a compromise: that companies could be forced to enfranchise indirect investors where they are responsible for the situation giving rise to the indirect holding (eg an ADR programme or participation in CREST) but not where it has arisen without their intervention (eg a family trust). However, he recognises that this is not an easy option and that there would inevitably be marginal cases on which difficult judgments might have to be made. He concludes that the difficulties involved in distinguishing between marginal cases brings into serious question any attempt to force companies to enfranchise indirect investors: 86 – 90.

[102] Nolan 'Indirect Investors' (n 74) 77.

[103] Pragmatic, sensible facilitative changes of this sort are now proposed in the draft Transparency Directive, art 13.

[104] That is, now putting to one side the problems that arise because modern equity investment structures can result in formal company law entitlements becoming separated from contractual or other private law rights in respect of shares.

attention. From the British perspective, the position is straightforward: it is those shareholders whose names appear on the register at a certain date (the record date) who are entitled to vote even if they subsequently sell their shares. However, some other EU states rely on blocking mechanisms to identify voting entitlements. Blocking mechanisms work by disabling any activity in the shares which means that investors can only participate in voting so long as they are willing to forgo the opportunity to sell their shares for the period of the block. This is a major discouragement to participation in voting. It has been described as a 'core' concern of major international institutional investors in relation to Italian corporate governance.[105] The Association of British Insurers regards inability to trade shares for extended periods around a meeting as a serious impediment to the exercise of voting rights.[106] Blocking requirements were also identified by respondents to the consultative document published by the Expert Group on Cross-Border Voting as a major impediment to effective cross-border voting by investors. It is therefore somewhat surprising that (so far as I can see) the Winter Group did not explicitly highlight the issue in its report, although it is swept up in the recommendation that the Commission should consider the recommendations of the Cross-Border Voting Group as a matter of priority. In my view, this issue deserves a high spot on the public policy agenda because it is a problem that can only be solved by regulatory intervention. The recommendation of the Cross-Border Voting Group that Member States should prohibit the application of a share blocking requirement as a condition for participation in the vote at the shareholders meeting merits serious and close attention.

3. Shareholder control outside the general meeting: special investigation rights

From the British perspective it is slightly odd that the Winter Group attaches particular importance to giving special investigation rights to minority shareholders. Although such a right exists in the UK, investigations conducted at the instigation of shareholders are rare. There has been no appointment of inspectors to conduct investigations under this power since 1990.[107] The circumstances in which the Secretary of State will appoint inspectors at the behest of shareholders are narrow: the Secretary of State must be satisfied that there is good reason

[105] Letter (September 2002) sent to the Chairman of the Italian Corporate Law Commission and published at <http://www.hermes.co.uk/pdf/sharcitaly.pdf>. Further on 'blocking' and wider issues arising in relation to cross border voting: Institutional Design *Cross Border Proxy Voting* (n 90).

[106] 'Position Paper' (n 98) para 3.2.

[107] *Company Investigations: Powers for the 21st Century* (London DTI) para 32 <http://www.dti.gov.uk/cld/company_investigations.pdf>.

(which is interpreted as meaning a strong public interest) for an investigation.[108] Applicants may have to pay for all or some of the costs of the investigation which could well be significant.[109] However, although they are very limited, it is notable that shareholder special investigation rights did not attract attention in the extensive policy discussions concerning shareholders' rights and remedies that took place in the UK in recent years. This omission that tends to suggest that there is no significant dissatisfaction with the current position or pressure to loosen the restrictions.

In principle there is nothing objectionable about shareholder special investigation rights. They appear to enhance shareholder control and so long as there are sensible thresholds conditions on their use to prevent them being used by shareholders in ways that would disrupt legitimate business activity, they should not constitute an unreasonable regulatory burden on companies. The different commercial and legal circumstances in other Member States may mean that across Europe there is greater need and investor demand for such rights than the UK position would suggest. Yet, even taking these considerations into account, it remains troubling that there should be singled out for special attention at the European level a right which, as the British experience demonstrates, can be devoid of meaningful practical effect. There is a danger that investors could misinterpret the extent to which their control rights would actually be improved by the enactment of special investigation rights (in various forms) across Europe. This distorting effect could be exacerbated because the issue of special investigation rights has now been presented in a way which removes it from what might be regarded as its appropriate context. Since special investigation rights are intended to be targeted at situations of suspected substantial impropriety and are not really concerned with facilitating discovery of more routine information, it would be preferable to consider them in the context of a more general assessment of the rights and remedies that should be afforded to shareholders in respect of managerial wrongdoing. This would focus attention on the priorities for European intervention. For example, is there a more pressing need for a pan-European special investigation right than there is for a pan-European right to bring a derivative action? The Winter Group appears implicitly to assume that there is, but this is a debate that should be brought out into the open.

[108] *Company Investigations – How They Work* (London DTI) <http://www.dti.gov.uk/cld/inv_htw.htm>.

[109] ibid – more than £1 million. This figure throws into question the statement that 'a special investigation procedure offers an efficient and overall not too costly form of enhanced shareholder information': Winter Report, 58.

E. A Concluding Observation

The last point in the preceding section blurs into a more general, concluding observation. Mechanisms for selecting and prioritising those issues which are most deserving of regulatory attention at the European level are surely crucial to the development of an effective and efficient company law regulatory framework. In this respect there remains work to be done to build upon the admirable start made by the Winter Report in spelling out the objectives of, and rationales for, regulation. The Winter Report expresses a preference for disclosure requirements over substantive rules, a preference which reflects mainstream, international thinking about how countries should frame their company laws and which is therefore likely to command wide support. Yet the Winter Group does not refrain from making recommendations for more substantive rules across a range of areas, some of which have been considered in this chapter. Quite why the Winter Report chose to focus on a particular issue or to suggest a particular substantive change is not always obvious. Whatever may be the merits of a particular substantive proposal looked at in isolation, it is important also to consider its place within the broader framework and to be satisfied that regulatory attention is being focused in the right direction. This implies that there is a need for a fuller statement of regulatory objectives and rationales than that which the Winter Group was able to formulate within the limited time that it was given to complete its work.[110] This statement should include a clear mechanism for regulatory selection and prioritisation, which will act as a discipline on the lawmaker in the lawmaking process and as a benchmark against which it can be held accountable. Adherence to a clear, full statement of regulatory objectives and rationales framed in this way should protect European lawmakers from charge that the European company law regulatory agenda simply reflects the personal preferences of those who are influential in the agenda-setting process and/or behind-the-scenes political compromises. To be sure, laws are shaped by political influences and it would be naïve to suggest otherwise. However, one can acknowledge the bruising reality that lawmaking on politically contentious issues can sometimes become (as witness the Takeover Directive), without detracting from the importance of striving for a lawmaking process that is grounded in coherent, consistent principles and which operates openly in accordance with clear, publicly-disclosed criteria.

[110] Modernising Company Law – European Commission Plan (Annex 1 in this volume) is a step in the right direction in that it attempts to define the key policy objectives which should inspire any future action to be taken at EU level in these areas and also to outline the guiding political criteria that should be respected in any new regulatory initiative.

Chapter 8: The Auditors

Gatekeeper Failure and Reform: The Challenge of Fashioning Relevant Reforms

JOHN C. COFFEE, JR.

Securities markets have long employed 'gatekeepers' – independent professions who pledge their reputational capital – to protect dispersed investors. This strategy of relying on reputational intermediaries to assess, verify and certify the corporate issuer's disclosures appears to have failed during the late 1990s, as accounting irregularities increased exponentially. Part I of this paper assesses the reasons for this failure, emphasizing both a shortfall in deterrence and the sudden shift from a cash-based to an equity-based system of executive compensation during the 1990s. Part II and III then survey the realistic regulatory options and the incomplete steps taken by the Sarbanes-Oxley Act. Breaking down these options into four categories – structural rules, prophylactic rules, procedural rules, and liability-enhancing rules, – Part III concludes that simply increasing the threat of liability could cause the market for gatekeeping services to fail. Instead, it proposes a shift towards stricter liability standards coupled with a ceiling on gatekeeper liability set at a level adequate to deter misconduct, but not to compensate investors. Finally, Part III proposes that the role of a new gatekeeper needs to be recognized and formalized: namely, the attorney who prepares a disclosure document, who should, it argues, be forced to provide a functionally parallel certification with regard to this issuer's non-financial disclosures to the certification provided by the auditor with respect to financial disclosures. The feasibility and scope of such a certification requirement, along with its impact on the attorney's other obligations to its client, are explored in Part III.

A. Introduction

Individual scandals – such as Enron or WorldCom – invite study in micro detail by the historian, the novelist, or the journalist, but a concentration of scandals over a short time period requires the broader macro perspective of the theorist. What caused the sudden outburst of scandals, involving a seeming epidemic of accounting and related financial irregularities that broke over the financial markets between late 2001 and mid-2002 – eg, Enron, WorldCom, Global Crossing, Tyco and others? To date, much commentary has broadly and loosely attributed these scandals to any or all of (1) a stock market bubble; (2) a decline in business morality; or (3) an increase in 'infectious greed.'[1] Without denying that any of these factors could have played some role, this article begins from the premise that such explanations are unsatisfactory because they depend on subjective trends that cannot be reliably measured.

Still others have blamed these scandals on a general failure of the board of directors[2] or on a 'few bad apples' – ie, a small group of 'rogue managers' who were corrupt and whose criminal prosecution will restore and rehabilitate American corporate governance. Again, this article dissents from these premises as well. While some boards certainly failed, the overall independence and power of outside directors has only increased over recent years, and the 2001-2002 epidemic of financial irregularity cannot be explained in terms of any recent decline in board performance. To explain an epidemic of irregularity, one must identify some force or factor that changed – either intensifying or weakening – so that its influence can explain the overall shift in behaviour, and clearly the board's performance, even if inadequate, did not decline materially over the relevant interval of the 1990s.

Similarly, the 'few bad apples' explanation overlooks the pervasiveness of the sudden surge in financial irregularities in the late 1990s. As will be seen, approximately 10% of all publicly listed U.S. companies restated their financial

[1] Federal Reserve Chairman Alan Greenspan coined this colourful phrase, saying that 'An infectious greed seemed to grip much of our business community.' See F Norris 'The Markets: Market Place: Yes, He Can Top That' *New York Times* (17 July 2002) A-l.

[2] For a representative such statement, see SL Gillan and JD Martin 'Financial Engineering, Corporate Governance and the Collapse of Enron' (SSRN Working Paper id=350040) (2002) at 3 (finding first cause of Enron's breakdown to have been 'a lack of board independence and board oversight'). In contrast, this paper doubts the adequacy of such an explanation. Admittedly, boards did fail, and even a special committee of Enron's own board has concluded that the Enron board failed to monitor officers for conflicts of interest adequately. See WC Powers, Jr and others 'Report of Investigation by the Special Investigative Committee of the Board of Directors of Enron Corp. (1 February 2002), 2002 WL 198018. Similarly, a Senate Subcommittee has assigned the principal blame to the Enron Board. See Report of the Permanent Subcommittee on Investigations of the Committee of Governmental Affairs, United States Senate 'The Role of the Board of Directors in Enron's Collapse' (Report 107-70) (8 July 2001). Nonetheless, such studies beg the larger question: why did these boards fail now and not earlier? Although board procedure or independence may have been deficient, they were almost certainly superior to a decade ago when such scandals were rare.

statements at least once between 1997 and June 2002,[3] and the annual rate of financial restatements soared during the latter half of the 1990s.[4] Such financial irregularity is, of course, characteristic of a bubble, and little doubt now exists that a large frothy bubble burst in 2000-2001.[5] As a historical matter, bubbles tend to produce scandals and, in turn, prophylactic legislation,[6] but this loose generalization leaves unanswered the critical questions: what caused this bubble and how does the growth of a bubble relate to the apparent breakdown of our once-confident system of corporate governance?

This article will focus on an alternative explanation for the wave of accounting and financial reporting irregularities that surfaced in 2001-2002: namely, that the gatekeepers failed. That is, the professionals who serve investors by preparing, verifying, or certifying corporate disclosures to the securities markets acquiesced in managerial fraud – not in all cases, to be sure, but at a markedly higher rate than during the immediately preceding period. While the concept of gatekeeper will be discussed and refined later, this term certainly includes the auditors, securities analysts, and securities attorneys who prepare, review, or analyse disclosure documents. Part I of this article develops competing, but complimentary, explanations for gatekeeper failure. The behaviour of gatekeepers cannot be examined in isolation, but rather appears to have been significantly influenced by the incentives that drove corporate managers over the same period. To this extent, the recent explosion of financial irregularity was less the product of ineffable factors – such as 'infectious greed' or mass irrationality – than the natural and logical consequence of trends and forces that had been developing for some time. Ironically, the blunt truth is that both the recent accounting scandals and the broader phenomenon of earnings management were the by-products of a system of corporate governance that has indeed made corporate managers more accountable to the market. Sensitivity to the market, however, can be a mixed blessing –

[3] See United States General Accounting Office, Report to the Chairman, Committee on Banking, Housing and Urban Affairs, US Senate, Financial Statement Restatements: Trends, Market Impacts, Regulatory Responses and Remaining Challenges' (October 2002) (GAO-03-138) at 4 (hereinafter, 'GAO Study').

[4] See text and notes at notes 18 to 24.

[5] While this bubble initially burst in 2000, an additional sharp price decline occurred in the late spring of 2002, as WorldCom and other crises appear to have further shaken market confidence. The S&P 500 index fell 26% between May 21 and July 23, 2002. See C Nicholls 'The Outside Director: Policeman or 'Policebo'?' (forthcoming 2002). Professor Nicholls, however, is sceptical that this market decline was caused by these corporate scandals. In his view, market downturns give rise to a 'post-hoc fallacy' that the scandals revealed in the wake of a market downturn caused that downturn.

[6] Professor Stuart Banner has argued that, over the last 300 years, most major instances of legislation regulating the securities markets have followed a sustained price collapse on the securities market. See S Banner 'What Causes New Securities Regulation?: 300 Years of Evidence' (1997) 75 Wash U LQ 849, 850.

particularly when the market becomes euphoric and uncritical. As a result, a corporate governance system that was adequate for a world in which the agents' incentives to act opportunistically were weaker failed when these same agents – managers, gatekeepers and financial intermediaries – responded to stronger incentives and rationally pursued their own self-interests to the detriment of shareholders.

Part I will conclude that the factor that most destabilized our contemporary corporate governance system was the sudden change in executive compensation during the 1990s. As executive compensation shifted to being equity-based, instead of cash-based, a greatly enhanced incentive arose for managers to manipulate earnings – and to induce their gatekeepers to let them. To this extent, blaming the board is a myopic theory of causation that leads nowhere, because it does not explain the sudden surge in irregularities. In truth, in most cases, boards cannot detect earnings manipulation in the absence of warnings from their professional gatekeepers.

While Part I offers a diagnosis, it proposes no prescription. Part II approaches this task by first mapping the range of strategies available to regulators. Basically, it groups the realistic regulatory options for dealing with conflicts of interest under four headings: (1) structural rules; (2) prophylactic rules; (3) procedural rules, and (4) liability-enhancing rules. Seeking to curb the conflicts of interest that compromised auditors and analysts, the Sarbanes-Oxley Act of 2002,[7] passed by Congress in response to the wave of corporate scandals that crested in 2002, utilizes all these strategies – except the last. Although enhancing liability rules is probably the most obvious and traditional response to scandals, this was also the one strategy that business interests effectively resisted during the enactment of Sarbanes-Oxley. Ironically, however, even though Congress has not used this technique, courts today appear to have enhanced the risk of legal liability on their own through the creative reinterpretation of ambiguous doctrines.

But therein lies a host of problems. Although gatekeepers need to face some legal threat to keep them faithful to shareholders, the optimal level of deterrence is much harder to estimate. An 'excessive' threat may both impair the financial viability of gatekeepers, even closing down the market for gatekeeping services, and impede the ability of many corporations to recruit qualified, outside directors. Part II therefore assesses the magnitude of the litigation 'threat' that is now developing as a prelude to suggesting other reforms that may be desirable because they seek to modify gatekeeper behaviour by means that do not threaten the solvency of gatekeepers.

Finally, Part III proposes alternative reforms intended to make gatekeepers more responsive to the interests of investors. Initially, Part III evaluates a possible model under which auditors should face heightened liability, but with their

[7] Technically, this statute is entitled the 'Public Company Accounting Reform and Investor Protection Act of 2002' 15 USC § 7201 ff, 107 Pub L No 204, 116 Stat 745.

maximum exposure capped at a multiple of their expected revenue from the client that would be sufficient to achieve adequate deterrence. The attraction of this combination is that it combines the better incentives of strict liability with a system that both places a realistic ceiling on the gatekeeper's aggregate liability and minimizes the transaction costs associated with enforcement. Concededly, this proposal subordinates the goal of compensation to that of deterrence, but gatekeepers are simply not of the economic scale to be able to fund significant compensation to investors, particularly in the new era of mega litigation. This proposed approach also reduces reliance that must be placed on courts for costly and unpredictable liability determinations. Most importantly, by moving towards a strict liability system, this proposal eliminates the incentive for auditors to rationalize or overlook fraud or irregularity and later assert that they were deceived by management. Thus, it enhances auditor performance without risking collapse of the market for auditing services.

Part III recognizes, however, that all gatekeepers are not alike, that critical distinctions exist between auditors and attorneys in terms of their typical functional activity, and that a model appropriate for one gatekeeper need not be appropriate for all. In that light, Part III does not propose strict liability for attorneys, but instead a structural reform: namely, imposing gatekeeper responsibilities on attorneys to monitor their corporation's disclosures, with a special emphasis on non-financial disclosures. In principle, the attorney should be given a functionally similar responsibility for non-financial disclosures as the auditor now has for financial disclosures. Easy as this is to say, the devil lies in the details. Specifically, Part III responds by outlining a certification requirement, an enhanced independence standard for special contexts, and a due diligence obligation under which the SEC could suspend or disbar securities attorneys who failed negligence or malpractice tests. To be sure, the SEC has already begun to move modestly and tentatively in this same direction by adopting an 'up-the-ladder' internal reporting requirement under which attorneys must report evidence of a material violation of law that they acquire in their representation of the corporation to the corporation's general counsel or, if necessary, its audit committee.[8] While important, this requirement deals only with a special context (violations of law) and does not create, as the proposed reforms would, a generalized obligation for at least a certifying attorney to monitor the accuracy of the corporation's non-financial disclosures.

Of course, any claim that the attorney is, or should be, a gatekeeper, will trigger predictable responses from the bar that such a role conflicts with the other roles that attorneys perform or that it will dry up the flow of information between attorneys and clients. Part III assesses and rejects these arguments, concluding that the principal consequence of expressly recognizing attorneys as gatekeepers will be instead to enhance their leverage with their clients. In short, the unrecognised conse-

[8] Securities Act Release No 33-8185 ('Implementation of Standards of Professional Conduct for Attorneys') (6 February 2003); see also text and notes at notes 126 to 130.

quence of expanded ethical or professional obligations is to empower the gatekeeper, thus responding appropriately to the phenomenon of 'gatekeeper failure.'

Part I

B. Gatekeepers: Past and Present

I. Defining the Concept

The term 'gatekeeper' has been widely used to refer to the outside professionals who serve the board.[9] The core idea underlying use of this concept is that the gatekeeper can be more easily deterred than the entity it serves because it receives a smaller share, if any, of the profits derived from corporate misconduct. Some also define the gatekeeper as 'a person or entity who provides a necessary service or certification without which the corporation cannot accomplish a transaction.'[10] This seems overly broad, because under it Microsoft might become a 'gatekeeper' for most of the business world (on the assumption that its basic Windows technology was indispensable). Instead, this article will use the term 'gatekeeper' more narrowly to mean a reputational intermediary who provides verification or certification services to investors. In so doing, the gatekeeper inherently pledges the reputational capital that it has built up over many clients and many transactions to assure investors as to the honesty and completeness of the issuer's statements or the fairness to them of a proposed transaction. The concept inherently presupposes the existence of reputational capital that can be pledged.

Obvious examples of gatekeepers who provide such verification or certification services would include: (1) the auditor providing its certification of the issuer's financial statements; (2) the debt rating agency certifying the issuer's creditworthiness (or relative creditworthiness); (3) the security analyst providing its objective assessment of the corporation's technology, competitiveness, or earnings prospects; (4) the investment banker providing its 'fairness opinion' as to the pricing of a merger; and (5) the securities attorney for the issuer providing its opinion to the underwriters that all material information of which it is aware

[9] The SEC regularly uses this term. See Securities Act Release No 7870 (30 June 2000) (noting that 'the federal laws ... make independent auditors 'gatekeepers' to the public securities markets'). 2000 SEC LEXIS 1389, *13; see also Securities Act Release No 7314 (25 July 1996) (discussing 'The Role of Gatekeepers in Maintaining the Quality of Disclosure').

[10] Professor Reinier Kraakman has defined 'gatekeepers' as private parties who are able to prevent misconduct by withholding their cooperation from wrongdoers. See R Kraakman 'Gatekeepers: The Anatomy of a Third Party Enforcement Strategy' (1986) 2 J L Econ & Org 53; see also Kraakman 'Corporate Liability Strategies and the Costs of Legal Controls' (1984) 93 Yale L J 857. This definition strikes me as much too broad, at least for purposes of discussing the role of professionals. It would potentially hold liable persons who sold pencils to Al Capone's gang on the grounds that one could not run a brewery and tavern business without using pencils to keep records.

concerning the issuer has been properly disclosed. The underwriter in an initial public offering is probably also a gatekeeper in the sense that its reputation is implicitly pledged and it is expected to perform due diligence services. Some professions (most notably, the auditor) provide services that consist primarily of gatekeeping, whereas other professions engage in such services only as an ancillary activity (for example, as discussed later, the attorney is primarily an advocate or a transaction engineer and only sometimes a gatekeeper).

Characteristically, the professional gatekeeper essentially assesses or vouches for the corporate client's own statements about itself or a specific transaction. This duplication is desired because the market recognizes that the gatekeeper has a lesser incentive to deceive than does its client and thus regards the gatekeeper's assurance or evaluation as more credible. Unavoidably, the gatekeeper as a watchdog is compromised to a degree by the fact that it is typically paid by the party that it is to monitor. Still, the gatekeeper's relative credibility stems from the fact that it in effect pledges a reputational capital that it has built up over many years of performing similar services for numerous clients. In theory, the gatekeeper as an entity would not rationally sacrifice its reputational capital for a single client or a modest fee. Nonetheless, here as elsewhere, logic and experience can conflict. Despite the clear logic of the gatekeeper rationale, experience over the 1990s showed that principal/agent problems can arise within gatekeeper firms with the result that agents can rationally decide to risk the firm's reputational capital to a degree that the firm as a whole would not. This decision may be rational for the agent, but not for the firm. As a result, professional gatekeepers do sometimes acquiesce in managerial fraud, even though the apparent reputational losses seem. to dwarf the gains to be made from the individual client.[11]

This paradox is illustrated by the facts of Arthur Andersen's fall in 2002. In theory, the firm should have resisted and not acquiesced in accounting irregularities, because it had many clients, each of whom pay a fee that was modest in proportion to the firm's overall revenues. Specifically, Arthur Andersen had approximately 2,300 audit clients.[12] On this basis, the firm seemingly had little incentive to risk its considerable reputational capital for any one client, even if that client paid a multi-million dollar fee.

During the 1990s, many courts bought this logic hook, line and sinker. For example, in *DiLeo v Ernst & Young*,[13] Judge Easterbrook, writing for the Seventh Circuit, outlined precisely the foregoing theory:

[11] This observation is hardly original with this author. See, for example, RA Prentice 'The Case of the Irrational Auditor: A Behavioral Insight Into Securities Fraud Litigation' (2000) 95 Nw U L Rev 1333.

[12] Michelle Mittelstadt 'Andersen Charged With Obstruction, Vows to Fight' *Dallas Morning News* (15 March 2002) 1.

[13] 901 F 2d 624 (7th Cir 1990); see also *Melder v Morris* 27 F 3d 1097, 1103 (5th Cir 1994); *Robin v Arthur Young & Co* 915 F 2d 1120, 1127 (7th Cir 1990) (mere $ 90,000 annual audit fee would have been an irrational motive for fraud).

> The complaint does not allege that [the auditor] had anything to gain from any fraud by [its client]. An accountant's greatest asset is its reputation for honesty, closely followed by its reputation for careful work. Fees for two years' audits could not approach the losses [that the auditor] would suffer from a perception that it would muffle a client's fraud .... [The auditor's] partners shared none of the gain from any fraud and were exposed to a large fraction of the loss. It would have been irrational for any of them to have joined cause with [the client].[14]

Of course, the modest fees in some of these cases (for example, the audit fee was only $ 90,000 in *Robin v Arthur Young & Co*)[15] were well less than the $ 100 million in prospective annual fees from Enron that Arthur Andersen & Co. explicitly foresaw. But this difference in magnitude cannot really explain Arthur Andersen's collapse. Even if Arthur Andersen saw Enron as a potential $ 100 million client, it must be remembered that Arthur Andersen generated over $ 9 billion in revenues in 2001 alone (so that its expected Enron revenues would total only around 1 % of its aggregate revenues).[16] Hence, a fuller explanation seems necessary.

II. The Auditing Profession During the 1990s: A Study in Transition

Once among the most respected of all professionals service firms (including law, accounting, and consulting firms), Andersen became involved in a series of now well-known securities frauds – eg, Waste Management, Sunbeam, HBOC-McKesson, The Baptist Foundation, and Global Crossing – that culminated in its disastrous association with Enron. Those who wish to view the recent corporate scandals as simply the work of a 'few bad apples' may seek to characterize Arthur Andersen as a deviant firm, in effect an 'outlaw' that masqueraded as an honest sheriff. This theory, however, simply does not hold water. The available evidence in fact suggests that, in terms of the percentage of accounting restatements experienced by its audit clients, Andersen was not significantly different from its peers and experienced the same (or lesser) rate of financial restatements.[17] To the extent it was different, the leading difference may have been only

[14] *DiLeo v Ernst & Young* 901 F 2d at 629.

[15] *Robin v Arthur Young & Co* 915 F 2d 1120, 1127 (7th Cir 1990).

[16] Arthur Andersen's website reports that revenues for 2001 were $ 9.34 billion. See <www.andersen.com>. Also. the $ 100 million figure was the expected revenue per year that Andersen partners foresaw in the future, when overall revenues would presumably also increase.

[17] Compared to its peers within the Big Five accounting firms, Arthur Andersen appears to have been responsible for a less than its proportionate share of earnings restatements. While it audited 21% of Big 5 audit clients, it was responsible for only 15% of the restatements experienced by the Big Five firms between 1997 and 2001. On this basis, it was arguably slightly more conservative than its peers. See 'Periscope: How Arthur Andersen Begs for

cont. ...

that it was less lucky. All in all, the more logical inference to draw from the 'accounting irregularity' scandals of 2001-2002 is that an erosion in the quality of financial reporting occurred sometime during the 1990s.

Indeed, this is the area where the data seems the clearest. During the 1990s, earnings restatements, long recognized as a proxy for fraud, suddenly soared. One study, conducted in 2001 by Moriarty and Livington, found that the number of earnings restatements by publicly held corporations averaged 49 per year from 1990 to 1997, next increased to 91 in 1998, and then skyrocketed to 150 and 156 in 1999 and 2000, respectively.[18] A later, fuller study conducted by the United States General Accounting Office in October, 2002, examined all financial statement restatements (not just earnings restatements) and also found a similarly sharp, discontinuous spike in 1999 that has continued through 2002.[19] The GAO Study's data shows the following trend line:[20]

Figure 1: Total Number of Restatement Announcements Identified, 1997-2002

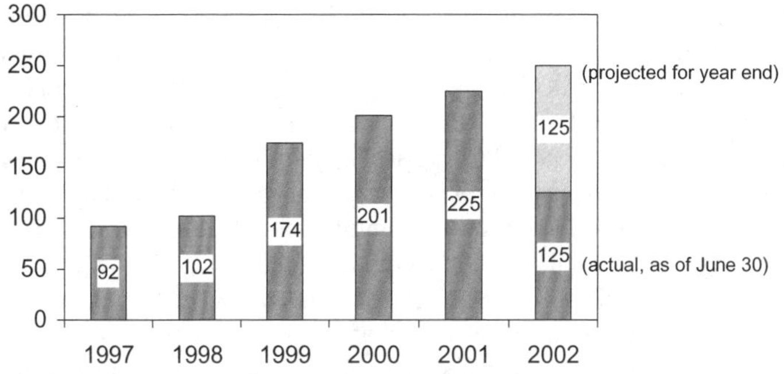

Business' Newsweek 18 March 2002, 6. In discussions with industry insiders, the only respect in which I have ever heard Andersen characterized as different from its peers in the Big Five was that it marketed itself as a firm in which the audit partner could make the final call on difficult accounting questions without having to secure approval from senior officials within the firm. Although this could translate into a weaker system of internal controls, this hypothesis seems inconsistent with Arthur Andersen's apparently below average rate of earnings restatements.

[18] Moriarty and Livingston 'Quantitative Measures of the Quality of Financial Reporting' (2001) 17 Financial Executive 53, 54.

[19] United States General Accounting Office, Report to the Chairman, Committee on Banking, Housing, and Urban Affairs, US Senate 'Financial Statement Restatements: Trends, Market Impacts, Regulatory Responses and Remaining Challenges' (October 2002) (GAO-03-138) at 4-5 (hereinafter, 'GAO Study').

[20] ibid at 15.

Not all restatements, however, are equal. Some may involve small, infrequently traded companies or involve only trivial changes or trigger only modest stock price reactions, while others may be on a scale with Enron or WorldCom. Therefore, it is useful to focus more precisely on financial statement restatements by companies listed on the NYSE, Amex, and Nasdaq, thereby excluding smaller companies that trade only on regional exchanges or over the counter. On this basis, between 1997 and 2001, the proportion of listed companies on the NYSE, Amex and Nasdaq that restated their financial statement approximately tripled, increasing from less than 0.89 percent in 1997 to approximately 2.5 percent in 2001.[21] Indeed, the GAO Study further predicted that this percentage would reach nearly 3 percent in 2002.[22] Overall, the GAO Study found that from January 1997 to June 2002, approximately '10 percent of all listed companies announced at least one restatement.'[23] Also noteworthy was the fact that the size (in terms of market capitalization) of the typical restating company rose rapidly over this period,[24] and in 2002, companies listed on the NYSE or Nasdaq accounted for over 85 percent of all restatements identified in that year.[25]

In theory, financial restatements could simply be the product of changes in regulatory rules and this could signify relatively little. But any possibility that issuers are indifferent to restatements can quickly be dispelled. In the real world, issuers resist restatements because they fear the stock price drops, securities class actions, and SEC investigations that generally follow in the wake of financial statement restatements. Indeed, the GAO Study found that stock prices of restating companies over the 1997 to 2001 period suffered an immediate market-adjusted decline of almost 10 percent on average, measured on the basis of the stock's three day price movement from the trading day before the announcement through the trading day after the announcement.[26] Between 1997 to 2002. restating firms lost over $ 100 billion in market capitalization just over this three trading day period surrounding a restatement announcement.[27] Given these significant and adverse stock price effects, it is implausible to read the sharp increase in restatements at the end of the 1990s as the product of any new tolerance for, or indifference to, restatements. Even if (as some audit firms have

[21] ibid at 4.

[22] ibid.

[23] ibid.

[24] Specifically, the average (median) size by market capitalization of a restating company rose from $ 500 million ($ 143 million) in 1997 to $ 2 billion ($ 351 million) in 2002. ibid.

[25] Of the 125 actual restatements identified through mid-2002, 54 were listed on Nasdaq, and 53 were listed on the NYSE (for a total of 107 or 85%). ibid.

[26] ibid at 5. The GAO Study also found a longer-term market-adjusted decline of 18% over the period from 60 trading days before the announcement to 60 trading days after the announcement. ibid at 29.

[27] ibid at 28.

contended) some portion of the change might be attributed to new SEC pronouncements or, more generally, to a SEC activism about 'earnings management,'[28] which became an SEC enforcement priority by 1998,[29] this explanation cannot carry us very far. Although SEC activism might trigger some increase in the number of restatements, it cannot explain the growth in the magnitude of restatements or the sharp stock price decline (averaging 10%) on their announcement.[30] 'Technical' restatements made simply to comply with new SEC interpretations should not produce these stock prices reactions. Clearly, such reactions show that the market was surprised.

The available data shows that, during the late 1990s, the magnitude of financial restatements increased, both in absolute terms (nearly doubling) and as a percentage of the issuer's rapidly increasing market capitalization.[31] This suggests that managers became progressively willing over this period to take greater risks. Moreover, as the decade of the 1990s wore on, earnings restatements were increasingly experienced by large, mature, publicly-held firms, rather than by smaller or newly public companies that might be expected to be more inexperienced or rash. Managerial behaviour within the largest firms then seems to have changed over this period.

In particular, the GAO Study's data corroborates this interpretation that managerial behaviour changed, because it shows a significant change in motive. Although there are many reasons why a company may restate its financial statements (eg to adjust costs or expenses or to recognize liabilities), one particular reason dominated during the period from 1997 to 2002. The GAO study found that issues involving revenue recognition accounted for almost 39 percent of the

[28] Accounting firms have sometimes attempted to explain this increase in restatements on the basis that the SEC tightened the definition of 'materiality' in the late 1990s. This explanation is not very convincing, in part because the principal SEC statement that tightened the definition of materiality – Staff Accounting Bulletin No 99 – was issued in mid-1999, after the number of restatements had already begun to soar in 1998. Also, SAB No. 99 did not truly mandate restatements, but only advised that any rule of thumb employed by auditors and issuers that assumed that amounts under 5% were inherently immaterial could not be applied reflexively. See Staff Accounting Bulletin No 99, 64 F R 45150 (19 August 1999).

[29] The SEC's prioritisation of earnings management as a principal enforcement target can be approximately dated to SEC Chairman Arthur Levitt's now famous speech on the subject in 1998. See A Levitt 'The Numbers Game' Remarks at NYU Center for Law and Business' (28 September 1998).

[30] See text and notes at notes 24 to 26.

[31] According to Moriarty and Livingston, supra note 18, companies that restated earnings suffered market losses of $ 17.7 billion in 1998, $ 24.2 billion in 1999, and $ 31.2 billion in 2000. ibid at 55. Expressed as a percentage of the overall capitalization of the market (which was ascendingly hyperbolically over this period), these losses for 1998 through 2000 came to 0.13%, 0.14% and 0.19%, respectively, of market capitalization. In short, however expressed, the relative size of the losses increased over this period.

919 announced restatements that it identified over the 1997 to 2002 period.[32] In effect, attempts by management to prematurely recognize income appear to have been the most common cause of restatements. Earlier in the decade and during prior decades, earnings management was more a game of 'smoothing out' the peaks and valleys in a corporation's income flow in order to reduce the apparent volatility in the corporation's returns. Thus, managements characteristically attempted to hide 'excess earnings' in 'rainy day reserves' in order to use such funds later to smooth out undesired declines in the firm's earnings.

Despite this earlier preference for income-smoothing, by the end of the 1990s, these same firms were robbing future periods for earnings that could be recognized immediately. In short, 'income smoothing' gave way to more predatory behaviour. Interestingly, restatements involving revenue recognition produced disproportionately large losses.[33] Seemingly, the market feared revenue-timing restatements more than others because of the apparent signal they carried that reported earnings could not be trusted. Yet, despite the market's antipathy for them, revenue recognition restatements became the most common form of restatement. At a minimum, this suggests that the interests of management and shareholders were not aligned, and gatekeepers appear to have been progressively caught in the middle.

III. Security Analysts During the 1990s

Before any attempt is made to generalize about the motivations that led managements to pressure their auditors for premature revenue recognition, it is useful to recognize that this pattern of increased acquiescence by the gatekeeper to its clients' demands during the 1990s was not limited to the auditing profession. Security analysts are probably the only other profession that has experienced equivalent (or harsher) criticism since the collapse of the high-tech bubble in 2000. Again, growing conflicts of interest appear to explain their change in behaviour.

Some of the evidence relating to gatekeeper failure involving analysts is anecdotal, but striking. As late as October 2001, shortly before Enron's bankruptcy, 16 out of the 17 securities analysts covering Enron maintained 'buy' or 'strong but recommendations on its stock.[34] Yet, months earlier as of December

[32] GAO Study, note 3, at 5. Revenue recognition was also the leading reason for restatements in each individual year over this period. ibid.

[33] While revenue recognition restatements accounted for 39 percent of restatements over the 1997 to 2002 period, they were associated with $ 56 billion (or roughly 56%) of the $ 100 billion in market capitalization that restating companies lost over this period. ibid. at 28.

[34] 'Statement of Frank Torres, Legislative Counsel, Consumers Union, Before the United States Senate, Committee on Governmental Affairs, on the Collapse of Enron: The Role Analysts Played and the Conflicts They Face' 27 February 2002 at 6 ('In the case of Enron, 16

cont. ...

31, 2000, Enron already had a stock price that was 70 times earnings and six times its book value, and had earned an 89% return for the year (despite a 9% decrease over the same period for the S&P 500 index).[35] Such a profile should have seemingly alerted any analyst who was even half awake to the possibility that Enron was seriously overvalued. Symptomatically, however, the first brokerage firm to downgrade Enron to a 'sell' rating in 2001 was Prudential Securities, which did not then engage in investment banking activities.[36] Prudential was also believed to have the highest proportion of sell ratings among the stocks it evaluated.[37] Perhaps, Prudential also woke up late, but it is still at least revealing that the least conflicted were the first to awake.

How close then are the similarities between analysts and auditors? Much like auditors, analysts are also 'reputational intermediaries,' whose desire to be perceived as credible and objective may often be subordinated to their desire to retain and please investment-banking clients. One statistic inevitably comes up in any assessment of analyst objectivity: namely, the curious fact that the ratio of 'buy' recommendations to 'sell' recommendations has recently been as high as 100 to 1.[38] In truth, this particular statistic may not be as compelling as it initially sounds because there are obvious reasons why 'buy' recommendations will normally outnumber 'sell' recommendations, even in the absence of conflicts of interest.[39] Yet, a related statistic may be more revealing because it underscores the apparent transition that took place in the 1990s and parallels the earlier noted

out of 17 analysts had a buy or a strong buy rating, one had a hold, none had a sell – even as the company stock had lost over half its value and its CEO suddenly resigned.'). 2002 WL 2011028; see also testimony of Frank Partnoy, Professor of Law, University of San Diego School of Law, Hearings before the United States Senate Committee on Governmental Affairs, 24 January 2002 (similar 16 out of 17 tabulation).

[35] PM Healy and K Palepu 'Governance and Intermediation Problems in Capital Markets: Evidence From the Fall of Enron' (Harvard NOM Research Paper No 02-27) (August 2002) at 2.

[36] L Young 'Independence Day' Smartmoney 1 May 2001, 28 Vol XI, No V, 2002 WL 2191410.

[37] ibid.

[38] A study by Thomas Financial/First Call has found that less than one percent of the 28,000 stock recommendations issued by brokerage firm analysts during late 1999 and most of 2000 were 'sell' recommendations. See Opening Statement of Congressman PE Kanjorski; Ranking Democratic Member, House Subcommittee on Capital Markets, Insurance, and Government Sponsored Enterprises, 'Hearing on Analyzing the Analysts' 14 June 2001 at 1 (citing and discussing study).

[39] A study by Thomas Financial/First Call has found that less than one percent of the 28,000 stock recommendations issued by brokerage firm analysts during late 1999 and most of 2000 were 'sell' recommendations. See Opening Statement of Congressman Paul E Kanjorski; Ranking Democratic Member, House Subcommittee on Capital Markets, Insurance, and Government Sponsored Enterprises, 'Hearing on Analyzing the Analysts' 14 June 2001 at 1 (citing and discussing study).

increase in accounting restatements during the 1990s. According to a by Thomson Financial, the ratio of 'buy' to 'sell' recommendations increased from 6 to 1 91 to 100 to 1 by 2000.[40]

Other evidence corroborates this picture of a systematic analyst bias towards optimism. Studying security analyst career patterns over the last two decades, Hong and Kubik find that career advancement for analysts depended more on a bias towards optimism than on the overall accuracy of their forecasts.[41] Although accuracy did matter, a tendency to be more optimistic than the consensus of analysts seemed to protect analysts from downward movement within their industry's hierarchy, and this tendency was most pronounced in the case of analysts who covered stocks underwritten by their own firms.[42] More importantly, this tendency for optimism to outweigh accuracy increased during the late 1990s.[43] They interpret their findings as at least consistent with the view 'that Wall Street lost any self-discipline to produce accurate research during the recent stock market mania.'[44] Perhaps, this assessment overstates, but the conclusion seems hard to escape that something happened during the 1990s that compromised the independence and objectivity of the gatekeepers on whom our private system of corporate governance depends.[45] Even before Enron, much evidence showed that the most sophisticated market participants understood the extent of these conflicts and had ceased to rely on 'sell side' analysts.[46]

IV. Explaining Gatekeeper Failure

The same observation has probably occurred to many: none of the watchdogs that should have detected Enron's collapse – auditors, analysts or debt rating agencies

[40] Opening Statement of Congressman PE Kanjorski, note 38, at 1. (citing study by First Call).

[41] H Hong and J Kubik 'Analyzing the Analysts: Career Concerns and Biased Earnings Forecasts' (2003) 58 J Fin 313.

[42] ibid at 341.

[43] ibid at 342 and 346 (finding that between 1996 and 2000, a strong bias towards optimism decreased an analyst's risk of downward movement in the industry).

[44] ibid at 345-46.

[45] Participants in the industry also report that its professional culture changed dramatically in the late 1990s, particularly as investment-banking firms began to hire 'star' analysts for their marketing clout. See G Morgenson 'Requiem for an Honorable Profession' *New York Times* (5 May 2002) at Section 3-1 (suggesting major change dates from around 1996).

[46] Although the empirical evidence is limited, it suggests that 'independent' analysts (ie, analysts not associated with the underwriter for a particular issuer) behave differently than, and tend to outperform, analysts who are associated with the issuer's underwriter. See R Michaely and K Wornack 'Conflict of Interest and the Credibility of Underwriter Analyst Recommendations' (1999) 12 Review of Financial Studies 653.

– awoke before the penultimate moment. This is the common denominator, not just in the case of Enron, but also in many of the other 'accounting irregularity' cases of 2001-2002. What plausible hypothesis can explain the collective failure of these gatekeepers? Here, several different, although ultimately complementary, stories can be told. Initially, this section will first review two generalized stories: the first will be called the 'general deterrence' story; and the second, the 'bubble' story. Then, it will focus on allocating responsibility among gatekeepers, managers, and investors.

1. The Deterrence Explanation: The Underdeterred Gatekeeper

The general deterrence story focuses on the decline in the expected liability costs associated with acquiescence by auditors in aggressive accounting policies favoured by managements. It postulates that, during the 1990s, the risk of auditor liability declined, while the benefits of acquiescence increased. Economics 101 teaches us that when the costs go down, while the benefits associated with any activity go up, the output of the activity will increase. Here. the activity that increased was auditor acquiescence.

Prior to the 1990s, auditors faced a very real risk of civil liability, principally from class action litigation.[47] Why did the legal risks go down during the 1990s? The obvious list of reasons would include:

(a) the Supreme Court's Lampf Pleva decision, which in 1991 significantly shortened the statute of limitations applicable to securities fraud;[48]

[47] As of 1992, Congress was advised that the securities fraud litigation costs for just the six largest accounting firms (then the 'Big Six') accounted for $ 783 million, or more than 14% of their audit revenues. Potential exposure to loss was in the billions. See Private Litigation Under the Federal Securities Laws: Hearings Before the Subcommittee on Securities of the Senate Committee on Banking, Housing and Urban Affairs, 103'dCon., 1st Sess No 103-431 (1993) (statement of Jake L Netterville), reprinted in Fed Sec L Rep (CCH) No 1696, (10 January 1996). One major auditing firm, Laventhol & Horwath, did fail and entered bankruptcy as a result of litigation and associated scandals growing out of the savings and loan scandals of the 1980s. See 'What Role Should CPA's be Playing in Audit Reform?' Partner's Report for CPA Firm Owners, April 2002 (discussing experience of Laventhol & Horwath). The accounting profession's bitter experience with class litigation in the 1980s and 1990s probably explains why it became the strongest and most organized champion of the Private Securities Litigation Reform Act of 1995.

[48] *Lampf Pleva, Lipkind & Petigrow v Gilbertston* 501 US 350, 359-61 (1991) (creating a federal rule requiring plaintiffs to file within one year of when they should have known of the violation underlying their action, but in no event more than three years after the violation). This one to three year period was typically shorter than the previously applicable limitations periods which were determined by analogy to state statutes and often permitted a five or six year delay – if that was the period within which a common law fraud action could be maintained in the particular state.

(b) the Supreme Court's Central Bank of Denver decision,[49] which in 1994 eliminated private 'aiding and abetting' liability in securities fraud cases;
(c) the Private Securities Litigation Reform Act of 1995 ('PSLRA'), which (i) raised the pleading standards for securities class actions to a level well above that applicable to fraud actions generally; (ii) substituted proportionate liability for 'joint and several' liability; (iii) restricted the sweep of the RICO statute so that it could no longer convert securities fraud class actions for compensatory damages into actions for treble damages; and (iv) adopted a very protective safe harbour for forward-looking information; and
(d) the Securities Litigation Uniform Standards Act of 1998 ('SLUSA'), which abolished state court class actions alleging securities fraud.[50]

The individual impact of each of these changes probably cannot be reliably measured, but their concurrent aggregate impact is clear: they greatly reduced the plaintiffs' incentives in securities class actions to sue secondary participants, such as auditors, analysts, and attorneys. As an SEC study noted, the number of audit-related suits filed against the then 'Big Six' accounting firms in 1990 to 192 was 192, 172, and 141, respectively.[51] Yet, in the first year following the passage of the PSLRA (1996), the SEC found that out of the 105 securities class actions it found to have been filed in that year, accounting firms were named in only six cases, corporate counsel in no cases, and underwriters in nineteen cases.[52] It concluded: 'Secondary defendants such as accountants and lawyers, are being named less frequently in securities class actions.'[53]

Not only did the threat of private enforcement decline, but also the prospect of public enforcement similarly subsided. In particular, there is reason to believe that, from some point in the 1980s until the late 1990s, the SEC shifted its

[49] *Central Bank of Denver NA v First Interstate Bank of Denver* NA 511 US 164 (1994).

[50] Pub L No 105-353, 112 Stat 3227 (codified in scattered sections of 15 USC). For an analysis and critique of this statute, see R Painter 'Responding to A False Alarm: Federal Preemption of State Securities Fraud Causes of Action' (1998) 84 Cornell L Rev 1.

[51] US Securities and Exchanges Commission, Office of the General Counsel, Report to the President and the Congress on the First Year of Practice under the Private Securities Litigation Reform Act of 1995. (April 1997) at 22 (available on SEC website at <http://www.sec.gov/news/studies/Ireform.txt>. The figures for the years 1990 to 1992 were reported to the SEC by the Big Six and include all class actions against them, which could include some non-securities class actions. Nonetheless, the number of such non-securities actions seems likely to have been small. As the above SEC study further notes: '[D]uring the period from 1991 through June 1996, accountants were defendants in 52 reported settlements (as opposed to complaints), ... and law firms were defendants in 7. Thus, there seems to be a real decline in the number of lawsuits against secondary defendants.' ibid at 22.

[52] ibid at 21 to 22.

[53] ibid at 4. As this study expressly noted, this decline could have been caused both by the PSLRA and the Supreme Court's decision in Central Bank of Denver in 1994 that ended private 'aiding and abetting' liability under Rule 10 b-5. See text and note at note 49.

enforcement focus away from actions against the Big Five accounting firms towards other priorities.'[54] In any event, the point here is not that any of these changes were necessarily unjustified or excessive,[55] but rather that their collective impact was to appreciably reduce the risk of liability. Auditors were the special beneficiaries of many of these provisions. For example, the pleading rules and the new standard of proportionate liability protected them far more than it did most corporate defendants.[56] Although auditors are still sued today, the settlement value of cases against auditors has gone way down.

Correspondingly, the benefits of acquiescence to auditors rose over this same period, as the Big Five learned during the 1990s how to cross-sell consulting services and to treat the auditing function principally as a portal of entry into a lucrative client. Prior to the mid-1990s, the provision of consulting services to audit clients was infrequent and insubstantial in the aggregate.[57] Yet, according to

[54] This point has been orally made to me by several former SEC officials, including Stanley Sporkin, the long-time former head of the Commission's Division of Enforcement. They believe that the SEC's enforcement action against Arthur Andersen, which was resolved in June 2001, was one of the very few (and perhaps the only) enforcement action brought against a Big Five accounting firm on fraud grounds during the 1990s. See *Securities and Exchange Commission v Arthur Andersen LLP*, SEC Litigation Release No 1703 9, 2001 SEC LEXIS 115 (19 June 2001). Although the Commission did bring charges during the 1990s against individual partners in these firms, the Commission appears to have been deterred from bringing suits against the Big Five themselves because such actions were extremely costly in manpower and expense and the defendants could be expected to resist zealously. In contrast, during the 1980s, especially during Mr. Sporkin's tenure as head of the Enforcement Division, the SEC regularly brought enforcement actions against the Big Five.

[55] Indeed, this author would continue to support proportionate liability for auditors on fairness grounds and sees no problem with the PSLRA's heightened pleading standards, as they have been interpreted by some courts. See, eg *Novak v Kasaks* 216 F.3d 300 (2[d] Cir 2000), cert denied, 531 US 1012 (2000).

[56] At a minimum, plaintiffs today must plead with particularity facts giving rise to a 'strong inference of fraud.' See eg, *Novak v Kasaks*, n 55. At the outset of a case it may be possible to plead such facts with respect to the management of the corporate defendant (for example, based on insider sales by such persons prior to the public disclosure of the adverse information that caused the stock drop), but it is rarely possible to plead such information with respect to the auditors (who by law cannot own stock in their client). In short, the plaintiff faces a 'Catch 22' dilemma in suing the auditor: it cannot plead fraud with particularity until it obtains discovery, and it cannot obtain discovery under the PSLRA until it pleads fraud with particularity.

[57] Consulting fees paid by audit clients exploded during the 1990s. According to the Panel on Audit Effectiveness, who was appointed in 1999 by the Public Oversight Board at the request of the SEC to study audit practices, 'audit firms' fees from consulting services for their SEC clients increased from 17% ... of audit fees in 1990 to 67% in 1999.' See the Panel on Audit Effectiveness, Report and Recommendations (Exposure Draft 2000) at 102. In 1990, the Panel found that 80% of the Big Five firms' SEC clients received no consulting services from their auditors, and only 1% of those SEC clients paid consulting fees exceeding their auditing fees to the Big Five. ibid at 102. While the Panel found only marginal changes during the 1990s, later

cont. ...

one recent survey, the typical large public corporation now pays its auditor for consulting services three times what it pays the same auditor for auditing services.[58] Not only did auditing firms see more profit potential in consulting than in auditing, but they also began during the 1990s to compete based on a strategy of low balling' under which auditing services were offered at, rates that were marginal to arguably below cost. The rationale for such a strategy was that the auditing function was essentially a loss leader by which more lucrative services could be marketed.

Although this argument that the provision of consulting services eroded auditor independence has considerable explanatory power, there is an obvious reply: those who defend the propriety of consulting services by auditors respond that the growth of consulting services made little real difference, because the audit firm was already conflicted by the fact that the client paid its fees. Put as bluntly as possible, the audit partner of a major client (such as Enron) is always conflicted by the fact that such a partner has virtually a 'one-client' practice. Whoever is the gatekeeper – attorney, auditor, or analyst – a 'one client' practice compromises the agent. Should the partner lose that client for any reason, the partner will likely need to find employment elsewhere. In short, both critics and defenders of the status quo tend to agree that the individual audit partner is already inevitably compromised by his or her desire to hold the client on whom the agent's career depends. From this premise, a prophylactic rule prohibiting the firm's involvement in consulting would seemingly achieve little.

Even if true in part, this rebuttal nonetheless misses one key point: namely, the difficulty faced by the client in firing the auditor in the real world. As discussed below, there are real costs associated with firing an auditor (but, in contrast, none to speak of in firing a consultant). Given this disparity, an unintended consequence of combining consulting services with auditing services in one firm is that the union of the two enables the client to more effectively threaten the auditing firm in a 'low visibility' way. To illustrate this point, let us suppose, for example, that a client becomes dissatisfied with an auditor who refuses to endorse an aggressive accounting policy favoured by its management. Today, the client cannot easily fire the auditor. Firing the auditor may result in public embarrassment, potential public disclosure of the reasons for the auditor's dismissal or

studies have found that consulting fees have become a multiple of the audit fee for large public corporations. See text and note at note 58.

[58] A survey by the Chicago Tribune this year finds that the one hundred largest corporations in the Chicago area (determined on the basis of market capitalization) paid consulting fees to their auditors that were on average over three times the audit fee paid the same auditor. See JK Stewart and A Countryman 'Local Audit Conflicts Add Up: Consulting Deals, Hiring Practices In Question' *Chicago Tribune* 24 February 2002 at C-1. The extreme example in this study was Motorola, which had over a 16:1 ratio between consulting fees and audit fees.

resignation, or a probable SEC intervention.[59] However, if the auditor also becomes a consultant to the client. the client can then easily terminate the auditor as a consultant (or reduce its use of the firm's consulting services) in retaliation for the auditor's intransigence. This low visibility response neither requires any disclosure, nor invites any SEC oversight, and yet incentivizes the audit firm to replace the intransigent audit partner. In effect, the client can bribe (or coerce) the auditor in its core professional role by raising (or reducing) its use of consulting services.

Of course, this argument that the client can discipline and threaten the auditor/consultant in ways that it could not discipline the simple auditor is based more on logic than actual case histories. But it does fit the available data. A recent study by academic accounting experts, based on proxy statements filed during the first half of 2001, finds that those firms that purchased more non-audit services from their auditor (as a percentage of the total fee paid to the audit firm) were more likely to fit the profile of a firm engaging in earnings management.[60]

2. The Market Bubble Story

Alternatively, Enron's and Arthur Andersen's downfalls, and the host of other sudden stock declines in 2001 to 2002, can be seen as the consequence of a classic bubble that overtook the equity markets in the late 1990s and produced a market euphoria. But what exactly is the connection between a market bubble and gatekeeper failure? Here, a hypothesis needs to be advanced that cannot be rigorously proven, but that is consistent with modern behavioural economics: in a bubble, gatekeepers become less relevant and hence experience a decline in both their leverage over their client and the value of their reputational capital. That is, in an atmosphere of market euphoria, investors rely less on gatekeepers, and managements in turn regard them as more a formality than a necessity. Gatekeepers provide a critical service only when investors are cautious and sceptical and therefore rely on their services. Conversely, in a market bubble, caution and

[59] Item 4 ('Changes in Registrants Certifying Accountant') of Form 8-K requires a 'reporting' company to file a Form 8-K within five days after the resignation or dismissal of the issuer's independent accountant or that of the independent accountant for a significant subsidiary of the issuer. The Form 8-K must then provide the elaborate disclosures mandated by Item 304 of Regulation S-K relating to any dispute or disagreement between the auditor and the accountant. See 17 CM 228.304 ('Changes in and Disagreements With Accountants on Accounting and Financial Disclosure').

[60] R Frankel, M Johnson and K Nelson 'The Relation Between Auditors' Fees for Non-Audit Services and Earnings Quality' MIT Sloan Working Paper No 4330-02 (available from Social Sciences Research Network at <www.ssrn.com> at id= 296557). Firms purchasing more non-audit services were found more likely to just meet or beat analysts' forecasts, which is the standard profile of the firm playing 'the numbers game'.

scepticism are by definition largely abandoned. In such an environment, auditors continue to be used more because SEC rules mandate their use (or because no individual firm wishes to call attention to itself by becoming the first to dispense with them) than because investors actually demand their use. As a result, because gatekeepers have reduced relevance in such an environment. they also have reduced leverage with their clients. Thus, if we assume that the auditor will be largely ignored by euphoric investors, the rational auditor's best competitive strategy (at least for the short term) was to become as acquiescent and low cost as possible.

Although this thesis assigns some causal responsibility to investors, themselves, for their own losses. it does not absolve gatekeepers from responsibility. For example, even if shareholders do not care much during a bubble about the auditor's reputation, it is still possible for an auditor to intervene effectively and prevent fraud, either by refusing to certify the issuer's financial statements, by withdrawing its certificate on a later discovery of the fraud, or by notifying the SEC.[61]

The key element in this story involves why investors cease to care about the gatekeeper's reputation. After all, the rise of auditing as a profession was the product of investors' own concerns about fraud and irregularity, not regulatory requirements. What then caused this concern to weaken? Here, behavioural economics supplies a plausible answer. Modern economics recognizes that individuals, including investors, have 'bounded rationality' and do not pursue all information relevant to an optimal decision.[62] The Nobel Prize-winning research of Professors Kahneman and Tversky has in particular demonstrated that individuals typically make decisions by using heuristics – that is, rules of thumb – rather than by incorporating all obtainable information. A heuristic that they find to be pervasively used by individuals and that has particular relevance to the context of securities markets is the 'availability heuristic.'[63] it asserts that individuals estimate the frequency of an event by recalling recent instances of its occurring (even if

[61] Section I OA of the Securities Exchange Act of 1934 requires the auditor of a public company to notify the Commission where the auditor discovers an 'illegal [that] has a material effect on the financial statements of the issuer' and management and the board of the issuer have not taken 'timely and appropriate remedial action' after notification by the auditor. See 15 USC §780)(A). Since its adoption in 1995, this provision has been seldom, if ever, employed.

[62] For overviews of behavioural economics, see C Jolis, C Sunstein and R Thaler 'A Behavioral Approach to Law and Economics' (1998) 50 Stan L Rev 1471; C Sunstein 'Behavioral Analysis of Law' (1997) 64 U Chi L Rev 1175. The term 'bounded rationality' was coined by Herbert Simon, a Nobel prize winner, and is broadly accepted by most economists. See HA Simon 'Rationality As Process and Product of Thought' (1978) 68 Am Econ Rev: Papers & Proceedings 1.

[63] Jolis, Sunstein and Thaler, note 62, at 1477-78. See also, A Tversky and D Kahneman 'Judgment Under Uncertainty: Heuristics and Biases' in D Kahneman, P Slovic and A Tversky (eds) *Judgment Under Uncertainty* (Cambridge University Press Cambridge 1982).

these instances are normally rare or infrequent, when viewed from a longer term perspective). Hence, if the stock market has recently experienced extraordinary returns for several years, it becomes predictable that individuals will overestimate the likelihood of such extraordinary gains continuing.[64] In effect, there is a status quo or persistence bias – what has recently occurred is expected to continue. Thus, as the market soared in the early and mid-1990s, investors, operating on heuristics, came to assume that this pattern would continue. Further aggravating this tendency is the deep-seated bias displayed by many individuals toward optimism in predicting future events.[65]

Thus, from the perspective of behavioural economics, 'bubbles' are not irrational moments of speculative excess or frenzy, but rather are the product of the predictable expectations of individuals who tend to assume that whatever has recently occurred will persist.

To trigger this persistence bias, it is arguably only necessary that market returns have in fact been extraordinary for a few successive years in order to cause investors to treat this phenomenon as normal and likely to continue. Such an explanation helps us understand why bubbles have re-occurred throughout history. Their re-occurrence is explained not by the hypothesis that investors are inherently gullible, but by the explanation that a period of extraordinary returns creates an expectation that such returns are normal and will persist.

Such heuristic biases are not, of course, the whole story. For the securities analyst, a market bubble presents a different and more serious challenge: during a bubble, those who are cautious and prudent will be outperformed by those who recklessly predict extraordinary returns. Hence, in a bubble, extreme optimism for analysts becomes less a heuristic bias than a competitive necessity. Put more bluntly, it is dangerous to be sane in an insane world. As a result, the securities analyst who prudently predicted reasonable growth and stock appreciation during the 1990s was increasingly left in the dust by the investment guru who prophesised a new investment paradigm in which revenues and costs were less important than the number of 'hits' on a website.

Institutional factors compounded this problem. As the initial public offering (or 61P099) market soared in the 1990s, securities analysts became celebrities and valuable assets to their firms;[66] indeed, they became the principal means by

[64] This is by no means the only way to explain bubbles without resorting to claims of mass delusion. An alternative theory is that institutional money managers have rational incentives to engage in 'herding behaviour', preferring a common wrong decision to a risky correct one. See text and notes at notes 74 to 76.

[65] See Jolis, Sunstein and Thaler, note 62, at 1524-25; see also ND Weinstein 'Unrealistic Optimism About Future Life Events' (1980) 39 J Personality & Soc Psychology 806.

[66] For the view that investment-banking firms changed their competitive strategies on or around 1996 and thereafter sought the 'popular, high-profile analyst' as a means of acquiring IPO clients, see Morgenson, note 45 at Section 3-1 (quoting chief investment officer at Trust Company of the West).

which investment banks competed for IPO clients, as the underwriter with the 'star' analyst could produce the greatest first day stock price spike in an EPO. But as their salaries thus soared, analyst compensation came increasingly from the investment banking side of their firms. Hence, just as in the case of the auditor, the analyst's economic position became progressively dependent on favouring the interests of persons outside their profession (ie, consultants in the case of the auditor and investment bankers in the case of the analyst) who had little reason to respect or observe the standards or professional culture within the gatekeeper's profession.[67]

One common denominator linking these examples is that, as auditors increasingly sought consulting income and as analysts became more dependent on an investment banking subsidy, these gatekeepers' normal desire to preserve their reputational capital for the long run become subordinated to their desire to obtain extraordinary returns in the short run by risking that reputational capital. Alternatively, the value of gatekeepers' reputational capital may have simply declined in a bubble, because investors in such an environment rationally reduce their reliance on gatekeeping services based on their false belief that extraordinary returns will persist. Under either story (or both together), it could have become more profitable for firms to realize the value of their reputational capital by trading on it in the short-run than by preserving it forever. Indeed, during the 1990s, to the extent that auditing became a loss leader for multi-service accounting firms eager to sell more lucrative consulting services and to the extent that securities analysts began to be subsidized by investment banking, each profession became less self-supporting and more dependent on those who wished to profit from the liquidation of their reputational capital.

3. Allocating Responsibility Among Gatekeepers, Managers and Investors

The foregoing explanations still do not fully explain the mechanisms by which reputational capital built up over decades might be sacrificed (or, more accurately, liquidated), once legal risks declined and/or a bubble developed. Here, an allocation of responsibility must be made among the various participants in corporate governance: managers, gatekeepers, and investors.

[67] This idea that professional gatekeepers became dominated by persons outside their profession is at the heart of a recent lawsuit initiated by the New York Attorney General against five chief executive officers of major US corporations. See P McGeehan 'Spitzer Sues Executives of Telecom Companies Over 'III Gotten' Gains' *New York Times* (1 October 2002) at C-1.

a) The Role of Managers

The pressure on gatekeepers to acquiesce in earnings management was not constant over time, but rather accelerated during the 1990s as managerial incentives changed. Executive compensation shifted during the 1990s from being primarily cash-based to being primarily equity-based. By 2001, equity-based compensation constituted approximately two thirds of the median annual compensation of chief executives of large public corporations, up from 8% in the 1990 and 0% in 1984.[68] Another measure of this shift is the growth in stock options. Over the last decade, stock options rose from five percent of shares outstanding at major U. S. companies to fifteen percent – a three hundred percent increase.[69] The value of these options rose by an even greater percentage and over a dramatically shorter period: from $ 50 billion in 1997, in the case of the 2,000 largest corporations to $ 162 billion in 2000 – an over three hundred percent rise in three years.[70] Stock options create an obvious and potentially perverse incentive to engage in short-run, rather than long-term, stock price maximization because executives can exercise their stock options and sell the underlying shares on the same day.[71]

The key problem here is not that stock options provide excessive compensation, but that they provide excessive liquidity. This excess liquidity was, in turn, partially the product of deregulatory reform in the early 1990s, which relaxed the rules under Section 16(b) of the Securities Exchange Act of 1934 to permit officers and directors to exercise stock options and sell the underlying shares without holding the shares for the previously required six month period.[72] Thus, if execu-

[68] Brian J Hall 'Six Challenges in Designing Equity-Based Pay' (2003) 15 Accenture Journal of Applied Corporate Finance 21, at 23 and Figure 1.

[69] G Morgenson 'Corporate Conduct: News Analysis; Bush Failed to Stress Need to Rein in Stock Options' *New York Times* (11 July 2002) at C -l; see also G Morgenson 'Market Watch: Time For Accountability At the Corporate Candy Store' *New York Times* (3 March 2002) Section 3, 1.

[70] Morgenson 'Corporate Conduct' note 69, at C-1 (citing study by Sanford C Bernstein & Co). Thus, if $ 162 billion is the value of all options in these 2,000 companies, aggressive accounting policies that temporarily raise stock prices by as little as ten percent create a potential gain for executives of over $ 16 billion – a substantial incentive.

[71] Hall, note 68, at 24-29 (surveying misincentives in stock options). This point has also been made by a variety of commentators who have called for minimum holding periods or other curbs on stock options. These include Henry M. Paulson, Jr, chief executive of Goldman, Sachs, and Senator John McCain of Arizona. See D Leonhardt 'Corporate Conduct: Compensation: Anger At Executives' Profits Fuels Support for Stock Curb' *New York Times* (9 July 2002) at A-l.

[72] Rule 16b-3(d) expressly permits an officer or director otherwise subject to the 'short-swing' profit provisions of Section 16(b) of the Securities Exchange Act of 1934 to exercise a qualified stock option and sell the underlying shares immediately 'if at least six months elapse from the date of the acquisition of the derivative security to the date of disposition of the ... underlying equity security.' See 17 CFR 240.16b-3(d). The SEC comprehensively revised its rules under Section 16(b) in 1991, in part to facilitate the use of stock options as executive

cont. ...

tives inflate the stock price of their company through premature revenue recognition or other classic earnings management techniques, they could quickly bail out in the short-term by exercising their options and selling, leaving shareholders to bear the cost of the stock decline when the inflated stock price could not be maintained over subsequent periods. Given these incentives. it became rational for corporate executives to use lucrative consulting contracts, or other positive and negative incentives, to induce gatekeepers to engage in conduct that assisted their short-term market manipulations. The bottom line is then that the growth of stock options resulted in gatekeepers being placed under greater pressure to acquiesce in short-term oriented financial and accounting strategies.

b) The Role of Investors

Investors cannot be fairly presented as entirely innocent victims in the recent epidemic of financial irregularities. At a minimum, a bubble reflects investors' acquiescence in unrealistic valuations. More importantly, conflicts of interest on the part of gatekeepers that might alarm investors in other circumstances may be accepted (or at least repressed) during a bubble. To be sure, many investors were likely misled by biased analyst research and overstated earnings, but this does not absolve the 'buy side' of all responsibility. Particularly in the case of institutional investors, who account for over half the ownership and seventy-five percent of the trading in NYSE-listed equities,[73] financial intermediaries may again have failed. According to one estimate, at the peak of the market, sixty percent of Enron stock was held by large institutional investors.[74] Why didn't they see that Enron was overvalued, at least once alarm bells began to sound? A plausible explanation for the failure of institutional investors to respond to warning signals in the case of Enron starts from the premise that professional money managers are principally motivated by the desire to perform no worse than their major institutional rivals; this pressure quickly leads to herding behaviour.[75] According to this analysis, fund managers attract investor funds and maximize their fees based on

compensation and to 'reduce the regulatory burden' under Section 16(b). See Securities Exchange Act Release No. 34-28869, 1991 SEC LEXIS 171 (8 February 1991). A premise of this reform was that 'holding derivative securities is functionally equivalent to holding the underlying equity security for purpose of Section 16.' ibid at *35 to *36. Hence, the SEC permitted the tacking of the option holding period with the stock's holding period, thereby enabling officers and directors to exercise options and sell on the same day (if the option had already been held six months).

[73] For these statistics, see JD Cox and R Thomas 'Leaving Money on the Table: Do Institutional Investors Fail to File Claims in Securities Class Actions?' (2002) 80 Wash U L Q 855 n 4.

[74] Healy and Palepu, note 35, at 22.

[75] The term 'herding' was coined over a decade ago by Scharfstein and Stein. See DS Scharfstein and J Stein 'Herd Behavior and Investment' (1990) 80 Amer Eco Rev 465; see also Healy and Palepu, note 35, at 26-27.

their quarterly reported performance relative to comparable funds or indices.[76] Thus. if a fund manager discovers that Enron is overvalued and sells his firm's investment, the manager and the managers clients do well – but only if the market agrees and Enron's stock price falls that quarter. If the market persists in over-valuing Enron or actually climbs based on biased 'sell side' research, the manager becomes an unfortunately premature prophet, and the manager's performance relative to his rivals falls. Precisely to the extent that this manager is accountable to the market, clients' funds flow out of their manager's account to those of rival fund managers, thereby collapsing like an accordion the funds under his management, so that this manager does not profit significantly even when Enron ultimately does collapse. In such an environment, there is little incentive to be ahead of the crowd and considerable incentive to ride the bubble to its top in order not to underperform rival investment managers. The result is 'herding' because, by following the herd, the fund manager will not underperform most of the manager's rivals. Put differently, the fund manager can survive mistakes that others also make, but will be more severely injured by correct decisions that the market only belatedly recognizes. In turn, this may explain why institutions would herd and follow 'sell-side' research that they know to be biased: that is, because they anticipated that others would follow it also, leaving them in the safe position of being part of the herd.

c) The Role of Gatekeepers

This conclusion that even sophisticated investors will follow and rely on 'sell-side' research that they know to be biased brings us back to the central role of gatekeepers. To some degree, gatekeepers will be followed even when they are not trusted, because it is expected that they will influence the market. In addition, there is evidence that gatekeepers 'herd' for careerist reasons. For example, career concerns appear to motivate security analysts not to deviate far from the consensus earnings forecasts, and particularly to avoid downward deviations.[77] As a result, it becomes predictable that some degree of bias will distort analyst recommendations (and that such advice will be followed), even when the market expects inflation. Moreover, ending the most obvious conflicts of interest (as Sarbanes-Oxley and related reforms attempt to do) will not solve this problem, because the careerist motives will remain.

[76] ibid at 26.

[77] H Hong, JD Kubik, and A Solomon 'Security Analysts' Career Concerns and the Herding of Earnings Forecasts' (2000) 31 Rand Journal of Economics 121. See also Hong and Kubik, note 41, at 341-46 (finding systematic tendency towards overly optimistic advice based on careerist considerations).

4. A Preliminary Evaluation

Does it matter which of the foregoing two stories – the deterrence story or the bubble story – is deemed more persuasive? Although they are complementary rather than contradictory, their relative plausibility may bear on whether particular reforms are necessary, desirable, or sufficient. To the extent one accepts the deterrence story, the logical prescription is legal change aimed at restoring an adequate legal threat. In principle, these changes could either raise the costs or lower the benefits of acquiescence to auditors (or both). To the extent one accepts the bubble story, the problem may be self-correcting. That is, once the bubble bursts, gatekeepers come back into fashion, as investors become sceptics who once again demand assurances that only credible reputational intermediaries can provide.[78] Alternatively, structural reforms may be desirable to enhance the independence of analysts, auditors, and other gatekeepers. Clearly, all gatekeepers are not alike. Thus, the deterrence story may work better for auditors than for analysts, while in the case of analysts, structural reforms aimed at increasing the independence of the gatekeeper may outperform litigation remedies.

Part II

C. The Near Future of Gatekeepers: Sarbanes-Oxley and the Looming Litigation Crisis

Historically, bubbles are followed by crashes, which in turn are followed by punitive legislation.[79] The 1999-2003 era is fully consistent with this pattern, and this section will focus on the likely impact of these reforms on gatekeepers. Initially, however, it is useful to categorize the range of strategies that Congress can follow in response to corporate scandals and conflicts of interest.

[78] Federal Reserve Chairman Alan Greenspan has indeed suggested that market corrections will largely solve the problems uncovered in the wake of Enron. See 'Remarks by Chairman Alan Greenspan, 'Corporate Governance' at the Stem School of Business, New York University, New York, New York, March 26, 2002' (available on the Federal Reserves website at <www.federalreserve.gov/boarddocs/speeches>. In his view, earnings management came to dominate management's agenda, and as a result: 'It is not surprising that since 1998 earnings restatements have proliferated. This situation is a far cry from earlier decades when' if my recollection serves me correctly, firms competed on the basis of which one had the most conservative set of books. Short-term stock price values then seemed less of a focus than maintaining unquestioned credit worthiness.' ibid at 4. He goes on to predict that: 'A change in behavior, however, may already be in train.' ibid at 5. Specifically, he finds that 'perceptions of the reliability of firms' financial statements are increasingly reflected in yield spreads of corporate bonds' and that other signs of self-correction are discernible. ibid.

[79] For a discussion of this cycle over history, see Banner, note 6.

I. A Typology of Conflict of Interest Reforms

There is a range of well-recognized strategies for responding to corporate financial scandals, each of which has well-known precedents. While other typologies can undoubtedly be constructed, the following four categories capture most of the realistic regulatory options:

1. Structural Reform

A new body or agency can be created, either public or private, to monitor conflicts and assure higher quality disclosure. The Securities and Exchange Commission, created by the Securities Exchange Act of 1934 in the wake of the 1929 market crash, is probably the clearest example of such a response, but the creation of the Public Company Accounting Oversight Board ('PCAOB') by the Sarbanes-Oxley Act to monitor auditing firms is a modern example that follows in its wake.[80]

Structural reforms can also change the obligations of private actors. For example, the law can create a new gatekeeper. In the 1930s, the federal securities laws and the SEC effectively made auditors into gatekeepers for the public (and not just for the clients who retained their services), and to a limited extent the SEC has already begun to impose gatekeeping responsibilities on attorneys and securities analysts. Part III will suggest that these initial steps should be generalized.

2. Prophylactic rules

Fiduciary law has long simply forbidden some forms of self-dealing between the fiduciary and the beneficiary. Thus, the trustee cannot transact business with the trust estate, because such transactions are either void or voidable. Over the course of the 201h Century, American corporate law largely relaxed the prohibition on self-dealing, provided that certain procedures were followed.[81] Offsetting this trend in state law, however, the federal securities laws introduced new prophylactic prohibitions, including a prohibition on a corporate officer or director

[80] Title 1 of the Sarbanes-Oxley Act creates the PCAOB as a regulatory body subject to SEC oversight, and Section 101(c) of the Act further directs the PCAOB to 'establish or adopt ... auditing, quality control, ethics, independence and other standards relating to the preparation of audit reports for' publicly held issuers. See 15 USC § 7211 (c).

[81] For a detailed discussion of the gradual relaxation over the last 150 years of American corporate law of the once standard prophylactic rule against self-dealing, see H Marsh, Jr 'Are Directors Trustees?' (1966) 22 Bus Law 35. Essentially, disclosure to, and approval by, disinterested directors replaced proof of the transaction's intrinsic fairness as the necessary precondition to sustaining a self-dealing transaction's validity.

retaining the proceeds of certain forms of short-term trading in his or her company's stock.[82] Sarbanes-Oxley has now introduced similar rules, most notably including a prohibition on a public company making or arranging for loans to its executives.[83]

3. Procedural rules

The core of American corporate law is full of procedural rules requiring disclosure of conflicts of interest by corporate officers to disinterested directors.[84] Indeed, American corporate law has largely substituted procedural rules for its former prophylactic prohibitions on conflict of interest transactions. Yet, events at WorldCom, Enron, Tyco and other companies suggest that such rules may not be adequately effective, either because outside directors have too little incentive to monitor diligently or because information costs are too high. Nonetheless, as discussed below, Sarbanes-Oxley also followed this time-honoured path and enacted new procedural rules.

4. Liability rules

The standard response to a corporate scandal is to enhance liability rules, either by increasing penalties, eliminating defences, or creating new private causes of action. The Securities Act of 1933 is here the classic example, as it creates virtual strict liability for the corporate issuer if issuer's registration statement contains a material misstatement or omission.[85] Yet, as discussed below, Sarbanes-Oxley

[82] Section 16(b) of the Securities Exchange Act of 1934, 15 U.S.C. § 78p(b), mandates that senior officers, directors and 10% shareholders must return to the corporation any profits they make, or losses they avert, on purchasing and selling the corporation's stock in any sequence within six months. The provision is a federal rule intended to discourage manipulation of the corporation's stock price by insiders.

[83] Section 402 of the Sarbanes-Oxley Act, which has been codified as Section 13(k) of Securities Exchange Act of 1934, forbids public companies 'directly or indirectly, ... to extend or maintain credit, to arrange for an extension of credit, or to renew an extension of credit in the form of personal loan to or for any director or executive officer ... of that issuer.' See 15 USC § 78m(k). This is in effect a throwback to the form of strict prophylactic rule that characterized 19th and early 20th Century American corporate law.

[84] For an overview of these rules that require disclosure and approval by disinterested directors of a self-dealing transaction, see J Choper, J Coffee and R Gilson *Cases and Materials on Corporations* (5th edn Aspen Publishers Gaithersburg 2000) at 112 to 130. For a representative cases, see: *Weinberger v UOP Inc* 457 A 2d 701 (Del 1983).

[85] Section 11 of the Securities Act of 1933 creates strict liability for the issuer (but grants a variety of affirmative defences to secondary participants) if the registration statement contains a material misstatement or omission of which the purchaser was unaware. See 15 USC § 77(k).

basically did not follow this path, except to the extent that it increased criminal penalties and SEC powers.

II. Congress's Response: The Sarbanes-Oxley Act

Passed almost without dissent, the 'Public Company Accounting Reform and Investor Protection Act of 2002' (popularly known as the Sarbanes-Oxley Act) essentially addresses the problem of accounting irregularities by shifting control of the accounting profession from the profession to a new body: the PCAOB, which is authorized to regulate the profession, establish auditing standards, and impose professional discipline.[86] Conceptually, this is not a new approach, as the PCAOB's authority largely parallels that of the National Association of Securities Dealers ('NASD') over securities brokers and dealers. What is new, however, is explicit recognition of the significance of conflicts of interest, because the Act expressly bars auditors from providing a number of categories of professional services to their audit clients and further authorizes the PCAOB to prohibit additional categories of consulting services.[87] Thus, to the extent that conflicts of interest compromised auditors, the Act responds with a relevant answer.

Yet, if accounting irregularities were more the product of a lack of general deterrence or the increased incentive of corporate executives to 'cook the books' because of the temptations created by stock options, the Act is less clearly responsive to these problems. For example, except in one minor respect, the Act does not seek to revise or reverse the PSLRA;[88] nor does it make gatekeepers liable in private litigation to investors where the gatekeeper knowingly aided and abetted a securities fraud. Finally, the Act never addresses stock options or executive compensation, except to the extent that it may require the forfeiture of such compensation to the corporation if the corporation later restates its earnings.[89] In short, while the potential benefits from acquiescing in accounting

[86] Section 10 1 (c) of the Act enumerates broad powers, including the authority to 'establish ... auditing, quality control, ethics, independence, and other standards relating to the preparation of audit reports for issuers....'

[87] Section 201 of the Act, which is to be codified as Section 10A(g) of the Securities Exchange Act of 1934, specifies eight types of professional services which the auditor of a public company may not perform for its audit client, and also authorizes the PCAOB to prohibit additional services if it determines that they may compromise auditor independence.

[88] Section 804 of the Act does extend the statute of limitation for securities fraud suits, thereby reversing a 1991 Supreme Court decision that had shortened the time period. See note 48.

[89] Section 304 of the Act requires the forfeiture of certain bonuses 'or other incentive-based or equity-based compensation' and any stock trading profits received by a chief executive officer or chief financial officer of an issuer during the 12-month period following the filing of an inflated earnings report that is later restated. This does cancel the incentive to inflate earnings and then bail out, but the enforcement methods applicable to this provision are unspecified and

cont. ...

irregularities appear to have been reduced for auditors, the expected costs to them. from gatekeeper failure also remain low because the level of deterrence that they once faced has not been restored.[90] Arguably then, the Sarbanes-Oxley Act represents an incomplete response. But assumes that courts have not largely filled this void.

III. The Judicial Response

Any assertion that gatekeepers face an inadequate deterrent threat assumes that all other factors affecting their total exposure to liability have remained constant, and this may not be the case. Although the Congress has been cautious about changing the balance of advantage in civil litigation involving gatekeepers, the judiciary may be rapidly shifting that same balance without waiting for legislative direction. The most obvious example of such a shift is the decision in late 2002 in *In re Enron Corp* Sec Derivative & ERISA Litig,[91] which seemingly has outflanked the Supreme Court's decision in Central Bank of Denver,[92] and largely restored private 'aiding and abetting' liability under a different name. In the Enron case, the district court denied the motions to dismiss filed by Enron's auditors, its principal outside law firm, and six major banks, all of whom asserted that they could not be deemed primary violators and so were immune from private suit under Central Bank. In response to their motions, the Court ruled that primary liability could extend to any person who contributes materially false or misleading information to persons who it understands to be preparing or drafting a report or press release to be filed with the SEC or disseminated to the investing public, even though this peripheral defendant neither solicited sales, participated in the actual drafting of the document, nor was otherwise identified in the document so filed or released.[93] The Enron decision not only rejected the majority rule in the federal courts, which seems to permit a private suit against the secondary participant only when the latter makes or authorizes an 'attributed statement' that specifically identifies it and its conclusion,[94] but also went well beyond the few cases that have allowed primary liability to extend to persons who 'substantially

the provision applies only if the earnings restatement is the product of 'misconduct' Ambiguities abound here.

[90] Prior to the 1990s, private litigation was a real (and arguably even excessive) constraining force on auditors. See text and note at note 47.

[91] 235 F Supp 2d 549 (SD Tex 2002).

[92] *Central Bank of Denver NA v First Interstate Bank of Denver* NA 511 US 164, 177 (1994).

[93] 235 F Supp 2d 549, 582-591.

[94] *Wright v Ernst & Young* LLP, 152 F 3d 169, 175 (2^d Cir 1998) (requiring that 'the misrepresentation must be attributed to the specific actor at the time of public dissemination').

participate' in the drafting of an SEC document.[95] Under the Enron ruling, almost anyone who could formerly be reached under 'aiding and abetting' liability now seemingly can be reached as a 'maker' or 'creator' of public statement.[96] Whether the Enron decision is correct can be (and is being hotly) debated. But the more relevant point for this article is that the decision seemingly signals a judicial shift – whether conscious or unconscious – toward imposing greater liability on gatekeepers. Moreover, Enro is not the only recent post-scandal decision to have expanded the scope of liability for secondary participants. In a series of decisions involving Lernout & Hauspie,[97] another federal court has refused to dismiss securities fraud allegations in private class actions against a variety of secondary defendants, including the firm's outside directors, auditors, stock analysts, and others. Unlike the Enron Court, the Lernout & Hauspie Court did not need to focus on whether the defendant corporation's audit committee members had substantially participated in the drafting of SEC reports or press releases. Rather, because each director had signed the defendant's Form 1 O-K, the Court found this fact alone sufficient to deem the audit committee members to have made a fraudulent statement.[98] In an even more sweeping conclusion, the Court further found that audit committee members could be held liable as 'controlling persons' under Section 20(a) of the Securities Exchange Act of 1934. Under long-established SEC rules, 'control' 'means the possession, direct or indirect, of the power to direct or cause the direction of the management and policies of a person.'[99] Although the Lernout & Hauspie Court acknowledged that outside directors were not inherently 'control persons,' it relied on an earlier decision to find that: '[A]n outside director and audit committee member who is in a position to approve a corporation's financial statements can be presumed to have the 'power to direct or cause the direction of the management and policies of the corporation, at least insofar as the 'management and policies' referred to relate to ensuring a measure of accuracy in the content of company reports and SEC registrations that they actually sign.[100] Although this conclusion did not rely on

[95] *In re Software Toolworks Secs Litig* 50 F 3d 615, 627 (9th Cir 1994) (using 'substantial participation' test).

[96] For this assessment, see W Gleeson and J Minier 'Financial Institutions and the Enron Whiplash: The Growing Pain of Rule 10 b-5 Liability' (2003) 22 Banking & Financial Services Policy Report 1.

[97] *In re Lernout & Hauspie Sec Litig* 286 BR 33, 2002 US Dist LEXIS 227089 2002 WL 31662595 (D. Mass. Nov. 18, 2002); see also *Bomberg v SG Cowen* 2002 US Dist LEXIS 23527 (D Mass 9 December 2002) (declining to dismiss action against security analyst who covered the issuer); *In re Lernout & Hauspie Sec Lifting 236 F Supp 2d 161 (D Mass 2003).*

[98] 2002 US Dist LEXIS 22708 at ** 11 to ** 13.

[99] See 17 CFR § 240.12b-2 (defining term 'control').

[100] BR 33; 2002 US Dist LEXIS 22708 at **14 (quoting *In re Livent, Inc Noteholders Sec Litig* 151 F Supp 2d 371, 437 (SDNY 2001); see also *In re Reliance Sec Litig* 135 F Supp 2d 480, 518 (D Del 2001).

the Sarbanes-Oxley Act, which cannot apply retroactively to the facts of Lernout & Hauspie, that statute only reinforces this mode of analysis because it greatly enhances the powers of the audit committee, thus making them look more like 'controlling persons.' As a result, audit committee members would now seem significantly more exposed to personal liability. Finally, although a plaintiff is still required to plead facts raising a strong inference of fraud, the Lernout & Hauspie Court found this last requirement satisfied by the fact that the audit committee members all allegedly had known that their corporation lacked an adequate system of internal controls and that its outside auditor had raised specific problems with its financial reporting.[101] Again, on this basis, many audit committee members could be held liable in the near future.

The net impact of these rulings is to substantially heighten the prospective liability of audit committee members. By signing a periodic report, by helping to draft such a report, or by acquiring knowledge of adverse facts as a 'controlling person,' audit committee members face a non-trivial risk of personal liability. From a public policy perspective, this may be counterproductive because one wants an active, hard-working audit committee to seek diligently to acquire such information. Thus, if the acquisition of adverse information were to make the audit committee potentially liable as 'controlling persons,' a disincentive arises, ironically created by legal rules, for the gatekeeper to do precisely what the law most desires.

On the state level, some signs of a similar, if milder, shift toward imposing heightened responsibilities on directors are also evident in Delaware, where respected members of its judiciary have called for new legislation and an expanded meaning to be given to the critical Delaware concept of 'good faith.'[102] These comments have warned that a conflicted director may not be found to have acted in 'good faith.' 'Good faith' is a key requirement under Delaware law, because, in its absence, a Delaware corporation cannot indemnify an officer or director; in addition, charter provisions eliminating monetary liability for breach of the duty of care (which most public companies in the US now have) are ineffective if the director did not act in 'good faith.'[103] In short, all the judicial straws in the wind point towards a higher risk of liability, although for the present the principal target of this new litigation appears to be directors, rather than gatekeepers.

[101] ibid at ** 8 to ** 10.

[102] WB Chandler III and LE Strine, Jr 'The New Federalism of the American Corporate Governance System: Preliminary Reflections of Two Residents of One Small State' (SSRN Working Paper No id=367720) (2003). Mr. Chandler is the Chancellor and Mr. Strine a Vice Chancellor of the Delaware Chancery Court. See also T Becker 'Delaware Judge Warns Boards of Liability for Executive Pay' *The Wall Street Journal* (6 January 2002) at A- 14.

[103] Delaware General Corporation Law Section 102(b)(7) (permitting charter provision to eliminate due care liability if director acted in 'good faith').

IV. The Prospective Litigation Impact of Reform

Little agreement exists about the overall impact of the Sarbanes-Oxley Act on civil litigation. Some critics have viewed it as more rhetoric than serious reform;[104] others contend that it is a sweeping intrusion into the US's existing system of corporate governance. Both perspectives miss, however, what it most important: Sarbanes-Oxley ushers in and accelerates a major and probably inevitable transition, which will move us from a rules-based system of financial disclosure to a principles-based system. In contrast to Europe, the US has long relied on a rules-based system in which generally accepted accounting principles (or 'GAAP') were precise, technical and limited. Typically, these narrow rules afforded safe harbours from liability for issuers and gatekeepers. In contrast, European accounting principles were broader, more generalized, and sometimes indefinite to the point of being ineffable. As discussed below, Europe could live with this imprecision because Europe is characterized by a relatively low rate of litigation, and thus its issuers did not need to fear American-style entrepreneurial litigation.

Precisely for this reason, however, a shift to a principles-based system exposes American issuers and their gatekeepers to a substantially heightened threat of liability. At the core of a principles-based system is the notion that the issuer must not only comply with GAAP, but must make a 'fair presentation' that provides a full, fair, and holistic picture of the issuer's financial condition and results of operations. In both Sections 302 and 906 of the Sarbanes-Oxley Act, Congress directed the chief executive officer and chief financial officer of every publicly held company to certify in every periodic report filed with the SEC 'that information contained in the periodic report fairly presents, in all material respects, the financial condition and results of operations of the issuer.'[105] This concept of 'fair presentation' is not limited by any reference to GAAP, and compliance with GAAP is clearly not dispositive of whether the issuer has provided a fair presentation. Instead, the standard seems to intend that the issuer provide full and fair disclosure in the form of a holistic picture of the company that reveals all material financial weaknesses, even if their disclosure were not required by GAAP.

[104] LA Cunningham 'The Sarbanes-Oxley Yawn: Heavy Rhetoric. Light Reform (and it Might Just Work)' (2003) 35 U Conn L Rev 915.

[105] The quoted language is from Section 906, which has been codified as 18 USC § 1350, a penal code provision (emphasis added). Section 302 of Sarbanes-Oxley Act uses slightly different language: 'the financial statements, and other financial information included in the report, fairly presents in all material respects the financial condition and results of operations of the issuer as of, and for, the periods presented in the report.' No difference in scope or meaning seems intended by this slight difference in phrasing.

Actually, this concept of 'fair presentation' was once the standard prescribed by Judge Henry Friendly for the Second Circuit in *United States v Simon*,[106] but over recent years Simon had seemingly become a forgotten decision, honoured more in the breach than in the observance.[107] Virtually overnight, however, Enron and related scandals have resuscitated Simon's concept of 'fair presentation' The reason for its revival is obvious: Enron showed beyond argument that a rules-based system of financial disclosure could be gamed and distorted to the point that investors could have little confidence in it. Even if newer and tighter rules were drafted, practitioners would predictably stay one step ahead of regulators by finding new ways to game and evade narrow and specific rules. As a result, Congress and the SEC framed the Sarbanes-Oxley Act's new certification requirements in terms of the Simon case, and in interpreting this new requirement, the SEC has cited Simon for the proposition that: 'Presenting financial information in conformity with generally accepted accounting principles may not necessarily satisfy obligations under the antifraud provision of the federal securities laws.'[108]

While this shift to a principles-based system is obviously consistent with the public's post-Enron mood, it poses significant risks for issuers and gatekeepers. Cases that might have been dismissed on summary judgment now seem more likely to survive, because the claim that full and fair disclosure was not provided is hard to resolve pre-trial. Here, the differences between the European and the American legal environment become starkly apparent. Lacking class actions, contingent fees, or the 'American rule' that generally precludes fee-shifting against the plaintiff, Europe experiences little securities litigation and hence can tolerate abstract generality in the formulation of its accounting rules. In contrast, US issuers are likely to encounter greater difficulty in any transition to accounting principles framed in broad-brush strokes. The combination of broad disclosure obligations and a legal environment that encourages class litigation means both a higher volume of litigation and higher settlement values to claims against gatekeepers and outside directors.

Nonetheless, this transition appears inevitable, not only because of recent scandals, but because of globalisation as well. Globalisation necessitates a common, world-wide accounting language. Under their 'Norwalk treaty,' the Financial Accounting Standards Board ('FASB') and the International Accounting

[106] 425 F 2d 796, 807-09 (2^{d} Cir 1969).

[107] No Circuit Court decision that I have found over the past twenty years appears to cite the Simon case in a decision upholding civil or criminal liability for securities fraud. The decision has been cited by dissenting judges who believed that a case should not have been dismissed or overturned. See, eg *In re K-Tel Int'l Sec Litig* 300 F 3d 881, 906 (8th Cir 2002). The last decision citing it favourably in a decision favouring private plaintiffs or the SEC appears to have been *SEC v Seaboard CM* 677 F 2d 1301, 1313 (9th Cir 1982).

[108] Securities Exchange Act Release No 33-8124 (9 September 2002) at *57279 n 55.

Standards Board ('IASB') are committed to developing international accounting standards that both US and European regulators will accept.[109] Europe has little interest in moving towards a rule-based regime, and the FASB cannot credibly push in this direction after Enron. As a result, the development of a common global accounting language will likely finish what Enron started: namely, the demise of a rules-based system.

So where do these trends leave us? The original issue was what level of legal threat would optimise deterrence. Too high a level of liability may cause the contemporary markets for gatekeeping services to fail, and too low a level invites future Enrons. This recognition has two implications that inform Part Hl. First, public policy should attempt to focus liability rules so that they punish laxity, but do not employ an overwhelming level of deterrence. Second, to the extent that it is impossible to define on a practical level the optimal level of legal threat and to the extent that courts appear to be increasing that threat on their own today, other types of legal rules – structural, prophylactic and procedural – may merit greater attention and should be blended into any overall policy response.

Part III

D. The Future Gatekeeper: Remedies for Gatekeeper Failure

Three linked problems dominate any attempt to redefine the role or restructure the obligations and liabilities of market gatekeepers:

First, public policy must strike an appropriate balance between excessive liability and an inadequate legal threat. Precise calibrations are probably impossible because volatile, exogenous factors – such as the public's mood, including both its scepticism of corporate actors and its desire for retribution – can quickly change the actual legal threat faced by gatekeepers. This is a uniquely American problem because the prospect of large class actions and jury decision-making is almost unique to the American legal system. On the practical political level, the most relevant and plausible reform would be to increase the legal threat that gatekeepers face by restoring to 'aiding and abetting' liability. Yet, if this were done at the same time as public (or judicial) attitudes became more sceptical of the business community generally (and gatekeepers specifically), the result arguably might be to generate overdeterrence. The dilemma here is that if the gatekeeper faces excessive risks that it cannot pass on to the client in its fees, the market for

[109] The two bodies – the FASB and the IASB – announced in October 2002 that they were committed to achieving convergence between their respective accounting standards by 2005 with an initial exposure draft being scheduled for late 2003. See 'Convergence of Global Accounting Standards; Regulatory Watch.' Accounting Today 25 January 2003, at 512 (describing memorandum of understanding between the two bodies).

gatekeeping services may simply fail. That is, established firms would cease to offer auditing services, and only smaller, less risk averse firms would undertake this role, gambling that they could reap a high return before litigation destroyed them.

Second, public policy must eliminate or minimize the impact of perverse incentives that give the gatekeeper an incentive not to investigate. For example, in securities litigation against auditors, the defence is frequently raised by the auditors that they were deceived by corrupt managements on whom they had justifiably relied. Often, this may be true, but it can still create an incentive not to inquire too closely – lest one acquire information that should place one on notice. More generally, the Private Securities Litigation Reform Act requires a particularized pleading at the outset of the case that gives rise to a 'strong inference of fraud.'[110] In the case of accountants, this standard means that more than reckless indifference must be shown and as of the very outset of the action, when typically little is known about the accountant's involvement. As a result, the auditor who remains ignorant of the fraud, even though reckless inattentive, probably escapes liability.

But how much can we realistically expect of the auditor? Auditors have long argued that there is an 'expectations gap' between what the public wants to do and their actual capacity.[111] This expectations gap is greatest, they assert, when it comes to the ability of auditors to detect fraud or illegal acts.[112] Of course, any profession has a collective self-interest in reducing its own risk of liability or public criticism. Still, the result may be that the accounting industry spends great time, effort, and expense in seeking to reduce the public's expectation that it should be able to detect fraud, rather than single-mindedly enhancing its capacity to do so. Courts in turn devote considerable time and resources seeking to distinguish those cases in which the auditor knew of the fraud from those in which it was merely negligent. This effort may, however, be socially wasteful if an alternative legal regime could be designed under which auditors were held liable for any undetected fraud without exposing them to penalties that caused the market to fail. Such an alternative system would be superior both because (i) it would not require courts to make often difficult and costly determinations as to whether the auditor was complicit in the fraud or merely negligent and (ii) it would maximize

[110] Section 21D(b)(2) of the Securities Exchange Act of 1934, 15 USC §78u-3 (requiring complaint to 'state with particularity facts giving rise to a strong inference that the defendant acted with the required state of mind').

[111] For an overview of asserted 'expectations gap', see C Pacini, MJ Martin and L Hamilton 'At the Interface of Law and Accounting: An Examination of a Trend Toward a Reduction In the Scope of Auditor Liability to Third Parties in the Common Law Countries' (2000) 37 Am Bus L J 171, 215-217 (discussing the 'expectations gap'); see also B Porter 'An Empirical Study of the Audit Expectation-Performance Gap' (1993) 24 Acct & Bus Res 49.

[112] Over 70% of investors questioned in one survey expected absolute assurance that material misstatements due to fraud would be detected. See M Epstein and M Geiger 'Investor Views of Audit Assurance: Recent Evidence of the Expectations Gap' (January 1994) J Acct 60.

the auditor's incentive to detect fraud (as opposed to explaining it away as undetectable). Of course, any shift in this direction of strict or negligence based liability also increases the prospect that the market for auditing services might collapse under the weight of excessive liability – unless a ceiling is placed on damages.

Third, public policy must also strike an acceptable balance between the obligation of client loyalty and the role of protecting the integrity of the market. This is the unique problem associated with asserting that securities attorneys owe gatekeeper obligations – either legal or ethical – to investors, as well as to their clients. Defenders of the traditional advocacy role of the lawyer find this conflict unbridgeable, and argue that imposing gatekeeper obligations on attorneys will simply 'dry up' the free flow of information between attorney and client, thus possibly resulting in greater illegality. This section finds this claim to be unsupportable. Rather, it concludes that the primary consequence of imposing gatekeeper obligations on attorneys will be to increase their leverage over their clients.

I. Striking the Balance on Liability

On the theoretical level, some commentators have proposed that gatekeepers should be held strictly liable for client misconduct.[113] Under such a system, for example, an auditor would pay damages whenever its client, the issuer, made a material misrepresentation or omission in its financial statements, without regard to whether the auditor knew, or was negligent in failing to detect, the misrepresentation or omission. The rationale for such a strict liability system is that it will induce auditors to implement the optimal combination of auditing, bonding, and other measures to detect financial irregularities (whether or not fraudulent) without imposing the considerable burden on courts that our current fault-based system does.[114] Obviously, under such a system, gatekeepers will raise their fees, but this increase is presented as one of the attractions of this approach because it forces the client that cannot convince its auditor that it presents a low risk of fraud or material error to bear a higher fee. In a perfect market, the issuer would thus bear the expected social cost of the fraud, which would in turn imply that the only issuers that could access the market would be 'those for whom the value of

[113] Frank Partnoy has proposed such a strict liability regime for underwriters, auditors and attorneys in light of Enron. See F Partnoy 'Barbarians at the Gatekeepers?: A Proposal for a Modified Strict Liability Regime' (2001) 79 Wash U L Q U91. See also A Hamdani 'Assessing Gatekeeper Liability' (Harvard Law and Econ Working Paper 2003).

[114] Partnoy, note 113, at 514.

the public financing exceeds the harm caused by fraud.'[115] Put more simply, very high audit fees should tend to deter the fraudulent actor.

Although possibly optimal in theory, enormous problems surround implementation of any such proposal. First, as even its proponents acknowledge, the gatekeeper may not be able to distinguish ex ante the 'honest' client from the 'fraudulent' one. Hence, it will charge both a single common fee – but a much higher one. Predictably, this inflated fee structure will allow the 'fraudulent' client still to access the market, but may well drive many honest clients from the market.[116] Even if we relax this assumption and assume that some broad risk classifications could be made, it still remains true that, to the extent these classifications are broad and general, then some clients within each category will pay too little and others too much.

Moreover, the increase in audit fees would have to be enormous in order to enable auditors to survive under a regime of strict liability. During the collapse of the high tech bubble in 2000 and 2001, publicly held firms audited by the Big Five fell by over $ 1 trillion in market value.[117] Under a strict liability regime, the auditor would be jointly and severally liable for this amount with the issuer, at least if a material misrepresentation or omission were shown. To protect itself against such exposure, the auditor would need to charge a fee that funded its expected liability costs – which loss could potentially reach into the tens of billions of dollars.[118] Most clients could simply not pay such an amount, and all would oppose such a fee increase with sufficient vigor as to make the adoption of strict liability politically infeasible.

[115] Hamdani, note 113, at 6. This analysis rests on a broader economic analysis that sees strict liability as superior to negligence-based liability in two respects: first, strict liability gives the principal actors optimal incentives to comply with legal requirements, while freeing courts from the need to make imperfect and error-prone liability determinations, and, second, it induces the principal actors to adopt an optimal level of activity. See S Shovel *Economic Analysis of Accident Law* (Harvard University Press Cambridge MA 1987) 6-7.

[116] This is, of course, the core consequence of a 'lemons market' in which the quality of the product cannot be easily determined. See G Akerlot 'The Market for Lemons: Quality Uncertainty and the Market Mechanism' (1970) 84 Q J Econ 488.

[117] Indeed, one survey of 33 public firms that restated their earnings finds that the Big Five audited companies that fell in value by roughly $ 1.3 trillion. See S Taub 'Big Five Gets Low Grades For Performance' <Economist.com> 12 July 2002 (noting fall from $ 1.8 trillion to only $ 527 billion in market capitalization).

[118] Of course, securities class actions today settle for a fraction of their asserted losses. But this fraction will certainly rise (and steeply) if we moved to a strict liability regime. Even today, neutral third parties have placed the likely settlement value of some outstanding securities class actions at $ 1 billion or higher. See M Peers 'Suits Cloud AOL's Optimism; Cost of Settling Holder Litigation May Hurt Effort to Cut Debt' *Wall Street Journal* (1 May 2003) B2 (estimating settlement cost of securities class action against AOL Time Warner Inc at $ 1 billion).

Given the risk of being rendered insolvent by a single client, some auditors also might simply cease to offer auditing services. Conceivably, their position in the market might be filled by smaller, risk-preferring 'fly-by-night' firms that would hope to charge very high fees for the short-term and then liquidate on an adverse determination (and protect their partners' assets through use of limited liability organizational forms, such as the limited liability company or partnership).

Finally, there still remains the possibility of litigation error. Even under a regime of strict liability, it would still be necessary to show that the issuer made a material misrepresentation or omission before the auditor could be held vicariously liable.[119] Given the potential of stock price drops resulting in damages of $ 100 billion or more, this means that litigation errors would be bankrupting to the auditor, which in turn means that the auditor would be under great pressure to settle such litigation. Such pressure in turn exacerbates the problem of 'extortionate' or 'frivolous' litigation. Stock prices can fall for a variety of reasons that are unrelated to fraud or misrepresentation. Yet, if the stock price decline is great enough, an almost irresistible incentive arises for the plaintiff s attorney to sue, as it has now been freed from the burden of alleging, pleading, or proving fraud or scienter. Hence, the prospect of 'frivolous' or 'extortionate' litigation increases in direct proportion to the degree to which one moves toward a strict liability regime.

II. Designing a 'Stricter' Liability Approach: A Proposal

For all these reasons, the 'real world' issue becomes whether a second-best substitute can be devised for a strict liability regime that sidesteps or minimizes the foregoing problems. The most practical means to this end may be to convert the gatekeeper into the functional equivalent of an insurer, but one who backs its own certification with an insurance policy that was capped at a realistic level. As a result, the gatekeeper's liability would be divorced from any showing of fault, but would also be limited to a level that achieves adequate deterrence without causing the market for gatekeeping services to unravel. Under this approach, for example, if the corporate client were found liable for $ 100 million, then the auditor would have to contribute toward that liability up to the amount of its policy. The one mandatory element in this proposal would be that the minimum floor on the gatekeeper's insurance policy would have to be an adequate multiple of the highest annual revenues received by the gatekeeper from its client over the last several years. For purposes of illustration, let's use a multiplier of ten. Now, on the facts

[119] In addition, it would be necessary for the plaintiff to prove loss causation, as otherwise in its absence the plaintiff would receive a seeming windfall. Thus, some complex litigation issues will still remain.

of the Enron case, where it has been widely reported that Arthur Andersen received roughly $ 52 million from Enron in its final year, Andersen's liability would be not less than $ 520 million (ie, $ 52 million times ten). This is a large number, but it does not approach the roughly $ 87 billion loss in market capitalization that Enron experienced and for which Andersen could conceivably be held liable under a strict liability regime. In a more typical case where the auditor receives only a $ 2 million audit fee from the client, the damages would be reduced to only $ 20 million. Hence, the market for gatekeeping services could easily function under this proposal. The auditor might also purchase insurance to cover its exposure, but to the extent it passed along this added insurance cost on to its clients, it would automatically increase the minimum required floor on its policy under the mandatory 10:1 ratio between minimum liability and direct or indirect revenues from the client.

Some will recognize this proposal as bearing considerable resemblance to Professor Partnoy's modified strict liability proposal.[120] Under his innovative proposal, the client and the gatekeeper would contract for the gatekeeper to bear a minimum percentage of the issuer's losses, possibly subject to a requirement that the gatekeeper must bear some specified minimum percentage.[121] Suppose the minimum percentage set by Congress in an amendment to the federal securities laws were 5%. If so, on the earlier Enron example, Andersen would be required to pay 5% of Enron's $ 87 billion loss or $ 4.35 billion.

There are essentially three practical differences between these two similar proposals: (1) Professor Partnoy's system is essentially contractual, while this proposal is essentially regulatory; (2) Professor Partnoy uses a percentage of the damages as its potential minimum floor, while this proposal uses a multiple of the gatekeeper's highest annual revenues from the client; and (3) while the potential damages, as calculated under Professor Partnoy's proposal, could often bankrupt the gatekeeper, bankruptcy would rarely follow when a multiple of the revenues from the client generated the required minimum floor on the gatekeeper's insurance obligation. Thus, this proposal could actually be supported by the relevant profession, once they recognized that their existing exposure to liability could be even higher. It thus falls (if only barely) within the range of political feasibility.

This proposal's refusal to accept private contracting (in contrast to Professor Partnoy, who relies primarily on contracting and disclosure) is based on three considerations: First, some gatekeeping professions (most notably, auditing) are extremely concentrated, and thus conscious parallelism in the pricing behaviour

[120] Partnoy, note 113, at 540-46; see also S Choi 'Market Lessons for Gatekeepers' (1998) 92 Nw U L Rev 916, 951-59. Professor Choi appears to have been the first to suggest that the issuer and the gatekeeper should contract over the share of the gatekeeper's liability for the losses experienced by the issuer's investors.

[121] Partnoy, note 113, at 540. Actually, Professor Partnoy does not clearly insist that there be a minimum floor placed on the auditor's liability below which they could not deviate by agreement, but notes that Congress could impose such a minimum percentage. ibid.

of the few actors in the industry becomes likely. Put more simply, if there are only four major auditing firms at present, it becomes unlikely that they would compete vigorously and accept liability significantly above any minimum required threshold.

Hence, it is simpler to specify that threshold (but also permit the parties to provide by contract for even greater liability). Second, in a bubble, investors might not care that their gatekeepers were accepting only a minimum liability, and thus the disclosure of the contract between the gatekeeper and the market might have little impact on the market. Third, a contractual approach overlooks that the corporate client may have little incentive to bargain for high liability on the part of the auditor. Not only will higher auditor liability not meaningfully reduce the liability of the client (given the typical relative disparity in their assets), but corporate managers may actually want the auditor to have a low ceiling on its liability in order to make it easier to induce the auditor to acquiesce in risky accounting practices favoured by management. Put more simply, if management wants to inflate earnings in order to maximize the value of their stock options, the lower the liability faced by their auditors, the easier it will be for management to convince them to acquiesce in dubious accounting policies.

The key conceptual difference between the two proposals involves this proposal's more explicit adoption of a deterrence framework. Prior proposals for making the auditor an insurer have relied on a tort law rationale, which tries to force the tort feasor to internalise the social costs of its actions by making it pay a higher fee. As earlier discussed, this is impractical, given the potentially astronomical liabilities involved. From a deterrence perspective, however, the goal of reform shifts from internalisation of the externalities to prevention. Under standard deterrence theory, prevention requires that the expected punishment cost exceed the expected gain.[122] Professor Partnoy's proposal to use a percentage of the issuer's losses as the minimum floor on contracting does not bear any functional relationship to the expected gain; nor does it increase the penalty to compensate for the limited risk of detection.

To illustrate the difference between the two proposals consider a very large issuer that experiences a sudden \$ 50 billion decline in its market capitalization as the result of accounting irregularities. Assume further that the issuer's auditor had received only \$ 10 million in fees, and that Professor Partnoy would limit the auditor's exposure to 10% of the total loss (or \$ 5 billion). Thus, there is here a 500:1 ratio between the auditor's projected liability (\$ 5 billion or 5% of the losses) and its own gain (\$ 10 million). This represents over deterrence – unless one thinks there is only a 5% chance of detection. In even a minimally efficient market, however, the prospect of detection of accounting irregularities seems far higher than that. In contrast, this article would impose a ceiling on auditor liabil-

[122] See generally, GS Becker 'Crime and Punishment: An Economic Approach' (1968) 76 J Pol Econ 169.

ity at $ 100 million (or 10 times its gain). Obviously, this article's proposal of stricter liability with a lower ceiling based on a multiple of the revenues from the client creates less liability, but still gives the gatekeeper ample incentive to utilize all monitoring controls (including closer monitoring of its own agents) that are reasonably likely to reduce the prospect of fraud or earnings manipulation. Also, this approach reduces the prospect of 'frivolous' or extortionate litigation directed against the auditor based only on the total amount of the investor losses. Above all, this approach prevents the market for gatekeeping services from unravelling.

How strict should a stricter system of liability be? Here, we enter the thicket of political realism. Pure strict liability might be the best rule, but it is probably not politically acceptable to auditors. Nor does it seem defensible to impose a significantly higher standard of liability on the auditor than on its client, the issuer. In this light, the highest standard of liability that might be politically attainable in the case of auditors would be that set forth already for auditors in Section II of the Securities Act of 1933, which requires the auditor as an expert to prove as an affirmative defence that the auditor 'had, after reasonable investigation, reasonable grounds to believe and did believe that it were true'.[123] In effect, the burden would be shifted to the auditor in all Rule 1 Ob-5 actions to prove its non-negligence and good faith belief in its statements.

III. Implementing the Gatekeeper Role of Attorneys

The foregoing proposal for 'stricter liability' has been primarily framed with auditors in mind. But should it apply to other gatekeepers, such as, for example, attorneys or stock analysts? Here, some basic distinctions among gatekeepers need to be recognized. While the auditor inhabits a relatively precise and rule-bound world, the analyst is essentially a prognosticator whose predictions about the future are frequently wrong. Thus, imposing strict liability on the analysts, given their necessarily higher rate of error, represents a virtual death sentence for the analyst. In addition, the analyst cannot pass on its higher exposure to liability to its client in the form of higher fees, because the analysts are not paid by the corporate issuer (but rather by investors through brokerage commissions). If brokerage commissions were increased, investors simply turn to discount brokers (or others), who did not use stock analysts.

The case of the attorney presents even greater differences: First, functionally, attorneys act only occasionally as gatekeepers, certifying or verifying information for investors, while auditors perform this function primarily (and increasingly exclusively). Second, the role of gatekeeper arguably conflicts with the more typical roles performed by attorneys as either advocates or transaction engineers for their clients. Third, asking attorneys to serve as gatekeepers may dry up the

[123] Section 1 1 (b)(3)(B) of the Securities Act of 1933, 15 USC § 77(k).

flow of confidential information between and client, thereby jeopardizing the ability of the attorney to serve the client. Based on these premises, the bar (and its academic defenders) have vehemently argued that, if the attorney were compelled to serve as a watchdog, instead of as an advocate or transaction engineer, for the client, the client could no longer depend on the attorney as a zealous advocate or transaction engineer.[124]

But even if there is an inconsistency between these roles, what does this imply? At least in theory, one could separate the roles of the attorney as gatekeeper from that of the attorney as transaction engineer by employing multiple counsels. That is, the corporation could use different law firms: one to plan and structure and the other to supervise disclosure. Obviously, this would be costly, because duplicative work would be performed. Yet, this is what Sarbanes-Oxley essentially did to the accountant, divorcing the roles of auditor and consultant because of the clear conflict of interest. Arguably, the same conflict is present in the case of the attorney. In any event, such a separation need not be legally mandated in the case of the attorney, because it could be left to the corporation to decide if it felt sufficiently threatened by an attorney who was under a legal obligation to make full disclosure that it wished to hire multiple counsels.

Although the SEC has long taken the position that any attorney who knowingly files a false or misleading statement or document with the SEC aids and abets the client's fraud,[125] it has never articulated a general statement of the attorney's gatekeeper role. In particular, the SEC's recent rules under Section 307 of the Sarbanes-Oxley Act, which authorizes the SEC to promulgate minimum standards of professional conduct for securities attorneys, focus only on the reporting of material violations of law and make no broader attempt to provide any conceptual overview of the attorney's responsibility to investors.[126] Although the SEC has commendably focused on the controversial issue of whether a securities attorney should ever be required to make a 'noisy withdrawal' that would warn investors of pending illegality, it has ducked the broader and seemingly prior issue of the attorney's overall obligations to these investors. For example, minimum standards of professional conduct could (1) require the attorney to perform reasonable due diligence with respect to the statements made in disclosure documents that the attorney drafts for the corporate client; (2) mandate standards of independence for attorneys performing certain sensitive tasks; and (3) subject the attorney to professional discipline for negligence or malpractice, thus giving the

[124] For a detailed exposition of this argument that the roles of the attorney and the gatekeeper are essentially inconsistent and that attorneys make poor informational and reputational intermediaries, see JE Fisch and KM Rosen 'Is there Role for Lawyers in Preventing Future Enrons?' (forthcoming in Villanova Law Review in 2003) (available on SSRN Electronic Library at id= 367661).

[125] eg *SEC v Fehn* 97 F3d 1276 (9th Cir 1995).

[126] Securities Release No 33-8185 (29 January 2003) (adopting final rule establishing standards of professional conduct for attorneys who appear or practice before the Commission).

SEC a useful enforcement tool in cases where it suggest misconduct but cannot easily prove scienter.

On the still undefended premise that securities attorneys should serve as gatekeepers for investors, this article will make three specific proposals. First, the SEC should adopt a limited certification requirement mandating that a securities attorney acknowledge that it has reviewed the non-financial disclosure in publicly filed reports; second, it should establish independence standards for attorneys performing certain tasks that require them to be independent of management, such as the conduct of internal corporate investigations for publicly held firms; and third, the SEC should deem negligence by attorneys in the preparation of SEC disclosure documents to amount to unprofessional conduct for which attorneys could be disciplined under the SEC's Rules of Practice (just as auditors can be disciplined today).[127] Uniting these proposals is the idea that the attorney should perform a due diligence investigation of the corporation's non-financial disclosures that roughly corresponds to the auditor's role with respect to financial disclosures.

1. A Negative Assurance Certification

A certification requirement applicable to attorneys can be justified simply on the grounds of consistency. Today, a publicly-held corporation's CEO and CFO must certify that each periodic report 'fairly presents in all material respects' the issuer's 'financial condition and results of operations.[128] Similarly, the securities analyst must also today certify that the analyst truly agrees with his or her research advice to investors.[129] Thus, managers, auditors and analysts all certify their work, but the corporation's principal counsel does not. Arguably, the attorney should not be able to escape a corresponding obligation, particularly because the auditor takes no responsibility for the textual portion of the disclosure document, which is independent of the financial statements that the auditor certifies. In effect, attorney certification mandates a parallel expert to review the non-financial disclosures of the public corporation, but the attorney as gatekeeper would not be asked to perform an audit or check facts in the manner that an auditor does.

[127] Rule 102(e)(1)(iv) of the SEC Rules of Practice, 17 CM § 2001.102(e)(1)(iv) (authorizing SEC to suspend or censure an accountant for 'a single instance of highly unreasonable conduct ... [or] ... repeated instances of unreasonable conduct.'

[128] See text and notes at notes 105 to 109 (discussing certification requirements under Sections 302 and 906 of Sarbanes-Oxley).

[129] Securities Act Release 33-8193 (20 February 2003) (adopting Regulation AC, which requires a research analyst employed by a broker or dealer to certify that the views expressed in the research report accurately reflect his or her personal views).

Specifically, the attorney principally responsible for preparing a document or report filed with the SEC should certify (1) that such attorney believes the statements made in the document or report to be true and correct in all material respects, and (2) that such attorney is not aware of any additional material information whose disclosure is necessary in order to make the statements made, in the light of the circumstances under which they were made, not misleading.'[130] The real thrust of this proposal is to require the issuer to subject its principal disclosure documents to the scrutiny of an attorney who would be under a professional obligation to exercise some level of 'due diligence' in their review.[131] Today, there is no barrier to the preparation and filing of such documents entirely by non-professionals.

In essence, this proposed certification simply tracks the language of Rule 10b-5. More importantly, however, this obligation would only generalize existing practices in the market because today, in most public underwritten offerings, issuer's counsel does deliver an opinion to the underwriters stating that it is not 'aware' of any material information required to be disclosed that has not been disclosed.[132] SEC rules would therefore simply be requiring for 1934 Act periodic filings what is already done in the primary market for 1933 Act disclosure docu-

[130] Issues could arise as to which attorney was principally responsible for preparing a document. The simplest answer to this issue is to require the corporation to disclose the identity of such attorney in the filing and then require that attorney's certification.

[131] An open question, on which this article takes no position, is whether such review should be by an attorney 'independent' of management – a term that additional SEC rules could define.

[132] For a description of this standard opinion in registered public offerings, see R Howe 'Rethinking Legal Opinion Letters: The Duties and Liabilities of Attorneys in Rendering Legal Opinions' [1989] Colum Bus L Rev 283, 287. The author of this article, a partner at the New York firm of Sullivan and Cromwell, properly observes that 'such opinions are not really 'legal opinions' at all in that they do not state any legal conclusion but only say that the attorney believed certain facts to be true.' ibid. Precisely for this reason, such an opinion is more a pledge of the law firm's reputational capital, which the underwriters demand. The counsel giving such opinion does not purport to conclude that all information required to be disclosed has been disclosed (as an auditor might by analogy), but only that it lacks personal knowledge or belief as to any such failure. See also RJ Gilson 'Value Creation by Business Lawyers: Legal Skills and Asset Pricing' (1984) 94 Yale L J 239, 291 (also describing such opinions); RW Painter 'Toward A Market for Lawyer Disclosure Services: In Search of Optimal Whistleblowing Rules' (1991) 63 Geo Wash L Rev 221, 226-27 and n 19 (discussing judicial interpretation of such opinions). The American Bar Association has characterized this type of opinion as a 'negative assurance' and finds such opinions to be 'unique to securities offerings.' See ABA Comm on Legal Opinions, Third-Party Opinion Report. Including the Legal Opinion Accord of the Section of Business Law, American Bar Association (1991) 47 Bus Law 167, 228. Although the ABA considers it generally inappropriate for attorneys to request such 'negative assurance' opinions from other attorneys, the special context of securities offerings is exempted, reflecting the fact that underwriters consider such an assurance to be necessary to them. That the A-BA, as the representative of the bar, 'disfavours' such opinions because of the demands they place on the attorney probably only underscores the value of such a reform.

ments; the real difference is that the case of periodic filings under the Securities Exchange Act, there is no analogue to the underwriter to demand such an opinion or certification from the attorney. Thus, SEC action would fill this void. In addition, such a requirement would have a profound symbolic and psychological effect on the bar because it would recognize the attorney's obligations as a gatekeeper. Ideally, the SEC should go even further and require the attorney to certify that the attorney so believed 'after making such inquiry that the attorney reasonably believed appropriate in the circumstances'; this would establish at least a minimal due diligence obligation.

Admittedly, limits need to be recognized on what an attorney can certify. Because the attorney does not audit its client, the attorney should not be asked to certify the accuracy and completeness of all information disclosed in SEC filings. Thus, the proposal here made requires only a negative certification that the attorney had no reason to believe, and did not believe, that the information was materially false or misleading. Legally, such a certification would trigger 'aiding and abetting' liability if the attorney was aware of materially false or misleading information, and it could even trigger criminal liability under various federal statutes. But its primary effect is to recognize that the securities attorney is a gatekeeper for investors.

2. Independence

Auditors, of course, must be independent of their client, and SEC rules have long defined tests for auditor independence. Increasingly, a new literature has warned that attorneys are becoming too economically interconnected with their client to exercise independent judgment, as the result in part of the increasing practice of law firms taking (and even demanding) equity stakes in the client in return for professional services.[133] If some level of independence is necessary for an attorney to function as a gatekeeper, SEC rules of professional conduct could define these limits. To illustrate, a law firm that holds in its portfolio 10% of the corporate client's equity (or, alternatively, equity in the client equal to 10% of its own net asset value) will probably be a poor, or at least a biased, monitor.

In any event, the context that is most sensitive and would most benefit from such rules is that of internal corporate investigations. Often, such investigations are mandated by the SEC, and typically the resulting reports are filed with the SEC. Should the corporation's normal outside counsel perform such an investigation? Or, should SEC rules define the level of independence necessary to conduct such a more sensitive inquiry? Absent SEC action, individual state bar asso-

[133] JS Dzienkowski and RJ Peroni 'The Decline in Lawyer Independence: Lawyer Equity Investments in Clients' (2002) 81 Texas L Rev 405; R de R. Baronies 'Professionalism Consequences of Law Firm Investments In Clients: An Empirical Assessment' (2002) 39 Am Bus L J 379.

ciations will either do nothing (the most likely outcome) or prescribe different and inconsistent standards, thereby creating needless disparities. Uniform standards for corporate internal investigations are desirable and as a practical matter can only come from the SEC. There is no need to offer precise rules here, but only to recognize that professionals are expected to be independent of their clients. Accordingly, the SEC should read Section 307 to grant it authority to define the point at which the attorney is not sufficiently independent of the client to perform certain sensitive tasks.

3. The Due Diligence Obligation

Certification is only a first step. The next logical step would be to mandate due diligence by the attorney in preparing or reviewing SEC filings as a minimum standard of professional conduct. Here, Sarbanes-Oxley changes the picture significantly, because Section 307 of Sarbanes-Oxley authorizes the SEC to establish 'minimum standards of professional conduct for attorneys appearing and practicing before the Commission'. This reference to 'professional conduct' would certainly seem to empower the SEC to adopt rules requiring the attorney both to conduct a minimal due diligence review before the attorney files a document or report with the SEC and to certify its good faith belief in the accuracy of the statements made therein. Indeed, in its existing Rules of Practice, the SEC already holds auditors to precisely such a standard and asserts the power to suspend or disbar them for merely negligent conduct.[134] If this can be done without special statutory authority, then it seems to follow a fortiori, after the enactment of Section 307, that the SEC could require attorneys to take reasonable steps to investigate the accuracy of statements made in documents that they prepare.[135]

The bottom line then is that the SEC is today empowered to adopt rules that could suspend or disbar an attorney for negligence as a form of professional misconduct. Negligence would clearly not support a private cause of action under Rule 1 Ob-5, but it may be the appropriate standard for the imposition of sanctions under Section 307.[136] Such a trade-off – ie public liability but not private

[134] See 17 CFR § 201.102(e)(iv) (specifying that two forms of 'negligent conduct'– either 'a single instance of highly unreasonable conduct' or 'repeated instances of unreasonable conduct' – could trigger sanctions under Rule 102(e).

[135] The attorney would, of course, be entitled to rely on the auditor with respect to financial information certified by the auditor, as in the case of the 'reliance on an expert' defence under Section 1 l (b)(3)(c) of the Securities Act of 1933. See 15 USC Section 77(k)(b)(3)(c).

[136] Historically, the SEC did once hold attorneys liable for professional negligence in 'aiding and abetting' cases. See *SEC v Spectrum Ltd* 489 F 2d 535, 536 (2d Cir 1973). This is no longer possible after the Supreme Court mandated a scienter standard in Hochfelder, but sanctions for professional misconduct could look to a similar standard.

liability for negligence – again seems desirable in that it enhances deterrence without threatening insolvency for law firms.

IV. Accessing Counter-Arguments: Can Attorneys Be Gatekeepers?

Any assertion that the SEC should compel the securities attorney to play a greater gatekeeping role inevitably runs into the argument that such a role is either inappropriate for attorneys or will reduce their clients' willingness to confide in them. The first claim that such a role is inappropriate depends largely on one' s vantage point. Litigators tend to view the attorney as an advocate for, and protector of, the client – a bulwark between the client and an oppressive state.[137] Securities attorneys are less ready to buy into this rhetoric, however, and do not have the same self- image of themselves. For the most part, they agree that they have at least an ethical responsibility to perform due diligence on documents they draft and file with the SEC. For over a quarter century, prominent securities attorneys have recognized that, as a result, their professional role is closer to that of the auditor than to that of the litigator.[138] The key elements that distinguish the attorney as advocate from the attorney as gatekeeper are: (1) a need for greater independence from the client; (2) a recognition of a duty to the public; and (3) professional

[137] EA Davis 'The Meaning of Professional Independence' (2003) Colum L Rev 1281 (arguing that the SEC's up-the-ladder reporting rules inhibit professional independence).

[138] The literature here is enormous, but one brief statement by a securities lawyer of iconic reputation stands out above the field. In 1974, in a famous and much quoted address, AA Sommer, Jr, then an SEC Commissioner, gave an address in which he initially described the securities attorney not as an advocate but rather as 'the field marshall who coordinate[s] the activities of others engaged in the registration process.' See AA Sommer, Jr 'The Emerging Responsibilities of the Securities Lawyer, Address to the Banking, Corporation & Business Law Section, N.Y. State Bar Ass'n' (24 January 1974), reprinted in LD Soderquist and T Gabaldon Securities Regulation (Foundation Press New York 4th edn 1999) 617. Then, based on his description of the attorney as more a transaction engineer than an advocate, he offered his normative assessment: 'I would suggest that in securities matters (other than those where advocacy is clearly proper) the attorney will have to function in a manner more akin to that of auditor than to that of the attorney. This means several things. It means that he will have to exercise a measure of independence that is perhaps uncomfortable if he is also the close counsellor of management in other matters, often including business decisions. It means he will have to be acutely cognizant of his responsibility to the public who engage in securities transactions that would never have come about were it not for his professional presence. It means that he will have to adopt the healthy scepticism toward the representation of management that a good auditor must adopt. It means that he will have to do the same thing the auditor does when confronted with an intransigent client – resign.' ibid at 317-319. Although Commissioner Sommer never used the term 'noisy withdrawal' in this speech, the same concept seems to have been, more or less, on his mind, and the elements that he does specifically enunciate – high independence, duty to public investors, professional scepticism – probably are the key elements that distinguish the attorney as advocate from the attorney as gatekeeper.

scepticism.[139] Exactly these differences need to be recognized by the SEC under Section 307.

The more important counter-argument to imposing gatekeeper obligations on securities attorneys is that attorneys will be unable to communicate as freely with their clients if gatekeeper obligations or 'noisy withdrawal' requirements were imposed. In response to this claim, it is first necessary to recognize that the ultimate goal of the law is to achieve law compliance, not to maximize uninhibited communications between the attorney and the client.[140] The norm of client confidentiality is a means to an end, not the end in itself.

Still, even with this concession, it remains true that lawyers can counsel most effectively when there is open, relatively unconstrained communication between their clients and themselves. Hence, the practical issue becomes whether gatekeeper obligations would necessary chill desirable attorney/client communications. The stress here should be on the word 'desirable.' What would be the likely impact of the SEC's proposed 'noisy withdrawal' standards on such communications? Here, a starting point for this analysis should be the recognition that the client knows little law and will almost always want to know if contemplated action is illegal. From this premise, it follows that the corporate official contemplating prospective action will still inquire of counsel whether the course of action under consideration is lawful. Indeed, the more the government pursues white-collar criminal prosecutions and punitive regulatory actions in the contemporary post-Enron environment, the more in turn that corporate officers are likely to inquire before they act. When then will communications be most likely to be chilled? The obvious answer is that the officer who has already acted may fear inquiring of an attorney if the officer's conduct was lawful – precisely because the officer fears that the attorney may be under an obligation to report unlawful actions to higher authorities or, indirectly, to the SEC. In short, it is the 'ex post' inquiry by the client of the attorney that is most likely to be chilled.

If one accepts this premise that ex ante communications between counsel and the client are less likely to be chilled than ex post communications, several implications follow: First, the impact of imposing gatekeeper obligations on attorneys may be socially desirable. In a well-known article, Professors Kaplow and Shavell have argued that the case for protecting ex ante communications between attorneys and clients is far stronger than the case for protecting ex post communi-

[139] AA Sommer, note 138, at 317-319.

[140] Thus, the 'crime/fraud' exception to the attorney/client privilege makes some communications between attorney and client discoverable, even though this result thereby arguably makes clients less ready to confide in their attorneys. The justification for this result, which applies similarly to this context, is that communications so excluded from the privilege are deemed socially undesirable. For the current status of this exception, see *In re Richard Roe, Inc* 168 F 3d 69 (2d Cir 1999). See also DN Zarnow and K Krakaur 'On the Brink of a Brave New World: The Death of the Privilege in Corporate Criminal Investigation' (2000) 37 Am Crim L Rev 147 (suggesting that the client/client privilege is already highly qualified in this context).

cations.[141] Advice before action leads individuals to comply with the law, they argue, whereas ex past advice does not provide a guide for action and may simply allow the defendant to reduce the expected penalty costs, thus encouraging illegality. It is not necessary to fully accept the Kaplow/Shavell analysis to see that its core distinction between ex ante and ex post advice suggests that we should be more concerned about chilling 'ex ante' communications between attorney and client. But this is not what most gatekeeper obligations do; rather, they may induce such communications by making 'ex post' advice less possible.

Second, requiring 'noisy withdrawals' and 'up-the-ladder' reporting also has a deterrent value that is independent of this issue of whether the initial corporate actor will still consult counsel. Few significant actions within a corporation can be taken by a single actor. Decisions made by one person still need to be implemented by others. Thus, even after the initial corporate actor has taken an irrevocable step (and will thereafter be arguably less willing to consult with counsel ex post), other corporate actors will need to be contracted and convinced to cooperate with the initial actor. They will have every incentive to consult with counsel because they are still at the 'ex ante' stage. In turn, knowledge that others are necessarily likely to learn of the original actor's conduct and to consult with counsel about its legality may deter the original actor. The modern public corporation is embedded with in-house attorneys, and even the possibility that they will report 'up the ladder' should deter some illegal conduct. Hence, even if under some conditions there may be less direct communication between corporate actors and counsel, knowledge that sooner or later counsel is likely to learn ex post can still deter corporate actors ex ante.

As a result, the principal practical effect that imposing gatekeeper obligations will have on clients is that a client who has been advised by an attorney that contemplated action is unlawful now has greater reason to heed that attorney's advice – again precisely to the extent that the client believes that the attorney may be under a legal obligation to report any misconduct (either inside the corporation or outside). Thus, even if it were true that clients would consult less, this impact could be more than fully offset by the fact that it would become more dangerous to disregard the lawyer's advice. Add to this mix the likelihood that 'ex ante' advice will not be chilled, and the net impact is to increase the attorney's leverage over the client by making it more dangerous to ignore the attorney's advice. If law compliance is the goal, such an impact seems socially desirable.

[141] L Kaplow and S Shavell 'Legal Advice About Information to Present in Litigation: Its Effects and Social Desirability' (1989) 102 Harv L Rev 565; see also R Posner 'An Economic Approach for the Law of Evidence' (1999) 51 Stan L Rev 1477, 1531-33.

E. Conclusion

The diagnosis of 'gatekeeper failure' made in Part I of this article leads naturally to a two-part prescription for gatekeepers: deterrence and empowerment. Deterrence is easy, but it can be overdone. Thus, although this article has favoured a shift towards stricter liability, it has coupled this recommendation with a proposed ceiling on liability set at the level necessary to deter the gatekeeper. In essence, this proposal subordinates compensation to deterrence – but only with regard to litigation against gatekeepers, who are seldom in any event in a position to fund full compensation to the investor class.

Empowerment is a trickier question. If we are to reduce accounting and financial reporting irregularities, the optimal strategy has to both motivate and empower gatekeepers to insist upon law compliance. In the case of the attorney, the first step toward making the securities attorney a gatekeeper should be to enhance their leverage over their clients in order to enable them to exert greater pressure for law compliance. A mandatory attorney certification standard, enforced by a due diligence obligation, does essentially this by forcing the client to seek the attorney's review. In addition, a 'noisy withdrawal' standard reduces the possibility that the client will disregard the attorney's advice or 'shop' for a favourable opinion from the most compliant attorney.

Gatekeeper empowerment necessarily requires intruding upon our existing guild-like structure of private self-regulation of the professions. Sarbanes-Oxley already does this in the case of the accounting and analyst professions, but the SEC has not yet compelled the legal profession to recognize that – like it or not – attorneys are also gatekeepers. To be sure, law firms cannot be insurers in the manner that accounting firms could, but their choice is not 'all or nothing.' Professions, like guilds, will predictably resist any increase in their responsibilities and liabilities to the public, but, if reforms are pressed, they will lose. Still, in the absence of gatekeeper reform, the certainty remains that recurrent gatekeeper failure will continue.

Corporate Governance and Auditor Independence: The Battle of the Private Versus the Public Interest

WERNER F. EBKE*

Recent high-profile cases of audit failures in the European Union and the United States illustrate that a professional audit of a public company's financial statements by an independent auditor is a cornerstone of any modern corporate governance system and an essential prerequisite for the proper functioning of the capital and securities markets. The European Union and the United States Congress have responded to the enormous challenges resulting from the high-profile audit failures by strengthening the rules on auditor independence. In addition, the public oversight of listed companies and their auditors has been increased. The present chapter throws some light on the role and position of the independent statutory auditor within the corporate governance system of public companies and then analyses key issues of auditor independence in light of recent statutory and regulatory developments on both sides of the Atlantic. The chapter concludes that accountants can discharge their public responsibility only if they are truly independent of their audit client – both in appearance and in fact.

A. Introduction

Financial accounting, auditing and disclosure of audited financial and non-financial information are essential prerequisites to the proper functioning of securities and capital markets.[1] Functioning securities markets, in turn, are a vital element

* I would like to thank John C. McGowan, J.D., Southern Methodist University Dedman School of Law, Dallas, Texas, for his valuable contributions to this paper.

[1] W Ebke 'Accounting, Auditing, and Global Capital Markets' in Th Baums, KJ Hopt and N Horn (eds) *Corporations, Capital Markets and Business in the Law. Liber Amicorum Richard M. Buxbaum* (Kluwer The Hague 2000) 113; W Ebke 'The Impact of Transparency Regulation on Company Law' in KJ Hopt and E Wymeersch (eds) *Capital Markets and Company Law* (OUP Oxford 2003) 173.

of the market for corporate control which, as we know, is one of the most effective means of any *external* corporate governance system.[2] In addition to their contribution to the effectiveness of the *external* corporate governance system,[3] financial accounting, auditing and disclosure contribute greatly to the effectiveness of the system of *internal* corporate governance. In its Report on a Modern Regulatory Framework for Company Law in Europe ('Winter Report'), the High Level Group of Company Law Experts ('High Level Group') recognizes that accounting and auditing are 'fundamental elements of a corporate governance system'.[4] The Group also emphasizes that requiring disclosure of financial and non-financial information can be a powerful regulatory tool in monitoring corporate management. Financial accounting aims at the presentation of the company's financial status and performance in meaningful and comparable terms on the basis of applicable laws, regulations, rules and generally accepted accounting principles (GAAP). Audits of financial statements by independent professionals are to ensure that a company's financial statements are prepared and presented by the company's executives in accordance with applicable laws, regulations, rules and GAAP. The disclosure of the company's certified financial and non-financial information enhances the accountability for, and the transparency of, the company's governance and its business and affairs.

Enron, WorldCom, FlowTex, ComRoad, Balsam Procedo, Bremer Vulkan, MLP, Crédit Lyonnais, Vivendi and similar high-profile cases of audit failures have revealed that a proper audit of a company's financial statements is a cornerstone of any modern corporate governance system. To remedy deficiencies in the audit practice and to close what is commonly referred to as 'expectations gap',[5] efforts have been made at a national, supranational, and international level to strengthen the role and position of those who are entrusted with performing independent audits of financial statements and other relevant information, to develop meaningful and reliable standards on auditing (Generally Accepted Auditing Standards – GAAS), and to enhance the professional qualifications of inde-

[2] eg KJ Hopt and E Wymeersch (eds) *European Takeovers. Law and Practice* (Butterworth London 1992); W Ebke 'Unternehmenskontrolle durch Gesellschafter und Markt' in O Sandrock and W Jäger (eds) *Internationale Unternehmenskontrolle und Unternehmenskultur* (Geburtstag Verlag JCB Mohr Tübingen 1994) 7, 21-28; B Grossfeld and W Ebke 'Controlling the Modern Corporation: A Comparative View of Corporate Power in the United States and Europe' (1978) 26 American Journal of Comparative Law 397, 425-426.

[3] eg Institut der Wirtschaftsprüfer *Wirtschaftsprüfung und Corporate Governance* (Düsseldorf and Frankfurt am Main 2002).

[4] The High Level Group of Company Law Experts, 'Report on a Modern Regulatory Framework for Company Law in Europe' (Brussels, 4 November 2002) 44 (hereinafter cited as 'Winter Report') (see Annex 3 in this volume).

[5] eg European Contact Group 'Responding to Market Expectations. An Action Plan to Reduce the Expectation Gap' (Brussels 1996); Fédération des Experts Comptables Européens 'Continuous Quality Assurance – Statutory Audit in Europe' (London 1998).

pendent auditors. At the centre of this development are the issues of the auditor's independence, the auditor's selection and compensation, the rotation of the key audit partner, the scope of statutory audits, the detection of management fraud and irregularities, audits of forecasts and risk assessments, audits of management's discussions and analysis, the reporting of the results of the audit, the interaction between the statutory auditor and the company's audit committee, the role and responsibilities of internal auditors, quality control and peer review and, last but not least, the auditor's civil liability to the client and third parties. The issues mentioned are the subject of intensive discussions, both in Europe and in the United States.

I. European Initiatives

In the European Union (EU), the issue of statutory auditors' independence was addressed as early as 1996 by the EU Commission's Green Paper on 'The Role, the Position and the Liability of Auditors in the European Union',[6] which received the support of the Council, the Economic and Social Committee, and the European Parliament. In its Green Paper, the Commission pointed out several areas that might lend themselves to improvement and further action at EU level. The Green Paper was intended to raise awareness of all interested parties in the issues at stake and to elicit their comments. The Commission itself launched a study on the role, the position and the liability of the statutory auditor, which was carried out by the Maastricht Accounting and Auditing Research Center (MARC).[7] The issues raised in the Green Paper were discussed at a conference held in Brussels on 5 and 6 December 1996.[8] It became evident that the member states' rules on statutory auditors' independence differ in several respects, such as: the scope of persons to whom independence rules apply, both within the auditing firm and outside the firm; the kind of financial, business and other relationships that a statutory auditor, an audit firm or an individual within the firm may have with an audit client; and the safeguards which need to be put in place. This situation makes it difficult to provide investors and other stakeholders in EU companies with a uniformly high level of assurance that statutory auditors perform their audit function independently throughout the EU. As a result of the EU Commission's 1998 Communication 'The Statutory Audit in the European

[6] Green Paper 'The Role, the Position and the Liability of Auditors in the European Union' OJ C 321 (28 October 1996) 1.

[7] W Buijink, S Maijoor, R Meuwissen and A van Witteloostuijn 'Final Report of a Study on the Role, Position and Liability of the Statutory Auditor within the European Union' (Brussels and Luxembourg 1996).

[8] The papers presented at the conference are published in European Commission (ed) 'Act of the Conference on the Role, the Position and the Liability of the Statutory Auditor within the European Union' (Brussels and Luxembourg 1997).

Union, the Way Forward',[9] the EU Committee on Auditing was created. The Committee established statutory auditor independence as one of its priorities. Finally, the Commission's Communication 'EU Financial Reporting Strategy: The Way Forward' underlines the importance of a statutory audit carried out in accordance with uniformly high levels across the EU, including a common approach to professional ethics standards.[10]

Agreement was reached in the Committee on Auditing that each Member State should provide statutory auditors, regulators, and the interested public with a common understanding of the independence requirement by the application of fundamental principles. This approach, the Committee believes, will bring about consistency in addressing facts and circumstances which threaten a statutory auditor's independence throughout the EU. In the opinion of the Committee, the existence of such principles should also help to provide a level playing field for the provision of statutory audit services within the single European market. The Committee emphasized that the principles should be comprehensive, rigorous, robust, enforceable and reasonable, and that they should be consistently interpreted and applied by statutory auditors and their clients as well as professional bodies, supervisors, regulators and other interested parties. The Committee also stressed the importance of common standards on auditors' independence for the creation of a single European capital market as outlined by the Financial Services Action Plan and endorsed by the Stockholm European Council.

On the basis of the Committee's work and proposals, the EU Commission published its Recommendation of 16 May 2002 on 'Statutory Auditors' Independence in the EU: A Set of Fundamental Principles'.[11] While it is not intended to provide an exhaustive list of all the circumstances in which threats to auditor independence might arise, the Recommendation deals, in an incredibly detailed fashion, with such subjects as non-audit services provided by auditing firms to their audit clients, the rotation of key audit partners and the employment of a former audit partner by the audit client. The Commission suggests that the

[9] EC Communication 'The Statutory Audit in the European Union, the Way Forward' OJ C 143 (8 May 1998) 3.

[10] Communication 'EU Financial Reporting Strategy: The Way Forward' COM (2000) 359.

[11] Commission Recommendation 'Statutory Auditors' Independence in the EU: A Set of Fundamental Principles (2002/590/EC)' OJ L 191 (19 July 2002) 22 (hereinafter cited as EU Recommendation). For a thorough analysis of the Commission's recommenations, see K van Hulle and G Lanfermann 'Mitteilung der Europäischen Kommission zur Stärkung der Abschlussprüfung' (2003) 58 Betriebs-Berater 1323; M Niehues 'Unabhängigkeit des Abschlussprüfers – Empfehlung der EU-Kommission – Hintergrund und Überblick' (2002) 41 Wirtschaftsprüferkammer-Mitteilungen 182. For a comparative analysis of the SEC's proposed rule 'Strengthening the Commission's Requirements Regarding Auditor Independence' see S Schmidt 'Neue Anforderungen an die Unabhängigkeit des Abschlussprüfers: SEC-Verordnung im Vergleich mit den Empfehlungen der EU-Kommission und den Plänen der Bundesregierung' (2003) 58 Betriebs-Berater 779.

Member States decide whether they want to apply the same independence standards to unlisted companies as applicable to listed companies.[12] In addition, the Commission suggests that the Member States determine whether or not its recommended auditor independence standards should also be applied to statutory audits of companies operating in regulated industries.[13] In the preamble of its Recommendation, the EU Commission strongly emphasizes the responsibility of the audit profession to uphold auditor independence as a means to assure audit quality. The Commission has announced that it will review the situation three years after the adoption of the Recommendation, 'taking into account international developments', to determine whether its Recommendation has brought about the desired harmonization within the EU.[14] Its review, the Commission states, will specifically address the question of to what extent the Recommendation has had an impact on auditor independence where auditors have provided non-audit services to audit clients. The Commission emphasizes that there is general agreement in the EU Committee on Auditing and in the Contact Committee on the Accounting Directives on the fundamental principles of the Commission's Recommendation.[15] In addition, the Commission has announced that it will produce a further Communication on policy issues which would deal with the role of independent auditors, a code of ethics for auditors, auditor's liability and the public oversight of the audit profession.[16]

The High Level Group supports the Commission's initiatives and has urged the Commission to proceed with its further Communication.[17] The High Level Group itself has focused primarily on the *internal* aspects of auditing, in particular on the responsibility of the board of directors for audits.[18] The High Level Group correctly emphasizes the management's responsibility for the company's financial statements.[19] While it does not express a view as to the structure of the board of directors (one-tier board versus two-tier board structure), the Group makes it clear that the responsibility for the audit of the company's financial statements should lie with non-executive or supervisory directors the majority of whom should be independent.[20] The audit committee which in practice is set up for this purpose, plays a key role in the relationship between the executives and the external auditor. The High Level Group sets forth provisions on the role and

[12] EU Recommendation (n 11) Preamble para 10.

[13] ibid.

[14] ibid para 15.

[15] ibid para 16.

[16] Winter Report (n 4) 70.

[17] ibid.

[18] ibid.

[19] ibid 67.

[20] ibid 70.

responsibilities of the audit committee[21] and recommends that the EU Commission include the provisions in the Commission's Recommendation on the role of non-executive and supervisory directors.[22]

II. The Sarbanes-Oxley Act

In the United States, Congress responded to the enormous challenges resulting from the various high-profile audit failures by enacting the Sarbanes-Oxley Act, which was signed into law by President George W. Bush on 30 July 2002.[23] Title II to that Act adds Sections 10A(g) through 10A(l) to the Securities Exchange Act of 1934 and requires that the Securities and Exchange Commission (SEC), within 180 days of enactment, adopt rules to carry out each of those sections. On 2 December 2002, the SEC proposed amendments to its existing requirements regarding auditor independence to enhance the independence of accountants who audit financial statements and prepare attestation reports filed with the SEC.[24] The proposed rule recognizes the need to enhance the independence of accountants who audit and review financial statements and prepare attestation reports filed with the SEC.[25] The proposed rule also emphasizes the critical role played by audit committees in the financial reporting process and the unique position of audit committees in assuring auditor independence.[26] As directed by the

[21] ibid 71.

[22] ibid 71.

[23] 107 Pub L No 204, 116 Stat 745.

[24] SEC, Proposed Rule, Strengthening the Commission's Requirements Regarding Auditor Independence, SEC Release 33-8154 (2 December 2002) (hereinafter cited as SEC Proposed Rule). The Final Rule 'Strengthening the Commission's Requirements Regarding Auditor Independence', SEC Release 33-8183A (26 March 2003) (hereinafter cited as SEC Final Rule on Auditor Independence), became effective 6 May 2003.

[25] Consistent with the SEC's Proposed Rule on auditor independence (n 24), the SEC's Final Rule on Auditor Independence applies to audit firms domiciled in the United States as well as to foreign audit firms.

[26] As directed by the Sarbanes-Oxley Act of 2002, the SEC adopted a new rule to direct the national securities exchanges and national securities associations to prohibit the listing of any security of an issuer that is not in compliance with the audit committee requirements mandated by the Sarbanes-Oxley Act of 2002. See SEC, Standards Relating to Listed Company Audit Committees, SEC Release 33-8220 (9 April 2003). The requirements of the new rule, which became effective 25 April 2003, relate to: the independence of audit committee members; the audit committee's responsibility to select and oversee the issuer's independent accountant; procedures for handling complaints regarding the issuer's accounting practices; the authority of the audit committee to engage advisors; and funding for the independent auditor and outside advisors engaged by the audit committee. Under the rule, listed issuers must be in compliance with the new listing rules by the earlier of their first annual shareholders meeting after January 15, 2004, or October 31, 2004. Foreign private issuers and small business issuers will have additional time to comply.

Sarbanes-Oxley Act of 2002, the proposed rule focuses on key aspects of auditor independence. The rule would

- revise the SEC's regulations related to the non-audit services that, if provided to an audit client, would impair an accounting firm's independence;
- define the circumstances whereby an issuer's audit committee can and should pre-approve all audit and allowable non-audit services provided to the issuer by the auditor of an issuer's financial statements;
- prohibit any partner on the audit engagement team from providing audit services to the issuer for more than five consecutive years;
- prohibit an accounting firm from auditing an issuer's financial statements if certain members of the management of that issuer had been members of the accounting firm's audit engagement team within the one-year period preceding the commencement of audit procedures;
- require that the auditor of an issuer's financial statements report certain matters to the issuer's audit committee, including 'critical' accounting policies used by the issuer;
- require disclosures to investors of information related to the audit and non-audit services provided by, and fees paid by the issuer to, the auditor of the issuer's financial statements.

In addition, the proposed SEC rule would define an accountant as not being independent from an audit client if any partner, principal or shareholder of the accounting firm who is a member of the engagement team received compensation based on any service provided or sold to that client other than audit, review and attest services.

Additionally, the SEC has proposed a Framework for Enhancing the Quality of Financial Information Through Improvement of Oversight of the Auditing Process.[27] The proposed rule would reform oversight and improve accountability of auditors of public companies, thereby enhancing the reliability and integrity of the auditing and financial reporting processes. Furthermore, moving to a different private sector regulatory structure, a new 'Public Company Accounting Oversight Board' (PCAOB) was created by the Sarbanes-Oxley Act[28] The PCAOB, a private, non-profit corporation made up of five full-time members, was established to oversee the audit of public companies that are subject to the federal securities laws, in order to protect the interests of investors and further the public interest in the preparation of informative, accurate, and independent audit reports for companies the securities of which are sold to, and held by and for, public investors. The PCAOB will also oversee the auditors of public companies and sanction accounting firms and individuals for violations of pertinent laws, regulations and rules.

[27] SEC Release 33-8109 (26 June 2002).

[28] Sarbanes-Oxley Act Sec 101(a).

III. Objectives

The various legislative and regulatory initiatives on both sides of the Atlantic emphasize the growing awareness among corporate lawyers, economists, legislatures, regulators, standard-setting bodies and others that statutory audits by independent professionals are a fundamental element of any corporate governance system and an essential prerequisite for the proper functioning of the securities and capital markets. In accordance with the directions given by the organizers of this conference, this chapter will throw some light on the role and position of the independent statutory auditor within the corporate governance system of public corporations (Section II). The paper will then focus on the complex and complicated issue of the external auditor's independence, in particular key aspects such as non-audit services provided by auditing firms to their audit clients, the rotation of key audit partners and the employment of a former audit partner by the audit client (Section III). Furthermore, this paper will briefly address the question of public oversight of the audit profession and statutory audits (Section IV). Throughout, the chapter will focus primarily on external auditors of listed companies (within the meaning of the Winter Report)[29] the shares of which are traded regularly in a regulated securities market, although references to 'open' companies and 'closed' companies (within the meaning of the Winter Report)[30] will also be made where appropriate.

B. The Role and Position of the Independent Auditor

The role, position and responsibilities of the independent auditor need to be seen in the broader context of the governance of large publicly-held corporations who, owing to their size, provide innumerable opportunities for far-reaching influence in social, economic, and political affairs.[31]

I. Exclusive Rights and Reciprocal Duties

A growing dissatisfaction with traditional internal control devices for public corporations, which had too often proved to be inefficient in view of the separation of ownership and control and the complexity of modern business practices, created a demand for external 'watchdog' devices. One of the most common and probably most effective external devices of control is the requirement of periodic

[29] Winter Report (n 4) 35.

[30] ibid.

[31] W Ebke 'In Search of Alternatives: Comparative Reflections on Corporate Governance and the Independent Auditor's Responsibilities' (1984) 79 Nw U L Rev 663.

presentation and disclosure of the company's status and performance in monetary terms. Today, large enterprises are required to summarize their status and performance in meaningful terms not only to their management, but also to their shareholders, employees, creditors, potential investors, and, because of their 'public function', to the public at large.[32] To give these parties access to the company's financial information, the financial statements (which include a balance sheet, an income statement and, in some countries, a statement of changes in financial position), together with management's discussion and analysis, generally must be sent to shareholders and must be filed with a special register, a government agency or other public or private regulatory body that oversees the securities markets. In addition, in several countries, the financial statements are required to be published in an official or semi-official bulletin, which is generally made available to the public.

Since shareholders, creditors, and other third parties ought to be able to rely on corporate financial statements, the laws of all EU member states and federal legislation in the United States now require that an independent auditors annually audit the financial statements at least of the listed companies and express an opinion as to the fairness and adequacy of their financial disclosures.[33] The legislatures on both sides of the Atlantic were careful to tailor the auditor's position vis-à-vis the corporation in such a way as to suit the auditor's function: Instead of making the external auditor an officer or agent of the audited company, the legislatures required the auditor to be independent of management, both in appearance and in fact.[34] The accounting profession was granted exclusive rights to perform the statutory audit function. Today, the audit function is generally performed by licensed professional accountants, known as 'Commissaire aux comptes' in France, 'Wirtschaftsprüfer' in Germany, 'Revisore contabile' in Italy or 'Registered Accountants' in the United Kingdom, to mention only a few of the presently fifteen member states of the EU, or 'Certified Public Accountant' in the United States. As a general rule, professional auditors are licensed by the government, provided they meet certain requirements of educational training and practical experience and pass a professional exam prepared and graded by either government authorities or the auditors' professional organization. Public accountants who audit financial statements are, as a general rule, subject to the ethical and professional standards of their professional organizations and, in some cases, to administrative as well as disciplinary measures of special governmental agencies or semi-official institutions.

[32] For a more detailed exposition of the 'public function' theory and its legal implications, see W Ebke *Die Arbeitspapiere des Wirtschaftsprüfers und Steuerberaters im Zivilprozess* (Otto Schmidt Cologne 2003) 39-41.

[33] W Ebke (n 31) 672-73. For the United States, see 15 USC 78j-1 (2003).

[34] For details, see, eg W Ebke 'Commentaries' in K Schmidt (ed) *Münchener Kommentar zum Handelsgesetzbuch* (CH Beck Munich 2001) § 316 annotations 26-28.

Although the accounting profession was granted exclusive rights to perform vital audit services, legislatures on both sides of the Atlantic were rather reluctant to define the reciprocal duties of the statutory auditor. Most importantly, most legislatures affirmatively decided to *not* set the standards that the external auditor is required to apply in conducting an independent statutory audit. Rather, legislatures typically require only that the auditor act with 'reasonable care' and 'impartially', and they leave the development of pertinent auditing standards to the profession or professional organizations, subject, at least in some countries, to the oversight by government agencies or private regulatory bodies and, eventually, the courts.[35] Historically, the accounting profession has also played a key role in shaping the standards on auditor independence. The standards vary, however, from country to country.[36] At present, there is no internationally accepted ethics standard for statutory auditors' independence that could be used as a benchmark for national independence standards. In view of the increasing role of the independent auditor for both internal and external corporate governance systems, scholars and, in light of recent audit failures, legislatures, securities commissions, policy makers and others recognize a need for greater auditor independence. As a result, the law, regulations and rules on auditor independence are being revised and refined to reflect the growing awareness that statutory auditors perform a vital public service to assure adequate corporate governance and financial market integrity.

II. 'Public Watchdog' Function

The view that financial statements are prepared and audited by an independent professional auditor not only for the use of the company that employs the auditor and pays his or her fees, but also for the benefit of shareholders and other stakeholders who have no contractual relationship with the auditor has long been recognized in Western legal systems. The view is most clearly expressed in the 1930 Draft of a German Corporation Code which, for the first time in the history of German corporation law, proposed a statutory audit for all public corporations ('Aktiengesellschaften'). The official Comment to the Draft states:

> Regular audits which are provided for by a number of foreign laws, can, as is especially demonstrated by the experiences in England, contribute considerably to the recovery of the corporate system and to its protection. Such a control appears also

[35] For a comparative analysis, see W Ebke and D Struckmeier *The Civil Liability of Corporate Auditors: An International Perspective* (Kluwer London 1994); W Ebke *Wirtschaftsprüfer und Dritthaftung* (Bielefeld 1983). For a discussion of the law of the member states of the EU, see W Ebke 'Die Haftung des gesetzlichen Abschlussprüfers in der Europäischen Union' (2001) 100 Zeitschrift für Vergleichende Rechtswissenschaft 62.

[36] For a recent comparative study, see N Demme *Die Unabhängigkeit des Abschlussprüfers nach deutschem, US-amerikanischem und internationalem Recht* (Baden-Baden 2003).

> to be necessary since numerous companies ... have become a central pool of national capital. A thorough audit is thus not only in the interest of the corporation, its creditors and shareholders, but also in the interest of the economy at large.[37]

A similar thought was expressed in the United States by the SEC, which over 45 years ago stated:

> The responsibility of a public accountant is not only to the client who pays his fee, but also to investors, creditors and others who may rely on the financial statements which he certifies.[38]

In England, too, it is argued that financial statements are prepared, audited and published not only for the benefit of the members and creditors of the audited company, but also for the public generally.[39]

In view of these statements one can hardly deny that professional auditors, once primarily engaged to inform management of irregularities and inefficiencies, have become independent external analysts of financial statements in the public interest. In the words of the United States Supreme Court, the statutory auditor

> assumes a public responsibility transcending any employment relationship with the client. The independent public accountant performing this special function owes ultimate allegiance to the corporation's creditors and stockholders, as well as the investing public.[40]

The 'public watchdog' function demands that the auditor maintain total independence from the audit client at all times, both in appearance and in fact, and requires complete fidelity to the public trust.

C. Auditor Independence

Independence in fact is maintained through 'direct evidence of the auditor's mental state.'[41] Independence in appearance 'recognizes that generally mental states can be assessed only through observation of external facts.'[42] An auditor is, as a general rule, considered to be not independent unless 'a reasonable investor, with knowledge of all relevant facts and circumstances, would conclude that the

[37] Reichsjustizministerium (ed) *Entwurf eines Gesetzes über Aktiengesellschaften und Kommanditgesellschaften auf Aktien sowie Entwurf eines Einführungsgesetzes nebst Erläuternden Bemerkungen* (Berlin 1930) 115 (my translation).

[38] *In Re Touche, Niven, Bailey & Smart* 37 SEC 629, 670 (1957).

[39] L Gower *Principles of Modern Company Law* (4th edn London 1979) 523.

[40] *United States v Arthur Young & Co* 104 S Ct 1495 (1984).

[41] AICPA Statements on Auditing Standards (SAS) No 1, AU 220-01-02 (1988).

[42] ibid.

auditor is not capable of exercising objective and impartial judgment.'[43] In the words of the EU Commission's Recommendation of 16 May 2002, '[p]rinciples and rules on statutory auditor independence should allow a reasonable and informed third party to evaluate the procedures and actions taken by the statutory auditor to avoid or resolve facts and circumstances that pose threats or risks to his objectivity'.[44] Objectivity, as a state of mind, and professional integrity should be the overriding principles underlying a statutory audit opinion on financial statements. Auditor independence both in appearance and fact builds trust and confidence. The lack of, or serious doubts as to, a statutory auditor's independence has far-reaching effects not only on those who rely on certified financial statements for their investment or other decisions, but also on the securities and capital markets, the corporate governance system and, ultimately, the public at large. Independence issues arise in a great variety of situations. As the EU Commission's Recommendation of 16 May 2002, points out correctly, '[s]tatutory auditors' independence can be affected by different types of threats, including self-interest, self-review, advocacy, familiarity or trust, and intimidation'.[45] Opinion shopping and compensation structures are 'classic' examples to illustrate the point.

I. Opinion Shopping

Although the auditor is primarily concerned with the audit client's financial accounting system, reports and internal controls, the auditor is also concerned with getting paid and retaining clients. If clients are not successful, the auditor will eventually lose the client. If the client is not satisfied with the audit, the auditor may lose the client or have collection problems. In many respects, audits are commodities. Without revenue generating clients, the auditor will not be able to operate, regardless of his adherence to independence standards and his duties to the public. This situation demonstrates the auditor's significant interest in promoting client success and satisfaction. The auditor's interest in maintaining successful and satisfied clients often conflicts with his or her duty to the public and create independence problems. When such a conflict arises, many commentators believe that the client's bargaining power outweighs that of the auditor because of the auditor's financial dependence on the client. In the United States, as many as eight hundred clients per year change auditors in what is known as 'opinion shopping'.[46] There are many documented cases of opinion shopping,

[43] ibid.

[44] EU Recommendation (n 11) A 1 (3).

[45] ibid A 3 (1).

[46] R Tucker and E Matsumura 'Going Concern Judgments: An Economic Perspective' (1998) 10 Behav Res in Acct 179, 181.

which suggest that it continues to be common despite mandatory SEC disclosure requirements.[47] By contrast, several European countries, including Germany, have adopted laws or rules that make it difficult, if not virtually impossible, for a listed company to terminate the audit engagement once the auditor has been elected by the general shareholders meeting and the audit agreement between the auditor and the company has been concluded.[48] Auditor swapping itself is not the main problem, however; the main problem is the client's ability to use the threat of auditor swapping to influence the audit and the auditor's opinion.[49] The threat may be so real as to result in an inadequate audit. As Louis Lowenstein noted recently, '[t]he SEC has been seeing a vast amount of cheerleading for clients by the very accountants on whose independence we rely. The accountants have come to see their auditing work less as a profit-centre guided by professionalism than as a lever for obtaining more lucrative consulting assignments.'[50] Despite the concerns by the SEC and several observers, the American Institute of Certified Public Accountants (AICPA), in the 1990s, continued to believe that there was 'no evidence that audit failure has been caused by a lack of independence.'[51]

II. Compensation Structure

Compensation structure also affects how individual accountants react to client influence. Although accounting firms have experienced incredible growth, fees from auditing have been relatively flat.[52] In order to increase earnings, the SEC reports, some accounting firms offered their professionals cash bonuses and other financial incentives to sell products or services, other than audit, review, or attest

[47] In re Broadview Fin Corp, Exch Act Release No 21,949 (Accounting and Auditing Enforcement Releases 1982-1987 Transfer Binder) Fed Sec L Rep (CCH) 73,454 at 63, 202 (17 April 1985). See also R Muoio 'An Independent Auditor's Suit for Wrongful Discharge' (1994) 58 Alb L Rev 413, 427.

[48] W Ebke and A Jurisch 'Der unerwünschte Abschlußprüfer: Ersetzungsverfahren (§ 318 Abs. 3 HGB) versus Anfechtungsklage (§ 243 Abs. 1 AktG)' (2000) 45 Die Aktiengesellschaft 208.

[49] R Prentice 'The Case of the Irrational Auditor: A Behavioral Insight into Securities Fraud Litigation' (2000) 95 Nw U L Rev 133, 143.

[50] L Lowenstein 'Corporate Governance and the Voice of the Paparazzi' (Working Paper no 132, February 1999) available at <http://www.law.columbia.edu/laweconomicstudies/paperps/wp132.pdf> (visited 1 March 2003).

[51] G Orren 'The Appearance Standard for Auditor Independence: What We Know and Should Know' in AICPA, *Serving the Public Interest: A New Conceptual Framework for Auditor Independence* (New York 1997) App A at 1, available at <http://www.aicpa.org/members/div/secps/isb/white.htm>.

[52] 'Accountants Should Stick to Auditing, Levitt Says' *Investor Rel Bus* (29 May 2000) 15.

services, to their audit clients.[53] As the consulting divisions of the major accounting firms have become more powerful, they often have pressured auditors into accommodating audit clients rather than focusing on audit issues. Studies have found that compensation structures supporting business development affect how individual auditors react to client influence. Thus, for example, Greg Trompeter studied several auditor compensation systems and found that if auditors' compensation was tied closely to client retention, the auditors would be more likely to succumb to client influence.[54] Furthermore, where accounting principles were more subjective, auditors were more likely to bend the principles in favour of clients.[55] The high level of subjectivity and the large degree of discretion resulting from many accounting principles as well as the profession's and regulators' inability to keep up with newly created, innovative financial and other transactions has allowed accountants many opportunities to bend the principles.[56] One should not forget that, after all, accounting is an art, not a science.

III. Non-Audit Services

In light of recent audit failures, it is generally recognized today that particularly serious independence issues arise where auditors provide non-audit services to an audit client. Most commentators seem to agree, however, that a categorical prohibition against the providing of non-audit services to an audit client is not necessary to ensure complete auditor independence.[57] In the United States, Congress seems to share this view. Instead of prohibiting the providing of non-audit services to audit clients, Section 201(a) of the Sarbanes-Oxley Act specifies nine non-audit services that are prohibited under the Act. The nine non-audit services included in the Act are:

[53] SEC Final Rule on Auditor Independence (n 24) at II.3 ('Compensation'). The new rule provides that an accountant is not independent if, at any point during the audit and professional engagement period, any audit partner, other than specialty partner, earns or receives compensation based on selling engagements to that audit client, to provide any services, other than audit, review, or attest services.

[54] G Trompeter 'The Effect of Partner Compensation Schemes and Generally Accepted Accounting Principles on Audit Partner Judgment' (1994) 13 Auditing: J Practice & Theory 56, 63-64.

[55] G Trompeter (n 54) 66.

[56] C Barbee 'Trends in Securities Litigation or Murphy's Law Applied to the World of D&O Underwriting' [September 2002] PriceWaterhouseCoopers, *Solutions* 6.

[57] eg SEC Final Rule on Auditor Independence (n 24) II.B. (at n 46); V Röhricht 'Unabhängigkeit des Abschlussprüfers' (2001) 54 Die Wirtschaftsprüfung 80, 83-84; W Ebke 'Anmerkung' (1998) 37 Wirtschaftsprüferkammer-Mitteilungen 76, 77.

- Bookkeeping or other services related to the accounting records or financial statements of the audit client;
- financial information systems design and implementation;
- appraisal or valuation services, fairness opinions, or contribution-in-kind reports;
- internal outsourcing services;
- management functions or humans resources;
- broker or dealer, investment adviser, or investment banking services;
- legal services and expert services related to the audit; and
- any other service that the Public Company Accounting Oversight Board determines, by regulation, is impermissible.

The SEC interprets the legislative history as indicating that Congress did not intend the provisions to contain broad categorical exceptions and that the scope of the prohibited services should be judged against overriding basic principles of auditor independence.[58]

Similarly, the EU Commission's Recommendation of 16 May 2002, makes it clear that providing non-audit services to an audit client does not render the audit or the auditor's opinion illegal or void *per se*. Rather, the Commission suggests that each specific situation should be analysed carefully, and provides a list of examples to illustrate the benchmarks against which such analysis is to be conducted.[59] Needless to say, the Commission views the preparation by the auditor of the audit client's accounting records and financial statements to constitute a 'self-review threat'.[60] Similarly, design and implementation of financial information technology systems and participation in the audit client's internal audit are also deemed to scarify auditor independence.[61] The Commission seems to take a slightly laxer view than the SEC, however, regarding recruiting services[62] or acting for the audit client in the resolution of litigation.[63] In addition, the Recommendation provides a list of fine, detailed provisions regarding the provision of non-audit services by the auditor to his or her audit client.[64]

[58] SEC Proposed Rule (n 24) 8.

[59] EU Recommendation (n 11) A. I.7.

[60] ibid A.I.7.2(1).

[61] ibid A.I.7.2.2.(1)-(2).

[62] ibid A.I.7.2.6.

[63] ibid A.I.7.2.5.

[64] ibid A.I.7.2.

1. Growth of Non-Audit Services

Although the major accounting firms experienced tremendous growth in the 1980ies and 1990ies, increasing their size and dominance, revenue growth for audit services began to stagnate. In 2000, fees for audit services accounted for less than one-third of the major accounting firms' total revenue.[65] Moreover, competitors began penetrating the major accounting firms' auditing monopoly by forming syndicates comprised of smaller accounting firms.[66] To counteract the lack of growth in audit revenue, the major accounting firms increasingly provided management consulting services to their audit clients and others. In 2001, the big accounting firms earned more than half their revenue from consulting, up from twelve percent in 1977.[67] Accounting firms were able to penetrate the management consulting service market since they were already familiar, through their audit engagements, with the corporate operations, management reporting mechanisms, and senior personnel.[68] With this knowledge, advising on how to improve control systems and information flow was a natural extension of their professional service offerings. The explosion in information technology in the 1990ies drove corporate demand for help in implementing or improving computer systems, ranging from material requirements planning to management information systems.[69]

In addition to consulting services, including technology and management consulting, the major accounting firms also began to provide tax consulting services to their audit client at a large scale. Tax work is a significant and traditional area of expertise of the major accounting firms. Although this area does not have the number of players that management and technology consulting have, competition is substantial. In the United States, for example, competitors include large tax shops like H&R Block and Jackson Hewitt, law firms, smaller accounting firms and computer software program providers like TurboTax.[70] A similar situation exists in most, if not all EU member states. In many EU member states, professional tax consultants in private practice ('Steuerberater') traditionally have held a large share of the market for tax consulting services. However, in the 1990ies, accounting firms succeeded in increasing their share of that market and began to enlarge their tax departments. An accounting firm's tax consulting is closely connected to its financial advising and financial planning area. Because the major accounting firms perform a variety of financial advising and planning services,

[65] N Byrnes 'Where Have all the Accountants Gone?' (27 March 2000) BusWk 203.

[66] 'A CPA Firm Goes Public' CPA J 8 (October 1999)

[67] 'Accountants Should Stick to Auditing, Levitt Says' (29 May 2000) Investor Rel Bus 15.

[68] R Thomas, S Schwab and R Hansen 'Megafirms' (2001) 80 N C L Rev 115, 152.

[69] R Thomas, S Schwab and R Hansen (n 68) 152.

[70] R Thomas, S Schwab and R Hansen (n 68) 156.

they also experience substantial competition from brokerage firms, such a Goldman Sachs and Merrill Lynch, banks and other financial institutions. Fierce competition also exists in the market for appraisal and valuation services (e.g., accounting for pensions or loss contingencies), fairness opinions, and contribution-in-kind reports. An equally important market for professional accountants is the market for comfort letters which are issued for numerous purposes, including IBOs.[71]

Finally, major accounting firms provide various legal services. The rise of multidisciplinary practices resulted in an aggressive competition with law firms for legal business.[72] Accounting firms provide legal services, such as tax, mergers and acquisition advisory, business planning, start-ups, securities advisory, litigation support and even dispute resolution.[73] Legal services may be related to the audit or unrelated to the audit. Accounting firms have slyly been referring to these services as 'consulting' since the law of numerous countries prohibits firms owned wholly or in part by non-lawyers to provide legal services. In spite of this fundamental rule, however, legal services provided by major accounting firms constitute a threat to the profitability and viability of law firms. In addition to legal services, accounting firms are in the business of providing expert services in connection with litigation, arbitration, administrative or regulatory proceedings. Until recently, very little was done to discipline accounting firms that had crossed the line into the practice of law.[74] Accounting firms and law firms have been going head to head for major corporate clients. Although this paper will not focus on dangers of accounting firms providing legal or expert services, the danger is systemic of accounting firms to expand constantly into new arenas. The growth of accounting firms into these new arenas is a consistent pressure since larger corporate clients demand a diverse range of services and one-stop shopping. Of course, there is an infinite number of other non-audit services an accounting firm may provide because such services do not pose an immediate threat as to their independence.. Yet, the question remains whether accounting firms should be permitted to provide non-audit services to their audit clients and, if so, to what extent such services may be provided by them and, most importantly, what services should be permitted and which ones should not.

[71] W Ebke and S Siegel 'Comfort Letters, Börsengänge und Haftung: Überlegungen aus Sicht des deutschen und US-amerikanischen Rechts' (2001) 55 Wertpapier-Mitteilungen 1 (spec. issue 2/2001).

[72] W Bower 'A Look at the Rise of Multidisciplinary Partnerships' (1998) 61 Phila Law 28, 32 n 1.

[73] G Morello 'Big Six Accounting Firms Shop Worldwide for Law Firms: Why Multi-Discipline Practices Should be Permitted in the United States' (1997) 21 Fordham Int'l LJ 190.

[74] L Fox 'Fighting for Independence' (1998) 61 Phila Law 28.

2. Separation of Audit and Non-Audit Services?

The SEC, the EU Commission and others, both in the United States and in Europe, have long argued that allowing auditing firms to provide management consulting to audit clients may affect the audit quality because consultants have an interest in expanding the service offering to audit clients, especially at times when audit revenues are stagnating or even declining. The natural desire to expand the service offerings to clients may result in the consulting division of an accounting firm pressuring the audit partner to accommodate a client's needs by potentially overlooking audit issues. If audit quality is reduced, investors and others will not have adequate reliable information. As a result, securities and capital markets will not function efficiently. In a market with perfect information, investors could vote against a corporation that hires low-quality, biased auditors by selling stock and reducing the corporation's valuation. By doing so, investors would urge companies to choose reliable and truly independent auditors. Unfortunately, however, markets are not perfect and investors cannot expect to measure auditor quality and independence using publicly available information. Therefore, some degree of separation between auditing and non-auditing within an audit firm is necessary.[75]

a) Conflicts of Interests

The EU Commission and the SEC have highlighted various ways that providing non-audit services to an audit client can create a conflict of interest. First, as auditors provide a broad array of services to their clients, they are viewed by clients and business associates as vendors committed to selling and not as sceptical and critical professionals who owe a duty of care and impartiality to the client and third parties. Recent studies have shown that the public senses that the focus of auditing firms has shifted. There is a growing perception that auditors are more and more concerned about expanding their consulting practice than performing independent statutory audits. In addition, recent studies suggest that compensation structures in auditing firms favour growing the consulting business.[76] PriceWaterhouseCoopers commented that '[i]n essence, we have become an organization trying to follow two missions at the same time. One goal has been to assure financial market integrity and provide investor protection. The other has been to help clients succeed by guiding them through complex, large-scale business transformations. One goal is objectivity and independence. The other

[75] To be sure, both the EU Recommendation (n 11) and the SEC Final Rule on Auditor Independence (n 24) do not limit the scope of non-audit services provided by an accounting firm to a non-audit client.

[76] Earnscliffe Research & Communications 'Report to the United States Independence Standards Board: Research into Perceptions of Auditor Independence and Objectivity' (November 1999) 14 (hereinafter cited Earnscliffe Report).

demands a direct interest in our client's success.'[77] Second, a broad service offering by the auditor to the audit client may align auditor and client interests. This is an issue if, for example, an auditor agrees to perform an audit of an early-stage company at a below-market fee on the thought that it will more than recoup the lost revenues through broad service offerings once the client is successful. In many ways, the auditor is merely investing in the client and is therefore tying itself to the client's success. Furthermore, if an auditor is hired by the audit client to perform consulting services, the auditor is, in effect, making management decisions. When an auditor acts as member of the client's management team, he may gain a 'mutuality of interest' with the client's management. Once this occurs the auditor is judged by the ultimate value he brings to the client. From this point forward, the auditor's allegiance will appear to be with management and not to the investing public. As a result, independence has been sacrificed.

Third, an increased offering of non-audit services may affect an auditing firm's internal culture. When non-audit services become more important to a firm than audit services, the core values and skills within the firm may give way to the growth of non-audit services. Furthermore, the compensation system within the firm may favour those who provide non-audit services over auditing services. Fourth, the public's recognition of problems related to non-audit services is growing. Earnscliffe reports that auditors, audit committee chairs, chief executive officers, analysts and regulators, to some degree, recognize the independence risks posed by broad relationships between auditors and their clients.[78] A majority of the Earnscliffe respondents felt that internal safeguards of accounting firms 'might ultimately be insufficient to sustain confidence in the independence of auditors'.[79] The respondents further noted that internal safeguards would be limited in achieving objectivity during the audit.[80]

b) A German Perspective

On the other hand, it is sometimes said that providing non-audit services, at least in some instances, may make economic sense and does not create too high a risk in terms of potential conflicts of interests; provided, of course, the auditor does not make decisions for the company that fall within the ambit of management, because an auditor must not exercise management functions for his or her audit client. Thus, for instances, in 1997 the German Supreme Court ('Bundesgerichtshof') held in *Allweiler* that a statutory auditor may provide technical expertise and

[77] *Wall Street Journal* (22 February 2000) A17.

[78] Earnscliffe Report (n 76) 28 and 37-41.

[79] ibid.

[80] ibid.

assistance to its audit client.[81] In the case at hand, the accounting firm of Ernst & Young had been engaged by its audit client to determine the amount of future pension liabilities for which the client had to make a provision in its balance sheet. The accounting firm had utilized its own valuation specialist to review the work done by the audit client itself and to determine the amounts recorded in the client's financial statements. Because the factual assumptions underlying the amounts on the balance sheet had been determined by the client, the audit partner did not review or audit his or her own work but rather provided consulting services.

The Court defined the term 'consulting' ('Beratung') within the meaning of Sec. 319(2) of the German Commercial Code ('Handelsgesetzbuch') to mean 'providing or debating recommendations by professionals concerning future decisions'.[82] In the opinion of the Court, a consultant 'points out a possible course of action and its consequences'.[83] According to the Court, the audit partner of the accounting firm cannot be considered to lack the independence required by Section 319(2) of the Commercial Code as long as the ultimate accounting decision (i.e., the determination of the factual assumptions underlying the amounts recorded in the client's financial statements) is made by management rather than the consulting partner of the accounting firm ('funktionale Entscheidungszuständigkeit'). Commenting on the Court's decision in *Allweiler* at the 1998 meeting of the German Institute of Public Accountants (Institut der Wirtschaftsprüfer) in Baden-Baden, Germany, Supreme Court Justice Volker Röhricht specified a list of professional services that, in his view, statutory auditors are permitted to provide under Germany's statutory rules on external auditor independence.[84] Section 319(2) and (3) of the Commercial Code contains broad categorical rules that specify situations in which an accountant ('Wirtschaftsprüfer') and an accounting firm ('Wirtschaftsprüfungsgesellschaft') cannot perform an audit. If the auditor is held to fall within the ambit of Section 319(2) or (3), his or her election by the client's general shareholders meeting is deemed void *ab initio*.[85]

While many commentators expected the German Supreme Court to take a more restrictive view in the post-*Enron* era, the Court expressly reconfirmed its

[81] BGHZ 135, 260. For a detailed analysis of the *Allweiler* decision, see, eg W Ebke (n 57); P Hommelhoff 'Abschlußprüfung und Abschlußberatung' [1997] Zeitschrift für Unternehmensrecht und Gesellschaftsrecht 550; N Neumann 'Abschlußprüfung und Beratung nach der Allweiler-Entscheidung des BGH' (1998) 28 Zeitschrift für Wirtschaftsrecht 1338.

[82] BGHZ 135, 260, 264.

[83] BGHZ 135, 260, 264.

[84] V Röhricht 'Beratung und Abschlußprüfung' (1998) 51 Die Wirtschaftsprüfung 153, 156-58.

[85] W Ebke (n 34) 319 annotations 16-18.

opinion in its *HypoVereinsbank* decision of 25 November 2002.[86] In the case at hand, the Court concluded that KPMG's appointment as statutory auditor of the 1999 financial statements of HypoVereinsbank, Germany's second largest private bank, was not void *ab initio* even though KPMG had provided a fairness opinion in connection with the 1998 merger of Bayerische Hypotheken- und Wechselbank AG and Bayerische Vereinsbank AG. However, the Court held that KPMG's 1999 appointment as external auditor of HypoVereinsbank was void *ab initio* as there was a 'reasonable concern' that KPMG was 'biased' ('Besorgnis der Befangenheit') within the meaning of Section 318(3) of the Commercial Code, due to KPMG's alleged failure, in the course of its previous fairness opinion engagement, to detect substantial value impairments of its client's commercial real estate assets which would have impacted KPMG's opinion on the adequacy of consideration in the merger transaction.[87]

The Court's decision in *HypoVereinsbank* is also important in that it allows every shareholder, irrespective of the number of shares owned by him or her, to bring a lawsuit against the corporation to challenge the appointment of the external auditor on grounds of a 'reasonable concern' that the auditor may be biased.[88] In view of the rather uncertain contours of the legal concept of a 'reasonable concern' that the auditor lacks the necessary independence ('Besorgnis der Befangenheit'), it is conceivable that shareholders will seek to utilize the 'nuisance value' attached to their individual right to bring a law suit against the corporation to remove the auditor.

c) The Four Factor Test

From the foregoing discussion it is evident that the nature and scope of non-audit services that an auditor may provide to his or her audit client should be limited and that a separation between auditing and non-auditing services within an auditing firm is necessary in the interest of efficient corporate governance and market integrity. As the SEC has pointed out correctly, the nature and scope of

[86] The Court's judgment in *HypoVereinsbank* is published in (2003) 58 Betriebs-Berater 462.

[87] ibid.

[88] The Court's holding that every shareholder is entitled to challenge the general shareholders meeting's election of the independent auditor irrespective of the number of shares held by that shareholder, is highly questionable in view of the fact that Sec 318(3) of the German Commercial Code seems to impose the requirement that the auditor can only be removed by shareholders holding a total of at least ten per-cent of the corporation's outstanding shares of stock. For a more detailed exposition of this view in light of the historical and legislative background of Sec 318(3) of the Commercial Code and its predecessors, see W Ebke and A Jurisch (n 48) 213-216; see also W Ebke (n 34) § 318 annotations 52-61 (with further references to court decisions and law review articles).

the prohibited services should be judged against four basic principles.[89] Those four principles are that an external auditor of a public, listed corporation cannot

- audit his or her own work (as he or she would if he or she provided bookkeeping services, actuarial services, appraisal or valuation services, internal audit outsourcing services or financial information systems design to an audit client);
- perform management functions or function as an employee of the audit client (as he or she would if he or she provided human resources services such as recruiting, hiring, and designing compensation packages for the officers, directors, or managers of an audit client);
- act as an advocate (lawyer) of the audit client (as he or she would if he or she provided legal services to an audit client or expert services to an audit client in judicial, administrative or regulatory proceedings); or
- be a promoter of the audit client's stock or other financial interests (as he or she would be if he or she served as a broker-dealer, investment adviser, or investment banker for the audit client).

To do so would clearly impair the auditor's independence. The following examples will illustrate this point.

d) Illustrations

An auditor's independence is impaired if he maintains or prepares the audit client's accounting records, prepares its client's financial statements or the information that forms the basis of the audit client's financial statements. When an auditing firm provides bookkeeping services for an audit client, the firm may be put in the position of later auditing the accounting firm's work.[90] If, during an audit, an accountant must audit the bookkeeping work performed by his or her accounting firm, it is questionable that the accountant could, or that a reasonable investor would believe that the accountant could, remain objective and impartial. If the accountant found an error in the bookkeeping, he or she could well be under pressure not to raise the issue with the client if raising the issue could jeopardize the firm's contract with the client for bookkeeping services or result in heightened litigation risk for the firm. In addition, keeping the books is a management function, which the accountant is not allowed to perform for his or her audit client. Similarly, an accountant is not deemed independent if the accountant designs or implements a hardware or software system that aggregates source data underlying the audit client's financial statements or generates information that is significant

[89] SEC Proposed Rule (n 24) 9. Cf EU Recommendation (n 11) B.I.7.1.

[90] SEC Final Rule on Auditor Independence (n 24) II.B.1; EU Recommendation (n 11) B.I.7.2.1.(1).

to the audit client's financial statements taken as a whole.[91] However, an audit firm should not be precluded from working on hardware or software systems that are unrelated to the audit client's financial statements or accounting records, as long as those services are pre-approved by the audit committee. Operating, designing or implementing systems affecting the financial statements may place the auditor in a management role, or result in the accountant auditing his or her own work or attesting to the effectiveness of internal control systems designed or implemented by that accountant. Similarly, the auditor is not independent if he or she provides appraisal or valuation services, or contribution-in-kind reports, to his or her audit client where there is a reasonable likelihood that the results of the service will be subject to audit procedures.[92] Appraisal and valuation services include any process of valuing assets, both tangible and intangible, or liabilities. They include valuing, among other things, in-process research and development, financial instruments, assets and liabilities acquired in a merger, and real estate. Fairness opinions and contribution-in-kind reports are opinions and reports in which the accounting firm provides its opinion as to the adequacy of consideration in a transaction. As the SEC has pointed out correctly, providing these services to audit clients raises several independence concerns:[93] Thus, when it is time to audit the client's financial statements, it is likely that the accountant would review his or her own work, including key assumptions or variables that underlie an entry in the financial statements. Also, if the appraisal methodology involves a projection of future results of operations and cash flows, the accountants may be unable to evaluate sceptically and without bias the accuracy of that valuation or appraisal. Accordingly, in the opinion of the SEC, accountants should not be permitted to provide any appraisal or valuation service or any service involving a fairness opinion or contribution-in-kind report for an audit client, unless it is reasonable to conclude that the results of these services will not be subject to audit procedures during an audit of the audit client's financial statements.[94]

Since the external auditor generally will rely, at least to some extent, on the internal control (internal audit) system when conducting the audit of the audit client's financial statements, the auditor is not independent when he or she performs internal audit services related to the internal accounting controls, financial systems, or financial statements, for an audit client.[95] If the internal audit function, or a part thereof, is outsourced to an accountant, the accountant assumes a management function and responsibility and becomes part of the company's con-

[91] For details, see SEC Final Rule on Auditor Independence (n 24) II.B.2; EU Recommendation (n 11) B.I.7.2.2.

[92] For details, see ibid II.B.3.

[93] ibid.

[94] ibid.

[95] For details, see ibid II.B.4.

trol system. The SEC's rules regarding auditor independence therefore prohibit the accountant from providing to the audit client internal audit services. The prohibition includes any internal audit service that has been outsourced by the audit client that relates to the audit client's internal accounting controls, financial systems, or financial statements unless it is reasonable to conclude that the results of these services will not be subject to audit procedures during an audit of the audit client's financial statements.[96]

Legal services also give rise to independence issues. An accountant is not independent of an audit client who, under circumstances in which the service is provided, could be provided only by someone licensed, admitted or otherwise qualified to practise law in the jurisdiction in which the service is provided.[97] A lawyer's core professional obligation is to advance his or her clients' interests. Rules of professional conduct require the lawyer to 'represent a client zealously and diligently within the bounds of the law'.[98] The lawyer must 'take whatever lawful and ethical measures are required to vindicate a client's cause or endeavour ... In the exercise of professional judgment, a lawyer should always act in a manner consistent with the best interests of the client'.[99] It follows that an individual cannot be both a zealous legal advocate for management or the client company, and at the same time maintain the objectivity and impartiality that are necessary for an audit. In *United States v Arthur Young*, the United States Supreme Court emphasized, '[i]f investors were to view the auditor as an advocate for the corporate client, the value of the audit function itself might well be lost'.[100] The same is true when the accountant provides expert opinions or other expert services to an audit client, or a legal representative of an audit client, for the purposes of advocating that audit client's interests in litigation, arbitration, regulatory or administrative proceedings.[101]

Tax services, by contrast, are often perceived differently. Thus, for example, Section 201(a) of the Sarbanes-Oxley Act provides that auditors may engage in tax services for the audit client when those services have been pre-approved by the client's audit committee; subject, of course, to the four factor test stated above.[102] It should be noted, however, that legal systems may disagree with the Act's basic proposition. This is particularly true in cases in which a legal system has established a 'tax-must-conform-to-book' requirement.[103] In such a case, the

[96] ibid.

[97] ibid II.B.9.

[98] eg D.C. Rules of Professional Conduct, Rule 1.3(a).

[99] ibid Rule 1.5.

[100] *United States v Arthur Young* 465 US 805, 819-20 n 15 (1984).

[101] Cf SEC Final Rule on Auditor Independence (n 24) II.B.10.

[102] See above, text accompanying n 89.

[103] For an excellent comparative analysis of the pertinent laws in the United States and Germany, see H Lischer and P Märkl 'Comformity between Financial Accounting and Tax

cont. ...

accountant's tax advise may directly impact the audit client's financial statements or information underlying the client's financial statements which may place the accountant in a position to audit his or her own work. In any event, an auditor's independence is clearly impaired where the accountant serves as an advocate for his or her audit client before a tax court or when the auditor provides a tax opinion concerning the audit client for the use by a third party in connection with a business transaction between the audit client and the third party. Under those circumstances, the auditor may be acting as an advocate for the audit client by actively promoting the client's interests. As a result, independence has been sacrificed.[104]

e) Some Final Comments

According to information available to the SEC, approximately 12,600 registrant companies did not purchase any non-audit (consulting) services from the auditor of their financial statements, whereas 4,100 registrants reported purchasing such services.[105] Based on the scrutiny that these services have received over the past two years, the SEC believes that the number of companies purchasing non-audit services from their external auditor might have decreased. The SEC's rules regarding auditor independence may cause accountants to lose one or more sources of revenue because they will no longer be permitted to sell certain non-audit services to their audit clients. Additionally, accounting firms may incur additional costs to market non-audit services with non-audit clients as well as additional learning costs to familiarize themselves with the operations of those non-audit clients. Finally, to the extent that there exist economies of scope in the provision of audit and non-audit service (as, for example, through the use of shared knowledge management systems and other infrastructure) and to the extent that the preclusion of certain non-audit services to audit clients results in the exit of personnel who provide such services from accounting firms, there may be an increase in the cost of both audit and non-audit services. The SEC believes, however, that in view of the comments by the largest four accounting firms, and others, that costs associated with its rules on auditor independence may be limited,[106] Also, to the extent that non-audit services are merely redistributed among the accounting firms, the SEC believes that there would be no net loss of revenue to public accounting firms as a whole.[107] Comparable data does not seem to be available for EU companies. Thus, it remains to be seen what impact on

Accounting in the United States and Germany' (1997) 36 Wirtschaftsprüferkammer-Mitteilungen 91 (spec issue June 1997).

[104] Accord SEC Final Rule on Auditor Independence (n 24) II.B.11.

[105] SEC Proposed Rule (n 24) V.C.1(a).

[106] ibid.

[107] ibid.

auditors' revenues the EU Commission's Recommendation of 16 May 2002, will have where auditors have provided non-audit services to audit clients.

Finally, one should stress an important point made by the EU Commission regarding the compensation of statutory auditors. In its Recommendation, the Commission correctly states that '[f]ee arrangements for audit engagements in which the amount of the remuneration is contingent upon the results of the service provided raise self-interest and advocacy threats which are considered to bear an unacceptable level of independence risk'.[108] Therefore, the EU Commission correctly insists that 'audit engagements should never be accepted on a contingent fee basis.'[109] While it should be absolutely clear that an auditor should not gain a financial interest in his or her audit client's success, there are cases in which auditors violated the rule against contingent fee arrangements. Thus, for example, in its 2003 report on the Swissair Group's debacle, Ernst & Young stated that, in the course of its investigations, it found a letter dated 21 January 1999 according to which PriceWaterhouseCoopers and its audit client Swissair agreed on a basic annual fee of CHF 2.6 million for PWC's audits of 1999 through 2001, subject to an increase or decrease, within a defined band, according to Swissair's earnings.[110]

IV. Audit Partner Rotation

Audit partner rotation is now a favourite subject, both in Europe and the United States.[111] The very concept of audit partner rotation is, however, not new. Thus, for example, audit partner rotation is common practice among the larger accounting firms in Germany.[112] In the United States, accounting firms that audit SEC registrants have been subject to internal audit partner rotation requirements, even before the Sarbanes-Oxley Act entered into force. The requirements of the AICPA's SEC Practice Section (SECPS) call for the engagement partner to rotate off the engagement after seven years and to remain off the engagement for two

[108] EU Recommendation (n 11) B.8.1.1.

[109] EU Recommendation (n 11) B.8.1.1(a).

[110] Ernst & Young *In Sachen Swissair. Untersuchungsbericht* (Zurich 2003) 243. On 26 June 2000, the fee arrangement of 21 January 1999 was revoked and replaced with a fixed fee agreement. Needless to say, contingency fee arrangements are illegal under both Swiss corporate law and Swiss professional standards. See J Kostkiewicz, U Bertschinger, P Breitschmid and I Schwander *Schweizerisches Obligationenrecht* (Zurich 2002) 892.

[111] eg N Herzig and C Watrin 'Obligatorische Rotation des Wirtschaftsprüfers – ein Weg zur Verbesserung der externen Unternehmenskontrolle? (1995) 47 Zeitschrift für betriebswirtschaftliche Forschung 775; for further references, see Ebke, (n 34) Vor § 316 annotation 3 n 10.

[112] W Ebke (n 34) § 319 annotation 50 n 142 (with a list of references).

years.[113] Section 203 of the Sarbanes-Oxley Act of 2002 now stipulates that the lead (or coordinating) audit partner (having primary responsibility for the audit), and the audit partner responsible for reviewing the audit, serve on the engagement in that capacity for no more than five consecutive years. Section 301 of the Sarbanes-Oxley Act specifies that the SEC is to direct the national securities exchanges and associations to adopt company listing standards stating that the company's audit committee has the responsibility for appointment, compensation, and oversight of the work of the company's audit firm. In that capacity, the audit committee has the responsibility for evaluating and determining that the audit engagement team has the professional competence necessary to conduct the audit engagement in accordance with GAAS. Additionally, the accountant is required to conduct the audit in accordance with GAAS. GAAS require that the accountant exercise due professional care in the conduct of the audit. In order to exercise due professional care, it is necessary to ensure that the engagement is properly staffed with individuals competent to understand the unique issues relevant to that audit. Additionally, the accounting profession's quality control standards require that the firm have processes in place to ensure that appropriate personnel are assigned to each audit engagement. In its proposing release of 2 December 2002, the SEC proposed that all partners on the audit engagement team, with the exception of certain 'technical services' or 'national office' partners be subject to internal rotation after five years and that after rotation, they would be subject to a five year time-out before they could return to that engagement.[114] The SEC stated that audit partners should not return to the audit engagement for five years in order to ensure investors and the public that there will be a periodic 'fresh look' at the accounting and auditing issues confronting the audit client. Similarly, since 1998 German law mandates an internal rotation of the lead audit partner if the auditor, within ten years prior to the current audit of the client, has signed the auditor's opinion ('Bestätigungsvermerk') in more than six years.[115]

While they differ somewhat, the audit partner rotation requirements in Germany and the United States ensure a continuity of knowledge and competence, especially in light of the fact that accounting firms would seem to be allowed to stagger the rotation of audit and review partners. Thus far, however, neither German law nor the law in the United States mandates a rotation of the audit firm (external rotation), which would mean that no partner of the auditing firm may provide audit services to the audit client after a certain number of years have passed, and that the auditors could not return to the audit engagement for a certain number of years. At first glance such a strict rule might appear appealing. In fact,

[113] American Institute of Certified Public Accountants, SEC Practice Section, Requirements of Members, item e.

[114] SEC Proposed Rule (n 24) II.C.

[115] German Commercial Code § 319(2) sent 2 & § 319(3) no 6. For details of these statutory provisions, see W Ebke (n 34) § 319 annotation 50.

several commentators, appointed commissions, and professional organizations that have researched and analysed the issue of audit firm rotation have suggested that the 'fresh look' can only be accomplished by requiring mandatory rotation of audit firms ('external rotation').[116] Upon a closer look, however, a mandatory audit firm rotation does not seem to be desirable as it creates an even greater risk to audit quality. As directed by Section 207 of the Sarbanes-Oxley Act, the issue of mandatory audit firm rotation will continue to be monitored by the SEC and the Comptroller General of the United States. In its final rule regarding auditor independence, the SEC tries to strike a balance between the need for a 'fresh look' on the engagement and the need for the audit team to be composed of competent accountants by requiring the lead and concurring partners to rotate off the audit engagement of SEC registrants after five years with a five year 'time out' period. The SEC believes that a five-year 'time out' period is appropriate for these two partners because of the importance of achieving a 'fresh look' to the independence of the audit function.[117]

V. Employment of a Former Audit Partner by the Audit Client

Another serious independence issue results from employment relationships of an auditor.

1. Previous SEC Rules

The SEC's previous rules on auditor independence deemed an accounting firm to be not independent with respect to an audit client if a former partner, principal, shareholder, or professional employee of an accounting firm had accepted employment with a client if he or she had a continuing financial interest in the accounting firm or was in a position to influence the firm's operations or financial policies.[118] Consistent with Section 206 of the Sarbanes-Oxley Act, the SEC has added a restriction on employment with audit clients by former employees of the accounting firm. The Act specifies that an accounting firm cannot perform an

[116] eg The Commission on Auditor's Responsibilities *Report, Conclusions, and Recommendations* (New York 1978) 109; United States General Accounting Office, Report to the Ranking Minority Member, Committee on Commerce, House of Representatives *The Accounting Profession, Major Issues: Progress and Concerns* (Washington DC 1996) 56; St Pierre, K Anderson and J Anderson 'An Analysis of Factors Associated with Lawsuits Against Public Accountants' [1984] Acct Rev 256. See also W Ebke (n 34) Vor § 316 annotation 3 and § 319 annotation 50 (with further references).

[117] SEC Final Rule on Auditor Independence (n 24) II.C. The SEC recognizes that the periodic replacement of audit partners might increase the costs of audits.

[118] SEC Final Rule on Auditor Independence (n 24) II.A.

audit for a registrant '... [i]f a chief executive officer, controller, chief financial officer, chief accounting officer, or any person serving in an equivalent position for the issuer, was employed by that registered independent public accounting firm and participated in any capacity in the audit of that issuer during the 1-year period preceding the date of the initiation of the audit.' Thus, the Act requires a 'cooling off' period of one year before a member of the audit engagement team can begin working for the registrant in certain key positions. Consistent with the Act's directive, the SEC has proposed that the employment of audit engagement team members of an accounting firm in a financial reporting oversight role at an audit client within one year prior to the commencement of procedures for the current audit engagement would cause the accounting firm not to be independent with respect to that issuer.

2. Final SEC Rules

The final rules of the SEC indicate that an accounting firm is deemed to be not independent with respect to an audit client if a former member of the audit engagement team is employed by the issuer in a 'financial reporting oversight role' unless the individual had not been a member of the audit engagement team during the one year period preceding the commencement of the audit.

The term 'financial reporting oversight role' refers to any individual who has direct responsibility for oversight over those who prepare the issuer's financial statements and related information (e.g., management's discussion and analysis) that are included in filings with the SEC. While the EU Commission's Recommendations of 16 May 2002, suggests that a period of 'at least' two years should have elapsed before a key audit partner can take up a key management position with the audit client, the one year cooling-off period required by the SEC seems to be sufficiently long to achieve an appearance of independence by the accounting firm. The concept of a 'cooling-off' period before an auditor can take a position at the audit client was previously considered by the Independence Standards Board.[119] In considering a cooling-off period, the Independence Standards Board noted that a mandated cooling-off period for partners and professional staff might create a greater appearance of independence between the accounting firm and the registrant.[120] Ultimately, however, the Independence Standards Board provided for an alternative to a strict cooling-off period. The Board concluded that '[a]n audit firm's independence is impaired with respect to an audit client that employs

[119] The Independence Standards Board was a private sector body that, from 1997 to 2001, was charged with the responsibility to set auditor independence standards for auditors of the financial statements of SEC registrants.

[120] Independence Standards Board 'Employment with Audit Clients' Discussion Memorandum 99-1 (12 March 1999).

a former firm professional who could, by reason of his or her knowledge of and relationships with the audit firm, adversely influence the quality or effectiveness of the audit, unless the firm has taken steps that effectively eliminate such risk.'[121] Independence Standards Board's Standard No. 3 specifically notes that additional caution is warranted when it has been less than one year since the profession disassociated him or herself from the firm.[122]

The provisions of the Sarbanes-Oxley Act reflect the view that the passage of time is the only appropriate safeguard to reduce the perceived loss of independence for the audit firm caused by the acceptance of employment by a member of the engagement team with an audit client. The Act specifies that the cooling-off period must be one year. In the opinion of the SEC the Act's cooling-off period does not apply only to partners on the audit engagement team but any member.[123] In its proposed rule of 2 December 2002, the SEC did not make a distinction based on the number of hours of audit, review, or attest services provided in determining who would be subject to the rule. In response to issues raised by several commenters, the SEC's final rule now requires that when the lead partner, the concurring partner, or any other member of the audit engagement team who provides more than ten hours of audit, review, or attest services for the issuer accepts a position with the issuer in a 'financial reporting oversight role' within the one year period preceding the commencement of audit procedures for the year that included employment by the issuer of the former member of the audit engagement team.

D. Public Oversight

Under Section 102 of the Sarbanes-Oxley Act of 2002, public accounting firms must register with the Public Company Accounting Oversight Board (PCAOB) in order to prepare or issue, or to participate in the preparation or issuance of any audit report with respect to any issuer. The PCAOB, a private, non-profit corporation made up of five full-time members, is to oversee and investigate the audits and auditors of public companies and sanction accounting firms and individuals for violations of pertinent laws, regulations and rules. The PCAOB, which is funded by public companies through mandatory fees as well as registration and annual fees of registered accounting firms (!), will issue standards or adopt standards set by other groups or organizations for audits of public companies. These standards include: auditing and related attestation, quality control, ethics, independence and 'other standards necessary to protect the public interest'. The Board

[121] Independence Standards Board 'Employment with Audit Clients' Standard No 3 (July 2000).

[122] ibid par 2(b)(iii).

[123] SEC Final Rule on Auditor Independence (n 24) II.A.

has authority to set and enforce audit and quality control standards for public company audits. The Board is empowered regularly to inspect registered accounting firms' operations and will investigate potential violations. Sanctions for failure to comply with pertinent standards will include revocation or suspension of an accounting firms' registration, prohibition from auditing public companies, and an imposition of civil penalties. During investigations, the PCAOB can require testimony or document production from the registered accounting firm, or request information from persons outside the accounting firm. Investigations can be referred, under certain circumstances, to the SEC or, with the SEC's approval, to the Department of Justice, state attorneys general or state boards of accountancy. Foreign accounting firms that 'prepare or furnish' an audit report involving U.S. registrants will be subject to the authority of the PCAOB. Additionally, if a registered accounting firm relies on the opinion of a foreign accounting firm, the foreign firm's audit work papers must be supplied on request to the PCAOB or the SEC. Section 105(a) of the Sarbanes-Oxley Act of 2002 directs the PCAOB to establish, by rule, standards for the investigation and discipline of registered accounting firms and individuals. On 21 April 2003, the PCAOB published a Working Paper Regarding Board Investigations and Disciplinary Proceedings to afford the SEC and the public an understanding of the board's plans with respect to the enforcement program and to provide a blueprint for the Board's staff. The PCAOB made it clear, however, that its proposal is subject to 'refinement and change' as the Board gains additional experience. Additionally, on 16 April 2003, the PCAOB held a public meeting regarding the process that it intends to use to establish auditing professional standards for registered accounting firms. It also discussed whether interim standards of auditing, attestation, quality control, ethics, and independence should be established.

Understandably, the reactions to the PCAOB, its powers and activities have been rather unfavourable in the EU.[124] This is particularly true with regard to the effects of the Board's authorities concerning foreign accounting firms. Thus, for example, Klaus-Peter Neumann, Chairman of the Board of the German Institute of Public Accountants (Institut der Wirtschaftsprüfer) recently criticized that European accounting firms now are not only subject to registration requirements and investigations and disciplinary proceedings of the professional associations of

[124] eg C Kersting 'Auswirkungen des Sarbanes-Oxley-Gesetzes in Deutschland: Können deutsche Unternehmen das Gesetz befolgen?' (2003) 24 Zeitschrift für Wirtschaftsrecht 233. For the view of the German *Wirtschaftsprüferkammer*, see Wirtschaftsprüferkammer 'Stellungnahme der WPK zum Sarbanes-Oxley Act of 2002 gegenüber dem Bundesministerium für Wirtschaft' (2002) 41 Wirtschaftsprüferkammer-Mitteilungen 290. The Joint Statement of the German *Institut der Wirtschaftsprüfer* and the *Wirtschaftsprüferkammer* to the Federal Attorney General: 'Stellungnahme von IDW und WPK zum Sarbanes-Oxley Act of 2002 gegenüber dem Bundesministerium der Justiz' is published in (2002) 41 Wirtschaftsprüferkammer-Mitteilungen 293.

their home state, but also of the PCAOB.[125] He has called for a concerted action by the EU to establish uniform European standards on auditing and related attestation, quality control, ethics, independence and other standards necessary to protect the public interest that would have to be implemented by the member states under the supervision of the EU Commission. The establishment of a European securities and capital market would seem, however, to call for not only a uniform set of professional auditing standards within the EU but also for a private sector regulatory body, such as an EU Public Oversight Board, for the enforcement of such standards. Most importantly, such a Board, if properly composed, would be best situated to develop uniform European standards on auditing and related attestation, quality control, ethics, independence and other standards necessary to protect the investing public's interests and to ensure public trust and confidence throughout the EU.

E. Conclusions

We must not forget that the accounting profession was granted exclusive rights, and reciprocal duties, to perform a vital public service. Affected by the public interest as much as any public utility, the accounting profession cannot be free from serious oversight or constraint – at least not in countries where check and balance is king. Given the sharpness of the current debate, and the transparency in this battle of the private versus the public interest, there is more at stake in the outcome than just the independence of the auditors. The proper functioning of the capital and securities markets and, consequently, the corporate governance system are being challenged by all those who bring political pressure to bear against proposals that cannot be defeated by argument on the merits. Auditors are the 'gatekeepers' to the securities and capital markets, and the law gives public accountants both an enormously valuable franchise and a bedrock public responsibility. Accountants will be able to accomplish their tasks only if they are truly independent – both in appearance and in fact.

[125] K Neumann 'Europa braucht dringend eine Antwort auf den PCAOB' (2003) 58 Betriebs-Berater I ('Die erste Seite').

Part III:

Corporate Governance: The Market for Corporate Control and the Level Playing Field

Chapter 9: American Experience and EU Perspectives

An American Perspective on Anti-Takeover Laws in the EU: The German Example

JEFFREY N. GORDON*

The new German Takeover Act contains anti-takeover provisions that reject the 'board neutrality/shareholder choice' of the defeated draft of the 13th Directive. These anti-takeover provisions may have a particular (albeit temporary) justification as part of negotiating strategy to obtain a Directive with a 'level playing field' approach to a wide variety of control barriers in the EU. This is because assent to cross-border mergers and the transnational economic integration associated with such mergers ultimately depends upon the control of economic nationalism. Mutual vulnerability to takeover bids by both acquirors and targets, in which acquirors who engage in value-reducing home country bias would face a control threat, can play a valuable role in restraining economic nationalism.

Nevertheless, the German anti-takeover provisions would have much more adverse impact than the US counterparts to which they are frequently compared. First, the favoured US defensive measure, the poison pill, is not available under prevailing German principles of pre-emptive rights and non-discrimination against any shareholder. German firms are likely to substitute irreversible, value-decreasing measures that were replaced in the US by the pill, such as capital structure changes or asset dispositions. Second, the typical US practice of annual shareholder elections of board members combined with heavy institutional investor ownership in large public firms means that managements are highly sensitive to public shareholder interests in considering a takeover bid. By contrast, German supervisory boards turn over much more slowly, and are co-determined. German management feels less legal and cultural pressure to adhere to public shareholder interests. Third, lucrative cash severance payments ('golden parachutes') and stock option-laden compensation packages make US managers quite receptive to high

* I am grateful for discussion and comments by Prof. Theodor Baums. I have elaborated on some of what follows in The International Relations Wedge in the Corporate Convergence Debate, forthcoming in JN Gordon and MJ Roe (eds) *Convergence and Persistence in Corporate Governance* (Cambridge University Press 2004), and a related working paper, 'An International Relations Perspective on the Convergence of Corporate Governance: The Evolution of German Shareholder Capitalism in the European Union: 1990-2000' available on SSRN. A somewhat different version of this paper was published as 'Das neue deutsche 'Anti'-Übernahmegesetz aus amerikanischer Perspektive' (An American Perspective on the New German Anti-takeover Law) [2002] Die Aktiengesellschaft 12.

premium bids, especially because a takeover typically triggers the accelerated vesting of such options. German compensation arrangements do not now and, as a matter of cultural constraint, are unlikely to imitate the US version. So if Germany insists too hard on a 13th Directive to its exact taste, it risks sacrificing internal and cross-border mergers that would produce efficiency gains and aid the EU transnational project.

A. Introduction

The hostile takeover bid is likely to become an increasingly important influence in the EU environment. Hostile takeover bids unsettle not only the managements of the particular targets but also the economic and political milieu because of their disruptive challenge to well-established business patterns. To take a German example, Krupp's thwarted hostile bid for Thyssen (1997) followed by Vodafone's successful bid for Mannesmann (1999) have been signature events in defining the corporate governance landscape. The success of the Vodafone bid represented a deep injection of shareholder capitalism into German business culture. Yet this event also seemed to provoke a backlash: In its aftermath, Germany rejected the 'board neutrality/shareholder choice' that characterized the EU's proposed 13th Company Law Directive and, instead, adopted a German takeover law that seems to license target board defensive measures in the face of a hostile bid.

Defenders of the German position (and, by extension, other opponents of the proposed 13th Company Law Directive) have invoked an impression of the US takeover regime under which targets purportedly have significant anti-takeover protection, to make two sorts of arguments. The first is that the greater vulnerability of EU firms will lead to an influx of US raiders, a trans-Atlantic 'level playing field' argument. The second is a harmonization argument: what's good for the US is good for the EU, or, more simply, if significant anti-takeover protection has not inhibited US mergers and acquisition activity, then it will not be a significant barrier in the EU either. This chapter contends first, that these arguments are founded on a misconception of how the American takeover regime works in practice. It is a mistake to think that, notwithstanding formal legal protections, US firms are functionally insulated from takeover bids; but it is also a mistake to think that the institutional factors that facilitate takeovers in the US would necessarily obtain in the EU. The second point, however, is that the US analogy is fundamentally misleading. The stakes for the EU in the hostile takeover debate, and by, extension, the debate over the 13th Directive more generally, are much greater than the stakes in the US debate. The key issue for the EU is not the efficiency question B whether hostile bids play an important role in shifting control over assets to higher valuing management teams B but rather the distinctively EU concern for the economic and political integration of the European Union. Hostile takeovers and, by extension, cross-border mergers generally, may have a crucial role in this project, so their benefits and costs must be assessed with a different set of parameters.

The common European misconception that US firms have effective anti-takeover protection is perhaps not surprising. Europeans observed that during the remarkable 'Deal Decade' of the 1980s, nearly half of the major US corporations received an unwanted, 'hostile' bid.[1] Even very large firms came under attack from financial buyers whose access to the 'junk bond' market meant they could engineer a highly leveraged transaction that would ultimately be repaid through the sale of various corporate divisions and other assets (a 'bust-up'). But this era of 'wild west capitalism' came to an abrupt halt in 1989, to be followed by a decade in which hostile deals seemed relatively uncommon.[2] What happened? Surely one thing that changed was the background legal rules that governed the defensive tactics available to a target board. Licensed by a 1987 US Supreme Court case,[3] states adopted anti-takeover statutes that would survive judicial scrutiny. In measuring the fiduciary duty of target directors, state courts adopted increasingly deferential attitudes toward defensive measures, and, in particular, sanctioned the remarkable lawyers' invention of the 'poison pill'. So, in 1992-93 a leading US corporate law academic could survey this landscape and write, 'The takeover wars are over. Management won.'[4]

As the 1990s unfolded, it became apparent that the reality was more complex. As I will discuss in more detail later, the formal takeover protections of statutes and poison pills have not produced functional takeover protection. Instead, US corporate governance institutions have adapted so that US managers rarely resist a premium bid. Acquisition activity in the US in the 1990s was, if anything, more intense than in the 1980s, measured both as a percent of market capitalization and in the number of transactions, and much greater if measured in real dollar terms or as a percent of GDP. The degree of reported 'hostility' declined across the

[1] M Mitchell and H Mulherin 'The Impact of Industry Shocks on Takeover and Restructuring Activity' (1996) 41 J Fin Econ 193.

[2] G Anrade, M Mitchell and E Stafford 'The New Evidence and Perspectives on Mergers' (2001) 15 J Econ Persp 103; B Holmstrom and S Kaplan 'Corporate Governance and Merger Activity in the United States: Making Senses of the 1980s and 1990s' (2001) 15 J Econ Persp 121. I will subsequently use quantitative evidence assembled by these two papers without further citation.

[3] *CTS Corp v Dynamics Corp of America* 481 US 69 (1987).

[4] JA Grundfest 'Just vote No: A Minimalist strategy for Dealing with Barbarians Inside the Gates' (1993) 45 Stan L Rev 857 (1993).

decades, but we have come to realize that in many cases 'hostility' is merely an artifact of when a deal becomes public.[5] Many transactions that start off as unwelcome overtures end up as 'friendly' rather than 'hostile' if target management decides that resistance is unsustainable and undesirable. There has been some change in the nature of the bidders: There are very few financial buyers pursuing highly-leveraged hostile bust-ups, but this is more because of the dearth of target for which this 1980s deal strategy now makes economic sense. During the 1990s, the hostile bidders were 'strategic buyers', including some of the most widely-respected firms, with access to internally-generated capital. The shift in the nature of the buyers helps to explain why the minuet of resistance and capitulation often played out privately.[6] Nevertheless the threat of 'going hostile' is still very important, because many 'friendly' deals are negotiated against a backdrop of the hostile bid possibilities. Thus insofar as the merger waves of the 1980s and 1990s have played a positive role in the reshaping of American business, in enhancing the competitive focus of American companies, the hostile bid has played an important role, perhaps an essential role.[7]

The anti-takeover provision of the German Takeover Act provides a good example of a measure that might be adopted by many EU states if the 13th Directive process breaks down. In general, the Takeover Act, adopted in late 2001, provided a mandatory legal framework for the regulation of the bid-making process.[8] But a specific provision, Section 33(1), added late in the legislative process,

[5] GW Schwert 'Hostility in Takeovers: In the Eye of the Beholder?' (2000) 55 J Finance 2599.

[6] On a broad definition of 'hostile', there were an average of 40 hostile deals a year over the period 1994-1998, many fewer earlier in the decade. Even in the really rambunctious 1980s, the era of the financial buyer, the maximum number of hostile bids in any given year was less than 100, against many hundreds of friendly bids. JC Coates 'Measuring the Domain of Mediating Hierarchy: How Contestable Are US Public Corporations?' (1999) 24 J Corp L 837, 856. On a narrower definition of 'hostile', where the target rejects not only the first bid but subsequent bids, there were many fewer hostile deals, typically well under a dozen. JH Flom 'Mergers and Acquisitions: The Decade in Review' (2000) 54 U Miami L Rev 754, 761.

[7] See generally JN Gordon 'Employees, Pensions, and the New Economic Order' (1997) 97 Colum L Rev 1519.

[8] The Act is formally cited as 'Wertpapiererwerbs- und Übernahmegesetz' v 20 Dezember 2001 (BGBl. I. S. 3822). A useful summary of its provisions are found in the Int'l Fin L Rev (March 2002). A more extensive, very useful account, including a legislative history, is provided by G Apfelbacher and others 'German Takeover Law – A Commentary (CH Beck Munich 2002). See also H Schmidt and S Prigge 'The New German Takeover Act: An Economic Perspective' (2003) 1 Int'l J of Disclosure and Governance Nos 1 and 2.

To be sure, the Act is more than an 'anti-takeover law'. It regulates all aspects of public bids in Germany, and insofar as it establishes clear rules and procedures and brings some useful innovations to German corporate law such as the freeze out merger, it may aid the making of offers for German firms, including hostile offers. Nevertheless its distinctive feature, the subject of extended debate during the legislative process, is the anti-takeover element.

allows management to take defensive measures merely upon approval of the supervisory board, without first going to shareholders for prior approval.[9] In other words, this German anti-takeover law has rejected the 'board neutrality'/'shareholder choice' position generally associated with the 13th Directive, which, like the UK City Code, would forbid board action that would tend to 'frustrate' a takeover bid.[10] Instead, management may, with board approval, have significant discretion to resist a hostile bidder. This opens a new era in the response of a German company to a hostile bid.

First I want to trace the history of this provision, at least a seen by an American observer, but then, more importantly, try to argue why the German anti-takeover law may have more negative consequences on mergers and acquisitions in Germany and the European Union than comparable laws in the United States. The general argument is that the institutional and cultural factors that disarm high-powered anti-takeover devices in the US, like the poison pill, may not operate in Germany, and, by extension, in other EU countries. Finally I bring these arguments to bear on the present versions of the 13th Directive.

B. Germany and the 'Level Playing Field': The Problem of Economic Nationalism

Mergers serve two general objectives for Germany. The first relates to the traditional purposes of industrial organization: to achieve optimal size and scope for business operations, to reconfigure business units into better structures with verti-

[9] S 33(1) reads: 'After announcement of a decision to make an offer, up to the publication of the results of the offer, the management board may take no actions that could frustrate the offer. This does not apply [to certain action] ... *as well as for actions which have been approved by the target's supervisory board.*' (Thaeter and Frederick transl) (emphasis added).

[10] Article 9 of the July 2000 draft of 13th Directive that was narrowly voted down in the European Parliament provided in relevant part:

'during the period [beginning when the offer is publicly noticed and ending when the results are announced or the bid is withdrawn] the board of the offeree company shall obtain the prior authorisation of the general meeting of the shareholders, given for this purpose, before taking any action which may result in the frustration of the bid, other than seeking alternative bids, and notably before the issuing of shares which may result in a lasting impediment for the offeror obtaining control of the offeree company.'

For the Council text and the proposed amendments of the European Parliament, see European Parliament, Recommendation for Second Reading, 8129/1/200 – C5-0327/2000-1995/0341 (COD). For the ill-fated history of the July 2000 proposal, see JN Gordon 'The International Relations Wedge in the Corporate Convergence Debate' forthcoming in JN Gordon and MJ Roe (eds) *Convergence and Persistence in Corporate Governance* (Cambridge University Press 2004).

This particular article is essentially unchanged in the October 2002 Commission draft, COM (2002) 534 final, 2002/0240(COD), web-posted at <http://europa.eu.int/eur-lex/en/com/pdf/2002/com2002_0534en01.pdf> (site visited 17 August 2003).

cal and horizontal efficiencies, to permit useful consolidation where there is overcapacity, and on some occasions, to replace one managerial team with one that may perform better. In these purposes mergers in Germany have much in common with those in the US.

But Germany is also part of the transnational project that is the European Union, and thus cross-border mergers serve a distinctive and especially important objective. Only through cross-border mergers can enterprises rapidly grow large enough to take advantage of the huge potential scale economies of EU-wide commerce. One of the great advantages of the US is its internal common market, which gives national businesses the immediate opportunity to move along the experience curve towards the lowest per unit output costs. This internal market is not only a substantial engine of local prosperity but makes those firms formidable competitors in international trade. The creation of EU-wide firms offers Europe similar potential.

But apart from efficient scale, cross-border mergers rapidly build businesses that are conduits for the transnational free flow of capital, good, services, and people, and, no less, a transnational attitude. Cross-border mergers are important for Germany and the EU generally, because the business organizations that result, trans-European firms, help bind the EU into a single economic entity and thereby serve the project of transnational economic and political integration. The creation of economic and monetary union lays the groundwork for this powerful change, but cross-border mergers must play a very large role as well.

Nevertheless cross-border mergers entail a special sort of risk, the problem of economic nationalism. The government of the state of the target's organization will be legitimately concerned that investment and divestment decisions will be influenced by economic nationalism benefiting the state of the acquiror's organization. Will the acquiror show home country bias in either facilities location decisions or in layoffs or downsizings? Another way to put the question: Will the minister insist that the new plant be located in Lyon rather than Düsseldorf?

What best protects against the potential for such economic nationalism is the mutual vulnerability to takeover bids by both of the firms in question. To see this, assume the acquiror begins to show significant home country bias. This inefficiency in the acquiror's operations will lead to a fall off in shareholder value that would create an opportunity for a control entrepreneur, if the acquiror was also exposed to the potential for a hostile bid. In other words, if firms in all countries are equally exposed to the threat of hostile takeover, this will help constrain the economic nationalism that is the greatest threat to the EU project while permitting very valuable cross-border merger activity.[11]

[11] This is not to say that exposure to takeovers is a complete solution to the economic nationalism problem. A government could make payments or provide subsidies to cover the costs to the firm of economic nationalism and thus protect shareholder value. But such payments might be fiscally infeasible, they could be matched by a competing government, and, of course, such payments could be forbidden by the transnational regime. Takeover vulnerability

cont. ...

With this argument in mind, I therefore have some sympathy for the articulated basis for German opposition to the 13th Directive's position on board neutrality, the problem of the 'level playing field.' The 13th Directive in its 2001 version addressed only the particular barrier to a hostile bid rooted in the board's defensive response. But other, perhaps more significant barriers might be found in the underlying corporate law or in the local pattern of ownership structure (including state retention of special control rights through 'golden shares'), or the distribution of voting rights.

In the years that the 13th Directive was debated, Germany moved from a closed to a more open system of corporate control; many of its extra-board barriers came down. This took place through significant corporate law changes, for example, the end of capped voting and new limitations on bank exercise of customer proxies. Also important was a tax law change, the phase out in January 2002 of the capital gains tax on the sale of corporate shareholdings, that would eliminate the financial lock-in of corporate cross-shareholdings. There were also ownership structure changes that produced over the 1990s a significant increase in the number of firms with dispersed ownership without a large blockholder.[12] Most importantly, there were cultural changes, reflected in the contrasting reactions to Pirelli's (unsuccessful) cross-border hostile bid for Continental in 1991, Krupp's (unsuccessful) bid for Thyssen (1997), and Vodafone (successful) cross-border hostile bid for Mannesmann in 1999. Germany had opened itself to the market for corporate control to a much greater extent than its EU partners, except for the UK, and, not unreasonably in my view, was concerned about potential harms from economic nationalism potentiated by an incompletely liberalized cross-border merger regime. Yes, undoubtedly there were concerns – some legitimate, many overblown – on the part of managers and employees about the adjustment costs of economic change that also motivate anti-takeover legislation in the US. But I would like to think that the crucial element in the German coalition against the 13th Directive and for section 33(1) of the new German anti-takeover law consisted of those who wanted to see Germany's tougher position as a bargaining chip in a kind of trade negotiation, a raising of barriers designed to precipitate a crisis and force a new round of negotiations that would lower trade barriers – here, takeover protections – across the board.

makes it harder for a government to promote economic nationalism simply by imposing the costs on shareholders. (Note that the temptations of this approach are increasing in the percentage of foreign stock ownership and that stock-for-stock cross border mergers will almost certainly increase the percentage of initial foreign ownership.)

[12] In 1991 approximately 10 percent of German publicly traded firms were either widely-held or had no large (25 percent or more) blockholder. T Jenkinson and A Ljungvist 'The Role of Hostile Stakes in German Corporate Governance' (2001) 7 J Corp Finance 397, 405. By 1999 the corresponding percentage was 25 percent. See C Van der Elst 'The Equity Markets, Ownership Structures and Control: Towards and International Harmonisation?' in KJ Hopt and E Wymeersch (eds) *Capital Markets and Company Law* (Oxford University Press Oxford 2003).

Thus, as I shall elaborate later, I commend the work of the Group of High Level Experts, the Winter Commission, whose report in January 2002 explicitly addressed the level playing field issue;[13] its proposals were the basis for the European Commission's revised 13th Directive of October 2002. Moreover, the European Court of Justice also seems newly sensitive to the risks of economic nationalism. A series of decisions in June 2002 created something like a rebuttable presumption against golden shares as notionally restricting the free movement of capital. A government must now show that the golden share legislation is a precisely tailored scheme for the protection of a legitimate national interest.[14] In particular the ECJ rejected a golden share retained by France in Elf-Acquitaine that permitted the Minister virtually unbounded discretion to block any significant accumulation in the company's shares.

C. The Different Impact of Anti-Takeover Measures, Germany vs US

The second part of my argument is to explain why the German anti-takeover law will have far more adverse consequences than its US counterparts. A popular defence/apologia for the German law is a harmonization-type argument: if target defensive tactics work out, all things considered, in the US, then they should work for Germany.[15] These arguments rest on a faulty factual premise: that defensive measures really protect US firms from hostile bids. They do not. Generally speaking, they merely structure a process in which the target board can negotiate a higher price for the shareholders. But that fortunate outcome is the result of institutions and practices that may not be easy to reproduce in Germany. Thus the same basic legal rules may lead to a radically different outcome in Germany.[16]

European are familiar with the 'poison pill' commonly adopted by US firms and think of it as the ultimate anti-takeover weapon. But even more potent is the synergistic combination of the poison pill and a 'classified' or 'staggered' board,

[13] Report of the High Level Group of Company Law Experts on Issues Related to Takeover Bids, January 10, 2002 (Annex 2 in this volume). Hereafter: Winter Report on Takeover Bids.

[14] Commission v France, C-483/99 (4 June 2002); Commission v Portugal, C-367/98 (4 June 2002); Commission v Belgium, C-503/99 (4 June 2002).

[15] An additional argument is a level-playing field argument. As should be apparent, I think the force of this argument in the EU setting does not work for the US, where control is quite contestable notwithstanding legally permitted defensive measures. The Winter Commission's empirical studies bear out the point that there is no legally-driven imbalance in cross-border merger activity between Germany and the US. (n 9, Annex 5).

[16] A general version of this point is why many academic lawyers are skeptical of the conclusions often drawn from the 'Law and Finance' literature.

available to perhaps 50 percent of large US firms.[17] The poison pill, is on its own, formidable. It operates by penalizing an unwanted acquiror that crosses an ownership threshold, say 15 percent, by giving the *other* shareholders the right to purchase target shares at a bargain price. To give an example based on the standard US pill: assume the target has 100 shares of stock outstanding. Then if a bidder were to acquire more than 15 shares, the remaining shareholders would have the right to acquire (from a stock issuance by the target) an additional 85 shares at a price equal to 50 percent of the bidder's per share acquisition price. In other words, the flip-in pill operates through a discriminatory issuance of cheap shares that would massively dilute the hostile bidder's stake. In light of this economic penalty, no poison pill has ever been triggered, meaning that, in a formal sense, no hostile bid has ever succeeded against a firm with a poison pill left in place.[18]

But the poison pill is not, in fact, an insuperable barrier, because an untriggered pill can be readily redeemed by the firm's board of directors (that's part of the point, after all). So the hostile bidder's countermove is to wage a proxy contest to elect a friendly slate of directors at the shareholders meeting, who will then redeem the pill to permit the conditional bid to go forward. This countermove is, as a practical matter, thwarted if the target board is 'classified', that is, subdivided into classes of directors with three year terms (the typical maximum in US law). This means that in order to gain control over the target board, the bidder would have to wage two election contests. The bidder's venture now becomes prohibitively risky: Not only must it bear the risk of holding together an electoral coalition across an additional 12-18 months period (remember that the bidder's own shareholdings are capped by the pill's trigger point), but also, more seriously, the market risk. A year later, the transaction may no longer make economic sense. Thus the classified board exponentially increases the real anti-takeover power of the poison pill.

Bebchuk, Coates, and Subramanian ('BCS') have demonstrated the theoretical power of the pill/classified board combination.[19] They examined all the hostile bids made for US firms in the 1996-2000 period, a total of 96 hostile bids. In this group, 47 firms had 'effective' classified boards;[20] 45 firms did not. All firms had

[17] For fuller accounts, see JN Gordon 'Just Say Never? Poison Pills, Deadhand Pills, and Shareholder-Adopted Bylaws: An Essay for Warren Buffett' (1997) 19 Cardozo Law Rev 511; LA Bebchuk, JC Coates IV and G Subramanian 'The Powerful Antitakeover Force of Staggered Boards: Theory, Evidence, and Policy' (2002) 54 Stan L Rev 887.

[18] It may be worth noting that the US 'poison pill' is structured under of the law of the state of incorporation of a US corporation and that the particular features may vary by state. There is no 'federal corporation law' in the US, in part because of important US Supreme Court cases that have in important ways confined some potentially expansive provisions of the US securities law to disclosure problems rather than substantive conduct or fiduciary duty.

[19] LA Bebchuk, JC Coates IV and G Subramanian (n 17).

[20] BCS use the locution 'staggered board' rather than 'classified board', and distinguish as well a category of 'effective' staggered, or classified, boards to take account of imperfectly

cont. ...

the poison pill. BCS determine that there was not 'a single ballot box victory' against a firm with an 'effective [classified] board'. In the whole group, 32 firms remained independent: 21 classified board firms, 11 others. This, BCS say, means that approximately 11 firms remained independent that otherwise would have been sold, because of the board classification.

What is remarkable, however, is how insubstantial this effect is in the overall scheme of the US takeover market. In the BCS study, 21 firms with this ultimate defensive power remained independent, and the losses to target shareholders were approximately $11 billion. But: there were over *40,000* acquisition transactions in the period, valued at $6.4 *trillion*; the accrued gains were *$1.9 trillion*. This means that the percentage of transactions where an 'effective [classified] board' made an ultimate difference was vanishingly small (0.03%); those cases account for 0.4% of the total m&a activity and 0.5% of the gains. Moreover, BCS present no evidence of a selection effect of targets and the sheer volume of acquisition activity combined with the ubiquity of classified boards (approximately half of public firms) makes a powerful selection effect unlikely. The BCS findings in the context of the overall US takeover market powerfully demonstrate the limited effect of anti-takeover measures in the US.

The point is hardly that the US has set the ideal legal tests for target takeover defensive measures, or that defensive measures are *necessarily* ineffective.[21] Rather, it's that a set of mitigatory institutions, or adaptive institutions,[22] of structure and culture means that high-powered defensive measures do not, in practice, systematically impede the US takeover market. In particular, US managers are subject to a governance structure that generally renders them roughly accountable to shareholders and are compensated through mechanisms that gives them powerful incentives to accept premium takeover bids. US managers are also embedded in a professional culture in which shareholder interests dominate stakeholder interests. My strong sense that equivalent institutions and cultural predispositions do not exist in Germany, and by extension the EU (except perhaps for the UK), so that defensive measures considerable milder than the poison pill

drawn charters or bylaws that let shareholders change or otherwise bypass the classified board protections.

[21] I have previously argued, as have BCS, that state courts should sharply limit the board's power to resist a hostile bid for a firm with a classified board where a potential acquiror has prevailed in a proxy contest for a class of directors coupled with a conditional takeover bid. See JN Gordon 'Just Say Never? Poison Pills, Deadhand Pills, and Shareholder-Adopted Bylaws: An Essay for Warren Buffett' (1997) 19 Cardozo Law Rev 511. As I shall discuss below, some of the mechanisms that have reduced the effect of high-powered defensive measures have been costly for shareholders. The point is simply that the US takeover market has proceeded relatively unimpeded nevertheless, because of institutions that are unlikely to prevail or arise in the EU.

[22] M Kahan and EB Rock 'How I Learned to Stop Worrying and Love the Pill: Adapative Responses to Takeover Law' (2002) 69 U Chi L Rev 871.

would have a much greater effect on the German (and EU) takeover market. So *formally* equivalent takeover protection will not be *functionally* equivalent.

Here are three examples of differences with far-reaching effects in the takeover arena: the poison pill, the composition of the board of directors, and particular executive compensation devices First, the favoured US defensive measure, the poison pill, will not be available to German managers, who are likely to substitute value-reducing defensive measures that, unlike the pill, are genuine deal breakers. As discussed above, the pill operates through discrimination against a disfavoured shareholder, a possible hostile bidder who crosses an ownership threshold without the board's approval. The threat of massive dilution freezes the disfavoured shareholder in its tracks. But it appears that a poison pill would not be feasible under German corporate law because its discriminatory feature would violate strong mandates for pre-emptive rights.[23] If so, German anti-takeover measures will resemble those used in the US in the 1970s and early 1980s, which were principally efforts to disrupt the economic logic of the acquisition. Favoured tactics included: defensive acquisitions to create competition policy problems for the acquiror; creating a blocking position for a 'white knight' through a sweetheart sale of securities; selling off assets that an acquiror might prize, the target's 'crown jewels'; reshaping the capital structure, as through additional leverage, to confound the acquiror's financing of the bid; entering into so-called 'tin parachute' agreements that promise large bonus payments to rank and file employees upon a control shift; exotic tactical moves, such as the so-called 'Pac-Man' defence of responding to a hostile bid with a counterbid for the putative acquiror.[24] In disrupting the acquiror's economic logic, however, these measures often reduce the value of the firm; they can destroy the firm in order to save it. Such self-destructive measures are now used by virtually no firm in the US, but they may be inevitable in light of the limited alternatives under German corporate law.[25]

[23] German law requires a 75 percent vote for the limitation of preemptive rights, AktG 186(4), and requires an explicit written explanation before the shareholder vote. If the US experience is any guide, shareholders would simply not approve. A poison pill has virtually never been put to shareholder vote in the US principally on the belief that the shareholders would reject it. Moreover, since the shares will be issued conditionally, a flip-in pill would be subject to additional, more limiting requirements for conditional increases in capital, AktG 192. Similar protection for preemptive rights and barriers to discriminatory share issuances are common in European corporate law and are buttressed by the Second Company Law Directive.

[24] For a useful catalogue, see RJ Gilson and BS Black *The Law and Finance of Corporate Acquisitions* (2d edn Foundation Press 1995) 734-773.

[25] Some might argue that existing German cases and statutes would limit management flexibility to act without shareholder approval in this possibly value-reducing way. For example, the *Holzmüller* doctrine [BGHZ 83, 122 ff] requires the Management board to obtain shareholder approval for a transfer of substantial assets. Moreover, the duty of conscientiousness and prudence required for Management board and the Supervisory Board decisions, AktG § 93, 116, may lead parties concerned about personal liability to seek shareholder approval for defensive

cont. ...

In terms of the comparative takeover market, there is an additional important point: Unlike the pill, which can be redeemed by the board to permit a bid proceed, these tactics are typically irreversible, and, if effective, will indeed fend off the acquiror, permanently. By contrast, the pill, because redeemable, has become a channelling mechanism that structures a bargaining process. It forces a bidder to negotiate with the board instead of its preferred strategy of making an offer directly to the shareholders. Indeed, US defenders of the pill claim that targets more typically use the pill to empower the board as a shareholder bargaining agent (thereby protecting dispersed shareholders against a 'low ball' tender offer) rather than for managerial entrenchment. Whatever the merits of that contestable claim, deploying a pill does not irrevocably commit the board to a rejectionist position. Thus the irreversible takeover defences open to German (and EU) boards are not simply substitutes for the pill. They could hamper the takeover bargaining process; if they reduce the value of the firm, they will produce lower takeover prices, and, in general, such defences are likely to have a much more disruptive effect on the takeover market.

Second, the typical US practice of annual shareholder elections of board members combined with heavy institutional investor ownership in large public firms means that managements and directors are highly sensitive to public shareholder interests in considering a takeover bid.[26] This of course affects how any particular defence tactics, eg, the poison pill, will be used. The fact that shareholders, and only shareholders, vote for directors establishes both legal and functional reasons for exclusive managerial accountability to shareholder interests. Moreover, most managers (and directors) of US firms are trained in a business school culture that typically emphasizes 'shareholder value'.[27] Thus management's understanding, a product of law and acculturation, that the firm is to be run for the shareholders, means that many bids, even if initially unwelcome, become friendly rather than hostile.

Compare Germany. The two-tier board structure under co-determination already reduces shareholder influence. Half the directors are labour representatives, often elected by unions with very broad goals. The dynamics of board composition mean there will be greater emphasis on stakeholder concerns in considering a takeover bid, or deciding whether to deploy defensive measures and to what pur-

measures. Nevertheless the courts may well decide to give broad scope to the legislative delegation of authority in [Takeover Act] § 33(1) to the Management and Supervisory Boards to act unilaterally in the face of a hostile bid. In any event the courts are likely to employ a form of 'business judgment rule' review, which in the US has meant a great deal of deference to board decisions taken in good faith after a reasonable process of investigation and deliberation. Boards may be reluctant to seek shareholder approval, either 'reserve authorization' within eighteen months of the offer, much less authorization after the offer, out of concern that shareholders will refuse and will thereby make subsequent unilateral management actions harder to justify.

[26] Even firms with classified boards run a highly visible annual election process.

[27] John Coates made this observation.

pose. Moreover, the co-determined structure of the board will lend itself to considerations beyond the welfare of a particular firm or its employees, much less its shareholders: how might a bid affect a particular industry (and employees at other firms) or the precedent that is set. Also important is the five year term for supervisory board members, which attenuates the board's sense of accountability to shareholders. Yes, under German law a 75 percent holder can remove and replace supervisory board members,[28] but observe how hard it can be to assemble 75 percent in a proxy contest for control and by, contrast, how easy it is to assemble a blocking coalition. So the German board structure and electoral pattern predicts for a more resistant use of defensive options in the face of a hostile bid.

On the cultural differences between US and German managements and boards, here is an interesting test case. As part of the wave of US state anti-takeover statutes enacted in the late 1980s, boards were often given explicit authority (though not a directive) to take account of stakeholder interests, called non-shareholder 'constituencies'.[29] Such constituency provisions buttressed the legal position of the board in refusing to redeem a poison pill, since its fiduciary duties now explicitly extended beyond shareholder interests. Indeed, in resisting a hostile bid, managements commonly invoked its concern for employee and other interests, citing the statutory permission. But such protestations almost invariably crumbled in the face of an improved bid B all the proceeds of which went to the shareholders. Indeed, insofar as a higher bid put additional financial pressure on the acquiror to reduce costs, arguably the invocation of the constituency provisions *reduced* employee welfare. Compare Germany again: German legal scholars have struggled to establish a mandate for shareholder primacy in the Aktiengesetz.[30] Would something like a constituency statute be sloughed off by German management and boards as a mere bargaining counter in the effort to extract a higher bid for the shareholders? Could managers and boards, having invoked such a statute on behalf of stakeholder interests in mounting a takeover defence, simply reverse course as the bidder sweetened the offer?

Third, perhaps the most important reason why takeover defences will play out differently in the US and Germany (and the EU generally) is the use of executive compensation devices in US that powerfully align managerial and shareholder interests in the takeover decision. Even if such devices are legally permitted in Germany (or the EU), their use is likely to run afoul of strong cultural constraints on managerial compensation. There are two important devices involved here: a 'golden parachute', which provides a large cash severance payment triggered by a

[28] AktG § 103.

[29] Delaware's antitakeover statute did not include such a provision.

[30] Compare eg P Mülbert 'Shareholder Value aus rechtlicher Sicht' [1997] ZGR 129-171 with, eg A v Werder 'Shareholder Value-Ansatz als (einzige) Richtschnur des Vorstandhandelns' [1998] ZGR 69-91.

change in control; and 'accelerated option vesting', which makes stock options granted over a long term immediately exercisable, upon a similar trigger.

Golden parachutes came into common usage in the US beginning in the mid-1980s on the basis of normative and practical considerations. Some argued that hostile takeovers could unfairly expropriate firm-specific human capital investments made by senior managers, and that a compensatory payment was both appropriate and necessary to encourage future such investments.[31] Others said that uncertainties created by an offer would make it easy for competitors to lure away key executives and that a generous severance package, forfeited upon resignation, was the necessary corrective. There was also the obvious, if less seemly, practical point that senior executives whose economic futures were made secure might give greater weight to shareholder interests in evaluating a hostile bid. In any event, there is now the well-developed compensation practice of a golden parachute package that commonly provides a cash payment of approximately three times the executive's salary and average bonus, plus other benefits-related protections (for heath insurance and pensions).[32]

Accelerated option vesting arises as a by-product of the use of stock grants as a significant component in the compensation of senior managers, especially the chief executive officer. Stock options have the feature that if the stock price significantly appreciates, the managers receive a correspondingly large payout. If used correctly, this can be a very useful incentive alignment mechanism with shareholder interests.[33] These stock option grants are typically structured to vest over time, a 5-10 year period, typically, both for retention purposes and also to give the managers long term incentives. However, upon a transfer of control, the vesting of the options will accelerate; they vest all at once, meaning they become immediately exercisable. There is a reason for the accelerated vesting: It would not necessarily be easy or desirable to convert options of the target into options of the acquiror, particularly since the acquiror may wish to install new managers. However, the practical effect is that the CEO of a target not only does well but can become genuinely rich. Why resist a takeover bid that is not only value increasing for the shareholders but also delivers a great payday for yourself and your management team?

[31] JC Coffee Jr 'Shareholders Versus Managers: the Strain in the Corporate Web' (1987) 85 Mich L Rev 1.

[32] See generally AD Chinn 'Change of Control Arrangements' in MS Sirkin and LK Cagney (eds) *Executive Compensation* (American Lawyer Media 2003). The US tax law effectively caps the salary and bonus multiple at three.

[33] As recent cases, such as Enron, in the US demonstrate, it is also possible to add so many stock options as to drive managers to prefer risks that shareholders would not countenance or to engage in outright fraud. See JN Gordon 'What Enron Means for the Management and Control of the Modern Business Corporation: Some Initial Reflections' (2002) 69 U Chi L Rev 1233; 'Governance Failures of the Enron Board and the New Information Order of Sarbanes- Oxley' (2003) 35 U Conn L Rev 1125.

Both of these compensation devices help explain why there are so many takeover bids in the US but few hostile bids. Golden parachutes provide managers with a very good payoff in event of a takeover; accelerated option vesting (whose importance varies with the use of stock options) can provide a bonanza. Note that these methods of incentive alignment impose costs on target shareholders. Indeed, one way to understand these devices is as a buyback by shareholders of the takeover-resistance endowment that managers were able to obtain from the legislatures and the courts during the 1980s. A first-best legal regime might avoid these costs by imposing greater restraint on target defences. Nevertheless, US institutions have made the necessary adaptations, so that the theoretical power of managers and boards to thwart a hostile bid is rarely invoked. To recall the prior statistics: less than 100 (of 40,000) acquisitions in the US takeover market of the late 1990s were reported as 'hostile'; in only 32 did managers press the point to the end.

It is unlikely that these compensation mechanisms would be available in Germany to overcome the resistance power that anti-takeover legislation would provide to German managements.[34] Stock option plans have only recently been introduced as a significant element of executive compensation. Until corporate reform legislation in 1998 (the 'KonTraG'), stock options could be issued only through a quite cumbersome method, and, apart from high tech companies that traded on the Neuer Markt, their usage has been far from ubiquitous. Large option grants, which should have the strongest pro-takeover effect, appear to run against the German tradition of a relatively narrow spread in the ratio of CEO and average worker compensation, 13-1 in Germany vs 34-1 in the US (in 1999). Some measure of the cultural constraint in executive compensation is reflected by the reluctance of German public companies to report individual compensation amounts.[35] Only the reporting of aggregate compensation to the management board is legally required. The 'best practices' code (the Crime Code) calls for individual reporting and a detailed breakdown by compensation type, as would be found in a typical US annual proxy statement. Nevertheless only a small minority of even the largest public firms make such disclosure, only 5 of the 24 German companies in the FTSE Eurotop 300.[36]

A good test for the plausibility of a executive compensation strategy that would overcome managerial resistance to takeovers is the reaction to Klaus Esser's receipt of a € 15 million bonus after the consummation of the Mannesmann takeover. From an American perspective, Esser is a hero: his negotiating

[34] See generally B Cheffins 'The Metamorphosis of Germany, Inc.: The Case of Executive Pay' (2001) 49 Am J Comp L 497, which is the basis for much of the description that follows.

[35] G Ferrarini, N Moloney and C Vespro 'Executive Remuneration and Corporate Governance in the EU: Convergence, Divergence and Reform Perspectives' chapter II. 5. herein.

[36] ibid. The Crome Code did, however, explicitly endorse the use of stock options and other performance based compensation approaches. See Cheffins (n 34).

strategy and his determination to let the shareholders decide delivered tens of billions of extra euros for the Mannesmann shareholders. The bonus he received would not be remarkable. In Germany, there is a criminal prosecution underway of Esser and of various notable Mannesmann supervisory board members. If the reshaping of executive compensation with devices like a golden parachute and significant stock options to counteract management's new capacity to protect power and perquisites is not feasible, then the German anti-takeover law will be a significant barrier to good deals as well as bad ones.

The difficulties have been deepened by the recent European Commission decision to require all firms listed on a European stock exchange to adopt International Accounting Standards within the next five years.[37] Unlike US GAAP, IAS requires the expensing of executive stock options. If the US executives who fought so hard against reform proposals in the early 1990s to require expensing are correct, then the IAS rule will independently stifle large stock option grants for European managers. In other words, the impact on reported earnings of large option grants may suppress their use independent of cultural factors. But the consequence will be a significant difference in management's incentives in the face of a hostile bid as compared with the US paradigm.

In sum, to give target management the prerogative to engage in defensive measures in Germany (or elsewhere in the EU) will play out quite differently than in the US. German (and other EU) managements are likely to employ defences that are far more disruptive of the firm's ongoing business and the overall takeover market. They would not be subject to the powerful institutional and cultural constraints that operate in the US. Formally similar legal rules on the use of defences will produce sharp functional differences in the takeover markets.

D. Prospects for a Revised 13th Directive?

In the aftermath of the defeat of the June 2001 version of the 13th Directive, the Commission convened a 'High Level Group of Company Law Experts' to address some of the open issues, in particular, the level playing field concerns that ultimately proved fatal. The High Level Group's answer to the level-playing field problem was a remarkable 'breakthrough' proposal that would override internal governance provisions (such as dual class common stock or capped voting) that could limit the control rights of a bidder who obtained a qualified majority of a firm's 'risk bearing capital'. The High Level Group was attacked from both sides. The 'levelers' objected that the proposal was too conservative, because it did not affect entrenchment schemes common in some EU countries, such pyramidal structures and shareholder agreements, that also protected the control rights of minority equity holders. The 'anti-levelers' objected even more

[37] v 13 February 2002, COM (2001) 80 endg 2001/0044 (COD).

vociferously that the scheme was too radical, because its 'breakthrough' of dual class structures abrogated voting schemes that had been bargained over and paid for.[38] The European Commission's revised proposal of October 2002 tried to make progress with the levelers without destroying the possibility of consensus by narrowing the breakthrough provision to restrictions on share transfers and shareholder voting.[39] The new proposal has met additional resistance from Germany, the UK, and other countries, probably because the changed economic and stock market circumstances since June 2001 have heightened concerns about the economic and political fallout out sometimes associated with hostile bids. What might be called the 'transition costs of capitalism' are easier to bear in prosperous, optimistic times. The prestige of the US model has also been undercut to some extent by Enron-related corporate governance problems.

The Portuguese have stepped into this breech, with a proposal (as of June 2, 2003) based on 'reciprocity'. Individual countries would have the right to opt in or opt out of the 13th Directive board neutrality/limited breakthrough regime of the October 2002 draft. Even in countries which opted out, individual firms could opt in. The twist is this: only firms that are subject to the 13th Directive regime (whether by country or individual choice) could obtain its benefits in making a takeover bid. So assume that Germany and the UK opt in, choosing to subject their firms to the 13th Directive regime, but France opts out. In a hostile bid by a UK firm for a German firm, the German firm must follow a board neutrality approach as defined in Article 9,[40] and the UK firm can break through protective stock transfer or voting rights restrictions under Article 11.[41] On the other hand,

[38] This of course assumes that such terms have been efficiently priced, a proposition rejected by the Winter Commission.

[39] COM (2002) 534(01), available through <http://europa.eu.int/comm/internal_market/en/company/company/news/index.htm> (last visited 20 August 2003).

[40] Article 9 of the October 2002 draft provides in the relevant part:

'During the [pendency of the bid], the board of the offeree company must obtain the prior authorisation of the general meeting of shareholders given for this purpose before taking any action other than seeking alternative bids which may result in the frustration of the bid and in particular before issuing any shares which may result in a lasting impediment to the offeror in obtaining control over the offeree company.'

[41] Article 11 of the October 2002 draft provides in relevant part:

> 2. Any restrictions on the transfer of securities provided for in the articles of association of the offeree company shall be unenforceable against the offeror during the period for acceptance of the bid.
>
> Any restrictions on the transfer of securities provided for in contractual agreements between the offeree company and holders of its securities or between holders of securities of the offeree company shall be unenforceable against the offeror during the period for acceptance of the bid.
>
> 3. Any restrictions on voting rights provided for in the articles of association of the offeree company shall cease to have effect when the general meeting decides on any defensive measures in accordance with Article 9.

cont. ...

the French hostile bidder (unless it separately subjects itself to the regime) could not object to defensive measures by the German firm or use the breakthrough powers. The goal of this proposal is to encourage a race to the top among countries and firms with respect to a 'high quality' takeover regime. For example, UK and German firms (and shareholders) will be doubly advantaged, through higher returns stemming from the efficiency-enhancing effects of greater exposure to control markets and through higher returns stemming from more combinations that achieve scale and scope economies. On the second advantage: since lower defensive barriers increase the likelihood of deal consummation, a UK bidder is more likely to investigate combinations with German firms than with French firms, all other things equal. So countries (or firms) that opt in will obtain greater benefits of the EU single market. It is a somewhat unusual proposal, with great deference to 'reciprocity' and volunteerism at the expense of simplicity, crafted in the effort to offer a 13th Directive that no one can refuse.[42]

E. Conclusion

Germany's rejection of the 13th Directive in July 2001 did indeed catalyse serious reflection on the level playing field problem, which bears importantly on the control of economic nationalism in cross-border merger activity. Yet a continued unwillingness to accept the 13th Directive under various proposed compromises and instead to push forward to permit target defensive measures will have serious costs. First, takeover defences will be much more effective in Germany (or most other EU countries) than in a country (the US) with background governance and cultural norms that favour shareholder interests. But even more important, adoption of the 13th Directive is tied up with the project of economic and political integration in the EU. At a minimum, the Directive establishes and clarifies procedures for the making of bids. This alone should enhance cross-border merger activity. Both the October 2002 Commission draft and the Portuguese proposal keep open a credible threat of a hostile bid, which will stimulate additional cross-

> Any restrictions on voting rights provided for in contractual agreements between the offeree company and holders of its securities or between holders of securities of the offeree company shall cease to have effect when the general meeting decides on any defensive measures in accordance with Article 9.
> 4. Where, following a bid, the offeror holds a number of securities of the offeree company which, under the applicable national law, would enable him to amend the company's articles of association, any restrictions on the transfer of securities and on voting rights referred to in paragraphs 2 and 3 and any special rights of shareholders concerning the appointment or removal of board members shall cease to have effect at the first general meeting following closure of the bid.
> To that end, the offeror shall have the right to convene a general meeting at short notice, provided that the meeting does not take place within two weeks of notification.

42 The proposal also contemplates that it will be revisited in five years.

border activity and help constrain economic nationalism. Without the 13th Directive, many fewer mergers will take place. Yet such mergers, especially cross-border mergers that achieve transnational scale, may be the key to greater economic competitiveness and to the EU project of economic and political integration that has stirred the hopes of the world.

Why Continental European Takeover Law Matters

ALLEN FERRELL*

This paper addresses the following question in the context of considering the recommendations of the High Level Group of Company Law Experts on Takeover Bids: Why does Continental European takeover law matter given the concentrated ownership structure of most Continental European firms? In answering this question, the paper discusses the interaction between takeover rules and ownership structure and the possible lessons that can be drawn from the British and American experience with takeover regulation. While a ban on the use of defensive tactics without shareholder approval (possibly in conjunction with a mandatory bid rule) can theoretically have the effect of either encouraging or discouraging the adoption of dispersed-ownership structures, the empirical evidence suggests that the former would be the more likely result. Moreover, the British and American experience highlights the importance of adopting a takeover regime earlier rather than later in time.

A. Why Worry About Continental European Takeover Regulation?

At first glance, it is not obvious why takeover regulation in Continental Europe is a particularly important topic. The ownership structure of firms in Continental Europe, compared to that of their U.S. and British counterparts, is very concentrated. While corporate ownership structures have seen changes over the last ten years, concentrated ownership is still the norm in Continental Europe. Berglof and Burkart, for instance, report that more than 50% of listed, non-financial companies in Austria, Belgium, Germany and Italy have a single control block with a majority of voting rights. In contrast, only 3% of companies in the United States

* Helpful comments and suggestions were provided by participants at the May, 2003 conference on 'A Modern Regulatory Framework for Company and Takeover Law in Europe – The Corporate Governance and Takeover Recommendations of the High Level Group of Company Law Experts to the European Commission.' I would like to thank the Harvard Law School John M Olin Foundation for Law, Economics and Business for financial support.

and the United Kingdom have a single control block with a majority of voting rights.[1]

Takeover rules governing the use of defensive tactics by target management, along with many other so-called 'technical barriers'[2], are critically important when there is a wide dispersion of ownership and control rights. If a company has a controller, whether that control is due to a large ownership stake or disproportionate voting rights, then these rules rapidly fade in importance. An acquisition will only occur when – and only when – the controller consents or has somehow lost control.

First impressions can be deceiving. The recommendations contained in the High Level Group of Company Law Experts on Takeover Bids (hereinafter, the Winter Report), an important set of recommendations produced by a distinguished committee of company law experts, would, after all, affect some European companies.[3] This would still be true even if the Winter Report's proposed 'break-through rule' – a rule that would permit a bidder that acquired a certain percentage of the risk-bearing capital of a firm to acquire control of that firm – were limited to only those bidders who obtain 75% of the risk-bearing capital of a firm.[4] Some recent empirical evidence, utilizing data on European firm ownership and control structures, indicates that the Winter Report's recommendations would, in fact, affect a nontrivial number of firms.[5] Even a small slice of the European Union's eight trillion dollar economy is surely worthy of sustained attention.

But there are perhaps even more compelling, if less straightforward, reasons why this is a timely and important topic. Part B will discuss the interaction between so-called 'technical barriers', the focus of the Winter Report's analysis, and 'structural barriers' to takeovers. 'Technical barriers' can have an effect on

[1] E Berglöf and M Burkart 'European Takeover Regulation' (2003) 36 Economic Policy 179. In more than 50% of non-financial, listed companies in Netherlands, France, Spain and Sweden there is, respectively, a single control block with 43.5%, 20%, 34.5% and 34.9% of the voting rights.

[2] 'Technical barriers' typically refer to those barriers to takeovers that are the result of various statutes and regulations that allocate power between various participants in the corporation. 'Structural barriers', on the other hand, refer to barriers resulting from such economic phenomena as ownership concentration.

[3] Report of the High Level Group of Company Law Experts on Issues Related to Takeover Bids, European Commission, Brussels, 10 January 2002 (hereinafter Winter Report on Takeover Bids). There was a second report issued on company law generally in November of 2002. See Report of the High Level Group of Company Experts on a Modern Regulatory Framework for Company Law in Europe, 4 November 2002 (see Annex 2 and 3 in this volume).

[4] At this point in time it looks as if the proposed 'break-through rule' will not be pursued by the European Commission.

[5] M Bennedsen and K Nielsen 'The Impact of a Break-Through Rule on European Firms' (2003) Working Paper Copenhagen School of Economics.

'structural barriers'. Part C will then consider some possible lessons the British and American experience with takeover regulation hold for why European takeover law matters despite its ownership structure and how European takeover regulation might profitably proceed. These discussions will provide a good vehicle for raising some of the issues that need to be addressed in evaluating the merits of the Winter Report's recommendations on takeover regulation.

B. Interaction Between Technical and Structural Barriers to Takeovers

The Winter Report goes out of its way to make clear that it does not take a position on either the general desirability of concentrated ownership nor the need for 'harmonizing' ownership structures in the European Union. But avoiding these topics entirely is not possible. The presence (or lack) of a market for corporate control of companies with dispersed ownership could have an effect on whether a concentrated ownership structure for some European firms will continue to persist. In other words, the interaction between 'technical barriers' to takeovers (such as the use of defensive tactics by target management) and 'structural barriers' (such as concentrated ownership) must be considered in an overall analysis of the Report's recommendations.[6]

Unfortunately, the sign of this interaction effect is theoretically unclear. 'Technical barriers' might either encourage continued concentrated ownership or promote dispersed ownership. Consider the first possibility. High, systematic levels of concentrated ownership is often attributed, at least in part, to poor corporate law which enables controllers to enjoy private benefits of control, often at the expense of minority shareholders.[7] If there are significant private benefits of control for controllers and an active market for corporate control in companies with dispersed ownership, then this could make it *less* likely that companies with a controlling share block will adopt a dispersed ownership structure via the controller selling his control block.[8] There is the possibility that a third party will acquire control of the company with a dispersed ownership structure, given the existence of an active market for corporate control, and thereby acquire the private benefits of control for himself. This possibility would make it less likely that a controller will agree to a dispersed ownership structure in the first place if

[6] Cf R Gilson 'The Political Ecology of Takeovers' in KJ Hopt and E Wymeersch (eds) *European Takeovers* (Butterworths London 1992) 49-75.

[7] See generally R La Porta, F Lopez de Silanes, A Shleifer, and RW Vishny 'Legal Determinants of External Finance' (1997) 52 J Fin. 1131; R La Porta, F Lopez de Silanes, A Shleifer, and RW Vishny 'Investor Protection and Corporate Governance' (2000) 58 J Fin Econ 3. As the Winter Report properly emphasized, however, concentrated ownership should not be viewed as a probem per se.

[8] See generally LA Bebchuk 'A Rent-Protection Theory of Corporate Ownership and Control' (1999) NBER Working Paper 7203 (modeling this effect).

such a decision will merely result in an uncompensated transfer of the private benefits of control from himself to a third party.

There is another story, however, one could tell. Concentrated ownership might be the result of high managerial costs resulting from a dispersed ownership structure rather than high private benefits of control associated with control blocks (or perhaps a combination of the two).[9] The high agency costs associated with the paradigmatic Berle and Means corporation might deter controllers from adopting such a structure in the first place. A market for corporate control, energized by a takeover-friendly regime, could reduce these managerial costs and thereby render a dispersed ownership structure more attractive than it otherwise would be to a controller considering relinquishing control.

So which is it? The balance of the evidence indicates that a more robust takeover market would render dispersed ownership structures more, rather than less, attractive. It is true that there is strong empirical evidence that controllers in Continental Europe, on average, enjoy substantial private benefits of control. This empirical evidence consists of the premiums paid for control blocks and voting shares. These premiums are widely interpreted as proxying for the size of the private benefits of control. The premium paid for a control block in Italy, for example, is 25% to 30% of firm value. The premium on shares with voting rights (with the baseline being shares without voting rights) is some 28% in France.[10] More generally, the size of the private benefits of control around the world do appear to be associated with ownership concentration.[11]

However, it is unlikely that the Winter Report recommendations on takeovers would deter controllers (more than they currently already are) from adopting a dispersed ownership structure for fear of a new controller extracting private benefits of control. A centerpiece of the Winter Report's recommendations is the proposal that target management be barred from taking 'actions frustrating a takeover bid' without shareholder approval.[12] It would obviously be in the interests of shareholders in a dispersed company to authorize management to block a bid by a party primarily interested in extracting private benefits of control. And it would be in the interests of target management to point this out if they wish to have the bid defeated.

The effects of the mandatory bid rule need to be addressed in assessing the probability that a new controller, rather than increasing firm value, would extract private benefits of control at the expense of minority shareholders. As is well know, a mandatory bid rule reduces the probability of a value-reducing takeover

[9] M Roe 'Corporate Law's Limits' (2002) 31 Journal of Legal Studies 233 discussion of this point.

[10] T Nenova 'The Value of Corporate Voting Rights and Control: A Cross-Country Analysis' (2003) 68 J Fin Econ 325.

[11] See generally R La Porta and others (1997 and 2000) (n 7).

[12] Winter Report, Recommendation 1.2.

as an acquirer, once the mandatory bid rule is triggered, will be unable to benefit at the expense of non-controlling shareholders.

All of this is to say that the Winter Report would be unlikely to deter the adoption of dispersed ownership structures. But would it encourage it through reducing managerial costs associated with dispersed ownership structures? The bulk of the evidence suggests that the threat of a hostile takeover does, in fact, operate to reduce managerial costs and thereby increase the value of firms with dispersed ownership structures.[13] For example, in a recent paper Gompers, Ishii and Metrick found that companies with more anti-takeover protections had a lower Tobin's Q (one commonly used measure of firm valuation) throughout the 1990s.[14] Moreover, they found that anti-takeover protection was associated with poorer firm performance in terms of their return on equity and sales growth. Studies measuring market reactions to the adoption of various state anti-takeover statutes have documented significant, negative market reactions.[15] Consistent with these studies are the findings by Bertrand and Mullinathan that more anti-takeover protection is associated with weakened managerial incentives to minimize labour costs.[16]

But this evidence also suggests the possibility that a mandatory bid rule has a serious downside if it increases the cost of takeovers, perhaps through increasing financing costs and increasing bidders' exposure to idiosyncratic firm risk, and thereby reduces their probability. There is a further cost if the mandatory bid rule is applied to firms with concentrated ownership as this might reduce sales of control blocks and thereby 'lock in' the current controller even if another controller would be able to add value. This is potentially a quite serious cost.

It is necessary to weigh this cost against the benefit of a mandatory rule in forcing potential controllers to internalise the costs of any private benefits of control they may wish to enjoy upon achieving control and, hence, make it more likely that a controller will be willing to move to a dispersed ownership structure in the first place. The importance of this benefit will be different for different countries. While private benefits of control do appear to be, on average, quite substantial in Continental Europe, there is significant variation across countries. For instance, the voting premium on shares with voting rights in Denmark is 1%, which is actually lower than that of the United States.[17] In the U.S. there is some

[13] I am using a very broad notion of 'managerial costs' covering a wide range of managerial conduct.

[14] P Gompers, J Ishii and A Metrick 'Corporate Governance and Equity Prices' (2003) 118 Quarterly Journal of Economics 107.

[15] eg M Swartz 'The Massachusetts Classified Board Law' (1998) 22 J Econ & Fin 29.

[16] M Bertrand and S Mullinathan 'Executive Compensation and Incentives: The Impact of Takeover Legislation' (1998) NBER Working Paper 6830.

[17] T Nenova 'The Value of Corporate Voting Rights and Control: A Cross-Country Analysis' (2003) 68 J Fin Econ 325.

empirical evidence suggesting that most block trades are not motivated by bidders wishing to extract large benefits of control.[18] However, in countries with high levels of private benefits of control, unlike Denmark and the U.S., the mandatory bid rule might play an important role in protecting shareholders in a takeover situation. Given the enormous variation in the private benefits of control, the trade-off in terms of what a mandatory bid rule should look like might very well vary as well. A one-size fits all approach, mandated at the European Union level, may therefore be inappropriate.

One final suggestive piece of evidence on the effects of having a market for corporate control on ownership structure is some recent research indicating that acquisition and merger activity in the United Kingdom was the primary mechanism by which ownership became dispersed.[19] Might the pattern of acquisition and merger activity in Continental Europe account for the different ownership structures? And would changing the pattern and incidence of acquisition and merger activity – via a more robust market for corporate control in dispersed corporations – affect ownership patterns in Continental Europe? There is still much research that needs to be done on the interaction between acquisition and merger activity and the mechanisms driving shareholder dispersion.

C. Standing the Test of Time? Two Case Studies

Putting aside the interaction between 'technical' and 'structural' barriers to takeovers, there is another important reason for why one should be interested in Continental European takeover regulation at this particular point in time. It is precisely when the number of companies potentially 'threatened' by a hostile takeover is relatively small that regulators have somewhat more leeway in the type of legal regime they can realistically consider. A takeover regime, for instance, that limits managers' ability to impede unwelcomed takeovers, as is proposed in the Winter Report, might well prove politically impossible to enact in a situation where management across the corporate universe view themselves as potentially on the receiving end of a hostile takeover bid.

Of course, regulatory regimes can change over time in response to new pressures. All of this leads to the following question: Which regulatory approaches have stood the test of time? And what lessons might they hold for Continental European takeover regulation? I will begin with a discussion of the U.S. and British experience with takeover regulation and then will draw some tentative lessons these experiences may hold for the European Union.

[18] E Berglöf and M Burkart (n 1) at 196-198 (discussing the empirical evidence on this point).

[19] JR Franks, C Mayer and S Rossi 'The Origination and Evolution of Ownership and Control' (2002) Working Paper.

I. The United States

The takeover regime in the United States is an example of a regime that has not clearly addressed the legality of most takeover defences (including, crucially, the 'poison pill' defence in the presence of a staggered board of directors) until relatively late in the game.[20] Indeed, some have suggested that it was not until the Delaware Supreme Court's 1995 opinion in *Unitrin v American General Corporation* that it became reasonably clear that corporate management has the right to maintain, with very little in the way of justification, a takeover defence against an unwanted takeover bid without the need to obtain shareholder approval. In *Unitrin* itself, target management's justification for not bringing the bid before the shareholders for consideration was the *claim* that shareholders, given their possible ignorance and confusion, were incapable of assessing the merits of the bid.[21] The Delaware Supreme Court found this justification to be a legally sufficient basis for target management's use of a defensive recapitalization to block the bid.

It is hard to see how this is a justification given the fact that management can always claim that shareholders are confused and ignorant. The sweeping nature of the *Unitrin* justification is troubling. As Vice Chancellor Strine of the Delaware Chancery Court put it, 'If stockholders are presumed competent to buy stock in the first place, why are they not presumed competent to decide when to sell in a tender offer after an adequate time for deliberation has been afforded them?'[22] One would like to see at least some evidentiary basis before such a presumption were made.

Regardless of whether the *Unitrin* case of 1995, or some point a few years earlier, is the exact date that the broad permissibility of defensive tactics became clear,[23] the important point is that corporate law in the United States only addressed this issue long after hostile takeovers had first appeared on the scene in a major way. Indeed, and not coincidentally, the 1980s saw the hostile takeover

[20] That is not to say that there were not takeover cases prior to the 1990s that provided some guidance. There obviously were. See *Unocal Corp v Mesa Petroleum Co,* 493 A.2d 946 (Del 1985); *Cheff v Mathes*, 199 A.2d 548 (Del 1964). But there was substantial uncertainty about the limitations these cases placed on the use of defensive tactics. See R Gilson and R Kraakman 'Delaware's Intermediate Standard for Defensive Tactics: Is there Substance to Proportionality Review?' (1989) 44 Bus Law 247 (describing this uncertainty).

[21] The Unitrin Board was concerned that 'Unitrin's shareholders might accept American General's inadequate Offer because of ignorance or mistaken belief regarding the Board's assessment of the long-term value of Unitrin s stock'. 651 A2d 1384 (Del 1995).

[22] *Chesapeake Corp v Shore*, 771 A.2d 293 (Del Ch. 2000).

[23] Other academics, myself included, read the Delaware Supreme Court's 1989 opinion in *Paramount Communications, Inc v Time*, 571 A2d 1140 (Del 1989) as the moment when it became reasonably clear that target management has broad authorization to use defensive tactics.

being commonly used by bidders interested in breaking up and streamlining companies. In those acquisitions, target management often lost not only their private benefits of control associated with running the target company but their jobs as well. In reaction to the 1980s boom in the use of the hostile takeover, corporate management (along with other groups) placed enormous pressure on states – regulators and legislators alike – to legitimise the use of defensive tactics regardless of shareholders' views.

While the question of how much discretion states would provide target management in the use of the 'poison pill' defence was left unresolved in the 1980s, states did adopt a series of anti-takeover statutes throughout the 1980s providing target management with more leeway in preventing and blocking unwanted bids. Once the constitutionality of the first wave of state anti-takeover statutes were called into question in the early 1980s in *Edgar v Mite*,[24] states substituted these constitutionally suspect laws with a new set of anti-takeover statutes.

The fact that a group disadvantaged by a particular practice would seek regulatory and legislative protection from that practice is neither surprising nor grounds for criticizing U.S. corporate law. Such is life. But what made corporate management's views on this matter particularly influential is the ability of corporations to select, through their (re)incorporation decision, which state's corporate law – including takeover law – will govern the corporation. More specifically, corporate management, under the law of every U.S. state, has a veto over whether reincorporation to another state will occur. States, such as Delaware, which care about maintaining (or increasing) their stock of incorporations will therefore give substantial weight to managerial interests. In other words, corporate management, in addition to whatever lobbying effort it undertook, was given leverage by the very regulatory structure of corporate law in the United States.

The end result of this process has been state takeover law that has placed relatively few discernable limits – as the *Paramount v Time* and *Unitrin* cases illustrate – on the use of takeover defences in the typical hostile takeover context.[25] The takeover defence that is the most potent, and therefore the most troubling, is the use of the 'poison pill' defence in conjunction with a staggered board. With a 'poison pill' in place, a bidder cannot acquire control of a target company without acquiring control of the target board first. And with a staggered board in place, a bidder cannot acquire control of the target board, given the staggered terms of directors, unless the bidder is willing to wait several years. The number of hostile takeovers in the 1990s, compared to the rate in the 1980s, dropped by approximately two-thirds. Tellingly, it was in the 1990s that it became clear that the

[24] 457 US 624 (1981).

[25] Few discernable limits does not mean none. The Delaware courts have, to their credit, prohibited the use of so-called 'dead-hand poison pills'. See *Camody v Toll Brothers*, 723 A.2d 1180 (1998). Moreover, when management puts a company up for sale, this will trigger heightened fiduciary duties to shareholders. *Revlon,* 506 A.2d 173 (1985).

'poison pill' defence would be permitted in a wide range of circumstances. Moreover, and equally telling, those companies that did not have a staggered board were unable to convince shareholders in the 1990s to adopt one. Most firms eventually gave up even trying.

This pessimistic interpretation of U.S. takeover law is not universally shared by legal academics or practitioners. One common defence is the observation that the explosion in stock option incentive compensation in the 1990s has made target management more likely to agree to a bidder's offer in the first place as stock options typically vest upon completion of a merger.[26] A value-maximizing Coasian bargain can now be struck whereby target management enjoys vested stock options, the bidder acquires the target, and target shareholders receive whatever market premium is being offered by the bidder. The empirical support for this claim, at least at this date, is lacking.[27]

It would be an overstatement to claim that there are no mitigating factors. The weakness of U.S. takeover law is offset somewhat by the fact that it is a commonly held view in the United States that the corporation should, at least ordinarily, be run in the interests of shareholders. The prevalence of this belief does make it more difficult, as a practical matter, for corporate management to block hostile takeovers regardless of shareholders' interests. Cultural norms and widely held attitudes can matter.

II. The United Kingdom

The United Kingdom's takeover regime, on the other hand, is an example of a regime that has taken – from an early point in the history of hostile takeovers – a clear position on the use of takeover defences that is much superior to the U.S. position.

Prior to World War II, merger and acquisition activity in Great Britain consisted of a bidder convincing the target's board of directors to sell their personal shares to the bidder. Target directors would then inform shareholders that they had sold their shares and that they recommended that shareholders follow suit. The bidder would then typically purchase shares from tendering shareholders on the same terms offered directors.[28] In short, takeovers were negotiated deals involving target management. Shareholders were encouraged to follow the lead of management.

[26] eg M Kahan and E Rock 'How I learned to stop worrying and love the pill' (2002) 69 U Chicago L Rev 871.

[27] See generally JC Coates IV and R Kraakman 'CEO Incentives and Merger Activity in the 1990s: Stock Options and Real Options' (2003) Working Paper.

[28] Franks, Mayer and Rossi (n 19).

It was only in the 1950s that hostile takeovers appeared on the scene as result of entrepreneurs like Sigmund Warburg and Charles Clore. Shortly after they gained notoriety with their use of hostile takeovers, the 'Notes of Amalgamations of British Business' was introduced in 1959 outlining the basic principles that were to govern takeover bids. Nine years later, in 1968, the first version of the City Code on Takeovers and Mergers was published. Right from the start the City Code contained General Principle 7 which bars target companies, once a bona fide offer has been made or is imminent, from taking action which would 'frustrate[ ]' the bid without first receiving shareholder authorization. This principle has remained a centerpiece of the City Code since that time. It has always been understood as seriously limiting the ability of target management to block unwelcomed bids.[29]

And what of defences adopted in the pre-bid period? There are a number of relevant statutory and London Stock Exchange rules that impede the adoption of certain types of defensive tactics. In addition to these provisions, there is a common law doctrine that managers may only use their corporate powers for 'proper purposes'. In the groundbreaking case of *Hogg v Cramphorn* it was concluded that placing a large block of stock in a trust fund established for the benefit of corporate employees was found to constitute an improper purpose under English common law given that the purpose of the managers in placing the shares was to block potential bidders.[30] As far as I am aware, the 'poison pill' has never been used in the United Kingdom. It would very difficult to articulate a purpose behind the 'poison pill' that did not consist of impeding or blocking unwanted bids.[31]

What accounts for the strong, persistent pro-shareholder position taken by British law in the takeover context? One factor might be that, unlike in the United States, a clear position on the role of shareholders in the context of a hostile bid was taken early on. Hostile takeovers first arrived on the scene in the 1950s. By the end of the 1950s, there was already a preliminary regulatory framework in place. By 1968 the City Code was firmly in place. Taking a sound position early on had two possible benefits. First, corporate managers did not see hostile takeovers as much a threat as they later on might have given their frequency at the time. This provided regulators with some space, in contrast to the situation in the United States, in crafting a regulatory regime. Second, once a regulatory position

[29] One commentator has summarized General Principle 7 as basically limiting the defensive tactics of management to 'providing information to the shareholders..., appealing to shareholder loyalty or patriotism, using their own and their supporters' resources to buy target company shares in the market..., and lobbying the government to have the bid referred to the Monopolies and Mergers Commission'. P Davies 'The Regulation of Defensive Tactics in the United Kingdom and the United States' in (KJ Hopt and E Wymeersch) *European Takeovers* (Butterworths London 1992) 200.

[30] See [1967] Ch. 254, [1966] 3 AER 420 Ch. 254.

[31] P Davies (n 29) at 210.

was adopted a certain degree of inertia inevitably set in. It is harder to change a regulation, generally speaking, than it is to enact one.

But surely inertia is not the entire explanation. How was it that the City Code, throughout all its revisions over the years, managed to retain General Principle 7 and its overall focus on shareholder empowerment? A partial answer might lay in the composition of the Takeover Panel, which is responsible for administering the City Code. The Takeover Panel is a self-regulatory body whose decisions, despite its traditional quasi-governmental status, have virtually never been ignored.

The membership of the Takeover Panel is diverse representing the interests of a number of different participants in the capital markets. This membership includes institutions representative of investors such as pensions funds and investments trusts. Members also include industry participants such as the British Merchant Banking and Securities House Association, the Stock Exchange, the London Investment Banking Association and the Institute of Chartered Accountants. In addition, companies themselves are represented by the Confederation of British Industry. Moreover, the Takeover Panel throughout its history has worked closely with the Bank of England.

The composition of the Takeover Panel, and its relationship with the Bank of England, ensures that the interests of all capital market participants are represented including investors as well as corporate managers. Any proposed change to takeover regulation, such as General Principle 7, would likely fail without first obtaining broad consensus across these different constituencies. Since the promulgation of the City Code in the 1960s, many commentators have noted that a strong culture has developed in the City emphasizing the important role played by shareholders in the running of the corporation, including their right to assess for themselves the merits of a bid. Indeed, the Confederation of British Industry has objected to proposals at the European Union level authorizing the use of defensive tactics as undermining the proper role of shareholders.

III. Lessons

So what lessons do these two (brief) case studies hold for how to approach the regulation of takeovers in Europe? I will draw attention to three tentative lessons that can be drawn from the British and American experience in takeover regulation that are worth considering when evaluating the Winter Report's recommendations.

1. The Desirability of Addressing Takeover Regulation Early

One way in which the United States and United Kingdom differ is when they addressed the legality of various defensive tactics. The United Kingdom addressed this issúe far earlier than the United States and has had since that time a widely admired takeover regime. Simple political economy considerations suggest that the two are not entirely independent. The earlier a takeover regime is erected the more leeway regulators have, all else being equal, in considering different possible approaches.

Timing might be especially important for Continental Europe where labour is particularly powerful politically.[32] If there is a hostile takeover that is widely perceived as resulting in layoffs (whether true or not) then this runs the risk of increasing the political pressure to adopt a takeover-hostile regime. The negative political reaction in many quarters to the hostile takeover by Vodafone of Mannesmann and the failure of the Thirteenth Directive is cause for concern on this score. Of course, there are no guarantees. If the political pressures are sufficiently strong, then a takeover-friendly regime, regardless of when it is adopted, will be unlikely to survive.

It might be helpful, in this regard, to emphasize that protection of various 'stakeholders' in the corporation, such as employees, is an analytically separate question from whether a mandatory bid rule, a break-through rule or a ban on the use of defensive tactics is good policy. Stakeholder protection, assuming that is one's goal, can be addressed separately from takeover regulation. Employee protection need not imply providing management with the means to block unwanted takeovers.

2. Participation in the Regulatory Process

Another lesson that can be drawn from the American and British experience is the importance of which market participants are given a voice in the regulatory process. The structure of regulatory competition in the U.S. has resulted in managers have a great deal of influence over the corporate law that governs their firm. The regulatory process in the United Kingdom, in contrast, ensures that investors and other market participants, in addition to corporate management, play an important ongoing role.

Naturally there are many ways that shareholders can be given a voice in the regulatory process. The United Kingdom's self-regulatory model is only one. Lucian Bebchuk and I have proposed for the United States a regime of regulatory competition in corporate law but one that empowers shareholders to make reincorporation decisions not subject to a managerial veto.[33] We labelled this 'choice-enhancing' competition. Criticism of U.S. takeover regulation need not imply a distrust for competition. Indeed, a 'choice-enhancing' approach emphasizes the need for a diversity of approaches that cover the spectrum of shareholder needs and preferences in a variety of settings.

[32] I would like to thank Mark Roe for pointing this out.

[33] LA Bebchuk and A Ferrell 'A New Approach to Regulatory Competition' (2001) 87 Virginia Law Review.

In contrast, the Winter Report states that shareholders should not be permitted to make a decision, prior to a bid occurring, on whether to provide management with the authorization to use defensive tactics. Shareholders' decisions must be made *ex post*; after a bid has been made. This is perhaps the most troubling aspect of the Winter Report's recommendations. This limitation of shareholder choice is in tension with shareholder decision-making, the first guiding principle of the Report. What shouldn't shareholders be able to make a decision *ex ante*? Under the 'choice-enhancing' proposal, shareholders could, if they wanted to, elect a regime where it is settled that takeover defences are unavailable to target management before a bidder ever arrives on the scene.

Under a range of circumstances, it is plausible that shareholders will conclude that the optimal arrangement entails some element of *ex ante* commitment on their part. It might be that shareholders *ex post* will find it in their interests to authorize the use of defensive tactics so as to enable management to extract a higher takeover premium from the bidder. But this might not be the optimal regime *ex ante* given the lower probability of a bid in the first place. Of course, this does not mean that what shareholders will decide to do *ex ante* is obvious. There is an extensive debate and discussion in the American legal academic literature over exactly when shareholders might find it in their interest to commit to a position on defensive tactics in the pre-bid period.

The only explanation the Winter Report provides for limiting shareholder choice to the post-bid period is the belief that shareholders will be better informed once they can assess the merits of a particular bid. But shareholders will know this when they are deciding whether to authorize management to use defensive tactics in the pre-bid period. And if shareholders are too confused or disinterested to make this calculation, then why assume that shareholders are sufficiently competent to make decisions on defensive tactics in the post-bid period? Surely an across-the-board assumption of shareholder incompetence in the pre-bid period is too sweeping.

3. The Importance of Substitutes

A third lesson that can be drawn from the American and British experience is the importance of considering substitutes when regulating. For example, if one is concerned about the use of takeover defences, it is unprofitable to focus on only one particular type of defensive tactic. When the first generation of state antitakeover statutes ran into constitutional difficulty in the United States, states just substituted those statutes with a new set of statutes.

In contrast, the City Code in addressing the issue of defensive tactics has taken a broad principle-based approach prohibiting the use of takeover defences once a bid has been made regardless of the particular form of the takeover defence. Throughout the City Code's existence, the Takeover Panel has not hesitated in ruling that new types of takeover defences are impermissible. While there are specific prohibitions in the City Code on the use of certain defensive tactics,[34] this does not mean that defensive tactics not on the list are off the hook. For example, the use of litigation by a target as a delaying tactic, commonly used in the United States, is subject to General Principle 7 despite not being listed in any specific Rule.[35]

Has the Winter Report cast its net wide enough to avoid the danger that the use of substitutes will undermine its regulatory goals? The break-through rule applies to dual class shares but not to pyramid schemes. As other commentators have pointed out, the two are substitutes in that they both separate voting and cash flow rights.[36] It is possible that if the Winter Report's recommendations are implemented, firms will merely switch from using dual class shares to pyramid schemes in order to separate ownership from control. If substitution does occur, it is unclear what has been accomplished. The Report cannot be blamed for not addressing this issue given its mandate but it does highlight the importance of considering substitutes.

D. Conclusion

In assessing the Winter Report, a variety of issues need to be considered. One such issue is the implications that takeover regulation has for ownership structures. In general, a takeover-friendly market for corporate control will likely make dispersed ownership structures more attractive on the margin. The bulk of the empirical evidence suggests that takeovers play a useful role in allocating assets and disciplining management of companies with dispersed ownership. Takeovers are likely to be especially important for the economy of the European Union given the recent emergence of a common market and the implications this has for the optimal structure and organization of firms.

In thinking through how (and when) one should proceed when crafting a takeover regime, it is helpful to look to the U.S. and British experience in regulating takeovers. This experience holds three tentative lessons: (1) the importance of timing when making the hard choices involved in crafting a takeover regime; (2) the importance of who has influence over the regulatory process as it evolves over time; and (3) the need to consider substitutes when considering the impact of a particular regulation or legal rule.

[34] Rules 21 and 37.3.

[35] *Consolidated Gold Fields* (Takeover Panel, 9 May 1989) at 4.

[36] eg LA Bebchuk and O Hart 'A Threat to Dual-Class Shares' *Financial Times* (31 May 2002).

The Economics of the Proposed European Takeover Directive

JOSEPH A. McCAHERY, LUC RENNEBOOG,
PEER RITTER, and SASCHA HALLER

This paper analyses the empirical evidence on the cross-border takeovers in the EU and the economics of the proposed takeover code. The authors favour the view that the policy debate on the proposed Directive should focus on the economic implications of the proposed legislation. The empirical evidence supports the view that competitive forces in the European capital markets will be strengthened by increased transparency. The authors note that reported findings show, moreover, that high takeover premiums are correlated to increased transparency and enhanced shareholder protection. The presence of good corporate governance rules has a direct impact on corporate performance through market prices. Empirical claims show that well-governed bidders find it easier to raise capital to finance an acquisition. Overall, there are substantial gains to be achieved by creating an integrated cross-border takeover market in the EU.

Although proponents claim that a break-through rule is needed to create a level playing field for takeovers, the article shows that, in fact, the weight of evidence does not warrant support of this view. Moreover, even if the break-through rule were adopted, the authors recommend that bidders should compensate the holders of dual- and multiple-class shares that have been broken through. To the extent that the break-through provisions affect acquired rights, the system by which compensation is calculated should be sufficiently flexible to take full account of the diverse circumstances of the deprived shareholders. A sell-out right given to the holders of dual- and multiple-class shares is found to be an ineffective a means for compensation. The authors favour grandfathering the existing dual- class and multiple class shares for a substantial period of time. The authors conclude by recommending that the Proposed Directive should include: (1) a mandatory bid rule requiring that a bidder must make an equitable offer to all shareholders; (2) a simple rule, that after the bid is made, restricts target management intervention beyond expressing its own view about the proposed takeover bid; and (3) a simple and efficient rule on squeeze outs.

A. Introduction

On October 2, 2002, the European Commission (EC) presented a new proposal for a Directive on Takeover Bids in an effort to harmonize takeover regulation across the European Union (EU). This is designed to 'contribute to the development and reorganisation of European firms' by integrating European markets, increasing legal certainty and providing protection for minority shareholders. Naturally facilitating the development of a takeover market is designed to have an impact on the corporate governance arrangements of continental European countries, which rely on a different set of financing and monitoring arrangements than the United Kingdom. In the context of the ongoing debate over the EU-wide harmonization of takeover regulation, this paper will evaluate recommendations of the High Level Group (HLG) Report and the Proposed Directive and use this evidence to derive conclusions about the necessity and rational for harmonization of takeover regulation.

The Proposed Directive focuses on three types of transactions: (1) takeovers in general; (2) mandatory bids; and (3) certain types of squeeze-outs. It aims at setting certain minimum guidelines for corporate conduct and transparency in the takeover context. The key area of national law the Proposed Directive deal with are: disclosure on the bid, board neutrality, mandatory bid, mini-break-through rule, squeeze-out and sell-out rights, employee rights, and transparency.

The purpose of this chapter is to evaluate the main components of the Proposed Takeover Bids Directive. It provides a detailed analysis of mandatory bid rule, taking into account both the ex ante and ex post trade-offs. We examine the valuable features of the mandatory bid rule in safeguarding against value-decreasing takeovers, and seek to understand whether the Commission's decision to allow member states to define the threshold for the mandatory bid is a sensible approach. Building on that analysis, we also outline the main elements of the break-through rule, which has been invented by the HLG to address corporate structures that are deemed to reduce the incidence of takeovers. Our analysis identifies a number of factors that supply good reasons for rejecting the break-through rule.

One view that has received considerable support is the fair compensation approach to compensate holders of dual class and multiple class shares. However, such an approach is unconvincing not because compensation is unnecessary but because the proposed mechanism would actually reverse causality: the compensation rule would determine the premium. As a consequence, we argue that it is very likely that the voting premium, which currently ranges from 5% to 80% across the EU, would move toward the proposed 15%. There are different compensation procedures, some better than others, to compensate holders of dual class and multiple class whose shares have been broken through. In our view, firm level compensation schemes are likely to prove more effective than proposed mechanisms.

We also present the case for strict board neutrality. Advocates argue that the management board of the target firm is restrained from taking actions that could frustrate the success of the takeover bid. Against this background, we show that when there is a choice between two alternative regulations (board neutrality vs managerial veto), the EU should adopt the rule that is more favourable to outsider shareholders. Thus, a simple European rule of board neutrality is likely to limit opportunism and reduce legal uncertainty for foreign bidders.

Finally, the paper also discusses the proposed squeeze-out rules. We show that the thresholds, beyond which a squeeze-out can be initiated, still reflect national legal history. Because these thresholds are to some extent arbitrary, it is desirable that these provisions should be harmonized for sake of simplicity. In addition to this argument, we show that it may be of little cost to streamline the rules such that an independent expert valuation is eliminated from the fair price determination. We conclude that the fair price presumption itself could also be streamlined.

The paper is comprised of three main parts. Part I provides a summary of the differences in the ownership and control structures in Europe. Part II supplies a brief history of takeover bids in the US and EU. Part III discusses the Proposed Directive, discussing the mandatory bid rule, the break-through rule, board neutrality, squeeze-out rules and the level playing field concept. To set the context of the discussion of the regulation of takeovers, this chapter commences in Section B with a discussion of the consequences of good corporate governance for the development of a strong and deep capital market. In Section C, we present the main features of the cross-country patterns of ownership and control in Europe. Our analysis of the differences in ownership patterns has important implications with regard to corporate governance. We show that shareholding concentration is much higher in Continental Europe than the UK, bank holdings are generally small in all countries unless they are part of a financial group, and that institutions and directors are the main shareholders in the UK, but do not hold much voting power.

As a backdrop, Section D provides explanations for the differences in concentrations across companies and countries. This section documents the corporate law mechanisms that allow controlling shareholders in Continental Europe to obtain greater premium for their shares. In Section E, we shift our focus to examine the main features of the takeovers in the United States and the European Union. In particular, we report on the value and size of deals in the EU during the fifth takeover wave as well as the means of payment. In Section F, we examine the determinants of bidder and target returns. In our analysis, we identify the variety of profitability drivers, noting that the main motive for mergers and acquisitions is the value created from buyer and seller synergies. In Section G we turn to examine the legislative history of the Proposed Takeover Bids Directive. We examine the key features of the High Level Group's recommendations. While the last sub-section of Section G.II. supplies a brief overview of the newly proposed legislation, Section H goes on to address the main features of the mandatory bid and break-through rule. In Section I, we shift our focus to board neutrality and consider whether there is a good case for boards to intervene ex post into the takeover process. In Section J, we examine the proposed squeeze-out rules with respect to the differences across countries. Finally, we discuss, in Section K, the concept of the level playing field for takeovers.

B. Corporate Governance and the Cost of Capital

Investors value good corporate governance. Discussions of corporate governance systems tend to identify a link between investor protection and the development of a country's capital market. Additionally, some argue that the greater the protection afforded to minority shareholders and creditors, the greater the probability that firms will receive external financing at a lower cost of capital. Not surprisingly, this issue has figured prominently in policy discussions in recent years regarding the corporate governance practices that companies should embrace.

Recent research explores the effect of corporate governance on stock market valuation. The work of La Porta, Lopez-de-Silanes, Shleifer and Vishny[1] is responsible for developing this new line of research to explain the differences in corporate governance systems by referring to the level of legal protection provided for minority shareholders and the degree of capital market development. La Porta et al. found that common law systems tend to outperform civil law systems by adopting legal rules that offer better protection both for expropriation of shareholders by management and the violation of the rights of minority shareholders by large shareholders. In their study of 49 countries, they classified these

[1] R La Porta, F Lopez-de-Silanes, A Shleifer and R Vishny 'Law and finance' (1998) 106 Journal of Political Economy 1113-1155; 'Ownership around the world' (1999) 54 Journal of Finance 471-517; 'Investor protection and corporate governance' (2000) 58 Journal of Financial Economics 3-27.

countries according to the origin of laws, quality of investor protection and quality of law enforcement. Moreover they investigated the extent to which a country adheres to the one-share-one-vote rule. A shareholder protection index was constructed which determined, inter alia, whether proxy voting by mail is allowed, whether minority protection mechanisms are in place and whether a minimum percentage of share capital entitles a shareholder to call for an extraordinary general meeting. Creditor rights are aggregated into an index that is higher when the creditor can take possession of the company in the case of financial distress, when there are no restrictions on workouts and corporate reorganizations and when the absolute priority rule is upheld. Finally, the rule of law index produced by the rating agency, International Country Risk, indicates the country risk and the degree to which laws are enforced. Both the shareholders and the creditors are best protected in common law countries and receive least protection in French civil law countries (see Table 1). The Scandinavian and German countries come somewhere in between. The implication of La Porta et al's work is that countries should move toward the more efficient common law system based on transparency and arm's length relationships.[2]

Table 1: Shareholder and creditor protection

	Shareholder protection	One-share-one-vote	creditor protection
UK	4	0	4
US	5	0	1
English origin average	3.39	0.22	3.11
France	2	0	0

[2] Some argue that theoretical framework developed by La Porta et al is too limited for analyzing governance issues in developing countries (E Berglöf and E-L von Thadden 'The changing corporate governance paradigm' (1999) in Pleskovic and Stiglitz (eds) *World Development Conference* (The World Bank) and SITE Working Paper No 99/03, Stockholm School of Economics). For instance, Berglof and von Thadden argue that La Porta et al's focus on protecting minority shareholders and creditors is far too narrow even to be applied to most European countries. Moreover, they also pay more attention to the protection of external finance and tend to ignore other important constraints on firm growth. By emphasizing the importance of dispersed ownership, the approach of La Porta et al. only appears relevant to the developing country context. Others argue that there have been significant changes, over the last twenty years, in the pattern of developing markets finance. The differences in corporate and legal rules cannot easily account for the differences in financial arrangements in emerging markets (J Glen, K Lee and A Singh 'Competition, corporate governance and financing of corporate growth in emerging markets' (2000) University of Cambridge Department of Applied Economics discussion papers in accounting and finance No AF46). There are also many companies that are not covered by the La Porta et al study.

	Shareholder protection	One-share-one-vote	creditor protection
Belgium	0	0	2
Italy	0	0	2
Spain	2	0	2
Portugal	2	0	1
Netherlands	2	0	2
French origin average	1.76	0.24	1.58
Germany	1	0	3
Austria	2	0	3
Switzerland	1	0	1
Japan	3	1	2
German origin average	2.00	0.33	2.33
Denmark	3	0	3
Finland	2	0	1
Norway	3	0	2
Sweden	2	0	2
Scandinavian origin average	2.50	0.00	2.00
Overall average	2.44	0.22	2.30

Source: La Porta et al[3]
Notes: One-share-one-vote is a dummy variable which equals 1 if one share carries one vote (no multiple class voting rights). The shareholder protection is index is higher if shareholders can mail their proxy votes, are not required to deposit their shares prior to the general meetings, cumulative voting is allowed, minority shareholders are protected and a minimum percentage of share capital allows a shareholder to call for an extraordinary general meeting. The creditor rights index is higher if absolute priority is followed in case of financial distress.

Other studies show analogous correlations. For example, the level of shareholder protection has been shown to relate inversely to the size of the premium over the market price paid for a majority voting block – higher premiums are commanded in countries with weak protections.[4] A direct connection between strong shareholder protections and the volume of initial public offerings has also been shown (see table 2). What these studies tend to confirm is the comparative advantage of

[3] Note 1 (1998).

[4] L Zingales 'The value of the voting right: A study of the Milan Stock Exchange experiment' (1994) 7(1) Review of Financial Studies 125-148.

countries that protect investors' interests. Recent empirical work by La Porta et al[5] found that firms operating in jurisdictions with strong shareholder protections have higher growth potential, as measured by Tobin's Q.

Table 2: External Finance and Legal Origin

	External Capital/GDP	Listed Domestic firms/Population	IPOs/ Population	Debt/GDP
UK	1.00	35.68	2.01	1.13
US	0.58	30.11	3.11	0.81
English origin average	0.60	35.45	2.23	0.68
France	0.23	8.05	0.17	0.96
Belgium	0.17	15.50	0.30	0.38
Italy	0.08	3.91	0.31	0.55
Spain	0.17	9.71	0.07	0.75
Portugal	0.08	19.50	0.50	0.64
Netherlands	0.52	21.13	0.66	1.08
French origin average	0.21	10.00	0.19	0.45
Germany	0.13	5.14	0.08	1.12
Austria	0.06	13.87	0.25	0.79
Switzerland	0.62	33.85		
Japan	0.62	17.78	0.26	1.22
German origin average	0.46	16.79	0.12	0.97
Denmark	0.21	50.40	1.80	0.34
Finland	0.25	13.00	0.60	0.75
Norway	0.22	33.00	4.50	0.64
Sweden	0.51	12.66	1.66	0.55
Scandinavian origin average	0.30	27.26	2.14	0.57
Overall average	0.40	21.59	1.02	0.59

[5] R La Porta, F Lopez-de-Silanes, A Shleifer and R Vishny 'Investor protection and corporate governance' (2000) 58 Journal of Financial Economics 3-27.

Source: R La Porta, F Lopez-de-Silanes, A Shleifer and R Vishny 'Legal determinants of external finance' (1997) 52 Journal of Finance 1131-50; 'Law and finance' (1998) 106 Journal of Political Economy 1113-1155; 'Investor protection and corporate governance' (2000) 58 Journal of Financial Economics 3-27.
Notes: External capital is defined as the equity capital held by shareholders other than the largest three shareholders. Initial public offerings are companies which are brought to the stock exchange. Debt is here defined as the sum of the issued corporate bonds and the funds provided by banks.

Furthermore, Lombardo and Pagano[6] find that better legal institutions influence equity rate of returns and the demand for equity finance by companies. They offer two reasons: good laws and efficient courts (1) curtail the private benefits of managers and (2) facilitate the contractibility of corporate relations with customers and suppliers and the enforceability of such contractual relations. In a context of better corporate legislation and more efficient courts, corporate profitability and growth will be higher which hence raises the amount of external financing. Better legislation leads in the Lombardo and Pagano model to a reduction of managerial benefits by introducing legal limits to transactions with other companies that may dilute the income rights of minority shareholders. Better legislation, ie class action suits or voting by mail, is also leading towards a reduction of the legal and auditing costs that shareholders must bear to prevent managerial opportunism. They conclude that the size of these effects on the equilibrium rate of return is increasing in the degree of international segmentation of equity markets.

For the most part, these studies document the effect of better corporate governance protection on financial market development.[7] Recent research looks at the effect of corporate governance rules on firm valuations within a single jurisdiction. In the context of market-based systems, that are characterized by dispersed equity holding, a portfolio orientation among equity holders and broad discretion of management to operate the business, shareholders are protected from abuse by an effective market for corporate control, a well-functioning board of directors, and strong fiduciary duties. Gompers, Ishii, and Metrick[8] create a

[6] D Lombardo and M Pagano 'Law and equity markets: a simple model' in J McCahery, P Moerland, T Raaijmakers and L Renneboog (eds) *Corporate Governance Regimes: Convergence and Diversity* (Oxford University Press Oxford 2002).

[7] Although these studies are provide evidence on the relation between legal rules and the cost of capital in a cross-section of developed and developing stock markets, some argue that the studies are limited because the direction of causality between legal system and financial structure runs in the opposition direction, viz. financial structure prompts transformations taking place in legal regime (P Bolton and E-L von Thadden 'Blocks, liquidity and corporate control' (1998) 53 Journal of Finance 1-25; LA Bebchuk and M Roe 'A theory of path dependence of corporate ownership and governance' (2000) 52 Stanford Law Review 775-808.

[8] P Gompers, J Ishii and A Metrick 'Corporate governance and equity prices' (2003) 118(1) Quarterly Journal of Economics 107-155.

governance index for US firms based on a large set of corporate governance provisions and focus on the relationship between governance and corporate performance. They provide evidence from 1500 US large firms that the firms with strong shareholders rights are associated with higher Tobin's Qs, higher profits, higher sales growth, lower capital expenditures, and undertook fewer acquisitions. Consistent with the theory of La Porta et al[9] firms that adopt stronger shareholders rights create substantial benefits for shareholders.

Similarly, Drobetz, Schillhofer and Zimmermann[10] further develop the one country approach pioneered by Gompers et al,[11] which links the relationship between strong shareholders rights and the long run performance of a cross-section of German firms. They classify corporate governance rules into five categories to construct a governance index, which is related cross-sectionally to leading measures, including dividend yields, price earnings ratios and book to market ratios. The evidence from Germany is broadly consistent with the central insights of Gompers et al study:[12] there is a significant relationship between strong investor protection rules and firm value. Using price to earnings ratios, dividend yields and historical returns to proxy the rate of return on capital, Drobetz, et al[13] provide evidence that for the sample period, from January 1, 1998 to March 1, 2002, the price earnings ratios and market to book ratios are positive, which implies, in turn, that better protection of shareholders leads to higher firm valuations.

The wealth of recent empirical studies that focus on the corporate governance system as the independent variable in a cross section of countries and evidence from Germany and the United States in support of the La Porta et al[14] theory suggests that good corporate governance is among the most important factors for determining the cost of capital.[15]

[9] R La Porta et al 'Investor protection and corporate governance' (2000) 58 Journal of Financial Economics 3-27.

[10] W Drobetz, A Schillhofer and H Zimmermann 'Corporate governance and expected stock returns: Evidence from Germany' (2003) University of Basel/Department of Finance working paper No 02/03.

[11] P Gompers, J Ishii and A Metrick Corporate governance and equity prices (2003) 118(1) Quarterly Journal of Economics 107-155.

[12] ibid.

[13] See note 10.

[14] La Porta et al 'Law and finance' (1998) 106 Journal of Political Economy 1113-1155.

[15] CP Himmelberg, RG Hubbard and I Love 'Investor Protection, Ownership, and Capital Allocation' (2002) Working Paper SSRN Feb 2002.

C. The Pattern of Ownership and Control in Europe

Figure 1: Percentage of Listed Companies Under Majority Control

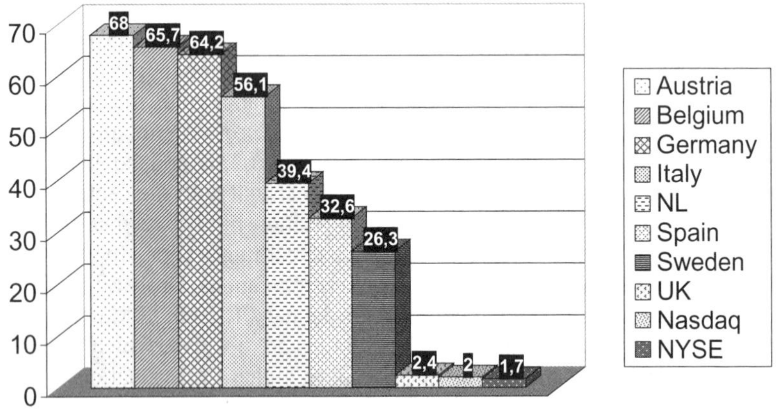

Corporate structures and ownership differ among countries and across economies. The recent empirical literature provides some international comparisons of ownership concentrations across western countries. Barca and Becht[16] analyze cross-country ownership patterns in Europe. Figures 1 and 2 show that most continental European countries are characterized by majority or near-majority holdings of stock held in the hands of one, two, or a small group of large investors. In contrast, the market-based system, which is found in the US and Commonwealth countries, is characterized by dispersed equity holding, a portfolio orientation among equity holders, and broad discretion on the part of management to operate the business.

[16] F Barca and M Becht *The Control of Corporate Europe* (Oxford University Press Oxford 2002).

Figure 2: Percentage of Companies with a Blocking Minority of at least 25%

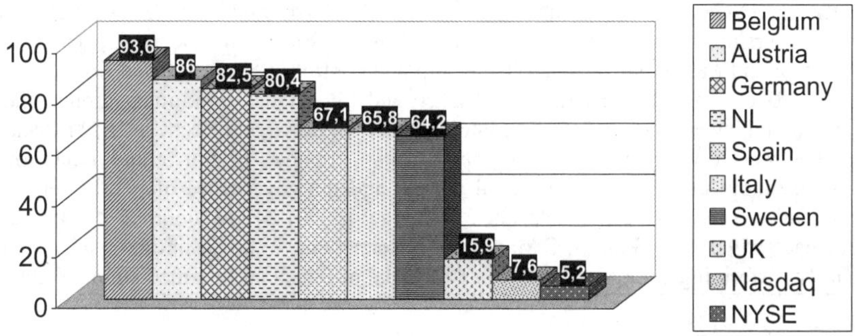

Table 3 shows further that the high degree of ownership concentration in continental Europe is striking; in French, German, Austrian, Belgian and Italian companies, a single shareholder (or a shareholder group) usually owns an absolute majority of shares. This stands in sharp contrast with the US and the UK where the largest shareholder owns an average stake of respectively 22.8% and 14%. Whereas a coalition of the three largest share holdings gives a cumulative share stake of more 60% in continental Europe (up to a super-majority of 75% in France and Austria), a similar coalition can vote a mere 30% of the shares in Anglo-American countries.

Table 3: Ownership distribution of largest shareholders in western economies

This table gives the size of the largest ownership stakes for European countries and the US. Ownership data are for 1996 (all countries) and 1994 (Belgium). The sample companies in all countries are listed, the Austrian sample consists of both listed and non-listed companies.

			Share holdings			
1996	Sample	Note	Largest	2nd largest	3th	4-10th
France	403	(1)	56.0	16.0	6.0	5.0
Austria	600	(1)	82.2	9.5	1.9	6.5
Italy	214	(1)	52.3	7.7	3.5	5.1
Netherlands	137	(2)	28.2	9.2	4.3	7.1
Spain	394	(1)	38.3	11.5	7.7	10.3
UK	248	(2)	14.0	8.3	6.1	9.2
			Largest	2nd + 3rd	4th + 5th	6-10th
Belgium	135	(1)	55.8	6.9	0.6	0.2
Germany	402	(1)	59.7	8.6	2.6	0.3

Note (1): both direct and indirect shareholdings are considered; (2): only direct shareholdings. Source: K Gugler et al 'The separation of ownership and control in Austria' in Barca and M Becht (n 16); M Becht, A Chapelle and L Renneboog 'Shareholding cascades: separation of ownership and control in Belgium' in Barca and Becht (n 16) 71-105; L Bloch and E Kremp 'Ownership and voting power in France' in Barca and Becht (n 16); R De Jong et al 'Ownership and Control in the Netherlands' in Barca and Becht (n 16) 188-206; R Crespi and M Garcia-Cestona 'Ownership and control of Spanish listed firms' in Barca and M Becht (n 16) M Bianchi, M Bianco and L Enriques 'Pyramidal groups and the separation between ownership and control in Italy' in Barca and Becht (n 16) M Becht and E Boehmer 'Ownership and voting power in Germany' in Barca and Becht (n 16) L Renneboog 'Ownership, managerial control and the governance of poorly performing companies listed on the Brussels stock exchange' (2000) 24 (12) Journal of Banking and Finance 1959-1995; J Franks, C Mayer and L Renneboog 'Who disciplines management of poorly performing companies?' (2001) 10 Journal of Financial Intermediation 209-248.

Furthermore, Table 4 shows that not only share concentration is different across countries, but that the main categories of owners also vary substantially across Europe and the US. The main shareholders are classified in (1) institutions (banks, insurance companies, investment and pension funds); (2) individuals (excluding directors) and their families; (3) directors and their families and trusts; (4) industrial, commercial and holding companies; and (5) the federal or regional governments. For each of these categories, we sum the voting shares they control directly (by owning shares directly in a target firm) as well as indirectly (as ultimate owners using intermediate ownership vehicles). In other words, we combine the voting shares controlled by an ultimate owner at the top of the ownership pyramid. Such pyramids or ownership cascades are frequently used in most continental European countries.

In France, the shareholder category of industrial and holding companies owns on average 34% of the shares. In Belgium, this number is even higher at 37%.[17] German industrial and commercial companies own an average stake of 21% in other German listed firms, or, from a different angle: in 52.4% of the sample companies, an industrial shareholder holds an average stake of 40%. This strikingly high concentration in hands of the corporate sector is also present in Spain, Italy, and Austria. In contrast, the industrial and commercial sector of the UK and the Netherlands owns less than 11% of the listed companies.

[17] The distinction between an industrial holding company (or conglomerate) and a financial holding company is often difficult to make across countries and therefore industrial companies and holdings companies are considered as one ownership category. The average cumulative ownership of share stakes in excess of 5%, held by French and Belgian holding companies is 21% and 27% respectively.

Table 4: Ownership distribution of largest shareholders in western economies

This table gives the total large share holdings (over >3% or >5%) held by different investors classes. For all countries the ownership data cover the year 1996, except for Belgium (1994) and UK (1993).

	Sample	Ownership	Individuals and families	Banks	Insurance companies	Investment funds	Holdings and industrial companies	State	Directors
France	402	(2)	15.5	16.0	3.5	0.0	34.5	1.0	0.0
Austria	600	(2)	38.6	5.6	0.0	0.0	33.9	11.7	0.0
Italy	(1)	(2)	68.6	7.2	0.0	0.0	24.2	0.0 (4)	0.0
Netherlands	137	(3)	10.8	7.2	2.4	16.1	10.9	1.3	0.0
Spain	394	(2)	21.8	6.6	8.8	0.0	32.6	0.0	0.0
Belgium	155	(2)	15.6	0.4	1.0	3.8	37.5	0.3	0.0
UK	248	(3)	2.4	1.1	4.7	11.0	5.9	0.0	11.3
Germany	402	(2)	7.4	1.2	0.2	0.0	21.0	0.7	0.0

Note (1): numbers for Italy refer to both listed and non-listed companies; for other countries only listed companies are taken; (2): both direct and indirect shareholdings are considered; (3): only direct shareholdings. (4): Of the listed Italian companies about 25% are directly and indirectly controlled by state holdings; this is classified in previous column under (State) Holdings and industrial holdings.
Source: Gugler, Stomper, Zechner and Kalls 'The separation of ownership and control in Austria' in Barca and Becht (n 16); Becht, Chapelle and Renneboog 'Shareholding cascades: separation of ownership and control in Belgium' in Barca and Becht (n 16) L Bloch and E Kremp 'Ownership and voting power in France' in Barca and Becht (n 16); De Jong, Kabir, Marra and Roell, 'Ownership and Control in the Netherlands' in Barca and Becht (n 16) Crespi and Garcia-Cestona 'Ownership and control of Spanish listed firms' in Barca and Becht (n 16); Bianchi, Bianco and Enriques 'Pyramidal groups and the separation between ownership and control in Italy' in Barca and Becht (n 16); Becht and Boehmer 'Ownership and voting power in Germany' in Barca and Becht (n 16); L Renneboog 'Ownership, managerial control and the governance of poorly performing companies listed on the Brussels stock exchange' (2000) 24 (12) Journal of Banking and Finance 1959-1995.

In Continental Europe, direct share holdings in the hands of banks are generally low. For example, in Germany, only 5.8% of the stakes of 5% or larger are held by banks. However, German banks' influence is higher than these numbers imply as investors depositing their bearer shares at the bank can allow the bank to exercise these proxy votes. Furthermore, the banks can as a result of the debt granted to companies also have additional influence on the (supervisory) board. Bank share holdings average between 0.5% and 11% in Belgium, Italy, Spain and the Netherlands and bank ownership in Anglo-American countries is negligible. Although direct French bank shareholdings above 5% in the French corporate sector average only to 2.7%, Table 4 shows that when the real bank voting power is taken into account by adding the indirect power of financial groups, bank voting power rises to 16%. Conflicts of interest constitute the main reason why direct bank share holdings in listed companies are low in most countries.[18] As banks owning corporate shareholdings frequently have also granted loans, the bank will have two different types of claims on the company. When there is a danger of bankruptcy and the bank faces a refinancing demand of the corporation, the creditor claims might encourage the bank to make the company file for receivership whereas the equity claims might entice the company to revolve the bank loans and increase the riskiness of the firm's investment projects. Such conflicts of interest might even be exacerbated by the fact that in countries like France, Belgium and Italy, part of the bank's equity is held by large industrial holdings owning also large shareholdings in listed companies to which that bank has granted bank loans.[19]

Investment and pension funds, and insurance companies hold important share holdings in the UK and the Netherlands, where such institutions are the main shareholders with an average of respectively 16% and 19%. Large stakes (of 5% or more) are rare in the other European countries, but this does not imply that the total percentage of shares owned by institutions is small. For example, in Belgium, insurance companies hold, in aggregate, more than 12% of the Brussels stock market capitalisation, and investment and pension funds account for about 20%. Still, such holdings are not required to be disclosed as individual stakes usually do not exceed the transparency thresholds of 5%. The foregoing point about the pattern of concentrated share ownership suggests that, in contrast to the Anglo-American countries, there is little in the way of 'shareholder activism' that can be expected from continental European institutions, given the insider trading legislation, the relative size of institutional shareholdings and the costs of corporate monitoring. Indeed, serious questions arise whether Anglo-American style institutional shareholder activism would have good results in such a context. For some scholars, minimal takeover activity is a precondition of relational engagement between institutional shareholders and managers.[20]

Table 4 reveals moreover that individuals and families account for about 15-25% of the large share stakes of listed companies in continental Europe.[21] In fact,

[18] M Goergen and L Renneboog 'Strong managers and passive institutional investors in the UK' in Barca and Becht (n 16) 259-284.

[19] L Renneboog 'Ownership, managerial control and the governance of poorly performing companies listed on the Brussels stock exchange' (2000) 24 (12) Journal of Banking and Finance 1959-1995.

[20] W Bratton and JA McCahery 'Comparative Corporate Governance and the Theory of the Firm: The Case Against Global Cross Reference' (1999) 38 (2) Columbia Journal of Transnational Law 213-297.

[21] The high number of family ownership in Italy and Austria is influenced by the fact that the sample consists of both listed and non-listed companies. Still, a majority of the listed Italian companies is family controlled.

Franks and Mayer[22] have found that large-scale family ownership is an especially pronounced feature of the largest German firms. This finding was also documented by Becht and Boehmer:[23] in 37% of their sample companies, individual (or family) shareholders own an average stake of 20%. In the case of the UK, directors' holdings (two thirds of which are executives) are, along with the institutional ones, the most important category of owners. The fact that in some UK companies, managers hold large share stakes, makes them somehow unaccountable to corporate control. For instance, Franks et al[24] show that voting rights in the hands of executive directors leads to managerial entrenchment and resistance to disciplinary actions undertaken against this management.

In this section, we have explained that the analysis of differences in ownership structures has important implications with respect to corporate governance. The basic picture is clear: (1) shareholding concentration is much higher in continental Europe than in the UK (and the US); (2) pyramidal and complex ownership structures are set up in continental Europe, mostly via intermediate holding companies, to retain control while relaxing the wealth constraints; (3) the continental European corporate sector owns a large stake in itself; (4) bank holdings are generally small in all countries unless they are part of a financial group; (5) institutions and directors are the main shareholders in UK, but do not hold much voting power in continental Europe; and (6) director ownership is high in the UK and leads to managerial entrenchment.

D. Explanations for Differences in Ownership and Control Concentration Across Companies and Countries

When a diffuse ownership structure coincides with weak shareholder voting power, there may be serious agency conflicts between management and shareholders as a result of a lack of monitoring. A shareholder bears the full cost of corporate monitoring whereas he only enjoys the potential increase in corporate value resulting from increased monitoring relative to his own share stake. Therefore, only a large share stake gives sufficient incentives to monitor a company. A diffuse ownership and control structure may therefore lead to insufficient monitoring as a consequence of free riding on control. The advantage of such a control structure is increased stock liquidity and the fact that the market for corporate control may assume a monitoring role. Strong ownership and voting power con-

[22] J Franks and C Mayer 'Ownership and control in Germany' (2000) 14 Review of Financial Studies 943-977.

[23] M Becht and E Boehmer 'Ownership and voting power in Germany' in Barca and Becht (n 16).

[24] J Franks, C Mayer and L Renneboog 'Who disciplines management of poorly performing companies?' (2001) 10 Journal of Financial Intermediation 209-248.

centration gives the opposite picture: liquidity is low but the presence of a large shareholder exercising strong voting power reduces managerial discretion to deviate from the principle of shareholder value maximisation. These base cases are panels A and D of table 5, which one would expect to represent most Anglo-American companies (dispersed ownership and control) and most Continental European and Japanese firms (concentrated ownership and control), respectively.

Table 5: Ownership and Voting Power

	Control	
Ownership	Panel A: Dispersed ownership and dispersed voting power	Panel B: Dispersed ownership and concentrated voting power
	Panel C: Concentrated ownership and dispersed voting power	Panel D: Concentrated ownership and concentrated voting power

Panel A: Dispersed Ownership and Dispersed Voting Power
- *where*: US, UK.
- *advantages*: a. portfolio diversification and liquidity; b. takeover possibility
- *disadvantages:* insufficient monitoring: free riding problem
- *agency conflicts*: management vs shareholders

Panel B: Dispersed Ownership and Concentrated Voting Power
- *where*: countries where a stakeholder can collect proxy votes and shareholder coalitions are allowed.
- *advantages*: a. monitoring of management, b. portfolio diversification and liquidity;
- *disadvantages*: a. violation of one-share-one-vote b. reduced takeover possibility
- *agency conflicts*: controlling block holders vs small shareholders

Panel C: Concentrated Ownership and Dispersed Voting Power
- *where*: any company with voting right restrictions
- *advantages*: protection of minority rights
- *disadvantages:* a. violation of one-share-one-vote b. low monitoring incentives, c. low portfolio diversification possibilities and low liquidity d. higher cost of capital e. reduced take over possibilities
- *agency conflicts*: management vs shareholders

Panel D: Concentrated Ownership and Concentrated Voting Power
- *where:* Continental Europe, Japan, in any country after take over.
- *advantages*: high monitoring incentives
- *disadvantages*: a. low portfolio diversification possibilities and low liquidity b. reduced takeover possibilities
- *agency conflicts*: controlling block holders vs small share holders

Panel B shows that it is possible to have a dispersed shareholding base with concentrated voting power. Concentrated ownership can be exercised to extract private benefits from minority shareholders. The corporate law regimes in most of

The case in which concentration of voting power is lower than that of ownership is exhibited in panel C. This can occur through the use of voting caps, which are designed to prevent large shareholders exercising control. Interestingly, the resort to use of voting caps, which disperses voting power, enables small shareholders to be protected, but it also may heighten the need to increase pressures on monitoring. In contrast to voting rights restrictions, the use of proxy voting can have a positive impact on the incentives for monitoring and control, while allowing the investors to diversify. Such voting caps were until recently used in Germany. When a company is in 'imminent danger', voting caps restrictions could be used. As such, corporate takeovers were affected by special voting rights measures designed to make the make the target more difficult to acquire. For example, Franks and Mayer[25] have show that in the three corporate takeover battles in Germany since WWII, voting rights restrictions were introduced. As a consequence, the voting power of several large share stakes was reduced from for instance 40% to 5%. The fact that these three takeover attempts failed, confirms our earlier observation that voting caps will likely result in a reduction of takeover activity and blockholder domination.

These countries include a number of mechanisms that allow controlling shareholders to be able to obtain greater premium for their shares. Such disparity between ownership and control is characteristic of countries that permit the exploitation of corporate opportunities. The most widely-used mechanism to accumulate control power with a limited investment are ownership pyramids or cascades which can enable shareholder to maintain control throughout multiple layers of ownership while at the same time sharing the investment with other (minority) shareholders at each intermediate ownership tier. Some European countries have traditionally allowed companies to design a pyramidal structure of share holdings which is one of the mechanisms that reduces the liquidity constraints of large shareholders while it allows those shareholders to retain substantial voting power. Whereas pyramids of share stakes require smaller investment of capital (smaller cash flow rights), the large shareholder can still control his target company. For instance, if a shareholder X owns 51% of the voting equity of firm Y which in turn owns 51% of the voting equity of firm Z, there is an uninterrupted control chain which gives shareholder X absolute majority control. Still, the cash flow rights of shareholder X are merely 26%.

Another solution for the reduced liquidity is the issuance of dual class voting shares to separate ownership and control. The costs of reduced liquidity for the large shareholder can be more than compensated by the value of control, as control can allow a large shareholder to transfer resources from the company. The private benefits of control are non-transferable benefits beyond the financial return on investment. For example, if a car producer attracts a subcontractor to

[25] J Franks and C Mayer 'Hostile takeovers and the correction of managerial failure' (1999) 40(1) Journal of Financial Economics 163-181.

supply him with car seats, a large share holding in the subcontracting company can yield an important (strategic) advantage. The large shareholder is usually allowed a seat on the board of directors and will thus receive non-public information on the firm's cost structure or on supply contracts of the competitors. The large shareholder could, for example, after obtaining such strategic information, renew negotiations about the subcontractor's price. Consequently, such transactions can lead to the creation of another kind of agency conflict, namely the oppression of minority shareholders rights. Another example illustrates the danger of expropriation of minority shareholders: suppose that a shareholder owns 51% of the voting shares in firm A and that this shareholder also owns 100% of the equity of firm B. If firm A is a supplier of firm B, the controlling shareholder may be tempted to reduce the transfer price of goods sold to firm B. This way profits are maximized in firm B of which the shareholder has full control and owns all the cash flow rights whereas profits are minimised in firm B at the expense of the minority shareholders. Other examples of tunnelling in the context of the transition economies are given in Johnson et al.[26]

A third common way to accumulate control with limited investment is the use of proxy votes. An example of proxy voting can be observed in Germany where banks use the voting rights deposited with them by shareholders. This is conditional upon the bank announcing how it will vote on specific propositions and upon a written confirmation by the depositing shareholders allowing proxy voting. Another example of proxy voting takes place in the US when the management makes propositions for the annual meeting and solicits proxy votes from the shareholders. A third mechanism to maintain control with a limited investment is by issuing dual class shares and holding the voting shares. Dual class shares are frequently used in Scandinavia, France, Spain, Italy and the US but are not present in the UK and recently abolished in Germany.

Dual class shares are commonly employed by European firms, but with large differences across EU member states. Faccio and Lang[27] document 5,232 firms in 13 Western European countries. For instance, in Finland, Italy, Denmark, Switzerland and Sweden the proportion of firms with outstanding dual class stocks ranges from around 35 percent to 65 percent. For Norway, Germany, UK, Austria and Ireland, the range varies from 13 percent to 24 percent. In Portugal, Spain and France the proportions are almost negligible (see Table 6).

The move toward firms being capitalized with dual and multiple classes of common stock is caused by the development of an integrated market for corporate control, which exposed even the largest firms to hostile bids. In the US, dual class shares have become an increasing important concern to investors since the 1980s

[26] S Johnson et al 'Tunnelling' (2000) NBER working paper.

[27] M Faccio and L Lang 'The ultimative ownership of Western European companies' (2002) 65(3) Journal of Financial Economics 365-395.

Table 6: Dual Class Shares in Europe

Country	# of Firms	# with Dual Class	in %	premium	period
Austria	99	23	23.23%		
Belgium	130	0	0.00%		
Denmark	210	70	33.33%	20-35%	1985-1991
Finland	129	47	36.43%		
France	607	16	2.64%		
Germany	704	124	17.61%	17.2% (-5%-35%)	1956-1998
Ireland	69	16	23.19%		
Italy	208	86	41.35%	82%	1987-1990
Norway	155	20	12.90%		
Portugal	87	0	0.00%		
Spain	632	1	0.16%		
Sweden	334	185	55.39%		
Switzerland	214	109	50.93%		
UK	1953	467	23.91%		
Total	5531	1164	21.05%		

Source: M Faccio and L Lang 'The ultimative ownership of Western European companies' (2002) 65(3) Journal of Financial Economics 365-395; and M Bennedsen and K Nielsen 'The impact of break-through rule on European firms' (2002) Copenhagen School of Economics working paper.)

as stock exchanges have liberalized their restrictive policy on multiple and dual class shares.[28] Dual Class shares provide equity finance without ceding control rights. In a dual class regime, one class (hencefore B) has lesser voting rights than the other class of shares (hencefore A).

The range of variation across Europe is considerable with regard to the specification of dual class shares. For example, the voting rights of B shares in Sweden are typically 1/10 of the voting rights of A shares, while in other countries the B class shareholders carry no voting rights. In principle, 1/10 voting shares are the same as non-voting shares because the B class has to abandon on a part of their voting rights proportional to the risk-bearing capital they represent. The scale of the surrender does not play a role in an economic analysis. Moreover, in Germany, but also in other countries, there exist preferred stocks (*Vorzugsaktien*). This is risk-bearing capital in the sense of non-voting stock, but also possesses dividend rights. Finally we find also multiple voting stocks. This is the case one

[28] J Gordon 'Dual class common stock and the problem of shareholder choice' in L Bebchuk (ed) *Corporate Law and Economic Analysis* (Cambridge University Press Cambridge 1992) 75-96, 75.

class (A) has additional voting rights compared to the other (B). A special case of a multiple voting stock is a so-called 'golden share' where one or more shareholders get a veto right for certain (well) defined situations. Against this background, it surprising that (at least) some of the European authorities do explicitly discriminate.

Table 7 displays the legal restrictions on dual class shares, the number of firms employing them for each country, and the average minimum percentage of stock needed to control 20 percent of the voting rights. We can see that Sweden and Finland, which have been shown to impose a lower limit on voting rights of shares, evidence higher concentrations of ownership than jurisdictions where there are no limits on voting rights. In contrast, the striking absence of firms using dual class shares in some jurisdictions is a direct consequence of the persistence of the one share-one vote rule.

*Table 7: Current regulation in Europe**

Country	Details	# of Firms	Own 20%	Dual class shares (%)
I. One-share-one-vote				
Belgium		130	20.00	0.00
Norway	Exception by government approval	155	19.05	13.16 / 12.90
II. Proportion on non voting (and limited voting) stocks capped				
France	< 25% of stock capital	607	19.93	2.64
Germany	< 50% of stock capital	704	18.83	17.61
Italy	< 50% of stock capital	208	18.38	41.35
Spain	< 50% of stock capital	632	20.00	0.16
Portugal	< 50% of stock capital	87	20.00	0.00
III. Minimum voting ratio				
Denmark	Minimum ratio:10%	102	n/a	51
Finland	Minimum ratio:10%	129	15.42	37.60 / 36.43
Sweden	Minimum ratio:10%	245	9.83	66.07
UK	Minimum voting rights**	1953	19.14	23.91
IV. Unrestricted				
Austria		99	18.96	23,23
Ireland		69	18.91	28.07 / 23.19
Switzerland		214	15.26	51.17 / 50.39
Luxembourg		n/a	n/a	n/a
Netherlands	Complex	n/a	n/a	n/a
Greece		n/a	n/a	n/a
Total		5334	18.74	19.91

*Legal restrictions on issuing dual class shares. 5232 publicly traded firms. 'Own 20%' is the average minimum percent of the book value of equity to control 20% of votes; 'Dual class shares' is the percentage of firms with outstanding dual class shares.
** in UK non voting shares are outlawed since 1968, but firms are free to issue 'preference stocks' given minimum rights are given. This includes voting (1) if the dividend is in arrears (2) if share capital should be reduced or the company should be winded-up (3) if the class rights will be affected.
*** relative premium mandatory bid rule installed since 1995/1996
Source: Faccio and Lang 'The ultimative ownership of Western European companies' (2002) 65(3) Journal of Financial Economics 365-395; M Bennedsen and K Nielsen 'The impact of break-through rule on European firms' (2002) Copenhagen School of Economics working paper; C Rose 'Corporate financial performance and the use of takeover defences' (2002) 13 European Journal of Law and Economics 91-112.

Meanwhile, corporate governance scholars have attempted to measure the size of private benefits of control. Beginning with Barclay and Holderness,[29] studies of private benefits have estimated the magnitude of private benefits empirically by measuring the privately negotiated acquisition of control blocks in publicly traded companies and the market price of a share after the announcement, corrected for bargaining power. Based on this analysis, Dyck and Zingales[30] propose to measure the private benefits of control in 39 countries based on 412 control transactions for the period 1990–2000. They find that the value of control ranges between –4% and +65% with an average of 14 percent. In some European countries, the size of private benefits appears to be very large. For example, the mean premium in Austria, Italy and Portugal, the mean premium was 38, 37, and 20 percent respectively. In contrast, they find that most other European countries show a mean premium below 10 percent.

In this chapter, we also employed the Barclay and Holderness method also to examine block transactions in Europe and US. We find that the value of control ranges between 1% and 58%, with an average 13% (Table 8).

Table 8: Block premium as percent of firm equity

This table presents descriptive statistics by country on the block premiums in the 412 control block transactions we study. The block premiums is computed taking the difference between the price per share paid for the control block and the exchange price two days after the announcement of the control transaction, dividing it by the exchange price two days after the announcement and multiplying the ratio by the proportion of cash flow rights represented in the controlling block.

[29] M Barclay and C Holderness 'Private benefits from control of public corporations' 25 (1989) Journal of Financial Economics 371-95.

[30] A Dyck and L Zingales 'Private benefits of control: An international comparison' (2002) Journal of Finance, forthcoming

Country	Mean	Median	Stand dev	Min	Max	Number of observ.	# obs. positive
Argentina	0.27	0.12	0.26	0.05	0.66	5	5
Australia	0.02	0.01	0.04	-0.03	0.11	13	9
Austria	0.38	0.38	0.19	0.25	0.52	2	2
Brazil	0.65	0.49	0.83	0.06	2.99	11	11
Canada	0.01	0.01	0.04	-0.02	0.06	4	2
Chile	0.15	0.12	0.18	-0.08	0.51	9	8
Colombia	0.27	0.15	0.34	0.06	0.87	5	5
Czech Republic	0.58	0.35	0.80	0.01	2.17	6	6
Denmark	0.08	0.04	0.11	-0.01	0.26	5	3
Egypt	0.04	0.04	0.05	0.01	0.07	2	2
Finland	0.02	0.01	0.06	-0.07	0.13	14	9
France	0.02	0.01	0.10	-0.10	0.17	5	3
Germany	0.10	0.10	0.13	-0.24	0.32	18	15
Hong Kong	0.01	0.03	0.05	-0.12	0.05	9	7
Indonesia	0.07	0.07	0.03	0.05	0.09	2	2
Israel	0.27	0.21	0.32	-0.01	0.89	9	8
Italy	0.37	0.16	0.57	-0.09	1.64	8	7
Japan	-0.04	-0.01	0.09	-0.34	0.09	21	5
Malaysia	0.07	0.05	0.10	-0.08	0.39	41	31
Mexico	0.34	0.47	0.35	-0.04	0.77	5	4
Netherlands	0.02	0.03	0.05	-0.07	0.06	5	4
New Zealand	0.03	0.03	0.09	-0.17	0.18	19	14
Norway	0.01	0.01	0.05	-0.05	0.13	14	9
Peru	0.14	0.17	0.11	0.03	0.23	3	3
Philippines	0.13	0.08	0.32	-0.40	0.82	15	11
Poland	0.11	0.08	0.11	0.02	0.28	5	5
Portugal	0.20	0.20	0.14	0.11	0.30	2	2
Singapore	0.03	0.03	0.03	-0.01	0.06	4	3
South Africa	0.02	0.00	0.03	0.00	0.07	4	2
South Korea	0.16	0.17	0.07	0.04	0.22	6	6
Spain	0.04	0.02	0.06	-0.03	0.13	5	4
Sweden	0.06	0.02	0.08	-0.01	0.22	13	12
Switzerland	0.06	0.07	0.04	0.01	0.15	8	8
Taiwan	0.00	0.00	0.01	-0.01	0.00	3	2
Thailand	0.12	0.07	0.19	-0.08	0.64	12	11
Turkey	0.30	0.09	0.55	-0.03	1.41	6	5
United Kingdom	0.02	0.01	0.05	-0.06	0.17	43	23
United States	0.02	0.02	0.10	-0.20	0.40	47	28
Venezuela	0.27	0.28	0.21	0.04	0.47	4	4
average/number	0.14	0.11	0.18	-0.04	0.48	412	300
Only Europe and the US:							
average/number	0.13	0.04	0.17	-0.03	0.44	200	140

Source: Dyck and Zingales[31]

[31] ibid.

Economists studying private benefits of control warn that estimating the value of the control premium is complicated. In trying to explain the size of private benefits, economists have argued that the control premium depends on a number of factors, including the competition in the market for corporate control, the size of the block sold, the distribution of shares in the target firm, the inequality of voting power, the nationality of the buyer, and the financially condition of the firm involved.[32] Almost invariably, the existence of large private benefits of control suggests that large shareholder may be able to obtain a large share of the rents. The control premium is lower in Anglo-American market-based corporate governance systems that have widely dispersed ownership structures and provide a high level of legal protection for minority shareholders. Finally, the factors explaining the differences in legal enforcement in the Dyck and Zingales study are tax compliance and product market competition.

Goergen and Renneboog[33] take a different approach to analyse why the levels of control are so different in two countries with strongly varying corporate governance regimes, Germany (a bank and blockholder based governance system) and the UK (a market-based regime). A first reason for shareholders to hold larger voting stakes in German firms is found in the differences in the regulatory and legal environment. A detailed analysis of the regulation of the German and UK stock exchanges, of the rules on minority shareholder protection, of informational transparency and of the takeover codes shows that there is lower shareholder protection in Germany. The voting practice at annual meetings, the composition of the board of directors and their fiduciary duties further reinforce this relative weakness of shareholder rights in Germany. As a consequence, control is more valuable to shareholders of German firms either to avoid expropriation of their investments or to take advantage of the higher levels of private benefits. Furthermore, holding large control stakes is less expensive in Germany relative to the UK because ownership pyramids, the possibility of issuing non-voting stock and the possibility to nominate one's representatives to the board of directors ensure that control can be maintained with relatively low levels of cash flow rights.

Although the legal environment predicts stronger levels of control in Germany, it does not explain how the difference in control concentration comes about. Both UK and German firms are floated on the stock exchange with high levels of initial control, and this raises the question as to what triggers subsequent changes in control. Goergen and Renneboog[34] investigate the economic factors

[32] E Berglöf and M Burkart, 'Break-through in European takeover regulation?' (2002) Stockholm School of Economics working paper; Dyck and Zingales (n 30).

[33] M Goergen and L Renneboog 'Why are the levels of control (so) different in German and UK companies? Evidence from initial public offerings' (2003) 19 Journal of Law, Economics and Organization 141-175.

[34] ibid.

that determine control retention by large initial shareholders, dissipation of control among many small shareholders, and control transfers whereby they distinguish widely-held and concentrated bidders. The paper uses a unique database of IPOs of which the control structure is tracked through time. They find that not only do the initial shareholders in the average German company own much larger stakes than their UK counterparts, but they also lose majority control only 6 years after the public offering. In contrast, initial owners in UK companies lose majority control already 2 years after going public.

Goergen and Renneboog[35] find strong evidence that corporate characteristics lead to differences in control evolution across companies within a country but also between the UK and German firms. Their Tobit models that estimate the percentage of control held by the initial and new large shareholders and the size of the free float 6 years subsequent to the flotation, show that corporate size is an important determinant of control concentration in the UK but not in Germany. Large UK companies evolve towards a more widely-held equity structure whereas in large German firms new shareholders hold significantly larger voting stakes. The reason is that wealth constraints become binding for UK shareholders whereas German ones can avoid this effect by leveraging control via pyramids. If the founder of a German firm is still a major shareholder at the initial public offering and if there are non-voting shares outstanding, control is likely to remain tight in the hands of the initial shareholders. This is not surprising as founding families often extract (non-pecuniary) private benefits of control and non-voting shares enable them to raise additional equity capital whilst maintaining control. Whereas they do not find any impact of growth on the control concentration of UK firms, strong growth in German firms leads to the initial shareholders transferring control to new large shareholders.

Finally, they estimate multinomial logit models that predict the occurrence of different states of control (initial shareholders retain control, control is diluted, control is transferred to a concentrated shareholder or to a widely-held firm). They show that specific corporate characteristics lead to different 'equilibrium' control states six years after the flotation. For the UK, the probability of a transfer of control to a concentrated shareholder increases when a company is risky, small and poorly performing. A UK firm is more likely to be taken over by a widely-held firm, if it is large, fast growing and profitable. So, for the UK, poor performance and high risk necessitate a high level of control and tight monitoring by a concentrated shareholder. High growth and profitability attract widely-held companies whose management may follow an 'empire building' acquisition program. The authors also document that high growth also leads to more diffuse control, which in turn is less likely when the founder family is still involved in the company. Founding families may be less inclined to dilute their stake in order to retain private benefits of control. When German firms are profitable and risky,

[35] ibid.

control is more likely to be acquired by a concentrated shareholder, but growth and low profitability increase the likelihood of being acquired by a widely-held firm.

E. Takeovers in the European Union and the US: Evolution

The clustering of mergers and acquisitions through time is a striking phenomenon. The first European merger wave started approximately in 1880 and ended in 1904. It was fuelled by the industrialisation started by the discovery of the steam engine. The prime incentive for these mostly horizontal mergers was the creation of monopolies. The introduction of anti-trust legislation played an important role in the second merger wave, which started in 1919 and continued throughout the 1920s. The old monopolies were broken up and mergers and acquisitions were used to achieve vertical integration. The third merger wave started in the 1950s, but reached its peak only in the mid-1960s. The focus turned towards diversification and the development of large conglomerates to face global markets. The development of new financial instruments and markets (e.g. the junk bond market) facilitated the financing of acquisitions and led to the fourth wave (1983-1989) that was fuelled by technological progress in biochemistry and electronics. The fifth M&A wave emerged in the early 1990s (1993-2000) and went hand in hand with a long economic boom period, stock exchange development and the growth in the internet- and telecommunications industries. In 2001, the collapse of consumer confidence in these industries as well as the overcapacity in the traditional sectors caused an abrupt reduction in merger activity.

Over 1993, the total dollar value paid for target firms in the US and Europe doubled after four consecutive years of reduction in M&A activity. Tables 9 and 10 exhibit a sharp rise as of 1996: the total value of US and European acquisitions rose to USD 840 million (with Europe accounting for 45%).[36] In the following years the M&A wave gained even more strength with a value of USD 1,186 million in 1997 (44% of which was realised in Europe), USD 1,957 million in 1998 (42% in Europe), and USD 2,567 million in 1999 (49% in Europe). The year 1999 was not only a remarkable year, because the European M&A market was now almost as large as the US market or because 12% of the total value was could be accounted by deals in excess of USD 100 billion, but also because an exceptionally high number of hostile takeovers took place in Europe. There were 369 hostile bids in Europe in 1999 compared to only 14 in 1996, 7 in 1997, 5 in 1998 and 35 in 2000.[37] The market for corporate control briefly sustained its momentum mainly as a result of European M&A activity as in 2000 the total

[36] The value total value of M&As excludes the acquisitions related to divestitures.

[37] As reported in an M&A report by Morgan Stanley using Thomson Financial Securities Data, April 2001.

value of all M&A deals amounted to USD 2,685 (53% in Europe). The stock market collapse of 2000 eroded shareholder confidence and brought about a significant decline in the M&A activity of 41% to USD 1,582. The year 2002 is expected to have known a further collapse of the takeover market by another 50%.

Table 11 shows that the most active M&A market consists of the UK which representing 31.4 % of the EU market for corporate control but only makes up 13.2% of EU GDP in 2001. In contrast, Germany (28.2% of EU GDP) only accounts for 16.3% of the M&A market. The third M&A market of the European Union consists of France with 13.5%. Whereas most takeovers are domestic, the number and percentage of cross-border takeovers have risen substantially, especially the number of foreign non-EU acquisitions (mostly by a US bidder or of a US target) (see Table 12). The percentage of domestic acquisitions within the member states of the EU decreased from 65.1% in 1991 to 56.4% in 1999, while the percentage of cross-border acquisitions remained relatively stable at about 15% of all M&A activity involving firms located in the EU. The percentage of EU firms taken over by non-EU corporations remained relative stable over the 1990s, but the relative activity of EU firms in cross-border acquisitions outside the EU more than doubled from 8.1% in 1991 to 17.4% in 1999.

Table 9: US acquisitions and divestitures from 1984 to Oct 2002

	Acquisitions		Divestitures		Divest./Acq. (in value)
Year	No. of Deals	Value ($bn)	No. of Deals	Value ($bn)	(%)
1985	1,713	148	767	50	34
1986	2,523	221	1,117	83	38
1987	2,517	211	1,014	77	36
1988	3,011	291	1,310	108	37
1989	3,828	324	1,660	89	27
1990	4,324	207	1,942	86	42
1991	3,642	141	1,829	54	38
1992	3,871	126	1,771	55	44
1993	4,436	179	2,052	77	43
1994	5,292	281	2,188	104	37
1995	6,706	391	2,598	143	37
1996	7,811	573	2,864	199	35
1997	9,059	784	2,970	219	28
1998	10,638	1,373	3,108	305	22
1999	9,546	1,438	2,841	289	20
2000	9,183	1,786	2,648	368	21
2001	6,224	1,143	2,331	245	21

Source: Various Annual Almanacs of Mergers & Acquisitions, S Sudarsanam *Creating value from mergers and acquisitions: The challenges* (Prentice Hall International 2003).

Table 10: EU acquisitions and divestitures from 1984 to Oct 2002

	Acquisitions		Divestitures		Divest./Acq. (in value) (%)
Year	No. of Deals	Value ($bn)	No. of Deals	Value ($bn)	
1984	41	1	7	0	2
1985	256	14	66	2	15
1986	553	40	142	16	40
1987	1,209	64	326	17	27
1988	2,356	108	602	36	33
1989	3,261	164	814	58	35
1990	3,407	175	1,228	73	42
1991	6,503	148	2,298	57	39
1992	6,056	159	2,267	59	37
1993	5,287	168	2,072	85	51
1994	5,902	156	2,063	63	41
1995	6,891	243	2,321	81	33
1996	6,281	267	2,274	98	37
1997	7,173	402	2,561	154	38
1998	7,744	584	2,421	173	30
1999	9,301	1,129	2,828	246	22
2000	10,405	899	3,016	313	35
2001	7,855	439	2,562	167	38
2002	4,709	224	1,557	117	52

Source: Thomson Financial SDC database, S Sudarsanam *Creating value from mergers and acquisitions: The challenges* (Prentice Hall International 2003).

Table 11: Distribution of M&A activity and GDP between EU Member States, 1991-2001

Member State	Share of EU M&A activity (%)	Share of EU GDP (%)
Belgium	2.8	3.2
Denmark	2.6	2.1
Germany	16.3	28.2
Greece	1.1	1.4
Spain	5.0	7.0
France	13.5	18.1
Ireland	1.7	0.9
Italy	6.2	12.6
Luxembourg	0.5	0.2
Netherlands	6.5	4.9
Austria	2.1	2.7
Portugal	1.2	1.3
Finland	3.9	1.6
Sweden	5.3	2.8
United Kingdom (UK)	31.4	13.2

Note: In calculating this table, cross-border intra-Community operations are counted twice, once for the bidder country and once for the target country. Percentage for EU may not add up to 100 because of rounding.
Source: Directorate General for Economic and Financial Affairs, European Commission, European Economy, Supplement A, Economic Trends, No 12, 2001.

Table 12: Evolution of National, Community and International M&A operations in the EU (% of all M & A transactions)

Year	National	Community	International EU-target	International EU-bidder	Total
1991	65.1	14.0	12.8	8.1	100
1992	67.9	12.9	12.2	7.1	100
1993	63.5	12.5	14.9	9.1	100
1994	62.7	13.6	13.5	10.2	100
1995	61.0	13.5	12.7	12.7	100
1996	57.9	13.5	14.8	13.8	100
1997	56.8	14.3	15.6	13.3	100
1998	55.0	14.5	15.5	14.9	100
1999	56.5	15.0	11.2	17.4	100

Source: Directorate General for Economic and Financial Affairs, European Commission, *European Economy*, Supplement A, Economic Trends, Table 9, 2000.

At the height of the fifth takeover wave, the total value of deals in the EU amounted to 12% of cumulative GDP (in 1999) as a consequence of an increase in the number of deals and individual deal size. The total value in the US even went to 16% of GDP (in 1998). Since then, M&A levels fell to more normal percentages of between 1-3% (see Figure 3). As depicted in Figure 4, the collapse of the stock market in 2000 caused the average size of takeover deals in 2002 to fall to 40% of the pre-collapse levels in both the EU and US.

Over the past 5 years, the means of payment in takeover bids consisted of cash in 47% of the EU offers and 37% of US bids (see Figures 7 and 8). All-equity bids were made in 10% and 24% in EU and US takeover cases. The remainder of the bids consisted of a combination of cash, equity and debt. Not only the number and average size of the takeover deals declined since 2000, but the financial composition of the takeover bids also changed. For both the EU and the US, the relative importance of cash deals increased by about 50% (see Figure 5). The declining market capitalizations of bidding firms and increased risk-aversion on the part of the target shareholders have reduced current relative importance of all-equity bids to one third of its level in 2000.

Figure 3: Total Acquisition Value as a % of GDP

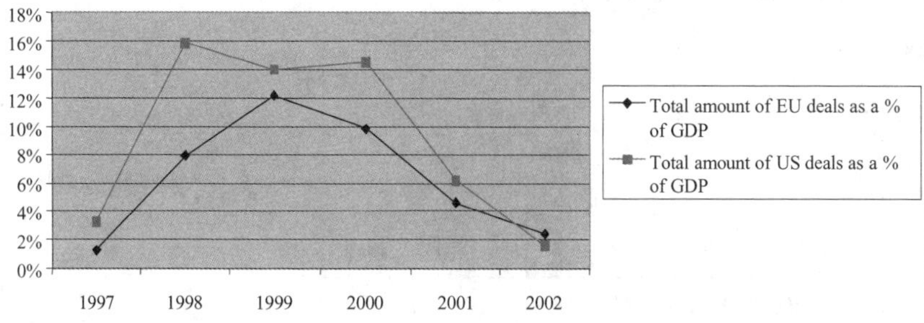

Figure 4: Average Size of Deals

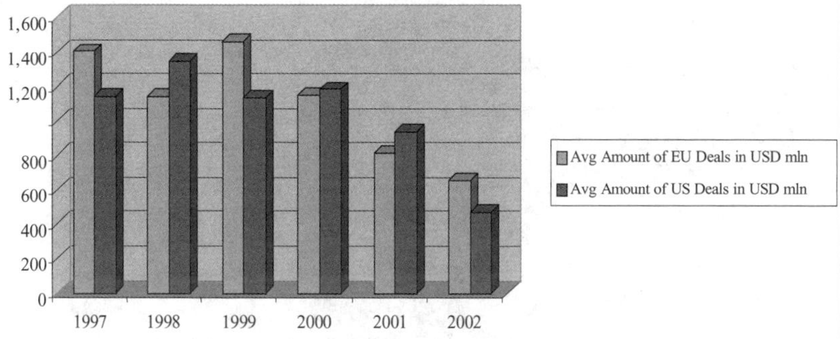

Figure 5: Pure Cash Deals as a % of Total Deals

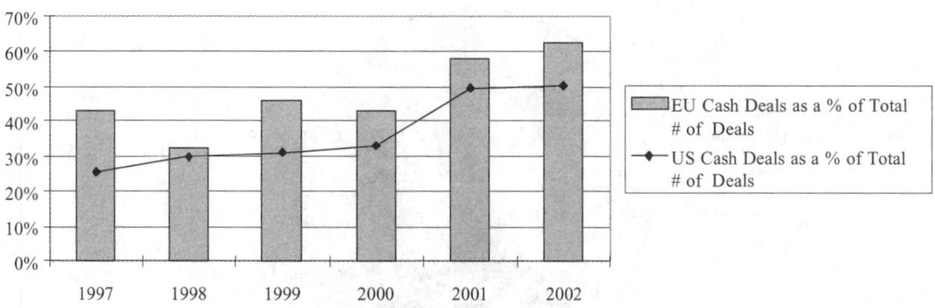

Figure 6: Pure Stock Deals as a % of Total Deals

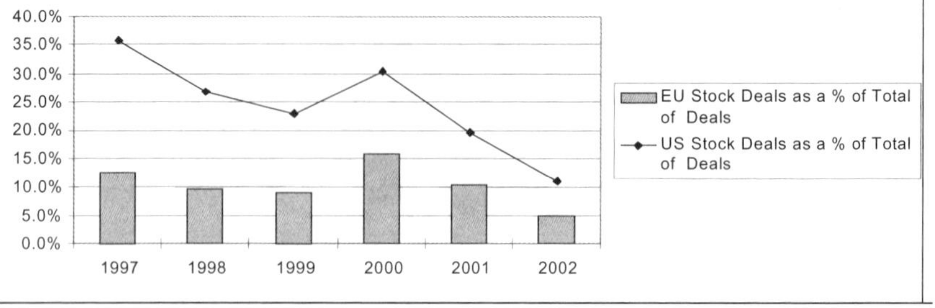

Figure 7: Avg. Structure of Payment EU (1997-2002)

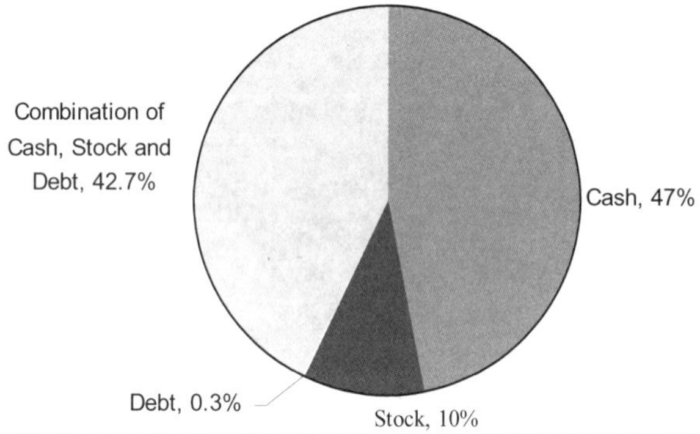

Figure 8: Avg. Structure of Payment US (1997-2002)

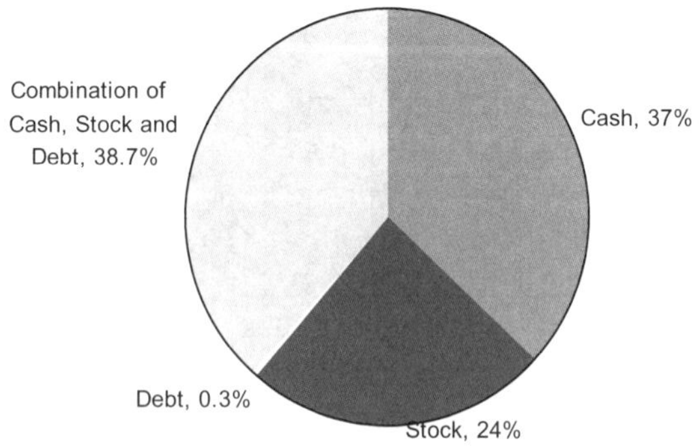

F. The Determinants of Bidder and Target Returns in the Economic Literature

The literature on the wealth effect of M&A announcements for target shareholders is unanimous: these shareholders receive an average premium within the 15 to 30% range over and above the pre-announcement share price (table 13). For the 1960s to 1980s, Jarrell and Poulsen,[38] Servaes,[39] Kaplan and Weisbach,[40] for instance, report average US target share price returns of 29% for 1963-86, 24% for 1972-1987 and 27% for 1971-82, respectively. In the 1990s, the US abnormal announcement returns remained at as similar level of 21%.[41] In contrast, there is little consensus about the announcement wealth effects for the bidding firms. About half of the studies report small negative returns for the acquirers[42] whereas the other half finds zero or small positive abnormal returns.[43] Considering that the average target is much smaller than the average acquirer, the combined net economic gain at announcement is positive, albeit small.

The findings for the UK are similar to those for the US although the target shareholders abnormal returns are somewhat higher (see Table 13). For the whole of Europe, Goergen and Renneboog[44] show that the announcement effect of a take-over including the price run-up which starts 40 trading days prior to the first public announcement cumulates to an abnormal return of 21.3% over and above the expected CAPM-return. The bidder returns are positive but close to zero.

[38] G Jarrell and A Poulsen 'The returns to acquiring firms in tender offers: evidence from three decades' (1989) 18 Financial Management 12-19.

[39] H Servaes 'Tobin's q and the gains from takeovers' (1991) 46 Journal of Finance 409-419.

[40] S Kaplan and M Weisbach 'The success of acquisitions: evidence from divestitures' (1992) 47 Journal of Finance 107-138.

[41] J Mulherin and A Boone 'Comparing acquisitions and divestitures' (2000) 6 Journal of Corporate Finance 117-139.

[42] See eg P Healy, K Palepu and R Ruback 'Does corporate performance improve after mergers?' (1992) 31 Journal of Financial Economics 135-175; M Mitchell and E Stafford 'Managerial decisions and long-term stock price performance' (2000) 73 Journal of Business 287-329; M Sirrower *The Synergy Trap: How Companies Lose The Acquisition Game* (The Free Press New York 1997); M Walker 'Corporate takeovers, strategic objectives and acquiring-firm shareholder wealth' [2000] Financial Management 53-66.

[43] See eg E Eckbo and K Thorburn 'Gains to bidder firms revisited: domestic and foreign acquisitions in Canada' (2000) 35 Journal of Financial and Quantitative Analysis 1-25; M Loderer a nd K Martin 'Corporate acquisitions by listed firms: the experience of a comprehensive sample' (1990) 19 Financial Management 17-33; G Schwert 'Hostility in takeovers: in the eyes of the beholder?' (2000) 55 Journal of Finance 2599-2640.

[44] M Goergen and L Renneboog 'Shareholder wealth effects of European domestic and cross-border wealth effects' (2003) European Financial Management Journal, forthcoming.

Previous research on cross-border M&A activity is largely confined to studies that involve US firms as targets or bidders. Similar to domestic acquisitions, the shareholders of US target firms can pocket large positive abnormal returns[45] in cross-border bids. Two studies analyze cross-border acquisitions between US and UK companies: Conn and Connell[46] for the period 1971-80 and Feils (1993) for the period 1980-90. Both studies conclude that the wealth effect for US target firms is substantially larger than for UK firms (40% versus 18% in Conn and Connell and 26% versus 16% in Feils). Danbolt[47] finds no statistical difference between short-run abnormal returns for UK targets of domestic mergers and acquisitions (18.46%) and those of cross-border takeovers (19.68%). Both Wansley[48] et al and Dewenter[49] suggest that the cross-border returns-effect for target US firms results from differences in the bid characteristics of domestic and cross-border acquisitions rather than from fundamental differences in the level of abnormal returns. Such a conclusion is also reached for UK target firms by Danbolt:[50] the target cross-border effect appears to be attributable to the method of payment, bid outcome and industrial sector.

[45] A Cebenoyan, G Papaioannou and N Travlos 'Foreign takeover activity in the US and wealth effects for target firm shareholders' (1992) 21 Financial Management 58-68; L Cheng and K Chan 'A comparative analysis of the characteristics of international takeovers' (1995) 22 Journal of Business Finance and Accounting 637-657; R Harris and D Ravenscraft 'The role of acquisitions in foreign direct investment: evidence from the US stock market' (1991) 46 Journal of Finance 825-844.

[46] C Conn and F Connell 'International mergers: returns to US and British firms' (1990) 17 Journal of Business Finance and Accounting 689-711.

[47] J Danbolt 'Target company cross-border effects in acquisitions into the UK' (2002) working paper University of Glasgow.

[48] J Wansley, W Lane and H Yang 'Shareholder returns to USA acquired firms and domestic acquisitions' (1983) 10 Journal of Business Finance and Accounting 647-656.

[49] K Dewenter 'Does the market react differently to domestic and foreign takeover announcements? Evidence from the US chemical and retail industries' (1995) 37 Journal of Financial Economics 421-441.

[50] Danbolt (n 47).

Table 13: Abnormal returns to shareholders surrounding successful takeover announcements

Study Sample period; sample size	Country	Event window (around announcement)	Benchmark return Model	Target abnormal return (%)	Bidder abnormal return (%)
Jensen & Ruback[51] (1983) (summary of 7 previous studies) 1958-81; 17 to 161	US	20 to 60 days	Market-adjusted	29	4
Jarrell & Poulsen[52] (1989) 1963-86; 526	US	31 days	Not reported	29	1
Jarrell, Brickley & Netter[53] (1988) 1960-85; 405	US	31 days	Not reported		2
Magenheim and Mueller[54] (1988) 1976-81; 78	US	1 month	Market		1
Bradley, Desai and Kim[55] (1988) 1963-84; 236	US	11 days	Market	32	1
Loderer and Martin[56] (1990) 1966-84; 274	US	6 days	Market		1
Schwert[57] (1996) 1975-81; 1814	US	42 days before 126 days after	Market	16 20	
Jensen & Ruback[58] (1983) (summary of 7 previous studies) 1962-79; 60 to 256	US (tender)	1 month	Market	16	1

[51] M Jensen and R Ruback 'The market for corporate control: The scientific evidence' (1983) 11 Journal of Financial Economics 5-50.

[52] Jarrell and A Poulsen (n 38).

[53] G Jarrell, J Brickley and J Netter 'The market for corporate control: The empirical evidence since 1980' (1988) 2 Journal of Economic Perspectives 49-68.

[54] E Magenheim and D Mueller 'Are acquiring firm shareholders better off after an acquisition?' in JC Coffee, L Lowenstein and S Ackerman (eds) *Knights, Raiders and Targets* (Oxford University Press Oxford 1988).

[55] M Bradley, A Desai and E Kim 1988 'Synergistic gains from corporate acquisitions and their division between the stockholders of target and acquiring firms' (1988) 21 Journal of Financial Economics 3-40.

[56] Loderer and Martin (n 43).

[57] G Schwert 'Markup pricing in mergers and acquisitions' (1996) 41 Journal of Financial Economics 153-192.

[58] Jensen and Ruback (n 51).

Study Sample period; sample size	Country	Event window (around announcement)	Benchmark return Model	Target abnormal return (%)	Bidder abnormal return (%)
Loderer and Martin (1990) 1966-84; 1135	US (tender)	6 days	Market	Not reported	1
Schwert[59] (1996) 1975-81; 959	US (tender)	42 days before 126 days after	Market	12 5	
Firth[60] (1980) 1969-75; 486	UK	1 month	Market	28	-6
Franks and Harris[61] (1989) 1955-85; 1445	UK	1 month	Market, market-adjusted & CAPM	22	0
Limmack[62] (1991) 1977-86; 462	UK	Bid period (3 months)	Market	31	-0
Sudarsanam, Holl & Salami[63] (1996) 1980-90; 429	UK	-20 to +40 days	Market	29	-4
Higson and Elliott[64] (1998)	UK	Bid period (3 months)	Size	38	0
Sudarsanam & Mahate[65] (2003). 1983-95; 519	UK	-1 to +40 days	Size, market-adjusted, book to market		-1 to –2
Baker and Limmack[66] 1977-90; 595	UK	1 month	8 methods		0

[59] Schwert (n 57).

[60] M Firth 'Takeovers, shareholder returns and the theory of the firm' (1980) 94 Quarterly Journal of Economics 235-60.

[61] J Franks and R Harris 'Shareholder wealth effects of corporate takeovers' (1989) 23 Journal of Financial Economics 225-249.

[62] R Limmack 'Corporate mergers and shareholder wealth effects' (1991) 21 Accounting and Business Research 239-51.

[63] P Sudarsanam, P Holl and A Salami 'Shareholder wealth gains in mergers: Effect of synergy and ownership structure' [1996] Journal of Business Finance and Accounting 23.

[64] C Higson and J Elliott 'Post-takeover returns: The UK evidence' (1998) 5 Journal of Empirical Finance 27-46.

[65] P Sudarsanam and A Mahate 'Glamour acquirers, method of payment and post-acquisition performance: The UK evidence' (2003) Journal of Business Finance and Accounting, forthcoming.

[66] R Baker and R Limmack 'UK takeovers and acquiring company wealth changes: the impact of survivorship and other potential selection biases on post-outcome performance' (2002) University of Stirling working paper, May 2002.

Study Sample period; sample size	Country	Event window (around announcement)	Benchmark return Model	Target abnormal return (%)	Bidder abnormal return (%)
Bergstrom, Hogfeldt & Hogholm[67] (1993); 1980-92; 94 targets, 149 bidders (tender offers)	Sweden	11 days	Market	17	0
Doukas and Holmen[68] (2000) 1980-95; 93 tender offers	Sweden	11 days	Market		1
Van Hulle, Vermaelen & de Wouters[69] (1991); 63 tender offers	Belgium	6 weeks	Market	38	-1
Van Hulle, Vermaelen & de Wouters[70] (1991); 76 acquirers & 48 acquired	Belgium	3 months	Market	6	-1
Eckbo and Langohr[71] (1989), 1966-82; 90 targets & 52 acquirers in public tender offers	France	16 weeks	Market	14	-3
Goergen and Renneboog,[72] 1993-2000: 136 target and 142 bidding firms	Europe	1 day 40 days prior + event day	CAPM	9.0 (1 day) 23.1 (40 days)	0.7 (1day) 0.4 (40 days)

Source: S Sudarsanam *Creating value from mergers and acquisitions: The challenges* (Prentice Hall International 2003) and M Goergen and L Renneboog 'Shareholder wealth effects of European domestic and cross-border wealth effects' (2003) European Financial Management Journal, forthcoming.

[67] C Bergstrom, P Hogfeldt and K Hogholm 'Strategic blocking, arbitrageurs and the division of the takeover gain: empirical evidence from Sweden' (1993) 3 Journal of Multinational Financial Management 217-249.

[68] J Doukas and M Holmen 'Managerial ownership and risk reducing acquisitions' in T Cooper and A Gregory (eds) *Advances in Mergers and Acquisitions 1* (JAI Press 2000) 183-203.

[69] K Van Hulle, T Vermaelen and G de Wouters 'Regulation, taxes and the market for corporate control in Belgium' (1991) 15 Journal of Banking and Finance 1143-1170.

[70] K Van Hulle, T Vermaelen and G de Wouters (n 69).

[71] E Eckbo and Langohr 'Information disclosure, method of payment and takeover premiums' (1989) 24 Journal of Financial Economics 363-403.

[72] M Goergen and L Renneboog 'Shareholder wealth effects of European domestic and cross-border wealth effects' (2003) European Financial Management Journal, forthcoming.

Table 14: Abnormal returns to acquirer and bidder shareholders in cross-border acquisitions

Study Sample period; sample size	Acquirer country - (Target country)	Benchmark abnormal return (%) (days)	Significant factors (effect on returns)
1.Cakici, Hessel & Tandon[73] (1996); 1983-92; 195	UK, GER, FR, NL, SWD, SWZ, IT, JP, AUS, CND – (USA)	2 (21 days) (market model)	Only AUS, JP, NL and UK (+) No tax effect
2. Eun, Kolodny & Scheraga[74] (1996); 1979-90; 103	AUS, CND, UK, FR, HK, JP, NL, NZ, SWD, SWZ, GER, OT – (USA)	-1.2 (11 days) (mean adjusted)	JP & CND acquirers (+); UK acquirers (-); Target's R&D Strength (+)
3. Kang[75] (1993); 1975-88; 119	JP – (USA)	0.59 (2 days)	Bank debt (+); strong yen (+) No tax effect
4. Markides & Ittner[76] (1994) 1975-88; 276	US – (CND, UK, Continental Europe, Pacific)	0.54 (5)	Strong $ (+); advertising intensity (+); oligopoly (+); No country effect
5. Cakici, Hessel & Tandon[77] (1996); 1983-92; 195	US – (UK, GER, FR, NL, SWD, SWZ, IT, JP, AUS, CND)	0 (21 days)	
6. Danbolt[78] (1995); 1986-91; 71	As above, Norway, US – (UK)	-10 (6 months post-acquisition) (market model)	

[73] N Cakici, C Hassel and K Tandon 'Foreign acquisitions in the United States: Effect on shareholder wealth of foreign acquiring firms' (1996) 20 Journal of Banking and Finance 307-329.

[74] C Eun, R Kolodny and C Scheraga 'Cross-border acquisitions and shareholder wealth: tests of the synergy and internalization hypotheses' (1996) 20 Journal of Banking and Finance 1559-1582.

[75] J Kang 'The international market for corporate control – mergers and acquisitions of US firms by Japanese firms' (1993) 11 Journal of Financial Economics 345-371.

[76] C Markides and C Ittner 'Shareholder benefits from corporate international diversification: Evidence from US international acquisitions' [1994] Journal of International Business Studies 343-366.

[77] N Cakici, C Hassel and K Tandon (n 73).

7. Conn & Connell[79] (1990); 1971-80; 35	US - (UK)	-2.5 (6 months post-acquisition)	
8. Goergen & Renneboog[80] (2003b); 1993-2000; 56	Europe (Europe)	2.4 (1 day) 1.5 (40 days)	cash payment (+); status of bid (hostility) (+);

Source: S Sudarsanam Creating value from mergers and acquisitions: The challenges, (Prentice Hall International 2003) and M Goergen and L Renneboog 'Shareholder wealth effects of European domestic and cross-border wealth effects' (2003) European Financial Management Journal, forthcoming.

The M&A literature has discovered a variety of profitability drivers. First, the announcement of tender offers and hostile takeovers generates higher target as well as bidder returns than the announcement of friendly mergers or acquisitions.[81] Second, when the bidding management owns large equity stakes, bidding firms obtain higher returns.[82] This suggests that managers are more likely to undertake value-destroying mergers, if they do not own equity in their firm. Third, all-cash bids generate higher target and bidder returns than stock-for-stock acquisitions.[83] The announcement that the takeover will be paid with equity may signal to the market that the bidding managers believe that their firm's shares are overpriced. This is in line with the fact that managers time the issues of shares to occur at the high point of the stock market cycle. Fourth, acquiring firms with

[78] J Danbolt 'An analysis of gains and losses to shareholders of foreign bidding companies engaged in cross-border acquisitions into the United Kingdom' (1995) 1 The European Journal of Finance 279-309.

[79] C Conn and F Connell (n 46).

[80] M Goergen and L Renneboog 'Shareholder wealth effects of European domestic and cross-border wealth effects' (2003) European Financial Management Journal, forthcoming.

[81] A Gregory 'An examination of the long run performance of UK acquiring firms' (1997) 24 Journal of Business Finance and Accounting 971-1002; L Lang, R Stulz and R Walkling 'Managerial performance, Tobin's Q and the gains from successful tender offers' (1989) 24 Journal of Financial Economics 137-154; T Loughran, and A Vijh 'Do long-term shareholders benefit from corporate acquisitions?' (1997) 52 Journal of Finance 1765-1790.

[82] eg P Healy, K Palepu and R Ruback 'Which takeovers are profitable: strategic or financial?' (1997) 38 Sloan Management Review 45-57.

[83] See eg J Franks, R Harris and C Mayer 'Means of payment in takeover: results for the United Kingdom and the United States' in A Auerbach (ed) *Corporate Takeovers: Causes and Consequences* National Bureau of Economic Research (University of Chicago Press 1988); J Franks and R Harris 'Shareholder wealth effects of corporate takeovers' (1989) 23 Journal of Financial Economics 225-249; Y Huang and R Walking 'Target abnormal returns associated with acquisition announcements: payment, acquisition form and managerial resistance' (1989) 19 Journal of Financial Economics 329-350; K Yook 'Larger return to cash acquisitions: signalling effect or leverage effect?' (2000) working paper Johns Hopkins University.

excess liquidities destroy value by overbidding. Several papers show evidence that free cash flow[84] is frequently used for managerial empire-building purposes.[85] Fifth, corporate diversification strategies destroy value.[86] This confirms that companies should not attempt to do what investors can do better themselves, ie creating a diversified portfolio. Sixth, the acquisition of value-companies leads to higher bidder and target returns. Rau and Vermaelen[87] show that the acquisition of firms with low market-to-book firms generates high returns (of about 12% on average) to the shareholders of the bidding firm whereas the acquisition of glamour firms (with high market-to-book ratios) leads to substantial negative returns.[88]

The main motive for mergers and acquisitions is the value creation resulting from synergies. These synergies are called operating synergies, if there are economies of scale or scope, and are called informational synergies, if the combined value of the assets of the two firms is higher than the value the stock market attributes to the assets. For example, informational synergies consist of the creation of an internal capital market: slack-rich firms with poor investment possibilities acquire slack-poor firms with outstanding growth opportunities.[89] Informational synergies can also consist in minimizing transaction costs or bankruptcy costs. However, Warner[90] shows that the reduction in direct bankruptcy cost (due to less than perfectly correlated earnings of the bidder firm and the target firm) is small. In Anglo-American markets, the role of hostile takeovers as a disciplinary force to remove poorly performing management is also often emphasized. This

[84] MC Jensen 'Agency costs of free cash flow, corporate finance and takeovers' (1986) 76 American Economic Review 323-329.

[85] See eg L Lang, R Stulz and R Walkling 'A test of the free cash flow hypothesis: The case of bidder returns' (1991) 29 Journal of Financial Economics 315-335; Servaes (n 39).

[86] PG Berger and E Ofek 'Diversification's effect on firm value' (1995) 37 Journal of Financial Economics 39-65; C Maquiera, W Megginson and L Nail 'Wealth creation versus wealth redistributions in pure stock-for-stock mergers' 1998 48 Journal of Financial Economics 3-33.

[87] PR Rau and T Vermaelen 'Glamour, value and the post-acquisition performance of acquiring firms' (1998) 49 Journal of Financial Economics 223-253.

[88] For an excellent overview of post-merger performance and of the motives for mergers and tender offers: see A Agrawal and J Jaffe 'The post-merger performance puzzle' in A Gregory (ed) *Advances in mergers and acquisitions* (volume 1 JAI Press Amsterdam 2000) 7-41.

[89] Still, the empirical evidence investigating the creation of an internal capital markets shows that diversified firms do not rely significantly less on the outside capital market than non-diversified firms (R Comment and G Jarrell 'Corporate focus and stock returns' (1995) 37 Journal of Financial Economics 67-87).

[90] JB Warner 'Bankruptcy costs: some evidence' (1977) 32 Journal of Finance 337-347.

market for corporate control seems to be more active in the US[91] than in the UK.[92]

G. Takeover Regulation in the European Union

This section begins by describing briefly the legislative history of 13th Directive in the EU and its problems. In particular we examine the High Level Group's reform proposals that have influenced the European Commission and the recent debates about the design of takeover legislation. Finally, the last part sub-summarizes the draft Takeover Bids Directive.

I. Legislative History of Takeover Bids Directive in the EU

The rapid integration of EU capital markets as a result of the euro has highlighted the remaining barriers to the realization of a single capital market. The proposal for a Takeover Bids Directive is regarded as a crucial element of the EU policy to create a truly integrated financial services market and in 1999 became part of the Financial Services Action Plan, which seeks to promote the adoption of certain pieces of legislation in this area by 2005. The March 2000 Lisbon European Council reiterated that the takeover directive is a crucial part in the economic strategy of improving the economic performance of European firms.

The efforts at harmonizing European takeover law focus on three types of transactions: takeovers in general, mandatory bids, and certain types of squeeze-outs. The initial proposal for a Takeover Directive[93] was a detailed document that specified required terms of the takeover bid. The proposal was seen by Member States as too detailed and, moreover, an unwarranted intrusion into their domestic policy. As a result, the European Commission announced in the declaration to Edinburgh European Council in December 1992 that it would revise the proposed directive which was reconfirmed at the Essen European Council in December 1994. The Commission introduced a second proposal, changing it into a framework proposal based on the British City Code on Takeovers and Mergers, in February1996.[94] In general the Commission, through the second proposal, in-

[91] A Bhide 'The causes and consequences of hostile takeovers' (1989) 2 Journal of Applied Corporate Finance 36-59; K Martin and J McConnell 'Corporate performance, corporate takeovers and management turnover' (1991) 46 Journal of Finance 671-687; R Morck, A Shleifer and R Vishny 'Managerial ownership and market valuation: an empirical analysis' (1988) 20 Journal of Financial Economics 293-315.

[92] J Franks, C Mayer and L Renneboog 'Who disciplines management of poorly performing companies?' (2001) 10 Journal of Financial Intermediation 209-248.

[93] OJ C 64, 14.3.1989, 8 with explanatory memorandum, Suppl 3/89 – Bull EC.

[94] OJ No C 162, 6.6.1996, 5; with explanatory memorandum, COM(95) 655 final.

tended to introduce some general principles designed to guide regulatory efforts, while allowing for minor variations in implementation of the principles by the competent authorities. The central elements of the 1996 proposal were the mandatory bid rule and the prohibition of frustrating actions by managers, the two provisions clearly reflected in the British City Code' approach to takeovers. While there was initial opposition to the second proposal, a common position was eventually agreed by the Council in June 2000.[95]

The text of the Common Position of the EU Council on the proposed Takeover Bids Directive was subsequently presented to the European Parliament for a second reading, after which the EP proposed amendments designed to allow directors to enact defensive measures and a requirement to safeguard workforce levels after a change of control. As a consequence, a conciliation process was necessary, which led to an agreement regarding the adoption of a joint text, along with a promise that a Group of Experts would examine, as part of a review to modernize European company law, the problem of equitable price and squeeze outs. When presented with the text on July 4, 2001, the European Parliament voted against the compromise text.

II. HLG Report on Takeovers and the Takeover Bids Directive

The failure to reach agreement on a common solution for takeover bids prompted the European Commission, in July 2001, to appoint a High Level Group of Company Experts (HLG),[96] chaired by Professor Jaap W. Winter, to examine the issues raised by the European Parliament and the EU's Council of Ministers during the last stage of negotiations on the common proposal for a Takeover Bid Directive. With respect to the High Level Group's mandate in relation to takeover bids, the Group considered three main issues: (1) the creation of a level playing field for takeover bids; (2) the definition of an equitable price for a takeover bid; and (3) the introduction of squeeze-out and sell-out procedure in the context of takeover bids.

The HLG Report (Annex 2 in this volume) recognizes the contribution of a well-developed securities market to the development of an integrated takeover market, but underlines the importance of Community interventions in specific company law mechanisms and structures to support the development of a level playing field for takeover bids. Against this background, the HLG Report identifies two principles, shareholder decision-making and proportionality between risk-bearing capital and control, needed to inform the regulation of corporate

[95] OJ No C 23, 24.1.2001, 1.

[96] Committee Members include: Jaap Winter, Jan Schans Christensen, José Maria Garrido Garcia, Klaus J. Hopt, Jonathan Rickford, Guido Rossi and Joëlle Simon along with Dominique Thienpont (Rapporteur) and Karel van Hulle (Secretariat).

acquisitions in Europe (Chapter 1, pp. 20-22). The HLG Report argues that the presence of differentiated voting rights, voting caps, golden shares, voting trusts, pyramid structures and circular and cross-shareholdings and other structures in the company law of Member States are generally inconsistent with the two principles.[97]

The HLG also advocates that target boards should be prevented from taking any defensive measures to frustrate a hostile takeover bid after it has become known unless it has received shareholder approval at a general meeting and this approval may not be obtained until the offer is presented. The only measure that target boards can take without authorization by shareholders is to seek separate bids.

Moreover to achieve a level playing field and the proportionality beween risk-bearing and controlling capital the HLG Report demands for a 'break-through rule,' which is applied after the acquisition of 75% of the risk-bearing capital. Under the proposed break-through rule, if the acquiring firm acquires a level of 75% of the risk-bearing capital of the company, then he should be able to exercise a corresponding share of total votes and therefore take control of the company. Furthermore the HLG Report is clear in denying that compensation should be extended to the holders of special control rights. The HLG Report also sought to clarify the notion of equitable price. In short, the HLG Report recommended a harmonized approach is necessary to allow offerors an effective and predictable way to determine the acquisition price for the target company. Finally, the HLG Report examined the approach to squeeze-outs of any shareholder who failed to tender their shares. Most Member States allow for large stockholders to eliminate a public target company's minority shareholders by squeezing them out.

The European Commission presented on October 2, 2002 a new proposal for a Directive on Takeover Bids, containing: (1) strict board neutrality rule on the part of the target board; a mandatory bid rule that ensures that an acquiring firm cannot obtain a controlling stake without making a controlling bid; (2) mini break-through rules which stipulate that, during the period of acceptance of a bid, any restrictions on the transfer of securities contained in the Articles of Association and contractual arrangements (but not in national legislation) are not enforceable against the offeror (this being more permissive than the HLG); (3) a set of disclosure rules in which the offer must announce his intention to make an offer and make public an offer document containing at least a minimum of information; and (4) 'squeeze-out' and 'sell-out' rules that would have to be implemented at a fair price.

[97] The HLG recommended also the improvement of disclosure requirements on such voting rights and structures (Chapter 1, 25-26).

H. The Market for Corporate Control and Tender Offers

To provide a context for the discussion of the Proposed Directive, we briefly describe how the tender offer process functions. As explained above, mergers between companies occur for several reasons: (1) to allocate assets more efficiently; (2) to solve problems of contracting on the product and input market (through vertical integration for example); (3) to gain access to know-how or new markets; and (4) to replace incumbent management teams. It is the latter aspect that has prompted a heated political debate about the Proposed Directive.

The market for corporate control is often viewed as a mechanism to correct managerial failure. As is well known, outside shareholders confront a fundamental agency problem. That is, as owners of the company, they have delegated the control over the use of their funds to managers. Formally, shareholders have the unconditional right to intervene in the company's course (unless their shares preclude voting). However, outside equity is often seen as rather powerless due to the collective action problem of dispersed ownership. Hostile takeovers are seen as one of the mechanisms for outside equity to overcome the collective action problem to give the management incentives. This implies that dispersed shareholders sell the control over the management to a large shareholder. The bidder has to incur the cost for collecting information on the target.

In case of takeover bids of companies with dispersed ownership, Grossman and Hart[98] explain why the cost of initiating a takeover may never be recovered viz., free-riding of dispersed shareholders. That is, when individual small shareholders take the success of a tender offer as given, they will not tender their shares as long as the bidder does not offer a bid price that is at least equal to the share price after the bid has succeeded. At any price lower, it is beneficial from the perspective of the individual shareholder not to sell, since in that case the minority shares of the firm after the takeover are worth more than the bid price.

The literature has outlined several solutions to the free-rider problem.[99] For example, a bidder could acquire a non-controlling toehold before the takeover bid becomes public. Also, private benefits from the merger to the bidder can finance the cost of a takeover. Furthermore, the free-rider problem is avoided in case where the target has a controlling shareholder. In this context, the transfer of control will be negotiated privately and success of the bid will depend on the controlling shareholder. Alternatively, the successful bidder could establish a 'dilution device' so as to exclude minority shareholders from participating in the full value of the company. Thus, in a world where equity finance is characterized by dispersed ownership, the frequency of takeovers increases if the target share-

[98] SJ Grossman and O Hart 'Takeover bids, the free-rider problem, and the theory of the corporation' (1980) 11(1) Bell Journal of Economics 42-64.

[99] L Bebchuk 'Efficient and inefficient sales of corporate control' (1994) 109(4) Quarterly Journal of Economics 957-993.

holders do not participate in the takeover gains. If the bidder sets the dilution device, however, this might lead to inefficient takeovers for companies with dispersed ownership.[100] This is the so-called 'pressure-to-tender' problem. In contrast to the free-rider problem, shareholders may feel a pressure to tender if they perceive that the minority share value, after a successful bid, is *lower* than the bid price. For example, this can occur if bidder is able to realize substantial private benefits of control after the takeover. As a consequence, theispersed shareholders will avoid tendering their shares if the bid price is less than the stand-alone public share value of the company. But, if an individual shareholder fears that the takeover bid will, nonetheless, be successful, he will be forced to tender since he expects other shareholders will tender. Naturally controlling shareholders are never under pressure to tender; thus this problem. In fact, this problem is less likely to arise in continental Europe as a consequence of the widespread blockholdings.

Bebchuk and Hart[101] propose a mechanism that can mitigate the free-rider problem and eliminate the pressure-to-tender problem. On this view, the bidder makes a binding offer on which shareholders hold a vote. If a majority agrees to the bid, then all shareholders would be required to tender their shares. This approach removes the uncertainty that shareholders will be left with shares that are worth less than the bid price, in case the bid succeeds against their will. Thus, a vote which is separate from the tendering process will serve to resolve the collective action problem. A vote with a simple majority may also, to some extent, remove the free-rider problem of Grossman and Hart.[102]

Similarly, Amihud, Kahan and Sundaram[103] develop a scheme, based on a squeeze-out mechanism, that avoids both free-riding and pressure-to-tender for dispersed shareholders. They propose squeeze-out legislation that guarantees target shareholders the highest price before the bid was made. Such a procedure is conditional on the bidder obtaining control but not based on further thresholds on capital holdings etc. The idea is that the bidder will offer a tender price equal to the stock market price before the bid was made public. As this will also be the price of minority shares in case of success, both free-riding and pressure-to-tender are eliminated.

[100] L Bebchuk 'Toward undistorted choice and equal treatment in corporate takeovers' (1985) 98 Harvard Law Review 1695-1808; M Burkart, D Gromb and F Panunzi 'Why higher takeover premia protect minority shareholders' (1998) 106 Journal of Political Economy 172-204.

[101] L Bebchuk and O Hart 'Takeover bids vs proxy fights in contests for corporate control' (2001) NBER Working Paper No 8633.

[102] SJ Grossman and O Hart (n 98).

[103] Y Amihud, M Kahan and R Sundaram 'The efficiency and welfare foundations of freezeout laws in takeovers' (2002) New York University Working Paper CLB-02-00.

Burkart and Panunzi[104] also show that an appropriately designed sell-out right could also eliminate the pressure-to-tender problem and preclude value-decreasing takeovers. They demonstrate that the price at which shareholders could demand a sell-out would correspond to the bid price. If the sell-out right applied already when the bidder's holdings have surpassed the control threshold, minority shareholders would no longer be afraid of being left with less than the bid price in case the takeover succeeds. Shareholders making this calculation will thus not sell their shares if the bid price was lower than the share price. The outcome would correspond to the squeeze-out right if designed along the lines proposed by Amihud et al.[105]

These models show that in order to increase the flow of takeover bids, it is necessary that minority shareholders do not participate in the full value of the firm. Thus, so long as there are safeguards for takeovers of widely held firms are not value decreasing, it will be efficient that the takeover gains accrue to the bidder. Against this background, it is clear that the proposed squeeze-out and the sell-out right should be reconsidered. The above arguments are based on the assumption that a bid succeeds or fails due solely to the discretion of shareholders. Often, however, the incumbent management has substantial discretion in determining whether a takeover bid can succeed. Board neutrality (Art. 9 of the proposed Directive) is meant to address the question whether shareholders should have the ultimate say in takeovers. Advocates of board discretion, however, argue that the board has superior information than shareholders. The implications of these claims are examined below.

In continental Europe, many takeovers will require that the incumbent controlling blockholder is willing to sell his shares. As noted above, controlling blockholders often enjoy private benefits, not least because the incur costs of controlling management. Notice that private benefits may comprise shifts between companies through transfer prices but also synergies between companies controlled by the same blockholder. Bebchuk[106] defines social efficiency in block transfers as an increase in the sum of the private and the security (ie the stock market) value of the firm. He notes that if the value of the company is distributed in a disproportional manner between controlling and minority shareholders, concerns may be raised about the value decreasing transfers. This occurs because incumbent blockholders wish to be compensated for his private benefits plus his share of the stock market value of the firm. It follows that the blockholder might agree to transfer control even in cases in which the buyer reduces the social value. Note this may take place if the buyer enjoys large private benefits but reduces the security value of the firm. A share of the cost of the reduced stock market value is

[104] M Burkart and F Panunzi 'Mandatory bids, squeeze-out, sell-out and the dynamics of the tender offer process', this volume.

[105] Amihud et al (n 103).

[106] Bebchuk (n 99).

borne by the minority shareholders, while for the controlling buyer the private benefits overcompensate.

Bebchuk examines the legal rules that might serve to limit inefficent sales of control. In the main, the mandatory bid rule functions to limit inefficient control transfers. Yet Bebchuk observes that the mandatory bid can impede efficiency-enhancing control transfers. Indeed, this may occur as a consequence of minority shareholders obtaining, notwithstanding the aims of blockholders, private benefits of control. Accordingly, an optimal solution may be to exclude the minority from the private benefits of the incumbent blockholder, so that the minority would not be worse off after a control transfer.[107] In principle, this could be achieved with a sell-out and a squeeze-out right. Thus, the task is to design an optimal set of rules. One proposal, for example, has been to use as a proxy the average stock market value in a time span before the bid has become public. But, since the precise value of private benefits is impossible to verify for outsiders, this may be a second-best solution.

The aim of takeover regulation must balance introducing rules that induce bidders to launch a bid and guarantee that small shareholders will be willing to sell their shares when it is efficient to do so. The available evidence suggests that policymakers must attempt to balance the tradeoffs between promoting policies that make takeovers less costly and thus produce more bids and encouraging equal treatment and the shareholder protection.[108] A recurrent theme in EU takeover policy discussions concerns the balance that policymakers must strike between protecting shareholders from the effects of managerial opportunism, represented in the form of pre and post bid defences, and deferring to the judgment of management. Against this background, the next section will examine the role of the mandatory bid rule, as set forth in the Proposed Directive, to ensure efficient takeovers.

I. Mandatory bid rule

Article 5 of the Proposed Directive is designed to trigger a mandatory bid when the bidder together with persons acting in concert with him acquires certain percentage of voting rights in the company that confers on him the control of the target. The Member States should determine both the percentage of voting rights conferring control and the method of its calculation.[109] The Member States should also adopt rules on information and particulars about the consideration to be offered.[110]

107 ibid.

108 E Berglöf and M Burkart (n 32); C Bergstrom, P Hogfeldt and J Molin (n 67).

109 See §§ 5(1), 5(3) of the Directive.

110 See § 6(3) of the Directive.

Under the proposal of the HLG, the mandatory bid rule is of crucial importance in protecting minority shareholders from the abuse of a majority blockholder. It provides the minority shareholders with adequate and fair terms of exit and eliminates any room for tendering in partial bids at less favourable prices.

The notion of the 'equitable price' is the key in the mandatory bid context proposed by the High Level Group and the Directive. Though the HLG does not give an exact definition of an equitable price, they argue that any definition should achieve adequate balance between flexibility in achieving minority protection and predictability of costs in the mandatory bid context.

The HLG argues that the introduction of a harmonized approach will allow '[offerors] to predict and ideally to determine the equitable price they will have to pay in a mandatory bid.'[111] The consideration must be offered at the highest price paid for the shares of the relevant class in a period between six to twelve months prior to the bid in market and over-the-counter transactions either in cash or in liquid securities.[112]

Based on the HLG recommendation, the highest price paid allows minority shareholders to obtain the benefits of any control premium to be paid on the one hand, while allows the bidder to predict his costs on the other hand. The HLG also acknowledges that the highest price rule may not achieve adequate treatment of the minority shareholders under certain circumstances. Following the recommendations of the HLG, the proposed Directive adopts the highest price rule. It allows member states to grant exemptions to the highest price rule under certain circumstances.

II. Implications of the mandatory bid rule

The mandatory bid rule can be broken down into two key components: (1) a full bid must be made; and (2) the consideration offered in the full bid. Requiring full bids alone offers some protection for minority shareholders. By restricting partial bids it is no longer possible to two prices for the front and back end of the dispersed shareholder base. In case the bid price is higher than the share price of the target company before the bid became known, mandatory bids can prevent value-decreasing takeovers. As Burkart and Panunzi[113] observe, however, it does not prevent value-decreasing bids when the bid price is below the share price before the offer (due to the pressure-to-tender problem).

However, the picture is altered if blockholders are introduced. Thus, if the bidder must obtain control from a blockholder, the equitable price rule will have

[111] Recommendation II.1 of the HLG Report.

[112] Recommendation II.2 of the HLG Report, See § 5(5) of the Directive.

[113] M Burkart and F Panunzi 'Mandatory bids, squeeze-out, sell-out and the dynamics of the tender offer process' this volume.

an impact.[114] Under the assumption that the blockholder has access to private benefits of control, the blockholder enjoys a disproportionately large segment of the company's stand-alone value. To transfer control, the incumbent blockholder demands compensation for the loss of enjoyment of the private benefits of control. If all shareholders must be treated alike (viz. shareholders of the same class), the blockholder's share will be proportionate to the value offered in the takeover. For the incumbent controlling shareholder, the proportionate value of the takeover can be less than the disproportionate share of the stand-alone firm value. In this case, takeover may fail even if the takeover were to create value. Based on the foregoing, the implication is that a mandatory bid rule decreases the number of takeovers. It avoids value-decreasing takeovers but may preclude some value-increasing takeovers. The ex-post efficient regulation would be designed to avoid all value-decreasing takeovers but encourage all value-increasing takeovers.

The Proposed Directive prescribes that the price to be offered in the mandatory bid does not allow any discounts to previous block trades. Hence, there is a danger that value-increasing takeovers are foregone. Thus, the question is how to describe an ex-post efficient pricing rule. While a prescribed percentage discount on previous block trades may permit more takeovers to proceed, nevertheless such a prescription may be too coarse grained given the variance of private benefits across firms.

The pure form of the equal opportunity rule would equal the mandatory bid rule price to the private sale of control. Other legal arrangements prescribe that the equal opportunity price should be related to the stock market price in a specified period prior to the bid. For example, the voluntary German Takeover Code in place before 2002 specified the highest stock market price in the three months prior to the bid as the equal opportunity price. This rule implies that the stock market price does not include any private benefits unless they are included in a subsequent squeeze out procedure. The stock market price rule can be seen as guaranteeing all shareholders the stand-alone value of the firm. This tends to imply a higher takeover incidence than under the proposed rule.

Taking into account ex ante efficiency involves more tradeoffs. On the one hand, the threat of takeovers is seen as an incentive mechanism for the incumbent managers. Since monitoring of management is costly, there must be a compensation for the shareholder that engages in monitoring. One of the ways to compensate the shareholder is to give him private benefits of control that can help to overcome the free-riding problem. In this view, blockholdings are thus beneficial from an ex ante perspective, because they encourage management to increase firm value. On the other hand, blockholders have an incentive to collude with the management. Thus private benefits are seen to be reducing firm value. Hence, takeovers under a mandatory bid rule function to distribute some of the future private benefits of the bidder to the target shareholders. From the viewpoint of

[114] Bebchuk (n 99).

allocative efficiency, this mechanism is valuable since the funds distributed may be reinvested by the shareholders in other projects. In addition, a participation in the private benefits of the incumbent controlling shareholder by a mandatory bid may enhance ex ante the willingness of small shareholders to buy stock at the IPO stage.[115] However, the more demanding the equitable price rule is, the lower the takeover threat with, perhaps, adverse effects on incumbent management's incentives.

The Proposed Directive leaves the definition of the trigger threshold for the mandatory bid to member states. Thus, not all aspects of the mandatory bid are regulated by harmonization. The idea is that effective control thresholds depend on national company law. In this regard, diversity is warranted as long as national company law differs. Since there are costs in terms of precluded value-enhancing takeovers, a harmonization of the equitable price rule precludes regulatory competition to minimize this cost. On the other hand, regulatory competition may not be strong if national equitable price rules would be complicated. However, it appears that regulators could in principle design simple rules that foreign shareholders (or 'the market') should be able to understand. Thus, shareholders from different jurisdictions would not benefit from the introduction of a harmonized rule. To be sure, the results of cost-benefit analysis of the proposed rule will depend on how effective it is in reducing value-increasing takeovers.

III. Break-through rule

As noted above, the HLG recommended in its January 2002 report a novel idea, called the break-through rule, designed to foster the incidence of takeovers in the EU. The proposal is intended to eliminate a wide variety of corporate governance arrangements that can have the effect of reducing the threat of takeovers. These pre-bid defenses are viewed as significant impediments to the emergence of a well-functioning cross-border takeover market in the EU. Thus, by stressing the need to create a transnational takeover market, the High Level Group advocates a policy designed to eliminate the control structures that impede takeovers – even if they have an impact on corporate governance beyond the specific context of a takeover bid – because they create barriers to the creation of an integrated market for corporate control and a mature capital market in Europe.

The HLG argues that a bidder should be permitted, immediately upon the acquisition of 75% of cash flow rights, or any relevant threshold not higher than 75% set forth by the Member States, to remove any arrangements that deviate from a one-share-one-vote. In the main, the HLG proposal is a scheme designed to answer the question: *who* (of the shareholders) should be allowed to vote.

[115] R Hecker *Regulierung von Unternehmensübernahmen und Konzernrecht* (Deutscher Universitäts-Verlag Wiesbaden 2000).

Certainly the rule implies that the very concept of ownership is redefined in the takeover context. Cash flow claimants become not only residual claimants of the company but also residual decision-makers. So, for example, upon reaching the required threshold, the bidder will be permitted to: (1) amend the articles of association and other constitutional documents; (2) remove any pre-bid takeover defenses approved by shareholders; (3) remove voting caps and differential voting rights; (4) remove provisions denying voting rights; (5) remove voting rights on non-risk bearing capital; (6) appoint, suspend, and dismiss the board members other than those appointed by third parties; (7) determine the composition of the board; (8) remove any staggered and/or fixed period provisions; and (9) override special control rights attached to golden shares.

The HLG provides a list of company charter devices that lead to deviations from a one-share-one-vote structure. However, it would be too great a task to review them one by one. The Proposed Directive considers only some of them in Art. 9. The device that is receiving most attention in the political debate is the multiple voting right share structure. For this reason, the break-through rule will be subsequently analyzed in the light of such a structure. Finally, we will move on to discuss the empirical evidence on the use of dual and multiple class shares among EU member states.

The effect of the break-through rule is to transform a bid on a company, which is held by a blockholder, into a bid with dispersed ownership. As conceptualized, it seems to have been implicitly assumed that the break-through rule would be applied only when the board of the target company formally rejects the takeover bid. It is clear, however, that the bidder may decide to pursue the break-through route of taking over a company even if the incumbent controlling shareholder would be prepared to negotiate on a transfer of control. Berglöf and Burkart[116] make this argument in their analysis of the break-through rule, which is detailed below.

IV. Implications of the break-through rule

The case for the one-share-one-vote rule is often justified by reference to the analysis of Grossman and Hart[117] and Harris and Raviv.[118] These models indicate that if the controlling shareholder can enjoy private benefits of control that rise when the security value of the firm rises, then it is optimal to concentrate voting rights in the hands of the controlling party. Takeovers are efficient (and will occur) if another controlling party appears with greater private benefits, and non-voting shareholders will automatically benefit as their shares gain in value too

[116] E Berglöf and M Burkart (n 32).

[117] SJ Grossman and O Hart 'One share-one vote and the market for corporate control' (1988) 20 Journal of Financial Economics 175-202.

[118] M Harris and A Raviv 'Corporate governance: voting rights and majority rules' (1988) 20 Journal of Financial Economics 203-235.

(even in absence of a mandatory bid rule). In contrast, if private benefits of the controlling party arise at the expense of the stock market value of the company, one-share-one-vote is optimal. The reason is that a controlling shareholder cares less about the security value the smaller his share in the cash flow rights. One share – one vote increases the share in the cash flow rights necessary to exercise control and thus reduces the negative externality on the remaining holders of cash-flow rights. This argument disregards the agency conflict between management and dispersed shareholders. Thus, concentrated shareholdings may solve this agency problem, leading to a better allocation of the company's funds. Yet control is costly for the blockholder. Whilst his reward may well be private benefits, it comes at a cost to dispersed minority shareholders.

Multiple voting rights or dual class – which are economically the same even though they may differ in dividend rights – are but one form of private contracting in the corporate charter. They are the outcome of prior shareholder decisions. Voting shareholders decided to issue them, and new shareholders agreed to purchase them. To override by regulation investment decisions that were made by shareholders in full knowledge of the rights attached to the investment securities, necessitates an analysis of whether there is a gain in efficiency to be expected from such regulatory measures.

Let's turn to examine dual class from the perspective of takeovers. The consequences of dual class viewed from a takeover defence perspective are well documented in the US.[119] Indeed, a number of empirical studies point out that anti-takeover provisions merely influence the takeover probability and the premium of the target firm.[120] Moreover, most empirical studies of takeover defenses have found that such structures have little or no impact on bid outcomes.[121]

However, to take account of the arguments propounded by the supporters of dual class shares, one is advised to look at the whole picture of corporate governance, not merely the event of takeovers. In terms of trying to isolate the firm value effects of dual class shares, Grullon and Kanatas[122] find that insiders in multiple class firms select their capital structure to defend against takeover threats. Using the unadjusted and industry-adjusted market-to-book ratio to assess how this behavior impacts firm value, they find that the average adjusted market-to-book value is ratio positive and significant at the 1 percent level, whereas the medium adjusted book-to-value ratio is negative and marginally significant at the

[119] JC Coates 'Explaining variations in takeover defenses: Blame the lawyers' (2001) 89 California Law Review 1301.

[120] S Hannes 'The Hidden Virtue of Antitakeover Defenses' (2002) Harvard University Center for Law, Economics, and Business working paper no 3.

[121] JA Brickley, JL Coles and RL Terry 'Outside directors and the adoption of poison pills' (1994) 35 Journal of Financial Economics 371.

[122] G Grullon and K George 'Managerial incentives, capital structure, and firm value: Evidence from dual-class stock' (2001) Rice University working paper.

10 percent level. Like previous studies, Grullon and Kanatas confirm that the company value consequence of dual class structures is ambiguous.[123] They find evidence that the returns on assets of dual class firms are significantly higher than the industry peers.

Unlike the US, there are few empirical studies in Europe that have sought to analyze the wealth effects of pre-bid defenses by shareholders. It is worth noting that some new studies are beginning to appear that seek to supply evidence about the effects of defenses on bids. For example, a recent paper by Rose[124] investigates the performance of Danish firms that adopted dual class shares for period between 1995 and 1999. Using Tobin's Q, share return, return on asset and return on equity, he shows that dual class stock firms are not outperformed by firms without dual class stock. Rose argues that other corporate governance mechanisms, including blockholder monitoring, appear to supply sufficient incentives to managers to persuade them to limit their opportunism and to invest in value-maximizing projects.

Based on the above, the efficiency implications of dual class stock are inconclusive. However, what the studies do indicate is that the market is able to differentiate between corporate governance arrangements. Recent anecdotal evidence about the status of multiple voting class shares indicates that capital cost considerations play an increasingly important role in the design of share class structures. For example, Ericsson is considering, in response to a recent decline in share performance, replacing its B class shares in order to lower its cost of raising new capital.

Berglöf and Burkart[125] observe that the break-through rule is inconsistent with the mandatory bid rule. This is due to the fact that the break-through rule is available as an option to bidders to bypass negotiations for private transfers of control with the incumbent management. As we have seen above, only in case of such negotiations will the mandatory bid rule lead to participation of the minority shareholders in the private benefits available to the controlling shareholder.

The effect of the break-through rule is to transform a bid for a company with a concentrated ownership structure into a dispersed bid. If the incumbent controlling shareholders have access to sufficient funds to launch a counterbid, the bidder will in turn be forced to bid at least as much as the incumbent shareholder. The maximum bid of the incumbent shareholder will include the sum total of his private benefits and the stock market valuation of the target firm. But, if the incumbent is financially constrained, the bidder will not offer more than the public value of the target firm after the completion of the takeover. The free-rider

[123] See also R Morck, A Shleifer and R Vishny 'Managerial ownership and market valuation: an empirical analysis' (1988) 20 Journal of Financial Economics 293-315.

[124] C Rose Corporate financial performance and the use of takeover defences (2002) 13 European Journal of Law and Economics 91-112.

[125] E Berglöf and M Burkart (n 32).

problem that arises in bids with widely dispersed ownership can be overcome by the private benefits available to the bidder. Hence to use the break-through rule, as a means of acquiring control, is the dominating strategy for the bidder even if the incumbent management is in principle willing to enter into negotiations.

In legal terms the break-through rule leads to the acquisition of control not by passing a threshold on voting share holdings but by effecting a change in a corporate charter. It is, however, unclear whether such a control transfer would trigger a mandatory bid. If it did not trigger a bid, then the problems associated with two-tier takeover bids would be reintroduced.

At the same time, under the assumption that the incumbent is not willing to tender, the break-through rule does not open up the possibility of affecting a squeeze out to the new controlling shareholder. Another important implication of the break-through rule is that it could alter the structures of ownership and concentration of voting rights. For example, Bebchuk and Hart[126] predict that break-through rule might induce firms – particularly new firms – to substitute a dual-class structure with a pyramiding structure. Such a step may in turn give rise, among other things, to problems related to monitoring, managerial incentives, and liquidity.

V. Compensation

This raises the issue how to compensate those shareholders that will be implicated by the introduction of the break-through rule. Whilst this issue was not addressed in the Proposed Directive, it has been discussed in a recent study issued by the European Parliament, which favoured the adoption of a fair compensation procedure. Proposals based on average European premiums for voting rights appear to suggest that in the event of a takeover bid, all outstanding shares would have the same voting right. Thus if the takeover were to proceed, the bidder would extend to voting shareholders an offer that is x per cent higher than to non-voting shareholders. As a value for x, 15 per cent has been proposed, deemed to be the European average premium. Given the importance of national circumstances in the determination of the premium, this (and any other) figure would be largely arbitrary. Moreover, imposing such a figure would change the relative share price. Its proponents overlook that this rule reverses causality: The compensation rule would determine the voting premium. The likely effect is that the voting premium would move towards the 15 per cent for all countries. A compensation scheme, derived from data equalizing jurisdictions, does not solve the compensation issue in an appropriate way.

There are other schemes that can be used to compensate the holders of dual and multiple class shares. The schemes fall into three categories: a mandatory

[126] L Bebchuk and O Hart A threat to dual-class shares *Financial Times* (31 May 2002).

level of compensation, independent expert valuation, and market-based compensation schemes (which may involve expert valuation as a remedy). We turn first to discuss mandatory schemes. The HLG Report explicitly recommended that the bidder should not be required to offer compensation as a public policy choice, in order to avoid appraisal proceedings and other costly legal proceedings. Some commentators, however, note that the mandatory rule exposes regulators to demands for compensation.

For an independent expert valuation, one may wonder whether the methods of appraisal proceedings involving parent-subsidiary contracts, squeeze-outs and cases where companies have abandoned their multiple voting shares could be employed. Taking examples from Germany, when courts employ appraisal methods to establish the 'intrinsic value' of the firm, they commonly use a free cash flow analysis.[127] This method involves a forecast of returns from the assets of the company. After making an initial forecast, the court will compare the forecast to the liquidation value of the company, which also takes non-substantive business assets into account. The crucial point is that the future business strategy is by and large taken as given and possibly an extrapolation of the current strategy. The discount factor for future returns is derived from a subjective judgement made by an accountant.[128] The evidence indicates that the application of accounting methods in appraisal proceedings is arbitrary to a significant degree,[129] (see also the section on squeeze-outs below).[130]

In cases of multiple voting rights or dual class with preference shares, measuring the 'intrinsic value' is not enough. The problem here is to ascertain the value of control as separate from the security value. Taking the business strategy as given seems counterintuitive, because the benefits of control are related to the controller's discretion over the use of the assets. This may even necessitate developing counterfactual business strategies (perhaps even including different dividend policies). For instance, Hering and Olbrich[131] propose a scheme under which a controlling shareholder would be denied compensation unless it was determined that his influence had a positive effect on firm value. They contend that a majority shareholder should only obtain compensated in those circumstances, after conversion, where the intrinsic firm value has decreased. Under this assumption, it may be necessary, in order to determine the level of compensation, compare business strategies that were altered in conjunction with the cessation of

[127] Hecker (n 115).

[128] Since recently, German accounting practice is turning to the discounted cash flow method (DCF), where the discount rate is derived from models built from capital market theory, which give a market valuation of the risk premium.

[129] Hecker (n 115).

[130] Her case study contained a sample of 16 compensation expertises.

[131] T Hering and M Olbrich 'Aktionärsabfindung und allgemeines Geschäftsrisiko' (2001) 53 Zeitschrift für betriebswirtschaftliche Forschung 726-727.

the multiple voting rights. Since the determination of firm value is forward-looking, it is assumed that a significant accounting judgement must be made about which changes in the business strategy should be pursued. Thus, given the circumstances, it may be quite difficult to accurately determine the appropriate compensation. As a corollary, they propose that that compensation should be denied to holders of multiple voting rights who are not de facto controlling shareholders. It is far from clear, however, that the argument favouring controlling shareholders is persuasive. Even if a large shareholder does not control the firm on his own terms, he could offer to sell his block to another large shareholder, who would as a consequence take control the firm. As a consequence, the non-controlling blockholder would be in a sufficiently strong position to bargain ex ante over the price of his shares and to receive some of the control benefits through the bargaining.

This confusion is evidenced by a recent case from Germany. In February 1999, the shareholders at the annual general meeting of Siemens AG voted to abolish a special class of shares (of small numbers), while denying their holders (the Siemens family) compensation for the loss of their additional voting rights. In response, the Siemens family sued for compensation. In October 2001, a Munich Court determined that the holders were entitled to receive compensation of approximately EUR 32 million. The court based its decision on a geometric mean of the relative price differences between common stock and preferred stock for a sample of German publicly listed companies over a period 12 years prior to the conversion. In addition, the court adjusted its calculations by considering special factors because the compensation to be found in this case was not for preferred stock but for multiple class stock with differing legal entitlements. For example, a discount for name shares was applied, and some contractual arrangements were priced, while others were not. In total, an additional vote was found to be worth EUR 0.70, which was multiplied by the number of additional votes of multiple voting shares the family had held.[132] In July 2002 the Higher Court of Bavaria reversed the lower court's decision, holding that it was not safe to conclude that the additional voting rights had a positive value.

We now turn to the proposal to couple compensation with a 'sell-out right.' It was proposed that a sell-out right would be given to the holders of multiple voting rights based on a fair price presumption.' Under this presumption, compensation would be regarded as equitable if it corresponded to the highest price paid by the bidder in a pre-specified period before the break-through. Obviously, this presumes that the bidder had to purchase some of the multiple voting shares either on the market or in a private negotiation. However, as explained above, the effect of the breakthrough rule is to bypass the incumbent multiple voting rights

[132] Landgericht München 'Entschädigung für die Abschaffung von Mehrstimmrechtsaktien: EGAktG § 5'; *Siemens AG* (Beschluss vom 14.9.2001 – 5 HKO 16369/99) (2002) 47 (2) Die Aktiengesellschaft 105-108.

holder. The bidder will only acquire multiple voting shares if they are necessary to reach the break-through capital threshold. However, in this case the break-through rule would be useless since the bidder would be required to enter into private negotiations with the incumbent controlling shareholder. Thus compensation by a sell-out right seems incompatible with the intention of the breakthrough rule.

Finally, let us turn to share class conversions that were negotiated at firm level. First, let us consider first evidence from Israel because there is a systematic study. Hauser and Lauterbach[133] examine Israeli stock unifications between 1990 and 1996. In 1989, 40% (104 of 260) publicly traded firms at the Tel-Aviv Stock Exchange (TASE) had outstanding dual class shares. Yet after the TASE – together with the Israeli Securities Authority – banned new issues of inferior class stocks in January 1990, more than 70 firms decided to unify voluntarily their existing dual class stocks. 67 unifications from 1990-1996, where compensation was paid (if at all) in the form of additional shares, are analyzed. The authors find that only in two unification processes did the majority shareholders surrender their controlling position. On average, the price (in new shares) for 1% of voting power was about 0.1% of firm's equity. Firms that decided to compensate and those that did not differed dramatically in their governance structure. The majority blockholder in firms that provide compensation owned a higher fraction of superior stock and a lower fraction of inferior stocks. Hauser and Lauterbach's findings are consistent with the hypothesis that majority blockholders dominate the unification process and especially determine the compensation scheme. The authors find, moreover, that the average share of majority holders in the firm's market value does not change significantly after unification.

Second, we turn to the German experience. In 1998, Germany decided to abolish multiple voting rights (but not non-voting preferred stock) with a transition period of 5 years. To do so, different routes were taken by two public utilities. After the IPO in 1922, RWE, a company that was founded as a public utility in 1905, had issued multiple class shares to several municipalities, which at the time were the main investors. In February 1998, the general assembly decided to abolish these special shares with a compensation of approximately EUR 600 million. This was the result of bargaining with the management, as the owners of the multiple voting shares originally asked for EUR 1000 million.[134] VEW, also public utility, decided to unify their share classes in mid 1999 and to offer compensation of EUR 9.00 for each additional vote. This calculation was based on the price differences of 29 companies between 1997 and 1998, adjusted to the price level of VEW shares and corrected by some 'special factors.'

[133] S Hauser and B Lauterbach 'The Value of Voting Rights to Majority Shareholders: Evidence from Dual Class Stock Unifications' (2000) UCLA Department of Finance working paper.

[134] Hering and Olbrich (n 131). At the official investor relationship site of RWE the compensation is not mentioned.

Several listed companies voluntarily altered their share structures in response to pressures emanating from the Deutsche Börse, which changed the rules for calculating its indices DAX and MDAX in June 2002. By permitting the free floating shares of only one class for a company's weight in the index, firms with multiple class structures saw their weight decrease in the index. As a consequence, large investment funds dropped their stocks. Since 2000 many of the major German companies have unified their preference shares with the common shares. Companies have employed a number of techniques. For instance, SAP and Südzucker AG used the equalization of dividends as the only measure of compensation. Before the conversion the superior voting shares of SAP were trade with a negative premium. The company was controlled by a group of founder who hold 63% of the votes. After a complete conversion this share decreased to 39%. Prior to conversion, Südzucker AG was controlled by three groups SVGZ[135] (60%), Deutsche Bank (13%), and an Austrian consortium (6%). As of January 2003, SVGZ controls 56%[136] and a new blockholder ZSG (NL) holds 10% of the votes. The free float has increased to 34%, but nevertheless a single block holder controls the firm. Interestingly, firms such as MAN Group and Metro decided to convert in a 1 to 1 ratio at a cash disbursement for the holder of inferior voting rights to be received by the company. In case of MAN, the payment was made at EUR 3.30, which corresponds approximately to 2/3 of the 3-month average price difference. At Metro the conversion was at cost of EUR 11.60 per preference share. There are only a few companies on the DAX, namely Volkswagen (VW), Bayrische Motorenwerke (BMW), Fresenius Medical Care and Henkel, which have preference shares outstanding. With the exception of Henkel, they have chosen to list the free float of common shares in the index.

VI. Conclusions

We have shown that the evidence on efficiency implications of dual class shares is inconclusive. Moreover, we have argued that market is able to attach different prices to competing corporate governance arrangements. Naturally a question arises about the benefits and costs of mandating European legislation on corporate arrangements that can have the effect of frustrating takeover bids. Some arrangements impact directly on corporate governance beyond the event of takeovers. This general impact may also depend on the national legislative context. It may be impossible to determine whether the costs of losing diversity outweigh the benefits attributed to the break-through rule. Could regulatory competition led to the introduction of the most efficient rule? As discussed above, such a projection depends on how effectively investors can evaluate the consequences of a

[135] Süddeutsche Zuckerrübenverwertungsgenossenschaft.

[136] Owner or holding in trust for another group.

particular corporate law rule on firm value. To be sure, not all arrangements that are classified as pre-bid defences by the HLG are equally transparent to investors. For example, the Dutch foundation model may be insufficiently transparent in its effects to foreigners. In contrast, the relative number of shares and votes in different classes may be easier ascertained. Nonetheless, their impact on the effectiveness of control will depend on country-specific factors that, as we have seen, give an inconclusive picture.

Given these tradeoffs, we find it difficult to make a clear-cut case in favour of an across the board elimination of corporate governance arrangements that can have the effect of frustrating takeover bids. Despite these considerations, the political process has isolated some corporate governance arrangements from the checklist of arrangements purportedly having the effect of frustrating takeover bids to be subject to a mandatory European break-through regulation.

The above discussion indicates that should the EU decide to adopt the break-through rule, the member states would be well advised grandfather the existing dual and multiple class shares for a significantly long period of time. We believe that this position has the advantage that the compensation takes place at company level and occurs only when the company itself decides to unify its share structure. Furthermore companies would have the flexibility to choose at least from a wide variety of alternatives, including the repurchase of their inferior voting shares, the allocation of additional shares to the formerly superior class, or an issue of a new single class share combined with a purchase right adjusted with a compensation in cash for the inferior shareholders.

While protecting the existing stock of dual and multiple class shares may limit in the near term the convergence toward the one-share-one-vote structure, it should provide an indirect mechanism to achieve this result. Indeed, if all new firms have de facto a one-share-one-vote structure an incumbent company with multiple classes may look 'old fashioned'. Shareholders can easily identify every company that have retained multiple classes (or indeed preferred stock). Thus, if investors favour particular corporate governance arrangements, we should anticipate the shareholders of old firms will actively campaign for management to unify share classes in order to obtain lower cost of capital. Firms that find their cost of capital is too high compared to the assumed advantages of their share structure will decide to strengthen their capital structure. We should, however, not expect that a small subset of firms that have controlling shareholders with few needs to return to the capital market would react quickly by altering the composition of their capital structure.

I. Board Neutrality

Article 9 of the proposed Directive stipulates that 'the board of the offeree company must obtain the prior authorization of the general meeting of shareholders given for this purpose before taking any action other than seeking alternative bids which may result in the frustration of the bid' and is mandatory in the time after a bid has been made. Commonly, this is termed as strict board neutrality. Next to the break-through rule, this provision has been much disputed.

The debate in corporate legal theory over takeovers falls into two broad schools of thought To begin, the shareholder choice perspective holds that boards are self-interested in their response to takeover bids and consequently should not be permitted to create defences.[137] Not only does board discretion reduce welfare by limiting the disciplinary effect of takeovers, but it also reduces shareholder value by attracting only friendly deals, allowing managers to extract a disproportionate share of rents produced by such transactions. While there is no doubt that shareholders are disadvantaged in ordinary day-to-day business decisions, proponents conclude that shareholders are best positioned to take the ultimate decision in a takeover bid.

In contrast, the board defence approach holds that shareholders are unable, due to limited experience, collective action and coordination problems, to make informed choices in the takeover context. These reasons appear to support claims that the board should be permitted to erect defences on the grounds that they are better placed to protect the interests of shareholders. This argument implies that managers may know better than shareholders what is best for the company. Furthermore, this claim presumes that managers have private information about the good state the company is in, which they are not able to convey either to the shareholder meeting of the company nor to market analysts.[138] Moreover, this claim supposes that when the company is in poor financial condition, the managers will bemore willing to concede this to shareholders and let the tender offer proceed.

Notice that *both* views claim that shareholders benefit from the respective rules. The problem with the management defense argument, however, is that it is difficult for shareholders to ascertain whether the management is not able or not willing to reveal the state of the company. As argued earlier, the collective action problem prevents small shareholders from collecting such information, while the takeover mechanism provide incentives for one party, the bidder, to become informed. Bebchuk and Hart[139] insist that it is unnecessary for their voting scheme to operate that every shareholder collects information. It suffices that there are a few informed traders. By observing market trading after the bid but prior to the vote, the uninformed shareholders can make an optimal decision, given the public information.

[137] L Bebchuk 'The case against board veto in corporate takeovers' (2002) 69 University of Chicago Law Review 973-1035.

[138] ML Wachter 'Takeover defense when financial markets are (only) relatively efficient' (2002) University of Pennsylvania Law Review, forthcoming.

[139] L Bebchuk and O Hart 'Takeover bids vs proxy fights in contests for corporate control' (2001) NBER Working Paper No 8633.

In the context of the debate on board neutrality, we argue that allowing deviations from a simple and strict board neutrality rule can easily raise legal costs in takeovers and create uncertainty for bidders. Complex national legislation and case law determine the allocation of intervention rights between management, supervisory boards and shareholder meetings outside the context of takeovers. In practice, management boards are not allowed to intervene at tender offers without any restrictions. They may have to ask shareholders in advance for an authorization to increase capital, for the introduction of a staggered board etc. In some countries, some of these authorizations can also be given by supervisory boards. We would briefly like to illustrate with the example of Germany that deviations from a simple board neutrality rule – although by themselves with some efficiency consideration – can lead to legal uncertainty.

I. Defences in Germany

In 2002, Germany adopted a new Takeover Code Act to replace the voluntary Takeover code. It is consistent with the general 'duty of neutrality' that prohibits the management from taking any unilateral action to frustrate the hostile takeover offer. Two exceptions are allowed. The first are so-called reserve authorizations, which are given *before a tender offer is received* by shareholders to explicitly enable the management to engage in defensive actions. The shareholder decision to waive their decision right in case of a tender offer has been justified with the freedom of contracting, shareholders would only do so if they believed that the management would subsequently act in their interest.

The second proposal is that management may engage in defensive action by permission of the supervisory board after a tender offer has been made. This effectively rests on the assumption that the management can and will share its superior private information with the supervisory board.[140]

Since the legislation was enacted, there have been no hostile takeovers where these above-stated provisions have been implicated.[141] With the German legal academy, scholars have attempted to delineate the scope of management discretion with or without shareholder or supervisory board approval. The range of actions that the management may undertake on its own is quite limited.[142] One constraint on management is that they prove that a particular action would also

[140] Whether the supervisory board would (or even should) feel responsible to shareholders, is a much debated question and beyond the scope of this paper. At present, German courts are venturing into what the responsibility of the supervisory board is worth in practice, taking the case of the Vodafone/Mannesmann takeover.

[141] In Germany the only hostile-turned-friendly takeover in 2002 was Kamps/Barilla.

[142] H Hirte Verteidigung gegen Übernahmeangebote und Rechtsschutz des Aktionärs gegen die Verteidigung' [2002] Zeitschrift für Unternehmens- und Gesellschaftsrecht 623-658.

have been undertaken in the absence of the bid. The second constraint is the provision that those actions that fall in the domain of the shareholder meeting do indeed require shareholder approval (see below). Finally, the third constraint is that many actions require supervisory board agreement.

A possibility for board discretion arises if the board has obtained, prior to a bid, permission by shareholders (*Vorratsbeschlüsse*). Reserve authorizations must generically describe the actions that the board may take. A reserve authorization, moreover, must obtain a majority of 75% of voting shares, and is only valid for a period of up to 18 months. Should a board decide to act upon such an authorization, it is required to obtain supervisory board permission. Importantly, there is no apparent agreement in the academic literature as to the scope of this provision.

Based on the foregoing, the management's room for action is the residual set of actions for which legislation, or the corporate charter, do not foresee shareholder decision-making or for which shareholders have given their authorization or for which supervisory board approval is not necessary. On this view, while boards have some discretion, they are restrained from taking actions that shareholders are required to decide. Moreover, they are not permitted to override shareholder decisions.

However, there is some dispute whether this is the only permissible interpretation of the German law. It is argued that supervisory board approval can be used to override shareholder decisions. Moreover, there is no agreement which decisions fall into the domain of shareholder decision-making. Actions that directly alter the shareholder structure fall into the domain of the shareholder meeting by law, other actions are permitted by case law. For example, a capital increase falls within the domain of the shareholder meeting. An abstract authorization (outside a takeover context) of the board to increase capital may be valid for five years, but scholars disagrees as to whether the use of this authorization is also permitted when the company has become a target, especially in conjunction with the exclusion of pre-emptive rights of the existing shareholders. Some argue that a supervisory board authorization would suffice.

Similar arguments can be made for share repurchase agreements.[143] The acquisition of shares of other companies may be seen as extra-ordinary business decisions by the management. It has been argued that these cannot be undertaken if they can be postponed until after the takeover process.[144] But it may be possible that a supervisory board agreement will suffice to allow management to adopt such strategies. It is thus debatable whether cross-holdings and defensive holdings require shareholder approval or only supervisory board agreement. Furthermore, it is questionable whether this only concerns the case when new share issues are used to finance this investment or when free cash flow is used.

[143] H Krause 'Die Abwehr feindlicher Übernahmeangebote auf der Grundlage von Ermächtigungsbeschlüssen der Hauptversammlung' [2002] Betriebs-Berater 1053-1061.

[144] Hirte (n 142).

It is worth pointing out that the literature cast doubt on whether reserve authorizations to defend takeovers would ever be used much in practice. That is, it is assumed that the management would, by resorting to a reserve authorization, reveal itself as a potential target and consequently trigger a fall in share price. Thus, it is argued that supervisory board agreement may be an easier mechanism for management to thwart bids.[145] However, we should expect that at least some management teams, fearing to become a takeover target, will chose to adopt share repurchases. Fostering takeover speculation in this way may raise the share price. Hence, the net effect in the stock price between decreased takeover probability due to shareholders' conferring of defensive powers to management and takeover speculation is unclear. Even though most assume that reserve authorisations will not be used in practice, it is noteworthy that some firms have argued that the provision is valuable.[146]

II. Conclusions

In this section we reported on the consequences of deviations from a simple board neutrality rule. The German example shows why it might be preferable to have a single, simple rule such as board neutrality. In order to facilitate cross-border transactions, a simple European rule might be preferable. This allows business parties to benchmark thediverse national provisions in a clearly defined circumstance without repercussions on the company's structures outside the context of takeovers. Moreover, this view is, compatible with schemes that ensure an efficient outcome of a bidding contest, even if not all shareholders are informed.

J. Squeeze-Out

The Commission embraced the HLG recommendation when it introduced the squeeze-out right in the Proposed Directive. A squeeze-out-right refers to the right (under specified conditions) of a majority shareholder to compel minority shareholders to sell their shares to him at an appropriate price. Although the squeeze-out procedure proposed in the Proposed Directive is uncontroversial, it is of interest for two reasons. Firstly, it constitutes one factor in the calculation of the minority shareholder when they determine to accept the mandatory bid or not. Secondly, the squeeze-out procedure deprives the concerned shareholders of their ownership rights against compensation.

[145] Krause (n 143); C Seibt and K Heiser 'Der neue Vorschlag einer EU-Übernahmerichtlinie und das deutsche Übernahmerecht' [2002] Zeitschrift für Wirtschaftsrecht 2193-2203.

[146] Max Dietrich Kley, CEO of BASF and chairman of the German Association of Publicly Listed Companies, quoted in the *Frankfurter Allgemeine Zeitung*, 23 October 2002.

The commonly supplied justification for providing a squeeze-out option is that retaining a small minority of shareholders can be costly (general assemblies would have to be arranged, shareholders notified etc). As a practical matter, small shareholders have, because control is no longer contestable, little hope of ever capturing the premiums from a control contest. Thus, the exclusion of the few remaining minority shareholders is efficient.

I. The proposed directive

Under Article 14 of the Proposed Directive, a majority shareholder can exert a squeeze-out under the constraint that he holds between 90% and 95% of the capital following a full bid (Art 14 1(a)). Alternatively,[147] a squeeze-out can be affected following a bid on the outstanding capital with the constraint that it has been accepted by shareholders representing more than 90% of the outstanding capital (Art 14 1(b)). Share classes are accounted for separately (Art 14 2). The equitable price in both cases can be determined in two ways. First, by a legal presumption on the 'fairness,' namely when the constraint is met that the bid attained 90% acceptances in terms of the share capital at which the bid was directed. In case of a prior mandatory bid, this threshold would not apply for the determination of an equitable price (Art 14 3). The time limit during which the equitable price presumption remains valid is set at three months. Second, in all other cases the squeeze-out price is to be determined by an independent expert (and in case of conflict, an appraisal proceeding) (Art 14 4).[148]

To be sure, this proposal may create considerable confusion as to when the appropriate compensation mechanism applies. Suppose a bidder had no stake in the target before launching the bid. Since at least 90% of the capital is needed to initiate a squeeze-out, this would correspond to at least 90% acceptances. However, if the bidder held an initial stake small enough that a mandatory bid became necessary, less than 90% acceptances would be needed to satisfy the 90% capital threshold and to ensure that the equitable price presumption applied. However, when the capital constraint is not satisfied – following a mandatory bid – the new controlling shareholder would need to launch a second bid in order to initiate a squeeze-out. Given that the acquirer already has a stake in the company, the 90% capital condition can be reached with less than 90% acceptances (as well as a 95% capital rule if the initial holding was at least 50%). But the equitable price assumption does not automatically apply. Rather, the price can be determined by an independent valuation as stricter conditions on the fair price presumption now

[147] It is not so clear whether member states are supposed to have the choice between these alternatives or a bidder.

[148] In the light of the arguments below, one may wonder how an appraisal procedure could be conducted for each class separately.

apply. Yet if the second bid were to have received a few more percentage points of acceptances, the fair price presumption could have been applied instead.

It is noteworthy that the proposal reflects a compromise between the traditions of different member states. However, it is submitted that a simple European rule would be preferable, particularly if the cost of harmonization is not too high. The question whether an expert valuation or the fair price presumption is applicable perhaps matters only at the margin. Appraisal proceedings are time-consuming and sometimes arbitrary. The Directive appears to have retained appraisal proceeding as a possibility by virtue of choosing not to fully harmonise the squeeze-out thresholds. However, there are costs involved for agreeing on a threshold that is not sufficiently high, as the threshold itself is somewhat arbitrary. An acceptance threshold only matters if there is an upward sloping supply of minority shares.

For an evaluation of the squeeze-out provisions, two considerations are important. In what follows, we will first discuss the fairness claim (the focus of the Directive) and go to consider the two methods of fairness determination. Second, we will discuss whether the proposed rules are efficient.

II. Fairness

As defined in Article 14, an equitable price presumption relies on the shareholders to evaluate their shares with the offered compensation. This is often referred to as a 'market mechanism.' A rule similar to the one proposed by the Directive is set forth in the UK Companies Act. Transaction costs is the main justification for embedding the equitable price presumption in the squeeze-out mechanism is transaction costs. Accordingly, the saving in transaction costs stems from avoiding the costs of negotiations with individual shareholders. To illustrate this insight, we consider three alternative situations of price determination where we assume that a shareholder may wish to initiate a full merger. In case (a), the bidder engages in individual negotiations; case (b) the bidder needs 100% acceptances for his proposal; and lastly (c) the bidder needs less than 100% acceptances to initiate the squeeze-out (which corresponds to the proposed Directive).

Suppose first that the majority shareholder would be forced to negotiate with each minority shareholder individually over the compensation. Since the minority shareholder would not be forced to give up his position at some point in time, he can always keep his shares as long as there is disagreement. In individual negotiations, his personal expectation of the future value of his shareholding would thus be the lower bound to his portion of the bargaining outcome. The distribution between the parties of the gain above this bound would depend on relative bargaining powers, for example the more patient party in the bargaining could be expected to attain a larger part. However, the majority shareholder may divert value from the controlled company as long as there is disagreement and thus weaken the minority shareholder's disagreement position. As a result, individual negotiations are, due to the large numbers of individual negotiations, very time-consuming and costly.

If the majority shareholder made a public offer to the outstanding shareholders conditional on a 100% acceptance rate, this would decrease transaction costs dramatically but would give every minority shareholder a veto right and thus the minority shareholder with the highest valuation would de facto decide on the outcome for all shareholders. Finally, we must assume that the shareholder is required to obtain an acceptance rate of less than 100%. The equitable price presumption in the directive thus constrains the veto power of minority shareholders, which makes the procedure fast and transaction cost saving.

Which procedure protects minority shareholders most effectively? To begin with, in circumstances in which all shareholders are homogeneous in their valuation of the company, the acceptance threshold would be irrelevant. As a consequence, the supply of minority shares would be flat (either all tender or none at a given price). Against this background, it is often argued that shareholders have different expectations of the future returns on their shares. However, in perfect capital markets, prices should reflect value. In case of companies with a large controlling shareholder, the low liquidity of the market for the outstanding shares may justify the assumption of an upward sloping share supply curve. It follows that the better- diversified shareholders become, the less important becomes such a threshold.

This does not imply necessarily that with individual bargaining minority shareholders would be better off than under the equitable price presumption. Broadly, one can expect that the total squeeze-out compensation determined in individual negotiations would reflect the average valuation across the minority shareholders of their minority shareholdings (their disagreement payoff). Under a 100% acceptance rule to a public offer, one would expect that the total cost to the offeror reflected the highest valuation by a minority shareholder of his minority shareholding. An acceptance threshold of less than 100% lowers the compensation, but not necessarily below the average of a series of individual negotiations.

It is thus clear that the equitable price presumption carries some arbitrariness with it. This does not necessarily allow the possibility of judicial remedy against it. Courts can only reconsider facts, not presumptions. The arbitrariness is in the thresholds that lead to the presumption. However, one may wish to resort to a different fair price determination procedure. It is argued that the alternative of an independent expert valuation does not fare any better in terms of arbitrariness, but instead adds costs.

III. Independent expert valuation

For every situation where Art 14 does not presume an 'equitable price' an independent expert valuation, based on accounting methods designed to determine the 'intrinsic value' of the firm, is coercive. Because the Directive does not explicitly specify the procedure we take in the following the appraisal procedures applied in Germany and US as examples to show the main problems that can arise. Broadly, in order to initiate a squeeze-out, the controlling shareholder should propose compensation based on independent expertise. If a minority shareholder considers this as inappropriate, the judicial remedy available is the appraisal proceeding, which re-evaluates the company's value by more independent expertise.

1. Germany

The German approach to expert valuation of a company is analysed in an extensive study by Hecker.[149] She focuses on parent-subsidiary contracts that must specify compensation for minority shareholders. The expert valuation in that case is similar to that used in squeeze-outs. When a shareholder (representing another company) has gained majority control, he could convene a general shareholder meeting to approve a contract between the parent and the subsidiary regulating the term of control. This contract must include a provision to compensate minority shareholders if they want to exit and a rent to be paid to them if the did not want to exit. The controlling shareholder would base the proposed compensation on a study by an external accountant. In case minority shareholders did not agree to the proposed compensation, the issue would be settled in an appraisal proceeding with additional accounting expertise.

During the time period of the study (1980s and 1990s), accountants would consider whether the subsidiary was as a going concern at the time when the shareholder meeting decided over the control contract with the parent company Synergies between the companies that might arise from a contract taking effect were not included.[150] Under this approach, information asymmetries between controlling shareholders and minority shareholders (for example due to lacking disclosure duties on hidden assets) are also taken as given. This use of this perspective[151] would lead accountants to understate, if the company had been independent under a sole owner, the intrinsic value of the company.

The valuation of profits is the method most commonly used in Germany for the ('Ertragswertmethode'). It is based on free cash flows ie, a forecast of returns on the assets of the company while maintaining its present substance. This can be

[149] Hecker (n 115). Her analysis concentrates on control contracts between parent and subsidiary. Other possibilities to exclude minority shareholders are mergers and going private transactions. German law did not provide for explicit squeeze-out procedures prior to the Takeover Act of 2002.

[150] The German Takeover Act of 2002 confirms this practice. The compensation should reflect the business as a going concern at the time when the general assembly decides on the squeeze-out.

[151] Hecker (n 115) 85-106.

set against the liquidation value of the company, which additionally takes non-substantive business assets into account. Unlike the asset-pricing model, the discount factor for future returns is essentially derived from the subjective judgements made by an accountant. Yet only recently has German accounting practice begun to accept the discounted cash flow method (DCF), where the discount rate is derived from models built from capital market theorywhich give a market valuation of the risk premium.

The evidence suggests that the application of the accounting methods is somewhat arbitrary in practice.[152] For example, the estimation of the reinvestment rates may involve subjective judgements on the part of accountants, which would, therefore, make it difficult to separate substantive from non-substantive business assets. Even when a business strategy of a firm is taken as given, the cash flow forecasts can differ in how uncertainty is taken into account. Finally, there may be problems finding the appropriate discount rate. In the valuation of profits method, the risk-free rate of return is augmented by the accountant's subjective evaluation of the risk premium (the compensation of the risk-averse investor for giving money to an uncertain project). The room for judgement is evidenced by the large differences between the initial expert studies and those commissioned in a subsequent judicial review.

2. United States

For squeeze-outs, theUS adopted the appraisal proceeding as a default rule. Because the US does not have a mandatory bid rule,[153] the US debate must be seen through a different lens. Coates[154] explains that Delaware law on company valuation in conflict transactions is non-binding. Companies are free to adopt 'fair price' charter provisions either to the benefit or to the disadvantage of minority shareholders in future squeeze-out procedures. However, companies make little use of this freedom despite the considerable variation in court decisions on appraisals.

Delaware law[155] stipulates that, in an appraisal proceeding, the fair value should be exclusive of any element of value arising from the accomplishment or expectation of the merger. The US debate thus attempts to establish criteria based on fairness grounds. Others note, however, that fair value can mean different

[152] Hecker (n 115). Her case study contained a sample of 16 compensation expertises.

[153] Of course, it is incorrect to speak of 'the US'. Indeed, only two US states have approved the mandatory bid rule. Moreover, Delaware, which is the focus of this section, has not followed the mandatory bid approach.

[154] JC Coates 'Fair value as an avoidable rule of corporate law: minority discounts in conflict transactions' (1999) 147 University of Pennsylvania Law Review 1251-1352.

[155] Delaware General Corporation Law, 262(h).

things. For instance, Booth[156] states that: 'In some case one may want to estimate the price at which one could buy or sell a controlling interest in a company. In other cases, one may want to estimate fair market value, that is, the value at which shares would trade in a completely undistorted market. Finally, in still other cases, one may seek to estimate the price at which a minority investor could actually sell shares.' Coates[157] attempts to ascertain the conditions under which a 'minority discount' would become unfair. In general, he argues that minority discounts constitute the difference between the value of control shares and the value of a minority share. 'Accordingly, 'minority discounts' and 'control premiums' are simply the inverse of one another.' Excluding synergies would be difficult, because it would require estimating the synergy value, the pure control value and the expropriation value, 'none of which, in isolation, is easy to observe directly.'

Both Coates and Booth, having reviewed the Delaware case law, conclude that the fair price proceedings can be expected to be arbitrary. In fact, Booth[158] explicitly considered the question whether the courts took account of control premiums that might have been paid in prior transactions. Booth suggests that the company should be evaluated as a whole in order to treat shares of the same class equally.[159] Recent case law[160] shows that 'premiums may arise from the (1) the potential for looting; (2) the right to direct business policies; or (3) synergistic gains'.[161] Since planned changes in the business strategy for the target are not considered in an appraisal, the courts would face the difficulty to disentangle from this an 'inherent value of control' that would be paid even in absence of the transaction in question. In the case referred to by Booth, the court argued that it was impossible to extract the factors that contribute to control premiums from the data. There the court took the data average of premiums paid in comparable company control transactions and reduced ten percentage points off the 40% average premium (as a proxy for the synergistic gains). This was added to the 'fair market value of the shares.' Booth concludes that this approach seemed to assume 'that *most* sources of premiums are part of the going concern value of the corporation that belongs to all stockholders.'

[156] RA Booth 'Minority discounts and control premiums in appraisal proceedings' (2001) 57(1) Business Lawyer 127-161.

[157] JC Coates 'Fair value as an avoidable rule of corporate law: minority discounts in conflict transactions' (1999) 147 University of Pennsylvania Law Review 1251-1352, 1278.

[158] n 156.

[159] According to the Delaware Supreme Court; RA Booth 'Minority discounts and control premiums in appraisal proceedings' (2001) 57(1) Business Lawyer 127-161.

[160] *Agranoff v Miller* No 16795, 2001 Del Ch LEXIS 71 (Del Ch 15 May 2001). Although this was not an appraisal proceeding, the issue was to determine whether there was expropriation of particular shareholders.

[161] Booth (n 156).

Analysis of the US evidence indicates that minorities participate to some extent in the takeover gains. As noted above, the US do not have a mandatory bid rule (and does allow for partial bids), so that in the initial takeover private benefits of control are usually not distributed to all shareholders. Plainly the American law on squeeze-outs provides a lower bound to the dilution of minority positions to overcome the free-riding problem. DeAngelo, DeAngelo and Rice[162] argue that minorities de facto have a veto right in squeeze-outs because the success of a judicial review of the compensation depended on whether the decision on the squeeze-out by the general assembly had been supported by a majority of the minority shareholders.

The company's market valuation is sometimes taken as the lower bound to the compensation offered by the controlling shareholder.[163] The market value of shares reflects the market's expectation of the present discounted value of the minority holding in the controlled company, thus potentially excluding private benefits of the controlling shareholder.[164] As noted above, low liquidity due to the few shares outstanding may depress the price somewhat. The market price also reflects the anticipated outcome of a squeeze-out procedure. Under the Proposed Directive, this would ensure with some probability that an appraisal procedure is initiated.[165]

To sum up, independent expert valuations and appraisal proceedings tend to be arbitrary in application of valuation methods. They are designed to arrive at a valuation independent of the market. Nonetheless, the valuations tend to include some market valuation, be it by estimating market discount rates, be it by taking the stock price as a lower bound to the compensation. In addition, they are time-consuming, for example, in Germany appraisal proceedings can well last for ten

[162] H DeAngelo, L DeAngelo and EM Rice 'Going private: minority freeze-outs and stockholder wealth' (1984) 27 Journal of Law and Economics 367-401, As quoted by E Wenger, C Kaserer and R Hecker 'Konzernbildung und Ausschluss von Minderheiten im neuen Übernahmerecht: Eine verpasste Chance für einen marktorientierten Minderheitenschutz' (2001) 13(5) Zeitschrift für Bankrecht und Betriebswirtschaft 317-334.324).

[163] This is common in the US. In Germany case law has accepted the market value as a lower bound since 1999. The market value contains the market expectation of the outcome of the appraisal procedure.

[164] This is not true of stock market prices before the takeover. The increase in the share price when a takeover is imminent is the anticipation of the distribution of private benefits (or synergies) in case control changes.

[165] There may be an additional problem as to when the majority shareholder initiates the squeeze-out procedure. The majority shareholder has an incentive to initiate the squeeze-out procedure when he knows that the shares are undervalued. This is an application of the 'lemons problem' in the economics of asymmetric information (L Bebchuk and M Kahan 'Adverse selection and gains to controllers in corporate freeze-outs' in R Morck *Concentrated Corporate Ownership* (University of Chicago Press 2000) 247-259.). This would create additional incentives to accept the mandatory bid, see below. This is not relevant when the squeeze-out compensation is tied to the takeover bid.

years.[166] Thus, it would be preferable to apply an equitable price presumption as often as possible because it lowers transactions cost and decreases the uncertainty over the outcome.

IV. Efficiency

In most cases, a squeeze-out is initiated as a consequence of a control change. Thus the squeeze-out should not be seen as independent from the actual takeover. As we discussed above, it is necessary, in order to overcome the free-riding problem, that minority shareholders do not participate in all the gains the takeover generates. The two mechanisms designed to overcome the free-rider problems are: (1) ex post expropriation of minorities ('dilution'); and (2) private benefits available to the new controlling shareholder. We noted that the degree of dilution is determined by the incentive effects of takeovers on the incumbent management of the target company.[167] We also discussed argued the efficient squeeze-out rule proposed by Amihud et al.[168] With Bebchuk[169] we outlined the issues that arise when an incumbent blockholder sells control privately. In sum, the optimal squeeze-out compensation may depend on the specific circumstances of the takeover, in particular whether the target was widely held, whether there were blockholders, whether there have been competing bidders, or whether there is a mandatory bid rule.

V. Conclusions

To sum up, the squeeze-out procedure is a legal mechanism to deprive shareholders of their ownership rights. Compensation is found either by allocating strong powers of rejection to the shareholders or by independent experts who take the use of funds in the controlled firm as given. There are strong caveats to use these methods to compensate for the break-through rule.

In principle, the squeeze-out rules proposed in the directive are acceptable. The proposed thresholds for a squeeze-out were designed to reflect national legal history. Since these thresholds are to some extent arbitrary, they may just as well be harmonized for simplicity. We suggest that little will be lost in terms of regulatory diversity because the squeeze-out regulation concerns a well-defined event and does not involve trade-offs with other areas of corporate governance. Further-

[166] Hecker (n 115).

[167] SJ Grossman and O Hart (n 98).

[168] Amihud et al (n 103).

[169] L Bebchuk 'Efficient and inefficient sales of corporate control' (1994) 109(4) Quarterly Journal of Economics 957-993.

more, it may be of little cost to streamline the rules such that an independent expert valuation will no longer be available for a fair price determination. Under the current proposal, it seems like a matter of chance for both the controlling and the minority shareholders whether the fair price presumption or the independent expert valuation has to be applied. The latter is inferior.

The fair price presumption itself could also be streamlined. Given that the change of control by a takeover triggers a mandatory bid that has its own – strict – fair price rule, the new controlling shareholder should be able to squeeze-out shareholders that have not tendered with no restrictions other than having to offer the takeover bid price, perhaps with a longer time horizon than three months.

The squeeze-out procedure is not a blueprint for compensation of groups of shareholders in other circumstances. First, it explicitly (in the appraisal proceeding) or implicitly (in the fair price presumption) allocates some bargaining power to the shareholders that are forced to tender their shares. The allocation of bargaining powers under circumstances other than a squeeze-out may be a different issue. Second, the independent expert valuation evaluates the company as a going concern. It does not evaluate the relative weights of different shareholder groups in the distribution (and determination) of the market value of the company. Attempts to do so on the basis of industry data are to some extent arbitrary.

K. The Level Playing Field Considered and Conclusions

The market for corporate control in Europe is underdeveloped and highly segmented. The takeover market needs to evolve in order to enhance productive and allocative efficiency and to ensure greater financial market integration. A harmonized approach to takeover regulation is now needed to promote minority shareholder protection and to handle systemically the barriers that limit the operation of the takeover market in several EU member states. There is a real need to reach agreement on a minimum common regulation that could reduce the price of takeovers and thus lead to the acceleration of takeovers. In addressing the regulation of takeovers at the European level, a more economic approach, based on economic efficiency, is required.

Yet fairness considerations have tended to overshadow economic efficiency concerns in the debate on the Proposed Directive. For example, the main contribution of the High Level Group was the claim that the EC takeover legislation should support the creation of a level playing field for takeovers. It becomes natural to ask whether the fairness claim is ultimately the basis upon which the European Union has to make its policy choices about the regulation of takeovers. In our view, the level playing field claim is at odds with the central idea that a harmonized takeover code should be evaluated in respect of whether it would achieve substantial welfare benefits and transparency.

As we have seen, the EU debate on takeover regulation begins with the unexamined assumption that firms competing in the same market should be governed by the same rules. The level playing field has been defined by the HLG as takeovers having 'an equal probability of success' across countries. However, in view of the previous discussion, takeover legislation should ensure that the probability of success is one if a particular takeover was to be efficient and zero otherwise. This already is difficult to establish and one might be sceptical as to whether legislation may ever be able to achieve this. Thus some systems competition to evolve towards a better system may be desirable. With the diversity of national takeover legislation currently in place, it is likely that in some countries the probability of efficient takeovers to succeed is smaller than in others. This in itself is not a sufficient reason for harmonization. Harmonization may be desirable in cases where the costs of having 15 rules preclude systems competition. In this paper, we have not dealt with the question whether our recommendations should be part of a mandatory European code or of a European code that provides a simple set of optional default rules. Firms deciding to opt out of an optional EU code may find its cost of capital rising. In some instances, it may be desirable to insert some mandatory safety devices in cases of unambiguous negative effects.

The creation of a level playing field with third countries is an idea we oppose. With the presumption that US state law allows for the board of directors of US companies to employ a range of ex post defensive measures without shareholder approval, this level playing field argument implicitly assumes that this type of measure will give US firms an unfair advantage in the international takeover market. But, mandating that the Proposed Directive does not operate in cases that involve a bidder outside the EU, may be difficult to justify on efficiency grounds. If the EU code is designed to protect shareholder value while other codes do not, so be it. It has nowhere been proven that the efficiency of the board neutrality rule depends on how many other firms also employ such a rule. If the focus of the proposed Directive is on efficiency, it should foresee tender offer rules that preclude value-decreasing takeovers. Whether the bidder and the target have different corporate charters, may be one point to consider for tendering (or voting) shareholders. As it is, it is not a concern for policy-makers and no reason for a rule of reciprocity.

Notice also that the reciprocity claim vis-à-vis the US is not based on a present competitive imbalance between US and EU corporations in the transatlantic market for corporate control. Rather, a careful evaluation shows that EU firms have greater market presence in the US corporate acquisition market than US firms have in the EU. It should be evident, as the empirical research suggests, that there is by no means a conclusive presumption in favour of reciprocity since there is little evidence that US state law rules are discriminatory in nature and do not serve European investors' interests. In addition, US stock markets are commonly seen as the world's most developed and efficient. There is little question that it would be wrongheaded to introduce regulatory protections against firms that are listed on such markets if the policy goal is to strive for more efficiency in Europe.

Similar arguments apply to proposals made by some Members of the European Parliament to allow the national securities regulator to frustrate takeover bids if the bidding company has some degree of market dominance in its home country. This would imply that the securities regulator would have to decide on market dominance. Inefficiencies arising from market dominance are a matter for merger control. To overload the takeover directive with issues of market dominance would create conflicts between the competition authorities and the securities regulator. Furthermore, if a company used (legal) monopoly profits to acquire foreign companies, the efficiency cost would accrue to its customers, not the shareholders of the target company, since they are free to reject the bid. Shareholders are not interested in perfect competition on the product market. Again, the level playing field argument proves to be systematically misleading.

As we have seen, the empirical research supports the view that good bidders originating from jurisdictions with good corporate governance regimes tend to have a lower cost of capital. Correspondingly, a firm may have inherent competitive advantages in the takeover market as a result of its ownership structure and the particular governance characteristics of the firm. The simple reason is that well-governed bidders find it easier to raise capital to finance their acquisitions. Moreover, this result is consistent with our earlier claim that corporate governance has a direct impact on corporate performance. In sum, the foregoing analysis suggests that there are gains to be achieved by creating an active cross-border takeover market that protects minority shareholders and promotes higher disclosure standards.

Reciprocity in Takeovers

MARCO BECHT*

The European Commission has proposed a directive on takeovers that will make the control of European corporations more contestable. The European Parliament and Germany will not adopt the directive unless it provides for reciprocity in takeovers, limiting access to new hostile takeover tools to bidders that are themselves open to hostile bids. These measures go beyond the formulation of common rules for takeovers. They involve direct regulatory intervention in the voting control of potential bidders and targets. To make the control of bidders and targets mutually contestable the challengers must be given the power to break the grip of blockholders and to oust the incumbent board. If reciprocity in takeovers is fully implemented, the European Union will conduct an untried experiment that will transform the control of corporate Europe on an unprecedented scale – and with uncertain outcomes. A more limited experiment that puts the new tools at the disposal of companies in all Member States would allow the creation of a pan-European market segment for companies that wish to embrace the advantages of high secondary market liquidity, managerial disciplining through hostile takeovers and related corporate governance instruments.

A. Introduction

After more than ten years of consultations, revisions and negotiation over related and unrelated issues[1] observers were confident that the European Parliament would adopt the European Commission's proposal for a Takeover Directive in the second round of its second reading. Like the first draft, the new proposal was closely modelled on the UK's City Code, but took into account concerns over

* I am grateful to Eilís Ferran, Guido Ferrarini and Jonathan Rickford for specific advice and comments. All mistakes and views they disagree with remain my own.

[1] At some stage Spain sought to 'trade' concessions on the Takeover Directive against concessions on to the future of Gibraltar.

employee involvement, 'tactical' litigation (greenmail) and the proper role of Member States (subsidiarity), among others.[2]

In the Commission's view a European Directive on takeovers was needed for facilitating corporate restructuring by having common rules and procedures applying to the takeover process throughout the single market and by providing equivalent protection for minority shareholders in takeover situations.

The proposed Directive had three essential features: one, a mandatory bid rule designed to protect minority shareholders; two, a squeeze-out provision allowing bidders to 'go private' after a successful bid; three, a board neutrality rule, putting the bid quickly to the target shareholders without giving the board a chance to bargain with the bidder, or to frustrate the bid. The mandatory bid rule effectively eliminated sales of control through partial share block trades; the board neutrality rule effectively banned post-bid takeover defences.

The draft adopted by Member States on 19 June 2000 seemed uncontroversial. Couched as a 'framework' (compromise) Directive, it gave Member States considerable freedom for implementing the mandatory bid rule. Indeed, some observers criticised the proposal for being too flexible, thereby undermining its objectives. Furthermore, while waiting, many Member States had already adopted national takeover legislation that exceeded the stipulations of the draft Directive, legislation that was successfully tested by the largest (hostile) deals in European history.[3] Final adoption of the compromise Directive by the European Parliament and the Council of Ministers appeared a foregone conclusion.[4]

To the European Commission's surprise, it transpired that a German led group of Members of the European Parliament were not satisfied with its proposal. The MEPs demanded 'reciprocity in takeovers', or allowing post-bid defences. It was unfair, so they argued, that some countries were depriving their corporations of all takeover protections while others were not, allowing their corporations to go

[2] The initial proposal for a 'Thirteenth Council Directive on Company Law Concerning Takeover Bids' was published on 19 January 1989 (COM(88)823 final – SYN 0186). It was followed by an opinion of the Economic and Social Committee (27 September 1989), an opinion of the European Parliament (17 January 1990) and an amended Commission proposal (COM(90) 416 final – SYN 0186). A second proposal was presented to the Council and Parliament on 8 February 1996 (COM(95)655 final), followed by an opinion of the Economic and Social Committee (11 July 1996) and a first reading of Parliament (26 June 1997), that resulted in twenty proposed amendments. The Commission's revised draft of the second proposal was retransmitted to Council and Parliament on 11 November 1997. At the same time the Commission published 'frequently asked questions', that tackled the concerns that had been raised in plain language <http://europa.eu.int/comm/internal_market/en/company/company/news/takeoverfaq.htm>. For links to the full text documents see <http://www.ecgi.org/takeovers>.

[3] The hostile bid of Olivetti for Telecom Italia during 1998/99 was driven by Italy's privatisation law. It is an important case because it was – to my knowledge – the first application of a 'breakthrough rule'.

[4] Indeed, the Council adopted, unanimously, a common position (19 June 2000) that was accepted by the European Commission (26 July 2000).

on hostile acquisition sprees in the neighbours' gardens wearing a bullet proof vest.

Germany formally joined the rebel MEPs position and it became apparent that the original move was motivated by a political inconsistency: The German 'Control and Transparency Law' (KonTraG) had just banned most pre-bid defences and led, indirectly, to the successful hostile bid of Vodafone plc for Mannesmann AG, the target not having bothered to replace its expiring pre-bid defences with a potent alternative.[5] Alerted to its vulnerability, the widely-held chemical industry (and others) extracted a promise for post-bid defences from Berlin, that Brussels was about to ban.[6] Put to a vote in the Parliament, the European Commission's proposal fell short of the required majority by one vote. The Parliament sent a message that without reciprocity in takeovers, also with companies from outside the EU, the proposed Directive would not pass.[7]

As a response to the impasse, the European Commission invited a 'high-level group of company law experts' chaired by Jaap Winter (the Winter Group) to suggest a technical solution to the reciprocity in takeovers challenge. The response of the Group is the so called 'breakthrough rule'. Inspired by the Italian privatisation law and a recommendation of the French Commission des Opérations de Bourse (COB), the breakthrough rule stipulates that a bidder acquiring 75% of the 'capital at risk' in a target can break through all statutory takeover defences.[8] Although the Winter Group proposals did not introduce full reciprocity, the 'breakthrough rule' made certain existing defences less effective, in particular pre-bid defences based on dual-class shares.

After intensive lobbying from Member States and companies with dual class share structures, the follow-up proposal of the European Commission did not

[5] Mannesmann had in place a voting right restriction of 5% that was due to expire a few months after the Vodafone bid was launched. When coupled with proxy vote support from German banks, voting right restrictions have traditionally provided a formidable takeover protection in Germany: J Franks and C Mayer 'Bank Control, Takeovers and Corporate Governance in Germany' (1998) 22 Journal of Banking and Finance 1385-1403.Without the voting right restriction, a rising proportion of votes in the hands of international investment funds and strategic change at the helm of Germany's large there was not much choice but to raise the white flag.

[6] For further details on the German takeover law see JN Gordon 'An American Perspective on the Anti-Takeover Laws in the EU: The German Example (chapter 9 in this volume)'.

[7] Reciprocity in takeovers (a 'level playing field') was only one of four issues the Parliament felt needed to be resolved, but the other three were less political and could be more easily resolved at a technical level: a procedure for a 'squeeze-out right'; a definition of the equitable price to be paid in the case of a mandatory bid; clarification of the rights of employees.

[8] The Group also recommended to ban share transfer restrictions and recommended the application of the breakthrough to 'golden shares'. It also recommended further study of pyramid structures, cross-holdings, circular shareholdings and the implications of imposing reciprocity on companies from outside the EU under international trade law principles and agreements. See Winter Group (2002) (Annex 2 in this volume).

adopt the full breakthrough rule (COM (2002) 534 final).[9] However, the report of the European Parliament's rapporteur (COM(2002) 534 – C5-0481/2002 – 2000/0240(COD), 11 March 2003) reinstated the original proposal. It imposed 'one-share-one-vote' for the breakthrough rule[10] and the shareholder vote on post-bid defences,[11] but granted an explicit breakthrough exemption to airlines,[12] central banks[13] and IPO companies.[14] The report also introduced a new article on 'international' and 'intra-European' reciprocity.[15]

Not surprisingly, the European Parliament's proposal was unacceptable for countries with dual-class share structures and a permanent stalemate was in sight (again). In May 2003 the Portuguese Presidency tabled a compromise proposal.[16] It foresees a reciprocal breakthrough regime companies can opt into (Option A), or not (Option B). Companies in the 'breakthrough club' allow other companies to use the breakthrough rule when making a hostile offer for acquiring their control. In return they can use the breakthrough rule when making bids for other companies in the club. Companies outside the club cannot use the breakthrough rule – but other companies cannot bid for them using the breakthrough rule either.

[9] The main arguments put forward were several legal problems and one economic consideration. Legal problems were: finding a definition of risk-bearing capital, the threshold for triggering the break-through; the dilution of the rights of ordinary shareholders from giving non-voting shares votes, the suspension of multiple voting rights without compensation (and resulting constitutional problems from such expropriation), breach of freedom of contract and undue interference with Member States' company law. The sole economic consideration was the well-documented theoretical insight that that dual class share structures actually makes it cheaper to acquire control (stimulating the market for corporate control). See the Commission's 'frequently asked questions' (MEMO/02/201, 02/10/2002).

[10] Amendment 29 (Article 11, Paragraph 4).

[11] Amendment 28 (Article 11, Paragraph 3a (new)).

[12] Airlines must be able to show that they are majority owned and/or controlled by the nationals of the member state in which they are registered, otherwise they can loose their landing rights outside the EU, that are often guaranteed through bi-lateral aviation agreements (Amendment 27).

[13] The Belgian Central Bank happens to be a listed company (Amendment 13, Article 1, paragraph 3 (new)).

[14] IPO companies are exempted from the breakthrough rule for up to five years (Amendment 30).

[15] A new Article 17a gives Member States the possibility of blocking bids from outside the EU, if 'important interests so require' and international legislation is respected (Amendment 36). Article 17b allows Member States to block bids from bidders deriving the bulk of their turnover from state guaranteed monopoly activity (Amendment 37). This amendment is motivated by Electricité de France's cross-border acquisition programme that is considered as unfair by some Member States, for example Italy, that has chosen to make the control of its privatised companies to contestable (see Section C.I).

[16] A revised Directive incorporating the Portuguese proposals was presented at the beginning of June 2003.

The latest report from the European Parliament has adopted the spirit of the Portuguese proposal.[17] Similarly, the Italian presidency has circulated a draft that allows Member States to opt-out of board neutrality (Article 9) and/or the break-through rule (Article 11), but it also allows companies in Member States that have opted-out to opt-in. Reciprocity is limited to board neutrality (Article 9), provided the target company has opted-in.

The remainder of this chapter is structured as follows: Section B provides a stylised map of corporate control arrangements in Europe. Section C argues that reciprocity in takeovers requires more radical measures than those proposed at the moment. Section D questions whether 'reciprocity in takeovers' doctrine as a policy objective in its own right. Section E concludes.

B. Models of Corporate Control[18]

The economics and finance literature distinguishes two basic models of corporate control and governance: the blockholder model (B) and the widely held corporation model (W). In the blockholder model an individual, a group of individuals or an organisation commands many (most) of the votes at the corporation's shareholder meetings. The blockholder has the power to appoint and/or remove the board of directors and the blockholder appointed board appoints and/or removes the CEO.[19] In contrast, the widely held corporation has a broad equity base with many small shareholders who, individually, command a small number of votes. The incumbent board nominates the new board, which is confirmed by the passive mass of small shareholders in a vote. Formally the board appoints the CEO. In practice, the CEO appoints the board, putting incumbent managers in control of the widely held corporation.

Empirically, most companies in Europe have a blockholder commanding at least a blocking minority of 25% (Figure 1) and often a majority of the voting rights (Figure 2). The United Kingdom is an exception. Here all but a few FTSE 100 companies have no blockholder larger than 100% (Figure 12).

[17] COM(2002) 534 – C5-0481/2002 – 2000/0240(COD), 3 September 2003, PE327.239/rev.

[18] For a more extensive treatment of corporate control issues see M Becht and C Mayer 2002, Introduction, in F Barca and M Becht *The Control of Corporate Europe* (Oxford University Press Oxford 2001); for a survey of takeover theory and evidence see M Burkart The Economics of Takeover Regulation (1999) Discussion Paper, Stockholm School of Economics, Stockholm.

[19] In some countries the ability of blockholders to appoint, remove or influence boards is limited by company law (Germany, Holland) or listing rules (in the United Kingdom). In Belgium a blockholder commanding 50% of the votes (plus one vote) can remove the board at any time ('*ad nutum*'), bringing the Belgian system very close to our stylised description of the blockholder model.

I. Two Models – Four Flavours

In practice, each of the main models comes with two flavours. In the blockholder model blocks of votes can be acquired with a proportional amount of capital ('one-share-one-vote'; Model B1) or with a less than proportional amount, through legal devices that give blockholders more than one vote for each Euro invested ('one-share-more-votes'; Model B2). Prominent examples are equity capitalisations with non-voting shares (Figure 3), shares with multiple voting rights (Figure 4) or issuance of certificates without votes.[20] The most complex of these devices are 'Chinese boxes', 'pyramids' or 'control cascades' that combine companies to control chains (Figure 5, Figure 6). At each level of the chain the controlling blockholder brings in outside capital while keeping control, thereby reducing the cost of control.[21]

For widely held companies we distinguish between those open to hostile takeovers (Model W1) and those that are not (Model W2).[22] In companies that are open to hostile bids, an outsider can purchase shares to form a controlling block, moving the company from the widely held to the blockholder model. The incumbent board (and/or CEO) is forced to hand control to the blockholder.

In well-defended companies, share blocks cannot be assembled without board and/or CEO approval. In Europe, pre-bid defences in widely held companies include devices like voting right restrictions (Figure 7), share transfer restrictions (Figure 8) and shares vested with special rights (Figure 9). The most potent post-

[20] A De Jong, R Kabir, T Marra and A Roëll 'Ownership and Control in the Netherlands' in Barca and Becht (eds) *The Control of Corporate Europe* (Oxford University Press Oxford 2001).

[21] Empirically we do not know with precision how much voting power leverage B2-type blockholders derive from the various devices. Under European disclosure rules only voting rights, not cash-flow rights are systematically disclosed throughout the European Union. Hence it is notoriously difficult to estimate how much leverage these instruments provide for blockholders across larger samples, at least outside of Scandinavia (F Barca and M Becht The *Control of Corporate Europe* (Oxford University Press Oxford 2001). It is possible, of course, to look at capital structures. Expanding on M Faccio and LHP Lang 'The Ultimate Ownership of Western European Corporations' (2002) 65 Journal of Financial Economics 3; M Bennedsen and K Nielsen 'The Impact of a Break-Through Rule on European Firms' (2002) CEBR Working Paper DP 2002-10, Copenhagen <http://www.cebr.dk>, have estimated that 1035 of 5162 listed firms in the EU (excluding Greece, Holland and Luxembourg) have dual class structures, with varying degree of importance in the firm's equity base. The disclosure situation for groups is even sketchier, making estimates of the control leverage in pyramidal structures even less reliable. Nevertheless, attempts have been made to estimate the extent to which the instrument is used. On the one hand they exaggerate the extent of pyramiding by counting complex holdings as a pyramid, on the other they might not be able to trace the full control chain (see, for example, Faccio and Lang (ibid) for a recent empirical study, subject to the limitations of current disclosure rules).

[22] At least in theory, the 'breakthrough rule' converts W2 into W1 companies by allowing bidders to overcome statutory takeover defences.

bid defence is 'blank cheque' preferred stock that can be placed with white knights, squires or other friendly party (see Figure 10).

To make the field even more colourful, some companies have special control structures that mix flavours or that are not straightforward to classify. For example, widely held companies with statutory pre-bid defences (Model W2) face the problem of bidders acquiring a supermajority (75%, 66.66%), allowing them to change the statutes and to remove the protections.[23] In this situation, 'lock-in' provisions are crucial. The simplest 'lock-in' is a Model B1 or B2-style minority block of 25% (or 33.33%).[24] The most sophisticated version is a priority share construction (Figure 9).

Both flavours can be found in privatised companies. The B2-style blocking minority is found in the case of Volkswagen AG (Figure 11), which is still governed by a special privatisation law. The law provides for a 20% voting right restriction. The arrangement is locked in through a blocking minority held through a dual-class share capitalisation by the Land of *Niedersachsen*, where the VW headquarters and its main plant are located.[25] The priority share lock-in is known as a 'golden share provision' in privatised companies.

More exotic are partnerships limited by shares that can be found in Germany (Henkel *KGaA*), France (Michelin *sociétés en commandite*) and Italy (Pirelli & C *Accomandita per Azioni*). The unlimited liability partners have full control over the company with a relatively small investment, with limited liability shareholders providing the bulk of the funds.[26]

C. Achieving Reciprocity

To achieve reciprocity in takeovers the Takeover Directive will have to ensure that the control of takeover targets is contestable and that the group of bidders that have access to the tools that make control contestable is limited to companies with voting control that is equally contestable. To achieve this aim the bidder and the target must be widely held and have no statutory takeover protections. Alternatively, a breakthrough rule must allow bidders to overcome such protections – and vice-versa.

[23] Indeed, this is the very mechanism the Winter Group baptised a 'breakthrough rule'.

[24] Under the original Winter Group proposal, only a Model B1-style block will provide the required 'lock-in'.

[25] Indeed, the Volkswagen law adds a further twist by raising the supermajority threshold to 80%, so only a smaller (cheaper) 20%, B2-style block is required for the lock-in.

[26] At least in the case of Michelin, the partnerships limited by shares as a corporate control structure is defended with great passion against the criticisms often voiced by institutional investors (see <www.michelin.com>).

The proposal put forward by the Winter Group does not achieve full reciprocity. For widely held companies the Group proposes to shrink the menu of available statutory defences[27] and to apply a breakthrough rule that is conditional on 75% acceptances. The latter raises the cost of locking in statutory defences, but it does not allow bidders to overcome statutory defences that are secured through a minority block.[28] The control of listed companies under majority control and the control of privately held companies remains incontestable, yet all these companies can continue to launch hostile bids on widely-held, open targets.

The Portuguese 'breakthrough club' proposal appears more promising. It ensures that the Winter Group's proposals will only apply with reciprocity. To use the breakthrough rule as a bidder, the bidder has to subscribe to the breakthrough rule, making the bidder a potential target. The trouble is that subscribing to the breakthrough rule alone does not make the control of a bidder contestable. Blockholder controlled companies and companies with statutory takeover protections locked in by minority blocks will happily opt into the 'breakthrough club'. Even with a breakthrough rule, their voting control is not contestable. Hence, even when combined with the Portuguese 'breakthrough club' proposal the breakthrough rule alone does not deliver full reciprocity in takeovers.

To achieve full reciprocity, more radical measures are required. To make blockholder control contestable, the Takeover Directive will have to convert blockholder-controlled companies into widely held companies, at least in terms of voting rights. To achieve this aim the Directive would have to (re)introduce the 'one-member-one-vote' (common law) principle that was the norm in early 19th century charters in Germany, France, the United Kingdom and the United States.[29] Irrespectively of the number of shares owned, each shareholder has one vote.[30] Voting right ceilings and voting scales achieve similar results.[31]

[27] The Group proposes, for example, to ban share transfer restrictions.

[28] The attention of the media has focused on the proposed 'one-share-one-vote' provision of the original breakthrough rule. This issue is important but is merely an extension of the more general observation. Dual-class share structures make it cheaper to put a 25.1% blocking minority in place, but there are close substitutes that are readily available. Companies that want to have 'one-share-one-vote' blocking minorities more cheaply can use pyramiding (L Bebchuck and OD Hart 'A Threat to Dual-Class Shares' (*Financial Times* 31 May 2002) and/or a dual-class holding company incorporated, for example, in Switzerland where dual-class blocking minority *cum* statutory takeover protection instrument will still be available.

However, there is an interesting contradiction in objectives. If the Takeover Directive aims at stimulating a European market for corporate control, it should explicitly allow dual-class share capitalisations. Dual-class structures make it cheaper.

[29] CA Dunlavy 'Corporate Governance in Late 19th Century Europe and the U.S.: The Case of Shareholder Voting Rights' in KJ Hopt, H Kanda, MJ Roe, E Wymeersch and S Prigge (eds) *Comparative Corporate Governance. The State of the Art and Emerging Research* (Oxford University Press Oxford 1998).

[30] Formal or informal voting agreements between shareholders could be used to assemble 'blocking minorities'. With 'one-member-one-vote' large coalitions would be needed, but to

cont. ...

However, voting right ceilings – on their own – does not fully open up the companies to hostile bids. On the contrary, voting right ceilings are themselves a powerful pre-bid takeover defence.[32] To eliminate this 'dark side' of the 'one-member-one-vote' rule, a radical ('Italian-style') breakthrough rule is required. When a bidder launches a full offer to acquire all the shares of a company, the voting right ceiling is not binding. All shares can be fully tendered, all statutory defences are suspended and the bidder, with 50% or more acceptances, can take full control of the target. After the takeover is complete the bidder can either take the company private, or the pre-bid reciprocity regime (voting ceiling plus 'Italian-style' breakthrough rule) applies, making control of the post-bid listed company contestable again.

Imposing a 'one-member-one-vote' rule and a full 'Italian-style' breakthrough rule would make the corporate control of listed companies contestable; adding the Portuguese 'breakthrough club' proposal would achieve reciprocity in takeovers, at least for a subset of listed companies.[33] The current proposal of the European Parliament, combining the Winter Group proposal and the Portuguese proposal, will not achieve full reciprocity. Companies controlled by a majority blockholder will continue to be shielded from hostile bids, but they can bid for the control of widely held companies using the breakthrough rule.[34]

I. Precedents

To my knowledge, a reciprocity system like the one I just described has not yet been implemented anywhere, but there are some important precedents that can be found in the laws and rules of certain Member States, and in selected company statutes.

The Italian privatisation law in force during in the hostile bid of Olivetti for Telecom Italia came close to what would be required for achieving reciprocity.

ensure that control is fully contestable it might be necessary to ban shareholder agreements altogether, or to limit the number of participants very severely.

[31] As a positive side-effect, voting right ceilings protect minority shareholders, another declared policy objective of the Takeover Directive.

[32] Voting right ceilings are statutory provisions and to be effective, they need to be locked in; with minority blocks (*Figure 11*) or priority shares. If 'one-member-one-vote' is imposed by regulation the provision does not need to be locked in, making the defence even more formidable.

[33] For minority shareholders of the target companies there would be a major shortcoming associated with this arrangement though. It would exclude non-listed companies from the group of potential bidders, reducing the chances of a bidding contest with multiple bidders.

[34] In terms of the stylised systems set out in the previous section, achieving reciprocity in takeovers requires moving all listed companies from systems B1, B2 and W2 to system W1 *and* restricting the group of potential bidders to W1 companies.

Telecom Italia had been privatised with a voting ceiling. Although they had entered into a shareholder pact, the core shareholders could not exert a dominant influence over the company. Olivetti could break through the ceiling by making a bid for 100% of the shares. The Italian breakthrough rule also suspended the shareholder pact, allowing individual core shareholder to tender their shares to Olivetti. The proposed Directive's restrictions on post-bid defences applied. Telecom Italia's board sought rival bidders (a White Knight) and to merge with a subsidiary, but this action required shareholder approval. However, the Olivetti/Telecom Italia bid fell short of the full reciprocity regime on two counts. One, the post-bid Telecom Italia continued to be listed, but its control was no longer contestable; Olivetti held a majority stake (Figure 6).[35] Two, the control of Olivetti and of Tecnost, the bidding vehicle, was not contestable; Telecom Italia could not use a 'Pac-Man' defence[36] and launch a counter-bid for Olivetti.[37]

In a more general sense the UK is already operating a system that combines a 30% voting power ceiling with managerial disciplining through hostile takeovers. The combination of the mandatory bid rule, the board neutrality rule and a (less well known) 30% 'arm's length' rule[38] create a system that explicitly prevents 30%+ blockholder from exerting control, while allowing a 'breakthrough' to full control of the company through a hostile bid, with squeeze-out provisions. In effect, the system is designed to generate a 'bang-bang' equilibrium of corporate control: *Plc*s are either listed, widely held and open to hostile takeovers, or they are not listed and privately held. The whole system has been designed to satisfy a general, overriding principle – ensuring the equal treatment of *all* shareholders. There are no explicit rules on reciprocity in takeovers. On the contrary, anybody can launch a hostile bid, provided they follow the rules governing the bidding process.

[35] However, through a series of consolidations and the need to reduce the debt-mountain Olivetti had to accumulate during the bid the stake Olivetti holds in Telecom Italia has been reduced to approximately 12%, making the control of Telecom Italia contestable again.

[36] In the Pac-Man defence the target launches a hostile counter-bid for the bidder (named after the classic arcade game, where the PAC-MAN, munching pills and being chased by ghosts that try to deflate him, can eat a power capsule, turn on the Ghosts and eat them, for extra points).

[37] Also, the Italian government, through the Italian Treasury, could have vetoed the hostile acquisition.

[38] Article 3.12 of the UK's Listing Rules prescribes that 'A company which has a controlling shareholder must be capable at all times of carrying on its business independently of such controlling shareholder [...] and all transactions and relationships between the company and any controlling shareholder (or associate) must be at arm's length and on a normal commercial basis.' Furthermore, Article 3.13 specifies that 'For the purposes of paragraph 3.12, a controlling shareholder is any person (or persons acting jointly by agreement whether formal or otherwise) who is: (a) entitled to exercise, or to control the exercise of, 30% or more of the rights to vote at general meetings of the applicant; or (b) able to control the appointment of directors who are able to exercise a majority of votes at board meetings of the applicant.'

Figure 12 shows a percentile plot of share blocks in FTSE 100, Midcap and Smallcap index companies. The mandatory bid/ 'arm's length' rule line at 30% is just visible, with few companies having large blockholders. Companies either have non-controlling shareholders holding blocks smaller than 30%, or they are privately held.

However, on several counts the UK system of voting control defies the general description and raises interesting questions for the reciprocity debate. One, the UK does not have reciprocity rules for takeovers and control contests are usually one-sided. Most listed UK plcs are open to hostile bids, but they are regularly taken over by bidders whose control is not contestable. Two, the UK's City Code does not actually ban pre-bid defences and some existing constructions go well beyond what is on offer in, for example, Germany and the Nordic countries (Figure 3).[39] Three, the 30% arm's length rule does not appear to have the same bite as, for example, a voting right ceiling. FTSE 100 companies like Associated British Foods plc and the Daily Mail and General Trust plc (DMGT, Figure 3) have majority blockholders and it is unclear how these companies can be run 'independently of such large shareholders at all times'. Moving down the scale, in the Midcap and Smallcap segments majority blockholders are more numerous and it is even harder to deny that they have the (voting) power to influence the way the companies are run, at all times.[40] Finally, the '30% rule' is

[39] Looking across to continental Europe this begs the question why so many UK plcs have done away with takeover defences voluntarily. The most plausible explanation appears to be the importance of institutional investor influence and power. After the first series of hostile bids in the 1960s, UK plcs did put into place pre-bid defences (Franks, Mayer and Rossi 2003). However, after some hesitation, the financial establishment of the City of London decided that it supported control structures that featured a broad shareholder base, share liquidity and external challenges to control via the hostile bid instrument. The dismantling of hostile takeover protections was forced through by institutional shareholders (JR Franks, C Mayer and S Rossi 'The Origination and Evolution of Ownership and Control' (January 2003). ECGI-Finance Working Paper No 09/2003 <http://ssrn.com/abstract=354381>, in some cases only fairly recently (BS Black and JC Coffee Jr 'Hail Britannia?: Institutional Investor Behavior under Limited Regulation' (1994) 92 Michigan Law Review 1997-2087). One is tempted to extrapolate and argue that the growth of institutional investors will force the convergence of continental European control patterns on those found in the UK. However, it is not clear that this will be the case: Switzerland and the Netherlands have large pension funds, yet companies can and do use a broad range of pre-bid defences. Looking from another angle, UK funds are increasingly investing in continental Europe, yet corporate control patterns in these countries have not changed dramatically, at least not yet.

[40] In the Midcap segment the Prudential and its subsidiaries hold a 79.3% stake in EGG Plc, its online banking arm. EGG's annual report states that 'The relationship between the Company and Prudential plc is documented in a relationship agreement, which has been approved by the Board of Directors. Under this agreement Prudential plc is entitled to nominate one person to be a director of the Company. [...] Prudential plc is also entitled to appoint any director to be Chairman of the Board (Annual Report at 34).' The Prudential has appointed two of its directors to the board of EGG plc but this is considered unproblematic because 'All the remaining non-

cont. ...

unlikely to explain why so many UK plcs are widely held;[41] UK plcs were widely held well before any formal listing rules were in force.[42]

Moving over to France, Alcatel S.A. has statutory control provisions that come closer to what one would expect to prevail if European corporations wanted to make their control more contestable. In accordance with a decision taken at the June 1989 annual meeting, Alcatel's statutes limit the voting power any shareholder, or group of shareholders, can exert to 8% of the total votes that can be cast at the company's annual meeting (Annual Report 2002, pg. 139). Furthermore, the voting right restriction falls if a bidder acquires 66.66% of the total number of shares in the company, after bidding for all shares issued and outstanding (*opus cit.*).[43] Alcatel is widely held with the largest shareholder owning 5.91% of the shares, exercising 6.14% of the total voting rights. The combination of a statutory breakthrough rule with a voting right ceiling brings out the best in both measures, at least in theory.

Although they are close to the full reciprocity benchmark, the Alcatel provisions fall short of on three counts. One, the voting right ceiling is raised to 16% when a shareholder has acquired double voting rights by holding shares in the company for more than three years. Hence, an informal coalition of two large long-standing and one tiny shareholder could block any breakthrough. Two, Alcatel has disclosure provisions that force potential raiders to notify minuscule changes in their holdings, essentially preventing them from building a toehold, a serious deterrent for a potential bidder.[44] Three, the Alcatel statutes do *not* state that only companies on which Alcatel can launch a hostile bid can take advantage of its breakthrough rule.

I have discussed three regulatory experiments that have sought to make the control of European companies more contestable, with the Italian privatisation programme coming closest to the mark. To my knowledge there are no precedents for reciprocity – limiting the pool of potential bidders to companies that are open to hostile bids themselves. Although not perfect, the existing experiments provide guidance for what would be required to create a market for hostile

executive directors are independent and accordingly the Board is of the view that throughout the period, a majority of the non-executive directors were independent (opus cit)'.

[41] M Becht and C Mayer 'Introduction' in F Barca and M Becht *The Control of Corporate Europe*, (Oxford University Press Oxford 2001) and M Goergen and L Renneboog 'Why Are the Levels of Control (So) Different in German and U.K. Companies? Evidence from Initial Public Offerings' (2003) 19 Journal of Law, Economics, and Organization 141-75) speculated that the 30% rule might act like a *de facto* voting right ceiling.

[42] JR Franks, C Mayer and S Rossi 'The Origination and Evolution of Ownership and Control' (January 2003). ECGI-Finance Working Paper No 09/2003 <http://ssrn.com/abstract =354381>.

[43] The threshold of 66.66% gives a supermajority in France.

[44] Toeholds are the most straightforward tools for overcoming the Grossman-Hart free-rider problem in hostile takeovers.

changes in control among listed companies through a European Takeover Directive. From a legal and intellectual perspective it is interesting to imagine such a European system being put in place. What ultimately matters though is whether a European market for corporate control would be conducive to fostering corporate restructuring, investment, employment and growth.

D. Reciprocity in Takeovers as a Policy Objective

The declared aim of the proposed Takeover Directive is to create a more vibrant market for corporate control in Europe while, at the same time, improving the protection of minority shareholders – without forgetting about the concerns of employees. A European market for corporate control is seen as an integral part of a single capital market and a major driver of European competitiveness, innovation and growth.

To be sure, reciprocity in takeovers is not required to create a European market for corporate control. At the European level, the creation of such a market only requires safeguards against discrimination of bidders and/or investors on the basis of nationality or location.[45] Reciprocity in takeovers is not required for minority protection either. Minority protection can be achieved through a mandatory bid rule or by rules that protect minorities directly, such as increased litigation rights.[46]

Reciprocity in takeovers is an issue because it was a latent aim of the Takeover Directive to make the voting control of European corporations more contestable. The proponents of reciprocity argue that in a market for *hostile* acquisitions of corporate control there should be a 'level playing field'; all targets should have access to the Pac-Man defence. Hence, two questions arise: One, is it beneficial to push European corporations towards the widely-held model of corporate control, accepting external challenges to blockholder and board control? Two, does a European market for corporate control have to have a 'level playing field' – does it require reciprocity in takeovers?

[45] In this context discrimination can take the form of exclusion and/or aiding national champions. Investors could be excluded from takeover offers based on their nationality and/or place of residence; or the acquisition programmes of national-champions could be subsidised through state aid.

[46] Indeed, as has been pointed out frequently, the mandatory bid rule is in contradiction to the first objective of creating a more active market for corporate control. The mandatory bid rule, and the mandatory disclosure of small toeholds, make the purchase of corporate control more expensive, discouraging the purchase of control blocks and corporate restructuring; see, for example, M Becht, P Bolton and A Roëll 'Corporate Governance and Control' in *Handbook of the Economics of Finance*, edited by George Constantinides, Milton Harris and René Stulz, North-Holland, *forthcoming* (ECGI – Finance Working Paper No 02/2002 available from <http://ssrn.com/abstract=343461>; J Franks (2003) 36 Economic Policy 209-211 and especially E Berglöf and M Burkart European Takeover Regulation (2003) 36 Economic Policy 171-208.

In theory there are substantial benefits the general endorsement of the widely-held model of the corporation could bring for Europe, in particular for Europe's capital markets. It is well documented that liquid markets are associated with lower transactions costs, lower expected returns and a lower cost of capital.[47] It is also documented that control blocks reduce liquidity, making it more difficult for investors to vote 'with their feet'.[48] Liquid stock markets also have the ability of carrying capital over 'long distances', both geographically and between sectors.[49] A more vibrant capital market, including hostile acquisitions, could help Europe move capital from sunset to sunrise industries.[50] In the United States, the hostile deals of the 1980s were associated with beneficial restructuring.[51]

Attractive as the widely-held model of the corporation may be, at least for some companies and sectors, the recent corporate governance scandals in the United States and elsewhere have reminded us that widely held corporations are open to major abuses of power. Celebrity managers drove forward 'visionary' plans under great market pressure and with very high-powered incentives, unchallenged by weak boards and passive shareholders. There is scientific support for this popular scepticism. In theory hostile takeovers can overcome the managerial disciplining problems in widely-held corporations. In practice, hostile takeovers in the UK hit companies with good performance and poor prior performance at roughly the same rate.[52] Good managers and poor managers are removed by hostile takeovers.[53] For tender offers more generally, target shareholders gain,

[47] See Becht, Bolton and Roëll (ibid), Section 7.2.3 for a survey.

[48] A number of commentators have pointed out that the Winter Group's breakthrough proposal, in its current form, might encourage the formation of larger blocks, as widely-held companies try to secure their statutory takeover protections through larger 'one-share-one-vote' blocks (eg M Becht 'Corporate Takeover Defences in Europe' (2002) Presentation at the ECGI Session of the Federation of European Securities Exchanges' 6th European Financial Markets Convention, Brussels, 31 May <http://www.ecgi.org/conferences/fese_efmc2002/efmc2002_becht_takeovers.ppt>, J Franks Comment (2003) 36 Economic Policy 209-211). Hence, a partial implementation of the breakthrough rule might result in a reduction of stock market liquidity.

[49] B Holmstrom and SN Kaplan 'Corporate Governance and Merger Activity in the United States: Making Sense of the 1980s and 1990s' (2001) 15 Journal of Economic Perspectives 121-44.

[50] E Berglöf, B Holmström, P Högfeldt, EM Meyersson Milgrom and HT Söderström 'Corporate Governance and Structural Change' (2003) SNS, Stockholm.

[51] A Bhide 'The Causes and Consequences of Hostile Takeovers' (1989) 2(2) Journal of Applied Corporate Finance 36-59

[52] J Franks, C Mayer and L Renneboog 'Who Disciplines Management in Poorly Performing Companies?' (2001) 10 Journal of Financial Intermediation 209-48.

[53] It is possible, of course, that the poorly performing targets are hit for disciplining reasons and the well performing targets for other reasons, for example product market considerations, but given the broad range of control variables in the study this is not very likely.

but the combined return for bidders and targets is zero or negative.[54] Comparisons of relative performance are even less encouraging. There is some evidence that the return on a portfolio of widely held firms open to hostile takeovers and is higher than on widely held firms shielded from hostile takeovers.[55] However, comparisons of blockholder controlled companies and widely held companies are less encouraging. Companies with blockholders perform as well or better than widely held companies,[56] with the latest studies finding that founder family controlled and operated firms in the United States show better performance than those in the hands of outsiders, or those under their *de facto* control.[57] In theory, innovations like independent directors, incentives pay and hostile takeovers themselves could overcome the managerial incentives problems associated with widely held-corporation but, on balance, these methods have not yet been proven to be effective, at least not in a recent reading of the scientific literature.[58]

Full reciprocity in takeovers goes even further than a general move to widely held corporations open to hostile bids. It would restrict the group of potential bidders to listed companies that are themselves open to hostile bid. From a theoretical perspective, this limitation is in conflict with the declared aim of protecting the minority shareholders of the target because it reduces the pool of potential

[54] G Andrade, M Mitchell and E Stafford 'New Evidence and Perspectives on Mergers' (2001) 15 Journal of Economic Perspectives 103-20.

[55] P Gompers, J Ishii and A Metrick Corporate Governance and Equity Prices (2003) 118 Quarterly Journal of Economics 107-55. Even here one can speculate if the higher returns do not simply capture.

[56] K Gugler *Corporate Governance and Economic Performance* (Oxford Oxford University Press 2001).

[57] RC Anderson and DM Reeb 'Founding-Family Ownership and Firm Performance: Evidence from the S&P 500' 2003 58 Journal of Finance 1301-28. However, due to the inherent econometric difficulties results from this line of empirical research should be treated with great caution (A Börsch-Supan and J Köke 'An Applied Econometricians' View of Empirical Corporate Governance Studies' (2002) 3(3) German Economic Review 295-326, M Becht, P Bolton and A Roëll (2003) Corporate Governance and Control, Handbook of the Economics of Finance, edited by George Constantinides, Milton Harris and René Stulz, North-Holland, *forthcoming* (ECGI – Finance Working Paper No. 02/2002 available from <http://ssrn.com/abstract=343461>, O Bohren and BA Odegaard 'Governance and Performance Revisited' (September 2003). ECGI – Finance Working Paper No 28/2003 <http://ssrn.com/abstract=423461>.

[58] M Becht, P Bolton and A Roëll 'Corporate Governance and Control' (2003) Handbook of the Economics of Finance, edited by George Constantinides, Milton Harris and René Stulz, North-Holland, *forthcoming* (ECGI – Finance Working Paper No. 02/2002 available from <http://ssrn.com/abstract=343461> See B Holmstrom and SN Kaplan ('Corporate Governance and Merger Activity in the United States: Making Sense of the 1980s and 1990s' (2001) 15 Journal of Economic Perspectives 121-44), for a positive assessment of the US corporate governance system that is dominated by widely held corporations, some open to hostile takeovers.

bidders.[59] Empirically, there is strong and consistent evidence that multiple bidders are associated with higher premia for target shareholders, in both the US[60] and in the UK.[61] Full reciprocity would also hinder restructuring. Large non-listed companies like JCB plc, Bosch GmbH, Bertelsmann AG or Bechtel Corporation would no longer have the ability to launch hostile bids for companies listed on a European stock exchange.

E. Conclusion

A significant number of European Parliamentarians and Member States have made it clear that a European Takeover Directive that makes the control of listed companies more contestable must achieve full reciprocity between targets and bidders, or they will refuse to adopt it. I have shown that the implementation of this condition requires radical measures that could result in a massive transformation of corporate control in Europe. To meet the reciprocity condition, outsiders launching a full bid for a listed company in the European Union must be given the unconditional power to break the grip of incumbent blockholders and to break through structural takeover defences that protect incumbent boards – provided the target can do the same in a 'pac-man' defence.

The benefits of such a transformation are not certain. Widely-held companies were the favourite corporate flavour during the late 1990s, but there is little scientific evidence to support this general preference. On the contrary, it has yet to be proven that independent directors, litigation, institutional shareholder activ-

[59] Multiple bidders in takeovers have been analysed theoretically by eg MJ Fishman ('A Theory of Preemptive Takeover Bidding' (1988) 19 Rand Journal of Economics 88-101.), M Burkart ('Initial Shareholdings and Overbidding in Takeover Contests' (1995) 50(5) Journal of Finance 1491-1515) and J Bulow, H Ming and P Klemperer 'Toeholds and Takeovers' (1999) 107 Journal of Political Economy 427-54.

[60] See Michel and Shaked (1988), M Bradley, A Desai and EH Kim 'Synergistic Gains from Corporate Acquisitions and Their Division between the Stockholders of Target and Acquiring Firms' (1988) 21 Journal of Financial Economics 3-40; A Banerjee and JE Owers 'The Impact of the Nature and Sequence of Multiple Bids in Corporate Control Contests' (1996) 3 Journal of Corporate Finance: Contracting, Governance and Organization 23-43; S De, M Fedenia and AJ Triantis 'Effects of Competition on Bidder Returns' (1996) 2 Journal of Corporate Finance: Contracting, Governance and Organization 261-82; CE Lefanowicz and JR Robinson 'Multiple Bids, Management Opposition, and the Market for Corporate Control' (2000) 35 Financial Review 109-21.

[61] JR Franks, RS Harris and C Mayer 'Means of Payment in Takeovers: Results for the United Kingdom and the United States' in Auerbach,-Alan-J (ed); *Corporate takeovers: Causes and consequences*. National Bureau of Economic Research Project Report series Chicago and London: University of Chicago Press 1988; 221-58, JR Franks and RS Harris 'Shareholder Wealth Effects of Corporate Takeovers: The U.K. Experience 1955-1985' (1989) 23 Journal of Financial Economics 225-49.

ism and hostile takeovers can overcome the governance problems the separation of ownership and control in the widely-held corporation brings about – and act as substitutes for traditional blockholder monitoring.

On the other hand, European stock markets do suffer from a lack of liquidity that is largely induced by the concentration of corporate equity bases. Broadening the shareholder base, at the expense of blockholders, would not doubt help in pumping up volumes and bringing down transaction costs. However, the benefits must be weighed against the potential cost. Introducing mandatory contestability and reciprocity for listed companies via a European Directive imposes severe restrictions on the freedom of contracting between shareholders and corporations across the European Union. In light of the limited and contradictory evidence on the benefits of hostile takeovers in the context of widely-held corporation, it is hard to justify such a public policy intervention. In this respect the often-cited example of the UK, the most hostile takeover friendly market in the world, is highly subversive. It suggests that widely-held companies arise 'naturally' over time and that the strengthening of institutional shareholder voice should have priority over breakthrough rules.[62] Furthermore, the available scientific evidence from the UK confirms that hostile takeovers, non-executive directors and institutional activism have – at least until recently – not solved all corporate governance problems of the widely-held public corporation.

In the light of the available evidence it would be equally hazardous to reject the idea of promoting contestable control outright. A politically and practically desirable way forward is a Directive (or Regulation) that broadens the menu of instruments for conducting hostile takeovers. Neither voting right ceilings nor a radical '0%' breakthrough rule are available in all Member States. German companies that wish to embrace a French-style or Italian privatisation-style arrangement of contestable control would have to re-register in France or Italy.[63] Instead of reducing the menu of available voting control structures the Takeover, or another Directive, should give companies access to additional tools that are needed for the adoption of widely-held contestable control structures. Backed by market pressure, such a Directive would facilitate the creation of 'revolutionary' pan-European market segments, for example a widely-held segment that combines voting right ceilings (explicit curbs on blockholder power), a full breakthrough rule and a procedure that gives minority shareholders the right to nominate candidates for election to the board.[64]

[62] Indeed, the evolution of ownership and control at Telecom Italia is an example of the pressures institutional investors are able to exert on large blue-chip corporations in Europe already.

[63] In addition, as I noted earlier, only the Italian privatisation model is close to being radical enough.

[64] The latter feature is highly controversial and the centre of debate in the United States at the moment; see LA Bebchuk 'Shareholder Access to the Ballot' (2003) Harvard Law and Economics Discussion Paper No 428. <http://ssrn.com/abstract=426951> for a forceful plead in

cont. ...

Against this background one has to wonder why some European politicians are pushing so hard for full mandatory contestability and reciprocity in takeovers for all listed companies, in particular those who have traditionally shown little interest in making the control of European corporations more contestable. Given the history of the Takeover Directive one cannot fail to suspect a Machiavellian plot most foul; by asking for everything, they hope to get nothing. Given the theoretical and empirical uncertainties surrounding an untried reciprocity experiment this might not be the worst possible outcome. Giving stock markets a tool for creating a pan-European market segment companies that want to embrace contestable control can list on, with or without reciprocity, is preferable. Implementing the current proposals as they stand will not achieve much, one-way or the other. If anything, they will add another level of complexity and confusion to the prevailing systems of corporate control in Europe.

favour of shareholder access to the corporate ballot box. For Europe's widely held corporations, a debate on corporate elections is bound to follow.

Figures

Figure 1. Percentage of Listed Companies with a blocking minority of at least 25%

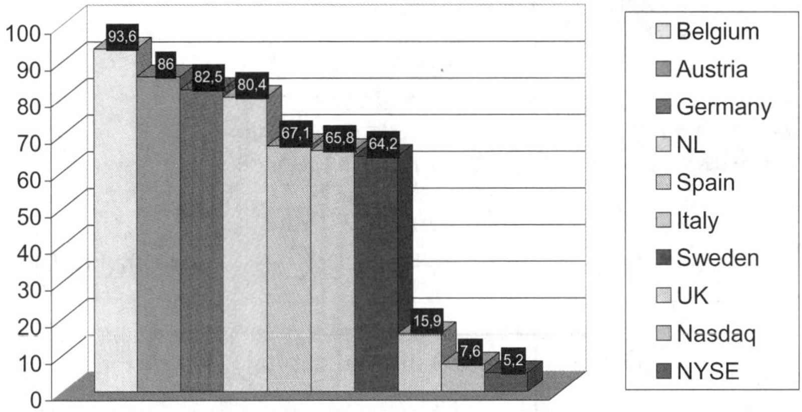

Source: Barca and Becht (2001), *The Control of Corporate Europe*, OUP.

Figure 2. Percentage of Listed Companies under Majority Control

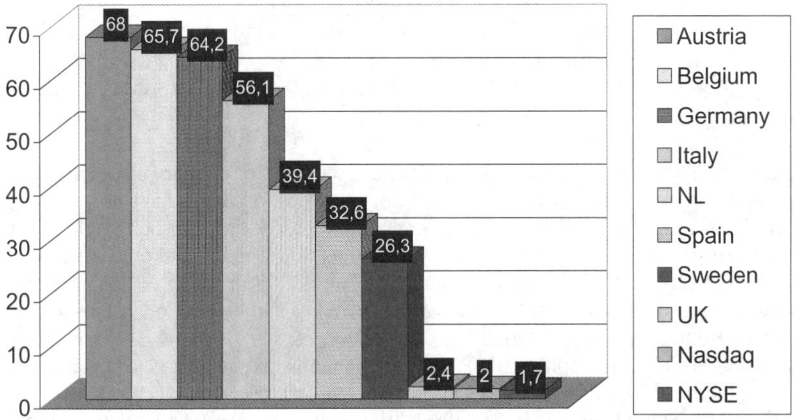

Source: Barca and Becht (2001), *The Control of Corporate Europe*, OUP.

Figure 3. Control Structure DMGT Plc

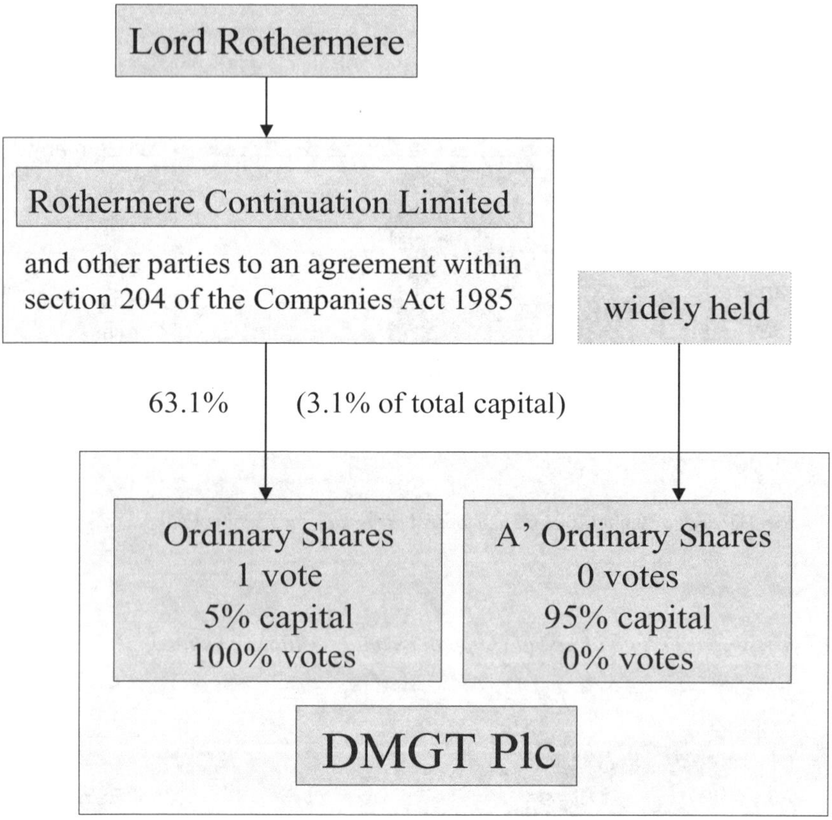

Note: DMGT Plc has a dual-class share structure with £2.5m ordinary shares and £47.6m 'A' non-voting ordinary shares allotted and fully paid up. 'A' shares have no voting rights, otherwise the shares are identical. Lord Rothermere has declared to be the ultimate controlling party of the Group, via Rothermere Continuation Limited and other parties to and agreement within section 204 of the Companies Act of 1985 holding 63.1% of the voting shares. A second block of 25.2% of the voting shares is held by the Codan Trust Company Ltd and Rothschild Trust (Bermuda) Ltd, trustees of the Esmond Harmsworth 1998 Settlement. Dual-class capitalisations are not common among listed companies in the U.K., although U.K. company law allows for substantial voting control leverage. In Germany, for example, no more than 50% of the equity capital can be issued as non-voting shares.

Source: DMGT Plc Annual Report 2002 and own calculations.

Figure 4. Control Structure of Novo Nordisk A/S

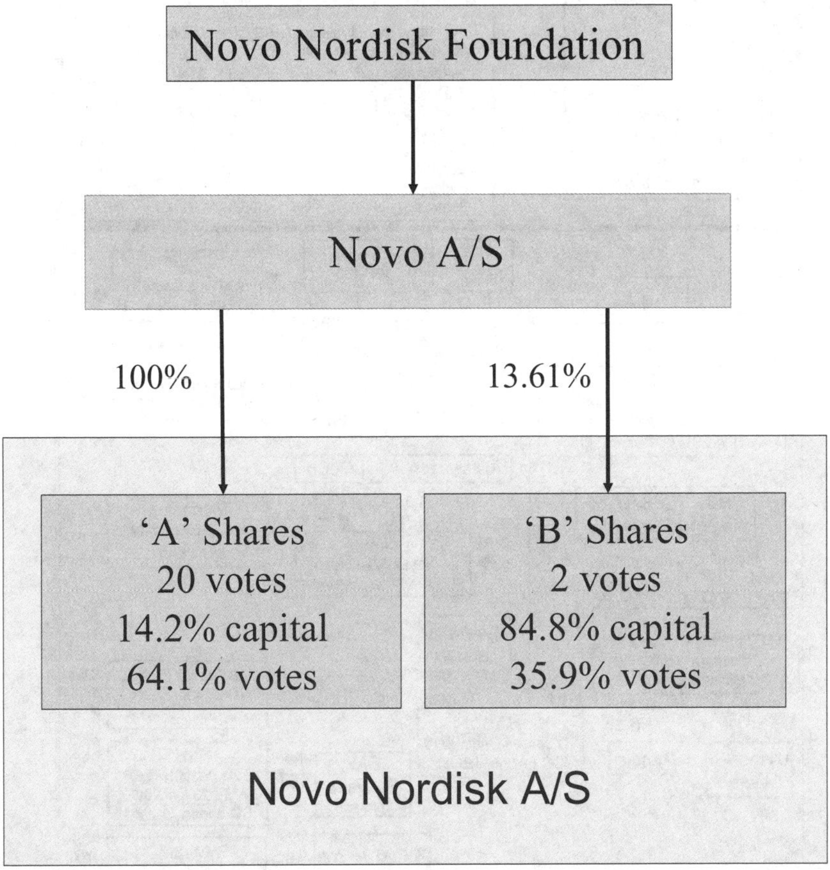

Note: Novo Nordisk A/S is controlled by the Novo Nordisk Foundation (via Novo A/S) that commands 64.1% of the votes with 14.2% of the capital by holding all 'A' shares, and an additional 4.95% of the votes by holding 13.61% of the 'B' shares. The other 'B' shares are widely held. Its statutes require the foundation to maintain material influence over Novo A/S and Novo Nordisk A/S and to protect the interest of the companies. The Foundation may not, for example, sell the 'A' shares it holds. Changes in the statues would require a two-thirds majority of the members of the Foundation's board and approval by the Danish foundation authorities.

Source: Form 20-F 2002 and Company Web-site <www.novonordisk.com>.

Figure 5. The Wallenberg Pyramid

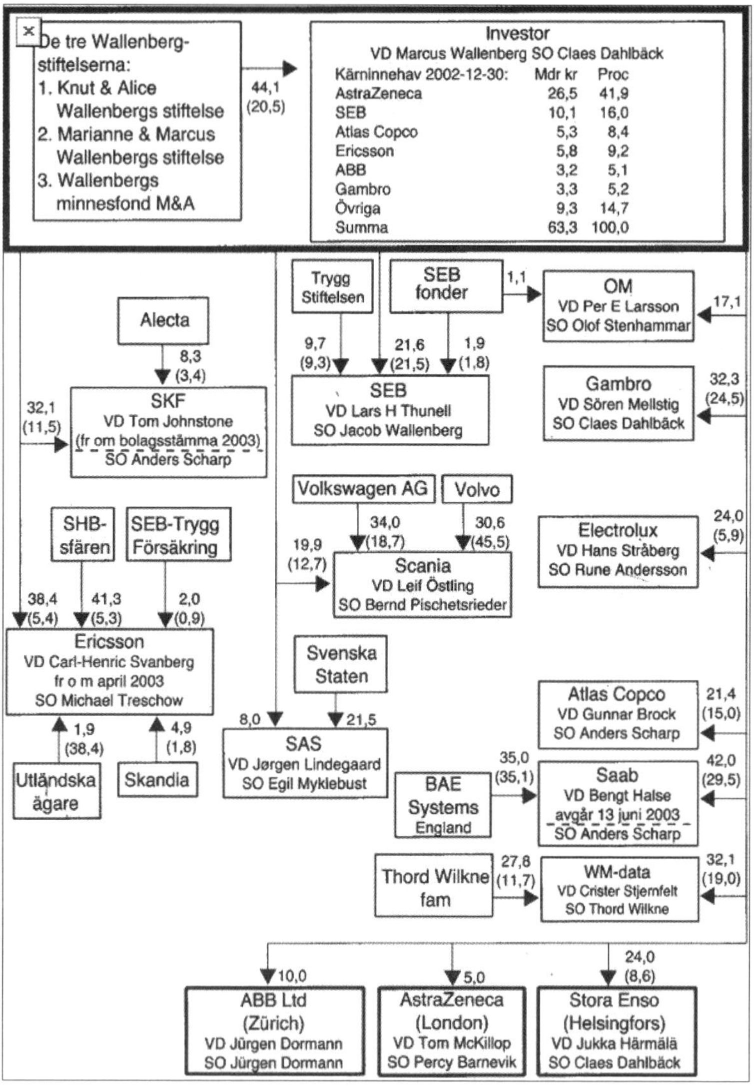

Note: Capital links in percent; corresponding percentage of votes in brackets.

Source: Fristedt, Sundin and Sundqvist (2003), Owners and Power in Sweden's Listed Companies (Ägarna Och Makten i Sveriges Börsföretag), Stockholm, SIS Ägarservice AB.

Figure 6. The Telecom Italia Pyramid

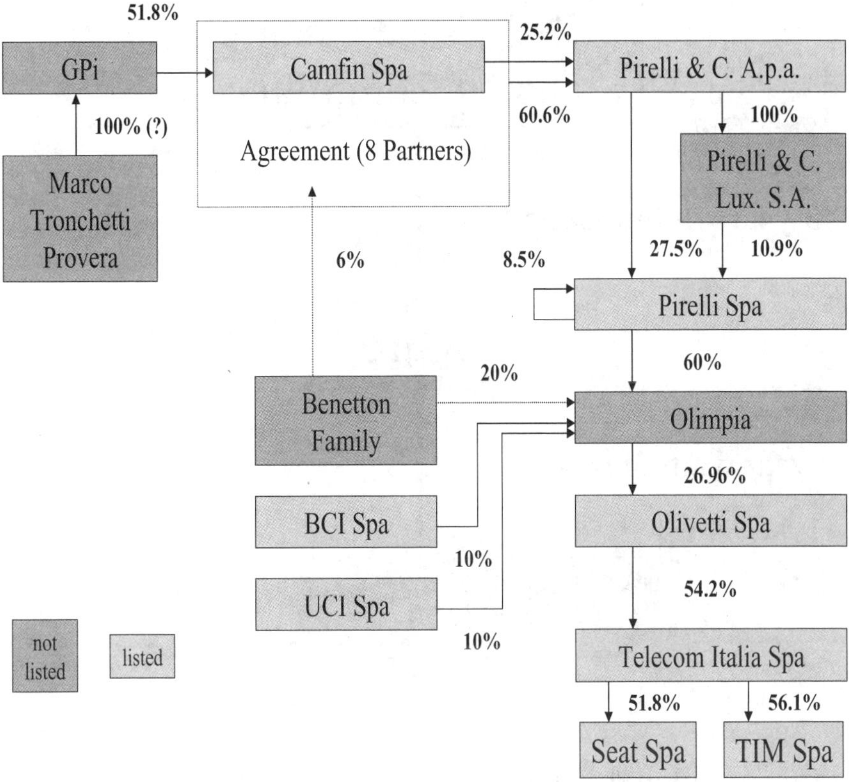

Note: The Telecom Italia pyramid is controlled by Marco Tronchetti Provera, with private equity from the Benetton family, two Italian banks (BCI and UCI) and other partners. The group originates with the leveraged hostile takeover of Telecom Italia by Olivetti. In 2003 the structure was simplified by merging Olivetti and Telecom Italia with Olimpia holding a mere 11.57% of the combined company in August 2003.

Source: Consob filings (June 2002) and <www.telecomitalia.it> (October 2003).

Figure 7. Former Control Structure of Banco Santander Central Hispano S.A.

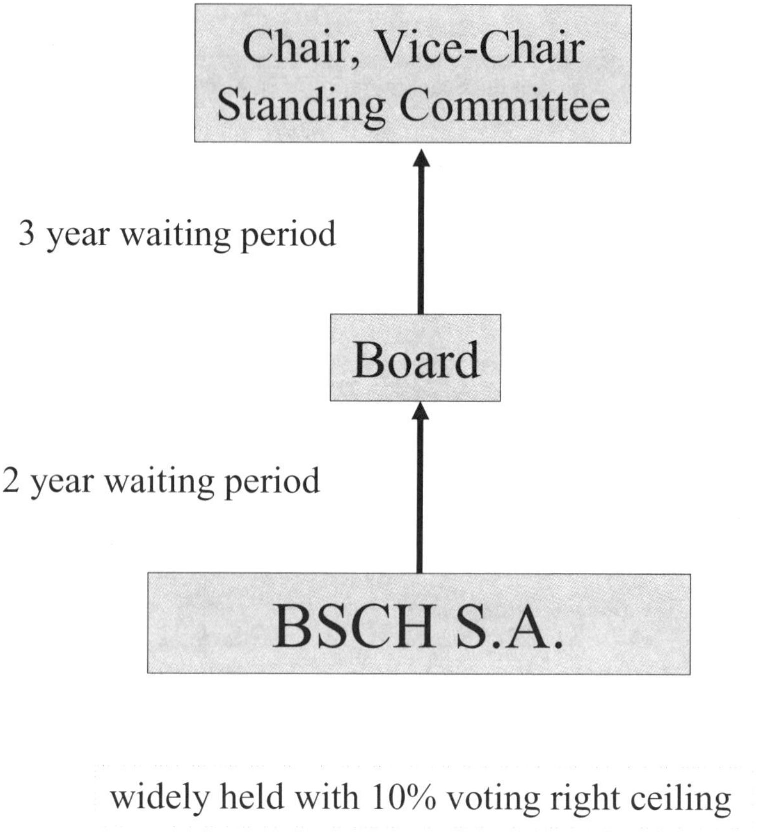

Note: The takeover defences at BSCH combines a 10% voting right restriction with waiting periods for gaining access to important board positions. A potential raider must have been a shareholder for two years to gain a board seat and a member of the board for three years before becoming eligible for election to key positions, like the chairmanship, vice-chairmanship or the powerful standing committee. The arrangement is secured through a 70% supermajority amendment, allowing a 30% coalition to prevent a raider from removing the statutory defences from the statutes. BSCH voluntarily dismantled these defensive structures in June 2003.

Source: Company Statutes, Company Web-site <www.bsch.es>.

Figure 8. Control Structure of Allianz AG and Munich Re AG

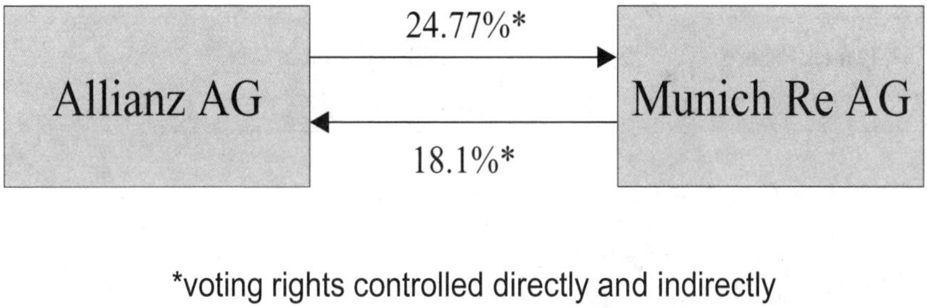

Notes: Allianz AG and Munich Re AG have a cross-holding that secures statutory provisions allowing the companies to refuse the transfer of shares. The companies can only refuse the transfer of shares 'in extraordinary circumstances when considered essential for the company' (Allianz AG Statutes, Article 2(2)). Share transfer restrictions are common among German insurance companies and often date back to their foundation, for example in the case of Munich Re.

Source: Company websites <www.allianz.de>, <www.munichre.de> and BaFin <www.bafin.de>.

Figure 9. Corporate Control of Royal Dutch/Shell

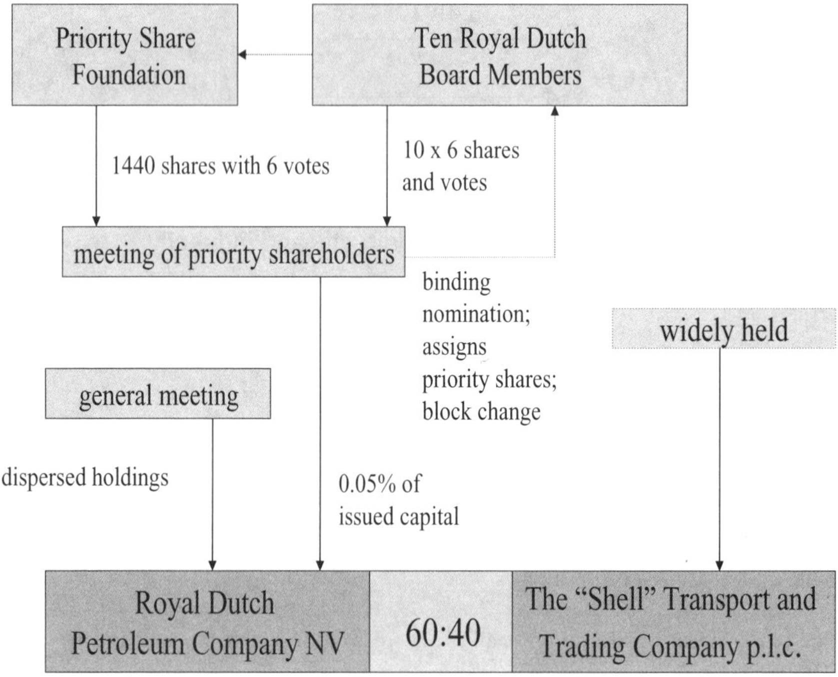

Note: Royal Dutch/Shell is an Anglo-Dutch company tied together through contracts and equalization agreements. The Shell Transport and Trading Company plc is widely held and controls 40% of the underlying assets of the group. The Royal Dutch Petroleum Company NV controls 60% of the underlying assets. The Dutch company has two classes of shares: ordinary shares that are widely held and constitute the bulk of the capital that has been issued and is outstanding; priority shares that make up a tiny proportion of the issued capital put have special rights. The most important rights include the drawing up of binding nominations consisting of two people for the managing and supervisory board, the right to veto changes to the Article of Association of Royal Dutch (lock-in) and a veto on the transfer of priority shares.

Source: Form 20-F 2002.

Figure 10. Takeover Defences of Royal Ahold N.V.

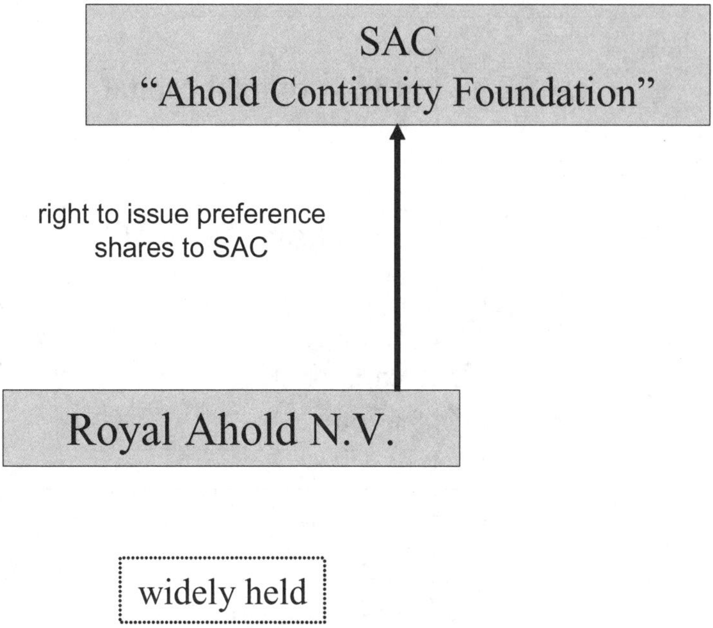

Note: Royal Ahold N.V. is widely held and uses authorized preference shares that can be issued to the friendly SAC 'Ahold Continuity Foundation' to defend against takeovers. In particular SAC has been granted an option to acquire from Ahold cumulative preferred shares 'up to a total par value that is equal to the total par value of all issued and outstanding shares of our capital stock, excluding cumulative preferred shares, at the time of exercising the option. The holders of the cumulative preferred shares are entitled to 2,000 votes per share and a cumulative dividend expressed as a percentage of the amount called-up and paid-up on the cumulative preferred shares. [...] We may stipulate that only 25% of the par value will be paid upon subscription for cumulative preferred shares until payment in full of the par value is later called by us.' In the fiscal years 2000 and 2001 no preference shares were issued or outstanding. The arrangement provides a very powerful takeover defence, despite a broad shareholder base and high secondary market liquidity in the ordinary shares.

Source: Form 20-F 2002, page 179.

Figure 11. Corporate Control of Volkswagen AG

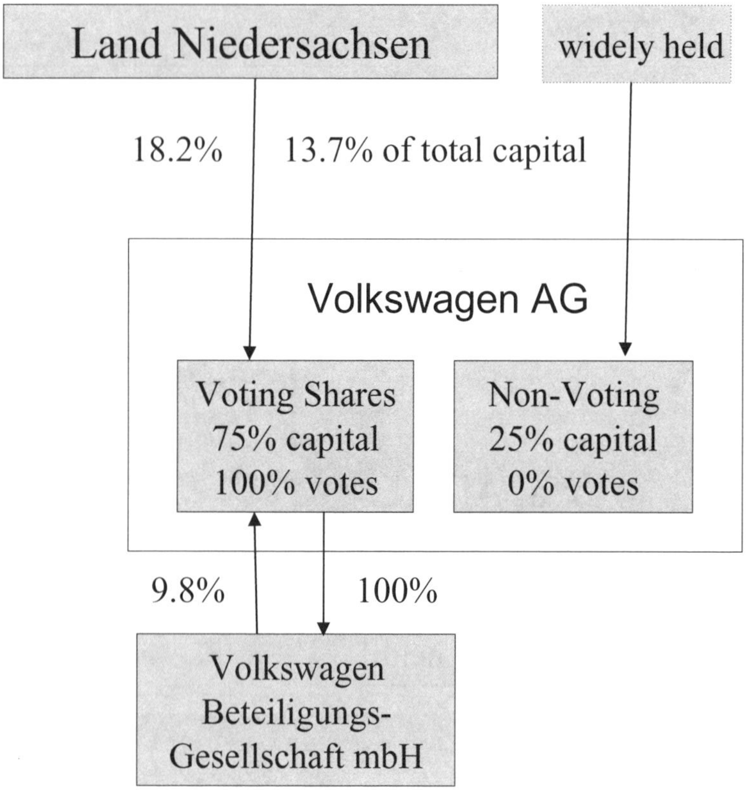

Note: Volkswagen AG combines an 80% supermajority amendment with a 20% voting right restriction and a blocking minority that is obtained with a dual-class share structure. In addition the state of *Niedersachsen* has the right to appoint two out of ten supervisory board members on the capital side.

Source: Volkswagen Annual Report 2002, Company Statutes.

Figure 12. Percentile Plot for Largest Block in FTSE 100, Midcap and Smallcap Index Companies

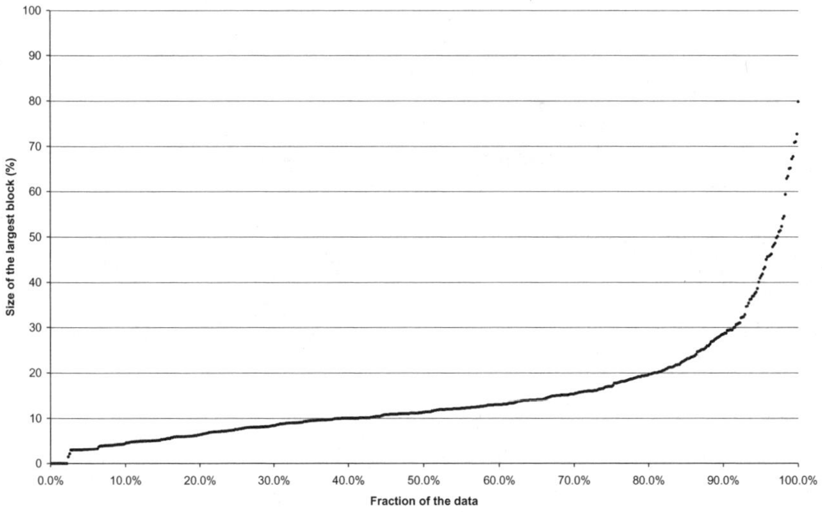

Note: The horizontal axis shows the fraction of UK listed companies in the FTSE 100, Midcap and Smallcap indices after sorting the companies by the size of their largest blockholder. The vertical axis plots the size of the largest shareholding.

Source: Hemscott REFS, July 2002 and own calculations.

Chapter 10: The Proposed 'Break-Through' Rule

Ownership, Takeovers and EU Law: How Contestable Should EU Corporations Be?

JOHN C. COATES IV*

In this paper, I draw on economic theory of ownership structure; empirical research on ownership, value and takeovers; and comparisons to US law to argue that the proposed break-through rule (BTR) is not clearly better than the *status quo*, from either a political perspective, or an economic perspective, with implications for any directive on takeover bids (DTB). The good (a step toward an integrated EU capital market) cannot wait on the perfect (ideal takeover rules), but neither should it be pursued without regard for the difference between the two. If the BTR is adopted, it should be kept flexible with a mixture of regulatory tools – sunsets, opt-outs, and industry-based exemptions – to reflect the fact that regulation will inevitably be both imperfect and difficult to modify once adopted. The best rationale for the BTR – that many ownership structures in EU firms reflect historic national market structures and may increasingly impede achievement of economies via cross-border mergers – would be better addressed by rules requiring control of such firms be made contestable on a periodic rather than a continual basis.

A. The DTB and the BTR

Six months ago, the European Commission (EC) presented a new proposal for a Directive on Takeover Bids (DTB).[1] The new DTB follows the European Parlia-

* I am grateful for comments and suggestions from Jennifer Arlen, Jack Coffee, Jeff Gordon, Yoshiro Miwa, Mark Ramseyer, Mark Roe, workshop participants at Harvard Law School, and participants at the May 2003 conference on 'A Modern Regulatory Framework for Company and Takeover Law in Europe – The Corporate Governance and Takeover Recom-
cont. ...

ment's surprise 'rejection' – 273 members of Parliament (MEPs) voting for, 273 against – of the prior proposal,[2] which was the culmination of over a decade of compromise, debate and conciliation dating back to 1989. Following this defeat, the EC created a group of 'High Level Company Law Experts' led by Professor Jaap Winter, and gave it the task of developing responses to three issues raised by the European Parliament.[3] The Winter group published two reports: one on takeover bids in January 2002 (Takeover Bid Report),[4] which formed the basis for the new DTB in October 2002, and a broader one on company (corporate) law in November 2002 (Company Law Report),[5] which formed the basis for a new company law 'Action Plan' released by the EC in May 2003.[6]

Perhaps because of the closeness of the vote by which the prior proposal (the old DTB) was defeated, the old DTB and the new DTB are remarkably similar. Their scope, organization, and overall goals are the same: to facilitate integration of European capital markets through takeovers, to 'offer transparent pan-European rules for the conduct of takeover bids to the benefit of shareholders', to 'facilitate company restructuring', and to 'contribute to making Europe more competitive'. In contrast to current law, which varies widely from country to country in the EU, the DTB would create a uniform floor of minority shareholder protection for takeover targets; create a framework for determining which legal authority will supervise takeovers and enforce the new rules; and impose disclo-

mendations of the High Level Group of Company Law Experts to the European Commission.' I thank David Marx for his research and assistance in compiling the data reflected in Figure 4 and the Appendix. All errors are mine.

[1] Proposal for a Directive of the European Parliament and of the Council on Takeover Bids (Presented by the Commission of the European Communities), Brussels, 2 October 2002, COM (2002) 534 final.

[2] OJ C 162, June 6, 1996, COM (95) 655 final (amended proposal for a 'framework' directive after consultations with Member States, setting out general principles but not attempting detailed harmonization of takeover rules); see also OJ C 64, 14 March 1989, Bull. EC Supp. 3/89 (original proposal for directive regarding takeover bids); OJ C 240, 26 September 1990, COM (90) 416 (amending 1989 proposal to reflect opinions of Economic and Social Committee and European Parliament).

[3] The three specific issues referred to the Winter group were: (1) how to create a 'level playing field' for shareholders in different countries within the EU, (2) the definition of an 'equitable price' to be paid to minority shareholders in takeovers, and (3) the right for a majority shareholder to buy out minority shareholders. Report of the High Level Group of Company Law Experts on Issues Related to Takeover Bids, European Commission, Brussels, 10 January 2002, at 1 (see Annex 2 in this volume).

[4] ibid.

[5] Report of the High Level Group of Company Law Experts on A Modern Regulatory Framework for Company Law in Europe, 4 November 2002 (see Annex 3 in this volume).

[6] Communication from the Commission to the Council and the European Parliament, Modernising Company Law and Enhancing Corporate Governance in the European Union – A Plan to Move Forward, 21 May 2003 (see Annex 1 in this volume).

sure and procedural requirements on bidders, including the requirement of a mandatory bid once a bidder acquires a control block, at a threshold to be specified by member states.

The most controversial portion of the new DTB also continues to be not the proposed rules governing bids per se, nor the rules governing bidders, but the rules governing targets. One proposed target rule comes straight out of the old DTB: the so-called 'neutrality rule' (NR) would forbid a target board from taking 'any action other than seeking alternative bids which may result in the frustration of the bid…' unless the board obtains prior shareholder approval of the action.[7] The NR closely tracks an established norm in the UK, enforced under the auspices of the London Stock Exchange.

A second element of the proposed target rules is new: the so-called "mini-break-through rule" (mini-BTR) provides that 'any restrictions on transfer of securities … shall be unenforceable….'[8] Likewise, any special rights of the shareholders concerning appointment or removal of directors cease to have effect following a bid in which the bidder obtains the requisite minimum. The mini-BTR would apply equally to restrictions in a company's charter, restrictions in agreements between the target and its shareholders, and restrictions in agreements among shareholders.

What the new DTB does not do, however, is include the full 'break-through rule' (BTR) proposed in the Takeover Bid Report. Arguably the most radical idea in the Takeover Bid Report, the BTR would allow any bidder acquiring more than a majority (or a required supermajority, but no more than 75%) of the target's cash flow rights to 'break through' any mechanism or structure that frustrates its control of the target. The BTR was directed at two types of defences: (1) multiple class capital structures, which limit the voting rights of some shareholders, and (2) capped or time-phased voting restrictions, which condition voting rights on holders not having, or not having recently acquired, control.[9] In general terms, the goal of the BTR is the same as the overall goal of the DTB – to

[7] DTB Article 9.

[8] DTB Article 11.

[9] The application of the BTR (and the mini-BTR in the new DTB) to golden shares – which provide one shareholder (usually a government) with a veto over transfers of control or other rights that interfere with such transfers – is unclear. However, on 4 June 2002, shortly after the Takeover Bid Report was issued, the European Court of Justice (ECJ) reversed prior opinions of the EU *Advocat Général* and significantly restricted the usefulness of golden shares as a generic form of takeover defense by limiting their legality to precisely tailored provisions justified by a compelling, current state interest, under Article 56 of the Treaty Establishing the European Community (Treaty of Rome, as supplemented by later treaties). Commission v France, C-483/99; Commission v Portugal, C-367/98; Commission v Belgium, C-503/99. These decisions were followed by two more on May 13, 2003 striking down 'golden share' legislation in Spain and the UK as incompatible with EC legal principle of the free movement of capital. Commission v United Kingdom, C- 98/01; Commission v Kingdom of Spain, C-463/00.

transform control of listed EU firms into a commodity available for purchase throughout (and outside) the EU.[10]

Instead of adopting the BTR, however, the new DTB specifically exempts 'securities carrying double or multiple voting rights.'[11] The DTB also provides that the mini-BTR does not apply to 'securities without voting rights which carry specific pecuniary advantages.' The EC explained the omission of the BTR as follows:

The [BTR recommendation] met with opposition from virtually all Member States and interested parties, notably because of the legal problems to which they may give rise (application threshold, concept of risk-bearing capital, compensation for rights foregone, etc.). Moreover, a large majority of those questioned were opposed to the inclusion in the proposal of measures that would have had far-reaching implications for company law.[12]

B. The High-Level Goals of the DTB

Before analysing the BTR, I should begin by acknowledging the importance and value of the high-level goals of the DTB. A unitary EU capital market would be a significant good for the EU and the global economy. A more unified system of regulating takeover bids would facilitate the development of an integrated capital market. Such a system of rules would itself improve transparency in a critical area of law.

A brief contrast to the US will make the point. US takeover law can be intricate at the firm level, requiring bidders and lawyers to analyse the precise control structure of a target before proceeding with a bid. Bidders nonetheless face a stable and relatively uniform scheme for regulation in analysing, planning, and implementing M&A transactions. Tender offers (bids) themselves are regulated by a uniform set of federal laws: the Williams Act, the SEC's rules, and relevant federal court decisions. Efforts by individual states to interfere with this scheme are constrained by the US Constitution's Supremacy and Commerce Clauses[13] and, more importantly, by the ability of corporations (with board and shareholder

[10] The Takeover Bid Report distinguished these 'technical' defenses from 'structural' defenses that arise by virtue of how ownership of normal one-share-one-vote common stock was dispersed or concentrated among individual holders (ie, control blocks), groups (ie, cross-holdings) or holding companies (ie, pyramids). Neither the mini-BTR nor the full BTR would apply to 'structural defenses. (n 24).

[11] The EC Company Law Action Plan recommends further study of whether Member States should be required to bar new listings of DC structures. Action Plan at 14.

[12] (n 1) at 4.

[13] JC Coates IV 'State Takeover Statutes and Corporate Theory: The Revival of an Old Debate' (1989) 64 NYU L Rev 806 (analyzing US Supreme Court jurisprudence under the Commerce Clause and the Supremacy Clause as it applies to state takeover statutes).

consent) to choose their state of incorporation regardless of the location of a company's headquarters. Freedom to reincorporate has created a stable equilibrium in which one state (Delaware) directly writes corporate law for about two-thirds of US public companies (and through mimicry writes most law for the rest),[14] with no pressure from local interest groups that have strong interests in impeding transfers of control.[15] Thus, contrary to the Takeover Bid Report's statement that 'the laws of the various states in the US regulating takeover bids differ widely',[16] takeover law for all practical purposes is quite similar for the vast majority of US public companies.

As important as this state of affairs is the fact that it can be cheaply communicated to business people. At the most general level, the business community 'gets it'. And 'it' does not change very much.[17] However much ink we US legal academics spill analysing and arguing the nuances of the fiduciary duties of corporate boards in the takeover context, a CEO who fell asleep in 1979 and woke like Rip Van Winkle in 2004 would not need many minutes or dollars to catch up on his practical and strategic grasp of the law-in-practice of M&A today.[18]

[14] See generally JC Coates IV 'Explaining Variation in Takeover Defenses: Blame the Lawyers' (2001) 89 Cal L Rev 1301, 1358, 1409 (reporting that of 62% of US firms going public 1991-1992 were incorporated in Delaware, increasing over the 1990s to 75% for IPOs in 1998-99; and analyzing state takeover laws relevant to proxy contests and finding them nearly uniform in effect); JC Coates IV 'Takeover Defenses in the Shadow of the Pill: A Critique of the Scientific Evidence' (2000) 79 Tex L Rev 271, 320-23 and n 203 (analyzing so-called 'shark repellents' and state takeover statutes and showing that, with the exception of the poison pill and the classified board, such provisions and statutes have little or no practical effect on takeovers when targets have already adopted poison pills or can adopt poison pills on short notice, as nearly all US public firms can do).

[15] See generally R Romano *The Genius of American Corporate Law* (AEI Press Washington DC 1993).

[16] (n 3) at 6.

[17] The remarkable, jingoistic assertion of the European Parliament's Committee on Legal Affairs and the Internal Market in its Draft Report on the new DTB (11 March 2003), at 28, that 'since 11 September 2001, the USA has enshrined in law a series of unilateral provisions that are a serious obstacle to investment in the USA by foreign companies is a gross exaggeration at best.

[18] Arguably, only one thing of importance has changed in US law regarding takeovers: the development of 'poison pills' (known to their defenders as 'shareholder rights plans') and their judicial approval in the mid-1980s. Pills had the effect of channeling takeover bids for US companies into one of two routes (transactions negotiated with a target's board or combination tender offer/proxy fights), and also had the effect of eliminating two-tier takeover bids and greenmail. Pills may also have reduced overall takeover bid activity, at least in the early 1990s, although the direct effect of pills on takeovers has not been nearly as important as their indirect effect, via staggered boards. See LA Bebchuk, JC Coates IV and G Subramanian 'The Powerful Antitakeover Force of Staggered Boards: Theory, Evidence and Policy' (2002) 54 Stan L Rev 887. Some US legal academics argue that even the combination of pills and staggered boards has had little overall effect, due to independent boards, active institutional shareholders, and

cont. ...

The stability and transparency of the overall US system of regulation is conducive to planning and execution of transactions. Stability and transparency are in my view more important to the ability of the US to sustain M&A booms like that of the 1990s than any particular rule affecting takeovers. As an example of the kind of principle or rule that one might think would be important, but turns out not to be, at least in the US, no authoritative legal doctrine or statute in the US affirmatively provides that protection of shareholders is in itself an overriding goal of the law. Shareholders in fact are protected in many ways by the US legal system, and target shareholders benefit directly from almost all M&A transactions. But shareholders are protected and benefited not because of any top-down articulation of shareholder-protection as an end to be pursued through the details of the legal system, but because their participation is essential in a capitalist economy and the net effects of the system of rules must benefit them overall, at least as they are enforced in practice, and as they are supplemented by norms and ideological consensus regarding the social value of profit-seeking and self-interest.[19] The more easily that fact can be convincingly communicated to shareholders, and the less frequently that fact can be brought into question by significant changes to the law (or scandals like Enron, Global Crossing, Tyco, Adelphia, WorldCom, and HealthSouth), the more likely shareholder participation will follow.

If US experience is any guide, then, achieving a unitary framework for regulating takeover bids in Europe would facilitate M&A transactions and the restructuring that they generally precede. By reducing country-by-country variation in how M&A is regulated, and by limiting the overall amount of potential change in the system, any plausible DTB would create an important set of conditions (stability, transparency) for an active M&A market. That 'high-level' goal should not be forgotten in an effort to perfect the details of the new DTB.

C. Doubts About the BTR

With that basic point in mind, I turn to the BTR. As articulated by the Takeover Bid Report, the BTR is primarily directed at provisions that interfere with 'proportionality' between cash-flow rights and control rights.[20] Proportionality raises important general questions about how firms should be governed. But why is proportionality important to the regulation of takeovers? The answer (pre-

executive compensation. eg M Kahan and EB Rock 'How I Learned to Stop Worrying and Love the Pill: Adaptive Responses to Takeover Law' (2002) 69 U Chi L Rev 871.

[19] This is why a spectacular failure like Enron did not in itself have much effect on US stock prices, but why the series of corporate scandals and failures that began the following January, from Global Crossing to Tyco to Adelphia to WorldCom, did send the US stock market into a long slide.

[20] (n 3) at 3-5.

sumably) is that disproportionality can facilitate barriers to takeover bids. Multi- or dual-class (DC) capital structures can make it easier for one shareholder to maintain control over a firm without paying for the cash-flow rights that accompany voting rights in single class structures. In the EU, at least, it is cheaper, ex ante, to create an absolute or near-absolute takeover defence using a DC structure than it is using a single-class structure. As takeover regulation, then, the BTR is directed primarily at companies that *both* (1) have DC structures and (2) have shareholders that could plausibly use high-vote shares to impede transfers of control.

I. BTR Will Make Less than 3-4% of EU Firms Vulnerable to a Bid

Recent empirical research, however, suggests that such companies are relatively rare in the EU. Bennedsen and Nielsen (2003) report that out of 5,162 public companies in the EU, 1,035 or 20% have DC structures.[21] Of those, however, only ~50 are currently invulnerable to a takeover and would be made vulnerable under the BTR, and only another ~150 would be vulnerable under the BTR and currently have a significant degree of disproportionality between the voting and cash flow rights held by their largest shareholders. The rest of the DC firms would either continue to be invulnerable to a takeover under the BTR or currently lack sufficient disproportionality for a DC structure to contribute meaningfully to takeover defence by a current control shareholder. In all, as reflected on Figure 1, only 4% of all public firms would even be potentially put at-risk of a takeover by the proposed BTR.

[21] M Bennedsen and K Nielsen 'The Impact of a Break-Through Rule on European Firms' Working Paper (2003). Bennedsen and Nielsen also show that DC structures are also common in the UK, a country where dispersed ownership is modal, takeovers are common, and minority shareholder protection is thought to be good. In the US, too, DC structures are not uncommon. See Figure 3 and n 41.

Figure 1: Effect of BTR and EU Public Firms

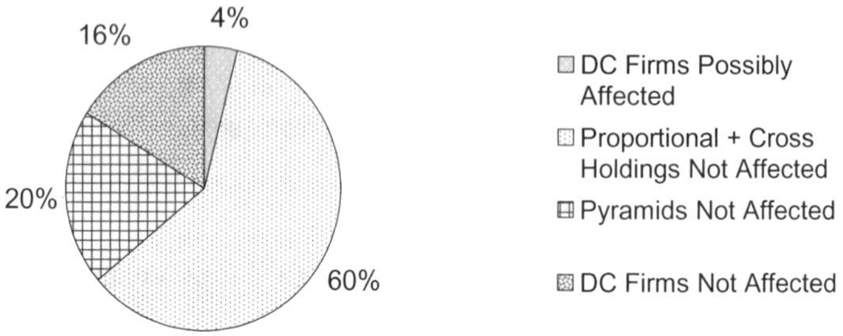

Sources for data: Bennedsen and Nielsen (2003) (DC data); Fiaccio and Lang (2002) (pyramid data)

But even this analysis overstates the potential value of the BTR to the creation of an EU-wide takeover market. That is because it implicitly assumes that companies would not dynamically respond to the adoption of the BTR, when they certainly would. Even the NR, as proposed in the DTB, could be deferred for up to three years by Member States; if the full BTR would to be included in the final DTB, political realities would require a deferral period. Thus, subject companies would have ample time to respond. They could do so in at least four ways. The first and simplest response is for large shareholders of currently vulnerable companies to increase their current holdings of cash-flow rights above the 25% threshold so that no bidder could acquire sufficient cash-flow rights to trigger the BTR. (This assumes as seems plausible that Member States most affected by the BTR established the highest permissible threshold.) Bennedsen and Nielsen's empirical analysis suggests that ~40 or 20% of DC firms that would be put at-risk by the BTR would plausibly be able to respond in this manner.[22]

For the remainder, the percentage of cash flow rights required to obtain such a veto block would be large enough that another, more costly alternative might be relatively more attractive: switching to a pyramid or cross-holding structure. Kraakman, Bebchuk, and Triantis (1999) have shown[23] – and the Takeover Bid

[22] ibid.

[23] R Kraakman, LA Bebchuk, and G Triantis 'Stock Pyramids, Cross-Ownership, and the Dual Class Equity: The Creation and Agency Costs of Separating Control from Cash Flow Rights' (1999) National Bureau of Economic Research Working Paper No 6951; also published cont. ...

Report acknowledges[24] – that from the perspective of both control and cash-flow rights, the same results produced by DC structures can be produced through either pyramids or cross-holding structures. Bebchuk and Hart (2002)[25] argue that firms will recognize this equivalence and that vulnerable DC structures will switch to pyramids or be forced to do so by bidders. Nothing in the DTB (or in the EC's subsequent Company Law Action Plan) would prevent firms from substituting these structures for DC structures.[26]

Gordon notes that the effects of a relatively common 10-to-1 super-to-normal vote DC structure could only be accomplished through a 3- or 4-level pyramid.[27] Further, the transaction costs associated with such a switch could be substantial. Another alternative response would be for at-risk firms to reincorporate outside the EU.[28] This, too, would be expensive, as the 'real seat' doctrine traditionally followed in the EU would require firms to not only reincorporate but to relocate their headquarters. Thus, not all at-risk DC firms would evade the BTR. At the same time, for many, the switch would be worth it to a controlling shareholder, when compared to the risk of a loss of control. On balance, the most one can confidently say about the net effect of the BTR is that it would make *less than 3-4%* of public firms in the EU more vulnerable to a takeover bid than they are now.

in RK Morck (ed) *Concentrated Corporate Ownership* (University of Chicago Press Chicago 2000). For related work that also notes the importance of substitutes in designing regulations, see J Arlen and E Talley 'Unregulable Defenses and the Perils of Shareholder Choice' Working Paper (15 April 2003) (various substitutes for takeover defenses common in the US); RJ Gilson 'Evaluating Dual Class Common Stock: The Relevance Of Substitutes' (1987) 73 Va L Rev 807 (leveraged buyouts as substitutes for dual class recapitalizations).

[24] n 3, at 6. In fact, the Takeover Bid Report singles out pyramids as 'difficult to justify from a general capital markets and company law perspective,' and candidly acknowledges that the only reason their proposed BTR would not apply to pyramids and cross-holdings is practicality. ibid at 38-39. The Company Law Report proposes that such structures be addressed with improved disclosure, rules on conflicts of interests in groups of listed companies with cross-holdings, and the delisting of holding companies whose 'sole or main assets are their shareholding in another listed company.' Company Law Report at 94-100. The EC Company Law Action Plan endorses the recommendations on disclosure and conflicts of interest, and recommends further study of the possibility of delisting 'abusive' pyramids, including the views of the Committee of European Securities Regulators (CESR). Action Plan at 18-20.

[25] LA Bebchuk and O Hart 'A Threat to Dual Class Shares' *Financial Times* (31 May 2002).

[26] n 23.

[27] JN Gordon 'Economic Nationalism and Corporate Governance: German Shareholder Capitalism in the European Union' Working Paper (2003), at n 151.

[28] Reincorporation would not need to go beyond Europe, of course: neither Switzerland nor Norway is part of the EU, and both are physically close to countries in which Bennedsen and Nielsen (n 21) find a high incidence of at-risk DC firms (Italy and Germany for Switzerland; Sweden and Denmark for Norway).

II. The BTR Will Not Create a 'Level Playing Field'

The fact that many firms could evade the BTR raises two further troubling issues. The likelihood of evasion only underlines the fact that the DTB – with or without the BTR – will not create or even meaningfully contribute to a true 'level playing field' for firms within the EU. The fact that DC firms are equivalent to pyramids and firms controlled through cross-holdings not only raises the risk of strategic evasion, but it means that disproportionality can make takeover defences cheaper at a range of public companies, some of which will, and most of which will not, be affected by the BTR. As reflected in Figure 1, Faccio and Lang report that roughly the same percentage (20%) of public firms in the EU have pyramid structures as have DC structures.[29] Likewise, the largest shareholders of many DC firms currently have what Bennedsen and Nielsen refer to as 'comfort' that their firms will not be taken over, even if the BTR were adopted, because they already own more than 25% of their firms' cash flow rights.[30] Even without considering the contribution of cross-holdings to disproportionality, these figures suggest that no more than 12.5% of EU public firms with disproportional capital structures will be affected by the BTR.

But the failure of the BTR (and the DTB more generally) to achieve a 'level playing field' would be worse than reflected by discrepancies among DC firms, or between DC firms and other firms with disproportional capital structures. As noted by Berglöf and Burkart in a recent survey of theory relevant to any evaluation of the BTR and the rest of the DTB:

In half of the listed non-financial firms in Austria, Belgium, Germany and Italy a single shareholder controls more than 50% of the votes (compared to 9.9% in the UK). In Dutch, Spanish and Swedish firms the median blockholder holds 43.5, 34.5, and 34.9%, respectively.[31]

Their conclusion is illustrated in Figure 2, which uses data from Barca and Becht (2001).

[29] Cf M Faccio and L Lang 'The Ultimate Ownership Of Western European Companies' (2002) 65 J Fin Econ 365 (reporting pyramid statistic) with Bennedsen and Nielsen (n 21) (reporting DC statistic).

[30] By some measures, Bennedsen and Nielsen estimate that nearly half or more of DC firms will fall into this category in Austria, Denmark, France, Germany, Italy and Sweden – precisely the countries in which DC firms currently pose the greatest impediment to takeover bids. (n 21, at Figure 2 Panel B). Put differently, the BTR will not achieve a level playing field for takeover bids even as regards countries in which DC structures have historically been most common.

[31] E Berglöf and M Burkart 'European Takeover Regulation' Economic Policy April 2003, at 179. They rely for data primarily on F Barca and M Becht (eds) Control of Corporate Europe (OUP London 2001).

Figure 2 Control Blocks in Public Companies

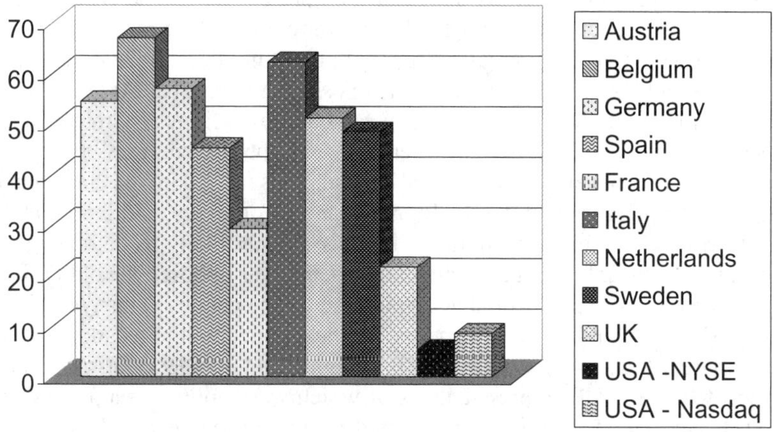

The bulk of the massive concentration of voting control among public firms in the EU, reflected in Figure 2, does not result from disproportionality. Rather, it simply reflects the fact that owners of a large percentage of public firms in a majority of countries in the EU have chosen to retain a control block in an ordinary one-share/one-vote capital structure. All these firms have an absolute defence to hostile takeover bids not supported by their controlling shareholders. Becht and Mayer understate the point when they say: 'Control may not be contestable, even under "one-share-one-vote."'[32] The BTR will have no effect on most takeover-proof EU public firms.

III. The Political Costs of the BTR

Thus, the BTR will do little to achieve a 'level playing field.' Since a level playing field is one of the key stated objectives of the DTB, one of the principal public-regarding political objections made to the old DTB by members of the Euro-

[32] Introduction, in Barca and Becht, (n 31) at 11. The Takeover Bid Report notes this point only in passing – lumping proportional control blocks in with a laundry list of 'general factors' that affect takeover bids, which it contrasts with 'company level factors' such as DC structures. (n 3, at 18). Nothing in the Company Law Report or the EC's Company Law Action Plan (other than proposals for improved disclosure) would address one-share/one-vote blocks.

pean Parliament,[33] and one of the three issues that the Winter group was asked to address, the BTR seems to be in need of further justification. Nor is the BTR likely to reduce political opposition to the overall DTB from specific Member States or specific constituencies within those Member States. Although the number of European DC firms that would be put at-risk by the BTR would be small in absolute terms, and very small relative to all public firms, some of those that would be put at-risk are quite large, with both the incentive and the capacity to organize and lead substantial political opposition to the DTB. At least 20 of the 500 largest firms in the EU, including such well-known firms as Groupe Danone, Telecom Italia, Fiat, Perelli, and Fresenius, would be placed at risk of takeover, using the criteria developed by Bennedsen and Nielsen.[34] Many of the companies that would be put at-risk by the BTR are located in Germany, and representatives from Germany are for many political reasons already likely to be among those opposing the new DTB, just as German representatives opposed the old DTB.

But the BTR's impact would not be limited to one country – many are located in Italy, Denmark and Sweden – and the political opposition to its adoption could be even larger than to the older proposal. A significant number of at-risk firms are also located in the UK, representatives of which were political supporters of the old DTB, and could otherwise be expected to support the new DTB. Because of the UK's robust public capital markets, at-risk companies in the UK are a small percentage of UK public companies, but for political purposes, that fact is not as helpful as the fact that a number of UK firms would be put at-risk is harmful: basic public choice or economic analysis of politics suggests that a small number of highly interested firms will tend to have a greater political impact than a large number of modestly interested firms, even if the theoretical sum of interest of the latter group is larger than that of the former group.

Some of the political currents swirling around the DTB and the BTR are opaque, at least to this US observer. One would think, for example, that representatives from the UK would be most in favour of rules helping to produce a 'level playing field', since UK firms are currently most vulnerable to hostile takeovers, both because of existing UK laws and because of the relatively dispersed ownership of most UK firms, as reflected in Figure 2. One would also think that representatives from Germany would be most inclined to accept either the old or the new DTB, which would facilitate cross-border bids generally without doing much to render vulnerable the majority of German firms (protected by state ownership, large blockholdings, pyramids, and DC structures). Yet in fact

[33] Of course, many members of the European Parliament may have opposed the old DTB anyway, for other reasons (eg, concerns about employees, ties to entrenched management, worries about the ability of US firms to buy EU firms on the cheap), even if it had done a better job of creating a 'level playing field' within Europe. But the political force of these other objections was surely enhanced by nationalist fears stimulated by the 'level playing field' argument.

[34] n 21.

political forces in the UK and Germany seem to be taking the opposite tacks: those from the UK favoured the old DTB, and are neutral or critical of the BTR (because the Takeover Bid Report did not include any compensation for holders of high-vote stock), and those from Germany favour the BTR as a step towards a level playing field, and opposed the old DTB. Perhaps these positions are political masks; perhaps the BTR is being supported by German MEPs in the hopes that it will function as a political poison pill that will reduce the odds that any DTB will be enacted. Or perhaps as with politics generally there is no simple mapping from publicly disclosed interests to publicly announced positions that can easily explain the facts.

Putting politics aside, if the DTB could be passed with the BTR, a large portion of public firms in the EU will remain outside the takeover arena, and to that extent the DTB will not directly facilitate Europe-wide restructuring, another stated goal of the DTB. Nevertheless, if the BTR were otherwise of clear benefit, with few costs, one might be inclined to respond with Voltaire's maxim: '*Le mieux est l'ennemi de bien*.'[35] But as I will now discuss, the BTR will in some ways make things worse than the status quo.

IV. The Economic Costs of the BTR

While the BTR will produce few certain benefits, it will produce sizeable certain costs. First, strategic reactions to the BTR discussed above – purchases of additional cash flow rights to achieve a takeover veto; switches to pyramids and cross-holding structures to replicate disproportionality without concern about the BTR; and reincorporations outside the EU – will generate transaction costs. In addition to substantial fees of lawyers, bankers and brokers needed to implement these strategic reactions, top management of affected firms will face significant distraction as they worry about preserving the control of their firms: if US takeover experience has any lessons, it is that top managers worry about few things more than loss of control. When top managers are distracted, ordinary business suffers. From a social perspective, these costs will be a pure loss, since no gain will be achieved in terms of making those firms more likely to be takeover targets.

Worse, as Bebchuk and Hart point out, *new* European firms that go public (including spin-offs of existing public firms) are likely to adopt pyramids and cross-holding structures at the outset if pre-IPO shareholders or other control persons wish to preserve their 'lock' on control while selling more than a majority of the cash flow rights to the public. To the extent more pyramids and cross-holdings result, either mid-stream (through switches) or from newly public firms seeking to avoid the BTR, matters will be made worse from the perspective of

[35] Voltaire *Dictionnaire Philosophique* ('the perfect is the enemy of the good').

transparency: while DC structures make takeover deterrence cheaper, pyramids and cross-holdings do that and also make it much more difficult for outside investors to understand, evaluate, and monitor existing controllers. As the Take-over Bid Report notes,

> Pyramid structures ... undermine the transparency of the ownership structure of listed companies; [and] ... affect the pricing mechanism with regard to listed shares at all levels in the structure....[36]

By inducing more pyramids or cross-holding structures, the BTR will reduce transparency and impair capital markets outside the scope of takeover bids.

Finally, both existing or new public firms that have both a conventional one-share/one-vote structure and a single (or small group) of controlling shareholders may simply turn down net present value projects if they would require the share-holders to put their control positions at risk.

D. Why Do Takeover-Proof Firms Exist?

To know whether the costs of the BTR are greater than its benefits – which as discussed above will be small – one needs, as a starting point, some basic theory about why concentrated ownership (through control blocks and disproportional structures) persist in public firms in the first place. While many things remain uncertain about ownership structure, one thing seems likely: concentrated owner-ship depends upon 'private benefits of control' (PBC).[37] As I use the term, PBC are any benefits that a control person derives from their control of a firm that are not shared proportionally with non-controlling shareholders.

The composition of PBC in practice is much less certain. At least three kinds of PBC can be distinguished: (1) transfers of value from minority shareholders to a controlling shareholder that are inefficient in the sense that the gain to the con-trol person from the PBC is less than the loss to the minority shareholder ('bad PBC');[38] (2) transfers of value that are efficient in the sense that the gain is no

[36] n 3, at 39.

[37] Other things may also be necessary, or may contribute to concentrated ownership. For example, control shareholders may profit when they sell shares to public investors if the latter may fail to 'price' properly the difference between contestable and non-contestable control structures. Or control shareholders may not internalize the full benefits of future takeover bids when choosing an ownership structure. LA Bebchuk and L Zingales 'Corporate Ownership Structures and the Decision to Go Public: Private versus Social Optimality' in Morck (n 23) at 55. In addition, as noted below, concentrated ownership may arise to control managerial agency cost problems, which can be viewed as an extreme form of private benefits of control.

[38] This seems implicit in the Winter Group's endorsement of proportionality, (note 3, at 21) and is consistent with some of the more prominent theoretical analyses of control blocks, which argue that control shareholders extract PBC from minority shareholders, lowering not only firm value but social welfare. eg LA Bebchuk 'A Rent-Protection Theory of Corporate Ownership

cont. ...

less than the loss ('good PBC,' called 'amenity potential' by Demsetz and Lehn[39]); and (3) value that is no meaningful sense a 'transfer' because it is inherent in control ('Inherent PBC').[40] Each type of PBC is discussed briefly below, but the key point for this analysis is the BTR can be expected to have only marginal effects on PBC of any type, and may reduce social welfare by interfering with contracts designed to protect good PBC or inherent PBC.

I. Bad PBC

Bad PBC are the sort of PBC that most commentators seem to have in mind when they talk of PBC: excessive (often hidden) compensation or perquisites of office, extraction of value through self-dealing transactions, excessive risk aversion, or choice of suboptimal business or operational strategies to satisfy some personal

and Control' (1999) NBER Working Paper 7203; R La Porta, F Lopez de Silanes, A Shleifer, and RW Vishny 'Legal Determinants of External Finance' (1997) 52 J Fin 1131; R La Porta, F Lopez de Silanes, A Shleifer, and RW Vishny 'Investor Protection and Corporate Governance' (2000) 58 J Fin Econ 3.

[39] H Demsetz and K Lehn 'The Structure of Corporate Ownership: Causes and Consequences' (1985) 93 J Pol Econ 1155; CG Holderness 'A Survey Of Blockholders and Corporate Control' [April 2003] Fed Res Bk of NY Econ Pol Rev 51. Olaf Ehrhardt and Erik Nowak, following Michael Jensen, argue that good PBC cannot exist, because a control shareholder will maximize the sum of PBC and his share of firm value, which will always diverge from firm value alone. Private Benefits and Minority Shareholder Expropriation – Empirical Evidence from IPOs of German Family-Owned Firms, Working Paper (March 2002) (citing M Jensen 'Value Maximization, Stakeholder Theory, and the Corporate Objective Function' (2001) 7 European Fin'l Mgt 297). This argument pushes logic beyond its limit. While actions that benefit a control shareholder may reduce firm value, many actions that produce PBC would also maximize firm value. Illegal insider trading could benefit a control shareholder on an expected basis (if enforcement is imperfect) and harm firm value on an expected basis (if there is a non-zero chance the insider is caught and any harm to the shareholder's reputation will also harm the firm) (eg, Martha Stewart); but if enforcement is good enough, or profit low enough, a shareholder will choose not to trade (for her own reasons), and that choice will (compared to the alternative) maximize firm value, too. Conversely, consider a high-profile, high-risk, and high-cost investment opportunity with positive expected value (eg. Berkshire Hathaway's purchase of Tyco convertible bonds). If the control shareholder pursues the opportunity through the firm, and the investment pays off, the shareholder will have benefited along with other shareholders, but will also added to his reputation in a way not shared with other shareholders.

[40] Ehrhardt and Nowak (n 39) use a different typology, distinguishing PBC in two dimensions: pecuniary vs non-pecuniary, and transferable vs non-transferable. They equate bad PBC with what pecuniary PBC. But not all bad PBC are pecuniary: a control shareholder choosing a low-risk strategy based on his risk preferences could harm minority shareholders more than the choice benefits him. And not all pecuniary PBC are bad: a shareholder could force the sale of a personal asset to a controlled firm at a price that exceeds his private valuation, producing pecuniary PBC, but if the sale price is below market price, neither the firm nor minority shareholders will have suffered. For a US legal case that plausibly illustrates the latter possibility, see *Cookies Food Products, Inc v Lakes Warehouse Distributing, Inc* 430 N W 2d 447 (Iowa 1988).

preference of control shareholders.[41] In each case, the PBC represent a reduction of firm wealth at the expense of minority shareholders, and what is more, a reduction that is greater than any benefit to control shareholders, resulting in social loss. (If the control shareholder valued the PBC more than the minority shareholders valued the loss to firm value they create, the PBC would be 'good PBC.') If bad PBC of this sort could be eliminated or reduced, social welfare would be enhanced.

II. Good PBC

At the time the firm sells shares to the public, existing controlling shareholders may value control (and the PBC it provides) more highly than anyone else would value those PBC. In standard neo-classical models of the firm, this is not possible, because control is not treated as a consumption good and no firm is unique, so control provides no unique PBC to any particular controlling shareholder. But casual observation suggests this picture is too simple.

Founding families often give their names to firms and work to inculcate a preference for maintaining control in the second- (or even third-) generation family members, who join the firm's management.[42] Thus, for example, Ford Motor Company continues to be dominated by the Ford family, and retains a disproportional capital structure. In the worlds of fashion, art, and music, creative entrepreneurs who produce new cultural products often (if not always) have a much greater psychic investment in control of the uses of their products than they can monetize on the capital markets. Recent research suggests that enough California vineyards are owned by hobbyists who enjoy producing high quality wines for its own sake that they lower the financial returns of, and discourage profit-maximizing owners from competing in, the high-end wine segment.[43] A similar effect is reported in high technology companies, where part of the incentive for innovators is their sense of ownership over the technology itself, in all its possible uses (or, more often, from their perspective, misuses), and the initial innovators are very plausibly the highest-valuing owners of the rights to dispose of the technology they have created.

Holdnerness notes that control shareholders are commonly corporations, or are individuals that control other businesses.[44] Where this is the case, synergies

[41] eg Bebchuk (n 38) at 16; S Johnson, R La Porta, F Lopez-de-Silanes and A Shleifer 'Tunneling' (2000) Am Econ Rev 22.

[42] DJ Denis and DK Denis 'Majority Owner-Managers and Organizational Efficiency,' (1994) 1 J Corp Fin 91 find that public firms with majority owners are more likely to have DC structures and family owners.

[43] FM Scott Morton and JM Podolny 'Love or Money? The Effects of Owner Motivation in the California Wine Industry' (2002) 50 J Ind Econ 431.

[44] Holderness (n 39) at 55.

can arise between the parent (or commonly controlled) companies and the firm in question. These synergies can benefit minority shareholders even if they are not shared on a purely pro rata basis, and are another type of good PBC.

Even if controlling shareholders are scrupulously honest and talented and work to maximize firm value, the presence of good PBC will give a reason to maintain a 'lock' on control.[45] And, if their capital needs are large enough, they may use DC structures to maintain their control while selling more than a majority of their firms' cash-flow rights to the public.[46] Any law – such as the BTR – that effectively taxes or prohibits such structures in such firms will reduce social welfare.

III. Inherent PBC

Some PBC, finally, are inherently non-contractible – they cannot be shared with minority shareholders, whether minority shareholders would (in theory) value those PBC more, less, or the same as control shareholders. Only one person can have final authority over the *New York Times* or *Le Monde*, for example. Indeed, media companies are often controlled by one shareholder, regardless whether they have public investors. Figure 3 shows that DC structures are more common in the media industry than in other industries, among mature US public firms and in US firms going public.[47] (The same is true of the firms listed in Appendix, discussed below, one of which is the firm that owns the *New York Times*.)

[45] Of course, many entrepreneurs are wealth constrained and risk-averse, and have other desires that lead them to sell control of their firms (and technologies) to the public. Thus, inside ownership is inversely correlated with firm size. CG Holderness and DP Sheehan 'The Role of Majority Shareholders in Publicly Held Corporations' (1988) 20 J Fin Econ 317. But some can be expected to (and do) retain control even if they take their firms public.

[46] Controllers typically follow a 'pecking order' when deploying capital: first rely on internal finance, then if external finance is needed, turn first to debt, then hybrid securities such as preferred stock, and only then voting equity. See SC Myers 'The Capital Structure Puzzle' (1984) 39 J Fin 581. This pattern illustrates the limitations of the Modigliani-Miller theorem that capital structure 'does not matter' with the implication that debt can always be used instead of equity. See F Modigliani and MH Miller 'The Cost of Capital, Corporate Finance and the Theory of Investment (1958) 48 Am Econ Rev 261. See also M Attari and S Banerjee 'Strategic Underinvestment, Managerial Entrenchment and Ownership Structure of a Firm' Working Paper (Tulane University) (2002) (insiders may 'underinvest' relative to first-best if investment requires issuing outside equity and risking control; DC structures may mitigate this problem).

[47] Figure 3 uses data on firms with dual class common stock in IRRC, Corporate Takeover Defenses (1998) (which includes the S&P 1500), excluding tracking stocks (based on Dow Jones News Reports), and data on firms with dual class common stock in sample of 1,019 firms that went public 1988-1992, from L Casares Field 'Control Considerations of Newly Public Firms: The Implementation of Antitakeover Provisions and Dual Class Shares Before the IPO' Working Paper (10 February 1999), subsequently published in slightly different form as L Casares Field and JM Karpoff 'Takeover Defenses of IPO Firms' (2002) 57 J Fin 1857. See

cont. ...

More generally, only one person can be the ultimate boss in a hierarchy, and thus only one person has no boss; this is an inherent feature of firms that cannot be plausibly changed by contract. True, even the ultimate boss of a public company must satisfy suppliers of capital and labour, and customers, and is thus constrained in many ways. But empirical evidence suggests that many entrepreneurs are consistently willing to 'pay' for formal autonomy by obtaining predictably lower average absolute (ie, not risk-adjusted) rates of return.[48]

As with good PBC, inherent PBC will motivate owners to retain a lock on control, even if they go public, and to use disproportional structures if their capital needs are sufficiently large and the discount on non- or low-voting shares is not too great. And again, any law that prohibits or taxes disproportional capital structures for such owners will reduce social welfare, either by discouraging pursuit of socially useful projects that could have been funded with the capital raised by selling low- or no-vote shares, or by inducing owners to forego control (and the inherent PBC that control protects) in order to pursue those projects.

Figure 3

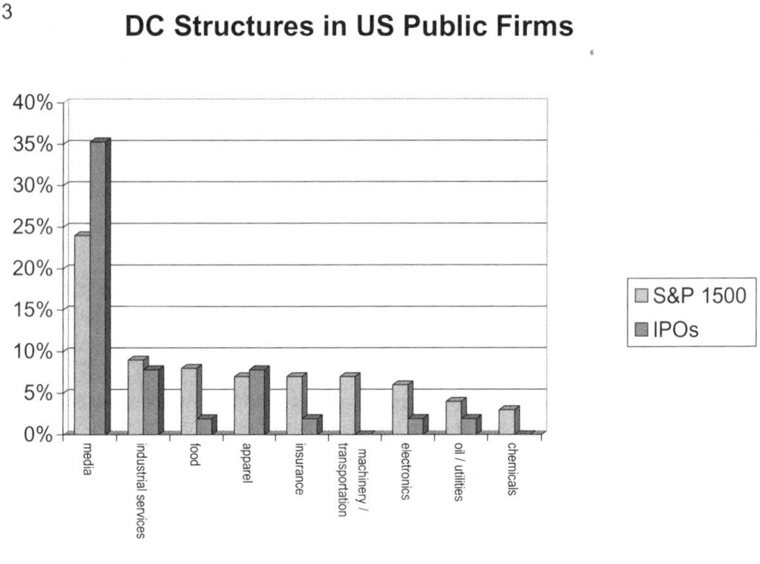

Data sources: IRRC (1998); DJNR; Compustat; Field (1999).

also SB Smart and C J Zutter 'Control as a Motivation for Underpricing: A Comparison of Dual- and Single-Class IPOs' (2003) 69 J Fin Econ 85, 105 (DC structures are disproportionately present in sports management, entertainment and media industries).

[48] BH Hamilton 'Does Entrepreneurship Pay? An Empirical Analysis of the Returns to Self-Employment' (2000) 108 J Pol Econ 604.

IV. Which Type of PBC Dominates? Do DC Firms Underperform?

Any rule that effectively reduces PBC in public firms generally might improve social welfare if the incidence of bad PBC was greater than the incidence of good and inherent PBC. Few attempts have been made to estimate the distribution of types of PBC.[49] As a simple, indirect test, the following analysis was conducted. From 206 US public firms listed by the Investor Responsibility Research Center as having DC structures, 30 were chosen randomly, and each firm's 2001 annual proxy statement was examined to verify that the firm was listed on a stock exchange or Nasdaq from 1995 to 2000, and that it in fact had a DC structure giving disproportionate voting rights to one or a small group of shareholders. Each firm was matched with a public firm with a proportional (one-share-one-vote) structure, from the same industry (2-digit SIC codes) and roughly the same size (1997 assets). Tobin's Q and return on assets were compared for each pair from 1997 to 2000. Results are summarized in Figure 4.

Figure 4

Figure 4: Effect of Disproportionality on Q and ROA in US Firms

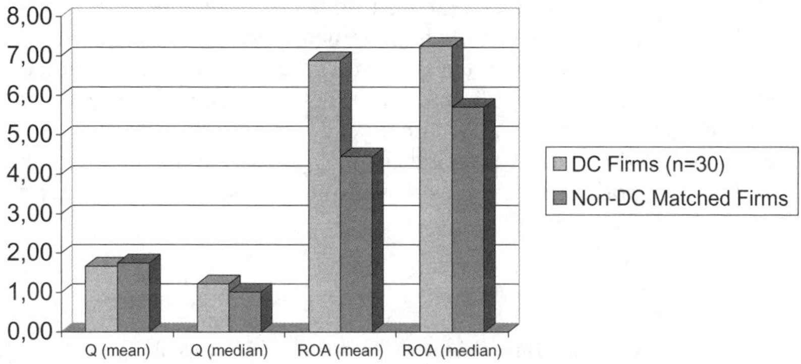

DC firms had larger median Q, mean ROA and median ROA, and smaller mean Q. For such a small sample, it is not surprising that none of these fairly small differences are statistically significant at a 95% confidence level, and the only difference that approaches statistical significance is for mean ROA ($p<.12$). From these (admittedly limited) data, one cannot conclude anything one way or another

[49] Studies of the existence and size of PBC exist, eg MJ Barclay and CG Holderness 'Private Benefits from Control of Public Companies' (1989) 25 J Fin Econ 371, but not the source of PBC. An exception is Ehrhardt and Nowak, discussed in n 39, and in the text below.

about the effect of DC structures on firm value or performance. Nor can one conclude that bad PBC outweighs good or inherent PBC, or vice versa.

These results are broadly consistent with those from other studies of US firms. Field and Karpoff study over 1,000 US firms going public in the early 1990s, and find no evidence that DC structures (or takeover defenses generally) 'degrade operating performance or are used to protect managers who are expected to perform badly.'[50] In fact, they find that raw ROA and ROA adjusted by comparison to an industry-matched firm with the same IPO-year ROA are actually higher for firms protected by DC structures and other defenses in the first two years after an IPO, although the difference falls to statistical insignificance thereafter. Dimitrov and Jain study 178 US firms that announced a new DC structure from 1979-1998, and find that conversion to the DC structures produces positive abnormal results for minority shareholders.[51] They further find that the positive abnormal returns (of 41.67% over 48 months) are concentrated in those firms where the control shareholder does *not* list the high voting stock; firms where the high voting stock is listed along with the low voting stock produce returns that are not statistically different from overall market model returns. Event studies of DC structures likewise find evidence generally consistent with the notion that conversions to such structures are not generally harmful to minority shareholders.[52]

Ehrhardt and Nowak study 44 German firms that went public with DC structures 1970-1991, and find that such firms underperformed relative to a size-matched portfolio of firms over the three years after the IPO (measured both by stock returns and operating performance).[53] They attribute the underperformance to bad PBC (as noted above, they do not believe good or inherent PBC exist).[54] They explain the difference between their findings and the findings from the US in Field and Karpoff to laxer protections of minority shareholders in Germany,

[50] n 47, at 1883.

[51] V Dimitrov and P Jain 'Dual Class Recapitalization and Managerial Commitment: Long-run stock market and operating performance' Working Paper (11 December 2001).

[52] Cf M Megan Partch 'The Creation of a Class of Limited Voting Common Stock and Shareholder Wealth' (1987) 8 J Fin Econ 313 (event study of 44 public US firms adopting DC structures midstream; finds a +1.2% average stock price reaction to announcement) and JN Gordon 'Ties that Bond: Dual Class Common Stock and the Problem of Shareholder Choice' (1988) 76 Cal L Rev 3 (finding similar results) with GA Jarrell and A Poulsen 'Dual-class Recapitalizations as Antitakeover Mechanisms' (1988) 20 J Fin Econ 129 (finding a –0.82% average stock price reaction in similar study of DC recapitalizations).

[53] n 39.

[54] Cf Smart and Zutter (n 47) who find that DC IPOs underperform single-class IPOs in the US not because of sub-par operating performance but because the shares are less underpriced in the IPO itself, because firms without DC structures have a greater need to underprice in order to disperse shares widely among small holders as partial substitute for the takeover defense offered by DC structures.

compared to the US, citing the now well-known comparative studies by LaPorta et al.[55]

But if weak shareholder protection is the explanation for Ehrhardt and Nowak's findings, German law must protect minority shareholders less well than they are protected in Denmark, as well in the US. Rose studies 102 firms listed on the Copenhagen Stock Exchange and finds that over half have DC structures.[56] Over the period 1995-1999, firms with high-levels of takeover protection (through DC structures or otherwise) perform no worse than those without such protection, whether measured by Tobin's Q, stock returns, ROA or ROE.

Even if it is true that more of the DC structures in the EU (or in Germany) are motivated by bad PBC than is the case in the US (or in Denmark), the BTR (and the DTB more generally) will do little to reduce bad PBC. The threat of takeovers reduces PBC only if a firm is a plausible takeover target. But as discussed above, only a minority of public firms in the EU are now takeover targets, and only a slightly smaller fraction will become takeover targets under the DTB, and an even smaller fraction would become takeover targets by virtue of the BTR. Other, more direct mechanisms would be necessary to reduce any bad PBC that induces concentrated ownership in the EU: better courts, better mechanisms to enforce shareholder rights outside the takeover context, more transparency, better audits, or better standards for ordinary governance of public firms. It is not necessary for this analysis to decide whether bad PBC is a big or small problem in the EU – and the contrasting results from the Denmark and Germany studies,[57] as well as studies showing large variations in premiums for voting shares and control blocks across countries,[58] suggest that bad PBC is probably a big problem in some countries and a small one in others. Whatever the case, the BTR itself will do little to reduce bad PBC.

V. Controlling Shareholders May Control Manager Agency Costs

In addition to these affirmative reasons for maintaining relatively concentrated ownership in a public firm (and for adopting DC structures if capital needs are

[55] See sources cited in n 40.

[56] C Rose 'Corporate Finance Performance and the Use of Takeover Defenses' (2002) 13 European J L & Econ 91.

[57] See sources cited in ns 39 and 51.

[58] Al Dyck and L Zingales 'Private Benefits of Control: An International Comparison' Harvard Business School and University of Chicago Working Paper (2001); F Modigliani and E Perotti 'Security versus Bank Finance: The Importance of a Proper Enforcement of Legal Rules' MIT Working Paper (2000); T Nenova 'The Value of Corporate Voting Rights and Control: A Cross-country Analysis' (2003) 68 J Fin Econ 325; cf Barclay and Holderness (n 49); L Zingales 'The Value of the Voting Right: A Study of the Milan Stock Exchange Experience' (1994) 7 Rev Fin'l Stud 125.

large enough), there is an important negative reason for concentrated ownership to persist in public companies: such ownership structures may better align the incentives of (or constrain through monitoring) managers. As the Takeover Bid Report acknowledges, 'a strong minority shareholder who controls the company from the inside may … overcome the problems related to disciplining management of companies with dispersed ownership.'[59] Even if concentrated ownership protects 'bad PBC,' any rule that forces a firm into a dispersed or proportional ownership structure may reduce bad PBC only by creating even larger manager agency costs. At the highest level of abstraction, one would expect manager agency costs to exceed bad PBC when managers own little stock, and bear a small share of the costs through ownership. Even if bad PBC outweighs good and inherent PBC in the EU, and even if the BTR could reduce bad PBC or PBC overall, it could come at the cost of increasing manager agency costs by a larger amount.

A component of the BTR does address manager agency costs: by imposing the 75% threshold for application of the BTR, the BTR would encourage control shareholders to retain at least 25% of a firm's cash-flow rights. Thus, the BTR can reasonably be defended as helping insure that a control shareholder is more like a sole owner and less like a manager. As a matter of theory, however, it remains far from clear that managers need to own anything like 25% of a company to have a strong incentive to maximize overall firm value, and there is some evidence, albeit disputed, that firm value rises in a controller's ownership only to a level of about 5%, and falls thereafter to a level of about 30% as block ownership enable managers to entrench themselves, and then rises again thereafter.[60] This evidence suggests that if the BTR encouraged more firms to hold 25% blocks, performance would be lower than if firms had either 5% blockholders or 50+% blockholders. In any event, the findings on DC structures reviewed above suggests that the link between ownership and value (or performance) is not confined to DC firms, but extends to one-share/one-vote firms, which are not addressed by BTR.

VI. US Law Permits Public Firms to Remain Takeover Proof

Consistent with the foregoing analysis, US law has never – and currently does not – prohibit takeover-proof companies. US firms can, and often do, ensure that they will never be subject to a hostile takeover in each of the ways used in the EU:

[59] n 3, at 24. See also MJ Roe 'Corporate Law's Limits' (2002) 31 J Legal Studies 233.

[60] R Morck, A Shleifer and RW Vishny 'Management Ownership and Market Valuation: An Empirical Analysis' (1988) 20 J Fin Econ 293. But see CP Himmelberg, R Glenn Hubbard and D Palia 'Understanding the Determinants of Managerial Ownership and the Link Between Ownership and Performance' (1999) 53 J Fin Econ 353 (arguing and presenting evidence that managerial ownership structure is endogenous and thus does not affect firm value).

retention of control blocks by pre-IPO owners, and use of disproportionate capital structures. Neither state corporate law nor federal securities law in any way prevents an entrepreneur from selling low- or even no-vote shares to the public. The only major constraint on DC structures occurs after a company has already gone public – at which point SEC Rule 19c-4 requires the stock exchanges (including Nasdaq) to impose a listing requirement that (in effect) no traded company may engage in a transaction that reduces or impairs the voting rights of already-issued stock, even with shareholder consent.[61] However, even this requirement can be 'evaded' (if that word is appropriate) by a company that is willing to go fully private (buying back all of its stock, or engaging in a cash merger with a new, privately held shell company), and then go public again, with low- or no-vote stock being sold to generate proceeds to pay off any debt used to engage in the buyout. (Likewise, although US tax law discourages pyramids, many US firms sell minority stakes in controlled subsidiaries to the public.)

It is true that shares of DC firms are thought to sell at a discount to what one-share-one-vote structures would produce in IPOs.[62] For that reason, only 5-10% of all new firms, on average, have DC structures in the US, as reflected in Figure 3. But the fact of that discount suggests that IPO investors are not being fooled (at least fully) into paying more than they should for shares of a firm that may never be taken over, even when a takeover would increase the value of the firm in the hands of outside investors. And the presence of the discount on new DC firms says nothing about whether those firms are adding to or reducing social welfare. In order to know that, one would have to know the size of the PBC that the control shareholders retain, and they idiosyncratic value that they place on those PBC; only if the discount was larger than those PBC would one be able to make any statement about the relative efficiency of DC structures.

[61] The current US regulation of DC structures was adopted after much public debate over mid-stream conversions of one-share-one-vote firms to DC structures during the hostile takeover wave of the 1980s. For a policy analysis that helped produce the current US rules, see Gilson (n 23). The current SEC rule was declared to be beyond the SEC's authority in *Business Roundtable v SEC*, 905 F2d 406, 416-17 (DC Cir 1990), thus theoretically enabling the NYSE or the Nasdaq to repeal their rules constraining midstream switches to DC structures, but both the SEC rule and the related NYSE and Nasdaq rules remain on the books.

[62] See Smart & Zutter (n 47) at 104-07 (DC firms have lower price/earnings multiples at IPO than similar single-class firms).

Figure 5: Bid Outcomes for US Firms, by ESB

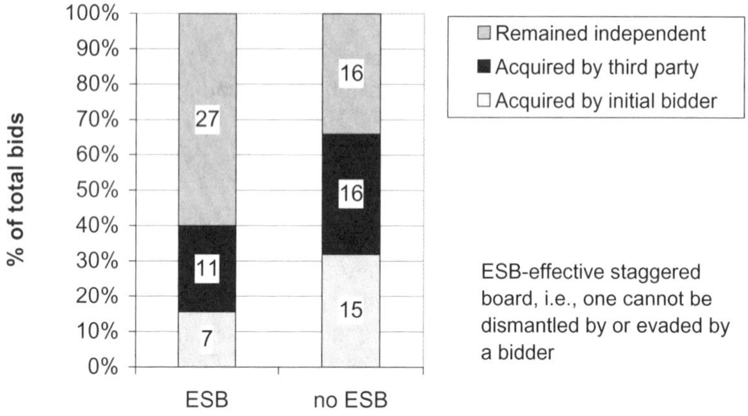

Source: Bebchuk, Coates & Subramanian (2002)

As illustrated by Figure 5, US firms can also greatly reduce the risk of being taken over on a hostile basis in one way not commonly found in the EU: adoption of a staggered board, which has its effect because of the poison pill.[63]

Thus, although contestable control can be found in about one-third to one-half of US public firms, many if not most US public firms do not leave themselves vulnerable to takeover bids. When viewed in that light, the US control market is no more or less contestable than the EU control market, despite the difference in ownership structures reflected in Figure 2.

Gordon points out that there may be other features of the US corporate control environment that could make it harder for managers of US firms to resist takeover bids even if they have the theoretical legal ability to do so.[64] Executive compensation, for example, is notoriously higher in the US than in Europe in large part because it consists of stock options, which in theory could provide managers with incentives to sell (to realize a deal premium, to accelerate vesting requirements, or to convert risky equity into cash). Preliminary analysis of cross-sectional

[63] Bebchuk, Coates and Subramanian (n 18) at 930. The results in Figure 5 are over the nine months following announcement of a bid, and reflect a sample of 92 takeover bids, which comprise all takeover bids for US public companies 1996-2000. Of the targets, 45 had ESBs, 47 did not.

[64] J Gordon 'An American Perspective on the New German Anti-takeover Law, With EU Implications' Working Paper (6 May 2003).

analysis of US firms in the S&P 500, however, suggests that CEOs with more stock option holdings are not, on average, any more likely to sell their firms than other CEOs, and theory also suggests that stock options can have either positive or negative effects on manager incentives to sell the company, depending on (among other things) the volatility of the stock underlying the options and thus the time value of the options relative to their intrinsic value.[65]

Likewise, more general worries that the 'culture' of Europe is less deal-, profit- or shareholder-oriented than in the US run up against the following facts:

- In 1999, 369 bids were reported for European firms, versus 20 for US firms.[66]
- In 1999, the dollar volume of EU hostile activity was 3x that in the US.[67]
- Overall European M&A grew rapidly in the '90s, faster than M&A in the US.[68]
- By 2002, 55% of worldwide M&A was European, more than double US levels.[69]

Whatever else one can say about corporate control in the EU, one cannot say that it is lagging the US in overall deal-making. Nor do the deals seem to harmful to shareholder-interests: Goergen and Reeneboog report that the stock market reaction to announcements of acquisitions of and by European firms are significantly positive for targets and neutral for bidders, as they are in the US.[70] The BTR

[65] JC Coates IV and R Kraakman 'CEO Incentives and Merger Activity in the 1990s: Stock Options and Real Options' Working Paper (7 March 2003).

[66] These data are drawn from the Thomson Financial Securities Data (formerly SDC) database. See also M Goergen and L Renneboog 'Shareholder Wealth Effects in Large European Takeover Bids' Working Paper (2 February 2002) (reporting similar data for Europe, based on a study by Morgan Stanley). My own analysis of data from SDC shows many fewer hostile bids in Europe (67), but still many more than in the US (12), even outside the UK (29).

[67] These data are drawn from the Thomson Financial Securities Data (formerly SDC) database.

[68] JA McCahery, L Renneboog, P Ritter and S Haller 'The Economics of the Proposed European Takeover Directive' Working Paper (May 2003), at 28-30. UK activity represented a disproportionate share of this increase, but nearly 70% of M&A in the EU took place outside the UK. ibid.

[69] These data are from a presentation by Robert Kindler of JP Morgan to the International Bar Association (12 June 2003).

[70] n 66 (tbl. 1). While stock market reactions to acquisitions of UK firms are about double those for non-UK European firms, reactions to acquisitions *by* UK firms have statistically similar stock price reactions as those by non-UK European firms. ibid. (tbl. 3). A minority of US analysts of the M&A market have long been concerned that the high deal premiums expected by US shareholders may impose an inefficient drag on the corporate control market, and have called for legal changes designed to reduce that drag. eg F Easterbrook and D Fischel *The Economic Structure of Corporate Law* (Harvard University Cambridge 1991) at 168-74 (criticizing legal impediments to hostile takeovers); A Schwartz 'Search Theory and the Tender

cont. ...

might stimulate additional M&A activity, and would probably shape the direction and nature of that activity, particularly by increasing cross-border M&A, which remains a non-trivial but minor part of M&A worldwide. Still, it seems hard to argue that the BTR (or the NR, for that matter) is in any sense a prerequisite for a robust M&A market.

E. Summary

In sum, the benefits of the BTR would not clearly be greater than its costs. Practically, the BTR will affect less than 3-4% of all public firms in the EU, leaving many more (more than half of public firms in many countries) outside the hostile takeover market. That is because the primary means by which EU firms remain invulnerable to takeovers is through blockholdings in one-share-one-vote structures. Even as a means of addressing disproportionality more generally (outside the takeover context), the BTR will only affect a minority of firms with disproportional structures, as it will leave intact pyramids and cross-holdings. The BTR will not contribute much to a level playing field, and it will produce dead-weight costs as firms strategically react or anticipate its effects.

More generally, the goals of the BTR – to reduce the incidence of disproportional structures by increasing the degree to which DC firms are exposed to the discipline of takeover bids – are themselves not clearly good from a societal perspective. Even if the BTR would create benefits for shareholders of some firms, or for shareholders in some countries, it will also impose losses on some control shareholders and on society more generally by preventing the use of DC structures to protect good or inherent PBC. Empirical studies of DC structures do not convincingly make the case that DC firms underperform on average. To the extent that some evidence is consistent with DC firms underperforming in some countries but not others, nothing in the BTR will reflect those distinctions. Worse, nothing in the BTR will address the underlying weaknesses in shareholder protection that allow bad PBC to arise in the first place, or that allow bad PBC to become so large in some countries and not others. Whatever one's instincts about disproportional structures, or about takeover-proofedness more generally, there is no clear answer to the question: would a ban on disproportional structures improve or harm social welfare?

These arguments are in addition to those advanced in the UK and elsewhere that the BTR would raise issues under the European Convention on Human Rights (would constitute a 'taking' in US legal parlance) if holders of high vote

Offer Auction' (1986) 2 J L Econ & Org 271 (same); but see LA Bebchuk The Case for Facilitating Competing Tender Offers (1982) 95 Harv L Rev 1028 (defending some legal impediments as adding to shareholder and social welfare).

stock were not compensated for the effects of the BTR.[71] Even if those distributional issues could be addressed with some form of compensation by Member States or by bidders (as recently argued in a draft report on the new DTB by the European Parliament's Committee on Legal Affairs and the Internal Market), the foregoing analysis suggests that the EC was correct to not include the BTR in the new DTB. Whether many of the same points could also be made about the lesser form of the BTR that is contained in the new DTB – the 'mini-BTR' that applies not to DC structures but to transfer restrictions that have similar effects – is an empirical question that depends both on the relative size of bad PBC in the EU, but also on the incidence and importance of firms with restrictions that would be affected by the mini-BTR.

F. Implications

Politics cannot wait on science. Science – particularly social science – is slow. The evidence reviewed above regarding DC structures and concentrated ownership in public firms more generally is inconclusive at best. The difficulties in social science of finding ideal natural experiments or designing and implementing well-specified studies of existing institutions are widely known. Corporate finance, corporate ownership, and the relationships between control and performance across variable political and economic environments are all highly complex and multi-dimensioned. It seems unlikely that any consensus will soon develop about the average (much less the distribution of) benefits of DC structures or other types of takeover defenses.

Yet politics moves in fits and starts, with laws adopted in windows of opportunity that can pass all too quickly. Above the level of details such as the BTR, a high-level need persists for political structures to harmonize and increase transparency of takeover regulation the EU. If there is a political opportunity for a new directive, that opportunity should not be missed. Given the intractable nature of the policy issues involved, the good cannot wait on the perfect. But the image of the perfect – as far in the future as it is – should affect the *way* the good is pursued in the present. With that in mind, I make three specific suggestions about how the BTR should be implemented if it is included in any BTR.

[71] eg City of London Law Society, Company Law Committee, Comments Submitted to the EC on the Text of the Draft Takeover Directive dated 2 October 2002 (December 2002) (comments to draft Arts 10 and 11); cf European Shadow Financial Regulatory Committee, Takeover Bids in Europe Statement No 13 (4 February 2002) (recommending five-year grandfathering to address concerns about 'property rights').

I. Opt-Outs

First, even during the initial period of application of the BTR, the DTB should provide an exemption from its application for companies that go public for the first time and include in their charters (with full disclosure) provisions opting out of the new takeover regime. So long as the disclosure system is working adequately, new investors put on notice as to the vulnerability (or lack thereof) of a firm to the takeover market should be presumed to be better positioned to weigh the costs and benefits of DC structures. This will allow owners of a DC firm that is currently publicly held to undertake (at some expense) a 'cleansing' process of raising sufficient private capital to buy out publicly held low or no vote stock, take their firm private, and then take it public again, with full disclosure. Because of the cost and public scrutiny that will attend such a process, DC firms that survive will be much more likely to be the kinds of firms that have good or inherent PBC motivating their concentrated control structures.

II. Sunsets

Second, the DTB should require EU-level *reenactment* of all of the controversial rules in the DTB, including the BTR (if it is included in the final version), as well as the mini-BTR and the NR. (In US legal parlance, controversial rules such as the BTR should contain 'sunset' provisions.) Currently, the new DTB proposes to require *reconsideration* of the DTB five years after its effectiveness.[72] But given the weight of political inertia in a system with as many checks and balances as the EU, it is likely that any rule that by its terms will remain in force unless altered will in fact remain in force, even if the rule could not then command a new and sufficiently broad enough majority in favor. But because the BTR can plausibly harm social welfare more than it can improve it, a heavier burden should be placed on the political system for it to be locked into place indefinitely.

This suggestion should apply particularly to the BTR. The Takeover Bid Report itself acknowledges that regulations should only cautiously limit contractual freedom (as the BTR does). But the BTR is justified as helping to complete the unification of the EU's internal capital markets, by facilitating ('jump-starting') the takeover market for companies that otherwise would remain invulnerable to a takeover bid. Once that market is up and running, however, the rationale for displacing contractual freedom will steadily diminish over time. Once the benefits (and costs) of a freer market for corporate control become apparent to observers and market participants, a continued willingness by investors to invest in low- or no-vote

[72] If a given rule is delayed in being implemented, of course, the sunset period should not begin to run until the rule is effective. Thus, if the DTB were adopted in 2004 but the BTR were to be effective in 2007, the sunset should occur in 2012.

stock, or otherwise to participate in disproportional structures, should no longer be taken as an uninformed or constrained form of participation, but an indication that such structures may provide sufficient benefits to allow their preservation.

III. Industry-Based Exemptions

Finally, if the BTR or the mini-BTR is adopted, consideration should be given to exempting, or modifying the rule as it applies to, firms in certain industries where good or inherent PBC are likely to be more common. This will necessarily be somewhat arbitrary in operation: not all firms in a given industry will have DC or other takeover-proof structures for the same reason, and some may well be dominated by bad PBC while others are cleanly run. But an industry-based approach seems no more arbitrary than adoption of the rule across the board, without any attempt to take into account the many DC structures that plausibly are adding to social welfare. An industry-based approach could look for guidance to the UK and the US, where DC structures are common but minority structures, and where they are concentrated in certain industries.

G. Alternatives to the BTR: Mandatory Re-Openings

Assuming these suggested modifications are insufficient to permit the adoption of a DTB with any form of the BTR (mini- or otherwise), what alternative rule might address some of the concerns that motivate the BTR? What, in fact, are the best rationales for the BTR? The political rationale – that the BTR is necessary to make more companies vulnerable to takeovers in Member States where DC structures substitute for other types of takeover defenses – is, as we have seen, not plausible unless political actors are (or believe their constituents are) badly informed about the details of the ownership structures of listed EU firms. What if any better rationale exists?

Perhaps the best rationale for the BTR is that many firms with DC structures were established long ago, when the firms had already achieved a then-efficient scale, and it was taken for granted that national borders imposed a high degree of constraint on further expansion of markets. Now that the EU has greatly reduced those constraints, scale economies are not being achieved in the most efficient manner (through M&A transactions) because controllers are unwilling or in some cases legally unable to sell or share control. Some DC structures, for example, include ultimate controllers who are trustees or similar agents who lack the legal power to alter their firms' control arrangements, or even if they have legal power, are so legally constrained in their ability to accept compensation for surrendering control that they have every incentive to resist doing so.[73] In instances where these structures were established several generations ago, the managers of these firms can fairly be said to be subject to the 'dead hand of the past.' To the extent these structures perpetuate national firms operating within national borders, they do in fact pose a barrier to the integration of the EU's internal market, with the political risks that continued fragmentation entails. These concerns, it should be noted, are distinct from those that arise from bad PBC – even if the trustees of a DC firm are perfectly honest and hard-working, taking nothing for themselves and serving solely the interests of shareholders, they could still be constrained by their existing control structure from pursuing efficient integration across national borders if that required giving up or sharing control.

Whether the BTR is the best remedy for such companies, however, is less clear. Instead of a continual prohibition on DC structures, as would be the case under the BTR, a better balance might be achieved with a periodic 're-opening' of control. Similar proposals have gotten some circulation in US legal academic circles in the last few years:[74] perhaps any structure that facilitates takeover-proofedness should be required to be revisited every ten or twenty years at a general meeting of shareholders, at which all shareholders should be given equal rights to vote on continuation of the structure. Such a rule would insure that control of every listed company would be put up for auction every so often, facilitating the integration of the EU's internal market, but would not immediately and permanently displace existing DC structures.

The logic for linking such a rule to the lifecycle of the firm – rather than to any arbitrary enactment date for a new DTB – is essentially the same as that supporting a sunset provision in the DTB itself, and to rationales for more conventional constraints on especially long-lived restraints on trade imposed by contract, certain forms of property, or other private law arrangements.[75] Humans are

[73] M Becht, for example, notes that in 1997, 30 (out of 117) listed firms in the Netherlands – including Royal Dutch / Shell, the 10th largest company in the world – used trust companies and other a DC structure to maintain control over the underlying listed firms. Report on Section 11 – The Proposed Break-Through Rule (May 29-31, 2003), at 8, 18.

[74] eg LA Stout 'Do Antitakeover Defenses Decrease Shareholder Wealth? The Ex Post / Ex Ante Valuation Problem' (2002) 55 Stan L Rev 845, 859.

[75] The rule against perpetuities, for example, has been justified on the ground that currently living persons may be reasonably thought to have legitimate, well-informed preferences regarding how assets will be used by the next generation, but not by the generation after the next. eg R Cooter and Th Ulem *Law and Economics* (2d edn Harper Collins New York 1995) at 133-36. Non-profit organizations, foundations, and trusts, too, are constrained in the US through tax law, which requires them to make current expenditures or grants at specified levels or face current taxation, which effects over time a redistribution of ownership and control over assets from the trustees of those organizations to others, facilitating economic activity and discouraging efforts to lock up assets in perpetuity. See, eg E Brody 'Charitable Endowments and the Democratization of Dynasty' (1997) 39 Ariz L Rev 873; E Brody 'Agents Without Principals: The Economic Convergence of the Nonprofit and For-Profit Organizational Forms'

cont. ...

fallible, particularly as regards the distant future.[76] The likelihood that shareholders (even sophisticated, well-informed shareholders) can adequately understand and price the effects of takeover-proof defenses seems likely to diminish rapidly as the defenses operate into the distant future. Many of the rationales for DC structures – particularly the kinds of good PBC that inhere in specific individuals, such as founders – will tend to fall or disappear entirely if the management team changes or dies. True, some founders want to preserve control in order to pass a company to their descendents, but it hardly seems unreasonable to require such persons to revisit the capital markets every generation as a check on the kind of bad PBC that many observers believe tend to develop in family-dominated firms over time. This would have the Jeffersonian effect of reopening the contestability of control at periodic intervals and putting a check on the worst forms of corporate sclerosis.

H. Conclusion

The BTR was an inspiring, radical idea. It has already had two clearly good effects, one political, one intellectual. Politically, it has helped re-ignite efforts to adopt a DTB, which if successful would have political and economic benefits by helping create a more stable, transparent, and integrated capital market across the EU. Odds remain long that a DTB will be adopted amidst EU efforts to adopt a constitution and add 10 new Member States, but the odds that some form of DTB will eventually be adopted are much higher today than they were prior to the release of the Takeover Bid Report.

Intellectually, the proposal for a BTR has helped stimulate much of the research reviewed in this paper, has shaped academic and governmental studies, and has thus produced information crucial to our still-feeble efforts to understand, predict and effectively regulate the market for corporate control – all forms of under-produced public goods. For this alone, the public owes the authors of the Takeover Bid Report a debt of gratitude. Ironically, however, these studies suggest that the BTR, as proposed, would have minimal effect, either politically or economically, and thus the EC was correct to not include it in its full form in the new DTB.

More broadly, however, the BTR is not, on reflection, clearly a good idea. That is true even if it were supplemented with effective rules addressing the full range of DC structures and the clear substitutes for DC structures (pyramids, cross-holdings), and even if the EC could somehow develop rules designed to disperse

(1996) 40 NYL Sch L Rev 457; H Hansmann 'Why Do Universities Have Endowments?' (1990) 19 J Legal Stud 3; JL Salmon 'Foundations Anxious Over Bill on Giving'; 'Forced Charity Would Hurt Groups' Stability, Some Say' *Washington Post* (8 July 2003) at A03.

[76] As put well by John Stuart Mill, in Principles of Political Economy: 'An exception … to the presumption that … individuals are the best judges of their own interest … is when an individual attempts to decide irrevocably now what will be best … at some … distant time.'

ownership of the bulk of EU listed firms in order to facilitate the development of a more vigorous market for corporate control in Europe. In the absence of that hypothetical world of complete capital markets, different ownership structures can respond to different preferences of owners, to different background conditions, and to different market forces (in the product, labor or ordinary capital markets), and mandatory rules impeding particular ownership structures will produce some degree of social loss. Until the case can be better made that the gains from the BTR (however supplemented) will outweigh those losses, the approach of a cautious, self-consciously fallible regulator would be to defer adopting the BTR. That is particularly true when the regulator (here, the EC) is unable to modify or amend rules easily and quickly in light of changing conditions.

Instead of endorsing the BTR as proposed, I have tentatively suggested two alternatives. The first alternative, or set of alternatives – opt-outs, sunsets, and industry-based exemptions – is designed to minimize the harm that the BTR will inflict, in light of existing and developing research on the varying conditions in which concentrated control of listed firms may be socially optimal. The second alternative – mandatory re-openings – would replace the continual effect of the BTR with a periodically imposed constraint on especially long-lived control structures. This second alternative seems, in my view, to achieve the most defensible goals of the BTR while imposing a much lower level of cost on existing firms and controllers. Even this second alternative is far from perfect – but it is more likely than any version of the BTR to achieve a modest amount of good.

Appendix

Firms used to generate the data reflected in Figure 4. The firms in the first column are 30 US public firms randomly selected from the 200+ firms identified by the Investor Responsibility Research Center as having DC structures in 1998. Proxy statements filed with the SEC were examined to verify that each in fact had a DC structure in which one or a small group of shareholders retained control through high-vote stock while selling low- or no-vote stock to the public. Each firm in the second column are in the same 2-digit SIC code industry group as the firm in the first column, and is approximately the same size in terms of 1997 fiscal year-end total assets.

Dual Class Companies	**2-Digit SIC Industry Group**	**Matched (Non-Dual Class) Companies**
Advanta	Nondepository financial	Green Tree Financia
Alberto Culver	Miscellaneous retail	Cole National
America West Holding	Air transportation	Alaska Airgroup
Brown & Sharpe	Industrial machinery	C-Cube Microsystems
Brown Forman	Food	Interstate Bakeries
Carter Wallace	Chemicals	Dial
Central Newspapers	Printing and publishing	Banta
Crawford	Insurance agents	White River
Dillard's	General merchandise stores	Costco
Dow Jones	Printing and publishing	Ziff-Davis
General Binding	Industrial machinery	Scotsman Industries
Hubbell	Electronics	Komag
Keane	Business services	Rational Software
Kelly Services	Business services	Adobe Systems
Lennar	General building contractors	Ryland Group
Meredith	Printing and publishing	Big Flower
New York Times	Printing and publishing	Gannett
Nike	Rubber and plastic products	Reebok International
Nortek	Lumber and wood products	Premdor
Oshkosh-B'Gosh	Apparel and textile products	Farah
Sotheby's	Business services	Compuware
Tecumseh Products	Industrial machinery	Pentair
Timberland	Leather and leather products	Wolverine
Times Mirror	Printing and publishing	Tribune
Tyson Foods	Food	Ralston Purina
Vishay Intertechnology	Electronics	LSI Logic
Wahington Post	Printing and publishing	McGraw-Hill
Marcus	Hotels and lodging	Four Seasons Hotels
Westwood One	Amusement and recreation	Ameristar Casinos
Wrigley William Jr.	Food	Earthgrains

Make It or Break It: The Break-Through Rule as a Break-Through for the European Takeover Directive?

PETER O. MÜLBERT

The break-through concept is the most recent idea to break the deadlock with respect to EU takeover legislation. As devised by the High Level Group of Company Law Experts, chaired by the Dutch Jaap Winter, the break-through concept would do away with two of the most important types of impediments to takeovers within EU member states. The first part of the paper explores the break-through concept in same detail, particularly with respect to its premises, its two guiding principles – exclusive shareholder decision-making and proportionality –, and the justifications given by the Group for the proposed interventionist rules. The second part of the paper is dedicated to an analysis of the economic effects of the two guiding principles, and in particular of the proposed 'one share one vote'-regime. While there is good reason to support the principle of exclusive shareholder decision-making with respect to takeovers the rationale for a strict 'one share one vote'-regime is more difficult to defend given the mandatory bid rule as an another core element of European takeover legislation. In all, the economic analysis presented in this paper supports the view that given a mandatory bid regime there is no need for European takeover regulation to incorporate an all-encompassing break-through concept based on 'one share, one vote'. On the other hand, apart from raising some difficult new problems the analysis does not identify any compelling argument against the introduction of such a rule either. Thus, it remains to be seen whether the break-through rule dead-ends all efforts of introducing a European takeover regulation or, on the contrary, acts as a catalyst that enables the EU finally to break through to the adoption of a Takeover Directive. The EU Commission, at least, because of strong political resistance from various interested parties only adopted a somewhat watered-down version of the break-through concept in its most recent proposal for a takeover directive of 2 October 2002.

A. Introduction

The concept of a break-through rule is the most recent idea to emerge in the long-standing discussion regarding EU takeover regulation. Broadly understood, the term 'break-through rule' refers to any provision that dispenses with either of two types of impediments to takeovers. The first of these impediments is legal structures and mechanisms that prevent shareholders from reacting to a takeover bid either by tendering their shares to the bidder or by voting on the authorization (or non-authorization) of defensive measures. The second impediment is legal structures that prevent a bidder from exercising control once he has successfully completed his bid and acquired a nominally controlling position in the firm. Both types of impediments are targeted in various ways by the different break-through rules that to date have been presented at the EU level.

The High Level Group of Company Law Experts, in its 'Report of the High Level Group of Company Law Experts on Issues Related to Takeover Bids,'[1] used the term 'break-through rule' with only the second of the above meanings, i.e., with respect to a post-completion break-through. In this vein, the Group recommended a post-completion rule requiring that, for the purpose of shareholder voting in a shareholder assembly, provisions in the articles of association and other constitutional documents of the target company deviating from the principle of 'one share, one vote' be overridden immediately upon the offeror having successfully completed the bid by acquiring at least 75% of all 'shares' (recommendations I.4 – I.7). Predictably, this proposal met with only partial approval. The EU Commission, in particular, adopted a watered-down version of the post-completion break-through rule in its new proposal for a takeover directive.[2] Art. 11 Para. 4, in its present form, deals only with private-law restrictions on the transfer of securities and the exercise of voting rights as well as with any special rights of shareholders concerning the appointment or removal of board members and renders them unenforceable or ineffective at the first general meeting following closure of the bid. Professors Dauner-Lieb and Lamandini, on the other hand, in a subsequent study[3] commissioned by the Committee on Legal Affairs and the Internal Market of the EU Parliament, endorsed the original version of the rule, at least in principle, and recommended an extension of the rule to include, *inter alia,* multiple voting rights and, within certain limits, non-

[1] Report of the High Level Group of Company Law Experts on Issues Related to Takeover Bids of 10 January 2002 (hereinafter referred to as the Winter Report on Takeover Bids) (see Annex 2 in this volume).

[2] Commission Communication on the proposal for a Directive of the European Parliament and the Council on takeover bids of 2 October 2002 <http://www.ecgi.org/takeovers/documents/european/proposal_english.pdf> The proposal itself is contained in the document COM (2002) 534 final and published in Official Journal C 45 of 25 February 2003, p. 1-17 <http://europa.eu.int/eur-lex/en/com/pdf/2002/com2002_0534en01.pdf>.

[3] B Dauner-Lieb and M Lamandini 'The New Proposal of a Directive on Company Law concerning Takeover Bids and the Achievement of a Level Playing Field with Particular Reference to the Recommendations of the High Level Group of Company Law Experts set up by the European Commission' <http://www.europarl.eu.int/comparl/juri/studies/study_complaw_en.pdf>.

voting shares carrying specific pecuniary advantages.[4] Since then, Klaus-Heiner Lehne, as rapporteur to the Committee on Legal Affairs and the Internal Market on the takeover directive, has adopted a similar position. In a preliminary draft of his report to the Committee, he recommended that Art. 11 Para. 4 be altered so that multiple voting rights – but not non-voting shares carrying specific pecuniary advantages – will also fall within the ambit of the break-through rule.[5]

With regard to the decision of the target's shareholders regarding the bid, the High Level Group recommended two rules: (i) that provisions in the articles of association and other constitutional documents deviating from the principle of 'one share, one vote' be overridden in the shareholder meeting required to authorize any defensive action by management that would frustrate the bid (recommendation I.3); and (ii) that provisions in the articles of association and related constitutional documents that restrict the transferability of shares not be enforceable against the selling shareholder or the buying bidder, respectively (recommendation I.9).[6] Furthermore, the Group concluded that the EU Commission should consider the introduction of a rule providing that shareholder agreements that prohibit the transfer of shares not be enforceable against the seller (recommendation I.10). With the exception of securities without voting rights that carry specific pecuniary advantages (Art. 11 Para. 5),[7] the Commission followed these recommendations to some extent. Art. 11 Para. 2 of the draft Takeover Directive provides for the unenforceability of all statutory or contractual transfer restrictions, whereas Para. 3 provides for the ineffectiveness of all statutory or contractual restrictions on voting rights in the case of a decision of the shareholder meeting regarding any defensive measures. In contrast, Professors Dauner-Lieb and Lamandini, as well as Klaus-Heiner Lehne as rapporteur, again sup-

[4] B Dauner-Lieb and M Lamandini (n 3) 36 ff, 59 (summary).

[5] Draft Report on the proposal for a European Parliament and Council directive of on takeover bids of 11 March 2003, PE 327.239 <http://www.ecgi.org/takeovers/documents/european/htsdesktakeover.pdf>.

[6] The recommendation refers only to restrictions on the transferability of non-listed shares, pointing out that the Council Directive of 5 March of 1979 coordinating the conditions for the admission of securities to official stock exchange listing (Official Journal L 66, 16.3.1979, 21) <http://europa.eu.int/smartapi/cgi/sga_doc?smartapi!celexapi!prod!CELEXnumdoc&lg=en&numdoc=31979L0279&model=guichett> requires for the admission of shares to the official stock exchange listing that the shares must be freely negotiable (Schedule A Chapter 2 para 2). However, while the Directive of 28 May 2001 on the admission of securities to official stock exchange listing and on information to be published regarding those securities (Official Journal L 184, 6.7.2001, 1 <http://europa. eu.int/eur-lex/pri/en/oj/dat/2001/l_184/l_18420010706en00010066.pdf> replaced the older listing directive, the admission of shares that may be acquired only subject to approval is still allowed provided that the use of the approval clause does not disturb the market (Art 46 para 3 of the Directive).

[7] The rationale underlying this provision is somewhat difficult to understand. Art 2 para 1 lit. E of the draft Takeover Directive defines 'securities' as transferable securities carrying specific voting rights in a company. Thus, non-voting preference shares are excluded anyway.

ported the extensions outlined above to, at a minimum, shares with double or multiple voting rights.

The mixed reception of the break-through concept, and in particular of the post-completion break-through rule, by Member States and by other interested parties as well as by academics[8] may be read as an indication that this interventionist approach is fraught with substantial problems. Indeed, apart from obvious political considerations,[9] critics have raised serious objections on economic grounds and, furthermore, have pointed to legal problems caused by the introduction of a post-completion break-through rule. A more detailed discussion of these problems, however, first requires some clarification with regard to the underlying rationale for, as well as the different contents of, the break-through concept.

The remainder of the paper is organized as follows: Section II examines the approach of the High Level Group in some detail. It describes core building blocks of the proposal and analyses the line of reasoning employed by the Group to derive the break-through concept. Sections III and IV discuss the two guiding principles employed by the Group in some detail, particularly with respect to their justification on efficiency grounds. Section V offers some concluding remarks.

B. The Break-Through Concept of the High Level Group

I. The Premise: the Creation of a Pan-European Level Playing Field

The High Level Group arrived at the post-completion break-through rule as well as the related rules in three steps.[10] The Group began with the premise that any European takeover regulation should aim at creating a level playing field for EU cross-border takeovers despite existing differences in national company law

[8] eg E Berglöf and M Burkhart '"Break-Through" in European Takeover Regulation?' Site Staff Paper no 02/03 (Stockholm School of Economics) 22 September 2002 <http://web.hhs.se/site/Publications/staffpapers/SP0203Sep.pdf>; L Bebchuck and OD Hart 'A threat to dual-class shares – The recommendation of the breakthrough rule fails to recognize its broader implications' *Financial Times* (31 May 2002) <http://www.ecgi.org/takeovers/media/articles/bebchuk_hart_ft.pdf>; A Khachaturyan 'Can Bolkestein Finally Break the Takeover Directive Deadlock?' CEPS Commentary March 2003 <http://www.ceps.be/Commentary/Mar03/Khachaturyan.php>; UH Schneider 'Die Break-through-rule und die holländische Poison Pill' *Börsenzeitung* (27 February 2002) 13. For a contrary view, see. Eg H Krause 'Der Kommissionsvorschlag für eine Revitalisierung der EU-Übernahmerichtlinie' (2002) 57 Betriebs-Berater 2341, 2347.

[9] The number of companies affected by the break-through rule is unevenly distributed among Member States. Scandinavian, Italian and German companies would be affected in disproportionate high numbers. See in more detail M Bennedsen and K Nielsen 'The impact of a break-through rule on European firms' (2002) Copenhagen Business School Working Paper 12 <http://www.cbs.dk/departments/econ/res/wpec122002.pdf>.

[10] As to the following, see Winter Report on Takeover Bids (n 1) 20, 26.

mechanisms and structures, as well as substantial differences in the capital and control structures of companies from different Member States. The Group then went on to postulate that this objective should be realized by the application of two guiding principles, namely shareholder decision-making and proportionality between risk bearing and control. Finally, it concluded that these two principles can only achieve a level playing field if a takeover regulation provides for far-reaching break-through mechanisms during a bid and after its completion.

Upon closer inspection, this line of reasoning appears somewhat problematic. Obviously, any set of principles can lead to a level playing field provided that the principles and the rules derived from them are applicable to all market participants in a uniform manner. Thus, the two guiding principles selected by the High Level Group to achieve a level playing field are in truth the (implicit) premises that underpin the rest of the Group's reasoning. In other words, given the premise that takeover regulation is governed by two principles – shareholder decision-making and proportionality – the creation of a level playing field for takeover bids requires, according to the High Level Group, that there be some break-through mechanisms at work. The fact that the two principles are far more fundamental than the aim of creating a level playing field becomes even more apparent in the report delivered by the High Level Group itself. Before working out the application of the two principles in the context of takeovers, the Group considered whether these two principles, being fundamental principles of company law in general, should be applied to all pre-bid structures and company law mechanisms that lead to a concentration of control rights in the hands of the board and/or shareholders. The Group refrained from going into details, however, pointing primarily to the short time given to produce to the report.[11]

The reason for the High Level Group's election to proceed from the starting point of creation of a level playing field instead of from the two guiding principles is probably to be found in the terms of the Group's mandate from the EU Commission. According to these terms, one of the three matters for the Group to examine was the measures necessary to ensure the existence of a level playing field in the EU with regard to the equal treatment of shareholders among Member States.[12]

The mandate's terms of reference did not, however, specify any guidelines with respect to the measures that might be considered in order to create a level playing field. By choosing two particular guiding principles – shareholder decision-making and proportionality – the Group made fundamental policy decisions of its own choosing. Admittedly, Art. 9 Para. 2 of the draft Takeover Directive, as approved by the Conciliation Committee on 6 June 2001,[13] already enshrined the

[11] Winter Report on Takeover Bids (n 1) 23 ff.

[12] Winter Report on Takeover Bids (n 1) 16, 70 (annex 1).

[13] Directive on company law concerning takeover bids, PE-CONS 3629/1/01 REV 1 of 19 June 2001 (annex 6 to the Winter Report on Takeover Bids).

principle of shareholder decision-making by providing that, in order to take defensive measures in the face of a bid, the board of the target company must first obtain the prior authorization of the general meeting of shareholders once a bid has been made. This provision, however, together with the lack of any break-through mechanisms as a means to create a level playing field, constituted one of the main reasons why the German rapporteur to the Committee on Legal Affairs and the Internal Market of the EU Parliament on the takeover directive, Klaus-Heiner Lehne, and the German government opposed the then-current draft of the directive and why the Parliament ultimately failed to adopt the directive by casting a tie vote.[14] Given this background, the Group could equally well have chosen another set of premises and could have come up with very different answers to the problem of establishing a level playing field. Therefore, an evaluation of the Group's break-through recommendations must start with a review of its premises, i.e., a review of the two guiding principles and the manner in which the Group applied them to takeover bids.

II. The Two Guiding Principles

1. Shareholder Decision-Making

Shareholder supremacy asserts itself primarily in the principle of shareholder decision-making. Applied in the context of a takeover bid, this principle, as developed by the High Level Group, has two meanings:

First, it is exclusively up to the shareholders of the target company – and not to its management – to decide on the outcome of a takeover bid (recommendation I.2). If takeover law or company law allows any authorization of defensive measures by shareholder resolution, the shareholder decision-making comes in two forms: the decision whether to tender the shares (recommendations I.9 – I.10) and the vote in the shareholder meeting on the approval of such defensive measures (recommendation I.3). Furthermore, if the bidder succeeds in acquiring a controlling position, it is up to him to choose the new management team that will run the company (recommendations I.4. – I.7).

Second, only decisions of the target company's shareholders taken in reference to an actual bid are to be decisive for the outcome of that bid. Thus, prior to a bid being received, shareholders are not able to vest in the board the power to take defensive actions (recommendation I.2). Once shareholders have received a bid, statutory restrictions on the transfer of shares are not enforceable against the

[14] The events leading up to the tie vote of Parliament are outlined in the Winter Report on Takeover Bids (n 1) 14 ff and in the Commission Communication (n 2) 2; for a more detailed account see JN Gordon 'An International Relations Perspective on the Convergence of Corporate Governance: German Shareholder Capitalism and the European Union 1990-2000' Working Paper No 108 49 ff (download at <www.uni-frankfurt.de/fb01/baums/>).

bidder or seller, respectively (recommendation I.9[15]). In the same vein, the Group recommends that the Commission at least consider a rule pursuant to which shareholder agreements that prohibit the transfer of shares to a bidder be unenforceable (recommendation I.10).

2. Proportionality

The principle of proportionality between risk-bearing and control in the context of a takeover bid as developed by the High Level Group has two meanings as well:

First, all holders of risk-bearing capital, i.e., holders of rights to residual profits and/or assets of the company,[16] are entitled to participate in shareholder decision-making with regard to takeover bids. Basically, that means that any holder of a residual right to the cash flow of the target company is entitled to take part in takeover-related decisions. This applies to decisions of the target company's shareholders on the outcome of a takeover bid – all holders of risk-bearing capital are entitled to vote on the authorization of defensive measures (recommendation I.3), and the unenforceability of transfer restrictions applies to all risk-bearing shares (recommendation I.9) – as well as to the vote on any shareholder resolution in a general meeting convened by the bidder after the successful completion of the bid (recommendation I.7[17]).

Second, all holders of risk-bearing capital are entitled to exercise votes in proportion to their holding of risk-bearing capital – for short, 'one share, one vote.' Again, this holds true for a shareholder resolution on the authorization of defensive measures[18] as well as for a vote on any shareholder resolution in a post-completion general meeting.[19]

III. The Justification of the Break-Through Concept

Accepting the two guiding principles and the aim of creating a level playing field as given still does not mean that, in order to reach this objective, European takeover regulation has to incorporate the broad break-through rules devised by the High Level Group. The Group itself dealt in a rather summary fashion with the fundamental question of whether its broad break-through concept is necessary,

[15] As to the erroneous restriction of this recommendation to non-listed shares see n 6.

[16] Winter Report on Takeover Bids (n 1) 21.

[17] Not only the bidder but also other holders of risk-bearing capital should be entitled to vote in proportion to their holdings. See Winter Report on Takeover Bids (n 1) 35.

[18] Winter Report on Takeover Bids (n 1) 28

[19] Winter Report on Takeover Bids (n 1) 32, 35.

justifiable or even advisable.[20] With regard to the principle of shareholder decision-making, the Group simply asserted that this is a necessary precondition for the full development of the European securities markets. Furthermore, it observed that, while a fully integrated and well-developed securities market might do without the principle of proportionality, such efficient markets do not currently exist across Europe. Given this factual and legal environment within the EU, the Group concluded that, in order to establish securities markets in the EU which both are efficient and provide an adequate level of investor protection, more detailed break-through rules at the EU level were needed. Aside from three exceptions – 'golden shares,' contractual arrangements,[21] and holding pyramids – these more detailed rules are designed to remove any deviation from the principle of 'one share, one vote' as elaborated by the High Level Group or, in other words, from the principle that 'holders of risk-bearing securities are to decide takeover-relevant questions on a strictly proportional basis in the present.'

In general, there are several levels on which to address the policy question of whether to introduce a break-through concept, e.g., political, economical and legal considerations. Apart from obvious fortunate coincidences on the political level – a full-scale break-through rule would to a large degree take account of Germany's objections with respect to board neutrality (Art. 9 of the draft Takeover Directive) the High Level Group argues on an economic level by suggesting that only efficient securities markets can do without the principle of 'one share, one vote,' while the European factual and legal environment requires the elimination of national laws that allow for statutory and/or contractual takeover barriers in order to achieve efficient securities markets within the EU and a high(er) level of investor protection.

This argument is somewhat difficult to evaluate. In particular, the implied relationship between the relative degree of market efficiency and the need to remove statutory or contractual takeover barriers seems unclear. Indeed, if at least some European markets were informationally less efficient, these obstacles might be less accurately reflected in stock prices. The deviations, however, might be randomly distributed – and in that case takeover barriers would probably curtail takeover activity no more than in an informationally efficient market. The Group's additional assertion that, in the long run, structures deviating from the two guiding principles should wither and die out in efficient markets, except to the extent that they are justified by the particular circumstances of a company, is at least not corroborated by circumstantial evidence (e.g., Ford Motor Company). More generally speaking, so far even US companies have been far more likely to introduce additional takeover defences than to abolish existing ones. In the same

[20] As to the following, see Winter Report on Takeover Bids (n 1) 20 ff.

[21] As to a possible exception with respect to shareholder agreements that prohibit the transfer of shares, see recommendation I.10.

vein, in the past decade, a considerable number of companies went public in the US securities markets with rather strong anti-takeover defences in place.[22]

It is even more difficult to see why allocatively less efficient markets would of necessity suffer more heavily from barriers to takeovers than more efficient ones. Admittedly, such obstacles might be the cause of additional allocative inefficiencies. But why should these additional inefficiencies be systematically higher in markets that are allocatively less efficient for other reasons? Indeed, the High Level Group seemed to have quite the opposite mechanism in mind:[23] European securities markets are less integrated than their US counterparts and, therefore, cross-border takeovers are less frequent, leading to allocatively less efficient markets. Removing barriers to takeovers will facilitate economically beneficial takeovers by making them less costly. This leads to a higher occurrence of takeovers and brings about allocatively more efficient securities markets.

In contrast to golden share-type restrictions, however, shareholders themselves – either the existing shareholders of the target company or the bidder after the successful completion of his bid – can in principle remove statutory and contractual obstacles to takeovers. Whether a sufficient number of shareholders are willing to eliminate the barriers, e.g., statutory restrictions on the transfer of shares, and/or are willing to tender their shares to the bidder depends, other things being equal, on the price the bidder offers. If a break-through rule is in place, however, shares carrying control rights that deviate from the principle of 'one share, one vote' will decrease in value and it will be less costly for a bidder to acquire a controlling stake in the company. Ultimately, thus, the break-through concept of the High Level Group can be sketched as follows: in order to facilitate takeovers and to increase their occurrence control rights are to be redistributed among all holders of risk-bearing capital according to the principle of 'one share, one vote' thereby making it less costly to acquire a controlling stake.

Upon closer inspection, however, this seemingly appealing concept becomes somewhat less obvious. Consider the following two numerical examples:

- Company X has issued 100,000 A shares with single voting rights that currently trade at 10 Euro, and 100,000 B shares with triple voting rights that currently trade at a premium of 20%. A bidder who wants to acquire a controlling stake, e.g., 75% of all voting rights, needs to buy only all of the

[22] See R Daines and M Klausner 'Do IPO Charters Maximize Firm Value? Antitakeover Provisions in IPOs' (2001) 17 Journal of Law, Economics and Organization 83, 95 ff; in particular with respect to dual-class share IPOs – ordinary common stock is issued to the public while insiders retain a class of shares with superior voting rights – see SB Smart and CJ Zutter 'Control as a motivation for underpricing: a comparison of dual- und single-class IPOs' Working Paper <www.ssrn.com> 5: by the late 1990s, about one in nine IPO firms adopted dual-class ownership, and those one in nine accounted for nearly 24% of aggregate IPO proceeds.

[23] See Winter Report on Takeover Bids (n 1) 22.

Class B shares, i.e., 50% of all cash flow rights, at a price of 1,200,000 Euro. If a break-through rule were in place, however, he would have to buy all of the Class B shares and an additional 50 % of the Class A shares. Assuming an even redistribution of the control premium among the two share classes, the bidder would have to pay 1,650,000 Euro, but would now be acquiring a total of 75% of the cash flow rights. Clearly, whether the bidder would prefer to obtain control by acquiring shares with multiple voting rights or under the 'one share, one vote' regime depends on the amount of private benefits the controlling shareholder is able to extract.

- Company X has issued 100,000 non-voting Class C shares that trade at 10 Euro and 100,000 Class D shares of common stock that currently trade at a premium of 20 %. Without a break-through rule in place, the bidder would only have to acquire 75% of the Class D shares at a price of 900,000 Euro; otherwise he would have to acquire all of class D shares as well as 50% of the Class C shares at a total price of 1,650,000 Euro. In the second case, the acquisition requires a much higher price – 1,650,000 Euro instead of 900,000 Euro – but the bidder also acquires a much higher percentage of residual cash flow rights – 75% instead of 37.5%. Again, the bidder's preference will, other things being equal, depend on the amount of private benefits a controlling shareholder is able to extract.

Both examples serve to illustrate a more general result:[24] from the perspective of a potential bidder the break-through rule does not necessarily work to his advantage. Whether he prefers to obtain control in a 'one share, one vote' regime, i.e., the acquisition of a corresponding number of voting rights and cash flow rights, or instead by acquiring a comparatively higher number of voting rights, depends, *inter alia*, on his ability as a controlling shareholder to extract private benefits. Thus, depending on the quality of the respective corporate law regime and, in particular, on the protection of minority shareholders the introduction of a break-through rule might even lead to a lower instead of a higher probability of takeovers occurring.

On the other hand, this (potential) problem does not exist within the confines of a mandatory bid regime. Put differently, a mandatory bid rule requiring the bidder to extend the bid to several – or even to all – classes of risk-bearing securities eliminates the bidder's option to obtain control by acquiring a comparatively higher number of voting rights. At present, Art. 5 of the draft Takeover Directive requires that the mandatory bid be addressed only to all holders of securities, i.e., to all holders of transferable securities carrying voting rights (Art. 2 Para. 1 (e)).[25] The High Level Group refrained from recommending an even

[24] For a more detailed discussion of the economic effects of the 'one share, one vote'-element of the break-through rule see D.II.3.

[25] This limitation is consistent with the scope of the break-through rule in Art. 11 that covers shares with multiple voting rights but not non-voting shares (Art. 11 para 5).

further extension of the mandatory bid rule. Arguably, the inclusion of other classes of risk-bearing capital would make a bid more costly and, thus, would lower the probability of takeover bids.

The upshot of the preceding discussion is that the economic effects of a break-through concept are difficult to assess, at best. In order to compare a takeover regime without a break-through rule and a takeover regime based on the principle of 'one share, one vote', one would have to calculate the costs and benefits of both designs. Apart from the relative change in takeover activity and the economic effects therefrom, one would also have to assess, for example, the effects that result from different possibilities for designing specific bundles of cash flow rights and voting rights. Given these difficulties the following sections will not undertake a comprehensive cost-benefit analysis of the break-through concept. Instead, they aim at reaching a more comprehensive assessment by separately analysing the different components of the two guiding principles – shareholder decision-making and proportionality – and the corresponding elements of the break-through concept derived from them.

C. Shareholder Decision-Making

I. Shareholders as Exclusive Decision-Makers

The shareholders of a target company – and not its management – are to decide on the outcome of a takeover bid. This postulate translates into the duty of a board and its members to remain passive respectively neutral in the face of a bid. To be more precise, baring the search for competing bids, the board has to abstain from all actions that may result in the frustration of a bid (Art. 9 Para.2 of the draft Takeover Directive).

Right from the start, the rule of passivity has been a central feature of the successive proposals for a EU Takeover Directive. Furthermore, until very recently, the duty of passivity seemed to become the uniformly accepted regulatory standard for all EU Member States. The consensus among Member States, however, broke down in 2001 once the EU Parliament, on a tie vote, had failed to accept the then-current draft of the Takeover Directive. As is well known, the German legislator used this development to do away with the hitherto hardly disputed all-encompassing rule of passivity. Due to a last minute revision of the 2002 Act on the Acquisition of Securities and on Takeovers (Wertpapiererwerbs- und Übernahmegesetz), Sect. 31 Para. 1 of the Act requires only in principle that the management board takes no actions that may frustrate the bid and allows for three exceptions: (i) actions that a prudent and diligent manager of a company that is not affected by a takeover bid would have taken similarly, (ii) the search for competing bids, (iii) actions to which the supervisory board of the offeree company has consented.[26] This reorientation, however, only reflects the influence of German industry and German labour unions, not a changed perception of the drawbacks and doubtful merits of unilateral resistance of the target company's board, i.e., of defensive measures without shareholder authorization. On the contrary, occasional exceptions notwithstanding, academics have continued to support the principle of passivity as a sound policy for regulating board behaviour in a takeover situation.[27]

Indeed, takeover regulation should not provide for unilateral defensive measures by the target company's board. Most participants in the extensive discussion on the benefits and drawbacks of defences have explicitly or implicitly acknowledged that defences can harm shareholders by increasing agency costs. This effect notwithstanding, some commentators have argued that defences may also benefit shareholders for any or all of the three following reasons:[28] (i) Anti-takeover mechanisms may alleviate the pressure on shareholders to tender by allowing managers to block coercively designed bids; (ii) the availability of defensive measures improves the bargaining position of the target management's board and allows the board to negotiate with the bidder for a higher premium and/or to search for a competing bid; (iii) defensive measures may allow managers to prevent shareholders from accepting inadequate bid price offers in certain situations, i.e., if the mispricing results from general market myopia or

[26] For two reasons, there is still uncertainty as to the ambit of this exception to the rule of passivity. First, the exact scope of the supervisory board's competence to allow defensive measures is disputed. A good number of academics claim that the supervisory board can only authorize such measures that do not fall within the ambit of s 33 para 2, ie if the shareholder meeting lacks the competence to authorize the defensive measure in question by way of a pre-bid resolution grounded in s 33 para 2 (see eg W Bayer 'Vorsorge- und präventive Abwehrmaßnahmen gegen feindliche Übernahmen' (2002) 31 Zeitschrift für Gesellschafts- und Unternehmensrecht 588, 602, 611 ff; H Hirte 'Verteidigung gegen Übernahmeangebote und Rechtsschutz des Aktionärs gegen die Verteidigung' (2002) 31 Zeitschrift für Gesellschafts- und Unternehmensrecht 623, 640 ff; also in H Hirte in: same (ed) *Kölner Kommentar zum WpÜG* (Cologne 2003) s 33 n 79 ff). Other commentators, most notably practitioners, are less restrictive arguing that the supervisory board can even authorize defensive measures that, in principle, could also be subject to a pre-bid authorization by the shareholder meeting (as to this debate, see the discussion report by Heinrich 'Bericht über die Diskussion' (2002) 31 Zeitschrift für Unternehmens- und Gesellschaftsrecht 659 ff). Second, even if one accepts the broader interpretation the supervisory board is still under a duty to act in the interests of the company as a whole ('Unternehmensinteresse') (see ie H Hirte 642 ff; also in Hirte, s 33 n 84). Thus, the approval of any wealth destroying transaction is excluded per se. Among the rather short list of permissible measures the supervisory board will primarily consider using an authorized capital by way of excluding preemptive rights and, to a lesser degree, buying back own shares of the company.

[27] Berglöf and Burkhart (n 8) 33.

[28] For an overview, see eg J Coates 'Explaining Variation in Takeover Defenses: Blame the Lawyers' (2001) 89 California Law Review 1301, 1329 ff.

from the target company undertaking projects the value of which is difficult to assess.

However, as argued elsewhere in considerable detail,[29] none of these three arguments justifies a default rule to the effect that the target board is allowed to employ defensive measures without the prior authorization of shareholders once a bid to the target's shareholders is imminent or has already been launched. As a general policy guideline, takeover regulation, because of diversified investor portfolios and the beneficial disciplinary effects of the takeover threat, should not necessarily be geared towards maximizing takeover premia. Furthermore, even if one were to adhere to the contrary view, allowing managers to resist to a bid without shareholder authorization does not seem a wise policy given the severe agency problems in a takeover situation and the availability of other mechanisms that are less harmful to shareholders. To be more specific: For one, because of the unavailability of the flip-in poison pill as a defensive mechanism in EU Member States,[30] managers may well have to resort to the type of wealth-destroying measures that were employed in the US before the introduction of the pill.[31] Moreover, from the European angle, the US solution to mitigate the conflict of interest between managers and shareholders in a takeover situation, i.e., the accelerated cash-out of high stock option-grants and/or other high severance payments may well be socially unacceptable or even illegal. In Germany, for example, Sect. 33 Para. 3 of the Act on the Acquisition of Securities and on Takeovers (Wertpapiererwerbs- und Übernahmegesetz) prohibits that the bidder, or any person acting in concert with him, grants unjustified benefits to any member of the target's boards in connection with the bid. Furthermore, on a more general level, Sect. 87 of the German Stock Corporation Act (Aktiengesetz) stipulates that the total compensation of management board members has to be appropriate in light of the tasks of the manager and the situation of the company. As of 21 May 2001, the Government Commission German Corporate Governance Code, giving in to popular demands in the press and governmental guidance by the German Ministry of Justice, even amended the German Corporate Governance Code to the effect that the supervisory board of a company shall determine a discretionary cap on stock options grants and comparable remuneration schemes for 'extraordinary, unforeseen developments'.[32] Finally, even the pressure to

[29] As to the following, see PO Mülbert and M Birke 'In Defense of Passivity – on the Proper Role of a Target's Management in Response to a Hostile Tender Offer' (2000) 1 European Business Organization Law Review 567, 584 ff, 589 ff.

[30] See Government Commission German Corporate Governance Code, Press Release of 21 May 2003 <http://www.corporate-governance-code.de/eng/news/presse-20030521. html>.

[31] As to this assessment, see J Gordon 'Das deutsche "Anti"-Übernahmegesetz aus US-Perspektive' (2002) 47 AG 670, 673.

[32] Pursuant to Art 25 para 1 of the Second Directive (Official Journal L 26 of 31 January 1977 <http://europa.eu.int/smartapi/cgi/sga_doc?smartapi!celexapi!prod!CELEXnumdoc&lg=en&numdoc=31977L0091&model=guichett>), the competence to decide on a raise of capital resides

cont. ...

tender target shareholders may experience does not warrant unilateral managerial resistance. All that would follow from accepting the premise of shareholders being subject to pressure to tender is that shareholders themselves should be allowed to resist takeover bids or to authorize target management to resist. Moreover, a mandatory full bid rule such as proposed in Art. 5 of the draft Takeover Directive would eliminate the threat of coercive bids by looters more effectively than allowing management resistance could ever do.

II. Post-Bid Shareholder Decision-Making

Shareholder decisions with respect to the outcome of a takeover bid are only relevant if shareholders decide after having received the bid, i.e., if they make their decision with full knowledge of the bid's terms. This restriction precludes an ex ante authorization of management to take defensive actions as well as the application of statutory or contractual restrictions on the transferability in a takeover situation.

However, even before the recommendation of the High Level Group many representatives of industry and some academics strongly argued in favour of allowing an anticipatory shareholder authorization of defensive actions.[33] In particular, the discussion in Germany prior to the enactment of the Act on the Acquisition of Securities and on Takeovers (Wertpapiererwerbs- und Übernahmegesetz) in its final stage almost exclusively centred on whether or not to allow the (in)famous 'Ermächtigungsbeschlüsse' respectively 'Vorratsbeschlüsse'. As is well known, in the end, the German legislature provided for a hitherto unlawful form of shareholder resolution that, within the next 18 months, allows management to take certain actions that aim at frustrating the success of takeover bids (Sect. 33 Para. 2 of the Act).[34]

Opponents of this shareholder choice-model will point to the obvious danger that management will make use of such a 'carte blanche' even if such a course of action is disadvantageous to the present shareholders and only serves the interests of the managers. Proponents of this model might respond by questioning why the legislator should be concerned by such inefficient outcomes. After all, as owners of the company, shareholders are free to make decisions that are potentially

solely with the shareholder assembly and never with the board alone. As to the several decisions of the European Court of Justice reinforcing this rule, see eg M Habersack *Europäisches Gesellschaftsrecht* (2nd edn Beck München 2003) [187 ff].

[33] eg UH Schneider and Burgard 'Übernahmeangebot und Konzerngründung – Zum Verhältnis von Übernahmerecht, Gesellschaftsrecht und Konzernrecht' (2001) 54 Betrieb 963, 968 ff.

[34] For an overview, see Lohrmann and C von Dryander in G Apfelbacher, S Barthelemess, TM Buhl and C von Dryander *German Takeover Law – A Commentary* (Beck Juristischer Verlag 2002) s 33 n 22 ff; for an in-depth analysis see H Hirte in ibid (n 26) s 33 n 95 ff.

detrimental to themselves, i.e., that allow management to frustrate a bid even if ex post shareholders will find it in their interest that management cannot interfere with the acceptance of the bid. In particular, the sole owner of a company could well state in advance his unconditional unwillingness to sell (sole owner standard). Furthermore, shareholders also benefit from the principle of private autonomy, i.e., within the general limits for private decision-making shareholders can make decisions even to their own disadvantage.[35]

The sole owner standard, however, does not go very far in justifying an ex ante shareholder authorization of defensive measures. As argued elsewhere,[36] a sole owner would not be bound by his own prior declaration. Given the favourable terms of an actual offer, he could still disregard his earlier statement and accept the offer. In contrast, allowing ex ante shareholder authorization of defensive measures would bind the shareholders insofar as they would have to repeal their former resolution in order to make sure that management would not interfere and prevent the shareholders from being able to accept the offer. Thus, even the sole owner standard requires that shareholders decide ex post in defending against a particular bid.

Upon closer inspection, even shareholder autonomy does not support an ex ante shareholder authorization of defensive measures. Obviously, management would have only to resort to a prior authorization of this kind if present shareholders, after having received a bid, were unwilling to allow defensive actions. Why, then, should the former majority of (past) shareholders be able to bind an unwilling majority of present shareholders with regard to an actual takeover bid? Proponents of the shareholder choice model fail to provide any convincing argument as to why company law should allow the majority of shareholders to protect their interests with regard to the ownership structure even after they have been reduced to a minority position. In particular, the pressure to tender-problem does not require the possibility of an ex ante authorization of defensive measures. Takeover law could sufficiently alleviate the pressure on shareholders to tender their shares to the bidder by providing for the possibility of a conditional acceptance, i.e., an acceptance on condition that the majority of shareholders unconditionally tender their shares.[37] Moreover, even if the bidder – in accordance with

[35] eg J McCahery 'Commentary on The Draft Takeover Directive' 2 ff <www.europarl.eu.int/hearings/20030128/juri/mccahery.pdf>.

[36] PO Mülbert and M Birke (n 29) 600.

[37] Rules such as s 16 para 2 of the German Act on the Acquisition of Securities and on Takeovers (*Wertpapiererwerbs- und Übernahmegesetz*) achieve a similar effect by allowing shareholders that have not accepted the bid within the acceptance period to still tender their shares within a certain period. The HLG Report recommends a technically similar solution in the form of a sell-out right setting the threshold for triggering the sell-out right at the 90% level for each class of securities (recommendation III.1./4./5.). However, this class-by-class requirement flatly contradicts the Group's concept of including all risk-bearing securities on a proportional basis. Furthermore, a severe inconsistency exists between the 90% threshold

cont. ...

recommendation I.3 of the HLG Report – were allowed to vote on the shareholder resolution on defensive measures, minority protection by way of an ex ante authorization of defensive measures would not be justified or even required. The votes exercised by the bidder could, other things being equal, only lead to a different outcome from the former vote on the ex ante authorization of defensive measures if the bidder acquired his shares from one of the shareholders having voted in favour of the former authorization – which would mean that the former majority of shareholders had already been reduced to a minority position.

Admittedly, this line of reasoning might ultimately lead to the conclusion that the legislator should ban all pre-bid defensive structures created by shareholders that deter a takeover bid or make it less likely to occur. However, even if one does not embrace such a sweeping prohibition the rule of post-bid decision-making by shareholders still seems to be the appropriate solution. The fact that shareholders willingly buy into a company with pre-bid defensive structures in place does not allow any conclusions as to the rule shareholders would prefer in the face of a concrete bid. Given the severe agency problems in takeover situations shareholders would clearly prefer to decide ex post on defensive measures unless they would substantially benefit from management acting independently from any actual shareholder authorization of defensive measures. However, it is hard to see, why this should be the case. In particular, even if the individual company in case is engaged in difficult-to-value projects shareholders would not decide on the outcome of the bid, i.e., would not be asked to evaluate the adequacy of the offer and react by either accepting or rejecting the offer. Instead, shareholders would only be called upon to decide whether to allow management to employ defensive actions, i.e., they would only need to evaluate whether the offer might be inadequate, and could leave any subsequent bargaining with the bidder to the management.

D. Proportionality

I. Holders of Risk-Bearing Securities as Decision-Makers

The extension of the break-through concept to encompass all holders of risk-bearing securities has the effect that non-shareholders are vested with a partial voting right. This redefinition of minimum property rights attached to all residual cash flow rights will cause a number of market participants to adapt their hold-

triggering the sell-out right and the 75% threshold triggering the conversion of the company to a 'one share one vote' regime. As an effective mechanism to alleviate the pressure to tender-problem the sell-out right would have to be triggered once the bidder obtains a majority of shares or, according to the concept of the HLG, a majority of all risk-bearing capital.

ings by buying or selling shares or other risk-bearing securities.[38] To this degree, the redistribution of voting rights is a costly measure and, if unnecessary, is to be avoided. Furthermore, there might be additional inefficiencies because of over-protection of some classes of risk-bearing securities or their holders.

Owners of residual cash flow rights are particularly vulnerable and prey to expropriation through opportunistic behaviour by the company or its management. Thus, holders of such securities need some mechanism that enables them to protect their investment effectively. Jurisdictions within the EU are aware of two very different mechanisms to address this problem:

- the market-based solution, pursuant to which the (future) holder of a residual cash flow right enters into a contractual relationship with the company; and
- the solution offered by company law proper, pursuant to which the holder becomes a member of the company and participates in the governance of the company by exercising the rights conferred on him as a member, e.g., by exercising his voting rights.

Given this dichotomy, the all-encompassing proportionality principle supported by the High Level Group may well result in overprotecting some classes of risk-bearing securities. Owners of residual cash flow rights that can resort to market-based contractual arrangements to protect their investments do not need any additional voting right as a (quasi-)member of the company,[39] i.e., a voting right with respect to the authorization of defensive measures. On the other hand, any break-through rule ought to include owners of (preferred) non-voting stock who are entitled to exercise a vote in the shareholder assembly if the company defaults on the payment of dividends or other (preferential) rights. Clearly, these types of securities correspond to common stock insofar as company law provides for a vote as the fundamental protective mechanism. Thus, if the EU were to introduce the break-through concept, Art. 11 Para. 3 (and 2) of the proposed Takeover Directive should be amended to the effect that (preferred) non-voting stock be included as well.

Admittedly, the foregoing argument applies primarily to the participation in the voting on the shareholder authorization of defensive measures. However, all classes of securities that are entitled to vote on this authorization should be entitled to vote as well if the post-completion break-through rule were triggered, i.e., in a shareholder assembly held after the successful completion of the bid. Otherwise, minority shareholders that were unable to block the transfer of control to the

[38] In the following analysis all types of risk-bearing securities will be referred to as 'shares'.

[39] For a parallel position with regard to the scope of the mandatory bid see H Baum, 'Vorzüge und Genussrechte in übernahmerechtlicher Sicht' (2003) 15 Zeitschrift für Bankwirtschaft und Bankrecht 9, 18 ff: the mandatory is to be addressed only to holders of securities carrying corporate law-specific membership rights.

bidder would in some cases still be in a position to prevent the bidder from exercising control. Again, if the EU were to introduce the break-through concept Art. 11 Para. 4 of the proposed Takeover Directive should be amended to the effect that (preferred) non-voting stock be included as well.

II. The 'One Share, One Vote' Voting Regime

1. General Observations

The takeover-specific application of the principle of 'one share, one vote' is clearly the most controversial part of the break-through concept recommended by the High Level Group. Depending on the capital structure of the company and in particular the structure of its share classes this principle could lead to a fundamental redistribution of control rights once a bid for the company is made. Furthermore, while this shift would only temporarily affect the 'normal' distribution of voting rights with respect to the vote on the authorization of defensive measures,[40] the post-completion break-through rule would invariably lead to a permanent alteration of the original distribution of control, and in particular of voting rights. Admittedly, according to recommendation I.7 the shift of control should only persist for so long as the acquirer retains the relevant majority. However, upon acquisition of at least 75% of all 'shares', the acquirer – to remove any uncertainty and confusion amongst shareholders as to their position[41] – would be empowered to amend the articles of association and other constitutional documents to the effect that, in the future, he would be able to exercise controlling rights in accordance with his acquired stake of risk-bearing capital. Practically speaking, upon reaching the trigger threshold, the acquirer would, e.g., be entitled to abolish double and multiple voting rights as well as voting caps and to transform non-voting stock into common stock.[42] Presumably, he should even be entitled to abolish statutory provisions that grant holders of a special class of shares or third parties the right to make binding nominations for the appointment, suspension or dismissal of board members.

Clearly, the break-through concept would not prevent a shareholder from using his controlling block of voting rights to extract private benefits. Put differently, the level of private benefits extracted by shareholders is not affected by the

[40] In one respect the Group advocates a permanent change already at the stage of the authorization of defensive measures. Holders of depository receipts of shares that represent risk-bearing capital should be free to exchange them for the underlying shares (Winter Report on Takeover Bids (n 1) 28). That means, though, that the holders could keep the shares even if the bid were completely defeated or if less than 75% of all shares were tendered to the bidder.

[41] Winter Report on Takeover Bids (n 1) 35.

[42] In case of preferred non-voting stock presumably without conserving the preference right.

break-through concept, but only determined by the quality of the applicable corporate law regime and, in particular, the rules for protecting minority shareholders. This observation holds true even if a company has been converted to the 'one share one vote' regime following a successful takeover bid reaching the 75% threshold for triggering the transformation. Still, a successful bidder holding at least 75% of the residual cash flow rights will internalise more of the external effects that result from his extraction of private benefits. Thus, once the company has been converted to the 'one share one vote' regime the external effects of a dual-class share structure will decrease. However, this internalisation does not result from the break-through rule as such but from the high ownership level of residual cash flow rights set for triggering the transformation. Seen from this perspective, a mandatory full bid rule could even be more effective in causing a successful bidder to internalise the external effects stemming from his extraction of private benefits. Thus, the assessment of the 'one share one vote' element on efficiency grounds warrants a somewhat broader discussion.

2. Legal Doctrine

So far, legal doctrine has treated the principle of 'one share, one vote' only in general terms, but not its takeover-specific application recommended by the High Level Group. This is particularly true with regard to multiple voting rights, which the German legislature completely abolished in 1998. Earlier contributions by German legal scholars, as well as the discussion accompanying the 1998 law reform, however, illustrate that legal doctrine does not have much to say on policy questions, i.e., whether the legislator should tolerate or, on the contrary, should ban multiple voting rights – and by extension: of deviations from the principle of 'one share, one vote'.[43] Instead, for good reasons, legal doctrine focuses on the questions whether and, more importantly, how the legislator can abolish multiple voting rights without infringing on shareholders' fundamental rights.[44]

3. Economic Theory

(1) The mandatory break-through concept and, in particular, the post-completion break-through rule interferes with the market process. According to standard economic theory legislative intervention of this type is only called for in order to prevent a market failure. The failure targeted by the High Level Group is a sub-

[43] For an illustrative example see W Zöllner and U Noack 'One share – one vote?' (1991) 36 Aktiengesellschaft 117, 118 ff (voting caps), 129 ff (multiple voting rights).

[44] For a short overview, see Dauner-Lieb and Lamandini (n 3) 42 ff.

optimal level of Pan-European cross-border takeovers. At first glance, the existence of statutory and contractual barriers to takeovers – as opposed to golden share-type restrictions – will not hamper takeover activity. As shareholders themselves are able to do away with these 'private' barriers, such impediments will only work to the effect that the total amount to be paid by the bidder will be distributed differently among shareholders than under a 'one share, one vote' regime.[45] This amounts to saying that the structure of the share classes issued by the company – as opposed to its ownership structure – does not affect its total market value because all bidders are indifferent to the particular share class structure of a company. As discussed below, however, economic theory disagrees. Moreover, the redistribution of control rights intended by the breakthrough concept aims at raising the probability of takeovers by reallocating the control premium among shareholders and, thus, by lowering the total amount to be paid by the bidder.

(2) Given dual-class share structures, shares with superior voting power nearly always trade at a higher price than shares with lower or no voting power. Economists generally cite three arguments to explain the existence of a control premium: (i) the possibility of a controlling shareholder to extract private benefits; (ii) the expected future payment of a takeover premium; and (iii) other reasons. The third category comprises, *inter alia*, the observation that in some cases the cash flows accruing to the holders of different classes of shares differ over time.[46] The second explanation, despite its popularity, does nothing to explain the existence of a control premium but rather only begs a reformulation of the problem: why is a bidder willing to pay a control premium?

The possibility for a controlling shareholder to extract private benefits, thus, turns out to be the pivotal explanation for the existence of control premia. Broadly speaking, private benefits comprise all pecuniary (gains from inequilibrate transfer prices etc.) and non-pecuniary (standing, etc.) advantages that – apart from dividend payments and other pro-rata distributions of the company's funds – accrue to a shareholder. Two types of private benefits deserve particular mention. Synergy gains on the part of the shareholder are special insofar as the company does not transfer any assets to him but receives no compensation for

[45] This at least true if the takeover regulation in place allows for price discrimination between the different classes of shares, eg between common stock with single and with multiple voting rights. Otherwise, ie if the bidder has to offer the highest price paid for any common stock or at minimum a certain percentage of this price, the effect of statutory or contractual takeover barriers becomes more difficult to evaluate. On the one hand, a highest price paid-rule will make bids more costly and, thus, lower takeover activity. On the other hand, stock prices may reflect reduced takeover activity respectively lower anticipated takeover premia. In the end, both effects may well cancel themselves out.

[46] Examples are provided, eg by Kunz 'Was beeinflusst den Wert des Aktienstimmrechts?' (1996) 10 Finanzmarkt und Portfolio Management 330, 332.

complying with his interests. Excessive management remuneration and other perquisites enjoyed by managers are special in case of managers being shareholders as well. Given this situation, lawyers tend to think in terms of private benefits extracted by the shareholder, whereas economists tend to think in terms of management entrenchment bolstered by a shareholding. Both perspectives are mutually compatible, though.

(3) The implications of private benefits for the principle of 'one share, one vote' have been analysed in a number of theoretical studies.[47] Their most relevant finding with respect to the present problem is that the existence of a dual-class share structure can be crucial if two types of bidders compete for (the management of) a company: bidder X, who manages the company's assets more efficiently and, thus, raises the future pro-rata cash flows to shareholders, and bidder Y, who, regardless of his ability to manage the company's assets more efficiently than incumbent management, is able to extract high private benefits. Given a dual-share class structure, bidder Y may be able to offer a higher bid premium for the higher voting shares and, thus, to acquire a majority of votes even if the additional value created by him – the higher value of the company plus the private benefits derived by him – is less than the higher company value that would result from a more efficient management of the company's assets by bidder X. A simple numerical example may illustrate the point: A company has issued 200 Class A shares with single voting rights and 101 Class B shares with double voting rights. Bidder X would increase the value of the company by 30 whereas bidder Y would be able to extract private benefits in the amount of 9. Bidder Y could out compete bidder X in a bid for all of the Class B shares and, thus, for control of the company as long as bidder Y were able to increase the value of the company by at least 6.

The intuition behind this somewhat surprising result is easy to understand. X is a pure value-enhancing bidder. At the margin, she can offer a bid premium for Class B shares that equals the additional discounted future cash flows per share generated by her more efficient management of the company's assets. In contrast, Y can use all of his private benefits in order to compete for the higher-voting Class B shares. Thus, if there are some private benefits, a type-Y bidder can offer a higher premium for the controlling share class even if he were to manage the company's assets (far) less efficient than a competing pure value-enhancing bidder.

[47] eg S Grossmann and O Hart, One share-one vote and the market for corporate control (1988) 10 Journal of Financial Economics 175 ff; M Harris and A Raviv 'Corporate Governance' (1988) 20 Journal of Financial Economics 203 ff; 'The Design of Securities' (1989) 24 Journal of Financial Economics ff; cf M Burkart, D Gromb and F Panunzi 'Why Higher Takeover Premia Protect Minority Shareholders' (1988) 106 Journal of Political Economy 172 ff.

Against this background, the effect of the 'one share, one vote'-element of the break-through rule is easy to discern. It serves to enhance the competitive position of type-X bidders relative to type-Y bidders. With a break-through rule in place, both types of bidders would have to acquire a higher number of shares in order to obtain control than without such a rule. This alteration of the takeover regime would not affect the marginal bid premium paid by bidder X. Bidder Y, however, would experience a decreasing marginal bid premium because he would have to use constant private benefits to buy more shares. Thus, while the 'one share, one vote'-element does not assure social optimality (in the sense that the company's assets are always managed by the most efficient user) the break-through rule would go some way towards this goal. Put differently, a break-through rule on the basis of 'one share, one vote' could be credited with increasing allocative efficiency.

(4) Within the framework of a mandatory full bid rule – a central feature of the successive proposals for an EU Takeover Directive now contained in Art. 5[48] with respect to shares carrying voting rights – the preceding analysis in favour of a break-through rule on the basis of 'one share, one vote' looses its persuasive power. The reason is straightforward: the mandatory full bid rule not only improves the competitive position of pure value-enhancing bidders but even puts the two types of bidders on an equal footing. If a bidder acquires all of a company's shares, he fully internalises the externalities caused by his extracting private benefits at the expense of the company and its shareholders, respectively. Thus, with respect to both bidders, their marginal bid premium is solely determined by the additional value they can create by managing the company's assets: additional value of the company (type-X bidder) vs additional value of the company plus private benefits (type-Y bidder). Put differently, even without a break-through rule in place, the mandatory full bid rule assures that the more efficient user will manage the company' s assets.

[48] To be sure, Art 5 of the draft Takeover Directive does not require the bidder to launch a single full bid. However, if the bidder obtains control due to a partial bid he has to launch a second bid, ie the mandatory bid, for all outstanding shares. So far, the draft Directive only provides for one exception to the mandatory full bid requirement: Pursuant to Art 5 para 2, the bidder is exempt from having to make a mandatory bid if he obtains control following a voluntary bid made in accordance with the Directive, and in particular in accordance with the equitable price requirement, to all holders of voting shares for all their holdings. However, the mandatory bid rule regimes already in place in different Member States provide for various additional exceptions (eg s 36 (excluding voting rights from determining whether the control threshold has been reached) and s 37 (exemption from the bid requirement) of the German Act on the Acquisition of Securities and on Takeovers). To avoid any uncertainty with respect to the implementation of the Directive the EU legislator should incorporate a provision delineating the possible scope for exceptions. So far, Member States, in implementing the Directive, could provide for additional exceptions only by arguing that 'the Directive itself does not attempt to specify the percentage of voting rights above which control can be deemed to have been acquired or the method of calculating such a percentage' (Commission Communication (n 2) 7).

Arguably, the bidder could try to mitigate this effect somewhat by offering a low enough bid price designed to attract as few shares as necessary to acquire a majority.[49] The minimum price requirement in Art. 5 Para. 1, 4 of the draft Takeover Directive – pursuant to Para. 4 the bidder has to offer an equitable price – renders this strategy at times difficult to implement, however. Furthermore, this strategy could only work in the absence of a rival bidder. Otherwise, competition between the two bidders would eliminate any chance of choosing a bid price to the effect that only the lowest number of shares required will be tendered to the bidder. However, with respect to a break-through rule based on 'one share, one vote', the possible benefits identified so far also depend on the existence of a rival bidder.[50]

A caveat is necessary, however. The just described effect of a mandatory full bid regime only holds true if, given a dual-class share structure, the mandatory bid rule extends to all share classes. Thus, in order to create a truly level playing field between the different types of bidders, Art. 5 of the draft Takeover Directive should be amended to the effect that the mandatory offer is to be addressed to the holders of non-voting shares as well, and preferably even to holders of non-voting shares carrying specific pecuniary advantages.

(5) Given a mandatory full bid regime (Art. 5 of the draft Takeover Directive), the introduction of a break-through rule based on 'one share, one vote' is sometimes said to lead to severe inconsistencies.[51] According to these critics, while the mandatory bid rule aims at distributing some of the private benefits of control to minority shareholders, the break-through rule conversely results in minimizing the control premium attached to higher-voting shares.

Obviously, this argument implicitly assumes the absence of a rival bidder. However, the incumbent holder of the higher-voting shares, in particular, is a (potential) rival unless the bidder acts in accordance with him. If the incumbent values his private benefits higher than the control premium offered by a third bidder he can protect his controlling position by making a counter-offer in order to prevent a switch from the dual-class voting regime to 'one share, one vote'. Thus, given a mandatory full bid regime the break-through rule would only deprive minority shareholders of a higher control premium if the incumbent controlling shareholder suffered from liquidity constraints.[52]

[49] In particular, Burkart, Gromb and Panunzi (n 47) heavily rely on this idea.

[50] For analytical purposes, the presence of a rival bidder does not require that a bidder contest actually does take place. All incumbents, eg a controlling shareholder, that derive private benefits can be conceptualized as (potential) rivals that will consider fending off a competing bid in order to protect their privileges. In reality, though, incumbents may suffer from liquidity constraints and, as a consequence, may not be able to make a competing offer. This particular problem will be addressed in a moment.

[51] E Berglöf and M Burkhart (n 8) 34; J McCahery (n 35) 4.

[52] E Berglöf and M Burkhart (n 8) 26 ff, 34.

On a more fundamental note, the decrease of the control premium, as a consequence of the break-through rule, is not an effect to take issue with. As already mentioned in Section IV.1, the maximization of takeover premia should not be among the objectives of takeover regulation policy. Proponents of bid premia maximization sometimes claim, however, that the ex ante premium maximization results in better ex post protection of remaining minority shareholders. Basically, they argue as follows:[53] A higher premium leads to the ex ante tender of more shares. Because of the resulting higher concentration of shareholdings the acquirer will internalise more of the externalities that result from his extraction of private benefits. In turn, this decrease in externalities will lead to a higher ex post share price. Upon closer inspection, however, this argument is flawed. While it is true that a higher concentration of shareholdings lowers the external effects due to the extraction of private benefits, the number of outstanding shares does decrease as well. Put differently, regardless of the number of shares acquired by the new controlling shareholder, per share, the external effect of private benefits remains constant. Thus, the amount of the bid premium and, in turn, the number of shares tendered does not affect the post-bid share price.

On the other hand, the reallocation of the control premium for higher-voting shares would only facilitate takeovers if the bidder, as a consequence of the dilution, could save on the amount of compensation he had to pay for all shares. The total amount to be paid crucially depends on the minimum price rule prescribed by the mandatory bid regime; i.e., on the reading of the equitable price rule contained in Art. 5 of the draft Takeover Directive. The dilution of the premium would not affect the amount to be paid for all shares if the rule allowed for price discrimination among the different share classes, e.g., among common stock with single voting rights and with multiple voting rights.[54] Conversely, the allocative effect of a break-through rule based on 'one share, one vote' had a beneficial impact on takeover incidence if the minimum bid price for all shares was determined by the highest price paid for any class of shares.

E. Concluding Remarks

The all-encompassing break-through concept as developed by the High Level Group consists of four core elements. Three of these are essential to the concept: exclusive shareholder decision-making, post-bid shareholder decision-making, and shareholder voting based on 'one share, one vote'. The fourth element – decision-making by all holders of risk-bearing securities – is expendable and, as a

[53] M Burkart, D Gromb and F Panunzi (n 47) 174.

[54] According to A Arnold 'Mehrstimmrechte und stimmrechtslose Vorzugsaktien in der Übernahmerichtlinie' (2003) 1 Der Konzern 173, 176, Art 5 of the draft Takeover Directive allows for bid price discrimination.

corollary, most difficult to defend. On the other hand, the narrow restriction of the draft Takeover Directive to transferable securities carrying voting rights in the company (Art. 2 Para. 1 lit. e) appears inadequate. At a minimum, ordinary non-voting shares should be included as well. Furthermore, non-voting shares carrying specific pecuniary advantages should at least be included if, as a consequence of a series of non-payments of preferential rights, shareholders obtained a voting right.

The preceding analysis of the essential elements of the break-through concept has shown that the High Level Group chose the appropriate starting point: the principle of shareholder decision-making. Shareholders – not managers – should decide on the fate of a bid, and they should only decide in full knowledge of the terms of an offer or, at the very least, in full knowledge that a concrete bid is imminent. The draft Takeover Directive adequately reflects this principle by banning any ex ante shareholder authorization of defensive measures (Art. 9). Furthermore, Art. 11 Para. 2, pursuant to which statutory and contractual restrictions on the transfer of securities are (only) unenforceable for the purpose of a shareholder vote on defensive measures, points in the right direction, at least.

'One share, one vote' shareholder voting in the takeover-related context is the key innovative feature of the break-through concept. For the concept to work, the 'one share, one vote' regime must apply to the vote on defensive measures as well as to all shareholder decision-making after the successful completion of the bid. That means that the company's voting regime must change permanently to 'one share, one vote' once the bidder holds shares in excess of a certain trigger threshold, i.e., the 75% threshold recommended by the High Level Group. Given the mandatory full bid regime in Art. 5 of the draft Takeover Directive, however, the effects of a break-through rule based on 'one share, one vote' are confined to diluting the control premium attached to higher-voting shares. Furthermore, this dilution would only facilitate takeovers if, as a consequence, the total amount to be paid by the acquirer were lower. This, in turn, depends on whether the minimum share price prescribed by the mandatory bid rule allows for price discrimination among the different share classes.

In all, the economic analysis presented in this paper supports the view that there is no need for European takeover regulation to incorporate an all-encompassing break-through concept based on 'one share, one vote'. On the other hand, apart from raising some difficult new problems – compensation (?) of holders of higher-voting shares;[55] adequate legal treatment of holding pyramids – the fore-

[55] One may doubt whether EU law requires that the holders of higher-voting shares, and in particular the holders of shares with double or multiple voting rights, are compensated for the loss of a control premium if the said financial advantage can be traced back to the ability of a controlling shareholder to extract private benefits at the expense of the company and other shareholders, respectively. But see A. Arnold 'Entschädigung von Mehrstimmrechten nach § 5 EGAktG' (2003) 41 Deutsches Steuerrecht 784, 785: private benefits in the form of synergy gains are to be compensated (with respect to German law).

going analysis did not identify any compelling argument against the introduction of such a rule either. In particular, the EU legislator should not be concerned by the possibility that some incumbent controlling shareholders may be financially constrained and, thus, may not be able to launch a counter-offer in order to protect their private benefits of control. At any rate, however, the legislator should clarify Art. 5 of the draft Takeover Directive to the effect that, for the purpose of fixing the minimum share price to be offered, the equitable price for each class of shares is to be determined independently.

Finally, even at the time of completing this paper, the future fate of EU takeover regulation remains unclear. This holds true for the break-through concept (Art. 11) as well as for board neutrality (Art. 9) as its 'twin' (on the political agenda, not in substance!), and even for the draft Takeover Directive as a whole. Thus, it remains to be seen whether the break-through rule dead-ends all efforts of introducing a European takeover regulation or, on the contrary, acts as a catalyst that enables the EU finally to break through to the adoption of a Takeover Directive. Even if the EU would fail to reach this major break through in the creation of a Pan-European level playing field the HLG Group ought to be credited with having paved the way to a mini break through: Without the intervention of the break-through concept the Takeover Directive would not have returned to the agenda of the European legislator.

Chapter 11: Mandatory Bids, Squeeze-Outs and Similar Transactions

Mandatory Bids, Squeeze-Out, Sell-Out and the Dynamics of the Tender Offer Process[*]

MIKE BURKART and FAUSTO PANUNZI

The European Commission's draft directive[1] proposes to introduce a squeeze-out right and a sell-out right and to set the price in a mandatory bid equal to the highest price paid in the 6 or 12 preceding months. Drawing on the existing literature, this paper analyses these three new provisions. In takeovers of widely held targets, the squeeze-out right and the sell-out right have the potential to resolve the collective action problem among shareholders, thereby ensuring the success of value-increasing takeovers and the failure of value-decreasing takeovers. Unlike the sell-out right, the mandatory bid rule requires competition by the incumbent to provide additional shareholder protection. In firms with a dominant shareholder, the mandatory bid rule eliminates inefficient control transfers at the cost of discouraging more efficient control transfers. The benefits but not the costs of the mandatory bid rule tend to disappear when control is consolidated via dual class shares or pyramids or when control benefits are determined by either environment or firm characteristics (but not by the blockholder's identity).

A. Introduction

A first attempt to harmonize takeover regulation in the European Union dates back to the early 1970s. At the time most Member States showed little interest,

[*] Paper prepared for the conference 'A Modern Regulatory Framework for Company and Takeover Law in Europe', Syracuse (Sicily), 29-30 May 2003. Financial support from
cont. ...

and the project was shelved a couple of years later. Subsequent attempts to create pan-European takeover rules also failed, notably in 2001 when the European Parliament put a stop to the proposed directive.[2] Although blocked by the smallest possible margin, the rejection by the Parliament came as a surprise since the proposal had been amended several times following readings in the European Parliament, negotiations within the Council, and the ensuing conciliation procedure.[3] Despite this defeat the European Commission did not abandon its idea of a European takeover regulation. In September 2001 the Commission appointed a 'High Level Group of Company Law Experts' under the chairmanship of Jaap Winter to provide independent advice on issues related to pan-European rules for takeovers and subsequently on key priorities for modernizing company law in the European Union.[4]

In October 2002 the Commission presented a new draft directive that embraces much of the previous proposal rejected by the European Parliament, such as the requirement that shareholders have to approve defensive measures once a takeover bid has been launched. Unlike its predecessor, the new proposal defines the 'equitable' price to be paid in a mandatory bid: it is the highest price paid by the new controlling party in the 6 or 12 months preceding the mandatory offer. (Henceforth, the term mandatory bid rule is meant to include this price requirement.) In addition, the new draft directive introduces a squeeze-out right and a sell-out right. These three additions to the directive are part of the recommendations of the Winter Group. But the Group made further suggestions aimed at neutralizing the effects of differentiated voting rights (dual class shares). More precisely, the Group proposed that differential voting power of shares should be voided in votes on defensive measures and – even more controversial – that a party owning a qualified majority (75 percent) of the equity capital can override any statutory defences to exercise core control rights.[5] Since this so-called break-

Riksbankens Jubileumsfond and Università Bocconi (ricerca di base) is gratefully acknowledged. We would like to thank Luca Enriques and conference participants for helpful comments.

[1] Proposal for a Directive of the European Parliament and the Council on Takeover Bids of October 2 2002 COM (2002) 534 final (Brussels).

[2] For an account of the various attempts to regulate takeovers at the EU level see R Skog *Does Sweden Need a Mandatory Bid Rule? A Critical Analysis* (Juristförlaget Stockholm 1995) and 'The Takeover Directive – an endless saga?' (2002) 13 (4) European Business Law Review 301, 302.

[3] In contrast, national regulation in most Member States evolved since the mid 1980s, many approximating in substance the UK City Code on Takeovers and Mergers.

[4] The Winter Group presented its first report on 'Issues Related to Takeover Bids' in January 2002 ('Winter Report on Takeover Bids', see Annex 2 in this volume), and its second report on 'A Modern Regulatory Framework for Company Law in Europe' (hereafter 'Winter Report', see Annex 3 in this volume) in November 2002.

[5] According to M Bennedsen and K Nielsen in 'The Impact of a Break-Through Rule on European Firms' mimeo Copenhagen Business School (2002), one-fifth of all listed firms in Europe use shares with differentiated votes. In a substantial number of these firms, the break-

cont. ...

through rule encountered tremendous opposition, the Commission did not include it in the new draft directive.[6] Influenced by this recommendation, the current proposal stipulates, however, that restrictions on voting rights and on the transfer of shares (directed against a potential acquirer) are rendered unenforceable once a bid has been launched (Article 11).

Applying the insights of the existing takeover literature, this paper provides an economic analysis of the three aforementioned new elements of the current draft directive; mandatory bid rule, squeeze-out right, and sell-out right.[7] Takeover regulation defines the rights and obligations of the acquiring and target firm, such as the content of information issued to shareholders, the terms of the offer, and the defensive measures available to the target firm. These rules affect how the gains from a takeover are shared between acquiring and target firm, and thereby the incentives to make and accept a tender offer. This holds true also for the mandatory bid rule, the squeeze-out right, and the sell-out right.

This paper shows that in takeovers of widely held targets the squeeze-out right and sell-out right have far-reaching implications for the dynamics of the tender offer process. This holds despite, or more accurately precisely because, these rights are triggered after the completion of the takeover. More specifically, the squeeze-out right allows the bidder to overcome the free rider problem, thereby making value-increasing takeovers feasible.[8] The sell-out right with a threshold at 50 percent eliminates the pressure to tender problem and hence prevents all value-decreasing takeovers. Unlike the sell-out right, the mandatory bid rule requires competition by the incumbent to provide additional shareholder protection. Hence, the mandatory bid rule never simultaneously secures a bid premium and provides effective protection. In firms with a dominant shareholder, the mandatory bid rule eliminates inefficient control transfers at the cost of discouraging

through rule would undermine the veto right of the controlling owner. Moreover, a large group of firms with multi-class shares would be constrained in raising new equity capital as the controlling block would fall below the break-through threshold.

[6] Some commentators characterized the break-through rule as an undue ex post intervention in contracts violating the very shareholder decision-making right that the Winter Group advocates (P Bolton Presentation at the ECGI Panel on the Winter Report at the Annual Meeting of the Federation of European Stock Exchanges 2002). Others argued that the proposal would affect existing corporate governance arrangements asymmetrically, in particular exempting and even promoting, for example, pyramids (LA Bebchuk and OD Hart *Financial Times* 31 May 2002).

[7] We do not discuss Article 11, another innovation of the current proposal. In essence, its provisions further reduce the discretion of management to frustrate a (hostile) takeover, thereby strengthening the principle that the ultimate decision over a takeover must be with the shareholders (E Berglöf and M Burkart, 'European Takeover Regulation' (2003) 18 Economic Policy 171).

[8] GK Yarrow 'Shareholder Protection, Compulsory Acquisition and the Efficiency of the Takeover Process' (1985) 34 Journal of Industrial Economics 3-16.

more efficient control transfers.[9] The benefits of the mandatory bid rule tend to disappear when control is consolidated via dual class shares or pyramids or when the size of the control benefits does not depend on the blockholder's identity.

Much of the takeover literature, eg, the seminal paper by Grossman and Hart[10], presupposes a publicly listed target firm with dispersed ownership and with no takeover barriers, making shares and their votes freely transferable. Clearly, this does not depict (Continental) European reality very accurately. Indeed, the available evidence on ownership structures demonstrates that dispersed ownership of large firms is not the prevalent organisational form outside the United States and the United Kingdom (La Porta et al 1999, Barca and Becht 2001). Most (Continental) European companies, even the listed ones, have a large (controlling) shareholder. The resulting concentration of control (votes), often enhanced through dual class shares, pyramiding, or cross-holdings, constitutes a considerable – if not insurmountable – obstacle to hostile takeovers.[11] In addition to these firm specific takeover barriers, hostile bids are further impeded by institutional arrangements such as the (German) co-determination, close bank-firm relationships, and the relatively small fraction of (Continental) European firms listed on stock markets.

Although widely held firms are frequent exceptions rather than the rule in Europe, our analysis is mainly carried out within the framework of Grossman and Hart[12]. Their model that we review (section 2) is central to the understanding of the tender offer process and its difficulties. It also lends itself particularly well to illustrate the fundamental conflict between promoting an active takeover market and protecting (minority) shareholder interests. In fact, the Grossman and Hart model is a point of reference for many issues in the takeover (regulation) debate. Moreover, a public tender offer is not a valid option if the target firm has a majority shareholder. Instead, outsider and incumbent majority owner negotiate a sale of the controlling stake. Hence, an analysis of takeover regulation can restrict attention to widely held target firms, with the important exception of the mandatory bid rule. The sale of a controlling stake is affected by whether or not the buyer is obliged to extend his offer to all remaining shareholders. We therefore examine the impact of the mandatory bid rule in case of a widely held firm

[9] LA Bebchuk 'Efficient and Inefficient Sales of Corporate Control' (1994) 109 Quartely Journal of Economics 957-993.

[10] SJ Grossman and OD Hart 'Takeover Bids, the Free Rider Problem, and the Theory of the Coporation' (1980) 11 Bell Journal of Economics 42-64.

[11] The purpose the break-through rule proposed by the Winter Group is to remove the (near) veto power of controlling shareholders over a control transfer in order to promote takeovers and restructuring. Burkart and Berglöf (n 7) provide a theoretical analysis of the break-through rule.

[12] n 10.

(section C) and in the case of a firm with a majority owner (section F).[13] Since the squeeze-out rule and the sell-out rule come into effect after the completion of a takeover, the pre-takeover ownership structure may seem inconsequential. As we will show, both rights have repercussions on the dynamics of the takeover outcome that are most pronounced for widely held targets. Hence, we discuss the squeeze-out rule (section D) and the sell-out right (section E) also within the Grossman Hart setting.

In the remainder of this section we briefly address two broader questions; first, why regulations is necessary, and second, what its objectives should be.

I. Rationale for Regulation

The position against mandatory (takeover) rules is based on the notion that a market economy achieves efficient outcomes without government intervention. If a certain provision, say an adequate shareholder protection, is in the interest of the firm, its founders providc it: Issuing claims in a competitive stock market is tantamount to efficient bargaining between founders and new investors. Since the founders are the residual claimants they choose claims (combination of return and control rights) that maximize total return. Hence, if it is efficient to protect shareholders adequately, provisions to this end will be included in the corporate charter.[14] Also, regulators lack the information to design efficient rules, let alone the problem that they may be captured by special interests.[15] Thus, it is clearly better to leave each firm the discretion to choose its own specific rules.

Obviously, private contractual agreements presuppose some minimum body of law, such as legal principles or default rules, as well as effective enforcement. Indeed, recent empirical work documents the limits to contractual solutions in

[13] Theoretical research has yet to answer how the presence of a minority blockholder who does not counter-bid but either accepts or rejects the offer affects the takeover outcome. Introducing a minority block in the Grossman and Hart framework does not alter the outcome because the mass of small shareholders remains pivotal. In a framework with a finite number of shareholders, B Holmström and B Nalebuff ('To the Raider Goes the Surplus? A Reexamination of the Free Rider Problem' (1992) 1 Journal of Economics and Management Strategies 37-62) show that large shareholders are willing to tender at lower prices than small shareholders. They do, however, not derive the mapping of ownership concentration (block size) into equilibrium bid prices.

[14] eg L Enriques *Mercato del Controllo Societario e Tutela degl Investitori* (Il Mulino Bologna 2002) 27.

[15] For instance, the Connecticut anti-takeover bill was not supported by broad political coalitions but promoted by a firm incorporated in Connecticut (R Romano 'The Political Economy of Takeover Statutes' (1987) 73 Virginia Law Review 111-199). In other cases, a firm that anticipated a takeover bid lobbied for the anti-takeover bill which was passed in an emergency session (M Bertrand and S Mullainathan 'Executive Compensation and Incentives: The Impact of takeover Legislation' (1999) NBER Working Paper no 6830.

poor legal environments (Nenova 2003). There are several arguments in support of more far-reaching regulatory intervention, ie, mandatory rules. First, even if founders and initial investors agree on a set of provisions that maximizes their joint return, these provisions are unlikely to be the socially efficient ones. The reason is that initial negotiations cannot feasibly include all parties that will in the future contribute to the value of the firm. Being self-interested, founders and initial investors deviate from the socially efficient rules in order to extract a larger share of future surplus. For instance, founders and initial investors adopt rules that maximize their expected takeover returns, while the social efficient rules maximize the sum of the expected returns to target and acquiring firm.[16]

The above argument against enabling rules seems to suggest that privately written rules are likely to be inefficient because these rules are agreed upon at the beginning of the life cycle of a firm, when many relevant future events are simply unknown. As the firm evolves over time these rules should be adjusted. But contrary to mandatory rules, enabling rules precisely provide the flexibility needed to make these adjustments. The discretion to adapt rules comes, however, with a considerable cost, the inability to commit not to change rules for purely opportunistic reasons. For instance, dispersed small shareholders do not engage in monitoring but remain passive, leaving control de facto to management or to controlling blockholders. Given such a powerful position, it is straightforward for these parties to change corporate charter provisions to its own advantages. Thus, the option to adapt may prove to be disadvantageous, even though the optimal rules change over time.

Collective action problems due to dispersed ownership are another argument in favour of mandatory rules. Economic theory provides numerous examples of how individually rational behaviour undermines the socially preferred outcome. We will discuss two well-known manifestations of this problem; the success of value-decreasing bids and the failure of value-increasing bids. Ownership concentration would overcome these problems, but is, in particular for large firms, not a feasible or realistic option because of individual investors' limited wealth, because of their desire to diversify risk, and because of their preference for liquidity.[17]

[16] In an extended Grossman and Hart model (SJ Grossman and OD Hart n 10) with endogenous private benefit extraction, Burkart et al (M Burkart, D Gromb and F Panunzi 'Agency Conflicts in Public and Negotiated Transfers of Corporate Control' (1998) 55 Journal of Finance 647-677) show that the socially optimally security-voting structure (fraction of non-voting shares) differs from the one that maximizes target shareholder return.

[17] M Becht, P Bolton and A Röell 'Corporate Governance and Control' (2002) mimeo Princeton University.

II. Regulatory Objectives

Once we accept the idea that takeover regulation is warranted, the question arises what its objective should be. The current draft directive pursues the same objectives as its rejected predecessor: to create a level playing field conducive to takeovers and to ensure the protection of minority shareholders. Abstracting from harmonization which is specific to supranational legislation, these objective are shared by other takeover regulations such as eg, the UK City Code.

The fundamental dilemma of takeover regulation is that (minority) shareholder protection and an efficient takeover market are conflicting objectives. Provisions that grant one side, say the acquirer, a larger fraction of the takeover gains necessarily translates into less protection of target shareholders as they receive less of the surplus.

In an efficiently functioning market for corporate control, a takeover succeeds whenever an outside party is able to generate more value than the incumbent management. Such an outcome is only ensured if the entire surplus accrues to the acquiring party and none to the target shareholders (zero takeover premium). Similarly, efficiency also demands that takeovers should fail if the outsider is not able to create additional value. This obtains if an acquiring party has to pay at least what the firm is worth under the incumbent management (no negative takeover premium).

This argument seems to suggest that legal provisions granting target shareholders part of the takeover gains provide undue minority shareholder protection. All what is needed are rules preventing that target shareholders realize a loss. But matters are definitely more complex. The willingness of an acquirer to pay the current firm value is by no means proof that he can generate additional value. It may equally well be a reflection of agency problems with the acquiring firm. That is, an acquisition may be motivated by managerial self-interest (empire-building) rather than value creation. Even in the absence of such agency problems, there is an economic rationale for letting target shareholders participate in the takeover gains. Anticipating the possibility of a takeover premium, a rational investor is willing to pay more for the shares or to invest in shares.[18] That is, better minority shareholder protection in takeovers has beneficial ex ante effects: it reduces the cost of equity capital, it increases the attractiveness for firms to be listed, and it ultimately encourages entrepreneurial activity.

[18] This argument is not restricted to takeovers but extends to the protection of outside investors in general. Recent empirical studies demonstrate clearly that the valuation and the breadth of capital markets (both equity and debt) increase with the quality of the legal investor protection (R La Porta, F Lopez-de-Silanes, A Shleifer and RW Vishny 'Legal Determinants of External Finance' (1997) 52 Journal of Finance 1131-1150; 'Law and Finance' (1998) 106 Journal of Political Economy 1113-55; 'Investor Protection and Corporate Governance' (2000) 58 Journal of Financial Economics 3-27.

This reasoning does, however, not specify how much investor protection should be provided at the cost of making takeovers less attractive for potential acquirers. It merely argues that both minority protection and an efficient market for corporate control have beneficial effects and that takeover regulation has to trade-off ex ante against ex post efficiency considerations.

Finally, European regulation is by definition supranational and hence harmonization (one of) its raison d'etre. With respect to takeovers, the Commission advocates harmonization because common takeover rules are a key element of an integrated market and promote the development of a level playing field for (cross-border) bids. Obstacles to or distortions in cross-border takeovers due to differences in national regulations are surely undesirable. However, common rules promote a level playing field only if the harmonized jurisdictions are sufficiently similar along other relevant dimensions. Given the considerable variations of ownership and control arrangements within the European Union, this condition is hardly satisfied in case of takeovers. As a result, specific rules can easily lead to different effects across Member States, making the playing field less levelled.[19] For example, the proposed mandatory bid rule impedes the takeover of a typical German firm with its controlling owner but not that of a typical UK firm with its dispersed ownership.

B. Economics of the Tender Offer Process

The role of ownership and control is a central theme in corporate finance. One of its important aspects concerns the dynamics of control allocation. Circumstances may and do arise in the evolution of a firm when the incumbent controlling party loses its comparative advantage in running the company and some other party is better suited for the task. For instance, the founder's heirs may not be as talented as the founder himself in managing the company. Yet, families often keep control rather than hiring a more able professional manager.[20] The family firm example shows that efficient transfers of control do not necessarily occur.

Takeovers are a key mechanism in the dynamic allocation of corporate control; they allow to remove inefficient managers (against their will) and to exploit synergies between firms. Moreover, the mere threat of a takeover affects the behaviour of those entrusted with control, ie, disciplines them. Consequently, a functioning takeover market is widely considered an important component of – if not prerequisite for – an effective governance system. However, takeover decisions are like any other managerial decision subject to agency problems. Takeovers may also be undertaking by inefficient management teams motivated by the prospect of further control benefits. In fact, most takeovers are not undertaken by

[19] E Berglöf and M Burkart n 7.

[20] M Burkart, F Panunzi and A Shleifer 'Family Firms' (2003) forthcoming Journal of Finance.

corporate raiders but by firms headed by professional managers.[21] Also, takeovers may redistribute rather than create value, transferring wealth from bondholders or other stakeholders to target shareholders.[22]

Clearly, highly concentrated share ownership, restrictions on share transferability, or other takeover defences hinder or even prevent tender offers. However, even in the absence of such barriers when ownership is dispersed and shares are freely transferable, the takeover market is plagued by a problem pointed to by Grossman and Hart (1980). We now review this so-called free-rider problem as it provides framework and foundation for our subsequent analysis of the mandatory bid rule, of the squeeze-out right, and of the sell-out right.

Grossman and Hart[23] consider a firm with a fully dispersed ownership that is approached by an outside buyer, henceforth the bidder, who does not own any shares prior to the tender offer. Let q denote the per-share value under the incumbent management and v the value under the bidder's control where $v > q$.[24] That is, we restrict attention here to the commonly considered case of a value-increasing takeover. In the next section, we also explore whether a value-decreasing takeover in which target sharcholders realize a loss can succeed.

In order to gain control, the bidder has to acquire at least 50 percent of the shares. (All shares carry the same number of votes.) The bidder makes an unrestricted offer with a price b for each share, conditional on getting (at least) 50 percent of the shares. The cost to the bidder of mounting a tender offer is $c > 0$ per share. Shareholders do not coordinate their response to the offer, and given the large number of shareholders each shareholder rightly presumes that his decision has a negligible impact on the outcome of the tender offer. To focus on the target shareholders' impact on the takeover outcome we abstract from both resistance by the incumbent manager and competition by another outside buyer.[25] For simplicity, we also assume that share values q and v and the takeover cost c are commonly known.

When deciding whether or not to accept an offer with a price b above the current share price q, each shareholder compares the benefits and costs of

[21] A Shleifer and RW Vishny 'Takeovers in the 60s and 80s: Evidence and Implications' (1991) 12 Strategic Management Journal 51-59.

[22] A Shleifer and LH Summers 'Breach of Trust in Hostile Takeovers' in AJ Auerbach (ed) *Corporate Takeovers: Causes and Consequences* (Chicago University Press Chicago 1988).

[23] n 10.

[24] For simplicity, we assume that the pre-takeover share price is not forward-looking, ie, does not incorporate the possibility of a takeover, but is equal to q the share value under the incumbent management. The qualitative arguments would not change if we were to include the impact that the prospect of a takeover has on the current share price.

[25] More generally, a successful bidder has to win the target shareholders' approval and (at least) match any competing offer. Effective competition among bidders by definition implies that the requirement to outbid any rival, rather than winning shareholder approval, determines the bid price.

tendering in case of success and failure of the takeover. If less than 50 percent of the shares (votes) are tendered, the offer becomes void and the individual shareholder's decision is immaterial. The incumbent management remains in control and share value is q. If the offer succeeds, the shareholder gets the offered price b when tendering, and the post-takeover share value v when retaining his share. Thus, for any price b below the post-takeover share value v, each individual shareholder prefers not to tender. As all shareholders behave in the same manner, the tender offer can only succeed if the bidder offers at least the post-takeover share value. Clearly, the bidder cannot make a profit at a price $b = v$, in fact he incurs a loss due to the takeover cost c. Thus, we have replicated the seemingly paradoxical result of Grossman and Hart[26]: A value-increasing takeover attempt of a widely held firm cannot succeed because of the small shareholders' free-riding behaviour. While the success of a value-increasing takeover is a public good for the target shareholders, each individual shareholder prefers to hold out to extract the maximum gains, and as a result the bid fails (is not undertaken).[27] This result neither depends on the amount of value improvement $v - q$ nor does it require that the target shareholders know the post takeover share value. Even if shareholders do not know the post-takeover share value, they can reasonable anticipate that it must exceed the offered price because the bidder would otherwise make a loss.[28]

The theoretical literature on takeovers suggests several ways how the bidder may overcome the free-rider problem. Of particular relevance in the context of takeover regulation is the proposal by Grossman and Hart[29] that provides for bidders to withhold part of the post-takeover share value from minority shareholders. This creates a wedge between the post-takeover share value to the bidder and that to minority shareholders, enabling the bidder to make a profit. More precisely, suppose that a successful bidder can divert a fraction $\phi \in (0,1)$ of the resources as private benefits. For instance, the bidder could pay minority shareholders only $(1 - \phi)$ of the dividends that he collects.[30] Due to this dilution of the

[26] n 10.

[27] With a finite rather than infinite number of shareholders, each individual shareholder takes into account that his decision is with positive probability pivotal, rather than negligible, for the aggregate outcome. Hence, he is willing to tender at a price (slightly) below the post-takeover share value, leaving the bidder some profits (Holmström and Nalebuff n 13).

[28] D Hirshleifer 'Mergers and Acquisitions: Strategic and Informational Issues' in RA Jarrow, V Maksimovic and WT Ziemba (eds) *Handbook of Operations Research and Management Science* (North-Holland 1995) vol 9.

[29] n 10.

[30] Discriminatory dividends are merely an illustrative example of diversion that should not be taken literally. Such outright theft of company profits is a blunt violation of the equal treatment principle, and would in most countries be prosecuted. In practice, there are, however, various more subtle forms of private benefit extraction that are either difficult to prove in court, or even not against the letter of the law. For instance, the bidder can sell at below market prices

cont. ...

return rights, each shareholder is willing to tender at a price $b \geq (1 - \o)v$ and the takeover succeed provided that the extracted private benefits cover the takeover cost $v\o > c$.

Clearly, the proposal to allow bidders to extract private benefits conflicts with equal treatment but makes the trade-off between protecting minority shareholder and promoting takeovers very transparent. In addition, it illustrates that maximum shareholder protection need not be in the shareholders' best interest. Banning all extraction, ie, imposing $\o = 0$, prevents the bidder from making a profit, thereby frustrating takeovers. This is also costly for the target shareholders as they forgo the takeover premium (provided that $\o$ is not too large such that $b \geq (1 - \o)v > q$ holds).

There are several other ways to (partially) solve the free-rider problem. First, granting the bidder a squeeze-out right circumvents the problem. We defer the discussion of how the squeeze-out right affects the shareholders' tendering decision to section 4. Second, the acquisition of a stake prior to the tender offer also mitigates the free-rider problem (Shleifer and Vishny 1986).[31] Suppose the bidder already owns an initial stake $\omega < 50\%$ before mounting the tender offer. Even if the bidder cannot extract any private benefits ($\o = 0$) and consequently has to offer a price $b = v$, the takeover may be profitable. While the bidder does not make a profit on the $1 - \omega$ shares acquired in the tender offer, the value improvement of his initial stake $\omega(v - q)$ accrues to him.[32] The essence of the Shleifer and Vishny argument is that the possibility to secretly acquire an initial stake prior to the tender offer is an important source of bidders' profits.[33] The regulatory implication is that disclosure rules are an important means to influence the prospective bidders' incentives and hence play a major role in shaping the level of takeover in the economy.[34]

output or assets of the target firm to another firm under his control. Other forms of dilution are excessive salaries to the executive, the consumption of perks, the appointment of friends or family members to management positions.

[31] In fact, most corporate governance mechanisms used in the world can be viewed as examples of large investors exercising their power (A Shleifer and RW Vishny 'Takeovers in the 60s and the 80s: Evidence and Implications' (1997) 12 Strategic Management Journal 51-59).

[32] The bidder's gain amounts to $\omega(v - q)$ only under the simplifying assumption that the bidder's purchase of his initial stake does not increase the pre-takeover share price. Accounting for this likely effect would reduce the bidder's profit and hence the likelihood that the takeover remains profitable.

[33] AS Kyle and J-L Vila 'Noise Trading and Takeovers' (1991) 22 Rand Journal of Economics 54-71, show that noise trading allows the bidder to acquire an initial stake at favourable prices so that a takeover can become profitable.

[34] M Burkart 'Economics of Takeover Regulation' (1999) mimeo Stockholm School of Economics.

Finally, Mueller and Panunzi[35] show how leverage may help to overcome the free rider problem. In a leveraged buyout shareholders anticipate that if they do not tender they will be minority shareholders in a highly leveraged company. Since debt is senior to equity, the post-takeover share value decreases with the amount of debt that the bidder issues. Thus, debt can be used to reduce the bid price, while the bidder gains because he can pocket (parts of) the proceeds from the debt issue.

These extensions and modifications of the Grossman and Hart model show that takeovers of widely held firms can be profitable. Thus, a more general restatement of the free rider problem is that the bidder's prospects of making a profit on the shares acquired in the tender offer are very limited, if not completely frustrated.[36] As a result, too few takeovers are undertaken, and if a takeover occurs, most of the gains accrue to the target shareholders.[37] The extensive evidence on bidder and target returns, in particular during the 1980s, is consistent with this latter implication of the free-rider result.[38]

C. Mandatory Bid Rule

Like its predecessor, the Commission's current draft directive obliges any party who has acquired control to make an offer to all remaining shareholders at an 'equitable price'. Following the recommendations of the Winter Report, Article 5(4) now defines the equitable price as the highest price paid by the bidder during the 6 or 12 preceding months. Though Article 5 allows for some flexibility, as Member States may adjust the price in circumstances and according to criteria that are clearly specified. The draft directive does not specify the control threshold, ie, the percentage of voting rights above which control has been acquired, but leaves this definition to the Member States.[39]

[35] H Mueller and F Panunzi 'Tender Offers and Leverage' (2003) mimeo University of Bologna.

[36] This holds true even in the setting where the bidder can extract private benefits at the expense of the remaining minority shareholders. Given the bidder has control and extracts private benefits, he values the shares (not needed for having control) at $v(1 - \phi)$, the price that he has to offer the shareholders.

[37] Other (complementary) reasons why a bidder may fail to make a profit are competition by other bidders and defensive actions by the incumbent management.

[38] Burkart n 34.

[39] Currently, the various mandatory bid rules in the Member States differ substantially; some countries refer to the highest price paid, others use different criteria such as average market value, and still others do not provide detailed provisions but only refer to general principles such as equal treatment of shareholders. By harmonizing the price to be paid in a mandatory offer, the Commission wants to improve legal certainty for cross-border takeovers. Given the perceived need for harmonization, it seems puzzling that the Commission does not also impose a common threshold for triggering mandatory bids.

As stated in the explanatory memorandum to the draft proposal, the Commission considers the mandatory bid rule to be indispensable for an adequate protection of minority shareholders. Thus, the Commission seems to subscribe to the view that the option to sell the shares protects each shareholder against potential expropriation by the bidder. This holds true if bids that are against the collective interests of the shareholders are deterred by a mandatory bid rule, or if the offered bid price exceeds the post-takeover minority share value. Otherwise, the option to sell would not offer any additional protection.

The preceding discussion of the free rider problem provides us with the analytical framework to examine to what extent the mandatory bid rule indeed protects minority shareholders. Extending this framework slightly, we now consider a widely held firm that is approached by a bidder who may be either value-increasing $((1-ø)v > q)$ or value-decreasing $((1-ø)v < q)$. For simplicity, we assume that the takeover costs are negligibly small. We continue to abstract from competition among bidders. For the evaluation of legal provisions aimed at protecting (minority) shareholders, the single bidder takeover is undoubtedly the more relevant case. When multiple bidders compete for a target, bids and counter-bids typically drive the price up beyond the level where regulatory provisions regarding minority protection would have an impact on the price.

As far as targets with dispersed ownership are concerned the mandatory bid rule amounts to a ban of bids restricted to the controlling stake, say 50 percent of the shares (votes). Thus, the impact of the mandatory bid rule is simply the difference between the outcome of an unrestricted bid and that of bid restricted to 50 percent. In case the restricted bid is oversubscribed we shall assume that the bidder purchases shares from all tendering shareholders on a pro rata basis.[40] We compare the two outcomes for a value-increasing bidder and value-decreasing bidder in turn.

From the shareholder's perspective, it is entirely irrelevant whether a value-increasing bidder makes an unrestricted or a restricted offer.[41] As argued above, an unrestricted offer wins the shareholders' approval only if the bid price b matches at least the post-takeover minority share value $(1-ø)v$. Moreover, the bidder does not voluntarily offer more than the price necessary to induce shareholders to tender. Thus, he offers $b = (1-ø)v$, and the bid succeeds.[42] The same reasoning applies to an offer restricted to 50 percent of the shares. No shareholder

[40] Indeed, Article 3 of the draft directive obliges bidders to treat shareholders equally. Thus, if partial bids would be admissible a bidder could not exclude some tendering shareholders from an oversubscribed partial offer.

[41] SJ Grossman and OD Hart 'One Share – One Vote, and the Market for Corporate Control' (1988) 20 Journal of Financial Economics 175-202.

[42] To be precise, each shareholder is indifferent at this price and may hence tender or retain his shares, and both success and failure can be supported as equilibrium outcomes. By swaying all shareholders into accepting the offer, an ϵ premium removes failure as an equilibrium outcome.

tenders unless $b \geq (1 - ø)v$ in which case each shareholder tenders since he gets the offered price for (at least) half of his shares. As with an unrestricted offer, the bidder offers $b = (1 - ø)v$, and the bid succeeds.

Thus, the argument that the mandatory bid rule protects shareholders against potential expropriation does not hold in case of value-increasing bidder. It overlooks that the ability to extract private benefits affects the bid price and the post-takeover minority share value to the same extent. With or without mandatory bid rule, the bidder offers neither more nor less than the post-takeover minority share value, and shareholders realize the same return on the shares that they (can) sell and on those that they (have to) retain. Furthermore, the argument also seems to ignore that an active takeover market relies on bidders' private benefits. Unless a bidder has some source of profits that is not eroded by the small shareholders' free rider behaviour, he has little incentives to launch a takeover in the first place.

As far as target firms with dispersed ownership are concerned, the mandatory bid rule has no impact in case of a value-increasing bidder. Consequently, the rationale for the mandatory bid as a means for minority shareholder protection must rely on the belief or argument that in its absence takeovers bids can succeed even though they are against the interest of the target shareholders as at least some of them realize a loss. A closer examination shows that the success of a value-decreasing takeover is indeed an equilibrium outcome of the Grossman and Hart[43] takeover model. If the bid fails, the tendering decision is immaterial. If the bid succeeds, each shareholder prefers to tender if the bidder offers at least the post-takeover share value, even if (or also when) the offered price is less than the pre-takeover share value under the incumbent management. Thus, a value-decreasing bid $q > b \geq (1 - ø)v$ can succeed against the collective interest of the shareholders. By offering (marginally more than) the post-takeover share value the bidder creates a pressure to tender.[44] That is, tendering becomes individually rational as a hedge against the unfavourable minority position, even though each shareholder prefers the bid to fail. This holds true irrespective of whether the bid is truly value-decreasing ($q > v$) or whether it is value-increasing but imposes a loss on the target shareholders ($(1 - ø)v < q < v$).

As has been pointed out in the literature,[45] the success of value-decreasing bids has the same cause as the failure of value-increasing bids: each shareholder bases his tendering decision only on a comparison between offered price b and post-takeover share value $(1 - ø)v$ without taking the current or pre-takeover share value q into account. As a result, a shareholder retains his shares even

[43] n 10.

[44] LA Bebchuk 'The Pressure to Tender: An Analysis and a Proposed Remedy' in JC Coffee, L Lowenstein and S Rose-Ackerman (eds) *Knights, Raiders, and Targets* (OUP New York 1988).

[45] LA Bebchuk and OD Hart 'Takeover Bids Versus Proxy Fights in Contest for Corporate Control' (2001) CEPR Discussion Paper No. 3073.

though he prefers the bid to succeed (free rider problem) or he tenders his shares even though he prefers the bid to fail (pressure to tender problem). It is to be noted, however, that failure of a value-decreasing bid is also an equilibrium outcome. Given that the bid fails, each shareholder may as well retain his shares, supporting failure as an equilibrium outcome.

Like in the case of value-increasing offers, neither the outcome nor the shareholders' return in a value-decreasing offer depends on the bid form. Given that the bidder offers $b = (1 - ø)v$ shareholders accept and realize the same loss $q - (1 - ø)v$ on the shares they (can) tender as on the shares they (have to) retain.[46] Thus, banning restricted offers through the mandatory bid does not by itself protect minority shareholder from value-decreasing bids. This conclusion implicitly assumes that shareholder approval, ie, the free-rider condition $b \geq (1 - ø)v$, is the sole constraint an offer has to satisfy in order to succeed. One may, however, argue that the current share value q imposes an additional constraint. Undoubtedly, a value-decreasing bid $b = (1 - ø)v < q$ would be beaten by a marginally higher offer from some third party. This counter-offer would also be profitable, even if neither incumbent management were replaced nor any changes made. The firm would simply be purchased at a price below its value. Such a risk free profit opportunity (arbitrage) cannot occur in equilibrium. Hence, competition by the incumbent[47] and the free-rider condition jointly determine the minimum price that a bidder has to offer to succeed, ie $b = \min[q,(1 - ø)v]$.

If the current share price imposes a lower bound on the bid price, the mandatory bid rule improves shareholder protection. In a regime with a mandatory bid rule, truly value-decreasing takeovers ($q > v$) are prevented, because the bidder would bear the entire value loss.[48] In addition, shareholders do not lose in value-increasing takeovers where the bidder is able to extract private benefits to an extent that the post-takeover value falls below the pre-takeover share value ($(1\ ø)v < q < v$).[49]

The above discussion shows that the mandatory bid rule improves minority shareholder protection if and only if competition by the incumbent forces bidders to offer at least the pre-takeover share value. Banning restricted bids has, however, no effect in case of value-increasing bids where the bid price is determined

[46] This is also true in the equilibrium in which the bid fails since in this case the bid form has obviously no impact on the shareholders' payoff.

[47] The requirement $b \geq q$ accords with the positive takeover premia reported in all empirical studies (M Burkart 'Economics of Takeover Regulation' mimeo Stockholm School of Economics (1999)).

[48] Grossman and Hart, n 41.

[49] The obligation to treat all (tendering) shareholders equal limits a bidder's ability to define the offer terms. For instance, it prevents a bidder from accepting tendering shares on a first-come first-serve basis that would generate a strong pressure to tender. Equal treatment does, however, not ensure the failure of (partial) bids that are against the collective interest of the shareholders. As shown above, shareholders can accept a partial bid $b = q > (1 - ø)v$.

by the post-takeover share value ($b = (1 - ø)v > q$). Overall, the mandatory bid rule never secures a bid premium and simultaneously provides effective shareholder protection: Since $b = \min[q,(1 - ø)v]$, effective shareholder protection through the mandatory bid rule requires $b = q > (1 - ø)v$, while a bid premium implies $b = (1 - ø)v > q$. Hence, the benefits of the mandatory bid rule depends on the (perceived) likelihood that value-decreasing bids are launched and not rejected by the shareholders. In addition, the mandatory bid rule is not without potential shortcomings, since it reduces the bidders' scope to recoup the takeover cost (or equivalently, increase the takeover costs). Suppose that the post-takeover share value $(1 - ø)v$ is substantially larger than the current share value q, but that the takeover cost c is of the same magnitude as $ø$. An unrestricted bid is feasible only if $ø > c$, while the condition for a restricted bid is $ø > c / 2$. Furthermore, it seems plausible that the (per-share) takeover cost are larger in a full acquisition because eg, the higher financing need increases the (marginal) borrowing cost. Thus, the mandatory bid rule may prevent some value-increasing takeovers, in particular those bids where the bidder is unable to extract large private benefits (small $ø$ values). Even if the mandatory bid rule does not prevent value-increasing takeovers, it can be to the target shareholders' disadvantage. In case multiple bidders compete for a target, the mandatory bid rule may lower the winning bid price.[50, 51]

Finally, there are alternative ways to prevent the success of value-decreasing takeovers. Like the failure of a value-increasing takeover, the success of a value-decreasing bid is a reflection of the discrepancy between collective interest and individually rational choice. Both problems can be resolved by the following mechanism:[52] First, a bidder seeking to buy a controlling stake asks all shareholders to vote on whether or not his offer shall be accepted or rejected. If the majority rejects, the offer is void. If a majority approves the offer, it becomes binding for all shareholders who are then treated equally, having to tender their shares on a pro-rata basis. The majority vote has to be binding to overcome the

[50] C Bergström, P Högfeldt, J Macey and P Samuelsson 'The Regulation of Corporate Acquisitions. A Law and Economics Analysis of European Proposals for Reform' (1994) Department of Finance, Stockholm School of Economics Working Paper no 62; F Cornelli and L Felli 'How to Sell a (Bankrupt) Company' (1998) Rodney L White Center Working Paper no 18-98, Wharton School, University of Pennsylvania.

[51] Consider two competing bidders, bidder 1 and 2 with respective (per share) firm value (in the absence of private benefit extraction) v_1 and v_2. For simplicity, there are no takeover costs and both bidders have the same ability to divert corporate resources, ie, the same $ø$ value. Effective competition implies that $v_2 > v_1 > v_2\,(1 - ø)$. If the bidders are forced by law to compete with unrestricted offers bidder 2 wins at a price equal to v_1 as this is bidder 1's maximum willingness to pay when acquiring all shares. If the bidders compete with offers restricted to 50 percent of the shares, bidder 2 has to offer $v_1\,(1 + ø)$ in order to outbid bidder 1. Given $ø < 1$ it follows that $1 / 2\ [(1 + ø)\ v_1 + (1 - ø)v_2] > v_1$ holds, ie, that target shareholders realize a higher return when bidders compete with restricted offers.

[52] Bebchuk and Hart, n 45.

free-rider problem. By contrast, the pressure to tender is also removed by a mechanism that requires approval by majority vote and (at least) a majority of shares tendered separately. If a majority of shareholders were to accept the offer, disapproving shareholders still have the option to tender. Thus, the latter have no incentives to distort their preferences in the vote due to hedging considerations. When voting on the offer, shareholder compare pre-takeover share value with the returns from tendering or retaining their shares and all value-decreasing bids get rejected in the vote.[53] A simple way to implement this mechanism is an extension of the offer period in case a takeover bid succeeds. It allows shareholders to tender once the bid has succeeded although they initially did not tender.[54] Thus, a regime with a pro rata requirement and an extension of the offer period protects target shareholders as effectively as the mandatory bid rule without discouraging as many value-increasing bids.

D. Squeeze-Out Right

Currently, most Member States grant majority shareholders the right to buy out remaining minority shareholders. The conditions under which this right can be exercised vary considerably, in particular with respect to the applicable threshold and the price to be offered.[55] The new draft directive (Article 14) introduces a common squeeze-out rule. Provided that the bidder owns 90 percent of the equity capital, he can compel the remaining minority shareholders to sell their shares at the price offered in the preceding takeover bid.[56] Member States have the discretion to apply a higher threshold with an upper limit of 95 percent (unless the bidder acquired 90 percent of the equity capital through the bid). In case the target firm has multiple classes of shares, the threshold applies separately to each class. Finally, the right to buy out minority shareholders can be exercised only after the threshold has been reached through a tender offer.

[53] While a value-increasing bidder would secure majority approval in the vote, he would fail to acquire the necessary amount of shares because shareholders prefer to free ride. Hence, the vote needs to be binding to ensure the success of value-increasing takeovers.

[54] The Swiss takeover regulation contains such a provision (Article 27.2 BEHG 1995).

[55] Draft Directive, n 1.

[56] When the market price is used as a proxy to set the squeeze-out price, the bidder's private information about the share value implies a lemon's problem (LA Bebchuk and M Kahan 'Adverse Selection and Gains to Controllers in Corporate Freezeouts' in R Morck (ed) *Concentrated Corporate Ownership* National Bureau of Economic Research Conference Volume (University of Chicago Press 2000) 295-315). This problem does not arise under the squeeze-out rule in the draft directive because the price is equal to the bid price if the squeeze-out right is exercised within three months after the end of the offer period of the takeover. Otherwise, the price is to be determined by an independent expert.

Besides harmonizing European takeover rules, the Winter Group advocates the squeeze-out rule on the grounds that the continued protection of the rights of a small minority imposes disproportionately high cost on the majority owner.[57] Minority shareholders may (threaten to) use their rights to jeopardize the majority owner's plans with the sole purpose of extorting undue concessions. Also in the absence of such hold-up problems, the continued presence of minority shareholders can be costly for the bidder.[58] For instance, the bidder cannot fully integrate the acquired firm with the activities and organization of his existing firm(s) and is hence unable to exploit all synergies.[59] Like the risk of obstruction, such forgone benefits make takeovers less attractive to prospective bidders. Furthermore, the squeeze-out right is more efficient and effective than de-listing procedures.

In sum, the Winter Group argues that the squeeze-out rule makes takeovers more attractive because full (100 percent) ownership has a higher value to bidders than an ownership of a large majority, say 90 percent (in per-share terms). Suppose that this is indeed the case and that the bidder owns 90 percent following a takeover bid. In order to buy out the remaining 10 percent, he would be willing to offer more than what he was willing to pay for the 90 percent. However, anticipating such a higher second offer, each shareholder would hold out and wait for the second offer. Hence, the initial bid would fail, unless the bidder already offered the higher price. This example indicates that the squeeze-out rule has the scope to influence the dynamics of the tender offer process. In fact, even when the bidder values (in per-share terms) full ownership and ownership of a large majority stake equally, the squeeze-out right affects the bidding and tendering decisions. To highlight these effects, we make the simplifying assumption of no such valuation differentials.

The squeeze-out right enhances the bidder's scope for action beyond the mere option to buy out possibly disruptive minority shareholders. As Yarrow[60] shows, the squeeze-out rule is 'a simple and elegant solution of the free rider problem'. To replicate this result, we introduce into our previous framework the squeeze-out right with threshold f, say $f = 0.9$. For simplicity, we assume that takeover costs c are negligibly small and set extraction $\o$ equal to zero. Suppose further that the bidder conditions his offer b on getting at least the fraction f of shares, ie, on being able to exercise the squeeze-out right.

[57] Draft Directive, n 1.

[58] The presence of minority shareholders also requires to maintain the infrastructure needed to enable them to exercise their rights, such as calling shareholder meetings and disclosing information.

[59] For instance, an acquiring firm with a controlling interest of less than 100 percent cannot transfer losses and profits between itself and the target firm to minimize the tax obligations (C Bergström, P Högfeldt and J Molin 'The Optimality of the Mandatory Bid Rule' (1994) 13 Journal of Law, Economics and Organization 433-451).

[60] GK Yarrow n 8.

Each shareholder continues to rightly presume that his tendering decision does not affect the outcome and compares the returns from tendering and retaining (for a given outcome). If less than f shares are tendered the offer is void, and the decision to tender is irrelevant. If f shares are tendered the shareholder receives the price b when tendering. If he retains his shares he either gets the price b or the post-takeover share value v, depending on whether or not the bidder exercises his squeeze-out right. The bidder will exercise the squeezes-out right when the price b is below the post-takeover share value v but not otherwise. As a result, the shareholder realizes at most a return equal to b when retaining his shares (in case the bid succeeds). Hence, provided that the bidder reaches the threshold f, each shareholder is indifferent between tendering and not tendering and may as well accept the offer even when the bid price is below the post-takeover share value ($b < v$).[61] The shareholders' indifference implies that failure, like success, is an equilibrium outcome.

Thus, the squeeze-out right makes takeovers feasible at a price below the post-takeover share value. Provided that the bid is conditioned on the squeeze-out threshold, it is impossible for target shareholders to become a minority shareholder, thereby solving the free rider problem. This has several implications. First, a takeover can be profitable even when the bidder owns no initial stake ($\omega = 0$) and when he is unable to dilute minority shareholders ($\phi = 0$).

Second, the result does not depend on whether or not the offer price is above or below the pre-takeover share value. To rule out the success of takeover bids at prices below the pre-takeover share value ($b < q$), we have again to invoke competition by the incumbent, thereby imposing the pre-takeover share value as the lower price limit for a successful bid. With the additional constraint $b \geq q$, all value-decreasing takeovers ($v < q$) are prevented, since the bidder would bear the entire value loss $q - v$. Since shareholders accept an offer $b = q$ conditioned on the threshold f, the bidder can extract the entire surplus $v - q$, and all value-increasing takeovers ($v \geq q$) occur.[62]

Third, the bidder can extract the entire surplus $v - q$, and thus all and only efficient takeovers occur whether the threshold triggering the squeeze-out right is 90 or say 60 percent. The threshold f becomes relevant only in a framework in which the supply of tendered shares is upward-sloping because target shareholders have for instance different liquidity needs or tax rates.[63] In such a setting,

[61] If the bidder were to offer a higher price in the squeeze-out than in the tender offer, he would re-create the free rider problem. All shareholders would want to participate in the squeeze-out, ie, would not accept the initial offer.

[62] A Yakov, M Kahan and R Sundaram 'The Foundations of Freezeout Laws in Takeovers' (2003) mimeo Department of Finance, Stern School of Business, New York University.

[63] D Hirshleifer and S Titman 'Share Tendering Strategies and the Success of Hostile Takeover Bids' (1990) 98 Journal of Political Economy 295-324; R Stulz 'Managerial Control of Voting Rights. Financing Policies and the Market for Corporate Control' (1988) 20 Journal of Financial Economics 25-54.

a higher threshold requires the bidder to offer a higher price in order to reach the threshold and squeeze-out the remaining minority shareholders. As this reduces the bidder's profits, the choice of the squeeze-out threshold involves a trade-off between promoting takeovers and protecting minority shareholders.

To conclude, the squeeze-out right leads to significant redistributions of the takeover gains. Rather than having to let target shareholders appropriate the bulk of the gains, the bidder can exclude them from the surplus. Hence, in regimes with a squeeze-out right, one would expect bidders to choose offers that are conditioned on the squeeze-out threshold level. Similarly, one would expect that bidders' returns in regimes with a squeeze-out right are (much) higher than in a regime without squeeze-out right.

E. Sell-Out Right

The new draft directive also introduces the sell-out right (Article 15). It is the quid pro quo for the minority shareholder of the squeeze-out right for the majority shareholder.[64]

Accordingly, the conditions under which the minority shareholders can exercise the sell-out right mirror those of the squeeze-out right. Provided that the majority shareholder owns 90 percent of the equity capital, the remaining minority shareholders can compel him to buy their shares at the price offered in the preceding takeover bid. Member States have the discretion to increase the threshold up to 95 percent of the equity capital. In case the target firm has multiple classes of shares, the threshold applies separately to each class.

In its report, the Winter Group motivates the introduction of the sell-out right with two kinds of arguments.[65] The first kind reverses the Group's arguments in favour of the squeeze-out right. After a takeover, the majority owner may abuse his dominant position, or in corporate finance parlance, extract private benefits at the expense of the minority shareholders. This problem becomes more severe once the majority stake becomes very large fraction, because the minority rights granted by law are in some Member States no longer available if minority holdings fall below a certain level. Furthermore, the market for shares becomes very illiquid in such situations, preventing an exit at a 'fair price'.

The second type of arguments on which we focus refers specifically to the tender offer process. The Winter Group argues that the sell-out right is a means to counter the pressure to tender. In particular, the sell-out right amounts to an extension of the offer period: Shareholders who have rejected the offer initially –

[64] About half the Member States provide a sell-out right and the national provisions vary along the same dimensions as the national squeeze-out provisions (Winter Report on Takeover Bids).

[65] ibid.

perhaps in the endeavour to make it fail – get the opportunity to tender their shares once the bidder has gained control (and reached the threshold triggering the sell-out right).

At first glance, the sell-out right looks like a toned-down version of the mandatory bid rule. The mandatory bid rule enables all shareholders to sell their shares, while the squeeze-out right grants this option only if the majority shareholder owns 90 percent following a takeover. Hence, it is hardly surprising that the sell-out right neither affects the outcome nor the shareholders' return in a value-increasing takeover. A value-increasing bidder offers a price equal to the post-takeover share value, and shareholders realize the same return whether they tender or not. Given that the price in the sell-out is the bid price, remaining minority shareholders do not benefit from the sell-out option.[66] Moreover, if a bidder is able to expropriate minority shareholders more when the minority becomes (very) small, as argued by the Winter Group, he can exploit this already in the tender offer. He simply makes an offer conditional on the sell-out threshold, thereby ensuring that in case of success the bid price is indeed equal to the further reduced post-takeover minority share value.

Another difference between sell-out right and mandatory bid rule concerns the timing. The sell-out right applies after the completion of a takeover, while the mandatory bid rule, being a condition on the offer, applies prior to the completion of the bid. Due to this difference, the sell-out right mitigates the pressure to tender problem, while the mandatory bid rule has no such effect. (The mandatory bid rule improves minority protection only to the extent that competition by the incumbent forces bidders to pay all shareholders at least the pre-takeover share value.)

Suppose that a value-decreasing bidder offers the post-takeover share value $b = (1 - \o)v < q$ and that no third party (incumbent) can finance a counter-bid. If the takeover succeeds and the bidder reaches the sell-out threshold, the sell-out right allows the shareholder to sell his shares at the same terms also after the takeover. Thus, there is no need to tender (accept the offer) only to avoid becoming a minority shareholder. This does, however, not hold for the outcome in which the takeover succeeds but the sell-out right is not triggered. Although this outcome is never reached in equilibrium, the mere possibility of it upholds the pressure to tender. The incentives to accept a value-decreasing bid are removed by setting the sell-out threshold such that only two outcomes are feasible, failure

[66] Abstracting from noise or irrationality, the sell-out right plays typically no role in the equilibrium of the takeover game. If shareholders are homogenous and the post-takeover share value does not depend on the fraction owned by the bidder, the bid either fails or all shareholders tender. In a framework with an upward-sloping supply curve, remaining minority shareholders do not want to exercise the sell-out option since their valuation of the minority share exceeds the bid price. This is the very reason why they preferred not to tender their shares in the first place.

or success where the sell-out right is triggered. Obviously, this is implemented by setting the threshold at 50 percent.

The sell-out right with a 50 percent threshold operates in the same manner as the aforementioned extension of the offer period following a successful takeover (section 3). Both rules allow shareholders to reject the offer without forgoing the option of selling their shares if the takeover happens to succeed. Given a second opportunity to sell there is no need to hedge against the minority position, and shareholder do not accept bids below the pre-takeover share value. In case a takeover succeeds, all remaining shareholders exercise their sell-out right if the bid price exceeds the post-takeover share value. Hence, all value-decreasing takeover are prevented.[67]

To conclude, the sell-out right is indeed equivalent to an extension of the offer period and has the potential to mitigate the pressure to tender. It, however, removes the pressure to tender effectively only at 50 percent threshold level.

F. Controlling Owners and Mandatory Bid Rule

As mentioned in the introduction, even listed (Continental) European firms typically have a controlling or dominant shareholder, rather than a dispersed ownership.[68] Therefore, an assessment of the new draft directive – or more precisely, of mandatory bid rule, squeeze-out right, and sell-out right – has to include the impact of these provisions on control transfers involving firms with controlling or dominant shareholders.[69]

The preceding analysis shows how in takeovers of widely held firms the squeeze-out right and the sell-out right can resolve the free rider problem and the pressure to tender problem respectively. Neither of these problems impairs the (in)efficiency of a control transfer involving firms with controlling shareholders. Hence, we can restrict our analysis of such control transfers to the mandatory bid rule. This does, however, not mean that minority shareholder protection is peripheral in the regulatory debate. In fact, the contrary applies.

Drawing on Kahan[70] and Bebchuk[71], we consider a firm controlled by an incumbent blockholder that is approached by an outside investor (henceforth

[67] Granting a second opportunity to sell does not change the free rider problem.

[68] R La Porta, F Lopez-de-Silanes and A Shleifer 'Corporate Ownership around the World' (1999) 54 Journal of Finance 471-517; F Barca and M Becht (eds) *Control of Corporate Europe* (OUP Oxford 2001).

[69] Control over a firm does not necessarily require a majority of votes, in particular, when the remaining shares are dispersed, a minority block may be sufficient. For instance, neither the Ford nor the Wallenberg families own a majority of votes.

[70] M Kahan 'Sales of Corporate Control' (1993) 9 Journal of law, Economics, and Organization 368-379.

[71] LA Bebchuk n 9.

rival) who would like to take control. The incumbent owns a fraction α of the return rights, and the remaining $(1-\alpha)$ is dispersed among small shareholders. The incumbent's block α may be larger or smaller than 50 percent. In the latter case, a dual class share structure ensures that the incumbent has nonetheless a majority of the votes. Under the incumbent's control, security benefits (total share value) are equal to X_I. In addition, the incumbent enjoys private benefits Z_I. If the rival gains control, security benefits are X_R and the rival's private benefits are Z_R. For simplicity, we do not explicitly consider that private benefits are (in part) extracted at the expense of the security benefits.[72] It also proves convenient to express all values in absolute terms rather than in per-share terms. The parameters X_I, X_R, Z_I, and Z_R are common knowledge. We refer to a control transfer as efficient (inefficient) if the sum of security benefits and private benefits under the rival's control exceeds (falls short of) the sum under the incumbent. Finally, it is useful to define $\Delta X = X_R - X_I$ and $\Delta Z = Z_R - Z_I$.

Subsequently, we identify the conditions under which efficient and inefficient control transfers takes place, first in a regime without the mandatory bid rule and then in a regime with the mandatory bid rule. The impact of the mandatory bid rule follows from a comparison of those conditions.

In the absence of a mandatory bid rule, incumbent and rival are not obliged to let the minority shareholders participate in the control transaction, and control can be transferred through a block trade at mutually agreeable terms. Since the subsequent arguments do not hinge on a specific block price, we abstract from its determination.[73] Having purchased the controlling block from the incumbent, the rival has always the option to make a voluntary tender offer to the dispersed small shareholders. Due to the free-rider behaviour, the rival does not gain from acquiring the remaining $1-\alpha$ dispersed shares and merely acquires the controlling block. Hence, a necessary and sufficient condition for a control transfer is that the block has a higher value under the rival's control than under the incumbent, or formally that $\alpha X_R + Z_R > \alpha X_I + Z_I$ holds.

By comparing this condition with the efficiency requirement ($\Delta X + \Delta Z > 0$) two conclusions emerge (Bebchuk 1994). First, an efficient control transfer may fail to take place. This inefficiency obtains in the parameter range $-[(1-\alpha)/\alpha]\Delta Z > \Delta X + \Delta Z > 0$. When the incumbent's private benefits are relatively large compared to the rival's private benefits, the incumbent does not want to trade. This may hold true even though a control transfer is efficient because the higher security benefits under the rival's control more than compensate his lower

[72] Transforming security benefits X_J and private benefits Z_J with $J = I, R$ into the previously used specification that explicitly accounts for this relationship yields $X_J = (1-\o)V_J$ and $Z_J = \o V_J$.

[73] In the theoretical literature, the block price is typically the outcome of a bargaining game between incumbent and rival that depends on the parties' outside options (see eg, Burkart and others 2000).

private benefits. The inefficiency arises because the incumbent and the rival do not take into account that a control transfer gives rise to a positive externality, ie, also benefits the small shareholders.

Second, an inefficient control transfer may occur. Being the mirror image of the above inefficiency, this outcome obtains whenever $0 > \Delta X + \Delta Z > -[(1-\alpha)/\alpha]$ ΔZ holds. When the rival's private benefits are relatively large compared to the incumbent's private benefits, incumbent and rival may want to trade the block even though the incumbent generates higher security benefits. The inefficiency is due the fact that incumbent and rival fail to internalise the negative impact that a control transfer has on the $1-\alpha$ widely held shares.

In the regime of the draft directive the rival cannot simply buy the controlling block from the incumbent but is obliged to offer all small shareholders the same conditions.[74] In such an environment, a control transfer takes place if, as before, it is mutually beneficial to rival and incumbent, and if the rival earns a profit when offering small shareholders the same per-share considerations. The incumbent agrees to sell control only if the rival compensates him for the security benefits of his stake αX_1 and the forgone private benefits Z_I (control premium). Having to extend these terms to the small shareholders requires the bidder to offer at least $X_I + Z_I / \alpha$ for the entire firm. Hence, a control transfer takes place under the mandatory bid rule if $X_R + Z_R > X_I + Z_I / \alpha$ holds. In this case, minority shareholders typically receive more than the security benefits under the rival's control, because they also get the incumbent's compensation for the forgone private benefits. (This holds true if $X_I + Z_I / \alpha > X_R$).

Comparing the condition $X_R + Z_R > X_I + Z_I / \alpha$ with the efficiency requirement yields the following two results. First, an efficient control transfer may not take place. This inefficiency obtains whenever $[(1-\alpha)/\alpha]Z_I > \Delta X + \Delta Z > 0$ holds. The mandatory bid rule obliges the rival to offer all shareholders the control premium that he pays the incumbent. When the incumbent's private benefits are large this requirement may inflate the price above the sum of security benefits and private benefits under the rival's control, even though the control transfer is efficient.

Second, the mandatory bid rule prevents all inefficient transfers. The price at which the incumbent is willing to sell the controlling block implies that the price for the entire firm exceeds the sum of private and security benefits under the incumbent's control ($X_I + Z_I / \alpha > X_I + Z_I$). Thus, block transfer and subsequent mandatory bid necessarily imply efficiency.

The mandatory bid rule redistributes part of the control transfer gains from the rival to the small shareholders. This redistribution has two opposing effects.[75] On

[74] Some national regulations are less stringent and allow for a discount relative to price paid in the block acquisition (Ferrarini 2002).

[75] Under less stringent rules that allow for some discrimination between per share price in the block trade and the tender offer, these two conflicting effects are both diluted. That is, fewer cont. ...

the one hand, it protects minority shareholders from inefficient control transfers.[76] On the other hand, the redistribution makes it more likely that an efficient control transfers fails to take place.[77] This is also to the disadvantage of the small shareholders when the rival is able to generate higher security benefits than the incumbent ($X_R > X_I$). Indeed, empirical studies on controlling block trades in the United States find that such trades are on average associated with abnormal share price increases.[78] This evidence suggests that improved management rather than extraction of private benefits is the primary source of gains in block trades. Further empirical work has to show to what extent these findings hold also in environments with weaker shareholder protection.

Overall, the mandatory bid rule strengthens minority shareholder protection at the expense of promoting efficient control transfers. Its merits therefore depend on the perceived likelihood that inefficient control transfers take place and that efficient control transfers fail. Two observations illustrate that the likely benefits and costs of the mandatory bid rule are sensitive to the environment.

First, the mandatory bid rule loses its advantage when private benefits are (predominantly) determined by the environment in which the firm operates or by the characteristics of the firm rather than by the identity of the controlling blockholder, ie, when $Z_I \cong Z_R > 0$.[79] In this case, inefficient control transfers do not take place in a regime without the mandatory bid rule, and fewer efficient transfers are discouraged. When the rival's and the incumbent's private benefits are of the same order of magnitude, both efficiency and surplus from a block trade only depend on the security benefits. This precludes the possibility that a block trade is beneficial but the control transfer is inefficient.

Second, a reduction in the size of the controlling block, ie, of the attached return rights, makes it more demanding to satisfy the condition for an efficient control transfer. This is true in a regime without and with the mandatory bid rule, but the effect is larger with the mandatory bid rule. In fact, the difference between

value-increasing control transfer are frustrated, but some value-decreasing transfers are not prevented.

76 In a framework where the bidder chooses the extent of inefficient private benefit extraction, the mandatory bid rule has an added beneficial effect. It increases the rival's final equity stake and thereby mitigates the private benefit extraction problem (M Burkart, D Gromb and F Panunzi n 16).

77 In the absence of the mandatory bid rule, a prerequisite for the failure of an efficient control transfer is $Z_I > Z_R$. Hence, the condition for a control transfer is stronger with the mandatory bid rule than in its absence, ie, $[(1 - \alpha) / \alpha]Z_I > -[(1 - \alpha) / \alpha]\Delta Z$.

78 CG Holderness 'A Survey of Blockholders and Corporate Control' (2003) Economic Policy Review, forthcoming.

79 In a sample of 412 controlling block transactions from 39 countries, A Dyck and L Zingales ('Private Benefits of Control: An International Comparison' (2002) forthcoming Journal of Finance) document considerable variation in the size of private benefits across countries. This finding suggest that national corporate governance plays an important role in shaping the size of private benefits of control.

the two conditions is $[(1-\alpha)/\alpha]Z_R$ which is decreasing in α. Thus, the adverse effect of the mandatory bid rule is exacerbated in environments where the controlling owner holds less return rights because of pyramiding or dual class shares. This suggests that such mechanisms for separating ownership and control should be removed prior to the introduction of a mandatory bid rule.

G. Conclusions

This paper provides an examination of the economic underpinnings of three new provisions of the draft takeover directive (October 2002), the squeeze-out right, the sell-out right, and the requirement that the price in a mandatory bid has to equal the highest price paid in the 6 or 12 preceding months. These provisions affect the distribution of the takeover gains, and thereby the incentives to make and accept a bid. Better (minority) shareholder protection lowers the ex ante cost of capital but reduces the takeover activity and hence ex post efficiency. This is the fundamental trade-off that any rule governing takeovers has to confront.

The focus of our analysis is how these new provisions affect the dynamics of the tender offer process in takeovers of widely held target firms. The squeeze-out right allows the bidder to overcome the free rider problem, while the sell-out right has the potential to eliminate the pressure to tender problem. By contrast, the mandatory bid rule has an effect only if competition by the incumbent constrains the acquirer from making a bid below the pre-takeover share value.

Taking a broader perspective, we want to comment on the Commission's apparent approach to a European takeover regulation. First, rather than merely emulating the UK City Code, we believe that a more open-minded approach should have been applied on some issues. Recent advances in corporate finance identify novel mechanisms to address known problems in takeovers. For instance, a combination of voting and tender offer overcomes the free rider problem and the pressure to tender problem.[80] Instead of retaining the mandatory bid rule, European corporate governance may have been better served through an adaptation of the Bebchuk-Hart scheme.

Second, harmonization undoubtedly facilitates many aspects of cross-border takeovers. However, in view of the considerable differences in control and ownership pattern across Europe, harmonization also has downsides. A specific rule likely to promote takeovers in one Member States may have the opposite effect in another Member State.[81] More generally, importing a takeover regulation developed within the Anglo-Saxon institutional setting into the current Continental European context may undermine rather than improve its current governance mechanisms.

[80] Bebchuk and Hart, n 45.

[81] E Berglöf and M Burkart n 7.

Finally, we would like to point out an omission in the current draft proposal. The Second Council Directive of the European Economic Community (1976) de facto severely impedes – or even prohibits – leveraged buyouts.[82] In view of the importance of leveraged buyouts for the United States' market for corporate control, this directive conflicts with the ambition of an active European takeover market. An amendment that explicitly allows for the possibility of financial assistance by the target firm to acquire its shares is called for as was recently done in Italy (Art. 2501-bis of the Italian Civil Code).

References

Amihud, Yakov, Marcel Kahan, and Rangarajan Sundaram, 2003, The Foundations of Freeze out Laws in Takeovers, mimeo Department of Finance, Stern School of Business, New York University.

Barca, Fabrizio and Marco Becht, 2001, (eds.), Control of Corporate Europe, Oxford University Press, Oxford.

Bebchuk, Lucien A., 1988, The Pressure to Tender: An Analysis and a Proposed Remedy, in J. C. Coffee, L. Lowenstein, and S. Rose-Ackerman (eds.), Knights, Raiders, and Targets, Oxford University Press, New York.

Bebchuk, Lucian A., 1994, Efficient and inefficient sales of corporate control, Quarterly Journal of Economics 109, 957-993.

Bebchuk, Lucian A. and Marcel Kahan, 2000, Adverse selection and Gains to Controllers in Corporate Freezeouts, in Randall Morck (ed.), Concentrated Corporate Ownership, National Bureau of Economic Research Conference Volume, University of Chicago Press, 295-315.

Bebchuk, Lucian A. and Oliver Hart, 2001, Takeover Bids Versus Proxy Fights in Contests for Corporate Control, CEPR Discussion Paper No. 3073.

Bebchuk, Lucian A. and Oliver Hart, 2002, A Threat to Dual-Class Shares, Financial Times, May 31.

Becht, Marco, Patrick Bolton, and Ailsa Röell, 2002, Corporate Governance and Control, mimeo Princeton University.

Bennedsen, Morten and Kaspar Nielsen, 2002, The Impact of a Break-Through Rule on European Firms, mimeo Copenhagen Business School.

Berglöf Erik and Mike Burkart, 2003, European Takeover Regulation, Economic Policy 18 (1), 171-213.

[82] Article 23 states that 'A company may not advance funds, nor make loans, nor provide security, with a view to the acquisition of its shares by a third party.'

Bergström, Clas, Peter Högfeldt, Jonathan Macey, and Per Samuelsson, 1994, The Regulation of Corporate Acquisitions. A Law and Economics Analysis of European Proposals for Reform, Department of Finance, Stockholm School of Economics Working Paper No. 62.

Bergström, Clas, Peter Högfeldt, and Johan Molin, 1997, The Optimality of the Mandatory Bid Rule, Journal of Law, Economics, and Organization 13, 433-451.

Bertrand, Marianne and Sendhil Mullainathan, 1999, Executive Compensation and Incentives: The Impact of Takeover Legislation, NBER Working paper 6830.

Bolton, Patrick, 2002, Presentation at the ECGI Panel on the Winter Report at the Annual Meeting of the Federation of European Stock Exchanges.

Bundesversammlung der Schweizerischen Eidgenossenschaft, 1995, Bundesgesetz über die Börsen und den Effektenhandel (BEHG).

Burkart, Mike, 1999, Economics of Takeover Regulation, mimeo Stockholm School of Economics.

Burkart, Mike, Denis Gromb, and Fausto Panunzi, 1998, Why takeover premia protect minority shareholders, Journal of Political Economy 106, 172-204.

Burkart, Mike, Denis Gromb, and Fausto Panunzi, 2000, Agency Conflicts in Public and Negotiated Transfers of Corporate Control, Journal of Finance 55, 647-677.

Burkart, Mike, Fausto Panunzi, and Andrei Shleifer, 2003, Family Firms, forthcoming Journal of Finance.

Cornelli, Francesca and Leonardo Felli, 1998, How to Sell a (Bankrupt) Company, Rodney L. White Center Working Paper No. 18-98, Wharton School, University of Pennsylvania.

European Commission, 2002, Report by the Group of High-Level Company Law Experts on Issues related to Takeover Bids, January 10 2002, Brussels.

European Commission, 2002, Directive of The European Parliament and of the Council on Takeover Bids, October 2 2002, Brussels.

Enriques, Luca, 2002, Mercato del controllo societario e tutela degl investitori, Il Mulino, Bologna.

Dyck, Alexander and Luigi Zingales, 2002, Private Benefits of Control: An International Comparison, forthcoming Journal of Finance

Ferrarini, Guido, 2002, Share ownership, Takeover Law and the Contestability of Corporate Control, Company Law Reform in OECD Countries. A Comparative Outlook of Current Trends. Conference Proceedings (forthcoming).

Grossman, Sanford J., and Oliver D. Hart, 1980, Takeover bids, the free rider problem, and the theory of the corporation, Bell Journal of Economics 11, 42-64.

Grossman, Sanford J., and Oliver D. Hart, 1988, One share-one vote, and the market for corporate control, Journal of Financial Economics 20, 175-202.

Hirshleifer, David, 1995, Mergers and Acquisitions: Strategic and Informational Issues, in Robert A. Jarrow, Vojislav Maksimovic, and William T. Ziemba (eds.), Handbook of Operations Research and Management Science, Vol 9, North-Holland.

Hirshleifer, David, and Titman, Sheridan, 1990, Share Tendering Strategies and the Success of Hostile Takeover Bids, Journal of Political Economy 98, 295-324.

Holderness, Clifford G., 2002, A Survey of Blockholders and Corporate Control, Economic Policy Review, forthcoming

Holmström, Bengt and Barry Nalebuff, 1992, To the Raider Goes the Surplus? A Re-examination of the Free Rider Problem, Journal of Economics and Management Strategies, 1: 37-62.

Kahan, Marcel, 1993, Sales of corporate control, Journal of Law, Economics, and Organization 9, 368-379.

Kyle, Albert S. and Jean-Luc Vila, 1991, Noise Trading and Takeovers, Rand Journal of Economics 22, 54-71.

La Porta, Rafael, Florencio Lopez-de-Silanes, Andrei Shleifer, and Robert W. Vishny, 1997, Legal Determinants of External Finance, Journal of Finance 52, 1131-1150.

La Porta, Rafael, Florencio Lopez-de-Silanes, Andrei Shleifer, and Robert W. Vishny, 1998, Law and Finance, Journal of Political Economy 106, 1113-55.

La Porta, Rafael, Florencio Lopez-de-Silanes, and Andrei Shleifer, 1999, Corporate Ownership around the World, Journal of Finance 54, 471-517.

La Porta, Rafael, Florencio Lopez-de-Silanes, Andrei Shleifer, and Robert W. Vishny, 2000, Investor Protection and Corporate Governance, Journal of Financial Economics 58, 3-27.

Mueller, Holger and Fausto Panunzi, 2003, Tender Offers and Leverage, mimeo Università di Bologna.

Nenova, Tatjana, 2003, The value of corporate voting rights and control: A cross-country analysis, Journal of Financial Economics 68 (3), forthcoming

Romano, Roberta, 1987, The Political Economy of Takeover Statutes, Virginia Law Review 73, 111-199.

Shleifer, Andrei and Lawrence H. Summers, 1988, Breach of Trust in Hostile Takeovers, in Alan J. Auerbach (ed.), Corporate Takeovers: Causes and Consequences, Chicago University Press, Chicago.

Shleifer, Andrei and Robert W. Vishny, 1986, Large Shareholders and Corporate Control, Journal of Political Economy 94, 461-488.

Shleifer, Andrei and Robert W. Vishny, 1991, Takeovers in the 60s and 80s: Evidence and Implications, Strategic Management Journal 12, 51-59.

Shleifer, Andrei, and Robert W. Vishny, 1997, A survey of corporate governance, Journal of Finance 52, 737-783.

Skog, Rolf,1995, Does Sweden Need a Mandatory Bid Rule? A Critical Analysis, Juristförlaget, Stockholm.

Skog, Rolf, 2002, The Takeover Directive – an endless saga?, European Business Law Review 13 (4), 301-312.

Stulz, René, 1988, Managerial Control of Voting Rights. Financing Policies and the Market for Corporate Control, Journal of Financial Economics 20, 25-54.

Yarrow, G. K., 1985, Shareholder Protection, Compulsory Acquisition and the Efficiency of the Takeover Process, Journal of Industrial Economics 34, 3-16.

The Mandatory Bid Rule in the Proposed EC Takeover Directive: Harmonization as Rent-Seeking?

LUCA ENRIQUES*

According to the new proposal for an EC takeover directive, anyone acquiring control of a listed company is required to make a bid, to be addressed to all holders of securities for all their holdings at a price at least equal to the highest price paid in the period preceding the acquisition, unless an exemption or a discount on price is granted by the supervisory authority. This paper provides an analysis of the mandatory bid rule as devised in the directive proposal and assesses whether there is a case for an EC rule of this kind. Five possible rationales are identified for the mandatory bid rule: the level playing field, the protection of minority shareholders, equality of treatment, companies' lower cost of capital, and efficiency and integration of European capital markets. Drawing from well-established economic analysis on transfers of control and the effects of the mandatory bid rule, the paper finds that harmonized rules such as those provided for in the proposal do not level the playing field and cannot be justified on this ground alone, have dubious effects on minority shareholders' welfare as a class and on firms' cost of capital, have no legal justification in terms of equal treatment, and can *possibly* be justified as rules enhancing the efficiency and integration of European capital markets, if other institutional arrangements such as low levels of enforcement of directors' duty of loyalty and the unavailability of the poison pill are taken into account. The paper concludes that *certainly* well-identified interest groups will gain from an EC mandatory bid rule provision. Corporate managers (and blockholders retaining working control) of widely-held European companies stand to gain from such provision, as it makes hostile takeovers more costly. Even more importantly, policy-makers and supervisory agency officials, to whom great power and discretion are granted in deciding whether the mandatory bid rule applies and what its price should be, are going to gain from its introduction. Finally, those providing advisory services in the market for corporate control, and above all lawyers specializing in mergers and acquisitions, stand to gain from having in place an EC mandatory bid rule.

* Paper prepared for the conference 'A Modern Regulatory Framework for Company and Takeover Law in Europe', Syracuse (Sicily), 29-30 May 2003. I wish to thank Matteo Gatti, Jeffrey Gordon, Roger Meservey, Fausto Panunzi, and conference participants for very helpful comments on earlier drafts. Usual disclaimers apply.

A. Introduction

According to its mandate from the EC Commission, the High Level Group of Company Law Experts (hereinafter, the High Level Group or simply the Group) had to deal with three issues regarding the EC takeover directive: (1) '[h]ow to ensure the existence of a level playing field in the European Union concerning the equal treatment of shareholders across Member States;' (2) '[t]he definition of the notion of an 'equitable price' to be paid to minority shareholders;' (3) '[t]he right for a majority shareholder to buy out minority shareholders ("squeeze-out right").'[1] This paper concentrates upon the second and third of these issues and also extends to the sell-out right, which the High Level Group, at its own initiative, treated somewhat in parallel to the squeeze-out right.[2] Given that the price in a mandatory bid lends substance to the mandatory bid rule itself and that in the Group's First Report the squeeze-out and sell-out rights are treated as a sort of corollary to the mandatory bid rule, it is only natural to dwell on the latter.

The paper proceeds as follows: section B summarizes the High Level Group's recommendations. Section 3 addresses the extent to which the Commission's new proposal for a takeover directive (hereinafter: the proposal)[3] has followed the Group's recommendations and documents (in footnotes) relevant proposed amendments by the European Parliament's rapporteur.[4] It describes in detail the provisions on mandatory bids and squeeze-out and sell-out rights, with some observations demonstrating that the proposal can achieve very little uniformity among Member States' regulations in this area and highlighting a few problems with the squeeze-out and sell-out rights as designed.

[1] *Report of the High Level Group of Company Law Experts on a Modern Regulatory Framework for Company Law in Europe* (European Commission November 2002) (Winter Report) (Annex 3 in this volume).

[2] Winter Report 62.

[3] Proposal for a European Parliament and Council Directive on takeover bids (COM (2002) 534) of 2 October 2002.

[4] European Parliament Draft Report on the proposal for a European Parliament and Council Directive on takeover bids, Committee on Legal Affairs and the Internal Market (Rapporteur: Klaus-Heiner Lehne) 2000/0240(COD) 11 March 2003.

Section D evaluates the provisions on mandatory bids, considering whether or not they are consistent with their possible rationales. It shows that harmonized rules such as those envisaged by the proposal do not level the playing field, have questionable effects on minority shareholders' welfare as a class and on firms' cost of capital, and have no legal justification in terms of equal treatment, but might *conceivably* be justified as enhancing the efficiency and integration of European capital markets.

In conclusion (section E), it is argued that an EC mandatory bid rule will *certainly* complicate and petrify the regulatory environment, leading to higher rents for lawyers. It will also grant wide discretion to securities agency officials, allowing them also to extract higher rents. The final outcome will be higher transaction costs for corporate takeovers.

B. The Group's Proposals on Mandatory Bid Price, Squeeze-Out and Sell-Out Rights

This section summarizes the High Level Group's proposals concerning the notion of equitable price and the squeeze-out and sell out rights for readers unfamiliar with the content of the Group's first Report.

I. Equitable Price

Self-evidently, there would be no substance to the mandatory bid rule, if the standards for setting the price were not determined by the legislator designing it. Essentially, the alternative for the EC legislator is either to fix the criteria itself or else to allow Member States wide discretion and, like the predecessor proposal, institute simply a broad standard, such as that of an 'equitable' price.[5] Of course, all sorts of intermediate solutions would be possible, such as providing the criteria and leaving Member States some degree of freedom to depart from them, either in transposition or case by case.

The trouble with the 'equitable price' formula, according to the Group, is that it would make the question of whether the price and the criteria are equitable 'a matter of European law, ultimately determinable by the European Court of Justice.'[6] This would imply delay and uncertainty that would 'have the effect of deterring transactions altogether.'[7] Having ruled out the sheer 'equitable price' formula on these grounds, the Report finds that a better solution must be devised

[5] Winter Report 45.

[6] ibid 48.

[7] Winter Report.

in a trade-off between the requirements of flexibility and predictability.[8] Flexibility is crucial, in light of the great diversity within the EU in rules, capital market characteristics, acquisition techniques and so on.[9] Predictability is essential to acquirers, who may otherwise be unable to plan their acquisitions, lacking a key piece of information for cost determination.[10]

Taking these two requirements into account, the Group's recommends to 'create a strong presumption in favour of a price established by application of a common rule and at the same time provide for sufficient flexibility in particular circumstances:'[11] hence, 'the price to be offered in the mandatory bid should, *in normal circumstances*, be equal to the highest price paid by the offeror for shares in that class … during a certain period [the length of which may be set by Member States between 6 and 12 months] preceding the date of the acquisition of securities by the offeror, which resulted in the change of control of the company.'[12]

The justification for this choice is twofold. First, this criterion is 'require[d]' by 'the principle of equivalent treatment of all holders of securities of the same class,'[13] since it 'offers the … benefit of allowing the minority shareholders to fully share the premium paid by the acquirer at any time in the period under consideration.'[14] I will come back to this justification for the highest-price-paid criterion in section D, in assessing the consistency of the proposal's provisions with their possible rationales.

Second, this criterion also 'giv[es] the offeror the certainty that he will not have to pay more in the mandatory bid than he has been willing to pay in the preceding period and as a result permit[s] him to determine himself at which maximum price he is prepared to acquire all securities of the company.'[15] This second rationale is hardly convincing: the acquirer will have the certainty of not paying more in the mandatory bid than he has been willing to pay in the preceding period whenever the criteria allow the mandatory bid price to be determined in advance and produce one that is no higher, but may well be lower. Moreover, it is also inconsistent with the Group's recommendation that the supervisory agency should have the power to impose a price higher than the highest one paid.[16]

[8] ibid 49.

[9] ibid.

[10] ibid.

[11] ibid.

[12] ibid. (emphasis added).

[13] ibid.

[14] Winter Report 50.

[15] ibid.

[16] Text corresponding to n 17.

The Group addresses flexibility by recommending that the Directive 'explicitly state that Member States are permitted to define both the situations in which … [the presumption that the highest price paid is equitable] may be displaced and the criteria which may be applied by supervisory authorities in their decision to retain a price higher or lower than the highest price paid.'[17] Hence, the presumption may be discarded not only in favour of the acquirer but also of the target shareholders, as when the highest price paid was set by collusion.[18]

In order to provide some guidance to the Member States, the Group argues, the directive should provide that: (a) 'the [highest price] rule can be deviated from only where it is demonstrated that its application would plainly result in an *unfair* price;'[19] (b) 'where deviation would lead to a lower price, the burden of proof should lie with the offeror;'[20] (c) 'in any areas of doubt, the judgement should be finally guided by the principle of "shareholder interest" – that is, all unclear cases should be solved by giving prevalence to the *fair* treatment of the target's shareholders.'[21] Of course, any decision to deviate from the highest price paid should be properly motivated by the supervisory authority.[22]

In a word, as the Group itself declares, in deciding whether to deviate from the default criterion, 'the main principle [would] be that of fairness.'[23] To concur that this guideline is vague indeed, one need not share Judge Easterbrook's view that '[f]airness is an empty concept into which agencies, courts, and lawyers pour a miscellany of unexamined and inconsistent premises:'[24] if not an empty concept, fairness is a very indeterminate standard, which definitely undermines predictability and can do little to set limits to policymakers' and supervisory authorities' discretion.

According to the Group, in case of deviation from the default criterion, the price should not be freely fixed, the directive having instead to provide a set of criteria from which Member States may choose. With the exception of the 'average market value over a certain period,'[25] all of these criteria would also leave ample discretion to the supervisory agencies: as is well known, 'the liquidation value of the company' and 'any other objective valuation criteria usually applied

[17] Winter Report.

[18] ibid.

[19] Winter Report (emphasis added).

[20] Winter Report.

[21] Winter Report (emphasis added).

[22] ibid 51.

[23] ibid 50.

[24] F Easterbrook 'Insider Trading As an Agency Problem' in JW Pratt and RJ Zeckhauser (eds) *Principals and Agents: The Structure of Business* (Harvard Business School Press Boston 1985) 81, 82-83.

[25] Provided that 'value' equals 'price'.

in financial analysis'[26] might well be 'objective' in the sense of being based on explicit assumptions but far from it in the sense of yielding one and only one possible result.

Finally, the Group's recommendations include a best price rule, to be applied not only during the bid period, but also to subsequent purchases (during a period of between 6 and 9 months after the mandatory bid), or, alternatively, a complete ban on purchases outside the bid in the same period.[27]

II. The Squeeze-Out Right

According to the Group, the squeeze-out right (ie, the right to buy minority shareholders' shares for a price set according to general criteria) should be granted at EC level to anyone having acquired, following a takeover bid, between 90 and 95 percent of the target's capital or having launched a takeover bid, when 90 or 95 percent of the outstanding shares have been tendered.[28] When there is more than one class of shares, the right should apply on a class-by-class basis, that is, it 'can be exercised only for the class(es) in which the applicable threshold (percentage of capital of the relevant class or percentage of acceptances of the relevant class) has been reached by virtue of a bid made in respect of the relevant class(es).'[29]

It should just be mentioned here that in its second Report the Group proposes generalizing the squeeze-out right, ie granting shareholders of all listed and open companies owning more than 90-95 percent of the shares, no matter how they have obtained this holding, the right to buy out minority shares.[30]

As to the consideration for the exercise of the squeeze-out right, the Group provides three alternative solutions:[31] (a) if a voluntary bid has been made, which has been accepted by shareholders holding 90 per cent or more of the shares in respect of which the offer was made, the bid price is *presumed* to be fair; but the presumption is rebuttable and can be challenged before courts or the supervisory authority; (b) if a mandatory bid has been made, the mandatory bid price is presumed to be fair, and the presumption is again rebuttable; (c) in all other cases, the price is set by an expert appointed by a court or by the supervisory authority. Alternative (c) also applies if the right is not exercised within a period ranging from 3 to 6 months following the bid.

[26] Winter Report 51.

[27] ibid 51-52.

[28] ibid 64.

[29] Winter Report 65.

[30] Winter Report 110.

[31] Winter Report 65-66.

III. The Sell-Out Right

The sell-out right (ie the right for minority shareholders to sell their shares to the majority shareholder for a price set by general criteria) is very similar in design to the squeeze-out right. The threshold for the sell-out right would be 90 to 95 percent of the capital, again if necessary class-by-class.[32] However, the sell-out right should 'not be exercisable in situations where the threshold is reached only on a temporary basis.' Further, in order to 'avoid the burden of multiple applications,' 'an adequate procedure [should] guarantee a fair treatment of all minority shareholders once one of them decides to exercise his sell-out right.'[33] The rules on consideration would be the same as for the squeeze-out right.[34]

The Group's second Report also recommends that a sell-out right be granted to minority shareholders of all listed and open companies, regardless of how the relevant threshold has been crossed.[35] In practice, such a right would indirectly impose a minimum 'floating' percentage on listed and open companies, like what such Member States as France and Italy already provide.[36]

C. The Proposal's Provisions on Mandatory Bids and Squeeze-Out and Sell-Out Rights: The Devil Is in the Details

Let us now scrutinize the proposal's provisions relating to mandatory bids and squeeze-out and sell-out rights. In short, the proposal grants Member States wide discretion, both at the time of implementation and in the practical administration of the rules as implemented, to set the mandatory bid price and, more important, to decide whether a bid must be made once the relevant threshold is crossed. Some features of the proposed squeeze-out and sell-out rights are questionable, raising concern as to the ability of the former to eliminate free riding and of the latter to protect minority shareholders against value-decreasing takeovers. Part of this section is again for readers unfamiliar with the proposal. Others may want to skip sections I, II.1, and III.1.

[32] ibid 66.

[33] ibid 67.

[34] ibid.

[35] Winter Report 110.

[36] eg A Viandier *OPA, OPE et autres offres publiques* (Editions Francis Lefebvre Levallois 1999) 417-18; R Costi *Il mercato mobiliare* (Giappichelli Torino) 97-98.

I. General Principles

Before describing the Commission choices directly relevant to this contribution, let us mention some of the definitions and broad principles set forth in Articles 2 to 4, which are essential to an understanding of the proposal's framework of rules.

Article 2(e) defines 'securities' as those 'carrying voting rights in a company' (reasonably, in its general meeting). Thus, when the directive uses this expression, it does *not* cover non-voting shares. Second, the term 'bid' includes both mandatory and voluntary offers. Third, Article 3 lays down a series of fundamental principles that Member States must follow in implementing the directive, at least one of which is worth citing: 'if a person acquires control of a company, the other holders of securities are to be protected' (para 1, letter (a)).

Most importantly for our analysis, Article 3(2), provides that Member States 'may lay down additional conditions and more stringent provisions than those required by this directive for regulating *bids*,' ie voluntary and mandatory bids. That is, the proposal only provides minimum safeguards for minority shareholders, Member States being free to devise further protections.[37] As is expressly stated in the Explanatory memorandum and in the Preamble,[38] Member States may decide, for instance, to apply rules on mandatory bids to other types of securities, such as non-voting shares.

Finally, according to Article 4(5), '[p]rovided that the general principles set out in Article 3(1) are respected, Member States may provide in their rules made or introduced pursuant to this directive that their supervisory authorities may, in certain types of cases determined at national level and/or in other special cases, grant derogations from these rules on the basis of a reasoned decision.' In other words, Member States may allow their supervisory authorities to decide, case-by-case, that the mandatory bid rule does not apply in certain special circumstances, whether specified by the national rules or not ('in other special cases'). To be sure, unjustified or over-ample use of this power may constitute a breach of Article 3(1)(a) (protection of minority shareholders in case of control transfer), unless of course some other equivalent form of protection is provided. In any event, the grey area in which a reasoned decision may be judged to be consistent with the directive is broad enough to leave Member State and local supervisory authorities considerable influence in the administration of the national mandatory bid regime.

[37] Compare Preamble n.(8).

[38] Explanatory Memorandum Article 2; Preamble n (10).

II. The Mandatory Bid Rule and the Equitable Price

As the Explanatory memorandum states, the proposal follows the Group's recommendations on the mandatory bid price and squeeze-out and sell-out rights.[39]

Article 5 contains the mandatory bid rule provisions, under which:

(1) 'Where a natural or legal person who, as a result of his own acquisition or the acquisition by persons acting in concert with him [as defined in Article 2(d)], holds securities of a company … which, added to any existing holdings and the holdings of persons acting in concert with him, directly or indirectly give him a specified percentage of voting rights in that company, conferring on him the control of that company [a concept to be defined by each Member State: para 3],[40] Member States shall ensure that this person is required to make a bid as a means of protecting the minority shareholders of that company. This bid shall be addressed at the earliest opportunity to all holders of securities for all their holdings at an equitable price' (para 1).

(2) 'The highest price paid for the same securities by the offeror, or by persons acting in concert with him, over a period of between six and twelve months prior to the bid referred to in paragraph 1 shall be regarded as an equitable price' (para 4).[41]

(3) However, 'Member States may authorize their supervisory authorities to adjust this price in circumstances and according to criteria that are clearly determined. To that end, they shall draw up a list of circumstances in which the highest price may be adjusted either upwards or downwards, for example [and hence not exhaustively] where the highest price was set by agreement between the purchaser and a seller [ie reasonably, in case of collusion], where the market prices of the securities in question have been manipulated, where market prices in general or certain market prices in particular have been affected by exceptional occurrences, or in order to enable a firm in difficulty to be rescued. They may also determine the criteria to be applied in such cases, for example the average market value over a particular period, the break-up value of the company or other objective valuation criteria generally used in financial analysis. Any decision by a

[39] Explanatory Memorandum 3.

[40] The European Parliament Draft Report contains an Amendment 16 which would set the threshold at '30% of the shares carrying most voting rights pursuant to Article (3) and (4).'

[41] The European Parliament Draft Report contains an Amendment 18 providing that, '[w]here this price cannot be ascertained because such securities have not been acquired by the offeror, the highest market price paid during the set period shall apply.' This amendment also requires Member States to define criteria for the determination of the price of multiple voting shares that are not publicly traded.

supervisory authority to adjust the equitable price shall be substantiated and made public' (para 4).

(4) 'The consideration offered by the offeror may consist exclusively of liquid securities. Where the consideration offered by the offeror does not consist of liquid securities admitted to trading on a regulated market, Member States may stipulate that such consideration has to include a cash consideration at least as an alternative. In any event, the offeror shall offer a cash consideration at least as an alternative where, either individually or together with persons acting in concert with him, over a period beginning at least three months before his bid is made … and ending before expiry of the period for acceptance of the bid, he has purchased in cash more than 5% of the securities or voting rights of the offeree company' (para 5).

(5) No obligation to launch a bid follows acquisitions through a voluntary bid to all holders of securities for all their holdings (para 2).[42]

(6) 'The Commission shall adopt, in accordance with the [comitology] procedure referred to in Article 17(2), the rules for the application of paragraphs 4 [price] and 5 [liquid securities]' (para 6).[43]

(7) 'In addition to the protection provided under paragraph 1, Member States [retain the freedom to] provide for further instruments aimed at protecting the interests of holders of securities in so far as these instruments do not hinder the normal course of the bid.'

III. Evaluation

Each of these provisions would well repay close scrutiny to draw a clear picture of their scope and content, but here I confine myself to some general observations providing a background for the assessment set out in the following section.

First of all, anyone familiar with national mandatory bid rules and practices will notice immediately that these provisions leave plenty of room for more or less ingenious ways to avoid the mandatory bid requirement, depending of course on how national implementing rules are drafted and enforced. As a matter of fact, in order to make the mandatory bid rule meaningful, Member States will have to supplement Article 5 with more specific rules on such matters as, to mention but

[42] The European Parliament Draft Report includes an Amendment 21 which aims at banning partial bids, following the German takeover law model (see WpÜG, Article 32).

[43] The European Parliament Draft Report contains an Amendment 20 proposing deletion of para 6 on constitutional grounds.

one, the treatment of control acquisitions of companies controlling a listed company, which do not seem to be covered.[44]

Second, the Directive only provides for one explicit derogation to the mandatory bid requirement, ie when the threshold is crossed following a 100 percent bid, while it is well known that legal systems imposing a mandatory bid upon change of control routinely identify a much broader set of derogations. For instance, in France a bid is not mandatory following the acquisition of a stake higher than the relevant threshold in case of: (1) gratuitous acquisitions, (2) acquisitions following a pro rata distribution by a corporation, (3) acquisitions through a capital increase in case of financial difficulty, (4) mergers or divisions approved by the general meeting of the relevant company, (5) reduction in the number of shares or votes, (6) a third party owning the majority of shares, alone or in concert with other persons, and (7) intra-group transfers of shares.[45] Some of these exemptions follow logically from the requirement in the proposal that the holding acquired must confer control. Some others do not. In any event, in implementing the directive, all Member States already providing for a mandatory bid rule will understandably confirm the variable range of derogations that they have in place today, while Member States now introducing it will also provide for more or less far-reaching derogations. This will presumably lead to considerable disparity of treatment of control changes around the EU.

With specific regard to the equitable price, the Commission has clearly adopted the High Level Group's proposal. However, instead of providing a general fairness guideline for deviating from the highest price paid, the proposal relies on the comitology procedure under Article 17 to 'spell out [the] circumstances and criteria justifying [departure from] it.'[46] Hence, unless the comitology procedure is scrapped, as the European Parliament suggests,[47] Member States will have less discretion in determining the equitable price than in carving out total exemptions. It will in turn depend on the regulations (if any) approved by the European Securities Committee whether national authorities will have more or less discretion in deciding whether such circumstances occur and how to apply the criteria.

[44] Compare B Dauner Lieb and M Lamandini 'The New Proposal of a directive on company law concerning takeover bids and the achievement of a level playing field' (2003) European Parliament Working Paper 57.

[45] eg A Viandier *OPA, OPE et autres offres publiques* (n 36) 288-98. Other legal systems provide for similar derogations. For the UK's City Code, see, eg C Pearson 'Mandatory and Voluntary Offers and Their Terms' in M Button and S Bolton (eds) *A Practitioner's Guide To The City Code on Takeovers and Mergers* (City & Financial Publ Old Woking 1999) 97, 104-07; for Italy, eg L Enriques *Mercato del controllo societario e tutela degli investitori* (il Mulino Bologna 2002) 147-210.

[46] Explanatory Memorandum 7.

[47] n 43.

In light of Member States' power to carve out exceptions to the mandatory bid rule altogether and of the supervisory authorities' power to derogate from the highest price paid rule, this framework will leave plenty of room for efforts by well paid legal advisers and investment bankers to design transactions in such a way as to minimize the acquirer's cost, whether because he will be exempted from the mandatory bid or because the supervisory authority grants him a discount.

Three further points are worth highlighting. First, as the European Parliament's Draft Report confirms, the directive does not ban partial bids,[48] and would-be raiders are in fact free to launch them. A bidder may seek a stake below the mandatory bid threshold, possibly because all he wants is working control, or he may want a larger stake. In either case, the partial bid is voluntary and must naturally comply with all the rules for bids in general. No mandatory bid requirement will of course follow a bid for a stake below the relevant threshold. If, instead, a bid for a larger holding is successful (ie if the bidder crosses the threshold through acceptance of the bid), then the bidder will have to make a mandatory bid according to Article 5 and offer to buy all the securities at the price paid in the partial bid (assuming this is the highest price paid in the relevant period). This two-step process may carry lower transaction costs than an initial bid for 100 percent of the shares, because financing can also be arranged in two steps, the mandatory bid being financed only once it is clear that control has been acquired. Note that partial bids followed by a mandatory bid such as that devised by the directive (ie with a price no lower than the partial bid price) are less coercive than 100 percent bids that carry exemption from the mandatory bid requirement.[49] As we know, shareholders face pressure to tender even in case of a 100 percent bid,[50] while in case of a partial bid to be followed by a mandatory bid for at least the same price, the pressure-to-tender problem is solved by the possibility of following the majority if the bid is successful.[51]

[48] n 42.

[49] Interestingly, such a two-step transaction would be almost identical to a takeover bid followed, as under the City Code and the Swiss and Austrian laws, by an extension of the offer period if the bid succeeds. See City Code, Rule 31.4 (UK); BEHG, Article 27(2) (Switzerland); ÜbG, Article 19(3) (Austria).

[50] See especially LA Bebchuk 'Toward Undistorted Choice and Equal Treatment in Corporate Takeovers' (1985) 98 Harvard Law Rev 1695, 1716-28 and 'The Pressure to Tender: An Analysis and a Proposed Remedy' (1987) 12 Delaware Journal of Corporate Law 911, 926-30.

[51] eg M Burkart and F Panunzi 'Mandatory Bids, Squeeze-out, Sell-Out and the Dynamics of the Tender Offer Process' (14 July 2003) ECGI – Law Working Paper No. 10/2003, 16-17. <http://ssrn.com/abstract=420940> (for a later version cf. chapter 11 in this volume).

Second, in light of the definition of 'securities' neither the exempting voluntary bid for 100 percent of the shares nor the mandatory bid must be extended to nonvoting shares. This, in turn, means that some value-decreasing acquisitions may well go through under the proposed regime: in the worst scenario, after the bid (voluntary or mandatory) the new controlling shareholder will be able to abuse his position to the detriment of holders of nonvoting shares, to whom the proposal gives no exit-option protection. Hence, if controlling shareholders really do prefer a world without mandatory bid rules, because they can sell out more freely and presumably at a higher price, then this feature of the EC proposed rule provides a clear incentive to issue nonvoting shares. This is patently at odds with the High Level Group's apparent aversion to deviations from one-share-one-vote.[52]

Third, and last, the proposal contains no prohibition of purchases outside the bid nor any best price rule to ensure equal treatment among shareholders and, more important, their undistorted choice.[53] While it can be easily argued that it would be a violation of the directive, and specifically of the general principle in Article 3(1) (equivalent treatment for all holders of securities of the offeree company), for a Member State not to ban purchases outside the bid or not to impose a best price rule, it is far from self-evident that it would violate the same principle, in either case, not to provide for a cooling-off period (the lack of which makes any ban or best-price rule readily avoidable).

IV. Squeeze-Out and Sell-Out Rights: The Proposal's Provisions

The provisions on squeeze-out and sell-out rights in the Directive strictly follow the High Level Group's recommendations.

Under Article 14, 'Member States shall ensure that, following a bid made to all the holders of securities of the offeree company for all their securities, an offeror is able to require the holders of the remaining securities to sell him those securities at a fair price in either of the following cases: (a) where he holds securities representing not less than 90% of the capital of the offeree company, or (b) where he has acquired, through acceptance of the bid, securities representing not less than 90% of the capital concerned by the bid.' Member States choosing alternative (a) may set 'a higher threshold that may not, however, be more than 95%

[52] Although the High Level Group finds that some deviations can be justified (Winter Report 24), the decision to make nonvoting shares useless in the case of a takeover battle (ibid 26) deprives them of their very function of protecting controlling shareholders from hostile takeovers, betraying the Group's negative view of them.

[53] On the best price rule's function see PL Davies 'The Notion of Equality in European Takeover Regulation' in J Payne (ed) *Takeovers in English and German Law* (Hart Publishing Oxford 2002) 9, 16-17.

of the company's capital' (para 1).[54] As recommended by the Group, '[w]here the offeree company has issued more than one class of shares, the rule laid down in paragraph 1 shall apply separately within each class' (para. 2). The price for the squeeze out has to be 'fair' and 'shall take the same form as the consideration offered in the bid.' A rebuttable presumption of fairness shall apply: (1) when the price 'corresponds to the consideration offered in [a voluntary] bid and the offeror has acquired, through acceptance of the bid, securities representing not less than 90% of the capital concerned by the bid;' (2) when the price corresponds to the consideration offered in a mandatory bid (para 3). These presumptions, however, 'shall apply only where the squeeze-out right is exercised within a period of three months after the end of the period for acceptance of the bid. In all other cases, the price shall be determined by an independent expert' (para 4).

Article 15 provides that 'Member States shall ensure that, following a bid made to all the holders of securities of the offeree company for all their securities, a minority holder of securities is able to require the offeror holding not less than 90% of the capital of the offeree company to buy his securities from him at a fair price. They may set a higher threshold, but this may not be more than 95% of the company's capital' (para 1). Again this rule applies separately for each class of shares for companies that have issued more than one (para 2). The provisions relating to the price for squeeze-outs shall apply also for sell-outs (para 3). Finally, 'the sell-out right may not be exercised where the specified threshold has been reached only for a short period' (para 1).

V. Assessment

In their contribution to this book, Burkart and Panunzi provide a very clear analysis of the effect of a squeeze-out option on takeovers. Assuming that the squeeze-out price equals the bid price and that the threshold is 90%, they demonstrate that when the bidder reserves the squeeze-out right in case of success and makes the bid conditional upon reaching the 90% threshold, shareholders are indifferent between tendering and not tendering.[55] This indifference implies that a bid may fail because not enough shareholders decide to tender, insofar as they assume that their tender is not pivotal and that the takeover is value-increasing (or at least not value-decreasing).[56]

[54] The European Parliament Draft Report contains an Amendment 32 allowing Member States to set a higher threshold, up to 95 percent, also when the threshold is calculated by making reference to acceptances of the bid. Amendment 34 suggests the introduction of an Article 15a providing a sell-out right in favor of holders of multiple voting securities who have been set aside in application of the modified breakthrough rule also proposed by the Parliament (see Amendment 29).

[55] Burkart and Panunzi (n 51) 18-19.

[56] ibid.

One qualification is needed here: under the proposal, the squeeze-out price is not necessarily equal to that of the previous bid: the right to buy minority holders' securities is exercised at a 'fair price' (Article 14(1)). More, 'the price shall be presumed to be fair where it corresponds to the consideration offered in [a voluntary] bid,' but only if 'the offeror has acquired, through acceptance of the bid, securities representing not less than 90% of the capital concerned by the bid' (para 3). If the presumption does not apply, 'the price will be determined by an independent expert' (para 4). Even excluding the possibility that shareholders hold out in order to challenge the presumption of fairness in court or before the supervisory agency,[57] where the bidder owns an initial stake (as is normally the case), for shareholders who perceive the bid as value-increasing the optimal outcome is that enough shareholders tender to put the bidder over the squeeze-out threshold but not enough to trigger the presumption of fairness of the bid price in the squeeze-out procedure. It is in fact at least possible, if not likely, that, in such a setting, the independent expert will determine a squeeze-out price higher than the bid price.

The proposal also provides that in the case of a mandatory bid, 'the consideration offered in the bid shall be presumed to be fair.' Hence, when the threshold is crossed following such a bid, the presumption applies regardless of the percentage of acceptances. Accordingly, an acquirer may find it convenient to use a two-step procedure: first, a voluntary partial bid allowing him to cross the mandatory bid threshold, then the mandatory bid at same price (or possibly a higher one, provided the increase is not announced in advance), to cross the squeeze-out threshold. Only in this case will minority shareholders be truly indifferent between accepting and not: the squeeze-out price will be the same as the mandatory bid (again leaving aside the possibility of a legal challenge). Of course, this procedure is more complex and so may entail higher transaction costs (two offers instead of one). This may not be the case, however, if supervisory authorities allow the acquirer to unify, so to speak, the two offers in terms of paperwork, by making them, as they truly are, two steps of a single takeover transaction.

Finally, note that the squeeze-out right in the proposal can only be exercised with regard to 'securities', ie shares with voting rights. Nonvoting shares are not covered, hence no harmonization will result for them: Member States will be free to decide whether to allow the acquirer to squeeze out minority holders of non-voting shares. This exclusion has two possible explanations: either it is just an inadvertent mistake or it may be considered consistent with the rationale for the squeeze-out right provided by the High Level Group in its first Report.

[57] According to the Winter Report the presumption is rebuttable (65) and it is plausible to assume that it is so also according to the proposal.

In fact, the Group provides three justifications for the squeeze-out right.[58] First, the continued existence of minority shareholders entails costs of various kinds to the majority shareholder. Second, and strictly related to this, ex ante, these costs will discourage takeover activity. Third, in some Member States a result similar to a squeeze-out can be achieved through delisting, but this is a more burdensome procedure which, to be sure, 'does not guarantee that minority shareholders transfer their shares.'[59]

In essence, these three justifications boil down to the first (the second one being the effect of the first on takeover activity and the third being merely evocative, since admittedly delisting does not lead to a compulsory sale of shares by minority shareholders). This first justification, in turn, centers upon the costs arising from the 'administrative' rights of minority shareholders, such as the 'direct costs for having to maintain the infrastructure for holding general meetings ... and in relation to other rights exercisable by minority shareholders (calling of meetings of shareholders, requests for information ...),'[60] and those stemming from 'abusive exploitation by the minority shareholders of their rights'[61] or the threat thereof.

If one assumes (although it is not necessarily true) that nonvoting shares cannot give rise to these costs, because they carry no voting nor other 'administrative' rights, then their exclusion may be justified. Economists, however, have made it abundantly clear that the problem with remaining shareholders after an acquisition is that they can free-ride on the acquirer's superior ability to manage the company by their very entitlement to their share of a company's *cash flow rights*, thus decreasing ex ante the incentives for takeovers.[62] This economic justification for the squeeze-out remedy applies to voting and nonvoting shares alike.

Finally, the sell-out right provision in the proposal is quite inconsistent with its economic justification within the framework of takeover regulation. Recall that the High Level Group gave four reasons for the sell-out right:

(1) after the bid, 'the majority shareholder may be tempted to abuse his dominant position' in many ways and '[i]n some Member States, the rights granted to minority shareholders by law to protect against such abuse are no longer available if the minority shareholdings drop below a certain level;'[63]
(2) minority shares may 'become illiquid as a result of the takeover bid;'[64]

[58] Winter Report 60-61.

[59] ibid.

[60] ibid.

[61] ibid.

[62] For references, see Burkart and Panunzi (n 51) 9-10 and 18.

[63] Winter Report 62.

[64] ibid.

(3) 'the sell-out right is an appropriate mechanism to counter the pressure on shareholders to tender in the takeover bid;'[65]

(4) it is also 'to be regarded as a fair counterpart for the squeeze-out right,'[66] which, to be sure, has in turn 'to be regarded as a compensation for the mandatory bid rule.'[67]

Leaving aside point (4), which is no more than an evocative analogy, among the other three only rationale (3) actually has to do with takeovers: rationales (1) and (2), in fact, could justify a sell-out right, even if the threshold has been crossed outside a takeover.[68] Once it is clear that only the rationale based upon the pressure to tender justifies a specific sell-out right following a takeover, it is also clear that at least two features of this right under the proposal are inconsistent with the rationale.

As others have already noticed,[69] if the pressure to tender is remedied by a sell-out right, ie essentially an extension of the offer period, then there is no reason why the right should be restricted to the most successful bids. Rather, it would be even more justified when the bidder gains just a 50 percent stake, because greater separation between ownership and control provides even stronger incentives to abuse control. The only way to justify such a high threshold would be to admit that the squeeze-out right as designed in the proposal cannot really solve the free-riding problem, so that some degree of pressure to tender remains justified.

A second feature of the sell-out right may be consistent with rationales (1) and (2) above, but definitely at odds with rationale (3). Following the Group's recommendations, the proposal provides that 'the sell-out right may not be exercised where the specified threshold has been reached only for a short period' (Article 15(1)). This should be taken to mean that a bidder may declare his intention to reduce his holding immediately to below the 90 percent threshold if this is crossed following the bid, and so frustrate the sell-out right.

[65] ibid.

[66] ibid.

[67] ibid 63.

[68] As previously noted, consistently with these rationales, in its second report the High Level Group recommends the introduction of a general sell-out right once a shareholder crosses a 90 to 95 percent threshold (text accompanying n 30).

[69] See PL Davies 'The Notion of Equality in European Takeover Regulation' (n 53) at 21 (according to whom a 90 percent threshold is not even consistent with rationale (a)); Burkart and Panunzi, cit., at 21-22.

D. The Uneasy Case for the Proposed EC Mandatory Bid Rule

Sections B and C have described the recommendations of the High Level Group and the proposal's choices, highlighting the incompleteness of the rules on mandatory bids and some inconsistencies in the provisions concerning the squeeze-out and sell-out rights. This section addresses the question of whether there is a case for an EC mandatory bid provision such as that designed by the proposal.

One may identify five possible justifications, not mutually exclusive, for an EC mandatory bid rule. These rationales are based on: level playing field, minority shareholder protection, equivalence of treatment, lower cost of capital, and efficient and integrated capital markets.

I. The Level Playing Field Rationale

In Professor Davies' words, '[t]he mandatory bid technique requires a number of consequential questions to be answered: what is control; should there be any exceptions to the mandatory bid requirement; if there are, how does one deal with reinforcement of control; at what level should the general offer be pitched and what type of consideration should be offered?'[70] As the previous section has shown, the proposal refers all these questions to the Member States, save the last (ie price), on which Member States will still have some degree of discretion (depending on the rules issued under the comitology procedure, if any) to deviate from the general rule.

This simply precludes the thesis that the proposal can produce any sort of 'level playing field'. When the directive is implemented, there will be twenty-five widely divergent mandatory bid rules around the EU, offering greater or lesser protection to minority shareholders and, correspondingly, being more or less burdensome to potential acquirers of control. There will also be twenty-five variations of the degree of discretion that supervisory authorities enjoy in granting exemptions or price discounts.

Regardless of how little or how much the proposed directive will achieve in terms of levelling the playing field, this rationale alone cannot justify an EC mandatory bid rule. In fact, a much simpler and more effective way to achieve a level playing field would be to *prohibit* mandatory bid rules within the EU. In other words, the level playing field rationale may indeed justify EC legislative intervention in this area, but can tell us nothing about the direction this intervention should take. Absent some other justification, there is no reason why harmonization should be achieved by imposing a 'positive' rather than a 'negative' obligation upon Member States.

[70] PL Davies, 'The Notion of Equality in European Takeover Regulation' (n 53) at 12-13.

II. The Minority Shareholder Protection Rationale

The proposal explicitly cites the protection of minority shareholders as the aim of the mandatory bid rule ('… this person is required to make a bid *as a means of protecting the minority shareholders of that company*:' Article 5(1)).[71] There is, however, broad consensus in the literature that, while obviously ex post (ie after a control acquisition materializes) minority shareholders are better off with a mandatory bid rule in place, ex ante the rule inevitably reduces the number of value-increasing control acquisitions.[72] It is far from certain that the benefits to minority shareholders from protection against value-decreasing acquisitions (in the worst scenario, by looters) are greater than the costs of lost opportunities for value-increasing acquisitions, the increased agency costs of reduced market discipline upon incumbent managers and blockholders,[73] and the efficiency loss deriving from the lesser adaptability of the industrial system to environmental changes.[74] And this is even more doubtful in the absence of any reason to believe that acquirers of control will on average tend to extract higher private benefits of control than incumbent shareholders.[75]

[71] See also Preamble n (8).

[72] See especially LA Bebchuk 'Efficient and Inefficient Sales of Control' (1994) 109 Quarterly Journal of Economics 957 *passim*.

[73] It is well known that, to use Eugene Fama's words, the market for corporate control provides the 'discipline of last resort' for managers (EF Fama 'Agency Problems and the Theory of the Firm' (1980) 88 J Pol Econ 288, 295).

[74] See RJ Gilson 'The Political Ecology of Takeovers: Thoughts on Harmonizing the European Corporate Governance Environment' (1992) 61 Fordham L Rev 161, 164-70. Compare also CJ Milhaupt and MD West 'Institutional Change and M&A in Japan: Diversity Through Deals' (18 November 2001), forthcoming in CJ Milhaupt (ed) *Global Markets, Domestic Institutions: Corporate Law and Governance in a New Era of Cross-Border Deals* (Columbia University Press New York) available at <http://ssrn.com/abstract =290744> (takeovers facilitate organizational change and diversity within firms, diversity being a virtue within a corporate governance system).

[75] eg E Wymeersch 'The Mandatory Bid: A Critical View' in KJ Hopt and E Wymeersch (eds) *European Takeovers* (Butterworths London 1992) 351, 358; Burkart and Panunzi (n 51) 25-26. This argument is also useful to counter the idea that in jurisdictions where courts are unable to curb minority shareholder expropriation, a mandatory bid rule is needed to protect minority shareholders against the risk of higher rent extraction following a change in control (see EC Rocha Gorga 'Does Culture Matter for Corporate Governance? A Case Study of Brazil' (23 May 2003), Stanford Law and Economics Olin Working Paper no 257, available at <http://ssrn.com/abstract=410701> 38; and compare RJ Gilson and JN Gordon 'Controlling Controlling Shareholders' (17 June 2003) Columbia Law and Economics Working Paper no 228, available at <http://ssrn.com/abstract =417181> at 11). In fact, there is no reason to suppose that in such jurisdictions incumbent controllers extract less value from their company than their prospective replacements. Or, to be more analytical, we can imagine three kinds of incumbents: bad incumbents, who

cont. ...

In fact, there are reasons to believe that in today's continental European market for corporate control the incumbents' private benefits of control are on average higher than potential acquirers': as Ehrhardt and Nowak argue, in equity markets dominated by founder- or family-controlled firms, 'reputation benefits … are of primary importance'.[76] These benefits 'are hardest to transfer to another owner, because they take time to build, are owner-specific, and in many cases require family or at least geographical membership.'[77] In such a setting, the chilling effect of the mandatory bid rule can be even worse than is usually considered.

Of course, there are quite a few ways to soften the chilling effect. The proposal relies upon the power of Member States and national supervisory authorities to grant general and specific exemptions from the mandatory bid as such or from the highest price paid rule. This solution is not without alternatives.

In case of an acquisition from the market (ie through a takeover bid), an exemption for partial bids may be granted either (1a) when shareholders are given the option to approve the bid as a separate decision from that of whether to tender or not,[78] as, with qualifications, in the Italian takeover law,[79] or, more simply,

already steal as much as they can; good ones, who do not steal as much as they can and who, no matter the price, will not sell to someone who may steal more than they do; good-but-mundane ones, who steal less than they can, because they have committed to do so (through any kind of binding commitment they may have been able to devise) at the IPO stage or later on in order to raise equity capital more cheaply, but who may be tempted to sell control for a premium. A mandatory bid rule can make a difference only to good-but-mundane incumbents, because in its presence they do not need to devise any contractual arrangement to commit themselves not to sell to potential looters (a commitment they need if they want to convince investors to pay a premium for their company's shares); that is, because they do not need to adopt the mandatory bid as a clause in their company's statute. But this also shows that, on closer inspection, the mandatory bid rule makes very little difference even for this category of incumbents, because they would opt for a contractual mandatory bid spontaneously in its absence.

[76] O Ehrhardt and E Nowak 'Private Benefits and Minority Shareholder Expropriation – Empirical Evidence from IPOs of German Family-Owned Firms' (22 March 2002) CFS Working Paper no 2001/10, available at <http://ssrn.com/abstract=302919> 9.

[77] ibid. See also at 23-25 for an illustration of this kind of benefit involving a company whose owner-manager 'became the most important citizen of a small south-German town called Trossingen … [t]hanks [also] to heavy monetary contributions' paid out of the company's coffers. In order to suggest that these benefits cannot be common to any potential acquirer of control, the authors aptly ask: 'Who else wants to be King of Trossingen and pay a premium for it?' (ibid 25).

[78] eg LA Bebchuk 'Toward Undistorted Choice and Equal Treatment in Corporate Takeovers' (n 50) 1760-61.

[79] PL Davies 'The Notion of Equality in European Takeover Regulation' (n 53) 27. For a more detailed description of this partial bid exemption see L Enriques *Mercato del controllo societario e tutela degli investitori* (n 45) 147-88.

(1b) when an extension of the offer period is granted once the offer is successful.[80] In case of acquisitions through block purchases, the possible alternatives are (2a) a lower price for the mandatory bid, such as, eg some form of average between the market and the highest price paid by the acquirer,[81] (2b) in the extreme case, a mandatory bid price equal to the pre-acquisition market price or to its average in a given prior period,[82] or finally (2c) an exemption triggered by a majority vote of the minority shareholders themselves.[83]

None of these alternatives, of course, is free of drawbacks.[84] They are mentioned here to show that endowing supervisory agencies with discretion is not the only way to mitigate the chilling effect. This is certainly the best solution from the point of view of supervisory agency officials, to whom so much discretion (power) is entrusted. Much less certain is that it is also the most effective solution for distinguishing value-increasing from value-decreasing acquisitions.

In fact, the more flexible the regime administered by supervisory agencies, the greater the risk that value-decreasing acquisitions avoid the mandatory bid. This is because the mandatory bid rule is a difficult one for any (public) supervisory agency to manage.[85] For every takeover, legions of high-priced lawyers and

[80] n 49 and accompanying text.

[81] This is the case in Italy, Switzerland, and Austria: see PL Davies 'The Notion of Equality in European Takeover Regulation' (n 53) 28.

[82] Justification for this approach can be found in FH Easterbrook and DR Fischel *The Economic Structure of Corporate Law* (Harvard University Press Cambridge 1991) ch 5, especially 124-25. This solution has been recently advocated by C Brescia Morra and C Salleo *A Simple Rule for Efficient Transfers of Corporate Control* mimeo (2002) 24-26.

[83] This is the solution advocated by YZ Stern 'The Private Sale of Corporate Control: A Myth Dethroned' (2000) 25 J Corp L 511, 541-45.

[84] Alternatives (1a) and (2c) give rise to a problem of vote sincerity, ie some rules have to be in place in order to ensure that only 'disinterested' shareholders take part in the approval procedure (eg rules prohibiting selective purchases and other forms of bribe) (see generally Z Goshen 'Voting (Insincerely) in Corporate Law' (2001) 2 Theoretical Inquiries in Law no 2 article 9 *passim*). Alternative (1b) may lead to the failure of value-increasing bids, as it makes it indifferent for a shareholder whether to accept the bid during the first stage or after it has succeeded. Alternative (2a) would only lower the number of value-increasing acquisitions which cannot go through and, if it relies on market price averages, could even lead to a price higher than the highest price paid (whenever prices have gone down considerably during the relevant time frame: see A Macchiati and G Siciliano 'Gli effetti economici dell'offerta obbligatoria successiva' (1999) Politica economica 169, 182-83). Finally, alternative (2b) exposes minority shareholders to the risk of manipulation of market prices by the acquirer, or, when a period long enough to rule out the possibility of manipulation is fixed, to the risk that the average price does not reflect the pre-acquisition market value of the company.

[85] In Member States in which the mandatory bid rule is the outcome of self-regulation and is administered by a self-regulatory body, notably the UK, there seems to be less risk

cont. ...

investment bankers will be available to acquirers (and sellers) willing to avoid its application by using loopholes and devising transaction forms as similar as possible to those eligible for exemptions or discounts. Predictably, with due exceptions, supervisory agency officials will not be on an equal footing in terms of incentives and skills with lawyers and investment bankers when they have to evaluate these complex deal structures. As a matter of fact, there is a risk that supervisory agencies may lack the skills and information to avoid false negatives. The unavoidable phenomenon of regulatory capture further increases this likelihood.

Even conceding that the mandatory bid is required to protect minority shareholders,[86] to justify its imposition upon Member States through a directive, one must show that without harmonized rules, no race to the top would arise. That is, one must still demonstrate that harmonization would not result spontaneously via adoption of the rule by Member States, especially if we take the passivity rule as a given.

that private parties will try to avoid the rule. The fact that it is self-regulation should in fact imply that rules of this kind are better internalized by market participants. Hence, the reputation of private parties and City Code Panel members is much more at stake than in jurisdictions where the rule is imposed by the State.

[86] Intriguingly, while economists stress that the mandatory bid rule comes at a cost to minority shareholders, sophisticated minority shareholders such as institutional investors appear to favor the mandatory bid rule even in countries where the private benefits of control are high and hence the chilling effect on takeover activity should be higher (eg, M Mulligan 'Minority investors' plight raises doubts over Latin American corporate reforms' *Financial Times* (27 May 2003) 3, reporting some institutional investors' view that Latin American countries should have a mandatory bid rule in place to protect minority shareholders). The reason for this preference is easy to understand. Institutional investors comparing a world with no mandatory bid rule and one with it have to choose between two scenarios. In scenario (1), absent a mandatory bid rule, if they experience a change of control, they see a lot of money being paid exclusively to a fellow shareholder (which no one likes, no matter how sophisticated one is or how high the stakes are: compare eg CR Sunstein and RH Thaler 'Libertarian Paternalism is Not an Oximoron' (9 May 2003) forthcoming in University of Chicago L Rev, available at <http://ssrn.com/abstract=405940> 10) and stand either to gain or to lose from the new controlling shareholder's management. In scenario (2), in the presence of a mandatory bid rule, if they experience a change in control, they can share the premium with the selling controller and do not have to worry whether the new controller will be better or worse than the selling one. Institutional investors may be perfectly well aware that scenario (2) is less likely than scenario (1), but as no precise estimate of this lower likelihood is possible, they probably tend to compare the two scenarios as such, in which case the superiority of scenario (2) is utterly self-evident. Of course, the minority shareholders' view of the mandatory bid rule is irrelevant to the question of whether the rule is justified on grounds of efficiency.

The question whether companies within the EC have enough room for regulatory arbitrage to permit regulatory competition in company and securities[87] law is clearly beyond the scope of this contribution. Of course, harmonization is justified if listed companies are captive, *i.e.* if they cannot shop around for their favorite national company law.

Assuming that there is indeed scope for regulatory competition (as a consequence of developments in European Court of Justice case law[88] or the introduction of the European Company),[89] in order to assess the need for a harmonized rule one should distinguish between companies whose control is uncontestable and widely held companies for which a hostile takeover is possible. It is easy to see why companies with controlling shareholders who are protected from hostile takeovers thanks to their majority holdings or to devices that are not neutralized by the proposal, such as pyramids and cross-holdings, would tend to opt for jurisdictions that do not impose a mandatory bid.[90] For them, the mandatory bid is useless as a defense against takeovers, but it could impede their freedom to sell, ie it could reduce the likely gains from a sale of control, which is to say their private benefits of control.[91]

[87] Most commonly, Member States impose the mandatory bid rule upon domestic companies listed on domestic markets (eg T Bonneau and L Faugérolas *Les offres publiques* (EFE Paris 1999) 43). Hence, in order for a company to choose one Member State's mandatory bid regime, it would have to reincorporate in that Member State (and hence also choose its company law) and list (also) in a domestic exchange.

[88] Case C-212/97 *Centros Ltd v Erhvervs-og Selskabsstyrelsen* [1999] ECR I-1459 and Case C-208/00 *Überseering BV v Nordic Construction Company Baumanagement (NCC)* [2002] OJ C323.

[89] L Enriques 'Silence Is Golden: The European Company Statute As a Catalyst for Company Law Arbitrage' (1 April 2003) ECGI – Law Working Paper no 07/2003, available at <http://ssrn.com/abstract=384801> *passim*.

[90] Issues affecting a company's position (as prey or predator) in the market for corporate control are key to its decision where to incorporate: see L Enriques 'Silence Is Golden: The European Company Statute As a Catalyst for Company Law Arbitrage' (n 89) 9, also for references.

[91] To illustrate this, suppose that company Alpha is incorporated in a State that does not have a mandatory bid requirement and that its shareholders face the choice whether to reincorporate in another State that does. Suppose that Alpha's market capitalization (P_1) is 100 and private benefits (B_1) for the controlling shareholder holding 30 percent of the shares equal 30; after reincorporation in the other State, thanks to the protection provided by the mandatory bid rule (we are assuming here that the mandatory bid rule is beneficial to minority shareholders), Alpha's market capitalization (P_2) would jump to 120, while private benefits (B_2) would go down to 20. A reincorporation of Alpha would not only make minority shareholders better off, but also result in an increase in social welfare (Alpha's value goes up from 130 to 140). However, the controlling shareholder would veto the reincorporation, because his controlling block, which is worth 30 + 30 = 60 when there is no mandatory bid rule, would be worth less (36 + 20 = 56) when there is one.

To the contrary, blockholders and managers of companies whose control is contestable have a strong incentive to incorporate or reincorporate in jurisdictions with mandatory bids, because it protects them against hostile takeovers.

To conclude, if one agrees that the mandatory bid protects minority shareholders, even where there is sufficient scope for regulatory arbitrage and an EC passivity rule is in place, there is still a case for an EC mandatory bid rule to protect minority shareholders of companies that are invulnerable to hostile takeover. To the contrary, there is no reason for interfering, at least on these grounds, with Member States' regulation of takeover bids concerning publicly-held targets. In fact, driven by the preferences of those making (re)incorporation decisions, Member States will spontaneously provide rules on bids that both protect minority shareholders from pressure to tender and, inevitably, by making acquisitions more costly, also protect managers from takeovers.[92] In other words, in such a scenario and on grounds of minority shareholder protection alone, there would be a case for an EC regulation of control *transfers* (and consolidations), but no case for EC regulation of *acquisitions* of control from the market.[93]

III. The Equal-Treatment Rationale

The High Level Group Report refers to equality of treatment as a justification for the highest-price-paid criterion, and the proposal includes it as a general principle (Article 3), in line with the traditional justification of the mandatory bid rule in the City Code[94] and legal scholarship.[95] Nevertheless, this rationale is far from convincing. In fact, it cannot be viewed as an application of the general principle that companies have a duty of equal treatment of shareholders, because in our setting the 'relationship between the shareholders horizontally' is involved, and European company laws have no principle imposing equal treatment horizontally.[96]

[92] If, for whatever reason, they do not provide such rules, they will face the migration of companies to other jurisdictions, making their rules on bids irrelevant to the protection of minority shareholders.

[93] In practice, it may be difficult to distinguish between transfers and acquisitions of control at the margin, but this does not mean that they cannot be separated conceptually. It only means that some anti-avoidance provisions should be in place if only transfers are regulated (at the EC level).

[94] eg JH Farrar and BM Hannigan *Farrar's Company Law* (4th edn Butterworths London 1998) 594.

[95] Compare E Wymeersch 'Takeovers from a comparative perspective' in Consob, Seminario internazionale in materia di Opa (1999) 32 Quaderni di Finanza 55, 62 ('Equality of treatment is the most traditional [argument for the mandatory bid]').

[96] ibid. See also GE Colombo 'La cessione dei pacchetti di controllo: considerazioni per una discussione' [1978] Rivista delle società 1443, especially at 1457-60.

IV. The Lower Cost of Capital Rationale

One may argue that equal treatment for minority shareholders in control transfers is like tips for waiters: as the latter accept lower wages if they can count on tips, minority shareholders will agree to buy shares at higher prices (incorporating the likelihood of receiving a 'tip' if control changes hands) if a mandatory bid rule is in place, so that ultimately firms' cost of capital is reduced (like restaurants' cost of labor). However, there is a problem with this line of reasoning.

As was argued with regard to the minority shareholder protection rationale, the mandatory bid rule results in less takeover activity. It is unclear why minority shareholders (the market) should not take this into account in pricing shares; again, it is impossible to state ex ante and in general (and even more so for all EC equity markets) whether the presumed 'tips' would offset the adverse effects of the mandatory bid rule on takeover activity and on managerial discipline.

V. The Mandatory Bid Rule as a Means to Integrate European Equity Markets and Make them More Efficient

One possible justification for mandatory bids is efficiency and integration of European equity markets, ie the very purpose of the takeover directive according to the Explanatory Memorandum.[97] As we know, for publicly held companies the mandatory bid rule is comparable to defensive tactics: both may solve the pressure-to-tender problem and may hence prevent value-decreasing acquisitions.[98] It may be argued that in Europe the mandatory bid is a superior alternative to managerial defenses, for two reasons: flip-in poison pills or like stratagems granting managers a veto power without harming the target company's operations are unavailable under EC law, meaning that European managers would have to resort to potentially harmful defensive tactics, which are now history in the US;[99] second, managers may be more likely in Europe than in the US to abuse their veto power by frustrating value-increasing bids, owing to laxer enforcement of fiduciary duties, greater insulation of managers from the risk of ouster by shareholders, and a cultural climate that rejects both hostile takeovers and compensation schemes aligning managers' interests to shareholders' in control contests.[100]

[97] Explanatory Memorandum at 3.

[98] eg PO Mülbert and M Birke 'In Defense of Passivity – on the Proper Role of a Target's Management in Response to a Hostile Tender Offer' (2000) 1 EBOR 445, 467-71.

[99] See JN Gordon 'An American Perspective on the New German Anti-takeover Law' (2002) ECGI – Law Working Paper no 02/2002, available at <http://www.ecgi.org/wp/l0202.pdf> 8 (see also chapter 9 in this volume).

[100] ibid at 9 (noting that stock option plans with features such as accelerated vesting upon a change of control provide substantial incentives for managers to accept hostile

cont. ...

In other words, in Europe the mandatory bid rule may have a less chilling effect on value-increasing acquisitions of publicly held companies than would allowing managers to undertake defensive tactics.

At the same time, it would be inadvisable to impose passivity without at least a mandatory bid rule in place, because public companies would be prey to looters, but also, and more importantly, ex ante, there would be fewer public companies: wherever control is valuable (as in many continental European countries), controlling shareholders would certainly resist relinquishing control to the market.[101]

In short, the mandatory bid rule may make it more convenient for blockholders to give up control through a direct sale to the market or through stock dilution (possibly to finance acquisitions), and impose lower costs than an alternative system in which defenses are allowed.[102] The positive outcome will be more consolidations, possibly cross-border, through exchange offers, and hence more continental-size global competitors,[103] an outcome which would be more difficult to attain without such a rule, because blockholders would find it even less acceptable to be diluted.

If one agrees that the mandatory bid rule would increase the efficiency and integration of European capital markets, in order to justify its imposition upon Member States through a directive, again one has to show that no harmonization would result from below. As we have argued in section 4.B, this outcome is impossible if companies are captive, ie not free to reincorporate in another Member State; if, instead, company law arbitrage is a viable option, then they would have every incentive to choose jurisdictions that do have the mandatory bid rule, possibly before controlling shareholders give up their control stake; hence, there would be no need for a harmonized rule.

takeovers). See also M Kahan and EB Rock 'How I Learned to Stop Worrying and Love the Pill: Adaptive Responses to Takeover Law' (2002) 69 U Chi L Rev 871, 896.

[101] Compare L Enriques 'Silence Is Golden: The European Company Statute As a Catalyst for Company Law Arbitrage' (n 89) 18-19. To be sure, majority shareholders would prefer a free defense regime to passivity, but they also prefer a passivity regime mitigated by the mandatory bid rule to nothing at all: only in the absence of a mandatory bid rule, in fact, do they risk losing *de facto* control also to looters. Note that, in any event, even in the presence of the mandatory bid rule, the incumbents would not be protected against value-increasing hostile takeovers, which would still leave them uncompensated for the loss of private benefits of control.

[102] PO Mülbert and M Birke 'In Defense of Passivity – on the Proper Role of a Target's Management in Response to a Hostile Tender Offer' (n 98) 469-71.

[103] Compare JN Gordon 'An American Perspective on the New German Anti-takeover Law' (n 99) cit 4-5.

VI. Conclusions

This section has shown that harmonized rules on mandatory bids such as those provided for in the proposal:

(1) fall short of leveling the playing field, because they cover only a tiny portion of the regulatory issues faced by policymakers,[104] deferring to Member States for the rest: the outcome will be twenty-five different mandatory bid regimes;
(2) have highly dubious effects on minority shareholders' welfare and on firms' cost of capital, when one takes their impact on the takeover activity into account;
(3) have no justification in terms of equal treatment;
(4) can perhaps be justified as enhancing the efficiency and integration of European capital markets. To make this case, however, one must demonstrate: first, that the passivity rule has positive effects on European capital markets (also compared to the potential alternative of the poison pill);[105] second, that the gains associated with minority shareholder protection from value-decreasing acquisitions and with greater willingness on the part of dominant shareholders to dilute their holdings would be higher than the loss from reduced takeover activity.

Even supposing that the mandatory bid rule improves minority shareholders' welfare and/or that it increases the efficiency and integration of capital markets, if we are heading to a world in which regulatory arbitrage is a viable option for listed companies, then in this scenario there is a case only for harmonized rules on control transfers: protective rules on takeover bids (ie legal systems providing

[104] To put it bluntly, mandatory bid rules will be no more uniform within Europe than legal capital rules would be if the Second Company Law Directive (merely stated that public limited liability companies have to have a legal capital and that distributions to shareholders cannot be made out of it. That legal capital rules also differ greatly from State to State (compare H Halbhuber 'National Doctrinal Structures and European Company Law' (2001) 38 CML Rev 1385, 1406-07), despite the Second directive's seemingly high degree of detail is, of course, quite another matter.

[105] If the main justification for defenses is to allow managers to protect minority shareholders from pressure to tender, one may design a rule that both preserves managerial passivity when it is justified and makes the mandatory bid rule useless: this outcome would be reached by a rule that allows defenses or even better a board veto against takeover bids (of course, in the exclusive interest of shareholders and subject to liability to the company in case the defenses adopted or the board veto are harmful to it), unless the bid is for all outstanding (voting or nonvoting) shares and its terms provide that the acceptance period is extended once the bid is successful, in which case, *i.e.*, in case the bid is noncoercive, Article 9 (the passivity rule) applies.

them) will be chosen spontaneously by listed companies, making harmonization in this area unnecessary.

E. Conclusions: A Lawyers' and Regulators' Plot?

The proposal provides for a very generic, vague rule that control transfers must be followed by a mandatory bid, but entrusts EC and national policymakers and, even more, national supervisory agencies with wide powers to grant partial and total exemptions.

In the European setting, with no poison pills available and a higher risk of abuse of defensive tactics, it may be that the mandatory bid rule (coupled with a passivity rule such as that designed in Article 9 of the proposal) is the lesser evil, as it protects minority shareholders (and managers) from value-decreasing bids and makes the prospect of (willingly) losing uncontestable control of companies by dominant shareholders more attractive. In other words, European capital markets might *possibly* be better off with such a rule in place and it might be good to have an EC directive imposing it, so long as European listed companies cannot freely choose the company and/or securities law applying to them.

What is *certain*, however, is that some interest groups will gain from such provisions. Corporate managers (and blockholders retaining working control) of widely-held European companies are the usual suspects, as they stand to gain from rules that make hostile takeovers more costly.[106] Less frequently cited, but even more suspect are the policymakers and securities agency officials to whom so much power and discretion is granted in deciding whether the rule applies and what the mandatory bid price should be. Finally, those providing advisory services in the market for corporate control, and above all lawyers specializing in mergers and acquisitions,[107] stand to gain from having in place a mandatory bid rule such as that designed in the directive: their services will in fact be available to buyers and sellers who want to evade the mandatory bid or at least to obtain a discount.

One may object that mandatory bid regimes very similar to the proposal are already in place in most Member States, so that there should be no increase in the rents securities agency officials and lawyers can extract, leaving them indifferent to its approval. The point, of course, is not that government officials and lawyers

[106] Compare eg E Wymeersch 'The Mandatory Bid: A Critical View' (n 75) 362.

[107] The inclusion of investment bankers among relevant interest groups would be more controversial, because the mandatory bid rule may increase their fees (due to the greater complexity of the transactions), but it also reduces the number of takeovers. It is far from certain that the net effect is favorable to investment bankers. Intuitively, the increase in fees and power respectively for lawyers and supervisory agency officials is of such magnitude as to offset the negative effect of fewer takeovers.

in Luxembourg, the Netherlands and Greece will now also be able to extract such rents.[108] Much more significantly, the directive would increase rents for government officials and lawyers across the EU in at least three ways. First, the proposed EC mandatory bid rule is more flexible in terms of price discounts (left to national supervisory authorities) than at least some of the Member State mandatory bid regimes now in place.[109] To put it bluntly, this greater flexibility would allow supervisory authority officials to make decisions that may be of great value to the powerful people involved in acquisitions (whether as sellers or buyers), while at the same time providing lawyers with a wider range of weapons to earn fees and hopefully please their clients. Second, the petrification effect typical of all directives[110] would keep Member States from scrapping their own mandatory bid rules, unless they agree to scrap the EC one. Finally, like any directive (at least in the company law area),[111] the takeover directive would add another layer of complexity to a regulatory picture that is already highly technical and complex in all jurisdictions. Questions of consistency between national provisions or decisions and the directive can be raised, a highly pleasing prospect from the point of view of at least one of the interest groups mentioned.

[108] The mandatory bid rule is already in place in 12 out of 15 Member States, Luxembourg, Greece and the Netherlands being the three exceptions (Willem Wiggers, e-mail to the author, 16 May 2003).

[109] For instance, in Italy no price discount can be granted by the supervisory authority.

[110] eg RM Buxbaum and KJ Hopt *Legal Harmonization and the Business Enterprise* (de Gruyter Berlin 1988) 243.

[111] Compare BR Cheffins *Company Law. Theory, Structure and Operation* (Clarendon Oxford 1997) 448; H Halbhuber 'National Doctrinal Structures and European Company Law' (n 104) 1407-08.

Annex 1

COMMISSION OF THE EUROPEAN COMMUNITIES

Brussels, 21.5.2003
COM (2003) 284 final

COMMUNICATION FROM THE COMMISSION TO THE COUNCIL AND THE EUROPEAN PARLIAMENT

Modernising Company Law and Enhancing Corporate Governance in the European Union - A Plan to Move Forward

COMMUNICATION FROM THE COMMISSION TO THE COUNCIL AND THE EUROPEAN PARLIAMENT

Modernising Company Law and Enhancing Corporate Governance in the European Union - A Plan to Move Forward

TABLE OF CONTENTS

INTRODUCTION

A dynamic and flexible company law and corporate governance framework is essential for a modern, dynamic, interconnected industrialised society. Essential for millions of investors. Essential for deepening the internal market and building an integrated European capital market. Essential for maximising the benefits of enlargement for all the Member States, new and existing.

Good company law, good corporate governance practices throughout the EU will enhance the real economy:

- An effective approach will foster the global **efficiency and competitiveness of businesses** in the EU. Well managed companies, with strong corporate governance records and sensitive social and environmental performance, outperform their competitors. Europe needs more of them to generate employment and higher long term sustainable growth.

- An effective approach will help to strengthen shareholders rights and third parties protection. In particular, it will contribute to rebuilding European investor confidence in the wake of a wave of recent corporate governance scandals. The livelihood of millions of Europeans, their pensions, their investments are tied up in the proper, responsible performance and governance of listed companies in which they invest.

Scope

This Communication outlines the approach that the Commission intends to follow specifically in the area of **company law and corporate governance.**

Achieving the objectives pursued (fostering efficiency and competitiveness of business, and strengthening shareholders rights and third parties protection) requires a **fully integrated approach**.

Related initiatives, forming part of this integrated approach but not part of this Action Plan, include:

- **The Financial Serv**ices Action Plan1 of 1999, which confirmed the overall objectives which should guide the financial services policy at EU level and set out a framework for an integrated capital market by 2005;

- The Financial Reporting Strategy2 of 2000, which seeks to achieve high quality financial reporting through the adoption of a common set of accounting standards and the development of a proper enforcement system, which led to the adoption in 2002 of the Regulation on the application of the international accounting standards;

- **The Communication on Corporate Social Responsibility[3] of 2002,** which addresses the social and environmental dimension of business in a global economy and led to the

---

1 Financial Services: Implementing the Framework for financial markets - Action Plan, Communication of the Commission, COM (1999) 232, 11.05.99.

2 EU Financial Reporting Strategy: the way forward, Communication of the Commission, COM (2000) 359, 13.06.00.

3 Corporate Social Responsibility: A business contribution to Sustainable Development, Communication of the Commission, COM (2002) 347, 02.07.02. The European Multi-Stakeholder Forum on CSR brings together representative organisations of business, trade-unions and civil

setting up of a European Multi-Stakeholder Forum with a view to promoting voluntary social and environmental practices of business, linked to their core activities, which go beyond their existing legal obligations;

- The Communication on Industrial Policy in an Enlarged Europe[4] of 2002, which addresses the need for EU industry to achieve a more sustainable production structure as a driver of growth and productivity.

- The Communication on the priorities for the statutory audit in the EU, which is published together with the present Communication and which covers an EU policy approach aimed at ensuring audit quality and public confidence in the audit profession. It covers issues like the use of ISA's (International Standards on Auditing), public oversight of auditors, and the modernisation of the Eighth Company Law Directive into a comprehensive principles-based approach.

Responding to the High Level Group's report

On 4 November 2002, **a High Level Group of Company Law Experts** appointed by Commissioner Bolkestein in September 2001 and chaired by Jaap Winter presented its Final Report on "A modern regulatory framework for company law in Europe". This report focused on corporate governance in the EU and the modernisation of European Company Law. **The Competitiveness Council** (30 September 2002) invited the Commission to organise an in-depth discussion on the forthcoming report and to develop – in co-ordination with Member States – an Action Plan for Company Law, including Corporate Governance, as soon as is feasible, declaring its intention to deal with the Action Plan as a matter of priority. The Ecofin Council has also shown a major interest in this work.

This Communication is the **Commission's response**. It explains why the European regulatory framework for company law and corporate governance needs to be modernised. It defines the key policy objectives which should inspire any future action to be taken at EU level in these areas. It includes an action plan, prioritised, over the short, medium and long term. It indicates which type of regulatory instrument should be used[5], and by when.

Guiding political criteria

In developing this Action Plan, the Commission has paid particular attention to the need for any regulatory response at European level to respect a number of guiding criteria:

- It should fully respect the **subsidiarity and proportionality** principles of the Treaty and the diversity of many different approaches to the same questions in the Member States, while at the same time pursuing clear ambitions (strengthening the single market and enhancing the rights of shareholders and third parties);

society. It will present in 2004 a report about its works to the Commission, which should then make an evaluation of its results, decide on its future and consider any other appropriate initiative.

4 Industrial Policy in an Enlarged Europe, Communication of the Commission, COM (2002) 714, 11.12.02.

5 When a legislative instrument is considered, this means that the action envisaged requires either the adoption of a new legislative proposal or the modification of one or several existing legislative instruments.

- It should be **flexible in** application, but firm in the principles. It should concentrate on priorities; be transparent; and subject to proper due process and consultation;

- It should help shape international regulatory developments. The EU must define its own European corporate governance approach, tailored to its own cultural and business traditions. Indeed, this is an opportunity for the Union to strengthen its influence in the world with good, sensible corporate governance rules. Corporate governance is indeed an area where standards are increasingly being set at international level, as evidenced by the recent developments observed in the United States. The Sarbanes-Oxley **Act**, adopted on 30 July 2002 in the wave of a series of scandals, delivered a rapid response. The Act unfortunately creates a series of problems due to its outreach effects on European companies and auditors, and the Commission is engaged in an intense regulatory dialogue with a view to negotiating acceptable solutions with the US authorities (in particular the Securities and Exchange Commission). In many areas, the EU shares the same broad objectives and principles of the Sarbanes-Oxley Act and in some areas robust, equivalent regulatory approaches already exist in the EU. In some other areas, new initiatives are necessary. Earning the right to be recognised as at least "equivalent" alongside other national and international rules is a legitimate and useful end in itself.

1. MODERNISING COMPANY LAW AND ENHANCING CORPORATE GOVERNANCE: THE EU ACQUIS AND THE NEED FOR NEW INITIATIVES

1.1. The EU Company Law Acquis

Historically, most of the initiatives taken at EU level in the area of company law have been based on **Article 44 (2) g (ex 54) of the Treaty** establishing the European Community. This Article, which appears in the Chapter devoted to the right of establishment, requires the European institutions to attain freedom of establishment, *"by co-ordinating to the necessary extent the safeguards which, for the protection of the interests of members and others, are required by Member States of companies or firms within the meaning of the second paragraph of Article 48 (ex 58), with a view to making such safeguards equivalent throughout the Community".*

This Article has been interpreted to include two important grounds for the adoption of EU initiatives in the area of company law:

a) **facilitating freedom of establishment of companies**: the harmonisation of a number of minimum requirements makes it easier for companies to establish themselves in other Member States where the regulatory framework is similar;

b) **guaranteeing legal certainty in intra-Community operations**, where the presence of a number of common safeguards is key for the creation of trust in cross-border economic relationships.

Over the years, the EU institutions have taken a number of initiatives in the area of company law, many leading to **impressive achievements**[6]. Between 1968 (adoption of the First Company Law Directive) and 1989 (adoption of the Twelfth Company Law Directive), nine Directives and one Regulation were adopted. Although the exact situation may differ from one Member State to the other, these European measures have had an **important impact** on national company law. Moreover, their influence was not limited to the types of companies expressly covered in the Directives, because many Member States decided to extend their provisions to other legal forms.

Over the last ten years, the EU company law legislative process has been characterised, in the wake of the Maastricht Treaty of 1992, by more political deference to national law (with a higher number of references to national rules in the legislative proposals). This **more flexible approach** to harmonisation made possible, in particular, the adoption of the European Company Statute (Societas Europaea), in October 2001.

1.2. Reasons for new initiatives at EU level

Now is the right time to give a fresh and ambitious impetus to the EU company law harmonisation process. New initiatives, aiming either at modernising the

6 See in Annex 2 the table of existing and proposed European legal instruments in the area of company law.

existing EU company law instruments or at completing the EU framework with a limited number of new, tailored instruments, are needed for the following reasons:

- **Making the most of the Internal Market**: the growing trend of European companies to operate cross-border in the Internal Market calls for common European company law mechanisms, inter alia, to facilitate freedom of establishment and cross-border restructuring.
- **Integration of capital markets**: dynamic securities markets are vital to Europe's economic future[7]. This requires giving both issuers and investors the opportunity to be far more active on other EU capital markets and to have confidence that the companies they invest in have equivalent corporate governance frameworks. Listed companies want a more coherent, dynamic and responsive European legislative framework.
- **To maximise the benefits of modern technologies** : the rapid development of new information and communication technology (video conferencing, electronic mail and above all the Internet) is affecting the way company information is stored and disseminated8, as well as the way corporate life is conducted (e.g. virtual general meetings, video-link board meetings, exercise of cross-border voting rights).
- Enlargement: the forthcoming enlargement of the EU to 10 new Member States is another gilt-edged reason to revisit the scope of EU company law. The new member countries will increase the diversity of the national regulatory frameworks in the EU, underlying further the importance of a principles-based approach able to maintain a high level of legal certainty in intra-Community operations. In addition to that, initiatives to modernise the EU Acquis will become more urgent than ever to ease the rapid and full transition of these countries to becoming fully competitive modern market economies.
- **Addressing the challenges raised by recent events:** Recent financial scandals have prompted a new, active debate on corporate governance, and the necessary restoration of confidence is one more reason for new initiatives at EU level. Investors, large and small, are demanding more transparency and better information on companies, and are seeking to gain more influence on the way the public companies they own operate. Shareholders own companies, not management - yet far too frequently their rights have been trampled on by shoddy, greedy and occasionally fraudulent corporate behaviour. A new sense of proportion and fairness is necessary.

---

7 See "Quantification of the Macro-Economic Impact of Integration of EU Financial Markets", Final Report to the European Commission – Directorate-General for the Internal Market by London Economics (in association with PricewaterhouseCoopers and Oxford Economic Forecasting), 12 November 2002, http://europa.eu.int/comm/internal_market/en/finances/mobil/overview.htm.

8 See in this respect the Proposal of June 2002 for a Directive amending the First Company Law Directive, as regards disclosure requirements in respect of certain types of companies, which introduces modern technologies in trade registers. The proposed modifications would allow full advantage to be taken of modern technologies: companies would be able to file their documents and particulars either by paper means or by electronic means, and interested parties would be able to obtain copies by either means.

2. KEY POLICY OBJECTIVES

The Commission considers that future actions at EU level in the area of company law should seek as much as possible to meet the following two policy objectives.

2.1. Strengthening shareholders rights and third parties protection

Ensuring effective and proportionate protection of shareholders and third parties must be **at the core of any company law policy**. A sound framework for protection of members and third parties, which properly achieves a **high degree of confidence** in business relationships, is a fundamental condition for business efficiency and competitiveness. In particular, an effective regime for the protection of shareholders and their rights, protecting the savings and pensions of millions of people and strengthening the foundations of capital markets for the long term in a context of diversified shareholding within the EU, is essential if companies are to raise capital at the lowest cost.

Maintaining efficient protection of members and third parties will be even more important in the future, in view of the **increasing mobility of companies** within the EU.

To allow European companies to reap the benefits of the unified Internal Market and of the integrating European capital market, ensuring adequate protection of members and third parties should be organised along the following lines:

- The Commission considers firstly that some new tailored initiatives should be taken with a view to enhancing shareholder rights and clarifying management responsibilities; and secondly the provisions related to the protection of creditors should be modernised with a view to maintaining a high quality framework (e.g. with respect to capital maintenance and alteration).
- A proper distinction should be made between categories of companies. A more stringent framework is desirable for listed companies9 and companies which have publicly raised capital. They should be subject to a certain number of appropriate detailed rules, in particular in the area of disclosure. With respect to other companies, regulatory initiatives should take full account of both their form and size, allowing a more flexible framework for SME's (in the same way as tailored deregulation initiatives have been taken at national level).
- Modern technologies can significantly help members and third parties to exercise their rights effectively. At a minimum, company law should enable and encourage as much as possible the use of up-to-date information and commu-

[9] The words "listed companies" used in the present Communication cover the companies whose securities are admitted to trading on a regulated market within the meaning of Council Directive 93/22/EEC (OJ L 41, 11.06.1993, p. 27, as last amended by Directive 2000/64/EC of the European Parliament and of the Council (OJ L 290, 17.11.2000, p. 27)) in one or more Member States. The present Action Plan provides where necessary explicit information on the scope of the various actions proposed. In short, the actions presented in the Corporate Governance Section in principle cover listed companies, although some of them are considered to be usefully applicable also to non listed companies. The actions presented in the other sections are generally applicable to all companies, except for the section on pyramids which by nature covers listed companies only.

nication technologies by companies in their various relationships with members and third parties. The Commission furthermore considers that proper attention must be paid to specific areas where the protection of shareholders and third parties may make it necessary to compel companies to use modern technologies. However, the time has not come yet where the use of modern technologies should be imposed by companies systematically on all members and third parties systematically without the necessary safeguards

- The development of a sound economy requires a high degree of confidence in the relationships between the various actors involved, so that the protection of members and third parties will be ensured by a limited number of measures aimed at **combating fraud and abuse** of legal forms. Such measures should be carefully designed, with a view to avoiding that they unduly hinder the development and use of efficient company law structures and systems, which the promotion of efficient and competitive business requires.

2.2. Fostering efficiency and competitiveness of business

Business efficiency and competitiveness, which are crucial components of economic growth and job creation, depend on many factors, one of which is a sound framework of company law. Key to the achievement of this objective is the setting up of a proper balance between actions at EU level and actions at national level. Some company law rules are likely to be best dealt with, and updated, more efficiently at national level, and some competition between national rules may actually be healthy for the efficiency of the single market.

With due respect of the subsidiarity and proportionality principles, business efficiency and competitiveness should be promoted along the following lines:

- EU initiatives in the area of company law should certainly address a number of specific **cross-border issues** (e.g. cross-border merger or transfer of seat, cross-border impediments to the exercise of shareholders rights...), where Community action may be the only way to achieve the pursued objectives.
- In addition to these specific cross-border issues, the necessary attention should be paid to the other initiatives which the promotion of business efficiency and competitiveness requires. As stated above, a certain degree of harmonisation of defined national issues reduces legal uncertainties and can thereby significantly enhance business efficiency and competitiveness.
- Flexibility should be available to companies as much as possible: where systems are deemed to be equivalent, maximum room should be left open to the freedom of the parties involved.

3. AN EU ACTION PLAN

Achieving the above policy objectives requires a number of initiatives to be taken at EU level in the coming years. The following approach is proposed:

- **Distinguishing the actions in three phases** (short term, medium term, long term), based on clear priorities.
- **Expert consultation** should be an integral part of the preparation of initiatives at EU level in the area **of** company law and corporate governance. The Commission therefore will regularly seek advice from representatives of Member States, as is the case of the current Group of Company Law National Experts, but also from representatives of the business and the academic sectors, to provide the necessary external input.
- This Communication will be open for public consultation until 31 August 2003. An **open, public consultation** will also be organised where appropriate in the future on the major initiatives following from the Action Plan.
- With respect specifically to corporate governance, a European Corporate Governance Forum will be convened once or twice a year to contribute to co-ordinating the corporate governance efforts of Member States, as is explained in Section 3.1.4. below.

The present Action Plan identifies the nature and the scope of the actions which appear necessary, proposes the type of regulatory instrument which should be used, and establishes clear priorities for the short, medium and long term.

3.1. Corporate Governance

Corporate Governance, which can be defined in many ways, is usually understood as **the system by which companies are directed and controlled**[10]. It is, in the light of the recent corporate scandals, now a major issue globally. Poor corporate governance performance, by some companies, has greatly undermined confidence in capital markets.

Within the EU, Member States have different systems of corporate governance, which reflect their different cultures and the various views about the roles of corporations and the way in which their industry should be financed. Over the last years, corporate governance has been the subject of an increasingly intense debate. **Forty or so corporate governance codes relevant to the European Union have been adopted over the last decade**, at national or international level, with the aim of better protecting the interests of shareholders and/or stakeholders.

Differences in national corporate governance arrangements may create uncertainty and costs for both issuers and investors, which need to be addressed to promote an efficient integration of EU capital markets. As announced in its 1999 Financial

[10] Cadbury Report, December 1992. For a more comprehensive definition, see for example the OECD Principles of 1999: "Corporate governance involves a set of relationships between a company's management, its board, its shareholders and other stakeholders. Corporate governance also provides the structure through which the objectives of the company are set, and the means of attaining those objectives and monitoring performance are determined." Corporate governance essentially focuses on the problems that result from the separation of ownership and control, and addresses in particular the principal-agent relationship between shareholders and directors.

Services Action Plan, the Commission launched in 2001 a review of the main corporate governance codes relevant to the EU. The **full comparative study**, prepared for the Commission by Weil, Gotshal & Manges LLP, was finalised in March 2002[11]and concluded **that the EU should not devote time and effort to the development of a European corporate governance code**: the study identified as a more valuable area for the European Commission to focus its efforts on the reduction of legal and regulatory barriers to shareholder engagement in cross-border voting ("participation barriers") as well as the reduction of barriers to shareholders ability to evaluate the governance of companies ("information barriers").

The need for a European code and for additional disclosure of corporate governance practices, as well as a series of additional issues raised by the **Oviedo Council in April 2002** in the wake of the US scandals (the role of non-executive directors and of supervisory boards, management remuneration, management responsibility for financial statements, and auditing practices), were also considered by the **High Level Group of Company Law Experts**. In its Final Report, it confirmed that there is no need for an EU corporate governance code.

In this line of thinking, the Commission observes, firstly, that the main differences between Member States are found in differing company law and securities regulation, as opposed to the corporate governance codes which, according to the March 2002 study, show a remarkable degree of convergence, and, secondly, that the existence of many codes in the EU is not generally perceived as a difficulty by issuers (many issuers continue to be active primarily on their domestic market; when they are active on other markets, they are faced with codes that are pretty similar; and in the rare instances where codes provisions are divergent, the "comply or explain" principle offers a satisfactory solution).

Moreover the Commission considers that:

a) the adoption of a European code would not achieve full information for investors about the key corporate governance rules applicable to companies across Europe, as these rules would still be based on - and part of - national company laws that are in certain respects widely divergent;

b) the adoption of such a code would not contribute significantly to the improvement of corporate governance in the EU, as this code would have either to allow for many different options or confine itself to abstract principles. Trying to harmonise all the elements of a European code would take years and would not be achievable in a reasonable timeframe.

There is nevertheless an active role for the EU to play in corporate governance, because some specific rules and principles need to be agreed at EU level in Directives or Recommendations and a certain co-ordination of corporate governance codes in the EU should be organised to encourage further convergence and the exchange of best practice.

[11] Comparative Study of the Corporate Governance Codes relevant to the European Union and its Member States : http://europa.eu.int/comm/internal_market/en/company/company/news/corp-gov-codes-rpt_en.htm

Therefore at this stage the Commission considers that:

- There is little indication that the development of a European corporate governance code as an additional layer between principles developed at the international level and codes adopted at national level would offer significant added value. In that respect, the Commission notes that corporate governance is now at the forefront of the activities of the OECD, which recently decided to revise its corporate governance principles of 1999 with the aim of adopting a modernised version of these principles in 2004. The Commission is taking an active part in this exercise.
- A self-regulatory market approach, based solely on non-binding recommendations, is clearly not always sufficient to guarantee the adoption of sound corporate governance practices. Only in the presence of a certain number of made-to-measure rules, markets are able to play their disciplining role in an efficient way. In view of the growing integration of European capital markets, **a common approach should be adopted at EU level with respect to a few essential rules and adequate co-ordination of corporate governance codes should be ensured.**

More specifically, the Commission, largely in line with the High Level Group's suggestions, intends to proceed along the following lines[12].

3.1.1. Enhancing Corporate Governance disclosure

Annual Corporate Governance Statement

Listed companies should be required to include in their annual report and accounts a coherent and descriptive statement covering the key elements of their corporate governance structure and practices, which should at least include the following items:

a) the operation of the shareholder meeting and its key powers, and the description of shareholder rights and how they can be exercised;

b) the composition and operation of the board and its committees13;

c) the shareholders holding major holdings, and their voting and control rights as well as key agreements;

d) the other direct and indirect relationships between these major shareholders and the company;

e) any material transactions with other related parties;

f) the existence and nature of a risk management system;

[12] In developing its approach, the Commission has paid particular attention to the following needs: considering where possible a) the use of alternatives to legislation, and b) the preference to be given to disclosure requirements (because they are less intrusive in corporate life, and they can prove to be a highly effective market-led way of rapidly achieving results).

[13] In this respect, it is considered essential for the restoration of public confidence that proper information is given on the way in which the company has organised itself at the highest level to establish and maintain an effective internal control system.

g) and a reference to a code on corporate governance, designated for use at national level, with which the company complies or in relation to which it explains deviations.

A proposal for a Directive containing the principles applicable to such an annual corporate governance statement, which should appear prominently in the annual documents published by listed companies, is regarded by the Commission as a priority for the short term, so as to rapidly allow market pressures to be better exerted. The definition of these principles will properly take into account the related requirements present in existing (e.g. major holdings[14]) or proposed (e.g. take-over bids) instruments.

Information about the role played by institutional investors

Institutional investors should be obliged:

a) to disclose their investment policy and their policy with respect to the exercise of voting rights in companies in which they invest;

b) to disclose to their beneficial holders at their request how these rights have been used in a particular case.

Such requirements would not only improve the internal governance of institutional investors themselves, but would also enhance participation by institutional investors in the affairs of the companies in which they invest. A requirement for institutional investors to systematically exercise their voting rights is not considered desirable, in view of its potential counterproductive effects (due to a lack of time or resources, institutional investors might simply vote in favour of any proposed resolution to fulfil the requirement).

Institutional investors have an important role to play in the governance of companies in which they invest. Fostering this role will require amendments to a series of existing legal texts (relating to insurance companies, pension funds, mutual and other investment funds, ...), and even more importantly the introduction of such a requirement would deliver its full effects only once the problems related to cross-border voting will have been solved. The Commission therefore intends to take the necessary steps in the medium term.

3.1.2. Strengthening shareholders' rights

Access to information

Shareholders of listed companies should be provided with electronic facilities to access the relevant information in advance of General Meetings. This issue is currently addressed by the Proposal for a Transparency Directive, which essentially enables listed companies to use electronic means to inform their

---

14 See Directive 2001/34/EC of the European Parliament and of the Council of 28 May 2001 on the admission of securities to official stock exchange listing and on information to be published on securities (Title IV – Chapter III "Obligations relating to the information to be published when a major holding in a listed company is acquired or disposed of").

shareholders[15] and contains specific provisions guaranteeing a timely access to regulated information when securities are listed in another Member State than the home Member State[16]. The Commission considers this solution as a significant and proportionate first step, which does not preclude the adoption of further measures (which would generally require listed companies to use electronic means to inform their shareholders) in the medium term, if this looks desirable in the light of the implementation of the Transparency Directive (which itself contains a revision clause).

Other shareholders' rights

There is a need for enhancing the exercise of a series of shareholders' rights in listed companies (right to ask questions, to table resolutions, to vote in absentia, to participate in general meetings via electronic means). These facilities should be offered to shareholders across the EU, and specific problems relating to cross-border voting should be solved urgently. The Commission considers that the necessary framework should be developed in a Directive, since an effective exercise of these rights requires a number of legal difficulties to be solved. In view of the important benefits expected from such a framework, the Commission regards the relevant proposal as a priority for the short term.

Shareholder democracy

Strengthening shareholders' rights should be based essentially on a) the provision of comprehensive information on what the various existing rights are and how they can be exercised and b) the development of the facilities necessary to make sure that these existing rights can be effectively exercised. This approach is fully consistent with the OECD Principles of Corporate Governance[17].

The Commission considers that there is a strong medium to long term case for aiming to establish a real shareholder democracy in the EU. The Comparative Study of Corporate Governance Codes relevant to the EU evidenced that corporate governance codes tend to support the one share / one vote principle, although many codes favour some flexibility in this respect. The hardest line is taken by the codes issued by bodies affiliated with investors, which clearly do not support the issuance of shares with reduced or no voting rights. The Commission nevertheless observes that any initiative in this direction, which would give further effect to the principle of proportionality between capital and control advocated by the High Level Group in its First Report on issues related to take-over bids, requires prior study. The Commission therefore intends to undertake a study, in the short to medium term, on the consequences which such an approach would entail.

---

15 The home Member State shall allow issuers the use of electronic means for the purposes of conveying information to shareholders, provided such a decision is taken in a general meeting and meets a series of conditions, including the individual consent of the shareholder concerned (See Article 13).

16 A host Member State may require issuers: a) to publish regulated information on their Internet sites, and b) to alert any interested person, without delay and free of charge, to any new disclosure or any change to regulated information which has already been published (See Article 17).

17 See the relevant statements, about disclosure (Capital structures and arrangements that enable certain shareholders to obtain a degree of control disproportionate to their equity ownership should be disclosed) and about exercise of rights (shareholders should have the opportunity to participate effectively and vote in general shareholder meetings).

3.1.3. Modernising the board of directors

Board composition

In key areas where executive directors clearly have **conflicts of interests** (i.e. remuneration of directors, and supervision of the audit of the company's accounts), decisions in listed companies should be made exclusively by **non-executive or supervisory directors** who are in the majority independent. With respect to the nomination of directors for appointment by the body competent under national company law, the responsibility for identifying candidates to fill board vacancies should in principle be entrusted to a group composed mainly of executive directors, since executive directors can usefully bring their deep knowledge of the challenges facing the company and of the skills and experience of the human resources grown up within the company. Non-executive directors should, nonetheless, also be included and specific safeguards should be put in place to deal with conflicts of interests when they arise, for example when a decision has to be made on the reappointment of a director.

These requirements should be enforced by Member States at least on a "comply or explain" basis. Certain minimum standards of what cannot be considered to be independent should be established at EU level. With a view to fostering a concrete and active role for non executive or supervisory directors, particular attention will be paid to the issue of the number of mandates that may be held concurrently. Moreover, the impact of interlocking directorships on the independence of directors should be properly addressed in the minimum standards to be established.

The Commission regards these measures as key to the restoration of confidence in the markets, and therefore intends to adopt a Commission Recommendation to this effect in the short term.

Such a Recommendation will define minimum standards applicable to the creation, composition and role of the **nomination, remuneration and audit committees**. In view of the recent accounting scandals, special emphasis will be placed on the audit committee (or equivalent body), with a view to fostering the key role it should play in supervising the audit function, both in its external aspects (selecting the external auditor for appointment by shareholders, monitoring the relationship with the external auditor including non-audit fees if any) and its internal aspects (reviewing the accounting policies, and monitoring the internal audit procedures and the company's risk management system)[18].

The High Level Group further recommended that at least listed companies in the EU should generally have the option between a **one-tier board structure** (with executive and non-executive directors) **and a two-tier board structure** (with managing directors and supervisory directors). The Commission welcomes the idea to offer additional organisational freedom to listed companies, but recognises that the implications of such a proposal should be carefully studied. Much has to be

---

18 In developing the minimum standards applicable to the audit committee, appropriate attention will be paid to a) the access it must have to the relevant information (there might be a scope for specific consideration of the need for greater legal protection for whistleblowers) and b) the extent to which transparency on its activities is desirable.

learned in this respect from the adaptation of national law to the Regulation and the Directive on the European Company Statute. The Commission therefore proposes that this recommendation from the High Level Group should be followed up in the medium term.

Directors' remuneration

Shareholders should be able to appreciate fully the relation between the performance of the company and the level of remuneration of directors, both ex ante and ex post, and they should be able to make decisions on the remuneration items linked to the share price. Agreeing with the High Level Group, the Commission considers that an appropriate regulatory regime should be composed of **four key items** (disclosure of remuneration policy in the annual accounts, disclosure of details of remuneration of individual directors in the annual accounts, prior approval by the shareholder meeting of share and share option schemes in which directors participate, proper recognition in the annual accounts of the costs of such schemes for the company).

In order to promote a swift application of such a regime, a Commission Recommendation should be adopted to this effect. The Commission regards this action as key to the restoration of confidence, and intends to adopt such a Recommendation in the short term and to closely monitor its application with a view to identifying whether any further additional rulemaking may be desirable in the medium term.

Directors' responsibilities

With a view to enhancing directors' responsibilities, the **collective responsibility** of all board members for financial and key non financial statements (including the annual corporate governance statement mentioned above in Section 3.1.1.) should be confirmed as a matter of EU law. The Commission considers that such a confirmation in framework provisions constitutes a first step which may be achieved rapidly, and intends to take the necessary initiatives in the short term.

The High Level Group made several other recommendations designed to enhance directors responsibilities: a) introduction of a **special investigation right**, whereby shareholders holding a certain percentage of the share capital should have the right to ask a court or administrative authority to authorise a special investigation into the affairs of the company; b) development of a **wrongful trading rule**, whereby directors would be held personally accountable for the consequences of the company's failure, if it is foreseeable that the company cannot continue to pay its debts and they don't decide either to rescue the company and ensure payment or to put it into liquidation; c) imposition of **directors' disqualification** across the EU as a sanction for misleading financial and non-financial statements and other forms of misconduct by directors. The Commission supports these ideas, whose implementation requires further analysis, and therefore intends to present the relevant proposal for a Directive in the medium term.

3.1.4. Co-ordinating corporate governance efforts of Member States

The Commission shares the view of the High Level Group that **the EU should actively co-ordinate the corporate governance efforts of Member States** through their company laws, securities laws, listing rules, codes, or otherwise. In particular, each Member State should progress towards designating a code of corporate governance, designated for use at national level, as the code with which listed companies subject to their jurisdiction are to comply or in relation to which they are to explain deviations. Co-ordination should not only extend to the making of these national codes, but also to the procedures Member States have in place to monitor and enforce compliance and disclosure. Member States should participate in the co-ordination process set by the EU, but the process itself should be voluntary and non-binding with a strong involvement of market participants.

The comparative study of codes relevant to the EU concluded one year ago that **these codes show a remarkable degree of convergence**. The Commission nevertheless observes that such a situation may change rapidly: several Member States are currently engaged in important policy initiatives, and the EU will soon be enlarged by 10 new Member States. In addition, standards are increasingly set at the international level and they should be implemented in Member States in a consistent way.

For these reasons, the Commission regards it important to encourage the co-ordination and convergence of national codes through regular high level meetings of the European Corporate Governance Forum. Participants to such a Forum, which could meet once or twice a year, will comprise representatives from Member States, European regulators (including CESR), issuers and investors, other market participants and academics. Interested MEP's will also be invited to present their views. The Forum will be chaired by the Commission.

3.2. Capital Maintenance and Alteration

The Second Company Law Directive adopted by the Council on 13 December 1976 in respect of the formation of public limited liability companies and the maintenance and alteration of their capital is one of the cornerstones of European company law. It imposes a minimum legal capital to public limited liability companies, and contains a number of detailed provisions aiming at protecting shareholders and creditors, which apply inter alia to the formation stage, to distributions to shareholders, to acquisitions of own shares, to increases in capital and to reductions in capital.

In 1999, a **Report by the Company Law SLIM Group** concluded that the capital maintenance regime organised by the Second Directive could be simplified on a limited number of points, and presented several proposals to this end[19]. From the discussions that followed the presentation of this SLIM Report, it appeared that the implementation of many of these recommendations required further examination.

The High Level Group of Company Law Experts confirmed that most of the SLIM Group proposals were indeed worth implementing and gave some guidance in this

[19] The topics covered by the SLIM Report were as follows: removal of the requirement for an expert opinion on contributions in kind in defined circumstances, introduction of no par value shares, simplification of the rules applicable to withdrawal of shares, simplification of the rules applicable to acquisition of own shares, reduction of the scope of the prohibition of financial assistance, simplification of the rules applicable to pre-emptive rights.

respect. In addition, the High Level Group formulated a few additional suggestions aiming at modernising the Second Directive. The Commission considers that a **simplification of the Second Directive** on the basis of these proposals and recommendations would significantly contribute to the promotion of business efficiency and competitiveness without reducing the protection offered to shareholders and creditors. A proposal to amend the Second Directive along these lines is therefore regarded as a priority for the short term.

The High Level Group further suggested that adequate protection of shareholders and creditors might be achieved, possibly even more effectively, with the introduction at a later stage of an **alternative regime** which would not be based on the concept of legal capital. This alternative regime, whose main lines are briefly outlined by the Group[20], could be offered as an option to Member States who should be able to freely decide to change to the new regime or to retain the Second Directive rules amended as suggested above.

The Commission considers that, before deciding to introduce an alternative regime which would fundamentally depart from the capital maintenance regime currently organised by the Second Directive, further work is needed as to both the exact characteristics of a possible alternative regime and its ability to achieve an effective protection of shareholders and third parties. **A study into the feasibility of an alternative to the capital maintenance regime** will be launched by the Commission in the medium term. The study will have to identify in particular the exact benefits that an alternative regime would offer in comparison with the Second Directive rules amended in the short term.

3.3 Groups & Pyramids

The High Level Group of Company Law Experts pointed out that groups of companies, which today are frequent in most, if not all, Member States, are to be seen as a legitimate way of doing business, but that they may present specific risks for shareholders and creditors in various ways. The Commission, following the Group's recommendation, takes the view that there is no need to revive the draft Ninth Directive on group relations[21], since the enactment of an autonomous body

---

20 Such an alternative regime would notably be based on the requirement for a solvency test before any payment of dividend or other distribution can be made.

21 A draft "Ninth Company Law Directive on the Conduct of Groups containing a Public Limited Company as a Subsidiary" was circulated by the Commission in December 1984 for consultation. According to its Explanatory Memorandum, the Directive was intended to provide a framework in which groups can be managed on a sound basis whilst ensuring that interests affected by group operations are adequately protected. Such a legal framework, adapted to the special circumstances of groups, was considered to be lacking in the legal system of most Member States.
Apart from its provisions dealing with the notification and disclosure of shareholdings in PLCs, which covered all PLCs, the Directive otherwise applied only when a PLC was the subsidiary of another undertaking (which could itself be a PLC, but could also be a natural person or a legal person).
The main features of the proposal were : a) a definition of a "subsidiary undertaking" which would oblige Member States to provide for "control contracts", b) rules about the disclosure of shareholdings in PLCs, c) detailed rules (Section 4) as to the conduct of a "parent undertaking" towards a PLC subsidiary (including the liability of the parent undertaking for damage to the PLC subsidiary and for its debts), d) detailed rules applicable when the parent undertaking had entered into a "control contract" with a PLC (Section 5), or when it had made a "unilateral declaration instituting a vertical group" (Section 6), which would contain similar safeguards to those

of law specifically dealing with groups does not appear necessary, but that particular problems should be addressed through specific provisions in three areas.

Financial and non financial information

Complete information and disclosure with regard to the group's structure and intra-group relations are a crucial pre-requisite to ensure that the functioning of groups remains compatible with the interests of shareholders and creditors at the different levels. The actual provisions of the Seventh Company Law Directive on consolidated accounts do not sufficiently address these concerns, in that consolidated figures do not reflect the financial situation of the various parts of the group and the degree of dependence of the subsidiaries on the parent company.

The need for better financial and non financial information about groups of companies is already addressed partly by a series of EU measures, whether adopted (application of IAS to consolidated accounts), pending (information to be provided under the proposed Thirteenth Directive), or envisaged (information to be provided in the annual corporate governance statement). The Commission nevertheless observes that the scope of these measures is limited to listed companies. The Commission therefore considers that additional initiatives aiming at improving to the extent necessary the financial and non financial information disclosed by groups are desirable when the parent company is not listed. Since transparency is felt as the most important area of intervention with regard to groups, whether they are listed or not, the Commission regards these additional initiatives as priorities for the short term.

Implementation of a group policy

Member States should be required to provide for a framework rule for groups that allows those concerned with the management of a company belonging to a group to adopt and implement a co-ordinated group policy, provided that the interests of that company's creditors are effectively protected and that there is a fair balance of burdens and advantages over time for that company's shareholders. The Commission sees the introduction of such a rule as an important step towards improved business efficiency and competitiveness, but stresses that appropriate safeguards have to be carefully designed. A proposal for a framework Directive to this effect will therefore be presented in the medium term.

Pyramids

Pyramids, defined by the High Level Group as chains of holding companies with the ultimate control based on a small total investment thanks to the extensive use of minority shareholders, raise a number of problems stemming from their lack of transparency. The Commission notes that the introduction of a requirement to

---

prescribed in Section 4 but with important additions (including a rights for the employee representatives on the subsidiary PLC's supervisory body to veto instructions from the parent undertaking).
The consultation on the draft Directive showed that there was very little support for such a comprehensive framework on group law: such an approach was largely unfamiliar to most Member States, and the business sector viewed it as too cumbersome and too inflexible. As a consequence, the decision was made not to issue an official proposal.

publish an annual corporate governance statement (as suggested in Section 3.1.1. above) would, together with the adoption of the proposed Thirteenth Directive, constitute a first significant improvement in this respect.

The Group stressed that pyramidal groups that include listed companies raise particular concerns. It recommended that national authorities should be required not to admit to listing companies belonging to abusive pyramids. The Group defined them as holding companies whose sole or main assets are their shareholding in another listed company, but made an exception for cases where the economic value of such admission is clearly demonstrated, thereby recognising that the definition of what constitutes an abusive pyramid required further consideration. It also suggested that operators of stock indices should properly take into account the free float in determining the respective weight of each company.

The Commission considers it necessary to give further examination to the risk inherent in abusive pyramids. In so doing, the Commission will take account of the need to avoid undue restrictions of companies' freedom to choose their appropriate organisation. The Commission therefore intends to obtain on this issue the expert opinion of the Committee of European Securities Regulators (CESR).

3.4. Corporate restructuring and mobility

The growing integration of the single market leads companies increasingly to do **business across national borders** within the Union. In order to be able to align their structure on their activities, European companies have repeatedly called for the adoption of legal instruments capable of meeting their needs for mergers between companies from different Member States and for transfer of their seat from one Member State to another.

The Commission intends to present in the short term a new proposal for a **Tenth Company Law Directive** on cross-border-mergers[22] as well as a proposal for a **Fourteenth Company Law Directive** on the transfer of the seat from one Member State to another[23]. Both proposals are faced with the task of solving difficulties relating to board structure and employee participation. In this respect, the Commission welcomes the approval in October 2001 of the European Company Statute, which opens up promising prospects for the solution of comparable issues

22 Although the laws of some Member States do not prohibit a company from one of those States from absorbing a company from another Member State or from taking part in the formation of a new company by merger with a company registered in another Member State, such an operation may be carried out only with companies from Member States where it is likewise not prohibited by law. The adoption of the European Company Statute offers one solution to these problems (a European Company may be created inter alia by merger of two or more public limited liability companies from different Member States). A proposal for a Tenth Company Law Directive is nevertheless desirable, since a) companies may wish to enter into a cross-border merger without creating a European Company, and b) other types of companies may wish to enter into a cross-border merger.

23 In the absence of legislation governing the cross-border transfer of seat, such an operation is currently impossible or at least contingent on complicated legal arrangements. This is because Member States laws do not provide the necessary means and, when a transfer is possible by virtue of simultaneously applying national laws, there are frequent conflicts between those laws because of the different connecting criteria applied in the Member States. A legislative effort is needed in this field in order to implement the freedom of establishment in the manner intended by the Treaty.

in the Tenth and Fourteenth Directives. In addition to these company law implications of corporate restructuring and mobility, which are covered by the present Communication, attention is paid to their social implications in other Commission initiatives (these social implications are addressed in the Multi-Annual Work Programme of the Social Partners 2003-2005).

The High Level Group made **other recommendations** relating to restructuring transactions, along the following lines : a) some of the requirements currently foreseen by the Third Company Law Directive (mergers of public limited liability companies) and by the Sixth Company Law Directive (division of such companies) should be relaxed in specific cases which make them superfluous; b) Member States should be required to create squeeze-out rights (for majority shareholders) and sell-out rights (for minority shareholders), at least in listed companies, subject to certain thresholds being reached. The introduction of such rights would complement the comparable provisions already contained in the current proposal for a Thirteenth Company Law Directive on take-over bids.

The Commission considers that the simplification of restructuring transactions pursued by the proposed relaxation of some of the requirements currently foreseen by the **Third Directive** and the **Sixth Directive** is desirable in so far as the necessary safeguards are ensured. The Commission notes that this simplification is not perceived by the Group as an immediate priority, and therefore intends to take the necessary initiatives in the medium term.

With respect to the introduction of **squeeze-out rights and sell-out rights**, proposed by the High Level Group in its Restructuring Chapter, the Commission observes that the same objectives are pursued by one of the recommendations made by the SLIM Group about the simplification of the Second Directive, which the High Level Group has endorsed. The Commission therefore intends to consider such an introduction as part of the modernisation of the Second Directive, which the Commission regards as a priority for the short term.

3.5. The European Private Company

The High Level Group noted that the Societas Europaea (SE), adopted in October 2001, may not meet all expectations of the business community, in particular SMEs, and referred to the development, from a private initiative, of a "European Private Company" (EPC) which, as a **new legal form at EU level**, would primarily serve the needs of SMEs which are active in more than one Member State. This concept has received **widespread interest and support** not only from the private sector, but also from the European Economic and Social Committee, and the introduction of such a form is regarded by many as easier to achieve than the European Company Statute.

The Group nevertheless observed that the first priority should be to adopt the **Tenth Directive** on cross-border mergers, which is expected to meet one of the purposes advocated for the EPC. Therefore, and in view of a number of issues which need to be solved (e.g. tax or co-determination issues), the Group recommended that before deciding to submit a formal proposal, the Commission should launch a **feasibility study** in order to clearly identify the practical benefits of – and problems related to – the introduction of an EPC statute.

The Group suggested that such a feasibility study should be launched in the medium term, i.e. after the adoption of the Tenth Directive. The Commission considers that the identification of most of the practical benefits of – and problems related to – the introduction of an EPC statute can be achieved independently from the progress hoped on the Tenth Directive. The Commission will therefore launch a feasibility study **in the short term**, with a view to presenting a proposal for an EPC statute (if the feasibility study confirms the need for such an initiative) in the medium term. The aim of this feasibility study is to evaluate the advantages and the problems generated by a possible European legal statute for small and medium enterprises in order to facilitate their internationalisation. To this end, the study should conduct an in-depth analysis of the legal, tax and social policy regimes relevant to SMEs in the 25 Member States of the enlarged Union.

3.6. The European Co-operative Society and other EU legal forms of enterprises

The European Council adopted last year a general orientation on the proposal for a Regulation on the **Societas Cooperativa Europaea** (SCE) and proposals of statutes for a **European Association** and a **European Mutual Society** are now examined by the European Parliament and the Council. The Commission observes that a majority of the responses received in the consultation organised by the High Level Group expressed positive views on the usefulness of these statutes.

The Commission intends to **actively support the ongoing legislative process engaged** on these statutes, in response to the explicit desire expressed by the European Parliament for giving significant attention to the development of new European legal forms of enterprises. Adoption by the Council of the Regulation on a European Co-operative Society is hoped for in the near future, while the discussion within the Council of the proposal for a European Association is actively going on. As soon as agreement on this proposal will have been reached, the necessary attention will be devoted to the proposal for a European Mutual Society.

With respect to the possible development of a proposal for a Regulation on a **European Foundation**, before deciding to submit a proposal, the Commission intends to launch a study aiming at assessing in depth the feasibility of such a statute. Such an assessment will have to take account of the lessons to be drawn from the adoption and use of the other European statutes, so that it should best take place in the medium term.

3.7. Enhancing the transparency of national legal forms of enterprises

Increased disclosure requirements for all legal entities with limited liability, are a need which stems from the necessity a) to preserve fair competition[24] and b) to prevent company law from being abused for fraud, terrorism or other criminal

24 The First Company Law Directive, which contains essential disclosure requirements (companies must file a series of documents and particulars with a register, and interested parties can obtain a copy thereof), applies only to limited liability companies, and not to a series of alternative forms of enterprise. The creation of a framework for disclosure of basic data on certain other legal entities engaged in economic activities is therefore perceived as a useful tool for trade and competition within the Internal Market.

activity[25]. The Commission is committed to respond to this need, but the scope and nature of this recommendation need to be further examined. In view of the numerous other priorities, the necessary actions will be taken in the medium term.

4. CONCLUSION

The present Communication explains why the European regulatory framework for company law and corporate governance needs to be modernised. It defines the key policy objectives which should inspire any future action to be taken at EU level in these areas. It includes an action plan, prioritised, to plan the various actions which appear necessary over the short, medium and long term. It determines which type of regulatory instrument should be used, and approximately by when.

Further to the conclusions adopted by the Brussels European Council of 20 and 21 March 2003, which requested the adoption of an Action Plan on Company Law and Corporate Governance, the Commission addresses this Communication to the European Parliament and the Council, and transmits it also to the European Economic and Social Committee and the Committee of the Regions.

Comments from all interested parties are invited by 31 August 2003. Comments should be sent to DG MARKT G3, European Commission, B-1049 Brussels (e-mail address: Markt-COMPLAW@cec.eu.int).

The Commission will publish a synthesis of the comments received, and they will be given adequate consideration when implementing the present Action Plan.

[25] See in this respect the study "Transparency and Money Laundering: A study of the regulation and its implementation, in the EU Member States, that obstruct anti-money laundering international co-operation (banking/financial and corporate/company regulative fields)", submitted to the Commission in October 2001 by the Transcrime Institute (University of Trento, Italy). This study, commissioned pursuant to conclusion n°58 of the Tampere Special European Council of 1999 and the joint ECOFIN/JAI Council of October 2000, presents recommendations to increase the transparency of limited liability companies as well as other vehicles (as trusts).

ANNEX 1

Modernising Company Law and Enhancing Corporate Governance in the European Union - A Plan to Move Forward ***List of Actions*** **SHORT TERM (2003-2005)**		
	Description of action	**Preferred type of initiative**[26]
Corporate Governance	Enhanced corporate governance disclosure requirements (including confirmation of collective responsibility of board members for key non financial statements)	Legislative (Directive amending existing legislation)
	Integrated legal framework to facilitate efficient shareholder communication and decision-making (participation to meetings, exercise of voting rights, cross-border voting)	Legislative (Directive)
	Strengthening the role of independent non-executive and supervisory directors	Non legislative (Recommendation)
	Fostering an appropriate regime for directors remuneration	Non legislative (Recommendation)
	Confirming at EU level the collective responsibility of board members for financial statements	Legislative (Directive amending existing legislation)
	Convening a European Corporate Governance Forum to co-ordinate corporate governance efforts of Member States	Non legislative (Commission initiative)
Capital Maintenance	Simplification of the Second Directive, on the basis of the SLIM recommendations as supplemented in the HLG Report (SLIM-Plus)	Legislative (Directive amending existing legislation)
Groups of companies	Increased disclosure of group structure and relations, both financial and non financial	Legislative (Directive amending existing legislation)
Restructuring	Proposal for a Tenth Directive on cross-border mergers	Legislative (Directive)
	Proposal for a Fourteenth Directive on cross-border transfer of the seat	Legislative (Directive)
European Private Company	Feasibility study in order to assess the practical needs for – and problems of – a European Private Company	Non legislative (Study)
EU legal forms	Active progress on current proposals (European Association, European Mutual Society)	Legislative (existing proposals)

[26] This column gives information about the type of regulatory instrument which should be used:
- When « Directive » is mentioned, this means that the action envisaged requires either the adoption of a new Directive or the modification of one or several existing Directives (in the areas of company law, securities law, financial reporting law...), in accordance with the regulatory powers of the various relevant bodies existing at EU level;
- To the extent possible, the necessary initiatives will be grouped with a view to avoiding a multiplication of legislative initiatives.

MEDIUM TERM (2006-2008)		
	Description of action	**Preferred type of initiative**
Corporate Governance	Enhanced disclosure by institutional investors of their investment and voting policies	Legislative (Directive)
	Choice for all listed companies between the two types (monistic/dualistic) of board structures Enhancing the responsibilities of board members (special investigation right, wrongful trading rule, director's disqualification)	Legislative (Directive) Legislative (Directive or Directive amending existing legislation)
	Examination of the consequences of an approach aiming at achieving a full shareholder democracy (one share / one vote), at least for listed companies	Non legislative (Study)
Capital Maintenance	Review of the feasibility of an alternative to the capital maintenance regime	Non legislative (Study)
Groups of companies	Framework rule for groups, allowing the adoption at subsidiary level of a co-ordinated group policy	Legislative (Directive)
Pyramids	Prohibition of stock exchange listing for abusive pyramids, if appropriate, following further examination and expert input	Legislative (possible Directive amending existing legislation)
Restructuring	Simplification of the Third Directive (legal mergers) and Sixth Directive (legal divisions)	Legislative (Directive amending existing legislation)
European Private Company	Possible proposal for a Statute for a European Private Company (depending on the outcome of the feasibility study)	Legislative
EU legal forms	Assess the need for the creation of other EU legal forms (e.g. European Foundation)	Non legislative (Study)
Transparency of national legal forms	Introduce basic disclosure rules for all legal entities with limited liability, subject to further examination	Legislative (Directive or Directive amending existing legislation)

LONG TERM (2009 onwards)		
	Description of action	**Preferred type of initiative**
Capital Maintenance	Possible introduction in the Second Company Law Directive of an alternative regime (depending on the outcome of the feasibility study)	Legislative (Directive amending existing legislation)

ANNEX 2
LIST OF EXISTING AND PROPOSED EUROPEAN COMPANY LAW INSTRUMENTS

Existing European Company Law Instruments	
REGULATIONS	
Title of Act	**Publication Reference**
Council Regulation (EEC) 2137/85 of 25 July 1985 on the European Economic Interest Grouping (EEIG)	[1985] OJ L 199/1
Council Regulation (2001/2157/EC) of 8 October 2001 on the Statute for a European Company SE *supplemented by* Council Directive (2001/86/EC) of 8 October 2001 supplementing the Statute for a European Company with regard to the involvement of employees	[2001] OJ L 294/1 [2001] OJ L 294/22
Regulation (EC) No 1606/2002 of the European Parliament and of the Council of 19 July 2002 on the application of international accounting standards	[2002] OJ L 243/1
DIRECTIVES	
Title of Act	**Publication Reference**
First Council Directive (EEC) 68/151 of 9 March 1968 on co-ordination of safeguards which, for the protection of the interests of members and others, are required by Member States of companies within the meaning of the second paragraph of Article 58 of the Treaty, with a view to making such safeguards equivalent throughout the Community	[1968] OJ L 65/8
Second Council Directive (EEC) 77/91 of 13 December 1976 on co-ordination of safeguards, which for the protection of the interests of members and others, are required by Member States of companies within the meaning of the second paragraph of Article 58 of the Treaty, in respect of the formation of public limited liability companies and the maintenance and alteration of their capital, with a view to making such safeguards equivalent throughout the Community	[1977] OJ L 26/1
Third Council Directive (EEC) 78/855 of 9 October 1978 based on Article 54(3)(g) of the Treaty concerning mergers of public limited liability companies	[1977] OJ L 295/36
Fourth Council Directive (EEC) 78/660 of 25 July 1978 based on Article 54(3)(g) of the Treaty on the annual accounts of certain types of companies	[1978] OJ L 222/11
Sixth Council Directive (EEC) 82/891 of 17 December 1982 based on Article 54(3)(g) of the Treaty concerning the division of public limited liability companies	[1982] OJ L 378/47
Seventh Council Directive (EEC) 83/349 of 13 June 1983 based on Article 54(3)(g) of the Treaty on consolidated accounts	[1983] OJ L 193/1

Eighth Council Directive (EEC) 84/253 of 10 April 1984 based on Article 54(3)(g) of the Treaty on the approval of persons responsible for carrying out the statutory audits of accounting documents	[1984] OJ L 126/20
Eleventh Council Directive (EEC) 89/666 of 21 December 1989 concerning disclosure requirements in respect of branches opened in a Member State by certain types of company governed by the law of another State	[1989] OJ L 395/96
Twelfth Council Directive (EEC) 89/667 of 21 December 1989 on single-member private limited liability companies	[1989] OJ L 395/40
RECOMMENDATIONS	
Title of Act	**Publication Reference**
Commission Recommendation (2001/256/EC) of 15 November 2000 on quality assurance for the statutory audit in the European Union: minimum requirements	[2001] OJ L 91/91
Commission Recommendation (2001/453/EC) of 30 May 2001 on the recognition, measurement and disclosure of environmental issues in the annual accounts and annual reports of companies	[2001] OJ L 156/33
Commission Recommendation (2002/590/EC) of 16 May 2002 on "Statutory Auditors' Independence in the EU : A Set of Fundamental Principles"	[2002] OJ L 191/22

Proposed European Company Law Instruments	
REGULATIONS	
Title of Act	**Publication Reference**
Amended Proposal for a Council Regulation (EEC) on a statute for a European Association	[1993] OJ C 236/1
Amended Proposal for a Council Regulation (EEC) on a statute for a European Co-operative Society	[1993] OJ C 236/17
Amended Proposal for a Council Regulation (EEC) on a statute for a European Mutual Society	[1993] OJ C 236/40
DIRECTIVES	
Title of Act	**Publication Reference**
Proposal for a Directive of the European Parliament and of the Council amending Council Directive 68/151/EEC, as regards disclosure requirements in respect of certain types of companies : COM (2002) 279	[2002] OJ C 227/377
Proposal for a Directive of the European Parliament and of the Council on take-over bids : COM (2002) 534 final	[2003] OJ C 45 E/1

Annex 2

REPORT

OF

THE HIGH LEVEL GROUP
OF
COMPANY LAW EXPERTS

ON

ISSUES RELATED
TO TAKEOVER BIDS

Brussels, 10 January 2002

THE HIGH LEVEL GROUP OF COMPANY LAW EXPERTS

Chairman : Jaap WINTER

Jan SCHANS CHRISTENSEN

José Maria GARRIDO GARCIA

Klaus J. HOPT

Jonathan RICKFORD

Guido ROSSI

Joëlle SIMON

Rapporteur : Dominique THIENPONT
Secretariat : Karel VAN HULLE

TABLE OF CONTENTS

Annex 6

European Parliament and Council Directive on Company Law concerning Takeover Bids : Joint text approved by the Conciliation Committee on 6 June 2001

PREAMBLE

This document constitutes the High Level Group of Company Law Experts' first report, in conformity with the Group's terms of reference which were defined by the European Commission on 4 September 2001 (see Annex 1).

The Group's first report based on Commission mandate

The Group has been set up by the European Commission to provide independent advice in the first instance on issues related to pan-European rules for takeover bids and subsequently on key priorities for modernising company law in the European Union. The High Level Group has been requested to "...deliver a preliminary report on its recommendations concerning rules for takeover bids by the end of 2001...".

First part of the mandate is related to Takeover Bids

Taking account of the positions of the EU's Council of Ministers and the European Parliament during the last stages of negotiation of the previous proposal for a Takeover Bids Directive, the Group has been asked to consider the following three issues :

The 3 main elements of the Takeover Bids mandate

- How to ensure the existence of a level playing field in the European Union concerning the equal treatment of shareholders across Member States;
- The definition of the notion of an "equitable price" to be paid to minority shareholders;
- The right for a majority shareholder to buy out minority shareholders ("squeeze-out right").

Acknowledgements

The Chairman, Jaap Winter, and Members of the Group would like to thank the Members of the European Parliament's Legal Affairs and Internal Market Committee; the European Commissioner Frits Bolkestein; and the Director General of the European Commission's Internal Market Directorate General, John Mogg, for their assistance and cooperation.

The Group would also like to thank all those who have taken part in the Group's hearings or otherwise have made their views known to the Group, often making themselves available at very short notice. A summary of the main comments the Group has received is included in Annex 3 to the present report.

Finally, the High Level Group would like to thank the rapporteur, the secretariat and their staffs for their constructive and efficient contribution to their work within the tight schedule given to the Group.

SUMMARY OF THE HIGH LEVEL GROUP OF COMPANY LAW EXPERTS' OBSERVATIONS AND RECOMMENDATIONS

CHAPTER I - *"Takeover bids : the need for a level playing field"*

An important goal of the European Union is to create an integrated capital market in the Union by 2005. The regulation of takeover bids is a key element of such an integrated market. The extent to which in a given securities market takeover bids can take place and succeed is determined by a number of factors. These factors can be of a general kind, often macro-economic, or company specific.

Currently there are many differences between the various Member States, in terms of such general and company specific factors. Annex [4] gives an overview of company specific barriers to takeover bids which are lawful or actually applied in the Member States and which the Group has reviewed. As a result, takeover bids cannot be undertaken with the same expectation of success in the different Member States and shareholders in Member States do not have corresponding opportunities to tender their shares. This is what is generally referred to as the 'lack of level playing field' in the area of takeover bids in the European Union.

In the light of available economic evidence the Group holds the view that the availability of a mechanism for takeover bids is basically beneficial. Takeovers are a means to create wealth by exploiting synergies and to discipline the management of listed companies with dispersed ownership, which in the long term is in the best interests of all stakeholders, and society at large. These views also form the basis for the Directive. This is not to say that takeover bids are always beneficial for all (or indeed any) of the parties involved.

The mandate of the Group is to review whether and to what extent a level playing field for takeover bids could and should be created with respect to the mechanisms and structures allowed and created under company law in Member States which may frustrate or inhibit takeover bids. These are by nature company related factors. The Group acknowledges that any approach on this basis would leave the various general differences existing in Member States untouched. It believes, however, that its recommendations with respect to company law mechanisms and structures would, in addition to market driven changes, mark an important step forward in developing a general level playing field for takeover bids in the European Union.

The Group believes that any European company law regulation aimed at creating a level playing field for takeover bids should be guided by two principles:

1. Shareholder decision-making

In the event of a takeover bid the ultimate decision must be with the shareholders. They should always be able to decide whether to tender their shares to a bidder and for what price. It is not for the board of a company to decide whether a takeover bid for the shares in the company should be successful or not. This is not to say that the board has no responsibility at all in the context of a takeover bid.

It is sometimes argued that allowing the board to frustrate a takeover bid can be justified as a means to help take into consideration the interests of shareholders and other stakeholders in the company, notably the employees. The Group rejects these views. Defensive mechanisms are often costly. Most importantly, managers are faced with a significant conflict of interests. Shareholders should be able to decide for themselves and stakeholders should be protected by specific rules (e.g. on labour law or environmental law).

2. Proportionality between risk-bearing capital and control

In the Group's view, proportionality between ultimate economic risk and control means that share capital which has an unlimited right to participate in the profits of the company or in the residue on liquidation, and *only* such share capital, should normally carry control rights, in proportion to the risk carried. The holders of these rights to the residual profits and assets of the company are best equipped to decide on the affairs of the company as the ultimate effects of their decisions will be borne by them. This report will use the term 'risk-bearing capital' to refer to this concept.

The holder of the majority of risk-bearing capital should be able to exercise control. Capital and control structures in a company which grant disproportionate control rights to some shareholder(s) should not operate to frustrate an otherwise successful bid for the risk-bearing capital of the company. The concept of risk-bearing capital used here does not include those preference shares which have no exposure to the surplus but only carry a limited right to distributions of profits and on liquidation.

It may well be that in a fully integrated and well developed securities market whether or not companies adhere to the proportionality principle should be left to the market itself. Similar arguments might be applied to the principle of shareholder decision-making, though the conflict of interest of the board may well lead to market failure in this context.

Currently, however, such efficient markets do not exist across Europe. The Group therefore considers it to be necessary to specify the two principles in more detailed rules which are binding in the Member States. The Group has investigated two possible approaches for such rules, i.e. the application of the guiding principles on a general basis and the application of the guiding principles limited to the context of a takeover bid.

Many of the company specific structures that the Group has reviewed not only deviate from the two guiding principles in a takeover context but are pre-bid structures, which more generally have the effect of concentrating control rights in the hands of the board and/or minority shareholders. It could be argued that it would be consistent to apply the two guiding principles generally, and not only in the context of takeover bids. The various mechanisms would then have to be assessed in the particular context in which they operate and judged to see whether and under what circumstances any justification still exists for them.

Such an exercise lies beyond the Group's terms of reference for this report and does not appear to be necessary if an effective solution addressing the takeover context can be devised. However, in the Group's view one type of general and permanent rule should be established: listed companies should generally be required to fully disclose their capital and control structures. Only on the basis of full disclosure can markets properly judge the efficiency of companies with different capital and control structures.

Whatever the virtues and justifications of company law mechanisms and structures deviating from the two guiding principles may be generally, the Group takes the view that they should not frustrate or unduly inhibit takeover bids or their successful execution. When a takeover bid is made two stages should be distinguished. The first stage commences when a bid is announced. The second is the stage commencing after the successful completion of the bid. The Group believes that a level playing field can only be achieved in this context if rules are in place to ensure effective application of the two guiding principles in both stages of a takeover bid.

With respect to the first stage, article 9 (1) (a) of the Directive essentially required the board of the offeree company to be "neutral" after a bid has been announced. Article 9 confirms the principle of shareholder decision-making in response to a takeover bid. It ensures that shareholders can decide on whether or not to tender in a bid and that any action to frustrate the bid requires the specific authorisation of the general meeting of shareholders at that time.

Article 9 as such does not ensure that the principle of proportionality between risk-bearing capital and control is adhered to once a takeover bid has been announced. Disproportionate control rights can be used to authorise the board to frustrate the bid if the board or the minority shareholder controlling the board wishes to oppose it. Application of the proportionality principle once a takeover bid is announced means that an authorisation by the general meeting of shareholders to take actions frustrating the bid would only be valid if made by a majority of votes exercised by the holders of the proportionate majority of the risk-bearing capital of the company.

For the second stage, after successful completion of the bid, the Group holds the view that a level playing field is only created if the two guiding principles apply with reasonable efficacy to company law mechanisms and structures which may frustrate a bid and which may already be in place prior to the bid. This can be achieved by introducing a rule which allows the bidder to break-through such mechanisms and structures, as defined in the articles of association and related constitutional documents, in the case of a takeover bid which achieves such a measure of success as clearly to justify this.

In the view of the Group a break-through rule applied after a successful takeover bid would strike an appropriate balance between, on the one hand, the need, at least for the time being, to allow differences in the capital and control structures of companies in view of the current differences between Member States, and, on the other hand, the need to allow and stimulate successful takeover bids to take place in order to create an integrated securities market in Europe.

The Group believes that the break-through rule should be available to a bidder who has made a general bid on all the risk-bearing shares of the company and who has acquired a certain threshold of risk-bearing capital as a result of the bid. The Group takes the view that the threshold should not be set at a percentage higher than 75% of the risk-bearing capital of the company. Member States should be allowed to set the threshold at a lower level sufficient to take special resolutions like amendments of the articles of association and corporate reconstructions.

After the bid has been announced, the general meeting of shareholders may have resolved or authorised the board to issue new risk-bearing share capital as a post-bid defence. So long as this resolution has been carried with the support of the appropriate majority of the risk-bearing capital, this decision is to be respected as it in itself does not violate the principles of shareholder decision-making and proportionality between risk-bearing capital and control. The bidder should be allowed, in case where invocation of the break-through rule is necessary to achieve effective control, to make his general bid for all the risk-bearing share capital of the company conditional upon reaching the threshold percentage of risk-bearing capital and the consequential ability to use the break-through facility.

The effect of the break-through rule should be to redress the deviations in the articles of association and other constitutional documents from the principles of shareholder decision-making and proportionality between risk-bearing capital and control. This implies two types of rules.

1. At least where the bidder acquires 75% or more of risk-bearing capital, he should be able to exercise a proportionate percentage of the total votes that can be cast in a general meeting of shareholders. In calculating the votes in a general meeting held after the bidder has reached the threshold, various provisions in the articles of association of the company (in particular voting caps, multiple voting rights or double voting rights, provisions completely denying voting rights, provisions conferring inappropriate voting rights (i.e. other than proper protective provisions) to non-risk-bearing capital) will have to be overridden.

2. The bidder acquiring 75% or more of risk-bearing capital should be able to exercise the core control rights that company law grants to shareholders. These rights include the right to appoint, suspend and dismiss board members and the right to determine the constitution of the company and the way in which it is to be operated and managed. Provisions in the articles of association that hinder the exercise of these rights should be overridden. An exception should be made for nomination or appointment rights of third parties which are mandatory in the company law of the Member States (e.g. co-determination rules).

From a company law and capital markets perspective, there is no justification to distinguish between companies in which special control rights are held by private persons and companies in which special control rights are held by states. From the perspective of the wider public interest, the Group believes that, where special control rights are attached to golden shares held by Member States, then, even if the European Court of Justice would rule they do not violate the Treaty of Rome as such, such rights should be exercisable in accordance with the principles of public law and not in accordance with private company law principles.

The break-through rule should apply regardless of whether the relevant provisions in the articles of association were already included prior to the bid being made or have been included as a post-bid defence after a bid was made. If, after having approved a post-bid defence, the shareholders decide to tender their shares to the bidder to such an extent that he acquires 75% of risk-bearing capital, they have clearly reversed their initial decision.

The effect of the break-through rule should be immediate upon the acquisition of the threshold percentage of risk-bearing capital by the bidder after a general takeover bid. A waiting period would create unacceptable uncertainty for the bidder, the company, the other remaining shareholders, the board and other stakeholders.

The exercise of control rights by the bidder in proportion to his holding of risk-bearing capital requires that a general meeting of shareholders be held. The bidder who has reached the threshold should have the right to convene a general meeting of shareholders at short notice. In the meeting, the bidder (and other holders of risk bearing capital) has the right to exercise voting rights in proportion to the holding of risk-bearing capital.

The Group has considered whether the holder of shares carrying disproportionate voting rights or special control rights should be compensated for the loss of these rights which results from the bidder reaching the break-through threshold after a general takeover bid. The Group agrees that the bidder should not be required to offer such compensation. The loss of these special rights would be the result of a public policy choice made by the European Union and the Member States in order to create a level playing field for takeover bids across the Union. There may be exceptional cases where compensation for loss of specific control rights is due and the holder of such rights demonstrates specific damage. The Group recommends that it be further reviewed whether an appraisal procedure should be provided for in these cases. Such a right of appraisal should in any case not prevent the bidder from using the break-through rule to exercise control.

Certain types of company specific barriers to takeover bids should remain outside the scope of the break-through rule, basically because the break-through rule appears to be an inadequate way to deal with them. This is not to say that these mechanisms should not be dealt with at all and should continue to be barriers to takeover bids. The Group has considered ways to deal with three types of barriers.

The first type consists of provisions restricting the transferability of shares. The Listing Directive of 1979 requires that listed shares must be freely transferable. However, it is not uncommon for listed companies to list only part of the risk-bearing capital or to have a separate class or classes of non-listed risk-bearing share capital. The requirement of free transferability does not apply to these non-listed shares. The Group believes that holders of non-listed risk-bearing shares should be able to sell to the bidder and the bidder should be able to acquire them. A specific example of this is where a company has issued risk-bearing shares to a trust or administration office, which in turn issues non-voting depository receipts. The depository receipts should be freely exchangeable into the underlying voting shares in case of a takeover bid.

The second type is the contractual barrier to takeover bids. A wide variety of arrangements exists in contracts to which the company is a party which cause the contract to take effect, alter or terminate as a result of a change of control of the company. The Group believes that these contractual arrangements should not be subject to a break-through rule as it would be very difficult to deal with the perfectly acceptable reasons the counterparty to the agreement may have for requiring such provisions, its good faith in relying on them and its entitlement to compensation if a break-through were to take place.

Another type of contractual barrier to takeover bids is the agreement between shareholders which prohibit the transfer of shares by these shareholders to a bidder, sometimes enforced by substantial financial penalties. There is a serious concern that shareholders entering into such an agreement lack sufficient information to judge whether tendering their shares in a potential future bid would be attractive or not and the Group recommends to review whether a rule whereby these agreements would be unenforceable when a general takeover bid is made, should be adopted in all Member States.

The third type is the pyramid structure. In some Member States a person exercises control over a company through a cascade of listed and unlisted holding companies. There are minority, non-controlling shareholders in every holding company in the chain. Pyramid structures in a different way achieve a similar disproportionality between ownership of risk-bearing capital and control rights as is, for example, achieved by multiple voting rights (similar concerns arise in the case of circular or cross-shareholdings between various listed companies). The Group believes pyramid structures should remain outside the scope of the break-through rule, because it is difficult to see how such a rule could deal with these structures and because they pose general problems also outside the context of a takeover bid. The Group recommends that it be reviewed whether pyramid structures including several listed companies should be regulated and what adequate measures of protection of minority shareholders (in group law, in listing rules or otherwise) should be enforced in all Member States.

In the debate about the Directive, the argument was put forward that it did not create a level playing field between the European Union and the United States. European companies would be severely restricted in putting up defences against takeover bids under Article 9 of the Directive, while American companies could use a number of devices to defend against a takeover bid. It has also been suggested that the US regime represents a desirable model for Europe.

First, it should be noted that the laws of the various states in the US regulating takeover bids differ widely. As a result there is no clear level playing field for takeover bids within the United States. But it is true that the board of American companies generally has a broad discretion to put up defensive devices under what is called the business judgement rule.

However, the Group believes that the American example should not be followed in Europe, for a number of reasons. The broad discretion of the board of US companies to put up defensive mechanisms operates in a general legal and capital market environment which differs widely from the European environment. The takeover activity on the American capital markets is intensive and, as Annex [5] shows, European companies benefit to a very large extent from that activity. The current anti-takeover rules in the United States are contested even there by a large body of both economic and legal literature arguing that the ultimate decision on takeover bids should be made by shareholders.

Second, as for the alleged relative advantage of US companies, the Group is not satisfied that, given the other aspects of the US environment, such an advantage arises in practice. If political concerns remain, consideration could be given to requiring the application of the proposed rules only to bids by European listed companies.

On the basis of these observations, the Group makes the following recommendations.

Subject	Recommendation
Item I.1 **General disclosure of capital and control structures**	Recommendation I.1. (see p. 25) Listed companies should be required to disclose complete information about their capital and control structures (except for those deriving from general applicable law), for instance in their annual reports, listing particulars and prospectuses. If important changes occur in this information, listed companies should be under a continuous obligation to disclose such changes. Disclosure of some of these elements is already required under existing Directives: the Group recommends that these elements be disclosed and presented in a combined, coherent way.
Item I.2 **Shareholder decision-making after announcement of the bid**	Recommendation I.2. (see p. 27) After announcement of the bid, the board of the offeree company should not be permitted to take actions frustrating a takeover bid on the basis of a general meeting authorisation given prior to the bid. Only when a bid is actually announced and the shareholders can really assess all relevant information, can they in fairness be asked to decide whether this takeover bid should be frustrated by the board or not.

Item I.3 **Proportionality between risk and control after the announcement of the bid**	Recommendation I.3. (see p. 28) After announcement of the bid, any authorisation by the general meeting of shareholders to take actions frustrating the bid should be given by a majority of votes exercised by the holders of the proportionate majority of the risk-bearing capital of the company. The bidder should also be allowed to vote in such a meeting to the extent he already holds risk-bearing capital in the company.
Item I.4 **Break-through right after completion of the bid -** **Principle**	Recommendation I.4. (see p. 29) A rule should be introduced, which allows the bidder to break-through mechanisms and structures which may frustrate a bid, as defined in the articles of association and related constitutional documents, after completion of a takeover bid for all the risk-bearing shares of the company, which achieves such a measure of success as clearly to justify this.
Item I.5 **Break-through right after completion of the bid -** **Threshold**	Recommendation I.5. (see p. 30) The threshold for exercising the break-through right should not be set at a percentage higher than 75% of the risk-bearing capital of the company on the date of completion of the bid. Member States should be allowed to set the threshold at a lower level sufficient to take special resolutions like amendments of the articles of association and corporate reconstructions. Member States should ensure that qualified majorities required for special resolutions do not exceed the level of risk-bearing capital they set as a threshold for the break-through rule. The bidder should be allowed to make his general bid conditional upon reaching the threshold percentage of risk-bearing capital, in case where invocation of the break-through rule is necessary to achieve effective control.
Item I.6 **Break-through right after completion of the bid -** **Effect**	Recommendation I.6. (see p. 32) Provisions in the articles of association and other constitutional documents deviating from the principles of shareholder decision-making and proportionality between risk-bearing capital and control should be overridden. Such provisions include 1. the rules affecting voting rights and 2. the rules relating to the composition of the board and the determination of the constitution of the company. These provisions should be overridden, regardless of the fact that such provisions were already included prior to the bid being made or have been included as a post-bid defence after a bid was made. In case shares with special control rights are in the hands of Member States, and to the extent they are permissible under community law, they should be subject to public law principles and not exercisable solely under the private law applicable to companies.
Item I.7 **Break-through right after completion of the bid -** **Timing and procedure**	Recommendation I.7. (see p. 34) The effect of the break-through rule should be immediate upon the acquisition of the threshold percentage of risk-bearing capital by the bidder after a general takeover bid. The bidder who has reached the threshold should have the right to convene a general meeting of shareholders at short notice, in which he has the right to exercise voting rights in proportion to his holding of risk-bearing capital. This control of the general meeting should persist for so long as the relevant majority is retained.
Item I.8 **Break-through right after completion of the bid -** **Compensation**	Recommendation I.8. (see p. 35) The bidder should not be required to offer compensation to the holder of shares carrying disproportionate voting rights or special control rights for the loss of these rights which results from the bidder reaching the break-through threshold after a general takeover bid. There may be exceptional cases where compensation is due and the holder of such rights demonstrates specific damages: the Group recommends that it be further reviewed whether an appraisal procedure should be provided in these cases.

Item I.9 Provisions restricting the transferability of shares	Recommendation I.9. (see p. 36) In the event a bidder makes a general takeover bid for the risk-bearing capital of the company, restrictions on the transferability of non-listed risk-bearing shares should not be enforceable against him. If depository receipts for risk-bearing shares are listed, they should be freely exchangeable into the underlying shares in the event of a general takeover bid.
Item I.10 Contractual arrangements	Recommendation I.10. (see p. 37) Contractual arrangements in general, which can form barriers to takeover bids, should not be subject to a break-through rule, but should be dealt with in general contract and company law. In the particular case of contractual agreements between shareholders which prohibit the transfer of shares to a bidder, sometimes enforced by substantial financial penalties, the Group recommends that the Commission review whether a rule whereby these agreements would be unenforceable when a general takeover bid is made should be adopted in all Member States.
Item I.11 Pyramid structures	Recommendation I.11. (see p. 38) The Group believes pyramid structures should remain outside the scope of the break-through rule and recommends that the Commission review whether pyramid structures including several listed companies should be regulated and what adequate measures of protection of minority shareholders (in group law, in listing rules or otherwise) should be enforced in all Member States.
Item I.12 Level Playing Field between the EU and the US	Recommendation I.12. (see p. 39) The Group's proposals, if implemented, would not result in company law rules for takeover bids applied in the European Union being broadly similar to those applied in the United States. The Group nevertheless believes for a number of reasons that the European Union should not use the controversial US rules as a model, but rather consider what type of regulation of takeover bids is best suited to enhance the development of efficient integrated capital markets in the Union. If, however, political concerns would remain, it could be considered whether to allow Member States to provide that the benefits of the application of the principles of shareholder decision-making and proportionality between risk-bearing and control as recommended in this report can only be enjoyed by European listed companies making general takeover bids for other European listed companies, to the extent this would not violate international agreements and could practically be enforced.

CHAPTER II – *"The equitable price to be offered in mandatory bids"*	
The notion of equitable price is included in Article 5(1) of the Directive, which seeks to harmonise the circumstances under which a mandatory bid has to be made and contains the following provision: "(...) This bid shall be addressed to all holders of securities for all their holdings at an equitable price. (...)". The Group considers that the requirement to offer an equitable price is of the utmost importance in the context of mandatory bids to achieve an adequate protection of the minority shareholders. In view of its mandate, the Group examines the notion of equitable price in the present report in relation to mandatory bids only. Apart from the limits on the Group's terms of reference, the exclusion of an equitable price requirement in voluntary offers is also justified on the ground that, in principle, the judgement on the adequacy of the offer price should be left to the market.	
The lengthy discussions on the Directive have illustrated the difficulty of defining common rules regarding the consideration that should be offered in a mandatory bid, with respect to both the level and the nature of such consideration. The Directive contains the following rules : - Article 5(1) refers to the situations in which a person acquires the control of a company and contains the principle of the mandatory bid, the notion of equitable price and some provisions (based on the "cash alternative" principle) related to the nature of the consideration which must be offered; - Article 6(3) requires Member States to adopt rules relating to the information which has to be stated in the offer document in any type of offer (whether it be voluntary or mandatory).	
In some of the Member States that currently apply a mandatory bid rule, the provisions on the consideration to be paid have a binding character, whereas a few Member States provide only recommendations. The provisions also differ widely with respect to both the level and the nature of the consideration to be offered. In a few Member States, the level of the consideration to be offered is determined by reference to general principles only (e.g. equal treatment of shareholders). However, a vast majority of Member States has adopted detailed provisions with respect to the consideration to be offered in a mandatory bid, but they vary considerably as to the nature and the number of the criteria used, and the way in which they are applied. In most Member States, a bidder is free to offer as consideration cash or securities.	
The effect of the wording of article 5(1) of the Directive is that the issue whether a price is equitable is a matter of European law, ultimately determinable by the European Court of Justice. In the view of the Group, it is not desirable that such a question should be determined by long drawn out court proceedings. The Group therefore considers that, at the very least, it should be made clear that it is for the Member States to satisfy the Directive requirement to provide for one or several equitable price criterion/criteria. The Group recognises that any sort of regulation on the consideration to be offered in a mandatory bid should allow for a reasonable degree of flexibility with the aim of effectively achieving an equivalent treatment of all holders of securities, but notes that an efficient functioning of the capital markets in the European Union requires a sufficient degree of predictability as to that consideration.	
On the basis of these observations, the Group makes the following recommendations.	
Subject	**Recommendation**
Item II.1 **Introduction of a harmonised approach to the equitable price**	Recommendation II.1. (see p. 48) A harmonised approach should be introduced at EU level with the aim of providing a means for offerors to predict and ideally to determine the equitable price they will have to pay in a mandatory bid. This approach should on the one hand create a strong presumption in favour of a price established by application of a common rule and at the same time provide for sufficient flexibility in particular circumstances.

Item II.2 Common rule applicable in normal circumstances	Recommendation II.2. (see p. 49) The price to be offered in the mandatory bid should, in normal circumstances, be equal to the highest price paid by the offeror for shares of the relevant class, whether on or off the market, during a certain period preceding the date of the acquisition of securities by the offeror, which resulted in the change in the control of the company. Member States should be free to set the length of this period between 6 and 12 months.
Item II.3 Flexibility in particular circumstances	Recommendation II.3. (see p. 50) Member States should be permitted to define both the situations in which the presumption above may be displaced and the criteria which may be applied by supervisory authorities in their decision to apply a price higher or lower than the highest price paid. With respect to the definition of the situations in which the presumption may be disproved, the Directive should contain the following principles: 1) the rule can be deviated from only where it is demonstrated that its application would plainly result in an unfair price, 2) where deviation would lead to a lower price, the burden of proof should lie with the offeror, 3) all unclear cases should be resolved by giving prevalence to the fair treatment of the target's shareholders. With respect to the criteria which may be applied in such circumstances, Member States should be permitted to retain: 1) the average market value over a certain period (ranging from 3 to 6 months) prior to the offer, 2) the liquidation value of the company, 3) any other objective valuation criteria usually applied in financial analysis. Any decision whereby a supervisory authority applies a price different from the highest price paid should be accompanied by the provision of complete supporting information.
Item II.4 Timing of the mandatory bid	Recommendation II.4. (see p. 51) The question of whether a price offered in the mandatory bid is equitable very much depends on the timing of the mandatory bid. The offeror should be required to make the mandatory bid within a short period (to be set by Member States at a maximum of 30 days) after having acquired control of the company through the acquisition of securities.
Item II.5 Acquisition of securities on more favourable terms outside of or after the mandatory bid	Recommendation II.5. (see p. 51) Member States could be required to implement either a) a system in which the acquisition of securities on more favourable terms is fully prohibited during the bid or for a certain period after the bid or b) a system whereby the acquisition of securities on more favourable terms during the bid or for a certain period after the bid obliges the offeror to pay the difference to the holders of securities who tendered their securities in the mandatory bid. Member States should be free to set the length of this period between 6 and 9 months.

CHAPTER III – *"The squeeze-out and sell-out rights after a takeover bid"*
The **squeeze-out right** basically refers to the right of a majority shareholder in a company to compel the minority shareholders to sell their shares to him at an appropriate price. Conversely, the **sell-out right** refers to the right of a minority shareholder to compel the majority shareholder to purchase his shares from him at an appropriate price. In the light of its mandate, the Group focuses in this report on the desirability of squeeze-out and sell-out rights in the context of a takeover bid.
Neither the squeeze-out right nor the sell-out right are currently regulated by any of the existing company law instruments adopted at EU level, so that Member States are free to decide whether and under which conditions such rights should be introduced in their national legislation. The vast majority of the Member States currently provide for a right of a majority shareholder to buy out the minority shareholders. However, the conditions under which that right may be exercised differ widely, in particular in the following areas : the types of companies for which the right exists, the link or lack of a link with takeover bids, the thresholds that have to be reached, and the determination of the consideration to be offered to the minority shareholders. About half of the Member States provide for a right to sell out to the majority shareholder. Here again, the conditions under which that right may be exercised differ widely, in the same areas as identified above in relation to the squeeze-out right.
The Group holds the view that the right of a majority shareholder to buy out the minority shareholders subsequent to a takeover bid can be justified on the following grounds: the presence of minority shareholders after a takeover bid leads to various costs and risks, the squeeze-out right makes takeover bids more attractive for potential bidders and may be viewed as a counterpart to the mandatory bid rule, and the squeeze-out right is more efficient than a delisting procedure. The Group notes that property rights are protected at national and international level, but observes that various courts in the Member States have ruled that the squeeze-out right is not to be regarded as incompatible with these protective provisions. The Group holds the view that the sell-out right of minority shareholders following a takeover bid can be justified on the following grounds : the majority shareholder may be tempted to abuse his dominant position after a takeover bid, minority shareholders cannot obtain appropriate compensation by selling their shares in the market if it has become illiquid, the sell-out right is an appropriate mechanism to counter the pressure on shareholders to tender in the takeover bid, and finally the sell-out right is to be regarded as a counterpart for the squeeze-out right.
On the basis of these observations, the Group makes the following recommendations.

Subject	Recommendation
Item III.1 **Availability of the squeeze-out and sell-out rights after a takeover bid**	Recommendation III.1. (see p. 63) In view of their justifications in the context of takeover bids, an initiative at EU level is necessary to ensure that the squeeze-out and sell-out rights exist in all Member States after a general takeover bid. With respect to both the definition of the applicable thresholds and the determination of the consideration to be offered, similar rules should be adopted throughout the EU while leaving sufficient room to Member States properly to take into account the peculiarities of their company law and the characteristics of their financial markets.
Item III.2 **Threshold for the squeeze-out right**	Recommendation III.2. (see p. 64) Member States should have the possibility to set the threshold for triggering the squeeze-out right by reference to the capital (between 90% and 95%). Alternatively, Member States should have the possibility to set the threshold by reference to the number of acceptances in the offer (at 90%). Where there are several classes of securities outstanding, the squeeze-out right should apply on a class by class basis, whichever of the two options mentioned above is retained at national level.

Item III.3 **Consideration to be offered in exercising the squeeze-out right**	Recommendation III.3. (see p. 65) With respect to the consideration to be offered in exercising the squeeze-out right, the price offered in the takeover bid should be presumed to be a fair price if the bid has been accepted by shareholders holding 90% or more of the share capital in respect of which the offer has been made. If a mandatory bid has been made, the mandatory bid price should be rebuttably presumed to be a fair price in the squeeze-out procedure even if the mandatory bid has not been accepted by shareholders holding 90% or more of the relevant share capital. In all other situations, the consideration should be determined by expert(s). Cash, or a cash alternative, should be offered if it was offered in the takeover bid.
Item III.4 **Threshold for the sell-out right**	Recommendation III.4. (see p. 66) Member States should set the threshold for triggering the sell-out right by reference to the capital (between 90% and 95%). Where there are several classes of securities outstanding, the sell-out right should apply on a class by class basis.
Item III.5 **Consideration to be obtained in exercising the sell-out right**	Recommendation III.5. (see p. 67) With respect to the consideration to be obtained in exercising the sell-out right, the Group recommends a mirroring of the proposals made above regarding the squeeze-out right.

INTRODUCTION

1. THE PROPOSALS FOR A TAKEOVER BID DIRECTIVE : A HISTORICAL PERSPECTIVE

1.1. The initial proposal

Takeover bid directive first envisaged in 1985

The Commission first announced its intention to propose a directive on the approximation of Member States' laws on takeover bids in its 1985 White Paper on completing the Internal Market.

Initial proposal presented by the Commission in 1989

Amended in 1990

On 19 January 1989, the Commission presented to the Council and the European Parliament a proposal for a Thirteenth Council Directive on company law concerning takeover and other general bids[1]. After having received the opinions of the Economic and Social Committee (27 September 1989)[2], and the European Parliament (17 January 1990)[3], the Commission presented an amended proposal on 10 September 1990[4].

This initial proposal was rather detailed

The initial proposal was rather detailed and it soon became clear that it would be difficult to obtain a qualified majority in the Council on this proposal. Some Member States were of the view that the text was overly detailed. Other Member States did not believe that a directive on takeover bids was really necessary, particularly in the absence of a level playing field for takeover bids in the EU.

Revision of the proposal decided on the ground of subsidiarity

In its declaration to the European Council in Edinburgh in December 1992 on subsidiarity, the Commission announced that it would revise its proposal. This intention was confirmed at the Essen European Council in December 1994. A consultation was launched with Member States on the basis of a questionnaire aiming at identifying those issues which could be included in a revised proposal on takeover bids.

1.2. The revised proposal

a) The Commission's proposal of 1996

Second proposal presented by the

On 8 February 1996, the Commission presented to the Council and to the European Parliament a second proposal for a Thirteenth Directive

1 OJ C 64, 14.3.1989, p. 8; with explanatory memorandum, Suppl. 3/89 - Bull. EC.
2 OJ C 298, 27.11.1989, p. 56.
3 OJ C 38, 19.2.1990, p. 41.
4 OJ C 240, 26. 9.1990, p. 7; with explanatory memorandum, COM(90) 416 final - SYN 186.

on company law concerning takeover bids[5]. This second proposal was drawn up in the form of a framework directive, following the consultation with Member States which showed a clear preference for a document that would only contain the general principles governing takeovers bids, leaving much scope for Member States and for the competent authorities to deal with the detailed implementation of those principles. For example, the 1996 proposal, unlike the 1989 version, does no longer define the threshold which must be reached for the launch of a mandatory bid. It is left for Member States to lay down such a threshold in accordance with their traditions and practices.

Commission in 1996, in the form of a framework directive

The Economic and Social Committee endorsed the second proposal on 11 July 1996.[6] The European Parliament delivered its opinion on the second proposal at its plenary session on 25 and 26 June 1997.[7] In its opinion, Parliament approved the second proposal by a large majority, while proposing some 20 amendments.

Endorsed by ECOSOC and approved by EP

An amended proposal was presented by the Commission at the end of 1997[8].

Amended proposal in 1997

b) The Council's common position

At its meeting of 21 June 1999, the Internal Market Council reached a political agreement on the Directive. This agreement was however made subject to a satisfactory outcome of the negotiations between Spain and the United Kingdom on the question of Gibraltar. As Article 4 of the Directive required Member States to designate a competent authority for the supervision of bids, Spain wanted to avoid any possibility of creating a separate authority for take-over bids in Gibraltar.

Council political agreement in 1999, subject to the outcome of negotiations on the Gibraltar issue

Almost one year later, an agreement was reached on the Gibraltar question and the Council finally adopted a common position on 19 June 2000[9].

Council common position adopted in 2000

c) Second Reading in the European Parliament

The text of the common position was presented to the European Parliament for a second reading. Discussions in the European Parliament, based upon the report prepared by Klaus-Heiner Lehne (PPE-DE) proved difficult. The Parliament adopted in the end 20

Second reading in Parliament identified three main problems :

5 OJ No C 162, 6.6.1996, p. 5; with explanatory memorandum, COM(95) 655 final.
6 OJ No C 295, 7.10.1996, p.1.
7 OJ No C 222, 21.7.1997, p.20.
8 OJ No C 378, 13.12.1997
9 OJ No C 23, 24.1.2001, p. 1.

amendments, proposing important changes to the text of the common position. The Parliament identified three main problems:

(1) the lack of harmonisation, particularly concerning the definition of the "equitable price" to be paid in the case of a mandatory bid;

- lack of harmonisation

(2) the introduction of the principle that shareholders must decide about defensive measures once a bid has been launched (so called principle of "neutrality" of the board);

- neutrality of the board

(3) the absence of specific measures aiming at the protection of employees in the case of a takeover bid.

- protection of employees

Furthermore, the Parliament also proposed to introduce into the text a harmonised procedure for squeeze-out.

and suggested introduction of squeeze-out

While the Commission could accept some of the amendments, several important amendments proposed by the Parliament were unacceptable to the Commission and to the Council. A conciliation procedure became therefore unavoidable.

Conciliation procedure became unavoidable

d) The Conciliation procedure

The conciliation procedure led to an agreement on most issues. As far as squeeze out and equitable price are concerned, the Commission declared that it would ask a Group of Company Law Experts to examine these issues as part of a broader mandate to review company law. Concerning employees' rights, the Council accepted most of the amendments presented by the Parliament to the extent that they related to the information to be presented to the employees and their representatives in the case of a takeover bid. The most difficult issue to resolve related to the question of board neutrality, which was put in the broader context of the lack of a level playing field for takeover bids within the EU and between the EU and the rest of the world, particularly the US.

Conciliation led to agreement on most issues

Equitable price and squeeze-out to be examined by Group of Experts

Level playing field heavily debated

Difficult negotiations led to the adoption of a joint text by the Conciliation Committee on 6 June 2001 (see Annex 6). This text is referred to in the present Report as "the Directive".

Joint text adopted in June 2001

When this text was presented to the European Parliament, it failed to obtain the required majority in the Plenary session on 4 July 2001 (273 members voted in favour and 273 members voted against the compromise text).

Rejection by the EP Plenary Session (July 2001)

2. PREPARATION OF A NEW PROPOSAL

Because agreement on a common solution for takeover bids is an essential feature of the Financial Services Action Plan, Commissioner Bolkestein announced at the ECOFIN Council meeting in July 2001 the Commission's intention to come forward with a new proposal as soon as possible. This new proposal would also have to address the issues raised by the European Parliament.

Commission's intention to come forward rapidly with a new proposal, announced in July 2001

Following a promise made to the European Parliament during the conciliation procedure, Commissioner Bolkestein decided in September 2001 to set up a High Level Group of Company Law Experts which should look at ways and means to modernise European company law. The mandate of the Group specifically includes the examination of the issues raised by the Parliament in relation to takeover bids. The Group would have to look at those issues as a matter of priority and report to the Commissioner by the end of 2001.

Creation in September 2001 of a High Level Group of Company Law Experts

Three issues were identified in the Group's mandate in relation with takeover bids: how to ensure a level playing field for shareholders in the EU; the definition of the equitable price to be paid in the case of a mandatory bid; the introduction of a squeeze out procedure.

Three takeover bids issues form first part of Group's mandate

3. PROTECTION OF THE RIGHTS OF THE EMPLOYEES

The Group does not specifically address the protection of employees' rights in the context of a takeover bid because it was only asked to look at a limited number of company law issues in relation to the Directive. Although the Group acknowledges that the interests of other stakeholders and in particular of employees may be at stake in the context of a takeover bid, it believes that this in itself does not justify defensive measures by the board which deny shareholders the opportunity to successfully tender their shares to a bidder who is willing to buy their shares.

Examination of the protection of employees' rights is not in the mandate of the Group

The Directive on takeover bids provided for extensive information requirements towards the employees. Further concerns for the interests of employees should be addressed by specific legislation providing for information and consultation of employees and for their protection in the event of a bid leading to restructuring. Many Member States already provide for these. An EU directive to harmonise information and consultation requirements is being prepared. Similar requirements are included in the Council Directive

Information and consultation rights are provided in the Directive on takeover bids and in several other instruments at EU level.

of 1994 on the establishment of a European Works Council[10] and in the Council Directive of 2001 supplementing the Statute for a European Company with regard to the involvement of employees[11]. The bidder will also be subject to these requirements after a successful bid. The decision to sell by target company shareholders does not affect the legal protections afforded to employees and other stakeholders.

Such protection is not affected by the completion of a takeover bid.

10 Council Directive 94/45/EC of 22 September 1994 on the establishment of a European Works Council or a procedure in Community-scale undertakings and Community-scale groups of undertakings for the purposes of informing and consulting employees, OJ No L 254, 30.9.1994, p. 0064

11 Council Directive 2001/86/EC of 8 October 2001 supplementing the Statute for a European company with regard to the involvement of employees, OJ No L 294, 10.11.2001, p. 0022

CHAPTER I

A LEVEL PLAYING FIELD FOR TAKEOVER BIDS

1. INTRODUCTION

Takeover bids regulation is key to an integrated EU capital market

An important goal of the European Union is to create an integrated capital market in the Union by 2005. The regulation of takeover bids is a key element of such an integrated market.

Takeover bids are influenced by a number of factors

The extent to which in a given securities market takeover bids can take place and succeed is determined by a number of factors. These factors can be of a general or structural kind, often macro-economic, or company specific.

General factors

General factors include the structure and stage of development of the securities market, the availability of alternative financial resources to the capital markets like long term credit and self-financing, the relative importance and role of the banking sector, share ownership patterns and the economic, social and cultural situation in a state.

Company specific factors

At company level, such factors include the extent to which the articles of association and other constitutive documents of the company prior to a bid confer voting rights on, or deny them to, shares acquired in a bid, or confer double or multiple voting rights or special control rights on other shares, the extent to which corporate structures confer majority rights on minority shareholders (pre-bid structures) and the availability of specific measures frustrating a bid once it is announced[1] (post-bid structures).

Many differences between Member States : lack of a level playing field

Currently, there are many differences between the various Member States in terms of such general and company specific factors. Annex [4] gives an overview of company specific barriers to takeover bids which are lawful and, in many instances, actually applied in the Member States and which the Group has reviewed. As a result, takeover bids cannot be undertaken with the same expectation of success in the different Member States and shareholders in Member States do not have equivalent opportunities to tender their shares. This is what is generally referred to as the 'lack of a level playing field' in the area of takeover bids in the European Union.

---

1 Art. 9 (1) (a) of the Directive allows Member States to provide that the authorisation of the general meeting of shareholders referred to in that article is required from an earlier time such as when the board of the offeree company becomes aware that the bid is imminent. For ease of reference this report only refers to 'when a bid has been announced or made' to indicate a post-bid situation.

In the light of available economic evidence, the Group holds the view that the availability of a mechanism which facilitates takeover bids is basically beneficial.

A takeover mechanism offers several benefits

Takeovers are a means for bidders to create wealth by exploiting synergies between their existing business and the target company. Many European companies will need to grow to an optimal scale to make effective use of the integrating internal market. The same is true for companies which compete on global markets. Takeover bids are a means to achieve this for those engaged in the business of both bidder and target.

Exploitation of synergies

Takeover bids also offer shareholders the opportunity to sell their shares to bidders who are willing to offer a price above the prevailing market price. Such a price will be offered where the bidders believe that the resources of the company can be better developed and exploited under their operation and control.

Opportunity to sell at a price higher than market price

Finally, actual and potential takeover bids are an important means to discipline the management of listed companies with dispersed ownership, who after all are the agents of shareholders. If management is performing poorly or unable to take advantage of wider opportunities the share price will generally under-perform in relation to the company's potential and a rival company and its management will be able to propose an offer based on their assertion of their greater competence. Such discipline of management and reallocation of resources is in the long term in the best interests of all stakeholders, and society at large. These views also form the basis for the Directive.

Discipline of management

This is not to say that takeover bids are always beneficial for the companies concerned, the target and the bidder, and their respective shareholders. As is the case for all types of mergers and acquisitions, takeover bids may be wealth-enhancing or wealth-destroying and benefits to shareholders of the target may be to the detriment of shareholders of the bidder. Whether or not the management of the bidder should undertake a takeover bid on the target company, and whether or not it should confer with its shareholders before executing the bid, is a matter of general corporate governance principles as applying to the bidder. It is outside the scope of the Directive.

This does not mean that takeover bids are always beneficial

The mandate of the Group is to review whether and to what extent a level playing field for takeover bids could and should be created with respect to the mechanisms and structures, allowed and created under company law in Member States, which may frustrate or inhibit takeover bids. These are by nature company related factors. The

Mandate of the Group concentrates on company specific factors (company law)

Group acknowledges that any approach on this basis would leave the various general and structural differences existing in Member States untouched. It believes, however, that its recommendations with respect to company law mechanisms and structures would, in addition to market driven changes, mark an important step forward in developing a general level playing field for takeover bids in the European Union.

Group's recommendations come in addition to market driven changes

2. TWO GUIDING PRINCIPLES

The Group believes that any European company law regulation aimed at creating a level playing field for takeover bids should be guided by two principles: shareholder decision-making and proportionality between risk bearing and control:

Level Playing Field : two principles

1. Shareholder decision-making

In the event of a takeover bid, the ultimate decision must be with the shareholders. They should always be able to decide whether to tender their shares to a bidder and at what price. This is an essential feature of companies listed on a stock exchange where shares can be acquired through purchases in the market and through public offers. The securities markets, and thus the capacity of European industry to finance itself, will only develop fully where this principle is generally adhered to.

In a takeover bid, the ultimate decision must always be with the shareholders

It is not for the board of a company to decide whether a takeover bid for the shares in the company should be successful or not. The board should not be able to frustrate or block a takeover bid and thereby deprive shareholders of the opportunity to tender in such a bid. Nor should it be free to take steps to facilitate a bid, or a preferred bid, if there is more than one, in a way which pre-empts the decision of the shareholders.

It is not for the board to decide whether a takeover bid should be successful or not

This is not to say that the board has no responsibility at all in the context of a takeover bid. Its insight into, and responsibility for, the strategy and day-to-day affairs of the company enable and require it to advise the shareholders on the takeover bid. The board should express its views on the consequences of the bid for the company and its business and on the attractiveness of the terms of the bid for the shareholders. If the board considers a particular bid not to be sufficiently attractive, it should be free and may sometimes be obliged to seek alternative bids from others. But then too, it is equally the case that the ultimate decision on the competing bids should be made by the shareholders. The board should not favour one of the bidders over another, for example by issuing shares to one of them.

Primary responsibility of the board is to advise the shareholders on the takeover bid

It is sometimes argued that allowing the board to frustrate a takeover bid can be justified as a means to help alleviate the pressure to tender that shareholders face, to increase the premium paid to them and to take into consideration the interests of other stakeholders in the company, notably the employees. The Group rejects these views. Even if board resistance to a takeover bid might in some circumstances help to achieve these goals, which is not always clear, any regime which confers discretion on a board to impede or facilitate a bid inevitably involves unacceptable cost and risk.

Various reasons are sometimes given to justify board discretion to frustrate a bid

The Group rejects these views

Defensive mechanisms are often costly in themselves, apart from the fact that they deny the bidder the opportunity to create wealth by exploiting synergies after a successful bid. Most importantly, managers are faced with a significant conflict of interests if a takeover bid is made. Often their own performance and plans are brought into question and their own jobs are in jeopardy. Their interest is in saving their jobs and reputation instead of maximising the value of the company for shareholders. Their claims to represent the interests of shareholders or other stakeholders are likely to be tainted by self-interest. Shareholders should be able to decide for themselves and stakeholders should be protected by specific rules (e.g. on labour law or environmental law).

Defensive mechanisms are often costly

Managers are faced with a conflict of interest

Interests of shareholders and stakeholders are better served otherwise

2. Proportionality between risk bearing and control

In open capital markets major (institutional) investors would normally prefer to invest where bearing the ultimate economic risk of the company confers proportionate control rights. The cost of capital of such companies is normally lower and they will be better able to raise capital on the securities markets. In the Group's view, proportionality between ultimate economic risk and control means that share capital which has an unlimited right to participate in the profits of the company or in the residue on liquidation, and *only* such share capital, should normally carry control rights. All such capital should carry control rights in proportion to the risk carried. The holders of these rights to the residual profits and assets of the company are best equipped to decide on the affairs of the company as the ultimate effects of their decisions will be borne by them. This report will use the term 'risk bearing capital' to refer to this concept.

Share capital which has an unlimited right to participate in the profits or residue on liquidation, and only such share capital, should normally carry control rights

Reference in the present Report to "Risk bearing capital"

The extent to which a shareholder holds risk bearing capital should determine the extent to which he is able to determine the affairs of the company and the operation of its business. The holder of the majority of risk bearing capital should be able to exercise control. Capital and control structures in a company which grant disproportionate control rights to some shareholder(s) should not operate to frustrate an otherwise successful bid for the risk bearing capital of the company.

The holder of the majority of risk bearing capital should be able to exercise control

The concept of risk bearing capital used here[2] does not include the normal form of preference shares which have no exposure to the performance of the company beyond their preferred rights but only carry a limited right to distributions of profits and/or on liquidation. Such preference share capital has a similar economic function to debt. On a strict and complete application of the proportionality principle, if it is to carry votes at all then its voting power should be related to risk, i.e. it should be brought into operation only when there is a default in the payment of the preferential dividend and to enable appropriate protections to be activated to respond to the default. Preference shares which have a preferred entitlement to part of the profits or assets and also carry rights to share with other shares in the rest of the profits or assets are included in the concept of risk bearing capital as used in this report. Similarly, participation rights which carry the ultimate unlimited right to participate in the profits or assets of the company, although formally not deemed to be share capital, should also be included in this concept of risk bearing capital.

Preference shares and participation rights are included in the "risk bearing capital", if they carry an unlimited right to participate in the profits or assets of the company

Rules specifying the guiding principles

These two principles should provide an overall guide for EU legislation on takeover bids for listed companies. The principles are not self-enforcing. The consequences of the principles must be specified.

The two principles are not self-enforcing

It may well be that, in a fully integrated and well developed securities market, whether or not companies should adhere to the proportionality principle should be left to the market itself. Such a market may be able to judge correctly the cost of capital of companies with capital and control structures which deviate from this principle and normally more efficient alternative investments are available to investors in such a market. In the long run, structures deviating from this principle should wither and die out except to the extent that they are justified by the particular circumstances of a company.

In efficient markets, enforcement of the proportionality principle might be left to market forces

Similar arguments might be applied to the principle of shareholder decision-making, though the conflict of interest of the board may well lead to market failure in this context.

The same might be true for the shareholder decision-making principle

Currently, however, such efficient markets do not exist across Europe. The securities markets in Member States differ widely in levels of development. In some Member States, they may be able

Such efficient markets currently do not exist across Europe

---

2 For the avoidance of doubt, the concept of risk bearing capital as used in this report is not identical to the concept of capital as used in the Second Directive on company law and in the company laws of the Member States nor does it correspond to the term "risk capital" as used in some member states to indicate peculiarly risky forms of investment such as venture capital.

efficiently to judge companies which do and do not adhere to these two principles. In most Member States, the Group believes that they cannot do so. These more and less developed markets must be integrated on a European level to enable the restructuring of European industry and the integration of European securities markets to proceed with reasonable efficiency and speed. Also, investor protection tends to be weaker in markets where the two principles are not generally followed.

In order to establish securities markets in the European Union which are both efficient and provide an adequate level of investor protection, the Group considers it to be necessary to specify the two principles in more detailed rules which are binding in the Member States. The Group has investigated two possible approaches for such rules, i.e. application of the guiding principles on a general basis and application of the guiding principles in a way which is limited to the context of a takeover bid.

Therefore the principles must be specified in detailed rules

Two possible approaches

3. GENERAL APPLICATION OF GUIDING PRINCIPLES

Many of the company specific structures that the Group has reviewed not only deviate from the two guiding principles in a takeover context but are pre-bid structures, which more generally have the effect of concentrating control rights in the hands of the board and/or minority shareholders.

Many structures deviate from the two principles on a permanent basis

Examples are control rights of board members relating to board appointments, the existence of various classes of shares with differentiated voting rights, e.g. a separate class of shares carrying a multiple of voting rights of another class of shares with the same nominal value and the same rights to participation in surplus, shares within the same class carrying double the voting rights of others within the class, classes of shares with limited voting rights, general voting caps for shareholders, special control rights, conferred on holders of a specific class (such as golden shares), or on the board, "voting trusts", "pyramid structures", and circular and cross-shareholdings.

Examples

It could be argued that it would be consistent to apply the two guiding principles generally, and not only in the context of takeover bids. On this approach all structures which deviate from the two guiding principles would have to be terminated and the capital and control structures of listed companies would have to be re-arranged accordingly.

It could be argued that the two principles should apply permanently

This would be a major operation, fundamentally affecting the ways listed companies in many parts of the Union are controlled, financed and operated. The various structures deviating from the guiding

Various structures have been developed in national contexts, principles in Member States have been developed in the respective national contexts, based on particular share ownership patterns and other factors affecting the control of companies. They often also serve purposes outside the scope of takeover bids. These have been and to some extent still are deemed to be justified in Member States.

where they often serve purposes outside takeover bids

Some structures, like special control rights for the board, voting caps and depository receipt structures have arguably been developed to protect a company with dispersed ownership against a small minority dominating the general meeting in the usual absence of the vast majority of shareholders. Structures like multiple voting rights and special control rights held by a minority shareholder often conform to particular ownership patterns in a Member State. By creating a strong minority shareholder who controls the company from the inside, such structures may have helped to overcome the problems related to disciplining management of companies with dispersed ownership. Structures deviating from the two guiding principles may also have been beneficial to companies and their shareholders at particular stages in their development, such as small and medium sized enterprises preparing for listing.

Examples of justifications

Other structures exist which appear to be difficult to justify from a general capital markets and company law perspective, like pyramid structures with multiple listings.

Other structures appear difficult to justify

In reviewing the effects of a general application of the two guiding principles, the various mechanisms deviating from them would have to be reviewed in detail. They would have to be assessed in the particular context in which they operate and judged to see whether and under what circumstances any justification still exists for them. It would then need to be decided how they are best dealt with if they are to be terminated. Such distortions in control structures may have been put in place to respond to defects in other governance mechanisms which would need in turn to be addressed before the distortion could be removed - for example in relation to the efficient and responsible operation of shareholders meetings.

A general application of the two principles would lead to a detailed examination of the various mechanisms deviating from them

This would constitute a major review which the Group was unable to undertake in the short time given to it to produce this report. But the Group also doubts whether such review would in the foreseeable future lead to general agreement on which structures could remain as acceptable deviations and under what circumstances, given the different stages of development of capital markets in the Member States, the different share ownership patterns and other general factors determining the level playing field among the Member States.

Such an ambitious exercise may prove to be difficult

Such an exercise might be feasible and useful in addressing other weaknesses in company governance structures, but a thorough

And it may simply not be necessary

examination of the issues lies beyond the Group's terms of reference for this initial report and does not appear to be necessary if an effective solution addressing the takeover context can be devised.

if a solution for takeovers can be devised

Duty to disclose

However, in the Group's view one type of general, permanent rule, should be established in order to help create an integrated capital market in the European Union. Listed companies should generally be required to fully disclose their capital and control structures. Such a disclosure requirement is also essential for the protection of investors in order to enable them to assess the value of and risks related to their investment. Only on the basis of full disclosure can markets properly judge the efficiency of companies with different capital and control structures.

However, listed companies should generally be required to fully disclose their capital and control structures

The Group recommends that listed companies in all Member States be required to disclose their capital and control structures, for instance in their annual reports, in their listing particulars and in prospectuses required to be published on the issue of new securities. If important changes occur in this information, listed companies should be under a continuous obligation similarly to disclose such changes. In the view of the Group, it should be encouraged to use a website dedicated to the company as an efficient and effective medium for providing this type of information to shareholders and others. The Group will come back to this in the second stage.

Disclosure in various places

Update is necessary

Use of website is encouraged

The information to be disclosed should include, inter alia:

Information to be disclosed

- direct and indirect significant shareholdings, including indirect holdings through pyramid structures and circular and cross-shareholdings
- shares and rights to acquire shares of board members and employees
- the system of control of any employee share scheme where the control rights are exercised on behalf of employees by another
- a description of classes of shares, including non-listed shares, the rights and obligations attached to each class of shares and the percentage of total share capital each class represents
- the holders of shares with special control rights and a description of their rights
- a description of the rules applicable to the appointment and removal of board members and the amendment of the articles of association
- a description of the powers of the board of directors, in particular whether or the board meeting has the power to issue and buy back shares

- significant agreements to which the company is a party and which take effect, alter or terminate upon a change of control of the company and the effects thereof.

Disclosure of some of these elements is already required under existing directives, such as the directive on disclosure of major shareholdings, and the first, second, fourth and seventh company law directives. The Group recommends that these elements be disclosed and presented in a combined, coherent way. However, companies should not be required to make reference to structures that arise under general applicable law.

Disclosure should be made in a coherent way

Disclosure does not encompass structures arising under general applicable law

4. APPLICATION OF THE GUIDING PRINCIPLES IN THE CONTEXT OF A TAKEOVER BID

Whatever the virtues and justifications of company law mechanisms and structures deviating from the two guiding principles may be generally, the Group takes the view that they should not frustrate or unduly inhibit takeover bids or their successful execution. In the context of a takeover bid, the principles of shareholder decision-making and proportionality between risk bearing capital and control should apply effectively to enable liquid and coherent markets in capital and corporate control to operate throughout the Union.

Whatever their virtues and justifications in general, deviating structures should not frustrate takeover bids

When a takeover bid is made two stages should be distinguished. The first stage commences when a bid is announced. Shareholders will have to consider how to respond to the bid and the question can arise whether a defence should be put up against the bid. Such a defence is generally referred to as a 'post-bid defence'. The second is the stage commencing after the successful completion of the bid. The bidder may then be frustrated in his ability to exercise control over the company both by post-bid defences as well as by barriers which were already in place prior to the announcement of the bid. These latter barriers are generally referred to as 'pre-bid defences'.

Takeover bids : two stages

First stage : a bid is announced

Second stage : a bid is completed

To ensure that the two guiding principles apply in both stages of a takeover bid, different regulatory approaches are required for each stage. The Group believes that a level playing field can only be achieved in this context if rules are in place to ensure effective application of the two guiding principles in both stages of a takeover bid. The recommendations the Group puts forward for rules to apply in each stage should therefore be understood and applied in combination. Neither of them would create a level playing field for takeover bids without the other.

Different regulatory approaches are required for each stage

Both are necessary to create a level playing field

4.1 Response to a takeover bid

Shareholder decision-making

Article 9 (1) (a) of the Directive essentially required the board of the offeree company to be "neutral" (in the special limited sense described above) after a bid has been announced. It must obtain the prior authorisation of the general meeting of shareholders, given for this purpose, before taking any action which may result in the frustration of the bid, other than seeking alternative bids, and notably before the issuing of shares which may result in a lasting impediment to the offeror obtaining control. This obligation to obtain the specific approval of the general meeting of shareholders is extended to the implementation of decisions taken before the bid has been announced but not yet fully implemented, article 9 (1) (b).

Article 9 of the Directive : Board neutrality principle

Specific approval of shareholders is necessary to frustrate the bid

Article 9 confirms the principle of shareholder decision-making in response to a takeover bid. It ensures that shareholders can decide on whether or not to tender in a bid and that any action to frustrate the bid requires the specific authorisation of the general meeting of shareholders at that time.

Article 9 confirms the shareholder decision-making principle in the first stage of a bid

The board can, and should under article 9 (1) (d), set out its opinion on the bid in a public document, explaining the reasons for its opinion, its views on the effects of implementation of the bid on all the interests of the company, including employment, and on the offeror's strategic planning for the offeree company and its likely impact on jobs and locations. The board has the explicit authority to seek alternative bids. The Group understands the obligation of the board under article 9 to include that it may not frustrate one bid to the benefit of a competing bid by, for example, issuing shares to the competing offeror, unless the general meeting of shareholders specifically authorises such issue of shares at that time. Nor should the board take steps to favour a bid which in any way pre-empts the right of shareholders to reject it.

Board must set out its opinion on the bid in a public document

Board may seek alternative bids

But shareholders must have the final word

The Group has considered whether Member States should be allowed to provide that the board can take actions frustrating a takeover bid if the general meeting of shareholders has authorised such actions in a period of for example eighteen months prior to the bid. The Group has come to the conclusion that this should not be allowed.

Frustrating actions based on an authorisation given prior to the bid should not be allowed

In the period prior to the bid shareholders will not be able to take into account and weigh all the circumstances which are relevant for their decision whether a takeover bid should be frustrated. They are not

Only when a bid is announced can shareholders really assess all

aware of the general market conditions prevailing at the time of a potential future bid, have no information on the performance of the company until that time, do not know whether and when a bid will be made and have no information on whether a potential future bid is attractive to the company and to them. The circumstances leading shareholders to authorise the board to frustrate a potential future bid may very well have changed fundamentally by the time a bid is actually made. Only when a bid is actually announced and the shareholders can really assess all relevant information, can they in fairness be asked to decide whether this takeover bid should be frustrated by the board or not.

relevant information and make an appropriate decision

Proportionality between risk bearing capital and control

Article 9 as such does not ensure that the principle of proportionality between risk bearing capital and control is adhered to once a takeover bid has been announced. If, prior to the bid, the capital and control structures of the company deviate from this principle, the disproportionate control rights can be used, and are likely to be used, to authorise the board to frustrate the bid if the board or the minority shareholder controlling the board wishes to oppose it.

Article 9 as such does not prohibit the use of existing disproportionate control rights

Application of the proportionality principle once a takeover bid is announced means that an authorisation by the general meeting of shareholders to take actions frustrating the bid would only be valid if made by a majority of votes exercised by the holders of the proportionate majority[3] of the risk bearing capital of the company. The Group believes that this principle should be applied once a takeover bid has been announced. It recommends that a rule to this effect be included in a future Directive on takeover bids.

Proportionality principle should apply in the general meeting convened in the first stage of a bid

The effect of this rule is that a shareholders meeting called to decide on whether a post-bid defence should be put up against a takeover bid should be held on a re-arranged, proportional basis. All holders of risk bearing capital must have the right to attend such meeting and to be able to exercise votes in proportion to their holding of risk bearing capital. The bidder should also be allowed to vote in such a meeting to the extent he already holds risk bearing capital in the company.

All holders of risk bearing capital (including the bidder) must be able to attend the general meeting and vote in proportion to their holding

In particular, holders of non-voting shares or participation rights should, to the extent they constitute risk bearing capital in the sense used in this report, be able to exercise voting rights. Holders of depository receipts of shares which represent risk bearing capital should be free to exchange them for the underlying voting shares. Holders of non-risk bearing shares should not be able to exercise

This rule applies to all holders of risk bearing capital

Voting rights

[3] The normal rules applicable in each company to determine the majority required for such a decision should be applied. Application of the proportionality principle does not as such imply a specific majority.

voting rights. General voting caps and limitations to voting rights applicable to risk bearing shares are to be overridden. Shares carrying double and multiple voting rights should only carry voting rights proportionate to their share in the risk bearing capital.

should be proportional to risk bearing capital

The concern could be raised that applying the proportionality principle in this way to the general meeting held in this stage of the takeover bid would affect defensive measures relating to voting in the general meeting of shareholders only and would leave others intact, and in that sense would not help to create a level playing field. The Group does not share this concern. Art. 9 of the Directive already ensured the application of the principle of shareholder decision-making as soon as a bid is announced. Mechanisms which would deviate from this principle can no longer be applied to frustrate a bid after it is announced, unless the shareholders specifically agree to them at that time. The Group believes that a level playing field can only be achieved if the principle of proportionality between risk bearing capital and control is applied to the general meeting which is called to discuss measures to frustrate the bid. If this requirement would not be imposed, it would be possible for the board or the shareholder with disproportionate or special control rights to put up such defences that the break-through rule the Group proposes after a bid has been completed successfully (see paragraph 4.2 below) would become ineffective.

Application of proportionality principle, together with the other principle already ensured by Article 9, to first stage of the bid is necessary to achieve a level playing field

The absence of such a requirement would have contestable consequences

4.2 Break-through after successful completion of a takeover bid

The Group holds the view that a sufficiently level playing field can only be created in the context of a takeover bid if the two guiding principles are applied with reasonable efficacy to company law mechanisms and structures which may frustrate a bid and which may already be in place prior to the bid. This can be achieved by introducing a rule which allows the offeror to "break-through" such mechanisms and structures in the case of a takeover bid which achieves such a measure of success as clearly to justify this. Such a break-through facility would leave these mechanisms and structures in place unless a general takeover bid is made and has become successful. The Group believes a successful bidder who has acquired a substantial part of the risk bearing capital in a general bid for all the shares of the company should have the ability to break-through any mechanisms which frustrate the exercise of proportionate control.

The creation of a level playing field requires that the two principles apply after successful completion of a bid

A successful bidder should be able to break-through any frustrating mechanism

In the view of the Group a break-through rule applied after a successful takeover bid would strike an appropriate balance between, on the one hand, the need, at least for the time being, to allow differences in the capital and control structures of companies in view of the current differences between Member States, and, on the other

A break-through rule applied after a successful takeover bid is a balanced approach

hand, the need to allow and stimulate successful takeover bids to take place in order to create an integrated securities market in Europe.[4]

When introducing a break-through rule, a number of issues need to be considered, in particular:

Four issues to consider

- the scope of a break-through rule
- the threshold to be reached by the offeror
- the effect of the break-through rule
- entitlement to compensation if special rights are lost as a result of the break-through

The Group reviews these issues below.

Scope

As is clear from the overview of company related defence mechanisms in Annex [4], these vary across a wide range. The Group believes that the break-through rule should apply to all provisions in the articles of association and related constitutional documents of the company which deviate from the principles of shareholder decision-making and proportionality. These provisions directly bear on the principles and the break-through rule can be applied to address them relatively easily. A number of barriers to takeovers fall outside this scope. Paragraph 4.3 below deals with some of these barriers.

Scope : provisions in the articles of association which deviate from the two principles

Some barriers fall outside this scope (see below 4.3.)

Threshold

The Group believes that the break-through rule should be available to an offeror who has made a general bid on all the shares of the company and who has acquired a certain threshold of risk bearing capital as a result of the bid, i.e. a certain percentage of the share capital which is entitled to the residual profits and assets of the company. Non-risk bearing capital in this sense should not be included in the calculation of the threshold.

Threshold should be defined by reference to the risk bearing capital

4 The concept of a break-through rule is not unknown in the European Union. In France, the COB has suggested in its 1992 report that limitations on voting rights no longer apply if a bidder succeeds in acquiring one half of the share capital of the company. The same principle is also the basis for a proposal for a law submitted to the Dutch parliament in which a bidder having acquired 70% of the share capital can ask the court to amend or nullify the provisions in the company's constitution which prohibit him from exercising control over the company. Such a request, however, can only be made by the bidder after a waiting period of one year. In Italy, the law of 1994 on privatisations introduced a rule that voting restrictions in privatised companies were automatically removed in any case of a takeover leading the bidder to acquire the majority of the share capital. This rule has been changed to the effect that now voting restrictions are removed as soon as a takeover bid is launched with respect to at least 60 % of the share capital, regardless of the success of the bid.

The Group takes the view that the threshold should not be set at a percentage higher than 75% of the risk bearing capital of the company. Member States should be allowed to set the threshold at a lower level sufficient to take special resolutions like amendments of the articles of association and corporate reconstructions. If the offeror acquires the applicable percentage (referred to below as 75% for convenience) of the risk bearing capital, he should be able to exercise the control rights which normally apply in proportion to his holding and thereby control the affairs of the company and the operation of its business.

Threshold should not be set at a level higher than 75%

Member States should ensure that qualified majorities required for special resolutions do not exceed the level of risk bearing capital they set as a threshold for the break-through rule. Generally, the effect should be to allow the bidder to exercise all the general shareholder rights of control of the company (without prejudice to the general law on the protection of minorities) including control over the appointment and removal of members of the company's board who are appointed under the control of shareholders and powers to change the constitution.

Qualified majorities required for special resolutions should not exceed the level set as a threshold for the break-through rule

After the bid has been announced, the general meeting of shareholders may have resolved, or authorised the board, to issue new share capital as a post-bid defence. If the newly issued share capital is non-risk bearing capital, this does not affect the threshold the bidder should reach to enjoy the break-through; the newly issued shares are ignored in calculating whether the bidder has acquired sufficient risk-bearing capital. If the newly issued share capital is risk bearing capital, the effect is that the bidder will have to acquire more of the risk bearing capital outstanding prior to the issue in order to enjoy the break-through.

Risk bearing capital issued after announcement of the bid will influence application of the break-through rule

If new risk bearing shares are issued to a third party determined not to sell to the bidder equalling more than one third of the risk bearing capital outstanding prior to the issue, it becomes impossible for the bidder to reach the threshold. This then is the result of a decision of the shareholders of the company taken in a meeting after the bid has been announced. But it should be noted, that in view of our recommendation above this can only be achieved with full application of the proportionality principle (see par 4.1 above). This decision is to be respected as it in itself does not violate the principles of shareholder decision-making and proportionality between risk bearing capital and control.

Such an issue may result in fully frustrating the bid

Which in itself does not violate the two principles

The desired effect of the break-through rule is not to squeeze-out and in that sense expropriate minority shareholders, but merely to redress deviations from the shareholder decision-making and proportionality principles (see further below under effect) after a successful takeover bid. A higher threshold similar to the 90% the Group recommends as

Threshold is lower than for the squeeze-out right, because effects are not the same

a minimum threshold for the squeeze-out right is therefore not justified as a threshold for the break-through facility.

The bidder should be allowed, in cases where invocation of the break-through rule is necessary to achieve effective control, to make his general bid for all the share capital of the company conditional upon reaching the threshold percentage of risk bearing capital (possibly increased as a post-bid defence with appropriate authorisation by the shareholders meeting after the bid has been announced) and the consequential ability to use the break-through facility.

Where necessary, the bidder should be allowed to make his general bid conditional upon reaching the threshold

Effect

The effect of the break-through rule should be to redress the deviations in the articles of association and other constitutional documents from the principles of shareholder decision-making and proportionality between risk bearing capital and control. The bidder acquiring 75% or more of risk bearing capital should be able to control the affairs of the company and the operation of its business. This implies two types of rules, each dealing with different mechanisms in the articles of association and other constitutional documents.

Break-through rule should allow to redress deviating provisions

Implies two types of rules

1. The bidder acquiring 75% or more of risk bearing capital should be able to exercise a corresponding percentage of the total votes that can be cast in a general meeting of shareholders. This means that, in calculating the votes and entitlement to participate in a general meeting of shareholders held after the offeror has reached the threshold, a number of provisions in the articles of association and other constitutional documents of the company will have to be overridden. For example:

1. Provisions preventing the exertion of proportional voting rights should be overridden, e.g. :

- provisions in the articles of association, or other constitutional document, installing general voting caps applicable to all shareholders or limitations on voting rights attached to a certain class of shares; to the extent these shares constitute risk bearing capital, they should carry voting rights proportionate to their stake in the total risk bearing capital of the company

Voting caps or other limitations

- provisions in the articles of association, or other constitutional document, granting multiple voting rights to the holders of a certain class of shares or double voting rights to certain holders within a class of shares; to the extent these shares constitute risk bearing capital, they should carry voting rights proportionate to their stake in the total equity capital of the company

Multiple or double voting rights

- provisions in the articles of association, or other constitutional document, completely denying voting rights to a certain class of risk bearing capital; these shares should carry voting rights proportionate to their stake in the total risk bearing capital of the company

Provisions denying voting rights

- provisions in the articles of association, or other constitutional

Voting rights

document, conferring voting rights on non-risk-bearing capital; these shares should be excluded from carrying voting rights, unless there is a default relating to their limited financial entitlements.

attributed to non risk bearing capital

2. The bidder acquiring 75% or more of risk bearing capital should be able to exercise the core control rights that company law grants in order to be able to control the conduct of the affairs of the company and the operation of its business. These rights include the right to appoint, suspend and dismiss board members and to set their conditions of appointment and the right to determine the constitution of the company by amending the articles of association and other constitutional documents. Provisions in the articles of association that hinder the exercise of these rights should be overridden. To the extent these provisions are not included in the articles of association but operate as default rules of general company law (e.g. a fixed term of appointment of board members as the default rule of company law), they should be overridden as well.

2. Provisions preventing the exertion of core control rights (board composition and constitution amendment) should be overridden

Such provisions include provisions that grant the holders of a special class of shares the exclusive right to make binding nominations for the appointment, suspension or dismissal of board members or that grant such rights to the board or third parties. An exception should be made for nomination or appointment rights of third parties which are mandatory in the company law of the Member States. These include the nomination or appointment rights of employees under mandatory national co-determination rules or, as to the European Company, under the Directive on the involvement of employees in the European Company[5]. The effect of the break-through should be that the bidder acquiring 75% or more of risk bearing capital is able to appoint, suspend and dismiss those directors that the general meeting of shareholders under applicable company law can appoint, suspend and dismiss. When the articles of association provide for staggered appointments of board members or appointments for a fixed period, these provisions should be overridden as well so as to allow the bidder immediately to dismiss the full board and appoint new members.

Various deviating provisions relating to the composition of the board should be overridden

Exception should be made for mandatory nomination or appointment rights of third parties

Similar provisions exist making the amendment of the articles of association subject to a prior proposal from the board or a meeting of holders of a specific class of shares. These should also be overridden after the offeror has reached the threshold. The bidder acquiring 75% or more of risk bearing capital should be able to amend the articles of association and any other constitutional document and thereby formalise reinstallation of the shareholder decision-making and proportionality principles on a permanent basis.

Various deviating provisions relating to the amendment of the constitution should be overridden

[5] Council Directive 2001/86/EC of 8 October 2001 supplementing the Statute for a European Company with regard to the involvement of employees.

Some Member States (or regional or local public authorities within Member States) hold shares with these control rights ('golden shares') in companies operating in certain economic sectors. Many of these companies are privatised former fully state-owned enterprises. State held golden shares may interfere with the free movement of capital (art. 56 Treaty of Rome) and the freedom of establishment (art. 43 Treaty of Rome). Several cases in which this is raised are currently under review by the European Court of Justice.

Some Member States hold such control rights in companies (golden shares)

From a company law and capital markets perspective, there is no justification for distinguishing between companies in which special control rights are held by private persons and companies in which special control rights are held by states. If a formerly state-owned enterprise is privatised and seeks to enjoy the benefits provided by the capital market, it should be subject to the same principles and rules of company law and capital market law as other companies. Therefore, the Group believes that the break-through rule should also apply so as to override special control rights attached to golden shares held by Member States, even if the European Court of Justice would rule they do not violate the Treaty of Rome as such. If Member States wish to retain control over a company for a legitimate public purpose, they should do so by legislation which is subject to public law principles. This would also help to ensure due process in the exercise of its powers by the state.

The break-through rule should also apply to golden shares

Legitimate control should be achieved by legislation subject to public law principles

The break-through rule should apply regardless of whether the relevant provisions in the articles of association were already included prior to the bid being made or have been included as a post-bid defence after a bid was made. The Group notes that, in its view, in the latter case the general meeting of shareholders can only have decided to include these provisions with due observance of the principles of shareholder decision-making and proportionality (see par. 4.1 above). If, nonetheless, thereafter the shareholders decide to tender their shares to the bidder to such an extent that he acquires 75% of risk bearing capital, they have clearly reversed their initial decision to put up a defence against the bid. Their later decision to tender their shares to such a large extent should prevail and the bidder should upon reaching the threshold be able to break-through the provisions in the articles of association that deviate from the two guiding principles.

The break-through rule should apply to deviating provisions, whether they were adopted as pre-bid or post-bid defences

The break-through rule should take effect immediately upon the acquisition of the threshold percentage of risk bearing capital by the bidder after a general takeover bid. If the break-through were only to take effect at the end of a certain period after reaching the threshold, this would create unacceptable uncertainty for the bidder, the company, the other remaining shareholders, the board and other stakeholders during such period. No reasonable interest is served by such a waiting period.

The break-through rule should apply immediately after successful completion of the bid

The exercise of control rights by the bidder in proportion to his holding of risk bearing capital, in particular to dismiss and appoint board members and amend the articles of association, requires that a general meeting of shareholders be held. The bidder who has reached the threshold should have the right to convene a general meeting of shareholders at short notice, provided that the meeting is not organised less than two weeks after its notification (cf. Art. 9 (1) (c) of the Directive for the convention of a general meeting at short notice to decide on defensive measures).

The break-through rule implies a general meeting

The successful bidder has the right to convene a meeting at short notice

In the meeting, the bidder (and other holders of risk bearing capital) has the right to exercise voting rights in proportion to the holding of risk bearing capital. The bidder can exercise his rights in order to cause the general meeting to dismiss and appoint board members and amend the articles of association of the company to make them consistent with his rights, thus removing any uncertainty and confusion amongst shareholders as to their position. Until such a meeting is held the board should be under an obligation not to frustrate the exercise of control by the bidder (cf. Art. 9 (1) (a) of the Directive for the obligation of the board not to frustrate the bid during the period of the bid).

In the meeting, the successful bidder can exercise the core control rights

Existing board must be neutral until that meeting

Compensation

The Group has considered whether the holder of shares carrying disproportionate voting rights or special control rights should be compensated for the loss of these rights which results from the bidder reaching the break-through threshold after a general takeover bid. The Group agrees that the bidder should not be required to offer such compensation. The loss of these special rights would be the result of a public policy choice made by the European Union and the Member States in order to create a level playing field for takeover bids across the Union. The holders of special rights lose them in a break-through situation basically because as a matter of public policy they should not be able to exercise those rights once a bidder has acquired 75% or more of risk bearing capital after a general takeover bid. The new regime may well lead to companies voluntarily restructuring their control provisions where they do not conform to the two guiding principles. There may be exceptional cases where compensation for loss of specific control rights is appropriate and the holder of such rights demonstrates specific damage. The Group recommends that it be further reviewed whether an appraisal procedure should be provided for in these cases. Such a procedure should in any case not prohibit the bidder from using the break-through rule to exercise control.

A bidder reaching the break-through threshold should not be required to offer compensation to the existing holders of special control rights

Group recommends to further review whether an appraisal procedure should be provided for in specific cases

Conclusion

The review of these issues results in a model for a break-through rule which should apply after a substantially successful takeover bid. The model will require further refinement in the Directive and may need to leave Member States some flexibility as to the way particular mechanisms (such as the basis and means of determining conclusively and assessing whether the threshold has been achieved) applied in the various Member States should be dealt with. The main principles of the model however should be laid down in a future directive on takeover bids.

Main principles of the break-through model should be laid down in a future directive on takeover bids

4.3 Other barriers to takeover bids

The Group takes the view that certain types of company specific barriers to takeover bids should remain outside the scope of the break-through rule, basically because the rule appears to be an inadequate way of dealing with them. This is not to say that these mechanisms should not be dealt with at all and should continue to be barriers to takeover bids. The Group has considered three types of barriers:

Some barriers should remain outside the scope of the break-through rule, and be dealt with otherwise

1. provisions in articles of association and related constitutional documents restricting the transferability of shares

The listing directive of 1979[6] requires that listed shares must be freely transferable. However, it is not uncommon for listed companies to list only part of the risk bearing capital (e.g. of the risk bearing ordinary shares only 50% is admitted to the listing) or to have a separate class or classes of non-listed shares of risk bearing capital. The requirement of free transferability does not apply to these non-listed shares. Companies can limit the transferability of these shares by imposing ownership caps or a right of first refusal or approval right for the company or other holders of these shares. If companies have issued a substantial amount of non-listed risk bearing shares which are subject to this type of transferability restrictions, it becomes effectively impossible for a bidder making a general takeover bid to reach the threshold of risk bearing capital required under the break-through rule.

Requirement of free transferability does not apply to non listed shares

Non listed risk bearing shares subject to transferability restrictions make it difficult to reach the break-through threshold

The Group believes that in the event that a bidder makes a general takeover bid for the risk bearing capital of the company, such restrictions on the transferability of non-listed risk bearing shares

Such restrictions should not be enforceable against the bidder

6 Council Directive 79/279/EEC of 5 March 1979 coordinating the conditions for the admission of securities to official stock exchange listing.

should not be enforceable against him. The holders of non-listed risk bearing shares should be able to sell to the bidder and the bidder should be able to acquire them.

A specific example of this is where a company has issued risk bearing shares to a trust or administration office, which has issued listed non-voting depository receipts in respect of those shares. It is not uncommon that the articles of association of the company or the documents regulating the depository receipts of shares, either fully exclude the possibility to exchange depository receipts for the underlying shares or limit such exchange to a small percentage of the underlying shares which can be held by each shareholder. If depository receipts for risk bearing shares are listed, they should be freely exchangeable into the underlying shares in the event of a general takeover bid.

Listed depository receipts for risk bearing shares should be freely exchangeable into the underlying shares in the event of a takeover bid

2. contractual barriers to takeover bids

A wide variety of arrangements exist in contracts to which the company may be a party which cause the contract to take effect, alter or terminate as a result of a change of control of the company. Examples are golden parachutes for directors, granting them substantial fees if they have to vacate their offices as a result of a takeover bid, change of control provisions triggering default clauses in loan and credit agreements, and change of control provision resulting in the winding up or change of control over a joint venture.

Many contractual arrangements can be linked to takeover bids

The Group believes that these contractual arrangements should not be subject to a break-through rule as it would be very complicated to deal with the perfectly acceptable reasons the counterparty to the agreement may have for requiring such provisions, its good faith in relying on the provisions and its entitlement to compensation if a break-through takes place.

These arrangements should not be subject to the break-through rule

The Group believes that these contractual arrangements, which can form barriers to takeover bids, should be dealt with in general contract and company law. Contractual arrangements which only cause damage to the company and do not appear to be justified by the legitimate needs of the counterparty normally can be addressed under contract law of the Member States. Even if contract law would not give an opportunity to address them with effect as against the counterparty, company law imposes duties on directors of a company who enter into them on behalf of the company. The risk of liability for breach of duty is a deterrent for directors against entering into these contracts.

They should be dealt with in general contract and company law

Another type of contractual barrier to takeover bids is the agreement

Another type of

between shareholders which prohibits the transfer of shares by these shareholders to a bidder, sometimes enforced by substantial financial penalties. If shareholders agreeing to such restrictions hold substantial stakes in the company, this effectively rules out a successful takeover bid.

arrangement consists of shareholders agreements

In principle, shareholders are free to agree with other shareholders not to tender their shares in a (specific) takeover bid or, in a mitigated form, to offer their shares to such other shareholders in the case of a takeover bid. However, there is a serious concern, analogous to that which arises in the case of an authorisation for defensive measures given by a shareholders' meeting prior to a bid actually having been made, that shareholders entering into such an agreement lack sufficient information to judge whether tendering their shares in a potential future bid would be attractive or not. The concern is even greater where the undertaking not to tender shares in a potential future bid is enforced by substantial penalties which prohibit shareholders from reviewing their decision in the light of changed circumstances. These concerns have led one Member State (Italy) to provide that this type of provisions in shareholders agreements is unenforceable when a general takeover bid is made. The Group recommends that the Commission review whether this could be a general rule in all Member States.

Shareholders agreements can be freely made

But they raise some concerns where they are linked to takeover bids

Group recommends to review whether they could be made unenforceable when a general bid is made

3. pyramid structures[7]

In some Member States, a person exercises control over a company through a cascade of listed and unlisted holding companies, each owning a controlling stake in the next one, with the company at the bottom of the hierarchy being ultimately controlled through a relatively small economic stake. There are minority, non-controlling shareholders in every holding company in the chain. The result is that the ultimate owner with a limited economic risk-bearing investment in the company can exercise de jure or de facto control over the company through this pyramid of holding companies which he can control. The more holding companies in the pyramid, the smaller the economic investment of the ultimate owner needs to be to retain control over such a company.

Pyramid structures : through a cascade of holding companies, the company at the bottom is ultimately controlled through a small economic stake

Pyramid structures in a different way achieve a similar disproportionality between ownership of risk bearing capital and control rights to that which is, for example, achieved by multiple voting rights. In each holding company, however, a strict proportionality between ownership of risk bearing capital and control rights can be maintained. The economic disproportionality can be achieved by holding just the minimum percentage required to retain control at each level and by having minority shareholders in each holding

Disproportionality created by pyramid structures is similar to that achieved by multiple voting rights

[7] Similar concerns arise in the case of cross- or circular shareholdings between various listed companies.

company to finance the exercise of control by the ultimate owner.

Application of the break-through rule to pyramid structures would be highly expensive and complicated

It is difficult to see how a break-through rule could deal with these structures. It would have to be applied to the pyramid structure as a whole and would have to assume that the percentage of risk bearing capital held in the company at the bottom of the hierarchy is to be determined on the basis of the proportionate aggregate holdings of shareholders at each level. In order to reach the threshold on an aggregate basis, the bidder must extend his bid to, and acquire, risk bearing capital in at least some of the holding companies in the pyramid. This is probably expensive and potentially impossible to achieve. It is certainly unattractive and highly complicated if the various holding companies in the pyramid, as sometimes is the case, not only hold shares in other holding companies in the specific pyramid structure but also hold shares in other, sometimes unrelated, companies. The offers the bidder would have to make to acquire sufficient risk bearing capital in the various holding companies would then have to include a price for an investment in other companies in which he is not interested at all.

Pyramid structures should remain outside the scope of the break-through rule

They pose general problems outside the context of takeover bids

Group recommends to review whether and how they should be regulated

The Group believes pyramid structures should remain outside the scope of the break-through rule. They pose general problems also outside the context of a takeover bid. They undermine the transparency of the ownership structure of listed companies; they affect the pricing mechanism with regard to listed shares at all levels in the structure; they make control over companies belonging to such groups substantially incontestable, even when they are listed, or at least they make the acquisition of control of such companies extremely expensive; and finally, they create minority shareholders at several levels who directly and indirectly in total hold the majority of the risk bearing capital but are unable to exercise control at any level. Whether or not this is unacceptable also depends on the level and effectiveness of the minority protections which apply to secure the protection of shareholders throughout the group. We recommend that the Commission review whether pyramid structures (including the possibility of more than one company within the same group having a listing) should be regulated and what adequate measures of protection (in group law, in listing rules or otherwise) should be enforced in all Member States.

5. LEVEL PLAYING FIELD BETWEEN THE EU AND THE USA

It has been argued that the Directive did not create a level playing field between the EU and the US

In the debate leading up to the rejection of the last proposal of the Directive in the European Parliament, the argument was put forward that the Directive did not create a level playing field between the European Union and the United States. European companies would be severely restricted in putting up defences against takeover bids under Art. 9 of the Directive, while American companies could use a number of devices to defend themselves against a takeover bid.

The Group would first like to point out that there is not one set of takeover rules generally applicable in the United States. Company law is a matter of state law in the United States and the laws of the various states regulating takeover bids differ widely. Federal securities regulation only has a limited relevance to the ability of companies to defend against takeover bids. As a result, there is no clear level playing field for takeover bids within the United States.

No clear level playing field in the US themselves, because state laws differ widely

Having said this, it is true that boards of American companies generally have a broad discretion to put up defensive devices under what is called the business judgement rule, which in some states has been modified in the takeover context. This discretion is used to employ a wide variety of defensive devices, like poison pills, selling crown jewels, green mail, control clauses and golden parachutes, to name only a few. The board has to remain neutral only if it has decided that the company is to be sold and what is needed is a process for choosing between two or more competing bidders. In that case, the only duty of the board is to ensure that shareholders get the best price for their shares.

However, American companies generally have a broad discretion to defend themselves, under the "business judgement rule"

In addition, many individual states have enacted laws specifically permitting the board to consider other interests than shareholders' interests (but not their own) when deciding how to respond to a takeover bid, or to prohibit the bidder from engaging the company in certain types of business combinations as long as he has not reached a certain threshold of the voting stock of the company. Some of these laws have been held unconstitutional or illegal by US courts, others are upheld and very commonly applied in practice. However, the US courts generally impose the burden of proving that the measures taken by the board were genuinely in the best interests of the company upon the directors and the obligations which arise are vigorously enforced by shareholders.

Boards are often permitted to consider other interests than shareholders' interests

But they must prove that their decisions were in the best interests of the company

The Group acknowledges that its proposals, if implemented, would not result in company law rules for takeover bids applied in the European Union being broadly similar to those applied in the United States. For a number of reasons, however, the Group believes that the American example should not be followed in Europe.

The American example should not be followed in Europe

1. The broad discretion of the board of US companies to put up defensive mechanisms operates in a general legal and capital market environment which differs widely from the European environment. American boards are subject to much more pressure to enhance shareholder value than their European counterparts typically are. They are judged by their performance on the capital markets. While in theory they can "just say no" to a potential bidder, they are subject

US board discretion operates in a widely differing general legal and capital market environment

to pressures from non-executive directors on the board, investment banks and advisors and in particular from institutional investors. Their behaviour is widely transparent under the legal transparency rules and the intense scrutiny of the media. They also have to reckon with being replaced in a successful proxy contest through which the bidder can have more friendly board members appointed, although in case of a staggered board only after some time. Finally, it is relatively easy for shareholders to take board members to court in derivative actions. Liability suits against directors are a common phenomenon of the American corporate practice. Even though the (modified) business judgement rule is in place, the risk of liability is definitely higher for board members of American companies than for board members of European companies. Moreover, the American judicial system is very open to claims like these and generally better equipped to deal with litigation in a takeover context than judicial systems in European Member States.

Takeover activity in the US is intensive, and European companies benefit to a large extent from that activity

2. The relatively broad discretion of the board to defend against takeover bids has certainly led to a number of takeover bids not being successful or not being made at all. Nonetheless, takeover activity in the American capital markets is intensive and forms an essential part of its financial and economical structure. Hostile takeover bids (i.e. bids not agreed to by the board of the target company) are made regularly and under pressure of the legal and capital market system often become friendly (i.e. the board of the target company recommends the bid to its shareholders or at least stops its opposition) at a later stage. As Annex [5] shows, defensive mechanisms and state defensive laws have not blocked European companies taking over American companies. European companies benefit to a very large extent from the takeover activity on the American capital markets. In many parts of Europe on the other hand, takeover barriers existing in various Member States more often tend to result in control over listed companies being incontestable. In the view of the Group, this is undesirable in the European context, as an integrated capital market has to be build up in order for business to fully benefit from and make effective use of the integrating internal market in Europe.

A number of anti-takeover mechanisms are prompted by the ability of the bidder to obtain control by making a partial bid, which is not possible in the system of the Directive

3. A number of anti-takeover mechanisms applied in the United States are prompted by the ability of bidders to obtain control over a company by making a bid on only a part of the company's share capital. In order to prevent shareholders being pressured to tender, these mechanisms force the bidder to make a general takeover bid for all the shares in order to be able to exercise control. In Europe on the other hand, the mandatory bid provision in the Directive would require a bidder to make a general takeover bid to all shareholders for all their holdings at an equitable price, if he wishes to acquire control of the company. In the system of the Directive, specific anti-takeover mechanisms are not needed to achieve this goal.

4. The current anti-takeover rules in the United States are by no means uncontroversial even within the United States. Some accept them as the outcome of regulatory competition among the states and effective lobbying by the business community, but there is a large body of both economic and legal literature arguing that directors should be prohibited from engaging in defensive actions and that the ultimate decision should be made by shareholders. The reasons for this latter view are identical to those the Group has put forward for its proposals to ensure the principles of shareholder decision-making and proportionality in the context of takeover bids.

Anti-takeover rules are contested in the US themselves by a large body of economic and legal literature

The Group believes the European Union should in the first place consider what type of regulation of takeover bids is needed to enhance the development of efficient integrated capital markets in the Union. In the view of the Group this objective is best served by introducing rules that ensure the operation of the principles of shareholder decision-making and proportionality between risk bearing and control in the context of a takeover bid, as recommended in this report. The controversial American anti-takeover rules are likely to be less beneficial to the development of efficient integrated capital markets in the European Union. Furthermore, the Group believes its proposals would not give American companies an unfair advantage when trying to exploit the European internal market by taking over European companies, as compared with the conditions which apply for European companies exploiting the American market by taking over American companies. If, however, political concerns remain, it could be considered whether to provide that the benefits of the application of the principles of shareholder decision-making and proportionality between risk bearing and control as recommended in this report, can only be enjoyed by listed European companies making general takeover bids for other listed European companies, to the extent that this would not violate international agreements and could practically be enforced.

The EU should not copy the US system, but implement the takeover bids regulation which is the best suited to its environment and objectives

If political concerns remain, benefits from two principles could be restricted to listed EU bidders

To summarise, listed companies should be required to disclose complete information about their capital and control structures (except for those deriving from general applicable law), for instance in their annual reports, listing particulars and prospectuses. If important changes occur in this information, listed companies should be under a continuous obligation to disclose such changes. Disclosure of some of these elements is already required under existing directives : the Group recommends that these elements be disclosed and presented in a combined, coherent way.

Summary: *Complete information about capital and control structures of listed companies should be disclosed in a coherent way*

After announcement of the bid, the board of the offeree company should not be permitted to take actions frustrating a takeover bid on the basis of a general meeting authorisation given prior to the bid. Only when a bid is actually announced and the shareholders can really assess all relevant information, can they in fairness be asked to decide whether this takeover bid should be frustrated by the board or

Frustrating actions cannot be taken by the board after announcement of the bid, on the basis of an prior

not. *authorisation*

After announcement of the bid, any authorisation by the general meeting of shareholders to take actions frustrating the bid should be given by a majority of votes exercised by the holders of the proportionate majority of the risk bearing capital of the company. The bidder should also be allowed to vote in such a meeting to the extent he already holds risk bearing capital in the company.

After announcement of the bid, any general meeting authorisation should be given with proportionate majority of the risk bearing capital

A rule should be introduced, which allows the offeror to break-through mechanisms and structures which may frustrate a bid, as defined in the articles of association and related constitutional documents, in the case of a takeover bid which achieves such a measure of success as clearly to justify this.

A rule allowing the successful bidder to break-through frustrating structures should be introduced

The threshold for exercising the break-through right should not be set at a percentage higher than 75% of the risk bearing capital of the company on the date of completion of the bid. Member States should be allowed to set the threshold at a lower level sufficient to take special resolutions like amendments of the articles of association and corporate reconstructions. Member States should ensure that qualified majorities required for special resolutions do not exceed the level of risk bearing capital they set as a threshold for the break-through rule. The bidder should be allowed to make his general bid conditional upon reaching the threshold percentage of risk bearing capital.

The break-through threshold should not be set at a percentage higher than 75%

Provisions in the articles of association and other constitutional documents deviating from the principles of shareholder decision-making and proportionality between risk bearing capital and control should be overridden. Such provisions include 1. the rules affecting voting rights and 2. the rules relating to the composition of the board and the determination of the constitution of the company. These provisions should be overridden whether or not a) such special control rights are held by private persons and companies or by states, and b) such provisions were already included prior to the bid being made or have been included as a post-bid defence after a bid was made. In the case of such provisions in the hands of member states, they should only be permitted if they are subjected to public law principles, and of course if they are justifiable under community law.

Provisions deviating from the principles of shareholder decision-making and proportionality between risk bearing capital and control should be overridden

The effect of the break-through rule should be immediate upon the acquisition of the threshold percentage of risk bearing capital by the bidder after a general takeover bid.

Effect should be immediate

The bidder who has reached the threshold should have the right to convene a general meeting of shareholders at short notice, in which he has the right to exercise voting rights in proportion to his holding of risk bearing capital.

Successful bidder should be able to convene a general meeting

The bidder should not be required to offer compensation to the holder of shares carrying disproportionate voting rights or carrying special control rights for the loss of these rights which results from the bidder reaching the break-through threshold after a general takeover bid. There may be exceptional cases where compensation is due if the holder of such rights demonstrates specific damage : the Group recommends that it be further reviewed whether an appraisal procedure should be provided for in these cases.

Bidder should not be required to offer compensation for loss of existing control rights

In the event that a bidder makes a general takeover bid for the risk bearing capital of the company, restrictions on the transferability of non-listed risk bearing shares should not be enforceable against him. If depository receipts for risk bearing shares are listed, they should be freely exchangeable into the underlying shares in the event of a general takeover bid.

Restrictions on transferability and exchangeability of shares should be overridden

Contractual arrangements in general, which can form barriers to takeover bids, should not be subject to a break-through rule, but should be dealt with in general contract and company law. In the particular case of contractual agreements between shareholders which prohibit the transfer of shares to a (certain) bidder, sometimes enforced by substantial financial penalties, the Group recommends that the Commission review whether a rule whereby these agreements would be unenforceable when a general takeover bid is made could be adopted in all Member States.

Contractual arrangements in general should not be subject to break-through rule

Shareholders agreements should be further examined

The Group believes pyramid structures should remain outside the scope of the break-through rule and recommends that the Commission review whether pyramid structures including several listed companies should be regulated and what adequate measures of protection of minority shareholders (in group law, in listing rules or otherwise) should be introduced in all Member States.

Pyramid structures should be further examined

The Group's proposals, if implemented, would not result in company law rules for takeover bids applied in the European Union being broadly similar to those applied in the United States. The Group, nevertheless, believes for a number of reasons that the European Union should not use the controversial US rules as a model, but rather consider what type of regulation of takeover bids is best suited to enhance the development of efficient integrated capital markets in the Union. If, however, political concerns remain, it could be considered whether to provide that member states are free to make provision that the benefits of the application of the principles of shareholder decision-making and proportionality between risk bearing and control as recommended in this report can only be enjoyed by listed European companies making general takeover bids on other listed European companies, to the extent that this would not violate international agreements and could practically be enforced.

The EU should not use the controversial US rules as a model

If political concerns remain, benefits from two principles could be restricted to listed EU companies

CHAPTER II

THE EQUITABLE PRICE TO BE OFFERED IN MANDATORY BIDS

1. INTRODUCTION

Notion of "equitable price" is included in Article 5(1) of the Directive

The notion of equitable price is included in Article 5(1) of the Directive, which seeks to harmonise the circumstances under which a mandatory bid has to be made and contains the following provision : "(...) This bid shall be addressed to all holders of securities for all their holdings at an equitable price. (...)".

Presence of an equitable price in mandatory bids is fundamental to achieve minority shareholders protection

The Group considers that the requirement to offer an equitable price is of the utmost importance in the context of mandatory bids to achieve an adequate protection of the minority shareholders. A mandatory offer made for a price which was not equitable would not only fail to achieve such a protection, in that it would deprive the minority shareholders of an opportunity to sell their securities on fair terms. The absence of an equitable price requirement in a mandatory bid may also induce minority shareholders to sell their securities in a voluntary partial bid for a price which they do not deem to be equitable.

The observations and recommendations made in the present chapter apply to mandatory bids only

In the hearings organised by the Group, the view has been expressed that it is also desirable to adopt rules on equitable price in the context of voluntary bids. However, in view of its mandate, the Group examines the notion of equitable price in the present report in relation to mandatory bids only. Apart from the limits on the Group's terms of reference, the exclusion of an equitable price requirement in voluntary offers is also justified on the ground that, in principle, the judgement on the adequacy of the offer price should be left to the market. The Group therefore considers that the recommendations it makes in the present chapter are applicable to mandatory bids only.

Long discussions on the Directive illustrate the difficulty of defining common rules on the consideration to be offered in mandatory bids

The lengthy discussions on the Directive have illustrated the difficulty of defining common rules regarding the consideration that should be offered in a mandatory bid, with respect to both the level and the nature of such consideration. In view of these difficulties, the Commission proposal of 1996 simply stated that the bid must be launched at a price which meets the objective of protecting the interests of minority shareholders. In its common position adopted in June 2000, the Council deemed it preferable to use the notion of equitable price, without defining it, and introduced a rule about the nature of the consideration to be offered. The Parliament resolution of December 2000 contained a rule defining the minimum level of the consideration to be offered, and added a further rule on the nature of that consideration. Only the latter of these two modifications was finally included in the text approved by the Conciliation Committee.

This Chapter covers the present situation, the desirability of some harmonisation and the Group's recommendations

This Chapter first outlines the rules relating to the notion of equitable price as they are provided for in the Directive, and gives a short overview of the rules on the same topic existing in the different Member States. The Group then observes that a definition of equitable price should achieve a proper balance between the competing objectives of flexibility and predictability, and examines whether some harmonisation at EU level seems desirable. The Group finally presents its recommendations as to the key characteristics of a European approach to the notion of equitable price.

2. THE PRESENT SITUATION

2.1. The rules provided for in the Directive

Two rules in the Directive :

The text approved by the Conciliation Committee on 6 June 2001 contains two rules relating to the consideration which must be offered in the context of a mandatory takeover bid :

Article 5(1) – determination of the consideration in a mandatory bid

- Article 5(1) refers to the situations in which a person acquires the control of a company and contains the principle of the mandatory bid, the notion of equitable price and some provisions (based on the "cash alternative" principle) related to the nature of the consideration which must be offered[12];

Article 6(3) – information about the consideration in any type of offer

- Article 6(3) requires Member States to adopt rules relating to the information which has to be stated in the offer document drawn up and made public by the offeror in any type of offer (whether it be voluntary or mandatory)[13].

[12] "..., Member States shall ensure that rules are in force, which oblige this person to make a bid as a means to protect the minority shareholders of that company. This bid shall be addressed to all holders of securities for all their holdings at an equitable price. When the consideration offered by the offeror does not consist of liquid securities admitted to trading on a regulated market, such consideration has to include a cash consideration at least as an alternative.

In any case, the offeror must provide a consideration in cash at least as an alternative, if he, alone or in conjunction with persons acting in concert with him, has, during a period commencing not less than 3 months before the bid was made public pursuant to Article 6(1) and ending on the expiry of the acceptance period, acquired for cash more than 5% of the shares or voting rights in the offeree company."

[13] "(d) the consideration offered for each security or class of securities and, in the case of mandatory bids, the basis of the valuation used in determining it, with particulars of the way in which that consideration is to be given;"

2.2. The great diversity of the national regimes

In some of the Member States that currently apply a mandatory bid rule, the provisions about the consideration to be paid have a binding character; a few Member States provide only recommendations. The provisions also differ widely with respect to both the level and the nature of the consideration to be offered, as explained below.

At Member State level, existing rules differ widely (both in nature and in substance)

a) The level of the consideration to be offered

In a few Member States, the level of the consideration to be offered is determined by reference to general principles only (e.g. equal treatment of shareholders). However, a vast majority of Member States has adopted detailed provisions with respect to the consideration to be offered in a mandatory bid, but they vary considerably as to the nature and the number of the criteria used, and the way in which they are applied.

With respect to the level of the consideration, Member States use different criteria in different ways.

A majority of the Member States refer to the highest price (or a percentage thereof) paid by the offeror, or a person acting in concert, over a certain period (ranging from 3 to 12 months) prior to the offer. However, many other criteria are found in the same or other Member States:
- the average market value over a certain period (ranging from 3 to 12 months) prior to the offer;
- the price paid for a block of shares the acquisition of which led to the modification in control;
- the "net worth" / "theoretical asset value" / "liquidation value" of the company;
- the "objective valuation criteria usually applied" and the characteristics of the company.

Criterion most often used : the highest price paid over a certain period prior to the offer

A few Member States use only one of these criteria, i.e. the highest price paid by the offeror. The other Member States use more than one (in most cases two or three - including often the highest price paid and the average market value - , but even more in one Member State).

Most Member States use more than one criterion

Most of the Member States which use more than one criterion apply them on a cumulative basis, which means that the consideration to be offered is the higher of the prices obtained. In some Member States however, a different approach is followed, whereby the different prices obtained have to be "averaged" or "balanced". Finally, a few Member States apply the different criteria on an alternative basis, the choice of the relevant rule depending on the circumstances.

Most Member States using more than one criterion apply them on a cumulative basis

The determination of the consideration to be offered in a mandatory bid may be further influenced by the following factors :

Other factors play a role :

- when different classes of securities exist, the criteria mentioned above must be applied on a class by class basis. In particular, where a mandatory offer arises out of the acquisition of control through a holding in one particular class, several Member States have specific rules applying to the other classes.

- existence of several classes

- in all Member States which have adopted detailed provisions, exceptions and derogations are allowed in specific circumstances provided that general principles are properly respected.

- presence of specific circumstances

- several Member States have rules which prevent the offeror from acquiring securities on better terms outside of or after (over a period ranging from 6 to 12 months) the mandatory offer. Such an acquisition may simply be prohibited, or in other Member States lead to a revision of the consideration paid in the mandatory bid.

- treatment of acquisitions on better terms outside of or after the offer

b) The nature of the consideration to be offered

In most Member States, the bidder is free to offer as consideration cash or securities (which, in some Member States, have then to be admitted to trading on a regulated market in a defined economic zone). In some Member States, when securities are offered, a cash alternative always has to be offered, whereas in a few other Member States, a cash alternative has to be offered in specific circumstances only. Finally, a few Member States generally require a cash offer and allow securities to be offered only in limited situations.

In most Member States, the consideration may consist freely of cash or securities

3. THE NEED FOR HARMONISATION

The effect of the wording of article 5(1) of the Directive is that the issue whether a price is equitable is a matter of European law, ultimately determinable by the European Court of Justice. In the view of the Group, it is not desirable that such a question - which will arise in the midst of a complex transaction where time is of the essence and where the issue will depend very much on particular circumstances if it is left undefined - should be determined by long drawn out court proceedings. The likelihood of such proceedings may well have the effect of deterring transactions altogether, which is undesirable.

The wording of Article 5(1) makes the issue whether a price is equitable a matter determinable by the European Court of Justice, which is not desirable

The Group therefore considers that, at the very least, it should be made clear that it is for the member states to satisfy the directive requirement to provide for one or several equitable price criterion/criteria, within the margin of appreciation laid down by a

It should at least be made clear that this issue is a matter primarily

broad requirement in the Directive that the mandatory bid must be made at an equitable price.

determinable by Member States

The great diversity of the national regimes applicable to the consideration to be offered in a mandatory bid indicates that it is difficult to conceive one single rule which could be used in all countries and in all situations to achieve an adequate level of protection of minority shareholders. Not only are the different criteria used in Member States not equally relevant because of the specific characteristics of their capital markets, but also the significance of particular circumstances must be properly taken into account when determining the price to be offered. For both reasons, any sort of regulation should allow for a reasonable degree of flexibility, with the aim of effectively achieving an equivalent treatment of all holders of securities.

Any sort of regulation should allow for a reasonable degree of flexibility

On the other hand, the Group notes that an efficient functioning of the capital markets in the European Union requires a sufficient degree of predictability as to the consideration to be offered in a mandatory bid. It is indeed a major disincentive to the acquisition of control if such acquisition imposes an obligation to bid but the price to be paid is not predictable. The Group therefore recognises the desirability of introducing at EU level a harmonised approach in providing a means for offerors to predict and ideally to determine the equitable price. This approach should on the one hand create a strong presumption in favour of a price established by application of a common rule and at the same time provide for sufficient flexibility in particular circumstances.

But an efficient functioning of the capital markets requires at the same time a sufficient degree of predictability

4. THE KEY CHARACTERISTICS OF A EUROPEAN APPROACH

The key issues to be addressed by a European approach to the equitable price in a mandatory bid relate to the determination of the consideration to be offered in the bid and to the treatment of acquisitions during or after the bid on better terms.

A European approach on two issues

4.1. The consideration to be offered in the mandatory bid

The Group holds the view that the principle of equivalent treatment of all holders of securities of the same class requires that the price to be offered in the mandatory bid should, in normal circumstances, be equal to the highest price paid by the offeror for shares in that class, whether on or off the market, during a certain period preceding the date of the acquisition of securities by the offeror, which resulted in the change in the control of the company. Member States should be free to set the length of this period between 6 and 12 months.

Criterion applicable in normal circumstances : the highest price paid over a period preceding the acquisition of control

Benefits associated to the highest price paid rule

The highest price paid rule offers the double benefit of allowing the minority shareholders to fully share the premium paid by the acquirer at any time in the period under consideration, while at the same time giving the offeror the certainty that he will not have to pay more in the mandatory bid than he has been willing to pay in the preceding period and as a result permitting him to determine himself at which maximum price he is prepared to acquire all securities of the company.

The highest price paid may not, in particular circumstances, achieve an equivalent treatment of holders of securities

The Group, nonetheless, considers that the highest price paid rule may not, in particular circumstances, achieve an equivalent treatment of holders of securities. Such circumstances include, but are not limited to, the following situations:
- the highest price paid was set by collusion (i.e. an agreement with the vendor aimed at evading the highest price paid rule);
- market prices in general have been affected by highly exceptional events;
- market prices for the relevant securities have been manipulated;
- a lower price may be a necessary condition to make it possible for companies in distress to be rescued from bankruptcy.

Member States should be permitted to define both the situations in which the above presumption may be displaced and the criteria which may be applied.

Based on these observations, the Group holds the view that the Directive should :
- on the one hand, contain a rule whereby the highest price paid, as defined above, by the offeror is assumed to be an equitable price in a mandatory bid in normal circumstances;
- on the other hand, explicitly state that Member States are permitted to define both the situations in which this presumption may be displaced and the criteria which may be applied by supervisory authorities in their decision to retain a price higher or lower than the highest price paid.

The Directive should contain the principles applicable to the definition of such situations

With respect to the definition of the situations in which the presumption may be displaced, the Group considers that the Directive should contain the following principles :
- the main principle should be that of fairness - that is, the rule can be deviated from only where it is demonstrated that its application would plainly result in an unfair price;
- where deviation would lead to a lower price, the burden of proof should lie with the offeror, meaning that the supervisory authority would not even consider the request if the argument provided does not appear sufficient;
- in any areas of doubt, the judgement should be finally guided by the principle of "shareholders' interest" - that is, all unclear cases should be solved by giving prevalence to the fair treatment of the target's shareholders.

With respect to the criteria which may be applied in such circumstances, the Group considers that Member States should be permitted to retain one or more of the following criteria :
- the average market value over a certain period (ranging from 3 to 6 months) prior to the offer;
- the liquidation value of the company;
- any other objective valuation criteria usually applied in financial analysis.

Member States should be permitted to retain one or more of the criteria to be mentioned in the Directive

The Group recommends that any decision whereby a supervisory authority retains a price different from the highest price paid be accompanied by the provision of complete information as to the exact nature of the particular circumstances invoked, the precise reason why under these circumstances the highest price paid is not equitable, and the detailed rationale (nature of the criteria, way in which they have been combined, ...) which led the supervisory authority finally to determine the price to be paid by the offeror.

Any decision to apply a price different from the highest price paid should be accompanied by complete supporting information

The Group observes that, when different classes of securities exist, the rules governing the determination of the equitable price must apply on a class by class basis. The Group furthermore considers that Member States should be required to adopt specific rules, where a mandatory offer arises out of the acquisition of control via a holding in one particular class, or some but not all classes, which apply in relation to the other classes in full conformity with the general principles of the Directive.

The rules governing the determination of the equitable price must apply on a class by class basis

The Group finally notes that the question of whether a price offered in the mandatory bid is equitable very much depends on the timing of the mandatory bid. Any reference to a price paid for or market value of the securities in a period preceding the acquisition of control by nature becomes less relevant the longer it takes after that moment before the mandatory bid is actually made. The Group believes therefore that the offeror should be required to make the mandatory bid within a short period (to be set by Member States at a maximum of 30 days) after having acquired control of the company through the acquisition of securities.

The question whether a price is equitable is linked to the timing of the mandatory bid

4.2. Rules applicable to the payment of a higher price during or after the mandatory bid

The Group considers that there are strong arguments that the principle of equivalent treatment of holders of securities of the same class should be regarded as requiring that a higher price may not be offered during the mandatory bid or for a certain period after the mandatory bid to holders of securities who do not sell in the bid. An additional benefit for minority shareholders of such a rule is that it acts as an incentive for the offeror to set the price offered in the

Acquisition on more favourable terms, outside of or after the mandatory bid, should be regulated

mandatory bid at a reasonably high level.

In this approach, Member States would be required to adopt rules aimed at achieving this objective, but could be free to choose between a) a system in which the acquisition of securities on more favourable terms is fully prohibited during the bid or for a certain period after the bid and b) a system whereby the acquisition of securities on more favourable terms during the bid or for a certain period after the bid obliges the offeror to pay the difference to the holders of securities who tendered their securities in the mandatory bid.

Member States could choose between two systems

As to the length of the period, the Group recommends that Member States should be required to adopt one of between 6 and 9 months.

Relevant period : between 6 and 9 months

To summarise, a harmonised approach should be introduced at EU level with the aim of providing a means for offerors to predict and ideally to determine the equitable price they will have to pay in a mandatory bid. This approach should on the one hand create a strong presumption in favour of a price established by application of a common rule and at the same time provide for sufficient flexibility in particular circumstances.

Summary: *A harmonised approach at EU level should combine predictability and flexibility*

The price to be offered in the mandatory bid should, in normal circumstances, be equal to the highest price paid by the offeror for shares of the relevant class, whether on or off the market, during a certain period preceding the date of the acquisition of securities by the offeror, which resulted in the change in the control of the company. Member States should be free to set the length of this period between 6 and 12 months.

Criterion applicable in normal circumstances : the highest price paid

Member States should be permitted to define both the situations in which the presumption above may be displaced and the criteria which may be applied by supervisory authorities in their decision to apply a price higher or lower than the highest price paid.

Member States are permitted to :

With respect to the definition of the situations in which the presumption may be displaced, the Directive should contain the following principles : 1) the rule can be deviated from only where it is demonstrated that its plain application would result in an unfair price, 2) where deviation would lead to a lower price, the burden of proof should lie with the offeror, 3) all unclear cases should be resolved by giving prevalence to the interest of the target's shareholders.

- define the situations in which the presumption may be displaced

With respect to the criteria which may be applied in such circumstances, Member States should be permitted to retain one or more of the following criteria : 1) the average market value over a certain period (ranging from 3 to 6 months) prior to the offer, 2) the

- and select one or more of the criteria mentioned in the Directive

liquidation value of the company, 3) any other objective valuation criteria usually applied in financial analysis.

Any decision whereby a supervisory authority applies a price different from the highest price paid should be accompanied by the provision of complete supporting information.

Complete supporting information must be presented

The question of whether a price offered in the mandatory bid is equitable very much depends on the timing of the mandatory bid. The offeror should be required to make the mandatory bid within a short period (to be set by Member States at a maximum of 30 days) after having acquired control of the company through the acquisition of securities.

The mandatory bid should be made within a short period after the acquisition of control

Member States could be required to implement either a) a system in which the acquisition of securities on more favourable terms is fully prohibited during the bid or for a certain period after the bid or b) a system whereby the acquisition of securities on more favourable terms during the bid or for a certain period after the bid obliges the offeror to pay the difference to the holders of securities who tendered their securities in the mandatory bid. Member States should be free to set the length of this period between 6 and 9 months.

Member States could choose between two systems to regulate the acquisition on more favourable terms outside of or after the bid

CHAPTER III

THE SQUEEZE-OUT AND SELL-OUT RIGHTS AFTER A TAKEOVER BID

1. INTRODUCTION

The **squeeze-out right** basically refers to the right of a majority shareholder in a company to compel the minority shareholders to sell their shares to him. Conversely, the **sell-out right** refers to the right of a minority shareholder to compel the majority shareholder to purchase his shares from him. Where squeeze-out and sell-out rights have been provided for in law, the relevant provisions usually determine certain thresholds the majority shareholder must have reached in order to trigger the squeeze-out and sell-out rights.

Both squeeze-out right (in favour of the majority shareholder) and sell-out right (in favour of the minority shareholders) usually depend on certain thresholds

Squeeze-out and sell-out rights can be relevant to majority shareholders and minority shareholders in both companies listed on stock exchanges and private companies, and regardless of whether the threshold has been reached by way of a general bid on shares or otherwise. In the light of its mandate, the Group focuses in this report on the desirability of squeeze-out and sell-out rights in the context of a takeover bid, i.e. a general bid for shares which are admitted to trading on a regulated market. In its second report, the Group will address squeeze-out and sell-out more generally.

Squeeze-out and sell-out rights may be offered in widely differing circumstances, but the Group focuses in this report on their desirability in the context of a takeover bid

This Chapter first gives a short overview of the existing rules related to the squeeze-out and sell-out rights, both at EU level and in the different Member States. The Group then examines on the one hand whether squeeze-out and sell-out rights produce significant benefits in the context of takeover bids, and on the other hand the extent to which some harmonisation at EU level seems desirable. The Group finally recommends that squeeze-out and sell-out rights should be generally available in the EU following takeover bids, and presents the key characteristics of a European approach to both rights.

This Chapter covers the present situation, the desirability of some harmonisation and the Group's recommendations

2. THE PRESENT SITUATION

2.1. The squeeze-out right

a) The present situation at EU level

The squeeze-out right is not regulated by any of the existing company law instruments adopted at EU level.

Squeeze-out right is not regulated at EU level

In particular, the Second Company Law Directive on formation and capital maintenance of public limited companies[14] does not contain provisions related to the squeeze-out right. The mechanisms provided for in Article 36 (compulsory withdrawal of shares) and in Article 37 (redemption of shares) of the Second Directive are different from the squeeze-out right, in that they are financed out of the funds of the company itself, as opposed to the funds of the majority shareholder.

The mechanisms provided for in the Second Directive are different from the squeeze-out right

In the context of the SLIM exercise[15], a Company Law Working Group on the simplification of the First and Second Company Law Directives recommended an easing of the conditions under which a compulsory withdrawal of shares may be made in the Member States which have not introduced a squeeze-out right in their national legislation. This recommendation, together with the other recommendations made by the SLIM Group, will be further examined by the Group in the second part of its mandate.

Modifications to the Second Directive proposed by the SLIM Group will be examined in the second part of the mandate

The Third Company Law Directive on mergers[16] does enable a majority of shareholders in an acquired company to agree that all the shares in that company including those in the hands of a dissenting minority should be replaced by shares in the acquiring company. However this provision, which does not apply to acquisitions of an undertaking by means of a takeover, is different from the squeeze-out right in that a) the shares of the minority shareholders are not transferred to the majority shareholders of the acquired company, and b) the Directive does not require that such mergers should be possible by means of cash consideration for the shareholders of the acquired company. The Group will consider such mergers in the second part of its mandate.

The merger by acquisition provided for in the Third Directive is different from the squeeze-out right

The Group will consider this mechanism in the second part of its mandate

A form of squeeze-out right was included in the draft 9th Directive on the conduct of groups[17], of which Article 33 would permit an

A form of squeeze-out right

---

[14] Second Council Directive of 13 December 1976 on co-ordination of the safeguards which, for the protection of the interests of members and others, are required by Member States of companies within the meaning of the second paragraph of Article 58 of the Treaty, in respect of the formation of public limited liability companies and the maintenance and alteration of their capital, with a view to making such safeguards equivalent (77/91/EEC).

[15] Report from the Commission to the European Parliament and the Council – Results of the Fourth Phase of SLIM – COM(2000)56 of 4 February 2000.

[16] Third Council Directive of 9 October 1978 based on article 54 (3) (g) of the Treaty concerning mergers of public limited liability companies (78/855/EEC).

[17] European Communities Draft Ninth Company Law Directive on the Conduct of Groups Containing a Public Limited Company as a Subsidiary

undertaking which had acquired directly or indirectly 90 % or more of the capital of a public limited company to make a declaration leading to the formation of a group and providing for the compulsory acquisition of the shares of the minority shareholders. The draft 9th Directive has however not given birth to an official proposal from the Commission.

was included in the draft 9th Directive

The Directive on takeover bids[18] does not include any provision related to the squeeze-out right.

No provision on squeeze-out right in the Directive on Takeover bids

In this situation where Community law remains silent on the squeeze-out right, Member States are free to decide whether and under which conditions such a right should be introduced in their national legislation.

The introduction of a squeeze-out right is currently a matter of national regulation

b) The great diversity of the national regimes

The vast majority of the Member States currently provide for a right of a majority shareholder to buy out the minority shareholders. However, the conditions under which that right may be exercised differ widely, in particular in the following areas : the types of companies for which the right exists, the link or lack of a link with takeover bids, the thresholds that have to be reached, and the determination of the consideration to be offered to the minority shareholders.

Squeeze-out right exists in most Member States, but national regimes differ widely

Only in a few Member States may the right to buy out minority shareholders be exercised in all limited liability companies. In most of the Member States, this right applies only to public limited companies. A few of these Member States limit this right to companies the securities of which are admitted to trading on a regulated market (or companies having publicly offered securities).

Squeeze-out right usually applies only to (listed) public limited companies

Some Member States establish a direct link between the right to buy out minority shareholders and takeover bids, in that such a right may be exercised only when the applicable thresholds have been reached by virtue of a public offer. In other Member States, the right to buy out minority shareholders is offered generally, regardless of how the applicable threshold has been reached. However, some of these Member States have special rules applicable to the situation in which the right to buy out is exercised subsequent to a takeover bid.

In some Member States, squeeze-out right is linked – directly or indirectly – to takeover bids

The threshold upon which the right to buy out the minority shareholders is conditional varies in most Member States between

Most Member States have set the threshold

[18] See the Joint Text approved by the Conciliation Committee on 6 June 2001 in Annex 6 to this Report.

90% and 95%, with an extreme high of 98% in one Member State. In most Member States, the threshold is set by reference to the amount of capital held or the number of voting rights held. Most of these Member States have opted for only one of these criteria, but some Member States set the threshold by reference to both criteria together (capital and voting rights). In one Member State, the threshold has to be reached in terms of either capital or voting rights.

between 90 and 95 %

Reference is usually made to capital and/or voting rights

In some of the Member States where the right to buy out minority shareholders may be exercised only when the applicable thresholds have been reached by virtue of a public offer, the threshold is set by reference to the proportion of acceptances of the offer : the offer must have been accepted by shareholders holding 90% or more of the share capital in respect of which the offer has been made. It should be observed that, in such a situation, the rights and obligations arise on a class by class basis (which means that the right to buy out is subject to the existence of separate bids for classes of shares, with separate application of the threshold).

In some Member States, the threshold is set by reference to the proportion of acceptances of the offer (on a class by class basis)

With respect to the determination of the consideration to be offered, three groups of Member States may be distinguished. In the first group (Member States where the right to buy out may be exercised only when the capital/voting rights thresholds have been reached by virtue of a public offer), the consideration offered cannot in most Member States be lower than the one offered in the takeover bid.

Where the squeeze-out right is directly linked to takeover bids, the consideration usually cannot be lower than in the bid

In the second group (Member States where the right to buy out may be exercised when the capital/voting rights thresholds have been reached by virtue of a public offer or otherwise), the most frequent situation is that the consideration to be offered must be determined by experts appointed by a Court[19]. The criteria to be used by these experts are not necessarily clearly stated in the law, but some of these Member States do recognise that, if the right is exercised subsequent to a recent takeover bid, the consideration offered in that takeover bid should be properly taken into account, in most cases as a minimum).

Where the squeeze-out right is indirectly linked to takeover bids, the consideration is usually determined by experts (and the price in the bid is used as one reference)

In the third group (Member States where the threshold is set by reference to the proportion of acceptances of the offer), the majority shareholder normally has the right to acquire the remaining shares in a class on the same terms as those of the offer for that class (by virtue of a rebuttable presumption that these terms are fair if the acceptance threshold has been reached. If the minority shareholder can show that the offer price was not fair, he may demand a court supervised appraisal instead).

Where the squeeze-out right is linked to the proportion of acceptances of the offer, the price in the bid is presumed to be fair

[19] In one Member State, the consideration to be offered is determined by the majority shareholder and based on a multicriteria analysis and an expert enquiry and report (the expert appointed by the majority shareholder must receive the approval of the securities regulator).

2.2. The sell-out right

a) The present situation at EU level

Sell-out right is not regulated at EU level

The sell-out right is currently not regulated by any of the existing company law instruments adopted at EU level.

The simplified procedure for a merger by acquisition provided for in the Third Directive is different from the sell-out right

The Third Company law Directive on mergers[20] does enable Member States to exempt from certain requirements set out in the Directive a merger by a company which holds 90 % or more, but not all, of the shares of another company if the minority shareholders of the company being acquired are entitled to have their shares acquired by the acquiring company and to receive consideration corresponding to the value of their shares. However this provision, which does not apply to acquisitions of an undertaking by means of a takeover, is different from the sell-out right in that it is subject to a decision by the acquiring company to carry out a merger under simplified procedures.

A form of sell-out right was included in the draft 9th Directive

A sell-out right was included in the draft 9th Directive on the conduct of groups, of which Article 39 would permit minority shareholders to request an undertaking which had acquired directly or indirectly 90 % or more of the capital of a public limited company to acquire their shares.

No provision on sell-out right in the Directive on Takeover bids

The Directive on takeover bids does not include any provision related to the sell-out right.

The introduction of a sell-out right is currently a matter of national regulation

As for the squeeze-out right, in this situation where Community law remains silent on the sell-out right, Member States are free to decide whether and under which conditions such a right should be introduced in their national legislation.

b) The great diversity of the national regimes

Sell-out right exists in half of the Member

About half of the Member States provide for a right to sell out to the majority shareholder[21]. Here again, the conditions under which that

[20] Third Council Directive of 9 October 1978 based on article 54 (3) (g) of the Treaty concerning mergers of public limited liability companies (78/855/EEC) : Articles 27 and 28.

[21] It should be noted that the Group deliberately restricted its examination to the national regimes providing for a sell-out right in normal circumstances. The special sell-out rights organised by the laws of several Member States in specific situations (e.g. where there has been an application by a shareholder or shareholders on the grounds of "oppression" ("unfairly prejudicial conduct of the company's affairs") by the controllers of the company, in which case the most frequent remedy is a court ordered buy-out of the complainants by the majority, or sometimes by the company) do not fall within the scope of the present Report.

right may be exercised differ widely, in the same areas as identified above in relation to the squeeze-out right.

States, but national regimes differ widely

Only in a small number of Member States may the sell-out right be exercised in all limited liability companies. In one of them, this right is open only to companies which are not admitted to trading on a regulated market. In most of the Member States where the sell-out right exists, this right applies only to public limited companies. A few of these Member States limit this right to companies the securities of which are admitted to trading on a regulated market (or companies having publicly offered securities).

Sell-out right usually applies only to (listed) public limited companies

In a small number of Member States, the sell-out right may be exercised only when the applicable thresholds have been reached by virtue of a public offer. In the majority of the Member States where the sell-out right exists, it is offered generally, regardless of how the applicable threshold has been reached. However, some of these Member States have special rules applicable to the situation in which the sell-out right is exercised subsequent to a takeover bid.

In some Member States, sell-out right is linked – directly or indirectly – to takeover bids

The threshold upon which the sell-out right is conditional varies in most Member States between 90% and 95%, with the exception of one Member State (in which this right is open only to limited liability companies which are not admitted to trading on a regulated market, and where the exercise of the right is not subject to any of the parties reaching any particular threshold but to the presence of appropriate reasons (e.g. a conflict of interests) to be presented to a court)[22].

Most Member States have set the threshold between 90% and 95%

In most Member States, the threshold is set by reference to the amount of capital held or the number of voting rights held. Most of these Member States have opted for both criteria cumulatively. In one Member State, the threshold has to be reached in terms of either capital or voting rights. However, a few Member States set the threshold by reference to the amount of capital only, and another one by reference to the number of ordinary (voting) shares).

Reference is usually made to capital and/or voting rights

In some of the Member States where the sell-out right may be exercised only when the applicable thresholds have been reached by virtue of a public offer, the rights and obligations arise on a class by class basis (which means that the sell-out right is subject to the existence of separate bids for classes of shares, with separate application of the threshold).

Where the sell-out right is directly linked to takeover bids, the rights and obligations sometimes arise on a class by class basis

With respect to the determination of the consideration to be offered, in some Member States the minority shareholders have the right to

The consideration to be offered may be linked –

[22] Similar anti-oppression remedies are found in many Member States.

sell the shares in a class on the same terms as in the offer for that class (by virtue of a rebuttable presumption that these terms are fair if the offeror holds more than 90% of the share capital in that class as a result of the offer. In this case either party may apply for a court-ordered appraisal instead). In the other Member States where the sell-out right exists, the consideration to be offered is most often determined by experts appointed by a Court, but is sometimes determined by the securities regulator or under its control. A small number of those Member States state that, if the right is exercised subsequent to a recent takeover bid, the consideration offered in that takeover bid should be properly taken into account.

directly or indirectly – to the terms of a takeover bid

3. THE JUSTIFICATION FOR THE SQUEEZE-OUT AND SELL-OUT RIGHTS AND THE NEED FOR HARMONISATION

3.1. The justification for the squeeze-out right

a) Grounds to justify the squeeze-out right

Justifications for the squeeze-out right :

The Group holds the view that the right of a majority shareholder to buy out the minority shareholders subsequent to a takeover bid can be justified on the following grounds :

Minority shareholders lead to costs and risks

- the continued existence of minority shareholders after the takeover bid creates various types of actual or opportunity costs and risks for the majority shareholder:

Inability fully to integrate the acquired company into the group

(i) the majority shareholder will incur costs related to his inability fully to integrate the acquired company into his group in terms of activities, use of assets, organisation and finance. The continued existence of minority shareholders inhibits efficient management by the majority shareholder of the company as a part of his group and thereby reduces the potential benefits of the takeover of the company;

Costs related to the rights exercisable by minority shareholders

(ii) the majority shareholder will incur direct costs for having to maintain the infrastructure for holding general meetings of shareholders with a view to the participation of minority shareholders (notices, meeting venue, disclosure, etc) and in relation to other rights exercisable by minority shareholders (calling of meetings of shareholders, requests for information, right to file a suit against the company, its directors, etc);

Risk of abusive exploitation of minority shareholders rights

(iii) the majority shareholder runs the risk of abusive exploitation by the minority shareholders of their rights. They may threaten to use their rights only to inflict costs and disturbance on the majority shareholder in order to induce him to agree to their wishes or to obstruct his development of the company's business ("hold-ups").

Minority shareholders

These costs and risks for the majority shareholder are caused by the rights of the remaining minority shareholders. The value of continued protection of these rights in public interest terms becomes disproportionate to the costs and risks for the majority shareholder when the remaining minority is reduced to a very low level.

rights may become disproportional

- without a squeeze-out right, takeover bids are less attractive to potential bidders because of the costs and risks related to the existence of minority shareholders after the bid. This will reduce the likelihood of voluntary bids and the prices offered in them and the range of circumstances in which such bids are economic. In the same way, the squeeze-out right may be viewed as a counterpart to the mandatory bid rule.

Squeeze-out right makes takeover bids more attractive for potential bidders

- an effect similar to squeeze-out can be achieved in some Member States by a delisting procedure. Delisting procedures generally entail an obligation to make a bid for the remaining minority shares, with the burdens and costs of delays and disclosure. This is inefficient where the majority shareholder has just made a takeover bid and it does not guarantee that minority shareholders transfer their shares. The squeeze-out right is a more efficient means to achieve the same end.

Squeeze-out right is more efficient than a delisting procedure

b) Compatibility with the right of property

The ability of one party to enforce the acquisition of the shares of another represents a significant infringement of the latter's vested rights. The Group therefore takes the view that this facility can only be justified in exceptional circumstances and where there are sufficient safeguards in place.

Infringement of vested rights can only be justified in exceptional circumstances

The Group notes that property rights are protected in most Member States at Constitutional level, and are furthermore guaranteed by the European Convention on Human Rights. The protection offered by these provisions makes it possible to deprive a person of his property only if this is justified by the public interest and if appropriate compensation is offered.

Property rights are indeed protected at national and international level

Various courts in the Member States[23] have ruled that the squeeze-out right is not to be regarded as incompatible with these protective provisions, in that this right is not exercised to satisfy private interests only. There is indeed a general and public interest in having companies efficiently managed on the one hand, and securities markets sufficiently liquid on the other hand. So long as the squeeze-out right applies only when the minority is fairly small and appropriate

Various courts have ruled that the squeeze-out right is not incompatible with these protective provisions

[23] See for example :
- Decision of the German Supreme Court of 7 August 1962, Feldmühle.
- Decision of the French Supreme Court of 29 April 1997, Association de défense des actionnaires minoritaires et autres against Société Générale et autres, Recueil Dalloz 1998, pages 334-338.
- Decision of the German Supreme Court of 27 April 1999, DAT/Altana.
- Decision of the German Supreme Court of 23 August 2000, Moto Meter.

compensation is offered, the use of squeeze-out to address these public interests is proportionate.

3.2. The justification for the sell-out right

The Group holds the view that the sell-out right of minority shareholders following a takeover bid can be justified on the following grounds:

Justifications for the sell-out right :

- after a takeover bid, the majority shareholder may be tempted to abuse his dominant position, e.g. by causing the company to enter into transactions with related parties on a not-at-arm's-length basis, through changes in the dividend policy, by changing the strategy of the company to fit the objectives of the wider group of companies controlled by the acquiring company, by reducing the information provided to minority shareholders, etc. In some Member States, the rights granted to minority shareholders by law to protect against such abuse are no longer available if the minority shareholdings drop below a certain level and the Group believes that in most, if not all, Member States the practical difficulties for minorities in continuously protecting their position are likely to be considerable;

Risk of abuse of his dominant position by the majority shareholder

Minority protection no longer available below a certain level

- in situations where the market has become illiquid as a result of the takeover bid, minority shareholders cannot obtain appropriate compensation by simply selling their shares in the market;

Fair price difficult to obtain in illiquid markets

- the sell-out right is an appropriate mechanism to counter the pressure on shareholders to tender in the takeover bid. In the consultations organised by the Group, the view has been expressed that there is no justification for a sell-out right in situations where a takeover bid has taken place, because the minority shareholders have the opportunity to sell in that bid. The Group does not share this view and considers instead that minority shareholders may have good reasons (unattractive price, promising perspectives for the company...) for not selling in the course of the bid, but should be entitled to modify their decision in view of the outcome of the bid. A rule whereby the consideration required in the sell-out procedure should normally not be higher than the consideration offered in the bid would help to prevent purely speculative behaviours.

Appropriate mechanism to counter the pressure to tender in the takeover bid

- the sell-out right is to be regarded as a fair counterpart for the squeeze-out right conferred on the majority shareholders and a component in the proportionality of the squeeze-out solution.

Counterpart for the squeeze-out right

Another view expressed in the consultations organised by the Group was that a sell-out right subsequent to a takeover bid creates unduly

Sell-out right is not an unduly heavy burden for

heavy financial burdens for the majority shareholder. The Group rejects this view. It sees grounds to justify a sell-out right following a takeover bid, i.e. a general bid for all the shares in the company. Such a bid may be voluntary or mandatory. The sell-out right does not require the majority shareholder to buy more than he was willing or required to buy when he made the takeover bid.

the majority shareholder

3.3. The need for harmonisation

In view of the justifications for the squeeze-out and sell-out rights following a general takeover bid, the Group takes the view that these rights should be offered throughout the European Union on a similar basis. Companies should have similar minimum opportunities everywhere in the EU to consolidate control and to support industrial restructuring, and an adequate level of protection of the holders of securities should be achieved on similar terms in all Member States.

Squeeze-out and sell-out rights after a takeover bid should be offered in all Member States

The Group considers that an initiative at EU level is necessary to ensure that squeeze-out and sell-out rights following general takeover bids exist throughout the EU and to harmonise the conditions under which the squeeze-out and sell-out rights may be exercised.

An initiative at EU level is necessary with respect to both rights in the context of takeover bids

The squeeze-out right may be regarded as a compensation for the mandatory bid rule included in the Directive. The absence of a squeeze-out right in some Member States is an impediment to voluntary bids, and the availability of a squeeze-out right is an incentive to launch a general bid. For these reasons, the introduction of a similar squeeze-out mechanism in all Member States should be favourable to the development of an efficient market for corporate control in the EU.

Squeeze-out right is a compensation for the mandatory bid rule, and is favourable to the development of an efficient market for corporate control

The sell-out right should be introduced everywhere in the EU under similar terms as a counterpart for the squeeze-out right. Transparent and harmonised rules on the protection of investors should contribute to increase their confidence and thereby the liquidity of the financial markets.

Sell-out right is a counterpart for the squeeze-out right and increases investors' confidence

The Group has not reviewed whether similar reasons justify offering squeeze-out and sell-out rights in other situations than where the applicable thresholds have been reached by virtue of a takeover bid. The Group will consider this question in its coming work on the second part of its mandate and reach appropriate conclusions in its second report.

Squeeze-out and sell-out rights outside the context of takeover bids will be examined in the second report

4. THE KEY CHARACTERISTICS OF A EUROPEAN APPROACH

The key issues to be addressed by a European approach to the squeeze-out right and sell-out right following a takeover bid relate to the definition of the applicable thresholds and the determination of the consideration. For these elements, similar rules should be adopted throughout the European Union, while leaving sufficient room to Member States properly to take into account the peculiarities of their company law and the characteristics of their financial markets.

Similar rules on thresholds and consideration should be adopted at EU level, while leaving sufficient room to Member States

4.1. The squeeze-out right

a) The criteria used to define the applicable thresholds

The Group considers that Member States should have the possibility to set the threshold for triggering the squeeze-out right of the majority shareholder by reference to the capital, held by the majority shareholder and any person acting in concert with him following his takeover bid, between 90% and 95%. Such a corridor would allow enough flexibility for Member States to take into account the characteristics of their financial markets (for example, a Member State where securities may be admitted to trading on a regulated market with only 10% of the capital might want to set the threshold at a figure higher than 90%).

Member States should have the possibility to set the squeeze-out threshold, by reference to the capital, between 90% and 95%

The minimum of 90% seems appropriate in view of the necessity to restrict any interference with the right of property to a reasonable degree. On the other hand, the maximum of 95% is justified in view of the practical difficulty in reaching a higher percentage through a takeover bid due to the presence in most companies of untraceable shareholders and the possible existence of an obdurate minority which refuses to accede to the bid even on reasonable terms.

Justifications for the minimum of 90% and the maximum of 95%

The Group reached the conclusion that Member States should alternatively have the possibility to set the threshold by reference to the number of acceptances in the offer, i.e. the offer must be accepted by shareholders holding 90% or more of the share capital in respect of which the offer has been made. The Member States which decide to apply this option would have to design appropriate rules dealing with the offeror's position at the commencement of the bid, for the purposes of determining which shares cannot be counted in calculating whether the 90% threshold has been achieved.

Alternatively, Member States should have the possibility to set the threshold by reference to the number of acceptances in the offer (at 90%)

The Group recognises that these two options produce different results, which depend on the initial shareholding held by the offeror.

The percentage of capital rule and the percentage of

As compared to a 90% of capital rule, the percentage of acceptances rule is always more exacting for the offeror. As compared to a 95% of capital rule, the percentage of acceptances rule is more exacting for the offeror when his initial shareholding was higher than 50% of the capital. On the other hand, this percentage of acceptances rule makes it possible to achieve progressive minority protection as minorities become smaller (which in turn is an incentive for launching early general bids) and to provide a robust valuation basis without the need for heavy reliance on appraisal procedures.

acceptances rule produce different results, but offer different advantages

The Group finally holds the view that, where there are several classes of securities outstanding, the squeeze-out right should apply on a class by class basis, whichever of the two options mentioned above is retained or introduced at national level. As a consequence, the squeeze-out right can be exercised only for the class(es) in which the applicable threshold (percentage of capital of the relevant class or percentage of acceptances for the relevant class) has been reached by virtue of a bid made in respect of the relevant class(es). The justification for such a class by class approach rests on it making possible a proportional application of the squeeze-out right, in the interest of both the majority shareholder (who need not reach the threshold for the company as a whole to be able to squeeze-out the minority shareholders in one class) and the minority shareholders (who cannot be squeezed-out from one class if the threshold is not reached in that particular class).

Where there are several classes of securities, the squeeze-out right should apply on a class by class basis, so as to guarantee a proportional application of the right

b) The consideration to be offered

The Group takes the view that, in both types of thresholds (percentage of capital or percentage of acceptances), the price offered in the takeover bid should be presumed to be a fair price for the shares of the minority shareholders if the bid has been accepted by shareholders holding 90% or more of the share capital in respect of which the offer has been made. This presumption would apply on condition that the squeeze-out right is exercised within a defined period following the bid. In the opinion of the Group, the length of this period should be set by Member States between 3 and 6 months, but this may need further testing with market experts. The presumption of the price of the bid as the fair price should be rebuttable, so that it could be challenged before courts or the authority supervising the takeover bid in particular circumstances.

Price offered in the takeover bid should be presumed to be a fair price in the squeeze-out procedure, if the bid has been accepted by 90% of the relevant shareholders

In the situation where a mandatory bid has been made, the Group considers that the price offered in that mandatory bid should be considered as fair in a subsequent squeeze-out procedure, even if the bid has been accepted by shareholders holding less than 90% of the share capital in respect of which the offer has been made, as the price offered in a mandatory bid has to be equitable. Here again, the presumption would be subject to a time limit and should be rebuttable

If this condition is not met but a mandatory bid has been made, the mandatory bid price should be presumed to be fair in the

in particular circumstances.

squeeze-out procedure

In all the other situations (i.e. where the 90% acceptance rate is not reached, or when no mandatory offer has been made, or when the time limit has expired), the Group recommends that the consideration to be offered is determined by an expert or experts appointed by a Court or the authority supervising the takeover bid.

In all other situations, the consideration should be determined by expert(s)

As far as the nature of the consideration is concerned, the Group takes the view that the shareholders who refused the offer should be treated no less favourably than those who originally accepted it. As a consequence, if cash, or a cash alternative, has been offered in the takeover bid, cash, or a cash alternative, should be offered in the squeeze-out procedure as well.

Cash, or a cash alternative, should be offered if it was offered in the takeover bid

4.2. The sell-out right

a) The criteria used to define the applicable thresholds

The Group considers that Member States should have the possibility to set the threshold for triggering the sell-out right of minority shareholders by reference to the capital, held by the majority shareholder and any person acting in concert with him after the takeover bid, between 90% and 95%. Here too, such a corridor would allow enough flexibility for Member States to take into account the characteristics of their financial markets. In the opinion of the Group, it would not be appropriate to set the threshold for exercising the sell-out right by reference to the number of acceptances in the bid, because this would unduly work against the interests of the minority shareholders.

Member States should have the possibility to set the sell-out threshold, by reference to the capital, between 90% and 95%

The Group holds the view that, where there are several classes of securities outstanding, the sell-out right should apply on a class by class basis. As a consequence, the sell-out right can be exercised only for the class(es) in which the applicable threshold (percentage of capital of the relevant class) has been reached by virtue of a bid made in respect of the relevant class(es). The justification for such a class by class approach rests on it making possible a proportional application of the sell-out right, in the interest of both the minority shareholders (who may exercise their sell-out right as soon as the threshold is reached for the relevant class) and the majority shareholder (who will not be forced to buy out the minority shareholders if the threshold is not reached in the relevant class).

Where there are several classes of securities, the sell-out right should apply on a class by class basis, so as to guarantee a proportional application of the right

In the view of the Group, it appears necessary that Member States adopt provisions which would make sure that :

Member States should adopt provisions with

- the sell-out right would not be exercisable in situations where the threshold is reached only on a temporary basis;
- an adequate procedure would guarantee a fair treatment of all minority shareholders once one of them decides to exercise his sell-out right, which procedure should avoid the burdens of multiple applications.

respect to temporary situations and co-ordinated fair treatment of all minority shareholders

b) The consideration to be offered

The Group recommends a mirroring of the proposals made above with respect to the squeeze-out procedure.

Rules on sell-out consideration should be similar to the rules on squeeze-out consideration

To summarise, the Group takes the view that, in view of their justifications in the context of takeover bids, an initiative at EU level is necessary to ensure that the squeeze-out and sell-out rights exist in all Member States after a general takeover bid. With respect to both the definition of the applicable thresholds and the determination of the consideration to be offered, similar rules should be adopted throughout the EU while leaving sufficient room to Member States properly to take into account the peculiarities of their company law and the characteristics of their financial markets.

Summary : *The squeeze-out and sell-out rights should be offered throughout the EU on a similar basis after a general takeover bid*

The Group considers that Member States should have the possibility to set the threshold for triggering the squeeze-out right by reference to the capital (between 90% and 95%). Alternatively, Member States should have the possibility to set the threshold by reference to the number of acceptances in the offer (at 90%). Where there are several classes of securities outstanding, the squeeze-out right should apply on a class by class basis, whichever of the two options mentioned above is retained at national level.

Squeeze-out threshold : two options

With respect to the consideration to be offered in exercising the squeeze-out right, the Group takes the view that the price offered in the takeover bid should be presumed to be a fair price if the bid has been accepted by shareholders holding 90% or more of the share capital in respect of which the offer has been made. If a mandatory bid has been made, the mandatory bid price should be rebuttably presumed to be a fair price in the squeeze-out procedure even if the bid has not been accepted by shareholders holding 90% or more of the relevant share capital. In all other situations, the consideration should be determined by expert(s). Cash, or a cash alternative, should be offered if it was offered in the takeover bid.

Squeeze-out consideration : reference to the takeover price where relevant

The Group considers that Member States should set the threshold for triggering the sell-out right by reference to the capital (between 90% and 95%). Where there are several classes of securities outstanding, the sell-out right should apply on a class by class basis.

Sell-out threshold set by reference to the capital

With respect to the consideration to be obtained in exercising the sell-out right, the Group recommends a mirroring of the proposals made above regarding the squeeze-out right.

Sell-out consideration : mirroring of the squeeze-out rules

Brussels, 10 January 2002

ANNEX 1

THE HIGH LEVEL GROUP OF COMPANY LAW EXPERTS' TERMS OF REFERENCE PRESS RELEASE OF 4 SEPTEMBER 2001

Company law: Commission creates High Level Group of Experts

The European Commission has set up a High Level Group of Company Law Experts that will help the Commission to prepare a new proposal for a Directive on the conduct of takeover bids and to define new priorities for the broader future development of company law in the European Union. The group comprises seven members, selected on the basis of their competence in company law and the Commission's desire that the members should have broad experience of the various legal and economic systems in the EU. The group will hold its first meeting on 11 September 2001. It is due to deliver a preliminary report on its recommendations to the Commission concerning rules for takeover bids by the end of 2001 and a final report concerning broader issues for the development of EU company law by mid-2002.

Internal Market Commissioner Frits Bolkestein said "This High Level Group has been set up because the Commission wants to get top quality independent advice from leading European experts in the first instance on pan-European rules for takeover bids and subsequently on key priorities for modernising company law in the European Union. A clear set of pan-EU rules for the conduct of takeovers stands to benefit European companies and shareholders, especially minority shareholders, by clarifying their rights and obligations. It would also facilitate the goal set by the Lisbon Summit of restructuring the European economy to make it the most competitive in the world by 2010. The European Parliament's vote of 4 July to not endorse a previous proposal for a Takeovers Directive was very disappointing. However, the creation of this Group demonstrates the Commission's determination to come forward as soon as possible in 2002 with a new proposal that takes account of the broadest range of views".

The group comprises:

- Chairman Jaap WINTER, Professor at the Erasmus University of Rotterdam and legal advisor UNILEVER, Netherlands
- José Maria GARRIDO GARCIA, Professor at the University of Castilla-La Mancha, Spain
- Klaus J. HOPT, Geschäftsführender Direktor Max Planck-Institut, Germany
- Jonathan RICKFORD, Consultant for the Department of Trade and Industry, United Kingdom
- Guido ROSSI, former President of the Italian stock exchange supervisory body CONSOB, Italy
- Jan CHRISTENSEN, Professor at the University of Copenhagen, Denmark
- Joëlle SIMON, Legal Affairs Director, French Business Confederation - MEDEF, France.

The Group will hold its first meeting on 11 September 2001. Taking account of the positions of the EU's Council of Ministers and the European Parliament during the last stages of negotiation of the previous proposal for a Takeovers Directive (see MEMO/01/255), the Group of High Level Experts will initially consider the following three issues:

- how to ensure the existence of a level playing field in the EU concerning the equal treatment of shareholders across Member States
- the definition of the notion of an "equitable price" to be paid to minority shareholders and
- the right for a majority shareholder to buy out minority shareholders ("squeeze-out procedure").

The Group is due to deliver a report on these issues, including possible solutions, to the Commission's services by the end of 2001.

During a second stage, the Group is due to provide recommendations for a modern regulatory European company law framework designed to be sufficiently flexible and up-to-date to meet companies' needs, taking into account fully the impact of information technology. The Group will examine best practice developed in the Member States (as well as in the USA) and consider a range of issues including the following:

- the creation and functioning of companies and groups of companies, co-operatives and mutual enterprises, including corporate governance
- shareholders' rights, including cross-border voting and virtual general meetings
- corporate restructuring and mobility (for instance, the transfer of the corporate seat)
- the possible need for new legal forms (for instance, a European Private Company, which would be of particular relevance for SMEs)
- the possible simplification of corporate rules in light of the SLIM report on the Second Company Law Directive of 13 December 1976 on the formation and capital maintenance of public limited liability companies.

The Group is due to deliver a final report to the Commission's services by mid-2002.

ANNEX 2

WORKING METHODS
OF
THE HIGH LEVEL GROUP OF COMPANY LAW EXPERTS

The Group began its work on 11 September 2001, and finished the first phase with the presentation of the report on 10 January 2002 in Brussels.

In spite of a very tight schedule, the Group considered it essential to canvass opinions from a number of institutions and organizations.

The Group appeared before the European Parliament Legal Affairs and Internal Market Committee in a hearing held on 5 November 2001.

The Group invited leading representatives of several organizations interested in the regulation applicable to takeover bids within the European Union to confidential hearings in Brussels. The Group had a total of 4 hearings on 5 November 2001, where representatives from the following organizations were heard :
- ETUC (European Trade Union Confederation)
- Euroshareholders
- FESE (Federation of European Stock Exchanges)
- UNICE (Union of Industrial and Employers' Confederations of Europe).

Others submitted comments to the Group at their own initiative.

A summary of the main comments submitted to the Group, either in the hearings or in written form, is included in Annex 3.

The report of the Group is submitted to the European Commission and presented to the Press on 10 January 2002 in Brussels.

ANNEX 3

SUMMARY OF COMMENTS TO THE HIGH LEVEL GROUP OF COMPANY LAW EXPERTS SUBMITTED IN THE ORGANISED HEARINGS AND OTHERWISE

Despite the tight time constraint, the Group decided to hold some hearings on 5 November 2001. It invited seven organisations representing at the European level the most interested parties in the debate about the Takeover bids Directive. Four of them accepted the invitation: UNICE (Union of Industrial and Employers' Confederations of Europe), ETUC (European Trade Union Confederation), Euroshareholders and FESE (Federation of European Securities Exchanges). Their views are summarised here under.

1. SQUEEZE-OUT

It was agreed that a common squeeze-out procedure would be useful to help companies to restructure themselves. A balance should be reached between the need for the fair treatment of minority shareholders and the competitiveness of the European capital market. Therefore, a new directive on takeover bids should allow a majority shareholder who has reached a sufficiently high threshold (90 or 95% of the share capital) to buy out the remaining shares at a defined price.

In order to achieve a balanced position, the majority of the participants was also in favour of the institution of the right for minority shareholders to sell out their shares to the majority shareholder.

One proposal was (i) the adoption of a procedure such that: if, for example, a 2/3 majority of the shareholders, excluding the dominant shareholder, decides to start a sell-out of the remaining shares, then a squeeze out procedure should be triggered, and (ii) an equitable price would be required.

2. EQUITABLE PRICE

It was agreed that the definition of the equitable price to be paid in the case of takeover bids, and above all in the case of a mandatory bid, is of the utmost importance. It should aim at the fair treatment of minority shareholders and the competitiveness of the European capital market, and should be based upon equal treatment of shareholders, at least in the same class of shares. A consensus seemed to be reached on the idea of the highest price paid by the offeror during a relevant period (to be indicated in the directive), although this price could be altered by the competent authorities in certain circumstances.

The following needs were also expressed: (i) that sufficient information should be provided to enable proper assessment of the price being offered, (ii) that shareholders should be offered the possibility to ask an independent institution to give its view about this price, and (iii) that due attention should be given to the marketability of the securities offered as a consideration.

3. LEVEL PLAYING FIELD

It was unanimously agreed (i) that the decision whether or not to sell a company belongs in essence to its owners, that is the shareholders and, in particular, not the managers of the company, and (ii) that there is a need for a level playing field for shareholders in the EU, and a directive on takeover bids is an important part of it.

On the other hand, there was a division on the content of the level playing field. Some suggested that attention should be given not only to take-over legislation but also to existing company law. Some proposed to reduce barriers to an absolute minimum and to prescribe the "one share-one vote" principle; others favoured the disclosure of the restrictions rather than the removal of these restrictions.

Proposals were made for (i) co-ordinating the rules on takeover bids with those on disclosure requirements and (ii) examining the possibility of establishing equivalent treatment between the US and the EU.

4. OTHER ISSUES

Some other ideas were submitted to the Group:

(i) introduction of a common threshold for the launch of a mandatory bid, with a preference for a fixed threshold system where the level to be fixed could be left up to national legislators within an established range;

(ii) re-examination of the social issues and recognition of the right for the employees to be consulted, and not only informed about the conditions of the bid; the Board should consult the employees before preparing its report on the bid, in order to have a joint evaluation of the bid and possible defensive measures.

ANNEX 4

OVERVIEW OF MOST IMPORTANT BARRIERS TO TAKEOVER BIDS

1. PRE-BID

1.1. BARRIERS TO THE ACQUISITION OF SHARES IN THE COMPANY

- Ownership caps
- Golden shares (some types)
- Restrictions to the transferability of shares (applicable to non-listed shares; listed shares may be subject to limitations in shareholders' agreements)
- Lack of access to the underlying shares (where depository receipts are traded instead of underlying shares)
- Dilution of the shares acquired by bidder or potential bidder (poison pills; certain classes of poison debt)
- Reduction of available shares by means of: acquisition of own shares; cross-shareholdings; pyramiding.

1.2. BARRIERS TO EXERTION OF CONTROL IN THE GENERAL MEETING

- Voting caps
- Shares with double or multiple voting rights
- Shares with limited or non-existent voting rights; participation rights carrying no votes
- Time lapse voting schemes
- Discriminatory quorum requirements
- Irrevocable proxies
- Binding voting agreements; voting trusts
- Supermajorities
- Golden shares (some types)

1.3. BARRIERS TO EXERTION OF CONTROL IN THE BOARD OF DIRECTORS

- Co-determination
- Other corporate structures that limit shareholders' control of the board (sociétés en commandite)
- Shares with special rights to appoint directors
- Staggered boards
- Fixed-term appointments for board members
- Qualifications for board membership (e.g. prior shareholding for a specified period)
- Golden parachutes
- Supermajority required to dismiss and/or elect the board

1.4. BARRIERS TO EXERTION OF CONTROL OVER THE ASSETS OF THE COMPANY

- Sale of assets ("scorched earth")

- Spin-offs
- Lock-ups of corporate assets ("crown jewels")
- Change of control clauses in non-financial agreements

1.5. CREATION OF FINANCIAL BURDENS AS A CONSEQUENCE OF THE TRANSFER OF CONTROL

- Poison debt
- Golden and tin parachutes
- Change of control clauses in loan agreements

1.6. CREATION OF REGULATORY PROBLEMS

- Defensive acquisitions creating antitrust problems or businesses subject to special regulation
- Defensive acquisitions invoking cross-holding rules

2. POST-BID (N.B. SOME PRE-BID BARRIERS MAY ALSO BE ADOPTED POST-BID)

2.1. REDUCTION OF SHARES ACQUIRABLE BY BIDDER

- Share buybacks; self-bid; delisting bid
- Issue of capital to a friendly party ("white squire")

2.2. INCREASE OF THE COST OF THE BID

- Issue of share capital with pre-emption rights

2.3. CREATION OF REGULATORY PROBLEMS

- Litigation (on the bid itself, or on antitrust or special regulatory problems, etc.)

2.4. SEARCH FOR ALTERNATIVE BIDDER

- "White Knight"

2.5. ACQUISITION OF THE BIDDER'S INTEREST IN THE COMPANY

- "Greenmail"

2.6. BID FOR THE BIDDER

- "Pacman" Defence

ANNEX 5

FINANCIAL FLOWS BETWEEN EUROPE AND THE US OVER THE RECENT YEARS

1. MERGERS AND ACQUISITIONS ACTIVITY 1995-1999 (SOURCE OECD 2001)

1.1. Inward cross-border M&As, Europe

USD billion

		Acquirer	
Year	Total	U.S.A	Europe
1995	85,9	25,7	53,9
1996	96,5	36,4	48,0
1997	139,4	41,1	83,9
1998	229,5	64,1	137,4
1999	390,5	83,1	282,2

Allocation among the biggest European acquirers

Year	France	U.K	Germany
1995	10,0	9,2	12,1
1996	8,6	6,3	5,6
1997	14,1	24,8	9,8
1998	25,9	19,8	16,0
1999	70,3	62,5	69,7

1.2. Outward cross-border M&As, Europe

USD billion

		Targets			
Year	Total	Europe		North America	
1995	93,4	53,9	57,7%	38,1	40,8%
1996	112,0	48,0	42,9%	53,4	47,7%
1997	158,1	83,9	53,1%	55,4	35,1%
1998	352,1	137,4	39,0%	171,9	48,8%
1999	553,0	282,2	51,0%	203,5	36,8%

1.3. Inward cross-borders M&As, United States

USD billion

		Acquirer
Year	Total	Europe
1995	55,2	34,7
1996	70,4	51,5
1997	86,0	52,8
1998	220,4	170,2
1999	253,1	202,0

Allocation among the biggest European acquirers

Year	U.K.	Germany	France
1995	13,8	11,1	2,2
1996	19,5	12,5	6,6
1997	13,7	4,7	8,8
1998	85,1	47,3	13,1
1999	110,9	16,3	22,6

1.4. Outward cross-border M&As, United States

USD billion

		Targets	
Year	Total	Europe	
1995	59,6	25,7	43,1%
1996	64,3	36,4	56,6%
1997	83,5	41,1	49,1%
1998	146,8	64,1	43,7%
1999	127,9	83,1	65,0%

2. NUMBER OF CASES NOTIFIED TO THE EU UNDER THE MERGERS REGULATION 1990-2000 (SOURCE EUROPEAN COMMISSION DG COMPETITION)

2.1 Total number of companies involved in notified cases by country

Number of Companies Involved In Notified Cases by Country (excluding Joint Ventures)
21.9.1990 - 10.5.2001

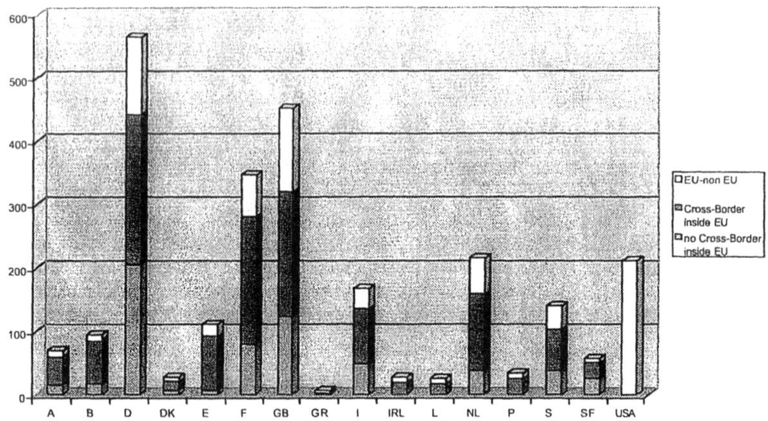

2.2 Total number of companies involved in takeover bids by country

Number of Companies Involved in All Take-over Bids by Country
21.9.1990 - 10.5.2001

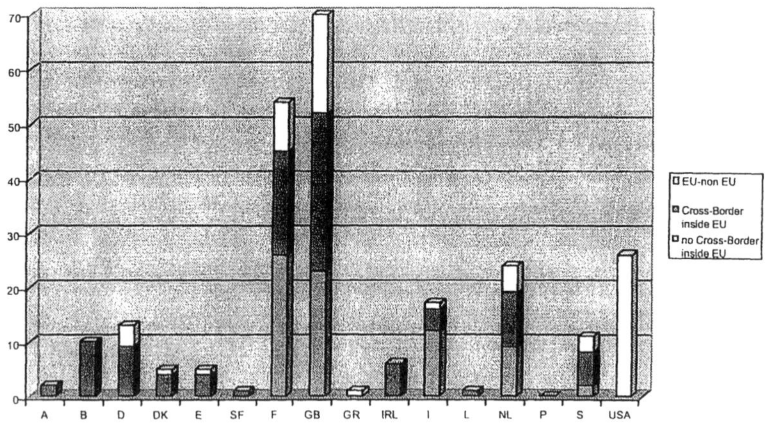

2.3 Number of companies involved in agreed takeover bids by country

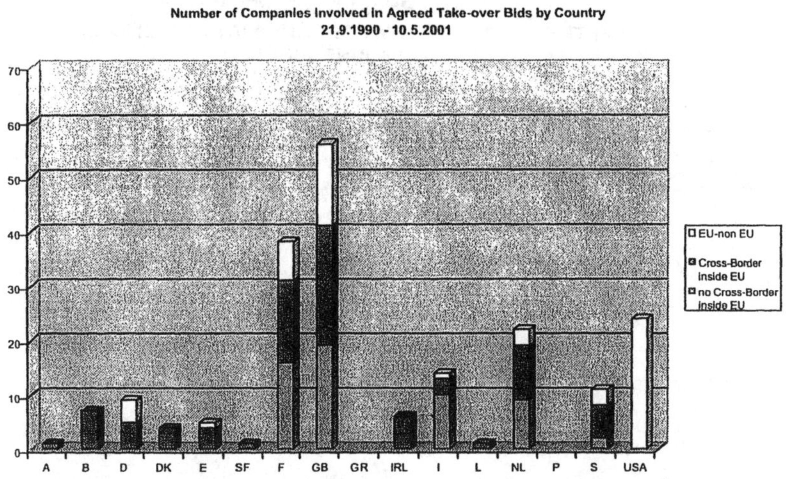

2.4 Number of companies involved in contested takeover bids by country

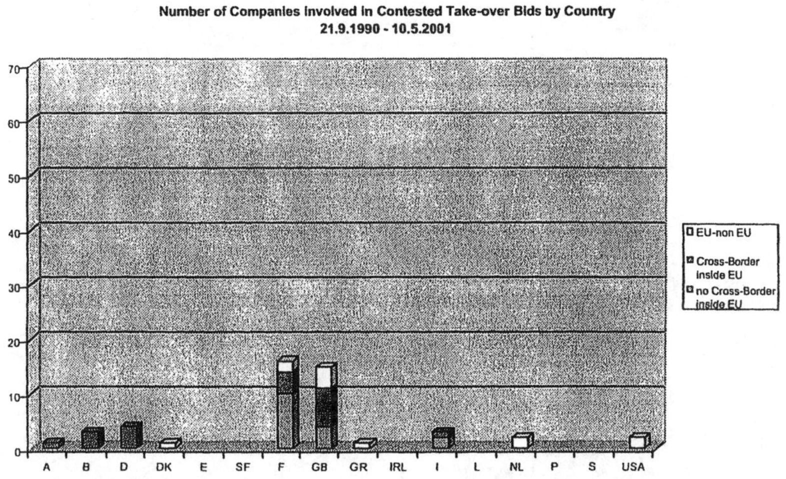

ANNEX 6

EUROPEAN PARLIAMENT AND COUNCIL DIRECTIVE ON COMPANY LAW CONCERNING TAKEOVER BIDS : JOINT TEXT APPROVED BY THE CONCILIATION COMMITTEE ON 6 JUNE 2001

EUROPEAN UNION

THE EUROPEAN PARLIAMENT **THE COUNCIL**

Brussels, 19 June 2001
(OR. en)

1995/0341 (COD)
C5-0221/2001

PE-CONS 3629/1/01
REV 1

DRS 27
CODEC 493

LEGISLATIVE ACTS AND OTHER INSTRUMENTS

Subject :	Directive of the European Parliament and of the Council on company law concerning takeover bids

Joint text
approved by the Conciliation Committee
provided for in Article 251(4) of the EC Treaty

DIRECTIVE 2001/ /EC OF THE EUROPEAN PARLIAMENT AND OF THE COUNCIL
of

on company law concerning takeover bids

THE EUROPEAN PARLIAMENT AND THE COUNCIL OF THE EUROPEAN UNION,

Having regard to the Treaty establishing the European Community, and in particular Article 44 thereof,

Having regard to the proposal from the Commission [1],

Having regard to the Opinion of the Economic and Social Committee [2],

Acting in accordance with the procedure referred to in Article 251 of the Treaty [3], in the light of the joint text approved by the Conciliation Committee on 6 June 2001,

Whereas:

(1) It is necessary to coordinate certain safeguards which Member States require of companies and firms within the meaning of the second paragraph of Article 48 of the Treaty for the protection of members and others, in order to make such safeguards equivalent throughout the Community.

(2) It is necessary to protect the interests of holders of securities of companies governed by the law of a Member State when these companies are subject to a takeover bid or to a change of control and their securities are admitted to trading on a regulated market within the scope of this Directive.

(3) Only action at Community level can ensure an adequate level of protection for holders of securities throughout the Community and provide for minimum guidelines for the conduct of takeover bids. Member States acting independently are not able to establish the same level of protection especially in the case of cross-border takeovers or acquisitions of control.

(4) The adoption of a directive is the appropriate procedure for laying down a framework consisting of certain common principles and a limited number of general requirements which Member States will be required to implement through more detailed rules according to their national systems and their cultural contexts.

---

1 OJ C 162, 6.6.1996, p. 5 and OJ C 378, 13.12.1997, p. 10.
2 OJ C 295, 7.10.1996, p. 1.
3 Opinion of the European Parliament of 26 June 1997 (OJ C 222, 21.7.1997, p. 20), confirmed on 27 October 1999, Council Common Position of 19 June 2000 (OJ C 23, 24.1.2001, p. 1) and Decision of the European Parliament of 13 December 2000 (not yet published in the Official Journal.) Decision of the European Parliament of and Decision of the Council of.

(5) Member States should take the necessary steps in order to protect holders of securities, and particularly those having minority holdings after the acquisition of control of their company. Such protection should be ensured by obliging the person who acquired control of a company to make a bid to all holders of securities for all of their holdings. It should be allowed, during a transitional period, to ensure this protection through other appropriate and at-least-equivalent means on condition that these means are specific to the transfer of control and include specific financial compensation for the minority shareholders. Member States may, in addition to the protection provided for by a mandatory bid or other equivalent means, provide for further instruments aimed at the protection of the interests of holders of securities.

(6) The obligation to make a bid to all holders of securities should not apply to those controlling holdings already in existence at the date when the legislation implementing this Directive enters into force.

(7) Member States may establish further instruments for the protection of the interests of holders of securities, such as the obligation to make a partial bid where the offeror does not acquire control of the company, or the obligation to make a bid simultaneously with the acquisition of control of the company.

(8) The obligation to launch a bid does not apply in the case of the acquisition of securities which do not carry voting rights in ordinary general meetings. Member States may establish that the obligation to make a bid to all holders of securities should include not only securities carrying voting rights but also securities only carrying voting rights in specific circumstances or carrying no voting rights at all.

(9) Each Member State should designate an authority or authorities to supervise the aspects of the bid governed by this Directive and to ensure that parties to takeover bids comply with the rules made pursuant to this Directive. The different authorities should cooperate with one another.

(10) In order to be effective, takeover regulation should be flexible and capable of dealing with new circumstances as they arise, and should accordingly provide for the possibility of exceptions and derogations. However, in applying any rules or exceptions laid down or in granting any derogations, supervisory authorities should respect certain general principles.

(11) Supervision may be exercised by self-regulatory bodies.

(12) In accordance with general principles of Community law, and in particular the right to a fair hearing, decisions of a supervisory authority will in appropriate circumstances be susceptible to review by an independent court or tribunal. However, this Directive leaves it to Member States to determine whether rights are to be made available which may be asserted in administrative or judicial proceedings, whether in proceedings against a supervisory authority or proceedings between parties to a bid.

(13) It is necessary to create Community-wide clarity and transparency in respect of legal issues to be settled in the event of takeover bids and to prevent patterns of corporate restructuring within the Community from being distorted by arbitrary differences in governance and management cultures.

(14) To reduce the scope for insider dealing offerors should be required to announce their decision of launching a bid as soon as possible and to inform the supervisory authority of the bid.

(15) The holders of securities should be properly informed of the terms of the bid by means of an offer document. Appropriate information should also be given at the same time to the representatives of the company's employees or, failing that, to the employees directly.

(16) It is necessary to regulate the period for the acceptance of the bid.

(17) To be able to perform their functions satisfactorily, supervisory authorities should at all times be able to require the parties to the bid to provide information on it and should cooperate and supply information in an efficient and effective manner without delay to other authorities supervising capital markets.

(18) To avoid operations which frustrate the bid it is necessary to limit the powers of the board of the offeree company to engage in operations of an exceptional nature without unduly hindering the offeree company from carrying out its normal business activities.

(19) The board of the offeree company should be required to make public a document setting out its opinion on the bid and the reasons on which it is based including its views on the effects of implementation on all the interests of the company and specifically on employment.

(20) It is necessary that Member States provide rules to cover the cases where the bid lapses, the right of the offeror to revise his bid, the possibility of competing bids for the securities of a company, the disclosure of the result of the bid and the irrevocability of the bid and the conditions permitted.

(21) It is important to entrust the Contact Committee set up by Article 20 of Council Directive 79/279/EEC of 5 March 1979 coordinating the conditions for the admission of securities to official stock exchange listing [4] with the task of assisting Member States and the supervisory authorities in the implementation of this Directive, particularly in areas such as cross-border takeover bids and the mutual recognition of offer documents, and to advise the Commission, if necessary, on additions or amendments to this Directive,

HAVE ADOPTED THIS DIRECTIVE:

---

4 OJ L 66, 16.3.1979, p. 21. Directive as last amended by Directive 88/627/EEC (OJ L 348, 17.12.1988, p. 62).

Article 1

Scope

1. The coordination measures prescribed by this Directive shall apply to the laws, regulations, administrative provisions, codes of practice or other arrangements of the Member States, including arrangements established by organisations officially authorised to regulate the markets (hereinafter "rules"), relating to takeover bids for the securities of a company governed by the law of a Member State, where such securities are admitted to trading on a regulated market within the meaning of Article 1(13) of Council Directive 93/22/EEC of 10 May 1993 on investment services in the securities field [5] in one or more Member States (hereinafter "regulated market").

2. The measures prescribed by this Directive shall not apply to takeover bids for securities is sued by companies the object of which is the collective investment of capital provided by the public, and which operate on the principle of risk spreading, and the units of which are, at the holders' request, repurchased or redeemed, directly or indirectly, out of the assets of those companies. Action taken by such companies to ensure that the stock exchange value of their units does not significantly vary from their net asset value shall be regarded as equivalent to such repurchase or redemption.

Article 2

Definitions

For the purposes of this Directive:

(a) "takeover bid" and "bid" mean a public offer (other than by the offeree company itself) made to the holders of the securities of a company to acquire all or part of such securities. A bid may be either mandatory or voluntary, and must follow or have as its objective the acquisition of control;

(b) "offeree company" means a company whose securities are the subject of a bid;

(c) "offeror" means any natural person or legal entity in public or private law making a bid;

(d) "persons acting in concert" means natural persons or legal entities who cooperate with the offeror or the offeree company on the basis of an agreement, either express or tacit, either oral or written, and aimed respectively at obtaining control of the offeree company or frustrating the successful outcome of a bid.

Persons controlled by another person within the meaning of Article 8 of Council Directive 88/627/EEC of 12 December 1988 on the information to be published when a major holding in a listed company is acquired or disposed of [6] shall be deemed to be persons acting in concert with such persons and with each other;

5 OJ L 141, 11.6.1993, p. 27. Directive as amended by Directive 95/26/EC (OJ L 168, 18.7.1995, p. 7).

6 OJ L 348, 17.12.1988, p. 62.

(e) "securities" means transferable securities carrying voting rights in a company;

(f) "parties to the bid" means the offeror, the members of the offeror's board, if the offeror is a company, the offeree company, holders of securities of the offeree company and the members of the board of the offeree company, or persons acting in concert with such parties.

Article 3

General principles

1. For the purposes of the implementation of this Directive, Member States shall ensure that the rules or other arrangements made or introduced pursuant to this Directive respect the following principles:

(a) all holders of securities of an offeree company of the same class are to be given equivalent treatment; in particular, if a person acquires control of a company, the other holders of securities are to be protected;

(b) holders of securities of an offeree company are to have sufficient time and information to enable them to reach a properly informed decision on the bid; when advising the holders of securities, the board of an offeree company shall present its views on the effects of implementation of the bid on employment, conditions of employment and the company locations.

(c) the board of an offeree company is to act in the interests of the company as a whole, and must not deny the holders of securities the opportunity to decide on the merits of the bid;

(d) false markets must not be created in the securities of the offeree company, of the offeror company, or of any other company concerned by the bid in such a way that the rise or fall in the prices of the securities becomes artificial and the normal functioning of the markets is distorted;

(e) an offeror shall announce a bid only after ensuring that it can fulfil in full any cash consideration, if so offered, and after having taken all reasonable measures to secure the implementation of any other type of consideration;

(f) an offeree company must not be hindered in the conduct of its affairs for longer than is reasonable by a bid for its securities.

2. In order to attain the objectives set out in paragraph 1, Member States:

(a) shall ensure that rules are in force which satisfy the minimum requirements set out in this Directive;

(b) may have additional conditions and more stringent provisions than those required by this Directive to regulate bids.

Article 4

Supervisory authority

1. Member States shall designate the authority or authorities, competent for supervising a bid for the purposes of the rules made or introduced pursuant to this Directive. The authorities thus designated shall be either public authorities or associations or private bodies recognised by national law or by public authorities expressly empowered for that purpose by national law. Member States shall ensure that these authorities exercise their functions impartially and independently of all parties to the bid. Member States shall inform the Commission of these designations and shall specify all divisions of functions that may be made.

2. (a) The authority competent for supervising the bid shall be that of the Member State in which the offeree company has its registered office if the securities of that company are admitted to trading on a regulated market in that Member State. When this is not the case subparagraph (b) or (c) shall apply.

(b) If the securities of the offeree company are not admitted to trading on a regulated market in the Member State in which the company has its registered office, the authority competent for supervising the bid shall be that of the Member State on whose regulated market the securities of the company are admitted to trading. If the securities of the company are admitted to trading on regulated markets in more than one Member State, the authority competent for supervising the bid shall be that of the Member State on whose regulated market the securities were first admitted.

(c) If the securities of the offeree company are first admitted to trading on regulated markets within more than one Member State simultaneously, the offeree company has to determine the competent authority for supervising the bid by notifying these regulated markets and their supervisory authorities on the first trading day.

If the securities of the offeree company are already admitted to trading on regulated markets in more than one Member State at the date referred to in Article 15(1) and were admitted simultaneously, the supervisory authorities of these Member States shall agree on who is to be the competent authority for supervising the bid within four weeks after the date mentioned in Article 15(1). Otherwise the competent authority shall be determined by the offeree company on the first trading day following the expiry of the period of time mentioned in the first sentence.

(d) Member States shall ensure that rules are in force requiring the decisions referred to in subparagraph (c) to be made public.

(e) In the cases referred to in subparagraphs (b) and (c) above, matters relating to the consideration offered in the case of a bid, particularly the price, and matters relating to the procedure of the bid, in particular the information on the offeror's decision to make a bid, the contents of the offer document and the disclosure of the bid shall be dealt with in accordance with the rules of the Member State of the competent authority. In matters relating to the information to be provided to the employees of the offeree company and in matters relating to company law, in particular the percentage of voting rights which confers control and any derogation from the obligation to launch a bid, as well as the conditions under which the board of the offeree company may undertake any action which might result in the frustration of the bid, the applicable rules and the competent authority shall be those of the Member State in which the offeree company has its registered office.

3. Member States shall ensure that all persons employed or formerly employed by the supervisory authorities shall be bound by professional secrecy. Information covered by professional secrecy may not be divulged to any person or authority except by virtue of provisions laid down by law.

4. The supervisory authorities of the Member States under this Directive and other authorities supervising capital markets, in particular in accordance with Council Directive 88/627/EEC, Council Directive 89/592/EEC of 13 November 1989 coordinating regulations on insider dealing [7] and Council Directive 93/22/EEC, shall cooperate and supply each other with information, wherever necessary for the application of the rules drawn up in accordance with this Directive and in particular in cases covered by Article 4(2) (b), (c) and (e). Information thus exchanged shall be covered by the obligation of professional secrecy to which the persons employed or formerly employed by the supervisory authorities receiving the information are subject. Cooperation should include the ability to serve the legal documents necessary to enforce measures taken by the competent authorities in connection with bids, as well as such other assistance as may reasonably be requested by the supervisory authorities concerned for the purposes of investigating any actual or alleged breaches of the rules made or introduced to implement this Directive.

5. Provided that the general principles referred to in Article 3(1) are respected, Member States may provide in their rules made or introduced pursuant to this Directive that their supervisory authorities may, on the basis of a reasoned decision, grant derogation from these rules in particular types of cases and in specific appropriate cases.6. This Directive does not affect the powers of the Member States to designate judicial or other authorities responsible for dealing with disputes and for deciding on irregularities committed in the bid procedure nor does it affect the power of Member States to regulate whether and under which circumstances parties to a bid are entitled to bring administrative or judicial proceedings. In particular this Directive does not affect the power which courts may have in a Member State to decline to hear legal proceedings and to decide whether or not such proceedings affect the outcome of a bid. This Directive shall not affect the powers of the Member States to determine the legal position concerning the liability of supervisory authorities or concerning litigation between the parties to a bid.

Article 5

Protection of minority shareholders; mandatory bid

1. Where a natural person or legal entity who, as a result of his own acquisition or the acquisition by persons acting in concert with him, holds securities of a company referred to

[7] OJ L 334, 18.11.1989, p. 30.

in Article 1(1) which, added to any existing holdings and the holdings of persons acting in concert with him, directly or indirectly give him a specified percentage of voting rights in that company, conferring on him the control of that company, Member States shall ensure that rules are in force which oblige this person to make a bid as a means to protect the minority shareholders of that company. This bid shall be addressed to all holders of securities for all their holdings at an equitable price. When the consideration offered by the offeror does not consist of liquid securities admitted to trading on a regulated market, such consideration has to include a cash consideration at least as an alternative.

In any case, the offeror must provide a consideration in cash at least as an alternative, if he, alone or in conjunction with persons acting in concert with him, has, during a period commencing not less than 3 months before the bid was made public pursuant to Article 6(1) and ending on the expiry of the acceptance period, acquired for cash more than 5% of the shares or voting rights in the offeree company.

2. Where a voluntary bid has been made in accordance with this Directive to all holders of securities for all their holdings and control has been obtained, the obligation to launch a bid no longer applies.

3. By way of derogation from paragraph 1, Member States, which provide at the time of adoption of this Directive for other appropriate and at-least-equivalent means in order to protect the minority shareholders of the company, may continue to apply such means for one year following the date mentioned in Article 15(1), on the condition that these means:

(a) are specific to the transfer of control, and

(b) include specific financial compensation for the minority shareholders.

4. In addition to the protection provided under paragraphs 1 and 3, Member States may provide for further instruments aiming at the protection of the interests of holders of securities insofar as these instruments do not hinder the normal course of the bid referred to in paragraph 1.

5. The percentage of voting rights which confers control for the purposes of paragraphs 1 and 3 and the method of its calculation shall be determined by the rules of the Member State in which the company has its registered office.

Article 6

Information

1. Member States shall ensure that rules are in force requiring that the decision to make a bid is made public without delay and that the supervisory authority is informed of the bid. Member States may require that the supervisory authority is informed before this decision is made public. As soon as the bid has been made public, the board of the offeree company shall inform the representatives of its employees or, where there are no such representatives, the employees themselves.

2. Member States shall ensure that rules are in force requiring the offeror to draw up and make public in good time an offer document containing the information necessary to enable the holders of securities of the offeree company to reach a properly informed decision on the bid. Before the offer document is made public, the offeror shall communicate it to the supervisory authority. When it is made public, the board of the offeree company shall communicate it to the representatives of its employees or, where there are no such representatives, to the employees themselves.

Where the offer document is subject to the prior approval of the supervisory authority and once it has been approved, it shall be recognised, subject to any translation, in the other Member State or Member States on whose markets the securities of the offeree company are admitted to trading, without its being necessary to obtain the approval of the supervisory authorities of that or those Member States and without their being able to require additional information to be included in the offer document. The supervisory authorities may, however, require that the offer document include information specific to the market of the Member State or Member States on whose markets the securities of the offeree company are admitted to trading concerning the formalities to be complied with for accepting the bid and for receiving the consideration due at the close of the bid as well as the tax arrangements to which the consideration offered to the holders of securities will be subject.

3. Those rules shall require that the offer document state at least:

(a) the terms of the bid;

(b) the identity of the offeror and, where the offeror is a company, the type, name and registered office of that company;

(c) the securities or class, or classes of securities for which the bid is made;

(d) the consideration offered for each security or class of securities and, in the case of mandatory bids, the basis of the valuation used in determining it, with particulars of the way in which that consideration is to be given;

(e) the maximum and minimum percentages or quantities of securities which the offeror undertakes to acquire;

(f) details of any existing holdings of the offeror, and of persons acting in concert with him, in the offeree company;

(g) all the conditions to which the bid is subject;

(h) the offeror's intentions with regard to the continuation of the business of the offeree company and, so far as affected by the bid, of the offeror company, and with regard to the continued employment of their employees and their management, including any material change in the conditions of employment. This relates in particular to the offeror's strategic planning for those companies and the likely impact on jobs and locations;

(i) the period for acceptance of the bid;

(j) where the consideration offered by the offeror includes securities of any kind, information about those securities;

(k) information on the financing for the bid;

(l) the identity of persons acting in concert with the offeror or with the offeree company, in the case of companies together with their type, name and registered office, and their relationship with the offeror and where possible with the offeree company.

(m) information on which national law will govern the contracts resulting from the bid between the offeror and the holders of securities of the offeree company.

4. Member States shall ensure that rules are in force requiring the parties to a bid to provide the supervisory authorities of their Member State at any time on request with all information in their possession concerning the bid which is necessary for the supervisory authority to discharge its functions.

Article 7

Period for acceptance

1. Member States shall provide that the period for acceptance of the bid to be specified by the offeror in the offer document in accordance with Article 6(3)(i) may not be less than two weeks or more than ten weeks from the date of publication of the offer document. Provided that the general principle referred to in Article 3(1)(f) is respected, Member States may provide that the period of ten weeks may be prolonged on the condition that the offeror gives at least two weeks prior notice of its intention to close the bid.

2. Member States may provide for rules modifying the period mentioned in paragraph 1 in specific appropriate cases. Member States may authorise the supervisory authority to grant derogation from the period mentioned in paragraph 1 in order to allow the offeree company to organise a general meeting to consider the bid.

Article 8

Disclosure

1. Member States shall ensure that rules are in force which require a bid to be made public in such a way as to ensure market transparency and integrity for the securities of the offeree company, of the offeror or of any other company affected by the bid, and which particularly avoid the publication or dissemination of false or misleading information.

2. Member States shall ensure that rules are in force which provide for the disclosure of all information or documents required in such a manner as to ensure that they are both readily and promptly available to the holders of securities at least in those Member States where the securities of the offeree company are admitted to trading on a regulated market and to the representatives of the employees of the offeree company or, where there are no such representatives, to the employees themselves.

Article 9

Obligations of the board of the offeree company

1. Member States shall ensure that rules are in force requiring the following:

(a) during the period set below, the board of the offeree company shall obtain the prior authorisation of the general meeting of the shareholders, given for this purpose, before taking any action which may result in the frustration of the bid, other than seeking alternative bids, and notably before the issuing of shares which may result in a lasting impediment for the offeror obtaining control over the offeree company. Such authorisation is required at all events after the board of the offeree company has received the information referred to in Article 6(1), first sentence, concerning the bid and until the result of the bid is made public or the bid lapses. Member States may provide that such authorisation is required from an earlier time such as when the board of the offeree company becomes aware that the bid is imminent;

(b) as regards decisions taken before the period referred to above and not yet partly or completely implemented, approval or confirmation by the general meeting of the shareholders is required if the decision was outside the normal course of business and its implementation may result in the frustration of the bid;

(c) for the purpose of obtaining prior authorisation of the general meeting of the shareholders as referred to above, Member States may provide for rules allowing a general meeting to be convened at short notice, provided that this meeting is not organised less than two weeks after its notification;

(d) the board of the offeree company shall draw up and make public a document setting out its opinion on the bid, together with the reasons on which it is based, including its views on the effects of implementation on all the interests of the company, including employment, and on the offeror's strategic planning for the offeree company and its likely impact on jobs and locations as set out in the offer document pursuant to Article 6(3)(h). The board of the offeree company shall at the same time communicate this opinion to the representatives of its employees or, where there are no such representatives, to the employees themselves. Where a separate opinion of the employees' representatives on the effects of implementation on employment is made available to the board of the offeree company in sufficient time, it shall be enclosed.

2. Member States may allow the board of the offeree company to increase the share capital during the period for acceptance of the bid on the condition that prior authorisation has been received from the general meeting of shareholders not earlier than 18 months before the beginning of the period of acceptance of the bid, with full recognition of the right of pre-emption of all shareholders as provided for in Article 29(1) of Second Council Directive 77/91/EEC of 13 December 1976 on coordination of safeguards which, for the protection of the interests of members and others, are required by Member States of companies within the meaning of the second paragraph of Article 58 of the Treaty, in

respect of the formation of public limited liability companies and the maintenance and alteration of their capital, with a view to making such safeguards equivalent [8].

Article 10

Rules applicable to the conduct of bids

In addition Member States shall ensure that rules are in force which govern the conduct of bids for at least the following matters:

(a) lapse of the bid;

(b) revision of bids;

(c) competing bids;

(d) disclosure of the result of bids;

(e) irrevocability of the bid and conditions permitted.

Article 11

Contact Committee

1. The Contact Committee set up by Article 20 of Directive 79/279/EEC shall also have as its functions:

(a) to facilitate, without prejudice to the provisions of Articles 226 and 227 of the Treaty, the harmonised application of this Directive through regular meetings dealing with practical problems arising in connection with its application;

(b) to advise the Commission, if necessary, on additions or amendments to this Directive.

2. It shall not be the function of the Contact Committee to appraise the merits of decision taken by the supervisory authorities in individual cases.

Article 12

Sanctions

Each Member State shall determine the sanctions to be applied for infringement of the measures taken pursuant to this Directive. The sanctions shall be sufficient to promote compliance with those measures.

[8] OJ L 26, 30.1.1977, p. 1. Directive as last amended by the 1994 Act of Accession.

Article 13

Revision of Article 4(2)

Three years after the date referred to in Article 15 (1), the European Parliament and the Council, acting on a proposal from the Commission, shall examine and if necessary revise Article 4(2) in the light of the experience acquired in applying Article 4(2).

Article 14

Amendment of Article 1(1) of Directive 88/627/EEC

Article 1(1) of Directive 88/627/EEC shall be replaced by the following:

"1. Member States shall make subject to this Directive natural persons and legal entities in public or private law who acquire or dispose of, directly or through intermediaries, holdings meeting the criteria laid down in Article 4(1) which involve changes in the holdings of voting rights in companies incorporated under their law the shares of which are admitted to trading on one or several regulated markets within the meaning of Article 1(13) of Directive 93/22/EEC.".

Article 15

Transposition of the Directive

1. Member States shall ensure that the laws, regulations, administrative provisions or other arrangements necessary for them to comply with this Directive are in force before *. Member States may however postpone compliance with Article 9 until **. They shall forthwith inform the Commission thereof.

When Member States adopt these measures, they shall contain a reference to this Directive or shall be accompanied by such reference on the occasion of their official publication. The methods of making such reference shall be laid down by the Member States.

2. Member States shall communicate to the Commission the provisions or other arrangements referred to in paragraph 1.

Article 16

Entry into force of the Directive

This Directive shall enter into force on the day of its publication in the Official Journal of the European Communities.

---

* Four years after the entry into force of this Directive.

** Five years after the entry into force of this Directive.

Article 17

Addressees of the Directive

This Directive is addressed to the Member States.

Done at ,

For the European Parliament	For the Council
The President	The President

EUROPEAN UNION

THE EUROPEAN PARLIAMENT **THE COUNCIL**

Brussels, 29 June 2001
(OR. en)

1995/0341 (COD)
C5-0221/2001

PE-CONS 3629/1/01
REV 1 COR 3
(it,nl,en,dk,el,es,pt,fi,sv)

DRS 27
CODEC 493

LEGISLATIVE ACTS AND OTHER INSTRUMENTS: CORRIGENDUM

Subject :	Directive of the European Parliament and of the Council on company law concerning takeover bids

Page 13, Article 4(5)

The following shall be inserted as a first paragraph:

"The supervisory authorities shall have all the powers necessary for the exercise of their functions which shall include the duty to ensure that the parties to the offer comply with the rules laid down pursuant to this Directive.".

Annex 3

REPORT

OF

**THE HIGH LEVEL GROUP
OF COMPANY LAW EXPERTS**

ON

**A MODERN REGULATORY FRAMEWORK
FOR COMPANY LAW
IN EUROPE**

Brussels, 4 November 2002

THE HIGH LEVEL GROUP OF COMPANY LAW EXPERTS

Chairman : Jaap WINTER

José Maria GARRIDO GARCIA

Klaus J. HOPT

Jonathan RICKFORD

Guido ROSSI

Jan SCHANS CHRISTENSEN

Joëlle SIMON

Rapporteur : Dominique THIENPONT
Secretariat : Karel VAN HULLE

TABLE OF CONTENTS

LETTER FROM THE CHAIRMAN

The High Level Group of Company Law Experts was set up by the European Commission in September 2001 to make recommendations on a modern regulatory framework in the EU for company law. In our First Report of January 2002, we dealt with issues related to the Takeover Bids Directive, which was rejected by the European Parliament in July 2001. Our original mandate was further extended in April 2002 by the Commission following the ECOFIN Council meeting in Oviedo to deal specifically with a number of corporate governance issues. Our Final Report is presented here.

A fundamental review of company law in Europe was certainly due. Many agree that EU company law has not kept up with developments which shape its role and application, in particular the creation of a single EU market which companies and their investors wish to use to the optimum, the development of European securities markets and their regulation, the development of modern information and communication technologies which should be facilitated and could be used to improve company law arrangements and the development of corporate governance practices and standards.

Indeed, we believe company law in Europe must catch up with these developments. We hope that our Report will stimulate this process, which will require concerted actions of many in the EU.

On behalf of the Group, I would like to thank Commissioner Frits Bolkestein who has always shown a genuine interest and support for our work. I would also like to thank his staff, in particular Karel Van Hulle, Dominique Thienpont and Erich Eggenhofer, who have been of tremendous support in the practical organisation of the work of the Group and in the production of our two Reports and the Consultative Document.

Within the limited time available, we have conducted an extensive consultation process, including a hearing in Brussels, which has received wide response. We are grateful for the numerous responses and comments we have received and highly appreciate the efforts made by many to respond in detail within a very short time. The responses were often of high quality and have greatly contributed to the shaping of views within the Group.

Many thanks are also due to the team of researchers of the Erasmus University in Rotterdam, led by professor Jan Berend Wezeman, which, again within a short time frame, has analysed and summarised in an extensive report for the Group the more than 2,500 pages of responses and comments made to our Consultative Document. This has proven immensely valuable for the Group in its efforts to analyse and take into account these responses.

Finally, I would like to express my personal thanks to all Members of the Group. We have worked closely together for over a year, with usually a very tight time schedule, and with limited resources and facilities for debate within the Group and with outside interested parties. The expertise each of you has brought to the Group, as well as your willingness and ability to identify and develop sound views that we could agree on, have been excellent. The continuous spirit of co-operation and good personal relations throughout the process have been key to our work. I am grateful for having been able to work with you so closely during the last year. It has been my pleasure and great honour to chair this Group.

Amsterdam, October 2002

Jaap Winter

SUMMARY OF
THE HIGH LEVEL GROUP OF COMPANY LAW EXPERTS' OBSERVATIONS AND RECOMMENDATIONS

CHAPTER I - *"Introduction"*
This document constitutes the High Level Group of Company Law Experts' Final Report, in conformity with the Group's terms of reference which were defined by the European Commission on 4 September 2001 and subsequently extended as a consequence of the Oviedo ECOFIN Council in April 2002.
The Group was set up by the European Commission to provide independent advice, in the first instance on issues related to pan-European rules for takeover bids, and subsequently on key priorities for modernising company law in the EU.
In pursuing its mandate, the Group has published a Consultative Document on the issues specified in the second part of its mandate, but including also general themes which appeared to be of importance for the future development of company law in Europe.
Based on the responses received in this consultation, on the discussions in the hearing held on 13 May 2002 and on its own discussions, the Group now presents its conclusions and recommendations to the Commission and to the public in this Final Report.

CHAPTER II - *"General Themes"*

In the Consultative Document, we raised a number of general themes that we believed followed from the mandate given to the Group "to provide recommendations for a modern regulatory European company law framework designed to be sufficiently flexible and up-to-date to meet companies' needs, taking into account fully the impact of modern technology". The themes and specific questions we raised triggered a range of responses, in which a number of suggestions have been made. Overall, the Group feels that respondents support the approaches taken, which we continue to regard as valid.

The EU approach to company law harmonisation has focused on the protection of members and third parties. Several instruments have been adopted, with a view to establishing an equivalent level of protection throughout the EU. Company law should primarily concentrate on the efficiency and competitiveness of business.

Proper protection of shareholders and creditors is necessary, but not all existing mechanisms are effective. This Report contains some recommendations to simplify current rules.

Particular attention should be given to the elimination of obstacles for cross-border activities. Responses to the consultation confirm the high importance of cross-border issues.

Responses to the consultation also call for a freedom of choice between alternative forms of organisation and structure, as is offered by the European Company Statute.

EU company law, once harmonised through Directives, is not easy to modify, whereas there is a growing need for continuous adaptation. Fixed rules in primary legislation offer both advantages and disadvantages, and we can see a movement in Member States to use alternatives for primary legislation, which include secondary regulation, standard setting and monitoring, and model laws. Responses to the consultation confirmed that directives should be restricted to setting principles and general rules, and that detailed rules should be left to secondary regulation and mechanisms for standard setting. There was more hesitation with respect to model laws, which seem difficult to use in different legal systems, but model documents and formats may be useful and the model approach may foster convergence of national legal forms.

For both primary legislation and any alternatives, proper consultation is indispensable.

Making use of alternative forms of regulation as suggested requires a new permanent structure to be built, which could provide the Commission with independent advice on future regulatory initiatives and be responsible for organising necessary consultations.

Disclosure can be a powerful regulatory tool : it creates an incentive to comply with best practice, and allows members and third parties to take necessary actions. Disclosure requirements can be more efficient, more flexible and easier to enforce. Information and disclosure requirements are at the intersection of company law and securities regulation, and responses to the consultation confirmed that disclosure was particularly suited in the area of corporate governance.

Company law traditionally distinguished between public and private companies, but this is often not fully relevant in practice. In today's reality, the Group sees three basic types of companies : listed companies (whose shares are regularly traded), open companies (whose shares could be regularly traded), and closed companies. The regulatory approach may vary for each type of companies, taking national differences into account.

Company law should provide a flexible framework for competitive business. Using company lax for other regulatory purposes may lead to an undesirable tightening of rules. Responses to the consultation confirmed that the development and use of efficient company law structures should not be hindered by anti-abuse provisions.

Due to its profound impact on our society, modern technology may require various types of changes to company law. As to the form of legal acts and of shares, most Member States have already implemented, or started processes of implementing, new rules. As to time, generally law should not force citizens to act quicker now that modern technology allows speedier actions and decisions. As to the place where the company is located and the function that existing company law mechanisms perform, the impact of modern technology is discussed in various chapters of the present Report. The impact of modern technology on disclosure and filing is an area where the EU could take initiatives, in addition to the recently published Proposal to amend the First Company Law Directive.

Company information is currently filed an disclosed at various places, which creates efficiency problems for both companies and interested parties. The Consultative Document suggested that companies could be required to maintain a specific section on their website, and/or a link with the register. Responses to the consultation were mixed.

Easy and cheap access to core information stored in public registers and filing systems should be ensured on a cross-border basis.

On the basis of these observations, the Group makes the following recommendations.

Subject	Recommendation
Item II.1 Facilitating efficient and competitive business in Europe	Recommendation II.1. (see p. 29) An important focus of the EU policy in the field of company law should be to develop and implement company law mechanisms that enhance the efficiency and competitiveness of business across Europe. Where mechanisms established so far to protect shareholders and creditors appear to be inappropriate impediments, they should be replaced by ones that are at least as – and preferably more – effective, and less cumbersome. In the future, the EU should concentrate primarily on the creation of the facilities necessary to operate and restructure across borders. Where various alternative systems exist in Member States for elements of the company's organisation and structure, the EU should as much as possible facilitate freedom of choice for companies across Europe.
Item II.2 Modern Company Law making	Recommendation II.2. (see p. 31) The EU should consider a broader use of alternatives to primary legislation (secondary regulation, standard setting and monitoring, model laws). The Group recommends that wide and expert consultation should be an integral part of any future initiative taken at EU level in the area of company law. There is a case for setting up a permanent structure which could provide the Commission with independent advice on future regulatory initiatives. The Commission, with the support of Member States, should investigate how best to set up such a structure.
Item II.3 Disclosure of information as a regulatory tool	Recommendation II.3. (see p. 33) The EU, in considering new – and amending existing – regulation of company law, should carefully consider whether disclosure requirements are better suited to achieve the desired effects than substantive rules. Any disclosure requirement should be based on the obligation to provide fair, relevant and meaningful information.

Item II.4 Distinguishing types of companies	Recommendation II.4. (see p. 34) The regulatory approach should be different for the three types of companies identified by the Group. Listed companies should be subjected to a certain level of uniform and compulsory detailed rules, whereas closed companies should benefit from a much higher degree of autonomy. The balance may be somewhere in between for open companies.
Item II.5 Increased flexibility vs. tightening of rules	Recommendation II.5. (see p. 36) The objective of combating fraud and abuse of companies should be achieved through specific law enforcement instruments outside company law, and should not be allowed to hinder the development and use of efficient company law structures and systems.
Item II.6 Modern technology	Recommendation II.6. (see p. 36) Listed companies should be required to maintain and continuously update a company information section on their websites, and maintain links with public registers and other relevant authorities. Other types of companies could be allowed to fulfil their filing and disclosure obligations by including such information on their websites, if appropriate links with public registers are established. Existing private initiatives to link the various registries that now contain formal company information should be encouraged by the EU. With respect to listed companies, the EU should at the minimum actively support Member States in their efforts to create national central electronic filing systems, and ensure that national systems are properly linked.

CHAPTER III - *"Corporate Governance"*
The original mandate of the Group included a review of whether and, if so, how the EU should actively co-ordinate and strengthen the efforts undertaken by and within Member States to improve corporate governance in Europe. In that light, we raised four general issues in our Consultative Document, together with general issues relating to the processes of shareholders information, communication and decision-taking. In reaction to the Enron case, the Commission and the ECOFIN have agreed to extend the mandate of the Group to review a number of specific issues related to corporate governance and auditing. In this Chapter, we address the original and newly added issues, under five themes, and we focus primarily on the internal corporate governance elements. Before, we stress that corporate governance is a system, having its foundations partly in company law and partly in wider laws and practices and market structures.
Disclosure has a pivotal role in company law, as we said in Chapter II and as we already underlined in our First Report. The high importance of disclosure for corporate governance was confirmed by responses to the consultation, at least as far as listed companies are concerned. Information should be given by listed companies on at least the key corporate governance items listed in the present Report.
Being the residual claimholders, shareholders are ideally placed to act as a watchdog. This is particularly important in listed companies, where minority's apathy may have harmful effects. Shareholders' influence will highly depend on the costs and difficulties faced. Shareholders' influence was traditionally exercised through the general meeting, which is no longer physically attended by many. Modern technology can be very helpful here, if it is introduced in a balanced way. In order to facilitate the move towards an integrated European capital market, equivalent facilities should be offered across the EU. Facilities developed for shareholders in listed companies are likely to benefit to other companies too.
Pre-meeting communication is frequently a one-way process. The biggest difficulties and costs arise with bearer shares, but registered shares also present some problems. Modern technology may offer a solution to many problems. Putting meeting materials and proxy forms on the company's website is efficient for both the company and its shareholders. Many responses to the consultation supported the enabling approach, but the Group believes that we should anticipate future normal practice. Mandatory bulletin boards and chat rooms are not recommended, because of the risks of abuse which require further review of many issues. Not all shareholders have access to electronic facilities, so that they should not be compelled at EU level to use them.
The rights to ask questions and table resolutions are often difficult to exercise, but responses to the consultation did not call for mandatory provisions at EU level in this area. In practice, the exercise of these important rights may be facilitated by modern technology, but companies should be able to take measures to keep the whole process manageable. The necessary flexibility for companies should be provided for at national level, but annual disclosure of how these rights can be exercised should be required at EU level. The right to table resolutions is linked to the squeeze-out right, and thresholds should be set consistently.
In view of the difficulties to attend meetings, shareholders should be able to vote in absentia. The necessary facilities should be offered, but not imposed, to shareholders, to the extent that cross-border holding problems have been solved.

Some companies offer participation to general meeting via electronic means, which increase shareholders' influence in an efficient way. Use of electronic means in meetings should be possible for companies, but not yet mandatory.
In cross-border situations, shares are typically held through chains of intermediaries, which make it difficult to identify the person entitled to vote. Cross-border voting is often almost impossible in practice, and the integration of financial markets calls for an urgent solution. A separate Cross-Border Voting Group has issued its own Report in September 2002, and proposed as primary rule that the right to determine how to vote should be recognised to ultimate accountholders, who should be granted all the voting options available in the company's Member State. The issues identified by this Group should be urgently addressed at EU level, in the interests of both European and non European shareholders.
Institutional shareholders have large shareholdings with voting rights, and tend to use them more frequently than before. Responses to the consultation were mixed about a possible formalisation of the institutional investors' role. The Group believes that good governance of institutional investors requires disclosure to their beneficiaries of their investment and voting policies, and a right of their beneficiaries to the voting records showing how voting rights have been exercised in a particular case. Responses to the consultation did not support an obligation to vote, and the Group agrees that there are no convincing reasons for imposing such an obligation.
In many cases, shareholders are inclined not to vote, due to a lack of influence and/or a lack of information. The special investigation procedure offered in several Member States is an important deterrent. A EU rule on special investigation right was supported by responses to the consultation. It should be open to the general meeting or a significant minority, and any authorisation by the court or administrative body should be based on serious suspicion of improper behaviour.
Many difficulties prevent dispersed shareholders from directly monitoring management, which calls for an active role of non-executive or supervisory directors. No particular form of board structure (one-tier/two-tier) is intrinsically superior : each may be the most efficient in particular circumstances.
The presence of (a group of) controlling shareholder(s) is likely to result in closer monitoring of management, but non-executive or supervisory directors then have an important role on behalf of the minority. Their general oversight role is of particular significance in three areas, where conflicts of interests may arise : nomination of directors, remuneration of directors, and audit of the accounting for the company's performance. The need for more independent monitoring is highlighted by the US regulatory response to recent scandals. The Group does not express views on the composition of the full (supervisory) board, but intends to promote the role of non-executive / supervisory directors. Nomination, remuneration and audit committees could be set up, and composed of a majority of independent directors. To qualify as independent, a non-executive or supervisory director, apart from his directorship, must have no further relationship, with the company, from which he derives material value. Certain other relationships with the company, its executive directors or controlling shareholders may also impair independence. Related parties and family relationships should also been taken into account. With respect to the competence expected from non-executive or supervisory directors, existing rules are generally abstract. Competence must be assessed together with the role a director has on the board. Basic financial understanding is always required, but other skills may be of relevance. Competence should be properly explained to shareholders, and they should be able to assess whether sufficient time is available for the director to fulfil his role.

Remuneration of directors is one of key area of conflict of interests. In order to align the interests of executive directors with the interests of the shareholders, remuneration is often linked to the share price, but this potentially has a series of negative effects. The Group considers that there is no need for a prohibition of remuneration in shares and share options, but that appropriate rules should be in place.
Recent corporate scandals and responses highlight the key importance of trust in financial statements. At national level, the board traditionally has a collective responsibility for the probity of financial statements, which avoids undue excessive individual influence. Collective responsibility must cover all statements on the company's financial position, except for ad hoc disclosure (where proper delegation must be organised), and also all statements on key non-financial data.
The introduction of a framework rule on wrongful trading was opposed by some respondents who argued that this is a matter of insolvency law. The Group rejects this view : the responsibility of directors when the company becomes insolvent has its most important effect prior to insolvency and is a key element of an appropriate corporate governance system. Various existing national rules make directors liable for not reacting when they ought to foresee the company's insolvency. The details of these national rules vary considerably, but they generally apply to group companies and do not interfere with on-going business decisions. The majority of responses to the consultation supported the introduction of a EU rule on wrongful trading. Without overly restricting management's decisions, such a rule would enhance creditors' confidence and introduce an equivalent level of protection across the EU.
Misleading disclosure by directors should be properly sanctioned, and applicable sanctions should be defined by Member States. Criminal and civil sanctions present some weaknesses, and the disqualification of a person from serving as a director of companies across the EU is an alternative sanction which may be easier to effectuate and has a powerful deterrent and longer disabling effect.
A proper audit is fundamental to good corporate governance. Some initiatives have already been taken by the Commission, among which the Recommendation on Auditor Independence. A new Communication on Audit is expected soon. In the present Report, the Group has focused on the internal aspects of auditing practices. As explained above, the Group believes that there is a key role to play for non-executive or supervisory directors who are in the majority independent. The main missions of the audit committee, which in practice is often set up for these purposes, are summarised in the present Report with respect to both the relationship between the executive managers and the external auditor, and the internal aspects of the audit function.
In the Consultative Document, the Group expressed reservations about the establishment of a EU corporate governance code : the adoption of such a code would not achieve full information for investors, and it would not contribute significantly to the improvement of corporate governance in Europe. A clear majority of responses to the Consultative Document rejected the creation of a European corporate governance code. However, the Group believes that there is an active role for the EU to play in corporate governance, apart from the various initiatives we suggested above. The EU should indeed co-ordinate the efforts of Member States to facilitate convergence, including with respect to enforcement, on a continuous basis and taking account of US developments.

On the basis of these observations, the Group makes the following recommendations.

Subject	Recommendation
Item III.1 **Annual Corporate Governance Statement**	Recommendation III.1. (see p. 45) Listed companies should be required to include in their annual report and accounts a coherent and descriptive statement covering the key elements of the corporate governance rules and practices they apply. This statement should also be separately posted on the company's website. The principles applicable to such an annual corporate governance statement should be set up in a framework Directive. The detailed rules should be set up by Member States in view of their national company laws, but the EU should ensure a certain level of co-ordination. Such a statement should contain a reference to the designated national code of corporate governance and/or company law rules with which the company complies or in relation to which it explains deviations. Responsibility for the annual corporate governance statement should lie with the board as a whole.
Item III.2 **Notice an pre-meeting communication – Use of websites**	Recommendation III.2. (see p. 49) Listed companies should be required to maintain a specific section on their website where they publish all information relevant for their shareholders, as recommended in Chapter II. This section should include all relevant materials relating to shareholders meetings, and should offer facilities for giving proxies or voting instructions on-line or for downloading and electronic transmission of proxy or instruction forms. Member States should however be able to require listed companies to provide hard copies of meeting materials and voting forms to shareholders who specifically request them.
Item III.3 **Notice and pre-meeting communication – Rights to ask questions and to submit proposals for resolution**	Recommendation III.3. (see p. 51) Listed companies should explicitly disclose to their shareholders how they can ask questions, how and to what extent the company intends to answer questions, and how and under what conditions they can submit proposals to the shareholders meeting. This should be an element of their mandatory annual corporate governance statement. With respect to the right to submit proposals for resolution by the shareholders meeting, there is a link with the squeeze-out right of a majority shareholder and sell-out right of minority shareholders. Member States should be required to set the applicable thresholds in a consistent way.
Item III.4 **Voting in absentia – Electronic facilities**	Recommendation III.4. (see p. 52) Listed companies should be required to offer all shareholders facilities to vote in absentia – by way of direct vote or proxies – by electronic means, and through hard copy voting instruction or proxy forms at their request. The Group recommends that such a requirement should not apply to cross border situations to the extent that any necessary solutions have not yet been found and implemented for the problems of cross-border holding of securities in Europe.
Item III.5 **General meetings – Participation via electronic means**	Recommendation III.5. (see p. 52) Listed companies should be permitted, but not required, to allow absentee shareholders to participate in general meetings via electronic means (such as internet or satellite). The permission to abandon the physical meeting should be a Member State decision, but such a decision should in any event be taken by – or with the consent of – the general meeting of shareholders with an appropriate strong qualified majority.

Item III.6 **Cross-border voting**	Recommendation III.6. (see p. 53) A separate Group of Experts set up in January 2002 by the Dutch Minister of Justice issued its Final Report on cross-border voting in September 2002. In that Report, it is recommended that the rights and obligations of accountholders and securities intermediaries be regulated at EU level, to ensure that accountholders across the EU can effectively exercise the voting rights on shares they hold. The issues identified by that Cross-Border Voting Group, combined with the relevant recommendations of the Group, should be considered by the Commission as a matter of priority, with a view to building a regulatory framework that facilitates the participation of shareholders across the EU and, where possible, outside the EU, in the governance of listed companies.
Item III.7 **Responsibilities of institutional investors**	Recommendation III.7. (see p. 56) Regulation of the relevant types of institutional investors by Member States should include an obligation on those institutional investors to disclose their investment policy and their policy with respect to the exercise of voting rights in companies in which they invest, and to disclose to their beneficial holders at their request how these rights have been used in a particular case.
Item III.8 **Minority shareholders' special investigation right**	Recommendation III.8. (see p. 61) Shareholders, in a general meeting or holding a maximum of at least 5 or 10 per cent of the share capital, should be given the right to apply to a court or appropriate administrative body to order a special investigation. A European framework rule should be adopted to this end, whereby this special investigation right should be guaranteed in all companies and as far as possible on a group-wide basis. Details of the procedure and determination of proper sanctions should be left to Member States.
Item III.9 **Board structures**	Recommendation III.9. (see p. 59) At least listed and other open companies across the EU should have the choice between the two types of board structure (one-tier / two-tier), so as to be able to elect the system which best suits their particular corporate governance needs and circumstances.
Item III.10 **Role of (independent) non-executive and supervisory directors**	Recommendation III.10. (see p. 60) Listed companies should be required to ensure that the nomination and remuneration of directors and the audit of the accounting for the company's performance within the board are decided upon by exclusively non-executive or supervisory directors who are in the majority independent. The Commission should rapidly issue a Recommendation to Member States that they should have effective rules in their company laws or in their national corporate governance codes to this end, which should be enforced on a "comply or explain" basis at the minimum. The Recommendation should include principles on independence, and could include a list of relationships which would lead a non-executive or supervisory director to be considered as not independent. Listed companies should be required to disclose in their annual corporate governance statement which of their directors they consider to be independent and on what grounds. Similar disclosure should be made when a new director is proposed for appointment. Listed companies should include in their annual corporate governance statement a profile of the board's composition, and should explain why individual non-executive or supervisory directors are qualified to serve on the board in their particular roles. Similar disclosure should be made in proposals for initial appointment. Listed companies should also be required to disclose what board positions in other companies their non-executive or supervisory directors hold.

Item III.11 Remuneration of directors	Recommendation III.11. (see p. 64) The remuneration policy for directors generally should be disclosed in the financial statements of the company, and should be an explicit item for debate on the agenda of the annual meeting. The individual remuneration of directors of the company, both executive and non-executive or supervisory directors, is to be disclosed in detail in the financial statements of the company. Schemes granting shares and share options and other forms of remuneration of directors linked to the share price should require the prior approval of the shareholders meeting, on the basis of a proper explanation by the remuneration committee of the applicable rules and of their likely costs. The costs of all share incentive schemes should be properly reflected in the annual accounts, and this accounting principle should be recognised in a European framework rule. The Commission should adopt a Recommendation defining an appropriate regulatory regime for directors' remuneration in listed companies, which should include the four elements outlined above.
Item III.12 Management responsibility for (financial) statements	Recommendation III.12. (see p. 67) Responsibility for the probity of financial statements should be attributed, as a matter of EU law, to all board members on a collective basis. This responsibility should extend to all statements made about the company's financial position, as well as to all statements on key non-financial data (including the annual corporate governance statement).
Item III.13 Wrongful trading rule	Recommendation III.13. (see p. 68) A rule on wrongful trading should be introduced at EU level, which would hold company directors (including shadow directors) accountable for letting the company continue to do business when it should be foreseen that it will not be able to pay its debts.
Item III.14 Sanctions – Director's disqualification	Recommendation III.14. (see p. 69) Appropriate sanctions for misleading financial and other key non-financial statements should generally be determined by Member States. The Commission should nevertheless review whether director's disqualification can be imposed at EU level as a sanction, at least for misleading financial and key non-financial disclosures or more generally for misconduct.
Item III.15 Audit committees	Recommendation III.15. (see p. 70) The responsibility for supervision of the audit of the company's financial statements should lie with a committee of non-executive or supervisory directors who are at least in the majority independent. Provisions on the role and responsibilities of audit committees (or any equivalent body), with respect to both the external and internal aspects of audit, should be included in the proposed Recommendation on the role of non-executive and supervisory directors.
Item III.16 Corporate governance codes – Co-ordination	Recommendation III.16. (see p. 72) The key input for codes of corporate governance should continue to come from the markets and their participants. Each Member State should designate one particular corporate governance code as the code with which companies subject to their jurisdiction have to comply or by reference to which they have to explain how and why their practices are different. A structure should be set up at EU level to facilitate the co-ordination of Member States efforts to improve corporate governance. Co-ordination should not only extend to the making of codes, but also to the procedures Member States have in place to monitor and enforce compliance and disclosure. Member States should be required to participate in the co-ordination process, but the results should be non-binding.

CHAPTER IV - *"Capital Formation and Maintenance"*

The concept of legal capital is seen as one of the cornerstones of European Company Law : its main function is seen to be creditor and shareholder protection. Many responses to the consultation stressed that legal capital is not in practice effective in attaining its objectives.

The European legal capital regime is generally not considered a competitive disadvantage for European companies, but it is no competitive advantage either. Legal capital is criticised for failing to protect creditors : it is a poor indication of the company's ability to pay its debts. The current regime is arguably inflexible and costly. Finally, annual accounts have become an inadequate yardstick for making decisions on distributions and for assessing the company's ability to pay its debts.

Most respondents agree that there is room for improvement of the current regime, although there is controversy on which is the best possible course to reform the present system.

In the Consultative Document, three alternative approaches were considered :
- a first approach based on the SLIM proposals, supplemented by further recommendations ("SLIM-Plus");
- a second approach inspired by the US experience, which would lead to a radical departure from the concept of legal capital, from many rules on capital formation and maintenance, and from the current balance of powers between shareholders and board of directors;
- a third approach based on the elimination of the concept of legal capital, but with retention of shareholders control.

Very few respondents expressed support for the second approach. A substantial number of respondents preferred the first and third approaches, with some of the respondents opting for one of them, but without excluding the other.

Any modernisation of the current capital formation and maintenance regime has to be selective : it should remove, where possible, the defects perceived in it, while maintaining its virtues. The SLIM Group made a number of suggestions for changing the Second Directive, which we discussed together with some other questions.

In considering the modernisation of the current regime ("SLIM-Plus"), the Group noted that :

a) the minimum capital requirement serves only one function, but it is not seen as a significant hurdle to business activity;

b) the introduction of no par value shares is widely demanded;

c) valuations of non-cash contributions by independent experts are expensive and do not offer a total guarantee of the assets' real value; responses to the consultation welcomed the possibility of allowing the provision of services as contribution in kind, with appropriate safeguards;

d) there is a case for simplifying the conditions under which listed companies can restrict or withdraw pre-emption rights when they issue new shares;

e) there is a case for applying the current regime - for creditor protection in the case of capital reduction - in all restructuring transactions; and for re-evaluating the need for such a protection when the capital is reduced to adjust to losses;

f) acquisition of own shares, and taking them as security, should be possible within the limits of the distributable reserves;

g) a majority of respondents believe that the prohibition of financial assistance should be relaxed;

h) the squeeze-out and sell-out rights should be introduced generally (and not only after a takeover bid);

i) the effectiveness of the legal capital regime could be improved by the introduction of rules on wrongful trading, and on subordination of insiders' claims.

Responses to the consultation supported the development of an alternative regime for creditor protection within a framework of shareholder control.
In considering such an alternative regime, the Group noted that : a) legal capital offers little protection for creditors against unconsidered distribution of assets, and no protection when the capital is reduced to account for, or write off, losses; creditors – and shareholders – can be better protected if an adequate solvency test is developed; b) the protection of shareholders can be substantially improved without the concept of legal capital.
On the basis of these observations, the Group makes the following recommendations.

Subject	Recommendation
Item IV.1 **Improvement of the current legal capital regime – Two step approach :** **1. SLIM-Plus** **2. Alternative regime**	Recommendation IV.1. (see p. 79) The Group agrees with most of the respondents to the consultation that there is room for improvement of the current legal capital regime, and proposes a two step approach. The Commission should, as a matter of priority, present a proposal for reform of the Second Company Law Directive, along the lines suggested by the SLIM Group, with the modifications and supplementary measures that are suggested in the present Report ("SLIM-plus"). Any modernisation of the current regime should remove, where possible, the defects perceived in it, while maintaining its virtues. The Commission should, at a later stage, conduct a review into the feasibility of an alternative regime, based on the third approach presented in the Consultative Document. The alternative regime need not replace the capital formation and maintenance rules of the Directive as amended according to the "SLIM-plus" proposals. Rather, the new regime could be offered as an alternative option *for Member States*, who should be able to freely decide to change to the new regime and impose it on companies subject to their jurisdiction or to retain the Second Directive rules as modified by the "SLIM-plus" reform. The alternative regime should at least be as effective in achieving the objectives of creditor and shareholder protection as the regime based on legal capital.
Item IV.2 **SLIM-Plus –** **Minimum capital**	Recommendation IV.2. (see p. 82) It is probably wise not to spend much time on minimum capital in a reform to make the current system more efficient, and to direct attention to issues which are more relevant. The minimum capital requirement should not be removed, nor increased.
Item IV.3 **SLIM-Plus –** **No par value shares**	Recommendation IV.3. (see p. 82) The Second Company Law Directive already allows for shares to have a fractional value (also referred to as "accountable par") rather than a nominal value (see for example Article 8 providing that shares cannot be issued below their nominal or fractional value). Such shares would have to include the appropriate fraction or the total number of shares, together with the date in which the fraction or the total number of shares was correct, and a reminder that the correct fraction can be obtained at any time from the company itself, or from the companies Register. It is debatable whether introducing shares without any reference to either nominal or fractional value would constitute a significant change in the system of the Second Company Law Directive. We recommend that, as part of SLIM-Plus, it is reviewed how no par value shares can be accommodated within the Second Company Law Directive.

Item IV.4 **SLIM-Plus – Contributions in kind**	Recommendation IV.4. (see p. 83) With respect to contributions in kind, the requirement for an expert valuation should be eliminated in certain cases where clear and reliable points of reference for valuation already exist (market price, recent evaluation, recent audited accounts). In addition, the Commission should review the possibility of allowing, with appropriate safeguards, the provision of services as contribution in kind.
Item IV.5 **SLIM-Plus – Pre-emption rights**	Recommendation IV.5. (see p. 84) As the SLIM Group has suggested, for listed companies it would be appropriate to allow the general meeting to empower the board to restrict or withdraw pre-emption rights without having to comply with the formalities imposed by Article 29 §4 of the Second Directive, but only where the issue price is at the market price of the securities immediately before the issue or where a small discount to that market price is applied. If real no par value shares are to be introduced, the suppression of pre-emption rights needs to be reconsidered as pre-emption rights may then be the only effective protection left at EU level for shareholders against dilution.
Item IV.6 **SLIM-Plus – Capital reduction**	Recommendation IV.6. (see p. 84) The current regime for creditor protection (right to apply to a court to obtain security for their claims) in the case of capital reduction should be applied in all restructuring transactions. The burden of proof should be on the creditors. In addition, there is a case for re-evaluating whether some safeguards are needed for creditors in the event of capital reduction to adjust legal capital to losses.
Item IV.7 **SLIM-Plus – Acquisition of own shares**	Recommendation IV.7. (see p. 84) Acquisition of own shares should be allowed within the limits of the distributable reserves, and not of an entirely arbitrary percentage of legal capital like the 10% limit of the current Directive. The same should apply to the taking of own shares as security. It should be possible to establish flexible requirements at least for unlisted companies.
Item IV.8 **SLIM-Plus – Financial assistance**	Recommendation IV.8. (see p. 85) Financial assistance should be allowed to the extent of the distributable reserves. A shareholders' resolution should in principle be required. The shareholders meeting should be allowed to authorise the board for a maximum period of time (e.g. five years) to engage the company in financial assistance within the limits of the distributable reserves. If this facility is to be allowed, there should be disclosure.
Item IV.9 **SLIM-Plus – Compulsory withdrawal of shares**	Recommendation IV.9. (see p. 85) The SLIM Group has recommended that a compulsory withdrawal of shares should be possible when a shareholder has acquired 90% of the capital, as an exception to the provision of Article 36 of the Directive that compulsory withdrawal is only possible if this is provided in the deed of incorporation or articles of association. The recommendations made in Chapter VI of this Report on squeeze-out and sell-out rights - for listed and open companies - would effectively deal with the issue addressed by the SLIM Group.
Item IV.10 **SLIM-Plus – Wrongful trading and subordination of insiders' claims**	Recommendation IV.10. (see p. 86) The responsibility of directors when the company becomes insolvent has its most important effect prior to insolvency and this is a key element of an appropriate corporate governance regime. We recommend that as an element of good corporate governance, a European framework rule should be introduced on wrongful trading, combined with the concept of "shadow" directors. The concept of subordination of insiders' claims could be considered as part of the development of an alternative regime for creditor protection (see below).

Item IV.11 **Alternative regime –** **Solvency test**	Recommendation IV.11. (see p. 87) In the alternative regime to be considered at a later stage, a proper solvency test should be required for any payment of dividend or other distribution. The solvency test should be based at least on two tests to be performed before making the distribution : a balance sheet test and a liquidity test. Further study is required in order to develop these two tests, as well as the valuation methods to be used. The study should also consider requiring a certain solvency margin and reviewing the relevance of the going concern concept. Directors of the company should issue a solvency certificate, in which they explicitly confirm that the proposed distribution meets the solvency test. Directors are responsible for the correctness of the solvency certificate and Member States should impose proper sanctions, which could be extended to "shadow" directors.
Item IV.12 **Alternative regime –** **Pre-emption rights**	Recommendation IV.12. (see p. 89) In the alternative regime to be considered at a later stage, exclusion or limitation of pre-emption rights should only be possible on the basis of an explicit shareholders' resolution, which is based on objective criteria.
Item IV.13 **Alternative regime –** **Issue of new shares**	Recommendation IV.13. (see p. 89) In the alternative regime to be considered at a later stage, a company should not be able to issue shares at a price that bears no relation to the real value of the existing shares. The alternative regime should provide that shares must be issued at fair value, which would substantially improve the protection of shareholders as compared to the current legal capital regime. When elaborating the effects of this principle, the case could be considered for making a distinction between listed and unlisted companies.
Item IV.14 **Alternative regime –** **Contributions in kind**	Recommendation IV.14. (see p. 89) In the alternative regime to be considered at a later stage, the issue of contributions in kind should be properly addressed. One possibility would be to require a shareholders resolution for any share issue for which a contribution in kind is made (subject to the exceptions already adopted in the Second Directive for such valuations). The directors could be required to certify the appropriateness of the issue in exchange for the contribution in view of the fair value of the shares. There would need to be appropriate protection for minorities.

CHAPTER V - *"Groups and Pyramids"*

Groups of companies today are frequent in most, if not all, Member States. Responses to the consultation supported the view that groups are a legitimate way of doing business, but recognised at the same time that there is a need for protection of some interests. The Group believes that the existence of risks does challenge neither the legitimacy of groups nor the limited liability principle. The Group takes the view that the enactment of an autonomous body of law, specifically dealing with groups, is not recommended at EU level, but that particular problems should be addressed in three areas.

Responses to the consultation have revealed that transparency is felt as the most important area of intervention with regard to groups. The consultation has confirmed that the actual provisions of the Seventh Company Law Directive do not sufficiently address these concerns, and respondents have suggested a number of areas where specific information should be provided.

The Group takes the view that increased disclosure with regard to a group's structure and relations is needed, and indicates areas where mandatory disclosure would be appropriate.

Some Member States do not recognise the interest of the group as such. The acknowledgement of the legitimacy of groups should actually lead to the recognition of the special position created by the membership of a group. In several Member States, a transaction made for the benefit of the group is legitimate, if the prejudice suffered by a particular company is justified by other advantages.

When groups become insolvent, the separate treatment of individual group companies' bankruptcies causes both procedural and substantive problems. In some Member States, a consolidated approach to group bankruptcies is possible under certain circumstances.

A pyramid is a chain of holding companies, with the ultimate control based on a small total investment. Pyramids extensively use minority shareholders, often through a series of separate stock exchange listings. Pyramids are a source of agency costs, and a number of problems stem from their lack of transparency.

Pyramids are difficult to regulate with specific rules, but the disclosure recommendations made in Chapter III are very relevant for dealing with pyramid structures. Pyramidal groups that include listed companies raise particular concerns, which should be properly addressed.

On the basis of these observations, the Group makes the following recommendations.

Subject	Recommendation
Item V.1 **Ninth Company Law Directive**	Recommendation V.1. (see p. 94) No new attempt to enact the Ninth Company Law Directive on group relations should be undertaken, but particular problems should be addressed through modifying existing provisions of corporate law in the following three areas.

Item V.2 **Transparency of group structure and relations**	Recommendation V.2. (see p. 95) Increased disclosure with regard to a group's structure and relations is needed, and the parent company of each group is to be made responsible for disclosing coherent and accurate information. The Commission should review the Seventh Company Law Directive's provisions in the light of the need for better financial disclosure, and consider whether improvements can be made consistent with International Accounting Standards. With respect to non financial disclosure, it should be ensured that – especially where listed companies are involved – a clear picture of the group's governance structure, including cross-holdings and material shareholders' agreements, is given to the market and the public. In addition, companies could be required to provide specific information when they enter into or exit from a group.
Item V.3 **Tensions between the interests of the group and its parts**	Recommendation V.3. (see p. 96) Member States should be required to provide for a framework rule for groups that allows those concerned with the management of a group company to adopt and implement a co-ordinated group policy, provided that the interest of the company's creditors are effectively protected and that there is a fair balance of burdens and advantages over time for the company's shareholders. The Commission should review the possibilities to introduce in Member States rules on procedural and substantive consolidations of bankruptcies of group companies.
Item V.4 **Pyramids**	Recommendation V.4. (see p. 98) The EU should require national authorities, responsible for the admission to trading on regulated markets, not to admit holding companies whose sole or main assets are their shareholding in another listed company, unless the economic value of such admission is clearly demonstrated. Finally, operators of stock indices should properly take into account the free float in determining the weight of each company.

CHAPTER VI - "*Corporate Restructuring and Mobility*"
Under this heading, the Group raised primarily five major topics in its Consultative Document : - change of corporate seat, or domicile; - the position of the acquiring company in a domestic merger under the Third Company Law Directive; - the acquisition of a wholly owned subsidiary by the same means; - creditor protection in restructuring transactions; - squeeze-outs and sell-outs.
The need for Community company law provisions facilitating cross frontier restructuring figured as a high priority in almost all the responses to the Document, and there were calls for the Commission urgently to bring forward revised proposals for a Tenth and a Fourteenth Company Law Directives.
Where a company moves its real seat but not its registered office between two states which attach no importance to that move ("incorporation doctrine states"), neither the sates concerned directly in the change nor third states have any interest in inhibiting the move.
There was almost unanimous agreement that for a Member State to adopt a version of the "real seat doctrine" which automatically denies recognition to a company which has its real seat in a country other than that of its incorporation was a disproportionate measure which can never be justified. Most respondents agreed that, in the case of a transfer of the real seat into a "real seat doctrine" state, there was a case for permitting the law of incorporation to be overridden to the extent necessary to respect requirements of the host state. The Group agrees with this view, but believes that any sanction inhibiting the freedom of movement should be subject to general EU principles, and it illustrates how they can be applied to various company law measures (capital maintenance; disclosure transparency and security of transactions; governance and company structure; employee participation).
A transfer of the real seat out of a state of origin may be regarded as a means of escaping the law of origin, but any sanctions imposed by that state should be subject to the same general principles. In addition, where the new host state seeks to impose its own law, a conflict of law may arise.
Third states are unlikely to be concerned in cases of moving real seat between a home and a host state, but a general rule should be developed with respect to the identification of the applicable law where necessary.
The Consultative Document noted that some provisions (e.g. special general meeting) of the Third Directive on domestic mergers serve no purpose for the acquiring company, given the nature and the effect of the transaction at issue, and therefore suggested that for domestic mergers such requirements should be removed at EU level and that for international mergers the Member State of the acquired company should be bound to accept the relaxation adopted by the Member State of the acquiring company. Similar considerations apply to the position of an acquiring company under the Sixth Directive. The great majority of responses agreed with these suggestions.
The case for relaxations of special requirements is even clearer for the acquisition by merger of a wholly owned subsidiary by its parent, and this was supported by almost all responses.

There is a wide diversity of practice in Member States in relation to creditor protection in restructuring transactions, while the policy considerations are the same and seem adequately met by the Second Directive provision on reduction of capital.	
Responses to the consultation showed widespread support for the introduction of a squeeze-out and a sell-out rights, which would not be limited to the acquisition of a majority by way of a takeover bid.	
On the basis of these observations, the Group makes the following recommendations.	
Subject	**Recommendation**
Item VI.1 Tenth and Fourteenth Company Law Directives	Recommendation VI.1. (see p. 101) There is a perceived need for Community action in the legislative field with regard to corporate restructuring and mobility, especially in the cross-border context. The Commission should urgently bring forward revised proposals for a Tenth Company Law Directive on Cross-Frontier Mergers and a Fourteenth Company Law Directive on Transfer of the Registered Office. Proposals in preparation are faced with the task of solving difficulties relating to board structure and employee participation. The solutions to these problems in the ECS may present a possible model for these issues.
Item VI.2 Transfer of real seat between Incorporation Doctrine States	Recommendation VI.2. (see p. 102) Where a company moves its real seat between two "incorporation doctrine states", there should be no room at Member State level or at EU level for attaching any sanctions to such a move which would be a wholly unnecessary interference with freedom of movement and operation of companies across the Community. This is likely to be found to be the effect of the Treaty. However, existing and proposed EU legislation should be aligned with this view.
Item VI.3 Transfer of real seat into Real Seat Doctrine State	Recommendation VI.3. (see p. 103) Where a company transfers its real seat to a real seat state, the law of the "host" state should be permitted to override the law of incorporation of the "guest" company, but only within the limits imposed by the principles of legitimate general interest, proportionality, minimum intervention, non-discrimination and transparency. External requirements of the "host" state, duly imposed on foreign companies with a view to these principles, should make any interference with internal governance of these companies redundant. This is especially true for the areas of capital maintenance, governance and company structure and employee participation. With regard to the latter, it is imperative that restructuring through liquidation and re-incorporation be only the ultimate step : any such remedy should allow the company and its organs sufficient time and opportunity to respond to the domestic requirements.
Item VI.4 Transfer of real seat out of Real Seat Doctrine State	Recommendation VI.4. (see p. 106) Where a company transfers its real seat out of a real seat state, any sanctions imposed by the "home" state should be subject to the above mentioned principles as well, and any conflict of law then still prevailing ought to be solved by reciprocity.
Item VI.5 Transfer of real seat – Position of Third States	Recommendation VI.5. (see p. 106) Third states, if concerned at all by a company's move of real seat, should be made to apply, in principle, the law of incorporation, with a renvoi to the law of the host state where appropriate.

Item VI.6 Third Directive Mergers – Position of the acquiring company	Recommendation VI.6. (see p. 107) With respect to domestic mergers, Member States should be allowed to relax special requirements of the Third Directive which are faced by the acquiring company. In order to facilitate international mergers, Member States of the acquired company should be required to accept such relaxation where it was adopted by the Member State of the acquiring company.
Item VI.7 Third Directive Mergers – Acquisition of wholly owned subsidiary	Recommendation VI.7. (see p. 108) Similar considerations apply to the acquisition by merger of a wholly owned subsidiary by its parent company. Consequently, relaxation of special requirements in domestic mergers should be permitted to the Member State of the acquiring company, and acceptance in international mergers of such relaxation, should be required from the Member State of the acquired company.
Item VI.8 Creditor protection in restructuring transactions	Recommendation VI.8. (see p. 109) A harmonised provision on creditor protection should be adopted at EU level to facilitate restructuring within the Community based on the Second Company Law Directive provision enabling a creditor to apply to the court where he can show that the company has not provided reasonable measures of protection.
Item VI.9 Squeeze-outs and sell-outs	Recommendation VI.9. (see p. 109) Member States should be required to create squeeze-out and sell-out rights at a level to be set at a 90% as a minimum and 95% as a maximum majority on a class by class basis, for listed and open companies. Before applying a similar regime to closed companies, further study into the relationship with contractual exit arrangements, etc. is required.

CHAPTER VII - *"The European Private Company"*
The Societas Europaea (SE) has been adopted in October 2001. The SE allows companies to merge and transfer their seat, across borders, and to do business as a "European company". But SEs may not meet all the expectations of the business community, in particular SMEs. A European form of private company is promoted by a private initiative, to facilitate SMEs business in Europe, in particular through joint ventures.
This private initiative resulted in a proposal for a European Private Company (EPC). The proposal has been supported by UNICE and Eurochambers, as well as by the European Economic and Social Committee. The proposal is based on contractual freedom, and is presented as an adequate vehicle for SMEs active in different Member States. On the other hand, it is argued by opponents that an EPC statute would be of little use if national companies were allowed to merge and transfer their seats across borders. Opponents also argue that the specific needs of SMEs could be met by a modernisation of national forms of private companies, in which process the proposal for a European Private Company could be used as a model for regulation at national level.
Responses to the consultation stressed that there are strong reasons to promote a European form dedicated to SMEs : a specific EU form should not be reserved to large companies, a flexible structure for joint ventures is necessary, the costs linked to the creation and operation of subsidiaries in other Member States would be greatly reduced, and the "European label" may be useful. Respondents generally did not perceive the adoption of a model law as an adequate answer to the needs expressed by SMEs.
Any proposal regulating the EPC will have to address the information, consultation and participation rights of employees. Opinions differ on how these issues should be regulated. Conclusions on these issues have been reached by the European Economic and Social Committee, and the Group has not considered these issues in further detail.
The SE can be set up in one of four ways; the requirements imposed on the formation of SEs are not sufficiently flexible for SMEs.
Contrary to the SE Statute, which often refers to national law, the EPC has been drafted as a genuine European company, not subject to national company laws, in order to facilitate its international use. In such a situation, the European Court of Justice would have an important role to play : some are concerned about the difficulties which might arise, whereas others are more confident. The majority of respondents, and the Group, find that a reference to national private law is unavoidable, since existing company laws in Member States are embedded in national bodies of private law.

On the basis of these observations, the Group makes the following recommendations.

Subject	Recommendation
Item VII.1 European Private Company – Need for an EPC statute	Recommendation VII.1. (see p. 113) The desire to have an EPC statute to serve the needs of SMEs in Europe has been clearly and repeatedly expressed. However, the first priority should be to adopt the Tenth Directive on cross-border mergers, which is expected to meet one of the purposes of the EPC statute. The Group recommends that, before deciding to submit a formal proposal, the Commission carries out a feasibility study in order to assess the additional practical need for – and problems related to – the introduction of an EPC statute.
Item VII.2 European Private Company – Incorporation	Recommendation VII.2. (see p. 116) When considering the introduction of an EPC statute, the requirements imposed on the formation of an EPC should be sufficiently flexible to facilitate proper development of such new form. The EPC should be open to individuals, and not only companies, and the founders should not be required to come from several Member States. A minimum requirement would however be that the EPC is undertaking activities in more than one Member State.
Item VII.3 European Private Company – Reference to national law	Recommendation VII.3. (see p. 117) When considering the introduction of an EPC statute, a proper connection with the law of the jurisdiction of incorporation is to be established, since many concepts of private law are also applicable in company law.

CHAPTER VIII - *"Co-operatives and Other Forms of Enterprises"*

The European Council recently adopted a general orientation on the Regulation on the Societas Cooperativa Europaea (SCE). The approach for the SCE has been to take advantage of the substantial work developed in the harmonisation of company law at EU level, and the Regulation therefore includes a high number of references to provisions in existing Company Law Directives.

In the Consultative Document, we asked questions on the need for and the usefulness of proposals for Regulations creating the European Association and the European Mutual Society. The questions elicited few answers, but a majority of the responses received express positive views on these proposals. In addition, respondents generally felt that the EU should not seek to harmonise the underlying rules for associations and mutual societies.

The Group fails to see how uniform regulations of the European Association and European Mutual Society could be achieved if there is no agreement on harmonisation of the underlying national rules. On the other hand, the Group acknowledges that the progress made on the SCE regulation represents an important precedent for the other proposed Regulations.

In the Consultative Document, we raised similar questions on the need for and feasibility of a regulation for the European Foundation. The Group notes that the differences in national regulation by Member States seem to be here even more profound.

There is a concern that alternative forms of enterprises are used in the governance of listed companies to avoid application of transparency requirements on controlling shareholders.

There is also a concern that other legal forms sometimes operate substantial businesses in competition with companies, without being subject to similar disclosure and general corporate governance standards, which may lead to unfair competition.

The Consultation Document sought views on the usefulness of an EU definition of the concept of enterprise. Respondents showed a clear opposition to such a European rule.

A substantial percentage of respondents agree that the lack of information on basic data of some of these alternative forms of enterprise causes problems, in particular when contracting across borders in the EU, and that it would be appropriate to introduce basic disclosure requirements for certain economic actors. A substantial harmonisation program is however rejected.

On the basis of these observations, the Group makes the following recommendations.

Subject	Recommendation
Item VIII.1 European Association / European Mutual Society	Recommendation VIII.1. (see p. 120) A European form of Association and a European form of Mutual Society are not regarded by the Group as priorities for the short and medium term. The impact of the forthcoming SCE Regulation on the co-operative enterprise should be studied closely before putting further efforts into creating these other European forms.
Item VIII.2 European Foundation	Recommendation VIII.2. (see p. 122) The Group reached the same conclusions about the need for and feasibility of a Regulation on the European Foundation, which might be even more difficult to achieve.

Item VIII.3 Alternative forms of enterprises – Model laws	Recommendation VIII.3. (see p. 122) The development of European legal forms for alternative forms of enterprises could benefit from a different regulatory approach : proponents of these European legal forms could consider themselves developing model laws for them. The EU could consider facilitating this work, which would contribute to basic convergence.
Item VIII.4 Alternative forms of enterprises – Disclosure	Recommendation VIII.4. (see p. 122) When alternative forms of enterprise are controlling shareholders, disclosure requirements, in particular relating to governance structures, should be extended to them. When these alternative forms operate substantial businesses, fair competition may require extension to them of disclosure and corporate governance standards.
Item VIII.5 General rules for enterprises – European definition	Recommendation VIII.5. (see p. 123) With respect to the usefulness of a European definition of the concept of enterprise, the Group recognises the difficulty of finding such a definition and therefore suggests that, if there is to be an EU initiative aimed at regulating entities regardless of their form, a list-based approach should be taken, in which every Member State lists the entities which would be subject to such a legislative instrument.
Item VIII.6 General rules for enterprises – Registration	Recommendation VIII.6. (see p. 123) In order to ensure access to basic information on alternative forms of enterprises, a framework Directive could require the registration of, at least, all limited liability entities with legal personality that engage in economic activities. Such a Directive should take advantage of technological developments, and linking of registries across the EU should be established.

CHAPTER IX - *"Priorities for Action"*

In this Report, we make a number of specific recommendations relating to various elements of the regulatory framework for company law in Europe.

If our recommendations are to be followed up, this will result in a substantial number of company law initiatives to be taken. Not all of this can be achieved simultaneously, and priorities will have to be set. The Group discussed possible priorities, and presents them in this Report.

The Group believes that much is to be gained from the setting up of a permanent structure to provide the Commission with independent advice on future regulatory initiatives in the area of EU company law.

The EU agenda for company law reform will be full the coming years, and it will require efforts of many. But the Group is confident that the results of these efforts will make them worthwhile.

On the basis of these observations, the Group makes the following recommendations.

Subject	Recommendation
Item IX.1 **Company Law Action Plan**	Recommendation IX.1. (see p. 125) The Commission should prepare a Company Law Action Plan which sets the EU agenda, with priorities, for regulatory initiatives in the area of company law and agree such an action plan with the Council and the European Parliament.
Item IX.2 **Permanent advisory structure**	Recommendation IX.2. (see p. 127) The setting up of a permanent structure to provide the Commission with independent advice on future regulatory initiatives in the area of EU company law should be duly considered.

CHAPTER I

INTRODUCTION

The Group's final report is based on Commission mandate

This document constitutes the High Level Group of Company Law Experts' Final Report, in conformity with the Group's terms of reference which were defined by the European Commission on 4 September 2001 and subsequently extended as a consequence of the Oviedo ECOFIN Council in April 2002.[1]

Second part of the mandate is related to modern company law

The Group was set up by the European Commission to provide independent advice in the first instance on issues related to pan-European rules for takeover bids and subsequently on key priorities for modernising company law in the EU.

Key priorities listed in second part of the mandate

According to the Group's mandate, these key priorities are :

- the creation and functioning of companies and groups of companies, co-operatives and mutual enterprises, including Corporate Governance;
- shareholders' rights, including cross-border voting and virtual general meetings;
- corporate restructuring and mobility (for instance, the transfer of the corporate seat);
- the possible need for new legal forms (for instance, a European Private Company, which would be of particular relevance for SMEs);
- the possible simplification of corporate rules in light of the SLIM-report on the Second Company Law Directive of 13 December 1976 on the formation and capital maintenance of public limited liability companies.

The Group published a comprehensive Consultative Document

In pursuing its mandate, the Group has published a Consultative Document on the issues specified in the second part of its mandate, but including also general themes which appeared to be of importance for the future development of company law in Europe.

Which covered both :

Thus, the Consultative Document eventually concentrated on the following topics:

[1] A copy of the Group's terms of reference is provided for in Annex 1.

a) General themes:

General Themes

- Facilitating efficient and competitive business in Europe
- Modern company law making
- Disclosure of information as a regulatory tool
- Distinguishing types of companies
- Increased flexibility vs. tightening of rules
- Modern technology

b) Specific topics:

And specific topics

- Corporate Governance
- Shareholder information, communication and decision-making
- Alternatives to capital formation and maintenance rules
- The functioning of groups of companies
- Corporate restructuring and mobility
- The European Private Company
- Co-operatives and other forms of enterprise

This Report presents the conclusions and recommendations of the Group

Based on the responses received in this consultation[2], on the discussions in the hearing held on 13 May 2002 and on its own discussions, the Group now presents its conclusions and recommendations to the Commission and to the public in this Final Report[3].

[2] A summary of the main comments received by the Group is included in Annex 3.
[3] The Group's working methods are further described in Annex 2.

CHAPTER II

GENERAL THEMES

In the Consultative Document, we raised a number of general themes that we believed followed from the mandate given to the Group "to provide recommendations for a modern regulatory European company law framework designed to be sufficiently flexible and up-to-date to meet companies' needs, taking into account fully the impact of modern technology". The themes and specific questions we raised triggered a range of responses, in which a number of suggestions have been made. Overall, the Group feels that respondents support the approaches taken, which we continue to regard as valid.

Consultative Document raised several general themes

Responses show overall support for the Group's approaches

1. FACILITATING EFFICIENT AND COMPETITIVE BUSINESS IN EUROPE

In the Consultative Document, we said that we believed that our mandate denotes a distinct shift in the approach the EU could take to company law. Until now, this approach has been mainly to co-ordinate the safeguards which, for the protection of the interests of members and others, are required by Member States of companies and firms with a view to making such safeguards equivalent throughout the Union (Art. 44 (2) (g) EC Treaty). Nine Company Law Directives have resulted so far[4]. "Meeting companies' needs" has not been a prominent feature of this harmonisation exercise. The exercise has been much more driven by establishing a proper level of protection - throughout the Union - for those who are involved in and affected by the affairs of the company, in particular shareholders and creditors, with a view to preventing a "race to the bottom" by Member States. Whether this effect actually has occurred or would have occurred in the absence of harmonisation is unclear, and some would argue that in some areas we have actually seen a "race to the top".

The EU approach to company law harmonisation has focused on the protection of members and third parties

Several instruments have been adopted, with a view to establishing an equivalent level of protection throughout the EU

In doing so, we may have lost sight of what the Group believes to be the primary purpose of company law : to provide a legal framework for those who wish to undertake business activities efficiently, in a way they consider to be best suited to attain success. Company law should first of all facilitate the running of efficient and competitive business enterprises. This is not to ignore that protection of shareholders and creditors is an integral part of any company law. But going forward the Group believes that an important focus of the

Company law should primarily concentrate on the efficiency and competitiveness of business

This should be an important focus of

[4] First, Second, Third, Fourth, Sixth, Seventh, Eighth, Eleventh and Twelfth Company Law Directives : for full citations, see Annex 4.

EU policy in the field of company law should be to develop and implement company law mechanisms that enhance the efficiency and competitiveness of business across Europe. Part of the focus should be to eliminate obstacles for cross-border activities of business in Europe. The European single market is more and more becoming a reality and business will have to become competitive in this wider arena. In order to do so, it will have to be able to efficiently restructure and move across borders, adapt its capital structures to changing needs and attract investors from many Member States and other countries.

company law policy at EU level

Particular attention should be given to the elimination of obstacles for cross-border activities

Proper mechanisms for the protection of shareholders and creditors add to the efficiency of company law regulation, as they reduce the risks and costs involved for those who participate in and do business with companies. But the effectiveness of the mechanisms to protect shareholders and creditors that have been established so far, for example in the area of capital maintenance and corporate restructuring, is questionable, and some of them appear to be real impediments to efficient financing and restructuring of business in Europe. Where possible, these mechanisms should be replaced by ones that are at least as - and preferably more - effective, and less cumbersome. In this respect, Chapter IV on capital formation and maintenance contains a number of recommendations to simplify the current rules of the Second Company Law Directive in order to make them less cumbersome, but also proposes a more in depth examination of an apparently more effective and less complex alternative approach. In Chapter VI on restructuring, we make a specific recommendation on the regime for creditor protection for legal mergers and other restructuring transactions where similar issues arise.

Proper protection of shareholders and creditors is necessary

But not all existing mechanisms are effective

This Report contains some recommendations to simplify current rules

There was general support for these views in the consultation. Many respondents commented that the EU should not so much continue with its efforts to harmonise the substance of company law, but should first of all create the facilities to operate and restructure across borders. This clearly comes out as an important priority for the EU.

Responses to the consultation confirm the high importance of cross-border issues

Some respondents have put forward another important approach to future development of company law in Europe which the Group fully supports. Where various alternative systems exist in Member States for elements of the company's organisation and structure, the EU should as much as possible facilitate freedom of choice between these alternative systems for companies across Europe , rather than trying to agree upon one specific EU system or leaving the option to Member States. The European Company Statute offers an example, in imposing an obligation on Member States to ensure that those who wish to establish an SE can choose between a unitary board structure

Responses also call for a freedom of choice between alternative forms of organisation and structure

Choice is offered by the European Company Statute

and a two-tier board structure. We believe that at least all listed and open companies in Europe should have such a choice, not just the SE, as we set out in the Chapter on corporate governance.

And should be extended to at least listed and open companies

2. MODERN COMPANY LAW MAKING

We noted in our Consultative Document that the system of harmonising company law through Directives - that have to be implemented by Member States - may have led to a certain 'petrifaction'. Once Member States have agreed to a certain approach in an area of company law and have implemented a Directive accordingly, it becomes very difficult to change the Directive and the underlying approach. Simultaneously however, there is a growing need to continuously adapt existing rules in view of rapidly changing circumstances and views. The "shelf life" of law tends to become more limited as society is changing more rapidly, and company law is no exception. Fixed rules in primary legislation may offer the benefits of certainty, democratic legitimacy and usually strong possibilities of enforcement. But this comes at the cost of little or no flexibility, and disability to keep pace with changing circumstances. EU Directives are in practice even more inflexible than primary legislation

EU company law, once harmonised through Directives, is not easy to modify

Whereas there is a growing need for continuous adaptation

Fixed rules in primary legislation offer both advantages and disadvantages

We can see a movement in Member States to use alternatives for primary legislation by government and parliament, which allow for greater flexibility. Such alternatives include:

Alternatives used by Member States include :

- Secondary regulation by the government, based on primary legislation in which broad objectives and principles are laid down; the secondary regulation can be amended more quickly when circumstances require change. (This process also often enables more effective consultation and reflection of an expert consensus.)

Secondary regulation

- Standard setting by market participants, or in partnership between government and market participants, through which best practices can be developed, adapted and applied; monitoring and reliance on market response and general governance powers on the basis of a "comply or explain" rule can often replace formal legal enforcement in company or securities law.

Standard setting, and monitoring

- Model laws, which can be used voluntarily and varied where the circumstances warrant this, e.g. where different types of companies are concerned (see also Section 3 below). A high level of uniformity in company law has been achieved by a process of "natural selection" on the basis of model laws in the United States of America, offering the benefits of more responsive adaptability and scope for variation.

Model laws

The efforts of the EU in the area of company law have so far been

The EU should

limited to primary legislation through Directives normally to be implemented in formal company law in the Member States. The Group believes the Union should consider a broader use of these alternatives to primary legislation when going forward. In many areas, company law in Member States can be modernised without agreeing on specific detailed rules in Directives. The Lamfalussy process has been set up in order to be able to promote the development of integrated financial markets in Europe by primary legislation of concepts and principles in Directives, secondary implementation legislation, and finally co-ordination between the securities regulators with respect to interpretation and enforcement. This is an example of an effort to introduce more flexible law making in an area closely related to, and to some extent overlapping with, company law.

consider a broader use of these alternatives

In many areas, Directives do not have to contain detailed rules

The Lamfalussy process is to be seen as an example

Many respondents commented that where primary regulation through a Directive would still be necessary, the Directive should be restricted to setting principles and general rules, leaving the detailed rules to secondary regulation. Where recourse is made to secondary regulation, democratic legitimacy must be ensured. Respondents agreed with us that secondary regulation and mechanisms for standard setting or co-ordination of standard setting would be most suitable in such areas as corporate governance and the operation of the general meeting of shareholders, in order to encourage the development of best practice.

Responses to the consultation :

Principles-based Directives, and

Encouragement of best practice

There was more hesitation with respect to the use of model laws. Respondents commented that due to the considerable differences in legal technique and substantive law, the development of model laws which could be applicable throughout Europe, although conceptually interesting, would be difficult. Some respondents did see room for a co-ordinated effort to produce model documents in certain areas, such as model (electronic) proxy forms for voting by shareholders in absentia. Model documents and formats may be particularly helpful where modern technology is needed and helpful to allow efficient co-ordination of transactions – e.g. voting of shares across different legal and business structures. The Group in addition believes that, where the EU would consider the introduction of new legal forms, the model approach may offer an alternative through which an informal and organic convergence of the national regulations of such legal forms may be achieved (see Chapter VIII below on the development of other European legal forms).

Model laws seem difficult to use in different legal systems

But model documents and formats may be useful

And the model approach may foster convergence of national legal forms

For all alternative forms of regulation that may be introduced, but also for any new primary company law legislation at EU level, it is important to ensure that full and proper consultation takes place with industry, commerce, services, professions and other interested

For both primary legislation and any alternatives, proper consultation is

parties. Ensuring proper procedures for wide consultation is one of the key elements of the Lamfalussy procedure for securities regulation. Where the aim is to make company law rules that facilitate efficient and competitive business in Europe, consultation with all parties involved in business is indispensable. The Group recommends that wide consultation be an integral part of any future legislative initiative taken at EU level in the area of company law.

indispensable

This should apply to any future EU initiative

Making use of alternative forms of regulation as suggested requires a new structure to be built. The first area where this is required is corporate governance. In Chapter III on corporate governance, the Group specifically recommends the Commission to issue Recommendations to Member States on aspects of the functioning of the shareholders meeting and the role of non-executive and supervisory directors, and the EU to actively co-ordinate the corporate governance efforts of Member States.

Alternative forms of regulation require a new structure

To use first in the area of corporate governance

In addition, the Group believes there is a case for setting up a more permanent structure which could provide the Commission with independent advice on future regulatory initiatives in the area of EU company law. Such advice should as much as possible be evidence based. Consultation with industry, commerce, services, professions and other interested parties is an important method of gathering evidence. The structure to be set up could be made responsible for organising such consultation.

A permanent structure is to provide independent advice

Based on proper consultation

We believe a structure in whatever form or shape performing these roles would be helpful for the future development of a modern and effective company law in the EU and recommend that the Commission investigate how such a structure can best be set up.

Commission should investigate how to set up such a structure

3. DISCLOSURE OF INFORMATION AS A REGULATORY TOOL

Requiring disclosure of information can be a powerful regulatory tool in company law. It enhances the accountability for and the transparency of the company's governance and its affairs. The mere fact that for example governance structures or particular actions or facts have to be disclosed, and therefore will have to be explained, creates an incentive to renounce structures outside what is considered to be best practice and to avoid actions that are in breach of fiduciary duties or regulatory requirements or could be criticised as being outside best practice. For those who participate in companies or do business with companies, information is a necessary element in order to be able to assess their position and respond to changes which are relevant to them. High quality, relevant information is an

Disclosure can be a powerful regulatory tool

It creates an incentive to comply with best practice

And allows members and

indispensable adjunct to the effective exercise of governance powers. It is for these reasons that the Group has, for example, recommended that capital and control structures of listed companies should be disclosed comprehensively and that such disclosure should be updated continuously[5].

third parties to take necessary actions

Information and disclosure is an area where company law and securities regulation come together. It is a key objective of securities regulation in general to ensure that market participants have sufficient information in order to participate in the market on an informed basis. Where the relevant security is a share in a company, the information required from a securities regulation point of view overlaps with the information to be provided from a company law perspective.

Information and disclosure requirements are at the intersection of company law and securities regulation

Disclosure requirements can sometimes provide a more efficient regulatory tool than substantive regulation through more or less detailed rules. Such disclosure creates a lighter regulatory environment and allows for greater flexibility and adaptability. Although the regulatory effect may in theory be more indirect and remote than with substantive rules, in practice enforcement of disclosure requirements as such is normally easier. The Group believes that the EU, in considering new - and amending existing - regulation of company law, should carefully consider whether disclosure requirements are better suited to achieve the desired effects than substantive rules. Overload of information should however be avoided.

Disclosure requirements can be more efficient, more flexible and easier to enforce

They should be considered before adoption of substantive rules

Many respondents agreed with this approach and almost all respondents took the view that disclosure was particularly suited as a regulatory tool in the area of corporate governance. In the Chapter on corporate governance, we make a number of specific recommendations on disclosure requirements. Some respondents rightly noted that increased emphasis on disclosure should not lead to simple box ticking exercises or automatic application of recommendations in order to be seen to be doing the right thing. Disclosure requirements should require companies to provide a fair, relevant and meaningful description of their arrangements in a form designed to bring this about.

Responses to the consultation :

Disclosure is particularly suited for corporate governance

If based on a fair and meaningful description

4. DISTINGUISHING TYPES OF COMPANIES

Company law in Member States usually distinguishes between two types of companies : the public company and the private or "closed" company. The existing Company Law Directives in most instances

Company Law traditionally distinguishes

[5] See the Report on Issues Related to Takeover Bids, p. 25-26; see also the new Proposal for a 13th Company Law Directive, in particular its Article 10.

also use this distinction to determine the scope of the Directives. However, the distinction between public and private companies in practice is often highly artificial. In some Member States, the regulation of the private company is merely a copy of the regulation of the public company with little real distinction. At the same time, in some Member States, a vast number of public companies in fact have a closed character, with a limited number of shareholders and restrictions on the transferability of shares.

between public and private companies

But this is often not fully relevant in practice

In today's reality, we see three basic types of companies:

Three basic types:

- **Listed companies,** which we define as those companies with registered office in one of the EU Member States whose shares are admitted to trading on a regulated market. For company law purposes, this group should also include companies whose shares are regularly traded outside regulated markets. Where we refer to listed companies in this Report, we refer to this broader category of companies. Listed companies are not only subject to company law but also to securities regulation (laws, secondary regulation, supervision, stock exchange regulation), which to some extent overlaps with company law. They tend to have dispersed ownership, or at least dispersed minority shareholders, and the markets on which their shares are traded provide an external disciplinary mechanism.

Listed companies (whose shares are regularly traded)

- **"Open" companies,** whose shares are not admitted to trading on a regulated market or otherwise regularly traded, but whose internal structures would allow for listing, free transferability of shares and dispersed ownership outside a securities market.

Open companies (whose shares could be regularly traded)

- **"Closed" companies,** whose shares are not freely transferable and which therefore cannot be admitted to listing on a stock exchange, and in the case of which dispersed ownership outside a securities market is inconceivable.

Closed companies

There may be good reasons why the regulatory approach in company law for these three types of companies should be different. For listed companies, a certain level of uniform, compulsory, substantive rules may be required to sufficiently protect both shareholders (investors) and creditors. On the other hand, disclosure requirements and market forces may provide powerful alternative disciplinary instruments. Respondents to the Consultative Document agreed that, for genuinely closed companies, generally speaking there should be a wider scope for the parties autonomously to determine the structure of the company and the rights, responsibilities and obligations of those participating in it. The balance of the regulatory approach for open companies may have to be somewhere between that for listed companies and that for closed companies, or it may be argued that the potential for open companies to tap the markets justifies regulating them as if they were listed in some or all cases. When

The regulatory approach may vary for each type of companies :

Detailed rules for listed companies

Broad autonomy for closed companies

Balanced approach for open companies

Taking national differences into

considering EU legislation, the different development of types of companies in Member States needs to be taken into account.

account

5. **INCREASED FLEXIBILITY VS TIGHTENING OF RULES**

If we consider that, in company law regulation, it is important to provide for a framework for competitive business, this calls for flexible rules and forms of rulemaking, for light regulatory regimes where possible, scope for party autonomy and for less cumbersome and burdensome procedures.

Company law should provide a flexible framework for competitive business

However, there is a tendency to use the traditional field of company law to achieve all sorts of other regulatory purposes, for example to combat tax fraud. Lately there is an, understandable, urge to suppress commercial and financial activities by terrorists and other criminals who use companies for these activities. This development leads to quite the opposite of company law as a framework for competitive business : more compulsory rules, heavier monitoring and enforcement regimes and slower, more cumbersome and burdensome procedures for all.

Using company law for other regulatory purposes may lead to an undesirable tightening of rules

As it does not follow that we should limit the right of all to acquire and use a mobile telephone because criminals use mobile telephones too, we should be very careful with burdening company law with detailed and cumbersome rules because some criminals make use of companies as well as the honest. The vast majority of respondents agreed with the Group that the objective of combating fraud and abuse of companies as accepted legal forms should be achieved through specific law enforcement instruments outside company law, and should not be allowed to hinder the development and use of efficient company law structures and systems.

Responses to the consultation :

The development and use of efficient company law structures should not be hindered by anti-abuse provisions

6. **MODERN TECHNOLOGY**

Modern information and communication technology has a profound impact on our society. Law should adapt to this in that, on the one hand, it should ensure that legal norms and values are also applied in a digital or virtual environment, and, on the other hand, it should facilitate exploitation of the new possibilities which modern technology offers. In the area of company law, basic concepts and goals may not necessarily change as a result of modern technology. It may , however, offer new and more efficient means to achieve these concepts and goals.

Due to its profound impact on our society, modern technology requires various types of changes to (company) law

In company law, modern technology can have an impact in various areas:

In company law, modern technology can have an impact in various areas

- The **form** of legal acts in company law, of shares, and of disclosure and filing of company information.
- The **time** within which information has to be produced and disclosed, actions have to be taken, etc.
- The **place** where the company is located through the concept of the corporate seat, in order to establish jurisdiction over the company, both in terms of applicable law and competent courts.
- The **function** that existing company law mechanisms perform. This may be particularly relevant in the area of financial reporting and the relationship with capital maintenance requirements and the process of ensuring information to, communication with and decision-making by shareholders.

As to **form**, most Member States have already implemented or started processes of implementing new rules which facilitate the use of electronic means to replace the paper form of legal acts in company law and to dematerialise shares. There does not seem to be a need for the EU to take specific steps in the company law area, besides the more general initiatives it has already taken (e.g. the E-commerce Directive).

As to form, no need for specific company law actions at EU level

As to **time**, the Group believes the EU should not take initiatives to shorten periods specified in the company laws of Member States. Generally, law should not force citizens to act quicker now that modern technology allows speedier actions and decisions. Law may even wish to protect citizens against overhasty actions and decisions that are prompted by faster communication methods. In any event, this does not seem to be an area of priority.

As to time, no justification for shortening the periods currently foreseen in company law

As to **place,** the impact of modern technology on the concept of the corporate seat is discussed in Chapter VI. As to **function,** the consequences of modern technology for the rules on the information of, communication with and decision-making by shareholders are discussed in Chapter III.

As to place and function, the impact of technology is discussed in various Chapters

The impact of modern technology on disclosure and filing is an area where the EU could take initiatives. This is the scope of the First Company Law Directive, on the basis of which companies are required to file certain documents and other information relating to the company in a register which is accessible to the public. A proposal to amend the First Directive in order to facilitate electronic filing and to ensure electronic access to such registers has recently been

Initiatives could be taken in the area of disclosure and filing, in addition to the Proposal to amend the First Company Law

published[6]. There are two additional areas where modern technology can offer benefits: the company's website and access to company information across borders.

Directive

6.1. The company's website

Information which companies, in particular those with stock exchange listings, have to file and disclose is currently scattered over various places: commercial or trade registers, notifications in newspapers, filings with stock exchanges and with securities regulators. Some, but not all, of the information thus filed and disclosed is accessible to the public, but normally at significant cost and with considerable effort. Efficiency, both for the company concerned and for those seeking information about the company, could be enhanced tremendously if the company were to put the information it is required to file and disclose on its own website.

Company information is filed and disclosed at various places, which creates efficiency problems for both companies and interested parties

The company could be required to maintain a specific section on its website, containing all legal and other information it is required to file and disclose, and to continuously update this information. The website is easily accessible to the public at low cost. Regulation would be required to ensure the quality of the content and the display of information in such a section on the website, and to provide that third parties relying on such information would be protected, as foreseen in the First Company Law Directive. The company could also be required to maintain two-way links with public registers that contain the relevant types of information.

The Consultative Document suggested that companies could be required to maintain a specific section on their website, and/or a link with the register

The responses to these proposals were mixed : some were in favour, others believed this should, at least at this stage, be a matter for companies to decide and not for the EU or national legislator. However, we believe that one should take into account that it will take a few years at the minimum for any legislation following our recommendations to be implemented and applied in Member States. By then, the use of a website by listed companies for formal information and disclosure purposes can be expected to have become a widely recognised best practice. The case for pressing ahead now with a co-ordinated approach is very strong.

Responses to the consultation were mixed

The Group believes that use of websites will be normal practice in a few years

In the light also of other EU legislative initiatives like the proposed Market Abuse Directive, the proposed Prospectus Directive and the forthcoming Directive on Ongoing and Periodic Transparency Requirements for Listed Companies, we believe that listed companies

Listed companies should be required to maintain a company

[6] Proposal for a Directive amending the First Company Law Directive, COM (2002) 279: for full citation, see Annex 4.

in Europe should be required to maintain and continuously update a company information section on their websites where the information they are required to file and disclose under company law and securities regulations is posted. If appropriate links are maintained from websites of public registers and other authorities where filings have to be made to the company's website, posting information on the company's website and notification thereof to the relevant public registers and authorities should be sufficient for meeting the filing requirements.

information section on their website, together with the appropriate links

The possibility should also be considered of at least allowing other types of companies to fulfil their filing and disclosure obligations under company law by including such information on their websites, if appropriate links from public registers are established[7].

The same system could be allowed to other types of companies

6.2. Access to company information across borders

In addition to companies' websites, public registries and filing systems remain important for investors, creditors and others dealing with companies, as central depositories where all relevant company information can be found. Modern technology enables easy and cheap access to core information stored in such public registries and filing systems relating to companies across the EU. Access to such information is essential in the light of the increasing international nature of business activities in Europe. An integrated system in which core company information is easily accessible across Europe should include the following elements -

Easy and cheap access to core information stored in public registers and filing systems should be ensured on a cross-border basis

a) Linking companies registries

There are private initiatives to link the various registries that now contain formal company information, like the European Business Register which companies registries join in order to exchange information (www.ebr.org) and crXML, a project to develop a document exchange standard for data in respect of enterprises (www.crxml.org/crxml). The EU could consider co-ordinating and supporting these initiatives, and where necessary facilitating them.

Private initiatives aiming at linking companies registries could be encouraged by the EU

[7] The Group already suggested in its First Report on Issues related to Takeover Bids that it should be encouraged that companies use their websites as an efficient and effective medium for providing information on the companies' capital and control structures (p. 25 of the Report). The company's website can also play an important role in the information of, communication with and decision-making by shareholders (see Chapter III).

b) National central electronic filing system

In the United States of America and in Australia, central electronic filing systems are operated by securities regulators, in which all information to be filed by companies listed on stock exchanges is filed electronically and to which the public has electronic access (the EDGAR-system in the USA and the EDGE- and *e*Register-systems in Australia). These systems offer the benefit that relevant information of all stock exchange listed companies is stored and easily accessible in one specific electronic register. This may improve on the function that publication in the national gazette traditionally has: to provide for a central and chronological access to company information. Such a system could be filled and updated efficiently by links to the websites of listed companies on which they post and update their relevant information.

Central electronic filing systems are operated in USA and Australia

They offer an easy access to information on listed companies

Links with companies' websites could be established

Although the responses to our Consultative Document were generally in favour of this suggestion, doubts were expressed as to its feasibility in the short term. The Group does believe that such central filing systems will be desirable as central repositories of all relevant information relating to listed companies. In the light of the strengthening of disclosure requirements for listed companies which results from our recommendations, but also from other EU legislative initiatives like the Market Abuse Directive, the Prospectus Directive and the forthcoming Directive on Ongoing and Periodic Transparency Requirements for Listed Companies, we also believe such central electronic filing systems in Europe will become inevitable and their creation is just a matter of time. There is a strong case for their development on a co-ordinated basis.

Such central filing systems are not only desirable

They will sooner or later become inevitable

The EU should at the minimum actively support Member States and co-ordinate their efforts in creating such central electronic filing system for listed companies, and should ensure that such systems are properly linked. It should then consider at what stage it is appropriate to require Member States to have such a central electronic filing system.

Such systems should be supported

And possibly required

c) European central electronic filing system

Out of the system of national central electronic filing systems for listed companies which are properly linked, in the future a European central electronic filing system can evolve. Such a system would benefit a truly integrated financial market in Europe. We agree however with the majority of responses to our Consultative Document that it does not seem to be worthwhile for the EU to actively try to set up such a

A European central system would benefit the markets

But the creation and linking of

system now, as the markets, their participants and the systems they apply may be too different. The creation of national central electronic filing systems and links between them is a necessary and desirable first step. *national central systems should be a priority*

To summarise, an important focus of the EU policy in the field of company law should be to develop and implement company law mechanisms that enhance the efficiency and competitiveness of business across Europe. ***Summary*** *: Focus on efficiency and competitiveness*

Where mechanisms established so far to protect shareholders and creditors appear to be inappropriate impediments, they should be replaced by ones that are at least as – and preferably more – effective, and less cumbersome. *Inappropriate mechanisms to be replaced*

In the future, the EU should concentrate primarily on the creation of the facilities necessary to operate and restructure across borders. *Importance of cross-border issues*

Where various alternative systems exist in Member States for elements of the company's organisation and structure, the EU should as much as possible facilitate freedom of choice for companies across Europe. *Organisation and structure : choice*

The EU should consider a broader use of alternatives to primary legislation (secondary regulation, standard setting and monitoring, model laws). *Alternatives to primary legislation*

The Group recommends that wide and expert consultation should be an integral part of any future initiative taken at EU level in the area of company law. *Consultation is key*

There is a case for setting up a permanent structure which could provide the Commission with independent advice on future regulatory initiatives. The Commission, with the support of Member States, should investigate how best to set up such a structure. *Permanent structure to be set up*

The EU, in considering new – and amending existing – regulation of company law, should carefully consider whether disclosure requirements are better suited to achieve the desired effects than substantive rules. *Disclosure requirements to be favoured*

Any disclosure requirement should be based on the obligation to provide fair, relevant and meaningful information. *Fair description*

The regulatory approach should be different for the three types of companies identified by the Group. *Three types of companies*

Listed companies should be subjected to a certain level of uniform and compulsory detailed rules, whereas closed companies should *Different regulatory approaches* benefit from a much higher degree of autonomy. The balance may be somewhere in between for open companies.

Company law not suited to fight against crime

The objective of combating fraud and abuse of companies should be achieved through specific law enforcement instruments outside company law, and should not be allowed to hinder the development and use of efficient company law structures and systems.

Mandatory use of website for listed companies

Listed companies should be required to maintain and continuously update a company information section on their websites, and maintain links with public registers and other relevant authorities.

Same possibility open to other companies

Other types of companies could be allowed to fulfil their filing and disclosure obligations by including such information on their websites, if appropriate links with public registers are established.

Links between registries to be encouraged

Existing private initiatives to link the various registries that now contain formal company information should be encouraged by the EU.

National central filing systems to be promoted

With respect to listed companies, the EU should at the minimum actively support Member States in their efforts to create national central electronic filing systems, and ensure that national systems are properly linked.

CHAPTER III

CORPORATE GOVERNANCE

1. INTRODUCTION

The original mandate of the Group included a review of whether and, if so, how the EU should actively co-ordinate and strengthen the efforts undertaken by and within Member States to improve corporate governance in Europe. In that light, we raised four issues relating to corporate governance in Section 3.1 of our Consultative Document:

Original mandate: need for a general EU approach ?

Consultative Document :

- Better **information** for shareholders and creditors, in particular better disclosure of corporate governance structures and practices, including remuneration of board members; *Information for shareholders and creditors*
- Strengthening **shareholders' rights** and minority protection, in particular supplementing the right to vote by special investigation procedures; *Shareholders' rights*
- Strengthening the **duties of the board,** in particular the accountability of directors where the company becomes insolvent; *Duties of the board*
- Need for a **European corporate governance code or co-ordination** of national codes in order to stimulate development of best practice and convergence. *European code or co-ordination*

We separately addressed issues relating to the processes of shareholder information, communication and decision-taking in Section 3.2 of our Consultative Document.

Plus shareholder information, communication and decision-taking

In a direct reaction to the Enron case, the Commission and the ECOFIN[8] have agreed to extend the mandate of the Group to review "issues related to best practices in corporate governance and auditing, in particular:

Extension of the mandate pursuant to the Enron case:

Four specific issues

- the **role of non-executive and supervisory directors**;
- the **remuneration of management**;
- the **responsibility of management for financial statements**;
- and **auditing practices**."

In this Chapter, we will address the original and newly added issues

All issues are covered here

---

[8] See Annex I

under the following themes:

Under five themes

- disclosure
- shareholders
- the board
- audit
- corporate governance regulation in the EU.

Before addressing these themes, we would like to stress that corporate governance is a system. It has its foundations partly in company law, setting out the internal relationships between the various participants in a company, and partly in the wider laws and practices and market structures which operate in different Member States. It follows that there are dangers in dealing with particular components of the corporate governance system in isolation from their wider context.

Corporate governance is a system, with roots partly in company law

In our First Report, we have dealt with the market for corporate control. This is one of the most important parts of external corporate governance or outside control.[9] Other market-oriented issues concern primarily securities regulation and are being dealt with in the framework of the Financial Services Action Plan of the Commission. Examples are the various disclosure obligations which securities laws impose on listed companies. But also the regulation of the services provided by investment banks and financial intermediaries of various kinds ("Institutional investors") and the work of securities analysts is crucial in the overall system of corporate governance. Finally, as we have seen over the last year, accounting and audit are fundamental elements of a corporate governance system.

Many external issues are related to the overall system of corporate governance

In this Report, we focus primarily on the internal corporate governance elements. We acknowledge that that is only part of the system of corporate governance, and appreciate that the EU is undertaking initiatives in other areas that contribute to the effectiveness of the corporate governance system in Europe.[10]

This Report focuses on internal corporate governance

---

[9] Report on Issues Related to Takeover Bids, 10 January 2002, http://europa.eu.int/comm/internal_market/en/company/company/news/02-24.htm .

[10] Cf. The Commission Recommendation of 16 May 2002 - Statutory Auditors' Independence in the EU: A Set of Fundamental Principles (2002/590/EC), *Official Journal L 191, 19/07/2002, p. 22*. The various initiatives under the Financial Services Action Plan include the Proposal for a Market Abuse Directive (COM 2001 281) of 30 May 2001, the consultation on ongoing transparency requirements for listed companies launched on 8 may 2002 (http://europa.eu.int/comm/internal_market/en/finances/mobil/transparency/index.htm#secondconsult), and the Proposal for a Prospectus Directive (COM 2002 460) of 9 August 2002.

2. DISCLOSURE

In our Chapter on General Themes, we take the view that disclosure has a pivotal role in company law (see Chapter 2, section 3, above). We underlined this when we recommended in our First Report that listed companies in all Member States be required to disclose their capital and control structures.[11] On the basis of information about potentially defensive structures established in a company, the market would be able to react by discounts and higher costs of capital.

Disclosure has a pivotal role in company law

As we already underlined in our First Report

In our Consultative Document, we took the view that corporate governance in general is a particular area where disclosure should be a key component of a regulatory regime. Corporate governance is of increasing importance for investment decisions and for interventionist action by investors. In the consultation, there was overwhelming support for better disclosure of corporate governance structures and practices in Europe (see Annex 3). There was agreement that this should at least be required for "listed companies" whose shares are admitted to trading on a regulated market or are regularly traded on a non-regulated market (see Chapter 2, section 4, above).

High importance of disclosure for corporate governance

Was confirmed by responses to consultation

At least for listed companies

As to whether this should also extend to "open companies", whose internal structures would allow for trading on a market, or even "closed companies", the reactions were mixed. The Group takes the view that this is a matter for Member States to decide. The population and relevance of open and closed companies differ from Member State to Member State. We do not see an overarching EU interest in imposing these disclosure requirements on open and closed companies across Europe as a matter of European law.

For "open" and "closed" companies, no need for establishment of disclosure requirement at EU level

Listed companies in all Member States should be required to include in their annual report and accounts a coherent and descriptive statement covering the key elements of the corporate governance rules and practices they apply, regardless of whether these elements arise from mandatory law, default provisions, articles of association, resolutions of company organs, codes or other company processes. The statement should also be separately posted on the company's website.

Listed companies should publish an annual corporate governance statement

And post it on their website

The principle rules relating to the disclosure requirement, and the key items to be disclosed, could be laid down in an EU Directive[12]. The

A framework Directive could

[11] See the Report on Issues Related to Takeover Bids, p. 25-26.

[12] We note that various existing and proposed EU Directives contain disclosure requirements relating to corporate governance, e.g. the Proposal for a Thirteenth Company Law Directive on Takeover Bids, the

Directive should not seek to regulate the details of the requirement to publish an annual corporate governance statement, as the views on what are the elements to disclose and the way they should be disclosed are likely to change over time. A system of flexible and efficiently adaptable subordinate rules should be created. We believe that the detailed rules should be set by the appropriate bodies within Member States in view of their national company laws, but the EU should ensure a certain level of co-ordination of the setting of these detailed rules by Member States. This should be part of the general framework to be set up in the EU to co-ordinate the corporate governance efforts of Member States (see Section 6).

set the applicable principles

Detailed rules would be set by Member States, with proper co-ordination at EU level

The annual corporate governance statement should at least include the following key items:

Information to be given at least on :

- The operation of the shareholders meeting, its key powers, the rights attached to shares, where applicable per class of shares, and how these rights can be exercised.

The shareholder meeting and the shares

- The operation of the board and its committees, the procedures for appointment of board members, the role and qualifications of individual board members and the direct and indirect relationships board members may have with the company beyond their board membership (see Section 4.1). Disclosure of directors' remuneration and other terms and conditions of appointment and removal should be required separately (see also Section 4.2).

The board's organisation and its individual members

- The shareholders holding major holdings as determined in Directive 2001/34/EC[13] and as foreseen in the Directive on Ongoing and Periodic Transparency Requirements, with a description of the voting rights and special control rights they can exercise, and, if they act in concert, a description of the key elements of the existing shareholder agreements.

The shareholders holding major shareholdings

And their voting and control rights

- The direct and indirect relationships between the company and holders of major holdings beyond the shareholding itself. This last element of disclosure is particularly important in many parts of Europe, as a substantial part of the share capital of European listed companies in those areas is held by large shareholders. The potential of conflicts of interests between these controlling

The other direct and indirect relationships with the major shareholders

---

forthcoming Proposal for a Directive or Regulation on Ongoing and Periodic Transparency Requirements (http://www.europa.eu.int/comm/internal_market/en/finances/mobil/transparency/index.htm), Directive of 28 May 2001 on the admission of securities to official stock exchange listing and on information to be published on securities (2001/34/EC). The Commission should ensure proper co-ordination between these various instruments, and that those subject to these requirements can make coherent disclosure of their corporate governance rules and practices.

[13] Directive of the European Parliament and of the Council of 28 May 2001 on the admission of securities to official stock exchange listing and on information to be published on securities (2001/34/EC), articles 85 to 97.

[14] See IAS 24 "Related Party Disclosures"; see also Articles 9 and 10 of the Fourth Company Law Directives.

[15] Particularly in the light of recent developments in the USA (see the Sarbanes-Oxley Act of 30 July 2002, and the Proposed Rule - issued by the SEC on 22 October 2002 - on Disclosure Required by Sections 404, 406 and 407 of the Sarbanes-Oxley Act).

shareholders on the one hand and the company and its minority shareholders on the other hand is well documented in legal and economic literature. We believe all material transactions that have taken place between the company and holders of major holdings should be reported separately in the audited financial statements, with an explanation as to what extent these transactions are at-arms-length (see also Chapter V on groups and pyramid structures).

In particular all material transactions, with due explanation

- Other material related party transactions, like transactions with subsidiaries and associate companies, unless already specifically disclosed in the company's financial statements[14].

Transactions with other parties

- The system of risk management applied by the company, describing the core strategy and activities of the company and the particular risks related thereto. Where such a system does not exist, this must be disclosed. Introducing a requirement in EU law for listed companies to have a developed system of risk management needs further study[15].

Existence and nature of risk management system

- A reference to a national code of corporate governance with which the company complies or in relation to which it explains deviations. As to national codes of corporate governance, see Section 6 below.

A reference to a national code of corporate governance

The responsibility for the correctness of the corporate governance statement lies with the board as a whole, as is the case with the responsibility for financial statements of the company (see further par. 4.3 below).

Responsibility for the statement should lie with the board as a whole

3. SHAREHOLDERS

3.1. Shareholder information, communication and decision-taking

In a proper system of corporate governance, shareholders should have effective means to actively exercise influence over the company. As we emphasised in our Consultative Document, shareholders are the residual claimholders (they only receive payment once all creditors have been satisfied) and they are entitled to reap the benefits if the company prospers and are the first to suffer if it does not. Shareholders need to be able to ensure that management pursues - and remains accountable to - their interests. Shareholders focus on wealth creation and are therefore, in the Group's view, very suited to act as "watchdog" not only on their own behalf, but also, in normal circumstances, on behalf of other stakeholders.

Being the residual claimholders

Shareholders are ideally placed to act as a watchdog

For which they should have the necessary means

There is a particular need for this in the case of listed companies

This is particularly

where shares are widely held, or at least in the minority widely held. From the viewpoint of a single shareholder, it may frequently seem appropriate to sell his shares if he is dissatisfied with - or lacks confidence in – incumbent management, rather than try to change things within the company. However, this "rational apathy" may prove very disadvantageous if adopted as a general attitude among shareholders.

important in listed companies

Where minority's apathy may have harmful effects

Reliance on shareholders performing this role presupposes that it is, indeed, possible for shareholders to influence the decisions of the company and, in addition, appears attractive for them to do so. This, in turn, depends on the costs and difficulties attached to exercising influence. The more costly and cumbersome it is to exercise influence, the more shareholders are likely to elect not to do so.

Shareholders' influence will highly depend on the costs and difficulties faced

The traditional means to exercise this influence is through the shareholders meeting, where shareholders can debate with management and each other, and vote on resolutions put forward to them. In the Group's view, the traditional shareholders meeting as a physical gathering of shareholders is unable in its present form to fulfil today's expectations. As a result of increasingly international shareholdings by both institutional and private investors, the vast majority of shareholders is unable to physically attend the shareholders meetings of their companies. The actual meeting can no longer offer a sufficient central forum for shareholder information, communication and decision-taking.

Influence was traditionally exercised through the general meeting

Which is no longer physically attended by many

The Group believes modern information and communication technology can be very instrumental in devising new concepts and methods for shareholder information, communication and decision-taking, and its potential should be fully explored and used. Many respondents to our Consultative Document stressed that, at the current stage of development and availability of new technologies, the use of modern technology should not be imposed but should merely be facilitated. We agree that an appropriate balance must be struck.

Modern technology can be very helpful

If introduced in a balanced way

In order to facilitate the move towards an integrated European capital market, it is important that shareholders across the EU have equivalent opportunities and facilities to participate in the information, communication and decision-making processes of shareholders. While the focus in this paragraph is on listed companies, non-listed companies are likely to benefit from the facilities developed for shareholders in listed companies.

Equivalent facilities should be offered across the EU

Non listed companies could benefit from them

a) Notice and pre-meeting communication

One set of issues relates to the preparation of general meetings of shareholders. The communication between a company and its shareholders prior to a general meeting (including sending notices of such meeting) is frequently a one-way process with limited, if any, feedback from the shareholders.

Pre-meeting communication is frequently a one-way process

Where bearer shares have been issued, communication will have to take place through the public media by means of advertisements or other costly means. Communication among shareholders is also costly: shareholders are not able to identify each other, and therefore frequently have to use the public media if they want to get points across to other shareholders. But also in registered share systems, communication to and among shareholders is increasingly difficult as substantial numbers of shareholders, particularly in cross-border situations, do not appear in the shareholders register, but hold shares through intermediaries.

The biggest difficulties and costs arise with bearer shares

But registered shares also present some problems

Many of the issues touched upon here may be resolved, at least in part, by using electronic means of communication, including the company's website and the internet. Companies could put all their meeting materials (notice, annual report and accounts, agenda including proposed resolutions, explanatory notes, shareholder circulars) on their website, to which shareholders can get access at their own initiative, rather than the company being required to send information to them. Proxy and voting instruction forms may be downloaded and submitted by electronic means. Also, the website can include a section where voting instructions or proxies can be lodged. This use of the company's website is efficient both for the company and its shareholders, and the practical evidence is that it leads to a huge reduction in costs as compared to postal mailings of meeting materials and proxy forms.

Modern technology may offer a solution to many problems

Putting meeting materials and proxy forms on the company's website

Is efficient for both the company and its shareholders

In our Consultative Document, we asked whether listed companies should not only be entitled to use modern technology as suggested above (i.e. that the use should be permitted by Member States' company laws – the "enabling" approach), but should be compelled to do so. Many respondents have expressed the view that use of modern technology should be a matter for the companies and their shareholders to decide and not for the Member States or the EU to determine.

Many responses to the consultation supported the "enabling" approach

As we have noted in Chapter II, however, the Group believes that the time is ripe to take this matter further. We should take into account

Group believes we should anticipate future

that it will take a few years at the minimum for any legislation following these recommendations to be implemented and applied in the Member States. By then, the use of a website by listed companies for formal information and communication purposes should, and in all likelihood will, be a widespread and recognised best practice.

normal practice

In Chapter II, we have recommended, also in the light of other Community initiatives like the proposed Market Abuse Directive, the proposed Prospectus Directive and the forthcoming Directive on Ongoing and Periodic Transparency Requirements for Listed Companies, that listed companies be required to maintain a specific section on their website where they publish all information they are required to file and publish (see Chapter 2, section 6). This section on their websites should include all relevant materials relating to shareholders meetings, and should offer facilities for giving proxies or voting instructions on-line or for downloading and e-mailing proxy or voting instruction forms.

In Chapter II, we recommended that a specific website section be maintained

This section should include all meeting materials and proxy forms

However, we would not want to recommend at this stage that such section should also include bulletin boards and chat rooms through which shareholders can directly communicate with management and other shareholders. Attractive as these facilities appear to be, chat rooms and similar devices, as many respondents have noted, are often abused to send irrelevant or improper messages. A particular risk is that they are used to manipulate share prices, e.g. by shareholders placing incorrect or misleading information in the chat room. Many issues have to be reviewed before companies could be required to offer these facilities, e.g. the ability to limit access to these devices to shareholders entitled to it and to filter irrelevant, abusive, misleading and improper messages, and the related costs and benefits.

Mandatory bulletin boards and chat rooms are not recommended

Because of the risks of abuse

Which require further review of many issues

While listed companies in our view should be required to offer shareholders electronic facilities to access information and to give proxy notifications or voting instructions, shareholders should, at least for the time being, not be required, as a matter of EU law, to use exclusively these electronic facilities. It is clear that for some time to come not all shareholders will have access to them. It is not yet appropriate for the EU to require shareholders to use electronic facilities in order to be able to participate in the information, communication and decision-taking. Listed companies may therefore be required under national law to provide hard copies of meeting materials and voting forms to shareholders who request them. On the other hand, we believe it is no longer appropriate for Member States' company laws to require listed companies to actively send hard copies of meeting materials to the shareholders they know, even

Not all shareholders have access to electronic facilities

Shareholders should therefore not be compelled at EU level to use them

Member States could require

without their specific request. Offering electronic access to the relevant information through the company's website, and sending hard copy materials to shareholders at their request where deemed appropriate at national level, gives sufficient access to the relevant information for all shareholders.

listed companies to send hard copies, but only on specific request

Information and communication are key issues for shareholders of any company. The legal requirements or restrictions with respect to the right to ask questions and submit proposals for decision-making often prevent small shareholders from being active. In the Consultative Document, we asked whether there is a need, at EU level, to provide for minimum standards regarding the right for shareholders to ask questions and submit proposals for decision-making at the general meeting. Many have responded that they see no grounds for doing so, and in general the Group would tend to agree that, at least for the time being, the case is not made out for substantive mandatory provisions at EU level.

The rights to ask questions and table resolutions are often difficult to exercise

But responses to the consultation did not call for mandatory provisions at EU level

As already indicated, adequate and correct information on the company and its business is key to shareholder motivation. It is important that shareholders are able to ask questions and have them answered properly. Also, the right for shareholders to submit proposals for general meeting decisions plays an important role in the corporate context.

In practice, exercise of these important rights may be facilitated by modern technology

On the other hand, use of modern technology may lead to practical problems if shareholders can raise questions (and require answers) and submit proposals without restriction, among other things via the company's website. The company could virtually be flooded with questions and proposals, which would make the whole process unworkable. A balance has to be struck between these rights of shareholders and the ability of the company to manage this aspect of communication with shareholders without undue burdens.

But companies should be able to take measures to keep the process manageable

We do not think measures to avoid such unintended use of influence on the part of shareholders should be taken at EU level. Member States differ significantly with respect to the regulation of shareholder rights, due to, at least in part, differences in markets, culture, and shareholder behaviour. Each Member State should consider whether its company law leaves adequate flexibility for companies to put in place measures against unintended exercise of shareholder influence. At this point, we would only recommend that at EU level it is ensured that listed companies explicitly disclose to their shareholders how they can ask questions, how and to what extent the company intends to answer questions, and how and under what conditions they can submit proposals to the shareholders meeting. This should be an element of their mandatory annual corporate

The necessary flexibility for companies should be provided for at national level

But annual disclosure of how these rights can be exercised should be required at EU level

governance statement.

With respect to the right to submit proposals for resolution by the shareholders meeting, there is a link with the squeeze-out right of a majority shareholder and sell-out right of minority shareholders (see Chapter VI). The protection company law offers to the minority shareholders that cannot be squeezed-out by the majority shareholder should include the right to submit shareholder proposals. A minority greater than the maximum squeeze-out minority should have this power. If for example, under a Member State's company law, a 95% shareholder can squeeze-out minority shareholders, the level of shareholding required for the submission of proposals should not exceed 5% of the share capital. The EU should consider imposing this as a minimum rule on Member States.

The right to table resolutions is linked to the squeeze-out right

Thresholds should be set consistently

Member States could be required to do so

b) General meeting, voting in absentia, electronic access

We have said that the traditional general meeting of shareholders, as a physical gathering of participants who discuss and decide, is today no longer a sufficient and effective means to perform the relevant governance functions. In order for shareholders to be able to participate in the decision-taking, they must be able to vote in absentia, either by way of direct vote outside the meeting (cf. the "vote par correspondance" in France) or by way of a voting instruction and proxy to be exercised in the meeting by somebody else (e.g. the chairman of the board, a representative from a bank or a notary).

In view of the difficulties to attend meetings, shareholders should be able to vote in absentia

The Group believes that listed companies should be required to offer all shareholders (or the intermediaries designated by them) facilities to vote in absentia - by way of direct vote or proxies - by electronic means, and through hard copy voting instruction or proxy forms at their request. However, the Group recommends that such an obligation should only be imposed on listed companies to the extent that solutions have been found and implemented for the problems of cross-border holding of securities (see Section 3.2). It would be inappropriate and would lead to an undesirable level of legal uncertainty to require companies to offer these facilities if they do not have the means to determine who are the shareholders entitled to vote.

The necessary facilities should be offered, but not imposed, to shareholders

But only to the extent that cross-border holding problems have been solved

Another means to enhance shareholders' participation in the information, communication and decision-making processes is to allow absentee shareholders to participate in traditional general meetings via electronic means, including via the internet (webcast) and satellite. In some Member States, systems are being developed through which shareholders following the meeting on their computer

Some companies offer participation to general meeting via electronic means

or television screens can participate by raising questions and exercise voting rights directly during the meeting. This can reinforce shareholder influence with little trouble and at low cost. Security and reliability however must be assured.

Which increase shareholder influence in an efficient way

The EU should ensure that the company law requirements of Member States as to e.g. the place where a meeting should be held may not impede such developments. There are however, in the Group's view, insufficient grounds for compelling Member States to require listed companies to establish the facilities required for such participation in the present stage of technological development and reliability.

Use of electronic means in meetings should be possible

But not yet mandatory

The development of technological means through which shareholders can communicate with management and each other and can take decisions without actually meeting, and the facilitating of these developments in law, inevitably lead to the question whether a physical meeting of shareholders still plays any useful role. If it is felt that the physical meeting of shareholders is no longer essential, it would seem sensible to allow companies who offer a comprehensive electronic process of information of, communication with and decision-making by shareholders to abandon the physical general meeting altogether. The responses in the consultation were mixed.

Comprehensive use of electronic means might make a physical meeting useless

Responses to the consultation were mixed

The Group finds that the answer to this question depends not only on the technical possibilities but also on the various features of Member States' company laws, including the basic shareholder rights, such as the right to face management and ask questions (and demand answers) at the general meeting of shareholders, as well as with respect to protection of minority rights. Therefore, it should be left to Member States to deal with this question, at least for the time being. The decision to abandon the traditional type of general meeting should in any event be taken by - or with the consent of - the general meeting of shareholders with an appropriately strong qualified majority.

The permission to abandon the physical meeting should be a Member State decision

But it should require a qualified majority decision by the general meeting

3.2. Cross-border voting

Investors in European listed companies face particular problems if they reside in countries other than where the company is registered. Nowadays, investors usually hold their shares in securities holding systems through accounts with securities intermediaries, who, in turn, hold accounts with other securities intermediaries and central securities depositories in other jurisdictions. In cross-border situations, shares are typically held through chains of intermediaries. These cross-border chains cause particular problems in the determination of the entitlement of shareholders to exercise the voting

In cross-border situations, shares are typically held through chains of intermediaries

Which make it difficult to identify the person

rights on shares held through the chains, and the process of communicating with - and actual voting by - such shareholders.

entitled to vote

In reality, it is often either very difficult and cumbersome or practically impossible for shareholders in one Member State or outside the EU, to vote on shares in a listed company in another/a Member State. This problem is becoming all the more urgent as the cross-border nature of equity investment is increasing and is actively stimulated by the drive to create integrated financial markets in Europe and beyond. Our recommendations on shareholder information, communication and decision-taking, if implemented, would have a very imperfect effect if the resulting systems could not be applied in cross-border situations.

Cross-border voting is often almost impossible in practice

Integration of financial markets calls for an urgent solution

The legal problems related to cross-border voting in Europe have been reviewed by a separate international Group of Experts set up in January 2002 by the Dutch Minister of Justice. The Cross-Border Voting Group has conducted its own consultation process and reported to the Minister in September 2002.[16] Two members of the High Level Group have participated in the Cross-Border Voting Group, whose Final Report was submitted to the High Level Group.

A separate Cross-Border Voting Group has issued its Report in September 2002

The Cross-Border Voting Group recommends that the rights and obligations of accountholders and securities intermediaries in the securities holding systems in Member States be regulated at EU level, to ensure that accountholders across the EU can effectively exercise the voting rights on shares they hold through these systems.

Rights and obligations of accountholders should be regulated at EU level

To that end, the Cross-Border Voting Group basically recommends that accountholders in European securities holding systems, who are not participating in these systems as securities intermediaries holding shares for their accountholders (such accountholders are defined as "Ultimate Accountholders" in the Final Report of the Cross-Border Voting Group), should be acknowledged across the EU to have the right to determine how to vote on shares they hold in their accounts (the primary rule). An Ultimate Accountholder should be granted the options available under the law of the Member State of the company in which he holds shares to be either recognised as the formal shareholder entitled to vote, or to receive a power of attorney from the securities intermediary who is formally entitled to vote, or to instruct that securities intermediary to vote according to his instructions. Securities intermediaries are to be prohibited from voting on shares they hold for their accountholders, unless explicitly instructed or authorised by their accountholders.

Primary rule :

The right to determine how to vote should be recognised to Ultimate Accountholders

Who should be granted the options available in the company's Member State

[16] The Final Report of the Cross-Border Voting Group has been posted on the website of the Dutch Ministry of Justice : http://www.wodc.nl

Where an Ultimate Accountholder is not a securities intermediary in the regulated European securities holding systems, but nonetheless holds shares on behalf of third parties (e.g. a US securities intermediary), such Ultimate Accountholder should be able to designate its clients to be recognised as entitled to determine how the shares are voted (the supplementary rule). These recommended rules are accompanied in the Final Report with further recommendations on the information, authentication and voting processes.

The Final Report contains also a supplementary rule

And further recommendations

Like the Cross-Border Voting Group, we believe that the issues identified by that Group urgently need to be addressed at EU level. A proper system for shareholder information, communication and decision-making in Europe facilitates the exercise of voting rights of all shareholders in European listed companies, regardless of the Member State in which they are located and whether they wish to vote on shares of companies in their own jurisdiction or in another jurisdiction. It is also important that such a system allows shareholders outside the EU to exercise their rights efficiently, as the Cross-Border Voting Group has recommended through the combination of the proposed primary and supplementary rule. Finally, such a system should operate efficiently for all parties concerned: shareholders, listed companies and securities intermediaries, with respect to both administrative and operational burdens and costs. Modern technology can be highly instrumental in achieving these ends and its use by all parties concerned should be stimulated to the maximum.

Issues identified by the Cross-Border Voting Group should urgently be addressed at EU level

In the interest of both European and non European shareholders

Efficiency for all parties would be enhanced by modern technology

We recommend that the Commission, as a matter of priority, consider the recommendations of the Cross-Border Voting Group - together with the recommendations in the previous paragraph on shareholder information, communication and decision-making - and in the light of these recommendations set up a specific project to build a regulatory framework for shareholder information, communication and decision-making that facilitates participation of shareholders across the EU and, where possible, outside the EU, in the governance of European listed companies.

A specific project should be set up at EU level to facilitate shareholders' participation

Some of the recommendations clearly need a Directive as a legal basis in order to work effectively, in particular relating to cross-border voting. Other elements, like the use of the company's website for communication with shareholders, and the requirement to offer electronic facilities for proxy voting, can and should be implemented quickly. Apart from a legislative initiative which may be appropriate, the Commission should consider issuing a Recommendation to Member States that they should adopt effective rules in their company

A Directive may be required for some issues, in particular cross-border voting

Whereas rapid use of websites and (electronic)

laws or other regulations ensuring that listed companies use their websites for communication with shareholders and offer electronic facilities for proxy voting.

proxy voting might be promoted by a Recommendation

3.3. Responsibilities of institutional investors

The increasing amounts of equity investments held by institutional investors within the EU has initiated a debate in certain Member States as to the role of institutional investors in the corporate governance of listed companies. Where traditionally, in companies with dispersed ownership, shareholders can produce little countervailing power against management, the rise of institutional investment may have changed this. The substantial holdings of institutional investors make the exit strategy (selling on the market) less attractive to them and they are increasingly inclined actively to engage in internal control within the company.

Institutional investors have large shareholdings with voting rights

And tend to use them more frequently than before

In the Consultative Document, we raised the question whether the role of institutional investors should be formalised by requiring them to disclose their policy regarding the investments they make and how they exercise their voting rights with respect to companies in which they invest. The views of respondents were mixed : some would be in favour of such an obligation, some would oppose it.

Responses to the consultation were mixed about the possible formalisation of institutional investors' role

The Group believes institutional investors have an important role to play in the governance of companies in which they invest. But there are also governance issues relating to the institutional investors themselves. Institutional investors are usually characterised as investors who invest on behalf of their beneficiaries, to whom they owe fiduciary duties as defined by law and the particular contractual relations between them. Pension funds invest contributions paid by employees (and often their employers) to fund their pensions; insurance companies invest premiums paid by policy holders to ensure payment of insurance claims, or to provide investment benefits on maturity of life policies; mutual and other investment funds invest contributions made by investors in the funds, etc. There are concerns about the potential for conflicts of interests of those who manage the investments on behalf beneficiaries, both in terms of their relationships with the companies they invest in and in terms of their internal reward schemes. This potential for conflicts of interests justifies, as a matter of good governance of institutional investors, their beneficiaries being entitled to know what their policies are with respect to investment and the exercise of rights attached to their investments. Beneficiaries are also entitled to demand to see the voting records showing how these rights have been used in a

Good governance of institutional investors requires

Disclosure to their beneficiaries of their investment and voting policies

And a right of their beneficiaries to the voting records showing how voting rights have been exercised in a particular case

particular case.[17]

Regulation of the relevant types of institutional investors should include an obligation on the institutional investor to disclose its investment policy and its policy with respect to the exercise of voting rights in companies in which it invests, and to disclose to beneficial holders at their request the voting records showing how these rights have been used in a particular case. The EU should ensure that Member States impose these rules in their regulation of the relevant types of institutional investors. We believe that such a requirement would not only improve the governance of institutional investors, but would also contribute to a considered participation by institutional investors in the affairs of the companies in which they invest for the benefit of corporate governance and company efficiency.

The EU should ensure that such rules are included in the regulations applicable at national level

Which should contribute to encourage active participation by institutional investors

We also raised the question whether institutional investors should even be required to use their voting rights in the companies in which they invest, as some institutional investors in the United States of America are required to do. The majority of the responses was negative and the Group agrees that such an obligation should not be imposed. We are doubtful as to the effect of such an obligation and fear that it may have counter-productive effects of institutional investors simply voting in favour of any proposed resolution to fulfil the requirement. We would not expect any additional value from the imposition of such mandatory voting once the requirement is imposed for institutional investors to disclose their voting policies and their actual use of their voting rights at the request of their beneficiaries.

Responses to the consultation did not support an obligation to vote

The Group agrees that there are no convincing reasons for imposing such an obligation

3.4. Special investigation rights of minority shareholders

Even if participating in shareholders meetings and voting are facilitated, many shareholders will refrain from doing so, often with good reason. This well-known phenomenon of "rational apathy" is not only common for private shareholders, but also for many institutional shareholders. In companies with one or more controlling shareholders, minority shareholders usually have no real influence, even if they vote. In groups of companies and particularly in multinational groups, the minority shareholders of the subsidiary, and even those of the parent, may just not know where the real problems are. In such cases, what is needed for shareholders is to first find out the facts (e.g. about related party transactions) and then to consider the appropriate course of action, which could be a shareholders'

In many cases, shareholders are inclined not to vote

Due to a lack of influence

And/or a lack of information

---

[17] See the relevant rules recently proposed by the SEC : Proposed Rule on Disclosure of Proxy Voting Policies and Proxy Voting Records by Registered Management Investment Companies (http://www.sec.gov/rules/proposed/33-8131.htm) and Proposed Rule on Proxy Voting by Investment Advisers (http://www.sec.gov/rules/proposed/ia-2059.htm).

resolution or even an action to hold directors or others liable.

A number of Member States have recognised the need for a special investigation procedure. The core provisions are rather similar, but the details vary considerably. In some Member States, special investigations are rare whereas, in others, they are much more common and used for a variety of purposes. In most of them, it is recognised that the special investigation procedure, even if it is rarely used, is an important deterrent or "fleet in being".

The special investigation procedure offered in several Member States is an important deterrent

In accordance with the vast majority of responses to the Consultation Document, the Group believes that the shareholders' right to vote and their standard right to information should be supplemented by a European framework rule on the right of shareholders to require a special investigation and the procedure for it. The Group recommends the extension of the special investigation right to all companies, whether listed, open or closed. Such rights are particularly relevant if the company structures are complex and not transparent, as is often the case in groups of companies and in multinational enterprises. Special investigation procedures should not be restricted to the single independent company, but should as far as possible be open to use group-wide, where the issues are sufficiently significant to justify this.

A EU rule on special investigation right was supported by responses to the consultation

The Group recommends it for all companies

And where possible on a group-wide basis

Shareholders, in a general meeting or holding a minimum of 5 or 10 per cent of the share capital, should be given the right to apply to a court or appropriate administrative body to order a special investigation. In companies subject to the squeeze-out procedure, the minimum minority holding should not exceed the squeeze-out minority (see further Chapter VI below). The order should only be given when there is a serious suspicion of improper behaviour, in order to avoid the procedure being used as a "fishing expedition" or as an instrument of harassment. The investigation should be conducted by the court or administrative body ordering the special investigation, or by professionals under its supervision. A special investigation procedure offers an efficient and overall not too costly form of enhanced shareholder information.

Investigation right should be open to general meeting or a significant minority

Authorisation should be based on serious suspicion

The European framework provision can be short and precise. The details should be left to the Member States in order to enable them to make the rule compatible with the procedural and administrative practice in their jurisdictions. Also, the European provision should refrain from indicating what the (potential) sanctions of the findings of special investigation should be, as sanctions are generally left to national law. But Member States should ensure that they have effective sanctions in place. Also, we note that director's disqualification is a particularly effective sanction which should be

Details of the procedure should be left to Member States

As well as the determination of proper sanctions

available in extreme cases (see further par. 4.5 below).

4. BOARD OF DIRECTORS

4.1. The role of non-executive and supervisory directors

a) Role

Good corporate governance requires a strong and balanced board as a monitoring body for the executive management of the company. Executive managers manage the company ultimately on behalf of the shareholders. In companies with dispersed ownership, shareholders are usually unable to closely monitor management, its strategies and its performance for lack of information and resources. The role of non-executive directors in one-tier board structures and supervisory directors in two-tier board structures is to fill this gap between the uninformed shareholders as principals and the fully informed executive managers as agents by monitoring the agents more closely.

Many difficulties prevent dispersed shareholders from directly monitoring management

Which calls for an active role of non-executive or supervisory directors

Board reform is at the core of corporate governance in the Member States as well as outside the EU. There is an extensive and ongoing academic discussion on the pros and cons of the one-tier and the two-tier board system. There is no clear evidence which of the two is a more effective monitoring body. Each of the two systems has its specific advantages and disadvantages and may be appropriate in particular circumstances. They have been developed along their specific paths of legal and cultural development. Good corporate governance structures can be created in both board systems.

No particular form of board structure (one-tier / two-tier) is intrinsically superior

Each may be the most efficient in particular circumstances

As the policy debates in Europe on the Fifth Company Law Directive and the European Company Statute have shown, it is not advisable to make one of the two systems mandatory in Europe. Rather, the Group believes that at least listed and open companies across the EU should have the choice between the two systems, as has been recently introduced for the European Company (SE). By offering companies the choice between the two systems, companies could elect the system which best suits their particular corporate governance needs and circumstances. This is a good example where the European variation in systems can be beneficial and less detrimental to facilitating efficient and competitive business in Europe.

None of the two systems should be made mandatory across Europe

But at least listed and open companies should be offered the choice to opt for the system best suited to them

As we have noted, listed companies in some parts of Europe are often controlled by one or a small group of large shareholders. These large shareholders usually are well informed about the affairs of the

The presence of (a group of) controlling shareholder(s) is

company and closely monitor the executive managers. This is generally seen as a benefit of controlling shareholder-structures. However, the position of the controlling shareholder(s) creates potential conflicts of interests with minority shareholders who, as in companies with fully dispersed ownership, lack sufficient information and resources to monitor management and the controlling shareholder(s). In this type of controlled company, there is a need for monitoring by non-executive directors or supervisory directors on behalf of minority shareholders.

likely to result in closer monitoring of management

But non-executive or supervisory directors then have an important role on behalf of the minority

Non-executive and supervisory directors, who are not involved in the day-to-day affairs of the company, normally have a role of oversight of the executive managers in areas like the financial performance of the company and major decisions affecting its strategy and future. Apart from these, there are three areas where there is a specific need for disinterested monitoring by non-executive and supervisory directors:

Non-executive and supervisory directors have a general oversight role

- The nomination of directors
- The remuneration of directors
- The audit of the accounting for the company's performance.

Of particular significance in three areas

In these three areas, executive directors clearly have conflicts of interests. Nomination is about the continuation of their own jobs and the jobs of their colleagues and potential new colleagues, and the persons who monitor them. Remuneration is about the rewards the executive directors receive for their services to the company. Audit is about the probity of the financial and non-financial accounting for the performance of the company by the executive directors who are responsible for its performance.

Conflicts of interests may arise about

Nomination,

Remuneration,

And audit

Lack of monitoring by independent, disinterested non-executive directors in these three areas has been a major cause for the various corporate scandals that we have witnessed this last year. An important element of the regulatory response in the USA therefore focuses on strengthening the independent monitoring by non-executive directors in these areas.

The need for more independent monitoring is highlighted by the US regulatory response to recent scandals

The Group does not express a view as to how the full one-tier board or supervisory board should be constituted, and to what extent independent non-executive or supervisory directors should be members of it. But we take the view that, for all listed companies in the EU, it should be ensured that within the board, and to the extent these are matters for the board and not for the shareholders to decide, the nomination and remuneration of executive directors and the audit of the accounting for the company's performance should be decided upon by exclusively non-executive or supervisory directors

Group does not express views on composition of the full (supervisory) board

But promotes role of non-executive / supervisory directors

who are in the majority independent.

Practically this may be effectuated by creating nomination, remuneration and audit committees consisting of non-executive or supervisory directors who are in the majority independent. Independent in this respect means independent of the operational business of the company and of those who take primary responsibility as executive directors, and also not receiving any benefit from the company other than their fully disclosed remuneration as non-executive or supervisory director.

Nomination, remuneration and audit committees could be set up

Composed of a majority of independent directors

The Group considered whether such committees should consist exclusively of independent non-executive or supervisory directors[18], but rejected this as a European rule. In Europe, we have to take account of particular situations relevant to board structures, like the existence of controlling shareholders and boards which are partly co-determined by employees. Employees of the company and representatives of controlling shareholders would normally not be considered to be independent, but it would go too far to exclude them completely from participating in these key areas. Requiring oversight by non-executive or supervisory directors who are in the majority independent would ensure a sufficient level of independent oversight, while accommodating these particular European situations.

In Europe, it seems neither appropriate nor necessary

To provide that such committees should consist exclusively of independent directors

Experience shows that producing binding EU legislation in the area of board structures is a lengthy process. The result is also generally likely to be inflexible and not responsive to local and changing needs and conditions. The Group takes the view that the EU should try to achieve a substantial result in the short term. The Group recommends that the Commission issue a Recommendation to Member States that they have effective rules in their company laws or in their national corporate governance codes ensuring that the nomination and remuneration of directors and the audit of the accounting of the company's performance is decided upon by non-executive or supervisory directors who are at least in the majority independent.

To achieve a substantial result in the short term

The Commission should issue a Recommendation on the role of (independent) non-executive / supervisory directors

By "effective rules", we mean that as a minimum this requirement should be enforced on a "comply or explain" basis, requiring listed companies to either fully comply with the requirement or to disclose in their annual corporate governance statement to what extent and why they deviate from it. Member States should be free to decide how to implement this in their jurisdiction, through company law, securities

Effective rules should be enforced at least on a "comply or explain" basis

---

[18] Cf. Sarbanes-Oxley Act of 30 July 2002, sec. 301-305;
New York Stock Exchange Listing Rules (http://www.nyse.com/about/report.html),
NASDAQ Listing Rules (http://www.nasdaq.com/about/ProposedRuleChanges.stm).

laws, listing rules or otherwise.[19] As in the Commission's Recommendation on Auditor Independence[20], the Commission should announce its intention to monitor to what extent Member States have and enforce these rules and to consider further rulemaking at EU level if their efforts and resulting levels of company compliance with the regime are insufficient.

Adoption and enforcement of these rules should be adequately monitored by the Commission

b) Independence

The Commission's Recommendation should include standards for what is considered to be independent in this respect. It is important that, to qualify as independent, the non-executive or supervisory director, apart from his directorship, has no further relationship, with the company, from which he derives material value. Certain relationships with the company, its executive directors or controlling shareholders may also impair independence. The Recommendation should include a list of relationships which would cause a non-executive or supervisory director to be considered not to be independent.

Recommendation should include principles on independence

Non independent relationships could be listed

In the view of the Group, such a list should at least include:

Minimum list :

- Those who are employed by the company[21], or have been employed in a period of five years prior to the appointment as non-executive or supervisory director; *(Former) employees*
- Those who receive any fee for consulting or advising or otherwise, from the company or its executive managers; *Advisors*
- Those who receive remuneration from the company which is dependent on the performance of the company (e.g. share options or performance related bonuses, etc.); *Performance related pay*
- Those who, in their capacity as non-executive or supervisory directors of the company, monitor an executive director who is non-executive or supervisory director in another company in which they are an executive director, and other forms of interlocking directorships; *Interlocking relationships*
- Those who are controlling shareholders, acting alone or in concert, or their representatives. Controlling shareholder for the purposes of this rule could be defined, as a minimum, as a shareholder who, alone or in concert, holds 30% or more of the *Controlling shareholders*

[19] Some doubt whether the proposed Prospectus Directive allows Member States to impose additional corporate governance requirements on listed companies through listing rules. Although it can be argued that the proposed Directive clearly does not prohibit Member States to do this, it would be helpful if this could be clarified, so as to put that position beyond any doubt.

[20] For complete references, see Annex 4.

[21] For the purpose of this list, the company should include any of its subsidiaries, holding companies, fellow group companies and possible other associates.

share capital of the company.

In defining relations which disqualify a non-executive or supervisory director from being considered to be independent, related parties and family relationships should be taken into account.

Related parties and family relationships to be taken into account

As a complement to these specific rules on independence of non-executive or supervisory directors, the Group believes listed companies should be required to disclose in their annual corporate governance statement which of their non-executive or supervisory directors they consider to be independent and on what grounds. Where they are not independent, the statement should explain what the dependency is. This would enhance the transparency of the actual role and position of non-executive and supervisory directors, and would enforce proper application of the independence rules. When a new director is proposed for appointment, similar disclosure should be made in the notice explaining the proposed resolution. The responsibility for the statement on independence is a collective board responsibility, but the individual director, or proposed director, with respect to whom the statement of independence is made carries a personal responsibility for its accuracy.

Information on individual independence should be given annually

And together with any proposal for appointment

Under an appropriate regime for (personal) responsibility

c) Competence

The company laws of all Member States include general rules on the competence which is expected of non-executive and supervisory directors. These rules are usually formulated in very abstract terms, like "the competence and skills which are to be expected from a director in his position". Whether or not a non-executive or supervisory director is competent generally is difficult to assess beforehand. It also depends on the role a director has on the board. In the light of the collective responsibility of all board members for the financial statements of the company (see Section 4.3 below), basic financial understanding is a fundamental skill all board members should possess or acquire upon their appointment. Apart from that, board members may be elected for their expertise in particular areas.

Existing rules on competence are generally abstract

Competence must be assessed together with role

Basic financial understanding is always required

But other skills may be of high relevance

In order for shareholders to be able to place sufficient trust in the non-executive or supervisory directors, they should be informed about their particular competencies in light of the board's composition. Listed companies should include in their annual corporate governance statement a profile of the board's composition, and should explain why individual non-executive or supervisory directors are qualified to serve on the board in the light of this profile. Again, there should be similar disclosures in proposals for initial

Competence should be explained annually against profile of board composition

And on appointment

appointment.

The increased importance attached to the role of non-executive or supervisory directors today requires them to make sufficient time available to fulfil their responsibilities. This should cause non-executive and supervisory directors to limit the number of non-executive or supervisory board positions they accept. What is an appropriate maximum number of non-executive or supervisory board positions will vary from person to person and according to the specific responsibilities involved in each position. In order to make this transparent to shareholders, listed companies should be required to disclose what board positions in other companies their non-executive or supervisory directors hold.

Shareholders should be able to assess whether sufficient time is available

Through proper disclosure of number and nature of board positions held in other companies

4.2. The remuneration of directors

Remuneration is one of the key areas where executive directors have a conflict of interests. In order to align the interests of executive directors with the interests of shareholders, modern systems of remuneration usually include performance-related remuneration, often through grants of shares, share options or other rights to acquire shares or by payments which vary with the share price. The result is that the remuneration of executive directors to a certain extent is dependent on the share price.

Remuneration is one key area of conflict of interest

To align interests, remuneration is often linked to the share price

Remuneration through grants of shares and rights to acquire shares does not take away fully the conflict of interests of executive directors and has some negative side effects. To the extent these forms of remuneration allow realisation of profits as a result of short term share price increases, they increase the pressures for executive directors to produce short term positive results according to the time contingency in their remuneration terms. These results may well not be sustainable in the long run. Furthermore, these forms of remuneration lead to a shift of monetary benefits and control rights of shareholders to executive directors. As the share price is related to the reported financial performance of the company, the executive directors, who are also primarily responsible for the accounting for the company's performance, have an incentive to produce accounts which overstate the performance of the company.

This has some negative effects :

Pressure for short term results

Shift of monetary benefits and control rights

Incentive to manipulate the accounts

The Group has considered whether remuneration in shares and rights to acquire shares should be prohibited altogether but has rejected this view. The form and level of remuneration of executive directors should be left to the companies and their shareholders themselves, and no particular form of remuneration should be generally prohibited. Within an appropriate regulatory regime, remuneration in shares and

No need for a prohibition of remuneration in shares and share options

But appropriate

rights to acquire shares can still make a useful contribution to the alignment of the interests of executive directors with the interests of the shareholders. However, because of the acute conflicts of interest inherent in such schemes, they must be subjected to appropriate governance controls, based on adequate information rights.

rules should be in place

An appropriate regulatory regime at least includes the following elements:

Including four elements at least

1. The remuneration policy for directors generally should be disclosed in the financial statements of the company, and should be an explicit item on the agenda of the annual general meeting. Shareholders should annually have the opportunity to debate the remuneration policy of the company on the basis of a comprehensive disclosure of the policy, without having to go through the process of tabling shareholder resolutions. Some Member States require, or are considering requiring, a form of mandatory or advisory vote by shareholders on the remuneration policy. We do not believe a shareholder vote on the remuneration policy generally should be an EU requirement, as the effects of such a vote can be different from Member State to Member State. The important thing is that shareholders annually have the opportunity to debate the policy with the board. See however n°3 below for prior approval by shareholders of share and share option schemes.

Remuneration policy for directors should be annually disclosed

And debated in the annual meeting

But requirement for a vote on the policy should not be imposed at EU level

2. The remuneration of individual directors of the company, both executive and non-executive or supervisory directors, is to be disclosed in detail in the annual financial statements of the company. This includes all financial and non-financial benefits derived from the company, including golden parachutes and pension rights and other perquisites. Disclosure of the individual remuneration of directors is important for shareholders in order to appreciate the relation between the performance of the company and the level of remuneration of the directors. It also takes away the possibility of hiding particular elements of remuneration of individual directors in aggregate numbers and thus puts up a barrier against excessive (elements of) remuneration. Some have argued that disclosure of individual director's remuneration will only lead to an increase of remuneration as a result of human nature of directors comparing their income with that of their competitors and peers. This may be a negative side effect but, on balance, the Group believes it is more important to give shareholders the information on the basis of which they can hold directors accountable for the remuneration they extract from the company.

Individual remuneration of directors should be disclosed in detail annually

To clarify the relation with company performance

And to prevent potential abuses

The requirement to disclose the remuneration of individual directors should extend to non-executive and supervisory directors. Usually,

This applies also to non-executive

their remuneration is more straightforward than that of executive directors. Shareholders should be able to judge to what extent the remuneration of non-executive and supervisory directors is justified in view of their performance, and to what extent (elements of) their remuneration render them non-independent. We believe that remuneration of non-executive or supervisory directors in shares or share options, or which is otherwise related to the company's performance, should not generally be prohibited, but such remuneration should disqualify the non-executive or supervisory director from being considered to be independent (see the previous Section).

and supervisory directors

Who should not be considered to be independent if their remuneration is linked to company's performance

3. Schemes under which directors are remunerated in shares, share options or any other right to acquire shares or to be remunerated on the basis of share price movements, and any substantial change in such schemes, should be subject to the prior approval of the shareholders meeting. The approval relates to the scheme as such, i.e. the system of remuneration and the rules applied to establish the individual remuneration under the scheme, and does not relate to the individual remuneration of directors under the scheme. Such remuneration should be set by the remuneration committee. When put to the shareholders meeting for approval, the remuneration committee must properly explain the scheme to shareholders in view of the intended application and should set out the relationship of the scheme to the overall remuneration policy. It should also provide an overview of the costs of the scheme to the company in view of the intended application.

Share incentive schemes should require a general meeting approval

Based on proper explanation, by remuneration committee, of the applicable rules and their likely costs

4. The annual costs to the company of share grant schemes, share options schemes and other share incentive schemes should be properly accounted for in the company's annual accounts. The present accounting standards are too loose and are under reform, both US GAAP and IAS. Mandatory accounting for the cost of share incentive schemes will reduce the distributable profits of the company and may pose particular problems for start-up companies. However, some major companies have already voluntarily started to implement such accounting. The Group believes such accounting is a major restraint on exorbitant share incentive schemes, and maybe the only one that is really effective. This has led the Group to recommend that the principle of accounting for the cost of share incentive schemes be recognised in a European framework rule. The accounting standards setting bodies and the accounting profession generally should develop the appropriate standards in more detail.

An important way to prevent abuses is to require full reflection of share incentive schemes in annual accounts

The appropriate framework rule should be adopted at EU level

These elements of an appropriate regulatory regime should apply to all listed companies across the EU. Again, their application should not be delayed by a lengthy legislative process. We propose that the

Recommendation to be adopted rapidly should cover all listed

Commission include these elements in a Recommendation to Member States and announces its intention to monitor compliance by - and within - Member States, and to consider further rulemaking if compliance is insufficient.

companies

And be duly monitored

4.3. Management responsibility for financial statements

The probity of financial statements is very much at the heart of the concerns raised by Enron and similar cases. Many of the regulatory responses in the US and in Europe are focused on ensuring that financial statements correctly reflect the financial position of the company and are not manipulated, whether or not to the personal benefit of directors or of holders of blocks of shares in the company. This is vital for shareholders, creditors and, more generally, the financial markets and the economy.

Recent corporate scandals and responses highlight the key importance of trust in financial statements

Under the company laws of Member States, the responsibility for the probity of financial statements of the company is primarily a collective responsibility of the board : in a one-tier structure, this is a collective responsibility of both executive and non-executive directors, and in a two-tier structure, this is the collective responsibility of both the managing directors and the supervisory directors. This is reflected in many Member States in the requirement that all executive, non-executive and supervisory directors sign the annual accounts of the company. The Group believes this collective responsibility is an appropriate mechanism to avoid a limited number of board members, in particular certain executive directors whose performance is to be reflected in financial statements, having a decisive role in determining their content.

At national level, board traditionally has a collective responsibility for the probity of financial statements

Which avoids undue excessive individual influence

The collective responsibility of the full board(s) should extend not only to the annual and consolidated accounts, but, in principle, to all statements regarding the financial position of the company, including quarterly result announcements (where applicable) and financial statements in prospectuses and other public documents. An exception can be made for mandatory ad hoc disclosure, where consideration by the full board(s) will often be practically impossible. However, it is the collective responsibility of the full board(s) to ensure that an appropriate authorisation system is in place for such ad hoc disclosures.

Collective responsibility extends to all statements on the company's financial position

Except for ad hoc disclosure, where proper delegation must be organised

The collective responsibility of the full board(s) should also extend to statements on key non-financial data, such as information on the company's risk management system, its business prospects and investment plans, and strategies in technical, organisational and human resources areas. It also includes in particular responsibility for

It also extends to all statements on non-financial data

Including the annual corporate

accuracy of the annual statement relating to the company's corporate governance structures and practices.

governance statement

The Group believes that the collective responsibility of the board for financial and key non-financial statements should be confirmed as a matter of EU law.

EU law should confirm collective responsibility

4.4. Wrongful trading

In our Consultative Document, we particularly addressed the need to strengthen the accountability of directors when the company is threatened by insolvency and suggested the introduction of a European framework rule on "wrongful trading". This is a matter all Member States' laws have to deal with, usually in a combination of company law and insolvency law. Some respondents argued that, as this is a matter of insolvency law, the EU should not interfere with it at all. The Group rejects this view. The responsibility of directors when the company becomes insolvent has its most important effect prior to insolvency and is a key element of an appropriate corporate governance system. From this perspective, it is irrelevant whether rules relating to this responsibility are laid down in company law or insolvency law.

The introduction of a framework rule on wrongful trading at EU level

Was opposed by some respondents on formal grounds

Which are not shared by the Group

The gist of the UK "wrongful trading" rules, the French and Belgian "action en comblement du passif", and other Member States laws is similar : if the directors ought to foresee that the company cannot continue to pay its debts, they must decide either to rescue the company (and ensure future payment of creditors) or to put it into liquidation. Otherwise, the directors will be liable fully or in part to creditors for their unpaid claims.

Existing national rules make directors liable for not reacting when they ought to foresee the company's insolvency

The details of the national rules vary considerably. In some Member States there are no specific provisions, but a similar effect is achieved through general rules on directors' liability, sometimes by tort law, though the general duty to file a petition for bankruptcy in the case of actual insolvency comes too late. The concept of wrongful trading applies both to independent companies and to companies within groups. The directors of a subsidiary company are subject to the rules, as well as the parent company and its directors if they operate as de facto or "shadow" directors of the subsidiary. The beauty of the rule is that it does not interfere with the on-going business decisions of directors, as long as an insolvency situation is not yet foreseeable. A general obligation to file for bankruptcy in case of actual insolvency usually comes too late.

National rules vary considerably

But they apply also to group companies

And do not interfere with on-going business decisions

The majority of responses supported the suggestion of the Group to introduce a European framework rule on wrongful trading, which would hold company directors (including "shadow" directors) accountable for letting the company continue to do business when it should be foreseen that it will not be able to pay its debts. This support strengthened the Group in its view that it should recommend that such a rule be introduced. It would be a considerable improvement in the functioning of companies and groups of companies.

Responses to the consultation supported the introduction of a EU rule on wrongful trading

Which the Group recommends

It would protect creditors without overly restricting companies and their directors, as they can and must make their own choice in case of – foreseeable, not yet actually imminent - insolvency whether to attempt to rescue the company or put it into liquidation. A European wrongful trading rule would enhance creditors' confidence and their willingness to do business with companies. This is even more important in Europe, since doing business across borders may be perceived to be more risky than in one's own jurisdiction where information on business partners may be easier to obtain. Finally, a wrongful trading rule would introduce an equivalent level of protection for creditors of companies across the EU, without any need to harmonise the whole body of directors' liability rules in all Member States.

Without overly restricting management's decisions

Such a rule would enhance creditors confidence

And introduce an equivalent level of protection across the EU

4.5 Sanctions, Director's disqualification

The responsibility for the company's financial and key non-financial disclosure should be properly sanctioned by Member States. Member States should ensure that all board members can be held accountable for misleading financial and other key non-financial statements, and that appropriate sanctions are in place. What sanctions should apply (criminal sanctions, civil liability for damages, forfeiture of bonuses and profits gained through share and share option grants) in the EU is a matter for Member States.

Misleading disclosure should be properly sanctioned

Applicable sanctions should be defined by Member States

Yet the Group believes that there is a case for examining whether one particular type of sanction should be introduced across the EU : director's disqualification. Criminal and civil liability sanctions are often very difficult to effectuate, may often come too late, may have substantially different applications in the various Member States, and may in practice not operate as a strong deterrent against misconduct by directors. The disqualification of a person from serving as a director of companies across the EU is an alternative sanction, which may be easier to effectuate and has a powerful deterrent and longer term disabling effect.

Criminal and civil sanctions have some weaknesses

Which may be addressed by the introduction at EU level of director's disqualification

We recommend that the Commission further review whether director's disqualification can be imposed as a sanction at least for misleading financial and key non-financial disclosures, or more generally for misconduct by directors. Such review should look into the director's disqualification systems that apply in some Member States and the "fit and proper" requirements for directors, as contained in European banking and insurance legislation. The constitutional aspects of the sanction in some Member States should be considered.

Adoption of such a rule should be considered by the Commission

After proper analysis of existing national and European rules

5. AUDITING PRACTICES

Enron, Worldcom and similar cases have revealed that a proper audit of financial statements of the company is a fundamental element of a corporate governance system. Audit, in an appropriate form, is also an important safeguard in non-financial reporting. A proper audit depends on the role and performance of the external auditor, as well as the internal audit process of the company.

A proper audit is fundamental to good corporate governance

The Commission has already undertaken initiatives to deal with particular issues relating to the role and performance of the external auditor. The Commission's Recommendation of May 16, 2002[22] deals with such subjects as:

- Non-audit services provided by audit firms to their audit clients;
- Rotation of key audit partners;
- Employment of a former audit partner by the audit client.

Some initiatives have been taken by the Commission,

among which the Recommendation on Auditor Independence

Furthermore, the Commission has announced that it will produce a further Communication on policy issues, which would deal with the role of public auditors, code of ethics, auditor's liability and public oversight of the audit profession.

A new Communication on Audit is expected soon

We support these initiatives of the Commission and urge it to proceed with its further Communication. The Group itself has focused on the internal aspects of auditing practices, in particular on the responsibility of the board for audit. As we have said, we believe that within the board the responsibility for the audit of the company's financial statements should lie with non-executive or supervisory directors who are at least in the majority independent (see Section 4.1 above). The audit committee, which in practice is usually set up for these purposes, has a key role to play in the relationship between the executive managers and the external auditor. To this end, the audit

Group has focused on internal aspects of auditing practices

Key role for non-executive or supervisory directors

Main missions of audit committee :

[22] For complete references, see Annex 4.

committee[23] should:

- be responsible for the selection of the external auditor for appointment by the shareholders meeting (as is the rule in most Member States) or the full board, and the terms and conditions of their appointment; *Selection of auditor*
- monitor the relationship of the external auditor with the company and its executive management, in particular to safeguard the external auditor's independence; *Monitoring of auditor's independence*
- monitor non-audit services provided by the auditor firm, if any. Non-audit services by audit firms to audit clients raise concerns generally, and the Group sees a case for prohibiting them altogether. As long as they are not prohibited, they should be closely monitored by the audit committee; *Monitoring of non audit services*
- meet with the external auditor at least every quarter, and at least once a year in the absence of executive managers; *Regular meetings with auditor*
- ensure that the external auditor has access to all information required to perform his role; *Ensuring access to information*
- receive the auditor's management letter with comments on the financial statements, and consider whether these comments should be disclosed in the financial statements. *Follow-up to management letter*

The audit committee should also be pivotal in the internal aspects of the audit function. To this end, the audit committee should: *And internal aspects of audit:*

- be responsible for reviewing the accounting policies of the company, and changes thereto; *Accounting policies*
- monitor the company's internal audit procedures and its risk management system; *Internal audit*
- meet regularly with those who are responsible for the internal audit procedures and risk management system; *Risk management*
- consider to what extent the findings of the risk management system should be reported in the company's financial statements;
- have access to all internal information relevant to performing its role. *With due access to information*

The Group recommends that the Commission include provisions on the role and responsibilities of audit committees in its Recommendation on the role of non-executive and supervisory directors, which we invite the Commission to issue. *Relevant provisions should be included in the proposed Recommendation*

[23] If no audit committee is set up, its role should be performed by the non-executive directors in the one-tier board or by the supervisory board as such, of which the majority then should be independent. For brevity sake, we will continue to refer here only to audit committee.

6. CORPORATE GOVERNANCE REGULATION IN EUROPE

In our Consultative Document, we addressed the issue how Europe should proceed with the regulation of corporate governance, and in particular whether a European code of corporate governance should be established. We expressed our reservations about a European corporate governance code.

Reservations were expressed in the Consultative Document about a EU corporate governance code

The adoption of such a code would not achieve full information for investors about the key corporate governance rules applicable to companies across Europe, as these rules would still be based on and part of national company laws that are in certain aspects widely divergent. We also doubted whether additional Europe-wide voluntary rules would contribute to the improvement of corporate governance, as Europe would either have to allow many alternative rules, depending on the various company law systems, or to confine itself to abstract, and perhaps largely meaningless, rules which would be compatible with all of these systems. Effective harmonising of corporate governance codes while leaving company law untouched is not feasible.

Such a code would fail to deliver full information

And would not be feasible

We finally emphasised that the key input for codes of corporate governance should come from the market and market participants. These codes are a means of building up reputation by voluntary compliance with rules of good behaviour. The market and its participants know best what rules enhance reputation. The EU as well as Member States should leave it to those who have an own interest in such codes, i.e. companies, investors, stock exchanges, etc. to take the initiative, while continuing to monitor the situation closely.

Key input for codes should come from the markets

And only be monitored by the EU and Member States

A clear majority of responses to our Consultative Document agreed with this approach and rejected the creation of a European corporate governance code.

Responses to the consultation reject a EU code

However, the Group does believe there is an active role for the EU to play in corporate governance, apart from the various initiatives we suggested in the previous Sections. The EU should actively seek to co-ordinate the efforts of Member States to improve corporate governance by changes in their company laws, securities laws (listing rules) or in their codes of corporate governance. Such a co-ordination is warranted in order to facilitate the convergence of the corporate governance efforts of Member States, which is already emerging, or at a minimum work to ensure that they do not unnecessarily diverge, and that Member States learn from each other's experiences. The co-ordination should not only extend to the

The EU should nevertheless co-ordinate the efforts of Member States

To facilitate convergence

Including with respect to enforcement

making of codes, but also to the procedures Member States have in place to monitor and enforce compliance and disclosure. This co-ordination structure should stimulate a continuous debate about what good corporate governance involves. In light of the recent regulatory initiatives in the USA, it is important that the EU also engages in a transatlantic debate on corporate governance, so that both the EU and the USA have a full understanding of each others' methods and practices.

On a continuous basis, and taking account of US developments

As the Weil, Gotschal & Manges Report[24] has shown, currently various corporate governance codes exist in Member States. We believe it is important that Member States designate one particular code of corporate governance as the code with which companies subject to their jurisdiction have to comply, or by reference to which they have to explain how and why their practices are different. This would also facilitate the co-ordination of the efforts of Member States.

Many codes currently exist

Each Member State should designate a reference code

We recommend that the Commission set up a structure which facilitates the co-ordination of the Member States' efforts to improve corporate governance. Member States should be required to participate in the co-ordination, but the process itself and the results of the process should be voluntary and non-binding. Market participants (including of course companies) should be invited to be actively involved in the co-ordination exercise.

A structure should be set up

To co-ordinate Member States efforts on a non-binding basis

Out of the co-ordination of the national corporate governance efforts of Member States over time, a general framework on corporate governance in Europe can be expected to emerge. The form and content of that framework, however, should not be determined beforehand, but should be left to the developments in Member States and in the wider business context and to co-ordination between them.

Co-ordination of national efforts may lead over time to a European general framework

To summarise, listed companies should be required to include in their annual report and accounts a coherent and descriptive statement covering the key elements of the corporate governance rules and practices they apply. This statement should also be separately posted on the company's website.

Summary : *Annual Corporate Governance Statement to be published*

The principles applicable to such an annual corporate governance statement should be set up in a framework Directive. The detailed rules should be set up by Member States in view of their national company laws, but the EU should ensure a certain level of co-

Based on common principles

[24] Comparative Study of Corporate Governance Codes relevant to the European Union and its Member States (http://europa.eu.int/comm/internal_market/en/company/company/news/corp-gov-codes-rpt_en.htm)

ordination.

Such a statement should contain a reference to the designated national code of corporate governance and/or company law rules with which the company complies or in relation to which it explains deviations.

Including reference to a national code

Responsibility for the annual corporate governance statement should lie with the board as a whole.

Under collective responsibility of the board

Listed companies should be required to maintain a specific section on their website where they publish all information relevant for their shareholders, as recommended in Chapter II. This section should include all relevant materials relating to shareholders meetings, and should offer facilities for giving proxies or voting instructions on-line or for downloading and electronic transmission of proxy or instruction forms.

All meeting materials and proxy forms to be contained in a specific website section

Member States should however be able to require listed companies to provide hard copies of meeting materials and voting forms to shareholders who specifically request them.

Sending of hard copies to be decided by MS

Listed companies should explicitly disclose to their shareholders how they can ask questions, how and to what extent the company intends to answer questions, and how and under what conditions they can submit proposals to the shareholders meeting. This should be an element of their mandatory annual corporate governance statement.

Rights to ask questions and to table resolutions to be explained

With respect to the right to submit proposals for resolution by the shareholders meeting, there is a link with the squeeze-out right of a majority shareholder and sell-out right of minority shareholders. Member States should be required to set the applicable thresholds in a consistent way.

Threshold to table resolution to be set consistently with squeeze-out and sell-out rights

Listed companies should be required to offer all shareholders facilities to vote in absentia – by way of direct vote or proxies – by electronic means, and through hard copy voting instruction or proxy forms at their request. The Group recommends that such a requirement should not apply to cross border situations to the extent that any necessary solutions have not yet been found and implemented for the problems of cross-border holding of securities in Europe.

Facilities to vote in absentia to be offered

To the extent that any necessary solutions have been found

Listed companies should be permitted, but not required, to allow absentee shareholders to participate in general meetings via electronic means (such as internet or satellite).

Electronic participation in meetings permitted

The permission to abandon the physical meeting should be a Member State decision, but such a decision should in any event be taken by – or with the consent of – the general meeting of shareholders with an

As well as abandonment of physical meeting

appropriate strong qualified majority.

A separate Group of Experts set up in January 2002 by the Dutch Minister of Justice issued its Final Report on cross-border voting in September 2002. In that Report, it is recommended that the rights and obligations of accountholders and securities intermediaries be regulated at EU level, to ensure that accountholders across the EU can effectively exercise the voting rights on shares they hold.

Consideration to be given to cross-border voting issues

The issues identified by that Cross-Border Voting Group, combined with the relevant recommendations of the Group, should be considered by the Commission as a matter of priority, with a view to building a regulatory framework that facilitates the participation of shareholders across the EU and, where possible, outside the EU, in the governance of listed companies.

With a view to building the appropriate regulatory framework

Regulation of the relevant types of institutional investors by Member States should include an obligation on those institutional investors to disclose their investment policy and their policy with respect to the exercise of voting rights in companies in which they invest, and to disclose to their beneficial holders at their request how these rights have been used in a particular case.

Institutional investors to disclose their investment and voting policies

Shareholders, in a general meeting or holding a maximum of at least 5 or 10 per cent of the share capital, should be given the right to apply to a court or appropriate administrative body to order a special investigation. A European framework rule should be adopted to this end, whereby this special investigation right should be guaranteed in all companies and as far as possible on a group-wide basis. Details of the procedure and determination of proper sanctions should be left to Member States.

Special investigation right to be offered in all companies

At least listed and other open companies across the EU should have the choice between the two types of board structure (one-tier / two-tier), so as to be able to elect the system which best suits their particular corporate governance needs and circumstances.

Permission for companies to freely adopt any of the two types of board structures

Listed companies should be required to ensure that the nomination and remuneration of directors and the audit of the accounting for the company's performance within the board are decided upon by exclusively non-executive or supervisory directors who are in the majority independent.

Key role to play by (independent) non-executive or supervisory directors

The Commission should rapidly issue a Recommendation to Member States that they should have effective rules in their company laws or in their national corporate governance codes to this end, which should

Based on a Recommendation to be issued rapidly

be enforced on a "comply or explain" basis at the minimum.

The Recommendation should include principles on independence, and could include a list of relationships which would lead a non-executive or supervisory director to be considered as not independent. Listed companies should be required to disclose in their annual corporate governance statement which of their directors they consider to be independent and on what grounds. Similar disclosure should be made when a new director is proposed for appointment.

Independence to be based on principles

And explained whenever necessary

Listed companies should include in their annual corporate governance statement a profile of the board's composition, and should explain why individual non-executive or supervisory directors are qualified to serve on the board in their particular roles. Similar disclosure should be made in proposals for initial appointment. Listed companies should also be required to disclose what board positions in other companies their non-executive or supervisory directors hold.

Disclosure about board's composition and qualifications

And other board positions held

The remuneration policy for directors generally should be disclosed in the financial statements of the company, and should be an explicit item for debate on the agenda of the annual meeting.

Remuneration policy to be disclosed and debated

The individual remuneration of directors of the company, both executive and non-executive or supervisory directors, is to be disclosed in detail in the financial statements of the company.

Individual director's remuneration to be disclosed

Schemes granting shares and share options and other forms of remuneration of directors linked to the share price should require the prior approval of the shareholders meeting, on the basis of a proper explanation by the remuneration committee of the applicable rules and of their likely costs.

Prior shareholder approval of share incentive schemes

The costs of all share incentive schemes should be properly reflected in the annual accounts, and this accounting principle should be recognised in a European framework rule.

Costs of these schemes to be accounted for

The Commission should adopt a Recommendation defining an appropriate regulatory regime for directors' remuneration in listed companies, which should include the four elements outlined above.

Appropriate regulatory regime to be included in a Recommendation

Responsibility for the probity of financial statements should be attributed, as a matter of EU law, to all board members on a collective basis. This responsibility should extend to all statements made about the company's financial position, as well as to all statements on key non-financial data (including the annual corporate governance statement).

Board to be responsible on a collective basis for financial and non-financial statements

A rule on wrongful trading should be introduced at EU level, which would hold company directors (including shadow directors) accountable for letting the company continue to do business when it

Introduction at EU level of a wrongful trading rule

should be foreseen that it will not be able to pay its debts.

Appropriate sanctions for misleading financial and other key non-financial statements should generally be determined by Member States. The Commission should nevertheless review whether director's disqualification can be imposed at EU level as a sanction, at least for misleading financial and key non-financial disclosures or more generally for misconduct.

Director's disqualification to be further reviewed as a possible sanction at EU level

The responsibility for supervision of the audit of the company's financial statements should lie with a committee of non-executive or supervisory directors who are at least in the majority independent. Provisions on the role and responsibilities of audit committees (or any equivalent body), with respect to both the external and internal aspects of audit, should be included in the proposed Recommendation on the role of non-executive and supervisory directors.

Role and responsibilities of audit committees to be defined in Recommendation on independent directors

The key input for codes of corporate governance should continue to come from the markets and their participants. Each Member State should designate one particular corporate governance code as the code with which companies subject to their jurisdiction have to comply or by reference to which they have to explain how and why their practices are different.

Each Member State to designate a reference code of corporate governance

A structure should be set up at EU level to facilitate the co-ordination of Member States efforts to improve corporate governance. Co-ordination should not only extend to the making of codes, but also to the procedures Member States have in place to monitor and enforce compliance and disclosure. Member States should be required to participate in the co-ordination process, but the results should be non-binding.

Co-ordination of Member States efforts to be co-ordinated by an EU structure, on a non-binding basis

CHAPTER IV

CAPITAL FORMATION AND MAINTENANCE

1. THE FUNCTION OF LEGAL CAPITAL AND THE COMPETITIVE EFFECT OF THE CURRENT RULES

The Consultation Document included a description of the traditional functions of legal capital in European Company Law, followed by three possible approaches for reform, and some special topics in the regulation of legal capital that deserved more detailed attention.

Consultation Document covered possible reforms of EU rules on capital, and special topics

The concept of legal capital is generally seen as one of the cornerstones of European Company Law. In the Consultative Document, the functions of legal capital, as described by orthodox legal and financial theory, were listed. A large majority of the respondents highlighted the fundamental functions of protecting creditors' and existing shareholders' interests. Many respondents highlighted this function of legal capital as a "retention figure" that prevents unlawful transfers of assets from the company to its members. Most respondents, and the Group itself, however do not believe that legal capital serves any function of indicating the adequacy of a company's assets for its entrepreneurial activity ("capital adequacy"), leaving aside the special regime of capital adequacy for certain regulated business activities.

Legal capital is seen as one of the cornerstones of European Company Law

Its main function is seen to be creditor and shareholder protection

But it does not reflect "capital adequacy"

In short, a considerable majority of the respondents agree that the most important functions developed by legal capital are the protection of creditors' and shareholders' rights. It is important to note, however, that many respondents added that the functions performed by legal capital are more important in theory than in practice: there is wide agreement that the concept of legal capital is not effective in attaining the objectives that are assigned to it.

Many responses to the consultation stressed that legal capital is not in practice effective in attaining its objectives

The rules on capital formation and maintenance have an impact on the cost of capital and credit, although that impact may be extremely difficult to assess. Most of the respondents do not believe that the peculiarities of the European legal capital regime put European companies at a competitive disadvantage in comparison with their competitors in other legal systems. Evidently, this question deserves thorough empirical research, which is difficult because the competitive effect of the legal capital regime is obscured by the presence of many other variables. However, none of the respondents argue that

European legal capital regime is generally not considered a competitive disadvantage for European companies

European companies enjoy an advantage thanks to the legal capital regime existing in the EU.

But it is no competitive advantage either

2. APPROACHES TO THE REFORM OF LEGAL CAPITAL IN EUROPE

In the Consultative Document, we referred to criticisms levelled against the legal capital regime in the Second Company Law Directive. The legal capital regime, it is argued, fails to adequately protect creditors, who are not so much interested in the capital of the company (and certainly not in the minimum capital) but much more in its ability to pay its short term and long term debts. It can also be said that the amount of legal capital, as shown in the articles of association, is a very primitive and inaccurate indication of the company's ability to pay its debts. There is an argument against the inflexibility and costs of the current regime, that could hamper in some way the ability of companies to obtain equity funding.

Legal capital is criticised for failing to protect creditors

Legal capital is a poor indication of company's ability to pay its debts

Current regime is arguably inflexible and costly

Finally, it is argued that the annual accounts have become an inadequate yard-stick for deciding whether the company has sufficient distributable reserves for it to make distributions to shareholders. As a result of changes in accounting standards, like standards on goodwill impairment and accounting for pension fund performance and costs of share and share option schemes, the accounts - and the reserves they show - become more and more volatile and less and less an indicator of the ability of companies to pay their current and future debts. Capital protection based on such accounts is becoming a delusion.

Annual accounts have become an inadequate yardstick for making decisions on distributions

And for assessing company's ability to pay its debts

Most of the respondents agree that there is room for improvement of the current regime, although there is controversy on which is the best possible course to reform the present system.

Current regime should be improved

In the Consultative Document, three alternative approaches were considered :

Consultative Document presented three approaches

- The first approach is based on the "SLIM" (Simpler Legislation for the Internal Market) proposals. This approach consists of an evolution of the current regime to a more simplified and modern capital regime. The purpose of the SLIM exercise was to simplify the Second Company Law Directive; as a consequence of this, more fundamental changes to the rules could not be considered by the SLIM Group, which proposed a number of measures intended to simplify and modernise the current legal capital regime. In the Consultative Document, this was suggested as one

First approach:

Simplification of the Second Directive

Based on the "SLIM" proposals

of the possible approaches to reform, supplemented by other recommendations that could be included in a wider reform of the Second Company Law Directive ("SLIM-plus").

Supplemented by further recommendations ("SLIM-plus")

- The second approach is roughly based on the experience of US jurisdictions that have passed statutes based on the Model Business Corporations Act. This approach would mean a radical departure from many of the features of European Company Law: the concept of legal capital does not exist in such a regime, and most of the rules related to capital formation and maintenance are different from the European rules, or even totally opposed to them. Apart from those basic features, in the US jurisdictions that follow this approach, the balance of powers between the general meeting of shareholders and the board of directors is usually tilted in favour of the latter, while the situation in Europe is different. In these US jurisdictions, the board of directors may issue new shares without any shareholders' involvement, but subject to the directors' fiduciary duties. Pre-emption rights are not recognised as basic shareholder rights, and they only exist where they are expressly recognised in the articles of association.

Second approach:

Inspired by US experience, it leads to a radical departure from:

- the concept of legal capital

- many rules on capital formation and maintenance

- the current balance of powers between shareholders and board of directors

- The third approach contemplated in the Consultative Document is also based on the elimination of the concept of legal capital, but seeks to integrate that fundamental change with some of the basic features of European Company Law, specifically the need for shareholder approval for operations that affect shareholders' equity.

Third approach:

Elimination of legal capital, but retention of shareholder controls

Very few respondents expressed support for the second approach. A substantial number of respondents preferred the first and third approach, with some of the respondents opting for one of them, but without excluding the other. Taking into account the consultation results, the Group recommends a two-step approach:

In view of support for the first and/or third approaches, the Group recommends two steps:

1. The Commission should, as a matter of priority, present a proposal for reform of the Second Company Law Directive, along the lines suggested by the SLIM Group, with the modifications and supplementary measures that are suggested in the present Report ("SLIM-plus").

First priority, to reform the Second Directive, based on "SLIM-plus"

2. The Commission should, at a later stage, conduct a review into the feasibility of an alternative regime, based on the third approach. The alternative regime need not replace the capital formation and maintenance rules of the Directive as amended according to the "SLIM-plus" proposals. Rather, the new regime could be offered as an alternative option *for Member States*, who should be able to freely decide to change to the new regime and

Later, to review the feasibility of an alternative regime, based on the third approach

impose it on companies subject to their jurisdiction or to retain the Second Directive rules as modified by the "SLIM-plus" reform. Obviously, the creation of a new regime will demand further study and consultation, but there is a very substantial and relevant percentage of answers to the Consultative Document that shows a strong interest in pursuing this alternative to the present capital formation and maintenance rules. In addition, the Group believes that the criticism directed at the current regime is so fundamental and serious that indeed an alternative regime aimed at efficient shareholder and creditor protection needs to be developed.

Such a regime could be offered as an option for Member States

Consultation indeed confirms strong case for the development of an efficient alternative regime

In the following pages, we give a brief overview of the SLIM-plus proposals and of an alternative regime that could be developed. The specific questions in the Consultative Document have been integrated in this overview. We acknowledge that the issues discussed here are complex and intricate. The nature of this Report does not allow a complete and exhaustive description of all necessary modifications. The aim of the Group here is to set the basic lines along which further work may proceed.

The basic lines of both approaches ("SLIM-plus" and alternative regime) are briefly presented in the following pages

3 MODERNISATION OF THE CURRENT CAPITAL REGIME IN THE SECOND COMPANY LAW DIRECTIVE ("SLIM-PLUS")

Any modernisation of the current capital formation and capital maintenance regime should remove, where possible, the defects perceived in it, while maintaining the virtues of the current regime.

A modernisation of the current regime has to be selective

The SLIM Group made a number of suggestions for changing the Second Company Law Directive:

"SLIM" proposals:

- elimination, in certain cases, of experts' valuations for contributions in kind; *- contributions in kind*
- further possibility of issuing shares without pre-emption rights when shares are issued at their market price, or slightly below; *- pre-emption rights*
- possibility for companies of acquiring own shares above the percentages set in the Directive, and allowing for longer authorisations to the board; *- acquisition of own shares*
- reduction of the prohibition of financial assistance; *- financial assistance*
- extension of the regime of compulsory withdrawal of shares. *- compulsory withdrawal*

We have discussed these proposals, and extended the consultation to some other questions, some of which had already been pointed at in the SLIM report.

We discussed these proposals, and some other questions

a) Minimum capital

The Group has reached the conclusion that the only function of the minimum capital requirement is to deter individuals from light-heartedly starting a public limited company. We are not convinced that minimum capital, at its present levels, performs any other useful functions, but there is no evidence that it constitutes a hurdle to business activity either. It is probably wise not to spend much time on minimum capital in a reform to make the current system more efficient, and to direct attention to issues which are more relevant. The minimum capital requirement should not be removed, nor increased.

Minimum capital serves only one function

But is not seen to be a significant hurdle

Requirement should not be removed, nor increased

b) No par value shares

Wide demand for no par value shares is being expressed by the financial industry and the legal professions. Not only the SLIM group favoured the introduction of no par value shares, but also the Giovannini Group in its report on *The Impact of the Introduction of the Euro on Capital Markets*[25].

The introduction of no par value shares is widely demanded

Offering the possibility to have no par value shares does not necessarily require major changes in the system. The Second Company Law Directive already allows for shares to have a fractional value (also referred to as "accountable par") rather than a nominal value (see for example Article 8 providing that shares cannot be issued below their nominal or fractional value). Shares would have to express numerically the fraction of the capital of the company that they represent or, alternatively, the total number of shares outstanding. In a system in which shares are dematerialised, the updating of the percentage or of the total number of shares should be relatively easy: there should be continuous disclosure of all shares outstanding, and, at the very least, companies should be required to update the fraction any time that there are relevant changes to it. As for "paper" shares, they would have to include the appropriate fraction or the total number of shares, together with the date in which the fraction or the total number of shares was correct, and a reminder that the correct fraction can be obtained at any time from the company itself, or from the companies Register.

The Second Directive already allows for shares to have a fractional value rather than a nominal value

Shares with fractional value require proper and continuous disclosure of relevant figures

Whether or not the shares are dematerialised

It is debatable whether introducing shares without any reference to either nominal or fractional value would constitute a significant

It is debatable whether shares without any

[25] See paragraph 2.2.2, letter D.

change in the system of the Second Company Law Directive. Many argue that Article 8 of the Directive - which prohibits issues with a discount to nominal value - is the only objection, and that a system of real no par value shares is consistent with the general approach of the Directive to capital formation and maintenance rules. Others take the view that real no par value shares would require a more fundamental change to the system of the Directive. We recommend that, as part of SLIM-Plus, it is reviewed how no par value shares can be accommodated within the Second Company Law Directive.

reference to either nominal or fractional value would be a significant change

Introducing them requires further review

c) Capital formation

As the SLIM Group diagnosed, one of the real problems of the system of capital formation created by the Second Company Law Directive is the valuation of non-cash contributions. Valuations performed by independent experts are expensive and do not offer a total guarantee of the assets' real value. The SLIM Group has proposed elimination of the need for an expert's valuation report where contribution consists of securities traded in a regulated market, which we fully endorse. Similarly, the idea of accepting a valuation that has been made in a preceding period should be considered, provided that the preceding valuation was made recently and there are no new qualifying circumstances that need to be taken into account. For other contributions in kind, there should be the possibility of relying on values derived from audited accounts, provided that the accounting principles used are still applicable to the assets. In that case, minority shareholders should have the right to apply to the court to require a valuation by an expert.

Valuations of non cash contributions are expensive and do not offer total guarantee

Requirement for expert valuation should be eliminated :

- where there is a market price

- where there is a recent evaluation

- where values derive from audited accounts

In the Consultation Document, we asked whether the possibility to allow the provision of services as valid contributions in kind should be introduced. A majority of the respondents are in favour of allowing services as contributions in kind, provided there are sufficient safeguards. The risk consisting of the lack of performance by the provider of services can be covered by placing shares in a escrow account, only to be released after the services have been provided, or, alternatively, by requiring the company to take an insurance policy to cover the absence of execution of services. Acceptance of services as a valid contribution in kind may be particularly useful for some types of companies (e.g. start-up companies, and technological or professional companies in which specialised services are an important asset to the company). We recommend that the Commission reviews the possibility of allowing the provision of services as contribution in kind in the revision of the Second Company Law Directive, with appropriate safeguards.

Responses to the consultation welcomed the possibility of allowing the provision of services as contribution in kind, with safeguards

This possibility should be further reviewed by the Commission

d) Pre-emption rights

Currently, Article 29 §4 of the Second Directive allows the right of pre-emption to be restricted or withdrawn only if stringent formalities (shareholders resolution adopted with qualified majority, presentation by the board of a specific written report) are observed. As the SLIM Group has suggested, for listed companies it would be appropriate to allow the general meeting to empower the board to restrict or withdraw pre-emption rights without having to comply with these formalities, but only where the issue price is at the market price of the securities immediately before the issue or where a small discount to that market price is applied.

For listed companies, additional freedom to suppress pre-emption rights should be allowed, but only if issue is made at market price or slightly below

If real no par value shares are to be introduced, the suppression of pre-emption rights needs to be reconsidered as pre-emption rights may then be the only effective protection left at EU level for shareholders against dilution.

Suppression of pre-emption rights to be reconsidered for real no par value shares

e) Capital reduction

In case of capital reduction, creditors have under the Directive the right to apply to the court to obtain security for their claims, unless the financial position of the company offers the creditor sufficient safeguards. It is up to Member States to provide for the conditions for creditors to exercise this right. In our Chapter on restructuring, we suggest that this model of creditor protection should be applied in all restructuring transactions where specific creditor protection arrangements are to be made (see Chapter VI, Section 5). The burden of proof should be on the creditors : creditors must show that they will be prejudiced by a capital reduction, instead of the company having to show that the creditor's position is secured. This would avoid creditors' hold-ups.

Current regime for creditor protection in case of capital reduction

Should be applied in all restructuring transactions

With the burden of proof on creditors

In addition, we believe that there is a case, if the capital maintenance scheme of the Second Directive is regarded as valid, for re-evaluating whether some safeguards are needed for creditors in the event of capital reduction to adjust legal capital to losses. If capital is reduced to adjust to losses, no assets are transferred to shareholders, but it allows future distributions to an extent that was impossible under the preceding legal capital.

In addition, the need for creditors safeguards when capital is reduced to adjust to losses should be reconsidered

f) Acquisition of own shares

As the SLIM Group suggested, there is a case for allowing acquisition

Acquisition of own

of own shares within the limits of the distributable reserves, and not to limit the acquisition to an entirely arbitrary percentage of legal capital, like the 10% limit of the current Directive. The same should apply to the taking of own shares as security. As to the design of share repurchase programs, the deregulating proposals made by the SLIM Group are to some extent countered by the need to control market manipulation. The Market Abuse Directive (presently at its second reading at the European Parliament) provides for a "safe harbour" for share repurchases, but the conditions to qualify for this exemption, to be set by comitology, will, in all probability, demand more stringent requirements than those included in the Second Company Law Directive. However, it should be possible to establish more flexible requirements for unlisted companies.

shares, and taking them as security, should be possible within the limits of the distributable reserves

This may not be compatible with Market Abuse Directive

But should at least be possible for unlisted companies

g) Financial assistance

The SLIM report proposed two alternative measures for financial assistance in the acquisition of the company's shares : either to allow financial assistance to the extent of distributable reserves, or to restrict the prohibition to subscription of new shares. A majority of respondents believe that the prohibition of financial assistance should be relaxed, but we note that some respondents' objections are based more on tax problems than on company law problems.

SLIM report proposed two alternative measures for relaxation of financial assistance rules

We would favour a solution whereby financial assistance is allowed to the extent of the distributable reserves. Such a solution would be consistent with the approach to the acquisition of own shares by the company. The distributable reserves should provide for full cover of the risk associated with the financial assistance. For example, the outstanding amount of a loan made by the company to acquire shares should be covered in full by the company's distributable reserves.

Group favours a solution whereby financial assistance is allowed to the extent of distributable reserves

In any case, a shareholders' resolution should be required, unless the assistance is given in the company's ordinary course of business as provided under Article 23 §2 of the Second Directive. We believe that there is a good case for allowing the shareholders meeting to authorise the board for a maximum period of time (e.g. five years) to engage the company in financial assistance within the limits of the distributable reserves. If this facility is to be allowed, there should be disclosure.

A shareholders' resolution should in principle be required

Shareholders meeting should be allowed to give authorisation to the board

h) Compulsory withdrawal of shares

The SLIM Group has recommended that a compulsory withdrawal of shares should be possible when a shareholder has acquired 90% of

SLIM report proposed

the capital, as an exception to the provision of Article 36 of the Directive that compulsory withdrawal is only possible if this is provided in the deed of incorporation or articles of association. In Chapter VI of this Report, we make general recommendations on squeeze-out and sell-out rights - for listed and open companies - where a shareholder has acquired, at the minimum, 90%, or, at the maximum, 95% of the capital of the company, where applicable on a class by class basis. These recommendations are in line with the recommendations we made in our first Report on squeeze-out and sell-out rights following a takeover bid. Such rights would effectively deal with the issue addressed by the SLIM Group.

extension of the situations in which compulsory withdrawal of shares is possible

This concern is met by our proposals in Chapter VI on squeeze-out and sell-out rights

i) Other topics

Other topics addressed in the Consultative Document included two concepts which could improve the effectiveness of the legal capital regime : the concept of wrongful trading - to enhançe the responsibility of directors when the company is threatened by insolvency - and the concept of subordination of insiders' (shareholders, directors) claims where the assets of the company are insufficient for its activities. The responses to the consultation are very interesting and reveal different ways of analysis for these matters. A substantial number of responses argue that these concepts belong to insolvency law and should be addressed in that area, and not as part of a reform of company law.

Consultative Document covered wrongful trading and subordination of insiders' claims

Responses argue that these concepts belong to insolvency law

As we say in Chapter III, Section 4.4, we reject this view, as the responsibility of directors when the company is becoming insolvent has its most important effect prior to insolvency and this is a key element of an appropriate corporate governance regime. It is irrelevant whether rules like these are laid down in company law or insolvency law. We then recommend that as an element of good corporate governance, a European framework rule should be introduced on wrongful trading, combined with the concept of "shadow" directors. The concept of subordination of insiders' claims could be considered as part of the development of an alternative regime for creditor protection (see Section 4 hereunder).

Group rejects this view, as responsibility of directors has it most important effect prior to insolvency

EU rules on wrongful trading to be introduced and insider subordination considered with the alternative regime

4 AN ALTERNATIVE REGIME FOR CREDITOR AND SHAREHOLDER PROTECTION

Respondents to the Consultative Document generally supported the approach of abandoning the current legal capital regime and rebuilding a regime which fits in the European company law structure.

Responses to the consultation supported the development of

The idea of integrating modern solutions for creditor protection into the European style of company where shareholder powers are retained has an obvious appeal. As we said above, the alternative regime to be developed is not necessarily to replace the current regime based on legal capital. It could be offered as an alternative to Member States, who could elect to impose the alternative regime on companies subject to their jurisdictions. In order for Member States to be allowed to abandon the current legal capital regime and replace it with an alternative regime, the alternative regime should at least be as effective in achieving the objectives of creditor and shareholder protection as the regime based on legal capital. We believe that, in fact, mechanisms can be created which are superior in achieving these objectives.

an alternative regime for creditor protection within a framework of shareholder control

Member States could be allowed to replace the current regime

With a new, at least as effective, regime

a) Creditor protection

In theory, creditors are protected by legal capital, but it is clear that legal capital may account for only a small fraction of the company's assets. It then offers little protection for creditors as the company enjoys ample freedom to distribute assets to shareholders, irrespective of its solvency. It should also be noted that capital can be reduced - without creditor protection - to account for, or write off, losses, which reduces the protection of creditors to a minimum in cases where there have been accumulated losses eliminating distributable reserves, which is the case in which the creditors most need protection.

Legal capital offers little protection for creditors against distribution of assets

And no protection when capital is reduced to account for, or write off, losses

Creditors can be better protected if an adequate solvency test is developed. According to a solvency test, a company can only make distributions to shareholders if the company remains solvent after the distribution. In a legal capital regime, it is possible that a solvent company is unable to make distributions, or, conversely, that an insolvent company is able to make distributions. In this sense, a system based on a proper solvency test is superior, as far as creditor protection is concerned (but also as far as shareholders' interests and the financing prospects of the company are concerned).

Creditors - and shareholders - can be better protected if an adequate solvency test is developed

A proper solvency test should be required for any payment of dividend or other distribution, including share buy-back and capital reduction (if the concept of a reserve for share capital which is not distributable is retained) against repayment to shareholders. The solvency test should be based at least on two different tests to be performed before making the distribution:

A proper solvency test should be required for any distribution

Based on at least two different tests:

a) *Balance Sheet test or Net Assets test*: according to the balance sheet test, assets must fully cover or exceed liabilities – excluding shareholders' equity – after the proposed dividend payment or

a) Balance Sheet test or Net Assets test

distribution. The valuation method applied in this test must be justified by the position the company is in (going concern, liquidation).

b) *Liquidity test or Current Assets/Current Liabilities test*: according to this test, the company must have sufficient liquid assets to make payments of the liabilities as they fall due in the following period, e.g. the forthcoming twelve months.

b) Liquidity test or Current Assets / Current Liabilities test

Further study will have to take place in order to develop these two tests, as well as the valuation methods to be used and the relationship with valuation methods applied in the audited accounts of the company. The study should also consider reinforcing the two tests by requiring a certain solvency margin and the relevance of the going concern concept. Such a margin would ensure that the assets after the proposed distribution exceed the liabilities by a certain margin and/or that the current assets after distribution exceed current liabilities by a certain margin. Although one respondent criticised this as a "one-size-fits-all" approach, it may offer a proper mechanism to integrate legal and statutory reserves into a regime in which there is no legal capital. In this way, the functions performed by reserves are also more effective than in the current regime, as the net assets test is reinforced by an additional solvency margin.

Further study is required to develop these tests and the valuation methods to be used

Such a study should consider the introduction of a solvency margin, and the relevance of the going concern concept

On the basis of the solvency test, the directors of the company should issue a solvency certificate, in which they explicitly confirm that the proposed distribution meets the solvency test. A valid distribution can only be made when the directors have issued a solvency certificate. Where the audited accounts of the company indicate that the proposed distribution cannot meet the solvency test, directors should not be allowed to issue a solvency certificate. Directors are responsible for the correctness of the solvency certificate and Member States should impose proper sanctions (personal liability, director's disqualification) if the certificate is proven to be misleading. Sanctions could be extended to "shadow" directors, as we recommend for the framework rule on wrongful trading, which should be part of the alternative regime as well.

Any distribution should require issuance by the directors of a solvency certificate

With adequate sanctions for misleading certificates

b) Shareholder protection

The abolition of legal capital, along the lines set above, does not necessarily reduce the level of shareholder protection. On the contrary, the protection of shareholders can be substantially improved without the concept of legal capital.

Shareholders protection can be improved without legal capital

In the alternative regime, pre-emption rights of shareholders in case of new share issues should feature as a fundamental mechanism to protect shareholders. Pre-emption rights should only be excluded or limited on the basis of a specific shareholders resolution, which is based on objective criteria.

In the alternative regime, pre-emption rights are a fundamental protection mechanism

Apart from this, a company issuing new share capital must take into account the fair value of the shares at that time. A company should not be able to issue shares at a price that bears no relation to the real value of the existing shares. This objective is only partly achieved in the legal capital regime, as shares can be issued at any price above nominal value and sometimes even below nominal value. The value of existing shares can be diluted by issuing capital at a price over nominal value, but well below their fair value. The alternative regime should provide that shares must be issued at fair value, which would substantially improve the protection of shareholders as compared to the current legal capital regime. When elaborating the effects of this principle, the case could be considered for making a distinction between listed and unlisted companies.

To better prevent dilution, issue of new shares should be made at fair value rather than nominal value

A distinction could be made between listed and unlisted companies

For listed companies, the market price is a clear indication of the fair value. The fair value could be calculated as the average market price in a period immediately preceding the new capital issue. At best, there should be a limited scope for issues below market price to allow for a marketable discount and underwriting activities.

For listed companies, fair value should be based on average market price

For unlisted public companies, a possible rule would be that the value of shares derived from the audited annual accounts should be presumed to be the minimum price for which new shares can be issued. This presumption would only be rebutted on the basis of clear evidence of a lower fair value of shares at the time of the proposed issue of new capital. Where accounts are not audited, directors should certify the appropriateness of the consideration for the shares to be issued, and the shareholders meeting should explicitly agree.

For unlisted companies, fair value should be based on audited accounts

Additional safeguards should be offered for non audited accounts

The alternative regime should also address the issue of contributions in kind. One possibility would be to require a shareholders resolution for any share issue for which a contribution in kind is made (subject to the exceptions already adopted in the Second Directive for such valuations). The directors could be required to certify the appropriateness of the issue in exchange for the contribution in view of the fair value of the shares. There would need to be appropriate protection for minorities.

The alternative regime should provide for necessary safeguards for contributions in kind

To summarise, the Group agrees with most of the respondents to the consultation that there is room for improvement of the current legal capital regime, and proposes a two step approach.

Summary : *Reform of legal capital to follow a two step approach*

The Commission should, as a matter of priority, present a proposal for reform of the Second Company Law Directive, along the lines suggested by the SLIM Group, with the modifications and supplementary measures that are suggested in the present Report ("SLIM-plus"). Any modernisation of the current regime should remove, where possible, the defects perceived in it, while maintaining its virtues.

Priority to be given to "SLIM-Plus"

The Commission should, at a later stage, conduct a review into the feasibility of an alternative regime, based on the third approach presented in the Consultative Document. The alternative regime need not replace the capital formation and maintenance rules of the Directive as amended according to the "SLIM-plus" proposals. Rather, the new regime could be offered as an alternative option *for Member States*, who should be able to freely decide to change to the new regime and impose it on companies subject to their jurisdiction or to retain the Second Directive rules as modified by the "SLIM-plus" reform. The alternative regime should at least be as effective in achieving the objectives of creditor and shareholder protection as the regime based on legal capital.

At a later stage, review to be conducted on the feasibility of an (optional) alternative regime

It is probably wise not to spend much time on minimum capital in a reform to make the current system more efficient, and to direct attention to issues which are more relevant. The minimum capital requirement should not be removed, nor increased.

Minimum capital requirement to stay unchanged

The Second Company Law Directive already allows for shares to have a fractional value (also referred to as "accountable par") rather than a nominal value (see for example Article 8 providing that shares cannot be issued below their nominal or fractional value). Such shares would have to include the appropriate fraction or the total number of shares, together with the date in which the fraction or the total number of shares was correct, and a reminder that the correct fraction can be obtained at any time from the company itself, or from the companies Register.

Use of fractional shares to be based on appropriate disclosure

It is debatable whether introducing shares without any reference to either nominal or fractional value would constitute a significant change in the system of the Second Company Law Directive. We recommend that, as part of SLIM-Plus, it is reviewed how no par value shares can be accommodated within the Second Company Law Directive.

Introduction of no par value shares to be considered as part of "SLIM-plus"

With respect to contributions in kind, the requirement for an expert valuation should be eliminated in certain cases where clear and reliable points of reference for valuation already exist (market price, recent evaluation, recent audited accounts).

Contributions in kind : valuation requirement to be relaxed

In addition, the Commission should review the possibility of allowing, with appropriate safeguards, the provision of services as contribution in kind.

Contribution of services to be considered

As the SLIM Group has suggested, for listed companies it would be appropriate to allow the general meeting to empower the board to restrict or withdraw pre-emption rights without having to comply with the formalities imposed by Article 29 §4 of the Second Directive, but only where the issue price is at the market price of the securities immediately before the issue or where a small discount to that market price is applied.

Suppression of pre-emption rights to be reviewed for listed companies

If real no par value shares are to be introduced, the suppression of pre-emption rights needs to be reconsidered as pre-emption rights may then be the only effective protection left at EU level for shareholders against dilution.

Pre-emption rights to be further considered if no par value shares are introduced

The current regime for creditor protection (right to apply to a court to obtain security for their claims) in the case of capital reduction should be applied in all restructuring transactions. The burden of proof should be on the creditors.

Current creditor protection to be extended

In addition, there is a case for re-evaluating whether some safeguards are needed for creditors in the event of capital reduction to adjust legal capital to losses.

And reconsidered when adjusting capital to losses

Acquisition of own shares should be allowed within the limits of the distributable reserves, and not of an entirely arbitrary percentage of legal capital like the 10% limit of the current Directive. The same should apply to the taking of own shares as security. It should be possible to establish flexible requirements at least for unlisted companies.

Acquisition of own shares to be facilitated

Financial assistance should be allowed to the extent of the distributable reserves. A shareholders' resolution should in principle be required. The shareholders meeting should be allowed to authorise the board for a maximum period of time (e.g. five years) to engage the company in financial assistance within the limits of the distributable reserves. If this facility is to be allowed, there should be disclosure.

Financial assistance to be facilitated

The SLIM Group has recommended that a compulsory withdrawal of shares should be possible when a shareholder has acquired 90% of the capital, as an exception to the provision of Article 36 of the Directive that compulsory withdrawal is only possible if this is provided in the deed of incorporation or articles of association. The recommendations made in Chapter VI of this Report on squeeze-out and sell-out rights - for listed and open companies - would effectively deal with the issue addressed by the SLIM Group.

Concern about compulsory withdrawal of shares to be addressed

The responsibility of directors when the company becomes insolvent has its most important effect prior to insolvency and this is a key element of an appropriate corporate governance regime. We recommend that as an element of good corporate governance, a European framework rule should be introduced on wrongful trading, combined with the concept of "shadow" directors. The concept of subordination of insiders' claims could be considered as part of the development of an alternative regime for creditor protection (see below).

Introduction of concept of "wrongful trading" recommended and "subordination of insiders' claims" to be considered

In the alternative regime to be considered at a later stage, a proper solvency test should be required for any payment of dividend or other distribution. The solvency test should be based at least on two tests to be performed before making the distribution : a balance sheet test and a liquidity test.

Alternative regime: Any distribution to be based on solvency test

Further study is required in order to develop these two tests, as well as the valuation methods to be used. The study should also consider requiring a certain solvency margin and reviewing the relevance of the going concern concept.

Further study to include net assets and liquidity criteria

Directors of the company should issue a solvency certificate, in which they explicitly confirm that the proposed distribution meets the solvency test. Directors are responsible for the correctness of the solvency certificate and Member States should impose proper sanctions, which could be extended to "shadow" directors.

With solvency certification by directors

In the alternative regime to be considered at a later stage, exclusion or limitation of pre-emption rights should only be possible on the basis of an explicit shareholders' resolution, which is based on objective criteria.

Alternative regime: Pre-emption rights to be protected

In the alternative regime to be considered at a later stage, a company should not be able to issue shares at a price that bears no relation to the real value of the existing shares. The alternative regime should provide that shares must be issued at fair value, which would substantially improve the protection of shareholders as compared to the current legal capital regime. When elaborating the effects of this

Alternative regime: Issue of new shares to be made at fair value

principle, the case could be considered for making a distinction between listed and unlisted companies.

Alternative regime: Appropriate safeguards to be designed for contributions in kind

In the alternative regime to be considered at a later stage, the issue of contributions in kind should be properly addressed. One possibility would be to require a shareholders resolution for any share issue for which a contribution in kind is made (subject to the exceptions already adopted in the Second Directive for such valuations). The directors could be required to certify the appropriateness of the issue in exchange for the contribution in view of the fair value of the shares. There would need to be appropriate protection for minorities.

CHAPTER V

GROUPS AND PYRAMIDS

1. THE EXISTENCE OF GROUPS OF COMPANIES AS A USEFUL AND LEGITIMATE ECONOMIC REALITY

As we pointed out in our Consultative Document, groups of companies represent today the main corporate reality for big companies in most, if not all, Member States. We also pointed out that groups are acknowledged as a legitimate way of doing business in most Member States and, at EU level, by the Seventh Company Law Directive and by various other legal provisions, such as banking, insurance, and antitrust laws. This view received consistent and almost unanimous support in the consultation.

Groups are frequent

And their legitimacy is recognised

On the other hand, it is also widely recognised that groups of companies may present specific risks for shareholders and creditors at the various levels, and the consultation process has revealed that a need for protection of those interests is felt in the business community.

But the need for protection of some interests is widely felt

At the outset, the Group wishes however to outline that, as a general matter, the risks related to the existence of groups should not impact on their legitimacy as a useful economic reality. Moreover, the Group believes that the existence of a group of companies should not be in itself a reason to abandon the limited liability principle, except perhaps in the most patent cases of abuse on the part of the group or the parent company leading to insolvency of a subsidiary.

Existence of risks does challenge neither groups' legitimacy nor limited liability principle

As to the instruments of intervention, the Group takes the view that the enactment of an autonomous body of law, specifically dealing with groups, is not to be recommended at EU level; we do not recommend the undertaking of a new attempt to bring about the Ninth Company Law Directive on group relations. Rather, the Group recommends that the Commission considers provisions within the existing range of corporate law to address particular problems.

No full Directive on groups appears necessary

But some problems should be addressed

The areas where intervention could be needed are considered in the following sections, and relate in particular to: (i) the transparency of the group's structure and relations; (ii) the tensions between the interests of the group and of its parts; and (iii) the special problems of

Intervention could be needed in three areas

pyramid structures.

2. TRANSPARENCY OF GROUP STRUCTURE AND RELATIONS

Responses to the consultation :

Transparency is the most important area of intervention

Complete information and disclosure with regard to groups' structure and intra-group relations are a crucial pre-requisite to ensure that the functioning of groups remains compatible with the interests of shareholders and creditors at the different levels. The consultation process has revealed that transparency is felt as the most important area of intervention with regard to groups.

Actual provisions of the 7th Directive are not sufficient

Respondents have suggested a number of areas where information is needed

The consultation has also confirmed the view that the actual provisions of the Seventh Company Law Directive on consolidated accounts do not sufficiently address these concerns, in that consolidated figures do not reflect the financial situation of the various parts of the group and the degree of dependence of the subsidiaries on the parent company. Respondents have suggested a number of areas where specific information should be provided, covering the group structure, the managing system and the persons effectively entrusted with the power of direction, intra-group transactions and the procedures and the activities through which the direction is exercised.

Some areas are covered by the 7th Directive Or addressed elsewhere in this Report

Some of these areas are already covered by the Seventh Company Law Directive (such as information about the control chain, at least downwards). Other areas - for example, the disclosure of governance structures and rights attached to shares - are addressed elsewhere in this Report (see Chapter III on corporate governance).

More information should be disclosed

By the parent company

In general, the Group takes the view that increased disclosure with regard to a group's structure and relations is needed. In order to ensure a consistent disclosure system, the parent company of each group is to be made responsible for disclosing coherent and accurate information relating to the group's structure and relations.

Group indicates areas where mandatory disclosure would be appropriate

The Group believes that a list of specific issues that are to be disclosed would not be useful here. Rather, we wish to indicate areas where mandatory disclosure would be appropriate, building as much as possible on existing rules. The recommendations provided in Chapter III on corporate governance are also to be considered fully applicable here.

First area : financial information

The first area is that of financial information. The consultation has indicated that the consolidated financial statements as regulated by the Seventh Company Law Directive should be accompanied by further financial information related to the group, covering for example the key financial figures of the major group's companies, the organisation of intra-group services and their allocation within the group's companies, intra-group and related party transactions, the group's policy with respect to supporting group members in distress and the group's internal and external debt structure and its financing and treasury policy.

Information contained in consolidated financial statements should be extended

The Group recommends that the Commission review the Seventh Company Law Directive's provisions in the light of the need for better financial disclosure, and consider whether improvements can be made consistent with International Accounting Standards.

Disclosure organised by 7th Directive should be extended

The consultation has also pointed out that a need for non financial disclosure, particularly with regard to the governance of groups of companies, is widely felt. Many of the suggestions received are covered by our recommendations on disclosure in Chapter III on corporate governance, and the Group believes that, were the relevant recommendations to be implemented, most issues related to the governance of groups would be sufficiently covered. The Group wishes only to recommend here that it is ensured that – especially where listed companies are involved - a clear and fair picture of the group's governance structure, including cross-holdings and material shareholders' agreements relevant to the control over the company, is given to the market and the public. This is also consistent with the disclosure recommendations in our First Report on Issues Related to Takeover Bids.

Second area : non financial information

Many issues already covered by Chapter III recommendations

A clear picture of the group's governance structure should be given

In addition, the Commission should review whether companies should be required to inform shareholders and the public when they enter into or exit from a group, including a statement by the company's directors as to the significance of the event with regard to the company's financial situation, governance, and performance.

A directors' statement might be required when entering or leaving a group

3. PROBLEMS FOR THE CREATION AND FUNCTIONING OF GROUPS OF COMPANIES: TENSIONS BETWEEN THE INTERESTS OF THE GROUP AND ITS PARTS

In some Member States, the creation and functioning of groups of companies is complicated by the fact that the management of the subsidiary may not take into consideration the common economic interests of the group of companies taken as a whole, unless this is in the particular interest of the subsidiary. Violations may make the directors liable both under criminal and private law. The result is regarded in some Member States as a clear impediment to the formation and functioning of groups of companies, nationally as well

Some Member States do not recognise the interest of the group as such

as within the EU.

In fact, the acknowledgement of the legitimate nature of groups of companies necessarily implies that the company law rules on conflicts of interest and on the duty to pursue the sole interest of each company's shareholders cannot be applied as such to groups, at least without taking account of the special position membership of a group creates. On the other hand, the protection of the interests of minority shareholders and creditors at the various levels has to be maintained, and it is therefore necessary to ensure that those interests are not prejudiced in the pursuit of the group's policy.

Group membership should lead to recognition of special position

With due protection of minority shareholders and creditors

A principle has been developed - with slight variations - in several Member States that tries to solve the conflict between the common interests of the group of companies taken as a whole and one or more of its members by providing that transactions which are beneficial for the group but are not in the direct interest of a single company can be considered as legitimate, provided that the interests of that company are safeguarded on balance. In other words, the prejudice suffered by a particular company in a certain transaction can be justified where the membership of the group ensures advantages to the same company so that its interests are safeguarded on balance. The work of the Forum Europaeum[26] in this field has been particularly helpful in clarifying the common principles underlying these rules in certain Member States.

In several Member States, a transaction made for the benefit of the group is legitimate

If the prejudice suffered by a particular company is justified by other advantages

The Group believes there is a case for requiring Member States to provide for a framework rule for groups that allows those concerned with the management of a group company to adopt and implement a co-ordinated group policy, provided that the interests of creditors of each company are effectively protected and that there is a fair balance of burdens and advantages over time for each company's (outside) shareholder. Such a regime would facilitate the creation and functioning of groups of companies. The details of the regime can be left to Member States.

A framework rule should allow the implementation of a group's policy

With necessary safeguards for creditors and minority shareholders

The adoption of such a framework rule would be all the more feasible when considering the improvement of the instruments to protect minority shareholders and creditors we recommend elsewhere in this Report, in particular the introduction of special investigation rights and sell-out rights for minority shareholders and the adoption of the concepts of wrongful trading and shadow directors (see par. 3.4 and 4.4 of Chapter III above, and par. 6 of Chapter VI below).

Other related recommendations in this Report would help such a rule to operate properly

[26] The Forum Europaeum Corporate Group Law consists of a steering committee composed of Academics from several European countries. For further information, see « Corporate Group Law for Europe », European Business Organization Law Review 1 (2000) : 165-264.

Another important area of possible intervention with regard to the proper functioning of groups is the law applicable to insolvent groups. When groups become insolvent, the separate treatment of individual group companies' bankruptcies causes both procedural and substantive problems, which are exacerbated when an insolvent group operates in different jurisdictions. In some Member States, a consolidated approach to group bankruptcies is possible under certain circumstances. We acknowledge that these problems are difficult to solve but this does not make a solution less desirable. Therefore, we recommend that the Commission takes the initiative to review the possibilities to introduce procedural and substantive consolidations of bankruptcies of group companies in Member States.

A consolidated approach to (cross-border) group bankruptcies is desirable

The introduction of rules on consolidated bankruptcies should be considered

4. PYRAMIDS

A group pyramid can be defined as a group structure characterised by a more or less long chain of control using several holding companies. The ultimate shareholders control each company in the chain by majority or controlling minority interests, leaving minority shareholders at each level. The result is that the ultimate shareholders may control the whole chain - up to and including the company at the bottom - on the basis of a small total investment. If, for example, the ultimate shareholders would own 50% at each level, in a chain of six companies including the company at the bottom only a total investment by the ultimate investor equivalent to 1.56% in the capital of the company at the bottom is required to have full control over the whole chain. This effect is created by having minority shareholders at each level finance the controlling stake of the ultimate shareholder in the level below. In order to facilitate this, often a number of the companies in the pyramid have separate stock exchange listings.

A pyramid is a chain of holding companies, with ultimate control based on a small total investment

Example

Pyramids use minority shareholders, often through a series of listings

Pyramidal structures may present specific problems. Pyramids are a source of agency costs in that they increase the private benefits of control and conflicts of interest, and therefore may come at an expense for the non-controlling shareholders. The lack of transparency of the ownership structure may have a number of problematic effects, such as lack of transparency in the group's operations and malfunction of the market for corporate control.

Pyramids are a source of agency costs

And a number of problems stem from their lack of transparency

The creation of specific rules for pyramids proves difficult, especially because the distinction between pyramidal groups and "normal groups" is hard in practice. At a minimum, the Group believes that full transparency with regard to the group's structure, governance, and operations (including material shareholders' agreements at the various levels relevant to the control of the group) is essential for

Pyramids are difficult to regulate with specific rules

But disclosure recommendations

solving the problems posed by pyramids. The disclosure recommendations made in Chapter III on corporate governance above are therefore very relevant for dealing with pyramid structures.

made in Chapter III are very relevant

The Group has particular concerns for those pyramidal groups that include listed companies, especially where these are placed at the lower levels of the chain. Where the sole or main asset of a holding company consists of shares in another listed company in the group structure, the stock exchange listing of the holding company usually does not have any additional economic value except to finance the control of the controlling shareholder.

Pyramidal groups that include listed companies raise particular concerns

In view of the weak position of the minority shareholders in such companies and the general concerns about lack of transparency and incontestability of control, we believe stock exchange listings should not be used for these purposes. We therefore recommend that the EU require the authorities in Member States, responsible for the admission to trading on regulated markets, not to admit to trading holding companies whose sole or main assets are their shareholding in another listed company.

Companies whose sole or main assets are controlling shareholdings should in principle not be admitted to trading

Exceptions should only be made where a strong case is made as to the economic value of such admission to trading beyond the financing of the control of the controlling shareholder. For existing pyramid structures that include such listed holding companies, a requirement should be considered for their delisting and offering minority shareholders shares in the controlled company in exchange for their shares in the holding company.

Exceptions only where economic value clearly demonstrated

Delisting could be used for existing pyramids

Finally, we note that additional pressure on pyramid structures is brought to bear by those who operate stock indices, by including only the free float in the weighing of companies in the index and excluding major shareholdings. Many operators of indices have already taken this approach, which the Group recommends.

Stock indices should properly reflect the free float of companies

To summarise, no new attempt to enact the Ninth Company Law Directive on group relations should be undertaken, but particular problems should be addressed through modifying existing provisions of corporate law in three areas.

Summary : *No need for a proposal for a Ninth Company Law Directive*

Increased disclosure with regard to a group's structure and relations is needed, and the parent company of each group is to be made responsible for disclosing coherent and accurate information.

Parent company responsible for

The Commission should review the Seventh Company Law Directive's provisions in the light of the need for better financial disclosure, and consider whether improvements can be made consistent with International Accounting Standards.

Better financial disclosure

With respect to non financial disclosure, it should be ensured that – especially where listed companies are involved – a clear picture of the group's governance structure, including cross-holdings and material shareholders' agreements, is given to the market and the public.

And better non financial disclosure

In addition, companies could be required to provide specific information when they enter into or exit from a group.

Entry or exit to be commented

Member States should be required to provide for a framework rule for groups that allows those concerned with the management of a group company to adopt and implement a co-ordinated group policy, provided that the interest of the company's creditors are effectively protected and that there is a fair balance of burdens and advantages over time for the company's shareholders.

Recognition of group's interest,

With appropriate safeguards

The Commission should review the possibilities to introduce in Member States rules on procedural and substantive consolidations of bankruptcies of group companies.

Need for rules on groups' bankruptcies

The EU should require national authorities, responsible for the admission to trading on regulated markets, not to admit holding companies whose sole or main assets are their shareholding in another listed company, unless the economic value of such admission is clearly demonstrated.

Specific rules for admission to trading of holding companies

Finally, operators of stock indices should properly take into account the free float in determining the weight of each company.

Stock indexes to reflect free float

CHAPTER VI

CORPORATE RESTRUCTURING AND MOBILITY

In Chapter 5.1 of our April Consultation Document, we described the various types of corporate restructuring transactions and raised possible proposals for reform on five major topics :

Under this heading, the Group raised primarily 5 major topics in its consultation document

- change of corporate seat, or domicile;
- the position of the acquiring company in a domestic merger under the Third Company Law Directive;
- acquisition of a wholly owned subsidiary by the same means;
- creditor protection in restructuring transactions;
- squeeze-outs and sell-outs.

We also invited comments on whether there were other aspects of corporate restructuring where reform at Community level was required.

1. PRIORITIES – RESTRUCTURING AND TENTH AND FOURTEENTH COMPANY LAW DIRECTIVES

The need for Community company law provisions facilitating cross frontier restructuring figured as a high priority in almost all the responses to the Document and, as we have indicated above (see Section 1 of Chapter II), we support this view. Almost all also took the view that the areas we had raised were the ones requiring attention, though there were calls for the Commission urgently to bring forward revised proposals for a Tenth Company Law Directive on Cross-frontier mergers and a Fourteenth Company Law Directive on Transfer of Registered Office (i.e. of corporate seat or domicile).

There is wide demand for Community law to facilitate cross frontier restructuring

We understand that such proposals are in preparation. Our recommendations on the issues listed above will be relevant in considering their final form. The most important remaining areas of difficulty relate to board structures and employee participation. We did not consult on these matters but, in the course of our work, the European Company Statute ("ECS") has been adopted. The solutions to these problems in the ECS – i.e. freedom of choice for public companies in their board structures and employee participation based on agreement or fall-back minimum rules applicable only in cases where there is a legitimate prior interest - may present a

The Commission has already taken steps to respond to this demand

Remaining areas of difficulty could be solved by analogy to the ECS

possible model for these issues. These are urgent matters for the additional reason that any necessary changes to domestic public company law may affect the mode of adoption of the ECS by the Member States.

2. CHANGE OF CORPORATE SEAT OR DOMICILE

2.1. Denial of recognition to a company moving its real seat

Broad application of "Real seat doctrine" to incapacitate companies is a disproportionate measure

There was almost unanimous agreement that for a Member State to adopt a version of the real seat doctrine which automatically denies recognition to a company which has its "real seat[27]" in a country other than that of its incorporation was a disproportionate measure which can never be justified. We agree with this view, and believe that it is likely to be against EU law to take such an approach.

2.2. Transfer of real seat between Incorporation Doctrine States

Any sanctions against transfer of real seat between incorporation doctrine states interferes unnecessarily with fundamental European freedoms

We similarly believe that, where a company moves its real seat but not its registered office between two states which attach no importance in terms of the law applicable to the company to that move ("incorporation doctrine states"), there should be no room at Member State law level (e.g. by a third state refusing to continue to recognise the company after such a change) or at EU law level, for attaching any sanctions to such a move which would be a wholly unnecessary interference with freedom of movement and operation of companies within the Community. Neither the states concerned directly in the change nor third states have any interest in inhibiting the move.

EU legislation (whether proposed or existing) should take this risk of interference into account

Again we believe that this is likely to be found to be the effect of the Treaty. However, existing and proposed EU secondary legislation should be aligned with this view. At present, the Regulations establishing the European Economic Interest Grouping and the European Company make it unlawful for such entities to have their "real seat" in a state other than their state of incorporation; this should be corrected. The contrary argument is that, for the sake of uniformity and simplicity, all EU legislation should always require conformity of the jurisdiction of registration with the place of the registered office; but this is an unnecessary interference with freedom of establishment.

[27] For the difficulties in defining this concept, and the consequent uncertainties and inhibition for companies which result, see the Consultation Document, page 33.

2.3. Transfer of real seat into Real Seat Doctrine State

a) General Principles

The law of a real seat "host" state should only be permitted to override the law of incorporation of a "guest" company, subject to the following conditions:

On the other hand, most respondents agreed that, where a company (a "guest" company) established its real seat in a state (a "host" state) where the effect of its law of incorporation was inconsistent with local mandatory requirements, there was a case for permitting the law of incorporation to be overridden to the extent necessary to respect those requirements of the host state. We agree with this view, but, consistently with the bar on refusing recognition on such grounds, we believe that the general EU law principles on freedom of movement must be applied – i.e. any sanction inhibiting such freedom of movement should :

- be imposed only to support a requirement of legitimate general interest; *- Legitimate general interest*
- not be disproportionate; *- Proportionality*
- require no more than is necessary and appropriate to secure the interest concerned; *- Minimum intervention*
- be non-discriminatory as between companies formed in the host state and the company concerned; *- Non-discrimination*
- be sufficiently transparent to inhibit to the minimum extent necessary the exercise in practice of the fundamental freedom of establishment. *- Transparency*

Where external requirements of the "host" state are sufficient, interference with internal governance of the "guest" company is inadequate

We believe that these are the general principles applicable to the imposition of local law inhibiting freedom of movement, consistent with the case law of the European Court of Justice[28]. Particularly close attention needs to be given to avoiding the application by the host state of domestic requirements which interfere with the internal governance of the company where external requirements are adequate measures of protection of the interest concerned – for example reporting requirements, provisions for external representation or other general obligations to protect creditors, such as wrongful trading duties. But such external requirements, while easier to justify as a less serious interference, still require to be justified against the general principles listed above.

[28] See for example case C-212/97, *Centros*; cases C-367/98, C-403/99 and C-503/99 (the "Golden Share cases); and the opinion of Advocate General Colomer in Case C-208/00, *Uberseering v Nordic Construction*..

b) Application of the principles

It is possible to illustrate the application of these general principles in the light of our views on the value of various company law measures and the present state of company law harmonisation.

Examples of application of these general principles :

Capital Maintenance

So far as minimum capital and capital maintenance requirements are concerned, for public companies these have been harmonised by the Second Company Law Directive; conclusions on the value and importance of the minimum capital requirements more widely will need to be reached in the light of the conclusions drawn from our recommendations above. But we doubt the justifiability of invoking these requirements as a justification for interference with the internal governance of companies, given that many states are well able to secure the general interests concerned by less interventionist external means (see for example our references to wrongful trading in par. 4.4 of Chapter III above)[29].

Capital requirements of the Second Directive should not be used as a justification for interference with internal governance

We conclude that there is no case for Member States imposing minimum capital and capital maintenance requirements on "guest" companies, whether they have their real seat within their territory or not. Moreover, capital maintenance requirements are now regarded in many quarters as ineffective in their present form (as the responses to our consultation have demonstrated), and their deliberate avoidance has been held not to justify the incapacitation, or disqualification from business activity, of a company in the country of its adopted real seat in the latest Court of Justice case on the subject[30].

Such non-interference should apply regardless of where the "guest" company has its real seat

Disclosure, Transparency and Security of Transactions

So far as disclosure and transparency is concerned, the effect of the First and Fourth Company Law Directives is to require adequate measures of disclosure and substantive rules on validity of transactions for all companies, and the Eleventh Company Law Directive secures adequate disclosure by "guest" companies operating through branches. Our own proposals for enhanced disclosure in Chapter III reinforce this.

First, Fourth and Eleventh Directive regulate disclosure by "guest" companies or their branches

---

[29] See too ECJ Case C-212/97, *Centros*, [1999] CMLR 551.

[30] Same references as above.

Governance and Company Structure

ECS-limits for interference with internal governance should apply generally

As for governance and structure of companies, the European Company Statute recognises the legitimacy of either one tier or two tier boards. We recommend in Chapters II and III of this Report that all companies in the EU should have this option. Other rules of internal governance are best regarded as a matter of agreement between company members and their organs. We do not believe that there is a case for interfering with the internal governance of "guest" companies by "host" state laws on such grounds.

Employee Participation

Interference by "host" state is justified, but total refusal to recognise a company because of its failure to comply with "host" state law on employee participation is disproportionate

Indeed the one area where such interference seems to be justified, recognised as a legitimate matter of general interest by the European Company Statute, is that of employee participation. However, any mandatory imposition of host state law in such a case must of course comply with the general principles. A total refusal to recognise a company on the ground that it fails to comply with the employee participation law of its place of real seat is clearly disproportionate; before a guest company should be subjected to sanctions on the ground of failure to comply with host state law on this matter, the connecting factor with the host state should be demonstrated to be sufficient and appropriate, and the remedy should be no greater than necessary to ensure the general interest in issue.

Interference by "host" state should be subject to certain conditions

At least where fewer than 50% of the employees are employed in the host state, any imposition of local law seems hard to justify, and, even where the connecting factor is sufficient, there should be provision to allow an agreed system of employee involvement to be adopted, analogous to that recognised by the ECS, and the company should be given time and opportunity to make the necessary changes in a way consistent with its law of incorporation. If our suggestion above for making domestic law more flexible on these questions is adopted, this solution is likely to be possible in most if not all cases.

Compulsory restructuring through liquidation and re-incorporation should only be last resort

Only where an adequate accommodation of employee rights cannot be achieved consistently with home state law, should the ultimate step of a compulsory restructuring through liquidation and re-incorporation be imposed. Any such remedy should be ex post, that is to say it should allow the company and its organs sufficient time and opportunity to respond to the domestic requirements. There should be no question of an incurable "legal ambush", disabling or fettering the company's activities, coming about.

2.4. Transfer of real seat out of Real Seat Doctrine State

A transfer of the real seat out of a state of origin may be regarded as a means of escaping the law of origin, and there is an argument that that state's interests are engaged. Any sanctions applied in such cases must comply with the principles set out above. Moreover, where the new "host" state applies the law of origin (as will be the case where that state applies the incorporation doctrine and thus recognises "home" state law), there can be no case for taking special measures on the ground of transfer of real seat. (We recommend below that third states should be required to apply the law of incorporation subject to recognising the legitimacy of measures permitted above.)

Sanctions, if any, imposed by the "home" state have to comply with the above mentioned principles

Where the new "host" state seeks to impose its own law, a conflict of laws may in theory arise; but the principle of reciprocity should discipline the sanctions which the state of origin may impose – that is to say the state of origin must recognise the right of the "host" state to impose the measures which it would itself impose in the converse case of a company moving its real seat into its, that is to say the "home" state's, territory. The "home" state should thus be obliged to accept the imposition by the "host" state of requirements which it, mutatis mutandis, would impose in the converse case.

A conflict of law between "home" state and "host" state can be solved with reciprocity

2.5. Third States

Third states are unlikely to be concerned in cases of moving real seat between a home and a host state, but the general rule should be that they should apply the law of the state of incorporation, with a *renvoi* to the law of the host state where appropriate.

If concerned, third states should apply law of incorporation

We believe that these conclusions are consistent with the general principles of European law, and are likely to be adopted by the European Court of Justice. We recommend that the Commission should keep this problem under review, and adapt actual and proposed Community legislation to reflect the above approach, i.e. consistency with the principles of legitimate general interest, proportionality, minimum intervention, non-discrimination and transparency. We doubt whether further action will be necessary, but recommend that the situation be kept under continuing review.

The Commission should adapt Community law to reflect the above mentioned principles

Ongoing review of the situation is needed

3. THIRD DIRECTIVE MERGERS – POSITION OF THE ACQUIRING COMPANY

We noted in the Consultation Document that the effect of a Third Company Law Directive merger on an acquiring company is not different, in its effect on shareholders and creditors, from normal trading transactions involving the incurring of liabilities and the issue of capital, and was similar in economic effect to a share-for-share takeover. Nonetheless, the Directive envisaged a special general meeting of shareholders of the acquiring company to authorise the transaction, or at least special publicity and minority protection measures. These requirements are not reflected, nor we believe justified, as a matter of EU law, in other transactions with the same or similar effect.

Some special provisions of the Third Directive serve no purpose for the acquiring company, given the nature and the effect of the transaction at issue

We suggested that :

Suggestions:

- for domestic mergers, such requirements should be removed at EU level, leaving it to the domestic law of the Member States, or the internal governance rules of the company concerned, to adopt the appropriate measures in relation to shareholder control of such mergers;
- for international mergers, the Member State of the acquired company should be bound to accept that relaxation, where it was adopted by the Member State of the acquiring company, and possibly further;
- there might be a particular case, for international mergers, for requiring Member States of acquiring companies to promote interstate restructuring by removing impediments in acquiring companies on a harmonised basis.

- removal of such requirements at EU level for domestic mergers

- acceptance of such relaxation in international mergers

- removal of impediments for international mergers, at EU level

Similar considerations apply to the position of an acquiring company participating in a division by fusion (scission) within the Sixth Company Law Directive.

These considerations apply also in a Sixth Directive division

The great majority of responses agreed with the first two of these suggestions, and many also supported the third. The objections seemed based mainly either on the argument that the provisions worked as they stood and should not be disturbed, or that the point was a minor one and not worthy of attention.

There is broad support for the first two of the above mentioned suggestions

We believe that there is a case for removing unnecessary formalities of this kind, which are costly and inhibit commerce, and we would recommend the removal of the special requirements for acquiring

Following this, the Group sees a case for relaxing requirements as

companies in domestic mergers at EU level and the imposition of the corresponding obligation on states of the acquired company to accept this in the international merger regime.

described

However, we are persuaded that it would not be appropriate to prohibit these acquiring company formalities, even in an international merger. This is because the case for the imposition of such formalities is a matter of scale and degree. There will be occasions where acquisitions by merger, in the same way as other acquisitions, are so important to the company that special formalities, even to the extent of shareholder approval, will be appropriate. Member States should not be deprived of the power to make such requirements mandatory in appropriate cases, and this is a matter for appreciation at Member State level according to the practices of corporate governance operating in such states. The arguments in favour of liberalising international mergers are not sufficiently strong to override this.

However, Member States should retain discretion about the scope of such relaxation, in line with their practices of corporate governance

4. THIRD DIRECTIVE MERGERS : ACQUISITION OF WHOLLY OWNED SUBSIDIARY

Similar considerations apply to the acquisition by merger of a wholly owned subsidiary by its parent company. Here the case for a relaxed view of what should be required of the acquiring company is even clearer and almost all responses, including those which opposed the change in relation to mergers of unrelated companies, believed that not only should the Directive protections be removed but that they should cease to operate as a mandatory matter, at least in relation to international mergers. However, we believe that similar considerations apply and that it should be a matter for the Member State of the acquiring company and/or its constitution, to impose the necessary formalities in such cases.

Here, the case for relaxation of special requirements is even clearer, but Member States' discretion should be respected here, too

Some responses argued that provision should be made, in the proposed Tenth Company Law Directive for cross-frontier divisions of companies, to enable a restructuring involving the undertaking of a company to be divided between companies in different Member States. We doubt the need for this, given the possibility for parts of a business to be hived off into separate subsidiaries preparatory to disposal by merger, but we recommend that further empirical research should be carried out on whether such a provision for international scissions is necessary.

The necessity to regulate cross-border divisions within the 10th Directive seems doubtful, but warrants research

We therefore recommend the removal of the Third and Sixth Company Law Directive requirements for general meeting approvals or mandatory minority protection in the acquiring company, leaving

Therefore, the above mentioned relaxations should be made possible

Member States to adopt such provisions if they wish, and that, in the forthcoming Tenth Company Law Directive on International mergers, acquired company states should be required to accept the exercise of this relaxation by acquiring company states.

And this should be reflected by the Tenth Directive

5. CREDITOR PROTECTION IN RESTRUCTURING TRANSACTIONS

We pointed out that there is a wide diversity of practice in Member States in relation to creditor protection in restructuring transactions, while the policy considerations were the same and seemed adequately met by the Second Company Law Directive provision on reduction of capital. The case for adopting such a solution on a general basis is strongest in the case of international mergers (including formation of a European Company by merger), but there is also a strong argument, which we are inclined to accept, in favour of adopting the same provision for all transactions for the sake of simplicity.

There is a case for harmonisation of creditor protection throughout all kinds of restructuring transactions

This suggestion was widely welcomed and we recommend the adoption of a harmonised provision on creditor protection to facilitate restructuring within the Community, based on the Second Company Law Directive provision enabling a creditor to apply to the court where he can show that the company has not provided reasonable measures of protection.

Creditors should be enabled at EU level to apply to the court to obtain reasonable protection

Where a creditor has the benefit of an intra-group guarantee arrangement under national provisions adopting Article 57 of the Fourth Company Law Directive, this fact should of course be taken into account, and this in many circumstances may well mean that in an intra-group merger the creditor is unaffected.

However, intra-group guarantee arrangements should be taken into account.

6. SQUEEZE-OUTS AND SELL-OUTS

Most responses favoured the creation of a facility, for an overwhelming majority shareholder with 90-95% of the capital, compulsorily to buy out the minority, not only after a takeover bid as proposed in our First Report[31], but generally regardless of how the majority was acquired. The price would be set on the basis of a right to demand appraisal of a fair value. The respondents almost all supported a corresponding right for the minority to require a sell-out.

There is widespread support for squeeze-out and sell-out rights generally, with an important majority shareholding

[31] See now Articles 14 and 15 of the Proposal for a Thirteenth Company Law Directive.

Some argued that these rights should be restricted to a limited period after the majority was acquired or announced, to remove uncertainty. While we see the force of this argument, we can also envisage cases where the circumstances may change after the acquisition in such a way as to justify the invocation of either right. Others argued that such rights were only needed after a takeover and that there were serious problems in providing independent appraisal of fair value in the absence of an agreed offer.

Sell-out and squeeze-out only for a limited period ?

Or only after takeovers, given the difficulty of appraisal ?

In some Member States, at least once the mandatory bid rule is in operation under the proposed Thirteenth Company Law Directive, there will be a takeover bid before such majorities are achieved in most cases involving listed companies. Nonetheless, we would propose that this provision should apply to all listed and open companies, and we believe that there is a case for enabling minority holdings of this kind to be removed by either side, regardless of how they arise.

Squeeze-out and sell-out rights should apply to listed and open companies

Regardless of how they arise

We considered whether these rules should also apply for closed companies. Few of the responses to our consultation addressed this issue. While there is a case for the adoption of such a rule in closed companies, as another form of exit may not be available to minority shareholders, we hesitate to recommend this without further study. We are aware that it is very common that special arrangements are adopted in such companies to protect minorities, in joint venture or family situations for example, and careful consideration would need to be given before overriding vested rights in such cases.

But not necessarily to closed companies, which often have special arrangements for minority protection

Views differed on whether any such right should be exercisable on a class by class basis or by reference to the aggregate of company capital. On balance, we believe that the class by class approach, which was supported by the majority of respondents who addressed the point, is the better one. The strength of the argument on expropriation as an argument against mandatory squeeze-out rights depends on the relevant majority being acquired over comparable rights. Each class of capital has its own protections.

A class by class approach for exercising any such right is preferable to a reference to the aggregate company capital

We therefore recommend that Member States should be required to create such squeeze-out and sell-out rights at a level to be set at a 90% as a minimum and 95% as a maximum majority on a class by class basis, for listed and open companies. Before applying a similar regime to closed companies, further study into the relationship with contractual exit arrangements is required.

Squeeze-out and sell-out rights as described here above ought to be created by Member States

To summarise, there is a perceived need for Community action in the legislative field with regard to corporate restructuring and mobility, especially in the cross-border context. The Commission should urgently bring forward revised proposals for a Tenth Company Law Directive on Cross-Frontier Mergers and a Fourteenth Company Law Directive on Transfer of the Registered Office.

***Summary**: Need for Community action, especially in the cross-border context (Tenth and Fourteenth Directives)*

Proposals in preparation are faced with the task of solving difficulties relating to board structure and employee participation. The solutions to these problems in the ECS may present a possible model for these issues.

ECS solutions to be considered as a possible model

Where a company moves its real seat between two "incorporation doctrine states", there should be no room at Member State level or at EU level for attaching any sanctions to such a move which would be a wholly unnecessary interference with freedom of movement and operation of companies across the Community.

Transfer of real seat between two incorporation states should not lead to any sanction

This is likely to be found to be the effect of the Treaty. However, existing and proposed EU legislation should be aligned with this view.

Where a company transfers its real seat to a real seat state, the law of the "host" state should be permitted to override the law of incorporation of the "guest" company, but only within the limits imposed by the principles of legitimate general interest, proportionality, minimum intervention, non-discrimination and transparency.

Transfer of real seat into real seat state should allow host state to take adequate measures, under strict conditions

External requirements of the "host" state, duly imposed on foreign companies with a view to these principles, should make any interference with internal governance of these companies redundant. This is especially true for the areas of capital maintenance, governance and company structure and employee participation. With regard to the latter, it is imperative that restructuring through liquidation and re-incorporation be only the ultimate step : any such remedy should allow the company and its organs sufficient time and opportunity to respond to the domestic requirements.

In particular, host states are to abstain, in principle, from interference with internal governance of a company

Where a company transfers its real seat out of a real seat state, any sanctions imposed by the "home" state should be subject to the above mentioned principles as well, and any conflict of law then still prevailing ought to be solved by reciprocity.

The same for transfer of real seat out of real seat state

Third states, if concerned at all by a company's move of real seat, should be made to apply, in principle, the law of incorporation, with a renvoi to the law of the host state where appropriate.

Third states to apply law of incorporation in any move of seat

With respect to domestic mergers, Member States should be allowed to relax special requirements of the Third Directive which are faced by the acquiring company.

Merger requirements to be relaxed for the acquiring company

In order to facilitate international mergers, Member States of the acquired company should be required to accept such relaxation where it was adopted by the Member State of the acquiring company.

Similar considerations apply to the acquisition by merger of a wholly owned subsidiary by its parent company. Consequently, relaxation of special requirements in domestic mergers should be permitted to the Member State of the acquiring company, and acceptance in international mergers of such relaxation, should be required from the Member State of the acquired company.

Similar relaxation even more important for acquisition by merger of a wholly owned subsidiary

A harmonised provision on creditor protection should be adopted at EU level to facilitate restructuring within the Community based on the Second Company Law Directive provision enabling a creditor to apply to the court where he can show that the company has not provided reasonable measures of protection.

Harmonisation of creditor protection with right to apply to the court is desirable

Member States should be required to create squeeze-out and sell-out rights at a level to be set at a 90% as a minimum and 95% as a maximum majority on a class by class basis, for listed and open companies.

Squeeze-out and sell-out rights should be introduced, for listed and open companies

Before applying a similar regime to closed companies, further study into the relationship with contractual exit arrangements, etc. is required.

CHAPTER VII

THE EUROPEAN PRIVATE COMPANY

1. A NEW LEGAL FORM COMPLEMENTARY TO THE SOCIETAS EUROPAEA (SE)

In October 2001, the "Societas Europaea" (SE) finally became a reality. The Statute of the SE and the corresponding Directive on the rights of employees of SEs were adopted by the Council of Ministers and the European Parliament[32]. The SE represents a major breakthrough, especially because it makes it possible for European companies to merge across borders and to transfer their seat from one Member State to another. Moreover, it may be important for a company to do business as a European company and not as an Italian, German or French company. This latter objective of the SE, however, is only partly achieved, as the Statute often refers to the law of the Member State of incorporation and, as a result, different types of SEs will come to exist depending on where they have been incorporated.

The Societas Europaea (SE) has been adopted in October 2001

The SE allows companies to merge and transfer their seat, across borders

And to do business as a European company

The SE has been designed for large enterprises and may not meet all the expectations of the business community, in particular small and medium sized enterprises (SMEs), both independent companies and group subsidiaries, which constitute the larger part of companies in Europe.

SEs may not meet all expectations of business community, in particular SMEs

A private initiative of business, supported by academics in some Member States, has argued that there is a specific need for a European legal form of private company, to facilitate SMEs' business in Europe. According to this initiative, the European Economic Interest Grouping (EEIG) only gives a partial solution, because its activity must be the continuation of its members' activity and it is an unlimited liability legal form. The initiative has specifically argued that the SE does not meet the expectations of companies who desire to establish joint ventures, as the SE Statute leaves little room for structuring the joint venture as the parties to it wish.

A European form of private company is promoted by a private initiative

To facilitate SMEs business in Europe, in particular through joint ventures

The private initiative has resulted in a specific, detailed proposal for a European Private Company – EPC –, complementary to the national forms of private companies in Member States and to the SE. The

This private initiative resulted in a proposal for a European Private

[32] For full citation of the Regulation and the Directive, see Annex 4.

proposal has been presented by the Paris Chamber of Commerce and Industry[33] and the French business confederation MEDEF (formerly CNPF)[34] in September 1998. The proposal has been drafted by a group of company representatives and specialists in company law from several nationalities, and has been supported by the Union of Industrial and Employers' Confederations of Europe (UNICE) and EUROCHAMBERS. More recently, in March 2002, the European Economic and Social Committee – EESC - has unanimously adopted an opinion on a European Company Statute for SMEs (own initiative opinion) stressing "the necessity for a European Company project for SMEs".

Company (EPC)

The proposal has been supported by UNICE and Eurochambers

And the European Economic and Social Committee

The proposal for a European Private Company statute is based on contractual freedom. This freedom covers the determination of corporate governing bodies, the organisation of relations among them, shareholders' rights, which might be unequal or specific, and the manner of access, withdrawal or removal of a shareholder, subject only to the limits of those rights laid down by the regulation. The EPC as proposed may not issue securities to the public or issue bearer shares. An EPC would, according to its supporters, offer an adequate vehicle for SMEs which are active in several Member States as well as for SMEs in several Member States merging their enterprises into a legal entity with a genuine European corporate identity.

The proposal is based on contractual freedom

And is presented as an adequate vehicle for SMEs active in different Member States

This opinion is challenged by those who argue that the only real benefit of the SE statute, and any possible EPC statute, is that it allows a cross-border merger of national companies and transfer of seats across borders that, in the absence of the Tenth and Fourteenth Directives, cannot otherwise be achieved by national companies. In this view, a specific European form – either SE or EPC – is of little use for business if national companies are allowed to freely merge and transfer their seats across borders.

But it is argued that an EPC statute would be of little use if national companies were allowed to merge and transfer their seats across borders

Opponents also argue that the European corporate environment should not be cluttered up with yet another legal form, if there is no specific need for it. If it is felt that national forms of private companies are insufficiently geared to facilitate SMEs and joint venture activity, an effort could be made to infuse more flexibility in the laws of Member States relating to private companies. This would not necessarily have to take the form of harmonisation through Directives, but could take a much lighter approach. Some think that the proposal for the European Private Company could be used as the starting point for a model for regulation of private companies in Europe. Such a

And that specific needs of SMEs could be met by a modernisation of national forms

In which process the proposal for a European Private

---

[33] http://www.ccip.fr/etudes/dossiers/spe/index.html
[34] http://www.medef.fr

model could be used by Member States to voluntarily amend their regulation of private companies. The EU should consider facilitating the adoption of a model for regulation of private companies in the Member States, including a mechanism to update the model if business needs so require.

Company could be used as a model for regulation at national level

Many respondents to our Consultative Document stressed that there are strong reasons to promote a European form dedicated to SMEs:

Responses to the consultation supported a EU form :

- Some respondents took the view that SMEs should also be entitled to the benefit of a European legal vehicle suitable to their needs and purpose, to compete on a level playing field. A specific European company form should not be reserved to big business only.

A specific EU form should not be reserved to large companies

- SMEs need a European structure to establish joint ventures, which leaves enough room for structuring the joint venture as the parties to it wish.

A flexible structure for joint ventures is necessary

- There is a significant cost argument in this context. An SME faces significant costs for in-house manpower and/ or outside counsel when setting up and operating subsidiaries of different shapes and forms in various Member States. The costs would be greatly reduced if the legal form of the subsidiaries in all Member States could be the same. With a view to EU enlargement, the creation of the EPC becomes even more important : with the accession of every new Member State, the advantages for the companies will grow exponentially.

Costs linked to the creation and operation of subsidiaries in other Member States would be greatly reduced

- It may be important even for SMEs to do business as European companies, and not as Italian, German or French companies.

The "European label" may be useful

Respondents generally did not perceive the alternative of adoption of a model law for regulation of private companies in Member States as an adequate answer to the needs expressed by SMEs.

Adoption of a model for national regulations was not supported

One issue that inevitably will have to be addressed in any proposal regulating the EPC is the information, consultation and, where applicable, participation of employees. In the MEDEF/ CCIP proposal, it was suggested that the rules relating to disclosure to and consultation of employees, and if applicable, their involvement in the corporate organs, should be determined by the law applicable to the registered office of the EPC. This does not address the concerns that may exist in some Member States that, by transforming or merging into an EPC national, companies could avoid application of, in

Any proposal regulating the EPC will have to address the information, consultation and participation rights of employees

Opinions differ on how these issues

particular, national participation rules. Some, mainly German respondents, raised this point. Other respondents took the view that this should not pose a problem. Some argued that the problem could be avoided completely by limiting the number of employees of the EPC (or its subsidiaries) below the thresholds for participation rights in Member States law. We note, however, that in some Member States, thresholds for employee participation are rather low (50 or 100 employees), and imposing a limit of numbers of employees related to these thresholds could therefore seriously restrict the application of the EPC by SMEs.

should be regulated

One solution could be to limit the number of employees of any EPC, but this may be overly restrictive

The EESC has addressed this issue as well and reached the following conclusions :

Conclusions of the EESC:

- The adoption of an EU Directive on the information and consultation of employees will address a number of issues for employees. It is intended to be applied above a threshold of 50 employees.

Information and consultation will be addressed by a Directive

- Concerning the participation of employees in the company's governing bodies, the solution adopted for the SE is not to be adapted for the EPC, because it is too cumbersome and complex. A realistic and pragmatic approach is required, aimed at maintaining acquired rights while avoiding an excessively cumbersome system.

Participation rights require a more pragmatic approach than in the SE

- If companies participating in the formation of an EPC already apply a form of participation, a negotiating group of employees should determine the conditions under which these could be extended. If no such rules existed and the number of employees was below a threshold of 250 as set in the Commission's Recommendation on the definition of SMEs, there should be no obligation to negotiate.

An obligation to negotiate should be imposed only in strictly defined circumstances

The Group has not considered the issues related to the involvement of employees in further detail, but just wishes to note that they have to be addressed if a regulation on the EPC is to be produced.

Group has not considered these issues in further detail

On balance, the Group acknowledges that the desire to have an EPC statute to serve the needs of SMEs in Europe has been clearly and repeatedly expressed. However, as priorities will have to be set, the first priority should be to adopt the Tenth Directive on cross-border mergers. We expect that one of the purposes of an EPC (to create cross-border joint ventures) can be met to a large extent by a facility for national companies to merge across borders. The Group recommends that, before deciding to submit a formal proposal, the Commission carries out a feasibility study in order to assess the additional practical needs for – and problems related to – the introduction of an EPC statute.

Desire to have an EPC statute has been clearly expressed

First priority should be the Tenth Directive

After which an EPC statute should be further considered

2. INCORPORATION OF THE EUROPEAN PRIVATE COMPANY

The SE can only be set up in one of four ways:

A SE can be set up :

- by the merger of two or more existing public limited companies, connected with at least two EU Member States; *By merger*
- by the formation of a holding company, promoted by public or private limited companies connected with at least two Member States; *By formation of a holding company*
- by the formation of a subsidiary, by companies connected with at least two Member States; *By formation of a subsidiary*
- by the transformation of a public limited company, which has for at least two years had a subsidiary in another Member State. *By transformation of a PLC*

Requirements imposed on the formation of SEs are not sufficiently flexible for SMEs

It has been noted that the requirement that only companies can incorporate an SE is particularly unhelpful for SMEs, many of which are incorporated and operated by individuals. It has also been noted that the requirement that companies from at least two Member States are to be involved in the incorporation of an SE is not suited for SMEs. When a statute for the EPC is being considered, access to it should in principle be unrestricted. It should be possible for one or more individuals or legal entities to form an EPC, whether or not they are nationals of one or more Member States. Some hold that the unrestricted access to the EPC is the only way to facilitate a full development of this form of company within the EU, and that the EPC should be available for every citizen of the Union. They stress the fact that it would enhance the "restatement" character of the EPC which should be an improved alternative to national forms of private companies, and as a result could trigger a process of convergence of national company laws.

The EPC should be open also to individuals, and regardless of the number of MS originally involved

An unrestricted access to the EPC would facilitate its development

Others argue that, without any link to a European dimension, as a matter of European Law there is no justification for the EU to be involved, and we agree. In this light, a minimum requirement would be that the EPC undertakes economic activities in more than one Member State. Thus when an EPC statute is being considered, access to its formation should be given to both individuals and legal entities who undertake activities in more than one Member State.

As a minimum requirement, EPCs should undertake economic activities in more than one MS

3. A GENUINE EUROPEAN COMPANY OR A STRUCTURE WITH A REFERENCE TO A NATIONAL LAW ?

As we have said, the SE Statute often refers to national laws of

Contrary to the

Member States applicable to public companies. The SE as a result only partly has a European character. The drafters of the proposal for the EPC intend this legal form to be governed only by the provisions of the regulation and the provisions of the articles of association which would not be inconsistent therewith. Of course, the EPC would remain subject to the general rules of Member States regarding accountancy law, tax law, penal law and bankruptcy law. One of the assumptions underlying the concept of the EPC is to create a genuinely European company, which is not subject to the company law of a Member State. This should facilitate the international use of this legal form, as those wishing to use it do not have to familiarise themselves with the company laws from other Member States.

SE Statute, which often refers to national law

The EPC has been drafted as a genuine European company, not subject to national company laws

In order to facilitate its international use

It is argued that this assumes an autonomous and exhaustive interpretation of the EPC regulation and the articles of association, ultimately by the European Court of Justice. This could raise concern about the strain this would impose on the European judicial system, and the delays and uncertainties for companies involved in resolving legal issues, but some respondents expect the SME practice to successfully deal with these issues. They argue that national courts and the European Court of Justice have demonstrated so far that they are able to interpret and develop further European company law from itself, and that they would be able to do the same with the EPC. This task, they say, is easier today than some decades ago when harmonisation of European company law started.

In such a situation, the European Court of Justice would have an important role to play

Some are concerned about difficulties

Whereas others are more confident

However, the Group notes that existing company laws in Member States are embedded in national bodies of private law. Many concepts of private law are also applicable in company law, e.g. concepts of legal acts, good faith, power of attorney, etc. The majority of respondents to the Consultative Document and the Group find it difficult to see how an EPC could operate completely outside such a national body of private law, in the absence of a European body of private law. For the proper operation of the company law applicable to the EPC, some connection will have to be made with the law of the jurisdiction of its incorporation. Such a reference to national law, it could be argued, would reduce to some extent the value of the EPC. But according to the supporters of the creation of an EPC, this does not reduce the strong need for it.

Majority of respondents and Group find that a reference to national private law is unavoidable

Which could reduce to some extent the value of the EPC, without removing the need for it

To summarise, the desire to have an EPC statute to serve the needs of SMEs in Europe has been clearly and repeatedly expressed. However, the first priority should be to adopt the Tenth Directive on cross-border mergers, which is expected to meet one of the purposes of the EPC statute. The Group recommends that, before deciding to

Summary : *Clear desire for an EPC statute*

First priority : Tenth Directive

submit a formal proposal, the Commission carries out a feasibility study in order to assess the additional practical need for – and problems related to – the introduction of an EPC statute.

To be followed by a feasibility study

When considering the introduction of an EPC statute, the requirements imposed on the formation of an EPC should be sufficiently flexible to facilitate proper development of such new form. The EPC should be open to individuals, and not only companies, and the founders should not be required to come from several Member States. A minimum requirement would however be that the EPC is undertaking activities in more than one Member State.

Formation requirements should be flexible

But any EPC should have activities in more than one MS

When considering the introduction of an EPC statute, a proper connection with the law of the jurisdiction of incorporation is to be established, since many concepts of private law are also applicable in company law.

A proper connection to national private law should be established

CHAPTER VIII

CO-OPERATIVES AND OTHER FORMS OF ENTERPRISES

1. REGULATION OF THE EUROPEAN CO-OPERATIVE, EUROPEAN ASSOCIATION AND EUROPEAN MUTUAL SOCIETY

The European Council recently adopted a general orientation on the Regulation on the Societas Cooperativa Europaea (SCE)

After the Consultative Document was published, the European Council adopted in July a "general orientation" on the Proposal for a Council Regulation creating the European Co-operative (Societas Cooperativa Europaea, SCE)[35]. According to Recital 2 of the Regulation, "it is essential that companies of all types the business of which is not limited to satisfying purely local needs should be able to plan and carry out the reorganisation of their business on a Community scale". In a similar vein, Recital 6 mentions the need to ensure "equal terms of competition".

This Regulation includes a high number of references to provisions in existing Company Law Directives

The number of rules in the Co-operative Regulation that apply provisions included in Company Law Directives is substantial. According to Recital 18 : "Work on the approximation of national company law has made substantial progress so that certain provisions, adopted by the Member State where the SCE has its registered office for the purpose of implementing Directives on companies, may be referred to by analogy for the SCE in areas where the functioning of the co-operative does not require uniform Community rules, such provisions being appropriate to the arrangements governing the SCE".

The SCE indeed takes advantage of the existing work on harmonisation of company law

The approach for the SCE has been to take advantage of the substantial work developed in the harmonisation of company law to the extent company law rules do not conflict with the peculiar traits of co-operatives[36]. The long list of articles[37] that call for the application of company law rules shows that the Company Law Directives can be used as instruments to complete many aspects of the Regulation on

[35] For full citation, see Annex 4.

[36] The European Co-operative Regulation expressly mentions the First Company Law Directive, the Fourth Company Law Directive, the Seventh Company Law Directive; the Eighth Company Law Directive and the Eleventh Company Law Directive.

[37] The articles including rules that refer to company law are the following: Article 4 (law applicable to appointment of experts); Article 10 (documents sent to third parties); Article 11 (registration and disclosure requirements); Article 12 (publication of documents in the Member States); Article 20 (law applicable in the case of merger); Article 26 (report of independent experts); Article 28 (laws applicable to formation of merger); Article 29 (scrutiny of merger procedure); Article 32 (publication of merger); Article 47 (power of representation and liability of the SCE); Article 68 (preparation of annual accounts and consolidated accounts); Article 70 (auditing); Article 71 (system of auditing).

the SCE.

In the Consultative Document, we asked questions on the need for and usefulness of proposals for Regulations creating the European Association[38] and the European Mutual Society[39]. The questions elicited few answers, which may be caused by general unfamiliarity with the problems affecting alternative forms of enterprise, but also by a different perception of the priority to be given to these initiatives. Whatever the explanation, a majority of the responses received express a positive view on these proposals, which are regarded as useful instruments for the development of economic activities on a European-wide basis by associations and mutual societies.

On the European Association and the European Mutual Society, the consultation elicited few answers

But a majority confirmed their usefulness

In the Group's view however, these proposals should not take priority in the short or medium term. We have not been convinced of the need for these forms in order for associations and mutual societies to be able to become active across Europe. In addition, respondents generally felt that the EU should not seek to harmonise the underlying rules for associations and mutual societies, as they are fundamentally different in the various Member States. Regulations on the European Association and the European Mutual Society will probably benefit less than the SCE Regulation from the harmonisation achieved by the Company Law Directives. We fail to see how uniform regulations of the European Association and European Mutual Society could be achieved if there is no agreement on harmonisation of the underlying national rules.

The Group does not view these proposals as high priorities

Respondents felt that the EU should not harmonise the underlying rules

Which makes the adoption of regulations difficult

On the other hand, we acknowledge that the progress made on the SCE Regulation represents an important precedent for the other proposed Regulations directed at alternative forms of enterprise. We believe the impact of the forthcoming SCE Regulation on the co-operative enterprise sector in Europe should be studied closely before putting further efforts into creating these other European entities. There are important questions deserving analysis in the future application of the SCE Regulation.

The forthcoming SCE Regulation is a precedent for other Regulations

Its impact should be studied prior to the creation of other EU entities

It will be interesting to see how the SCE relates to the national forms of co-operatives. Will the SCE indeed be used for transnational restructurings and joint ventures? If so, this may enhance the competitiveness of co-operatives. But it might well be that the SCE will result in a *de facto* harmonisation, given the fact that the national forms are still subject to mainly national rules. In other words, the SCE will compete with national forms in being the most effective instrument to organise a business activity. This could also lead,

Particularly interesting will be the extent to which the SCE will compete with national forms of co-operatives

[38] Proposal for a Council Regulation on the European Association : for full citation, see Annex 4.
[39] Proposal for a Council Regulation on the European Mutual Society : for full citation, see Annex 4.

potentially, to a lack of balance between national legal forms of co-operatives and the SCE.

In the Consultative Document, we raised similar questions about the need for and feasibility of a regulation for the European Foundation. In this respect we have basically come to the same conclusions as we reached for the European Association and the European Mutual Society. For foundations, the differences in national regulation by Member States seem to be even more profound, making the drafting of a EU Regulation on a European Foundation without any form of harmonisation of national laws on foundations all the more difficult.

The Group reached the same conclusions on a Regulation for the European Foundation, which seems even more difficult to achieve

This said, it seems to us that this area of developing European legal forms for alternative forms of enterprise could benefit from a different regulatory approach. Instead of trying to produce Regulations for these alternative European legal forms, the proponents of these European legal forms themselves could consider developing model laws for them as indeed is already being done for foundations[40]. The EU could consider facilitating this work on model laws by those who could benefit from them. The work on such model laws would need to reach agreement on the basic characteristics the European legal form should have, and thus contribute to agreement on a certain level of harmonisation of these national legal forms. Once that level of agreement is reached, the introduction of alternative European legal forms could become feasible.

Instead of EU Regulations, the proponents of these legal forms could consider developing model laws

The EU could facilitate this work on model laws, which would contribute to basic convergence

The Group would like to make two further, related, comments on these alternative legal forms of enterprise. There is a concern that such forms are used in the governance of listed companies to avoid application of transparency requirements on controlling shareholders. Where foundations, associations, mutual societies or other legal forms are indeed controlling shareholders, it must be ensured that the disclosure requirements, in particular relating to governance structures, are extended to these legal forms as well.

When alternative forms of enterprise are controlling shareholders, disclosure requirements should be extended to them

Apart from this, there is also a concern that other legal forms sometimes operate substantial businesses in competition with companies, without being subject to similar disclosure and general corporate governance standards. This may lead to unfair competition and to an undesirable use of these other legal forms to escape appropriate disclosure and corporate governance requirements. When disclosure and corporate governance standards are being formalised, the EU and Member States should seriously consider how and to what extent they should be extended to other legal forms

When these forms operate substantial businesses, fair competition may require extension to them of disclosure and corporate governance standards

[40] See the international Bertelsmann Foundation project on a European Foundation, which is expected deliver recommendations by 2004.

which operate substantial businesses.

2. GENERAL RULES FOR ENTERPRISES

In the Consultative Document, we finally asked questions on the usefulness of a European definition of the concept of enterprise, and the appropriateness of an "Enterprise Directive" aimed at regulating several key aspects of every business activity carried out by legal entities, regardless of their form.

Consultation sought views on the usefulness of an EU definition of "enterprise"

Respondents showed a clear opposition to a European rule defining the basic elements of what it is to be considered to be an enterprise. The Group recognises the difficulty of finding such a definition, and would therefore suggest that, if there is to be an EU initiative in this area, a list-based approach should be taken, in which every Member State lists the entities which would be subject to the legislative instrument.

Respondents showed clear opposition

Groups suggests that a list-based approach is used in any initiative

A substantial percentage of respondents agree that the lack of information on basic data of some of these alternative forms of enterprise causes problems, in particular when contracting across borders in the EU, and that it would be appropriate to introduce basic disclosure requirements for certain economic actors. A substantial harmonisation program is rejected, both because of its inherent difficulties and because no need for it is perceived. However, the creation of a framework for disclosure of basic data related to different types of certain legal entities engaged in economic activities is perceived as a useful tool for trade within the EU Internal Market. The need for this would, in the Group's view, be most prominent with respect to legal entities which confer limited liability on those controlling and participating in them.

Respondents agree that the lack of information on basic data creates problems

A substantial harmonisation is rejected

But a framework for disclosure of basic data would be useful

A framework Directive could require the registration of, at least, all limited liability entities with legal personality that engage in economic activities, and could ensure access to basic data like the entity's name, address and contact details, directors or others controlling its external existence. Powers of representation should also be published. Such a Directive should take advantage of technological developments in the area of registration and filing as described in Section 6 of Chapter II. It could be left to Member States to decide whether this basic registration needs to be included in their commercial registries or special registries are to be set up for these purposes. Linking of such registries across the EU should again be established.

Registration of all limited liability entities engaging in economic activities could be required

In a way that takes advantage of technological developments

To summarise, a European form of Association and a European form of Mutual Society are not regarded by the Group as priorities for the short and medium term. The impact of the forthcoming SCE Regulation on the co-operative enterprise should be studied closely before putting further efforts into creating these other European forms.

***Summary** : No urgent need for a European Association, and a European Mutual Society*

The Group reached the same conclusions about the need for and feasibility of a Regulation on the European Foundation, which might be even more difficult to achieve.

The same for a European Foundation

The development of European legal forms for alternative forms of enterprises could benefit from a different regulatory approach : proponents of these European legal forms could consider themselves developing model laws for them. The EU could consider facilitating this work, which would contribute to basic convergence.

Development of model laws to be encouraged

When alternative forms of enterprise are controlling shareholders, disclosure requirements, in particular relating to governance structures, should be extended to them.

When these alternative forms operate substantial businesses, fair competition may require extension to them of disclosure and corporate governance standards.

Company disclosure requirements to be extended where necessary

With respect to the usefulness of a European definition of the concept of enterprise, the Group recognises the difficulty of finding such a definition and therefore suggests that, if there is to be an EU initiative aimed at regulating entities regardless of their form, a list-based approach should be taken, in which every Member State lists the entities which would be subject to such a legislative instrument.

No need for a European definition of "enterprise"

In order to ensure access to basic information on alternative forms of enterprises, a framework Directive could require the registration of, at least, all limited liability entities with legal personality that engage in economic activities. Such a Directive should take advantage of technological developments, and linking of registries across the EU should be established.

Registration of all limited liability entities engaging in economic activities to be considered

CHAPTER IX

PRIORITIES FOR ACTION

In this Report, we make a number of specific recommendations relating to various elements of the regulatory framework for company law in Europe. If our recommendations are to be followed up, this will result in a substantial number of company law initiatives to be taken, in the first instance by the Commission. We realise that not all of this can be achieved simultaneously. We would advise the Commission to make a Company Law Action Plan which sets the EU agenda for regulatory initiatives in the area of company law, and to agree such an action plan with the Council and the European Parliament.

This Report contains many recommendations

Proper follow-up would require establishment of an Action Plan

In this light, the Group has discussed which of its recommendations it believes should have priority in such an EU Company Law Action Plan. We have ranked the various recommendations into three categories of actions, to be undertaken on the short term, medium term and long term.

Group discussed priorities

And ranked them in 3 categories

SHORT TERM:

- improve the EU framework for corporate governance, specifically through:

Corporate Governance

  - enhanced corporate governance disclosure requirements;
  - strengthening the role of independent non-executive and supervisory directors, particularly in three areas where executive directors have conflicts of interests, i.e. nomination and remuneration of directors and audit of the company's accounts;
  - an appropriate regime for directors' remuneration, requiring disclosure of the company's remuneration policy and individual director's remuneration, as well as prior shareholder approval of share and share option schemes in which directors participate, and accounting for the costs of those schemes to the company;
  - confirming as a matter of EU law the collective responsibility of board members for the company's financial and key non-financial statements;
  - an integrated legal framework to facilitate efficient shareholder

information, communication and decision-making, on a cross-border basis, using where possible modern technology;

- setting up a structure to co-ordinate the corporate governance efforts of Member States;

– simplify the Second Company Law Directive on capital formation and maintenance, on the basis of the SLIM recommendations as supplemented in this Report ("SLIM-Plus"); *Second Directive*

– offer efficient mechanisms for cross-border restructuring and mobility of companies, specifically by adopting proposals for the Tenth Company Law Directive on cross-border mergers and the Fourteenth Company Law Directive on transfer of the seat. *Tenth and Fourteenth Directives*

MEDIUM TERM:

– require Member States to set up central electronic filing systems for listed companies; *Electronic filing systems*

– introduce an EU framework rule on special investigation rights for minority shareholders; *Special investigation right*

– introduce an EU framework rule on wrongful trading by directors and "shadow" directors; *Wrongful trading*

– review the feasibility of director's disqualification across the EU as a sanction for director's misconduct; *Director's disqualification*

– review the feasibility of an alternative to the capital formation and maintenance rules of the Second Company Law Directive, as amended according to the SLIM-Plus proposals; *Alternative to capital formation and maintenance*

– provide a framework rule for groups, allowing the adoption at subsidiary level of a co-ordinated group policy with proper protections of creditors and shareholders; *Rule allowing group policy*

– prohibit stock exchange listing, except where permitted after special economic justification, of holding companies whose sole or main asset consists of shares in another listed company, as a measure to restrict the use of pyramid structures; *Restriction of pyramids*

– simplify the current Third and Sixth Company Law Directives on legal mergers and divisions, to avoid superfluous formalities; *Third and Sixth Directives*

– introduce general squeeze-out and sell-out rights with a threshold of at a minimum 90% and at a maximum 95% of the company's share capital; *Squeeze-out and sell-out rights*

– launch a feasibility study in order to assess the practical needs for - and problems of - a European Private Company statute. *European Private Company Statute*

LONG TERM:

- assess the need for the creation of other European legal forms;
- introduce basic disclosure rules for all legal entities with limited liability.

Other legal forms

Disclosure for all legal entities

The Group believes that much is to be gained from the setting up of a more permanent structure to provide the Commission with independent advice on future regulatory initiatives in the area of EU company law.

A permanent structure should provide advice on future initiatives

The EU agenda for company law reform will be full the coming years, and it will require efforts of many involved to achieve results. But a lot of work needs to be done so that company law in Europe can make a proper contribution to the conditions for productive enterprise and the creation and maintenance of competitive and efficient economic and financial markets in Europe. The Group is confident that the results of these efforts will make them worthwhile.

Company Law reform will require significant effort

But expected results will justify this

To summarise, the Commission should prepare a Company Law Action Plan which sets the EU agenda, with priorities, for regulatory initiatives in the area of company law and agree such an action plan with the Council and the European Parliament.

***Summary** : A prioritised Company Law Action Plan to be prepared*

The setting up of a permanent structure to provide the Commission with independent advice on future regulatory initiatives in the area of EU company law should be duly considered.

Creation of an advisory structure to be considered

ANNEX 1

THE HIGH LEVEL GROUP OF COMPANY LAW EXPERTS' TERMS OF REFERENCE

PRESS RELEASE OF 4 SEPTEMBER 2001 (Extract)

Company law: Commission creates High Level Group of Experts

The European Commission has set up a High Level Group of Company Law Experts that will help the Commission to prepare a new proposal for a Directive on the conduct of takeover bids and to define new priorities for the broader future development of company law in the European Union. The group comprises seven members, selected on the basis of their competence in company law and the Commission's desire that the members should have broad experience of the various legal and economic systems in the EU. The group will hold its first meeting on 11 September 2001. It is due to deliver a preliminary report on its recommendations to the Commission concerning rules for takeover bids by the end of 2001 and a final report concerning broader issues for the development of EU company law by mid-2002.

Internal Market Commissioner Frits Bolkestein said "This High Level Group has been set up because the Commission wants to get top quality independent advice from leading European experts in the first instance on pan-European rules for takeover bids and subsequently on key priorities for modernising company law in the European Union.".

The Group will hold its first meeting on 11 September 2001. Taking account of the positions of the EU's Council of Ministers and the European Parliament during the last stages of negotiation of the previous proposal for a Takeovers Directive (see MEMO/01/255), the Group of High Level Experts will initially consider the following three issues:

- how to ensure the existence of a level playing field in the EU concerning the equal treatment of shareholders across Member States
- the definition of the notion of an "equitable price" to be paid to minority shareholders and
- the right for a majority shareholder to buy out minority shareholders ("squeeze-out procedure").

The Group is due to deliver a report on these issues, including possible solutions, to the Commission's services by the end of 2001.

During a second stage, the Group is due to provide recommendations for a modern regulatory European company law framework designed to be sufficiently flexible and up-to-date to meet companies' needs, taking into account fully the impact of information technology. The Group will examine best practice developed in the Member States (as well as in the USA) and consider a range of issues including the following:

- the creation and functioning of companies and groups of companies, co-operatives and mutual enterprises, including corporate governance
- shareholders' rights, including cross-border voting and virtual general meetings
- corporate restructuring and mobility (for instance, the transfer of the corporate seat)

- the possible need for new legal forms (for instance, a European Private Company, which would be of particular relevance for SMEs)
- the possible simplification of corporate rules in light of the SLIM report on the Second Company Law Directive of 13 December 1976 on the formation and capital maintenance of public limited liability companies.

The Group is due to deliver a final report to the Commission's services by mid-2002.

PRESS RELEASE OF 18 APRIL 2002 (Extract)

Financial services: Commission services publish analysis of repercussions of Enron collapse

The European Commission's services have published online an initial analysis of the repercussions for the EU of the collapse of Enron. The paper, entitled "A first response to Enron related policy issues" outlines steps that need to be taken to guard against similar events in Europe. It was presented by Internal Market Commissioner Frits Bolkestein to the informal meeting of Economics and Finance Ministers in Oviedo on 12-14 April (see also MEMO/02/72). Ministers welcomed the paper and endorsed the Commission's proposal to ask its High Level Group of Company Law Experts to review further corporate governance and auditing issues in the light of the Enron case. The paper emphasises that the EU is already working on most Enron-related regulatory issues through the Financial Services Action Plan, which aims to establish an efficient and competitive capital market that deserves investors' trust. The full text of the paper can be found on the Commission's Europa site.

The mandate of the High Level Group of Company Law Experts (see IP/01/1237) will be expanded to review further corporate governance and auditing issues. These will include the role of non-executive directors and of supervisory boards; management remuneration; and the responsibility of management for the preparation of financial information.

Ministers decided in Oviedo that the Group's preliminary conclusions and proposals for reform would be discussed at the June Council of Finance Ministers and subsequently at the Seville European Council in June. The final conclusions will be presented to the informal meeting of EU Finance Ministers in September.

ANNEX 2

WORKING METHODS
OF
THE HIGH LEVEL GROUP OF COMPANY LAW EXPERTS

The High Level Group of Company Law Experts comprises:

- Chairman Jaap WINTER, the Netherlands, Partner at De Brauw Blackstone Westbroek and Professor at the Erasmus University of Rotterdam
- José Maria GARRIDO GARCIA, Spain, General Counsel to the Comision Nacional del Mercado de Valores and Professor at the University of Castilla-La Mancha
- Klaus HOPT, Germany, Geschäftsführender Direktor Max Planck-Institut and Professor at the Anton Philips chair of the Tilburg University
- Jonathan RICKFORD, United Kingdom, Unilever Professor at Leiden University and Member of the UK Competition Commission
- Guido ROSSI, Italy, former President of the Italian stock exchange supervisory body CONSOB
- Jan SCHANS CHRISTENSEN, Denmark, Professor at the University of Copenhagen
- Joëlle SIMON, France, Legal Affairs Director, French Business Confederation – MEDEF

The Group began its work on 11 September 2001. After the presentation of its "Report on Issues Related to Takeover Bids" on 10 January 2002 in Brussels, the Group took up its work on the second part of its mandate, according to which the Group was to provide recommendations for a modern regulatory European company law framework.

To this end, the Group held meetings in Brussels every month from January 2002 to September 2002.

In order to include in its work the broadest possible spectrum of opinions, the Group published a Consultative Document on 25 April 2002, in which it asked those interested in and concerned with company law in Europe to comment on the issues specified in the second part of its mandate.

Before submitting its Consultative Document to the public, the Group appeared before the European Parliament Legal Affairs and Internal Market Committee on 16 April 2002, on which occasion the Chairman gave a basic overview of the main content of the Consultative Document.

Following the publication of the Consultative Document, a hearing was held in Brussels on 13 May 2002 with representatives of mainly European business and professional organisations for the purpose of obtaining first opinions on the Group's considerations contained in the Consultative Document.

The comments received on the Consultative Document were analysed and summarised for the Group by a team of researchers from the Company Law Department of the Faculty of Law of the Erasmus University in Rotterdam led by Professor J.B. Wezeman.

A summary of the main comments, prepared by the team, is included in Annex 3 (for respondents' nationality and sector of activity, see the overview on the following pages).

The Final Report of the Group is submitted to the European Commission and presented to the Press on 4 November 2002 in Brussels.

Overview of nationality and sector of activity of respondents:

a) Full text contributions (number received: 119):

Nearly two thirds of all responses came from organisations representing various parts of industry, services and professions at national, European and international level (referred to by "L" in the following graph). About 10% of all contributions came from private entities (enterprises or individuals), while governments or government agencies accounted for more than 8 % of responses (referred to in the graph by "PRI" and "G" respectively). Less than 8% of the responses were received from academics ("U" in the graph). Slightly less than 7% were received from practitioners ("PRA"). The remainder (2,5%) was received from non-governmental organisations ("NGO").

Graph 1: Full text responses - respondents by sector of activity

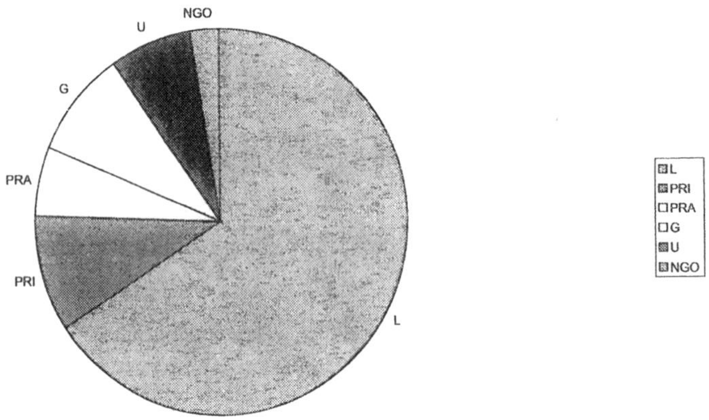

In terms of nationality (or, as in the case of organisations, in terms of context of activity, be it European or even global), contributions from EU Member States accounted for more than three quarters of the total, whereby the greatest number of contributions was received from Germany (about one quarter of all contributions), followed by the UK (more than one fifth of all contributions) and by contributions received from a predominantly European context (slightly less than one sixth of all contributions).

Graph 2: Full text responses - respondents by country

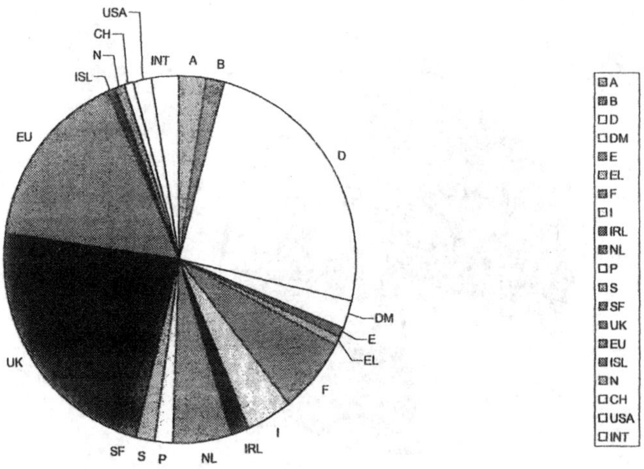

b) On-line contributions (number received: 48):

Here, more than one quarter of all contributions came from private entities (enterprises or individuals) and from academics respectively. One quarter of all responses came from representative organisations. Practitioners accounted for about one tenth of responses. The remainder was received from governments or government agencies (about 6%) and non-governmental organisations (about 4%).

Graph 3: Online responses - respondents by sector of activity

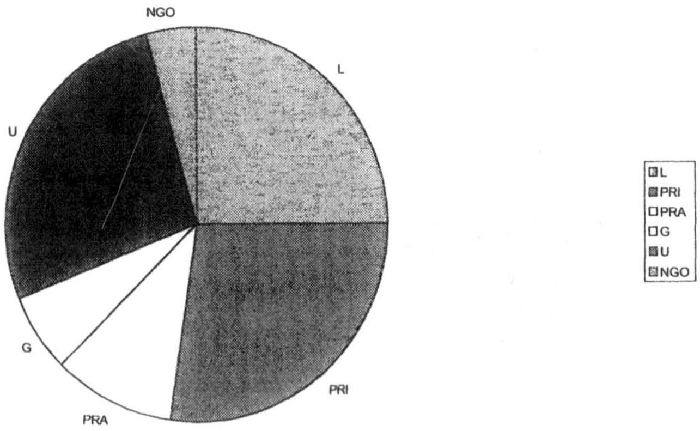

In terms of nationality (or, as in the case of organisations, context of activity, be it European or even global), contributions from EU Member States accounted for more than 80% of the total, whereby the greatest number of contributions was received from Germany (nearly half of the contributions), followed by the UK (one sixth of all contributions).

Graph 4: Online responses - respondents by country

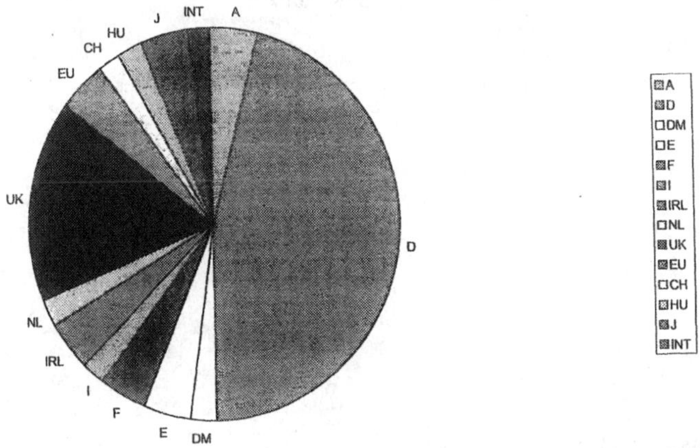

ANNEX 3

SUMMARY OF COMMENTS
SUBMITTED TO THE HIGH LEVEL GROUP OF COMPANY LAW EXPERTS
IN RESPONSE TO ITS CONSULTATION DOCUMENT

Erasmus University Rotterdam
October 2002

Professor Jan Berend Wezeman
Martijn Bras
Ageeth Klaassen
Michelle Reumers
Maarten Verbrugh

TABLE OF CONTENTS

INTRODUCTION

The European Commission has asked the company law department of the Faculty of Law of the Erasmus University in Rotterdam (the Netherlands) to support the High Level Group of Company Law Experts in analysing and summarising the comments the Group has received in response to its Consultation Document on a Modern Regulatory Framework for Company Law in Europe. The team of the Erasmus University was led by Professor Jan Berend Wezeman and included Martijn Bras, Ageeth Klaassen, Michelle Reumers and Maarten Verbrugh.

The team has prepared a number of detailed analyses, summaries, tables and charts for the Group. The summary of responses in this Annex is based on these analyses and summaries. This summary, with further tables and charts (on a no-names basis), can also be accessed at the Erasmus website at www.frg.eur.nl/pri/har/HLGannex.pdf

In total, the team has analysed responses from 119 respondents, excluding responses received on-line (which were analysed directly by the Commission services).

On the whole, respondents tended to support the proposals of the Group put forward in the Consultative Document. The following graph gives an impression of the thrust of the answers of respondents to the questions on the specific subjects raised in the Consultative Documents. Questions 11a, 12b, 14d , 15a, 15b and 16a stand out as questions with a high number of no-answers. Of these, the Group itself had indicated in the Consultative Document to favour a negative answer to questions 11a, 12b, 15b and 16a.

The following gives a summary and short statistical analysis of the various comments made in response to the questions in the Consultative Document.

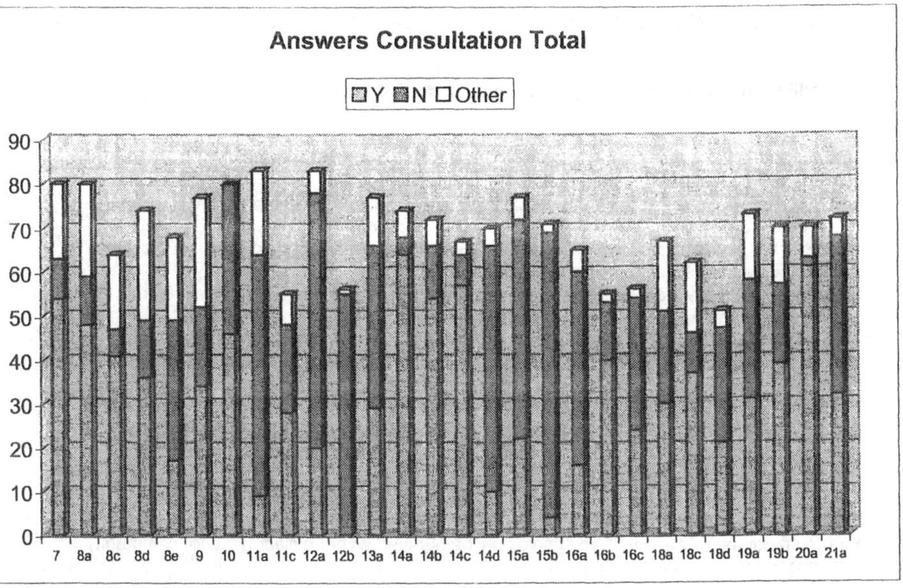
Answers Consultation Total
Y N Other
0 10 20 30 40 50 60 70 80 90
7 8a 8c 8d 8e 9 10 11a 11c 12a 12b 13a 14a 14b 14c 14d 15a 15b 16a 16b 16c 18a 18c 18d 19a 19b 20a 21a

1.1.

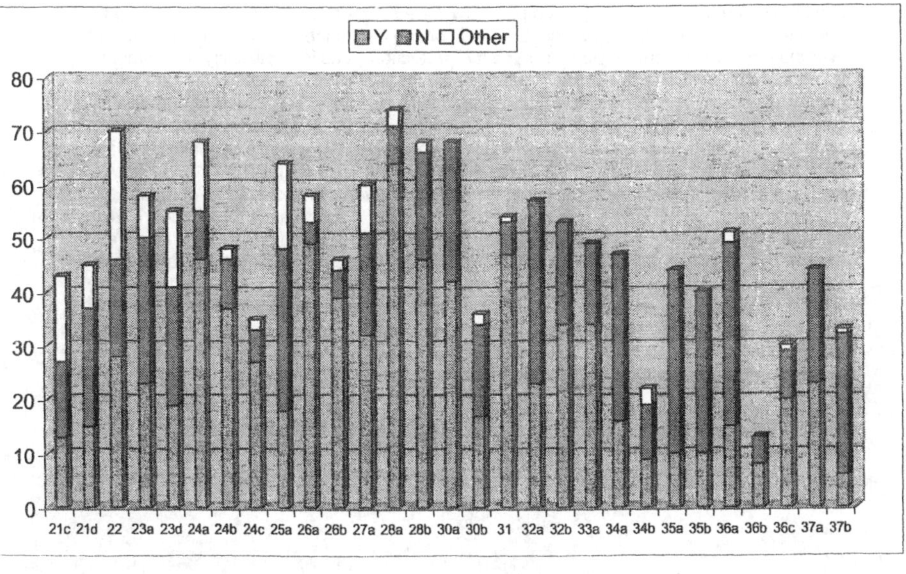
Y N Other
0 10 20 30 40 50 60 70 80
21c 21d 22 23a 23d 24a 24b 24c 25a 26a 26b 27a 28a 28b 30a 30b 31 32a 32b 33a 34a 34b 35a 35b 36a 36b 36c 37a 37b

I - GENERAL THEMES (CHAPTER 2 of the Consultative Document)

1. Facilitating efficient and competitive business in Europe

Most respondents to question 1a agree that the European Union, moving forward in the area of company law, should primarily focus on developing company law, which facilitates the efficient and competitive operation of business across the Union, especially by deregulation and by creating more flexibility and permitting more variation. Often the capital rules of the 2nd Directive are seen as an unnecessary burden. For example: the suggestion is made to regulate the payment of dividend solely by means of a solvency test. Today's business practice demands a legal framework flexible in form.
Nevertheless, many respondents emphasise that the protection of shareholders and creditors remains important, although other ways of protection might be possible.
Also the remark that the EU should focus on general framework rules is often made.
Several respondents suggest a step-by-step approach, in view of the differences between the Member States, and not a general reform, respecting the different national cultures. These respondents emphasise the principle of subsidiarity, while some others express the need of further consultation with the business community before launching new proposals.
A few respondents think that the protection of investors and creditors remains the most important aim of company law.
Some respondents express that – apart from cross-border merger and transfer of the seat - there is no real need for further harmonisation, or that - due to the principle of subsidiarity - European company law initiatives should only be pursued where a clear need for community wide action can be demonstrated.

A large majority of the respondents think that progress should be made, as a matter of priority, in the areas of cross-border merger and transfer of the seat of the company (question 1b). In relation to this, also de-mergers and similar restructuring operations are sometimes mentioned and the need for efficient reorganisation procedures in order to avoid liquidation.
Other often mentioned topics are the need to harmonise insolvency procedures. A part from these topics, the following areas of company law were mentioned where progress should be made as a matter of priority by one or a few of the respondents: information needs of stakeholders/shareholders, including minority protection; public availability of company information across the EU; social law/collective labour law/safety at work; (a uniform structure of) commercial registers; a European private company; integration of participation of workers into company law; provisions on personal liability of the management; capital market law; uniform structure of the powers of representation, especially abolition of any ultra vires doctrines; availability of EU company law instruments (e.g. SE) to companies not residing in the EU; disclosure of payments ("publish what you pay"); creating a company law framework which first and foremost caters for small and medium sized companies ("think small first"); easy dissolution of companies (as in e.g. Denmark); co-ordination of the issue of sanctions in the area of company law, especially by recommendation to favour civil sanctions; requirement for every public company to state its objects; adequate debt/equity leverage; hybrid securities and voting bonds; mutual recognition of companies; environmental regulation; banking law applying to company financing; joint ventures and inter-company agreements; unification of partnership law. Tax rules, especially taxation of cross-border transactions, were mentioned as well.

2. Modern company law making

The majority of the respondents to question 2a agree to the concept of making more use of alternatives as indicated by the HLG to primary legislation in directives. Most respondents agree that directives are inflexible and can lead to petrifaction and should therefore be limited to principles with a global focus. The differences between national systems can be respected better in secondary regulation. Others think a pragmatic combination of all ways is preferable, mainly because "comply of explain"-rules can not replace enforcement in full. A few respondents, whilst not against alternatives, do not believe that model laws will prove particularly useful.
Some respondents recognise, however, that secondary legislation can lack transparency and democratic legitimacy and should only be used by way of exception and with care. An important group of the respondents – mostly German respondents - think that mainly for these disadvantages, the EU should in principle make use of directives. Some of these respondents think the procedure for modifying directives should be simplified.

The areas of corporate governance (e.g. conduct of general meetings) and accounting (and in general: disclosure) are mentioned often as areas of company law, which are particularly suited for an alternative regulatory approach (question 2b). Other areas mentioned by some are the use of IT or other fast changing or newly emerging topics; an optional uniform model law, especially for listed companies (cf. U.S.A); a framework for a whole legal entity (e.g. European Private Company); fundamental organisational rules and rules on share registers; listing rules (and content of prospectuses etc.) or other areas with capital market relevance.

3. Disclosure of information as a regulatory tool

Almost all respondents to questions 3a and 3b agree that disclosure requirements can sometimes provide a more efficient regulatory tool than substantive rules, especially in the area of corporate governance, disclosure of structures of groups of companies, conflict of interest, financial affairs, share options/board compensation/payments or other dealings with directors, substantial shareholders and related parties, and the capital structure of listed companies.
A few respondents only agree in case of listed companies.
Several respondents emphasise, however, that disclosure is only effective as long as there are clear rules concerning the information itself and as long as disclosure is enforceable. Disclosure requirements cannot fully replace regulation. Furthermore, costs and benefits of disclosure have to be carefully balanced and flooding the public with information of no relevance should be prevented. C.f.: "Moreover disclosure leads to an effect like in a football stadium: if everybody gets up, no one has a better view any more".
To avoid overload, co-ordination at EU-level for consistency and materiality is important. As for the dividing line between disclosure and more substantive regulation, one of the respondents refers to the ideas as set out in the Final Report of the Company Law Review in the UK (CLR). Also, disclosure requirements based on a definitive code of best practise have proven to be effective in improving corporate governance in the UK.
Some respondents think that there are already enough (or to many) disclosure requirements or that disclosure requirements cannot provide an efficient regulatory tool.

4. Distinguishing types of companies

A lot of the respondents to questions 4a and 4b express that there are good reasons to distinguish between three kinds of companies: listed companies, public (open) companies and private (closed) companies, since the interests involved are actually different. A large

group of others think only a distinction is necessary between listed and non-listed companies. The definition of "listed company", however, needs to be considered carefully as the structure of the securities markets is changing.
In general, the respondents feel that the rules applying to private companies can mainly be dealt with at national level and that these rules can be more flexible and less mandatory, especially in the areas of incorporation, corporate governance (e.g. the communication with shareholders, the holding of general meetings and shareholder decision making), the internal organisation of these companies, accounting, alternative dispute resolution. Company law should not impose a corporate governance regime on small companies, which is designed to solve issues that are specific to listed companies, but should recognise the significance of a company's financial size. Cf. the answer of one of the respondents: "think small first", referring to the Report of the UK Company Law Review.

Some respondents believe no new categories should be created but we should use the existing distinction between private and public companies, with additional requirements for listed public companies. Rigid legislative distinctions between types of company based upon size or other criteria can create problems when a company changes from one category to another. They may also prove to be a barrier to growth. Some respondents stress the fact that it is not advisable to create two different legal forms, i.e. one for listed companies and one for closed companies, because the existence of two such forms might discourage closed companies' access to the market.
Company law for listed companies should facilitate the efficient operation of the securities markets in Europe, whilst providing appropriate safeguard for investors (e.g. by means of stricter disclosure rules). A single respondent thinks, however, that the existence of markets suggest that there should be less mandatory legislation for the listed company than for the private company. Another respondent states that it should not be a question of more regulation for listed companies but a question of different regulation which for listed companies would underline the importance of transparency.
A few respondents think all companies, listed or not, who make a public call for financial resources, should be governed by the same rules. A few respondents think that it should be left to individual markets to provide further regulatory mechanisms appropriate to a publicly traded company or that basically one type of limited company is sufficient. Others think that only a distinction between private and public companies is necessary, as additional rules of a stock exchange will apply to listed companies. On the other hand, some respondents don't see the need for distinction between public (open) and private (closed) companies, or think that it is not really a matter to be dealt with at EU level.

5. Increased flexibility vs. tightening of rules

In principle, almost all respondents to question 5 agree with the statement of the HLG, that company law should not be burdened with rules to combat fraud and terrorism. A few respondents, however, express that also company law should contribute in these areas, at least if there are no other options. Cf. the work of the FAFT concerning Corporate Vehicles. Also it might be envisaged to generally dematerialise shares, in order to enable Government authorities to know the identity of the shareholders. One respondent suggests that the HLG should consider whether implementation in national requirements of the provisions of the OECD Convention on Combating Bribery and Corruption has been an effective mechanism.

6. Modern technology

Almost all respondents to questions 6a and 6b encourage the use of modern information and communication technology, especially for listed companies. Some of the German respondents refer on this topic to the German Corporate Governance Codex.

Quite a few respondents think listed companies should be required to maintain a specific section on their website as the single place where they publish all relevant information (if proof can be given of what information was effectively present on the website at any given moment in time). Some of these respondents are nevertheless of the opinion that to file with the relevant national register should remain the primary obligation and that privately-controlled websites cannot replace – at least not for the time being - public registers when it comes to the protection of third parties. Some make the suggestion that a neutral third party should provide the required information on a website.
Most respondents, however, are of the opinion that website publication should not be compulsory. It is felt that not everyone has unlimited access to internet; that the legal, practical and technical risks and implications should first be investigated thoroughly; that technology is fast-evolving; that an obligation would lead to a significant increase of costs and risks for companies; that the security aspect of the electronic information published needs special attention since it is open for manipulation; that the idea of two-way links with public registers is questionable as Member States – but also accession countries – will probably have difficulties to offer such online-registers; that public registers have the advantage that once information has been disclosed it cannot be altered by companies; that an obligation to ensure that the information on the website is correct and up to date appears problematic; that it will extend a company's liability. Furthermore, most respondents think publication on a website cannot replace the official registers; therefore it has to be ensured that information available both in a public register and on a company website are properly synchronised.
The view that also non-listed companies are allowed to file and publish information on their website is broadly shared, as long as there is no obligation to do so and this kind of publication does not replace the official registers.

A large group of the respondents to questions 6c and 6d believe that a single central electronic filing system within the EU, where all public information on companies can be found, should be facilitated, but is not really feasible in the near future. Some respondents refer to the EDGAR-system in the USA, to the SOPHIE-system in France for listed companies, to the Australian Commercial Register ("Firmenbuch") as models worth copying, or propose to start with setting up, like e.g. Germany, national central electronic registers. One of the difficulties mentioned is the language question, where lessons may be learned from the multilingual Swedish Commercial Register.
Other respondents are more optimistic and more strongly support the idea of a single central commercial register for all companies or only for listed companies.
Several suggestions are also made by one of the respondents, referring to the national system linking Italy's 103 Chambers of Commerce through a high-speed/high-security electronic network and to the project to devise a European Business Register (EBR), financed by the European Commission, as well as to the European Commercial Registers Forum (ECRF).
Some respondents are opposed to the idea of creating a central register; they think that this can be left to the member states, that a central register would only lead to multiple notifications, or that a central register is not necessary if there would be a common standard for the national registers.
Most respondents agree that the European Union should facilitate or provide for the co-ordination of public company registers in the Member States, e.g. by introducing a uniform standard. However, a few respondents think there is no tasks here for the EU or that links between the filing systems in the member states will be sufficient. The technology is available to link existing registers into a virtual single system from a user perspective.

II - SPECIFIC TOPICS (CHAPTER 3 of the Consultative Document)

1. CORPORATE GOVERNANCE

1.1 The role of the European Union in corporate governance for European business

A majority (ca. 66%) of the 82 respondents to question 7 agree with the HLG that efforts to improve or strengthen corporate governance are necessary and important for efficient business activities in the EU and for an integrated European securities market. Nevertheless, many respondents are of the opinion that there is no need for legislation or a European Code. A small minority (11% of the 82 respondents) gave a negative response and is of the opinion that corporate governance systems will develop and progress in a natural way under pressure from the financial markets. Two respondents notice that competition among national jurisdictions in this area is preferable to the development of EU-wide standards.

1.2 Better information for shareholders and creditors, in particular better disclosure of corporate governance structures and practices including remuneration of board members

That there should be more disclosure on corporate governance structures and practices of companies in Europe, is expressed by a majority (60% of the 80 respondents) to question 8a. Elements to be disclosed are for example: shareholder rights and structures of company organs and defensive instruments, including voting agreements. Transparency is good for the confidence of the shareholders and it is an essential criterion in investment decisions. Several respondents, however, believe that regulation is not needed at European level. Only a small minority (ca. 14%) of respondents believe that more disclosure is not necessary and that this matter can be left to the market.

A majority of the 60 respondents to question 8b is of the opinion that more disclosure should only be given by listed companies and not by all "open" or "closed" companies. Only a minority thinks that open or even closed companies should give more disclosure as well. One respondent thinks that disclosure requirements are more needed for mutual and co-operative societies than for listed companies.

To question 8c a majority (ca. 64%) of the 64 respondents answers that disclosure should include an indication whether a certain corporate governance code is followed and where and why the code is not complied with. Several respondents prefer a "comply or explain" rule. A number of respondents are of the opinion that a European rule is not required. Only a small minority (ca. 9%) does not agree with the statement in question 8c.

Of the 74 respondents to question 8d a large group (ca. 49%) agrees with the idea that remuneration of individual board members should be disclosed, in particular if it is linked to the share price performance. Only 13 respondents (ca. 18%) do not agree. Some believe that the disclosure must be limited to listed companies. More respondents are of the opinion that disclosure should not be regulated at European level. The respondents give less information about how detailed remuneration information should be. Some respondents mention fixed salary, variable income, cash bonus, stock options, fringe benefits, and golden parachutes.

Arguments against disclosure are based on of privacy-concerns.

68 respondents answered question 8e; 25% is of the opinion that shareholders have a role in fixing the principles and limits of board remuneration. A large group of the respondents (ca. 47 %) believe, however, that this topic does not fall within the powers and scope of the general meeting. A few respondents suggest that this task must be entrusted to a remuneration-committee.

1.3 Strengthening shareholders' rights and minority protection, in particular supplementing the right to vote by special investigation procedures

Of the 77 respondents to question 9, 34 (ca. 44%) agree that shareholders' rights and decision-making, including minority protection, should be enhanced by European law, in particular by enabling the general meeting of shareholders, by resolution, or a qualified minority of shareholders to apply to a court or an appropriate administrative body for the ordering of a special investigation. A minority of ca. 23% (18 respondents) does not agree.
A number of respondents suggest that the German rule of "Sonderprüfung" can be used as a model for European regulation. All kinds of thresholds are mentioned, e.g. 1%, 5%, 10%, 25 %, a total of the share capital with a market value of Euro 100,000. An alternative for minority shareholders in family companies would be not a specific percentage but the minority shareholding following the biggest shareholder. Two respondents are in favour of enhancing the civil liability of members of the board towards their shareholders. Another remark is that the authority to implement the general principles in the light of the different types of companies and ownership structures should be left to EU members. Several respondents bring up the problem of abuse.
A few respondents are of the opinion that there is no need for harmonisation because the special investigation procedures in the individual Member States have proved successful in practice. Other respondents believe that national law should regulate the subject.

1.4 Strengthening the duties of the board, in particular the accountability of directors where the company becomes insolvent

A majority (56%) of the 81 respondents to question 10 feel that the European Union should introduce a framework rule which would hold company directors accountable for letting the company continue to do business when it is foreseeable that it can no longer pay its debts. Some respondents of this majority, however, believe that such a wrongful trading rule should be restricted, very general or should (also) be dealt with in insolvency law.
An important minority of ca. 40%, however, does not agree. Arguments against a wrongful trading rule are that company law should not deal with insolvency law, that this is not a topic for harmonisation but a topic of national law or that several practical problems would arise. Several respondents state that efficient rules already exist, in e.g. Germany, Sweden, Iceland and Ireland.

1.5 Need for a European corporate governance code or co-ordination of national codes in order to stimulate development of best practice and convergence

Against a small minority (ca. 11%) the majority (ca. 66%) of the 83 respondents to question 11a believe there is no need for a voluntary European corporate governance code in addition to or instead of the various national corporate governance codes, because corporate governance questions are strongly determined by socio-economic differences in Member States. Differences in company law are also a reason to be against a European corporate governance code. It should be worked out by or left to the market Two respondents believe it is too early. Many respondents refer to the study of Weil, Gotshal & Manges or mention the OECD-code.
The 25 respondents who answered question 11b give examples of what rules and recommendations a European corporate governance code should contain: rules concerning disclosure and communication with shareholders, equitable treatment of shareholders, the function, responsibilities, independence of the directors, non-executives and auditors and the relation between them, disclosure and transparency, company policy on remuneration and information about conflict of interest.
A small majority (ca. 51% of 55 respondents) agree that the EU should facilitate the co-ordination of national codes in order to stimulate development of best practices and

convergence (question 11c). A minority of 36% believes that this should be left to the market; the market will provide or encourage the co-ordination.

2. SHAREHOLDER INFORMATION, COMMUNICATION AND DECISION-MAKING

2.1 Notice and pre-meeting communication

A majority (ca. 70%, versus a minority of 24%) of the 83 respondents think that listed companies should not be required to establish on their website electronic devices (bulletin boards, chat rooms or similar devices) that allow for electronic communication between shareholders and the company and among shareholders prior to general meetings, including with respect to notices of general meetings, submissions of proposals and questions and solicitations of proxies (question 12a).
Most respondents, however, feel that this is a matter that should be encouraged as a voluntary action. Generally, the use of chat rooms is not recommended due to the potential for abuse. Some respondents note that establishing communication between shareholders is not a responsibility of the company.
None of the 56 respondents to question 12b think that, if listed companies are required to establish electronic devices on their websites, shareholders should be required to communicate by electronic means and thus be compelled to abandon the use of traditional means of communication. It should be an alternative to those interested. To make this a requirement at this moment would inconvenience and disenfranchise a significant amount of shareholders.

Only a minority (ca. 38%) of the 77 respondents to question 13a think that there is a need, at the European level, to provide for minimum standards regarding the right for shareholders to ask questions and submit proposals for decision-making at the general meeting. It could encourage greater cross-border share ownership. Some note that all shareholders must have the right to ask questions. Many of these respondents see problems that would arise if a lot of irrelevant questions would be asked and the management would be obliged to answer. Solutions for this might be a maximum amount of questions to be asked be a single shareholder. Others think that minimum standards must be set and not all shareholders should be able to ask questions and submit proposals. Among those against harmonisation (48%), a lot of respondents note that this issue is a matter for national law.
Question 13b was answered by ca. 29% of respondents. Some standards that are thought to be sufficient are the following: shareholders should be able to ask 3 questions and have 5 minutes to speak, to submit proposals, the shareholder must own 5% of the shares; the right to put items on the agenda should require no more than an aggregate of 10% of the shares; no minimum for raising questions, not more than 250.000 Euro for submitting proposals, maximum time for submitting proposals should be 4 weeks.

2.2 The meeting, electronic access, proxy voting

A large majority (ca. 87% of 74 respondents) think that listed companies should be required to provide facilities for proxy voting by all shareholders (question 14a). However, caution has to be taken. Abuse of a proxy solicitation system by management and opposing shareholders is not unthinkable. Proxy contests can make the system very costly. Many respondents note that this matter should not be regulated on a European level.
A majority (ca. 73% of 72 respondents) think that listed companies should be enabled to offer to their shareholders electronic facilities for proxy voting (question 14b). A few respondents even think this should be required. None of the respondents think that shareholders should be compelled to use electronic proxy voting and that traditional proxies should be abolished.

Question 14c was answered by 67 respondents, of which ca. 85% agree that companies should be enabled to allow absentee-shareholders to participate in traditional general meetings via electronic means, including via the internet (webcast) and satellite. None think a requirement to do so is appropriate. Of the few respondents against enabling companies to provide these means, most think that the technology at this moment is not advanced enough to make this possible.

A majority of 80% of the 70 respondents who answered question 14d think that companies which offer a comprehensive electronic process of information to, communication with and decision-making by shareholders should not be enabled to abandon the traditional type of general meeting. Most think abandoning the traditional type of meeting is premature. Others think the ability to come face-to-face with the management can never be substituted by a virtual meeting.

2.3 Voting by institutional investors

A majority of ca. 66% (of 72 respondents) does not think that institutional investors in Europe, or alternatively all shareholders holding a certain percentage of the share capital, should be required to disclose their policy as regards to the investments they make, and as to how they exercise their voting rights (question 15a). Among those who object to this requirement, some respondents do note, however, that institutional investors should have to report to their beneficiaries on the way they exercise their votes. Arguments against the disclosure of policy are that confidentiality of business strategy from a competitive standpoint and equality of shareholders must prevail and that institutional investors should not be burdened with the extra costs.

A large majority (ca. 92% of 71 respondents) think that institutional investors should not be required to exercise their voting rights with respect to the shares they hold (question 15b). Some respondents feel that exercising of voting rights should be encouraged but not compelled. Others note that an obligation to vote would distort the voting process, unconsidered votes can be swamped by 'required' votes, that it would create a 'box-ticking compliance culture', it would lead to an unwanted dominance of institutional investors and to under-informed decision-making. The mere fact that they have fiduciary duties is not sufficient to oblige them to vote.

3. ALTERNATIVES TO CAPITAL FORMATION AND MAINTENANCE RULES

3.1 The functions of legal capital and the competitive effect of the current rules

The majority (ca. 68%) of the 65 respondents to question 16a does not think that legal capital effectively protects the interests of creditors and shareholders, and ensures capital adequacy. Many note that legal capital mainly serves as protection for creditors and secondly for shareholders and that it must not be abolished because it gives the best safeguards. Others note that it does not reflect the size of the company. Some respondents think that a more flexible regulation is needed in relation with further issues such as directors' duties, insolvency law and creditor protection. A few respondents note that legal capital 'more or less' serves the four functions. A minority (ca. 25%) of the respondents firmly believes in the current system.

A large majority (73%) of the 55 respondents to question 16b think that there are possibilities of reaching the same results by means of other techniques than legal capital. The most popular option is a solvency test and a regulation on the liability/duties of directors. The solvency test should be linked to a declaration of solvency by the directors with appropriate penalties. Other possibilities are: financial reporting and disclosure requirements, equity regulation and a provision of guarantees by shareholders and directors to take over the company's liability in case of insolvency. Of those (ca. 24%) who do not think that there are

other possibilities, most note that the current regime should be maintained and is appropriate.
A small majority (ca. 54%) of respondents does not think that European companies are at a disadvantage as against companies in jurisdictions with a more flexible capital regime (question 16c). Half these negative responses are from German respondents. Some respondents note that although the regime is strict, there is no real reason for radical reform. However, some improvements are welcome. Some respondents also think that the strict rules provide a better reputation for European companies. Respondents who do think that European companies are at a disadvantage blame this on the restrictive character and complexity of the system, in particular to issues such as financial assistance for the purchase of own shares, increasing capital by way of contributions in kind, issuing convertible bonds, no par-value shares and the weak protection of creditors.

3.2 Three approaches to the reform of legal capital in Europe

Of the 57 respondents to question 17a a large majority thinks a new approach to the reform of legal capital in the EU is needed. Ca. 10% of the respondents mention that there is no need for a new approach on a European level.
As to question 17b, a large group (ca. 45%) of those who think a new approach is needed, opt for the evolutionary approach 1: the SLIM-approach. They argue that the other approaches are too radical and not pragmatic. Advantages of the SLIM proposals as they are and as they might become, mentioned by respondents, are the possibility of no par-value shares, a solvency test, eased formalities, personal liability of directors a reduction of mandatory valuations, the extension of the period in which own shares can be purchased (licensed up to 5 years), purchasing own shares for more than 10 %, the possibility to exclude pre-emptive rights for a period of 5 years and a reduction of reporting obligations.
After the SLIM-approach, the revolutionary approach that rebuilds the US capital regime from a European point of view (the third approach in the Consultative Document), is favoured by 26% of respondents. The supporters of this approach argue that a tailored approach can eliminate legal capital and can combine the best aspects of the different systems. Finally, ca. 9% of the respondents favour the revolutionary US-approach (the second approach in the Consultative Document). It provides a helpful basis for further analyses, but should not be adopted wholesale.
A small group of the respondents (ca. 10%) mentioned other approaches or did not clarify their favourite approach.

3.3 Specific topics

Many respondents to questions 18a-18e were of the opinion that minimum capital should be kept, whereby the level should strike a balance between an appropriate impediment to set up a company on the one hand, and not setting the barrier too high on the other hand. Some would favour a minimum capital, which would be linked to the kind of activity of the company. Often respondents made a distinction between SME and other companies. Most respondents (of the ones that responded) think that "wrongful trading" is an effective instrument for creditor protection and about half consider that subordination is not an effective and desirable way of enhancing creditor protection.

Almost half (ca. 45%) of the 67 respondents to question 18a see the minimum capital requirement as an appropriate impediment to starting up a company, whereas 21 respondents (ca. 31%) do not agree. According to several respondents, the level is too low to be an impediment. Some respondents made a distinction between SME and other (listed or open) companies, whereby the impediment exists for SME; some answered that there should be no impediment at all.
Of the 66 respondents to question 18b, almost half would not abolish the minimum capital requirement or impose a stricter minimum capital requirement than the one presently in

force. Some respondents are in favour of abolishing (ca. 18%) or lowering the level of minimum capital, whereas ca. 15% feels for stricter requirements. Some of the other comments (positive, negative or other) to this question were: the level should be re-examined at least every ten years, one should distinguish between regulated and financial companies and other companies, the question of abolition or relaxation should take other forms of creditor protection into consideration (e.g. directors liability, insolvency law, etc.), the new Basel II standard shows that the legal capital should be much higher in most companies, no (additional) minimum capital for SME, effective rules on debt/equity should be in force, abolition with additional maintenance rules in place.

The majority (ca. 60%) of the 62 respondents to question 18c considers that "wrongful trading" is an effective instrument for creditor protection, only 15% disagreed. More than once the effectiveness is made dependent on the enforcement, with sometimes a reference to the difficulty of the burden of proof. And more than once the national situation was explained. Some (German respondents) were of the opinion that it should not be used outside insolvency law. Other comments (positive, negative or other) to this question were: the triggering effect should not be too late, if it does not require a proof of intent, it depends if it is applied to a financial sector, it should be compatible with the legal system, next to other instruments, it leads to endless debates on their application, it might lead to the management staying in charge too long, the experience is rather mixed, comes into play rather late in the life of a company, states should fix the rules, it has proved beneficial, the procedure is more difficult for smaller structures, It should be linked to the degree of guilt, it should not be harmonised, if introduced then it should look at the possibility of reorganisation rather than liquidation, it has a deterrent effect, the UK concept of fraudulent trading (sic) provides further safeguards, it is expensive.

About half of the 51 respondents to question 18d consider that subordination is not an effective and desirable way of enhancing creditor protection, while 21 respondents (ca. 41%) think it is. Some respondents stress the need of full disclosure, and some fear a deterrent effect on insiders to finance the company. Other comments (positive, negative or other) to this question were: it should not depend on the identity of the creditor but on the nature of the claim, it should be dealt with in insolvency law, any distinction should be left to the choice of the parties or to the member states, "capital-replacing-loans" (German case law) seem to have worked well, it would deter shareholders loans for troubled companies.

Question 18e (are there any other possibilities worth considering to protect creditors) was answered by 26 respondents. The comments made include: creditor protection would be improved by a shift of the burden of proof to show that the value attributed to contributions reflect the real value; Belgium has introduced the rule whereby the founders of the company can be held liable –jointly and severally- for "manifest under-capitalisation" for a two years period; disclosure should be improved; there is a case for allowing other forms of consideration for capital, including the provision of services and for simplifying the rules dealing with acquisitions of own shares; the prohibition of financial assistance could be changed; it may be appropriate to extend the scope of share capital, for example to cover services; alongside a claim for damage, a responsibility of criminal law should be envisaged; compulsory indemnity insurance, to be held by directors; new directors should: a) make a standard solemn oath that they understand their duties and responsibility, or b) take a test of their understanding of their duties and responsibility; the 'New Money' rules applied in the UK seem to work reasonable well; directors accountability rule should not only be triggered when the company is insolvent, but should be replaced by an "early intervention approach"; the formation of a rule based on the English common law rule of "doubtful solvency"; one could oblige companies to make a financial plan, whereby failing to do so could be the basis for a personal liability in case of insolvency; the financial early warning system in case of the loss of half of the guaranteed capital could be strengthened, if it is applied earlier; disqualification for a certain period, also as founder; one should think about introducing a common regulation on "lifting the corporate veil".

Of the 73 respondents to question 19a ca. 43% agree that other forms of consideration, such as services, should be allowed as valid forms of consideration for capital, whereas ca. 37% do not. The advocates as well as the opponents often observe that allowing services as a valid form of consideration for capital would probably lead to valuation problems. Some of the advocates state that other forms of consideration for capital should be allowed, provided proper creditor protection and valuation procedures are introduced, or provided there are measures to protect minority shareholders. Some respondents to this question argue that other forms of consideration for capital should (at least) be allowed for private companies, provided that a clear creditor protection procedure and evaluation procedure are considered. Some of the opponents state that claims for services to be rendered are not enforceable and that future services, as opposed to services rendered, should therefore not be allowed as consideration for capital. Others mention that capital paid for by services and the like should not compete with the registered capital. Furthermore respondents notice that there might be accounting difficulties in case the services will be activated.

A majority (ca. 56%) of the 70 respondents to question 19b believe that the prohibition of financial assistance for the acquisition of own shares should be eliminated or at least that financial assistance should be allowed if it complies with the general rules for distributions to shareholders. Ca. 26% (18 respondents) don't agree. Advocates propose that financial assistance for the acquisition of own shares should be allowed, provided that creditor protection and evaluation procedures are introduced, or that the prohibition should be eliminated, subject to a solvency test where such assistance is given. Moreover, a few respondents refer to the exemption model for private companies under UK law, that is the so-called "whitewash procedure". Some of the opponents believe that, although the prohibition should not be eliminated, it deserves further investigation whether financial assistance should be allowed if it complies with general rules for distributions to shareholders. Furthermore some respondents compare financial assistance for the acquisition of own shares with the repurchase of own shares by the company itself, and believe that the rules governing such assistance should be configured accordingly.

4. THE FUNCTIONING OF GROUPS AND COMPANIES

4.1 The existence of groups of companies as a useful and legitimate economic reality

Groups of companies appear to be frequent in most – if not all – Member-States. Only 2 of the 68 respondents to question 20a gave a negative answer. These negative answers state that groups of companies are not frequent in their respective countries.

Most of the 62 respondents to question 20b state long lists of advantages of groups. Disadvantages and risks are also stated, but the lists are shorter. All the other responses varied. Frequently mentioned advantages are amongst others: (increased) possibilities to allocate risks, to obtain better financing conditions and tax advantages, to foster synergies and to increase management efficiency and flexibility. Group structures also facilitate restructuring of businesses, and the applicability of the principle of limited liability encourages risk taking. Another frequently mentioned advantage is the possibility to maintain minority shareholders in subsidiaries, because this will strengthen the business' capital base. Frequently mentioned disadvantages or risks are: minority and creditor protection problems, creditor reliance problems, lack of transparency (in relation to intra-group dealing), problems arising from conflicts of interests between the (boards of the) subsidiaries and the (board of) the parent, complex and laborious management, audit problems and the lessening of competition, violation of fair competition rules, some companies may be sacrificed for the greater good of other companies in the group, problems regarding the distribution of responsibility among directors and statutory auditors within the group, and cascades.

4.2 Transparency of group relations

Half of the 72 respondents to question 21a do not feel that the 7th Company law Directive should be supplemented by rules that require greater transparency of group relations and possible risks arising from them both to the subsidiary and to the parent, while ca. 44% of the respondents do. Some of the adversaries argue that the risks arising for the subsidiary should be dealt with in the accounts of that subsidiary rather than in the consolidated accounts. Any additional requirements in this regard may therefore more appropriately be included in the 4th Company Law Directive. Others argue that supplementation is not warranted, because the IAS (or IFRS) will be implemented for listed companies (see especially IAS 24). Member-States may allow or require other companies to also use IAS. More generally it is sometimes stated that if enhanced transparency is required, details should be a matter for the accountancy standard bodies rather than be dealt with by further regulation at EU level.

If rules enhancing transparency were to be implemented they should – according to the 40 respondents that answered question 21b – include information on: the group structure, ownership, the managing system, the activities of the subsidiary and the group strategy behind it, intra-group transactions, related party transactions, cross guarantees and liabilities, siphoning of risks, interlocking directorships, remunerations to management, audit and compliance procedures, intra-group competition rules, conditions of trading, etc. Also reference is made to IAS 24 and IAS 34. It is furthermore stated that information rights of the supervisory board and the shareholders of the parents should be enlarged to activities at least in consolidated subsidiaries.

Question 21c was answered by 43 respondents; ca. 33% of these respondents is of the opinion that enhanced transparency rules should not be applied to listed companies, while ca. 30% do agree to the implementation of such rules for listed companies. The reason mostly stated for non-implementation of enhanced transparency rules for listed companies is that the IAS will be implemented in 2005, which will suffice in this regard. See especially IAS 14, 24 and 34. Some respondents remark that full transparency should relate to all companies, whether listed or not, because these rules not only benefit shareholders but also creditors.

Almost half of the 45 respondents to question 21d is of the opinion that special transparency rules for banks and other financial institutions are not needed. Arguments mentioned by the adversaries are amongst others that the Insurance Group Directive 98/78 already regulates the matter, that the Directive on the supervision of financial conglomerates will enter into force by the end of 2002 and that rules should be framed as to render special rules unnecessary. 33,3% of the respondents answered question 21d in the affirmative. These respondents mainly argue that special rules are necessary because financial institutions fulfil a public function. Rules should be implemented with respect to capital requirements, special qualifications for directors, holding company issues, risk analysis, etc.

4.3 Problems for the creation and functioning of groups of companies: tensions between the interests of the group and its parts

Ca. 59% of all respondents answered question 22; 40% of these respondents belief in the need of a "safe harbour" (which allows those concerned with the management of the companies within a group to adopt a co-ordinated group policy provided that creditors are protected and there is a fair balance of advantage for shareholders over time). A smaller minority (ca. 26%) argues that there is no need for such a "safe harbour". Some advocates argue that European legislation will lead to harmonisation, which will in turn allow for the creation of cross-border groups of companies. One respondent argues that at EU level only general principles should be implemented, which then can be filled in by the Member States. Some German respondents argue that the German "Konzernrecht" in this regard has proven to be so successful and that EU rules could be modelled after the German rules, while others prefer the French solution or refer to the proposals from the Forum Europaeum on

Corporate Group Law. Opponents argue that rules at EU level are not necessary. Member States should deal with this problem. Also a general principle is not necessary, because this would leave the present situation – e.g. different rules in each Member State – in tact.

4.4 Pyramids

Ca. 49% of all 58 respondents answered question 23a. Ca. 47% of these respondents state that pyramids are not frequent in their country (A, DE, DK, F, IR, IS, NL, PL, SC, SE, SU & UK). Ca. 40% answered the question in the affirmative (B, DE, EL, IT & UK). Some answers are contradictory. 10 respondents for example state that in Germany pyramids are frequent, while 6 others say they are not. But respondents seem to agree that in Italy pyramids are frequent.
42% of the respondents answered question 23b; 30% of these respondents find pyramids useful, 38% find them harmful, 8% find them indifferent and 16% state that the answer to the question depends on the way pyramids are organised and managed.
The respondents that find them useful state for example that pyramids can be advantageous because they allow integration into a group of a company with minority shareholders, which helps to finance activities. Pyramids may also be helpful for supervisory reasons, as they avoid the whole group from becoming subject to supervisory measures outside the EU, and they have for a long time ensured a high rate of development.
Ca. 25% of all the respondents answered question 23c. Respondents considering pyramids to be harmful mention, amongst others, the following risks: lack of transparency, maximising control with a minimal investment, asymmetrical risk-sharing, the cascade-effect e.g. the transfer of legal capital from parent to subsidiary and then to the subsidiary of the subsidiary and problems with creditor and minority shareholder protection. Some respondents argue that the problems presented by pyramids are similar to those presented by groups.
55 Respondents answered question 23d. 40% of these respondents is of the opinion that specific measures beyond group transparency are not desirable for pyramids. It can be argued that special rules can be omitted if potential investors will be able to ascertain whether special rights are attached to a particular class of shares, which could affect their investment. Ca. 34% of the 19 respondents to this question believes special rules beyond transparency are necessary for pyramids. Among the proposed measures are: provisions avoiding company directors from mala gestio, provisions ensuring the independence of directors and cumulative voting for directors, and provisions providing a minimum disclosure of indirect holdings through pyramids and circular and cross-shareholdings.

5. CORPORATE RESTRUCTURING AND MOBILITY

On questions 24a – 29, a vast majority answered positive. In general, respondents are in favour of freedom of cross border mobility (transfer of seat, mergers, etc.) and relaxation of (unnecessary) requirements, but without loosing sight of the position of the shareholders and creditors (and in question 24, workers). According to a few responses, there should be no distinction between national and international transactions. Some stressed the subsidiarity principle, but overall a task for the EU was envisaged, either for minimum standards in the EU, or for harmonisation on specific topics. Often reference was made to national laws, and often with further explanations.

5.1 Change of corporate seat, or domicile

57% (68 respondents) answered question 24a. Of these 67% (46 respondents) answered positive, ca. 13% negative (9 respondents) and 19% (13 respondents) gave an answer other than yes or no. The majority (of the ones that responded) is in favour of the incorporation doctrine, which is more than 5 times the negative response. Of the positive answers, many argued for a (general) freedom of mobility across borders and abolition of barriers. Some negative respondents saw the question in light of the different legal systems. More than once reference was made to an international transfer of seat without losing legal personality and to the 14th Directive. And more than once, case law of the ECJ (Centros, Überseering) was given, with sometimes the advise to wait for a judgement of the ECJ on this question. Some other comments (positive, negative or other) were: most cases of cross border transfer of seat are "smelly", the two systems are influenced by the available remedies, one should also look at competition law and civil law in general, the topic should also address transfer of registered office, the real seat is not easy to determine, uniform approach is needed to protect shareholders and creditors.

Ca. 40% (48 respondents) answered question 24b. Of these, 77% (37 respondents) answered positive, ca. 19 % negative (9 respondents) and 4% (2 respondents) gave an answer other than yes or no. A big majority (of the ones that responded) agrees that the Member States should be free to apply mandatory requirements, which is more than 4 times the negative response. Of the positive answers, many agreed with the proposition of the HLG, since there are no minimum common standards (e.g. shareholders rights, creditor protection, workers participation, tax) in the EU, which could lead to abuse of freedom of establishment or circumvention of rules. There was a call for uniform mandatory rules. Many respondents mentioned social laws and workers participation as examples of mandatory rules. Some respondents feared new barriers, uncertainty or discrimination. Some other comments (positive, negative or other) were: a European judicial institution should review these rules, reference was made to the Dutch law on "pseudo-foreign companies", several actions should no longer fall under company law, but under torts etc., a race to the bottom is feared if no mandatory rules would apply, a proportionality test should be introduced, the UK 'over sea companies' seem to work well, (partly) replace articles of company, conflicting rules might then be applicable, wait for decision ECJ.

The question on the connecting factor is not always answered. Answers were: an activity of the company, permanent operational presence, where management team de facto runs day-by-day operation, registered in their territory.

Ca. 29% (35 respondents) answered question 24b. Of these, 77% (27 respondents) answered positive, 17% negative (6 respondents) and ca. 6 % (2 respondents) gave an answer other than yes or no. A big majority (of the ones that responded) found that other Member States should be bound to recognise such provisions. Most respondents (ca. 71%) did not answer this question. The responses differ widely and not always seem to answer the question.

5.2 Third Directive Mergers – position of the acquiring company

Ca. 54% (64 respondents) answered question 25a. Of these, 28% (18 respondents) answered positive, ca. 47% negative (30 respondents) and 25% (16 respondents) gave an answer other than yes or no. A minority (of the ones that responded) found that the EU requirements for special provisions governing merger decisions in acquiring companies should be removed, which is 1.6 times less as the negative response. Most negative responses replied that this protection of shareholders was needed and a few also spoke about the protection of creditors. Some respondents did not answer the question in full, but merely replied that unnecessary provisions should be abolished. The difference between a merger and a takeover bid is stressed more than once. Other comments (positive, negative or other) were: the 3rd Directive already provides for relaxation, except in a 'reverse takeover'; the questionnaire does not take up the rule of Article 8, 3rd Directive (max. 10% in cash), it should be examined; often it is possible to change the acquiring company for the acquired company.

Ca. 39% (46 respondents) answered question 25b. Of these, ca. 30% answered positive (14 respondents: 5 for a simple yes, 2 for a yes for all mergers and 7 for a yes for all international mergers), ca. 28% negative (13 respondents) and ca.41% (19 respondents) gave an answer other than yes or no. Of the one-third positive responses, the majority found that the relaxation should be mandatory for an international merger (7), a minority for all

mergers (2) and a big number found that Member States should be bound to accept such relaxations in an international merger (5). Around one-third of the respondents did not find that Member States of an acquired company should be bound to accept any such relaxation in respect of an acquiring company in an international merger, or that the relaxation should be made mandatory for all international mergers, or even for all mergers. A big number (especially compared with other questions) gave an answer other than yes or no.
Many stress the necessity of a uniform regulation and the need to facilitate international mergers, some do not want to make a distinction between national and cross-border mergers. Other comments (positive, negative or other) were: Member States should be free to decide on domestic mergers, the scope of the 3rd Directive should be extended to international mergers, if the 10th Directive is adopted, then application of national laws is prevented, relaxation should be standardised to avoid distortion of competition, uniformity is needed for the internal market.

5.3 Third Directive – acquisition of a wholly owned subsidiary

Ca. 49% (58 respondents) answered question 26a. Of these, ca. 85% (49 respondents) answered positive, ca. 7% negative (4 respondents) and 8% (5 respondents) gave an answer other than yes or no. A big majority (of the ones that responded) found that Member States should be permitted to relax the directive requirements in the case of acquisitions of 100%-subsidiaries, which is more than 12 times the negative response.
An argument often mentioned is that no minorities are affected. Some argue that one still has to consider the position of stakeholders.
Ca. 39% (46 respondents) answered question 26b. Of these, ca. 85% (39 respondents) answered positive, ca. 11 % negative (5 respondents) and 4% (2 respondents) gave an answer other than yes or no. A big majority (of the ones that responded) found that the Member State of the acquired subsidiary should be required to accept such relaxation by the Member State of the holding company in an international merger, which is almost eight times the negative answer. Examples of comments given are: what about reciprocity, co-ordination is necessary, it is of no concern to the acquired company state, if it does not lead to tax avoidance and reduction of the position of the third party.
Ca. 26% (31 respondents) answered question 26c. Of these, ca. 65% (20 respondents) answered positive, 29% negative (9 respondents) and 7 % (2 respondents) gave an answer other than yes or no. A majority (of the ones that responded) found such requirements should be removed in all cases (13 respondents), international not, or in all such international cases (4 respondents). Most respondents (74%) did not answer this question.

5.4 Creditor protection in restructuring

Ca. 50% (60 respondents) answered question 27a. Of these, ca. 53% (32 respondents) answered positive, ca. 32% negative (19 respondents) and 15% (9 respondents) gave an answer other than yes or no. A (slight) majority (of the ones that responded) found that the creditor protection requirements for reductions of capital, mergers and transfers of registered office should be aligned as proposed by the HLG. Some others simply state that this is not necessary, or should be left to the Member States. Other comments (positive, negative or other) were: it may well be that an international merger affects the creditor's position more severely than a national one, a mixed (administrative and judicial) control is proposed, one only has to apply the 2nd Directive to all capital reorganisations, there should be a solvency test, insolvency law should be taken into account, Article 32, 2nd Directive should be clarified.
Ca. 25% (30 respondents) answered question 27b. Of these, 60% (18 respondents) answered positive, 3% negative (1 respondents) and ca. 37% (11 respondents) gave an answer other than yes or no. A big majority (of the ones that responded) found that such alignment should be confined to international mergers and transfers of corporate domicile (2 respondents), or that it should apply to all EU restructuring provisions (16 respondents). Most respondents (ca. 75%) did not answer this question. Comments (positive, negative or

other) were: yes, for the sake of equity and certainty, to avoid forum shopping, there is no reason to distinguish between national and international restructurings, etc.

5.5 Squeeze-outs and sell-outs

Ca. 62% (74 respondents) answered question 28a. Of these, ca. 87% (64 respondents) answered positive, ca. 9% negative (7 respondents) and 4% (3 respondents) gave an answer other than yes or no. A big majority (of the ones that responded) found that Member States should be required to introduce provisions enabling a majority shareholder (the majority to be set at not less than 90% nor more than 95%) in a company to buy out the minority for a fairly appraised price. Many respondents referred to the laws of their country, which enables squeeze-outs, with sometimes a different threshold. Overall, a practical need was found to be served with the rule. Some respondents only favoured a squeeze-out for listed (and de-listed) companies. A few responded that this should not be regulated at EU-level.

Other comments (positive, negative or other) were: it applies since 2002 in Germany and a quorum of 95% seems fair, one should consider a "Reversed Triangular Takeover", the proposed threshold differs significantly from the one in the UK, is there a need to express the maximum of 95%?, in France the price is decided by a multi-criteria test, we favour 90% to create a level playing field, consider a lower threshold where consideration in shares is offered, the market price of the last three month should be taken, valuation should be done by an expert and in case of unlisted companies by the tribunal, the price should not be higher than the takeover price, one-person company may not be valid in all Member States, Member States should be allowed to introduce lower thresholds, anti-embarrassment rules should be established in case of non-quoted companies, etc.

Ca. 57% (68 respondents) answered question 28b. Of these, ca. 68% (46 respondents) answered positive, ca. 29% negative (20 respondents) and 3% (2 respondents) gave an answer other than yes or no. A majority (of the ones that responded) found that minority shareholders should have a corresponding right to be bought out where the 90-95% threshold has been reached.

Other comments (positive, negative or other) were: minorities already have the right to sell their shares, the UK Company Law Review rejected it, under certain conditions, for an equal treatment, etc.

Ca. 47% (56 respondents) answered question 28c. Of these, 55% (31 respondents) answered positive, 25% negative (14 respondents) and 20% (11 respondents) gave an answer other than yes or no. A majority (of the ones that responded) found that in companies with more than one class of share the rule should operate on a class-by-class basis. Other comments (positive, negative or other) were: it should operate in terms of voting rights rather than ownership of capital, attention should be given to convertible bonds, a two tier approach is suggested, depends on the threshold, it will make takeover bids more attractive for potential bidders, etc.

5.6 Other issues

Only a few respondents answered question 29 whether there is a need for legislation at the EU level providing for restructuring in ways not already discussed. Some of the answers were: there should be a European regulation on winding up, on material and procedural insolvency law and on recovery of companies in crisis; the possibility of "Reverse Triangular Mergers" (in line with Delaware law); the introduction of a squeeze-out rule below 90-95% in case minority shareholders of a subsidiary receive shares in the holding company; the restructuring measures that form part of the Financial Service Action Plan should form the priority focus of EU company law initiatives; legislation for an easy dissolution of private limited companies; the tax and stamp duty rules on share for share exchanges and de-mergers in separate jurisdictions; statutory, contractual and security rights of lenders.

6. THE EUROPEAN PRIVATE COMPANY

6.1 An initiative to establish a European Private Company

Ca. 57% (68 respondents) answered question 30a, ca. 62% positive, 38% negative. A majority thinks an EPC will or can be useful. SME's play an important role in the European economy, account for more than 90 percent of all European firms and should be facilitated with a fitting European form. The Regulation should not be complicated but it should deal with matters like directors liability and make use of the notaries expertise. It can be argued that if the legal form of subsidiaries were the same, the cost when setting up and operating subsidiaries would be reduced.

Some respondents suggest that it is better to monitor the further development of the SE before an EPC should be founded, others disagree. Some arguments mentioned by the minority against a new European form are the issue of co-determination, the lack of a need or interest for an EPC, a lack of predictability, an EPC cannot be governed exclusively by the Regulation, harmonisation is preferable.

Ca. 30% (36 respondents) answered question 30b, 47,2% of which positive, 47,2% negative, 5,6% other. Half of the respondents think that the model for regulation of a private company is an appropriate way to encourage flexible regulation in Member States. Some consider it to be a more interesting possibility than an EPC (at this moment). It could amount to a benchmark which all Member States would be encouraged to aspire. A minimum set of standards in the model law would be appropriate with reference to the first and second EU company law directives. Arguments against a model law are that it cannot be a substitute for an EPC and that this is no priority. One respondent notes that there is no hard evidence of the inefficiency of the laws of Member States at facilitating SME's.

6.2 Incorporation of the European Private Company

Ca. 45% (54 respondents) answered question 31, 87 % of which positive, 11% negative, 2% other. A big majority of the respondents conclude that it should be possible for an EPC to be set up by both individuals and legal entities and by one or more nationals of one Member State as long as the EPC undertakes economic activities in two or more Member States.

A small group of respondents do not agree with the element 'economic activities in two or more Member States'. Easy access and contractual freedom are mentioned as important factors. European governance will have to ensure equal positions for the shareholders in each Member State.

6.3 A genuine European company

Ca. 48% (57 respondents) answered question 32a, 40% of which positive, 60% negative. A minority thinks that the EPC, with respect to the company law applicable to it, could be exclusively governed by the provisions of the Regulation and the provisions of its articles which are not inconsistent therewith, with autonomous interpretation ultimately by the ECJ. Most think it is hard to see how an EPC could operate outside a body of national law or in the absence of a European body of private law and implementation will be very difficult. It would leave great legal uncertainty and would damage the credibility of the EPC. On the other hand one respondent notes that high costs for advice and information, uncertainties and accountability risks can only be reduced when reference to national law will be abolished. Shareholders must be able to regulate all important issues in the memorandum of association. Standard forms of articles of association should assist those forming an EPC. In the case of problems with interpretation, judges and arbitrators will decide. In the case of a legal vacuum, which according to some seems highly unlikely, referral to national law is unavoidable. The EPC should then be treated like one of the corporate forms in existence in the relevant Member State. Concerning the role of the ECJ some respondents note that an increase of its competence will be unjustifiable and it will lead to an unmanageable burden

for the ECJ. A few respondents note that tax harmonisation is the key for European companies.
Ca. 45% (53 respondents) answered question 32b, 64% of which positive, 36% negative. A majority thinks it is necessary to refer to the law applicable to the private companies in the Member States of incorporation where a question is not answered in the Regulation of the EPC or its articles of association. This would be an easy, efficient and transparent solution. Parties could freely choose the most efficient system.

7 CO-OPERATIVES AND OTHER FORMS OF ENTERPRISE

7.1 Regulation of the European Co-operative, European Association and European Mutual Society

Ca. 41% (49 respondents) answered question 33a, 69% of which positive, 31% negative. A big majority of the respondents considers the enactment of the proposed Regulations necessary or desirable. However, most respondents do not see this as a top priority. Those who are positive mainly support the proposal for co-operatives and secondly for mutual societies. One respondent was very positive about the high quality of the proposal for the European Co-operatives. The quality of the proposals for the European Association and the European Mutual Society are not up to par yet. The least desirable Regulation appears to be is that for the European Association.
Ca. 28% (33 respondents) answered question 33b, 58% of which positive, 33% negative, 9% other. The majority makes a positive assessment of the potential these Regulations have in the solution of the problems affecting co-operatives and other forms of enterprise in the European Union. A level playing field is necessary. However, a group of respondents notes that the proposals do not meet the expectations. If there is a need for a European Mutual Society or a European Association, the proposals for these forms are impractical. The proposed rule on employee participation devaluates the proposal for a European Co-operative to a great extent.

7.2 Harmonisation of national laws on co-operatives, associations and mutual societies

Ca. 40% (47 respondents) answered question 34a, 34% of which positive, 66 % negative.
A big majority does not think that there is a need to harmonise rules for the alternative forms of enterprise in Europe. Harmonisation is considered to be very difficult because of the diversity of the forms of enterprise and their specific role. Their impact is mainly local, so harmonisation is not necessary.
Ca. 19 (22 respondents) answered question 34b, 41% positive, 46% negative, 14% other. Less than half of the respondents think that it is satisfactory that the regimes in the proposed Regulations are completed by application of the Company Law Directives, which do not apply to the national forms of these enterprises. In the UK this system works for the building societies legislation, which mainly follows company law. Adversaries mention that this would bring forth a complicated system that will hollow out the regimes. Specific regulations should be drafted for different types of activity.

7.3 Foundations in Europe

37 % (44 respondents) answered question 35a, 23% of which positive, 77 % negative.
A big majority opposes the introduction of a European Foundation. Foundations are mainly locally rooted, a European form for foundations should not have priority and the principle of subsidiarity must prevail. In Germany even the federation does not have legislative power concerning foundations. Tax problems for foundations and its donors should however be abolished to promote cross-border donations. One respondent, who is very enthusiastic

about a European Foundation based on endowment contributions, is doing extensive research. One respondent notes that a European Foundation would be preferable to promote transparency.
Ca. 34% (40 respondents) answered question 35b, 25 % of which positive, 75 % negative.
A big majority is against harmonisation of national rules applicable to foundations. Harmonisation would limit the grown diversity of frameworks, which is an asset for founders and foundations. Two respondents note that the European Foundation and not harmonisation of national legislation should be the priority. However, harmonisation can also be a step towards a European Foundation and vice versa. Harmonisation in relation to key matters and tax law are mentioned as pros by a couple of respondents.

7.4 Enterprise law

Ca. 43% (51 respondents) answered question 36a, 29% of which positive, 67% negative, 4% other. A big majority of the respondents does not think a definition of 'enterprise' would be useful. Different legal structures need different legislation. A coherent definition will be difficult, is not needed and not yet possible.
Ca. 11% (13 respondents) answered question 36b, 62% of which positive, 38% negative. The majority thinks that 'economic activity' and 'organisation' should be the main elements in the definitions of enterprise. The formula should be broad. Durability should also be an element. One should be aware of the fact that the element 'economic' is not typical for non-profit organisations. Suggestions as elements are: marshalling of resources in an organised manner for the pursuit of a defined common purpose and co-ordinated and continuous organisation of assets existing in any Member State.
Ca. 25% (30 respondents) answered question 36c, 67% of which positive, 30% negative, 3% other. A big majority thinks basic harmonised rules should only apply to limited liability entities. Regulations for all forms of enterprise do not meet the specific needs for all forms of enterprise. Harmonising regulations on partnerships would be against the principle of subsidiarity.

37 % (44 respondents) answered question 37a, 52% of which positive, 48% negative. A small majority thinks there is a need to introduce harmonised rules in Europe for registration, access to core data and powers of representation relating to enterprises as defined in the document. Harmonisation of these areas is essential for cross-border trade, freedom of movement and the reduction of costs and risks. Whether harmonisation is possible at this moment is not clear. One respondent thinks that these issues should apply to all legal persons. Another respondent explains in his extensive answer that a common technological platform for the consultation and interpretation of national registers is preferable to a European register. The internet could be a useful tool. Those who are against harmonisation note that easier cross-border access should be ensured.
Ca. 28% (33 respondents) answered question 37b, 18% of which positive, 79% negative, 3% other. Most respondents do not see a need for other issues like financial reporting, branches, groups of enterprises, transformation and transfer of seat to be addressed in an Enterprise Law Directive.
An Enterprise Law Directive should be limited to constituting a general legal framework.

ANNEX 4

EXISTING AND PROPOSED EUROPEAN COMPANY LAW INSTRUMENTS

LIST OF EXISTING EUROPEAN COMPANY LAW INSTRUMENTS

Regulations

- Council Regulation (EEC) 2137/85 of 25 July 1985 on the European Economic Interest Grouping (EEIG), [1994] OJ L 199/1;
- Council Regulation (2001/2157/EC) of 8 October 2001 on the Statute for a European Company (SE), [2001] OJ L 294/1 *supplemented by* Council Directive (2001/86/EC) of 8 October 2001 supplementing the Statute for a European Company with regard to the involvement of employees, [2001] OJ L 294/22;
- Regulation (EC) No 1606/2002 of the European Parliament and of the Council of 19 July 2002, OJ L 243/1 on the application of international accounting standards.

Directives

- 1st Council Directive (EEC) 68/151 of 9 March 1968 on co-ordination of safeguards which, for the protection of the interests of members and others, are required by Member States of companies within the meaning of the second paragraph of Article 58 of the Treaty, with a view to making such safeguards equivalent throughout the Community, [1968] OJ L 65/8;
- 2nd Council Directive (EEC) 77/91 of 13 December 1976 on co-ordination of safeguards, which for the protection of the interests of members and others, are required by Member States of companies within the meaning of the second paragraph of Article 58 of the Treaty, in respect of the formation of public limited liability companies and the maintenance and alteration of their capital, with a view to making such safeguards equivalent throughout the Community, [1977] OJ L 26/1;
- 3rd Council Directive (EEC) 78/855 of 9 October 1978 based on Article 54(3)(g) of the Treaty concerning mergers of public limited liability companies, [1977] OJ L 295/36;
- 4th Council Directive (EEC) 78/660 of 25 July 1978 based on Article 54(3)(g) of the Treaty on the annual accounts of certain types of companies [1978] OJ L 222/11;
- 6th Council Directive (EEC) 82/891 of 17 December 1982 based on Article 54(3)(g) of the Treaty concerning the division of public limited liability companies, [1982] OJ L 378/47;

- 7th Council Directive (EEC) 83/349 of 13 June 1983 based on Article 54(3)(g) of the Treaty on consolidated accounts, [1983] OJ L 193/1;
- 8th Council Directive (EEC) 84/253 of 10 April 1984 based on Article 54(3)(g) of the Treaty on the approval of persons responsible for carrying out the statutory audits of accounting documents, [1984] OJ L 126/20;
- 11th Council Directive (EEC) 89/666 of 21 December 1989 concerning disclosure requirements in respect of branches opened in a Member State by certain types of company governed by the law of another State, [1989] OJ L 395/96;
- 12th Council Directive (EEC) 89/667 of 21 December 1989 on single-member private limited liability companies [1989] OJ L 395/40;

Recommendations

- Commission Recommendation (2001/256/EC) of 15 November 2000 on quality assurance for the statutory audit in the European Union: minimum requirements, [2001] OJ L 91/91;
- Commission Recommendation (2001/453/EC) of 30 May 2001 on the recognition, measurement and disclosure of environmental issues in the annual accounts and annual reports of companies, [2001] OJ L 156/33.
- Commission Recommendation (2002/590/EC) of 16 May 2002 on "Statutory Auditors' Independence in the EU : A Set of Fundamental Principles", [2002] OJ L 191/22.

Green Paper

- The role, the position and the liability of the statutory auditor within the European Union [1996] OJ C 321/1.

Communications

- Commission Communication "Accounting Harmonisation: A New Strategy vis-à-vis International Harmonisation", November 1995, COM (1995) 508;
- Commission Communication "Financial Services: Implementing the Framework for Financial Markets: Action Plan" of 11 May 1999, COM (1999) 232;
- Commission Communication (98/C143/03) "Statutory Audit in the European Union, the way forward", [1998] OJ C 143/3;
- Commission Communication of 13 June 2000, "EU Financial Reporting Strategy: the way forward", COM (2000) 359;

- Interpretative Communication (98/C16/04) Concerning Certain Articles of the Fourth and Seventh Council Directives on Accounting, [1998] OJ C 16/4.

LIST OF PROPOSED EUROPEAN COMPANY LAW INSTRUMENTS

Regulations

- Amended Proposal for a Council Regulation (EEC) on a statute for a European Association, [1993] OJ C 236/1;
- Amended Proposal for a Council Regulation (EEC) on a statute for a European Co-operative Society, [1993] OJ C 236/17;
- Amended Proposal for a Council Regulation (EEC) on a statute for a European Mutual Society, [1993] OJ C 236/40;

Directives

- Proposal for a Directive of the European Parliament and of the Council amending Council Directive 68/151/EEC, as regards disclosure requirements in respect of certain types of companies, COM (2002) 279, 3 June 2002, OJ C 227/377;
- Proposal for a Directive of the European Parliament and of the Council amending Council Directives 78/660/EEC, 83/349/EEC and 91/674/EEC on the annual and consolidated accounts of certain types of companies and insurance undertakings COM(2002) 259/2 final, 24 September 2002, OJ C 227/336;
- Proposal for a Directive of the European Parliament and of the Council on take-over bids, COM (2002) 534 final, 2 October 2002.

Cases

Australia

Canada

European Human Rights Court

European Union

Germany

France

Switzerland

United Kingdom

United States

Index